RETIREMENT PLANNING
AND EMPLOYEE BENEFITS

James F. Dalton

Michael A. Dalton

12th Edition

3116 5TH STREET
METAIRIE, LA 70002
888-295-6023

Printed in the U.S.A.

ISBN-13: 978-1-936602-39-1

ABOUT THE AUTHORS

James F. Dalton, MBA, MS, CPA/PFS, CFA®, CFP®

- Adjunct professor at George Mason University (2014 - present)
- Adjunct professor at Georgetown University (2002 - 2014)
- Former Executive Vice President, Assessment Technologies Institute LLC
- Former Senior Vice President, Kaplan Professional
- Former President, Dalton Publications LLC
- Former Senior Manager of KPMG, LLP, concentrating in personal financial planning, investment planning, and litigation consulting
- MBA from Loyola University New Orleans
- Master of Accounting in Taxation from the University of New Orleans
- BS in accounting from Florida State University in Tallahassee, Florida
- Member of the CFP Board of Standards July 1996, Comprehensive CFP® Exam Pass Score Committee
- Member of the AICPA and the Louisiana Society of CPAs
- Member of the Financial Planning Association
- Member of the *Journal of Financial Planning* Editorial Review Board
- Author of *Money Education's Quick Sheets*
- Co-author of *Cases in Financial Planning: Analysis and Presentation (1st - 2nd Editions)*
- Co-author of *Retirement Planning (1st - 12th Editions)*
- Co-Author of *Fundamentals of Financial Planning (1st - 4th Editions)*
- Contributing Author of *Insurance Planning (1st - 4th Editions)*
- Contributing Author of *Estate Planning (1st - 9th Editions)*
- Author of Kaplan Schweser's Personal Financial Planning Understanding Your Financial Calculator
- Author of Kaplan Schweser's Understanding Your Financial Calculator for the CFA® Exam
- Co-author of BISYS CFA® Study Notes Volumes I and II
- Co-author of Kaplan Schweser's Personal Financial Planning Cases and Applications
- Co-author of the Kaplan Schweser Review for the CFP® Certification Examination, Volumes I–VIII and Kaplan Schweser's Financial Planning Flashcards

Michael A. Dalton, Ph.D., JD, CPA, CLU, ChFC, CFP®
- Former Chair of the Board of Dalton Publications, L.L.C.
- Associate professor of Accounting and Taxation at Loyola University in New Orleans, Louisiana (retired)
- Adjunct professor at George Mason University (2014 - present)
- Adjunct professor at Georgetown University (2002 - 2014)
- Former Senior Vice President, Education at BISYS Group
- Ph.D. in Accounting from Georgia State University
- J.D. from Louisiana State University in Baton Rouge, Louisiana
- MBA and BBA in Management and Accounting from Georgia State University
- Former board member of the CFP Board's Board of Examiners, Board of Standards, and Board of Governors
- Former member (and chair) of the CFP Board's Board of Examiners
- Member of the Financial Planning Association
- Member of the *Journal of Financial Planning* Editorial Advisory Board
- Member of the *Journal of Financial Planning* Editorial Review Board
- Member of the LSU Law School Board of Trustees (2000 - 2006)
- Author of *Dalton Review for the CFP® Certification Examination: Volume I – Outlines and Study Guides, Volume II – Problems and Solutions, Volume III - Case Exam Book, Mock Exams A-1 and A-2 (1st - 8th Editions)*
- Author of *Retirement Planning and Employee Benefits (1st - 12th Editions)*
- Author of *Estate Planning (1st - 9th Editions)*
- Author of *Fundamentals of Financial Planning (1st - 4th Editions)*
- Author of *Insurance Planning (1st - 4th Editions)*
- Co-author of *Income Tax Planning (1st - 9th Editions)*
- Co-author of *Cases in Financial Planning: Analysis and Presentation (1st - 2nd Editions)*
- Co-author of *Dalton CFA® Study Notes Volumes I and II (1st - 2nd Editions)*
- Co-author of *Dalton's Personal Financial Planning Series – Personal Financial Planning Theory and Practice (1st - 3rd Editions)*
- Co-author of *Dalton's Personal Financial Planning Series – Personal Financial Planning Cases and Applications (1st - 4th Editions)*
- Co-author of *Cost Accounting: Traditions and Innovations* published by West Publishing Company
- Co-author of the *ABCs of Managing Your Money* published by National Endowment for Financial Education (NEFE)

ABOUT THE CONTRIBUTING AUTHOR

Randal R. Cangelosi, JD, MBA

- Practicing litigator throughout Louisiana, in business/commercial law and litigation, products liability litigation, wills and trust litigation, environmental law and litigation, medical malpractice defense, and insurance law and litigation
- Has successfully defended numerous corporations, businesses, and doctors in jury and judge trials
- Juris Doctorate from Loyola University New Orleans
- Masters of Business Administration from Loyola University New Orleans
- BS in Finance from Louisiana State University
- Member of the American & Federal Bar Associations
- Member of the Bar of the State of Louisiana
- Member of the New Orleans and Baton Rouge Bar Associations
- Board Member of La Lupus Foundation
- Board Member of Baton Rouge Chamber of Commerce
- Former Board Member of the Baton Rouge Area Chapter of the American Red Cross
- Admitted to practice before US District Courts, Western, Eastern & Middle Districts of Louisiana
- Admitted to practice before the Federal 5th Circuit Court of Appeals
- Admitted to practice in USDC, Southern District of Iowa (Pro Hac Vice)
- Admitted to practice in Circuit Court of Wayne County, Mississippi (Pro Hac Vice)
- Admitted to practice in Circuit Court of Barbour County, Alabama (Pro Hac Vice)
- Admitted to practice in Court of Common Pleas, Darlington County, South Carolina (Pro Hac Vice)
- Admitted to practice in Los Angeles County Superior Court, California (Pro Hac Vice)
- Admitted to practice in Superior Court of New Jersey: Morris County (Pro Hac Vice)
- Admitted to practice in 17th Judicial Court, Broward County, Florida (Pro Hac Vice)
- Former Chairman of New Orleans Bar Association, Community Service Committee
- Former Chairman of New Orleans Bar Association, Food and Clothing Drives
- Co-author of *Personal Financial Planning: Theory and Practice (1st - 3rd Editions)*
- Co-author of *Professional Ethics for Financial Planners*

ACKNOWLEDGEMENTS & SPECIAL THANKS

We are most appreciative for the tremendous support and encouragement we have received throughout this project. We are extremely grateful to the faculty members and program directors of CFP Board-Registered programs who provided valuable comments during the development stages of this text. We are fortunate to have dedicated, careful readers at many institutions who were willing to share their needs, expectations, and time with us.

We owe a special thanks to the following reviewers for their constructive feedback throughout this and previous editions. Their thorough editing, detailed calculation reviews, helpful suggestions for additional content, and other valuable comments, improved this text. To each of these individuals we extend our deepest gratitude and appreciation.

Brad Childs is an Associate Professor of Accounting at Belmont University, where he does research in the fields of taxation and financial planning. He has a Ph.D. from Purdue University and a J.D. from Suffolk University. Mr. Childs is currently a licensed attorney in Tennessee, a licensed CPA in Ohio, and a CFP Certificant.

Randall Martinez is a Personal Financial Planner specializing in personal financial planning, estate, and individual income tax planning. He teaches retirement planning, estate planning, and income tax planning through various universities as well as comprehensive reviews for the Certified Financial Planner Examination.

Kristi Tafalla is an attorney and personal financial planner specializing in income tax and estate planning. She teaches estate planning, income tax planning and comprehensive case courses through various CFP® Board-Registered Programs as well as comprehensive reviews for the CFP® certification. She is a contributor to Money Education's *Estate Planning for Financial Planners*.

Bill Yurkovac has a private practice in Florida focusing on asset management and estate planning considerations for his clientele. Mr. Yurkovac holds a Master's Degree in Education, has more than twenty-five years experience in the financial services arena, and enjoys serving as an instructor for candidates preparing for the CFP® Certification Examination. Current community involvement includes assisting and counseling several nonprofit organizations and a chair on the local Estate Planning Council's Board of Directors.

We would also like to pay special thanks to **Donna Dalton** and **Robin Meyer** for their significant contribution to this textbook. Developing a textbook that is aesthetically pleasing and easy to read is a difficult undertaking. They worked diligently with the authors and reviewers to manage the project, performed numerous reviews, and provided invaluable feedback throughout the entire project. This book would not have been possible without their extraordinary dedication, skill, and knowledge.

We have received so much help from so many people, it is possible that we have inadvertently overlooked thanking someone. If so, it is our shortcoming, and we apologize in advance. Please let us know if you are that someone, and we will make it right in our next printing.

PREFACE

Retirement Planning and Employee Benefits is written for graduate and upperdivision undergraduate level students interested in acquiring an understanding of retirement planning from a professional financial planning viewpoint. The text is intended to be used in a Retirement Planning course as part of an overall curriculum in tax or financial planning. The text is also intended to serve as a reference for practicing professional advisors.

This textbook was also designed to meet the educational requirements for a Retirement/Employee Benefits Course in a CFP Board-Registered Program. Therefore, one of our goals is to assure CFP Board-Registered Program Directors, instructors, students, and financial planners that we have addressed every relevant topic covered by the CFP Board Exam Topic List and the most recent model curriculum syllabus for this course. The book will be updated, as needed, to keep current with any changes in the law, exam topic list, or model curriculum.

Special Features

A variety of tools and presentation methods are used throughout this text to assist the reader in the learning process. Some of the features in this text that are designed to enhance your understanding and learning process include:

- **Learning Objectives** – At the beginning of each chapter is a list of learning objectives to help you focus your studying of the material. These learning objectives will provide a preview of the important topics covered in the chapter.

- **Key Concepts** – At the beginning of each subsection are key concepts, or study objectives, each stated as a question. To be successful in this course, you should be able to answer these questions. So as you read, guide your learning by looking for the answers. When you find the answers, highlight or underline them. It is important that you actually highlight/underline and not just make a mental note, as the action of stopping and writing reinforces your learning. Watch for this symbol:

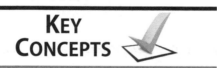

- **Quick Quizzes** – Following each subsection you will find a Quick Quiz, which checks and reinforces what you read. Circle the answer to each question and then check your answers against the correct answers supplied at the bottom of the quiz. If you missed any questions, flip back to the relevant section and review the material. Watch for this symbol:

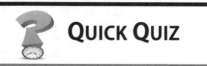

- **Examples** – Examples are used frequently to illustrate the concepts being discussed and to help the reader understand and apply the concepts presented. Examples are identified in the margin with the following symbol:

EXAMPLE
1.1

- **Exhibits** – The written text is enhanced and simplified by using exhibits where appropriate to promote learning and application. Exhibits are identified with the following symbol:

EXHIBIT
1.1

- **Cases** – Most chapters contain real world case summaries to help the reader appreciate the application of particular topics being discussed in the chapter.

- **Key Terms** – Key terms appear in **boldfaced type** throughout the text to assist in the identification of important concepts and terminology. A list of key terms with definitions appears at the end of each chapter.

- **End of Chapter Questions** – Each chapter contains a series of discussion and multiple-choice questions that highlight the major topics covered in the chapter. The questions test retention and understanding of important chapter material and can be used for review and classroom discussion.

- **Quick Quiz Explanations** – Each chapter concludes with the answers to the Quick Quizzes contained in that chapter, as well as explanation to the "false" statements in each Quick Quiz.

- **Glossary** – A compilation of the key terms identified throughout the text is located at the end of the book.

Additional Information Available on Money Education's Website (money-education.com)
- Resourceful Websites
- Cost of Living Adjustments (COLA) Increases
- Nondiscriminatory Classification Test

Visit our website at
money-education.com
for updates to the text &
information on Money Education's
Quick Sheets

This book is dedicated to

the many members of the United States Armed Forces

including our family members

Lt. Col. James J. Dalton, U.S. Army (1912-1981)
Lt. Col. James J. Dalton II, USMC Retired
Lt. Col. Brian J. Dalton, USAF Retired
William "Billy" Delle, U.S. Navy
Major Edwin C. Marotte, U.S. Army (1919-2009)
Laurence R. Means, U.S. Navy

for protecting our unalienable rights,

including Life, Liberty and the pursuit of Happiness.

Michael A. Dalton & James F. Dalton

Table of Contents

CHAPTER 1 - INTRODUCTION TO RETIREMENT PLANNING

CHAPTER 2 - RETIREMENT PLANNING ACCUMULATIONS AND DISTRIBUTIONS

CHAPTER 3 - QUALIFIED PLAN OVERVIEW

CHAPTER 3 APPENDIX - SPECIAL TOPICS OF QUALIFIED PLANS

CHAPTER 4 - QUALIFIED PENSION PLANS

CHAPTER 5 - PROFIT SHARING PLANS

CHAPTER 6 - STOCK BONUS PLANS & EMPLOYEE STOCK OWNERSHIP PLANS

CHAPTER 7 - DISTRIBUTIONS FROM QUALIFIED PLANS

CHAPTER 8 - INSTALLATION, ADMINISTRATION, AND TERMINATION OF QUALIFIED PLANS

CHAPTER 9 - IRAS AND SEPS

CHAPTER 10 - SIMPLE, 403(b), AND 457 PLANS

CHAPTER 11 - SOCIAL SECURITY

CHAPTER 12 - DEFERRED COMPENSATION AND NONQUALIFIED PLANS

CHAPTER 13 - EMPLOYEE BENEFITS: FRINGE BENEFITS

CHAPTER 14 - EMPLOYEE BENEFITS: GROUP BENEFITS

CHAPTER 15 - ITEM SETS AND THE MIKE & MARIA ROMAN CASE

APPENDIX

INTRODUCTION TO RETIREMENT PLANNING

LEARNING OBJECTIVES

After reading this chapter, you should be able to:
1. Define financial independence.
2. Explain why employers are interested in retirement planning.
3. Identify all the groups interested in the study of retirement planning.
4. Identify the factors that explain why some Americans have high confidence about their ability to retire comfortably.
5. Articulate the myths and realities about what people think in comparison to what they actually do regarding working during retirement and picking a retirement age.
6. Explain why employers establish employee benefits and retirement plans.
7. Describe how the government can influence social policy.

INTRODUCTION

Retirement planning and employee benefits are challenging, but fascinating areas of study. Although complex, they provide tremendous career and intellectual opportunities for a wide variety of interested parties. Most individuals are interested in achieving financial security, which means achieving **financial independence** so that they are able to maintain their desired lifestyle without employment income. To become financially independent, one must generally forgo a certain level of immediate consumption to provide an opportunity for discretionary funds to grow and accumulate over time while avoiding catastrophic financial occurrences that could result in financial dependence. Retirement planning and employee benefits play an essential role in satisfying the need to save for future consumption and toward the goal of financial independence.

Employers are keenly interested in the areas of retirement planning and employee benefits because they consider and select employer-sponsored benefit plans. As a result, they are impacted by both current and future benefits costs and the limitations of such plans. Employees are also interested because benefits are generally considered a part of an overall compensation package. Another significant group interested in this area of study is the diverse group of professionals and members of the financial services industry because of the professional opportunities and the sheer dollar size of retirement assets in the market. Lastly, the U.S. government has a public, social, and tax policy interest in the area. When the government wants to promote social policy, such as health care benefits or promoting home ownership, it frequently utilizes tax policy to encourage plan selectors to adopt the programs desired by the government.

Be forewarned, the topics of study are neither simple nor entirely intuitive. Determining funding requirements for retirement requires an in-depth understanding of life expectancies, work life expectancies, retirement life expectancies, the projection of inflation and investment returns, and the determination of expenditure needs for particular persons far in advance of their occurrence. When a person reaches retirement age, the optimal distribution amount must be determined given a probability element that the distribution amount will provide sufficient income to maintain the retiree's lifestyle for the entire retirement period while having little or no risk of being depleted during the retiree's life.

A vast amount of study is needed to initially master the subject of qualified retirement plans because of the complexity of the federal legislation controlling the area. In addition, as one might expect, the rules governing qualified retirement plans are frequently amended by new legislation. Therefore, current rules and optimal choices today may change at any time. Thus, continuing study in the area is essential to maintain and improve your skill level. Tax-advantaged plans, other than qualified plans, are also government created or approved, have similar complexities, and also run the risk of legislative change.

While the first pension plans in the United States were established by the railroad industry in the 19th century, Congress has been legislating them since 1921. Because of the importance of retirement planning, Congress has provided oversight for these plans in an attempt to increase the protection of retirement benefits of workers. The most recent significant law change is the Pension Protection Act of 2006, which is intended to provide greater protection for workers with defined benefits and came after the bankruptcy and subsequent termination of United Airline's pension plan. It is important to stay abreast of legislation affecting pension and retirement plans.

This textbook also covers Social Security legislation and benefits, both of which are large and complex topics. Furthermore, after the implementation of employee benefit plans, the costs and benefits, as well as the employee censuses (age, income, length of services, etc.), do not remain static. Therefore, there will always be a need for monitoring, making changes, or terminating plans. As a result, one must learn the myriad of federal rules and stay current with changes in law and practice to become a master of the retirement planning field.

INTERESTED PARTIES

EMPLOYEES

Retirement plans and employee benefits provide an essential role in the pursuit of financial security. Retirement plans, whether employer or employee funded, offer employees an opportunity to accumulate assets that can later be used to provide a stable standard of living and financial security during retirement.

Funding of retirement benefits has changed significantly over the last thirty years. Years ago, many large employers provided employees with a retirement benefit, typically in the form of a fixed pension that would continue for the life of the retiree. Over time these plans, which were generally noncontributory by employees and costly to employers, have been replaced by plans that place more of the burden of funding on employees and shift the investment risk and responsibility from the employer to the employees. Reasons for this trend include the costliness of defined benefit plans compared to defined contribution plans and the attractiveness of defined contribution plans with the addition of IRC 401(k) plans resulting from the Revenue Act of 1978. The following exhibit illustrates these trends.

EXHIBIT
1.1

TOTAL RETIREMENT PLANS, PLAN PARTICIPANTS, & PLAN ASSETS (1975-2013)[1]

Year	Total Plans			Total Plans Participants (in thousands)			Total Plan Assets (in millions)		
	Total	Defined Benefit	Defined Contribution	Total	Defined Benefit	Defined Contribution	Total	Defined Benefit	Defined Contribution
1975	311,094	103,346	207,748	44,511	33,004	11,507	259,963	185,950	74,013
1980	488,901	148,096	340,805	57,903	37,979	19,924	563,551	401,455	162,096
1985	632,135	170,172	461,963	74,665	39,692	34,973	1,252,739	826,117	426,622
1990	712,308	113,062	599,245	76,924	38,832	38,091	1,674,139	961,904	712,236
1995	693,404	69,492	623,912	87,452	39,736	47,716	2,723,735	1,402,079	1,321,657
2000	735,651	48,773	686,878	103,329	41,613	61,716	4,202,672	1,986,177	2,216,495
2005	679,095	47,614	631,481	117,406	41,925	75,481	5,061,622	2,254,032	2,807,590
2006	694,550	48,579	645,971	121,995	42,146	79,849	5,684,302	2,468,142	3,216,160
2007	707,787	48,982	658,805	123,854	42,280	81,574	6,090,473	2,646,603	3,443,870
2008	717,530	48,374	669,156	124,851	42,342	82,509	4,703,461	2,040,925	2,662,537
2009	706,667	47,137	659,530	129,268	41,820	87,448	5,511,060	2,193,983	3,317,076
2010	701,012	46,543	654,469	129,724	41,423	88,301	6,281,749	2,448,361	3,833,388
2011	683,647	45,256	638,390	129,581	40,876	88,705	6,345,595	2,516,109	3,829,487
2012	676,622	43,601	633,021	130,584	39,809	90,775	6,966,261	2,701,856	4,264,405
2013	681,154	44,163	636,991	131,631	39,084	92,547	7,870,897	2,866,392	5,004,505

EXHIBIT
1.2

DEFINED CONTRIBUTION VS. DEFINED BENEFIT PLANS

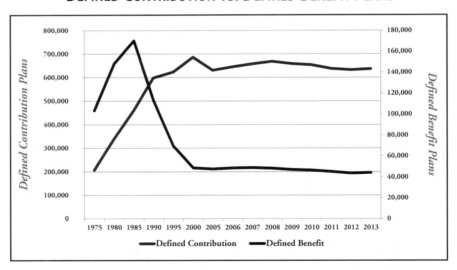

As employer funding has decreased and as life expectancy has increased, employees have begun to realize the importance of planning for retirement in hopes of achieving financial independence through their own savings and investments. Employees are also becoming more interested in risk management benefit plans (health insurance, disability insurance, life insurance, and long-term

1. Form 5500 filings with the U.S. Department of Labor.

care insurance) because they are beginning to understand the risk and potential negative financial impact of a catastrophic event on their financial security. While it is the employer's responsibility to communicate employer-sponsored employee benefit and retirement plans provided to employees so that the employees have an opportunity to fully understand such benefits, the employee must take an active role in choosing and evaluating benefits available.

Many employees view retirement plan benefits and employee benefits (where employer contributions are present) as part of their overall compensation package. For example, employees realize that premiums paid for group health insurance are generally less costly than premiums paid for an individual plan with the same coverage and exclusions. Employees also realize that to the extent the employer contributes to the payment of such premiums, this value is not included in the employee's taxable income and, therefore, is less costly to the employee, who would have to purchase health insurance with after-tax dollars without such a plan.

Unfortunately, not all workers are covered by employee benefit plans, nor are they covered by retirement plans sufficient to produce adequate retirement income. While 90 percent of state and local government employees had access to retirement benefits, only 69 percent of all private industry employees had access to retirement benefits. In addition, the participation rates are lower than they should be at 81 percent for state and local government employees and only 53 percent for private industry employees.[1] Exhibit 1.3 also illustrates the difference in retirement benefit access and participation for private industry employees of different size firms. While 86 percent of workers in private companies with 100 or more employees had access to retirement benefits, only 52 percent of workers in companies with less than 100 employees had access to retirement benefits. It is worth noting that the participation rate for employees in small companies is significantly lower at 36 percent compared to the participation rate for larger companies at 69 percent.

RETIREMENT BENEFITS: ACCESS, PARTICIPATION, AND TAKE-UP RATES; NATIONAL COMPENSATION SURVEY, MARCH 2015

EXHIBIT 1.3

	PRIVATE INDUSTRY			STATE AND LOCAL GOVERNMENT		
	Access	Participation	Take-Up Rate	Access	Participation	Take-Up Rate
1 to 99 Workers	52	36	70	78	70	89
1 to 49 Workers	46	33	71	70	63	90
50 to 99 Workers	67	46	69	91	80	89
100 Workers or More	86	69	81	91	82	90
100 to 499 Workers	81	61	75	88	80	91
500 Workers or More	91	79	87	93	83	89

Source: U.S. Department of Labor, BLS, National Compensation Survey, March 2015

Meanwhile, Americans' overall confidence in their ability to retire comfortably has increased slightly. The 2015 Retirement Confidence Survey by the Employee Benefit Research Institute indicates that approximately 58 percent of workers (up from 55 percent in 2014) are "somewhat" to "very confident" that they will have sufficient assets to live comfortably throughout retirement (a 17 percent decline since 2007, when the percentage was 70% confident).

1. US Department of Labor, Bureau of Labor Statistics "National Compensation Survey: Employee Benefits in Private Industry in the United States, March 2015"

EXHIBIT
1.4

CONFIDENCE SURVEY[1]

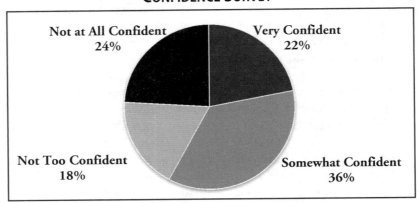

Not at All Confident
24%

Very Confident
22%

Not Too Confident
18%

Somewhat Confident
36%

Mathew Greenwald's statement regarding the prior year's Retirement Confidence Survey (March 19, 2013) provides an insightful summary of the preparedness for retirement of the U.S. population:

> "Savings rates of workers are disturbingly low and many are not saving at all. Only two-thirds of workers say they, or their spouse, have saved any money for retirement. At this point in time only 57% are actively saving money for retirement. As a result, the accumulated savings of many workers are quite low. Almost 3 in 5 (57%) of workers have financial assets that total to less than $25,000, not including their primary residence. Even when we just look at workers ages 45 and over, just under half (47%) have less than $25,000. Clearly, many are way behind in their financial preparation for retirement."

He also went on to discuss that the explanation most often given for not saving is the cost of living and the day-to-day expenses. However, many of the same participants agreed that there are expenses that could be cut out of their budgets, which would allow them to save more for retirement. The two expectations that contribute to not saving, even though there is an awareness of the need, are the expectation of working longer and the expectation of working during retirement.

However, these two expectations are fraught with peril. There has historically been a significant difference between the expectation of working during retirement and actually working during retirement.

The 2015 study indicates that the poor economy has delayed the expected retirement age for many workers. The percentage of workers who expected to retire after age 65 increased from 11 percent in 1991 to 36 percent in 2015. The increase in the expected retirement age indicates the severity of the economic problems and the real issues that retirees have in today's economic conditions.

---

1. Employee Benefit Research Institute, 2015 Retirement Confidence Survey.

The 2015 study also points out the following myths and realities:

Myth: 67 percent of respondents say they plan to work during retirement.

Reality: Only 23 percent of retirees actually work during retirement.

Myth: 8 percent of respondents expect to retire before age 60 and 26 percent expect to retire at age 70 or later.

Reality: The average worker retires at age 62, which has remained constant for many years. 49 percent of retirees retired earlier than expected for some reason that was beyond their own control (e.g., due to health or changes in employment). 36 percent of workers retired before age 60 and only 6 percent actually waited until at least age 70 to retire.

It is also concerning that workers have very little saved for retirement, despite the dramatic trend away from traditional defined benefit pension plans that provide annuitized income for life. The survey provides the following facts:[1]

- Only 67 percent of workers have saved for retirement.
- 57 percent of workers have less than $25,000 in total savings and investments (excluding defined benefit plans and the value of their home).
- 28 percent (down from 36 percent) of workers have less than $1,000 in total savings and investments.
- 48 percent of workers have completed a retirement needs analysis or calculation.[2]

Unfortunately, even where employer-sponsored retirement plans exist, many of these plans are employee self-reliant plans requiring the participant to determine both the amount to save and the investments to choose from those offered. The ongoing need for assistance in the form of competent financial advice regarding retirement planning cannot be overemphasized.

COMMON EMPLOYEE PERSPECTIVES OF RETIREMENT	EXHIBIT 1.5

- Employees view benefits as part of overall compensation.
- Employees would rather pay costs with pretax dollars.
- Employees generally understand retirement plans, and employee benefits are part of their overall financial plan.
- Employee confidence regarding their ability to retire comfortably is high, but inconsistent with reality.
- Employees generally do not really know the cost of retirement or how to achieve financial security.

---

1. EBRI 2015 Retirement Confidence Survey.
2. The topic of calculating needs is discussed in Chapter 2.

EMPLOYERS

Employers view employer-sponsored retirement plans and employee benefits as part of overall compensation costs. Employers are sensitive to the fact that once these plans are put into place, it is the employer that will have to manage these costs in the future, in spite of increasing rates of inflation associated with some of these benefits.

According to the 2015 Employer Health Benefit Survey, "in 2015, the average annual premiums for employer-sponsored health insurance are $6,251 (up from $6,025 in 2014) for single coverage and $17,545 (up from $16,834 in 2014) for family coverage. The single premium is four percent higher and the family premium is also four percent higher than the 2014 average premiums. During the same period workers' wages increased 1.9 percent and inflation decreased by 0.2 percent. Over the last 10 years, the average premium for family coverage has increased 61 percent" as indicated in the following chart:

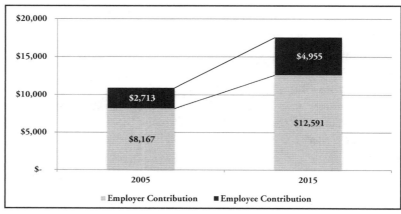

EXAMPLE 1.1

The following is an example of how basic employee benefits (including health, life, and disability insurance; a 401(k) match; and reasonable vacation, personal, and holiday time) can increase employer payroll costs. In this case, the employer paid the employee a $40,000 salary and incurred $14,998 in additional benefits. These costs vary depending on the benefits offered, the age of the employee (insurance), and the salary received. There may also be other expenses, such as worker's compensation insurance and unemployment taxes (not intended to equal averages above).

	Amount	% of Compensation
Salary	**$40,000**	
Social Security	$3,060	7.65%
Health Insurance Premiums Paid	$6,500	16.25%
Life and Disability Insurance Premiums Paid	$700	1.75%
401(k) Employer Match	$1,200	3.00%
Vacation Time - 10 Days	$1,538	3.85%
Personal Time - 5 Days	$769	1.92%
Holiday Time - 8 Days	$1,231	3.08%
	$14,998	37.50%

The reasons that employers establish employee benefits and retirement plans are principally business related. Such plans have a positive impact on the ability to attract, reward, and retain qualified employees. The two leading reasons employers do not sponsor such plans are affordability and a lack of faith that such plans would have a positive effect on production and profitability.

Unfortunately, most small business owners are no more well informed about retirement plans and employee benefits than the workers they employ. There are a number of retirement plans that cost the employer little or nothing and would greatly benefit both the owner and the employees. Such plans are widely available but unknown or not understood by small business owners. Approximately one-third of small business owners have never heard of a SIMPLE plan, which has low costs and a positive impact on retirement planning.

Large employers are more likely than small employers to have a wide variety of employee benefits and a retirement plan. These employers have human resource departments that help select and administer employee benefit and retirement plans. The human resource departments make use of outside professional institutions and experts in plan selection, plan communication, and plan administration. The professionals include actuaries, pension experts, ERISA attorneys, employee benefit consultants, investment advisors, and plan administrators.

COMMON EMPLOYER PERSPECTIVES OF RETIREMENT PLANS	EXHIBIT 1.6

- Employers view retirement plans and employee benefits as part of overall compensation costs.
- Employee benefit expenses may add 30% - 40% to payroll costs.
- Employers use employee benefit plans to recruit, hire, and retain qualified workers.

PROFESSIONALS AND INSTITUTIONS

There are a wide array of professionals and experts providing services in the areas of retirement planning, retirement plans, and employee benefits. There are also large financial institutions that manage plan assets (investments), administer plans, and communicate plan information to plan participants. Professionals within these financial institutions include personal financial planners or advisors who assist individuals and small business owners; actuaries whose primary role is in defined benefit or target benefit pension plans; pension experts and ERISA attorneys who assist in plan selection or creation, implementation, and communication; valuation experts who are used to value closely-held stock held in retirement plans; pension administrators who manage plan assets and communicate plan information to participants; Certified Public Accountants and other tax preparers who file required tax compliance reports; insurance planning professionals; and investment advisors who may advise either employers, plan participants, or both.

Major financial institutions play a role in the retirement plan area by providing prototype retirement plans for the convenience of customers, taking assets under management, and serving as custodians of assets. These institutions may also provide employee benefit plans and include insurance companies, banks, investment houses, and mutual fund companies.

Because of the complex nature of the entire field, any one of these experts may only be an expert in a small portion of the whole field. However, it is essential that advisors have a solid working knowledge of all of the areas and understand what each expert contributes so they can advise both employees and employers accordingly.

Case Study 1.1

WWL is a talk radio station in New Orleans, Louisiana, broadcasting on 870 AM to the gulf coast and is now owned by Entercom Communications. The station has its beginnings at Loyola University, a Jesuit university that sought permission and was granted permission from the Vatican to own a radio station. It first began broadcasting in March 1922 and was finally sold in 1989 by Loyola to build the university's endowment fund.

From a tax perspective, WWL is an interesting example of how the government creates laws that may help or hinder certain industries or businesses. Internal revenue Code (IRC) §512 deals with unrelated business taxable income (UBTI). IRC §512(b)(15) is reproduced below:

Except as provided in paragraph (4), in the case of a trade or business -

512(b)(15)(A) **w**hich consists of providing services under license issued by a Federal regulatory agency,

512(b)(15)(B) **w**hich is carried on by a religious order or by an educational organization described in §170(b)(1)(A)(ii) maintained by such religious order, and which was so carried on before May 27, 1959, and

512(b)(15)(C) **l**ess than 10 percent of the net income of which for each taxable year is used for activities which are not related to the purpose constituting the basis for the religious order's exemption, there shall be excluded all gross income derived from such trade or business and all deductions directly connected with the carrying on of such trade or business, so long as it is established to the satisfaction of the Secretary that the rates or other charges for such services are competitive with rates or other charges charged for similar services by persons not exempt from taxation.

Notice that the first word for IRC §512(b)(15)(A),(B) and (C) begin with the letters WWL. The drafting of this code section was no accident. Nor is the code section an accident. The exclusion in this section was intended to benefit Loyola University specifically and its ownership of WWL and was attributed to Senator Russell Long of Louisiana. It also serves as an example of how the government can and does create laws that can help or hinder specific businesses or industries.

PROFESSIONALS AND INSTITUTIONS INTERESTED IN RETIREMENT PLANNING

EXHIBIT
1.7

INTERESTED PROFESSIONALS

- Actuaries
- Pension Consultants
- Valuation Experts
- Financial Planners
- Employee Benefit Consultants
- ERISA Attorneys
- Certified Public Accountants
- Plan Administrators
- Insurance Professionals

INTERESTED INSTITUTIONS

- Banks
- Mutual Funds
- Insurance Companies
- Wirehouses and Brokerage Firms

According to the Investment Company Institute, there was approximately $23 trillion in retirement assets in the U.S. as of the third quarter of 2015. This includes Individual Retirement Accounts (IRAs), SEP IRAs, Roth IRAs, employee-sponsored defined contribution plans, state and local government plans, private and federal defined benefit plans, and annuities, with the largest areas of growth being defined contribution plans and IRAs.

RETIREMENT ASSETS IN THE U.S., 2015 (THIRD QUARTER)[1]

EXHIBIT
1.8

IRAs (including rollovers)	$7.27 Trillion
Defined Contribution Plans	$6.52 Trillion
State and Local Government Retirement Plans	$3.56 Trillion
Private Defined Benefit Plans	$2.81 Trillion
Federal Pension Plans	$1.44 Trillion
Annuities	$1.87 Trillion
TOTAL	$23.46 Trillion (**rounded**)

1. ICI.org.

EXHIBIT
1.9

RETIREMENT ASSETS 1975-2015 (THIRD QUARTER) (IN BILLIONS OF DOLLARS)

	1975	1980	1985	1990	1995	2000	2005	2006	2007	2008	2009	2010	2011	2012	2013	2014	3Q2015
Series1	$469	$991	$2,320	$3,923	$6,979	$11,56	$14,41	$16,47	$17,73	$13,94	$16,13	$17,94	$18,15	$19,83	$22,79	$24,16	$23,46

GOVERNMENT

The U.S. Government has a fundamental interest in employer-sponsored private retirement plans and privately-sponsored employee benefit plans. The government, as sponsor of the Social Security program and its benefits (retirement, disability, and survivorship) and health care benefits for retirees over age 65 through Medicare, is greatly concerned that Social Security contributions (funded through payroll taxes) may be insufficient to meet promised benefits. The government has a vested interest in promoting employee benefits such as employer-sponsored health care plans and retirement plans to mitigate the risk of more people ending up in the public welfare system. The government uses tax policy to make retirement plans and employee benefit plans sufficiently attractive so that a large number of employers will adopt them.

Keep in mind, however, that what the government gives out with one hand, it may take back with the other. Consider when studying these areas that while there are advantages to all these plans, usually in the form of current tax relief, there are also disadvantages, usually in the form of compliance, costs, and future taxes. The trillions in retirement assets combined with the annual contributions to retirement plans, is expected to grow significantly and will produce trillions in tax revenues. Both the Department of Labor and the Internal Revenue Service play an important role in these areas as does the Pension Benefit Guaranty Corporation (PBGC).

GOVERNMENT PERSPECTIVE OF RETIREMENT

EXHIBIT 1.10

- The government promotes social changes through tax legislation.
- The government sponsors the Social Security and Medicare systems, which act as a safety net for individual workers.
- The government has a vested interest in taxing deferred accounts.

PERSPECTIVE OF THE TEXT

The perspective of this text is that of a professional advisor who is providing professional services to workers and employers in the following areas:

- retirement funding
- retirement plan selection
- Social Security benefits
- employee benefits

In order to provide the highest level of service to the client, the advisor must have a thorough knowledge of retirement funding and forecasting. The advisor must also have a working knowledge of which qualified plans are appropriate for large employers given the goals and the employees census, which qualified plans are appropriate for small to medium size businesses, and which qualified plans are appropriate for single or few employee professionals.

The advisor needs to know the advantages and disadvantages of qualified plans and other tax-advantaged plans. The advisor needs to know when to use a nonqualified plan and how nonqualified plans fit into an employer's executive compensation plan.

Advisors need a deep understanding of retirement, disability, and survivorship benefits provided by Social Security and the benefits provided by Medicare to properly advise clients of the government sponsored safety net programs and to determine any gaps that need to be filled to meet client goals or needs.

EXHIBIT
1.11

OVERVIEW OF TEXT

The text covers retirement funding issues, a thorough understanding of qualified plans, other tax-advantaged plans, as well as Social Security, deferred compensation arrangements and employee benefits. It is organized as follows:

Chapter(s)	Topic
2	Retirement Accumulations and Distributions
3	Qualified Plan Overview
4	Qualified Pension Plans
5	Profit Sharing Plans
6	Stock Bonus Plans and Employee Stock Ownership Plans
7	Distributions from Qualified Plans
8	Installation, Administration, and Termination of Qualified Plans
9	IRAs and SEPs
10	SIMPLEs, 403(b) Plans, and 457 Plans
11	Social Security
12	Deferred Compensation and Nonqualified Plans
13	Employee Benefits: Fringe Benefits
14	Employee Benefits: Group Benefits
15	Item Sets & the Mike and Maria Roman Case

HISTORY OF THE EMPLOYMENT-BASED RETIREMENT SYSTEM

EXHIBIT
1.12

Employers established retirement plans in the late 19th century in the absence of any tax advantages, although the government began granting tax-favored treatment to plans in the 1920s. After the Social Security system was established in 1935, employment-based retirement plans became widespread. In recent years, Congress has enacted legislation to regulate retirement plans more carefully and to allow employees to actively participate in certain types of employment-based plans.

Retirement Plans Prior to Tax Incentives

Formal retirement plans in the United States developed in tandem with shifts in family ties and in the nature of the business world. Urbanization weakened the extended family, which formerly had helped support those who were too old to work. In addition, the number of elderly people grew rapidly as earlier immigrants aged and life spans increased.

Large corporations needed systematic, publicly acceptable ways of moving elderly workers out of their jobs. Pensions were considered one solution that also provided an incentive to younger employees to stay with an employer throughout their working life. By 1929, about 15 percent of private-sector employees were covered by employment-based plans, which were concentrated in large corporations and in sectors in which government oversight tended to be the strongest.

The Government Gets Involved

The Revenue Acts of 1921, 1926, and 1928 initiated tax advantages for employment-based retirement plans. The 1921 law allowed employers to deduct contributions to profit-sharing and stock bonus plans from their taxable income. Employees, in turn, were allowed to delay recognizing contributions to those plans as taxable income until the contributions were withdrawn. The legislation also exempted the investment earnings of such plans until withdrawal. The 1926 law extended those advantages to pensions, while the 1928 law allowed sponsoring employers to deduct contributions for past as well as current service.

On the basis of the reported debate, it appears that Congress's exempting of the earnings of stock bonus and profit-sharing plans from taxation in 1921 was primarily intended to motivate workers to be more productive; increasing saving was a secondary consideration. Lawmakers' intentions in exempting pension plans in 1926 are less clear because there was no floor debate or discussion documented in committee reports. The provisions might have been intended to assist employers' nascent benefit plans or to resolve, in a purely technical way, the difficult problem of assigning trust income to a taxable entity.

Whatever the intent of those provisions, their enactment had little effect on the development of employment-based retirement plans in those years. Low tax rates held down the value of the benefits, so employers had little incentive to use them. Moreover, the provisions were barely in place when the Great Depression reversed the evolutionary trend of retirement plans: many employers terminated their plans, and a number of them failed to pay the benefits they had already promised to their workers.

Because employers' failure to pay promised benefits was exceptionally disruptive to the railroad industry, the federal government stepped in and established the Railroad Retirement system in 1935 to enable the depleted pension funds to meet their obligations. In that same year, lawmakers enacted the first Social Security legislation (although initially it covered only a portion of the labor force). Symptomatic of the general decline of employer-sponsored plans was the nearly total absence of any mention of them in the report of Congress's Committee on Economic Security in 1935.

By the late 1930s, however, retirement plans had revived enough to generate concerns about their being used primarily as tax-avoidance schemes for the wealthy. Accordingly, Congress passed the Revenue Act of 1938, which made pension and profit-sharing trusts irrevocable. The Revenue Act of 1942 established conditions that employer-sponsored plans had to meet before they qualified for tax-favored treatment. The 1942 law introduced the concepts of nondiscriminatory coverage and nondiscrimination in benefits and contributions, provisions that form the core of today's regulation of employment-based retirement plans. During World War II, pensions became a desirable form of compensation for two reasons: first, tax rates were very high and, second, contributions to pensions were exempted from wage controls. After the war, more and more employers began to offer pensions because tax rates remained high, Social Security benefits had been eroded by wartime inflation, and labor unions were successful in making pensions subject to collective bargaining.

Developments in the 1970s and 1980s

Changes in the tax code in recent years reflect evolving standards of adequacy and fairness in allocating the tax benefits associated with retirement plans. Lawmakers enacted plans in 1962 for self-employed workers and other noncorporate employers that were more tightly restricted than corporate plans. The Employee Retirement Income Security Act of 1974 (ERISA) considerably tightened the qualification rules for employers' plans. ERISA gave the federal government authority to prescribe a uniform meaning for plan rules and legislated minimum standards for participation, investing, the accrual of benefits, and funding.

Between 1974 and 1986, Congress pursued two different lines of policy. On one hand, it enhanced access to the tax-advantages of qualified plans in ways that emphasized individual decision making. The Revenue Act of 1978 sanctioned so-called salary-reduction arrangements in profit-sharing plans - now known as 401(k) plans - and in the state and local government sectors (§457 plans). Similarly flexible arrangements had already been possible in the nonprofit sector under §403(b) of the tax code. Then, in the Federal Employees Retirement System Act of 1986, Congress extended salary-reduction opportunities to all federal civilian employees. Although operated by employers, salary-reduction arrangements shift several key decisions from employers to workers, allowing participants to determine how much will be contributed and, in many cases, how that money will be invested.

On the other hand, lawmakers enacted changes that further constrained employer practices by emphasizing the collective or forced-saving aspects of pensions. Examples are the top-heavy plan rules in the Tax Equity and Fiscal Responsibility Act of 1982 (TEFRA) and the protections extended to widows in the Retirement Equity Act of 1984. TEFRA also eliminated differences between qualified plans maintained by corporate and noncorporate employers.

The Tax Reform Act of 1986 (TRA-86) reversed the trend toward individual control over retirement saving by lowering the maximum amount of compensation that could be deferred under 401(k) plans: whereas earlier law allowed annual deferrals of up to $30,000, TRA-86 limited them to only $7,000. But the law also extended a trend toward greater sharing of benefits among a firm's employees, primarily through stricter requirements for the inclusion of employees in retirement plans, faster vesting of benefits, and smaller offsets of plan benefits because of Social Security. Separately, the law's lowering of tax rates reduced the value of the tax advantages.

Recent Legislative Activity

During the 1990s, lawmakers sounded a theme of simplification. The various restrictions that the tax code placed on employers offering retirement plans were seen as placing an undue burden on small businesses that would probably discourage them from setting up plans. The Small Business Job Protection Act of 1996 established two new options (called SIMPLEs) for employers of 100 or fewer workers. Those plans allowed eligible employers to contribute to their employees' 401(k) plans or IRAs without being subject to nondiscrimination rules and the other tests that qualified plans must meet. In return for exempting employers from those requirements, the law specified formulas as the basis for employers' contributions.

In 2001, Congress passed the Economic Growth and Tax Relief Reconciliation Act (EGTRRA), which contained a variety of provisions that liberalized employment-based retirement plans. The law allows employers to contribute more to the retirement plans of high-income employees and to deduct more of what they contribute to all retirement plans. Employees are also allowed to contribute more to 401(k)-type plans on their own behalf. Additional provisions establish a credit for expenses incurred by small businesses in starting up a retirement plan and administering it for the first three years. They also enhance portability by permitting rollovers from one type of employment-based plan to another and from IRAs to employment-based plans.

In 2006, Congress passed The Pension Protection Act of 2006 (PPA), which was signed into law on August 17, 2006. The PPA 2006 is the most sweeping pension legislation in over 30 years and includes a number of significant tax incentives to enhance and protect retirement savings for millions of Americans. One of its primary focal points is to force companies to fully fund obligations under defined benefit plans.

The Small Business Jobs Act of 2010 provided for Roth Accounts in 457 Plans and created the in-plan Roth rollover, which allows plan balances in traditionally deferred accounts within qualified plans to be converted to Roth accounts.

The American Taxpayer Relief Act of 2012 made permanent many of the provisions in EGTRRA 2001 and increased the funds that could be converted in an in-plan Roth rollover.

RETIREMENT PLANNING ACCUMULATIONS AND DISTRIBUTIONS

LEARNING OBJECTIVES

After reading this chapter, you should be able to:

1. Identify the factors affecting retirement planning.
2. Draw the exponential graph representing the required investment assets as a percent of gross pay at various ages to age 65.
3. Explain why saving early is usually better than saving later.
4. Explain the impact of inflation on purchasing power.
5. Identify the costs that may decrease and those that may increase from pre-retirement to retirement.
6. Distinguish between the top down and the bottom up approaches in determining the wage replacement ratio.
7. Identify the various sources of retirement income.
8. Calculate the capital needs analysis using an annuity approach.
9. Calculate the capital needs analysis using a capital preservation approach.
10. Calculate the capital needs analysis using a purchasing power approach.
11. Discuss the various methods for sensitivity analysis as it is applied to capital needs analysis.
12. Compare two of the common approaches to managing withdrawals for retirement income.

FACTORS AFFECTING RETIREMENT PLANNING

Individuals face many decisions regarding retirement planning. In particular, they must decide what retirement means to them. Does retirement mean withdrawing from the workforce when financially able, or does it mean changes in lifestyle and family situations? For most, it is a momentous lifestyle change resulting from a significant shift in how they spend their time, money, and energy.

Adequate retirement planning requires an understanding of the factors that affect retirement planning and the proper interrelationships of these factors. While this chapter discusses the major factors affecting retirement planning, it does not examine every factor that affects retirement planning. The most significant factors are:

- the remaining work life expectancy (RWLE)
- the savings amount and rate
- the wage replacement ratio (WRR)
- inflation expectations
- and other qualitative factors

- the annual income needed (needs) during retirement
- the retirement life expectancy (RLE)
- the sources of retirement income
- investment returns

A retirement plan based on these factors must produce sufficient income at retirement to ensure that a comfortable pre-retirement lifestyle is maintained throughout the retirement period. A discussion of each factor, its associated risks, and the calculations essential to retirement planning (capital needs analysis) is presented below.

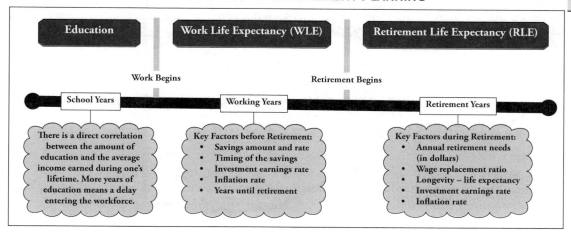

FACTORS AFFECTING RETIREMENT PLANNING

EXHIBIT
2.1

REMAINING WORK LIFE EXPECTANCY (RWLE)

Work life expectancy (WLE) is the period of time a person is expected to be in the work force. This time period may be as long as 30 to 40 years and is essential in retirement planning because it is the period during which one saves and accumulates funds to use during retirement. Increasing or decreasing the work life expectancy impacts the time period over which individuals can save for retirement. The United States has seen a substantial decline in the overall WLE in the last several decades primarily due to individuals pursuing advanced education (undergraduate and graduate degrees), delaying their entry into the workforce, and those taking early retirement, which hastens their exit from the workforce.

Normal retirement has historically occurred at age 65 primarily because Social Security designated it as such and other employer provided retirement plans followed suit. The age at which recipients of Social Security can begin receiving benefits is age 62, but they must wait until Full Retirement Age to receive their full benefits under the system. Until recently, the average retirement age in the United States had steadily decreased since the 1970s due to a variety of factors including early retirement options from employer plans, early retirement under Social Security, and to some extent, positive investment performance during the 1980s and 1990s increasing retirees' wealth.

However, Census Bureau data show that the trend of earlier retirement is reversing and the age at which people are retiring has risen over the last several years. For example, in 2010, 35.8 percent of men aged 65 to 69 were employed, compared with 27.9 percent in 1990 and 30.2 percent in 2000. Among women 65 to 69 years old, 26.4 percent were working in 2010, compared with 16.9 percent in 1990 and 19.9 percent in 2000.[1]

This trend of delaying retirement is due to a variety of factors, but heavily impacted by economic issues. The stock market crash of 2008 and the lingering recession beginning in 2008 has severely impacted the wealth of those that are contemplating retirement.[2] There also appears to be a trend

---

1. U.S. Census Bureau: Labor Force Participation and Work Status of People 65 Years and Older, January 2013.

of partial retirement, where an employee will continue working but on a reduced schedule. This transition allows employers to reduce cost but maintain experienced employees. The Pension Protection Act of 2006 provided an opportunity for employees to begin receiving pension benefits while employed after the attainment of age 62.

The trends discussed above are illustrated in the following chart.

EXHIBIT
2.2

LABOR FORCE PARTICIPATION FOR WORKERS 65 AND OLDER

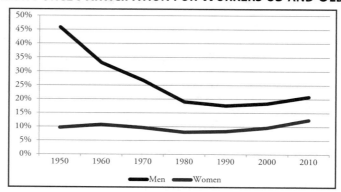

U.S. Bureau of Labor Statistics

Exhibit 2.2 illustrates the retirement age steadily declining over the last six decades, but increasing in the most recent years. According to research done by the Center for Retirement Research, based on US Census data, the average retirement age for men increased from age 62 to age 64 over the last 20 years. In addition, they found that the average age of retirement for women is age 62.[3] It is important for advisors to understand this information because it can provide them with a benchmark to use when calculating retirement needs. Thus, the advisor needs to talk with the client to determine the age the client is planning to retire.

KEY CONCEPTS

1. What are the major factors affecting retirement planning?

2. Define work life expectancy and retirement life expectancy.

3. When will most clients retire?

4. Explain the work life expectancy/retirement life expectancy dilemma.

The **remaining work life expectancy (RWLE)** is the work period that remains at a given point in time before retirement. For example, a 30-year-old client who expects to retire at age 65 has a RWLE of 35 years. Determining the RWLE is important for the advisors because it tells the advisor the remaining number of years the client has to save for retirement.

---

2. It should be noted that retirement assets were $17.9 trillion in 2007 and dropped to $13.9 trillion in 2008, but have increased to over $23 trillion at the end of the third quarter of 2015. (http://www.ici.org)
3. What is the Average Retirement Age?, Alicia H. Munnell, Center for Retirement Research at Boston College, August 2011.

RETIREMENT LIFE EXPECTANCY (RLE)

Retirement life expectancy (RLE) is the time period beginning at retirement and extending until death. Currently, many retirees live as long as 20 to 40 years in retirement. However, this longevity has not always been the case. In 1900, the average life expectancy for a newborn child was 47 years[4], and many individuals worked as long as they were able. During this time, the country was more agrarian and families lived together. As family members aged, they were cared for by the younger members of the family. There was not an official "retirement period." The concept of retirement, as we know it today, did not exist. Exhibit 2.3 presents data depicting the increase in life expectancy at birth from 1949 to 2013 and Exhibit 2.4 depicts the increase in life expectancy at age 65.

Population trends provide the advisor with a good understanding of how long a person may live in their retirement. Women born in 2013 are expected to live on average 81.2 years, while men born in 2013 are expected to live on average 76.4 years. The average woman retiring in 2013 at age 65 would be expected to be in retirement for 20.5 years. Similarly, a man

QUICK QUIZ 2.1

1. Approximately 80% of men work past age 65.
   a. True
   b. False

2. The RLE is the time period beginning at retirement and extending until death.
   a. True
   b. False

3. As the RLE increases because of early retirement, there is generally an increased need of funds to finance the RLE and a shortened WLE in which to save and accumulate assets.
   a. True
   b. False

False, True, True.

retiring in 2013 at age 65 would have a life expectancy of 17.9 years. The problem with this information is that the average life expectancy is just that - an average. Fifty percent of women who were age 65 in 2013 are expected to live longer than 20.5 years and 50 percent of men who were age 65 in 2013 are expected to live longer than 17.9 years. In addition, the older an individual gets, the more likely they are to live beyond their average life expectancy at birth. Proper planning is needed because if the retired individual lives longer than planned for, there is a risk of running out of money. This risk is known as superannuation.

---

4. It should be noted that the life expectancy in 1900 is biased due to a high infant death rate at the time.

EXHIBIT
2.3

LIFE EXPECTANCY AT BIRTH (U.S. 1949 - 2013)

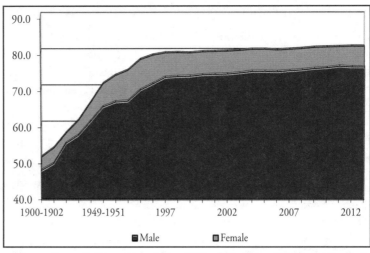

Source: Centers for Disease Control, Trend Tables, United States 2014 (www.cdc.gov)

EXHIBIT
2.4

LIFE EXPECTANCY AT AGE 65 (U.S. 1949 - 2013)

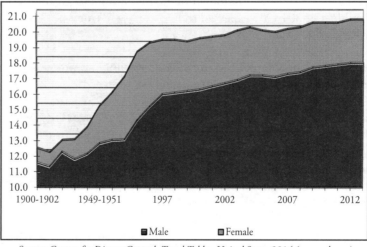

Source: Centers for Disease Control, Trend Tables, United States 2014 (www.cdc.gov)

THE WLE AND THE RLE RELATIONSHIP

It is important to understand the WLE and the RLE relationship. Since there is a fixed time between life and death, each period of time changes inversely with the other. If the WLE increases or decreases, the individual must shorten or lengthen the pre-work life expectancy (PWLE) or RLE. Thus, the advisor must estimate each period to determine the ability to save and the financial needs while in retirement. When clients are unable to save adequately, the advisor and the client can adjust the periods in order to meet the client's needs. For example, if a client is unable to meet the needed retirement goal at age 62, the advisor can discuss lengthening the WLE by continuing to work and, thus, shortening the RLE in order to meet the retirement need. Exhibit 2.5 visually depicts this relationship.

THE WLE/RLE DILEMMA

EXHIBIT
2.5

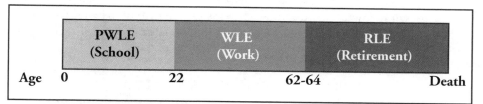

The area to the left of WLE represents the prework life expectancy (PWLE), which continues until the person enters the work force on a full time basis. Generally, the PWLE ends between the ages of 18 to 26, with the average age at 22. The middle area, the work life expectancy (WLE), represents the period of working years prior to retirement. This period begins at the end of the PWLE and ends at the beginning of retirement. The retirement life expectancy (RLE) usually begins around age 62 and ends around age 85 but may continue beyond age 100. Notice that as the RLE period increases due to early retirement and longer life expectancy, there is an increased need to finance the RLE and a shortened WLE in which to save and accumulate assets. Careful planning is needed long before the attainment of the desired retirement age to meet the funding requirements for a financially secure retirement.

SAVINGS AND INVESTMENT ISSUES

The savings amount, the savings rate, the timing of savings, and investment decisions are important concepts in retirement planning. If people were adequately saving for retirement beginning at an early age (25 to 35), they would need to save approximately 10 to 13 percent of their gross annual income and invest in a broad portfolio of growth investments over their entire work life to adequately fund their retirement goal (see the following exhibit). They would need to be ever mindful of investment returns and inflation to ensure sufficient savings and accumulations. Unfortunately, as demonstrated later in this chapter, most of our society saves at a much lower savings rate than is necessary to adequately fund retirement, is not investment savvy, and is insensitive to the impact of inflation over long periods of time.

SAVINGS BALANCE FROM AGE 25 TO AGE 100

EXHIBIT
2.6

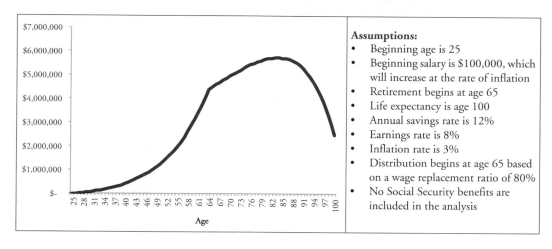

THE SAVINGS AMOUNT

If individuals do not begin saving at an early age, then they must save a greater amount of their gross earnings to compensate for the missed years of contributions and compounding of investment returns. Exhibit 2.7 illustrates the amount individuals must save if they begin saving at different ages.

EXHIBIT
2.7

REQUIRED SAVINGS RATE FOR RETIREMENT
(ASSUME $0 OF ACCUMULATED SAVINGS AT THE BEGINNING AGE)

Age Beginning Regular and Recurring Savings*	Savings (as percent of gross pay) Rate Required to Create Appropriate Capital*
25 - 35	10 - 13%
35 - 45	13 - 20%
45 - 55	20 - 40%**

*Assumes appropriate asset allocation for reasonable-risk investor through accumulation year; also assumes normal raises and an 80 percent wage replacement ratio at Social Security normal retirement age and includes Social Security retirement benefits.

** At age 55, the person will realistically have to delay retirement until age 70.

Exhibit 2.7 illustrates a significant problem with delaying saving for retirement, namely, the need to save large amounts because there is less savings time to accumulate a sufficient amount of capital to retire. Saving requires foregoing current consumption and most individuals find it difficult to decrease consumption by 20 to 30 percent, especially when they have been accustomed to maintaining a certain standard of living.

Consider Exhibit 2.8 that depicts the required annual savings percentage based on the time until retirement and the rate of return earned on invested assets.[5] Notice that if the RWLE is shortened from 40 years to 30 years and the portfolio continues to earn 8 percent that the contribution increases from 12 percent to 22 percent. This example helps illustrate the importance of beginning a savings program early.

KEY CONCEPTS

1. What are the savings and investment concepts that are important to retirement planning?

2. Why is it important to begin to save early for retirement planning?

3. Why is it important to understand investment decisions and their consequences in retirement planning?

4. How is inflation relevant to retirement planning?

5. Exhibit 2.6 used future dollars whereas Exhibit 2.8 uses today's dollars. The inflation rate remains at 3 percent, so the real rate of earnings at 8 percent is 4.8544 percent. The target future value is $1,399,103, which is the future value (in today's dollars) based on the same assumptions as Exhibit 2.5.

REQUIRED ANNUAL SAVINGS PERCENTAGE[6]

EXHIBIT
2.8

Based on Exhibit 2.6 Assumptions		Number of Years Until Retirement						
		40	35	30	25	20	15	10
Rate of Return	4%	29%	34%	40%	50%	64%	87%	134%
	5%	23%	28%	35%	44%	58%	81%	128%
	6%	19%	24%	30%	39%	53%	76%	123%
	7%	15%	19%	25%	34%	48%	70%	117%
	8%	12%	16%	22%	30%	43%	66%	112%
	9%	9%	13%	18%	26%	39%	61%	107%
	10%	7%	11%	15%	23%	35%	57%	102%
	11%	6%	9%	13%	20%	31%	52%	98%
	12%	4%	7%	11%	17%	28%	49%	93%

As an alternative to Exhibit 2.7, consider Exhibit 2.9, which assumes that each person is saving 10 to 13 percent of gross pay, including any employer retirement plan contributions. Assuming that the person saves 10 to 13 percent and also has an investment account balance equal to what they need at each age, they are making adequate progress toward the goal of financial security. If the person does not have the appropriate investment assets or has a lower savings rate, the problem will eventually surface. Therefore, both investment assets and the savings rate are relevant.

BENCHMARK FOR INVESTMENT ASSETS AS A PERCENTAGE OF GROSS PAY

EXHIBIT
2.9

Age	Investment Assets as a Ratio to Gross Pay Needed at Varying Ages
25	0.20 : 1
30	0.6 - 0.8 : 1
35	1.6 - 1.8 : 1
45	3 - 4 : 1
55	8 - 10 : 1
65	16 - 20 : 1

The benchmarks as calculated consider incomes between $50,000 and $350,000, inflation at approximately two to three percent, a balanced investment portfolio of 60 / 40 equities to bonds returning five percent over inflation, a savings rate of 10 to 13 percent of gross pay, and a wage replacement ratio of 80 percent of gross pay. To the extent that any of these assumptions are incorrect for a particular person, the results may be misleading and require a specific personal calculation. These benchmarks are only a beginning.

Note that Exhibit 2.9 illustrates that a person planning to retire at age 65 will need investment assets approximately 16 to 20 times the pre-retirement gross pay. A person at age 55 who plans to

---

6. The exhibit above uses the same assumptions as Exhibit 2.5. This result is the same as in Exhibit 2.5. Note also that as the time until retirement decreases, the required savings percentage increases significantly. Remember that this example includes zero savings at the beginning of the problem (PV = $0.00).

retire at 65 will need investment assets equal to eight times their current gross pay and will need to continue to save 10 to 13 percent of gross pay, including any employer contributions, to achieve adequate retirement funding. More precise calculations are addressed throughout this chapter. While this is only a benchmark, it works well for incomes between $50,000 and $350,000, inflation at two to three percent, and a balanced portfolio earning about five percent over inflation.

Exhibit 2.9 also illustrates that a tremendous amount of the retirement asset accumulation occurs toward the end of the working years (ages 55 to 65). This increase is attributable to the compounding that occurs during the last ten years based on the accumulation at age 55. Assuming that returns during this ten-year period are average, the accumulated assets should be what was expected. However, if the last ten years under perform from an investment return perspective, the investor may have to delay retirement or reduce his needs during retirement.

Assume Carrie, age 45, comes to you and is currently earning $100,000 per year. She has $350,000 (3.5 times her annual earnings) of investment assets (cash, mutual funds, retirement funds, etc.), not including personal use assets (equity in personal residence) and is saving $10,000 of her gross pay (10%). Carrie is concerned about making adequate progress towards her retirement goals. Assuming that Carrie is invested in an appropriate investment portfolio, she appears to be making adequate progress towards retirement if that is her only goal. Note that she will have to save more if she wants to spend longer in retirement. Assume she can earn 8% with inflation of 3%. She will run out of money at age 89.

Step 1: Determine Future Income at Age 65	
Current Earnings - PV	$100,000
Inflation - I	3%
WLE - N	20 years
Future Earnings - FV	$180,611
Step 2: Determine Needs at Retirement	
WRR	80%
Retirement Payment	$144,489 ($180,611 x 80%)
Step 3: Project Savings at Retirement	
Current Assets - PV	$350,000
Annual Savings - PMT	$10,000
Earnings Rate - I	8%
Work Life Expectancy - N	20 years
Assets at Retirement - FV	$2,088,955
Step 4: Determine Period of Time Funds will Last	
Asset at Retirement - PV	($2,088,955)
Annual Inflation Adjusted Annuity Payment - PMT_{AD}	$144,489
Inflation Adjusted Earnings Rate - I	4.85437 ((1.08/1.03)-1) x 100
Funds at End - FV	$0
Years in Retirement that Funds will Last (Approximate)	24 Years

*Note that savings amount will increase each year with raises.

SAVINGS RATE

The **savings rate** identifies the average savings amount in the U.S. based on consumption. The savings rate is interpreted as personal saving as a percentage of disposable personal income. According to the Bureau of Economic Analysis, the personal savings rate has declined significantly since the 1980s. In fact, the personal savings rate fell to 2.6 percent in 2005, but has increased since that time. Exhibit 2.10 illustrates the sharp decline. The growth in personal expenditures may be the cause of the drop in savings over the past few years and suggests that individuals are not saving enough for retirement. This low savings rate identifies a major concern for all advisors. Recall that in order to meet just the retirement goal, a savings rate of 10 to 13 percent of gross pay over a long period is necessary. Unfortunately, most people are not well prepared for retirement, in terms of accumulated savings.

U.S. PERSONAL SAVINGS RATE (1961-2015)

EXHIBIT 2.10

TIMING OF SAVINGS

The earlier a person saves, the greater the number of future compounding periods available prior to retirement. A greater number of compounding periods leads to a lower required savings rate and a larger accumulation of capital at retirement. When saving is delayed, the power of compounding is lost and individuals must compensate by saving a greater percentage of their disposable income.

> Lori saves $2,500 a year from age 25 until age 34 (inclusive) and invests the money in an account earning eight percent annually. Lori stops investing at age 34, but does not withdraw the accumulation until age 65. Lori's accumulation at age 65 is $393,588 even though she only deposited $25,000. In contrast, Peter saves $2,500 a year from age 35 until age 65 inclusively and invests in a similar account to Lori, earning eight percent annually. Even though Peter saved $52,500 more than Lori, he will have accumulated $85,223 less than Lori at age 65. The deposits and balance at age 65 for Lori and Peter are presented in Exhibit 2.11.

EXAMPLE 2.2

EXHIBIT
2.11

TIME/SAVINGS EXAMPLE (ACCUMULATION AT AGE 65, ORDINARY ANNUITY)

	Lori	Peter
Total Invested (10 Years)	$25,000	$77,500 (30 Years)
Balance at age 65	$393,588	$308,365
Earnings Rate	8%	8%

While Peter invested more than three times as much as Lori, Lori has 22 percent more than Peter at age 65. This result demonstrates the power of compound earnings over the longer period of 41 years versus 31 years. Exhibit 2.12 illustrates this phenomenon graphically.

EXHIBIT
2.12

ACCUMULATION OF UNEQUAL DEPOSITS OVER VARYING TIME PERIODS

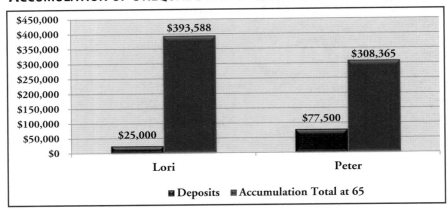

INVESTMENT CONSIDERATIONS

A successful retirement plan is dependent on a successful investment plan. A retirement plan is dependent on savings over time, but is also dependent on the earnings and growth of those funds during the asset accumulation phase and throughout retirement. In Exhibit 2.6, with the 25-year old saving 12 percent of his income for 40 years earning 8 percent, approximately 80 percent of the savings balance at retirement is from investment earnings.

An investment plan must take into consideration the risk tolerance of the investor as well as the time horizon of the goal. In addition, consideration must be given to historical and expected returns from the various asset classes, diversification, and the types of assets included in tax-deferred accounts versus taxable accounts. All of these factors go into constructing a portfolio to achieve specific goals, such as retirement planning.

The risk tolerance of an investor is essentially the willingness and ability to accept risk for potential returns. As indicated below, assets with larger returns typically have larger risks or larger variations in returns. Risk tolerance is typically assessed through questionnaires, an understanding of the investor's experience with risky assets and with the time horizon of the investment goal. If both the willingness and the ability to accept risk are high, the risk tolerance is high. If both the willingness and the ability are low, then the risk tolerance is low. If, however, there is a mismatch between ability and willingness (one high and the other low), then it suggests that the investor may need additional education.

The **suitability** of an investment or portfolio is greatly impacted by the time horizon of an investment goal. Longer-term goals can generally tolerate higher amounts of risk than shorter-term goals. Investments for the accomplishment of short-term goals should generally consist of relatively safe or stable assets, such as short-term debt instruments. Investments for the accomplishment of long-term goals can consist of assets that generate higher returns, but have a tendency to fluctuate more sharply when markets or the economy changes.

When investors are young, their investment portfolio should typically be dominated by common stocks because, due to long time horizons, young investors can generally afford the additional risk of common stocks. As investors near retirement, their asset allocation generally begins to shift so that it becomes less risky while still maintaining some growth component to mitigate against the risk of inflation. It is important to keep in mind that more than 50 percent of individuals who reach the age of 65 will live for more than 20 years. Therefore, equities are a critical ingredient in an investor's (retiree's) portfolio because they provide for growth over longer-term time horizons.

A fundamental understanding of investment choices and their consequences is essential to successful retirement planning. All asset classes do not have the same historical investment returns nor risks. When planning for retirement, it is important to have a historical perspective of investment returns and risks for a wide variety of asset classes. Exhibit 2.13 provides an 82-year perspective on historical investment returns, inflation-adjusted returns, and risk as measured by standard deviation.

HISTORICAL RETURNS, INFLATION-ADJUSTED RETURNS, AND STANDARD DEVIATION OF ASSET CLASSES (1930 - 2012)

EXHIBIT 2.13

Asset Class	Historical Returns	Inflation-Adjusted Returns	Standard Deviation	Real Return After-Tax and Inflation
Small-Capitalization Stocks	12.0%	9.0%	32.0%	5.4%
Large-Capitalization Stocks	10.0%	7.0%	20.0%	4.0%
Long-Term Government Bonds	6.0%	3.0%	10.0%	1.2%
U.S. T-Bills	3.6%	0.6%	3.0%	(0.50%)
Consumer Price Index (CPI)	3.0%	N/A	N/A	N/A

Exhibit 2.13 illustrates the need to choose investments wisely for inclusion within a portfolio based on the risk and return of the asset class. Notice that after inflation, real economic returns are extremely low for fixed-income securities and Treasuries, and these returns are further reduced by the effects of taxation. This suggests that the only way to have real investment growth in an investment portfolio over a long term is to invest at least some portion of the portfolio in common stocks. Common stocks also provide the best hedge against inflation (the loss of purchasing power).

The risk tolerance and time horizon of the investor, as well as the expected risk and returns from various investment choices is considered in constructing an asset allocation and portfolio. The asset allocation is responsible for the majority of variation in returns within the portfolio and is a critical element in retirement planning.

QUICK QUIZ 2.2

1. Our society tends to save at a rate that is adequate for retirement planning.
   a. True
   b. False

2. Fixed-income securities generally provide the best hedge against inflation and loss of purchasing power.
   a. True
   b. False

3. Individuals must consider the impact of inflation when projecting retirement needs.
   a. True
   b. False

False, False, True.

Appropriate Assets for Tax Advantaged and Taxable Accounts

In addition to the asset allocation decision, investors should consider the appropriateness of assets for the different types of investment accounts. Income earned in a taxable account, such as a brokerage or bank account, is subject to current taxation, whereas income earned in a tax-deferred account, such as an IRA, is not subject to current taxation. Because there is a significant difference in the tax rates of capital gains and dividends compared to income from fixed income securities, such as bonds, it is logical to hold fixed income assets in tax-deferred accounts. This decision results in all fixed income securities residing in tax-deferred accounts. However, investors must also consider liquidity needs that are better met through fixed income investments and more easily accessed in taxable accounts. Therefore, there must be a balance between tax efficiency or optimization and the liquidity needs of the investor.

In addition to the asset allocation decision and deciding where to hold fixed income and equity securities, an investor must consider limitations on the types of securities that can be held in various retirement accounts. Some of these issues and limitations are discussed in Chapter 3 on qualified plans, as well as in Chapter 9 for IRAs. Investors managing assets held in IRAs and qualified plans should also be aware of the rules relating to unrelated business taxable income, discussed below.

Unrelated Business Taxable Income

Unrelated business taxable income (UBTI) is a term used to describe income earned by a tax-exempt entity that is subject to taxation. The tax on unrelated business income applies to most organizations exempt from tax under §501(a). These organizations include charitable, religious, scientific, and other corporations described in §501(c), as well as employees' trusts forming part of pension, profit-sharing, and stock bonus plans described in §401(a). In addition, the following are subject to the tax on unrelated business taxable income:

1. Traditional IRAs
2. Roth IRAs
3. Simplified Employee Pensions (SEP-IRAs)
4. Savings Incentive Match Plans for Employees (SIMPLE IRAs)
5. State and municipal colleges and universities
6. Qualified state tuition programs
7. Medical savings accounts (MSAs)
8. Coverdell savings accounts

Because of the UBTI rules, IRAs and qualified plans, in addition to the other entities listed, are impacted if UBTI is earned within the entity. The impact is that the entity has to pay income tax on the UBTI and file Form 990-T if UBTI exceeds $1,000. The purpose of these rules is to prevent a tax-exempt entity from unfairly competing against businesses subject to tax. This concept is reflected in the following excerpt from Treas. Reg. §1.513-1.

> "The primary objective of adoption of the unrelated business income tax was to eliminate a source of unfair competition by placing the unrelated business activities of certain exempt organizations upon the same tax basis as the nonexempt business endeavors with which they compete."

The term "unrelated business taxable income" generally means the gross income derived from any unrelated trade or business regularly carried on by an exempt organization, less the deductions directly connected with carrying on the trade or business. If an organization regularly carries on two or more unrelated business activities, its unrelated business taxable income is the total of gross income from all such activities less the total allowable deductions attributable to all the activities.

Generally, an unrelated trade or business includes one that meets the following three requirements:

1. It is a trade or business,
2. It is regularly carried on, and
3. It is not substantially related to furthering the exempt purpose of the organization.

EXAMPLE 2.3

BU, an exempt scientific organization, enjoys an excellent reputation in the field of biological research. It exploits this reputation regularly by selling endorsements of various items of laboratory equipment to manufacturers. The endorsing of laboratory equipment does not contribute importantly to the accomplishment of any purpose for which exemption is granted BU. Accordingly, the income derived from the sale of endorsements is gross income from unrelated trade or business.

Generally, income in the form of dividends, interest, payments with respect to securities loans, and annuities are excluded in computing unrelated business taxable income. In addition, royalties and rental income are generally not included in determining UBTI. However, investment income that is generally excluded from UBTI must be included to the extent it is derived from debt-financed property. The amount of income included is generally proportionate to the debt on the property.

Typically, a qualified plan, or an IRA, will be subject to the UBTI rules if it:

- Operates a trade or business,
- Owns an interest in a pass through organization, such as a partnership or S corporation, that is operating a trade or business,
- Owns an interest in a master limited partnership, or
- Uses debt to generate portfolio income, as in the case of margin debt.

Bob's IRA owns an interest in Sushi & Saki LLC, a restaurant. The LLC is taxed as a partnership. Because the LLC interest is held in an IRA, the IRA's share of income from the LLC will be subject to UBTI tax.

INFLATION

Inflation causes a loss of purchasing power. If a retiree has a fixed retirement income beginning at age 65 and inflation is three percent, the retiree has a loss of purchasing power of 26 percent in 10 years, 45 percent in 20 years, and 59 percent in 30 years. While Social Security retirement benefits are inflation adjusted, most private pension plans are not. Thus, the advisor must consider the impact of inflation when projecting retirement needs and advise clients to save accordingly. Exhibit 2.14 illustrates the decline in purchasing power over a 50-year period of a $100,000 fixed income with a three percent inflation rate.

Parker is 65 years old and spends $300 per month on groceries. If inflation is 3 percent, he can expect to spend over $540 when he is 85 years old on the same groceries. While an annual 3 percent increase is hardly noticeable in the short term, it amounts to an 80 percent increase over 20 years.

EXHIBIT 2.14

IMPACT OF INFLATION: PURCHASING POWER OF $100,000 OVER 50 YEARS

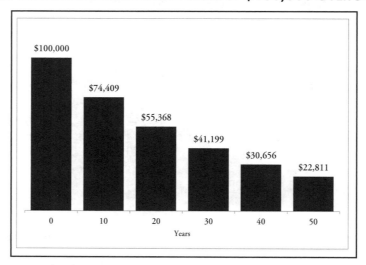

As illustrated, in year 10 the $100,000 has lost 26 percent of its purchasing power. After 10 years, one can only buy $74,409 worth of items using $100,000 of today's dollars. More disturbing is the fact that in year 20, the same person would only be able to purchase $55,368 worth of assets for that same $100,000. Imagine the client that expected to have a carefree retirement in 20 years with the $100,000 income they have today.

IMPACT OF INFLATION OVER 100 YEARS

EXHIBIT 2.15

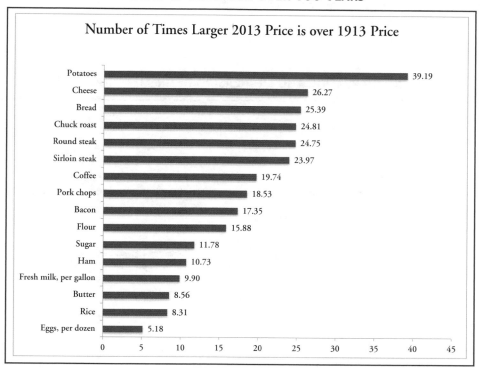

Number of Times Larger 2013 Price is over 1913 Price

Item	Value
Potatoes	39.19
Cheese	26.27
Bread	25.39
Chuck roast	24.81
Round steak	24.75
Sirloin steak	23.97
Coffee	19.74
Pork chops	18.53
Bacon	17.35
Flour	15.88
Sugar	11.78
Ham	10.73
Fresh milk, per gallon	9.90
Butter	8.56
Rice	8.31
Eggs, per dozen	5.18

The exhibit above provides an additional perspective of inflation over long periods of time. It depicts how many times greater the cost of an item is in 2013 compared to the price 100 years earlier. For example, cheese is 26.27 times more expensive in 2013 compared to 1913. Inflation over many years can be a significant obstacle to overcome as retirees attempt to manage their finances and is an important factor to consider in retirement planning.

RETIREMENT NEEDS ANALYSIS

How much money and/or income does a person need to be financially independent? Most people entering retirement intend to maintain the same lifestyle they had immediately prior to retirement. People do not generally reduce their expenses radically during retirement unless it is necessary. When preparing a retirement budget, the budget should have similar expense categories and amounts as the pre-retirement budget with a few adjustments. There are expenses that may increase and there are expenses that may decrease as a person moves into the retirement phase of life. Expenses that may decline in retirement include: (1) costs associated with employment

KEY CONCEPTS

1. List the common factors that increase and decrease retirement income needs.

2. What is the wage replacement ratio?

3. Identify the two alternative methods for calculating the wage replacement ratio.

4. How is the WRR calculated utilizing the two applicable methods?

(certain clothing costs, parking, some meal costs); (2) mortgage costs if the mortgage debt is scheduled to be repaid by retirement; (3) costs of children (tuition, clothes); (4) payroll costs (e.g., FICA); and (5) the cost of savings because the plan will require the use of accumulated savings. For some people, retirement can bring increased spending on travel and other lifestyle changes. Some retirees are also at risk for increases in health care costs. Exhibit 2.16 presents lists of potential decreasing and increasing costs when entering retirement.

EXHIBIT 2.16

BALANCING INCREASING AND DECREASING RETIREMENT INCOME NEEDS

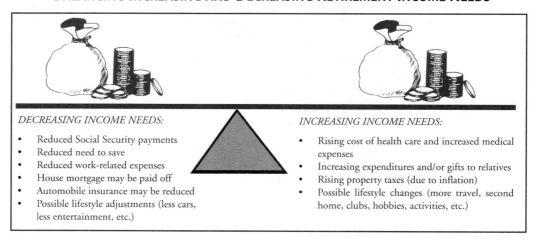

DECREASING INCOME NEEDS:

- Reduced Social Security payments
- Reduced need to save
- Reduced work-related expenses
- House mortgage may be paid off
- Automobile insurance may be reduced
- Possible lifestyle adjustments (less cars, less entertainment, etc.)

INCREASING INCOME NEEDS:

- Rising cost of health care and increased medical expenses
- Increasing expenditures and/or gifts to relatives
- Rising property taxes (due to inflation)
- Possible lifestyle changes (more travel, second home, clubs, hobbies, activities, etc.)

PLANNING FOR RETIREMENT - PRETAX OR AFTER-TAX

It is possible to plan for retirement needs either on a pretax or an after-tax basis. Most advisors who are not certified public accountants (CPAs) plan in pretax dollars believing that a pretax approach is what their clients best understand. The implicit assumption associated with the pretax approach is that clients are more likely to know their gross income rather than to know their net after-tax cash flow. Therefore, advisors establish retirement plans pretax with the expectation that the clients will simply pay whatever income taxes they have out of their gross retirement income, similar to what clients do during pre-retirement years. Many CPAs think in terms of after-tax dollars and, therefore, plan for retirement on an after-tax basis. After-tax planning assumes that income taxes are paid before other retirement needs. Planning can be effective either way as long as the client and the advisors understand the pretax or after-tax planning choice. Throughout the text, we generally use a pretax approach.

WAGE REPLACEMENT RATIO (WRR)

The **wage replacement ratio (WRR)** is an estimate of the percent of annual income needed during retirement compared to income earned prior to retirement. The wage replacement ratio or percentage is calculated by dividing the amount of money needed on an annual basis in retirement by the pre-retirement income. For example, if a client in the last year of work (prior to retirement) makes $100,000, and that client needs $80,000 in the first retirement year to maintain the same pre-retirement lifestyle, the wage replacement ratio (WRR) is 80 percent ($80,000 ÷ $100,000).

CALCULATING THE WAGE REPLACEMENT RATIO

There are two alternative methods to calculate the wage replacement ratio: the top-down approach and the bottom-up approach (also called the budgeting approach).

Top-Down Approach

The top-down approach is frequently used with younger clients where income and expenditure patterns are unlikely to remain constant over time. As clients approach retirement age, a more precise wage replacement ratio should be calculated using a budgeting approach. The top-down approach estimates the wage replacement ratio using common sense and percentages.

> To illustrate the top-down approach, assume a 40-year-old client earns $50,000 a year, pays 7.65 percent of his gross pay in Social Security payroll taxes, and saves 10 percent of his gross income. If we assume that any work-related savings resulting from retirement are expected to be completely offset by additional spending adjustments during retirement and that the client wants to maintain his exact pre-retirement lifestyle, we would expect that the client would need a wage replacement ratio of 82.35% (100% - 7.65% - 10%).
>
> | | | | |
> |---:|:-:|---:|:---|
> | $50,000 | = | 100.00% | of salary in % terms |
> | (5,000) | = | (10.00%) | less: current savings in % terms |
> | (3,825) | = | (7.65%) | less: payroll taxes in % terms (not paid in retirement) |
> | $41,175 | = | 82.35% | wage replacement ratio in % terms |
>
> The client is currently living on 82.35 percent of his gross pay. The remaining 17.65 percent is paid to FICA taxes and savings. Therefore, the 82.35 percent is a reasonable estimate, or proxy, of the amount necessary, as a percentage of current income, to maintain the (current) pre-retirement lifestyle.

Bottom-Up (Budgeting) Approach

The bottom-up approach used to calculate the wage replacement ratio is also called the budgeting approach. It is often used with older clients because as a person nears retirement age, it is possible to examine the actual current expenditure patterns of the person and to more accurately forecast the retirement expenditure patterns. Working with the client, the advisor can determine which costs in the current (pre-retirement) budget will change (increase or decrease) in the retirement budget, allowing the advisor to determine a wage replacement ratio with greater precision than the top-down approach of estimating retirement needs.

EXAMPLE 2.7

Assume you had two clients, Anna and Bart, who had identical income and expenses each year. Anna and Bart each make $120,000 in pre-retirement income. Anna has arranged her financial affairs in such a way that she will have no mortgage payment or car payment while in retirement. Bart, on the other hand, expects to continue to have both a mortgage payment and a car payment throughout the majority of his retirement years. Both of them expect some expenses to decrease during retirement. The following chart illustrates that, while Anna will need a 64.75 percent WRR, Bart will need a 84.75 percent WRR. The difference is due to Bart's $18,000 annual mortgage payments and $6,000 annual car payments.

	CLIENT ANNA & BART	CLIENT ANNA	CLIENT BART
	Current Budget	**Retirement Budget**	**Retirement Budget**
Income (Current) Budget	$120,000	***	***
Expenses:	Current	Retirement	Retirement
Income Taxes (28%)	$33,600*	$33,600	$33,600
Food	5,400	5,400	5,400
Utilities/Phone	6,000	6,000	6,000
Mortgage	18,000**	0	18,000
Social Security Taxes	2,500	0	0
Health Insurance	2,000	2,000	2,000
Auto Insurance	1,200	1,200	1,200
Entertainment	6,000	6,000	6,000
Clothing	4,000	2,500	2,500
Auto Maintenance/Operation	1,000	750	750
Auto Payment	6,000	0	6,000
Church	2,400	2,400	2,400
Savings	12,000	0	0
Miscellaneous	19,900	17,850	17,850
Total Expenses (Needs)	**$120,000**	**$77,700**	**$101,700**
Wage Replacement Ratio (WRR)		64.75%	84.75%

*Assume for this example that Anna and Bart's income tax liability remains the same during retirement.

**Note that the mortgage of both is 15% of current income before retirement, but 0% for Anna and 18% of needs for Bart after retirement.

*** The current budget at retirement will be equal to the needs.

Does a person really need the same inflation-adjusted income throughout the entire retirement period? The answer is generally no. There are indications that consumption slows somewhat as people age. The 70 to 80 percent wage replacement ratio is probably most appropriate from the beginning of retirement (regardless of age) until the retiree reaches his or her late 70s. It appears that a person's consumption past the age of 80 declines primarily due to lessened mobility. While this may be correct for society at large, certain individuals will incur dramatic medical costs during the latter part of their retirement period. Therefore, while most people who study retirement expenditures would suggest a consumption function similar to the one provided in Exhibit 2.17, such a model may or may not apply to a particular individual.

QUICK QUIZ 2.3

1. The WRR is an estimate of the percentage of annual income needed during retirement compared to income earned prior to retirement.
   a. True
   b. False

2. The two methods for calculating WRR are the top-down approach and the budgeting approach.
   a. True
   b. False

True, True.

AVERAGE ANNUAL EXPENDITURES BY AGE

EXHIBIT 2.17

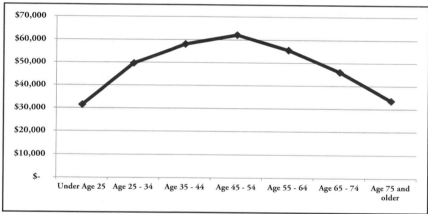

Bureau of Labor Statistics: Consumer Expenditures Study 2012

Many expert advisors conclude that most clients need approximately 70 to 80 percent of their pre-retirement income to retire and maintain their pre-retirement lifestyle. While many clients fall into this range, there are also those particularly frugal clients who may need as little as 40 percent of their pre-retirement income and others who may need substantially more than the 80 percent wage replacement ratio (usually due to corporate perks that are no longer received during retirement).

EXHIBIT 2.18

ADJUSTMENTS FROM PRE-RETIREMENT INCOME TO RETIREMENT INCOME NEEDS

From Pre-retirement Income to Retirement Income Needs Adjustments to Expenditures	
Adjustments which decrease income needs:	Amount or Percent Saved:
• No longer pay Social Security taxes	7.65% to 15.3%
• No longer need to save	10% to 15%
• No longer pay house mortgage	Maybe
• No longer pay work-related expenses	*
• Auto insurance may be reduced	*
• Possible lifestyle adjustments	*
Adjustments which may increase income needs:	
• Increasing cost of health care	*
• Lifestyle changes	*
• Increase in travel	*
• Second home	*
• Clubs and activities	*
• Expenditures on family/gifts/grandchildren	*
• Increased property taxes	*

Amounts must be estimated for each individual

Exhibit 2.18 presents common adjustments from pre-retirement to retirement in terms of estimated percentages. Notice that most of the adjustments in Exhibit 2.18 are client-specific.

SOURCES OF RETIREMENT INCOME

Most retirees rely on a combination of funds to finance retirement, including Social Security, private and company-sponsored retirement plans, income from personal retirement plans, and income from personal savings. These sources of funds are intended to complement each other to provide adequate retirement income. Exhibit 2.19 illustrates the average percent of income for the average retiree in 1962 and 2012 from each of these sources.

RETIREMENT INCOME SOURCES FOR THE ELDERLY

EXHIBIT
2.19

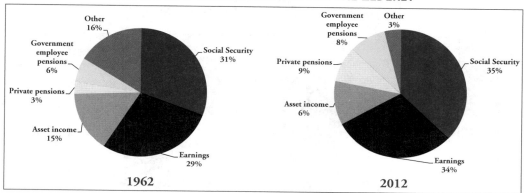

1962   2012

Source: Social Security Administration

Notice that the average retiree receives approximately 35 percent of retirement income from Social Security. Social Security will only provide a wage replacement ratio of 16 to 24 percent for a worker with income of $200,000 (see Exhibit 2.21). Therefore, such a worker will need to look to other sources of funds to make up the amount of short-fall in wage replacement to maintain the worker's desired lifestyle.

SOCIAL SECURITY

Social Security provides a foundation of retirement income. Social Security covers almost all occupational groups (except 25 percent of state and local government employees) with retirement benefits

KEY CONCEPTS

1. Identify the main sources of retirement income.

2. How does Social Security factor into retirement income?

3. Discuss the importance of personal savings to an individual's retirement income needs.

adjusted for inflation. It is considered the safety net of a secure income, but for most income levels, it is an insufficient source of income replacement during retirement. According to the Social Security Administration, 90 percent of individuals aged 65 or older received Social Security benefits. As Exhibit 2.20 illustrates, Social Security was the major source of income for retired individuals. Historically, Social Security was the only source of income for approximately 21 percent of retirees.

EXHIBIT
2.20
PERCENTAGE OF RETIRED INDIVIDUALS RECEIVING SOCIAL SECURITY BENEFITS BY RELATIVE IMPORTANCE TO TOTAL RETIREMENT INCOME

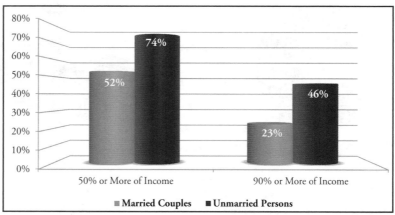

Source: Social Security Administration, Social Security Basic Facts (April 2, 2014)

Most middle to higher income individuals planning for retirement should, therefore, consider Social Security as a foundation of income rather than depending on Social Security as their main source of retirement income. Social Security retirement benefits provide a wage replacement ratio ranging from less than 20 percent (for high-income earners) to approximately 80 percent (for low-income earners who have a same age, nonworking spouse). As illustrated in Exhibit 2.21, Social Security is an adequate wage replacement for lower wage earners, but is clearly inadequate to provide sufficient replacement income for middle-to-higher-wage earners. Keep in mind that Social Security was never meant to be the only source of income upon retirement. President Franklin D. Roosevelt implies this reality in his statement while signing the Social Security Act on August 14, 1935:

"We can never insure one hundred percent of the population against one hundred percent of the hazards and vicissitudes of life, but we have tried to frame a law which will give some measure of protection to the average citizen and to his family against the loss of a job and against poverty-ridden old age."

SOCIAL SECURITY AS A WAGE REPLACEMENT PERCENTAGE (FOR INDIVIDUALS HAVING VARIOUS EARNINGS)

EXHIBIT
2.21

Current Earnings	Worker Benefit %*	Worker with Same Age, Nonworking Spouse Total Benefit %	Comment
$15,000	70%	105%	Low Income
$20,000	61%	91%	(WRR Good)
$25,000	55%	82%	
$30,000	51%	77%	
$35,000	48%	73%	Middle Income
$50,000	43%	65%	(WRR Adequate)
$75,000	36%	54%	
$100,000	31%	46%	High Income
$200,000	16%	24%	(WRR Poor)

Estimated based on single person at normal retirement age (2015).
At same age, nonworking spouse would receive 50 percent of the benefits of the covered worker.

PRIVATE PENSION AND COMPANY-SPONSORED RETIREMENT PLANS

Private pension plans are the second source of retirement income. According to a 2014 report by the U.S. Bureau of Labor Statistics, 65 percent of private-industry workers had access to a pension or retirement plan, and almost 48 percent of those workers participated in the plans.[7] Qualified retirement plans have dramatically changed over the last few decades from employer-sponsored funded plans to employer-sponsored employee self-reliant plans, increasing the emphasis on personal savings as the primary source of retirement income for middle-to-upper-wage workers.

PERSONAL ASSETS AND SAVINGS

Personal assets and savings is the third source of retirement income and is the one source that has traditionally been the most influenced by the individual. This is a more difficult way to accumulate savings for retirement because savings may have to accumulate in a taxable account instead of a tax deferred account. While there are some tax deferred alternatives, such as traditional and Roth IRAs, there are limitations regarding how much can be contributed to these accounts. However, personal

QUICK QUIZ 2.4

1. Retirees generally rely on Social Security, private pension plans, and personal savings to fund their retirement income.
    a. True
    b. False

2. Social Security is an adequate wage replacement for most individuals.
    a. True
    b. False

3. Personal savings is the source of retirement income most influenced by the individual.
    a. True
    b. False

True, False, True.

7. US Department of Labor, Bureau of Labor Statistics "National Compensation Survey: Employee Benefits in Private Industry in the United States, March 2014."

savings can be a significant source of retirement income. The more personal savings an individual puts aside for retirement, the larger the accumulation at retirement and the larger the retirement income for the individual.

Exhibit 2.10 illustrates the significant decrease in the personal savings rate since 1990. As illustrated, the savings rate fell from 1990 to 2005, with the trend reversing since then.

Whenever a retiree has income from invested assets, it can mean a substantially higher overall retirement income. The median income of those retirees with asset income is more than twice as large as the income of retirees with no asset income. As the two charts in Exhibit 2.22 illustrate, retirees without personal asset income are concentrated in the lowest income categories. Notice in Exhibit 2.22 that, of retirees having income from personal assets and savings, 65 percent have income of $30,000 or more, whereas for those retirees without personal assets and savings, only 28 percent have income of $30,000 or more in retirement. There is a noticeable difference between retirees who have income from personal assets and those who do not.

EXHIBIT 2.22

INCOME OF RETIREES WITH AND WITHOUT INCOME FROM PERSONAL ASSETS

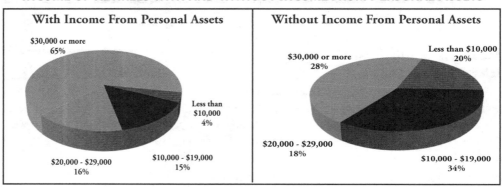

Source: Social Security Administration: Income of the Aged Chartbook 2012

QUALITATIVE FACTORS IN RETIREMENT - ADVISING CLIENTS

Qualitative factors associated with retirement may be more important than the financial or quantitative factors. Qualitative factors include involuntary versus voluntary retirement; emotional and psychological factors, such as loss of self esteem with loss of job and boredom in retirement; and the decision to relocate or to do things that were postponed during the work life (i.e., travel or pursue another vocation).

The best overall advice for clients is to have a strong support system, a well-planned qualitative side to retirement, and a system in place to maintain ego and self-esteem. Many persons in our culture define themselves by what they do at work. The mere act of going to work may be a ritual or habit that provides that person with a sense of self-worth and reason to live. A trusted colleague at the workplace may be a source of support and personal gratification. Voluntary retirement, even when well-planned, means change - and change can be difficult.

Involuntary retirement, if perceived as undesirable, can have a devastating emotional impact on an individual including shock, anger, and denial. Financial planning professionals need to recognize the emotional state of clients and realize that when someone is emotionally troubled, major decisions (financial or otherwise) are sometimes best delayed. Rather than abruptly making important financial decisions, it may be better to do the minimum financial maneuvering necessary during a grieving period. Such grieving may last for a period of a year or longer. Trying to optimize the financial situation when the client is emotionally unable to determine goals or priorities is probably counterproductive and may add stress to the situation.

KEY CONCEPTS

1. Why are qualitative factors important considerations in retirement planning?

2. What are some of the common factors that negatively affect retirement planning and what impact do they have on the planning process?

A client's decision to relocate after retirement (for example, move to another state) should be carefully considered over a long period of planning. Some retirees do not realize that when they move, they will have a completely new environment to adjust to, as well as a substantial loss of their former support system of friends and family. Someone considering moving should conduct a trial transition over a number of years, spending increasingly longer periods at the desired location. This gradual adjustment can help determine if the potential permanent relocation will actually enhance retirement. People considering retiring abroad will encounter even more change, thereby necessitating even more detailed planning.

SUMMARY OF FACTORS AFFECTING RETIREMENT PLANNING

Advisors may encounter clients who subjectively "feel" they are financially secure because they have a good job and/or a good net worth. If a good job is lost through premature death, disability, lay off, job termination, unexpected illness, etc., or if net worth decreases dramatically, the client's financial security is impaired. Thus, the actual determination of financial security is objective rather than subjective. Regardless of how people feel subjectively, in the real, objective world, there is a certain quantitative percentage of people who will become disabled, die untimely, or become unemployed.

Other complications that affect the retirement planning process include at least two societal issues. Our society has become more mobile with the deterioration of the traditional family unit. Having lost the close connection to family, older persons may not be able to depend on family to provide retirement assistance. Thus, there is a greater need for financial independence for each individual. Additionally, because our society seems to place more value on youth than on age and wisdom in the workplace, retirees have less chance of being hired for part-time employment, which could supplement retirement income.

Many people begin planning for retirement too late in life and save too little to effectively meet retirement capital accumulation needs. Some people do not give retirement funding any thought until they are well into their forties. Even when people do save, many of them make poor investment choices and, therefore, have poor investment returns and insufficient accumulations.

Inflation reduces an individual's purchasing power. To recipients of fixed incomes, inflation is like a progressive tax which causes declining purchasing power.

Exhibit 2.23 lists the factors that frustrate effective retirement planning and the negative impact associated with each factor.

QUICK QUIZ 2.5

1. Qualitative factors associated with retirement are of less importance than the financial or quantitative factors.
   a. True
   b. False

2. Many people begin planning too late in life and save too little to effectively meet their retirement income needs.
   a. True
   b. False

3. Factors that positively impact retirement planning include reduced WLE and increased RLE.
   a. True
   b. False

False, True, False.

EXHIBIT 2.23

FACTORS THAT NEGATIVELY AFFECT RETIREMENT PLANNING AND THEIR IMPACT ON THE PLANNING PROCESS

Factors	Impact
Reduced WLE	Insufficient savings period
Increased RLE	Increases capital needs
Reduced family reliance	Fewer alternatives in retirement
Reduced ability to work	Fewer alternatives in retirement
Planned too late	Fewer compounding periods
Low savings rate	Unable to meet capital requirements
Inflation	Reduces purchasing power
Poor earnings rate and asset allocation	Unable to meet capital requirements

Long-term financial security does not happen automatically. It requires careful planning, a clear understanding of the quantification of the goal, and identification and management of the risks that are present. Retirement planning requires the collection and projection of data and must be conducted meticulously and conservatively.

RISKS TO FINANCIAL INDEPENDENCE

There are many risks on the way to achieving financial independence. Selected risks are identified in Exhibit 2.24. It is a wise idea to save early, save a sufficient amount, invest prudently, and not underestimate retirement needs or the impact of inflation.

SUMMARY OF SELECTED FACTORS AFFECTING RETIREMENT PLANNING

EXHIBIT 2.24

FACTOR	RISK	MITIGATOR
Work Life Expectancy (WLE)	Shortened due to untimely death, disability, health, unemployment	Life insurance, disability insurance, health insurance, education, training, experience
Retirement Life Expectancy (RLE)	Lengthened	Adequate capital accumulation
Savings rate, amount, and timing	Too low and too late	Save enough; start early
Inflation	Greater than expected	Conservatively estimate inflation and needs
Retirement needs	Underestimated	Use wage replacement estimators; don't include Social Security benefits in the calculation
Investment returns	Inadequate to create necessary retirement capital	Knowledge of and investments in broad portfolio of diversified investments and proper asset allocation
Sources of retirement income	Overestimation of Social Security benefits, private pension plans, or personal income (or adverse changes in taxation of such income)	Conservatively estimate and plan for such income, as well as monitor income projections and tax policy

RETIREMENT FUNDING (CAPITAL NEEDS ANALYSIS)

Capital needs analysis is the process of calculating the amount of investment capital needed at retirement to maintain the pre-retirement lifestyle and mitigate the impact of inflation during the retirement years. It uses both objective and subjective criteria to determine retirement income needs. Below are three methods for analyzing capital needs: the basic annuity method, the capital preservation model, and the purchasing power preservation model.

ACCURATE ASSUMPTIONS

Before calculating the capital needs analysis, the advisor must first make several assumptions. Assumptions are made for the wage replacement ratio, work life expectancy, retirement life expectancy, inflation, earnings, Social Security, and any other benefits. If these assumptions are inaccurate, the projection using those assumptions will be flawed. The wage replacement ratio should be calculated carefully, especially for a client near retirement. Estimating life expectancy usually begins with the IRS tables and is conservatively estimated at age 90 to 93, due to the risk of outliving retirement money. Where family history indicates a particularly long life expectancy, that age should be increased. The estimate of the work life expectancy is critical, as one less year of work means one less year of saving and one more year of retirement funding. Conversely, working one additional year may make an otherwise unworkable retirement plan work quite nicely due to the additional year of savings, the additional year of compounding, and one less year of consumption.

The assumptions regarding inflation and earnings rates are essential ingredients in capital needs analysis. Historical data is available for inflation; however, future inflation is difficult to predict. Perhaps the best estimate is the long run inflation rate for a period equal to the remaining WLE plus the RLE. Earnings rates are dependent on the client's asset allocation and the markets; however, returns can be estimated for a well-diversified portfolio over a long period. It is wise to conservatively estimate inflation (up a little) and conservatively estimate earnings (down a little). Such estimation provides conservatism in case one or more of the assumptions are not realized. Social Security benefits and pension benefits that are inflation

KEY CONCEPTS

1. What is capital needs analysis and why is it important in retirement planning?

2. What are the three most common methods for analyzing capital needs?

3. How do each of these methods differ?

4. What assumptions must be made in capital needs analysis?

protected should be carefully determined and documented. The retirement plan and capital needs analysis can be adjusted on an annual basis as information becomes more certain.

BASIC PLANNING - CAPITAL NEEDS ANALYSIS / ANNUITY METHOD

The **annuity method** is the simplest way to determine retirement needs. The annuity method assumes the individual saves for a period of time, begins taking distributions at retirement, and then dies with a zero accumulation balance on the projected life expectancy date. The following steps are used to determine the capital necessary at the beginning of retirement to fund the retirement period:

1. Calculate the WRR. Determine the wage replacement ratio (WRR) today using one of the two methods identified earlier (top-down or budgeting).

2. Determine the gross dollar needs. Determine the wage replacement amount in today's dollars from Step 1.

3. Determine the net dollar needs. Reduce the result from Step 2 by any expected Social Security benefits in today's dollars or other benefits that are indexed to inflation.

4. Calculate the inflated pre-retirement dollar needs. Inflate the result from Step 3 to the retirement age at the CPI rate to determine the first annual retirement payment.

5. Calculate the capital needed at retirement age. Calculate the present value at retirement of an annuity due for an annual payment equal to the result from Step 4 over the full retirement life expectancy (estimate life expectancy conservatively at age 90 to 93) and use the inflation-adjusted earnings rate. It is important to note that a conservative approach should be used when estimating the life expectancy, as this will allay any shortfall in funding.

To determine the amount to save during the work life expectancy, discount the capital needed at retirement using the savings rate, being mindful as to whether the client is expected to save annually or more frequently and whether the client is expected to save under an annuity due or an ordinary annuity scheme.

Jordan, age 42, currently earns $70,000. Her wage replacement ratio is determined to be 80 percent. She expects that inflation will average 3 percent for her entire life expectancy. She expects to earn 9.5 percent on her investments and retire at age 62, possibly living to age 90. She has sent for and received her Social Security benefit statement, which indicates that her Social Security retirement benefit in today's dollars adjusted for early retirement is $15,000 per year. It is reasonable to subtract the Social Security benefit from today's needs because it is inflation adjusted.

1. Calculate Jordan's capital needed at retirement at age 62.

Step 1	80% WRR			
Step 2	($70,000 x 0.80)	=	$56,000	Total needs in today's dollars
Step 3			- 15,000	Less Social Security in today's dollars
			$41,000	Annual amount needed in today's dollars
Step 4	N	=	20 (62 - 42) Work Life Expectancy	
	i	=	3% (inflation)	
	PV	=	$41,000 (Step 3) Retirement needs in today's dollars	
	PMT	=	0	
	FV	=	74,050.56 (Step 4) First year needs for retirement	
Step 5	N	=	28 (90 − 62) Retirement Life Expectancy	
	i	=	6.3107 [(1 + earnings rate ÷ 1 + inflation rate) − 1] x 100 [(1.095 ÷ 1.03) − 1] x 100	
	FV	=	0 Annuity model is 0 at life expectancy	
	PMT_{AD}	=	$74,050.56 (from Step 4) this is also an annuity due	
	$PV_{AD@62}$	=	$1,022,625.84 (Step 5 - amount needed at age 62)	

Note: The math in this example assumes unrounded numbers are used throughout the calculation. If the calculator is cleared at each step and a rounded number for i is used, the results will be slightly lower.

2. Calculate the amount Jordan must save monthly, at month end (an ordinary annuity), assuming she has no current savings to accumulate the capital needed for retirement at age 62.

$FV_{@62}$	=	$1,022,625.84 (from Step 5)
N	=	240 (20 years x 12 months)
i	=	0.79167 (9.5% ÷ 12)
PV	=	0
PMT_{OA}	=	$1,436.43 (monthly savings necessary) at month end

3. Calculate the amount she must save monthly, at month end, assuming she presently has $50,000 in current retirement savings.

$FV_{@62}$	=	$1,022,625.84
N	=	240
i	=	0.79167
PV	=	- $50,000
PMT_{OA}	=	$970.36 (monthly savings necessary) at month end

EXHIBIT
2.25

ASSET ACCUMULATION AND DISTRIBUTION (USING DATA FROM EXAMPLE 2.8)

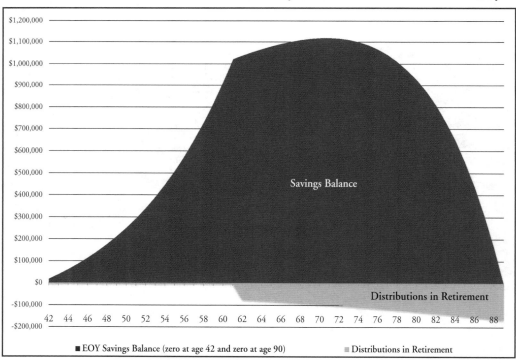

■ EOY Savings Balance (zero at age 42 and zero at age 90)   ■ Distributions in Retirement

To mitigate against the risk of the assumptions being overly optimistic, the advisor can adjust inflation upward, the earnings rate downwards, or make use of a capital preservation model or a purchasing power preservation model rather than a simple annuity model to determine capital needs. These two additional models help to overcome the risks of the pure annuity model (primarily the risk of running out of money).

ADVANCED FINANCIAL PLANNING - CAPITAL PRESERVATION MODEL (CP)

The basic capital needs analysis is a **pure annuity concept**, generally prepared on a pretax basis. The annuity concept means that if all assumptions happen exactly as expected, the person will die exactly at the assumed life expectancy with a retirement account balance of zero. There is some risk that clients could outlive their assets under the annuity approach. Therefore, they may actually need greater accumulations at retirement. Two models used to mitigate the risk of outliving money are the capital preservation model and the purchasing power preservation model. The **capital preservation model** assumes that at life expectancy, as estimated in the annuity model, the client has exactly the same account balance as started with at retirement. The purchasing power preservation model assumes that the client will have a capital balance of equal purchasing power at life expectancy as he did at retirement. In spite of any conservatism that the advisor may have built into the annuity model, it is always possible that one or more assumptions will be unrealized. Therefore, there is the need to consider one of the alternative models.

The capital preservation model maintains the original capital balance needed at retirement for the entire retirement life expectancy.

QUICK QUIZ 2.6

1. Capital needs analysis is the process of calculating the amount of investment capital needed at retirement to maintain the pre-retirement lifestyle.
   a. True
   b. False

2. The annuity method assumes that the individual will die at the expected life expectancy with a retirement account balance of zero.
   a. True
   b. False

3. The capital preservation model and the purchasing power preservation model are used to mitigate the risk of outliving retirement funds.
   a. True
   b. False

True, True, True.

EXAMPLE
2.9

Recall that the amount needed for Jordan at age 62 calculated from Example 2.8 was $1,022,625.84. If we discount that amount at the expected earnings rate of 9.5 percent, we can determine the additional amount of capital necessary to leave an estate of exactly $1,022,625.84 at life expectancy.

N	=	28
i	=	9.5
$FV_{@90}$	=	$1,022,625.84 (amount at life expectancy)
PMT	=	0
$PV_{@62}$	=	$80,560.37
$1,103,186.21	=	$80,560.37 + $1,022,625.84
		(amount needed for capital preservation model)

Thus, the capital preservation model will require an additional accumulation at retirement of $80,560.37 greater than the pure annuity model but will reduce the risk of running out of money (superannuation). Such an increase in capital accumulation also requires that savings be increased for calculations 2 and 3 in the Jordan example (Example 2.8).

The following chart compares the capital preservation model with the annuity model for our example.

	Capital Preservation Model		Annuity Model	
	Beginning Balance of Zero Savings Calculation 2	Beginning Balance of $50,000 Calculation 3	Beginning Balance of Zero Savings Calculation 2	Beginning Balance of $50,000 Calculation 3
$FV_{@62}$	$1,103,186.21	$1,103,186.21	$1,022,625.84	$1,022,625.84
N	240	240	240	240
i	0.79167	0.79167	0.79167	0.79167
PV	0	- $50,000	0	- $50,000
PMT_{OA}	$1,549.59	$1,083.52	$1,436.43	$970.36

The capital preservation model requires additional savings of $113 per month, but mitigates against many of the risks

in the traditional capital needs annuity approach.

ADVANCED PLANNING - PURCHASING POWER PRESERVATION MODEL (PPP)

An even more conservative approach to capital needs analysis is the **purchasing power preservation model**. This model essentially maintains the purchasing power of the original capital balance at retirement.

Again recall Example 2.8. The capital balance of $1,022,625.84 is used as the future value, and then the entire calculation made in the original capital preservation model is repeated. By doing this, the $1,022,625.84 is simultaneously inflated at the rate of inflation and discounted at the earnings rate.

EXAMPLE 2.10

N	=	28
i	=	6.3107
FV	=	$1,022,625.84
PMT_{AD}	=	$74,050.56 (amount needed the first year of retirement)
$PV_{@62}$	=	$1,206,939.24 (if i is not rounded, it will be $3 more) capital needed for purchasing power preservation model

The additional accumulation at retirement using a purchasing power model is $184,313.40 greater than the pure annuity approach.

The answers to calculation 2 and 3 in the Jordan example would again change. The chart below compares the purchasing power model with the annuity model for our example.

	Purchasing Power Model		Annuity Model	
	Beginning Balance of Zero Savings Calculation 2	Beginning Balance of $50,000 Calculation 3	Beginning Balance of Zero Savings Calculation 2	Beginning Balance of $50,000 Calculation 3
$FV_{@62}$	$1,206,939.24	$1,206,939.24	$1,022,625.84	$1,022,625.84
N	240	240	240	240
i	0.79167	0.79167	0.79167	0.79167
PV	0	- $50,000	0	- $50,000
PMT_{OA}	$1,695.33	$1,229.25	$1,436.43	$970.36

EXHIBIT
2.26

CAPITAL NEEDS ANALYSIS COMPARISON FOR JORDAN EXAMPLE[8]

	Annuity Model	Capital Preservation Model	Purchasing Power Preservation Model
Capital needed at retirement (calculation 1)	$1,022,625.84	$1,103,186.21	$1,206,939.24
Monthly savings with no initial balance (calculation 2)	$1,436.43	$1,549.59	$1,695.33
Monthly savings with $50,000 initial balance (calculation 3)	$970.36	$1,083.52	$1,229.25

RANGE ESTIMATES, SENSITIVITY ANALYSIS, SIMULATIONS, AND MONTE CARLO ANALYSIS

As one might expect, small changes in the assumptions regarding earnings, inflation, life expectancy, and retirement funding needs can have a dramatic impact on the retirement plan. One of the problems with traditional capital needs analysis is that advisors use deterministic estimates (i.e., the estimate is predetermined as opposed to a probability estimate) for each of the variables (needs, inflation, portfolio returns, life expectancies, etc.). While point estimates help the advisor create a plan for the client, it is unrealistic to think that these variables are really predictable to an exact deterministic point (given) and instead may vary. Generally, point estimates used in deterministic models are the mean expectancy. For example, 10 percent on large capitalization common stocks is the mean expected return. While it is true that over the last 80 or so years large-cap stocks' average returns were 10 percent, there were only a few years out of 80 when the actual return was close to the mean expected return. It is unlikely that for any period going forward the investment return will replicate the historical return. A plan that only uses deterministic assumptions is likely to produce results that may range far from the original forecast. The advisor can employ various techniques to help begin to understand the effect of the range of probable outcomes for each variable in a plan. These techniques include range estimates, sensitivity analysis, and simulations such as Monte Carlo Analysis.

KEY CONCEPTS

1. Explain how sensitivity analysis is used.
2. What is a Monte Carlo Analysis?

Range Estimates

Using range estimates allows the advisor to project what outcome will occur if we use a range of assumptions (e.g., 2.5% to 3.5% inflation) for a variable as opposed to a single mean expectation (three percent inflation). A range estimate approach produces multiple outcomes that allow us to gain insight into the impact of a change in one variable or changes in a set of variables. Range

---

8. Although we concentrate on the Annuity Model, Capital Preservation Model, and Purchasing Power Model in this textbook, the capital needed at retirement can also be calculated based on complex actuarial assumptions. In order to verify our results in the Jordan example, we sought the advice of an actuary who used a different approach (but one that we verified was competent), which assumed no particular start balance. He calculated the capital needed at retirement to be approximately $1,245,000. We do not present the details of this calculation due to the complexity of the assumptions and calculations. Suffice it to say that the capital needed is $1,200,000 to $1,250,000 regardless of the assumptions. If you are looking for a rule of thumb, it is 10% more for the Capital Preservation Model and 20% more for the Purchasing Power Preservation Model as long as you have similar factors (e.g., 28 years and 3% inflation), but there is no substitution for exact calculations.

estimate assumptions are usually conducted around the mean estimate, both lower and higher than the mean point estimates. If an advisor wanted to rotate the assumed coefficient of the variable toward the risk of an adverse outcome (e.g., an investor who is more concerned with down side losses than upside potential returns may use semivariance analysis or alternatively, the number of months returns that were less than T-bill returns), then the technique to employ is sensitivity analysis rather than range estimating.

Sensitivity Analysis

Sensitivity analysis consists of rotating each variable assumption toward the undesirable side of the risk to determine the impact of a small change in that variable on not achieving the overall plan. Small deviations in one variable may significantly impact the entire plan.
For example:

1. One additional year of employment often makes the retirement plan work because there is one more year of savings, one more year of earnings accumulation, and one less year of consumption. The opposite is also true; one less year of work may destroy an otherwise achievable plan.
2. Small changes in the spread between the earnings rate and the inflation rate can have a significant impact on a plan, both positively and negatively.
3. A small increase in inflation can have a significant negative impact on an otherwise achievable retirement funding plan.

Understanding the importance of each individual variable and the risk involved if there is a change from the assumed number to a more conservative number allows the advisor to use sensitivity analysis to build a slightly worse case scenario and then determine the impact of these more conservative assumptions on the overall plan.

Recall the assumptions given in the Jordan annuity calculation (Example 2.8). The left columns below identify the given variables while the right columns below identify alternative variables that could be used.

EXAMPLE 2.11

Deterministic Example 2.8 Selected Assumptions		Sensitivity Analysis Conservative Assumptions
N	20 years to retirement	• Try 19 years
i	3% inflation	• Try 3.5% inflation
PV	$41,000 current needs	• Try $42,000 needs
PMT	$0	
FV	$74,050.56 future needs	

Deterministic Example 2.8 Selected Assumptions		Sensitivity Analysis Conservative Assumptions
N	28 years in retirement	• Use 30 years in retirement instead of 28
i	$[(1.095 \div 1.03) - 1] \times 100 = 6.3$	• Use a real rate of 5.75 instead of 6.3
PMT_{AD}	$74,050.56 future needs	• Use $80,745 as future needs rather than $74,050.56
$PV_{@62}$	$1,022,625.84 needed at retirement	
FV	$0	

Notice that slightly more conservative assumptions were used for the sensitivity analysis than were used in the original example in order to determine the robustness, or alternatively the sensitivity, of the previously calculated solution. If the retirement plan was recalculated using all of the sensitivity analysis assumptions previously identified, Jordan would need $200,000 more at retirement than originally expected, an increase of 20% just for the annuity model.

Annuity Model Solution with Conservative Assumptions Using Sensitivity Analysis	
N	19 years to retirement
i	3.5 inflation
PV	$42,000 current needs
PMT	$0
FV	$80,745 future needs
N	30 years in retirement
i	5.75 real rate of return
PMT_{AD}	$80,745 real payment (future dollars)
$PV_{@62}$	$1,207,472 (compared to $1,022,625) needed at age 62
FV	$0

Approximately $160,000 of the $200,000 change was caused by the inflation assumption being 3.5% instead of 3%.

Approximate Cause of Change		Explanation
1. Inflation 3.0 to 3.5	$158,916	1. Drives up future needs and drives down real return.
2. Change years 20 to 19	$15,857	2. Drives future needs higher, but over a shorter term.
3. Change years 28 to 30	$25,902	3. Makes more annuity payments.
Total	$200,676	4. The reconciliation cannot be exact because of the changes in terms and rates.
Actual Change	$184,847	

Simulations and Monte Carlo Analysis

There is uncertainty associated with any retirement funding projection. The assumptions can be analyzed using the latest retirement planning software packages that incorporate simulations, such as Monte Carlo Analysis (MCA). As illustrated below, most retirement projections are based on fixed (deterministic) assumptions. While useful during retirement planning, deterministic projections do not account for variations. A **Monte Carlo Analysis** is a mathematical tool that can be used to illustrate the unpredictability of the "real" world and its effects on an individual's retirement plan. MCA uses a random number generator for inputs into a software package that will provide an output with specific probabilities of outcomes. MCA provides insight into the most likely outcome, but also provides other possible outcomes. It allows for a variety of alternative assumptions, such as changes in investment rates of return, the variability of inflation, adjustments to life expectancy, and many other market-condition scenarios. Such a method is invaluable to the advisor, as it allows the advisor to observe a large number of projections illustrating a potential range of future outcomes based on changing variables. Various software programs are available that allow the advisor to run simulations projecting various scenarios, thereby increasing the probability that the individual's retirement plan will be successful.

QUICK QUIZ 2.7

1. Sensitivity analysis eliminates the risk of retirement planning.
   a. True
   b. False

2. Monte Carlo analysis predicts particular events.
   a. True
   b. False

3. Simulations allow for an unlimited number of simultaneous ranging variables.
   a. True
   b. False

False, False, True.

A simulation calculates multiple scenarios of a model by repeatedly sampling values from probability distributions for uncertain variables. Traditional range estimates calculate outcomes on a best case, expected case, and worst case basis. Sensitivity analysis allows the model user to manipulate variables usually one at a time or one set of variables at a time. Simulations allow for an unlimited (or very large) number of simultaneous ranging of variables, possibly leading to more insight into the problem and into the impact of interacting variables.

Because retirement is frequently 20 to 30 years or longer and there are many historical patterns of investment returns for selected 20 to 30 year periods, the advisor simply does not know what the market conditions will be when the client retires, nor does the advisor know the pattern of market returns that will follow a particular retirement date. Monte Carlo Analysis helps the advisor to understand the possibilities and probabilities. However, Monte Carlo Analysis cannot predict particular events. An excellent discussion of the problems with Monte Carlo Analysis was written in the Journal of Financial Planning by David Rawrocki (November 2001, Article 12) and is summarized in Exhibit 2.27.

EXHIBIT
2.27

SELECTED PROBLEMS WITH MONTE CARLO ANALYSIS

- Assumes normal distributions, serial independence, and linear relationships for investment returns (none of which are true).
- Stock returns are not normally distributed - kurtosis is higher than expected. (Stock returns are actually **lepto-kurtic**, meaning that they do not have a normal distribution.)
- Means and standard deviations for stock returns vary over time rather than remain static.
- Many Monte Carlo Analysis ignore income tax consequences.

Monte Carlo Analysis is a valuable tool and an interesting exercise. However, as with any analytical tool, it should not be used in a vacuum. It is useful to provide insight, but should not take the place of professional judgment. As with most financial planning, retirement planning is a process that includes regular monitoring and adjustments to the plan as needed. Clients should visit their advisor regularly (at least annually) to modify and update their retirement plan to adjust for changes in the preselected variables so that their retirement objectives can be met.

ALTERNATIVES TO COMPENSATE FOR PROJECTED CASH-FLOW SHORTFALLS

There are many times when a retirement projection simply works. Occasionally, a person's assets are significantly greater than their needs, and they may actually need encouragement to spend some of their money or they may need assistance transferring it to loved ones or donating it to charity. These situations are generally easier to deal with than those involving unrealistic expectations and shortfalls.

Situations can be challenging where the required annual savings amount is unrealistically high or the expressed needs of a client greatly exceed the assets available. In these situations, the plan simply does not work. There are several alternatives to consider, some of which have already been discussed briefly in this chapter. However, many of these alternatives are closely linked to the variables that are quite sensitive in the capital budgeting model. These include the amount of retirement needs, the amount of the required savings, the length of the WLE, the length of the RLE, the earnings rate, and the rate of inflation. With that in mind, the plan may work if one or more of the following adjustments can occur:

1. The annual or monthly retirement needs are reduced
2. The annual or monthly savings amount is increased
3. Expected investment earnings are increased
4. Expected inflation is reduced
5. The WLE is increased
6. The RLE is decreased

Obviously, there are implications and limitations to each of the possibilities listed above. However, there is often a combination of these adjustments that may help to resolve the budget shortfall. For example, a solution might entail refining the needs a bit more precisely, resulting in a decrease in what is actually needed combined with working a few additional years and increasing the portfolio risk slightly, assuming of course that the portfolio is not already heavily weighted toward equities. This solution reduces needs, increases the years of savings, decreases the years of needs, and increases the expected return from the portfolio.

Caution should be taken when adjusting the expected investment returns and inflation. The expected investment return should be based on reasonable expectations about the returns from risky assets and should generally be an output from an asset allocation model that incorporates the investor's risk tolerance and time horizon. Capital budgeting models are extremely sensitive to changes in expected return and inflation and care should be taken when adjusting these input variables.

EXAMPLE 2.12

BJ is 45 years old and plans on retiring at age 65 and living until age 95. Assume that he currently earns $100,000 and his wage replacement ratio is 70 percent and Social Security will provide $20,000 (in today's dollars) in retirement benefits. Also assume that he expects inflation to be 3 percent and expects that he can earn 6 percent on his investments.

Scenario 1: Step 1 of this problem is to determine the needs to be funded in today's dollars. His current income adjusted for the WRR and Social Security result in a funding need of $50,000 ($100,000 x 70% - $20,000) in today's dollars. Step 2 inflates this need until retirement. Based on inflation and when he is retiring, he will need $90,306 his first year of retirement. Step 3 determines the balance he needs in his investment accounts at retirement, which is $1,842,331. Finally, Step 4 calculates the required annual savings of $50,083. The annual funding is problematic because it is 50 percent of his income.

As would likely be the case, assume that Scenario 1 does not work for BJ. Scenarios 2, 3, 4, and 5 illustrate how changing the assumptions will impact the annual funding requirements:

Scenario 2: Requires BJ to work an additional three years. This adjustment increases his savings by three years and decreases his needs by three years.

Scenario 3: Requires a greater investment return from his portfolio increasing the return during his savings years from 6 percent to 9 percent. It does not change the return during retirement.

Scenario 4: Combines Scenarios 2 and 3.

Scenario 5: Combines Scenarios 2 and 3 and requires that he sell an asset, such as land or a boat, for $75,000 and uses the proceeds as the initial fund for his retirement plan.

		Scenario 1 (original projection)	Scenario 2 (work 3 more years)	Scenario 3 (increase investment return)	Scenario 4 (Scenarios 2 & 3 combined)	Scenario 5 (Scenario 4 & sale of asset)
Step 2: Inflate funds to retirement age	PV	($50,000)	($50,000)	($50,000)	($50,000)	($50,000)
	N	20	23	20	23	23
	i	3.00%	3.00%	3.00%	3.00%	3.00%
	PMT	0	0	0	0	0
	FV	$90,305.56	$98,679.33	$90,305.56	$98,679.33	$98,679.33
Step 3: PV of retirement annuity	PMT	$90,305.56	$98,679.33	$90,305.56	$98,679.33	$98,679.33
	N	30	27	30	27	27
	i	2.9126%	2.9126%	2.9126%	2.9126%	2.9126%
	FV	0	0	0	0	0
	PV	($1,842,330.85)	($1,880,625.32)	($1,842,330.85)	($1,880,625.32)	($1,880,625.32)
Step 4: Annual funding amount	FV	$1,842,330.85	$1,880,625.32	$1,842,330.85	$1,880,625.32	$1,880,625.32
	N	20	23	20	23	23
	i	6.00%	6.00%	9.00%	9.00%	9.00%
	PV	$0.00	$0.00	$0.00	$0.00	($75,000.00)
	PMT	($50,082.95)	($40,016.86)	($36,011.07)	($27,046.93)	($19,218.29)

The impact of these changes is that his annual savings requirement decreases from $50,083 in Scenario 1 to $19,218 in Scenario 5, which is certainly more reasonable based on his income. These changes may or may not be acceptable to BJ, nor are they necessarily the best choices. However, they illustrate how a plan can be adjusted to more realistically achieve the level of funding desired. One obvious choice that was not included was to decrease the annual needs, which would result in a lower savings requirement. Another alternative is to maintain the same 9 percent investment assumption throughout his life. This adjustment combined with Scenario 5 results in an annual savings amount of $15,905.

There are numerous other ways one might adjust a plan to help with its viability. Other considerations might include potential inheritances that would offset future costs or reduce spending needs toward the later part of retirement, which is consistent with the spending patterns of many retirees (see Exhibit 2.17). Part time work may also be a desire or possibility for those who are in good health. Finally, paying off mortgage debt (which often represents 20 percent of a budget) prior to retirement can significantly reduce required expenses during retirement. The examples above are not an exhaustive list. Instead, they should be considered as a starting point for situations in which a retirement plan initially does not work. Investors will generally have to make a choice of sacrificing today, working longer, or sacrificing during retirement when there are projected shortfalls.

IMPLICATIONS OF CAPITAL NEEDS ANALYSIS

Once the question of how much money will be needed at retirement is determined, consideration must be given to how that goal will be achieved. Individuals have several sources of funding for retirement including personal savings, retirement plans from work Social Security, and working while in retirement. Personal savings can be accomplished through banks and brokerage accounts. However, these accounts are not "tax-advantaged," meaning that income earned on accumulated assets will be subject to current taxation. It is generally accepted that in most cases, deferral of taxation is beneficial to the taxpayer. Taxpayers with earned income may be able to fund individual retirement accounts (IRAs) with pre-tax dollars up to $5,500 ($6,500 for those over age 50) for 2016. IRAs, which are covered in Chapter 9, are beneficial because they defer taxation until retirement. However, the IRA contribution limit is relatively small compared to what may need to be saved on an annual basis.

The other method to save on a pre-tax basis is through employer-sponsored retirement plans that permit employee salary deferrals, such as 401(k) plans, 403(b) plans, SARSEPs, 457 plans and SIMPLEs, which each permit employees to defer significantly more than can be contributed to an IRA. These plans, pension plans and other qualified plans are discussed in Chapters 3 through 8 with other tax-advantaged plans discussed in Chapter 9 and 10.

Social Security benefits act as a base source of retirement funding and the amount received is influenced by the number of years that are worked as well as the amount of earnings. Social Security is discussed in Chapter 11.

MANAGING RETIREMENT DISTRIBUTIONS

One of the biggest challenges for retirees is determining how to manage their wealth once they retire. How much can they spend every year or week? How long will their money last? The risk of running out of money is referred to as superannuation, which is one of the primary concerns for most retirees. This issue is of paramount concern more today than in past due to the decreased pensions and the increased number of defined contribution account type plans (e.g., 401(k) plan).

When defined benefit plans were prevalent, the risk of superannuation was pooled together. The defined benefit plan was responsible for paying a pension for as long as the retired participants lived. Naturally, some retirees would live longer than others and some would not live very long. Actuaries could mathematically estimate the average life expectancy of the pool of employees and determine the funding necessary to meet those needs. However, the pooling of risk ceased as defined benefit plans were replaced with defined contribution plans. No longer is the risk of outliving resources mitigated with shared risk. Now, retirees are responsible for the funds they have accumulated and must determine how to make those funds last throughout their retirement. While self-reliance is generally a great attribute, the reality is that many, if not most, retirees are ill-equipped to manage their portfolio themselves and will need the assistance of financial advisors. This responsibility can be daunting to retirees.

While managing one's assets in retirement has its challenges, there are ways to mitigate against superannuation. The simple answer is to shift the risk instead of retaining the risk. This risk shifting can be accomplished with annuities. Annuitized income is equivalent to the stream of income that was paid from defined benefit plans.

The simple fact is that annuities reduce the risk of superannuation. Whether from corporate or government pensions, insurance companies, or Social Security, annuities provide a base of cash flow that allows retirees to meet a certain percentage of necessities. There is published research that indicates a positive correlation between annuitized income and happiness. That correlation is not an endorsement for all annuities. Instead, it is a reflection of the risk averse nature of many investors and retirees and the simple fact that annuities reduce one aspect of risk. Those retirees who are extremely risk averse should have a larger portion of their assets annuitized compared to retirees who are less risk averse. While annuities have advantages, they also have disadvantages that must be considered by investors.

One of these disadvantages of purchasing an annuity or choosing an annuity is that the funds used for the annuity are no longer available. The funds are no longer available for unexpected emergencies or unexpected desires. In addition, if the retiree does not live to at least his or her life expectancy, then the purchase of the annuity reduced the assets that would have been available to transfer to heirs. Annuities are by no means a panacea. However, they are a prodigious solution that can be partially implemented without much difficulty.

Assuming that a retiree is going to retain the risk or some of the risk, there are many different approaches that can be utilized to reduce the risks of outliving retirement accumulation. Two of the more common approaches are:

1. *4 percent per year approach*: Limit withdrawals from the capital accumulation to four percent per year.
2. *Money-for-life approach*: Divide capital into unequal tranches with each tranche representing five years of retirement. Invest the funds for each tranche in varying asset classes expected to produce inflation adjusted returns of about five to six percent per year.

4 PERCENT OF CAPITAL BALANCE APPROACH

Conceptually, this approach is relatively simple to understand and implement. It provides for distributions equal to four percent of the capital balance each year and generally has a very high success rate, especially when the assets are invested in a balanced portfolio, such as one with 60 percent equities and 40 percent fixed income. Such a portfolio should generally provide a good balance between income, growth, and downside protection.

However, one scenario that is a risk for retirees is when the retirement portfolio is subjected to several years of relatively large losses combined with distributions of four percent or more of the portfolio. In this scenario, the portfolio balance may decline so fast that it is irreparably impacted, without the retirees dramatically changing their lifestyle or going back to work.

It should be noted that some advisors and clients might choose to use a 3.5 percent model or a 4.5 percent model. Adjustments such as these will provide more confidence or less confidence in the funds lasting through the retirement time period.

A four percent level of withdrawal initially indicates an account balance that is 25 times the income needed and implies a needed earnings rate of only 1.310 percent to pay out at a four percent rate for 30 years, assuming no inflation and annuity due payments. A four percent inflation adjusted withdrawal rate (assume inflation is 3 percent) would require an earnings rate of 4.349 percent annually for 30 years.

REQUIRED EARNINGS RATE			
Withdrawal Rate	Fixed Payment Required Earnings Rate	Inflation Adjusted Required Earnings Rate	Portfolio Allocation
3%	-0.711%	2.268%	Very Conservative
4%	1.310%	4.349%	Conservative
5%	3.079%	6.171%	Moderate Conservative
6%	4.696%	7.837%	Moderate
7%	6.218%	9.405%	Moderate Aggressive
8%	7.678%	10.908%	Aggressive

As mentioned above and implicit in the chart above, the investment of the retirement assets is critical to successfully managing the risk of superannuation. The four percent withdrawal rate is an appropriate approach that will generally achieve the objectives of clients as long as the beginning retirement portfolio is large enough.

MONEY-FOR-LIFE APPROACH

This approach divides assets into six five-year tranches and funds each tranche with sufficient money and the correct investment choices to provide retirement income for that period. The schedule below is an example that indicates the percent of capital necessary in each tranche, the expected investment return required for that tranche, and the type of asset class necessary to sustain this return.

Years	% of Capital	Rate of Return Required	Investments
1-5	28%	2%	Money Markets
6-10	26%	4%	Treasuries
11-15	20%	6%	Corporate Bonds
16-20	13%	8%	Balanced Fund
21-25	7%	10%	Large Cap & International Stock
26-30	6%	12%	Small Cap & International Stock

This approach is expected to produce a real overall return between five percent and six percent. The goal of this approach is to replenish the first five-year increment (the immediate income) every five years.

It should be noted that this method is not a significant deviation from historical methods of managing assets. In fact, the overall portfolio allocation is similar to that of a moderately allocated portfolio. This model is a different way of accounting for the funds and retirement needs. It should also be noted that the investor and advisor might choose to change the percent of capital percentages as well as the number of tranches. For example, seven five-year tranches might be used in lieu of six. This approach helps the client focus on the current needs, which are funded by the most stable types of investments, while longer term investments are invested to provide for growth and future needs.

These two approaches are effective for developing retirement income distribution strategies for clients. It is important to keep in mind that not all models will work with all clients, and clients often have unique goals or needs that must be accounted for specifically.

KEY TERMS

ANNUITY METHOD - Determines how much a client needs to fund their retirement based on the assumption that the person will die exactly at the assumed life expectancy with a retirement account balance of zero.

CAPITAL NEEDS ANALYSIS - The process of calculating the amount of investment capital needed at retirement to maintain the pre-retirement lifestyle and mitigate the impact of inflation during the retirement years.

CAPITAL PRESERVATION MODEL (CP) - A capital needs analysis method that assumes that at client's life expectancy, the client has exactly the same account balance as he did at the beginning of retirement.

LEPTO-KURTIC - A distribution that appears to be normal but has more area under the two tails than a normal distribution (i.e., fat tails).

MONTE CARLO ANALYSIS - A mathematical tool used to calculate the success of an individual's retirement portfolio using changing variables.

PURCHASING POWER PRESERVATION MODEL (PPP) - A capital needs analysis method that assumes that at a client's life expectancy, the client will have a capital balance with purchasing power equal to the purchasing power at the beginning of retirement.

PURE ANNUITY CONCEPT - The basic capital needs analysis approach, generally prepared on a pretax basis.

REMAINING WORK LIFE EXPECTANCY (RWLE) - The work period that remains at a given point in time before retirement.

RETIREMENT LIFE EXPECTANCY (RLE) - The time period beginning at retirement and extending until death; the RLE is the period of retirement that must be funded.

SAVINGS RATE - The average savings amount in the U.S. based on consumption.

SENSITIVITY ANALYSIS - A tool used to understand the range of outcomes for each variable in a retirement plan by rotating each variable toward the undesirable side of the risk to determine the impact of a small change in that variable on an overall plan.

SUITABILITY - Having a reasonable basis to believe that a recommended transaction or investment strategy is appropriate for a client, after considering the client's age, other investments, financial situation and needs, tax status, investment objectives, investment experience, investment time horizon, liquidity needs, risk tolerance and other relevant issues. See FINRA Rule 2111.

KEY TERMS

WAGE REPLACEMENT RATIO (WRR) - An estimate of the percent of income needed at retirement compared to earnings prior to retirement.

WORK LIFE EXPECTANCY (WLE) - The period of time a person is expected to be in the work force, generally 30-40 years.

DISCUSSION QUESTIONS

1. List the major factors affecting retirement planning.

2. Define work life expectancy.

3. Define retirement life expectancy.

4. What is the median retirement age for individuals in the U.S.?

5. Explain the work life expectancy/retirement life expectancy dilemma.

6. List the major savings and investment concepts that are important to retirement planning.

7. Explain the importance of beginning a retirement savings plan early.

8. Explain the importance of understanding investment decisions and their consequences in retirement planning.

9. How is inflation relevant to a retirement plan?

10. Why do an individual's needs increase or decrease during retirement?

11. List some of the common factors that increase an individual's retirement income needs.

12. List some of the common factors that decrease an individual's retirement income needs.

13. Define the wage replacement ratio.

14. What is the most common estimate range (in percentage terms) for the wage replacement ratio?

15. Describe why a person may or may not need the same wage replacement percentage dollar amount or purchasing power amount throughout their entire retirement period.

16. List the two alternative methods for calculating an individual's wage replacement ratio.

17. How is the WRR calculated utilizing the top-down approach?

18. How is the WRR calculated utilizing the budgeting approach?

19. List the three most common sources of an individual's retirement income.

20. Explain how Social Security affects an individual's retirement income.

21. Describe the importance of personal savings to an individual's retirement income needs.

22. List some of the qualitative considerations that are important in retirement planning.

23. List some of the common factors that negatively affect retirement planning.

24. Explain capital needs analysis and its importance to retirement planning.

25. List the three most common methods for analyzing an individual's capital needs.

26. Identify the main assumptions necessary for capital needs analysis.

27. Describe how Monte Carlo Analysis can be used in retirement planning.

28. Explain how the annuity model calculates retirement needs.

29. What assumption does the capital preservation model make to mitigate the risk of an individual outliving their retirement savings?

30. Why is sensitivity analysis important to retirement planning?

MULTIPLE CHOICE PROBLEMS

1. Which of the following expenditures will most likely increase during retirement?

    a. Clothing costs.
    b. Travel.
    c. FICA.
    d. Savings.

2. Margaret, a 35-year-old client who earns $45,000 a year, pays 7.65% of her gross pay in Social Security payroll taxes, and saves 8% of her annual gross income. Assume that Margaret wants to maintain her exact pre-retirement lifestyle. Calculate Margaret's wage replacement ratio using the top-down approach (round to the nearest %) and using pre-tax dollars.

    a. 70%.
    b. 80%.
    c. 84%.
    d. 90%.

3. Ralf, a 40-year-old nurse who earns $80,000 a year, saves 14% of his annual gross income. Assume that Ralf wants to maintain his exact pre-retirement lifestyle. Calculate Ralf's wage replacement ratio using the top-down approach (round to the nearest %) and using pre-tax dollars.

    a. 70%.
    b. 78%.
    c. 86%.
    d. 92%.

4. Danny would like to determine his financial needs during retirement. All of the following are expenditures he might eliminate in his retirement needs calculation except:

    a. The $200 per month he spends on drying cleaning for his work suits.
    b. The $1,500 mortgage payment he makes that is scheduled to end five years into retirement.
    c. The FICA taxes he pays each year.
    d. The $2,000 per month he puts into savings.

5. Susie has the following expenditures during the current year:

Expense	Amount
1. Health Care	$800
2. Savings	$4,000
3. Travel	$500
4. Gifts to Grandchildren	$1,000

Which of these expenditures would you expect to decrease during Susie's retirement?

    a. 2 only.

    b. 1 and 3.

    c. 2 and 4.

    d. 1, 2, 3, and 4.

6. Tiffany, a self-employed dentist, currently earns $100,000 per year. Tiffany has always been a self proclaimed saver, and saves 25% per year of her Schedule C net income. Assume Tiffany paid $13,000 in Social Security taxes. Tiffany plans to pay off her home mortgage at retirement and live debt free. She currently spends $25,000 per year on her mortgage. What do you expect Tiffany's wage replacement ratio to be at retirement based on the above information?

    a. 37.00%.

    b. 59.70%.

    c. 65.30%.

    d. 84.70%.

7. Which factors may affect an individual's retirement plan?

    1. Work life expectancy.

    2. Retirement life expectancy.

    3. Savings rate.

    4. Investment returns.

    5. Inflation.

        a. 1 and 2.

        b. 1, 2, and 3.

        c. 1, 2, 3, and 4.

        d. All of the above.

8. Contributing $1,500 to his retirement fund at the end of each year beginning at age 18 through age 50, with an average annual return of 12%, how much does Juan have in his retirement account at this time to use toward a possible early retirement?

    a. $346,766.42.

    b. $399,987.65.

    c. $457,271.58.

    d. $541,890.55.

9. Steve and Roslyn are retiring together today and they wish to receive $40,000 of income (in the equivalent of today's dollars) at the beginning of each year from their portfolio. They assume inflation will be 4% and they expect to realize an after tax return of 8%. Based on life expectancies, they estimate their retirement period to be about 30 years. They want to know how much they should have in their fund today.

    a. $698,457.24.

    b. $728,299.37.

    c. $731,894.20.

    d. $813,529.88.

10. Tyrone, age 25, expects to retire at age 60. He expects to live until age 90. He anticipates needing $45,000 per year in today's dollars during retirement. Tyrone can earn a 12% rate of return and he expects inflation to be 4%. How much must Tyrone save, at the beginning of each year, to meet his retirement goal?

    a. $3,980.76.

    b. $4,585.46.

    c. $4,879.29.

    d. $5,132.33.

11. Roy and Barbara are near retirement. They have a joint life expectancy of 25 years in retirement. Barbara anticipates their annual income in retirement will need to increase each year at the rate of inflation, which they assume is 4%. Based on the assumption that their first year retirement need, beginning on the first day of retirement, for annual income will be $85,000, of which they have $37,500 available from other sources, and an annual after-tax rate of return of 6.5%, calculate the total amount that needs to be in place when Roy and Barbara begin their retirement.

    a. $743,590.43.

    b. $859,906.74.

    c. $892,478.21.

    d. $906,131.31.

12. Cathy and her twin sister Carley, both age 25, each believe they have the superior savings plan. Cathy saved $5,000 at the end of each year for ten years then let her money grow for 30 years. Carley on the other hand waited 10 years then began saving $5,000 at the end of each year for 30 years. They both earned 9% on their investment and are 65 years old today and ready to retire. Which of the following statements is correct?

    a. Both strategies are equal as they have equal account balances at age 65.

    b. Cathy's strategy is better because she has a greater account balance at age 65.

    c. Carley's strategy is better because she has a greater account balance at age 65.

    d. Neither strategy is better because Carley has a greater account balance but Cathy contributed less.

13. Shelley saves $3,000 per year, for ten years, at the end of each year starting at age 26 and ending at age 35. She invests the funds in an account earning 10% annually. Shelley stops investing at age 35, but continues to earn 10% annually until she reaches the age of 65. In contrast, Kevin saves $3,000 per year at the end of the year between the ages of 36 and 65 inclusively and invests in a similar account to Shelley, earning 10% annually. What is the value of Shelley's and Kevin's separate accounts at age 65?

	Shelley	Kevin
a.	$710,861	$387,212
b.	$710,861	$493,482
c.	$834,296	$387,212
d.	$834,296	$493,482

14. Kwame and Omarosa, both age 40, have $80,000 of combined retirement assets. They both expect to retire at the age of 65 with a life expectancy of 100 years old. They expect to earn 10% on the assets within their retirement accounts before retirement and 8% during their retirement. If they did not make any additional contributions to their account and they receive a fixed monthly annuity benefit for life, what is the monthly benefit (annuity due) amount they will receive during retirement?

    a. $4,775.30.

    b. $4,984.20.

    c. $6,115.60.

    d. $6,156.37.

15. Charlie would like to retire in 11 years at the age of 66. He would like to have sufficient retirement assets to allow him to withdraw 90% of his current income, less Social Security, at the beginning of each year. He expects to receive $24,000 per year from Social Security in today's dollars. Charlie is conservative and assumes that he will only earn 9% on his investments, that inflation will be 4% per year and that he will live to be 106 years old. If Charlie currently earns $150,000, how much does he need at retirement?

    a. $1,955,893.

    b. $2,049,927.

    c. $3,011,008.

    d. $3,155,768.

16. Bowie, age 52, has come to you for help in planning his retirement. He works for a bank, where he earns $60,000. Bowie would like to retire at age 62. He has consistently earned 8% on his investments and inflation has averaged 3%. Assuming he is expected to live until age 95 and he has a wage replacement ratio of 80%, how much will Bowie need to have accumulated as of the day he retires to adequately provide for his retirement lifestyle?

    a. $726,217.09.

    b. $784,314.45.

    c. $1,050,813.28.

    d. $1,101,823.40.

17. Assuming the same facts as Question 15, approximately how much must Bowie save at the end of each year, from now until retirement, to provide him with the necessary capital balance assuming he has a zero balance today?

    a. $67,163.98.

    b. $70,424.36.

    c. $72,537.10.

    d. $76,058.31.

18. Utilizing the facts given in Question 15, how much more will Bowie need at retirement to have the same amount at his death as he will have (calculated in #15) at his retirement?

    a. $82,897.54.

    b. $86,921.67.

    c. $109,496.29.

    d. $230,545.40.

19. Utilizing the facts given in Question 15, how much more will Bowie need at retirement to have the same amount at his death with an equal purchasing power as he will have (calculated in #16) at his retirement?

    a. $82,897.54.

    b. $86,921.69.

    c. $109,496.29.

    d. $230,545.41.

20. Robin is planning for her retirement. She is currently 37 years old and plans to retire at age 62 and live until age 97. Robin currently earns $100,000 per year and anticipates needing 80% of her income during retirement. She anticipates Social Security will provide her with $15,000 per year at age 62, leaving her with required savings to provide $65,000 ($100,000 x 0.80 - $15,000) annually during retirement. She believes she can earn 11% on her investments and inflation will be 2% per year. How much must Robin save at the end of each year, if she wants to make her last savings payment at age 62 to meet her retirement goal?

    a. $10,846.78.

    b. $10,899.37.

    c. $11,861.07.

    d. $13,414.60.

21. Assume the same facts as in question 19 except that Robin would like to have the same amount in retirement savings at age 97, as she does at age 62, when she retires. How much must Robin save at the end of each year, if she wants to make her last savings payment at age 62, and maintain the original account balance needed at retirement for the entire retirement life expectancy?

    a. $2,379.57.

    b. $10,899.37.

    c. $11,181.92.

    d. $11,280.51.

22. Assume the same facts as in question 19 except that Robin would like to have the same purchasing power in retirement savings at age 97, as she does at age 62, when she retires. How much must Robin save at the end of each year, if she wants to make her last savings payment at age 62 to meet her retirement goal, assuming she wants to maintain the original purchasing power of her capital balance?

    a. $4,758.88.

    b. $10,899.37.

    c. $11,464.44.

    d. $11,565.52.

23. Which of the following statements is false?

   a. To be more conservative in planning for an individual's retirement, extend the individual's life expectancy.

   b. A Monte Carlo Analysis uses a random number generator to provide the advisor with an array of possible outcomes utilizing the same fact pattern.

   c. A sensitivity analysis helps the advisor determine the single most effective factor in a retirement plan.

   d. The capital preservation model assumes that at life expectancy the client will have exactly the same account balance as he did at retirement.

QUICK QUIZ EXPLANATIONS

QUICK QUIZ 2.1
1. False. The average age men retire is age 64. Labor force participation for men over age 65 is under 30 percent.
2. True.
3. True.

QUICK QUIZ 2.2
1. False. Given that a savings rate of 10% to 13% of gross pay over a long period of time is necessary to meet the retirement goal, the savings rate in the U.S. is insufficient for retirement planning.
2. False. Common stocks provide the best hedge against inflation. The real economic returns for fixed-income securities are low and are not a good hedge against inflation.
3. True.

QUICK QUIZ 2.3
1. True.
2. True.

QUICK QUIZ 2.4
1. True.
2. False. Social Security is not a sufficient source of income replacement during retirement for most income levels. Social Security provides 100% of income to only 20% of individuals aged 65 or older receiving Social Security benefits.
3. True.

QUICK QUIZ 2.5
1. False. Qualitative factors associated with retirement may be more important than the financial or quantitative factors.
2. True.
3. False. A reduced WLE and an increased RLE will negatively impact retirement planning because a reduced WLE will result in an insufficient savings period and an increased RLE will result in an increased capital need.

QUICK QUIZ 2.6
1. True.
2. True.
3. True.

QUICK QUIZ EXPLANATIONS

QUICK QUIZ 2.7

1. False. While sensitivity analysis does not eliminate all risk associated with retirement planning, it does allow the advisor to build a slightly worse case scenario and to determine the impact of more conservative assumptions on the overall plan.
2. False. Monte Carlo Analysis does not predict particular events. Rather, it provides insight into the most likely outcome while also providing other possible outcomes, both good and bad.
3. True.

QUALIFIED PLAN OVERVIEW

LEARNING OBJECTIVES

After reading this chapter, you should be able to:
1. Understand the history of employer-sponsored retirement plans.
2. Understand the primary differences between pension plans and profit sharing plans.
3. Understand the primary differences between defined benefit plans and defined contribution plans.
4. Be able to explain the advantages of a qualified plan.
5. Describe the requirements for a plan to be classified as a qualified plan under IRC §401(a).
6. Calculate whether a plan meets the coverage tests for a qualified plan.
7. Determine whether an employee is classified as highly compensated or as a key employee.
8. Identify employees who meet plan eligibility rules and those that can be excluded from the plan.
9. Explain the impact of top-heavy status on defined benefit and defined contribution plans.
10. Compare the vesting schedules for defined contribution, defined benefit and cash balance plans.
11. Explain the funding limitations for defined contribution plans, defined benefit plans, and the limits on employers who sponsor both.

HISTORY

Employer-sponsored pension and retirement plans have grown in terms of prevalence, protection and benefits over the last 100 years. In the United States, the first employer-sponsored pension plans were found in the railroad industry in the late 19th century. Pensions were not protected as they are today and were often paid out of current cash flow. Congress first provided preferential treatment to pension, profit sharing, and stock bonus plans in the Revenue Act of 1921. During the 1930s and 1940s, Congress provided that pension funds had to be used exclusively for the benefit of employees and their beneficiaries and that plans could not discriminate in favor of highly compensated employees.

Over time, with the number of plans increasing, Congress realized that it was critical to further regulate pension and profit sharing plans. At the time, there was no legal recourse for employees of companies who did not pay pension benefits. ERISA[1] (Employee Retirement Income Security Act) was signed into law by President Ford on September 2, 1974 and was designed to provide greatly enhanced protection for pension and retirement benefits. Congress wrote in §1001 of ERISA:
- the Congress finds that the growth in size, scope, and numbers of employee benefit plans in recent years has been rapid and substantial;
- that the operational scope and economic impact of such plans is increasingly interstate; that the continued well-being and security of millions of employees and their dependents are directly affected by these plans; that they are affected with a national public interest; that they have become an important factor affecting the stability of employment and the successful development of industrial relations;
- that they have become an important factor in commerce because of the interstate character of their activities, and of the activities of their participants, and the employers, employee organizations, and other entities by which they are established or maintained;

---

1. Chapter 18 of Title 29 of U.S. Code.

- that a large volume of the activities of such plans are carried on by means of the mails and instrumentalities of interstate commerce; that owing to the lack of employee information and adequate safeguards concerning their operation, it is desirable in the interests of employees and their beneficiaries, and to provide for the general welfare and the free flow of commerce, that disclosure be made and safeguards be provided with respect to the establishment, operation, and administration of such plans;

- that they substantially affect the revenues of the United States because they are afforded preferential Federal tax treatment; that despite the enormous growth in such plans many employees with long years of employment are losing anticipated retirement benefits owing to the lack of vesting provisions in such plans;

- that owing to the inadequacy of current minimum standards, the soundness and stability of plans with respect to adequate funds to pay promised benefits may be endangered;

- that owing to the termination of plans before requisite funds have been accumulated, employees and their beneficiaries have been deprived of anticipated benefits; and

- that it is therefore desirable in the interests of employees and their beneficiaries, for the protection of the revenue of the United States, and to provide for the free flow of commerce, that minimum standards be provided assuring the equitable character of such plans and their financial soundness.

Congress believed that pension plans and the welfare of Americans was too important not to regulate employer-sponsored retirement plans. ERISA also set forth rules on disclosure, reporting, standards for fiduciaries, vesting, minimum benefits and provides for pension plan termination insurance, as afforded by the Pension Benefit Guarantee Corporation.

There is a large overlap of rules between ERISA and the Internal Revenue Code. Both ERISA and the IRC provide rules that employer-sponsored plans must comply with in the operation of retirement plans.

INTRODUCTION

Employers have many choices when selecting a retirement plan for the benefit of their company and its employees. Each retirement plan may have unique benefits and characteristics, but if the plan is to be a **qualified plan**, it must follow a standard set of rules and requirements to attain "qualified" status under Internal Revenue Code (IRC) §401(a). Once a plan has achieved qualified status, (provided it maintains the qualified status per §401(a)) the plan sponsor and the participants will benefit from tax deferral, asset protection, and several other advantages as discussed throughout this chapter and in Chapters 4, 5, and 6. Keep in mind that some employer-sponsored plans, such as 403(b) plans and SEPs, are tax-sheltered retirement arrangements, but are not "qualified" under IRC §401(a).

To help understand the unique advantages of each available qualified retirement plan and the specific requirements for the plans to attain qualified status, the universe of available qualified plans can be divided into four categories. Each of these four categories can be defined by its specific combination of certain qualities, benefits, and rules. First, qualified plans consist of **pension plans** and **profit sharing plans**. These plans are further divided into either **defined benefit** or **defined**

contribution qualified plans, as depicted at Exhibit 3.1. (Note that "defined benefit" and "profit sharing" are category titles as well as plan names.)

As Exhibit 3.1 illustrates, a qualified plan will always possess the characteristics of either a pension plan or a profit sharing plan with the characteristics of either a defined benefit plan or a defined contribution plan. For example, a money purchase pension plan has the qualities, advantages, disadvantages, and requirements of both a pension plan and a defined contribution plan, whereas a cash balance pension plan has the qualities of a pension plan and a defined benefit plan.

KNOW THE NUMBERS (2016)	
Covered Compensation	$265,000
Defined Benefit Maximum Limit	$210,000
Defined Contribution Maximum Limit	$53,000
401(k) Plan Deferral Limit	$18,000
Highly Compensated Employee	$120,000
Key Employee	$170,000
Social Security Wage Base	$118,500

EXHIBIT 3.1

QUALIFIED PLANS

		Pension Plans (4 Types)	Profit Sharing Plans (7 Types)	
DEFINED BENEFIT PENSION PLANS (2 Types)		Defined Benefit Pension Plans Cash Balance Pension Plans	Profit Sharing Plans Stock Bonus Plans Employee Stock Ownership Plans 401(k) Plans Thrift Plans New Comparability Plans Age-Based Profit Sharing Plans	**DEFINED CONTRIBUTION PROFIT SHARING PLANS (All 7)**
DEFINED CONTRIBUTION PENSION PLANS (2 Types)		Money Purchase Pension Plans Target Benefit Pension Plans		

Note: The DB(k) plan is not listed as it is a combination of a DB plan and a 401(k) plan.

PENSION PLANS VS. PROFIT SHARING PLANS

Historically, a retirement plan paid benefits to retired employees until death. Some retirement plans continued the payment of retirement benefits even after the employee's death until the surviving spouse's death. Generally, the employee did not contribute to the plan, bear any responsibility for investment decisions for the plan, or participate in the management of the plan. The employee was simply promised a guaranteed benefit at retirement. Over the past 30 years, however, the number of these types of plans (noncontributory defined benefit plans) has

KEY CONCEPTS ✓

1. Explain the reason for the change from pension plans to profit sharing plans.

2. From a global perspective, what are the differences between defined benefit and defined contribution plans?

decreased substantially as some employers have not fulfilled the promise of paying the retirement benefit and as employees have begun changing jobs frequently throughout their work life. In fact, between 1980 and 2010 the number of defined benefit pension plans declined from 148,096 to fewer than 50,000. Changing jobs even a few times in a lifetime could result in significantly limiting the growth of retirement benefits payable from these types of plans, which generally require many years of continuous service with the same employer to attain the expected or desired retirement benefit.

With the decline of these "guaranteed" type plans, commonly known as defined benefit pension plans, came the addition of profit sharing plans. Under profit sharing plans, plan participants usually become responsible for the management of the plan's assets (investment decisions) and sometimes even responsible for personal contributions to the plan (contributory plans). The profit sharing plan also changed the employer's funding requirement and began to permit, subject to limitations, in-service withdrawals from qualified plans and investments in the employer's securities. Exhibit 3.2 compares the basic characteristics between pension and profit sharing plans, which are discussed further in Chapters 3, 4, 5, and 6.

THE DIFFERENCES BETWEEN PENSION PLANS AND PROFIT-SHARING PLANS

EXHIBIT 3.2

CHARACTERISTIC	PENSION PLAN	PROFIT-SHARING PLAN
Legal promise of the plan	Paying a pension at retirement	Deferral of compensation and taxation
Are in-service withdrawals permitted?	No*	Yes (after two years) if plan document permits
Is the plan subject to mandatory funding standards?	Yes**	No
Percent of plan assets available to be invested in employer securities	10%	Up to 100%
Must the plan provide qualified joint and survivor annuity and a qualified pre-survivor annuity?	Yes	No

* Under the Pension Protection Act of 2006, pension plans can provide for in-service distributions to participants who are age 62 or older.
** For plan years beginning in 2008, the funding rules under IRC §412 have been amended by the Pension Protection Act of 2006.

Pension Plan (Treas. Reg. 1.401-1(b))	• A pension plan within the meaning of §401(a) is a plan established and maintained by an employer primarily to provide systematically for the payment of definitely determinable benefits to his employees over a period of years, usually for life, after retirement. • Retirement benefits generally are measured by, and based on, such factors as years of service and compensation received by the employees. • A plan designed to provide benefits for employees or their beneficiaries to be paid upon retirement or over a period of years after retirement will, for the purposes of §401(a), be considered a pension plan if the employer contributions under the plan can be determined actuarially on the basis of definitely determinable benefits, or, as in the case of money purchase pension plans, such contributions are fixed without being geared to profits.
Profit Sharing Plan (Treas. Reg. 1.401-1(b))	• A profit-sharing plan is a plan established and maintained by an employer to provide for the participation in his profits by his employees or their beneficiaries. • The plan must provide a definite predetermined formula for allocating the contributions made to the plan among the participants and for distributing the funds accumulated under the plan after a fixed number of years, the attainment of a stated age, or upon the prior occurrence of some event such as layoff, illness, disability, retirement, death, or severance of employment. • A formula for allocating the contributions among the participants is definite if, for example, it provides for an allocation in proportion to the basic compensation of each participant. • A plan (whether or not it contains a definite predetermined formula for determining the profits to be shared with the employees) does not qualify under §401(a) if the contributions to the plan are made at such times or in such amounts that the plan in operation discriminates in favor of officers, shareholders, persons whose principal duties consist in supervising the work of other employees, or highly compensated employees.
Defined Contribution Plan (IRC 414(i))	• The term "defined contribution plan" means a plan which provides for an individual account for each participant and for benefits based solely on the amount contributed to the participant's account, and any income, expenses, gains and losses, and any forfeitures of accounts of other participants which may be allocated to such participant's account.
Defined Benefit Plan (IRC 414(i))	• The term "defined benefit plan" means any plan which is not a defined contribution plan.

DEFINED BENEFIT VS. DEFINED CONTRIBUTION

As illustrated in Exhibit 3.1, qualified plans can be further divided into defined benefit plans and defined contribution plans. All defined benefit plans are pension plans, but defined contribution plans can be either pension or profit sharing plans. The primary differences between the classification of the plans as defined benefit or defined contribution are the assumption of the investment risk, the allocation of plan forfeitures, coverage under the Pension Benefit Guaranty Corporation (PBGC), the calculation of the accrued benefit or account balance, and the availability to grant credit to employees for prior service. Each of these differences is illustrated in Exhibit 3.4 and discussed in detail below.

Under the Pension Protection Act of 2006, defined contribution plans that hold publicly traded securities of the employer must allow plan participants to diversify their pre-tax deferrals, after-tax contributions, and employer contributions that have been invested in those employer securities. The defined contribution plan must offer a choice of at least three investment options, other than employer securities, each of which must be diversified and have materially different risk and return characteristics (e.g., a money market fund, a bond fund, and a stock fund).

All plan participants must be allowed to diversify the investment of their elective deferrals and after-tax contributions. In addition, plan participants with three or more years of service must be allowed to diversify the investment of employer contributions made on their behalf. These requirements do not, however, apply to an ESOP if there are no contributions to the ESOP that are subject to the 401(k) nondiscrimination tests and the ESOP is a separate plan from any other qualified retirement plan.[2] As described in Chapter 6, ESOPs already require diversification under certain circumstances.

QUICK QUIZ 3.1

1. Pension plans are more common than profit sharing plans because individual workers remain longer with one employer and, therefore, can receive more benefits.
   a. True
   b. False

2. All pension plans are defined benefit plans.
   a. True
   b. False

False, False.

---

2. Pension Protection Act of 2006, §901.

EXHIBIT
3.4

CHARACTERISTICS OF DEFINED BENEFIT VS. DEFINED CONTRIBUTION PLANS

CHARACTERISTICS	DEFINED BENEFIT	DEFINED CONTRIBUTION
What is the Annual Contribution Limit?	The greater of (1) the sum of the plan's funding target, target normal cost, and a cushion amount over the value of the plan asset, or (2) the minimum required contribution for the plan year.*	25% of covered compensation
Who assumes the investment risk?	Employer	Employee
How are forfeitures allocated?	Reduce plan costs	Reduce plan costs or allocate to other participants
Is the plan subject to Pension Benefit Guaranty Corporation (PBGC) coverage?	Yes (except professional firms with less than 25 employees)**	No
Does the plan have separate investment accounts?	No, they are commingled	Yes, they are usually separate
Can credit be given for prior service for the purpose of benefits?	Yes	No

This is the annual contribution limit for defined benefit plans beginning in 2008 as a result of the PPA 2006. See Chapter 4 for more detail.
** ERISA §4021, 29 U.S.C. §1321.

Pension plans can be either defined benefit or defined contribution, while all profit sharing plans are defined contribution plans. The differences among various pension plans are discussed in more detail in Chapter 4.

ADVANTAGES OF QUALIFIED PLANS

The U.S. government offers several income tax advantages to both employers and employees who elect to maintain and participate in a qualified retirement plan. The plan must be designed and adopted in a fashion "approved" by the government, and the plan must meet certain requirements enumerated in IRC §401(a). Most of these requirements are established to ensure that a qualified plan is designed to protect and benefit rank-and-file employees. As distinguished from senior executives and owners, the rank-and-file are employees, such as the factory workers, counter clerks, mechanics, staff accountants, associate attorneys, etc. The government's primary motivation for the IRC requirements of §401(a) is to prevent employers from adopting qualified retirement plans that solely benefit executives and owners of the business. When a plan meets the qualification requirements and is considered a "qualified plan" under §401(a), the employer and the plan participants will benefit from income tax deferrals, payroll tax savings, and federally provided creditor asset protection. Each of these advantages is discussed below. The trade-offs for the tax advantages of qualified plans are the cost of the plan (both the operational expenses and contributions) and the compliance requirements, including vesting, funding, eligibility, non-discrimination testing, IRS reporting, and employee disclosure.

TAXATION OF CONTRIBUTIONS TO PLANS

Income Tax

In almost all cases in the field of income taxation, when one individual or entity has a tax deductible expense, another entity or individual will have taxable income. This concept is referred to as the matching principle and is prevalent throughout the IRC. Consider an office supply store that sells office supplies to a publishing company for $600. The office supply store has revenue, or taxable income, of $600 (subject to its costs), and the publishing company has a tax deductible expense of $600. This matching of income and expense especially holds true when an employer pays employees' wages, salaries, or bonuses for performance of services. The employees have taxable income and the employer has a tax deduction for the same amount. This concept is referred to as the matching principle because of the matching of income and deductions.

> **KEY CONCEPTS** ✓
>
> 1. Explain the matching principle as between expenses and income and its application to qualified retirement plans.
>
> 2. How does the imposition of payroll taxes on contributions impact qualified retirement plans?
>
> 3. How are the investment earnings within a qualified plan taxed?

> Carla works 40 hours a week at Best Feed Supply for $6.00 per hour. In addition, if Carla sells more than 200 pounds of feed during the week, she receives a bonus of $200. In a week that Carla works 40 hours and sells 300 pounds of feed, Carla has taxable income of $440 (($6.00 x 40) + $200), and Best Feed Supply has a tax deductible wage expense of $440.

EXAMPLE 3.1

Contributions by employers to qualified plans, however, do not have to comply with this "matching" of taxable income with tax deductible expense. An employer may deduct an amount up to 25 percent (or as actuarially determined for defined benefit plans) of the total covered compensation paid to its employees as a contribution to a qualified plan. The employer will immediately have a deductible expense for income tax purposes, but the employee will not have taxable income related to the plan contribution until the funds are later distributed from the plan. This timing "mismatch" of income and expense is provided for in the IRC as a governmental incentive to entice employers to establish and fund qualified retirement plans for their employees. This mismatch is significant as it reduces the current tax revenue for the U.S. Treasury and defers the taxation of the funds until the plan participant receives a distribution from the qualified plan, generally many years later (during retirement).

This tax deferral is a benefit both to the participant and to society as it encourages the accumulation of assets specifically for retirement. As demographics have changed over the last several decades and life expectancies have increased, this tax deferral has become more important. However, because of this tax benefit and its potential abuse, the government has established, and continues to establish, certain limits for funding and deducting contributions to qualified retirement plans to minimize the reduction of tax revenue and to ensure that a substantial portion of the benefits are available to rank-and-file employees.

EXAMPLE
3.2

Computer Connection, a C Corporation, employs fifteen service technicians, each earning $40,000 per year. The sole-shareholder of Computer Connection, Jason, who is also a service technician and employee, pays himself $120,000 per year. For 2016, Computer Connection contributed 20 percent of each employee's salary to a qualified profit sharing plan. For 2016, Computer Connection will have a deductible business expense for contributions to the profit sharing plan of $144,000 ((15 x $40,000) x 20% + 20% x ($120,000)). Neither the employees nor Jason will have current taxable income related to the contribution to the qualified profit sharing plan, but any distributions from the plan are taxable as ordinary income (and may be subject to penalties) to the recipients at the time of distribution. However, neither the employer contributions nor the distributions will ever be subject to payroll tax.

QUICK QUIZ
3.2

1. Contributions to qualified retirement plans follow the IRC matching principle of the inclusion of income and the deduction of the expense at the same time.
   a. True
   b. False

2. The employer and employee are each responsible for their share of payroll taxes on the employee's compensation.
   a. True
   b. False

3. Distributions from a qualified retirement plan are generally taxable as ordinary income.
   a. True
   b. False

False, True, True.

Payroll Taxes

In addition to income taxes, an employee who receives compensation for services rendered to an employer also incurs **payroll taxes** equal to 6.2 percent for Old Age Survivor and Disability Insurance (OASDI) on compensation up to $118,500 for 2016 and 1.45 percent for Medicare tax on 100 percent of the employee's compensation. The employer is also required to match any payroll taxes paid by the employee, creating a combined total payroll tax of 12.4 percent for OASDI up to $118,500 and 2.9 percent for Medicare on 100 percent of employee compensation.[3]

However, when the employer makes a contribution to a qualified retirement plan on behalf of its employees, the employer's contribution is not subject to payroll tax even though the contribution was on account of services rendered. This payroll tax savings acts to entice employers to fund qualified retirement plans and to view the combination of a qualified retirement plan and an employee's salary as part of an overall compensation package. Since the employee is not subject to payroll taxes on an employer's contribution to a qualified retirement plan either, a total savings of up to 15.3 percent (12.4 percent OASDI and 2.9 percent Medicare tax) on the employer contribution may be realized. In Example 3.2, the alternative would have been to pay the $144,000 to the employees as additional salary instead of making the contribution to the qualified retirement plan. In that case, both the employer and the employee would have paid combined payroll taxes of up to 15.3 percent on most of the $144,000.

---

3. Chapter 11 discusses the new Medicare taxes resulting from the Affordable Care Act for years 2013 and beyond.

> If Butcher Block paid its two employees $50,000 each in wages and did not contribute to a qualified profit sharing plan for the year, Butcher Block would incur payroll taxes relating to the wages of $7,650 ($100,000 x 7.65%). Butcher Block's employees would have also incurred payroll taxes of $7,650 for total payroll taxes of $15,300.

> In comparison, if Butcher Block would have paid its two employees $45,000 each in wages and contributed $5,000 to a qualified profit sharing plan for each employee, Butcher Block would incur total payroll taxes relating to the wages and profit sharing plan contribution of $6,885 ($90,000 x 7.65%). In this case, Butcher Block's employees would also only incur $6,885 of payroll taxes for a total of $13,770 of payroll taxes. The combined payroll tax savings would be $1,530 ($15,300 - $13,770); however, Butcher Block's employees received total payments for services rendered equal to $50,000, $45,000 as cash compensation and $5,000 in contributions to a qualified profit sharing plan. Note that even at the time distributions are taken from the qualified profit sharing plan, the distributions will not be subject to any payroll taxes. The $1,530 of payroll tax that was saved is permanently avoided.

The payroll tax exclusion for contributions to qualified retirement plans does not pertain to employee elective deferrals to 401(k) plans, 403(b) plans, SIMPLEs, SARSEPs, and 457 plans. Therefore, if an employee defers income by making a pretax elective deferral contribution into one of these plans, then amounts deferred by the employee are subject to payroll taxes. However, if these employee contributions have employer-matching provisions, or the employer is making other contributions (such as profit sharing), the employer-matching contribution is not subject to payroll taxes. Note that 403(b) plans are not qualified plans and will be discussed in more depth in Chapter 10.

> Joseph earns $166,667 and is a participant in his employer-sponsored 401(k) plan that offers a 75 percent match for contributions up to three percent of salary. Joseph elects to defer three percent of his salary, or $5,000, into the qualified 401(k) plan, and his employer matches the contribution with a $3,750 (75% x $5,000) contribution into the plan. Joseph's contribution of $5,000 is subject to payroll taxes, but the employer's contribution of $3,750 is not subject to employee or employer payroll taxes. Note that because Joseph's earnings are in excess of the Social Security wage base and the OASDI of 6.2 percent is only paid on compensation up to the Social Security wage base, the employer and the employee are only saving the Medicare tax portion of 1.45 percent on the matching contribution to Joseph's 401(k) plan. However, in other cases where the employee's earnings are below the Social Security wage base, the employer and the employee are saving the full payroll taxes of 7.65 percent of the contribution by the employer.

TAX DEFERRAL OF QUALIFIED PLAN EARNINGS AND INCOME

Assets contributed to a qualified retirement plan are held in a tax exempt trust by a fiduciary, the plan sponsor, or an appointee of the plan sponsor. The plan assets are invested per the direction of the fiduciary or the employee (as determined at the creation or by amendment of the qualified plan), and the earnings on the plan investments are not subject to current income tax.

EXAMPLE 3.6

Mark's employer contributed $4,000 to a money purchase pension plan on his behalf. The funds were invested in a mutual fund that earned $300 in income during the year. The $300 is paid to Mark's money purchase pension plan account and reinvested in the mutual fund. Neither Mark nor his employer will currently recognize any taxable income resulting from the $300 of income from the mutual fund. Only upon distribution will the contribution ($4,000) and earnings ($300) be subject to income tax.

When funds are distributed from a qualified retirement plan, the recipient of the distribution will have taxable income. With a few exceptions (as discussed below), the entire distribution is taxed at the recipient's ordinary income tax rate at the time of the distribution regardless of whether the plan distributes cash, municipal bonds, Treasury bonds, or even stocks with "built-in" or unrealized capital gains.

KEY CONCEPTS

1. What protection does ERISA provide to participants in qualified plans?

2. Describe the special taxation options available for lump-sum distributions from a qualified plan.

It should be noted that because of the decrease in income tax rates over the last few decades, the advantages of tax deferral have been reduced. Specifically, the highest marginal income tax rate in 1986 was 50 percent while today's highest marginal income tax rate is 39.6 percent. Also, the tax rate on dividends and capital gains has been reduced to 15 percent (or less) for many equity investments and other capital assets.[4] By deferring taxes today, an employee saves current income tax, but gives up favorable tax treatment on dividends and capital gains. For most employees, dividends and capital gains will be a large part of their earnings on funds used for retirement. These changes in tax rates should be considered as part of the analysis of whether a qualified plan is appropriate.

ERISA PROTECTION

Because of various abuses by plan sponsors, Congress enacted the **Employee Retirement Income and Security Act (ERISA)** in 1974 to provide protection for an employee's retirement assets, both from creditors and from plan sponsors. Title I of ERISA ensures the employee's right to receive their dedicated benefits and is enforced by the Department of Labor.

Anti-Alienation Protection[5]

Because a qualified plan is designed to provide individuals with income during their retirement, ERISA provides **anti-alienation protection** over all assets within a qualified retirement plan. This anti-alienation protection prohibits any action that may cause the plan assets to be assigned, garnished, levied, or subject to bankruptcy proceedings while the assets remain in the qualified retirement plan. Assets in a retirement plan covered by ERISA can only be seized to pay federal tax liens. This protection is to ensure that the individual has income during retirement.

---

4. The American Taxpayer Relief Act of 2012 increased the 15% rate to 20% on dividends and capital gains for individuals and taxpayers filing married filing jointly for AGI over $400,000 and $450,000, respectively. These limits are indexed annually.

5. 29 U.S.C. §1056.

George has $4,000,000 in qualified retirement plan assets. George's business failed and George personally filed for federal bankruptcy (Chapter 7). At the time of the bankruptcy filing, George had other assets totaling $250,000 and debts totaling $650,000. The court awarded George's creditors $0.38 on the dollar and discharged George of any remaining creditor claims. This judgment left George with nothing except his qualified retirement plan assets. Because of ERISA afforded anti-alienation protection, the court could not award any of George's $4,000,000 of qualified retirement plan assets to his creditors. George will continue to have full rights over the assets of his qualified retirement plan.

EXAMPLE 3.7

Nicole Brown Simpson's family and Ron Goldman's family won a civil judgment that exceeded $30 million dollars against O.J. Simpson in 1997. However, most of O.J.'s remaining assets (after the trial and his subsequent bankruptcy) were qualified retirement plan assets that are protected under ERISA. Because of the ERISA protection, the Brown and Goldman families have been unable to collect much, if any, of the $30 million dollar judgment even though the value of O.J.'s retirement assets is large enough to defray some of the debt.

EXAMPLE 3.8

Once funds are distributed from a qualified retirement plan, the distributed assets are no longer protected by ERISA. Additionally, qualified retirement plan assets are not protected from alienation due to a **qualified domestic relations order** (QDRO - a court order related to divorce, property settlement, or child support), a federal tax levy, or from a judgment or settlement rendered upon an individual for a criminal act involving the same qualified plan. Individual Retirement Accounts (Traditional, Roth, SEP, or SIMPLE) are not afforded the same anti-alienation protection under ERISA, but as a result of the Bankruptcy Abuse Prevention and Consumer Protection Act of 2005 (BAPCPA 2005), IRAs are afforded similar creditor protection under Federal Bankruptcy law. Prior to the BAPCPA 2005, it was unclear whether IRAs were exempt from the debtor's estate. The Act clarifies that retirement accounts that are exempt from tax under the Internal Revenue Code are also exempt from the debtor's estate (up to $1 million).[6] See Chapter 9 for more details.

QUICK QUIZ 3.3

1. ERISA protects qualified plan assets from all creditors.
   a. True
   b. False

2. One disadvantage of a qualified plan is that it does not protect the employee from the employer's wrong doings.
   a. True
   b. False

3. A lump-sum distribution from a qualified retirement plan may be eligible for special income tax treatment.
   a. True
   b. False

False, False, True.

---

6. Bankruptcy Abuse Prevention and Consumer Protection Act of 2005, §224. This exemption is indexed to $1,245,475 as of April 2013. This limit was not indexed for 2016 as of the time of printing.

Protection from Employers

ERISA provides the laws, rules, and enforcement provisions to protect employees from abuse and misuse of qualified plan assets by employers as plan sponsors. Specifically, employers are prohibited by ERISA from discriminating against employees based on the benefits payable to the employee under the plan, from substantially altering the plan document without appropriate approval and notice, and from managing the qualified plan in a manner that is not in the best interest of the qualified plan participants and their beneficiaries.

SPECIAL TAXATION OPTIONS FOR LUMP-SUM DISTRIBUTIONS

As briefly discussed above (and thoroughly discussed in Chapter 7), the full value of a distribution from a qualified plan is usually subject to ordinary income tax at the date of the distribution (except for the return of a participant's adjusted basis from certain types of after-tax contributions). However, in certain circumstances, when an employee takes a lump-sum distribution from a qualified plan, that **lump-sum distribution** may be eligible to receive favorable income tax treatment. A lump-sum distribution is a complete distribution of a participant's account balance within one taxable year of death, disability, attainment of age 59½, or separation from service. Specifically, a lump distribution may be eligible for ten-year forward averaging, pre-1974 capital gain treatment, or net unrealized appreciation treatment (discussed in detail in Chapter 7). The beneficial tax treatment of these distribution options is intended to lower the overall income tax payable by the distribution recipient (but also functions to accelerate the tax revenue for the current administration by encouraging the participant to take a full distribution rather than just the yearly annuity amount needed during retirement). It is important to recognize that due to various changes in the tax laws over the years, these lump-sum distribution options do not always create the lowest overall income tax and may not be the best choice for taxpayers eligible for these options.

Only lump-sum distributions from qualified plans qualify for the ten-year forward averaging taxation option. Distributions from an IRA, SEP IRA, or SIMPLE IRA do not qualify as lump-sum distributions for the purposes of ten-year averaging, pre-1974 capital gain treatment, or NUA, and are taxed at ordinary income tax rates.

EXHIBIT 3.5

ADVANTAGES OF QUALIFIED PLANS

Advantages to the Employer
• Employer contributions are currently income tax deductible
• Employer contributions to the plan are not subject to payroll taxes

Advantages to the Employee
• Availability of pretax contributions
• Tax deferral of earnings
• ERISA protection
• Lump-sum distribution options (ten-year averaging, NUA, Pre-1974 capital gain treatment)

DISADVANTAGES OF QUALIFIED PLANS

EXHIBIT
3.6

- Limited contribution amounts
- Contributions cannot be made after money is received
- Plans usually have limited investment options
- No or limited access to money while an active employee
- Distributions usually taxed as ordinary income (Basis = $0)
- Early withdrawal penalties may apply (prior to age 59½)
- Mandatory distributions at age 70½ (unless still employed)
- Only ownership permitted is by the account holder
- Cannot assign or pledge as collateral
- Limited enrollment periods (plan entrance dates)
- Considered to be an Income in Respect of a Decedent asset, subjecting distributions to both income and estate taxes with no step-up in basis
- Costs of operating the plan

QUALIFICATION REQUIREMENTS

To benefit from the advantages of qualified plans, the IRC and ERISA impose requirements regarding eligibility, coverage, vesting, and plan funding limits for employers sponsoring qualified retirement plans. These requirements protect rank-and-file employees and ensure that qualified plans are not being used solely to provide additional benefits to owners and senior executives of the employer.

PLAN DOCUMENT

When a qualified plan is adopted, the terms of the plan are identified and described in the plan document. In order for the plan to maintain its qualified status, the plan document and the administration of the plan must be consistent with the IRC qualification requirements, which are discussed in this chapter. In some cases, plan adopters may choose between several options (such as vesting schedules and loans) and still maintain their qualified status. These selections must be identified and described in the initial plan document and the plan document must be amended if different options are later selected. The plan document is discussed in more detail in Chapter 8.

ELIGIBILITY

A qualified retirement plan must provide rules regarding when an employee becomes eligible for participation in the plan. The IRC provides **standard eligibility requirements** that state that an employee must be considered eligible to participate in the plan after the employee has completed a period of service with the employer extending beyond the later of either the date on which the employee attains the age of 21 or the date on which the employee completes one year of service (defined as a 12 month period in which the employee works at least 1,000 hours).[7] Any employer-provided qualified retirement plan may be more generous and provide that an employee is eligible

7. IRC §410(a)(1)(A).

to participate before one year of service or before the attainment of age 21, but this generally only occurs with 401(k) plans because a majority of contributions to 401(k) plans consist of employee elective deferrals and, thus, may only cost the employer a minimal matching amount. In fact, a plan that requires an employee to attain any age or term of service less than the standard eligibility requirements of the IRC will meet the eligibility requirements necessary to be a qualified retirement plan.

Note that an eligible employee is not automatically a participant in a qualified retirement plan. Other provisions of the plan may limit an employee's participation in the plan. Eligibility rules requiring age and service are established to ensure that employers are not requiring excessive years of service by employees or only allowing older employees to be eligible for the plan.

KEY CONCEPTS

1. What are the eligibility rules for qualified plans?

2. Explain the special two-year election for eligibility in a qualified plan.

3. How are tax exempt educational institutions encouraged to establish qualified plans?

Plan Entrance Date

The eligibility rules could create an administrative burden for employers, requiring them to track eligible employees each day of the year. However, the IRC provides an elective grace period for the employer that states that even if an employee meets the requirements for eligibility listed above, an employer can make the employee wait until the next **plan entrance date** after the date on which the employee meets the eligibility requirements. The employer is allowed to follow this plan entrance date rule as long as the next available entrance date is not more than six months after the date of eligibility as determined above.[8] Because of this rule, most qualified retirement plans establish two plan entrance dates per year so that no eligibility date requires an employee to wait more than six months to enter the plan once the eligibility requirement has been met. However, a qualified retirement plan with quarterly or monthly entrance dates will also meet the grace period requirement because it is more generous than twice per year and would always meet the six month requirement set forth by the IRC.

EXAMPLE 3.9

Helium Limited operates a money purchase pension plan on behalf of its employees. The plan has entrance dates of January 1 and July 1 of each year. On April 12, 2016, Bob turned 21 years old and celebrated three years of service. On November 15, 2016, Cathy, age 25, celebrated her one-year anniversary of employment. Helium Limited considered Bob a participant in the plan at July 1, 2016 and Cathy a participant in the plan at January 1, 2017. Both employees were required to wait for entrance into the qualified retirement plan past their exact eligibility date, but neither was required to wait more than six months past their exact eligibility date. Thus, the plan meets IRC entrance requirements.

8. IRC §410(a)(4).

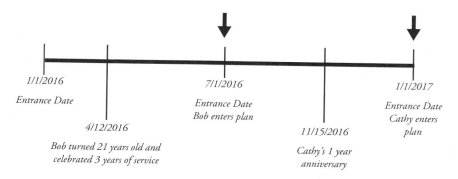

Special Eligibility Rules

Two Year, 100 Percent Rule[9]

As an exception to the above eligibility rule, a qualified retirement plan could require that an employee complete two years of service to be eligible for participation into the qualified retirement plan. When an employer elects this special requirement for its qualified retirement plan, there are consequences. The plan must provide the plan participants with 100 percent immediate vesting of their accrued benefit or account balance upon completion of two years of service for the retirement plan to be considered qualified under §401(a). With this exception, the employer may still require that the employee attain the age of 21. Thus, such a plan would have an age 21 and two years of service requirement. The two-year eligibility election may be beneficial to employers that have high employee turnover during the first two years of employment. If the employer experiences higher turnover during the first two years, the two-year eligibility election can help the employer avoid covering employees who are not likely to remain with the employer for a significant amount of time.

> Doctor's Resource sponsors a stock bonus plan (a qualified plan) that requires that its employees be 21 years old and complete two years of service before being considered eligible to participate in the stock bonus plan. To retain qualified status for the stock bonus plan, Doctor's Resource's stock bonus plan must provide its plan participants with a 100 percent immediate vested account balance after completing two years of service. Therefore, any employer contributions to the plan will automatically be fully vested for the employee as of age 21 and 2 years of service.

EXAMPLE 3.10

The special **two-year eligibility election** is not available for 401(k) plans because most contributions to 401(k) plans are employee elective deferral contributions. As will be discussed in Chapter 5, a 401(k) plan may have employer-matching contributions, but these employer contributions usually account for a smaller portion of the total 401(k) account balance as compared to the employee elective deferral contributions. Because the government wants to provide employees with the maximum ability to save for their retirement and the 401(k) plan provides the employees with such a device, the government statutorily prohibits 401(k) plans from requiring two years of service for eligibility.[10]

---

9. IRC §410(a)(1)(B)(i).
10. IRC §401(k)(2)(D).

Educational Institution

A tax-exempt educational institution with a qualified retirement plan maintained exclusively for its employees may delay eligibility in its qualified retirement plan until the later of the employee attaining age 26 or the completion of one year of service.[11] The IRC allows for this delayed age requirement to provide an incentive for tax-exempt institutions to establish and fund qualified retirement plans to benefit their employees. Otherwise, a tax-exempt institution is unlikely to establish a qualified plan for its employees because the tax-exempt institution does not, by nature, benefit from the tax deductions created by the contributions to a qualified retirement plan. From the organization's standpoint, a contribution to a qualified plan only creates additional costs to maintain the plan. It does not create additional tax deductions as a tax-exempt educational institution does not pay tax on its earnings but it may save payroll taxes. The organization's age requirement of 26 allows the tax-exempt educational institution, most of whose employees are teachers, the ability to deny eligibility to those new teachers that do not spend many years with the school. As discussed above, the employer could be more generous and consider employees eligible before attaining age 26 and one year of service, but unless the employer permits eligibility based on the general rule of completing one year of service and attaining the age of 21, the employees must be 100 percent vested in their account balance or accrued benefit after meeting the eligibility requirements of age 26 if that eligibility requirement is selected.

QUICK QUIZ 3.4

1. Using the standard eligibility rules, an employee must be allowed to enter a qualified plan on the day they attain the age of 21 and have completed one year of service.
   a. True
   b. False

2. If a company elects the two year eligibility rule, it can still require the employee to attain the age of 21 before being eligible for participation in the qualified retirement plan.
   a. True
   b. False

3. Tax-exempt educational institutions can require participants to attain the age of 26 before being eligible to participate in the qualified retirement plan.
   a. True
   b. False

False, True, True.

EXAMPLE 3.11

A qualified profit sharing plan of a tax-exempt high school permits its employees to be eligible for the profit sharing plan after completing six months of service and attaining the age of 20. The qualified retirement plan follows a three-year cliff-vesting schedule. In this case, the profit sharing plan retains its qualified status under §401(a) even though participant account balances are not 100 percent vested after they complete one year of service because the plan did not increase the age requirement for eligibility to 26.

EXAMPLE 3.12

A tax-exempt middle school sponsors a qualified money-purchase pension plan. To be considered eligible for the money purchase pension plan, the employees must complete one year of service and attain the age of 24. Because the money-purchase pension plan does not permit eligibility based on the general rule of completing one year of service

---

11. IRC §410(a)(1)(B)(ii).

and attaining the age of 21, the money purchase pension plan must provide 100 percent vesting to participant's accrued benefits.

COVERAGE

As described above, an employer is only required to consider those employees that meet the eligibility requirements (age and years of service) for participation in the plan. In addition, all employees covered under a collective bargaining agreement and nonresident alien employees who do not perform services in the U.S. are also excludable from the plan.[12] All other employees, those deemed **nonexcludable**, must be considered for participation in the qualified plan. However, even after this

KEY CONCEPTS

1. Which employees may be excluded from a qualified plan?

2. Which employees are highly compensated?

determination, an employer is not required to adopt a plan that benefits each and every nonexcludable employee. In fact, many employer-provided plans are designed to benefit only select classes of the nonexcludable employees. Provided the employer's selection of the beneficial class is not discriminatory (as defined below), the employer-provided plan may still be considered qualified if it meets the IRC coverage tests described below.

Participation in a qualified retirement plan counts as coverage in the plan. Specifically, an employee is **covered** under a qualified retirement plan when the employee receives a benefit from the plan.[13] For example, if the qualified retirement plan is a profit sharing plan, the employee is considered covered if he receives a contribution to his profit sharing plan account for the year. If the plan is a defined benefit plan, the employee is covered if the employee accrues a benefit for the plan year. Also, an employee who makes an employee elective deferral contribution under a 401(k) plan arrangement or an employee who receives a forfeiture allocation is considered covered under a qualified retirement plan.

Nondiscriminatory Classification

The selection of the class of nonexcludable employees who will benefit under a qualified retirement plan must be reasonable and established based on the facts and circumstances of the business using objective business criteria. A few classifications considered reasonable are those based on whether the employee is hourly or salaried, the geographic location of the employee, or the employee's job description. For example, many law firms exclude their associate attorneys while some businesses exclude commissioned sales people from coverage under the qualified retirement plan. In these examples, the employers are excluding all employees who share a common job description from coverage. Provided the exclusion is uniform, the exclusion will be treated as nondiscriminatory. If, however, an employer bases coverage on age (other than according to the eligibility rules discussed above), sex, or any other non-business determination such as color of hair, eyes, or an employee's height, the classification will be considered discriminatory and the retirement plan will be disqualified, thus losing the tax benefits of qualified status.

12. IRC §410(b)(3).
13. Treas. Reg. §1.410(b)-3.

When selecting the criteria to determine which employees benefit from the qualified retirement plan, an employer should always consider that a retirement plan is part of an employee's overall compensation package and should be viewed as a method of attracting, rewarding, and retaining employees. For example, if an employer chooses not to benefit those employees in its Atlanta office, the employees within that office may seek employment with competing employers in the local market who offer retirement plan benefits to their Atlanta employees. In this case, the employer may lose qualified employees to its competitor. The cost of the lost employees will likely far outweigh the cost of covering the employees under a qualified retirement plan.

Coverage Tests

The ability to determine which employees benefit under a qualified retirement plan is further governed by IRC requirements that a certain number of nonhighly compensated employees (defined below) must benefit from the plan for the plan to retain its qualified status. Specifically, to be qualified, the retirement plan must meet one of the three following coverage tests:

1. the general safe harbor test,
2. the ratio percentage test, or
3. the average benefits test.[14]

(As discussed below, a defined benefit plan must also satisfy another coverage test known as the 50/40 test.) Each of these tests only considers nonexcludable employees (as defined above), and each employer-provided retirement plan must only satisfy one of these tests (except defined benefit plans, which must also satisfy the 50/40 test) to meet the coverage requirements of the IRC.

Highly Compensated Employees

For purposes of several coverage test calculations, all nonexcludable employees are further divided into two classifications, **highly compensated** (HC) and nonhighly compensated (NHC).[15] The definition of a highly compensated employee provided by the IRC is an employee who is either:

- A more than five percent owner (defined below) at any time during the plan year or preceding plan year, or
- An employee with compensation in excess of $120,000 for the prior plan year (2016).

If the plan uses a fiscal year, calendar year compensation is used for the plan year that includes December 31. Notice that under this definition, an employee who meets either one of these requirements is considered a highly compensated employee. So, any owner with more than a five percent interest is a highly compensated employee, even if his compensation is the lowest of any employee.

QUICK QUIZ 3.5

1. Qualified plans can exclude employees who are nonresident aliens that do not perform services in the U.S.
   a. True
   b. False

2. A qualified plan can exclude (as a class) all women from the plan.
   a. True
   b. False

3. A person who earns $70,000 during 2016 is highly compensated for the 2017 plan year.
   a. True
   b. False

True, False, False.

14. IRC §410(b).
15. IRC §414(q).

5-Percent Owner Defined

Although the term "5-percent owner" seems relatively self-explanatory, it is actually a bit complicated. The IRC defines a "5-percent owner" as anyone who owns more than five percent of a company's stock or capital.[16] Therefore, if an employee owned exactly 5 percent of his employer's stock, that employee would not be considered a 5-percent owner, nor would he be considered highly compensated under this definition.

In addition to direct ownership, family attribution rules direct that an individual is considered as owning the shares of stock of certain relatives, including stock owned by the individual's:[17]

1. Spouse
2. Children
3. Grandchildren
4. Parents

Ownership of corporations, partnerships, estates, and trusts can also be attributed to individuals in the determination of whether one meets the definition of a 5-percent owner.

> Harold, his wife Wanda, and his son Steve, each own one-third of the stock of the Great Corporation. For purposes of determining the amount of stock owned by Harold, Wanda, or Steve, the amount of stock held by the other members of the family is added together. Thus, for coverage testing, each of them is deemed to own 100 percent of the stock of the Great Corporation.

EXAMPLE 3.13

> Bob, his wife Wilma, his son Sam, and his grandson (Sam's son) George, own the 100 outstanding shares of BWSG, Inc. stock, each owning 25 shares. Bob, Wilma, and Sam are each considered as owning 100 shares of BWSG, Inc. George is considered as owning only 50 shares (his own and his father's).

EXAMPLE 3.14

> Jeanette and her husband Don started Trophy Shop, Inc. many years ago. Together they owned 95% of the business and their only employee at that time, Cheryl, owned the remaining 5%. Don died last year and left his shares to Jeanette. Jeanette wanted to give up a majority of her responsibilities at the trophy shop and spend more time with her grandchildren. In the current year, Jeanette sold all but a 5% interest to Cheryl. Jeanette now owns 5% of the business and Cheryl owns 95%. Cheryl recently had a baby and no longer wants to work full time. Cheryl and Jeanette each receive a salary of $50,000 for the limited amount of work they do. Cheryl hired Delano, a successful salesman, to run the day-to-day operations and grow the business. Delano's salary is $150,000. Which of the three employees are considered highly compensated based on the qualified plan rules?

EXAMPLE 3.15

16. IRC §416(i)(1)(B).
17. IRC §318(a).

EMPLOYEE	SALARY	OWNERSHIP % CURRENT YEAR	OWNERSHIP % LAST YEAR
Jeanette	$50,000	5%	95%
Cheryl	$50,000	95%	5%
Delano	$150,000	0	0

In this example, all three individuals are considered highly compensated for the current year. Even though Jeanette does not own more than 5% in the current year, she is considered highly compensated because she owned greater than 5% last year. Cheryl is highly compensated because she is a greater than 5% owner in the current year. Delano is highly compensated because his income exceeds the compensation limit.

Highly Compensated Election

An employer election is available to reduce the number of employees considered highly compensated. This election allows an employer to only count those employees whose compensation is in excess of the dollar limit as highly compensated if that employee is also in the top 20 percent of all paid employees as ranked by compensation.[18] This exception will not exclude employees who are more than five percent owners because such employees will be considered highly compensated based on ownership. An employer would consider this election when it would reduce the number of highly compensated employees as compared with the general highly compensated definition. An employer's overall goal is to reduce the number of employees classified as highly compensated and, thus, have more nonhighly compensated employees because the plan will be more likely to pass a coverage test and may help comply with the ADP test described in Chapter 5.

EXHIBIT 3.7

DETERMINATION OF HIGHLY COMPENSATED

Owner Employees	Nonowner Employees
Either An owner of > 5%* for current or prior plan year *or* Compensation in excess of $120,000 for 2016** for prior plan year	Compensation in excess of $120,000 for 2016** for prior plan year

5% ownership may include ownership by spouse, children, grandchildren, or parents.

**If special employer election is made, add "and in top 20% of employees ranked by salary."*

---

18. IRC §414(q)(1)(B)(ii) and IRC §414(q)(3).

EXAMPLE
3.16

Desk Emporium has the following 10 employees.

EMPLOYEE	SALARY	OWNERSHIP %
A	$200,000	65%
B	$150,000	35%
C	$145,000	-
D-J	$30,000	-

Utilizing the general definition of highly compensated (greater than five percent owner or compensation greater than $120,000 for 2016), employees A and B are highly compensated because both are greater than five percent owners of Desk Emporium. Employee C is also a highly compensated employee because his salary is in excess of $120,000 for 2016. So, in this example, three of the 10 employees are highly compensated.

If Desk Emporium elected to only count those employees as highly compensated if they were also in the top 20 percent of employees ranked by compensation, only employees A and B would be highly compensated. Employee C would not be highly compensated because he is not an owner of the company and if ranked by salary, C is not in the top 20 percent. In a company with 10 employees, only the top two ranked by salary would be in the top 20 percent. In this case, employee C is ranked third by salary and is therefore not highly compensated. By making the election, Desk Emporium reduced the number of highly compensated employees to two of the 10 employees. In a situation like this, the employer might make the 20 percent election and reduce the number of highly compensated employees to help pass the coverage tests.

	DESK EMPORIUM HIGHLY COMPENSATED TEST			
	General Rule		20% Election	
Employee	> 5% Owner	> $120,000 Compensation	> 5% Owner	Top 20% (ranked by compensation)
A	✓	✓	✓	✓
B	✓	✓	✓	✓
C		✓		
D - J				

General Safe Harbor Coverage Test

The general **safe harbor coverage test** is a straightforward test that considers the number of nonhighly compensated employees covered by the qualified retirement plan. A qualified retirement plan satisfies the general safe harbor coverage test if the plan benefits 70 percent or more of the nonexcludable, nonhighly compensated (NHC) employees.[19] Notice that this test only considers the nonhighly compensated employees, often called the rank-and-file, to determine the percent covered by the plan. The safe harbor test is not concerned with the percentage of highly compensated employees covered by the retirement plan.

KEY CONCEPTS

1. What is the general safe harbor test for coverage in a qualified plan?

2. What is the ratio percentage test for coverage in a qualified plan?

3. What is the average benefits test and what are its component parts?

4. What is the defined benefit 50/40 test?

EXAMPLE 3.17

Gerard's Automotive has 125 employees (26 highly compensated and 99 nonhighly compensated). 100 of these employees are nonexcludable and 25 of those are highly compensated (75 are nonhighly compensated). The company's qualified profit sharing plan benefits 21 of the highly compensated employees and 55 of the nonhighly compensated employees. The profit sharing plan meets the general safe harbor coverage test because it benefits 73.33 percent (55/75) of the nonhighly compensated eligible employees.

	Nonexcludable Employees		Excludable	Total
	Covered	Not Covered	(Not 21&1, Union, etc)	All
NHC	55	20	24	99
HC	21	4	1	26
Total	76	24	25	125

General Safe Harbor Coverage Test			
	Nonexcludable Employees	Covered Employees	(%) Covered Employees
NHC	75	55	73.33%
HC	25	21	N/A
Total	100	76	General Safe Harbor Test % of NHC covered = 73.33% ≥ 70%

---

19. IRC §410(b)(1)(A).

Only those employees considered nonexcludable were considered for the calculation of the safe harbor coverage test. Keep in mind that the plan does not cover each of those nonexcludable employees. In fact, 20 (75-55) of the nonexcludable NHC employees and four (25-21) of the nonexcludable HC employees are not covered by the plan. All of these employees meet the eligibility rules of the qualified retirement plan yet are not covered under the plan. Provided that the selection of the beneficial class was based on a nondiscriminatory classification (for example, the plan only benefits Gerard's Automotive's mechanics), the plan will satisfy the safe harbor coverage test because it covers at least 70 percent of the NHC employees. If an employer only has HC employees, the plan will automatically meet the coverage test.[20]

Ratio Percentage Test

In the event a plan does not meet the safe harbor coverage test, the plan must meet one of two other coverage tests available or the plan risks disqualification. The first of these two tests is the ratio percentage test. The **ratio percentage test** compares the percentage of covered nonhighly compensated employees to the percentage of covered highly compensated employees. A plan satisfies the ratio percentage test if the plan covers a percentage of nonexcludable nonhighly compensated employees that is at least 70 percent of the covered nonexcludable highly compensated employees. The coverage percentage of each class is calculated simply by dividing the number of covered employees from that class by the total number of nonexcludable employees of that class. After these calculations are performed, the percentage of covered nonhighly compensated employees divided by the percentage of covered highly compensated employees equals the plan's ratio percentage test. If this percentage is at least 70 percent, the retirement plan satisfies the ratio percentage test.[21]

EXAMPLE 3.18

A qualified profit sharing plan covers 60 of the 100 (60%) nonexcludable NHC employees and 40 of the 50 (80%) nonexcludable HC employees. This profit sharing plan's ratio percentage is 75 percent (60%/80%), and, thus, satisfies the ratio percentage test.

Ratio Percentage (%) Test			
	Nonexcludable Employees	Covered Employees	(%) Covered Employees
NHC	100	60	60%
HC	50	40	80%
Total	150	100	

$$\text{Ratio \% Test} = \frac{\text{\% of NHC Covered}}{\text{\% of HC Covered}} = \frac{60\%}{80\%} = 75\% \geq 70\% \quad \text{Pass}$$

In this example, the plan would not pass the general safe harbor coverage test because the plan only covered 60 percent (not 70%) of the nonhighly compensated employees. Remember, the plan only has to pass one coverage test and this one passed the ratio percentage test.

---

20. IRC §410(b)(6)(F).
21. IRC §410(b)(1)(B).

EXAMPLE 3.19

A qualified profit sharing plan covers 40 percent of the nonexcludable (80 out of 200) NHC employees and 60 percent of the nonexcludable HC employees (30 out of 50). The plan's ratio percentage is 66.67 percent (40%/60%), failing the ratio percentage test. The plan also fails the safe harbor test because the plan does not cover ≥ 70 percent of the NHC.

Note: If the plan meets the general safe harbor test, then it will always meet the ratio percentage test.

Ratio Percentage (%) Test			
	Nonexcludable Employees	Covered Employees	(%) Covered Employees
NHC	200	80	40%
HC	50	30	60%
Total	250	110	

$$\text{Ratio \% Test} = \frac{\text{\% of NHC Covered}}{\text{\% of HC Covered}} = \frac{40\%}{60\%} = 67\% \leq 70\% \text{ Fails}$$

If a qualified plan fails to meet all of the coverage tests, it is subject to disqualification. The above plan has failed two tests, but gets a chance to pass the third test (the average benefits test).

Average Benefits Test

The third coverage test, the **average benefits test**, determines whether the plan adequately benefits the nonhighly compensated employees compared with the benefits received by the highly compensated employees and determines whether the employee classification is nondiscriminatory.[22] As such, the average benefits test actually consists of the following two tests:

1. The average benefits percentage test, and
2. The nondiscriminatory classification test.

A plan must pass both of these two tests, as described below, to be considered as passing the average benefits test and fulfilling the coverage requirement. If a plan does not pass both of these tests, it fails the average benefits test and must pass either the requirements of the general safe harbor coverage test or the ratio percentage test to satisfy the coverage requirements.

Average Benefits Percentage Test

A retirement plan satisfies the **average benefits percentage test** if the following ratio is at least 70 percent.[23]

$$\frac{\text{Average Benefit Percentage of Nonhighly Compensated Employees}}{\text{Average Benefit Percentage of Highly Compensated Employees}} \geq 70\%$$

The average benefit percentage of each class of employees is determined by first calculating the benefit percentage for each nonexcludable employee. To do this, the benefit provided to each

22. IRC §410(b)(2).
23. IRC §410(b)(2)(B).

nonexcludable employees is divided by that employee's annual compensation (i.e., an employee who has a $100,000 salary and receives a $10,000 benefit has a 10 percent average benefit). A benefit percentage is also determined for each nonexcludable employee who does not benefit from the plan (thus, a benefit percentage of zero). The calculated benefit percentages are then summed according to the employee's class (HC or NHC) and an average is calculated to determine the average benefit percentage. As expressed in the above formula, the average benefit percentage for the nonhighly compensated employees is then divided by the average benefit percentage of the highly compensated employees to arrive at a ratio that must be equal to or greater than 70 percent for the plan to pass the average benefits percentage test portion of the average benefits test.

Employee	Status	Salary	Benefit $	Benefit %	Avg. Benefit %
A	HC	$150,000	$15,000	10%	10.00%
B	HC	$140,000	$14,000	10%	
C	NHC	$50,000	$3,000	6%	5.33%
D	NHC	$50,000	$5,000	10%	
E	NHC	$50,000	$0	0%	

HC = Highly Compensated
NHC = Non Highly Compensated

$$\frac{NHC\%}{HC\%} = \frac{5.33\%}{10.00\%} = 53\% \text{ (Fails Average Benefits Percentage Test)}$$

Waggaman's Meat Market employs 400 people and sponsors a money purchase pension plan for its employees. Of the 350 nonexcludable employees, 50 are HC employees and 300 are NHC employees. The HC have a calculated average benefit percentage of 10 percent, and the NHC have a calculated average benefit percentage of eight percent. This money purchase pension plan satisfies the average benefit percentage test of the average benefits test because the ratio of the average benefit of the nonhighly compensated (8%) to the average benefit of the highly compensated (10%) is 80 percent (8%/10%), which is greater than the requirement of 70 percent. This plan must also satisfy the nondiscriminatory classification test to satisfy the average benefits test.

Average Benefit Percentage (%) Test		
	Covered Employees	Average Benefit %
NHC	300	8%
HC	50	10%
Total	350	

$$AB\%Test = \frac{\% \text{ of NHC Covered}}{\% \text{ of HC Covered}} = \frac{8\%}{10\%} = 80\% \geq 70\% \text{ Pass}$$

Nondiscriminatory Classification Test

The second requirement of the average benefits test is the nondiscriminatory classification test. To satisfy this requirement, the method in which an employer chooses employees to cover under a qualified plan must meet both of the following requirements:

1. The classification must be reasonable and established, based on the facts and circumstances of the business, under objective business criteria that identify the category of employees who benefit under the plan (i.e., hourly or salaried, geographic location), and

2. The classification must be nondiscriminatory. In order for the classification to be nondiscriminatory, the plan must meet one of the following two tests:
   - **Safe harbor test**
   - **Facts and circumstances test**

The nondiscriminatory classification test is designed to guarantee that a plan truly provides benefits to a substantial group of the nonexcludable nonhighly compensated employees. If this nondiscriminatory test were not part of the average benefits test, it would be possible to satisfy the average benefits percentage test by benefiting only a very small group of nonhighly compensated employees with a substantial benefit. For example, if an employer chose to only provide a benefit to the janitors and the executives, the classification would satisfy the general nondiscrimination rule discussed above because it is a classification based on job description. The employer could then provide the janitors with a benefit sufficient enough to satisfy the average benefits percentage test and the plan would be considered qualified. This second nondiscriminatory classification test is included to protect against a classification selection such as this by requiring the employer to provide a benefit to at least a certain number of nonexcludable nonhighly compensated employees.

QUICK QUIZ 3.6

1. A plan must pass the general safe harbor, the ratio percentage test, and the average benefits test.
   a. True
   b. False

2. The average benefits test is comprised of two tests and at least one of them must be passed.
   a. True
   b. False

3. Defined benefit pension plans must pass the 50/40 test in addition to at least one of the other coverage tests.
   a. True
   b. False

False, False, True.

For a plan to satisfy the average benefits test, it must actually satisfy three requirements, the average benefits percentage test and the two nondiscriminatory classification requirements. If the plan satisfies the average benefit percentage test, the reasonable classification requirement, and the classification is nondiscriminatory, it will satisfy the coverage requirements and it will not be required to satisfy the general safe harbor coverage test or the ratio percentage test. Otherwise, if a plan does not pass the average benefits test, it must pass either the general safe harbor test or the ratio percentage test for it to satisfy the coverage requirement.[24]

A retirement plan is required to pass only one of these three coverage tests (general safe harbor, ratio percentage test, or average benefits test) to be a qualified retirement plan. Once it is determined that the plan passes one of these tests, the coverage requirement is met and no other test is

---

24. More detailed information on the nondiscriminatory classification test, as well as other resources for the Retirement Planning textbook, can be found at money-education.com.

performed. It is possible for a plan to fail one test and still meet the requirements of another and, thus, pass the coverage requirements.

COVERAGE TESTS SUMMARY

EXHIBIT
3.8

A retirement plan must annually satisfy at least one of the following tests to be considered a qualified retirement plan.*

General Safe Harbor Test	% of NHC Covered $\geq 70\%$
Ratio Percentage Test	$\dfrac{\% \text{ of NHC Covered}}{\% \text{ of HC Covered}} \geq 70\%$
Average Benefits Test (Both Tests)	1. Average Benefit % Test $\dfrac{AB\% \text{ of NHC}}{AB\% \text{ of HC}} \geq 70\%$ 2. Nondiscriminatory Test

A defined benefit plan must also pass the 50/40 test described below.

Defined Benefit 50/40 Test

A defined benefit plan must satisfy the **50/40 coverage test** in addition to one of the other three coverage tests described in Exhibit 3.8.[25] The 50/40 coverage test requires the defined benefit plan to benefit the lesser of 50 nonexcludable employees or 40 percent of all nonexcludable employees on each day of the plan year. In the case of a defined benefit plan that has four or fewer nonexcludable employees, the plan must benefit at least two employees (or if there is only one nonexcludable employee, that employee must benefit from the defined benefit plan). This 50/40 coverage test does not segregate the calculation between highly compensated employees and nonhighly compensated employees.

50/40 COVERAGE TEST

EXHIBIT
3.9

Number of Nonexcludable Employees	How Many Must Be Covered
1	1 Employee
2 - 4	2 Employees
< 125	40% of Employees
≥ 125	50 Employees

A defined benefit plan sponsored by an employer with 125 nonexcludable employees must benefit at least 50 of the employees. This is calculated by determining the lesser of 50 employees or 40 percent of the employees. In this case, either calculation provides a requirement of exactly 50 employees. Note: A plan does not ever need to cover more than 50 employees to meet this test, but must still pass one of the other previously discussed coverage tests.

---

25. IRC §401(a)(26).

EXAMPLE 3.23

A defined benefit plan being sponsored by an employer with 100 nonexcludable employees must benefit at least 40 employees. The determination is calculated by determining the lesser of 50 employees or 40 percent of the employees – in this case 40 employees (0.40 x 100 employees).

EXAMPLE 3.24

A defined benefit plan being sponsored by an employer with three nonexcludable employees must benefit at least two employees. The determination is calculated based on the rule that states that a plan with less than four employees must benefit at least two of the employees.

EXAMPLE 3.25

A defined benefit plan being sponsored by an employer with 5,000 nonexcludable employees must benefit at least 50 employees. The determination is calculated by determining the lesser of 50 employees or 40 percent of the employees – in this case 50 employees is less than 2,000 employees (40 percent of 5,000).

A defined benefit plan must satisfy either the general safe harbor test, the ratio percentage test, or the average benefit test and must also satisfy the 50/40 rule to satisfy the coverage requirements imposed by the IRC.

EXAMPLE 3.26

Walker Brothers sponsors a defined benefit plan for its employees. Walker Brothers has 200 employees, 20 of which are excludable because they do not meet the age and service requirements set forth in the plan document. 15 of the nonexcludable employees are HC, and the remaining 165 are NHC employees. 10 of the HC employees are covered under the defined benefit plan, and 150 of the NHC employees are covered under the defined benefit plan. The average benefit percentage for the HC is 15 percent, and the average benefit percentage for the NHC is six percent. The selection of the covered class is determined to be nondiscriminatory. To be considered as passing the coverage test, Walker Brothers' defined benefit plan must pass either the general safe harbor test, the ratio percentage test, or the average benefits test and must also pass the 50/40 coverage test.

Employees	Nonexcludable	Covered	% Covered	AB%
NHC	165	150	90.91%	6%
HC	15	10	66.67%	15%
Total	180	160		

Coverage Test	Required to Pass	Plan Specific	Pass/Fail
Safe Harbor Test	$\geq 70\%$ of NHC covered	90.91% of NHC covered	Pass
Ratio Percentage Test	$\dfrac{\% \text{ of NHC Covered}}{\% \text{ of HC Covered}} \geq 70\%$	$\dfrac{90.91\%}{66.67\%} = 136.36\%$	Pass
Average Benefits Test	$\dfrac{\text{AB \% of NHC}}{\text{AB \% of HC}} \geq 70\%$	$\dfrac{6\%}{15\%} = 40\%$	Fail
50/40 Test	Plan must cover the lesser of: • 50 Employees • 40% of Employees	Plan covers 160 Employees	Pass

Note: Since the plan passed the safe harbor test, it does not have to pass the ratio percentage test or the average benefits test. However, because it is a defined benefit plan, it is required to also pass the 50/40 test.

VESTING

Historically, some employers would require their employees to have many years of service for the employee to **vest** or receive ownership of employer benefits (employer contributions and the earnings on those contributions) provided by a retirement plan. The stringency of these requirements reduced the employer's final cost of providing the benefit to its employees because the employee did not receive the otherwise full benefit as determined without meeting the vesting requirement. In other words, the employer would segregate and deduct the employer contribution made on behalf of the employee to the plan each year as determined under the plan document, but unless the employee continued employment for a period of time equal to or greater than the vesting requirement, the employee would

KEY CONCEPTS

1. What vesting schedules are available for qualified plans?

2. How is the vesting schedule of a qualified plan affected by the plan's top-heavy status?

3. At what point must the employer be 100% vested?

4. Define years of service.

only receive a portion, if any, of the intended benefit. The loss of benefit upon termination would act as an incentive for employees to continue employment with the plan sponsor. Often, if the employee terminated employment before retirement, the employee would not receive any benefit at retirement. If the benefit was not paid to the participant, it was forfeited. In such a case, the employer used these "forfeited" funds to contribute to the remaining employees' future benefits; thus, reducing the employer's overall future retirement plan costs (the expense of funding the employees' benefit). The IRC continues to allow qualified retirement plans to maintain a vesting requirement but limits the number of years of service that can be required by the employer for an employee to fully vest in employer contributions and associated earnings.

An employee's elective deferral contributions to a qualified plan and the earnings attributable (pro rata) to the employee's elective deferral contributions are not subject to any vesting requirements. Those contributions and earnings are always 100 percent vested in the employee's account. These funds are always the employee's funds because they are part of a salary reduction plan and were always owned by the employee.

Employer contributions will often vest using a cliff or graduated vesting schedule. A **cliff vesting schedule** provides an employee full rights to the plan's assets immediately upon the passage of a certain number of years of service, usually three years. A **graduated vesting schedule** provides an employee with full rights to a certain percentage benefit (less than 100%) after completing a certain number of years of service and provides the employee with an additional percentage for additional years of service.

In 1974, the year ERISA was enacted, employer contributions could vest under a 15-year graduated schedule, a 10-year cliff-vesting schedule, or under a method referred to as the "Rule of 45." However, since then, Congress has continued to reduce the years required for employees to fully vest in employer contributions.

Since the passage of the Pension Protection Act of 2006 (PPA 2006), all defined contribution plans (not defined benefit plans) must vest employer contributions under a 2 to 6 year graded or 3-year cliff schedule.[26] As a result, all employer contributions to defined contribution plans, including those made to top-heavy plans, are subject to a uniform set of vesting requirements (see Exhibit 3.10).

Minimum vesting in defined benefit plans remains at either 5-year cliff or 3 to 7 year graded vesting (see Exhibit 3.11), except when a defined benefit plan is classified as top-heavy, in which case the minimum vesting will be the same as for defined contribution plans.[27] Note that the vesting schedules defined here do not replace or modify the 100 percent vesting requirements for a plan that elects the two years of service for eligibility (as previously discussed).

Cash balance plans are a special type of defined benefit plan with hypothetical accounts. These plans are required to provide a 3 year cliff vesting schedule.[28] Thus, after three years of service, a participant has a nonforfeitable right to 100 percent of benefit derived from the employer contributions in a cash balance plan.

A plan must also vest an employee 100 percent in any accrued benefit or account balance when the employee attains normal retirement age (for vesting purposes, normal retirement age is the later of the age specified by the plan or the employee becoming age 65) or upon termination of the plan.[29]

---

26. Prior to the Pension Protection Act of 2006, the IRC required that the employer's contributions and the earnings attributable (pro rata) to the employer's contributions follow a vesting schedule that provides a vested benefit to the employee at least as rapidly as a 5-year cliff vesting schedule or a 3 to 7 year graduated vesting schedule. When a plan was considered a top-heavy plan or when the employer's contributions were made as part of a matching contribution (such as in a 401(k) plan), the employee's accrued benefit or account balance under the plan had to vest at least as rapidly as a 3-year cliff or a 2 to 6 year graduated vesting schedule.

27. Pension Protection Act of 2006, §904; IRC §411.

28. IRC §411(a)(13)(B).

29. Treas. Reg. §1.411(d)-2(a)(1).

DEFINED CONTRIBUTION PLAN VESTING SCHEDULES

EXHIBIT
3.10

YEARS OF SERVICE	ALL EMPLOYER CONTRIBUTIONS			EMPLOYEE CONTRIBUTIONS
	2 TO 6 YEAR GRADUATED	3-YEAR CLIFF	2-YEAR ELIGIBILITY ELECTION*	
1	0	0	0	100%
2	20%	0	100%	100%
3	40%	100%	100%	100%
4	60%	100%	100%	100%
5	80%	100%	100%	100%
6	100%	100%	100%	100%

Note: The two-year vesting schedule also applies to employer contributions under a 401(k) plan that makes use of an Automatic Enrollment Feature, as outlined in PPA 2006 (effective for years after 2007).

DEFINED BENEFIT PLAN VESTING SCHEDULES

EXHIBIT
3.11

YEARS OF SERVICE	ALL EMPLOYER CONTRIBUTIONS						
	NON-TOP-HEAVY DB PLANS		2-YEAR ELIGIBILITY ELECTION	TOP-HEAVY DB PLAN		CASH BALANCE PLAN*	
	3 TO 7 YEAR GRADUATED	5-YEAR CLIFF		2 TO 6 YEAR GRADUATED	3-YEAR CLIFF		
1	0	0	0	0	0	0	
2	0	0	100%	20%	0	0	
3	20%	0	100%	40%	100%	100%	
4	40%	0	100%	60%	100%	100%	
5	60%	100%	100%	80%	100%	100%	
6	80%	100%	100%	100%	100%	100%	
7	100%	100%	100%	100%	100%	100%	

Note that under IRC §411(a)(13)(B), a cash balance pension plan provides for 100% vesting of employer contributions after three years of employee service.

EXAMPLE
3.27

Marcus has been employed by Blue Cliff Supply Stores for two years. After meeting the plans eligibility rules, he is a benefiting participant of Blue Cliff's qualified profit sharing plan, which consists of employer contributions only and follows a 3-year cliff vesting schedule. The current balance of Marcus' profit sharing plan is $14,000. The $14,000 will be forfeited if Marcus terminates employment before reaching three years of service. Any forfeited funds will then be used by the plan to either reduce current plan costs or to increase the benefit provided to remaining participants.

EXAMPLE
3.28

Craig has attained three years of service with Stone Corporation. Over those three years, Craig has received employer contributions to a qualified profit sharing plan in the amount of $60,000. If the plan follows a 2 to 6 year graduated vesting schedule, Craig has a vested account balance of $24,000 (40% of $60,000).

EXAMPLE 3.29

Mallory has attained four years of service with Pharmex Corporation. Pharmex sponsors a defined benefit plan that is not top-heavy and does not permit employee contributions. Mallory has an accrued benefit to date under the plan of $30 per month at retirement. If the plan follows a 3 to 7 year graduated vesting schedule and Mallory terminates her employment today, she would be entitled to a benefit of $12 (40% x $30) per month at her normal age retirement.

Vesting Schedule Options

Vesting schedules ensure that nonhighly compensated employees will benefit under the plan and that it does not require an unreasonable amount of time to become vested. The employer may always elect to provide the employee with a vested benefit faster than the standard schedules. For example, a defined contribution plan may vest an employee's benefit 100 percent after 18 months of service, or the vesting schedule may be based on a 3-year vesting schedule that provides for equal vesting in each of the three years. When an employer elects a faster vesting schedule, however, the vested benefit must always be comparatively better than one of the statutory vesting schedules and cannot provide a greater vested percentage as compared to one of the schedules in some years and in other years fulfill the requirement by providing a greater vested percentage as compared to another vesting schedule. The charts that follow list several examples of permitted vesting schedules and non-permitted vesting schedules for qualified plans. The first example below illustrates permitted vesting schedules for a defined contribution plan and the second example below illustrates permitted vesting schedules for a defined benefit plan.

EXAMPLE 3.30

The following chart illustrates four various sample vesting schedules for a *defined contribution plan* and whether they meet the qualified plan vesting requirements.

Years of Service	Permitted 2 to 6 Graduated	Permitted 3-Year Cliff	Permitted Schedule (A)	Not Permitted Schedule (B)	Permitted Schedule (C)	Not Permitted Schedule (D)
1	0	0	5%	5%	33%	0
2	20%	0	25%	25%	66%	**0**
3	40%	100%	45%	**35%**	100%	50%
4	60%	100%	75%	60%	100%	75%
5	80%	100%	100%	80%	100%	100%
6	100%	100%	100%	100%	100%	100%
7	100%	100%	100%	100%	100%	100%

The permitted vesting schedules (A and C) for a defined contribution plans are at least as rapid as either the 2 to 6 year graduated vesting schedule or the 3-year cliff vesting schedule. The "not permitted" vesting schedules (B and D) provide a vesting schedule that is at least as rapid in some years as one of the schedules and at least as rapid as other vesting schedules in other years. Specifically, Vesting Schedule A provides a greater vested percentage in every year compared to the 2 to 6 year graduated vesting schedule. Vesting Schedule B provides a greater vested percentage than the 2 to 6 year graduated vesting schedule in years 1 and 2, but it is not as rapid as the 2 to 6 year vesting schedule in Year 3.

Vesting Schedule C provides vesting at least as rapid as compared to the 3-year cliff; therefore it meets the requirements and is considered a permitted vesting schedule. Vesting Schedule D provides a better benefit than the 2 to 6 year graduated schedule except for year 2. Therefore, it is not permissible.

The following chart illustrates four various sample vesting schedules for a *defined benefit plan* and whether they meet the qualified, non-top-heavy plan vesting requirements.

EXAMPLE 3.31

YEARS OF SERVICE	PERMITTED 3 TO 7 GRADUATED	PERMITTED 5-YEAR CLIFF	PERMITTED SCHEDULE (A)	NOT PERMITTED SCHEDULE (B)	PERMITTED SCHEDULE (C)	NOT PERMITTED SCHEDULE (D)
1	0	0	5%	5%	0	0
2	0	0	10%	10%	5%	5%
3	20%	0	20%	15%	10%	20%
4	40%	0%	60%	60%	15%	30%
5	60%	100%	80%	80%	100%	60%
6	80%	100%	100%	100%	100%	80%
7	100%	100%	100%	100%	100%	100%

Note that under IRC §411(a)(13)(B), a cash balance pension plan provides for 100% vesting of employer contributions after three years of employee service.

The permitted vesting schedules (A and C) for a defined benefit plan that is not top-heavy are at least as rapid as either the 3 to 7 year graduated vesting schedule or the 5-year cliff vesting schedule. Whereas, the "not permitted" vesting schedules (B and D) provide a vesting schedule that is at least as rapid in some years than one of the schedules and at least as rapid as other vesting schedules in other years. Specifically, Vesting Schedule A provides a greater vested percentage in every year compared to the 3 to 7 year graduated vesting schedule. Vesting Schedule B provides a greater vested percentage than the 5-year cliff vesting schedule in years 1 to 4, but in years 5 to 7 its vesting schedule is only as rapid as the 3 to 7 year graduated vesting schedule. To provide a vested benefit at least as rapid as the permitted vesting schedules, Schedule B must be compared in a blended fashion to both the 3 to 7 year graduated and the 5-year cliff; thus, it is not a permitted vesting schedule. Vesting Schedule C provides a greater vested percentage in each year as compared to the 5-year cliff; therefore it meets the requirements and is considered a permitted vesting schedule. Vesting Schedule D meets the requirements compared to the 5-year cliff for years 1 to 4 and then only meets the requirements for years 5 to 7 in comparison to the 3 to 7 year graduated vesting schedule. Since Vesting Schedule D does not meet the minimum vesting requirements of either schedule, it is not a permitted vesting schedule.

Lisa works for Pacific United and was hired three and a half years ago. She is a participant in her company's cash balance plan and has a hypothetical account balance of $12,000. If she were to leave today for another job, she would be able to take 100 percent of her account balance because cash balance plans must vest at least as rapidly as three-year cliff vesting.

EXAMPLE 3.32

Years of Service

As illustrated in Exhibits 3.10 and 3.11, employees earn a certain percentage benefit based on the applicable vesting schedule and after the employee attains a certain number of years of service. The **years of service** determination is based on the number of years, defined as a 12-month consecutive period with at least 1,000 hours worked for the employer. The determination is based on the employee's beginning date of employment and not on the date the employee becomes eligible to participate in the plan. For example, an employee who has worked 1,200 hours within a 12 month period has attained one year of service for purposes of vesting even though they may have just become eligible to participate in a qualified retirement plan that follows the general eligibility rule. This means that an employee will generally accrue years of service from the beginning of employment even though the employee is not yet eligible for the plan.

An employer does not have to count for purposes of vesting: (1) years of service the employee acquired with the employer before reaching the age of 18 if the employee was not participating in the plan at that time, (2) years of service the employee attained before the employer sponsored a qualified plan, or (3) years of service the employee attained during years when he did not contribute to an employee-contributory qualified plan.[30] If the employer desires, the employer can count any of these otherwise excludable years towards the employee's vesting requirement as long as all employees are treated the same.

EXAMPLE 3.33

Taters Restaurant sponsors a defined benefit plan that does not permit employee contributions. Brian has been employed by Taters Restaurant for the past five years and has an accrued benefit to date under the plan of $20 per month at retirement. The Tater Restaurant's defined benefit plan is considered top-heavy and follows the least generous graduated vesting schedule. If Brian terminated his employment with Taters Restaurant today, he would be entitled to a benefit of $16 ($20 x 80%) per month at his retirement, an 80 percent vested accrued benefit. Taters Restaurant follows the 2 to 6 year graduated vesting schedule and not the 3 to 7 graduated vesting schedule because Taters Restaurant's plan is considered top-heavy (see below for more information on top-heavy plans) and is a defined benefit plan.

---

30. IRC §411(a)(4).

EXAMPLE
3.34

The employees of Tax Heaven are given the opportunity to contribute to a 401(k) plan after six months of continuous service. As part of the benefit, Tax Heaven matches employee elective deferral contributions with an amount equal to 25 percent. The plan maintains the least generous graduated vesting schedule for the employer matching contributions. Mike has four years of service with Tax Heaven and has contributed $18,000 to his 401(k) account over those four years. Mike has received $4,500 (25% of $18,000) of employer matching contributions to the 401(k) plan, has earnings of $9,500, and has a current balance of $32,000. As of today, Mike has a vested balance of $29,440 as illustrated in the chart below.

Calculation of Mike's vested account balance:

CONTRIBUTIONS		VESTED PERCENTAGE	VESTED BALANCE
Employee	$18,000	100%	$18,000
Employer	$4,500	60%*	$2,700
Total Contributions	$22,500		
EARNINGS ($32,000 - $22,500 = $9,500)			
Employee	$9,500 \times \dfrac{18,000}{22,500} = \$7,600	100%	$7,600
Employer	$9,500 \times \dfrac{4,500}{22,500} = \$1,900	60%*	$1,140
Earnings Total	$9,500		
TOTAL ACCOUNT BALANCE	**$32,000**	**Total Vested Balance**	**$29,440**

* Employer matching contributions for a 401(k) plan must vest at least as rapidly as 2 to 6 year graduated or 3-year cliff vesting schedules.

TOP-HEAVY PLANS

The **top-heavy** rules were designed to ensure that qualified plans that significantly benefit owners and executives of the company must provide some minimum level of benefits for the rank-and-file employees. The top-heavy requirements are most commonly applicable to small employer plans, age-based profit sharing plans, and any other plans that provide owners and executives with a disproportionate level of benefit from the plan. Most often the top-heavy rules are not applicable because the benefits provided to the non-key employees are generally greater than the required minimums of the top-heavy rules. The impact of the top-heavy rules has been lessened as a result of the PPA 2006's shortened vesting schedules. A plan is considered top-heavy under either of the following two definitions:

KEY CONCEPTS

1. What is a top-heavy plan?

2. Which employees are considered key employees?

3. If a qualified plan is deemed top-heavy, how does it affect the vesting and funding of a plan?

- A defined benefit plan is considered top-heavy when the present value of the total accrued benefits of key employees (defined below) in the defined benefit plan exceeds 60 percent of the present value of the total accrued benefits of the defined benefit plan for all employees.[31]
- A defined contribution plan is top-heavy when the aggregate of the account balances of key employees in the plan exceeds 60 percent of the aggregate of the accounts of all employees.[32]

When a qualified retirement plan is determined to be top-heavy, the plan must: (1) use top-heavy vesting schedules[33] and (2) provide a minimum level of funding to non-key employees.[34] These top-heavy provisions attempt to ensure that non-key employees are actually benefiting from the qualified retirement plan and that the key employees are not benefiting in a disproportionate way.

Key Employee

A **key employee** is any employee who is any one or more of the following:

- A greater than five percent owner,[35] or
- A greater than one percent owner with compensation in excess of $150,000 (not indexed), or
- An officer (defined below) with compensation in excess of $170,000 for 2016 as determined last year.[36]

John owns five percent of the stock of Market Resources, Inc. and receives an annual salary of $110,000. Even though John is an owner, he is not considered a key employee because his ownership percentage is not greater than five percent, and even though he is a greater than one percent owner, his income is not greater than $150,000.

Maurice is an officer of Whinny National Bank. He earns $500,000 per year in annual compensation. Maurice is a key employee because he is an officer with compensation in excess of the annual limit.

Officer

Whether an individual is an officer is determined upon the basis of all the facts, including the source of his authority, the term for which elected or appointed, or the nature and extent of his duties. Generally, the term "**officer**" means an administrative executive who is in regular and continued service.[37]

An employee who merely has the title of an officer but not the authority of an officer is not considered an officer for purposes of the key employee test. Similarly, an employee who does not have the title of an officer but has the authority of an officer is an officer for purposes of the key employee test.

---

31. IRC §416(g)(1)(A)(i).
32. IRC §416(g)(1)(A)(ii).
33. IRC §416(b)(1). Note that under the PPA 2006, all defined contribution plans must vest on a 3 year cliff or 2 to 6 year graded vesting schedule, without regard to the plan's top-heavy status.
34. IRC §416(c).
35. The definition of a five-percent owner under top-heavy rules is the same as it is for determining whether an employee is highly compensated and includes family attributions.
36. IRC §416(i)(1).
37. Treasury Regulation §1.416-1, Q&A T-13.

No more than 50 employees must be treated as officers. If the number of officers, as defined above, exceeds 50, then only the first 50 ranked by compensation will be considered officers under the key employee definition.

Top-Heavy Vesting

If the qualified defined benefit retirement plan is top-heavy, the plan must accelerate the vesting from the standard vesting schedules to either a 2 to 6 year graduated or a 3-year cliff vesting schedule. All qualified defined contribution retirement plans now vest on a 3-year cliff or 2 to 6 year graduated vesting schedule, without regard to the plan's top-heavy status.[38] Therefore, the impact of the top-heavy rules regarding vesting is now limited to defined benefit plans. The employer may provide a vesting schedule that provides a vested benefit to its employees faster than that required by the top-heavy rules, but if so, the employer must utilize a vesting schedule that is always comparatively more rapid than one of the permitted vesting schedules.

Top-Heavy Funding

The sponsor of a top-heavy plan must also provide its non-key employees with a minimum level of funding. The amount of the minimum level of funding depends on whether the plan is a defined contribution plan or a defined benefit plan. These differences are discussed below.

Minimum Funding for Defined Contribution Plans

A defined contribution plan that is considered top-heavy must provide each of its nonexcludable, non-key employees a contribution equal to at least three percent of the employee's compensation. The benefit is payable to all eligible employees of the plan sponsor. An exception to the three percent minimum funding requirement occurs when the largest funding made on behalf of all key employees is less than three percent.[39] In such a case, all of the non-key employees must receive a minimum benefit percentage equal to the funding for the key employee with the highest percentage benefit for the year.

> The qualified profit sharing plan of MakeUps, LLP is considered top-heavy for the year. James, a plan participant, has annual compensation equal to $65,000 and James is not a key employee. The minimum amount that MakeUps, LLP must contribute to the qualified profit sharing plan on James' behalf is $1,950 ($65,000 x 3%) assuming that they contribute at least 3% to key employees.

> Erasers, Inc. sponsors a qualified age-based profit sharing plan. For the plan year, Eraser made contributions to its two key employees of one percent of compensation to Key Employee A and two percent of compensation to Key Employee B based on the formula provided under the plan document. The qualified profit sharing plan is top-heavy; therefore, all eligible nonexcludable, non-key employees must receive at least a two percent contribution to the qualified age-based profit sharing plan on their behalf because this is the largest funding percent made to a key employee (Employee B).

---

38. Pension Protection Act of 2006.
39. IRC §416(c)(2)(B)(i).

Defined Benefit Plan

A top-heavy defined benefit plan must provide a benefit to its non-key employees equal to two percent per the employee's years of service multiplied by the employee's average annual compensation over the testing period.[40] A participant's testing period shall be the period of consecutive years (not exceeding five) during which the participant had the greatest aggregate compensation from the employer.[41] The maximum top-heavy requirement is a minimum benefit of 20 percent (or 10 years of service at two percent each year) of the employee's average annual compensation for the period of consecutive years not exceeding five. If the employer's benefit funding equation provides a greater percentage than the minimum funding level calculated for the year, the employer's funding equation will be used to determine the employee's benefits. See Example 3.38 for an illustration of possible funding schedules compared with the minimum funding requirements of top-heavy plans.

Boudreaux, Kadeaux, and Thibodeaux Corporations sponsor defined benefit plans providing benefits based on years of service and an employee's average annual salary. Boudreaux, Kadeaux, and Thibodeaux provide benefits of 1%, 1.5%, and 3% respectively for each year of service.

DEFINED BENEFIT PLANS ACCRUED BENEFIT PERCENTAGE AFTER YEARS OF SERVICE - MINIMUM FUNDING FOR TOP-HEAVY PLANS				
Years of Service	Funding Schedules			Minimum Funding Requirement for Non-Key Employees if the Plan is Top-Heavy (D)
	Boudreaux Corp. (A)	Kadeaux Corp. (B)	Thibodeaux Corp. (C)	
1	1.0%	1.5%	3.0%	2.0%
2	2.0%	3.0%	6.0%	4.0%
3	3.0%	4.5%	9.0%	6.0%
4	4.0%	6.0%	12.0%	8.0%
...				
10	10.0%	15.0%	30.0%	20.0%
11	11.0%	16.5%	33.0%	20.0%
12	12.0%	18.0%	36.0%	20.0%
13	13.0%	19.5%	39.0%	20.0%
14	14.0%	21.0%	42.0%	20.0%
15	15.0%	22.5%	45.0%	20.0%

Beyond 20%, the top-heavy rules no longer apply.

---

40. IRC §416(c)(1).
41. IRC §416(c)(1)(D).

If the plans are top-heavy, Boudreaux Corp. and Kadeaux Corp. must provide a benefit of 2.0% per year of service up to 20% (D) for non-key employees, rather than the 1.0% (A) and 1.5% (B) per year of service, as defined in their plan documents. Notice that in Year 14, the funding schedule for non-key employees of Kadeaux Corp. reverts back to the original schedule (B). Key employees with Boudreaux Corp. and Kadeaux Corp. will not be impacted and will simply receive the benefits provided for in their plans (A) and (B). Thibodeaux Corp. benefits are more generous than those provided by the top-heavy rules; therefore, the top-heavy rules would not apply and both key and non-key employees would receive benefits as provided under their plan.

Entertainment Hourly, Inc. sponsors a defined benefit plan for its employees. The plan benefit formula is 1.5 percent multiplied by the employee's years of service multiplied by the average of the employee's three highest consecutive years of compensation. The plan is determined to be top-heavy for the year. Charlotte, a participant of the plan, has been employed by Entertainment Hourly, Inc. for eight years. Under the current benefit formula, Charlotte should have an accrued benefit in the defined benefit plan of 16 percent (2% x 8 years) times her three highest consecutive years of compensation. The defined benefit plan funding formula is based on two percent times years of service in this case because the defined benefit plan is considered top-heavy and the benefit provided under the plan is less than that provided by the top-heavy rules.

EXAMPLE 3.40

QUICK QUIZ 3.8

1. An officer with compensation of $120,000 is a key employee.
   a. True
   b. False

2. Qualified defined benefit plans that are considered top-heavy must use a 3 to 6 year graduated vesting schedule or a 3-year cliff vesting schedule.
   a. True
   b. False

False, False.

A defined benefit plan's benefit formula is 25 percent of an employee's average three highest consecutive years compensation at retirement. The plan has been determined to be top-heavy for the year. An employee with 30 years of service and an average three highest consecutive years of compensation of $40,000 has an accrued benefit equal to $10,000 (25% x $40,000). In this case, the top-heavy formula is not applicable because it would have only provided the employee with a 20 percent benefit (the minimum funding formula always tops out at a 20 percent benefit). When the plan benefit formula provides a greater benefit than the top-heavy benefit formula, the plan benefit formula is used.

EXAMPLE 3.41

Case Study 3.1

In the case of ***Snyder v. Elliot W. Dann Co.***, Inc., top-heavy minimum benefits were at issue.[1] In the case, Snyder, a vested participant in an employee pension plan, filed a lawsuit against the Plan, its administrators, and its fiduciaries seeking, among other things, minimum top-heavy benefits.

The court first addressed whether the Plan was top-heavy. Section 416(c) of the Internal Revenue Code of 1986 and Section 7.3 of the Plan provided that a member of the Plan who was not a "key employee" was entitled to a "top-heavy minimum benefit," also referred to as a "minimum annual pension," equal to the product of two percent of compensation multiplied by his or her "years of service."[2] The Plan was deemed to be "top-heavy" because the present value of the cumulative accrued benefits under the plan for key employees exceeded 60 percent of the present value of the cumulative accrued benefits under the plan for all employees. Snyder was not a "key employee" as defined by IRC §416(i)(1) and §2.18 of the Plan.

The court next addressed whether Snyder was entitled to top-heavy minimum benefits for his last incomplete year of service. Dann Co. conceded that Snyder was entitled to top-heavy minimum benefits under the Plan for prior years, but contested his claim for his final year of employment on the basis that Snyder did not complete a "year of service." Snyder had been actively employed by defendant Dann Co. during all of 1984 and 1985. Snyder resigned from his employment on September 15, 1986, but he continued to render service to Dann Co. on a regular basis through December 15, 1986.

Snyder submitted evidence indicating that he conducted extensive efforts, including series of telephone conferences, correspondence, and meetings that culminated in a property sale on December 10, 1986, which generated a fee of $475,000 to Dann Co., one-half of which was paid to Snyder on December 15, 1986. The court reasoned that because Snyder was compensated on a commission basis, he may be considered employed for Plan purposes through the final date of his remuneration. Because Snyder put forth sufficient evidence to establish his claim that he worked past September 1986 and into December 1986, the court granted top-heavy minimum benefits for all three years at issue, including 1986.

---

1. ***Snyder v. Elliot W. Dann Co., Inc.***, 854 F.Supp. 264 (S.D.N.Y. 6/8/1994).
2. See IRC § 416(c)(1)(A)-(B).

TOP-HEAVY PLAN SUMMARY

EXHIBIT
3.12

	Defined Benefit Plan	Defined Contribution Plan
Definition	More than 60% of the total accrued benefits of the defined benefit plan are for the benefit of key employees.	More than 60% of the total account balances of the defined contribution plan are for the benefit of key employees.
Funding	Must be at least 2% x years of service x compensation factor (up to 20%)	3% minimum to all eligible non-key employees or less if less provided to the key employees
Vesting	The plan participant's benefits must vest at least as rapidly as a 2 to 6 year graduated vesting schedule or a 3-year cliff vesting schedule. This only impacts defined benefit plans for years after 2006.	

ACTUAL DEFERRAL PERCENTAGE/ACTUAL CONTRIBUTION PERCENTAGE

Any qualified plan that includes a cash or deferred arrangement (CODA), such as a 401(k) plan, must also satisfy each of the two following tests:

- the Actual Contribution Percentage (ACP) Test for employer matching contributions (and employee after-tax contributions), and
- the Actual Deferral Percentage (ADP) Test for employee elective deferrals.

Both of these tests compare the benefits derived from the CODA plan by the nonhighly compensated employees to the benefits attributable to the highly compensated employees to ensure that the plan is not benefitting the highly compensated employees by an impermissible disproportionate amount.

As these tests are specific to CODA-type plans, the requirements of the ADP and ACP tests are explained and discussed in detail in Chapter 5.

PLAN LIMITATIONS ON BENEFITS AND CONTRIBUTIONS

To retain its qualified status and to benefit from the qualified plan advantages discussed earlier, an employer-sponsored qualified plan is limited in the benefits and/or contributions that it is permitted to provide to its employees. The various types of plans (defined benefit or defined contribution) have different methods by which the plan's benefits are provided to its participants. A defined benefit plan promises a definable payment at retirement whereas a defined contribution plan provides a contribution to a plan for each year of employment or at least on a regular basis. For this reason, the contribution limits differ for each type of plan. Defined benefit plans limit the distributions provided at retirement, and defined contribution plans limit the annual contributions to each employee's account for the year.

KEY CONCEPTS

1. What is the covered compensation limit for qualified plans?

2. What are the plan limits for defined benefit plans?

3. What are the plan limits for defined contribution plans?

4. What are the plan limits for combined qualified plans?

Covered Compensation[42]

The benefits payable under a qualified plan are based on the employee's compensation from the employer. However, the maximum amount of compensation that can be considered for the plan year is $265,000 for 2016, and is referred to as the **covered compensation limit**. Before applying any of the rules or limitations discussed below, the covered compensation limit must be taken into account. For example, an employee whose compensation is $350,000 for the year may only consider compensation up to the limit of $265,000 for 2016. As such, any plan funding formula that requires the use of the employee's compensation cannot consider any compensation above the covered compensation limit.[43]

EXHIBIT 3.13

COVERED COMPENSATION LIMIT

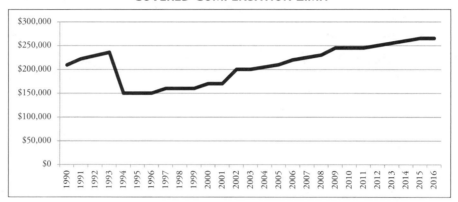

Defined Benefit Plans

As will be fully discussed in Chapter 4, a defined benefit plan is designed to provide a benefit to an employee at normal retirement age, approximately age 65, and will not provide the employee with any benefit during the term of employment or prior to his separation from service with the employer. As such, the employer determines when designing the plan the amount of benefit desired to provide to employees for this future date. The statutory requirements generally limit the employer to providing an employee with the following maximum annual expected benefit at retirement:

The lesser of:
- $210,000 for 2016, or
- 100 percent of the average of the employee's three highest consecutive years compensation during the time of plan participation (considering the covered compensation limit).

42. In 1993, Congress enacted the Omnibus Budget Reconciliation Act of 1993, which reduced the annual compensation limit from $235,840 in 1993 to $150,000 in 1994. This change was an attempt by Congress to limit contributions to higher income employees and/or increase contributions to rank-and-file employees. It has taken almost twenty years to return to the compensation limits from 1993.
43. IRC § 401(a)(17).

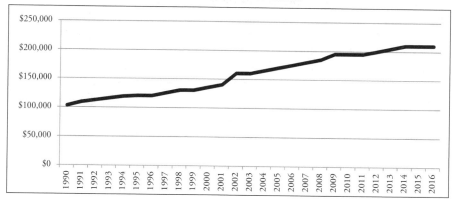

DEFINED BENEFIT LIMIT

EXHIBIT
3.14

Accordingly, the greatest annual amount an employee can expect to receive as a benefit from a defined benefit plan will never exceed the lesser of $210,000 (adjusted periodically for inflation) or the average of the employee's three highest consecutive years compensation. A defined benefit plan may always provide a lesser benefit based on its formula but can never provide a greater benefit than $210,000 per year for 2016.

> Trinity Audio has employed Ronald for 12 years. Trinity Audio operates a defined benefit plan that provides a benefit to its employees equal to one percent per year of service of the average of employee's three highest consecutive years compensation. Ronald has earned $275,000, $325,000, and $350,000 for the past three years, his highest consecutive years of compensation. The maximum benefit Trinity Audio can provide Ronald with at retirement considering the plan formula and the 2016 covered compensation of $265,000 is $31,800 (1% x 12 x $265,000) annually.

**EXAMPLE
3.42**

To ensure that qualified retirement plans do not benefit only certain employees with very few years of plan participation, an individual who participates in a defined benefit plan for less than 10 years must reduce the calculated maximum benefit by 10 percent for every year of participation less than 10.[44]

> Charlie begins employment with Employer Avant on January 1, 2009, at the age of 58. Avant maintains a noncontributory defined benefit plan, which provides for a straight life annuity beginning at age 65 and uses the calendar year for the plan year. Charlie becomes a participant in Avant's plan on January 1, 2009, and works through December 31, 2015, when he is age 65. Charlie begins to receive benefits under the plan in 2016. Charlie's average compensation for the period of Charlie's high-3 years of service is $40,000. Furthermore, under the terms of Employer A's plan, Charlie has only 7 years of service with Avant (2009 through 2015).
>
> Because Charlie has only 7 years of service with Avant at the time he begins to receive benefits under the plan, the maximum permissible annual benefit payable with respect to Charlie is $28,000 ($40,000 multiplied by 7/10).[45]

**EXAMPLE
3.43**

---

44. IRC §415(b)(5).

Distributions from defined benefit plans should begin at the normal retirement age of the employee. However, employers may provide in the plan document that the benefit be payable to the employee before the normal retirement age, perhaps as a method to encourage early retirement. In these situations where the benefit payments begin prior to normal retirement age, the calculated maximum benefit is actuarially reduced to an equivalent maximum benefit for the payment year. Other circumstances may create the need for an employer to establish an incentive to continue employment past the normal retirement age and allow the employee to accrue additional benefits in the defined benefit plan. Accordingly, where an individual's benefit payments begin after the normal retirement age, the maximum payment can be actuarially increased to an equivalent maximum benefit for the payment year. The depth and detail of these actuarial calculations are reserved for an advanced course in retirement planning.

Jose, age 68, has been employed by Whole Drinks Store for 39 years. He began employment as a grocery clerk and is now the President of the company. Jose has calculated that under the company's defined benefit plan, he will receive $210,000 per year after his retirement. However, because Jose has continued to work past his normal retirement age, his benefit will be increased to an amount actuarially equivalent to what it would have been if he had taken it at his normal retirement age.

Defined Contribution Plans

Similar to the defined benefit plan, the defined contribution plan also has a maximum benefit it may provide to its participants. However, the maximum benefit of a defined contribution plan is the maximum amount that may be contributed to an employee's defined contribution account for the year, not the amount payable to the employee at retirement, as in the case for defined benefit plans. This "annual additions limit" is a statutory ceiling that consists of employee deferrals, employer matching contributions, employee discretionary contributions, employee after-tax contributions, and forfeitures.[46]

In general, the maximum contribution per participant to a defined contribution plan is the lesser of:

- 100 percent of an employee's compensation for the plan year, or
- $53,000 for 2016.[47] Catch-up contributions increase this limit to $59,000 for 2016.

Only those employees whose compensation is less than $53,000 (2016) are affected by the percentage limitation of 100 percent of compensation. For example, an employee whose compensation for the plan year is $30,000 could potentially receive a $30,000 contribution to a defined contribution plan. However, an employee whose compensation for the plan year is $150,000 could only receive a maximum $53,000 contribution to a defined contribution plan in 2016.

---

45. Treas. Reg. §1.415(b)-1.
46. IRC §415(c).
47. Does not include the catch-up contribution for those 50 and older, which is $6,000 in 2016. Therefore, the limit for these individuals is $59,000 for 2016.

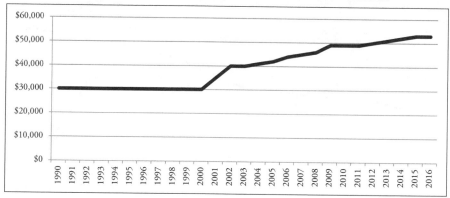

The maximum contribution is an aggregate amount consisting of:
- The employer contributions to the plan, plus
- The employee contributions to the plan, plus
- Any forfeitures allocated from non-vested employees who terminated employment during the year.

The maximum contribution discussed here should not be confused with the employer's maximum tax-deductible amount of 25 percent of the employer's total covered compensation paid (discussed below). The limit under IRC §415(c) is an individual limit, while the 25 percent limit is a plan limit. Both limits must be complied with while operating the qualified plan.

Employer Contributions to the Plan

The total employer contributions to a defined contribution plan include any mandatory contributions, discretionary contributions, and matching contributions. If the employer maintains multiple defined contribution plans, the limit is based on the aggregate of all contributions to all of the qualified retirement plans.

Employee Contributions to the Plan

The total employee contributions to a defined contribution plan include any mandatory contributions, elective deferral contributions, and any after-tax contributions. The maximum employee elective deferral, as discussed in Chapter 5, is included within the defined contribution account maximum annual contribution. The limit for employee salary deferrals is $18,000 for 2016. This limit is an individual annual limit and includes 401(k) plans, 403(b) plans, SARSEPs and SIMPLEs[48]. Therefore, if an individual has access to more than one of these plans during a year, the maximum that could be contributed to all the combined plans is $18,000 for 2016.[49] Catch-up contributions made by the participant are not limited by the $53,000 for 2016 limit and allow an individual over the age of 50 to contribute up to $59,000 for 2016.[50]

---

48. SIMPLEs have a lower limit than the 401(k) plans, 403(b), plans and SARSEPs, but deferrals to a SIMPLE will count against the annual deferral limit.

49. Note that 457(b) plans have the same deferral as the plans mentioned. However, the deferrals to the 457(b) plans are not counted against the salary deferral limit. Therefore, someone with a 401(k) plan and a 457(b) plan could defer twice the annual limit – see Chapter 10 for more on 457 plans.

50. Catch up contributions (IRC §402(g)(1)(C)) are discussed in Chapter 5 relating to contributions to a 401(k) plan.

EXHIBIT
3.16

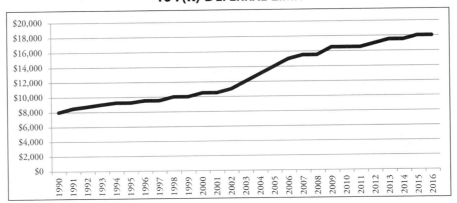

401(k) Deferral Limit

Forfeitures from Non-Vested Employees

If an employee terminates employment prior to being fully vested, the employee's benefits or a percentage of the employee's benefits will be forfeited and may then either be used to reduce future plan costs or increase the other plan participants' account balances. Any **forfeiture** allocated to an employee's defined contribution plan account during the year is included as a contribution to the plan when determining the maximum annual additions limit.

**EXAMPLE
3.45**

Pretzels, Inc. sponsors a defined contribution plan for its employees. Ashley, age 46, a long-term employee with compensation of $135,000 for 2016, has received a $33,500 profit sharing plan contribution and $2,000 of forfeiture allocations. Ashley could still defer $17,500 ($53,000 - $33,500 - $2,000) in the 401(k) plan to maximize her annual contribution limit of $53,000 for the plan year.

**EXHIBIT
3.17**

MAXIMUM PLAN LIMITATIONS

	DEFINED BENEFIT	**DEFINED CONTRIBUTION**
Covered Compensation	$265,000 for 2016	$265,000 for 2016
Maximum Benefit	Lesser of: • $210,000 for 2016 or • Average of 3 highest consecutive years of compensation	Lesser of: • 100% of compensation or • $53,000 for 2016

**EXHIBIT
3.18**

COORDINATION OF MAXIMUM DEFINED CONTRIBUTION LIMIT (2016)

 Employer Contributions
+ Employee Contributions
+ Plan Forfeitures
= Lesser of $53,000 or 100% of compensation

Employer Contribution Limit

In addition to the limits per employee as detailed above, another limit applies to the maximum tax deductible amount allowed by an employer. Generally, an employer cannot deduct contributions to defined contribution plans in excess of 25 percent of the employer's total covered compensation. Covered compensation includes compensation up to $265,000 (2016) for all those employees included in the plan. The 25 percent rule does not apply to defined benefit pension plans because the employer is required to fund the defined benefit plan to the minimum funding standard determined by the actuary.

Multiple Plan Limitations

When an employer maintains both a defined benefit plan and a defined contribution plan, the general rule[51] is that the total amount deductible in a taxable year under such plans shall not exceed the greater of:

- 25 percent of the compensation otherwise paid or accrued during the taxable year to the beneficiaries under such plans, or
- the amount of contributions made to or under the defined benefit plans to the extent such contributions do not exceed the amount of employer contributions necessary to satisfy the minimum funding standards.

QUICK QUIZ 3.9

1. The covered compensation limit for 2016 is $265,000.
   a. True
   b. False

2. The defined benefit plan limit is $210,000 for 2016.
   a. True
   b. False

3. The defined contribution plan limit is the lesser of 25% of compensation or $53,000 for 2016.
   a. True
   b. False

True, True, False.

Effectively, the defined benefit plan must be funded, even if the contributions exceed 25 percent of covered compensation. If the funding does not exceed 25 percent of covered compensation, then additional contributions can be made to the defined contribution plan. However, PPA 2006 made the rules less stringent with several exceptions introduced. This combined limit does not apply in the following cases:[52]

1. If there are no employees who benefit under both the defined benefit and defined contribution plans, then the combined limit does not apply.
2. If the plan is subject to PBGC insurance, the combined limit does not apply. The defined benefit plan would be subject to the minimum funding standards and the defined contribution plan would be limited to 25 percent.
3. If one or more of the plans is a multiemployer plan, then that plan is not considered for purposes of these rules.
4. Salary deferrals are not considered for purposes of determining the combined limits.[53]
5. If contributions do not exceed six percent of the compensation otherwise paid or accrued during the taxable year to the beneficiaries under the plans, then these limitations do not apply.

51. IRC §404(a)(7).
52. IRC §404(a)(7)(C).
53. IRC §404(n).

Regarding exception number 5 above, if the defined benefit plan is not covered by PBGC and if contributions do exceed 6 percent, then only the excess beyond the six percent limit will be subject to the limitation.[54] In essence, when employer contributions to a defined contribution plan exceed six percent of compensation, then the combined limit would apply. Another way to view these limits is that if the contribution to the defined benefit plan exceeds 19 percent of covered compensation, then the defined contribution plan is limited to six percent.

EXAMPLE 3.46

Mary's Carpentry Supplies (MCS) operates a defined benefit plan not covered by PBGC insurance and a defined contribution plan. The annual covered compensation for MCS is $1,000,000. The actuary has determined that a contribution of $120,000 must be made to the defined benefit plan. In this case, MCS can make a tax deductible profit sharing plan contribution on behalf of its employees up to $130,000 (($1,000,000 x 25%)-$120,000) for the current year. Notice that the contributions to the defined contribution plan are in excess of 6%.

EXAMPLE 3.47

Consider the same facts as above except that the actuary determined that a contribution of $400,000 had to be made to the defined benefit plan. In this case, MCS can make a tax deductible contribution to the profit sharing plan of up to 6% or $60,000 for a total deduction of $460,000 or 46%.

EXAMPLE 3.48

Cheryl owns Notlad, which sponsors both a defined benefit plan (not covered by the PBGC) and a profit-sharing plan. The covered compensation for Notlad is $500,000. If the required funding for the defined benefit plan is $50,000, then how much can be contributed to the profit-sharing plan? The answer is $75,000, or the difference between 25% of $500,000 and the $50,000 for the defined benefit plan.

EXAMPLE 3.49

Saben LLC sponsors both a defined benefit plan and a profit sharing plan with a cash or deferred arrangement. The defined benefit plan is covered by the PBGC. The covered compensation for Saben LLC is $900,000. Salary deferrals total $50,000. If the required funding for the defined benefit plan is $200,000, then how much can be contributed to the profit-sharing plan? The answer is $225,000 since the plan is covered by the PBGC and the multiple plan limits do not apply. If the plan was not insured with the PBGC, then $54,000 (6% of $900,000) could be contributed to the profit sharing plan.

On March 13, 2007, the Internal Revenue Service issued Notice 2007-28, which provides guidance with regard to the 2006 changes. Notice 2007-28 states that the 2006 changes exclude multiemployer plans from consideration and provide that the combined limit only applies in the case of employer contributions to one or more defined contribution plans to the extent that such contributions exceed six percent of the compensation otherwise paid to or accrued during the taxable year to the beneficiaries under the plan. The Notice further states that matching contributions and nonelective employer contributions are taken into account for the purpose of applying the limits of §404(a)(7), but elective deferrals are not.

---

54. IRC §404(a)(7)(C)(iii)(II).

CONTROLLED GROUP

A controlled group consists of two or more commonly owned corporations. These commonly owned entities generally take one of two forms. A controlled group will be classified as a parent-subsidiary group or as a brother-sister group. However, a group of related entities may be classified as a combined controlled group of corporations.

There are a variety of tax benefits that are available to corporations and other taxable entities, such as lower tax brackets, expensing of depreciable business assets (IRC §179), and tax deductions for contributions to qualified plans. Except for the controlled group rules under IRC §1561, savvy business owners could double or even triple these and other tax benefits by splitting current companies into two or three companies and still maintaining complete ownership. The controlled group rules cause multiple entities that are commonly owned to be treated as one entity for purposes of certain tax limits and tax benefits. The controlled group rules are intended to prevent business owners from simply splitting a company into separate companies with identical ownership so as to double or even triple certain benefits that are provided under the Internal Revenue Code.

Fully understanding the controlled group rules may allow a family to structure entity ownership in such a way as to avoid falling within the controlled group rules, thus being able to benefit by having multiple entities.

The Internal Revenue Code (specifically IRC §414(b)) also provides that companies belonging to a controlled group be treated as a single employer for purposes of qualified plans, specifically for purposes of:

- IRC §401 – qualification
- IRC §404 – deductions
- IRC §410 – participation
- IRC §415 – contribution and benefit limitations
- IRC §416 – top-heavy rules

It should also be noted that while the controlled group rules under IRC 1563 relate specifically to corporations, IRC §414(c) provides for similar treatment for purposes of qualified plans, SEPs, and SIMPLEs as it relates to non-incorporated businesses (such as partnerships and LLCs).

Therefore, companies belonging to a controlled group must comply with the qualification rules, participation rules, and the other rules relating to qualified plans as if the companies were a single employer. In the event that such businesses fail to meet these requirements, the qualified plan(s) will be subject to disqualification. More information on the controlled group rules can be found in the Appendix to this chapter.

If two or more corporations, trades or businesses are part of a controlled group of businesses, the controlled group members are treated as a single employer when applying certain employee plan benefits requirements. These requirements are:

1. Nondiscrimination, IRC §401(a)(4),
2. Compensation dollar limit under IRC §401(a)(17),
3. Minimum participation test under IRC §401(a)(26),
4. Eligibility, IRC §401(a)(3) and §410(a),
5. Coverage, IRC §410(b),
6. Vesting, IRC §401(a)(7) and IRC §411,
7. Section 415 limits,
8. Top heavy rules IRC §416, and
9. SEP's under 408(k) and SIMPLE-IRA plans under IRC §408(p).

IRC Sections 414(b) & (c) were added to the Code because, in the words of the Senate Committee Report on ERISA: "The Committee, by this provision, intends to make it clear that the coverage and nondiscrimination provisions cannot be avoided by operating through separate corporations instead of separate branches of one corporation." A plan that is maintained by an employer, within a group of employers that are under common control, must meet the requirements of IRC Section 401(a) as if a single employer employed all employees of the group.

EMPLOYEE PLANS COMPLIANCE RESOLUTION SYSTEM (EPCRS)

If a qualified plan does not meet any one of the necessary requirements discussed throughout this chapter, the plan could lose its qualified status and its tax-favored status. In this case, the employer will lose its tax deductions for contributions to the plan, and the employees (usually only highly-compensated and key employees) would be taxed on the value of the plan's assets, including any earnings in their accounts.

To avoid the total loss of its tax advantages, a plan sponsor may voluntarily correct any problems with its qualified plan following the **Employee Plans Compliance Resolution System** (EPCRS) before two years from the end of the plan year in which the problem occurred. By voluntarily correcting the problem, the IRS will be more lenient and, provided the plan sponsor retroactively benefits all employees as if the problem had not occurred, will more likely than not allow the continuance of the plan's qualified status.[55]

---

55. More information on the EPCRS can be found on the IRS website, IRS.gov.

CHAPTER
3
APPENDIX

LEASED EMPLOYEES

Qualified and other tax-advantaged retirement plans, such as SEPs and SIMPLEs, have specific guidelines as to which persons must benefit under the plan. Generally, only an employee of the sponsor organization will benefit under the plan. Independent contractors and temporary or leased employees are usually not covered by a company's retirement plan. However, there are specific rules that determine when a leased employee must be treated as an employee for purposes of the plan. If these rules were not in place, a company could simply hire temporary employees (leased employees) to fill the majority of positions within the company and avoid having to provide them with retirement benefits. This would create the illusion of a nondiscriminatory plan even though such a plan would be discriminatory. To avoid this possibility, the IRC provides guidance on who is to be considered leased employees and the employer's (sponsor) requirements as it relates to these employees.

Any person who provides services to the employer and is not an employee will be considered a leased employee if the following criteria are met:
- The services provided are pursuant to an agreement between the employer and a leasing organization;
- Such person has performed services for the employer on a substantially full-time basis for a period of at least one year; and
- Such services are performed under the primary control of employer.[56]

The significance of these rules is that leased employees must be considered a common law employee for purposes of meeting coverage rules, top-heavy rules, contribution and benefit rules, as well as a variety of other rules.[57]

---

56. IRC §414(n)(2).
57. IRC §414(n)(3) states that a leased employee is considered an employee for purposes of the following code sections: §§401(a)(3), (4), (7), (16), (17), and (26); §408(k); §408(p); §410; §411; §415; §416; §79; §106; §117(d); §120; §125; §127; §129; §132; §137; §274(j); §505; and §4980(B).

EXAMPLE 3.50

ABC company, sponsor of a qualified plan, hires a receptionist, Diana, through a temporary service and employs Diana for a period in excess of one year. In such a case, Diana is treated the same as any employee of the organization for certain requirements related to qualification of the retirement plan. For example, Diana must be considered for purposes of meeting the coverage rules if she was otherwise eligible (e.g., 21/1). Although the general rule is that only 70 percent of the non-highly compensated employees must be covered, the addition of Diana may cause the plan to violate the coverage rules.

The IRC provides that if certain requirements are met (safe harbor rules) by the leasing organization, someone meeting the definition of a leased employee will not have to be treated as an employee. The leased employee(s) must be covered by a plan that is maintained by the leasing organization and the leased employee(s) must not represent more than 20 percent of the employer's nonhighly compensated work force. However, the plan that is sponsored by the leasing organization must also meet certain requirements, including:

- The plan must be a money purchase pension plan with a nonintegrated employer contribution rate for each participant of at least 10 percent of compensation;
- Such plan provides for full and immediate vesting; and
- Each employee of the leasing organization (other than employees who perform substantially all of their services for the leasing organization) immediately participates in such plan.[58]

Although the above rules provide a safe harbor for an employer who uses leased employees, the requirements are so stringent that they are unlikely to be met.

CONTROLLED GROUP (ADDITIONAL INFORMATION)

There are a variety of tax benefits that are available to corporations and other taxable entities, such as lower tax brackets, expensing of depreciable business assets (IRC §179), and tax deductions for contributions to qualified plans. Except for the controlled group rules under IRC §1561, savvy business owners could double or even triple these and other tax benefits by splitting current companies into two or three companies and still maintaining complete ownership. The controlled group rules cause multiple entities that are commonly owned to be treated as one entity for purposes of certain tax limits and tax benefits. The controlled group rules are intended to prevent business owners from simply splitting a company into separate companies with identical ownership so as to double or even triple certain benefits that are provided under the Internal Revenue Code.

However, fully understanding the controlled group rules may allow a family to structure entity ownership in such a way as to avoid falling within the controlled group rules, thus being able to benefit by having multiple entities.

The Internal Revenue Code (specifically IRC §414(b)) also provides that companies belonging to a controlled group be treated as a single employer for purposes of qualified plans, specifically for purposes of:

- IRC §401 – qualification

---

58. IRC §414(n)(5).

- IRC §404 – deductions
- IRC §410 – participation
- IRC §415 – contribution and benefit limitations
- IRC §416 – top-heavy rules

Therefore, companies belonging to a controlled group must comply with the qualification rules, participation rules, and the other rules relating to qualified plans as if the companies were a single employer. In the event that such businesses fail to meet these requirements, the qualified plan(s) will be subject to disqualification. In addition to the rules for qualified plans, the rules under IRC §408(k) relating to Simplified Employee Pensions (SEPs) are also subject to the same limitations.

DEFINITION OF A CONTROLLED GROUP

A controlled group consists of two or more commonly owned corporations. These commonly owned entities generally take one of two forms. A controlled group will be classified as a parent-subsidiary group or as a brother-sister group. However, a group of related entities may be classified as a combined controlled group of corporations.

Parent-Subsidiary Controlled Group[59]

A parent-subsidiary controlled group of businesses consists of a group of entities with common controlling ownership and a common parent. A controlling interest generally implies an 80 percent ownership interest. However, for purposes of IRC §415 (limitation on contributions and benefits), the 80 percent limit is reduced to 50 percent. The following examples will help to illustrate the point.

P corporation owns stock representing 80 percent of the total combined voting power of all classes of stock entitled to vote of S corporation. P is the common parent of a parent-subsidiary controlled group consisting of member corporations P and S.

Assume the same facts as above. Assume further that S owns stock representing 80 percent of the total value of shares of all classes of stock of T Corporation. P is the common parent of a parent-subsidiary controlled group consisting of member corporations P, S, and T. The result would be the same if P, rather than S, owned the T stock.

59. Treas. Reg. §1.1563-1(a)(2).

EXAMPLE 3.53

Corporation owns 80 percent of the only class of stock of M Corporation, and M, in turn, owns 40 percent of the only class of stock of O Corporation. L also owns 80 percent of the only class of stock of N Corporation, and N, in turn, owns 40 percent of the only class of stock of O. L is the common parent of a parent-subsidiary controlled group consisting of member corporations L, M, N, and O.

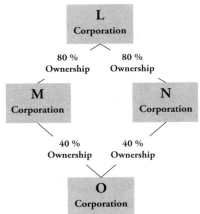

Brother-Sister Controlled Group

A brother-sister controlled group consists of two or more companies that share common owners. There are two tests that must be met for a group of entities to be considered a controlled group: the 50 percent test and the 80 percent test. Two or more entities are a brother-sister controlled group if the same five or fewer persons who are individuals, estates, or trusts own stock possessing:

- At least 80 percent of the total combined voting power of all classes of stock entitled to vote or at least 80 percent of the total value of shares of all classes of the stock of each corporation; and
- More than 50 percent of the total combined voting power of all classes of stock entitled to vote or more than 50 percent of the total value of shares of all classes of stock of each corporation, taking into account the stock ownership of each such person only to the extent that such stock ownership is identical with respect to each such corporation.

These tests are best understood through an example.

Assume that individuals A, B, C, D, and E own corporations P, Q, R, S, and T as follows. Are these corporations or some of these corporations considered a controlled group? The answer to this question depends on whether or not both the 80 percent test and the 50 percent test are met.

EXAMPLE 3.54

	CORPORATIONS					
Individuals	P	Q	R	S	T	Identical Ownership
A	55%	51%	55%	55%	55%	51%
B	45%	49%	-	-	-	45%*
C	-	-	45%	-	-	
D	-	-	-	45%	-	
E	-	-	-	-	45%	
Total	100%	100%	100%	100%	100%	

* *(P & Q only)*

The 50 percent test is met for all five corporations (P through T). However, corporations R, S, and T are not members of a controlled group because at least 80 percent of the stock of each of the corporations is not owned by the same five or fewer individuals whose ownership is considered for purposes of the 50 percent test. Only corporations P and Q are classified as a controlled group in the above example.

Consider the following example:

EXAMPLE 3.55

	SCENARIO 1		SCENARIO 2		SCENARIO 3	
Individuals	P	Q	P	Q	P	Q
A	100%	-	80%	20%	70%	30%
B	-	100%	20%	80%	30%	70%
C	-	-	-	-	-	-
D	-	-	-	-	-	-
E	-	-	-	-	-	-
Total	100%	100%	100%	100%	100%	100%

Clearly, Companies P and Q in Scenario 1 are not a controlled group. A owns 100 percent of the stock of Company P, while B owns 100 percent of the stock of Company Q. In Scenario 2, the 80 percent test is met; however, the 50 percent test is not met. A has 20 percent common ownership of Companies P and Q and B has 20 percent common ownership of Companies P and Q. Thus, the identical ownership is 40 percent, not the required greater than 50 percent. In Scenario 3, both tests are met, which means that Companies P and Q are members of a brother-sister controlled group.

AFFILIATED SERVICE GROUPS

Affiliated service groups are groups of entities that perform services together on a regular basis. The importance of affiliated service groups to retirement planning is that the entities that constitute an affiliated service group are treated as one organization or entity for purposes of the qualified plan rules. Prior to these rules, elaborate structures of entities could be established to provide higher qualified plan benefits to certain groups of owners at the expense of the rank-and-file employees. The affiliated service group rules were enacted to prevent such abuses.

A classic example of an affiliated service group is a two person law firm that is structured as a partnership with two corporations as the partners. Each corporation is solely owned by an individual attorney, who is also the only employee of such corporation. The three organizations, the partnership and the two corporations, constitute the affiliated service group.

An "affiliated service group" is a particular type of group of related employers. The affiliated service group designation refers to two or more organizations that have a service relationship and, in some cases, an ownership relationship.[60] There are three types or categories of affiliated service groups, including A-Organization groups, B-Organization groups, and management groups.

A doctor is the 100% shareholder of Corporation X, a medical corporation that specializes in sports injuries. He also owns a 40% interest in Corporation Y, which performs such medical diagnostic services as X-rays and MRIs. The doctor regularly refers patients to Y for such services. Under the attribution rules of §318(a)(3), the doctor's 40% ownership interest in Corporation Y is attributed to Corporation X. The corporations are regularly associated in providing medical services to patients; thus, constitute an affiliated service group. Under the A-Org test, Corporation Y is the FSO and X is the A-Organization. Y has ownership interest in X and the organizations regularly perform services for patients.

Jones, an attorney, is a 25% shareholder in a law firm. Jones also has a 25% interest in corporation X, which provides word processing and other clerical and secretarial services. The law firm engages the services of corporation X on a regular basis. X derives at least 10% of its gross receipts from this relationship. The law firm and corporation X constitute an affiliated service group.

Mike is the former owner of Company P. He sells his interest in the company but continues to provide management consulting services to Company P through a new wholly owned entity, Company Q. Company Q provides management functions to P on a regular basis with all of the income for Company Q derived from Company P. Companies P and Q constitute an affiliated service group.

---

60. IRC §414(m).

EXAMPLE
3.59

Assume the same facts as above except that Company Q also provides management functions to 2 other businesses (total of 3) and that the revenue received from each of the companies is approximately equal. In this case, there is not an affiliated service group. Since no one company is the principal business of Company Q, there is no affiliated service group.

IMPACT OF AFFILIATED SERVICE GROUPS

As with the controlled group rules, when a group of companies are classified as an affiliated service group, the group of companies is treated as a single employer for purposes of qualified plans rules. The qualified plan rules that are impacted include eligibility, coverage, vesting, non-discrimination (including ADP and ACP), contribution/benefit limits under IRC §415, top-heavy rules, and other rules.

SEPARATE LINE OF BUSINESS

Eligible employees within the same company are generally required to be treated uniformly with regard to qualified retirement plans. However, companies that maintain separate lines of business may be permitted to treat the employees of one line of business different than employees of another line of business.[61]

Usually, a separate line of business will have a separate organizational unit, separate accounting, separate employee group, and separate management. A firm can provide different benefits, including qualified retirement plan benefits, to employees of a separate line of business than to other parts of a business. This provision may allow a firm to reduce company expenses.

For an employer to treat various parts of a business as separate lines of business, there must be a valid business purpose and certain rules must be met. The employer must have at least 50 employees within a line of business and notify the Secretary (IRS) that such line of business is going to be treated as a separate line of business for purposes of IRC §129(d)(8) and 410(b). Form 5310-A (Notice of Merger or Consolidation, Spinoff, or Transfer of Plan Assets or Liabilities; Notice of Qualified Separate Line of Business) is used to notify the IRS that a company intends to maintain separate lines of business. In addition, such lines of business must meet certain guidelines prescribed by the Secretary or the employer must receive a determination letter permitting the line of business to be treated as a separate line of business.

Certain safe harbor provisions will satisfy the previous requirement of meeting prescribed guidelines established by the Secretary.[62] A line of business will meet the safe harbor requirements if the percentage of highly compensated employees is not less than one-half and not more than twice the percentage that highly compensated employees are of all employees of the employer. There are also a variety of administrative safe harbor rules that will permit a separate line of business.

---

61. IRC §414(r).
62. IRC §414(r)(3).

BREAK IN SERVICE RULES

In some cases an employee may leave their job and return at a later time. This may occur because an individual quits and then is later rehired, or the individual may take a leave of absence due to the birth of a child or for military service. These types of leaves from the employer may create what is referred to as a "break in service." The consequences of a break in service depend on the length of time the employee is away, whether their retirement benefit was fully vested, and, in some cases, the reason that the employee took the leave.

A one year break in service is defined as a "calendar year, plan year, or other 12-consecutive-month period designated by the plan during which the participant has not completed more than 500 hours of service."[63] In the case of a plan utilizing the elapsed time method, the term "1-year break in service" generally means a 12-consecutive month period beginning on the severance from service date or any anniversary thereof and ending on the next succeeding anniversary of such date.

Fischer and Company maintains a qualified plan. The plan requires 2 years of service to become eligible for the plan. Paul was hired on January 1, 2016 and works 40 hours per week for the rest of the year. Paul takes a leave of absence from February 1, 2018 to December 31, 2018 to care for his aging father. Paul returns to work January 1, 2019. Since Paul only worked 160 hours in 2018, a one year break in service occurred for 2018.

In general, a qualified plan must count all of the employee's years of service for eligibility purposes since the employee's date of hire. However, for an employee who has incurred a 1-year break in service, years of service completed before such break are not required to be taken into account until the employee has completed one year of service after his return to service.[64] In addition, if a plan requires two years of service before an employee can enter the plan, then the plan can, if properly elected in the plan document, disregard years of service before a "one year break" in service.

EXAMPLE 3.61

In the example above, Paul had one year of service before he had a one year break in service. Since the plan requires two years of service for eligibility the plan is not required to take into account Paul's service for 2016. Thus, when Paul returns to work in 2019 his years of service for eligibility will start over.

If an employee is already eligible for the qualified plan then a break in service can affect the employee's vesting in the plan. In the case of a nonvested participant who has incurred a 1-year break in service, years of service completed before such break are not required to be taken into account with regard to vesting if the employee has the greater of five consecutive one year breaks in service or the participant's years of service before the break.

---

63. IRC §411(a)(6)(A).
64. IRC §1.411(a)-6.

Fischer Company maintains a qualified plan. The plan utilizes a calendar year 3-year cliff vesting schedule. Paul was hired on January 1, 2016. After 2 years of service Paul separated from service. One year later Paul returns to Fischer Company and reenters the plan. If Paul completes one year of service after reentering the plan then the plan must credit Paul for his previous years of service. Thus, when Paul has completed one year of service after reentering the plan, he will have 3 years accumulated toward meeting the vesting requirement.

EXAMPLE 3.62

Assume instead Paul returns five years later instead of one year later. Since Paul has five one year breaks in service, the plan is not required to credit Paul for his previous years of service. Therefore, when Paul has completed one year of service after reentering the plan, he will only have 1 year towards the 3 year requirement.

EXAMPLE 3.63

In the case of a participant in a defined contribution plan who has incurred a 1-year break in service, years of service completed after such break are not required to be taken into account for purposes of determining the nonforfeitable percentage of the participant's right to employer-derived benefits that accrued before the break if the employee has five consecutive one year breaks in service or receives a distribution of the account balance.

Fischer Company maintains a defined contribution plan. The plan utilizes a calendar year 2 to 6 year graduated vesting schedule. Paul was hired on January 1, 2016. After 3 years of service Paul separated from service with a vested balance of 40% that was not distributed from the plan. One year later Paul returns to Fischer Company and reenters the plan. If Paul completes one year of service after reentering the plan, then the plan must credit Paul's pre-break in service account for years of service after the break. Thus, Paul's account balance will be 60% vested in all funds in the account at his initial separation. In addition, the contributions made by Paul after he reenters the plan will benefit from the prior years of service. Thus, when Paul has completed one year of service after reentering the plan, he will also be 60% vested in that year's contributions.

EXAMPLE 3.64

Assume instead Paul returns five years later instead of one year later. Since Paul has five one year breaks in service, the plan is not required to credit Paul's pre-break in service account for years of service after the break. Thus, the 60% unvested portion in his pre-break account is forever lost. In addition, contributions made after Paul's return do not benefit from Paul's prior service. Therefore, when Paul has completed two years of service after reentering the plan, he will only be 20% vested in his post break account balance.

EXAMPLE 3.65

For purposes of determining the employee's accrued benefit under a plan, the plan may not disregard service due to distribution unless the plan provides an opportunity for the participant to repay the full amount of the distribution after returning to service. A defined benefit plan can also require the repayment to include interest no greater than 120 percent of the federal midterm rate on the first day of the plan year that the repayment occurs. The plan provision required may provide that such repayment must be made in the case of a withdrawal because of separation from service, before the earlier of 5 years after the first date on which the participant is subsequently re-employed by the employer, or the close of the first period of 5 consecutive 1-year breaks in service commencing after the withdrawal; or in the case of any other withdrawal, 5 years after the date of the withdrawal.

Fischer Company maintains a defined contribution plan. The plan utilizes a calendar year 2 to 6 year graduated vesting schedule. Paul was hired on January 1 of this year. After 3 years of service Paul separated from service with a vested balance of 40%, which was distributed from the plan. One year later Paul returns to Fischer Company and reenters the plan. Since Paul took the distribution from the plan, the plan does not have to credit Paul for post break service unless he repays the distribution.

Employees wanting to take a leave of absence should carefully examine their plan document so that they do not inadvertently and unnecessarily lose retirement benefits.

MILITARY SERVICE

If an employee leaves employment for qualified military service and is then reemployed after such service, then the employee is treated as not having incurred a break in service. The term "qualified military service" means any service in the uniformed services (as defined in Chapter 43 of Title 38, United States Code) by any individual if such individual is entitled to reemployment rights under such chapter with respect to such service. Each period of qualified military service served by an individual is, upon reemployment, deemed to constitute service with the employer maintaining the plan for the purpose of determining the nonforfeitability of the individual's accrued benefits under such plan and for the purpose of determining the accrual of benefits under such plan.[65]

There is no requirement for the employer to make contributions to the military employee's defined contribution plan while they are on active duty. However, once the military employee returns from military duty and is reemployed, the employer must make the employer contributions that would have been made if the military employee had been employed during the period of military duty. If employee contributions are required or permitted under the plan, the employee has a period equal to the lesser of three times the period of military duty or five years, whichever ends first, to make up the contributions. If the employee makes up the contributions, the employer must make up any matching contributions. There is no requirement that the employer contributions include earnings or forfeitures that would have been allocated to the employee had the contributions been made during their military service.[66]

MATERNITY/PATERNITY LEAVE

For vesting and eligibility purposes, an employee who is absent from work due to pregnancy or the birth or adoption of a child is treated as having completed the number of hours that would have been credited but for the absence up to 501 hours of service. The credit for hours of service during the absence is only for determining if a break in service has occurred.[67]

---

65. IRC §414(4)(8).
66. IRC §414(a)(2)(A).
67. http://www.irs.gov/retirement/article/0,id=135692,00.html

Donna works 10 hours a week for Mad Scientist Inc. Mad Scientist Inc. has a qualified plan and Donna participates in the plan. For the current year Donna worked 36 weeks and was on maternity leave for 16 weeks. While Donna only worked 360 hours for the year, for purposes of the break in service rules she is credited with the 160 hours she would have worked had she not been on maternity leave. Therefore, Donna will not have a break in service since she is deemed to have worked 520 hours for the year.

KEY TERMS

ANTI-ALIENATION PROTECTION - An ERISA-afforded protection for qualified plans that prohibits any action that may cause a qualified plan's assets to be assigned, garnished, levied, or subjected to bankruptcy proceedings. Exceptions to the anti-alienation rule apply for tax levies and QDROs.

AVERAGE BENEFITS PERCENTAGE TEST - One part of the average benefits coverage test that requires the average benefit percent of the nonhighly compensated employees to be at least 70 percent of the average benefit percentage of the highly compensated employees.

AVERAGE BENEFITS TEST - A qualified plan coverage test that determines whether the plan adequately benefits the nonhighly compensated employees by comparing the benefits received by the nonhighly compensated to the benefits of the highly compensated employees and also determines whether the employee classification is nondiscriminatory. The test consists of the Average Benefits Percentage Test and the Nondiscriminatory Classification Test.

CLIFF VESTING SCHEDULE - A vesting schedule that provides the participant's full rights to the plan's assets immediately upon the passage of a certain number of years.

COVERED COMPENSATION LIMIT - The maximum employee compensation that may be considered for contributions to qualified plans or the accrual of benefits to a qualified plan. For 2016, the covered compensation limit is $265,000.

COVERED EMPLOYEE - An employee who benefits from a qualified plan during the year.

DEFINED BENEFIT PLAN - A qualified retirement plan that provides its participants with pre-determined calculated benefits at retirement.

DEFINED CONTRIBUTION PLAN - A qualified retirement plan that provides its participants with either a contributory or noncontributory retirement account, which benefits from tax-deferred growth for contributions and earnings in the plan.

EMPLOYEE PLANS COMPLIANCE RESOLUTION SYSTEM (EPCRS) - The system provided by the IRS that allows plan sponsors to voluntarily correct any disqualifying actions within two years of the plan year end in which the problem occurred.

EMPLOYEE RETIREMENT INCOME AND SECURITY ACT (ERISA) - Legislation enacted by Congress in 1974 as a result of various abuses by plan sponsors to provide protection for an employee's retirement assets, both from creditors and from plan sponsors.

50/40 COVERAGE TEST - A coverage test applicable only to a defined benefit pension plans that requires the plan to cover for every day during the plan year the lesser of 50 employees or 40% of all eligible employees.

KEY TERMS

FORFEITURES - The percentage or amount of a participant's accrued benefit that was not vested to the employee at the employee's termination from the plan sponsor. The forfeited amount stays in the plan and may be allocated to the other plan participants (defined contribution plan) or reduce future plan costs (defined contribution plan or defined benefit plan).

GRADUATED VESTING SCHEDULES - A vesting schedule that provides an employee with full rights to a certain percentage (less than 100%) of benefits after completing a number of years of service and provides the employees with an additional percentage for each additional years of service.

HIGHLY COMPENSATED EMPLOYEE - An employee who is either a more than 5 percent owner at any time during the plan year or preceding plan year, or had compensation in excess of $120,000 for the prior plan year (2016). A special election can be made to count only those employees whose compensation is in excess of $120,000 and are in the top 20% of employees as ranked by compensation.

KEY EMPLOYEE - Any employee who is a greater than five percent owner, a greater than one percent owner with compensation in excess of $150,000 (not indexed), or an officer with compensation in excess of $170,000 (2016).

LUMP-SUM DISTRIBUTION - A complete distribution of a participant's account balance within one taxable year on account of death, disability, attainment of age 59½, or separation from service. Lump-sum distributions from qualified plans are eligible for special taxation options.

NONEXCLUDABLE - An employee who must be considered as eligible to participate in a qualified plan.

OFFICER - An administrative executive who is in regular and continued service and has the executive authority normally associated with an officer.

PAYROLL TAXES - The combination of OASDI and Medicare tax paid by an employee and employer on an employees compensation.

PENSION PLAN - A qualified retirement plan that pays a benefit, usually determined by a formula, to a plan participant for the participant's entire life during retirement.

PLAN ENTRANCE DATE - The date an eligible employee becomes a participant in a qualified plan.

PROFIT SHARING PLAN - A qualified retirement plan established and maintained by an employer where the employer makes deductible contributions on behalf of the employees, the assets grow tax-deferred, and if there is a CODA feature, the employee also makes pretax contributions.

QUALIFIED DOMESTIC RELATIONS ORDER (QDRO) - A court order related to divorce, property settlement, or child support that can divide a participant's interest in a qualified plan.

KEY TERMS

QUALIFIED PLAN - A retirement plan that meets the qualifications of IRC §401(a).

RATIO PERCENTAGE TEST - A coverage test that compares the ratio of nonhighly compensated covered by a retirement plan to the ratio of highly compensated covered by the plan. The comparative ratio must be at least 70%.

SAFE HARBOR COVERAGE TEST - A coverage test that requires the employer to cover at least 70% of the nonhighly compensated employees.

STANDARD ELIGIBILITY REQUIREMENTS - IRC eligibility rules for participation in a qualified plan. Provides that an employee must be considered eligible to participate in the plan after completing a period of service with the employer extending beyond the later of the date on which the employee attains the age of 21 or the date on which the employee completes one year of service (1,000 hours of service within 12 months).

TOP-HEAVY - Rules that were designed to ensure that plans established primarily to benefit the owners and executives of the company also provided some minimum level of benefits for the rank-and-file employees. A plan is top heavy if more than 60 percent of either the account balance or accrued benefits are for the benefit of key employees.

TWO-YEAR ELIGIBILITY ELECTION - A special election that overrides the standard eligibility requirements and permits the employer to only consider those employees who have two years of service as eligible to participate in a plan. If the employer elects the two year requirement, than the employer must also provide 100% vesting at the completion of two years of service. This exception is not available for 401(k) plans.

VEST - To give an employee rights to employer contributions and earnings in their retirement plan benefits.

YEAR OF SERVICE - At least 1,000 hours of service for an employer and 12 months of continuous employment.

DISCUSSION QUESTIONS

1. Describe the historical change from pension plans to profit sharing plans.

2. Describe the overall differences between defined benefit and defined contribution plans.

3. Explain the matching principle of expenses and income and its impact on qualified plans.

4. What are payroll taxes and how do they impact qualified retirement plans?

5. How are contributions to, earnings within, and distributions from qualified plans taxed?

6. Describe the anti-alienation protection afforded to qualified plans.

7. How are assets of a qualified plan protected for employees from the employer?

8. List the special taxation options available for lump-sum distributions.

9. Explain the standard eligibility rules for qualified plans.

10. What is the "Two-Year" eligibility rule?

11. Explain how eligibility rules are used to encourage tax-exempt educational institutions to sponsor qualified plans.

12. Which employees may be excluded from a qualified plan?

13. Define "highly compensated."

14. Describe the general safe harbor coverage test.

15. Describe the ratio percentage coverage test.

16. Describe the average benefits test and its component parts.

17. Describe the defined benefit 50/40 coverage test.

18. Explain the available vesting schedules for qualified plans.

19. Define "years of service" for qualified plans.

20. Define a "top-heavy qualified plan."

21. Define "key employee."

22. How are the vesting and funding requirements of a qualified plan affected by it being a top-heavy status plan?

23. What is the current covered compensation limit?

24. What is the maximum annual benefit that may be provided to an employee from a defined benefit plan?

25. What is the maximum allowable contribution to an individual's account under a defined contribution plan for 2016?

26. What are the funding limits when a company sponsors a defined benefit plan and a defined contribution plan?

MULTIPLE CHOICE PROBLEMS

1. Which of the following is not an example of a qualified retirement plan?

    a. ESOP.

    b. Age-based profit sharing plan.

    c. ESPP.

    d. 401(k) plan.

2. Dole Electronics, a C Corporation, has 4 employees. The company sponsors a profit sharing plan and contributed 10% of employee compensation for the current year to the plan. The company has the following employee information. There is no state income tax and federal withholding is 15% of gross pay.

EMPLOYEE	GROSS SALARY	PROFIT SHARING CONTRIBUTION
Andy	$50,000	$5,000
Candy	$40,000	$4,000
Mandy	$30,000	$3,000
Sandy	$20,000	$2,000

    Which of the following statements is true?

    a. Dole Electronics will not be able to take a deduction for the contribution to the profit sharing plan.

    b. After payroll taxes and withholding, Andy will only receive $38,675 in take home salary.

    c. Dole electronics will pay FICA payroll taxes of $11,781.

    d. Candy must include the $4,000 contribution to the profit sharing plan made on her behalf in her gross income for the current year.

3. Steve has a qualified plan with an account balance of $2,000,000. In which of the following circumstances would a third party be able to alienate the assets within Steve's qualified plan?

    1. A QDRO in favor of a former spouse.
    2. A federal tax levy.
    3. Creditors in a personal bankruptcy.

    a. 3 only.

    b. 1 and 3.

    c. 1 and 2.

    d. 1, 2, and 3.

4. Barry's Graphic Arts Studio sponsors a qualified profit sharing plan. The plan requires employees to complete one year of service and be 21 years old before entering the plan. The plan has two entrance dates per year, January 1st and July 1st. Assuming that today is December 15, 2017 and the Studio has the following employee information, which of the following statements is correct?

EMPLOYEE	AGE	START DATE
Barry	35	1/1/2016
Del	34	8/1/2016
Karen	24	6/1/2017
Jenn	18	5/1/2016

   a. Two people have entered the plan.
   b. The qualified plan must provide participants with 100% vesting upon entering the plan because of the eligibility requirements of the plan.
   c. Del has not yet entered the plan.
   d. Jenn entered the plan on July 1, 2017.

5. Organic Inc. sponsors a qualified plan that requires employees to complete one year of service and be 21 years old before entering the plan. The plan also excludes all commissioned sales people and all other allowable exclusions allowed under the code. Which of the following employees could be excluded?

   1. Sarah, age 32, who has been a secretary for the company for 11 months.
   2. Andy, age 20, who works in accounting and has been with the company for 23 months.
   3. Erin, a commissioned sales clerk, who works in the Atlanta office. Erin is 25 years old and has been with the company for 4 years.
   4. George, age 29, who works in the factory. George has been with the company for 9 years and is covered under a collective bargaining agreement.

   a. 1 only.
   b. 1 and 3.
   c. 1, 2, and 4.
   d. 1, 2, 3, and 4.

6. Which of the following people would be considered a highly compensated employee for 2016?

    1. Kim, a 1% owner whose salary last year was $150,000.

    2. Rita, a 6% owner whose salary was $42,000 last year.

    3. Robin, an officer, who earned $105,000 last year and is the 29th highest paid employee of 96 employees.

    4. Helen, who earned $132,000 last year and is in the top 20% of paid employees.

       a. 1 and 4.

       b. 1, 2, and 4.

       c. 1, 3, and 4.

       d. 1, 2, 3, and 4.

7. Wanka Factory has 100 nonexcludable employees, 10 of whom are highly compensated. Eight of the 10 highly compensated and 63 of the 90 nonhighly compensated employees are covered under Wanka's qualified plan. The average accrued benefits for the highly compensated is 4% and the average accrued benefit for the nonhighly compensated is 1.5%. Which of the following statements is true regarding coverage?

    1. The plan passes the ratio percentage test.

    2. The plan passes the average benefits test.

       a. 1 only.

       b. 2 only.

       c. Both 1 and 2.

       d. Neither 1 nor 2.

8. Cheque Company has 100 eligible employees and sponsors a defined benefit pension plan. The company is unsure if they are meeting all of their testing requirements. How many employees (the minimum) must be covered by Cheque Company's defined benefit pension plan for the plan to conform with ERISA?

       a. 40.

       b. 50.

       c. 70.

       d. 100.

9. Billy's company sponsors a 401(k) profit sharing plan with no employer match, but the company did make noncontributory employer contributions because the plan was top-heavy. Billy quit today after six years with the company and has come to you to determine how much of his retirement balance he can take with him. The plan uses the least generous graduated vesting schedule available. What is Billy's vested account balance?

	EMPLOYER	**EMPLOYEE**
CONTRIBUTIONS	$2,000	$2,000
EARNINGS	$600	$600

   a. $2,600.
   b. $4,160.
   c. $4,680.
   d. $5,200.

10. WHR, LLC sponsors a defined contribution plan. Vaughn, age 44, has compensation of $160,000 for the year. WHR has made a $15,000 profit sharing plan contribution on Vaughn's behalf and $4,000 of plan forfeitures were allocated to Vaughn's profit sharing plan during the year. How much can Vaughn defer into his CODA plan (401(k)) to maximize his annual contributions to the qualified plan for 2016?

   a. $18,000.
   b. $24,000.
   c. $30,000.
   d. $34,000.

11. SJ, Inc. covered the following employees under a qualified plan.

   1. Joan, a 9% owner and employee with compensation of $30,000.
   2. Lind, a commissioned salesperson with compensation of $160,000 last year (the highest paid employee).
   3. Reilly, the chief operating officer, who had compensation of $137,000 last year but was not in the top 20% of paid employees.
   4. Garner, the president, who was in the top 20% of paid employees with compensation of $195,000.

   Assuming the company made the 20% election when determining who is highly compensated, which of the following statements is correct?

   a. Exactly three people are key employees.
   b. Exactly two people are highly compensated.
   c. Lind is a key employee but is not highly compensated.
   d. Reilly is neither highly compensated nor a key employee.

12. Which of the following vesting schedules may a top-heavy defined benefit plan use?

YEARS OF SERVICE	(A)	(B)	(C)	(D)
1	5%	10%	0	0
2	10%	20%	0	0
3	15%	45%	0	20%
4	20%	65%	100%	40%
5	60%	100%	100%	60%
6	100%	100%	100%	80%
7	100%	100%	100%	100%

13. Charles earns $400,000 per year at Home Cleaning Services, Inc. where he has been employed for the last ten years. Home Cleaning Services sponsors a defined benefit plan that provides its employees with a benefit equal to 1.5% per year of service of the employees final compensation. At the current time, what is Charles' retirement benefit payable from the defined benefit plan?

    a. $39,750.

    b. $60,000.

    c. $210,000.

    d. $265,000.

14. Milton, age 38, earns $170,000 per year. His employer, Dumaine Consulting, sponsors a qualified profit sharing 401(k) plan and allocates all plan forfeitures to remaining participants. If in the current year, Dumaine Consulting makes a 20% contribution to all employees and allocates $4,000 of forfeitures to Milton's profit sharing plan account, what is the maximum Milton can defer to the 401(k) plan in 2016?

    a. $0.

    b. $15,000.

    c. $18,000.

    d. $24,000.

15. Mouse Emporium sponsors a single-employer defined benefit pension plan that is covered by the PBGC and a qualified profit sharing plan. Mouse's annual covered compensation is $2,000,000 and the actuary has determined that a $600,000 contribution must be made to the defined benefit plan for the year. If Mouse would like to contribute the maximum to their defined contribution plan, how much could Mouse contribute to the defined contribution plan in 2016?

    a. $0.

    b. $53,000.

    c. $100,000.

    d. $500,000.

16. SK owns SK Ltd, which is a professional firm with five employees that sponsors both a defined benefit plan and a profit sharing plan with a cash or deferred arrangement. The covered compensation for SK Ltd is $600,000. Salary deferrals total $30,000. If the required funding for the defined benefit plan is $120,000, then how much can be contributed to the profit-sharing plan?

    a. $0.
    b. $30,000.
    c. $36,000.
    d. $150,000.

17. Which of the following vesting schedules may a top-heavy qualified cash balance plan use?

    a. 1 to 4 year graduated.
    b. 35% after 1 year, 70% after 2 years, and 100% after 3 years.
    c. 2 to 6 year graduated.
    d. 4 year cliff.

18. Qualified plans have many benefits to the employee and the employer. However they must satisfy many tests and comply with many limits to maintain their qualified status. Which of the following is correct regarding coverage tests?

    a. Profit sharing plans must satisfy only the three coverage tests.
    b. Defined benefit plans must satisfy any two of the four coverage tests.
    c. Coverage testing can include leased employees as part of the calculation.
    d. Employees who do not meet the eligibility requirements are still included in the determination of at least one of the coverage tests.

19. Andrew is a small business owner and wants to install a qualified plan that has specific requirements. Which of the following plans meets the following list of requirements?

    1. Qualified under IRC Section 401(a).
    2. Permits at least 25 percent of employer securities to be invested in the plan.
    3. Can use forfeitures to reduce plan contributions.
    4. Does not require a joint and survivor annuity distribution option.
        a. Profit sharing plan.
        b. 403(b) plan.
        c. Money purchase plan.
        d. Cash balance plan.

20. Aztec clay distributor is a family owned business that is owned by Alice, Bill, Chad and Zion. Zion is not an employee, rather a silent or somewhat silent partner. Alice and Bill are married and Chad is their 25-year-old son who has a degree in Soil Science from Dhaka University in Bangladesh. The employee census information is in the chart below.

Employee	Ownership	Salary	DeferralPlan	Balance	Status
Alice	30%	$330,000	$20,000	$400,000	Officer
Bill	3%	$210,000	$20,000	$600,000	
Chad	4%	$80,000	$10,000	$150,000	
Dave	0%	$180,000	$15,000	$150,000	Officer
Erin	0%	$140,000	$15,000	$100,000	
Frank	0%	$50,000	$8,000	$50,000	
Ginger	0%	$40,000	$0	$10,000	
Haley	0%	$30,000	$2,000	$30,000	
Irish	0%	$20,000	$1,000	$10,000	
Jen	0%	$20,000	$0	$5,000	
		$1,100,000	$91,000	$1,505,000	

What is the most that could be contributed to a profit sharing plan and deducted by Aztec if they set up a profit sharing plan (ignoring any issues with salary deferrals)?

   a. $187,500.
   b. $252,250.
   c. $258,750.
   d. $275,000.

21. Aztec clay distributor is a family owned business that is owned by Alice, Bill, Chad and Zion. Zion is not an employee, rather a silent or somewhat silent partner. Alice and Bill are married and Chad is their 25-year-old son who has a degree in Soil Science from Dhaka University in Bangladesh. The employee census information is in the chart below.

Employee	Ownership	Salary	Deferral Plan	Balance	Status
Alice	30%	$330,000	$20,000	$400,000	Officer
Bill	3%	$210,000	$20,000	$600,000	
Chad	4%	$80,000	$10,000	$150,000	
Dave	0%	$180,000	$15,000	$150,000	Officer
Erin	0%	$140,000	$15,000	$100,000	
Frank	0%	$50,000	$8,000	$50,000	
Ginger	0%	$40,000	$0	$10,000	
Haley	0%	$30,000	$2,000	$30,000	
Irish	0%	$20,000	$1,000	$10,000	
Jen	0%	$20,000	$0	$5,000	
		$1,100,000	$91,000	$1,505,000	

Who are the highly compensated employees, assuming Aztec does not use the exception as part of the definition of highly compensated employee?

    a.   Alice and Bill.

    b.   Alice, Bill, Dave, and Erin.

    c.   Alice, Bill, Chad, and Dave.

    d.   Alice, Bill, Chad, Dave, and Erin.

QUICK QUIZ EXPLANATIONS

QUICK QUIZ 3.1

1. False. Pension plans are now less common than profit sharing plans. Pension plans are less common because workers tend to not stay as long with one employer.
2. False. Pension plans can be either defined contribution or defined benefit plans.

QUICK QUIZ 3.2

1. False. Contributions by employers to qualified plans do not have to comply with the matching principle. When a contribution is made, the employer has a current deduction, but the employee does not have taxable income related to the contribution until the funds are distributed from the plan.
2. True.
3. True.

QUICK QUIZ 3.3

1. False. ERISA does not protect qualified plan assets from alienation due to a QDRO, a federal tax levy, or from a judgment or settlement rendered upon an individual for a criminal act involving the same qualified plan.
2. False. An advantage of a qualified plan is that ERISA provides the laws, rules, and enforcement provisions to protect employees from the employer's wrong doings.
3. True.

QUICK QUIZ 3.4

1. False. Using the standard eligibility rules, an employee must be allowed to enter a qualified plan within six months becoming eligible.
2. True.
3. True.

QUICK QUIZ 3.5

1. True.
2. False. The selection of a class of excludable employees must be reasonable and established based on the facts and circumstances of the business under objective business criteria.
3. False. In 2016, a highly compensated employee is one who earned at least $120,000 in the previous plan year.

QUICK QUIZ 3.6

1. False. To be a qualified retirement plan, a plan only needs to pass one of the coverage tests. A qualified retirement plan is not required to pass all three coverage tests.
2. False. The average benefits test is comprised of two tests and both tests must be passed.
3. True.

QUICK QUIZ EXPLANATIONS

QUICK QUIZ 3.7
1. True.
2. True.
3. False. The employee does not attain one year of service until he has worked for a 12-month period with at least 1,000 hours.

QUICK QUIZ 3.8
1. False. In 2016, an officer must have compensation in excess of $170,000 to be considered a key employee.
2. False. Qualified defined benefit plans that are top-heavy must use a 2 to 6 year graduated or 3-year cliff vesting schedule.

QUICK QUIZ 3.9
1. True.
2. True.
3. False. The defined contribution plan employer contribution limit is 25% of covered compensation. The maximum annual additions limit for an employee under a defined contribution plan is the lesser of 100% of compensation or $53,000 for 2016.

QUALIFIED PENSION PLANS

LEARNING OBJECTIVES

After reading this chapter, you should be able to:

1. Explain the characteristics of pension plans.
2. Differentiate between pension plans and profit sharing plans.
3. Explain the difference between defined benefit pension plans and defined contribution pension plans.
4. Evaluate the appropriateness of each of the pension plans discussed in the chapter relative to the needs and goals of a specific company.
5. Describe the limitations of using life insurance within qualified plans and the tax impact when life insurance is included in these plans.
6. Understand how the Pension Benefit Guarantee Corporation helps to protect the pensions of workers who are participants or beneficiaries of defined benefit plans.

INTRODUCTION

The traditional **pension plan** pays a formula-determined benefit beginning at retirement, usually in the form of an annuity, to a plan participant for the participant's remaining life. In some cases, a lump-sum option may be available. Historically, pension plans were offered by many employers; however, over the last 30 years, many employers have replaced their pension plans with profit sharing plans in an attempt to reduce employers' costs, eliminate mandatory funding requirements, and shift the investment responsibility from the employer to the employees.

The legal promise of a pension plan is to pay a pension. There are defined benefit pension plans, including both defined benefit and cash balance pension plans, characterized by annual funding requirements, actuarial needs, Pension Benefit Guaranty Corporation (PBGC) insured benefits, and investment risk retained by the employer. There are also two defined contribution pension plans characterized by separate individual accounts, investment risks borne by the participants, and no government-insured benefits. All of these issues will be discussed in this chapter.

PENSION PLANS (4 TYPES)	
DEFINED BENEFIT PENSION PLANS (2 TYPES)	Defined Benefit Pension Plans
	Cash Balance Pension Plans
DEFINED CONTRIBUTION PENSION PLANS (2 TYPES)	Money Purchase Pension Plans
	Target Benefit Pension Plans

Recall from Chapter 3 that there are numerous dollar limits that qualified plans must comply with including contribution limits, limits on distributions, limits on covered compensation and others. Many of these limits are illustrated below in the "Know The Numbers" table.

KNOW THE NUMBERS (2016)	
Covered Compensation Limit for Qualified Plans	$265,000
Defined Benefit Maximum Limit	$210,000
Defined Contribution Maximum Limit	$53,000
401(k), SARSEP, 457, 403(b)	$18,000
PBGC Monthly Benefit at Age 65	$5,011.36
PBGC Yearly Benefit at Age 65	$60,136

Traditional defined benefit pension plans continue to exist today but are primarily used in mature, well-established companies (often publicly traded) that have not changed to profit sharing plans.[1] The PBGC pays monthly retirement benefits to approximately 744,000 retirees in 4,000 pension plans that no longer exist.[2] Fewer new pension plans are being established today because employers have shifted the retirement planning burden from the employer to the employee. As illustrated in Exhibit 4.1, the number of defined benefit plans has decreased dramatically since 1985, while there has been a substantial increase in defined contribution plans.

Despite the expense associated with pension plans, most governmental agencies continue to provide pensions plans (although these are not qualified plans) as the predominant form of retirement benefit, but the benefits payable from these pension plans have been reduced over the years. Many governmental agencies have begun to include profit sharing type plans in conjunction with the traditional pension plan in an attempt to shift some of the responsibility for retirement funding and planning to the individual employee through self-reliant contributory plans. For example, the Federal government Thrift Savings Plan, which is discussed in more detail in Chapter 5, is extremely similar to a 401(k) plan.

Traditional pension plans promise a certain defined benefit amount available at the time of a participant's retirement. This benefit, the present value of which can be calculated at any given point during an employee's service, is commonly based on a combination of the participant's years of service and salary with the company and the participant's salary.[3] A participant's salary for these purposes is usually defined as the participant's final salary, the average of the participant's highest salaries, or the average of the participant's salaries over their career. If, however, a career average salary is used in the formula, there will be a significant loss of purchasing power when the benefit is received as compared to the final salary method. The following is an example of a common pension plan benefit formula.

1.5%	x	# of Years of Service	x	The Average of the 3 Highest Consecutive Years Salary	=	Annual Pension Benefit Amount ($)

---

1. It should be noted that there are many planning opportunities with defined benefit plans for small businesses. Some of these are discussed in this chapter.
2. www.pbgc.gov/about/how-pbgc-operates.html.
3. It may also be based on years of participation in the pension plan and the participant's salary.

TOTAL PLANS BY TYPE 1975 - 2013

Year	TOTAL PLANS		
	Total	Defined Benefit	Defined Contribution
1975	311,094	103,346	207,748
1980	488,901	148,096	340,805
1985	632,135	170,172	461,963
1990	712,308	113,062	599,245
1995	693,404	69,492	623,912
2000	735,651	48,773	686,878
2005	679,095	47,614	631,481
2006	694,550	48,579	645,971
2007	707,787	48,982	658,805
2008	717,530	48,374	669,156
2009	706,667	47,137	659,530
2010	701,012	46,543	654,469
2011	683,647	45,256	638,390
2012	676,622	43,601	633,021
2013	681,154	44,163	636,991

Source: Form 5500 filings with the U.S. Department of Labor

EXAMPLE 4.1

Assume that Eric works for ABC company, which sponsors a defined benefit plan with a benefit formula of 1.5% times the years of service times the final salary. Assuming that Eric worked for ABC for 40 years and that his final salary is $100,000, he would be entitled to an annual benefit of $60,000 per year (1.5% x 40 x $100,000) during retirement. If Eric were to live for 30 years in retirement, ABC would have to pay a total of $1.8 million ($60,000 x 30 years) in retirement benefits to Eric. (Note that corporate pension benefit payments are not usually adjusted for inflation.)

There are many possible variations for the benefit formula of a pension plan resulting in a promise to pay the employee a defined benefit during retirement. Generally, pension plans do not include employee contributions (**noncontributory plans**). However, it is possible, especially in a not-for-profit or governmental institution, to have a defined benefit plan with mandatory employee contributions. In the more general case of a noncontributory plan, the full funding burden is on the employer. The plan document defines the formula that will be used to determine the pension benefit.

PENSION PLAN CHARACTERISTICS

An employer who establishes a pension plan promises to pay a defined benefit to an employee. In some cases, the funds necessary to pay benefits are not available upon the employee's retirement. If this occurs, it is usually the result of the employer's bankruptcy, cash flow problems, poor investment decisions, or some combination of the above. In any case, the employee will not receive the promised retirement benefit. As a result of the employer's promise to pay a retirement benefit and the employee's reliance on this expected retirement benefit, the government established several requirements to increase the likelihood that a pension plan has the funds required to pay the promised defined benefit throughout the employee's retirement.

> ## KEY CONCEPTS
>
> 1. Explain the mandatory funding requirement and how it is different for defined contribution plans and defined benefit plans.
>
> 2. Define an "in-service withdrawal."
>
> 3. What are the investment limitations for pension plans?

For qualified pension plans, the government requires mandatory annual funding, disallows most in-service withdrawals,[4] limits the investment of the plan assets in employer's securities, and limits the investment of plan assets in life insurance. Each of these requirements is designed to provide protection for the employee's promised benefit. In addition, the Pension Benefit Guaranty Corporation (PBGC) was established in 1974 as part of ERISA to provide additional protection for lower-wage participants of defined benefit plans. The PBGC is discussed in more detail later in this chapter.

EXHIBIT 4.2

PENSION PLAN REQUIREMENTS

1. Mandatory annual funding
2. Disallow most in-service withdrawals
3. Limited investment in employer securities
4. Limited investment in life insurance

ANTI-CUTBACK RULE

ERISA provides a rule prohibiting a plan sponsor from amending a plan such that the accrued benefit of an employee is decreased or reduced by such amendment or change.[5] This rule is intended to protect employees and participants from changes made by the employer with the intent of simply reducing the cost of the plan. However, this rule does not prevent the plan from freezing benefits, reducing future benefits, or eliminating future benefits. It simply provides that benefits already accrued cannot be retroactively reduced through amendment. This rule is referred to as the anti-cutback rule.

---

4. Under the Pension Protection Act of 2006, pension plans may allow in-service withdrawals for workers age 62 or older.
5. 29 U.S.C. §1054(g).

MANDATORY FUNDING

ERISA and the IRC provide rules to ensure that there are or will be sufficient assets available to pay the promised benefits from pension plans to participants and their beneficiaries. The PPA 2006 significantly enhanced these rules in an attempt to provide better protection to participants and their beneficiaries. These changes followed and were likely a result of several high profile corporate bankruptcies, especially in the airline industry in the early 2000s. There continues to be a balance between insuring that the promised pension benefits are properly funded and limiting the employer's ability to over-fund retirement plans as a means of sheltering current taxable income. However, it appears that the pendulum has swung toward protecting benefits with these changes, as one of the primary themes of PPA 2006 was to ensure that pension plans were working toward fully funding their pension liabilities by 2015.

There are many issues regarding defined benefit funding that must be considered by plan sponsors and actuaries that are also contemplated by ERISA. The liabilities of a defined benefit plan or pension plan are long-term in nature and should therefore be funded over a longer period of time. As with any long period of time, there is uncertainty regarding future costs of pension plans due to unknown information, including information about earnings, inflation, mortality, disability, and salary increases. Each of these factors impacts the actual cost of funding pension plan obligations.

A good example of this uncertainty is the recent investment market and economic declines beginning in 2008. These declines resulted in many pension plans, including government pension plans, being currently underfunded. However, there are also periods in which investment returns significantly exceed assumptions built into pension liability projections.

The calculation of the **mandatory funding requirement** differs for defined benefit pension plans and defined contribution pension plans, but in both cases, the employer is required to fund the plan with the determined amount (or within a range of amounts for defined benefit pension plans) regardless of the current investment market situation. The application of the mandatory funding standard requirement for both defined benefit pension plans and defined contribution pension plans is described below.

Defined Benefit Pension Plans

A **defined benefit plan** is a plan that focuses on the benefit payable to participants during retirement. Based on those expected payments, an actuary determines the amount of current funding necessary when compounded to the retirement period to fund that future benefit. The mandatory funding requirements of a defined benefit pension plan, either a defined benefit plan or a cash balance pension plan, require that the plan sponsor fund the plan on an annual basis with an amount within the range provided by an actuary (whose services are required annually). The range provided by the actuary is statutorily defined in the IRC as an amount that is between the accumulated funding deficiency and the full funding limitation.

ERISA requires companies sponsoring defined benefit pension plans to fully fund the plans every year. The minimum required contribution to a single-employer defined benefit pension plan for a plan year generally depends on a comparison of the value of the plan's assets with the plan's funding target and target normal cost.

Funding Target

A plan's funding target for a plan year is the present value of all benefits accrued or earned under the plan as of the beginning of the plan year. For this purpose, all benefits (including early retirement or similar benefits) are taken into account. Benefits accruing during the plan year are not taken into account in determining the plan's funding target.

Target Normal Cost

The minimum required contribution for a plan year generally includes the plan's target normal cost for the plan year. A plan's target normal cost is the present value of all benefits expected to accrue or be earned under the plan during the plan year (the "current" year). For this purpose, an increase in any benefit attributable to services performed in a preceding year by reason of a compensation increase during the current year is treated as having accrued during the current year.

The minimum required contribution for a plan year, based on the value of plan assets compared to the funding target, is shown in the following table:

If the value of plan assets	The minimum required contribution is:
is <u>less than</u> the funding target,[1]	the sum of: (1) target normal cost; (2) any shortfall amortization charge; and (3) any waiver amortization charge.
<u>equals or exceeds</u> the funding target,	the target normal cost, reduced (but not below zero) by the excess of: (1) the value of plan assets, over (2) the funding target.

1. The value of the plan assets is generally reduced by any prefunding balance and funding standard carryover balance. These balances may be used to offset the minimum contribution for the current year.

If the plan assets are greater than the funding target or PV of accrued benefits at the beginning of the year, then the minimum contribution equals the target normal cost reduced by the excess of the plan assets over the funding target. However, if the assets are less than the funding target, then the shortfall will generally have to be amortized over a seven-year period. Therefore, the minimum contribution equals the target normal cost plus any shortfall amortization charge.

In addition, contributions in excess of the required minimum contributions generally are credited to a prefunding balance that may be used in certain circumstances to reduce otherwise required minimum contributions in the future. The value of the prefunding balance is usually deducted from the plan assets when determining if a plan has met the funding target.

While comparing assets to liabilities should be rather straight forward, that is not always the case when the valuation of those assets or liabilities involves discounted cash flows. ERISA and the IRC provide rules for determining the funding target, which is the process of determining the present value of the accrued benefits at the beginning of the year. Specifically, plans are required to discount future benefits using three separate discount rates based on when the benefits are expected to be paid:

1. Benefits in the first five years: plans will use a short-term interest rate.
2. Benefits in the next fifteen years: plans will use a mid-term interest rate.
3. Benefits beyond twenty years: plans will use a long-term interest rate.

These three interest rates are determined by the Treasury and are derived from an average of yields over a 24-month period from an investment grade corporate bond yield curve. The objective of using the separate discount rates is to more accurately value future liabilities while taking into consideration the uncertainty of future earnings rates.

At-Risk Plans

As part of the new rules, plans that are not current with their funding obligations and are thus deemed to be at risk of defaulting on their liabilities must use specific actuarial assumptions and may have increased current liabilities. In other words, plans that do not maintain funding are penalized. These rules are intended to be an incentive to keep funding of pension obligations current.

A plan is in at-risk status for a plan year if it does not meet either of two tests.[6] Under the first test, a plan is at-risk unless the funding target attainment percentage for the preceding plan year is at least 80 percent. Under the second rule, a plan is at-risk unless the funding target attainment percentage for the preceding plan year (determined by using additional "worst case" actuarial assumptions in computing the funding target) is less than 70 percent.

There is an exception to the at-risk rules for smaller plans. Plans with 500 or fewer participants on each day of the preceding year are not treated as in at-risk status for the plan year.

Plans that have been in at-risk status for at least two of the preceding four years are subject to an additional cost referred to as a loading factor. This loading factor increases the current cost of the plan and equals four percent of the plan's liabilities plus $700 per participant. This penalty for not maintaining the funding status is consistent with the theme from the PPA 2006 of providing more protection for participants and beneficiaries.

For plan years beginning in 2010 and later, a combined plan is permitted with elements of a defined benefit pension plan together with a 401(k) plan arrangement. The combined single plan is known as a DB(k) plan and is discussed further in Chapter 5.

Defined Contribution Pension Plans

There are two types of defined contribution pension plans, money purchase pension plans and target benefit pension plans. The mandatory funding requirements for a defined contribution pension plan, either a money purchase pension plan or a target benefit pension plan, require that the plan sponsor fund the plan annually with an amount as defined in the plan document.

An employer who establishes a money purchase pension plan requiring a 17% annual contribution must make an annual contribution of 17% of each employee's covered compensation to the money purchase pension plan to meet the mandatory funding requirement.

Underfunding

The plan sponsor of a pension plan that does not meet the mandatory funding requirements may apply to the IRS for a funding waiver. The IRS grants the waiver in most cases when the employer

---

6. IRC §430(i).

is temporarily experiencing hardships that limit the availability of funding and when not waiving the requirement would negatively impact the interests of the plan participants. For example, if the requirement was not waived, the company may become bankrupt. Any funding waiver merely postpones the employer's required contribution (as determined under the mandatory funding requirements) but does not eliminate the funding requirement of the plan. In fact, the employer will be required to fund the plan with the "waived" amount and any additional amounts that accrue during the waiver period.

> If an employer receives a waiver to fund the plan when the funding requirement contribution is $40,000 and the employer has not funded the $40,000 by the following year, the employer will be required to fund the plan with the $40,000 and also fund the current year's determined mandatory funding amount.

EXAMPLE 4.3

Long periods of poor investment performance in the equity market may cause pension plans to become underfunded, but the underfunded status may change because of reversing market conditions.

DISALLOWANCE OF IN-SERVICE WITHDRAWALS

An **in-service withdrawal** is any withdrawal from the plan while the employee is a participant in the plan other than a loan (which requires a defined term, interest accrual, and repayment provisions as discussed in Chapter 7). Because the fundamental promise of a pension plan is to pay the employee a benefit at retirement, the plan cannot permit in-service withdrawals or it would risk not having enough money to pay the retirement benefit. Any such provision would be inconsistent with the promise to pay the pension benefit at retirement. Plan loans are not in-service withdrawals because they are required to be paid back. Although loans are allowed by the IRC, most pension plans do not permit plan loans because the contributions are generally funded exclusively by the employer.

Under the Pension Protection Act of 2006, pension plans can now provide for in-service distributions to participants who are age 62 or older.[7] This type of distribution, also known as phased retirement, is intended to enable older workers to become part-time employees and receive partial benefits to maintain their current earnings level. This provision is effective for plan years beginning after 2006 and is a beneficial option for employees and plan sponsors.

LIMITED INVESTMENT IN EMPLOYER SECURITIES

The assets of a pension plan may be invested in the securities of the employer/plan sponsor provided the aggregate value of the employer securities does not exceed 10 percent of the fair market value of the pension plan assets at the time the employer securities are purchased.[8] Employer securities are any securities issued by the plan sponsor or an affiliate of the plan sponsor, including stocks, bonds, and publicly traded partnership interests.

The purpose of this limitation is to protect the ability of the plan to pay the promised retirement benefit. The value of the plan sponsor's securities are tied to the value of the company. If the company performs poorly, its securities will likely decrease in value. In the case where there was no

7. IRC §401(a)(36).
8. ERISA §407(a)(2); 29 U.S. Code §1107(a)(2).

limit on investment in the employer's securities, the defined benefit plan assets would also decrease substantially. Any such decrease could subsequently create a large funding requirement from the same employer that is in the financial difficulty (the cause of the plan's decrease in value).

If the company is struggling financially and the pension plan assets were heavily invested in the employer's securities, several problems may occur. The company would already have cash flow problems due to the financial situation and the reduction in the plan assets attributable to the decrease in the company's stock price would further exacerbate the cash flow problem by increasing the minimum amount necessary to fund the plan. Therefore, it is not reasonable to have a significantly large percentage of plan assets in a pension plan invested in employer securities. The 10 percent limitation of investment of a pension plan's assets in the employer's securities is designed to protect the employer's promise to pay a pension to the employee.

A significant exposure to any one security is inconsistent with the concept of asset allocation and portfolio diversification. A basic understanding of asset management and portfolio management supports the notion of limiting the exposure to the employer's securities to promote risk reduction through diversification in the investment portfolio.

DIVERSIFICATION

In addition to the 10 percent limitation, the Pension Protection Act of 2006 requires defined contribution plans holding publicly traded employer securities to allow plan participants to diversify their pre-tax deferrals, after-tax contributions, and employer contributions that have been invested in employer securities. The defined contribution plan must offer a choice of at least three investment options, other than employer securities, each of which must be diversified and have materially different risk and return characteristics. This requirement is consistent with that found in ERISA and generally implies that a plan must provide at least one type of stock, bond, and cash fund as investment options. All plan participants must be allowed to diversify the investment of their elective deferrals and after-tax contributions. In addition, plan participants with three or more years of service must be allowed to diversify the investment of employer contributions made on their behalf. This investment diversification requirement is now fully phased in.[9]

QUICK QUIZ 4.1

1. A pension plan that is unable to deposit the mandatory funding amount may apply for a one time waiver eliminating the funding needed for that particular year.
    a. True
    b. False

2. Pension plans do not permit in-service withdrawals for individuals less than 62 years old.
    a. True
    b. False

3. Pension plans may only invest up to 15 percent of plan assets in employer stock.
    a. True
    b. False

False, True, False.

9. IRC §401(a)(35).

LIMITED INVESTMENT IN LIFE INSURANCE

One exception to the retirement benefit promise is the ability to use the assets of a pension plan to provide incidental death benefits to a participant's beneficiary through the purchase of life insurance.[10] In fact, any qualified plan may purchase life insurance (subject to these limitations). As long as life insurance is not the primary focus of the pension plan, the government allows this exception from the ultimate retirement benefit promise because the death benefit of the life insurance policy is payable to the employee's spouse and other survivors at the employee's death. The beneficiaries of the policy are usually the same beneficiaries who would receive the remainder of the employee's retirement benefits at the employee's death; therefore, purchasing life insurance allows employees to leverage the amount they will leave to their survivors in the event of an untimely death.

Whether the life insurance is the primary focus of the qualified plan or is an incidental death benefit is determined by a series of tests that limit the amount of life insurance coverage provided by a qualified plan or the cost of the life insurance provided by the plan. To maintain its qualified plan status, a qualified plan that includes life insurance must pass either the (1) 25 percent test or (2) the 100 to 1 ratio test.

25 Percent Test[11]

The 25 percent test consists of two tests, a 25 percent test and a 50 percent test. The test used depends upon the type of life insurance provided by the plan. If a **term insurance** or **universal life insurance** policy is purchased within the qualified plan, the aggregate premiums paid for the life insurance policy cannot exceed 25 percent of the employer's aggregate contributions to the participant's account. If a **whole life insurance policy** is purchased within a qualified plan, the aggregate premiums paid for the whole life insurance policy cannot exceed 50 percent of the employer's aggregate contributions to the participant's account. In addition, for any permanent life insurance policy, the entire life insurance policy must be converted to cash or an annuity at or before retirement. In the case of term insurance, the policy cannot be maintained in a qualified plan after retirement. The IRS treats whole life policies different from term and universal life policies. Term and universal policies must meet the 25 percent rule while whole life policies must meet the 50 percent rule, and the mortality cost alone cannot exceed 25 percent of the contributions. In general, the 25%/50% rule will be applied to defined contribution plans, including defined contribution pension plans. A qualified plan that meets the 25 percent test (either the 25 percent test or the 50 percent test) does not have to meet the 100 to 1 ratio test to retain its qualified status.

> Joe is a participant in a qualified plan sponsored by his employer. The employer has made aggregate contributions for Joe of $100,000. His plan holds a $90,000 term life insurance policy on his life. The total premiums that have been paid for the policy are $4,000. Because this is a term life insurance policy, the premiums paid cannot exceed $25,000 ($100,000 x 25%) per the 25% test. Since the premiums for this policy have been $4,000, the plan meets the 25% test.

EXAMPLE 4.4

---

10. Treas. Reg. §1.401-1(b)(1)(i).
11. Revenue Ruling 74-307.

100 to 1 Ratio Test

A defined benefit plan may have life insurance in the plan and retain its qualified status by meeting the 100 to 1 ratio test, which provides limits based on the benefits provided by the life insurance protection rather than the cost of the life insurance protection. Specifically, the 100 to 1 ratio test limits the amount of the death benefit of life insurance coverage purchased to 100 times the monthly-accrued retirement benefit provided under the same qualified plan's defined benefit formula. It is quite common to use the 100 to 1 ratio test for a defined benefit pension plan because of the ease of calculating the monthly accrued retirement benefit. Most qualified defined contribution plans, including pension and profit sharing plans, will use the 25%/50% tests. Although, if the defined contribution plan benefit is an annuity, it would be possible to use the 100 to 1 ratio test (unusual). In any case, the objective of these rules is to insure that life insurance death benefits are incidental to the retirement benefit and not the primary focus of the plan.

As a participant in her employer's defined benefit plan, Becky has accrued a retirement benefit of $4,000 per month. Based on the 100 to 1 ratio test, the plan is limited to utilizing plan assets to purchase life insurance up to a face amount of $400,000 ($4,000 x 100).

Tax Issues with Life Insurance in Qualified Plans

The proceeds from life insurance policies are typically not subject to income tax to the beneficiary and funds in a qualified plan are typically contributed on a pre-tax basis. Therefore, premiums paid by the employer for the life insurance policy are taxable to the employee at the time the premium is paid.[12] The premium cost of life insurance protection provided by a qualified plan is considered to be the one-year term premium for the amount of insurance provided for the participant. According to IRS Notice 2002-8, the one-year term premiums may be determined from Table 2001, which shows the premium per $1,000 of life insurance.[13]

---

12. Treas. Reg. §1.72-16(b)(2).
13. Note: Table 2001 premiums effectively replace the older P.S. 58 rates set forth in Rev. Rul. 55-747.

TABLE 2001: TABLE OF ONE-YEAR TERM PREMIUMS FOR $1,000 OF LIFE INSURANCE PROTECTION

EXHIBIT
4.3

Attained Age	Section 79 Extended and Interpolated Annual Rates	Attained Age	Section 79 Extended and Interpolated Annual Rates	Attained Age	Section 79 Extended and Interpolated Annual Rates
0	$0.70	35	$0.99	70	$20.62
1	$0.41	36	$1.01	71	$22.72
2	$0.27	37	$1.04	72	$25.07
3	$0.19	38	$1.06	73	$27.57
4	$0.13	39	$1.07	74	$30.18
5	$0.13	40	$1.10	75	$33.05
6	$0.14	41	$1.13	76	$36.33
7	$0.15	42	$1.20	77	$40.17
8	$0.16	43	$1.29	78	$44.33
9	$0.16	44	$1.40	79	$49.23
10	$0.16	45	$1.53	80	$54.56
11	$0.19	46	$1.67	81	$60.51
12	$0.24	47	$1.83	82	$66.74
13	$0.28	48	$1.98	83	$73.07
14	$0.33	49	$2.13	84	$80.35
15	$0.38	50	$2.30	85	$88.76
16	$0.52	51	$2.52	86	$99.16
17	$0.57	52	$2.81	87	$110.40
18	$0.59	53	$3.20	88	$121.85
19	$0.61	54	$3.65	89	$133.40
20	$0.62	55	$4.15	90	$144.30
21	$0.62	56	$4.68	91	$155.80
22	$0.64	57	$5.20	92	$168.75
23	$0.66	58	$5.66	93	$186.44
24	$0.68	59	$6.06	94	$206.70
25	$0.71	60	$6.51	95	$228.35
26	$0.73	61	$7.11	96	$250.01
27	$0.76	62	$7.96	97	$265.09
28	$0.80	63	$9.08	98	$270.11
29	$0.83	64	$10.41	99	$281.05
30	$0.87	65	$11.90		
31	$0.90	66	$13.51		
32	$0.93	67	$15.20		
33	$0.96	68	$16.92		
34	$0.98	69	$18.70		

In effect, the use of funds from a qualified plan to purchase life insurance is deemed a distribution.[14] This taxation does create taxable basis in the plan, which is further discussed in Chapter 7.

---

14. IRC §402(a). However, this distribution is not subject to any penalties.

EXAMPLE 4.6

George works for Appletosh, which sponsors a qualified plan. The plan purchased a life insurance policy on George's life. The cost of the insurance (from Table 2001) purchased in the plan is taxable to George.

As mentioned, generally the proceeds from life insurance are not taxable to a beneficiary. Qualified plans are permitted to purchase cash value life insurance in qualified plans. The limit for whole life insurance is 50 percent because part of the premium is used to fund the cash value of the policy, similar to deferred compensation. Because of this, the beneficiary of a life insurance policy purchased within a qualified plan must include into taxable income the proceeds of life insurance to the extent of cash value of the policy.[15]

EXAMPLE 4.7

Jay died suddenly in a freak accident. Fortunately for his girlfriend, Toni, there was a life insurance policy payable to her that was purchased in Jay's qualified plan. The face amount of the policy is $25,000 and the cash value of the contract just before his death was $11,000. Therefore, $14,000 is treated as life insurance paid by reason of the death of the insured, and $11,000 is a death benefit, which is taxable to Toni. However, the taxable portion may be reduced by Jay's basis, that is, the aggregate of the amounts that were currently taxable to him because they represented the portion of premiums paid by employer for the life insurance protection. This aggregate amount represents the employee's contribution to the plan. Assuming that the basis is $1,000, it reduces the taxable portion from $11,000 to $10,000.

As mentioned and will be discussed further in Chapter 7, distributions from qualified plans are generally taxable as ordinary income.[16] The distribution of life insurance is subject to taxation except to the extent that, within 60 days after the distribution of the contract, all or any portion of such value is irrevocably converted into a contract under which no part of any proceeds payable on death at any time would be excludable as life insurance proceeds under IRC §101(a).[17] In other words, the contract must be converted to an annuity contract.

412(e) PLAN (FORMERLY 412(i) PLAN)

A "section 412(e) plan," set forth in IRC §412(e), is a specific type of defined benefit pension plan that is funded entirely by a life insurance contract or an annuity. The employer claims tax deductions for contributions that are used by the plan to pay premiums on an insurance contract covering an employee. The plan may hold the contract until the employee dies or it may distribute or sell the contract to the employee at a specific point, such as when the employee retires.

The typical candidate for this type of plan is a sole proprietor with only a few employees. The 412(e) plan allows greater contributions to the plan than a traditional defined benefit plan because of the need to fund the life insurance or annuity. In addition, the plan is easier to explain to employees because the insurance/annuity is fixed and provides less risk due to the certainty of the insurance/annuity. The plan is also less costly than a traditional defined benefit plan. Because of the exclusive use of life insurance or annuities as a funding vehicle, no actuarial calculations are necessary, reducing administrative requirements and associated expenses. Unfortunately, the plan

---

15. Treas. Reg. §1.72-16(c)(2).
16. IRC §402(a).
17. Treas. Reg. §1.402(a)-1(a)(2).

does not provide alternative investment choices, thus sacrificing the opportunity for significant long-term appreciation. In addition, the employer does not have much flexibility with regard to plan design and the plan cannot permit loans.

Although originally thought to be beneficial, some advisors have determined that 412(e) plans generally are not growth or cash flow beneficial. The lack of growth potential for 412(e) plans often overshadows the ability for greater funding. In addition, 412(e) plans have been the focus of IRS controversy over the last few years, prompting narrowing regulations and rulings.

In 2004, the IRS and the Treasury Department issued guidance intended to shut down abusive transactions involving 412(e) plans. The guidance covers three specific issues. First, a new proposed regulation states that any life insurance contract transferred from an employer or a qualified plan to an employee must be taxed at its full fair market value. This provision was designed to counteract arrangements in which an employer establishes a 412(e) plan, makes contributions to the plan (which are then deducted by the employer), purchases life insurance, and then sells the policy to the covered employee for less than the full fair market value of the policy.

Second, Revenue Ruling 2004-20 states that an employer cannot buy excessive life insurance in order to claim large tax deductions. These arrangements are considered listed transactions for tax-shelter reporting purposes.

Third, Revenue Ruling 2004-21 states that a 412(e) plan cannot use differences in life insurance contracts to discriminate in favor of highly paid employees. While 412(e) plans may initially appear beneficial to defer taxes, costs and cash flow requirements have slowed their growth. While caution should be taken when considering this type of plan, it remains a viable tool in certain circumstances.

DEFINED BENEFIT PENSION PLANS vs. DEFINED CONTRIBUTION PENSION PLANS

The defined benefit pension plan and the cash balance pension plan are both defined benefit pension plans whereas the money purchase pension plan and the target benefit pension plan are both defined contribution pension plans. Each of these plans share the characteristics attributable to pension plans but differ between the categorization of defined benefit and defined contribution. The primary differences between the two categorizations of the plans include the following:
- the use of an actuary (annually, at inception, or not needed)
- assumption of the investment risk (to the employer or to the employee)
- the disposition of plan forfeitures (reduce plan costs or allocate to remaining employees)
- coverage under the Pension Benefit Guaranty Corporation (PBGC)
- the use of Social Security integration (offset or excess)
- the calculation of the accrued benefit or account balance
- the ability to grant credit for prior service for funding
- the use of commingled funds versus separate, individual investment accounts

THE ACTUARY

Defined benefit and cash balance pension plans require the use of annual actuarial services to determine the proper annual funding of the plan. The target benefit pension plan uses actuarial assumptions only at the inception of the plan and does not require annual actuarial work. The money purchase pension plan has no need for actuarial services because the annual contribution is predefined (usually as a percentage of covered compensation) in the plan documents.

ACTUARY

Plan Type	Actuary Required
Defined Benefit & Cash Balance	Annually
Target Benefit	At Inception Only
Money Purchase	Not Used At All

The **actuary** makes assumptions about future inflation, expected wage increases, life expectancy of the assumed retirees, expected investment returns on plan assets, expected mortality rates for retirees, and expected forfeitures resulting from termination. Each of these assumptions has an impact and relationship to plan costs and plan funding.

ACTUARY ASSUMPTIONS AND RELATIONSHIP TO PLAN COSTS

Actuarial Assumption About	Direct Relationships			Indirect Relationships		
	Expected Inflation	Expected Wage Increases	Life Expectancy	Expected Investment Returns	Expected Mortality	Expected Forfeiture / Employee Turnover
Change	↑	↑	↑	↑	↑	↑
Impact on Plan Costs	↑	↑	↑	↓	↓	↓

Inflation affects plan costs directly and includes such costs as actuarial services, plan supplies, and the cost of providing service and summary plan documents for the plan. As wages increase, plan costs increase because benefits are almost always paid as an annuity derived from a formula that includes some measure of the last or highest salaries. Because the pension is a life or joint life annuity, any increase in life expectancy will increase plan costs. On the indirect side, plan costs are reduced when actual investment returns are higher than what was assumed. If the retiree's mortality rate increases faster than expected, payouts are lessened and plan costs are reduced. In addition, if there are more forfeitures than originally expected, plan costs are reduced because forfeitures in defined benefit plans must be used to reduce future plan costs.

INVESTMENT RISK

A defined benefit pension plan is designed to pay a promised benefit to a plan participant at the participant's retirement, whereas a defined contribution pension plan only guarantees that contributions based on a defined formula will be made to the plan per the plan document. In other words, the participant in a defined contribution plan is entitled to the value of the defined contribution plan account balance at retirement, including any investment gains or losses. The participant in a defined benefit plan is entitled to the promised defined benefit at retirement, regardless of the actual investment performance. Consider employees A and B who earn equal salaries, are the same age, and have the same length of service. Each will receive exactly the same pension benefit as calculated under any one of the defined benefit funding formulas at their retirement. If, however, A and B were participants in a defined contribution plan, they would have each received the same contribution each year to their defined contribution accounts, but their individual investment performance may vary widely based on their investment selections, resulting in different account balances at their retirement. Because of the nature of the benefit to be provided (a promised benefit or a promised contribution), the investment risk while the plan assets are within the qualified plan is borne by the plan sponsor for a defined benefit pension plan and generally borne by the individual plan participant for a defined contribution pension plan.

KEY CONCEPTS

1. How does the investment risk differ for defined contribution plans as compared with defined benefit plans?

2. How are forfeitures treated in defined benefit and defined contribution plans?

3. Which types of qualified plans are covered by the PBGC?

4. How is the accrued benefit of a defined benefit plan calculated?

5. Which qualified plans allow credit for prior service?

INVESTMENT RISK

Plan Type	Burden of Investment Risk
Defined Benefit & Cash Balance	Employer
Target Benefit & Money Purchase	Employee

EXHIBIT 4.6

Defined Benefit Plan

The plan sponsor of a defined benefit plan must ensure that the guaranteed benefit as provided in the plan document is available to pay the employee at the time of the employee's retirement. After meeting the mandatory funding standards as required for all pension plans (as discussed above), plan assets are invested and will experience investment returns dependent upon the investment selections made by the plan sponsor or investment manager. If the plan's investments experience positive returns and the assets grow to a level exceeding the plan's mandatory funding requirement, the plan is said to be overfunded, and the employer benefits from the excess growth by being able to offset the required funding amount for future years by the excess growth. Conversely, if the value of the plan's assets decrease due to less than expected investment returns, the employer is responsible for contributing additional amounts to maintain the mandatory funding requirement.

Any deficiency in funding is the employer's responsibility regardless of how low the value of the plan's assets have decreased in comparison to the minimum required funding amount as determined by the actuary.

EXAMPLE 4.8

If an employer funds a defined benefit pension plan with the required mandatory funding for 2016 of $100,000, and subsequently the fair market value of the pension plan assets declines in value to $80,000, the employer is required to contribute additional funds to restore the pension assets to the required level. However, any deficit will generally be amortized over a period not to exceed seven years.

EXAMPLE 4.9

If an employer funded a defined benefit pension plan with the mandatory funding standard amount of $100,000 for 2016 and the fair market value of the pension plan assets grows to $180,000, the plan sponsor can utilize the growth of the assets to offset future plan funding requirements. If, in the subsequent year, the mandatory funding amount was $190,000, the employer would only be required to contribute $10,000 to meet the requirement. Any excess investment growth reduces the employer's future plan costs.

EXAMPLE 4.10

If an employer sponsors a defined benefit pension plan with a target normal cost of $100,000 for 2016 and the plan's assets are less than the plan's funding target, the plan sponsor would have a minimum required contribution of $100,000 plus any shortfall amortization charge. If the value of the plan assets exceeds the plan's funding target, then the $100,000 minimum contribution is reduced by the amount that the value of the plan assets exceed the plan's funding target. Therefore, any excess investment growth will still offset future plan funding requirements.

One advantage for participants of a defined benefit pension plan is that they do not bear any of the investment risk. Their benefit is guaranteed to be the amount determined by the benefit formula in the plan document.[18] The fact that the employer bears this investment responsibility is viewed as a disadvantage for the employer because it is required to fund whatever amount as determined by the actuary to meet the mandatory funding requirements. This funding requirement increases the cost of providing retirement benefits to employees in years when the market performs poorly and, thus, could disrupt the projected cash flows of the employer.

Within the last two decades, several Fortune 500 companies' defined benefit pension plans that had not previously required any employer contributions to meet the mandatory funding requirements in several years, required large contributions to meet the mandatory funding standards because of the continuously poor performing investment market. In the summer of 2003, General Motors' defined benefit pension plan was so underfunded that the company issued bonds worth $17 billion. The proceeds were solely directed to fund the deficiency in its pension plan. Even though General Motors filed for Chapter 11 bankruptcy protection in 2009, its two defined benefit plans continue under the company's sponsorship and are currently insured by PBGC.

---

18. Assuming the company has the requisite funds to pay the benefit. Even though defined benefit plans are generally covered by the PBGC, participants may not receive full benefits, especially if they have higher incomes.

Defined Contribution Pension Plans

The investment risk of plan assets within a defined contribution pension plan is generally borne by each participant in the plan. To a large extent, the plan sponsor's responsibility ends after the contribution required in the plan document is made to the defined contribution plan account on behalf of the participant. As such, if the value of the investments in the account increases, the plan participant benefits from all of the increase in the account value. Conversely, if the value of the account decreases, the plan participant bears the sole responsibility and risk for this decrease. The employer is not required to subsequently contribute any additional amounts to make up for any decline in value of the account.

Defined contribution pension plans require the employer to fund the plan annually per the plan document, but the employer is not required to continuously maintain any minimum value in an individual participant's account. After the employer contribution is made, a defined contribution pension plan generally permits the individual employee participant to select investments. A poor performing investment market will not affect the employer's cash flows in the same way they might be affected under a defined benefit pension plan.

The shift from defined benefit pension plans to defined contribution pension plans has gradually resulted in a shifting of investment risk to employees, who may not be in the best position to manage their own investments.

Amelia's Flight School sponsors a 15% money purchase pension plan. In the current year, Amelia's contributed $15,000 to the plan on behalf of Joann. If the value of the $15,000 contribution decreases to $10,000 in the subsequent year, Amelia's is not responsible for the loss. If Joann is still employed by Amelia's at the end of the subsequent year, Amelia's must make another contribution of 15% of covered compensation on Joann's behalf for that subsequent year.

ALLOCATION OF FORFEITURES

When an employee terminates employment before being fully vested (discussed in Chapter 3), those benefits allocated to the employee that are not yet vested are known as **forfeitures**. For a defined benefit pension plan, the forfeited funds can only be used to reduce future plan funding costs of the employer. The forfeitures within a defined benefit plan cannot increase the benefit of any other plan participant, nor may the forfeited funds be allocated for any other purpose. The plan sponsor of a defined contribution pension plan, however, can choose to utilize plan forfeitures in one of two ways, either by reducing future plan funding costs or by allocating the forfeitures to other remaining participants in a nondiscriminatory manner; thus increasing the participants' account balances. The total contributions to a participant's defined contribution plan, including any forfeitures, are limited to the maximum annual contribution as discussed in Chapter 3.

Tony has an accrued benefit from his employer's defined benefit plan equal to $6,000 per month at retirement. However, based on the plan's vesting schedule, Tony has a vested accrued benefit equal to $4,800 per month at retirement. If Tony terminates employment today, the non-vested assets in the defined benefit plan must be used to offset future plan funding costs.

EXAMPLE 4.13

Carmela has a defined contribution pension plan with an account balance equal to $100,000, but she is only 20% vested in the account balance. If Carmela terminates employment today, the nonvested amount (forfeiture amount) of $80,000 could be allocated to the other plan participants or it could be used to reduce future plan costs.

EXHIBIT 4.7

FORFEITURES

Plan Type	Forfeitures
Defined Benefit & Cash Balance	Must Reduce Plan Costs
Target Benefit & Money Purchase (and all other Defined Contribution Plans)	Can Reduce Plan Costs or Allocate to Remaining Participants

PENSION BENEFIT GUARANTY CORPORATION INSURANCE

The **Pension Benefit Guaranty Corporation (PBGC)** was established in 1974 when President Gerald R. Ford signed the Employee Retirement Income Security Act (ERISA) into law. The PBGC acts, just as its name implies, to guarantee pension benefits. It is a federal corporation that acts as an insurance provider to maintain the benefits promised to employees by their defined benefit pension plans. The plan sponsors of defined benefit and cash balance pensions plans pay premiums for the insurance coverage, but the PBGC only provides plan participants with a limited retirement benefit if the plan completely or partially terminates with an unfunded or underfunded liability.

The PBGC does not insure defined contribution pension or profit sharing plans, nor does it insure defined benefit pension plans of professional service corporations with 25 or fewer participants. The PBGC does insure all other defined benefit plans and covered plans are required to pay a flat-rate, per participant premium. In addition, previously underfunded plans must pay a variable-rate premium equal to 3.0 percent (or $30 per $1,000 for 2016) of unfunded vested benefits. The Pension Protection Act of 2006 limits the variable-rate premiums owed by employers with 25 or fewer employees to $5 per participant for plan years after 2006. Note that this limitation only applies to employers that are not professional service corporations because the PBGC does not insure the plans of professional service corporations with 25 or fewer participants. Additionally, there is a flat-rate premium for all defined benefit plans of $64 per participant for single-employer pension plans (for 2016) with indexing based on increases in average wages.

EXAMPLE 4.14

Daniel is one of three partners in SueMe Law Corporation, which employs five other attorneys and 6 staff members. A defined benefit plan sponsored by SueMe would not be covered by the PBGC because it is a professional services corporation with less than 25 employees.

EXAMPLE 4.15

ABC has a defined benefit pension plan with 1,000 participants, and it has unfunded liabilities payable to the plan of $2 million dollars. The PBGC insurance premium is $64,000 ($64 x 1,000) + $60,000 ($30 per $1,000 of underfunding) for a total of $124,000.

MAXIMUM PBGC PENSION GUARANTEE FOR 2016

EXHIBIT 4.8

	Guarantee Limit at Age 65	Guarantee Limit at Age 62	Guarantee Limit at Age 60	Guarantee Limit at Age 55
Monthly	$5,011.36	$3,958.97	$3,257.38	$2,251.11
Yearly	$60,136	$47,508	$39,089	$27,061

In the event that a defined benefit plan terminates or partially terminates with an unfunded amount, the calculation of the benefit payment is not equal to the calculation under the terminated plan document. Instead, the PBGC benefits have a maximum limit that is indexed to inflation. As discussed in Chapter 3, a defined benefit pension plan may provide a benefit to a plan participant with a maximum of $210,000 for 2016 at retirement. However, the maximum benefit paid to plan participants at retirement by the PBGC is $60,136 per year for 2016. This lower amount can create a significant deficiency in expected retirement benefits for employees with higher compensation levels. Earning the maximum benefit based on the terminated pension plan document does not equate to the plan participant earning the maximum under a plan managed by the PBGC. The payment from the PBGC is based upon:

1. the form of the benefit as payable under the terminated plan,
2. the participant's age, and
3. any amounts that PBGC recovered from the employer in the case that the plan was under-funded.

In April of 2003, the PBGC became the trustee of the defined benefit pension plan for the US Airways pilots. Many of these pilots had salaries in excess of the covered compensation limit and had accrued benefits at their retirement equal to the maximum defined benefit pension plan amount of the plan. However, the PBGC will only pay out the maximum amount based on the termination date. For plans terminated in 2003 (as US Airways was), the max benefit at age 65 was $43,977, and $28,585 for age 60. Age 60 was the mandatory retirement age for pilots in 2003. These amounts are significantly less than what the pilots would have expected from their defined benefit plan.

In July 2009, the Pension Benefit Guaranty Corporation announced it will assume responsibility for the pension plans of 70,000 workers and retirees of Delphi Corp., the nation's largest producer of automotive parts. The PBGC took on unfunded liabilities in excess of $6 billion. Delphi was spun off from General Motors in 1999.

PBGC INSURANCE

EXHIBIT 4.9

Plan Type	PBGC Insurance
Defined Benefit & Cash Balance	Yes
Target Benefit & Money Purchase	No

As discussed, the objective of the PBGC is to insure pension benefits for participants and beneficiaries of defined benefit plans. However, it only insures benefits up to the annual limit. In addition, it has taken over many defined benefit plan over the last ten years such that the liabilities of the PBGC exceed its assets by billions of dollars. In response to this situation, the PBGC has increased annual premiums and has increased the risk within its asset portfolio.

EXHIBIT 4.10

PBGC NET POSITION (ASSETS MINUS LIABILITIES) OVER TIME

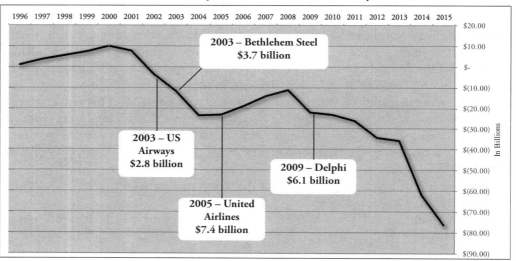

BENEFITS - ACCRUED BENEFIT/ACCOUNT BALANCE

At any given time, based on the provisions of each specific plan, a plan participant has accrued a benefit within his qualified pension plan. How the accrued benefit is calculated depends upon the type of plan sponsored by the participant's employer. A participant in a defined benefit plan has an accrued benefit roughly equal to the present value of the expected future payments at retirement (discussed further below). In contrast, a participant in a defined contribution plan has an accrued benefit equal to the account balance of the qualified plan consisting of any combination of employer and employee contributions plus the earnings on the respective contributions reduced by any non-vested amounts.

Accrued Benefit

A defined benefit plan is subject to the mandatory funding requirement as calculated by an actuary. An employee who terminates participation in the plan, usually through termination of employment before full retirement age, will be entitled to a benefit payable from the plan equal to the retirement benefit earned to date. This benefit is the actuarial equivalent of the benefit that would have been provided to the participant had the participant waited until retirement to receive the payments. As each plan document will detail the plan benefit formula (as discussed below), the calculation of the participant's accrued benefit utilizes all information at the date of termination. Communicating the value of the accrued benefit to the participants of a defined benefit plan is difficult because participants generally do not understand the funding process and the plan benefit formula. Also, an employee who is far from retirement and whose accrued benefit is quite small, will likely not grasp the true value of the ultimate benefit.

Account Balance

Calculating the accrued benefit for the participant in a defined contribution plan is usually much easier than calculating the accrued benefit for the participant of a defined benefit plan because the benefit in a defined contribution plan is simply the participant's account balance reduced by any non-vested amounts. The participant's account balance is the sum of the employer contributions to the plan and the employee contributions to the plan plus or minus any investment earnings or losses. This balance is communicated to the plan participants with periodic investment statements. These statements explain to the participants the exact amount of any plan benefit.

BENEFITS

EXHIBIT 4.11

Plan Type	Benefits
Defined Benefit & Cash Balance	Accrued Benefit
Target Benefit & Money Purchase	Account Balance

CREDIT FOR PRIOR SERVICE

At the creation of a retirement plan, every employee's accrued benefit or account balance is zero. However, an employer who establishes a defined benefit plan may elect to give employees credit for their service prior to the establishment of the plan. A defined benefit plan can easily incorporate the prior years of service into the defined benefit formula. If the plan is established in the current year, an owner who is also an employee can be credited for all of his years of service since the inception of the company. Granting **credit for prior service** must be nondiscriminatory, but in any case may benefit an older owner employer who does not have many long-term employees. The benefit of giving oneself credit for prior years of service may outweigh the additional cost of giving the other short-term employees' credit.

EXAMPLE 4.18

Danny started Dirty Day Car Wash 12 years ago. His company is finally profitable, and he would like to establish a defined benefit plan to benefit himself and his employees. The plan will provide the employees with a benefit equal to 1.5% x years of service x final salary. If Danny elects when he establishes the plan to give credit for prior service, immediately Danny's benefit would be based on 12 years of service; however, the plan must then count prior years of service for all employees. Alternatively, Danny could choose not to count prior years of service in the calculation of the benefit, but then his benefit would only be calculated on years of service after the establishment of the defined benefit plan.

A defined contribution plan cannot grant credit for prior service.

EXAMPLE 4.19

Washboard Industries, Inc. established a defined contribution plan today that provides for a 20% of compensation annual contribution to all of its employees. As a defined contribution plan, contributions can only be made to participants' accounts based on compensation for plan years after the establishment of the plan.

EXHIBIT
4.12

CREDIT FOR PRIOR SERVICES

Plan Type	Credit for Prior Service
Defined Benefit & Cash Balance	Yes
Target Benefit & Money Purchase Pension Plan	No

INTEGRATION WITH SOCIAL SECURITY - PERMITTED DISPARITY FOR DEFINED BENEFIT PLANS

The Social Security system is intentionally designed to be discriminatory towards lower income workers. The system, which is discussed in detail in Chapter 11, replaces a higher percentage of income for lower income workers than for higher income workers.[19] Qualified plans have been able to provide higher benefits to higher paid workers to offset the structure of the Social Security system since the Revenue Act of 1942 through what is know as Social Security integration or permitted disparity.

Permitted disparity (often referred to as Social Security Integration) is a technique or method of allocating plan contributions or benefits to employees that provides higher contributions to those employees whose compensation is in excess of the Social Security wage base for the plan year. All qualified pension plans may utilize permitted disparity as a method of allocating benefits to plan participants.[20] Permitted disparity allows the qualified plan to consider the Social Security benefits that will be provided to plan participants in the calculation of the participant's accrual of benefit or contribution amount.

The two primary parts of the Social Security system are OASDI (Old Age Survivor Disability Insurance) and Medicare taxes. Both employers and employees each contribute to the system through FICA[21] payments that consist of 6.2 percent for OASDI and 1.45 percent for Medicare.[22] The OASDI portion of 6.2 percent applies to income up to the Social Security wage base ($118,500 for 2016), while the Medicare portion applies to all income with no limit. In effect, the Social Security system does not consider income that exceeds the wage base for purposes of retirement benefits. Therefore, an individual who earns $118,500 will be treated exactly the same as someone who earns $1,000,000 for purposes of retirement benefits and for purposes of the amount of income that is subject to the 6.2 percent OASDI tax.

---

19. This disparity is due to two factors: income over the wage base is not considered for purposes of benefits and income at the lower level is counted at a higher percentage through the PIA (primary insurance amount) calculation.
20. All qualified plans can make use of permitted disparity except ESOPs and CODAs.
21. FICA stands for Federal Insurance Contributions Act.
22. Beginning in 2013, there is an additional Medicare tax of 0.9 percent on all earned income above $125,000 for single tax payers and $250,000 for taxpayers filing jointly.

Consider Employee A who earns $118,500 for 2016 and Employee B who earns $234,000 (twice the Social Security wage base). In this case, their employer will make a 6.2 percent contribution to the governmental retirement plan (OASDI) on 100 percent of Employee A's income and only a 3.1 percent contribution on Employee B's total income. Stated another way, the 6.2 percent contribution or payment applies to 100 percent of Employee A's income and only 50 percent of Employee B's income. Social Security taxes are only paid on earned income up to the wage base and Social Security benefits are only based on Social Security covered earnings. However, because of this disparity in treatment between lower and higher paid workers in the Social Security system, the IRC permits qualified plans to provide higher contributions or benefits to employees with income that exceeds the Social Security wage base.

The two methods of permitted disparity are the offset method and the excess method. Defined benefit plans can utilize the excess method or the offset method (discussed below), while defined contribution plans are only permitted to utilize the excess method (see Chapter 5).

Excess Method – Defined Benefit Pension Plans

The excess method provides an increased percentage benefit, referred to as the excess benefit, to those plan participants whose earnings are in excess of an average of the Social Security wage bases over the 35 year period prior to the individual's Social Security Retirement Age. This average is called the covered compensation limit, which is $75,180 for 2016.[23] The covered compensation limit can be found in an annual Revenue Ruling from the IRS.

The increased percentage benefit only applies to income that exceeds the covered compensation limit and is limited to the lesser of (1) 0.75 percent per year of service or (2) the benefit percentage for earnings below the covered compensation limit per year of service. This additional benefit only applies up to 35 years. Therefore, the maximum increase in benefits for compensation over the covered compensation limit is 26.25 percent, which is found by multiplying 0.75 percent by 35 years.

QUICK QUIZ 4.2

1. The plan participant bears the investment risk of the assets in a defined benefit pension plan.
   a. True
   b. False

2. Defined benefit and defined contribution plans allocate all plan forfeitures in the same manner.
   a. True
   b. False

3. If a company cannot pay a plan participant the benefit promised from a defined benefit pension plan, the PBGC will pay the plan participant the full defined benefit amount.
   a. True
   b. False

4. Defined benefit plans can give plan participants credit for service prior to the establishment of the plan.
   a. True
   b. False

False, False, False, True.

---

23. Revenue Ruling 2016-5.

Katy is a participant of Button World's defined benefit pension plan, earns $50,000 per year, and has been employed with Button World for 30 years. The base funding formula for Button World's defined benefit plan is 1 percent per year of service multiplied by final salary. Under this formula, Katy would have a benefit equal to $15,000 (1% x 30 x $50,000).

In addition, Button World also provides an additional benefit of 0.75 percent per year of service for income that exceeds the covered compensation limit. Assuming that the covered compensation limit is $40,000, Katy would be entitled to an additional benefit of $2,250 (0.75% x 30 x $10,000). Therefore, by integrating the plan with Social Security, Katy receives $2,250 more during retirement than she would have received if the plan had not been integrated.

Offset Method – Defined Benefit Pension Plans

To provide an increased benefit to those individuals whose earnings are in excess of the covered compensation limit, the offset method applies a benefit formula to all earnings and then reduces the benefit on earnings below the covered compensation limit. It simply takes a different approach compared to the excess method, which provides additional benefits for earnings above the covered compensation limit. The reduction of the benefit is limited to the lesser of (1) 0.75 percent per year of service up to 35 years or (2) 50 percent of the overall benefit funding percentage per year of service. As with the excess method, the total reduction is limited to 26.25 percent of the earnings below the covered compensation limit.

Consider the same facts as above, except that Button World's defined benefit funding formula is 1.75 percent per year of service multiplied by final salary and includes an offset reduction that reduces the benefit for earnings below the covered compensation limit by 0.75 percent. In this case, Katy would receive a benefit equal to $17,250 [(1.75% x 30 x $50,000)-(0.75% x 30 x $40,000)].

The above examples were designed to illustrate that the same outcome could be reached whether you followed the excess benefit method or the offset method. However, the important concept is that defined benefit plans can be structured in such a way as to provide higher benefits to those employees who have compensation above the Social Security wage base.

Jen has worked for Ex-On for the last 30 years.[24] Ex-On's basic formula is 1.6% times years of service times final salary minus the Social Security offset. The Social Security offset amount equals 1.5% times years of service (up to a maximum of 33 ½ years) times the Social Security benefit. Jen's salary is $70,000 and she expects to receive $2,000 per month from Social Security. Her benefit is as follows:

1.6% x 30 years x $70,000 = $33,600

Less Social Security offset (1.5% x 30 years x $2,000 x 12 months) = $10,800

Annual pension benefit = $22,800

---

24. Example is adapted from the ExxonMobile Pension Plan Formula detailed in the 2012 summary plan description.

There are several reasons to justify permitted disparity or Social Security integration. The first is that employers pays half of FICA and being able to offset the benefits provided under Social Security allows employers to reduce part of the cost of offering a pension plan. This accommodation provides an incentive to establish and offer pension plans. In addition, permitted disparity allows for higher benefits for those higher paid workers, which is a method of attracting, retaining and rewarding key employees.

While integration can help employees and employers, it can add to the confusion of the value of the benefit to be received during retirement, specifically with defined benefit plans. Participants may believe that they are receiving a higher benefit and not realize that their pension is being offset by benefits provided under the Social Security system.

INTEGRATION

EXHIBIT 4.13

Plan Type	Method of Integration
Defined Benefit & Cash Balance	Excess or Offset
Target Benefit & Money Purchase (and all other Defined Contribution Plans)	Excess Only

COMMINGLED VS. SEPARATE INDIVIDUAL INVESTMENT ACCOUNTS

Defined benefit pension plans use a commingled investment account, but send individual summaries to participants showing their accrued benefit to a certain date. Most defined contribution plans, including target benefit and money purchase pension plans, utilize separate, individual investment accounts and require that the individual participant invest his own retirement assets. In some cases in a defined contribution plan, the employer will direct the investments or hire an outside investment advisor to manage the investments, in which case the funds may be commingled.

COMMINGLED VS. SEPARATE ACCOUNTS

EXHIBIT 4.14

Plan Type	Accounts
Defined Benefit & Cash Balance	Commingled
Target Benefit & Money Purchase (and all other Defined Contribution Plans)	Usually Separate

EXHIBIT
4.15

SUMMARY OF CHARACTERISTICS OF DEFINED BENEFIT PENSION PLANS VS. DEFINED CONTRIBUTION PENSION PLANS

Characteristic	Defined Benefit Plans	Defined Contribution Plans
Actuary (Annually)	Yes	No (Except Target Benefit at Inception)
Investment Risk Borne by	Employer	Employee
Treatment of Forfeitures	Must Reduce Plan Costs	Reduce Plan Costs or Allocate to Other Plan Participants
PBGC Insurance	Yes	No
Credit for Prior Service	Yes	No
Social Security Integration	Offset or Excess	Excess Only
Separate Investment Accounts	No - Commingled	Yes - Separate (Usually)

DEFINED BENEFIT PENSION PLANS

The various qualified retirement plans have been initially divided into pension and profit sharing type plans and further subdivided into defined benefit and defined contribution plans. Beyond the requirements and characteristics detailed above, the defined benefit pension plan is unique as compared to the other pension plans.

ESTABLISHING THE FORMULAS FOR BENEFITS

To determine the retirement benefit provided by a defined benefit pension plan, first the plan funding and allocation formula must be established. The IRC offers several methods of calculating the participant's ultimate retirement benefit, but the most common benefit formulas are:

1. the flat amount formula
2. the flat percentage formula
3. the unit credit formula

Regardless of which formula is used, it is important to keep in mind that in order to receive the maximum benefit under a defined benefit pension plan, the employee must have at least 10 years of participation in the plan. If an employee has less than 10 years of participation in the plan, then the maximum benefit is determined by multiplying $210,000 (the 2016 maximum benefit permissible for defined benefit plans) by the employee's number of years of participation divided by 10.[25]

Rudy has worked for Nicholas Toy Corporation for eight years. Nicholas Toy Corporation sponsors a defined benefit pension plan. The maximum benefit that Rudy is eligible to receive under the defined benefit pension plan is $210,000 x (8 years/10 years) or $168,000.

---

25. IRC Section 415(b)(5). However, IRC Section 415(b)(4) states that such reduction is not required for total annual benefits that do not exceed $10,000.

Charlie begins employment with Employer Alpha on January 1, Year 1, at the age of 58. Alpha maintains only a noncontributory defined benefit plan that provides for a straight life annuity beginning at age 65 and uses the calendar year for the plan year. Charlie becomes a participant in Alpha's plan on January 1, Year 2, and works through December 31, Year 7, when Charlie is age 65. Charlie begins to receive benefits under the plan in Year 8. Charlie's average compensation for the period of Charlie's high-3 years of service is $40,000. Furthermore, Charlie has only 7 years of service with Employer Alpha (Year 1- Year 7).

Because Charlie has only 7 years of service with Alpha at the time he begins to receive benefits under the plan, the maximum permissible annual benefit payable with respect to Charlie is $28,000 ($40,000 multiplied by 7/10).[26]

EXAMPLE 4.24

Flat Amount Formula

A defined benefit pension plan that provides its participants with a benefit calculated under the **flat amount formula** provides each participant with an equal dollar benefit at retirement. The formula provides an amount that each plan participant will receive at retirement, such as $250 per month. The formula is not based on years of service with the employer or the participant's salary. From the highest paid plan participant to the lowest paid plan participant, each participant will receive the same amount at retirement.

A plan that utilizes the flat amount formula protects the employer from having to provide increased benefits as salaries increase. Such a plan does not provide the participant with any incentive to attain additional years of service with the employer because the benefit will not increase with any additional years of service beyond the minimum number required to receive the benefit. This formula is used more commonly in union plans and collective bargaining agreements.

An employer wishing to utilize a defined benefit plan to improve employee retention would generally not choose a flat amount formula. Also, highly paid employees, usually the persons selecting the qualified plan for the employer, are unlikely to choose a flat amount formula because, as a proportion of income, they would benefit less than the lesser paid employees. However, a flat amount formula may be used in combination with a unit credit formula or some other benefit formula.

26. Treas. Reg. §1.415(b)-1.

Flat Percentage Formula

The **flat percentage formula** provides all plan participants with a benefit equal to a specific percentage of the participant's salary, usually the final salary or an average of the participant's highest salaries. The percentage remains the same throughout participation in the plan and does not increase based on additional years of service or age. The flat percentage formula will provide a plan participant with an increasing benefit as salary increases simply based on the fact that the benefit will be calculated based on the increased salary. Usually the participant must attain a required minimum number of years of service to be eligible to receive the benefit. This type of benefit formula is not widely used because it does not give credit for long service. However, flat percentage formula can be used to provide benefits to older owners who are attempting to fund defined benefit plans with larger amounts of additional cash flow.

KEY CONCEPTS

1. What are the common funding allocation methods for a defined benefit plan?

2. How are participant accounts treated within a defined benefit plan?

3. Which age group benefits more from the establishment of a defined benefit plan?

Unit Credit Formula

When a defined benefit plan utilizes both a participant's years of service and salary to determine the participant's accrued benefit, the plan is using a **unit credit formula**. Unit credit formulas provide a fixed percentage of a participant's salary multiplied by the number of years (the unit) the participant has been employed by the employer. Examples include 2 percent per year of service multiplied by the participant's annual compensation or 1.5 percent per year of service multiplied by the average of the participant's three highest annual consecutive salaries. A unit credit formula gives credit for both a participant's term of employment and salary in the awarding of the benefit. A participant without substantial years of employment will not accrue a benefit comparable to the participant's annual salary. Generally, a unit credit formula is more likely to retain employees than the flat amount formula or the flat percentage formula. The unit credit formula approach is widely used in defined benefit pension plans.

CE Corporation uses a unit credit formula for calculation of benefits as follows:

2%	x	# of Years of Service	x	The Average of the 3 Highest Consecutive Annual Salaries

Kevin, Brian, Jimmy, and Michael are retiring this year. Each person's benefit is calculated below based on their years of service and compensation.

	Years of Service	Average of 3 Highest Years of Compensation	Annual Benefit	Wage Replacement Ratio
Kevin	28	$100,000	$56,000	56%
Brian	30	$120,000	$72,000	60%
Jimmy	40	$150,000	$120,000	80%
Michael	33	$60,000	$39,600	66%

SUMMARY OF DEFINED BENEFIT PLAN FUNDING FORMULAS

EXHIBIT 4.16

Funding Formula	Benefit Calculation	Example	Comments
Flat Amount Formula	Flat amount per month	$250 per month	No incentive for participants to continue employment after attaining maximum flat amount
Flat Percentage Formula	Flat percentage based on compensation	10% of compensation per year at retirement	Incentive to increase compensation through raises but not to continue employment after attaining a desired benefit
Unit Credit Formula	Benefit determined on a combination of service and compensation	2% x years of service x average 3 highest consecutive years of pay	Incentive to attain additional years of service and additional compensation to increase ultimate benefit

BENEFIT ACCRUAL

Defined plans may use a flat amount, flat percentage, unit credit formula or a combination of these methods in structuring the benefit to participants. However, ERISA and the IRC provide for three primary methods of benefit accrual for defined benefit plans to ensure against what is referred to as **back loading**.

Back loading is a practice of delaying the accrual of benefits until late in someone's career so that, if they were to leave the company, they would forfeit all or a large portion of their benefits. Consider the following example:

EXAMPLE
4.26

Consider BackLoad Inc. that sponsors a defined benefit plan. Assume that the earliest someone could enter the plan is age 21, normal retirement is age 65 and the benefit accrual rate is as follows:

Years of Service (YOS)	Benefit Accrual
Age 21 through 60	0.1% x YOS
Age 61 through 65	15% x YOS

In this example, an employee who worked for 40 years and terminated would accrue a benefit of just four percent (0.1% times 40 years), whereas if that employee worked five more years, the benefit would be 79 percent. This is an example of extreme back loading.

The three permitted benefit accrual methods provided for in the IRC are:

1. 3 Percent Method
2. 133⅓ Percent Rule
3. Fractional Rule

All defined benefit plans, other than excluded 412(e) plans, must satisfy one of the above accrual methods.

3-Percent Method

A plan will satisfy the 3-percent method if the accrued benefit to which each participant is entitled upon the participant's separation from the service is at least three percent of the normal retirement benefit to which the participant would be entitled if he or she commenced participation at the earliest possible entry age under the plan and served continuously until the earlier of age 65 or the normal retirement age specified under the plan, multiplied by the number of years (not in excess of 33⅓) of participation in the plan.

This rule means that at any point a participant separates from service, the participant should receive a benefit that is at least three percent per year of participation times the full benefit assuming that the participant entered the plan at the earliest point and left at normal retirement.

QUICK QUIZ 4.3

1. The unit credit formula helps retain employees more than either the flat benefit formula or the flat percentage formula.
   a. True
   b. False

2. Defined benefit plans have separate accounts for each plan participant.
   a. True
   b. False

3. The establishment of a defined benefit pension plan generally benefits older employees more than the younger employees.
   a. True
   b. False

True, False, True.

X corporation's defined benefit plan provides an annual retirement benefit, commencing at age 65, of 2% of the average of the 3 highest consecutive years of compensation (AC) for each year of service (YOS) in the Plan (not to exceed 30). As a condition of participation, the plan requires that an employee should have attained age 21 and has one year of service. Does the plan formula satisfy the "3% rule?"

EXAMPLE
4.27

Answer:

For a plan to satisfy the 3% method, as of the end of each year, the employee's accrued benefit should equal to 3% x YOS x normal retirement benefit (NRB), which is calculated as if the participant entered the plan at the earliest possible entry age and terminated from service as of the earlier of the plan's normal retirement age (which in this case is 65) or age 65.

In this case, at the end of the first year of participation, the participant would have accrued a benefit of two percent of AC. Under the three percent method, if the employee had entered the Plan at age 21 and terminated from service at age 65, the employee would have had 44 years of service. Based on that, the NRB provided by the Plan is two percent of AC x 30 YOS = 60% of AC.[27]

At the end of year 1, the participant's accrued benefit should be at least as great as 3% x 1 x 60% of AAC = 1.8% of AC. At the end of year 1, the participant's accrued benefit (2% of AAC) is greater than what is required under the three percent method (1.8% of AC). The participant's accrued benefit would exceed the accrued benefit required under the three percent method for all other years. For example, in Year 5, the participant's accrued benefit would be 10 percent of AC. Under the three percent rule, the participant would be required to have an accrued benefit that is at least as great as 3% x 5 x (60% of AC)= 9% of AC. Therefore, the Plan accruals comply with the "3% method."

133 $\frac{1}{3}$ Percent Rule

A defined benefit plan satisfies the requirements of the 133⅓ rule if the accrued benefit payable at the normal retirement age is equal to the normal retirement benefit and the annual rate at which any participant can accrue the retirement benefits payable at normal retirement age under the plan for any later plan year is not more than 133⅓ percent of the annual rate at which the participant can accrue benefits for any prior plan year.

Y corporation's defined benefit plan provides an annual retirement benefit based on years of participation and AC. The plan provides that a participant will accrue his benefits as follows:

EXAMPLE
4.28

- 2% of AC for the first 15 years of participation
- 3% of AC for the next 15 years of participation

---

27. Note that years in excess of the maximum 30 years are ignored because the plan benefit limits benefit accrual to 30 years.

> The Normal Retirement Benefit payable at age 65 will be equal to the accrued benefit calculated for the participant based on the accrual rates provided above.
>
> Answer:
>
> For the plan to comply with the $133\frac{1}{3}$ percent rule, a subsequent year's accrual cannot exceed $133\frac{1}{3}$ percent of a prior year's accrual. Because 3% is 1.5 times 2%, the plan does not pass the $133\frac{1}{3}$ percent rule. If however the first accrual rate was 1.5% and the second accrual rate was 2%, then the plan would meet the $133\frac{1}{3}$ percent rule.

Fractional Rule

A defined benefit plan satisfies the Fractional Rule if the accrued benefit to which any participant is entitled upon separation from the service is not less than a fraction of the annual benefit commencing at normal retirement age to which he or she would be entitled under the plan as in effect on the date of separation if the participant continued to earn annually until normal retirement age the same rate of compensation upon which the participant's normal retirement benefit would be computed under the plan, determined as if the participant had attained normal retirement age on the date on which any such determination is made. The fraction cannot exceed 1.

This rule is satisfied if the benefit is proportional to the years of participation relative to the full benefit that would have been received if the participant had remained in service until normal retirement.

> ABC defined benefit plan provides for a Normal Retirement Benefit of 60% of high-3 consecutive years' average compensation (AC) payable in the form of a life annuity at the Plan's NRA of 65. The Plan provides that the participant's Accrued Benefit will be based on the fractional rule. Employee A commences participation in the Plan at age 35 and separates from service at age 50. Assume his AC is $40,000.
>
> Answer:
>
> Benefit at NRA = 60%
>
> Years of participation 15 (50 – 35)
>
> Years of participation until NRA 30 (65 – 35)
>
> Accrued benefit = 60% benefit x 15/30 x $40,000 = $12,000

COMMINGLED ACCOUNTS

Even though a participant in a defined benefit pension plan may have a calculated accrued benefit, a defined benefit pension plan does not have separate accounts for each participant. All of the assets of a defined benefit plan are managed as a group, and it is impossible to segregate any individual participant's funds. Benefits are simply paid from the pool of assets.

YOUNGER/OLDER

A defined benefit pension plan is generally considered to benefit older participants because at the creation of the plan, the largest percentage of the overall contribution to the plan will often be attributable to the older participant(s). Older employees entering the plan require higher accrued benefits because of fewer compounding periods to retirement.

ELIGIBILITY/COVERAGE/VESTING

Defined benefit plans follow the eligibility, coverage, and vesting rules described in Chapter 3.

DISTRIBUTIONS

Distributions from defined benefit pension plans are subject to the rules for distributions from qualified plans described in Chapter 7.

CASH BALANCE PENSION PLANS

A **cash balance pension plan** is a defined benefit pension plan that shares many of the characteristics of defined contribution plans, but provides specific defined retirement benefits. From the participant's perspective, a cash balance pension plan is a qualified plan that consists of an individual account with guaranteed earnings attributable to the account balance. However, the account that the employee sees is merely a **hypothetical account** displaying hypothetical allocations and hypothetical earnings. The accounts are hypothetical because the cash balance pension plan assets are managed by the plan sponsor in the same manner as a defined benefit pension plan. This commingled account consists of the assets that will be used to fund the benefits promised to the plan participants on their account statements.

> ## KEY CONCEPTS
>
> 1. Explain how participant accounts are treated in cash balance pension plans.
>
> 2. Which age group usually benefits the most from the establishment of a cash balance pension plan?
>
> 3. Define "interest rate whipsaw" with regard to cash balance pension plans.

Because the cash balance pension plan is a defined benefit pension plan, it is subject to all of the requirements of defined benefit plans and pension plans. Most notably, the plan sponsor of a cash balance pension plan is subject to mandatory funding (the guarantee that the participant will have a benefit at retirement), insurance from PBGC, the investment risk of the plan's assets, and must obtain an annual actuarial valuation of the plan.

CONTRIBUTIONS AND EARNINGS

When a cash balance plan is established, the plan sponsor must develop a benefit formula. A cash balance formula typically includes two elements – a pay credit and an interest (or earnings) credit:

Pay credit – the plan specified amount that is contributed in the hypothetical account, which is generally stated as a percent of compensation. The pay credit will often be a fixed percent of compensation, such as four percent or five percent. However, the pay credit may also be different for different age groups, employee classifications, or by other methods. Pay credits may be designed to benefit older employees or higher paid employees or owners. However, benefits must be non-discriminatory. In addition, benefits can be integrated with Social Security.

Interest credit – the amount of earnings applied to the balance in the hypothetical account. The interest credit may be a fixed rate, such as three percent, or a variable rate tied to an index, such as the one-year Treasury bill rate. The formula for the interest credit can certainly be more complicated including a minimum interest rate combined with a variable component that is higher or lower than a specified rate by a specified number of basis points.

The PPA 2006 provided new rules for cash balance plan interest credits. These rules, described in Treasury Regulation §1.411(b)(5)-1(d) (market rate of return) provide that a cash balance plan cannot provide an interest credit rate in excess of a "market rate of return." This term permits a cash balance plan to base the crediting rate on actual rates of return assuming diversification, the returns of a mutual fund assuming the returns are not more volatile than the market, certain fixed percentage rates, other fixed income rates, and combinations of permitted rates.[28]

Participants will receive annual statements detailing the additions to the account during the year. The statement will look very much like that of a defined contribution plan in that it will have an opening balance and include the contributions during the year. The opening balance simply equals the ending value from the prior year. The contributions include the pay credit and the interest credit. The sum of the three will equal the ending value for the year. Below are examples of different benefit formulas for cash balance plans.

---

28. Applies to plan years that begin on or after January 1, 2016.

CASH BALANCE STATEMENT

EXHIBIT
4.17

January 01, 20XX – December 31, 20XX

For Information Contact:
Vanguard Participant Services
In the USA (800) 523-1188
Or via the internet at *www.vanguard.com*

THE RETIREMENT
PLAN FOR THE ALPHA
COMPANIES

THE RETIREMENT
PLAN FOR THE ALPHA
COMPANIES

Participant's
Name & Address

John Smith
123 Main Street
New Town, USA 12345

Company
Plan Name
& Number

THE RETIREMENT PLAN FOR THE
ALPHA COMPANIES - CASH
BALANCE RETIREMENT PROGRAM
Plan No.:   02
Division: Delta
Division No.:   04

FROM YOUR PLAN SPONSOR

We are pleased to provide you with your Cash Balance Retirement Program statement. This statement is presented in two sections. The second section shows the beneficiary information on record.

You have a non-forfeitable right to the balance in your cash balance account only if you are 100% vested (generally after you have completed 3 years of service). The "Vested Balance" line indicates whether or not you are currently 100% vested.

PLAN BENEFIT SUMMARY

	Year 20XX
Opening Balance	$23,000.00
Employer Contribution Credit	3,500.00
Interest Credit	333.50
Ending Balance	$26,833.50
Vested Balance (100% vested)	$26,833.50

Pay Credit: 3.5%
of $100,000

The interest credit rate for the year was: 1.45%

Interest Credit: 1.45%
of Opening Balance

Glatfelter Cash Balance Plan SPD Example[29]

The Glatfelter pay credit (contribution credit) equals 5.5 percent of pay contributed on a monthly basis. The interest credit is based on the Moody's Aa nominal bond yield, also credited monthly.

---

29. Glatfelter SPD Glatfelter Retirement Plan for Salaried Employees Cash Balance Benefit Effective January 1, 2007.

University of Pittsburgh Medical Center Cash Balance Plan Example[30]

The retirement benefit under this plan is based on a "point system" determined by adding age and years of service. The formula benefits older participants and those with more years of service. The pay credit is based on the following table:

If Your Age Plus Benefit Service Equals:	Annual Retirement Credit
Less than 36 points	2.5% of pay
36 to 49 points	3.0% of pay
50 to 69 points	4.0% of pay
70 or more points	5.0% of pay

The interest credit for this plan is based on the 30-year Treasury bond rate.

Esterline Retirement Plan Cash Balance Formula Example[31]

The Esterline cash balance formula provides pay credits based on the age of the employee as follows:

Age on December 31st	Pay Credit %
Less than 30	2%
At least 30, but less than 40	3%
At least 40, but less than 50	4%
At least 50, but less than 60	5%
60 or more	6%

The plan is also integrated with Social Security and provides for an additional pay credit of 2% for compensation that exceeds the Social Security wage base.

Interest credits for the Esterline plan are based on the highest IRS safe harbor rate based on IRS Notice 96-8.[32]

Note that the above examples are real and that these companies will certainly be reviewing their plans for compliance with the interest credit rules provided for by PPA 2006.

Practical Considerations

Cash balance plans are often found in large companies and may have been established to provide a pension benefit that is easier to communicate to employees and easier to manage costs of the plan. These plans are often found in large publicly traded companies and may be a result of a company converting its traditional defined benefit plan to a plan with a cash balance formula.

Small businesses may establish a cash balance plan, often in conjunction with a profit sharing plan such that the combination of plans benefits the owners of the business at a significantly higher rate than for the rank-and-file employees. While the plans require relatively advanced actuarial testing,

---

30. UPMC Retirement Summary Plan Description Spring 2003.
31. Summary plan description (SPD) for the Esterline Technologies Retirement Plan updated 1/01/2011.
32. Notice 96-8 provided for use of several "Safe-Harbor" interest rates to project Hypothetical Allocations.

it is important to know that these types of plans can provide significantly higher benefits than what is permitted under the IRC 415(c) limits.[33]

When a cash balance pension plan is established, the plan sponsor develops a formula to fund the cash balance hypothetical allocation. Usually, the promised funding is based on a percentage of a participant's salary, such as four percent of salary, and earnings on the contributions are guaranteed to be at least a fixed amount, such as two percent earnings per year, or may be tied to a variable rate, such as the U.S Treasury Bond rate. The contributions may be integrated with Social Security to produce a higher benefit percentage to those participants who earn a salary above the Social Security wage base or may be based on a combination of age and years of service – thus rewarding participants for longer service.

In any case, participants receive a statement each year detailing the additions to their account, which are equal to the promised contribution and the promised earnings for the plan year. This statement communicates the participant's benefit to the employee in an understandable format, but this account statement only portrays a hypothetical account. The value detailed to the participant is the benefit that will be payable to the participant based on the funding formula set forth in the plan document by the plan sponsor but not until the participant's retirement.

The plan sponsor does not fund a cash balance pension plan with the full benefit as detailed by the participant's hypothetical account; instead, the plan sponsor will fund the cash balance pension plan with the actuarial equivalent of the benefit (allocations plus earnings) that will be payable from the cash balance pension plan to the participant at the participant's normal retirement age. This actuarial equivalent is calculated by an actuary (whose services are required annually) considering mortality, disability, turnover, and salary growth.

Like all defined benefit plans, the plan sponsor is responsible for the investment performance of the plan's assets and earnings. The benefit, as determined under the plan document, will be payable to the participant at retirement regardless of the plan's true earnings, whether greater than or less than the benefit provided by the plan formula.

QUASI-SEPARATE ACCOUNTS

A cash balance pension plan does not have a separate account for each participant even though the plan participant receives a statement detailing a separate account in his name. A cash balance pension plan consists of a commingled account that has a value equal to the actuarial equivalent of the present value of the expected future benefits that will be paid from the cash balance pension plan to the participants (the promised contribution and earnings).

---

33. Treas. Reg. §1.401(a)(4)-9(b)(2)(v)(D)(3) discusses non-discrimination rules for plan aggregation (two or more plans tested together) and provides that a plan is deemed to satisfy the minimum aggregate allocation gateway of this paragraph (b)(2)(v)(D) if the aggregate normal allocation rate for each NHCE is at least 7 1/2% of the NHCE's compensation within the meaning of §415(c)(3), measured over a period of time permitted under the definition of plan year compensation.

YOUNGER/OLDER

A cash balance pension plan is generally more beneficial for younger participants because the formula is generally based on the number of years the participant is employed by the plan sponsor with a guaranteed rate of return. Younger participants have more years of contributions and earnings than older participants. However, benefits under a cash balance plan can be structured such that older employees receive higher pay credits than younger employees.

ELIGIBILITY/COVERAGE/VESTING

The cash balance pension plan follows the rules and requirements for eligibility, coverage, and vesting required under the Pension Protection Act of 2006 and described in Chapter 3. You should recall that cash balance plans must use a 3 year cliff vesting formula or a vesting schedule that is at least as generous as a 3 year cliff formula.

DISTRIBUTIONS

The available and required distribution options of qualified plans are discussed in Chapter 7, but of particular concern for lump-sum distributions from cash balance pension plans is the guaranteed interest rate used to determine the value of the participant's accrued lump-sum value. Under prior law, where the hypothetical earnings credit rate was greater than the interest rate required by ERISA (to calculate the lump-sum payment), the required payment to the participant was greater than provided under the plan benefit formula. As a result of the Pension Protection Act of 2006, however, this calculation discrepancy has been eliminated.

To determine the value of the lump-sum payment under prior law, first calculate the annuity that the participant would have received for continued employment through retirement using the interest rate provided under the plan document. This is the hypothetical account balance. Second, the present value of this annuity is then calculated utilizing the interest rates provided under ERISA, usually a rate tied to the 30-year Treasury rate. A number of courts concluded that the participant entitled to a lump-sum distribution must be paid the greater of the present value calculated under the ERISA rate or the hypothetical account balance. A cash balance pension plan with interest credits tied to the same rate provided by ERISA or with a rate lower than the ERISA rate would not experience a difference in the calculation value of the lump-sum distributions. But those cash balance pension plans that utilize a higher (more generous) guaranteed earnings rate credit under the above formula may be required to provide a lump-sum payment greater than the payment calculated under the plan document. This effect on the distribution is sometimes referred to as "interest rate whipsaw." The whipsaw results in terminating employees being paid amounts far in excess of their hypothetical account balance. This, of course, is detrimental to the plan and plan sponsor.

Under the PPA 2006, for distributions after August 17, 2006 (the date of enactment), no distribution in excess of a participant's hypothetical account balance is required.

CONVERSIONS TO A CASH BALANCE PLAN

A cash balance "conversion" occurs when an employer changes from a traditional defined benefit pension plan into a cash balance plan. Current law does not prevent companies from converting to cash balance plans. The law does prevent an employer from taking away or reducing the value of a pension benefit that has already been earned by a worker, whether or not there is a cash balance conversion.[34] This law is referred to as the anti-cutback rule and prohibits an employer from amending a plan such that employees loose benefits accrued to date or benefits are reduced. A cash balance plan conversion has no effect on current retirees.

During the 1990s, a number of companies converted their defined benefit plans into cash balance plans, prompting charges from older workers that the change violated age-discrimination laws. The Treasury proposed regulations in December 2002 to address this issue. The proposed regulations provided guidance under the statutory age-discrimination rules for all qualified plans, including cash balance pension plans. The proposed regulations set forth specific conditions under which cash balance plans and cash balance conversions would not be considered to violate these age-discrimination rules. Thousands of comment letters were submitted on the proposed regulations, including comments from older and longer-service employees who stated that they had been adversely affected by cash balance conversions. Other comments set forth employer concerns that the regulations would create issues for certain traditional defined benefit plans that had not previously been considered age-discriminatory.

Section 205 of the Consolidated Appropriations Act, 2004, Pub. L. 108-199, eliminated funding to implement the proposed age-discrimination regulations or any regulations reaching similar results. Additionally, the Act required the Secretary of the Treasury propose legislation providing transition relief for older and longer-service participants affected by cash balance conversions. In response, the Treasury set forth a proposal addressing cash balance plans and conversions to cash balance plans. The legislative proposal would require companies converting to cash balance plans to protect current employees through a five-year "hold harmless" period and would prohibit any benefit wear-away. The proposal also would provide rules under which cash balance formulas would not be considered age-discriminatory. The proposal would eliminate the "whipsaw" effect, which acts as a cap on the interest credits that cash balance plans can provide to workers. This would permit companies to give higher interest credits, allowing larger retirement accumulations for workers.[35] The proposal would provide similar rules for other types of hybrid plans and hybrid plan conversions.[36]

---

34. http://www.ustreas.gov/press/releases/js172.htm.
35. http://www.ustreas.gov/press/releases/js1132.htm.
36. http://www.irs.gov/irb/2004-27_IRB/index.html.

In July of 2004, the Treasury withdrew the proposed age-discrimination regulations issued in December 2002 to provide Congress an opportunity to review and consider the Administration's legislative proposal and to address cash balance and other hybrid plan issues through legislation. The PPA 2006 sets forth the circumstances under which hybrid plans can avoid discrimination claims. In addition, the PPA 2006 also sets forth the standards for conversions from defined benefit plans to hybrid plans. The new provisions apply to hybrid plan conversions or hybrid plans adopted after June 29, 2005. Under the PPA 2006, a hybrid plan must meet three main requirements.

The first requirement is that a participant's accrued benefit, as determined as of any date under the terms of the plan, would be equal to or greater than that of any similarly situated, younger participant. For this purpose, an individual is similarly situated to a participant if the individual and the participant are (and always have been) identical in every respect (including period of service, compensation, position, date of hire, work history, and any other respect) except for age.

QUICK QUIZ 4.4

1. Participants in a cash balance pension plan have separate accounts.
   a. True
   b. False

2. The establishment of a cash balance pension plan generally benefits the younger employees more than the older employees.
   a. True
   b. False

3. A cash balance plan can be structured to benefit owners and higher compensated employees under certain circumstances.
   a. True
   b. False

False, True, True.

The second requirement is that the interest rate used to determine the interest credit on the account balance in the hybrid plan must not be greater than a market rate of return, to be determined under regulations to be issued.

The third requirement is that for plan years beginning after 2007, the hybrid plan must provide 100 percent vesting after three years of service.

The PPA 2006 also addresses the "whipsaw" effect by providing that the distribution of a participant's hypothetical cash balance account is sufficient to satisfy the participant's benefit entitlement from distributions after the date of enactment. Thus, employers are no longer penalized for using a higher interest credit.

Case Study 4.1

In ***Cooper v. IBM Personal Pension Plan***, a class action suit was filed against the IBM Personal Pension Plan ("IBM Plan").[1] Various plaintiffs claimed that IBM's defined benefit plan violated the age discrimination prohibitions of ERISA.[2] Plan amendments were made that converted the IBM defined benefit plan to a cash balance plan. The court calculated that a 49-year-old employee with 20 years of service would accrue $8,093 in age-65 annuity benefits in 2000 under that employer's cash balance plan, an additional $622 in benefits in 2001, and $282 per year in benefits by 2010.[3] Thus, the employee's benefit accrual is reduced for each year he ages.

The court acknowledged that a defined benefit plan violates ERISA's age discrimination prohibition if "an employee's benefit accrual is ceased, or the rate of an employee's benefit accrual is reduced, because of the attainment of any age."[4] The court explained that the theory that cash balance plans violate this provision is based on a series of premises. The court said that when evaluating defined benefit plans, ERISA directs that accrued benefits are calculated in terms of "an annual benefit commencing at normal retirement age,"[5] or in other words, in terms of a traditional annuity beginning at age 65. In order to apply this definition to a cash balance plan, the current hypothetical balance in an employee's account must be translated into the equivalent age-65 annuity that those sums could purchase. The court reasoned that age discrimination arises because money contributed to a younger employee will be worth more (when expressed as an annuity starting at age 65) than the same amount of money contributed to an older employee because the contribution to the younger employee will have more years to accrue interest before normal retirement age.[6] Stated another way, if any employer contributes the same amount to an employee's cash balance account every year, the value of those annual benefits when expressed as an annuity starting at age 65 decreases with every passing year.[7] This inevitably results in a declining benefit accrual rate as an employee ages, an apparent violation of ERISA.

The court ultimately ruled that IBM's cash balance plan conversion was a violation of ERISA because it impermissibly discriminated against participants based on age. Under the ruling of the case, all cash balance plans per se violate the ERISA age discrimination provision by virtue of their design. Interestingly, there are other cases in the federal case law that lead to a different result. See for example ***Eaton v. Onan Corp.***, 117 F.Supp.2d 812, 817 (S.D.Ind.2000)(finding cash balance plan did not violate ERISA); see also ***Campbell v. BankBoston***, N.A., 327 F.3d 1, 9-10 (1st Cir. 2003) (noting problems with the age discrimination theory to attack cash balance plans).

1. ***Cooper v. IBM Personal Pension Plan***, 274 F.Supp.2d 1010 (S.D.Ill. July 31, 2003).
2. Employee Retirement Income Security Act, 29 U.S.C. Sections 1001-1461.
3. ***Cooper***, 274 F.Supp.2d at 1021-22.
4. 29 U.S.C. §1054(b)(1)(H)(i). See also ***Cooper***, 274 F.Supp.2d 1010, 1021-22.
5. 29 U.S.C. §1002(23)(A).
6. ***Cooper***, 274 F.Supp.2d at 1021.
7. ***Cooper***, 274 F.Supp.2d at 1021-22.

PENSION EQUITY PLANS

Pension equity plans (PEP) are a type of hybrid plan similar to a cash balance plan. These plans have not received the attention of cash balance plans and are certainly less popular. However, they become more popular when RJR Nabisco implemented one in 1993 recognizing that its work force had become more mobile and it wanted to attract more experienced employees that would not benefit as much under a traditional defined benefit plan.

Two important distinctions of pension equity plans compared to cash balance plans are the salary used as part of the benefit and interest credits. The final lump-sum benefit for a PEP is based on a final average salary, whereas cash balance plan pay credits are effectively career average since they are credited each year. The second issue is that PEPs do not typically provide for interest credits prior to termination. Rather, the benefit is structured in such a way that it references years of service and final pay. Both types of plans define the benefits in terms of lump-sum benefits.

Colin is a participant in the Davidson plan and retires after 30 years of service. The plan provides for a benefit equal to 5 percent per year of service multiplied by the final pay average. If Colin's final pay was $100,000, then the lump-sum benefit would be equal to 150 percent or $150,000.

Similar to cash balance plans, PEPs can provide more complicated benefit formulas that provide higher benefits to those workers with a greater number of years of participation.

Jackie works for Pearson and is a participant in the Pearson Pension Equity Plan. It provides for the following benefits:

Age	PEP Percentage
Under 30	3%
30 - 39	4%
40 - 49	5%
50 - 59	6%
60 and over	8%

Jackie started working at age 40 and continued until last year when she retired at age 65. Her benefit is determined as follows:

Age	Benefit				
Under 30	3%	x	0 years	=	0%
30 - 39	4%	x	0 years	=	0%
40 - 49	5%	x	10 years	=	50%
50 - 59	6%	x	10 years	=	60%
60 and over	8%	x	5 years	=	40%
				Total	150%

Benefit = PEP Percentage x Years of Service

> Assuming Jackie's final average salary is $60,000, her lump-sum benefit is $90,000 or 150 percent of her final average salary.

These examples should help to clarify how PEPs are presented to employees and how they are differ from cash balance plans and traditional defined benefit plans.

MONEY PURCHASE PENSION PLANS

A **money purchase pension plan** is a defined contribution pension plan that provides for a contribution to the plan each year of a fixed percentage of the employees' compensation. Specifically, the employer promises to make a contribution to the plan for the plan year, but the employer is not required to guarantee a specific retirement benefit. The limitations and characteristics of money purchase pension plans are discussed below.

CONTRIBUTION LIMIT

As a defined contribution plan, money purchase pension plans are limited in the amount of contributions that an employer can make on behalf of the participants. An employer cannot deduct contributions to the plan in excess of 25 percent of the employer's total covered compensation paid. As discussed in Chapter 3, a defined contribution plan is limited in the contribution to the plan each year on behalf of each participant to the lesser of 100 percent of the participant's compensation or $53,000 for 2016. This limit is an aggregate per person limit for all contributions to defined contribution plans for the year and includes employer contributions, employee contributions, and any forfeitures allocated to a participant's account for the year.

> ## KEY CONCEPTS ✓
>
> 1. What is the contribution percentage limitation for money purchase pension plans?
>
> 2. How are participant accounts treated in money purchase pension plans?
>
> 3. At the establishment of a money purchase pension plan, which age group generally benefits the most?
>
> 4. Describe the impact of EGTRRA 2001 on money purchase pension plans.

The funding formula of the money purchase pension plan is stated in the plan document. A common funding formula is a percentage of a participant's salary, similar to the cash balance pension plan but without the promise of a guaranteed earnings rate. For example, a money purchase pension plan might promise a contribution of 10 percent of each participant's salary per year. The plan may be integrated with Social Security (as detailed in Chapter 5) or otherwise designed in such a way to provide disproportionate contributions to a certain class of participants, perhaps based on a combination of age and years of service.

SEPARATE ACCOUNTS

When the employer makes a contribution on behalf of each participant to a money purchase pension plan, the contribution is made to a separate account on behalf of each participant. As such, participants know exactly the value of their benefit from the stated value on the account statement – allowing the plan benefits to be communicated to the plan participants more easily than with a defined benefit pension plan.

The plan sponsor can choose to manage the funds of each participant but usually does not do so. The plan usually requires that participants manage their own investments. In either case, employees retain their own separate account.

YOUNGER/OLDER

A money purchase pension plan, like all defined contribution plans, benefits younger participants more than older participants because of the increased number of contributions and compounding periods. The younger participants will have the benefit of receiving more contributions to the account over time and the benefit of the tax-deferred growth. An older participant simply has fewer years to accumulate assets within the retirement plan.

IMPACT OF THE ECONOMIC GROWTH AND TAX RELIEF RECONCILIATION ACT OF 2001 (EGTRRA 2001)

After the enactment of EGTRRA 2001, most employers interested in establishing a defined contribution plan would establish a profit sharing plan instead of a money purchase pension plan. Before EGTRRA 2001, employers could deduct contributions to money purchase pension plans up to 25 percent of the total employer's compensation paid but could only deduct contributions to profit sharing plans up to 15 percent of the total employer's compensation paid. Under these old limits, some employers (especially single practitioner professionals) would establish two plans, a money purchase pension plan and a profit sharing plan. Commonly, the employer would set the funding limit of the money purchase pension plan at 10 percent (the mandatory component) and would have discretionary contributions to the profit sharing plan up to 15 percent for a total 25 percent limit. This combination of the pension plan and the profit sharing plan is known as a **Tandem Plan** and would provide the employer with the maximum deductibility for contributions to employee retirement plans with the greatest flexibility in the funding for the plans. With the Tandem plan, the employer was only required to make a 10 percent contribution to the money purchase pension plan each year, but because the profit sharing plan contributions are discretionary, the employers' contributions to the profit sharing plan only have to be "substantial and recurring" allowing the employer to forego contributions in certain years (discussed fully in Chapter 5).

QUICK QUIZ 4.5

1. A plan sponsor cannot deduct more than 25 percent of their covered compensation as a contribution to a money purchase pension plan.
   a. True
   b. False

2. Each participant has a separate account in a money purchase pension plan.
   a. True
   b. False

3. The establishment of a money purchase pension plan generally benefits older employees more than younger employees.
   a. True
   b. False

4. EGTRRA 2001 increased the popularity of money purchase pension plans.
   a. True
   b. False

True, True, False, False.

EGTRRA 2001 increased the contribution limit for profit sharing plans to 25 percent and created an equal deduction limit for both defined contribution pension and profit sharing plans of 25 percent. Employers now wishing to establish a defined contribution plan will likely establish a profit sharing plan because they will be able to deduct the maximum amount in any given year (25 percent of employer compensation), but the contribution will not be mandatory as is the case of money purchase pension plans. Consequently, some employers with money purchase pension plans converted their plans to profit sharing plans (or terminated their money purchase pension plans) to avoid the future mandatory funding requirements.

Many of EGTRRA 2001's provisions were schedule to sunset for tax years beginning after 2010. However, the Pension Protection Act of 2006 has made the provisions of EGTRRA 2001 permanent.

ELIGIBILITY/COVERAGE/VESTING

The money purchase pension plan is subject to all of the eligibility, coverage, and vesting rules applicable to defined contribution pension plans, which are described in Chapter 3. Note that because money purchase pension plans are a type of defined contribution plan, they are subject to the shorter vesting requirements for defined contribution plans under the PPA 2006. In other words, employer contributions to a money purchase pension plan must vest at least as rapidly as a 2 to 6 year graduated or 3-year cliff vesting schedule.

DISTRIBUTIONS

Chapter 7 describes the distribution options, availability, and requirements for all qualified plans.

TARGET BENEFIT PENSION PLANS

A special type of money purchase pension plan, known as a **target benefit pension plan**, determines the contribution to the participant's account based on the benefit that will be paid from the plan at the participant's retirement. The plan formula may be written to provide a contribution to each participant during the plan year that is actuarially equivalent to the present value of the benefit at the participant's retirement. An actuary is required at the establishment of the target benefit pension plan, but unlike a defined benefit plan or a cash balance

KEY CONCEPTS

1. List the benefits of a target benefit pension plan.

2. What are the eligibility and coverage rules for a target benefit pension plan?

pension plan, an actuary is not required on an annual basis. The actuary will create a funding formula for participants entering the plan at various ages. Once established, the funding formula is generally not recalculated for changes in assumptions. The target benefit pension plan considers the formula as the "target," the benefit the employer hopes the employee will have at retirement. Instead of funding the plan with the amount necessary to attain the target and ensuring that the target is met, the employer promises a contribution to the participant's individual account based on the original actuarial assumptions. Once the contribution has been made, the participant is responsible for choosing investments. Like any defined contribution plan, the participant, at retirement, is entitled to the plan balance regardless of its value, be it greater than or less than the intended target benefit.

The actuarial equivalent contribution will vary from participant to participant because of age and salary differences. In fact, the contribution will be greatest for the oldest participants because the discounting period (contribution date to retirement date) is less than the discounting period for younger participants. Accordingly, target benefit pension plans are utilized to disproportionately benefit older participants because the target benefit funding formula will allocate a greater contribution to the older participants.

The target benefit pension plan is a form of money purchase pension plan; consequently, the target benefit pension plan is subject to all of the same contribution, eligibility, coverage, vesting, and distribution limitations as the money purchase pension plan.

QUICK QUIZ
4.6

1. A target benefit pension plan is a defined benefit pension plan.
   a. True
   b. False

2. Target benefit pension plans have the same coverage and eligibility rules as money purchase pension plans.
   a. True
   b. False

False, True.

Mainly due to the increase of the profit sharing deductibility limits to 25 percent under EGTRRA 2001, target benefit pension plans have lost some of their attractiveness. Instead, employers are establishing age-weighted profit sharing plans (see Chapter 5) so that the contributions to the plan each year are discretionary rather than mandatory but still favor older employees.

EXAMPLE 4.35

Ken, a business owner, is age 50 and earns $265,000 per year. The company's target benefit plan has a benefit formula equal to 132.075% of compensation reduced by 1/25th for each year of participation less than 25 years. Therefore, since Ken plans to retire at age 65, his contribution is reduced by 40% because he only has 15 years until retirement (15/25 = 60%). The plan also benefits Melissa, an employee age 25 earning $25,000 per year. Melissa has more than 25 years until retirement, so her contribution is not reduced. The first year contribution is determined as follows, assuming a normal retirement age of 65 and 8% interest:

	Ken	Melissa
Age	50	25
Compensation	$265,000	$25,000
Target Benefit (134.615% of compensation)	$210,000	$33,019
Actuarial Factor for Age	2.338	0.304
PV of Benefit	$490,980	$10,038
Factor	0.1075	0.0812
Theoretical Contribution	$52,780	$815.06
Annual Additions Limit (100% of payroll or $53,000)	$53,000	$25,000
Top-Heavy Minimum (3% of compensation)	$0	$750
Actual Contribution	$52,780	$815.06
Contribution Rate	19.92%	3.26%
Percent of Contribution	98.5%	1.5%

* The benefit for the business owner is 132.075% x $265,000 x (15 ÷ 25) = $210,000.

** The benefit for the employee is 132.075% of $25,000 = $33,019.

The plan permits the benefits to be principally contributed to Ken, the owner. The target benefit plan can still be used to reduce overall plan costs. However, as you will see in Chapter 5, profit sharing plans allow contributions up to 25% of covered compensation and discretionary funding. In some cases, age-based profit sharing plans and new comparability plans can produce similar results to the target benefit plan without the mandatory funding and compliance issues.

KEY TERMS

ACTUARY - An expert professional who makes quantitative calculations and assumptions about inflation, wage increases, life expectancy of the assumed retirees, investment returns on plan assets, mortality rates for retirees, and forfeitures resulting from termination in order to determine funding for a retirement plan.

BACK LOADING - A practice of delaying the accrual of benefits until late in someone's career so that if they were to leave the company they would forfeit all or a large portion of their benefits.

CASH BALANCE PENSION PLAN - A defined benefit pension plan that shares many of the characteristics of defined contribution plans but provides specific defined benefits based on a mandatory contribution and earnings rate.

CREDIT FOR PRIOR SERVICE - To give employees credit for years of service (with the plan sponsor) prior to the establishment of the qualified plan.

DEFINED BENEFIT PLAN - A qualified retirement plan that provides its participants with pre-determined formula-based benefits at retirement.

DEFINED CONTRIBUTION PLAN - A qualified retirement plan that provides its participants with either a contributory or noncontributory retirement account which benefits from tax-deferred growth for contributions and earnings in the plan.

FLAT AMOUNT FORMULA - A benefit formula of a defined benefit pension plan that provides each of its participants with an equal dollar benefit at retirement.

FLAT PERCENTAGE FORMULA - A benefit formula of a defined benefit pension plan that provides all plan participants with a benefit equal to a fixed percentage of the participant's salary, usually the final salary or an average of the participant's highest salaries.

FORFEITURES - The percentage or amount of a participant's accrued benefit that was not vested to the employee at the employee's termination from the plan sponsor. The forfeited amount stays in the plan and may be allocated to the other plan participants (defined contribution plan) or reduce future plan costs (defined contribution plan or defined benefit plan).

HYPOTHETICAL ACCOUNT - The account statement that displays hypothetical allocations and hypothetical earnings. The accounts are hypothetical because the cash balance pension plan assets are managed by the plan sponsor in the same manner as a defined benefit pension plan.

IN-SERVICE WITHDRAWAL - Any withdrawal from a qualified retirement plan other than a loan while the employee is a participant in the plan.

KEY TERMS

MANDATORY FUNDING REQUIREMENT - An amount or percentage that must be contributed to a qualified pension plan by the employer each plan year.

MONEY PURCHASE PENSION PLAN - A defined contribution pension plan that provides for mandatory employer contributions to the plan each year of a fixed percentage of the employees' compensation. The employer does not guarantee a specific retirement benefit.

NONCONTRIBUTORY PLANS - Qualified retirement plans that do not include employee contributions.

PENSION BENEFIT GUARANTY CORPORATION (PBGC) - Established in 1974 when President Gerald R. Ford signed the Employee Retirement Income Security Act (ERISA) into law. The PBGC guarantees qualified pension benefits. It is a federal corporation that acts as an insurance provider to maintain the benefits promised to employees by their defined benefit pension plans.

PENSION PLAN - A qualified retirement plan that pays a benefit, usually determined by a formula, to a plan participant for the participant's entire life during retirement.

TANDEM PLAN - Combination of a money purchase pension plan and a profit sharing plan.

TARGET BENEFIT PENSION PLAN - A special type of money purchase pension plan that determines the contribution to the participant's account based on the benefit that will be paid from the plan at the participant's retirement rather than on the value of the contribution to the account. Requires an actuary at inception.

TERM INSURANCE POLICY - A life insurance contract which states if the insured dies within the term of the contract, the insurance company will pay a stated death benefit.

UNIT CREDIT FORMULA - A benefit formula of a defined benefit pension plan that utilizes a combination of the participant's years of service and salary to determine the participant's accrued benefit.

UNIVERSAL LIFE INSURANCE - A term insurance policy with a cash accumulation account attached to it.

WHOLE LIFE INSURANCE POLICY - A permanent life insurance policy that guarantees that the policy will remain in force as long as the premium is paid. The life insurance policy has a cash account that grows tax deferred.

DISCUSSION QUESTIONS

1. Explain the mandatory funding requirement and its impact on defined contribution plans and defined benefit plans.

2. Define "in-service withdrawal."

3. Explain the investment limitations for pension plans.

4. Compare the investment risk of defined contribution plans to the investment risk of defined benefit plans.

5. Compare the treatment of forfeitures within defined benefit plans and defined contribution plans.

6. What is the PBGC and what plans are covered by the PBGC?

7. How is a participant's accrued benefits calculated for defined benefit and defined contribution plans?

8. List and describe the common funding formulas of a defined benefit plan.

9. How are a participant's accrued benefits managed in defined benefit plans?

10. Which age group generally benefits the most from the establishment of a defined benefit pension plan?

11. List the advantages of cash balance pension plans.

12. Which age group generally benefits the most from the establishment of a cash balance pension plan?

13. What is the contribution limit for money purchase pension plans?

14. How are participant account balances managed in money purchase pension plans?

15. Which age group generally benefits the most from the establishment of a money purchase pension plan?

16. What impact did EGTRRA 2001 have on money purchase pension plans?

17. List the characteristics of a target benefit pension plan.

MULTIPLE CHOICE PROBLEMS

1. Which of the following is not a characteristic of pension plans?

    a. Mandatory funding.

    b. In-service withdrawals for employees under the age of 62.

    c. Limited investment in life insurance.

    d. A limit of 10 percent investment in the employer's securities.

2. Which one of the following statements is true for a defined benefit plan?

    a. A defined benefit plan generally favors older age entrants.

    b. The maximum retirement benefit payable from a defined benefit plan is the lesser of 100 percent of the participant's compensation or $210,000 for 2016.

    c. A defined benefit plan with 100 employees is required to pay PBGC insurance premiums.

    d. All of the above are true.

3. If a participant's accrued benefit from a qualified defined benefit pension plan is $2,000 per month, what is the maximum life insurance death benefit coverage that the plan can provide based on the 100 to 1 ratio test?

    a. $0.

    b. $2,400.

    c. $200,000.

    d. $240,000.

4. Which of the following statements regarding defined benefit plans is true?

    a. A defined benefit plan can allocate forfeitures to other plan participants.

    b. A defined benefit plan can use forfeitures to reduce future plan costs.

    c. A defined benefit plan cannot give credit for prior service.

    d. Each participant of a defined benefit plan has an individual account.

5. Which of the following actuarial assumptions is not used by the actuary who determines the mandatory funding range for a defined benefit plan?

    a. Mortality.

    b. Turnover.

    c. Divorce rate.

    d. Disability rate.

6. Which of the following is not a common defined benefit plan funding formula?

    a. Flat amount formula.

    b. Flat percentage formula.

    c. Unit credit formula.

    d. Excludible amount formula.

7. Which of the following statements is true regarding the anti-cutback rule, as it is referred to?

    a. The anti-cutback rule prohibits the plan sponsor from making changes to the plan that are retroactive to the beginning of the year.

    b. The anti-cutback rule prohibits the plan sponsor from freezing the benefits under the plan.

    c. The anti-cutback rule prohibits the plan sponsor from terminating the plan.

    d. The anti-cutback rule prohibits the plan sponsor from amending the plan such that prior accrued benefits are reduced.

8. Which of the following statements is true?

    a. A cash balance pension plan usually benefits older employees the most.

    b. A defined benefit plan promises a contribution to a hypothetical account each year for a plan participant.

    c. Cash balance pension plan participants under age 62 may take a withdrawal from the plan during employment with the plan sponsor.

    d. A cash balance pension plan does not have individual separate accounts for each participant.

9. Which of the following statements regarding the plan sponsor of a money purchase pension plan is correct?

    a. The plan sponsor is required to make an annual contribution to the plan.

    b. The excess earnings of a money purchase pension plan are returned to the plan sponsor.

    c. The plan sponsor generally bears the investment risk of the plan assets.

    d. A plan sponsor with fluctuating cash flows would adopt a money purchase pension plan.

10. Which of the following statements regarding EGTRRA 2001 is false?

    a.   EGTRRA 2001 increased the employer's deductible contribution limit for profit sharing plans to 25 percent of employer compensation.

    b.   After the enactment of EGTRRA 2001, money purchase pension plans adoptions have increased.

    c.   Many Tandem Plans were terminated and/or converted after the enactment of EGTRRA 2001.

    d.   Prior to EGTRRA 2001, an employer could deduct contributions to a money purchase pension plan up to 25 percent of employer covered compensation.

11. Of the following statements regarding target benefit pension plans, which is true?

    a.   A target benefit pension plan is a money purchase pension plan with a funding formula that considers age and salary.

    b.   The plan sponsor of a target benefit pension plan does not guarantee that the participant will receive an amount, expected to be the "target benefit" amount, at his retirement.

    c.   Plan participants of a target benefit pension plan do not have separate accounts.

    d.   The plan sponsor guarantees an earnings rate for the contributions made to target benefit pension plans.

12. Which of the following pension plans would allocate a higher percentage of the plans' current costs to a certain class or group of eligible employees?

    1.   Defined benefit pension plan.

    2.   Target benefit pension plan.

    3.   Money purchase pension plan with permitted disparity.

        a.   1 only.

        b.   1 and 2.

        c.   2 and 3.

        d.   1, 2, and 3.

13. A defined benefit pension plan has a funding formula equal to 1% x years of service x final salary. If Jim's final salary is $600,000 and Jim has earned 30 years of service, what is Jim's retirement benefit in 2016?

    a. $79,500.

    b. $180,000.

    c. $210,000.

    d. $265,000.

14. Accent, Inc. sponsors a 25% money purchase pension plan for its eligible employees. Carlos earns $200,000, Kevin earns $60,000, Kelly earns $300,000, and Rick, who is ineligible, earns $27,000. What is Accent's required deductible contribution for the year? All employees are under age 50.

    a. $118,000.

    b. $131,250.

    c. $138,000.

    d. $140,000.

15. Bobby is the owner of Ideal Mechanics, Inc. He would like to establish a qualified pension plan and would like most of the plan's current contributions to be allocated to his account. He does not want to permit loans and he does not want Ideal to bear the investment risk of the plan's assets. Bobby is 47 and earns $300,000 per year. His employees are 25, 29, and 32 and they each earn $25,000 per year. Which of the following qualified pension plans would you recommend that Bobby establish?

    a. Defined benefit pension plan.

    b. Cash balance pension plan.

    c. Money purchase pension plan.

    d. Defined benefit pension plan using permitted disparity.

16. Which of the following statements regarding target benefit pension plans is true?

    a. A target benefit pension plan cannot allocate plan forfeitures to remaining plan participant accounts.

    b. Target benefit pension plans may not be established after 2001.

    c. Assuming equal salaries, a target benefit pension plan would allocate a higher percentage of its current contributions to an older employee.

    d. A target benefit pension plan may always exclude any participant who has not attained the age of 26 and completed one year of service.

17. Ashley is a participant in her law firm's defined benefit plan. Ashley, who is an aggressive attorney, is 44 years old and earns $150,000. She has four years of service for purposes of the plan and has worked at the firm for four years. The plan provides a benefit of 1% for the first three years of service and a benefit of 1.5% for all additional years of service. The plan has the least generous vesting schedule possible. Almost eighty percent of the accrued benefits are attributable to the two equal owners, Martin and Bob, who have been working at the company for decades. If Ashley were to leave, what percent of her salary (as defined by the plan) could she expect to receive at normal retirement?

    a. 3.6%.

    b. 4.8%.

    c. 5.5%.

    d. 6.4%.

18. Rick, who is age 45, is having a few leadership issues and must resign from his current position as CEO. He worked for A-Send, which sponsors a cash balance plan and a standard 401(k) plan. Each of the plans uses the longest permitted vesting schedule and neither plan is top heavy. He has a balance of $80,000 in the cash balance plan, has deferred $40,000 into the 401(k) plan and has employer matching contributions of $20,000. If he has been employed for two and a half years, but only participating in the plans for the last two years, how much does he keep if he resigns and terminates his employment today?

    a. $44,000.

    b. $60,000.

    c. $124,000.

    d. $140,000.

19. Knowledge Star is a 30-year-old company that has grown significantly in terms of revenue and product offerings. They sponsor a pension plan that provides a benefit of 2% times years of participation times the average of the final three years of salary less an offset. The offset equals 1% times years of service times income below the covered compensation limit of $40,000 (assumed). Roberto has worked with Knowledge Star for the last 30 years and earned $90,000 two years ago, $110,000 last year, and $130,000 this year. If he is retiring this year, how much should he expect to receive as a pension benefit?

    a. $45,000.

    b. $54,000.

    c. $66,000.

    d. $78,000.

QUICK QUIZ EXPLANATIONS

QUICK QUIZ 4.1

1. False. While a pension plan may request a funding waiver, such a waiver only postpones the employer's funding obligation. The funding waiver does not eliminate the funding needed for that particular year.
2. True.
3. False. Only ten percent of a pension plan's assets may be invested in employer securities.

QUICK QUIZ 4.2

1. False. In a defined benefit pension plan, the employer bears the investment risk.
2. False. Defined benefit pension plans must use forfeitures to reduce plan costs. Defined contribution pension plans can use forfeitures to either reduce plan costs or the forfeitures can be allocated to the other remaining plan participants.
3. False. In the event that a defined benefit pension plan cannot pay the promised amount, the PBGC will pay the employee an amount based on (1) the form of the benefit as payable under the terminated plan, (2) the participant's age, and (3) any amounts the PBGC recovered from the employer in the case that the plan was underfunded. The PBGC benefit is not guaranteed to be equal to the amount of the benefit that would have been paid under the defined benefit pension plan.
4. True.

QUICK QUIZ 4.3

1. True.
2. False. Defined benefit plans do not maintain separate accounts for each participant. All of the assets of a defined benefit plan are managed as a group and it is impossible to segregate any individual participant's funds.
3. True.

QUICK QUIZ 4.4

1. False. Participants in a cash balance pension plan do not have separate accounts even though the plan participant receives a statement detailing a separate account in his name. Rather, the account balance on the statement is a hypothetical amount that has a value equal to the actuarial equivalent of the present value of the expected future benefit that will be paid to the participant.
2. True.
3. True.

QUICK QUIZ EXPLANATIONS

QUICK QUIZ 4.5

1. True.
2. True.
3. False. The establishment of a money purchase pension plan generally benefits younger employees because younger employees have the benefit of a greater number of contributions and compounding periods.
4. False. EGTRRA 2001 increased the popularity of profit sharing plans by increasing the contribution limit for profit sharing plans to 25 percent of the employer's total compensation paid.

QUICK QUIZ 4.6

1. False. A target benefit pension plan is a defined contribution pension plan, not a defined benefit pension plan. A target benefit pension plan is a special type of money purchase pension plan.
2. True.

PROFIT SHARING PLANS

LEARNING OBJECTIVES

After reading this chapter, you should be able to:
1. Explain the basic purpose of profit sharing plans.
2. Understand the primary differences between pension plans and profit sharing plans.
3. Discuss the various methods of allocating profit sharing contributions to employee accounts including advantages and disadvantages of each method.
4. Explain why Social Security integration is permitted and how to apply it to a profit sharing plan.
5. Illustrate the impact of an age based formula on the allocation of contributions to a profit sharing plan.
6. Describe the basic elements of a new comparability plan.
7. Recommend an appropriate allocation method for a profit sharing plan based on a desired outcome.
8. Explain what a 401(k) plan is and when it would be an appropriate retirement plan for a business.
9. Explain the 401(k) deferral limits and how they impact the limits under IRC §415(c).
10. Describe the differences between Roth accounts and Roth IRAs.

PROFIT SHARING PLANS

Profit Sharing Plans (7 Types)
Profit Sharing Plans
Stock Bonus Plans
Employee Stock Ownership Plans
401(k) Plans
Thrift Plans
Age-Based Profit Sharing Plans
New Comparability Plans

The term profit-sharing plan is defined in Treasury Regulation §1.401-1(b) as follows:
A **profit-sharing plan** is a plan established and maintained by an employer to provide for the participation in profits by employees or their beneficiaries. The plan must provide a definite predetermined formula for allocating the contributions made to the plan among the participants and for distributing the funds accumulated under the plan after a fixed number of years, the attainment of a stated age, or upon the prior occurrence of some event such as layoff, illness, disability, retirement, death, or severance of employment. A formula for allocating the contributions among the participants is definite if, for example, it provides for an allocation in proportion to the basic compensation of each participant. A plan (whether or not it contains a definite predetermined formula for determining the profits to be shared with the employees) does not qualify under Section 401(a) if the contributions to the plan are made at such times or

in such amounts that the plan in operation discriminates in favor of officers, shareholders, persons whose principal duties consist in supervising the work of other employees, or highly compensated employees. For the rules with respect to discrimination, see §§1.401-3 and 1.401-4. A profit-sharing plan within the meaning of IRC §401 is primarily a plan of deferred compensation, but the amounts allocated to the account of a participant may also be used to provide for him or his family incidental life, accident, or health insurance.

KNOW THE NUMBERS (2016)	
Covered Compensation Limit	$265,000
Defined Contribution Maximum Limit	$53,000
401(k), SARSEP, 457, 403(b) Catch-Up	$6,000
401(k), SARSEP, 457, 403(b) Employee Deferral Limit	$18,000
Highly Compensated Employee	$120,000
Social Security Wage Base	$118,500

BASIC DIFFERENCES BETWEEN PENSION PLANS AND PROFIT-SHARING PLANS

EXHIBIT
5.1

CHARACTERISTIC	PENSION PLAN	PROFIT-SHARING PLAN
Legal Promise of the Plan	To pay a pension at retirement	To defer compensation and thus tax deferral
Are in-service withdrawals permitted?	No*	Yes (after two years)
Is the plan subject to mandatory funding standards?	Yes	No
Percent of plan assets allowed to be invested in employer securities	10 percent	100 percent
Employer annual contribution limit of covered compensation	25 percent**	25 percent***

* Pension plans may allow in-service withdrawals for participants age 62 or older as a result of the PPA 2006.
** The plan must meet minimum funding standards. Defined benefit pension plans may exceed 25%.
*** Increased from 15 percent by the EGTRRA 2001 for years after 2001.

Profit-sharing plans allow employers to make contributions to a qualified plan on behalf of employees of the company. A pure profit sharing plan is a noncontributory plan (employees do not contribute). As with all qualified plans, earnings within a profit sharing plan are not subject to income tax until the funds are distributed from the plan. Because profit sharing plans are not subject to mandatory funding requirements, contributions can be, and generally are, made on a discretionary basis from year to year. However, any contributions made to the plan must be made to participant's accounts on a nondiscriminatory basis. In other words, contributions cannot discriminate against the rank-and-file employees for the benefit of shareholders, officers, and highly compensated employees. That, however, does not mean that the contributions to rank-and-file employees have to be equal to the contributions to shareholders, officers, and highly compensated employees.

KEY CONCEPTS

1. Define "profit sharing plan" as per Treasury Regulation §1.401-1(b).

2. Identify the key differences between pension and profit sharing plans.

3. When is the deadline for establishing and funding a profit sharing plan?

4. What is the maximum annual percentage contribution to a profit sharing plan considering the covered compensation limit?

Although contributions must be made on a **nondiscriminatory** basis, there are types of profit sharing plans available that provide for larger allocations of contributions to shareholders, officers, and highly compensated employees. Among these types of plans are age-based profit sharing plans, integrated plans, and new comparability plans. The use of such plans is permitted by the IRS because they are within the anti-discrimination permissible limits.

CONTRIBUTIONS AND DEDUCTIONS

As with all qualified plans, profit-sharing plans must be established by the end of the tax year (December 31 for calendar year entities) for which the employer will be contributing to the plan. However, contributions can be made to the plan as late as the due date of the company income tax return (including extensions).

XYZ partnership, a calendar year taxpayer, wants to establish a profit sharing plan for the current year. It must do so by December 31 of this year. However, it can fund the plan after December 31, but no later than September 15 of next year assuming that it has properly filed all extensions for its tax return.

Contributions to profit sharing plans are generally discretionary but funding must be "substantial and recurring."[1] Contributions can be in the form of employer stock, but proxy voting rights remain with the plan trustee.[2] A plan that does not make any contributions for an extended period of time risks disqualification.

---

1. Treasury Regulation §1.401-1(b)(2). As a rule of thumb, contributions during 3 out of 5 years or 5 out of 10 years will usually gain IRS approval. See Revenue Ruling 80-144.
2. IRC §401(a)(22) provides that, to qualify under IRC §401, a defined contribution plan other than a profit-sharing plan (i.e., a stock bonus plan or a money purchase pension plan) must satisfy the pass-through voting requirements of IRC §409(e).

Although most contributions to profit sharing plans are made in cash and are related to profits of the company, there is no requirement that a company must contribute to the plan in a year in which it has profits nor is there a prohibition against contributions to the plan in years in which the company does not have profits.[1]

Profit sharing plans have an employer contribution limit of 25 percent of covered compensation.[2] Covered compensation is considered to be the compensation of all eligible employees.[3] Therefore, if an employer's total covered compensation paid to its employees is $1,000,000, then the largest income tax deduction that can be taken by the employer for contributions to the plan is $250,000 ($1,000,000 x 25%).[4]

In some cases, an employer may contribute more than the permitted 25 percent. In such a case, the employer will currently deduct the 25 percent (on the tax return) and may carry forward the contribution amount in excess of the 25 percent limit and deduct this amount in a future year. However, the amount carried forward when added to the contribution made for the future year cannot exceed 25 percent. Additionally, the employer is required to pay a 10 percent excise tax on the portion of the contribution that exceeds 25 percent of covered compensation for the current year.[5]

QUICK QUIZ 5.1

1. A profit sharing plan is a plan established and maintained by an employer to provide participation in the profits of the company solely for officers and shareholders.
   a. True
   b. False

2. A pension plan can be funded using 100% employer securities.
   a. True
   b. False

3. Profit sharing plans must be established by the end of the tax year for which the employer wants to make contributions, and contributions must be made by the due date of the income tax return including extensions.
   a. True
   b. False

False, False, True.

ALLOCATIONS

Standard Allocations

A profit sharing plan must provide a definite predetermined formula for allocating plan contributions to employee's accounts. The standard method of allocating contributions to a profit sharing plan is to simply allocate the contribution based on a percentage of each employee's covered compensation. Example 5.2 illustrates this method.

---

1. The determination of whether the plan under which any contributions are made is a profit sharing plan shall be made without regard to current or accumulated profits of the employer and without regard to whether the employer is a tax-exempt organization. IRC §401(a)(27).
2. IRC §404(a)(3).
3. The compensation considered cannot exceed the compensation limit for each covered employee - $265,000 for 2016.
4. The overall plan compensation limitation does not include employee 401(k) deferrals after EGTRRA 2001. However, prior to EGTRRA 2001, employee deferrals, such as in a 401(k) plan, counted against the plan limit.
5. IRC §4972(a).

EXAMPLE
5.2

There are 7 employees (A-G), ages 25-55 with compensation ranging from $30,000 to $200,000.

Employee	Age	Covered Compensation*	Contribution Percent	Overall Contribution	Percent of Total Contribution
A (owner)	55	$200,000	11%	$22,000	42%
B	45	$60,000	11%	$6,600	13%
C	40	$60,000	11%	$6,600	13%
D	35	$50,000	11%	$5,500	11%
E	30	$40,000	11%	$4,400	8%
F	25	$35,000	11%	$3,850	7%
G	25	$30,000	11%	$3,300	6%
		$475,000		$52,250	100%

STANDARD PROFIT SHARING ALLOCATION

* Recall that there is a covered compensation limit.

In this example, each employee receives a contribution of 11% of their covered compensation. The 11% was selected by the employer based on what the employer wanted to contribute to the plan ($52,250). Note that the contribution percentage could have ranged from 0% to 25% of the total covered compensation, or an overall maximum contribution of $118,750 (25%). Assuming that employee A is the owner of the business as well as an employee, A receives a contribution of $22,000 or 42% of the total plan contribution.

This methodology benefits the highly compensated more than the non-highly compensated in terms of absolute dollars but is nondiscriminatory with regard to percentages of the total contribution because the contributions are based on a straight percentage of total covered compensation.

Permitted Disparity (Social Security Integration)

Social Security retirement benefits are designed to replace a greater percentage of wages for lower-income workers than for higher-income workers. For a low income worker, Social Security replaces a large percent (50% to 75%) of pre-retirement earnings, while for a higher wage earner, it will replace a smaller percent (10% - 25%) of pre-retirement earnings. With the Revenue Act of 1942, private pension plans are permitted to provide larger benefits to higher paid workers than to lower paid workers in an attempt to reduce the gap in total wage replacement. Plans may consider the benefits provided by Social Security in the design of their benefit formula. Plans can integrate their retirement benefit formulas with Social Security under an "offset method" or an "excess method." However, a defined contribution plan may only use the "excess method."

Permitted disparity (often referred to as **Social Security Integration**) is a technique or method of allocating plan contributions to employees' accounts that provides higher contributions to employees whose compensation is in excess of the Social Security wage base for the plan year. In the standard allocation example (Example 5.2), all plan participants received a contribution of 11 percent of their covered compensation. However, an integrated (permitted disparity) formula provides an even higher percentage contribution for the higher compensated employees (those above the Social Security wage base) when compared to lower compensated employees (those below the Social Security wage base).

For defined contributions plans, such as profit sharing plans, an integration level is chosen by the plan sponsor (employer). This integration level is usually the Social Security wage base, which is $118,500 for the year 2016.[1] With an integrated formula, there are two profit sharing plan contribution rates established, the base contribution percentage rate and the excess contribution percentage rate. The base rate is applied on income earned up to the integration level, while the excess rate is applied to income earned above the integration level but only up to the maximum **covered compensation limit** for the year, $265,000 for 2016. The excess rate is generally 5.7 percentage points higher than the base rate.[2] The excess rate is limited to the lesser of twice the base rate or a maximum difference of 5.7 percent. In other words, the maximum disparity equals the lesser of the base rate or 5.7 percent. Consider the following table:

Base Rate	Excess Rate	Maximum Disparity
1.0%	2.0%	1.0%
2.0%	4.0%	2.0%
3.0%	6.0%	3.0%
5.0%	10.0%	5.0%
5.7%	11.4%	5.7%
8.0%	13.7%	5.7%
10.0%	15.7%	5.7%
12.0%	17.7%	5.7%

---

1. The integration level may be less than the Social Security wage base; however, if so, the excess percentage will be reduced.
2. If the base rate is less than 5.7 percent, then the excess rate cannot be more than twice the base rate. If the base rate is equal to or greater than 5.7 percent, then the excess rate can be no more than 5.7 percentage points greater than the base percentage rate. In addition, if the integration level is not at the Social Security wage base, then the 5.7 percent rate will generally be lower.

EXAMPLE
5.3

Assume that Tantalus Inc. sponsors an integrated profit sharing plan that provides for a 10 percent base contribution percentage and an excess contribution percentage of 15.7 percent. If Dave earns $50,000, he would receive a contribution of $5,000 (10% x $50,000). If Mike earned $200,000 and the Social Security wage base was $118,500, then Mike would receive a contribution of $24,646 [10% x $118,500 plus 15.7% x ($200,000 - $118,500), rounded to the nearest dollar]. It is important to understand that integration has increased Mike's contribution by $4,646 ($24,646 - $20,000) over a straight 10 percent plan. This higher contribution is a result of the higher excess contribution rate for compensation above the integration level.

TANTALUS INTEGRATED PROFIT SHARING PLAN								
Employee	**Covered Comp.**	**Base Comp.**	**Excess Comp.**	**Base Cont. 10%**	**Excess Cont. 15.7%**	**Total Cont.**	**Percent of Comp.**	**Percent of Total Cont.**
Mike	$200,000	$118,500	$81,500	$11,850	$12,796	$24,646	12.32%	83.1%
Dave	$50,000	$50,000	$0	$5,000	$0	$5,000	10.00%	16.9%
Totals	$250,000	$168,500	$81,500	$16,850	$12,796	$29,646		100.0%

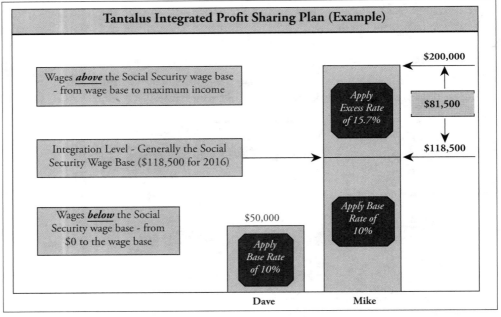

Tantalus Integrated Profit Sharing Plan (Example)

EXAMPLE
5.4

Consider the same facts as in Example 5.2 (they want to contribute about $52,000), except with an integrated profit sharing plan and a base contribution rate chosen by the employer of 10% (the excess rate is 15.70% (10 + 5.7 = 15.7)).

	INTEGRATED PROFIT SHARING PLAN							
Employee	Covered Comp.	Base Comp.	Excess Comp.	Base Cont. 10.0%	Excess Cont. 15.7%	Total Cont.	Percent of Comp.	Percent of Total Cont.
A (Owner)	$200,000	$118,500	$81,500	$11,850	$12,796	$24,646	12.32%	47.26%
B	$60,000	$60,000	$0	$6,000	$0	$6,000	10.00%	11.51%
C	$60,000	$60,000	$0	$6,000	$0	$6,000	10.00%	11.51%
D	$50,000	$50,000	$0	$5,000	$0	$5,000	10.00%	9.59%
E	$40,000	$40,000	$0	$4,000	$0	$4,000	10.00%	7.67%
F	$35,000	$35,000	$0	$3,500	$0	$3,500	10.00%	6.71%
G	$30,000	$30,000	$0	$3,000	$0	$3,000	10.00%	5.75%
Totals	$475,000	$393,500	$81,500	$39,350	$12,796	$52,146		100.00%

Figures are rounded to the nearest dollar.

Base compensation ($)– represents compensation up to the integration level, $118,500 for 2016.

Excess compensation ($)– represents compensation above the integration level, (over $118,500 for 2016) but below the covered compensation limit ($265,000 for 2016).

Base contribution ($)– represents the contribution for compensation up to the integration level (10% in this example).

Excess contribution ($)– represents the contribution for compensation above the integration level [rate of 15.7% (10 + 5.7)] and below the covered compensation limit.

Total contribution ($)– represents the sum of the base contribution and the excess contribution. The total amount contributed ($52,146) is close to what would have been contributed using a standard allocation of 11% ($52,250). This amount was chosen by management as what they could afford to contribute to the plan.

In this example, the base rate equals 10%. Therefore, all employees will receive a contribution of 10% of their own compensation earned up to $118,500, the integration level for 2016. Notice that the column "Percent of Comp" is the same for employees B through G; all have a contribution of 10% of their compensation. None of them have compensation above the integration level, so none will have a contribution at the higher excess contribution rate of 15.7%.

Because employee A has compensation in excess of the integration level, he will have a contribution for both the base compensation and an additional contribution for the excess compensation. His base contribution equals $11,850 ($118,500 x 10%), while his excess contribution equals $12,796 [($200,000 - $118,500) x 15.7%]. His excess contribution is based on the $81,500 ($200,000 - $118,500) of compensation over the integration level.

> Notice that in this example, the company has contributed $52,146 to the plan and the owner A receives an allocation of $24,646; whereas in the first example, the total contribution was $52,250 and the owner A received $22,000. Integration has allowed the owner to increase his contribution by $2,646. The $2,646 has come from reducing the contributions of B-G from 11% to 10% each to reflect that employer contributions to Social Security are part of the overall retirement plan and by increasing the total contributions only slightly.

Although the integration level is generally equal to the Social Security wage base, it can be reduced to allow for larger amounts of income to be subject to the higher excess rate. However, as the integration level is reduced, so is the maximum difference between the base rate and the excess rate. Higher income employees will generally have higher contributions as the integration level is reduced, but this may also result in additional contributions for other employees.

If the integration level is less than the Social Security wage base, but more than 80 percent of the wage base, then the 5.7 percent is reduced to 5.4 percent. If the integration level is less than or equal to 80 percent of the wage base and greater than 20 percent of the wage base, then the 5.7 percent is reduced to 4.3 percent. At 20 percent or less, the rate remains at 5.7 percent.[1]

EXHIBIT 5.2

INTEGRATION LEVEL AND MAXIMUM EXCESS PERCENTAGE

Social Security Integration Level	Excess Percentage
100% of wage base	2 times the base limited to 5.7%
More than 80% of wage base but less than 100% of wage base	2 times the base limited to 5.4%
More than 20% of wage base but less than 80% of wage base	2 times the base limited to 4.3%
Below 20% of wage base	2 times the base limited to 5.7%

Integration is generally used when the owner wants to increase or skew the contributions toward higher paid employees (those whose earnings are above the wage base) or himself. Social Security integration is not considered discriminatory because the employees who are receiving the excess contributions are not receiving Social Security retirement contributions on their wages in excess of the Social Security wage base.

AGE-BASED PROFIT SHARING PLANS

Age-based profit sharing plans use both age and compensation as the basis for allocating contributions to an employee's account. An age-based plan is chosen when the employee census is such that the owner or key employee is older than most or all other employees and the company wants to tilt the contribution toward those older employees. The concept of using an age-weighting formula in the allocation of benefits is based on a theory of comparable benefits for employees at normal age retirement (usually 65). Because older employees are closer to normal retirement age, current contributions must be higher than those for younger employees. While this initially

---

1. Treas. Reg. §1.401(l)-2.

appears to be discriminatory when comparing the current contributions to the plan, it seems relatively fair after comparing the ultimate benefits derived from the plan at the time of each of the employee's retirement.

It is possible that employees may perceive an inequity in the contributions to the plan under an age-based profit sharing formula. For example, if two employees are performing the same duties and are paid the same salary but are of different ages, the older employee will receive a higher current contribution to the plan than the younger employee. An illustration of an age-based profit sharing plan is provided in Example 5.5.

There are seven employees (A-G), ages 25-55 and with compensation ranging from $30,000 to $200,000.

EXAMPLE 5.5

AGE-BASED PROFIT SHARING PLAN						
Employee	Age	Covered Comp	PV of $1**	Allocation Factor (age-weighted compensation)	Percent of Total Contribution**	Dollar Contribution**
A (Owner)	55	$200,000	0.4423	$88,457	0.755305	$39,465
B	45	$60,000	0.1956	$11,737	0.100218	$5,236
C	40	$60,000	0.1301	$7,806	0.066650	$3,482
D	35	$50,000	0.0865	$4,326	0.036937	$1,930
E	30	$40,000	0.0575	$2,302	0.019652	$1,027*
F	25	$35,000	0.0383	$1,339	0.011436	$598*
G	25	$30,000	0.0383	$1,148	0.009802	$512*
		$475,000		$117,114	1.000000	$52,250

Note that this plan is most likely a top-heavy plan. Therefore, employees E, F, and G would have to be allocated 3% of their salary ($1,200, $1,050, and $900 respectively). This would reduce the amount available to the owner or increase the overall cost of the plan.

** Rounded

The initial step in calculating the contribution under an age-based profit sharing plan is to determine the present value of one dollar of benefit at the normal retirement age, usually age 65. For example, to determine this present value factor for employee A, the following calculation is performed:

FV = 1.0

N = 10 (65–55) (difference in current age from normal age retirement 65)

i = 8.5

PMT = 0

PV = 0.44229 (the contribution factor for this employee)

The term (N) is determined by subtracting the current age from the normal retirement age. In this case, the employee (A) has 10 years until he attains the age of 65. The interest factor is generally permitted by the IRS to be between 7.5% and 8.5%. This calculation, using 8.5%, results in a present value of 0.4423, which means that for employee A to receive a benefit of $1.00 at age 65, the plan sponsor would have to contribute $0.4423 today.

Notice that the present value factor decreases for younger age participants reflecting the longer period until retirement. For example, employee C's present value factor is 0.1301, whereas employee E's factor is 0.0575. The result is that contributions are higher for those employees who are older because the present value factor increases each year for each employee as they approach retirement.

The next step in the calculation is to weight the present value factor by the employee's compensation to arrive at an age-weighted compensation. For employee A, the allocation factor equals $88,457 ($200,000 x 0.4423). Once this process is completed for each employee, the resulting allocation factors are used to prorate the total contribution to the plan to the individual employees. Employee A's allocation factor over the total age-weighted compensation equals 75.53 percent ($88,457 ÷ $117,114), a significantly higher percentage relative to the other employees. The percentage of total age-weighted compensation is then multiplied by the total dollar contribution to the plan ($52,250).

The age-weighted profit sharing formula provides an amazing result. The owner, employee A, increases his allocation of the $52,250 contribution from $22,000 in our first example to $39,465 (recall that the 2016 limit for any particular employee is $53,000). This method of allocating contributions works extremely well when the owner is older than the other employees and when his compensation is relatively high. We could even calculate the total amount of employer contribution necessary to give A the maximum contribution for profit sharing plans in 2016 of $53,000 ($53,000 ÷ 75.5305% = $70,170.35). As illustrated in Exhibit 5.3, if the census data were as presented, the owner employee can allocate a high percentage of the total contribution to his account balance utilizing the two available age-weighted options illustrated.

COMPARISON OF STANDARD, INTEGRATED, AND AGE-BASED PROFIT SHARING PLANS

EXHIBIT 5.3

Technique for Plan Contributions	Allocation of Contribution to Owner	Total Employer Contribution to Plan	Owner's Percentage of Contribution	Impact of the Change Over Standard Allocation (%)
Standard Allocation (Equal %)	$22,000	$52,250	42.11%	N/A
Permitted Disparity (Integration)	$24,646	$52,146	47.26%	+ 12.03%
Age-Weighted Plan	$39,465	$52,250**	75.53%	+ 79.39%
Age-Weighted - Maximum contributions to owner	$53,000	$70,170	75.53%	+ 140.91%

Figures are rounded to the nearest dollar.
*** Employer will need to increase the contribution to comply with the top-heavy 3% rule - total additional contribution equals $1,013.*

Unfortunately, most business owners are unaware of the availability of these favorable contribution methods for a retirement plan. This provides advisors and pension experts who are knowledgeable with an opportunity to add significant value to the professional/client relationship.

NEW COMPARABILITY PLANS

A **new comparability plan** is a profit sharing plan in which contributions are made to an employee's account based on their respective classification in the company as defined by the plan sponsor (employer). The contributions for the "owner" category classification will always be higher than the contributions for other employee classifications.

The higher contributions are based on the concept of cross-testing, in which contributions to a defined contribution plan are determined to be non-discriminatory in terms of benefits, rather than contributions. IRC §401(a)(4) states that, for a plan to be qualified, the contributions or benefits provided under the plan must not discriminate in favor of highly compensated employees.[1] The key word in that sentence is the word "or." Either the contributions or the benefits must be non-discriminatory, not both.

QUICK QUIZ 5.2

1. Permitted disparity is a method of allocating plan contributions that allows the employer to make contributions only to highly compensated individuals because they do not receive Social Security.
   a. True
   b. False

2. Age-based profit sharing plans use both age and compensation as the basis for allocating contributions to employee accounts.
   a. True
   b. False

3. New comparability plans are safe, flexible plans that allow the employer to allocate all benefits to the owner(s).
   a. True
   b. False

False, True, False.

1. IRC §401(a)(4).

The regulations provide several methods for a new comparability plan to meet the non-discrimination rules.[1] The regulations provide that a plan will meet the non-discrimination rules if the plan conforms to one of the two "minimum allocation gateways." The general rule is that a plan satisfies the minimum allocation gateway if each NHCE has an allocation rate that is at least one third of the allocation rate of the HCE with the highest allocation rate. The second gateway provides that a plan is deemed to satisfy the minimum allocation gateway if each NHCE receives an allocation of at least five percent of the NHCE's compensation (within the meaning of IRC §415(c)(3)).

EXHIBIT
5.4

MINIMUM ALLOCATION GATEWAY

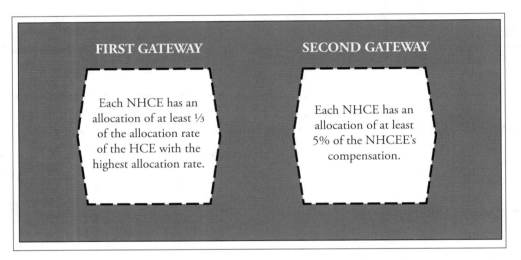

FIRST GATEWAY

Each NHCE has an allocation of at least ⅓ of the allocation rate of the HCE with the highest allocation rate.

SECOND GATEWAY

Each NHCE has an allocation of at least 5% of the NHCEE's compensation.

In addition, the regulations provide that if a plan does not meet either of the minimum allocation gateways, then it can still meet the non-discriminatory requirements if the plan has "broadly available" allocation rates or if the plan has age-based allocation rates that are based on either a gradual age or service schedule. These alternatives are discussed in detail within the Treasury regulations.

While new comparability plans are generally more expensive to administer, they allow for higher contributions for owners. Below is an example of a business with seven employees in which an owner would benefit from a new comparability allocation compared to a traditional profit sharing plan or an integrated profit sharing plan.

---

1. Treas. Reg. §1.401(a)(4)-8.

Employee	Age	Salary	Profit Sharing Plan 13.36% Allocation	Integrated Profit Sharing Plan with Base Percentage of 11.57%	New Comparability Allocation
Owner	50	$265,000	$35,412	$39,003	$53,000
Manager	45	$150,000	$20,044	$19,146	$15,000
Staff 1	30	$40,000	$5,345	$4,627	$2,000
Staff 2	25	$35,000	$4,677	$4,048	$1,750
Staff 3	20	$30,000	$4,009	$3,470	$1,500
Staff 4	20	$25,000	$3,341	$2,892	$1,250
Staff 5	20	$20,000	$2,673	$2,313	$1,000
Totals		$565,000	$75,500	$75,500	$75,500

Notice that the total employer contribution is the same in all three examples. The difference is in how that contribution is allocated among the seven employees. In the case of the new comparability plan, the owner would receive $53,000, while he would receive less using the other allocation methods. As indicated, new comparability plans are more complicated, but provide an effective option for small businesses to benefit higher paid owners.

OTHER ALLOCATION METHODS

A highly compensated owner can fund his plan with the annual additions limit, $53,000 for 2016, using profit sharing plans with or without a cash or deferred arrangement (CODA). In many cases, the use of a CODA may enable an owner to reach the maximum contribution limit of $53,000 (2016) with a lower total employer contribution. 401(k) profit sharing plans are used in most cases to fulfill this need.

FORFEITURES

When employment is terminated and the employee has funds in a profit sharing plan that are less than 100 percent vested, the employee forfeits the amount not vested. **Forfeitures** in a profit sharing plan may either be used to reduce future plan contributions or be reallocated to the remaining participant's accounts.[1] However, any such reallocation of the forfeiture amounts must not be discriminatory in favor of highly compensated employees, owners, or officers.

KEY CONCEPTS

1. What are the vesting schedules available for profit sharing plans?

2. When are distributions allowed from profit sharing plans?

Forfeitures can be allocated to remaining employees' accounts based on account balances as long as the allocation method does not discriminate. Alternatively, the forfeitures could be allocated on current year compensation – the same as normal contributions to the plan. Forfeitures cannot be reallocated to participants' accounts that have already reached their annual additions limit for the year. Therefore, an owner who has managed to have current contributions of $53,000 for 2016

---

1. IRC §401(a)(8).

made to his account will likely consider having forfeitures reduce future contributions to the plan since he cannot personally benefit from forfeitures. Alternatively, a forfeiture policy of reallocation can be combined with integration or an age-based approach to assist the owner in receiving the maximum contribution allowed.

EXAMPLE 5.6

George has a $30,000 account balance and is 80% vested in his profit sharing plan when he terminates employment. George's vested balance in the profit sharing plan is $24,000, and he will forfeit the remaining $6,000. This forfeiture could be used to reduce future plan contributions. For example, the $52,250 contribution to the age-based profit sharing plan in the previous example could be reduced to $46,250 ($52,250 - $6,000). Alternatively, in the previous example demonstrating the profit sharing plan that utilized the standard allocation formula, the $6,000 could be distributed to the remaining participants with $2,526 ($200,000/$475,000 x $6,000) allocated to employee A. In this case, employee A, the owner, would have total contributions to the profit sharing plan in the amount of $24,526 ($22,000 + $2,526) rather than the $22,000.

ELIGIBILITY

Profit sharing plans are subject to **standard eligibility** rules of other qualified plans. Therefore, the standard eligibility of age 21 and one year of service will generally apply to profit sharing plans. As discussed before, plan sponsors may always relax the eligibility requirements.

In addition, profit sharing plans may also require a two year waiting period before an employee is eligible; however, all employer contributions must then be 100 percent vested. The two year eligibility rule is not a common choice for most businesses due to the 100 percent vesting requirement.

VESTING

The vesting rules for profit sharing plans are the same as for defined contribution plans. The standard 3-year cliff or 2 to 6 year graduated vesting apply unless the plan requires a two-year waiting period, in which case all contributions must then be 100 percent vested.[1] As discussed before, the plan sponsor is always permitted to be more generous but may not exceed these vesting requirements.

QUICK QUIZ 5.3

1. A profit sharing plan can require the participants to wait three years before entering the plan, but all contributions must then be 100% vested.
   a. True
   b. False

2. Under PPA 2006, profit sharing plans must use a 5-year cliff vesting schedule or a 3 to 7 year graduated vesting schedule.
   a. True
   b. False

3. Profit sharing plans may permit in-service withdrawals after a participant has attained two years of service in the plan.
   a. True
   b. False

False, False, True.

---

1. PPA 2006 increased the vesting for all defined contribution plans beginning in 2007.

DISTRIBUTIONS

Generally, profit sharing plans do not permit employees to receive distributions from the plan except upon termination, hardship, disability, or retirement. However, profit sharing plans may permit in-service withdrawals after the participant has fulfilled two years of service in the plan. Chapter 7 fully explains the taxation of distributions from qualified plans and the application of any penalties for early withdrawal.

CASH OR DEFERRED ARRANGEMENTS [401(k) PLANS]

A **cash or deferred arrangement (CODA)**, generally referred to as a 401(k) plan, is a feature that attaches to certain types of qualified plans to create a contributory component to the plan. Specifically, a CODA is permitted with profit sharing plans and stock bonus plans.[1] The CODA permits employees to defer a portion of their salary on a pretax basis to the qualified plan, thereby reducing their current income tax liability. These employee elective deferral contributions are tax-deferred - meaning that the earnings are not subject to income taxation until such time as the employee receives a distribution from the plan. Note that in the case of a Roth account, the deferral contribution occurs on an after-tax basis. It is referred to as a cash or deferred arrangement because employees are given the option to receive their current salary in cash (in their payroll) or make an elective deferral contribution into the 401(k) plan.

KEY CONCEPTS

1. What are the general characteristics of a cash or deferred arrangement?

2. List the advantages for employees to have a 401(k) plan.

3. Which type of entities may establish a 401(k) plan?

Cash or deferred arrangements were introduced to the Internal Revenue Code in The Revenue Act of 1978 with an effective date of January 1, 1980. Since then, the number of 401(k) plans has increased dramatically. 401(k) plans are attractive to employers because these plans are employee self-reliant plans and provide a means of establishing a qualified retirement plan for employees without requiring the employer to make contributions to the plan (although employer contribution matches are a common option).

---

1. CODAs can also be used with pre-1974 money purchase pension plans.

EXHIBIT
5.5

GROWTH OF 401(k) PLANS FROM 1984 TO 2013[1]

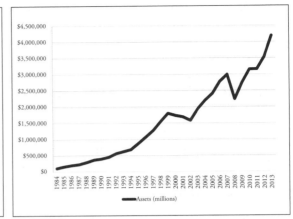

EXHIBIT
5.6

ADVANTAGES OF 401(k) PLANS

TO EMPLOYEES	TO EMPLOYERS
• Shelter current income from taxation in a qualified plan • Self-directed investments • Earnings grow tax-deferred until distributed	• Minimal expense • No annual contribution commitment required • Owner employees may participate

401(k) plans are the most popular type of newly installed qualified retirement plans today. Cash or deferred arrangements are so prevalent because employers have begun to shift from plans in which the employees are dependent on the employer for the funding of retirement benefits to plans in which the employees are responsible for the funding of retirement benefits. Employers can provide contributions to such plans (usually in the form of a match based on the employee's deferral); nonetheless, as with any profit sharing, such employer contributions are discretionary.

ESTABLISHING A 401(k) PLAN

As with any qualified plan, plan sponsors may use prototype plans (see Chapter 8) or custom designed plans to establish a cash or deferred arrangement. Because these cash or deferred arrangements are qualified plans, the procedures to establish one are similar to other qualified plans. However, there are certain differences in terms of which types of entities can establish CODAs.

---

1. Form 5500 filings with the U.S. Department of Labor.

Which Entities May Establish a 401(k) Plan?

Only certain types of entities are permitted to establish and sponsor a 401(k) plan. Employers, such as corporations, partnerships, LLCs, and proprietorships may establish such a plan. In addition, for years after 1996, tax-exempt entities are permitted to establish 401(k) plans. Traditionally, tax-exempt entities (such as 501(c)(3) organizations) have established tax sheltered annuities (403(b) plans), but today, these types of entities may establish either the traditional tax sheltered annuity (403(b) plan) or a 401(k) plan. Over the past few years, these two types of plans have become very similar in nature. A governmental entity may no longer establish a 401(k) plan;[1] however, certain grandfathered government plans that were in existence prior to May 6, 1986 may continue to be maintained. In addition, self-employed individuals and owner-only businesses with no employees may establish individual 401(k) plans, which will be discussed below.

QUICK QUIZ 5.4

1. A tax-exempt organization cannot establish a 401(k) plan.
   a. True
   b. False

2. Employers can establish 401(k) plans with minimal expense.
   a. True
   b. False

3. Governmental entities cannot establish 401(k) plans today.
   a. True
   b. False

False, True, True.

A 401(k) plan is typically a profit sharing plan (although it may be arranged as a stock bonus plan) that permits employees to make contributions from their salary to the plan on a pretax basis.

Entities Which May Establish a 401(k) Plan
Corporations
Partnerships
LLCs
Proprietorships
Tax-exempt entities

Because of its qualified status, 401(k) plans must comply with the rules discussed in Chapter 3 regarding eligibility, coverage, nondiscrimination, vesting, etc. However, some of the rules that relate to 401(k) plans are different than the standard rules relating to qualified plans. These differences are discussed below.

---

1. IRC §401(k)(4)(B).

ELIGIBILITY

401(k) plans, like other qualified plans, have rules regarding who is eligible to participate in the plan. As you recall, the standard eligibility rules for qualified plans are that the employee must have attained the age of 21 and worked **one year of service** (defined as 1,000 hours within a 12 month period).[1] The exception to the one year of service rule is that an employer may make an employee wait two years to enter the plan if upon entrance into the plan, all benefits are fully vested. This two year exception is

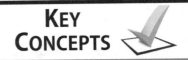
not available for 401(k) plans because an employee cannot be required to complete more than one year of service as a condition of participation in a section 401(k) arrangement.[2] The reason for this exception is that the employee elective deferral contributions are already 100 percent vested.

As with any qualified plan, the eligibility rules may always be more liberal to benefit the employees but cannot be more restrictive.

Once the eligibility requirements are met, the employee will enter the plan upon the next plan entrance date. As discussed in Chapter 3, most qualified plans have two entrance dates or more to meet the qualification requirement, which limits the waiting period to six months or less after eligibility.

EXAMPLE 5.7

Dirk, age 35, has just taken a job at Advanced Technologies, which sponsors a 401(k) plan that requires one year of service and has entrance dates on January 1 and July 1. If Dirk started work on February 15, 2016, he will be entering the plan on July 1, 2017.

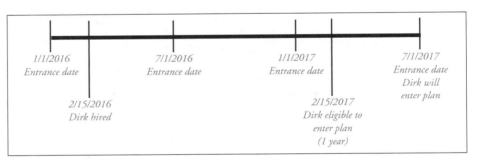

VESTING

The vesting requirements for 401(k) plans are the same as those for other defined contribution plans. Contributions to 401(k) plans consist of employee elective deferrals and if applicable, employer matching contributions. If the 401(k) plan is sponsored in conjunction with a profit sharing plan or stock bonus plan, contributions to those plans are considered separate from the 401(k) plan contributions. For vesting purposes, all employee deferral contributions and the earnings on those contributions are always 100 percent vested. The employer matching

---

1. Rule is generally referred to as "21 and 1."
2. IRC §401(k)(2)(D).

contributions, employer discretionary profit sharing contributions, and the earnings on employer contributions must vest under a schedule at least as generous as the 2 to 6 year graduated or 3-year cliff schedules.

EXAMPLE
5.8

The total balance of Wallace's 401(k) profit sharing plan is $200,000. Of this balance, $60,000 is attributable to employer profit sharing plan contributions and $40,000 is attributable to earnings on the employer profit sharing plan contributions. $39,000 consists of Wallace's elective deferral contributions to the 401(k) plan and $21,000 is the earnings on Wallace's elective deferral contributions. The remainder of the balance consists of employer matching contributions and the earnings on the employer match. If the 401(k) plan uses a graded vesting schedule and Wallace has completed two years of service with his employer, what is his vested balance in this 401(k) profit sharing plan?

To calculate this, first separate all of the contributions to determine the proper type of vesting schedule to use with each type of contribution, and then apply the appropriate vesting percentage.

Profit Sharing Plan		Vested %		Vested Amount
Employer contribution	$60,000	20%	2 to 6 graduated vesting	$12,000
Earnings or employer contributions	$40,000	20%	2 to 6 graduated vesting	$8,000
Total	$100,000	20%	Vested profit sharing plan	$20,000
401(k) Plan				
Wallace's deferral contributions	$39,000	100%	100% vested	$39,000
Earnings on Wallace's contributions	$21,000	100%	100% vested	$21,000
Employer matching contributions and earnings	$40,000	20%	2 to 6 year graduated vesting	$8,000
Total 401(k)	$100,000			$68,000
Total	**$200,000**		**Vested 401(k) Account Balance**	**$88,000**

PARTICIPATION

Employee enrollment meetings are typically held after the establishment of a 401(k) plan to inform the employees of the plan details and to encourage participation in the plan.[1] These educational meetings also help the plan sponsor comply with their ERISA 404(c) fiduciary requirements.[2] The most popular form of election under a CODA is a salary reduction agreement in which the employee agrees to reduce compensation in exchange for the elective deferral contribution into the plan. The salary reduction agreement may apply to current salary; to a salary increase; or to a bonus, commission, or other form of compensation for services. The employee's election to defer is generally made as a percentage of income or a dollar amount that will be contributed to the plan for the current year and usually directs the funds to be invested in a specific manner.

EXAMPLE 5.9

Sam agrees (elects) to reduce her $50,000 salary by 20% ($10,000) if the funds are deposited in the 401(k) plan. She receives a W-2 showing taxable compensation of $40,000 with the remainder ($10,000) of her salary contributed to the 401(k) plan. Typically, she will choose how the funds are invested – whether stocks, bonds, cash, or other investments.[3] Plans that provide for employee self-direction of plan assets generally permit the employees to change their investments on a regular basis, in many cases on a daily basis.

EMPLOYEE CONTRIBUTIONS

Contributions to 401(k) plans can be made as employee elective deferral contributions (either as a traditional elective deferral or as a contribution to a Roth account), employee after-tax contributions, employer matching contributions, employer profit sharing contributions, or employer contributions used to solve an ADP/ACP problem (discussed below).

Employee Deferrals

Employee elective deferral contributions are limited per year to the amounts in Exhibit 5.7.

---

1. Participation is encouraged for the benefit of the employee and for ADP/ACP testing.
2. ERISA 404(c).
3. While most 401(k) plans provide for self-direction, some plans may provide for outside management of the plan assets.

401(k) ANNUAL ELECTIVE DEFERRALS LIMITS

EXHIBIT
5.7

Year	Annual Elective Deferral Limit	Catch-Up Contributions **	Total Elective Deferral Limit
2016	$18,000	$6,000	$24,000

* The same limits apply to SARSEPs, 403(b) Plans, and 457 Plans.
** Age 50 or older.

Tax Impact

Besides the mere accumulation of benefits towards retirement, pre-tax funds deferred in a 401(k) plan are not currently subject to federal income tax and are not currently subject to state income tax. This tax deferral reduces current tax payments and allows for greater compounding of the funds contributed and the earnings over time.

Although employee elective deferrals (other than to a Roth account) are not subject to income tax, these deferral amounts are subject to payroll taxes. This means that the employee and the employer must pay payroll taxes on the employee elective deferral amounts contributed to a 401(k) plan. This will result in a Form W-2 that has different amounts in the various boxes on the form.

W-2 EXAMPLE

EXHIBIT
5.8

a Employee's social security number 123-45-6789	OMB No. 1545-0008
b Employer identification number (EIN) 35-1234567	**1** Wages, tips, other compensation 132,000.00 **2** Federal income tax withheld 34,000.00
c Employer's name, address, and ZIP code Best Employer 99 Company Drive City, GA 12345	**3** Social security wages 118,500.00 **4** Social security tax withheld 7,347.00
	5 Medicare wages and tips 150,000.00 **6** Medicare tax withheld 2,175.00
	7 Social security tips **8** Allocated tips
d Control number 35-1234567	**9** **10** Dependent care benefits
e Employee's first name and initial Last name Suff. Greatest Employee 100 Greatest Drive City, GA 12345	**11** Nonqualified plans **12a** C | 81.28
	13 Statutory employee ☐ Retirement plan ☒ Third-party sick pay ☐ **12b** D | 18,000.00
	14 Other **12c**
	12d
f Employee's address and ZIP code	
15 State Employer's state ID number GA | 9876543210	**16** State wages, tips, etc. 132,000.00 **17** State income tax 6,800.00 **18** Local wages, tips, etc. **19** Local income tax **20** Locality name

Form **W-2** Wage and Tax Statement   Department of the Treasury—Internal Revenue Service
Copy 1—For State, City, or Local Tax Department

Notice, in the Form W-2 above, Medicare wages (box 5) represents the total income for the employee. Subtracting the 401(k) deferral of $18,000 (box 12b) from Medicare wages results in the taxable wages found in box 1. Box 4 (Social Security tax withheld) equals 6.2 percent of box 3 (Social Security Wages) and box 6 equals 1.45 percent of box 5 (Medicare wages). Recall that the Medicare tax applies to all wages, while the Social Security tax (OASDI) is limited to the Social

Security wage base ($118,500 for 2016).[1] (Box 12a indicates the taxable component of the insurance premiums for the employee's group term life coverage.)

Employer Deposits of Employee Deferrals

Employee elective deferrals must be deposited and segregated from the employer's assets by the earliest date that is reasonably possible. However, the segregation of the funds must be completed by the 15th day of the month following the deferral from the employee's compensation. It is important to note that the 15th day is not a safe harbor. The employer has a responsibility to deposit the funds as soon as it is reasonably possible.

Catch-Up Contributions

One of the helpful provisions that came out of the EGTRRA 2001 was the allowance for higher contributions for older workers, which provides the opportunity to better prepare and save for retirement. Employees who are at least 50 years old during the plan year may increase their elective deferral limit by up to $6,000 for 2016. The additional deferral is called a **"catch-up" contribution** and allows those nearing retirement to increase their deferral contributions to improve their financial situation for retirement.

KEY CONCEPTS

1. Identify the methods employees can contribute to 401(k) plans and the applicable deferral contribution limits.

2. What is the income tax impact of 401(k) employee deferral contributions?

3. When must the employer deposit employee deferral contributions into the 401(k) plan?

4. Discuss the application of the catch-up contribution rules and the limits on catch-up contributions.

5. Identify the participation rules and negative elections.

In 2016, the employee elective deferral catch-up contribution may increase an employee's deferral limit from $18,000 to $24,000. In addition, these employee deferral catch-up contributions are not limited by plan limits, limits on annual accumulations, or by the ADP/ACP testing (discussed below). In other words, as long as the plan provides for equal treatment among participants (both HC and NHC), there are virtually no restrictions on using these catch-up contributions for employees 50 and older.

Employee deferrals are included as part of the employee's annual funding limit of the lesser of 100 percent of income or $53,000 for 2016. However, the catch-up contributions do not count against this limit and, therefore, allow a participant who is age 50 or older to increase the maximum contributions to qualified plans to $59,000 for 2016.

---

1. One of the helpful provisions that came out of the EGTRRA 2001 was the allowance for higher contributions for older workers, which provides the opportunity to better prepare and save for retirement.

Andrea, age 50, has a salary of $160,000. She chooses to defer $24,000 for 2016 into the 401(k) plan. The employer may also contribute up to $40,000 ($160,000 x 25%) to the plan (not her account). Note that the employer's contribution to her account will be limited to $35,000 due to the maximum annual contribution limit of $53,000. In total for the year, Andrea would have contributions to qualified plans totalling $59,000 ($53,000 + $6,000 catch-up).

It is important to note that the catch up provision is only employee funded. An employer cannot make the contribution for the employee and an employee that did not have access to a cash or deferred arrangement could not exceed the IRC §415(c) limit.

Employee After-Tax Contributions - Thrift Plans[1]

Although much less popular today, some 401(k) plans still permit employees to make after-tax contributions to the plan. These types of contributions have typically been called **thrift plan** contributions and were utilized by those persons who wanted to save more than the elective deferral limit or more than the amount allowed under the ADP/ACP test (discussed below). Any earnings on the after-tax contribution grow tax-free until distribution just as the earnings on pretax contributions. As will be discussed in Chapter 7, these after-tax contributions (Thrift Plan) give the plan participant an adjusted basis in their 401(k) plan.

Roth Contributions (Roth Accounts)[2]

Roth accounts were first introduced by EGTRRA 2001 for years beginning after 2005. IRS regulations for designated Roth contributions under qualified cash or deferred arrangements described in Section 401(k) were adopted effective January 3, 2006 and apply to plan years beginning on or after January 1, 2006. However, even today, Roth accounts are not widely adopted.

Under IRC §402A, a plan may permit an employee who makes elective contributions under a qualified cash or deferred arrangement to designate some or all of those contributions as Roth contributions. Designated Roth contributions are elective contributions under a qualified cash or deferred arrangement that are:

1. designated irrevocably by the employee at the time of the cash or deferral election as designated Roth contributions that are being made in lieu of all or a portion of the pre-tax elective deferral contributions the employee is otherwise eligible to make under the plan;
2. treated by the employer as includible in the employee's gross income at the time the employee would have received the contribution amount in cash if the employee had not made the cash or deferral election; and
3. maintained by the plan in a separate account.

The same dollar limits that apply to employee pretax deferrals also apply to Roth contributions in total. Therefore, for 2016, an employee could contribute up to $18,000 to a 401(k) plan Roth account or to a pre-tax account, but not to both. Similarly, a catch-up contribution can be

---

1. These thrift plans are different than the governmental Thrift Savings Plan (TSP), which is a retirement savings and investment plan for Federal employees and members of the uniformed services, including the Ready Reserve. It was established by Congress in the Federal Employees' Retirement System Act of 1986 and offers the same types of savings and tax benefits that many private corporations offer their employees under 401(k) plans.
2. IRC §402A.

contributed to a Roth account or to the pre-tax account of a 401(k) plan. This treatment is the same for catch-up contributions for 403(b) plans and governmental 457(b) plans.

Designated Roth contributions to a 401(k) account bear some similarity to contributions to a Roth IRA (discussed in Chapter 9). Contributions to either type of account are after-tax contributions and qualified distributions from either type of account are excludable from gross income. In addition, both Roth IRAs and Roth 401(k) plans are subject to the qualified distribution rules under IRC §408A(d)(2)(A).

However, there are several differences between these types of arrangements. For example, contributions to a Roth account (unlike contributions to a Roth IRA) are not subject to modified adjusted gross income limitations. In addition, the contribution limit for designated Roth account contributions is $18,000 in 2016, which is significantly higher than the limits for contributions to traditional and Roth IRAs. Furthermore, distributions from a Roth account are not subject to the same favorable ordering rules that apply to Roth IRA distributions. Instead, distributions from a Roth account are subject to the rules under IRC §72, which provide for a pro-rata distribution of income and basis in the event the distribution fails to be a qualified distribution. Finally, unlike Roth IRAs, Roth 401(k) account balances are subject to minimum distributions requirements and are available for loans.

EXHIBIT 5.9	COMPARISON OF ROTH IRA AND ROTH ACCOUNTS (2016)		
Characteristic	**Roth IRA**	**Roth Account**	
Participation	Anyone with earned income under limit	Anyone who is a participant in a 401(k), 403(b) or 457 plan that permits Roth contributions	
Contribution Limits	IRA Annual limit - for 2016, $5,500 plus $1,000 catch up if age 50 or older. Subject to AGI limit: Single ($117,000-$132,000); MFJ ($184,000-$194,000)	Deferral limit - for 2016, $18,000 plus $6,000 if age 50 or older. No AGI limits.	
Rollover Recharacterization Permitted	Yes - permitted[1]	No - not permitted. Once the rollover takes place, it cannot be undone.	
Minimum distributions	Only after death of participant	Yes - required	
Requirements for qualified distribution	5 years & on account of death, disability, age 59 ½ or first time home purchase (up to $10,000)	5 years & on account of death, disability or age 59½	
Tax for nonqualified distributions (early distributions penalties may apply to part of the distribution)	Nonqualified distributions are distributed in order: contributions (basis), conversions (basis), then earnings (taxable)	Nonqualified distributions are prorated between Roth contributions (basis) and earnings (taxable)	

1. The taxpayer can "reconvert" the later of: (1) the beginning of the following year after conversion, or (2) 30 days after the recharacterization.

Under the final regulations, there are a number of requirements that must be met by an employer sponsoring a qualified cash or deferred arrangement in which employees may make designated Roth contributions. First, if the employer/plan sponsor offers designated Roth elections, it must also offer pre-tax elective contributions (i.e., traditional contributions). Second, separate accounting must be maintained for any contributions designated as Roth contributions. Consequently, no contributions other than designated Roth contributions and certain rollover contributions may be allocated to a designated Roth account. In other words, matching contributions and forfeiture allocations may not be allocated to a designated Roth account.[1] Third, a designated Roth contribution must satisfy the requirements applicable to any other elective contributions made under a qualified cash or deferred arrangement (e.g., nonforfeitability and distribution restrictions) and is taken into account under the actual deferral percentage test (ADP test) in the same manner as pre-tax contributions.[2]

The Small Business Jobs Act of 2010

The Small Business Jobs Act (SBJA) of 2010 signed by the President on September 27, 2010 made several changes to the IRC §402A, which sets forth the rules for elective deferrals to Roth accounts. SBJA 2010 added IRC §402A(c)(4) to the Code, effective for distributions made after September 27, 2010, to permit plans that include a qualified Roth contribution program to allow individuals to roll over amounts from their accounts other than designated Roth accounts to their designated Roth accounts in the plan. This option, which can be accomplished as a direct rollover or as an indirect rollover, is akin to converting funds in a traditional IRA to a Roth IRA. In addition, SBJA 2010 permits governmental 457(b) plans to include designated Roth accounts for years after 2010. These rules are discussed in greater detail in Chapter 7.

Individual 401(k) Plan (Also Known As Solo 401(k))

An **individual 401(k) plan** is an easy-to-administer, low-cost retirement plan designed for self-employed individuals and owner-only businesses. An individual 401(k) may also be known as a self-employed 401(k), solo 401(k), or a 401(k)I. An individual 401(k) plan offers many of the same advantages of a traditional 401(k), but has fewer administrative costs and requirements due to its

QUICK QUIZ 5.6

1. The employee 401(k) plan deferral limit is indexed for inflation after 2006.
   a. True
   b. False

2. Employee deferral contributions to 401(k) plans are subject to payroll taxes at the time of contribution.
   a. True
   b. False

3. An employer is not required to deposit the employee's 401(k) plan deferral contributions until the 15th day of the month following the deferral.
   a. True
   b. False

4. As a maximum, an individual over 50 years old can defer $24,000 in 2016 to a 401(k) plan.
   a. True
   b. False

5. A negative election is an election the employee can make that states that they want to participate in the plan.
   a. True
   b. False

True, True, False, True, False.

---

1. Treasury Regulation §1.401(k)-1(f)(2).
2. IRC §402A, Treasury Regulation §1.401(k)-1(f).

small size. An individual 401(k) may be used by a sole proprietorship or business owner (including S and C corporations and partnerships) with no employees other than a spouse. Note that business owners must have at least a five percent ownership share to be eligible for an individual 401(k). Individual 401(k) plans are subject to the same elective deferral limits as traditional 401(k) plans, but annual funding is not required. Individual 401(k) plans are also eligible for the Roth account feature.

EMPLOYER CONTRIBUTIONS

Matching Contributions

Employers and plan sponsors often provide a matching contribution based on the **employee elective deferral contributions** to the 401(k) plan. These **employer matching contributions** act as an incentive for plan participants to defer larger portions of their compensation than they may have otherwise contributed. Examples of methodologies for matching contributions are:

- 50 percent match up to six percent of compensation. If an employee contributes six percent or more of his compensation, the employer would match with a three percent contribution.
- Dollar-for-dollar match up to four percent. For every dollar of employee elective deferral, the employer will contribute (match) equally up to four percent of the employee's compensation.

In 2016, Rita elects to defer 8% of her $40,000 salary to a 401(k) plan. Her employer matches 50% of her deferral up to a maximum of 6%. For the year, Rita contributes $3,200 and her employer contributes 3% (50% of 6%), or $1,200, for a total contribution of $4,400.

In 2016, Rita elects to defer 8% of her $40,000 salary to a 401(k) plan. Her employer matches 50% of her deferral up to a maximum of 6%. For the year, Rita contributes $3,200 and her employer contributes 3% (50% of 6%), or $1,200, for a total contribution of $4,400.

Assume Joyce is 50 and attempting to maximize her employee deferral contributions. She has a $50,00 salary and her employer matches dollar for dollar up to 4% of salary. Joyce can elect to defer $18,000 (2016) and she can elect to defer the catch-up of $6,000 (2016). Joyce's total elected deferral contribution to the 401(k) plan would be $24,000. In addition, the employer match would be $2,000 ($50,000 x 4%) for a total contribution of $26,000. Rita's W-2 would show $26,000 ($50,000 - $24,000) subject to federal income tax, although she and her employer would pay payroll taxes on the full $50,000. The employer match would not be subjected to payroll tax or current income tax.

While employee elective deferral contributions are always 100 percent vested, employer matching contributions must vest at least as rapidly as either a three-year cliff vesting schedule or a 2 to 6 year graduated vesting schedule. These are the same maximum vesting schedules that are required for all defined contribution plans. Remember, plan sponsors can always be more generous by reducing years of service requirements for employees to achieve full vesting but may not extend the vesting period. Some matching contributions are applied simultaneously

KEY CONCEPTS

1. What are matching contributions and their allowed vesting schedules?

2. How can profit sharing plan contributions be used with the 401(k) plan?

3. What are the requirements for a 401(k) plan to offer a Roth Account?

with employee deferral contributions. Other plans may require active employment as of December 31 to qualify for the employer match, so matching contributions occur after year end.

Profit Sharing (Stock Bonus) Contributions

Because 401(k) plans consist of a CODA attached to a profit sharing plan or stock bonus plan, employers may also make a contribution to the profit sharing (or stock bonus) plan. These contributions are often referred to as the nonelective employer contribution. The employee elective deferral contributions do not count against the plan contribution limit of 25 percent, so large contributions can be made as a nonelective profit sharing contribution. The total contributions to qualified plans for the year is still limited to $53,000 per person for 2016 ($59,000 if the participant is age 50 and over).

The following example illustrates how profit sharing contributions, employee deferral contributions, and catch-up contributions work in unison. This example also illustrates how the annual additions limit works in harmony with the 401(k) limit and plan contribution limit.

> Assume that each employee wants to maximize his employee deferral contributions and the employer is already making a 25% of employee compensation contribution to a profit sharing plan on behalf of each employee.
>
> Consider Employees A through D with compensation ranging from $40,000 to $265,000. Also assume that each employee is over the age of 50.

EXAMPLE 5.13

401(k) PLAN

EXHIBIT 5.10

PROFIT SHARING, ELECTIVE DEFERRALS, AND CATCH-UP CONTRIBUTIONS				
	Employee A	**Employee B**	**Employee C**	**Employee D**
Salary	$40,000	$100,000	$150,000	$265,000
Catch-up contribution	$6,000	$6,000	$6,000	$6,000
401(k) plan deferral	$18,000	$18,000	$15,500	$0
P/S contribution (25%)	$10,000	$25,000	$37,500	$53,000
Total Contributions	$34,000	$49,000	$59,000	$59,000

Notice, if you assume the employer is going to make a 25% contribution, that will limit the elective deferral for C and D but will not affect the catch-up contribution.

The profit sharing contribution is assumed to be 25% of the employee's salary limited to the annual additions limit of $53,000, as in the case of Employee D. The 401(k) deferral is assumed to be limited to the lesser of the difference between the annual additions limit or the maximum deferral for the year. In the case of Employee A, he cannot reach either the $53,000 limit or 100% of his annual compensation because of how the limits work together. Notice that because the profit sharing contribution for Employee C is so high, Employee C is only allowed to defer $15,500 in the 401(k) plan. In the case of Employee D, the profit sharing contribution is limited to the $53,000 limit and thus Employee D is unable to contribute to the 401(k) plan with the exception of the catch-up contribution.[1]

Now assume that each employee maximizes their employee deferral contributions and the catch-up provision, and then the employer makes the maximum profit sharing plan contribution allowed after the deferral.

	Employee A	**Employee B**	**Employee C**	**Employee D**
Salary	$40,000	$100,000	$150,000	$265,000
Catch-up contribution	$6,000	$6,000	$6,000	$6,000
401(k) deferral	$18,000	$18,000	$18,000	$18,000
P/S contribution	$10,000	$25,000	$35,000	$35,000
Total Contributions	$34,000	$49,000	$59,000	$59,000

In this case, the profit sharing contributions are limited for C and D rather than the employee deferral contributions, but each employee (C and D) still reaches the maximum contribution to qualified plans for the year.

---

1. IRC §401(a)(22) provides that, to qualify under IRC §401, a defined contribution plan other than a profit-sharing plan (i.e., a stock bonus plan or a money purchase pension plan) must satisfy the pass-through voting requirements of IRC §409(e).

NONDISCRIMINATION TESTING

All qualified plans are required to meet certain nondiscrimination tests, but qualified plans that maintain a CODA must also meet two special nondiscrimination tests known as the actual deferral percentage test (ADP) and the actual contribution percentage test (ACP). However, because of the burdensome nature of annually complying with these rules, the IRC provides a safe harbor provision that eliminates the requirement of annual testing. In addition, the Pension Protection Act of 2006 has provided an optional nondiscrimination safe harbor for automatic enrollment plans. Thus, after December 31, 2007, employers will have three options with respect to 401(k) nondiscrimination testing. They can:

1. perform the ADP and ACP tests and take corrective action if the plan fails the test;
2. institute a qualified automatic enrollment feature and comply with the new safe harbor;[1] or
3. comply with the old safe harbor.

ACTUAL DEFERRAL PERCENTAGE TEST (ADP)

The **Actual Deferral Percentage (ADP) test** limits employee elective deferrals for the highly compensated employees (HC) based on the elective deferrals of non-highly compensated employees (NHC). A qualified plan with a CODA does not fail the ADP test simply because all eligible employees are highly compensated.[2]

IRC §401(k)(3) states that the actual deferral percentage for eligible highly compensated employees for the plan year is limited by the actual deferral percentage for all other eligible employees for the preceding plan year and must meet either of the following tests:

- **Test 1:** The actual deferral percentage for the group of eligible highly compensated employees is not more than the actual deferral percentage of all other eligible employees multiplied by 1.25 (the 1.25 requirement).
- **Test 2:** The excess of the actual deferral percentage for the group of eligible highly compensated employees over that of all other eligible employees is not more than two percentage points, and the actual deferral percentage for the group of eligible highly compensated employees is not more than the actual deferral percentage of all other eligible employees multiplied by 2 (the 200% / 2% test).

1. IRC §401(k)(13).
2. IRC §401(k)(3).

Although the ADP test above may appear rather convoluted and difficult to follow, the test can be interpreted rather easily with the following exhibits.

EXHIBIT
5.11

ADP SCHEDULE

ADP SCHEDULE	
If the ADP for NHC Employees is:	**The Permissible ADP for HC Employees is:**
0% to 2%	2 times ADP for NHCs
2% to 8%	2% plus ADP for NHCs
8% and over	1.25 times ADP for NHCs

EXHIBIT
5.12

EXPLANATION OF ADP SCHEDULE

The Rule	ADP of NHC	ADP Limit for HC
2 times ADP of NHC	1%	2.00%
	2%	4.00%
Plus 2 percentage points of ADP of NHC	3%	5.00%
	4%	6.00%
	5%	7.00%
	6%	8.00%
	7%	9.00%
	8%	10.00%
1.25 times ADP of NHC	9%	11.25%
	10%	12.50%
	11%	13.75%
	12%	15.00%
	13%	16.25%
	14%	17.50%
	15%	18.75%

As indicated in the above exhibits, the elective deferral contributions of the highly compensated employees are limited based on the elective deferrals of the nonhighly compensated employees. Generally, the current plan year ADP for the highly compensated employees is tested against the ADP of the nonhighly compensated employees for the prior plan year. Using this approach will generally minimize excess contributions by highly compensated employees. In other words, knowing the ADP for the nonhighly compensated employees for the prior plan year will allow the highly compensated employees to comply with the ADP test for the current plan year.

Plans can choose either the Current Year Method or Prior Year Method for ADP testing. The Prior Year Method calculates the maximum permissible deferral for highly compensated employees by using the nonhighly compensated employee's ADP from the previous year. Although the highly compensated employees have less certainty in knowing their deferral limits by using the Current Year Method, this approach may give the highly compensated employees a slightly higher deferral ceiling. The Current Year Method also provides more flexibility to the plan sponsor in the event of ADP failures.

In the first year of a 401(k) plan or the year that such plan is established, there is obviously no prior year on which to base the ADP for the highly compensated employees. In the first plan year, the ADP for the nonhighly compensated employees will be either three percent (as provided for in the regulations) or the actual ADP for the current year.[1]

KEY CONCEPTS

1. What are the ADP tests, and how are they calculated?

2. What remedies are available if a company fails the ADP test?

3. What are the safe harbor rules?

How is the ADP Calculated?

To determine whether the requirements of the ADP test have been met, the first step is to separate the eligible employees into highly compensated and nonhighly compensated groups. The only employees included in the calculation are those who meet the eligibility requirements of the 401(k) plan. It is important to note that this also includes those employees that have met eligibility but have chosen not to defer any of their compensation.

Next, calculate the actual elective deferral ratio (ADR) for each of the eligible employees by dividing the elective deferral contribution by the employee's compensation. Once the ADR is determined for each eligible employee, the amount of the ADP is calculated by averaging the ADRs for the employees within each group (HC or NHC). Once the ADP for each group is determined, they are compared to determine that the qualified plan complies with either the 1.25 test or the 200%/2% test.

> Boo Company sponsors a 401(k) plan with ten eligible employees. Each employee can defer up to 70 percent of their compensation limited to the annual deferral limit. The employees made the following deferral elections:

EXAMPLE 5.15

BASIC DATA				
Employee	Ownership	Compensation	Elective Deferral	ADR
A	60%	$200,000	$11,000	5.5%
B	30%	$160,000	$11,200	7.0%
C	5%	$150,000	$15,000	10.0%
D	3%	$80,000	$8,000	10.0%
E	2%	$50,000	$2,500	5.0%
F	-	$30,000	$3,000	10.0%
G	-	$25,000	-	0.0%
H	-	$25,000	$1,000	4.0%
I	-	$25,000	-	0.0%
J	-	$20,000	$500	2.5%

---

1. Treas. Reg. §1.401(k)-1(g)(11).

| Employee | ALTERNATIVE A | | ALTERNATIVE B | |
| | HC definition without 20% election* | | HC definition with 20% election* | |
	HC	NHC	HC	NHC
A	5.5%		5.5%	
B	7.0%		7.0%	
C	10.0%			10.0%
D		10.0%		10.0%
E		5.0%		5.0%
F		10.0%		10.0%
G		0.0%		0.0%
H		4.0%		4.0%
I		0.0%		0.0%
J		2.5%		2.5%
Average	7.5%	4.5%	6.25%	5.19%

Election to include only top 20% of employees as determined by compensation as HC.

Who is highly compensated in the example?

- Employee A and B are clearly highly compensated because of their ownership percentage.
- Employee C is highly compensated based on his income of $150,000. However, if the definition for highly compensated includes the election of being in the top 20 percent of paid employees, then Employee C would be classified as a NHC. Although Employee C owns 5% of the company, he is not a "5% owner" because he is not a more than 5% owner of the company.[1]
- Employees D through J are all NHC employees.

Alternative A and Alternative B demonstrate the difference of treatment depending upon whether the top 20% election is made or not.

Following Alternative A (without the top 20% election), the ADP of the HCs is 7.5%, while the ADP for the NHCs is 4.5%. Referring to the table above, with the NHCs ADP equal to 4.5%, the ADP for the HCs should be no greater than 6.5% - two percentage points more than the ADP for the NHCs. Therefore, the plan fails the ADP test.

---

1. IRC §416(i)(1)(B).

See the discussion below for remedies.

HC	NHC
ADP of HC - 7.5	ADP of NHC must be equal to 6.5 = 4.5% + 2%

Following Alternative B (with the top 20% election), the ADP of the HCEs is 6.25%, while the ADP for the NHC employees is 5.19%. Based on these figures, the plan complies with the ADP test. Notice that in this example, the difference between passing the ADP and not passing is how the plan defined the definition of highly compensated. By electing the top 20% of paid employees, Employee C shifted from the HC category to the NHC category. This example illustrates one reason an employer might choose the 20% election as the definition of highly compensated.

Failing the ADP Test

If the ADP test is not met, then there has been an excess elective deferral contribution by the highly compensated employees. An excess contribution occurs when the HCs defer more than is permitted under the ADP test. When this happens, there are four alternative remedies that the plan may use to bring the plan into compliance:

- corrective distributions,
- recharacterization,[1]
- qualified nonelective contributions (QNEC), or
- qualified matching contributions (QMC).

If a plan does not meet the ADP test, there are two explanations on why the plan did not meet the nondiscrimination test:

- the highly compensated employees deferred too much, or
- the non-highly compensated employees deferred too little (or some combination of the two).

This is a question of whether the "glass is half full or half empty." As discussed below, the negative election is often used to entice participation and increase the deferral for the NHC. In either case, the plan must be corrected to meet the ADP test by either reducing the HC employees elective deferral contributions or by increasing the NHC employees elective deferral contributions. Corrective distributions and recharacterizations are methods to reduce the HC employees elective deferrals, while QNECs and QMCs are methods to increase the ADP of the NHC employees.

When there are excess contributions, the 401(k) plan must correct the situation within 2½ months (75 days) after the plan year for which the contributions were made. If the correction is not made, then the employer is subject to a 10 percent penalty on the excess deferral contribution amount. In addition, if the correction is not made within twelve months, the plan may be deemed disqualified.

If the employer chooses to use a QNEC or QMC, then these contributions can be made beyond the 2½ month period.

---

1. IRC §401(k)(8)(A).

Corrective Distribution

When a plan fails the ADP test, the most common method of correcting the situation is to reduce the elective deferrals of the HCs by distributing or returning funds to the HCs. This distribution is referred to as a **corrective distribution** because it corrects the elective deferrals with regard to the ADP test. Corrective distributions must be completed within 2½ months after the end of the plan year; otherwise, a 10 percent excise tax is imposed on the amount that should have been distributed.

EXAMPLE 5.16

Recall Alternative A of the Boo Company example above in which the ADP for the HC was 7.5% while the ADP for the NHCs was 4.5%. With the NHC's ADP equal to 4.5%, the ADP for the HCs must equal 6.5%. Therefore, the plan would have to distribute enough from the HCs to reduce the ADP to 6.5% from 7.5%. The leveling method is used to determine the total excess contributions based on the dollar amount of the deferrals.

	Employee A	Employee B	Employee C	Total
Compensation	$200,000	$160,000	$150,000	$510,000
Deferral	$11,000	$ 11,200	$15,000	$37,200
Initial ADR	5.50%	7.00%	10.00%	7.50%
Initial Deferral	$11,000	$11,200	$15,000	$37,200
First reduction <1>	-	-	($3,800)	($3,800)
Net	$11,000	$11,200	$11,200	$33,400
Next reduction <2>	-	($200)	($200)	($400)
Net	$11,000	$11,000	$11,000	$33,000
Final reduction <3>	($100)	($100)	($100)	($300)
Corrected deferral	**$10,900**	**$10,900**	**$10,900**	**$32,700**
Corrective distribution	($100)	($300)	($4,100)	($4,500)
Compensation	$200,000	$160,000	$150,000	$510,000
Deferral	$10,900	$10,900	$10,900	$32,700
Corrected ADR	**5.45%**	**6.81%**	**7.27%**	**6.51%**

* Rounded

Under the leveling method, the elective deferral of the HC employee with the highest deferral, Employee C is reduced by the amount, <1>, necessary to reduce the deferral to the highest deferral to the next highest dollar deferral, $11,200. The process continues to reduce to the next highest deferral, <2>. If the total excess contribution is not fully allocated, the process continues, <3>, until the full amount is distributed.

This process results in Employee A reducing his deferral by $100, Employee B reducing his deferral by $300, and Employee C reducing his deferral by $4,100. Averaging the ADR for each HC employee results in an ADP of 6.51% rounded to 6.5% – a deemed acceptable level.

In addition to the excess contributions being returned to the HC employees, any earnings on those contributions must also be returned or distributed to the HC employees.

Tax Treatment of Corrective Distributions

Corrective distributions are intended to properly adjust the HC's deferral amount. Therefore, if the HC deferred too much, the corrective distribution returns the excess deferral back resulting in a lower deferral, which corresponds with the ADP test. However, the distribution may be taxable in the year in which the deferral was taken or the following year, depending on when the distribution is received by the HC.

If the distribution is received within 2½ months after the plan year end, then the distribution will be taxable to the HC in the year in which the deferral was taken. In effect, it is as if the HC deferred the proper amount. However, if the distribution is received after the 2½ month period, then it is taxable in the following year. Thus, the HC would have received a larger deduction than should have been allowed in one plan year and more income the next.

> Randy defers $10,000 in the current year. However, after the ADP test is calculated, Randy is determined to have deferred $2,000 more than permitted under the test. Therefore, Randy needs to receive a corrective distribution of the $2,000 by March 15 of the next year. If this happens, then the $2,000 will be included in Randy's taxable income for the previous year. If the distribution is received after March 15 of the next year, then it is taxable to Randy in the next year and the employer must pay a 10 percent penalty on the amount not distributed within 2½ months after the plan year end, in this case $2,000.

EXAMPLE
5.17

Recharacterization

If a plan fails the ADP test, the plan sponsor may choose to recharacterize the excess deferrals (pretax) as after-tax employee contributions. This **recharacterization of deferrals** must be completed within 2½ months after the end of the plan year, at which time these recharacterized contributions are taxable to the employee.[1] If the excess contributions are not recharacterized within 2½ months of the plan year end, then the employer is subject to a 10 percent excise tax (penalty) on the amount of excess contributions (the amount that should have been recharacterized).

One potential problem with recharacterization is that the pretax contributions that are recharacterized to after-tax contributions may cause the plan to fail the actual contribution percentage (ACP) test. The ACP test is the exact same mathematical test as the ADP test except that instead of testing employee elective deferrals (actual deferral percentage, ADP), it tests employer matching contributions and employee after-tax contributions (actual contribution percentage). In addition, these after-tax contributions will be counted against the employee's annual additions limit of the lesser of $53,000 for year 2016 or 100 percent of compensation.

---

1. These after-tax employee contributions would then be subject to the ACP test.

Qualified Nonelective Contributions

An employer may choose to make a **qualified nonelective contribution (QNEC)** to NHC employees CODA plan accounts to increase the ADP of the NHC employees for purposes of passing the ADP test. The QNEC is made by the employer without regard to any elective deferral election made by the employee, so the contribution is made on behalf of all eligible employees. The contribution is treated as if deferred by the employee and therefore is included in the calculation of the ADP test to increase the ADP of the NHC. Since the contribution is treated as an employee elective deferral, it is also 100 percent vested in the employee.

EXAMPLE 5.18

The ADP of the HC employees is six percent and the ADP of the NHC is 3.75%. To pass the ADP test, the NHC employees must have an ADP at least equal to 4%. To increase the ADP of the NHC, the plan sponsor may elect to make a QNEC to all eligible employees that will increase the ADP of the NHC to 4%. Whatever amount of QNEC contributions is made will be considered 100% vested in the NHC employees.

Qualified Matching Contributions

A **qualified matching contribution (QMC)**, like a QNEC, increases the ADP of the NHC employees. However, unlike the QNEC, the QMC is only made to those eligible employees who had elected to defer during the plan year. Essentially, the QMC is an additional match from the employer to increase the deferral percentage of the NHC. Because the contributions are treated as being made by the employee, the QMC is 100 percent vested.

EXAMPLE 5.19

The ADP of the NHC employees was 6% for the plan year, and the ADP of the HC employees was 8.20% for the year. To pass the ADP nondiscrimination test, the plan sponsor would make QMC to all NHC employees who had elected to defer during the plan year to increase the ADP of the NHC to 6.20%. Those employees who had not deferred during the year would not receive any QMC. The QMC is 100% vested in the employee.

ACTUAL CONTRIBUTION PERCENTAGE (ACP)

The **actual contribution percentage test (ACP)**[1] is calculated the same way as the ADP test except that instead of testing the employee elective deferral contributions, the ACP test calculates a contribution percentage based on the sum of the following:

1. employee after-tax contributions, and
2. employer matching contributions.

After calculating the ACP for both NHC employees and HC employees, the two are compared using the same scale as the ADP test. If the plan does not pass the ACP test, the same corrective measures as used for the ADP test are used to either reduce the ACP of the HC or increase the ACP of the NHC.

SAFE HARBOR 401(k) PLANS

Plans that provide for a CODA are subject to the nondiscrimination rules discussed above as well as the top-heavy rules discussed in Chapter 3. For many employers and plan sponsors, the annual testing required to comply with these rules is administratively burdensome and costly. Fortunately, the IRC provides a **safe harbor** provision whereby the employer is not required to comply with the ADP test, the ACP test, or the top-heavy testing if the plan meets the safe harbor test.

An election must be made 60 days prior to the beginning of the plan year to convert a 401(k) plan to safe harbor status. To comply with safe harbor status, the plan must provide a minimum contribution that must be immediately 100 percent vested. The permissible contributions can either be a three percent minimum nonelective contribution or a matching contribution (discussed below). Under the nonelective contribution, all eligible employees would receive a 100 percent vested contribution equal to three percent of their compensation from the employer.

If the employer elects to use a match rather than the nonelective contribution, the standard safe harbor match formula requires the employer to match 100 percent of the first three percent of employee elective deferrals and 50 percent of employee elective deferrals greater than three percent and less than five percent.

SAFE HARBOR MATCH	
Employee Elective Deferral	**Employer Safe Harbor Match**
0%	0.0%
1%	1.0%
2%	2.0%
3%	3.0%
4%	3.5%
5% or more	4.0%

---

1. IRC §401(m).

Alternatively, the employer can provide for any formula that is at least as generous as this formula and satisfy the safe harbor provisions. A common formula found in many CODA safe harbor adoption agreements is a match of 100 percent up to four percent of compensation. This formula is slightly more generous than the one discussed above and is easier to communicate to employees.

Although matching contributions or nonelective contributions are required to be 100 percent vested, safe harbor plans allow the employer to avoid the ADP test, the ACP test, and the top-heavy rules and thus have become quite popular over the last few years.

KEY CONCEPTS

1. Why would an employer want to elect to convert a 401(k) plan to a safe harbor status?

2. What are the permissible employer contributions necessary to comply with safe harbor status?

3. What are the features of a Qualified Automatic Contribution Arrangement (QACA)?

Automatic Enrollment Safe Harbor 401(k) Plans

Some 401(k) plans have an "automatic enrollment" or "negative election" feature. Such plans provide that elective contributions by the employee are made at a specified rate unless the employee elects otherwise (i.e., elects not to make contributions or to make contributions at a different rate). However, the employee must have an effective opportunity to elect to receive cash in lieu of contributions. This feature has been approved by the IRS and is used to increase the elective deferrals of the NHC in an attempt to meet the nondiscrimination tests applicable to 401(k) plans.

The negative election can apply to both current employees as well as recently hired employees or employees who meet eligibility requirements.

> **EXAMPLE 5.20**
>
> After one year of service, Adrian meets the eligibility requirements for the ABC company 401(k) plan. The plan provides for a negative election in which the employer will deposit five percent of participants' compensation to the 401(k) plan. If Adrian earns $40,000, the plan sponsor will contribute $2,000 of her compensation to the plan unless she affirmatively elects to increase or decrease the contribution.

Under the Pension Protection Act of 2006, plans that contain a "qualified automatic enrollment feature" are eligible for a new nondiscrimination safe harbor and are treated as meeting the ADP test and the ACP test, and are not subject to the top-heavy rules. This type of plan is known as a **Qualified Automatic Contribution Arrangement (QACA).** The new automatic enrollment provisions are effective for plan years after 2007. A qualified automatic enrollment feature must meet certain requirements with respect to:
1. automatic deferral
2. matching or nonelective contributions
3. notice to employees

Automatic Deferral

To satisfy the automatic deferral requirement, a qualified automatic enrollment feature must provide that, unless an employee elects otherwise, the employee is treated as making an election to make elective deferrals equal to a stated percentage of compensation not in excess of 10 percent and at least equal to: three percent of compensation for the first year the deemed election applies to the participant; four percent during the second year; five percent during the third year; and six percent during the fourth year and thereafter. The stated percentage must be applied uniformly to all eligible employees.

QUALIFIED AUTOMATIC ENROLLMENT FEATURES

EXHIBIT 5.13

ELECTIVE DEFERRALS	
Period	Required Deferral Percentage
Year 1	At least 3%
Year 2	At least 4%
Year 3	At least 5%
Year 4 and thereafter	At least 6%

The automatic enrollment feature satisfies the contribution requirement if the employer either:
- meets the matching contribution requirement detailed below; or
- makes a nonelective contribution to a defined contribution plan of at least three percent of an employee's compensation on behalf of each nonhighly compensated employee who is eligible to participate in the automatic enrollment feature.

Matching Contribution Requirement

A plan generally satisfies the matching contribution requirement if, under the arrangement:
1. the employer makes a matching contribution on behalf of each nonhighly compensated employee that is equal to 100 percent of the employee's elective deferrals up to one percent of compensation and 50 percent of the employee's elective deferrals between one and six percent of compensation; and
2. the rate of match with respect to any elective deferrals for highly compensated employees is not greater than the rate of match for nonhighly compensated employees.

Any matching or other employer contributions taken into account in determining whether the requirements for a qualified automatic enrollment feature are satisfied must vest at least as rapidly as under two-year cliff vesting. In other words, employees with at least two years of service must be 100 percent vested with respect to such contributions.

Notice Requirement

To satisfy the notice requirement, each employee eligible to participate in the qualified automatic enrollment feature must receive notice of the feature informing the employee of such rights and obligations and is written in a manner calculated to be understood by the average employee. The notice must explain:
1. the employee's right under the arrangement to elect not to have elective contributions made on the employee's behalf or to elect to have contributions made in a different amount; and
2. how contributions made under the automatic enrollment arrangement will be invested in the absence of any investment election by the employee.

The employee must be given a reasonable period of time after receipt of the notice and before the first election contribution is to be made to make an election with respect to contributions and investments.

With this new additional safe harbor created by the PPA 2006, plan sponsors have three methods of dealing with the ADP / ACP nondiscrimination testing: either perform the tests and take corrective measures (if necessary), adopt a Safe Harbor Plan, or use the automatic enrollment provisions provided for in PPA 2006 (see Exhibit 5.9).

Reduction of Safe Harbor Contributions

In November 2013, the IRS issued regulations for 401(k) plans that provide guidance on permitted mid-year reductions or suspensions of safe harbor nonelective contributions in certain circumstances.[1] Companies are permitted to reduce contributions if the business is operating at an economic loss for the plan year[2] or the company provides specific a statement in the required notification to employees that the plan may be amended during the year to reduce or suspend safe harbor matching contributions and notice is actually provided prior to any reduction or suspension.

ELIGIBLE AUTOMATIC CONTRIBUTION ARRANGEMENT[3]

Under an eligible automatic contribution arrangement (EACA), a participant is treated as having elected to have the employer make contributions in an amount equal to a uniform percentage of compensation. This automatic election will remain in place until the participant specifically elects not to have such deferral percentage made (or elects a different percentage). There is no required deferral percentage and there is no required matching or non-elective contribution as is required with a qualified automatic contribution arrangement.

KEY CONCEPTS

1. Under what circumstances may individuals take distributions from their 401(k) plan?

2. Define "hardship distributions."

Under an EACA, participants are permitted to withdraw their automatic contributions to the plan if there is an election to do so no later than 90 days after the date of the first elective contributions under the EACA. In addition, the participant must withdraw the entire amount of EACA default contributions, including any earnings thereon.

If the plan allows withdrawals under the EACA, the amount of the withdrawal other than the amount of any designated Roth contributions must be included in the employee's gross income for the tax year in which the distribution is made. The additional 10 percent tax on early distributions will not apply to the distribution.

---

1. Under Treas. Reg. §1.401(k)-3.
2. As described in IRC §412(c)(2)(A).
3. IRC 414(w).

401(k) NON-DISCRIMINATION TESTING

EXHIBIT
5.14

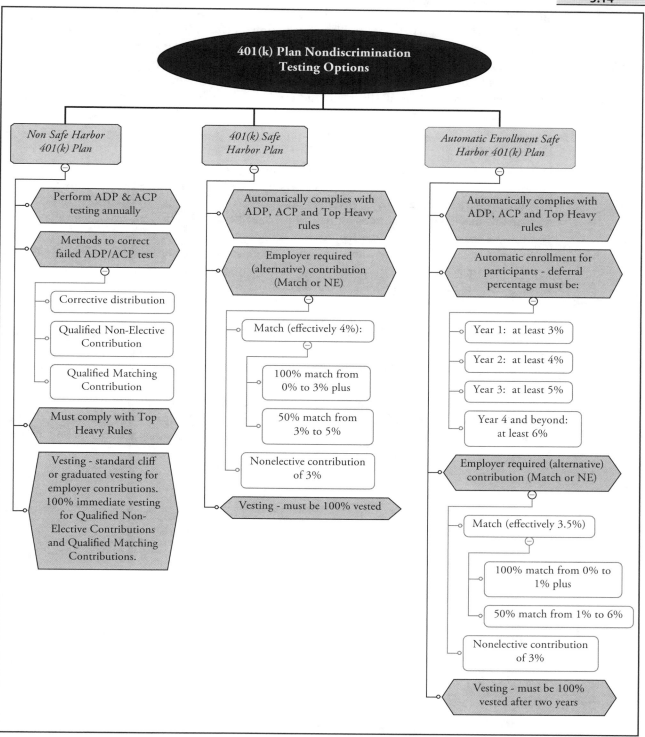

401(k) Plan Nondiscrimination Testing Options

Non Safe Harbor 401(k) Plan

- Perform ADP & ACP testing annually
- Methods to correct failed ADP/ACP test
  - Corrective distribution
  - Qualified Non-Elective Contribution
  - Qualified Matching Contribution
- Must comply with Top Heavy Rules
- Vesting - standard cliff or graduated vesting for employer contributions. 100% immediate vesting for Qualified Non-Elective Contributions and Qualified Matching Contributions.

401(k) Safe Harbor Plan

- Automatically complies with ADP, ACP and Top Heavy rules
- Employer required (alternative) contribution (Match or NE)
  - Match (effectively 4%):
    - 100% match from 0% to 3% plus
    - 50% match from 3% to 5%
  - Nonelective contribution of 3%
- Vesting - must be 100% vested

Automatic Enrollment Safe Harbor 401(k) Plan

- Automatically complies with ADP, ACP and Top Heavy rules
- Automatic enrollment for participants - deferral percentage must be:
  - Year 1: at least 3%
  - Year 2: at least 4%
  - Year 3: at least 5%
  - Year 4 and beyond: at least 6%
- Employer required (alternative) contribution (Match or NE)
  - Match (effectively 3.5%):
    - 100% match from 0% to 1% plus
    - 50% match from 1% to 6%
  - Nonelective contribution of 3%
- Vesting - must be 100% vested after two years

PLAN LOANS

Although distributions to employees are generally not permitted until retirement or termination, qualified plans are permitted to make loans to plan participants. However, plan loans must be made available to all participants and beneficiaries on an effectively equal basis, must be limited in amount, must be paid back within a certain time period, must bear a reasonable rate of interest, must be adequately secured, and the administrator must maintain proper accounting for the loans. Although any qualified plan could establish a loan provision, they are generally only found in CODA type plans, such as 401(k) plans and 403(b) plans. Chapter 7 includes a full discussion of the rules related to qualified plan loans.

DISTRIBUTIONS

Participants of 401(k) plans can generally take distributions from the plan following the same rules as provided to other qualified plans (discussed in Chapter 7). However, all CODA type plans, including 401(k) plans, provide that in addition to the normal distribution options, plan participants may take distributions for hardships. Specifically, distributions may occur after:

- the retirement, death, or separation of service of the participant,
- the termination of the plan without the establishment of another plan,
- certain acquisitions of the company or company assets,
- the attainment of age 59½ by the participant, or
- certain hardships.

Distributions on account of any of these items are taxable as ordinary income to the extent the participant does not have an adjusted basis in the 401(k) plan and may also be subject to a 10 percent penalty. The full distribution rules and the application of the 10 percent early withdrawal penalty are discussed in Chapter 7.

It is important to note that distributions of elective deferrals from a 401(k) plan cannot take place merely by reason of the completion of a stated period of participation or the lapse of a fixed number of years. Profit sharing plans may permit distributions after a stated period of time; however, this is not the case for 401(k) plans.[1]

---

1. IRC §401(k)(2)(B)(ii).

Case Study 5.1

In **Sternberg v. IRS**,[1] the plaintiff, Irwin Sternberg ("Sternberg") brought an action against the Internal Revenue Service ("IRS") seeking a refund of taxes he paid for the 1997 tax year and a release from taxes still owed for that year.

In 1990, Sternberg retired from the Harris Company. In July 1990, Sternberg received a lump-sum distribution of $147,512 from his employer's 401(k) plan and timely rolled over this distribution into an IRA.

In 1997, Sternberg withdrew $211,007 from his IRA, representing the original roll-over of $147,512 plus deferred earnings from 1990 to 1997. On his 1997 tax return, Sternberg showed a tax liability of $40,956, primarily the result of a withdrawal of $211,007 from his IRA. Thereafter, Sternberg re-read the printed instructions accompanying IRS Form 1040 and "became aware of IRS Publication 590 and Form 8606 which were to be used in the determination of taxable distributions" from IRAs. On Form 8606 for "Nondeductible IRAs," Sternberg treated the original rollover of $147,512 as a nondeductible contribution to his IRA. After following the remaining instructions on Form 8606, Sternberg calculated his taxable IRA distribution for 1997 as being $83,347, not $211,007.

Based on this new number, Sternberg then filed an amended Form 1040 tax return in June 2000 that reported a total tax assessment of only $1,819 for the 1997 tax year. Accordingly, Sternberg claimed that the IRS owed him $36,741 in overpaid taxes. By letter, the IRS disallowed Sternberg's amended tax return on the grounds that, under IRC §408(d), the IRA distribution taken in 1997 was fully taxable.

Both parties agreed that Sternerg rolled over $147,512 from his employer's 401(k) into an IRA in 1990 without having to pay tax on the 401(k) distribution. Both parties also agreed that Sternberg received a distribution of $211,007 in 1997 (the original rollover plus earnings from 1990 to 1997) from the IRA, and reported the distribution as taxable on his 1997 tax return. The court found that Sternberg erroneously characterized his $147,512 rollover in 1990 as a nondeductible contribution to his IRA, when the relevant statutes, regulations, and publications establish that the rollover only deferred the taxes that he would have owed had he elected to keep the 401(k) distribution.

Under the Internal Revenue Code, if "any amount ... distributed from an individual retirement or individual retirement annuity" is paid to the owner of the annuity, and the entire amount is then rolled over into an individual retirement account within 60 days, the amount distributed is not subject to income tax at that time.[2]

---

1. **Sternberg v. Internal Revenue Service**, 2004 WL 790219 (E.D.N.Y.), 93 A.F.T.R.2d 2004-1388 (Feb. 9, 2004).
2. IRC §402(c); 26 C.F.R. §1.408 4(b).

Hardship Distributions

Distributions on account of hardship must be limited to the maximum distributable amount. The maximum distributable amount is equal to the employee's total elective deferral contributions as of the date of distribution, reduced by the amount of previous distributions of elective contributions. Thus, the maximum distributable amount does not include earnings, Qualified Nonelective Contributions (QNECs) or Qualified Matching Contributions (QMCs), unless certain grandfather rules apply. These grandfather rules relate to amounts that were credited to an employee's account prior to December 31, 1988.[1]

EXHIBIT 5.15

MAXIMUM HARDSHIP DISTRIBUTIONS

Employee Deferral Contribution at Date of Distribution
less: (Previous Distributions)
equals: Maximum Distributable Amount

EXAMPLE 5.21

Hardy defers $5,000 of his annual compensation into the company 401(k) plan every year. He has been doing so for the last ten years. Therefore, his maximum distributable amount is equal to his total elective deferrals, or $50,000. If he had previously received a hardship distribution, then the amount of that distribution would reduce the $50,000 maximum distributable amount.

Hardship distributions can only be provided if there is an immediate and heavy financial need and the withdrawal is necessary to satisfy such need. Whether an employee has an immediate and heavy financial need is to be determined based on all the relevant facts and circumstances. Generally, for example, the need to pay funeral expenses of a family member would constitute an immediate and heavy financial need. A distribution made to an employee for the purchase of a boat or television would generally not constitute a distribution made on account of an immediate and

1. Treas. Reg. §1.401(k)-1(d)(3).

heavy financial need. A financial need may be immediate and heavy even if it was reasonably foreseeable or voluntarily incurred by the employee.[1]

A distribution is deemed to be on account of an immediate and heavy financial need of the employee if the distribution is for any of the following:

- expenses for medical care described in IRC §213(d) previously incurred by the employee, the employee's spouse, or any dependents of the employee (as defined in IRC §152) or necessary for these persons to obtain medical care described in IRC §213(d);
- costs directly related to the purchase of a principal residence for the employee (excluding mortgage payments);
- payment of tuition, related educational fees, and room and board expenses for up to the next 12 months of post-secondary education for the employee or the employee's spouse, children, or dependents (as defined in IRC §152); or
- payments necessary to prevent the eviction of the employee from the employee's principal residence or foreclosure on the mortgage on that residence.

A distribution is treated as necessary to satisfy an immediate and heavy financial need of an employee only to the extent the amount of the distribution is not in excess of the amount required to satisfy the financial need. For this purpose, the amount required to satisfy the financial need may include any amounts necessary to pay any federal, state, or local income taxes or penalties reasonably anticipated to result from the distribution.

A distribution is not treated as necessary to satisfy an immediate and heavy financial need of an employee to the extent the need may be relieved from other resources that are reasonably available to the employee. This determination generally is to be made on the basis of all the relevant facts and circumstances. For these purposes, the employee's resources are deemed to include those assets of the employee's spouse and minor children that are reasonably available to the employee. Thus, for example, a vacation home owned by the employee and the employee's spouse, whether as community property, joint tenants, tenants by the entirety, or tenants in common, generally will be deemed a resource of the employee. However, property held for the employee's child under an irrevocable trust or under the Uniform Gifts to Minors Act (or comparable State law) is not treated as a resource of the employee.

An immediate and heavy financial need generally may be treated as one not capable of being relieved from other resources that are reasonably available to the employee. An employer can rely upon the employee's written representation, unless the employer has actual knowledge to the contrary, that the need cannot reasonably be relieved from any of the following:

- through reimbursement or compensation by insurance or otherwise,
- by liquidation of the employee's assets,
- by cessation of elective contributions or employee contributions under the plan,
- by other distributions or nontaxable loans (at the time of the loan) from plans maintained by the employer or by any other employer, or
- by borrowing from commercial sources on reasonable commercial terms in an amount sufficient to satisfy the need.

---

1. Treas. Reg. §1.401(k)-1(d)(3).

Hardship distributions are taxed as ordinary income and may be subject to the 10 percent early withdrawal penalty. Distributions are not subject to the 20 percent statutory withholding requirements since hardship distributions are not eligible for rollover treatment. Those taking a hardship distribution are suspended from making future contributions to the plan for six months.

EXAMPLE 5.22

Dalmart Co. maintains Plan Y, a profit sharing plan that includes a CODA that does not permit participant loans. However, Plan Y provides that elective contributions under the arrangement may be distributed to an eligible employee on account of hardship using the deemed immediate and heavy financial need provisions. Amanda is an eligible employee in Plan Y with an account balance of $50,000. The total amount of elective deferral contributions made by Amanda, who has not previously received a distribution from Plan Y, is $20,000. Amanda requests a $15,000 hardship distribution of her elective deferral contributions to pay six months of college tuition and room and board expenses for her dependent child. At the time of the distribution request, Amanda's sole asset (that is reasonably available to Amanda within the meaning of the code) is a savings account with an available balance of $10,000.

A distribution is made on account of hardship only if the distribution is made both on account of Amanda's immediate and heavy financial need. A distribution for payment of up to the next 12 months of post-secondary education and room and board expenses for Amanda's dependent child is deemed to be on account of an immediate and heavy financial need of Amanda.

However, the distribution is only treated as necessary to satisfy Amanda's immediate and heavy financial need to the extent the need may not be relieved from other resources reasonably available to Amanda. Since Amanda has a $10,000 savings account as a reasonably available resource, it must be taken into account in determining the amount necessary to satisfy Amanda's immediate and heavy financial need. Thus, Amanda may only receive a distribution of $5,000 ($15,000 - $10,000) of her elective deferral contributions on account of this hardship plus an amount necessary to pay any federal, state, or local income taxes or penalties reasonably anticipated to result from the hardship distribution.

EXAMPLE 5.23

The facts are the same as in Example 5.22. Doug, another employee of Dalmart Co. has a vested account balance of $25,000. The total amount of elective deferral contributions made by Doug, who has not previously received a distribution from Plan Y, is $15,000. Doug requests a $10,000 distribution of his elective deferral contributions to pay six months of college tuition and room and board expenses for his dependent child. Doug makes a written representation (with respect to which Dalmart Co. has no actual knowledge to the contrary) that the need cannot reasonably be relieved:

- through reimbursement or compensation by insurance or otherwise,
- by liquidation of the employee's assets,
- by cessation of elective contributions or employee contributions under the plan,

- by other distributions or nontaxable (at the time of the loan) loans from plans maintained by the employer or by any other employer, or
- by borrowing from commercial sources on reasonable commercial terms in an amount sufficient to satisfy the need.

A distribution for payment of up to the next 12 months of post-secondary education and room and board expenses for Doug's dependent child is deemed to be on account of Doug's immediate and heavy financial need. In addition, because Dalmart Co. can rely on Doug's written representation, the distribution is considered necessary to satisfy Doug's immediate and heavy financial need. Therefore, Doug may receive a $10,000 distribution of his elective contributions on account of hardship plus an amount necessary to pay any federal, state, or local income taxes or penalties reasonably anticipated to result from the distribution.

DB(k) RETIREMENT PLANS

COMBINED DEFINED BENEFIT AND QUALIFIED CASH OR DEFERRED ARRANGEMENTS PLAN

A **DB(k) retirement plan** incorporates, under one single plan with a single trust, a defined benefit plan combined with a 401(k) arrangement. For plan years beginning in 2010 and later, a DB(k) plan can be established by a sponsoring employer who employs an average of 2 to 500 workers in the preceding calendar year and employs at least two workers at the beginning of the plan year (for a new employer the determination is based on the average number of employees anticipated to employ during the current calendar year). The defined benefit and defined contribution components must meet the benefit, contribution, vesting, and nondiscrimination requirements under IRC §414(x). Note: Under IRC §414(x), after three years of service the employee has a nonforfeitable right to 100 percent of employee's accrued benefits derived from employer contributions under the defined benefit portion of the plan, and to employer nonelective contributions made under the defined contribution portion of the plan.

DEFINED BENEFIT COMPONENT OF DB(k)

The minimum benefit provided by the defined benefit portion of the plan, must provide each participant with an annual retirement amount that is not less than the worker's final average pay times the lesser of: (1) one percent multiplied times the participant's years of service, or (2) 20 percent. The participant's final average pay is computed by averaging up to five consecutive years of the worker's highest compensation. A plan participant must be fully vested in the defined benefit plan after completion of three years of service.

DB(k) plans are permitted to offer a cash balance formula as the defined benefit part of the plan. In such a case, the pay credits must not be less than the following table, which is based on the age of the employee:

30 or less 2%
Over 30 but less than 40 .... 4%
40 or over but less than 50 .... 6%
50 or over 8%

The DB(k) plan design will either provide a normal defined benefit or one with a hypothetical account (i.e., cash balance).

DEFINED CONTRIBUTION COMPONENT OF DB(k)

The 401(k) portion of the combined plan is considered an automatic contribution arrangement if it meets notice and election requirements and if the plan provides that each worker eligible to participate is treated as having elected to participate in a contribution amount equal to four percent of the worker's compensation (unless the employee elects out or selects a lower rate of contribution). Employer matching contributions must be made in an amount equal to 50 percent of the employee elective contributions up to four percent of compensation. Participants must be immediately fully vested in any required employer matching contributions. After completion of three years of service, a participant is fully vested in any employer nonelective contributions. A DB(k) plan is deemed to satisfy the top-heavy rules, as well as the rules for ADP and ACP.

Small companies that are currently managing both a benefit pension plan and a 401(k) plan may consider the DB(k) plan to reduce plan costs and paperwork. In addition, small companies that employ skilled workers, such as engineering, law, and accounting firms, may consider the plan to competitively attract talented employees. In order to offer the plan, a small company needs adequate cash to pay the costs of adopting the DB(k). Because the DB(k) retirement plan may have limited application, the individual 401(k) (covered earlier in this chapter) may be an attractive alternative to the DB(k) plan.

QUICK QUIZ 5.9

1. A distribution from a 401(k) plan is not available until the plan participant either retires or dies.
   a. True
   b. False

2. A hardship distribution can be taken from a 401(k) plan for an amount equal to the employee's total elective contribution less the value of any previous hardship distributions.
   a. True
   b. False

3. Hardship withdrawals are available if there is an immediate and heavy financial burden even if the participant has other assets available to satisfy the need.
   a. True
   b. False

False, True, False.

DB(k) Plans

EXHIBIT
5.16

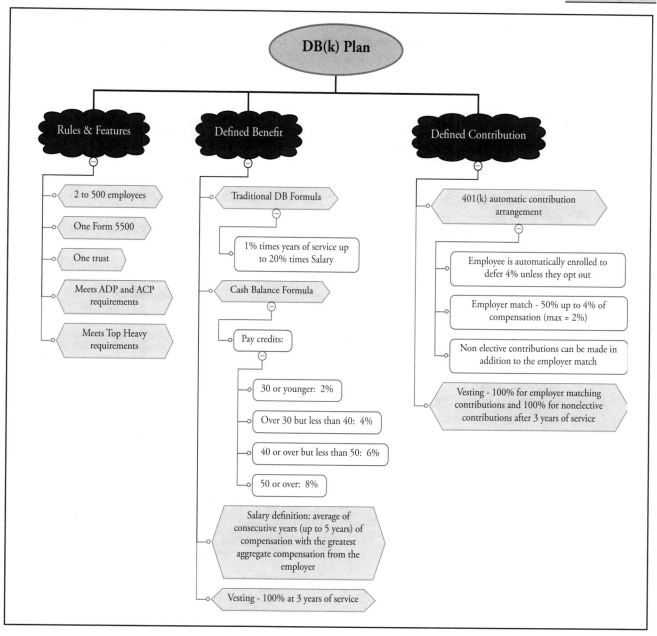

DB(k) Plan

Rules & Features

- 2 to 500 employees
- One Form 5500
- One trust
- Meets ADP and ACP requirements
- Meets Top Heavy requirements

Defined Benefit

- Traditional DB Formula
  - 1% times years of service up to 20% times Salary
- Cash Balance Formula
  - Pay credits:
    - 30 or younger: 2%
    - Over 30 but less than 40: 4%
    - 40 or over but less than 50: 6%
    - 50 or over: 8%
- Salary definition: average of consecutive years (up to 5 years) of compensation with the greatest aggregate compensation from the employer
- Vesting - 100% at 3 years of service

Defined Contribution

- 401(k) automatic contribution arrangement
  - Employee is automatically enrolled to defer 4% unless they opt out
  - Employer match - 50% up to 4% of compensation (max = 2%)
  - Non elective contributions can be made in addition to the employer match
- Vesting - 100% for employer matching contributions and 100% for nonelective contributions after 3 years of service

US GOVERNMENT THRIFT SAVINGS PLANS

The **Thrift Savings Plan** (TSP) is a retirement savings and investment plan for Federal employees and members of the uniformed services, including the Ready Reserve. It was established by Congress in the Federal Employees' Retirement System Act of 1986 and offers the same types of savings and tax benefits that are provided in 401(k) plans.

CONTRIBUTIONS

There are three sources of contributions to the TSP:
1. employee contributions
2. agency automatic contributions
3. matching contributions

The employee contributions are the same as 401(k) salary deferrals and have the same limit, including catch up contributions for those who have attained the age of 50 within the year. The TSP includes an automatic enrollment into the plan such that a three percent contribution is automatically deducted from salary and contributed to the plan. This negative election can be changed by the participant.

Employees covered by the Federal Employees' Retirement System (FERS) automatically receive contributions of one percent of basic pay to the TSP. These contributions are called Agency Automatic (1%) Contributions and generally vest after three years.

The third type of contribution is a matching contribution. Employee deferrals are matched dollar-for-dollar up to three percent of pay and 50 percent from three percent to five percent.[1] With an employee deferral of five percent or more, the match is four percent of compensation. Matching contributions are always fully vested.

The contribution limit is the same as with 401(k) plans at $18,000 (2016)[2] with a maximum deferral of $24,000 (2016) for those who have attained age 50. Total contributions are also limited to the IRC §415(c) limit of $53,000 (2016).

Other similarities of the TSP and 401(k) plans are rollover rules, both in and out of the plan, loan provisions, and hardship withdrawals. In addition, participants in the TSP have an array of investment options to choose from ranging from government securities to international equities. Ultimately, the TSP is very much a government version of the standard safe harbor 401(k) plan.

---

1. This is the same formula as for a safe harbor 401(k) plan.
2. Contributions to the TSP by uniformed service members in a combat zone are contributed to the TSP as "tax-exempt" are not subject to the IRC elective deferral limit, but are considered for purposes of the IRC §415(c) limit. The term "uniformed services" means the Armed Forces, the Army National Guard and the Air National Guard when engaged in active duty for training, inactive duty training, or full-time National Guard duty, the commissioned corps of the Public Health Service, and any other category of persons designated by the President in time of war or national emergency.

KEY TERMS

ACTUAL CONTRIBUTION PERCENTAGE TEST (ACP) - A nondiscrimination test that limits the sum of employee after-tax contributions and employer matching contributions for the HC based on the sum of employee after-tax contributions and employer matching contributions for the NHC.

ACTUAL DEFERRAL PERCENTAGE TEST (ADP) - A nondiscrimination test that limits employee elective deferrals for the highly compensated employees (HC) based on the elective deferrals of non-highly compensated employees (NHC).

AGE-BASED PROFIT SHARING PLAN - A qualified profit sharing plan that uses a combination of age and compensation as the basis for allocating the contribution to a participant's account.

CASH OR DEFERRED ARRANGEMENT (CODA) - Permits an employee to defer a portion of his salary on a pretax basis to a qualified plan or receive the salary as current taxable income.

CATCH-UP CONTRIBUTION - A contribution that allows those nearing retirement to increase their deferral contributions to improve their financial situation for retirement. An elective contribution for employees 50 and over that allows them to increase their elective deferral limit by up to $6,000 for 2016.

CORRECTIVE DISTRIBUTION - A distribution to satisfy the ADP or ACP test that reduces the elective deferrals or contributions of the HC employees by distributing or returning the funds to the HC employees.

COVERED COMPENSATION LIMIT - The maximum employee compensation that may be considered for contributions to qualified plans or the accrual of benefits to a qualified plan. For 2016, the covered compensation limit is $265,000.

DB(k) RETIREMENT PLAN - For plan years beginning in 2010 and later, a DB(k) retirement plan incorporates, under one single plan with a single trust, a defined benefit plan combined with a 401(k) arrangement.

EMPLOYEE ELECTIVE DEFERRAL CONTRIBUTIONS - Pretax employee contributions to a qualified retirement plan with a CODA. The employee must chose to defer the compensation before earning the compensation.

EMPLOYER MATCHING CONTRIBUTIONS - Employer provided contributions to a qualified retirement plan, usually a 401(k) plan that are based on the employee contributions.

FORFEITURES - The percentage or amount of a participant's accrued benefit that was not vested to the employee at the employee's termination from the plan sponsor. The forfeited amount stays in the plan and may be allocated to the other plan participants (defined contribution plan) or reduce future plan costs (defined contribution plan or defined benefit plan).

KEY TERMS

HARDSHIP DISTRIBUTIONS - A distribution from a 401(k) plan because the employee has an immediate and heavy financial need and the withdrawal is necessary to satisfy the need. The distribution is taxable and subject to penalties to the extent the participant has other resources to have satisfied the financial need.

INDIVIDUAL 401(k) PLAN - An easy-to-administer, low-cost retirement plan designed for self-employed individuals and owner-only businesses.

NEW COMPARABILITY PLAN - A qualified profit sharing plan in which contributions are made to employees' accounts based on their respective classification in the company as defined by the plan sponsor.

NONDISCRIMINATORY - A requirement of all qualified plans. The eligibility rules, coverage requirements, and contributions allocations of a qualified plan cannot discriminate against the rank-and-file employees for the benefit of shareholder, officers, and highly compensated employees.

ONE YEAR OF SERVICE - 1,000 hours of service with an employer within a 12 month period.

PERMITTED DISPARITY (SOCIAL SECURITY INTEGRATION) - A technique or method of allocating qualified plan contributions to an employee account that provides a higher contribution to those employees whose compensation is in excess of the Social Security wage base ($118,500 for 2016) or selected integration level for the plan year.

PROFIT SHARING PLAN - A qualified retirement plan established and maintained by an employer where the employer makes deductible contributions on behalf of the employees, the assets grow tax-deferred, and if there is a CODA feature, the employee also makes pretax contributions.

QUALIFIED AUTOMATIC CONTRIBUTION ARRANGEMENT (QACA) - A plan that contains a "qualified automatic enrollment feature" and is eligible for a new nondiscrimination safe harbor under PPA 2006.

QUALIFIED MATCHING CONTRIBUTION (QMC) - Additional matching contributions made by the employer to satisfy the ADP or ACP test that increases the ACP or ADP of the NHC employees by who had deferred compensation during the plan year.

QUALIFIED NONELECTIVE CONTRIBUTION (QNEC) - A contribution made by the employer to satisfy the ADP or ACP test that increases the ADP or ACP of the NHC employees by making additional contributions to all NHC eligible employees without regard to any elective deferral election made by the employees.

RECHARACTERIZATION OF DEFERRALS - To change the nature of any excess employee deferrals from pretax employee contributions to after-tax employee contributions.

KEY TERMS

SAFE HARBOR 401(k) PLANS - A 401(k) plan that satisfies a minimum contribution or matching test and allows the plan sponsor to bypass the ADP test, the ACP test, and the top-heavy tests.

SOCIAL SECURITY INTEGRATION (PERMITTED DISPARITY) - A technique or method of allocating qualified plan contributions to an employee account that provides a higher contribution to those employees whose compensation is in excess of the Social Security wage base ($118,500 for 2016) or selected integration level for the plan year.

STANDARD ELIGIBILITY - The general eligibility requirement that requires an employer to consider an employee eligible when the employee attains 21 years of age and has completed one-year of service (defined as 1,000 hours of service with an employer within a 12-month period).

THRIFT PLAN - A qualified retirement plan that permits employees to make after-tax contributions to the plan. Although the contributions are taxable before being contributed to the plan, the account still benefits from tax-deferred growth on earnings.

THRIFT SAVINGS PLAN (TSP) - A retirement savings and investment plan for Federal employees and members of the uniformed services, including the Ready Reserve.

DISCUSSION QUESTIONS

1. Describe the key elements of a profit sharing plan as discussed in Treasury Regulation 1.401-1(b).

2. List the differences between pension plans and profit sharing plans.

3. When is the last date during the year that a profit sharing plan may be established and by when must contributions be made to the profit sharing plan?

4. Explain the differences between the standard allocation formula, permitted disparity, age-based profit sharing plans, and new comparability plans.

5. How can forfeitures be used within a profit sharing plan?

6. What are the eligibility requirements for profit sharing plans?

7. What are the applicable vesting rules for profit sharing plans?

8. When may distributions be taken from a profit sharing plan and how will they be taxed?

9. Describe the characteristics of a cash or deferred arrangement.

10. List the advantages of 401(k) plans to both employees and employers.

11. Which entities may establish a 401(k) plan?

12. Describe the eligibility rules for 401(k) plans.

13. What are the entrance dates rules for 401(k) plans?

14. Define "participation" and "negative elections" with regard to 401(k) plans.

15. How can employees make contributions to a 401(k) plan and what are the applicable limits?

16. What is the income tax impact of employee elective deferrals?

17. When must the employer deposit employee elective deferrals?

18. Describe the catch-up contribution available for some employees.

19. How are employee after-tax contributions taxed?

20. Describe matching contributions and their associated vesting schedules.

21. How can a profit sharing contribution be used with a 401(k) plan?

22. What is the purpose of the ADP test and how does it work?

23. How is the ADP test calculated?

24. What are the remedies available if a company fails the ADP test?

25. What are corrective distributions and how are they used to correct the ADP test?

26. What is recharacterization and how is it used to correct the ADP test?

27. What are qualified nonelective and matching contributions and how are they used to correct the ADP test?

28. Explain the pre-PPA 2006 safe harbor rules and how they affect 401(k) contributions.

29. When may distributions be taken from a 401(k) plan?

30. Describe the hardship distribution rules.

MULTIPLE CHOICE PROBLEMS

1. Which of the following is not true regarding profit sharing plans?

    a. The plan is established and maintained by the individual employee.

    b. Allows employees to derive benefit from profits of the company.

    c. Profit sharing plans cannot discriminate in favor of officers and shareholders.

    d. Profit sharing plans provide a definite predetermined formula for allocating the contributions made to the plan among the participants and for distributing the funds accumulated under the plan.

2. Which of the following statements is true?

    a. Profit sharing plans may not offer in-service withdrawals.

    b. Pension and profit sharing plans are both subject to mandatory funding requirements.

    c. Profit sharing plans allow annual employer contributions up to 25 percent of the employer's covered compensation.

    d. The legal promise of a profit sharing plan is to pay a pension at retirement.

3. Andi, the 100 percent owner of Andi's Day Care, would like to establish a profit sharing plan. Andi's Day Care's tax year ends July 31 to coincide with the school year. What is the latest day Andi can establish and contribute to the plan?

    a. Andi must establish and contribute to the plan by December 31 of the year in which she would like to establish the plan.

    b. Andi must establish the plan by July 31 of the year in which she would like to have the plan and contribute by May 15 of the following year assuming she filed the appropriate extensions.

    c. Andi must establish the plan by July 31 of the year in which she would like to establish the plan and contribute by December 31.

    d. Andi must establish the plan by December 31 of the year in which she would like to establish the plan and contribute to the plan by April 15 of the following year.

4. Mikael opened a fabulous restaurant ten years ago. The food is so exceptional that the restaurant has become one of the top spots in the city. Mikael, age 55, is the sole owner with compensation of $265,000. Mikael's son Jamel, age 28, is the master chef with compensation of $100,000. Jamel has been with the restaurant full time since he turned 18. Mikael also employs 15 other individuals whose ages range between 25 and 35 and have compensation on average of $40,000 per year. Mikael wants to establish a profit sharing plan. Which of the following statements is true?

    a. If Mikael selected the standard allocation method and the plan contributes 10 percent per individual, the plan will contribute $53,000 to Mikael's account.

    b. If Mikael selected the permitted disparity method and the plan contributes 10 percent per individual, the contribution the company makes for Mikael will be increased.

    c. Considering the needs and wants of Mikael and Jamel, an age-based profit sharing plan is the best plan for both of them.

    d. A new comparability plan is the least expensive, simplest way to meet both Mikael and Jamel's retirement needs.

5. Kathi's Cheerleading Uniforms has 4 employees. The company has a profit sharing plan that has made contributions every year. The plan is designed to maximize the contribution to Kathi and has reached Kathi's 415(c) limit each year. The company made a 20 percent contribution yesterday on behalf of all employees. The employee census and account balances are as follows:

EMPLOYEE	OWNERSHIP	COVERED COMPENSATION	CURRENT BALANCE	NONVESTED PLAN BALANCE	VESTED PLAN BALANCE
Kathi	100%	$265,000	$201,000	$0	$201,000
Darrin	0%	$30,000	$15,600	$10,800	$4,800
Carroll	0%	$20,000	$8,000	$6,400	$1,600
Lee	0%	$20,000	$8,000	$6,400	$1,600
Total	100%	$335,000	$232,600	$23,600	$209,000

Today, after a huge blow up, Kathi fired Carroll. Which of the following statements regarding forfeitures is correct (assume the plan meets all necessary testing requirements)?

    a. If the plan document permitted allocation of forfeitures based on compensation, then Kathi would receive $5,062.69 of Carroll's unvested plan balance.

    b. If the plan document permitted reduction of plan contributions for forfeitures, Carroll's $8,000 balance could be used to offset future plan contributions.

    c. Since Kathi fired Carroll, Carroll becomes 100 percent vested in her plan assets and there is no forfeiture of plan assets.

    d. Given the company census and plan information, the appropriate plan choice for forfeitures is to use them to reduce future plan contributions.

6. Skatium, the city's most popular roller skating rink, has a profit sharing plan for their employees. Skatium has the following employee information:

EMPLOYEE	AGE	LENGTH OF SERVICE
Brett	62	14 years
Greer	57	14 years
Jennifer	32	6 months
Dan	22	2 years
Karen	19	2 years
Mike	17	6 months
Craig	16	1 year

The plan requires the standard eligibility and the least generous graduated vesting schedule available. The plan is not top-heavy. All of the following statements are correct except:

    a. Dan and Karen are 20 percent vested in their benefits.

    b. Brett and Greer became 100 percent vested when they had been employed for six years.

    c. Three of the seven people are eligible to participate in the plan.

    d. Craig is not eligible for the plan.

7. Which of the following statements is true regarding CODAs?

    a. A 401(k) can only be established as a stand alone plan.

    b. A CODA is allowed with a profit-sharing plan, stock bonus plan, and a cash balance pension plan.

    c. Contributions can only be made after-tax.

    d. CODAs are employee self-reliant plans.

8. All of the following are advantages of a 401(k) plan except:

    a. Employees are permitted to shelter current income from taxation in a 401(k) plan.

    b. Employers can sponsor 401(k) safe harbor plans without committing to annual contributions and without creating a deferred liability.

    c. Earnings grow tax-deferred until distributed.

    d. Employers can establish 401(k) plans with minimal expense.

9. Which of the following entities is unable to establish a 401(k) plan?

    a. Government entity.

    b. LLC.

    c. Partnership.

    d. Tax-exempt entity.

10. Ansley's Art Gallery has a profit sharing plan. The plan requires employees to be employed two years before they can enter the plan. The plan has two entrance dates per year, January and July 1st. Assume today is December 1, 2018 and the Gallery has the following employee information.

EMPLOYEE	AGE	START DATE
Ansley	42	1/1/2016
Ginny	37	5/1/2016
Max	31	8/12/2016
Alex	29	6/4/2017

Which of the following statements is true?

   a. As of today, three individuals have entered the plan.

   b. Ginny entered the plan on 5/1/2017.

   c. Alex will enter the plan on 1/1/2019.

   d. As of today, three individuals are eligible for the plan.

11. Which of the following is true regarding negative elections?

   1. A negative election is a device where the employee is deemed to have elected a specific deferral unless the employee specifically elects out of such election in writing.

   2. Negative elections are no longer approved by the IRS.

   3. Negative elections are only available for employees who enter the plan when it is first established and are not available for new employees.

   a. 1 only.

   b. 1 and 2.

   c. 2 and 3.

   d. 1, 2, and 3.

12. Rex, age 47, an employee at Water Waste, is considering contributing to a 401(k) plan during 2016. Which of the following statements are true?

   a. Rex can make a $24,000 elective deferral contribution to a 401(k) plan for 2016.

   b. If Rex does make an elective deferral contribution, the amount is not currently subject to income or payroll taxes.

   c. Rex can contribute $18,000 to a 401(k) plan and an additional $18,000 to a 401(k) Roth account in the current year.

   d. Water Waste must deposit Rex's elective deferral contribution to the plan as soon as reasonably possible.

13. Tyler's Bike Shop has a 401(k) plan that offers an employer match of dollar-for-dollar up to four percent of employee compensation. Although the plan provides for the least generous graduated vesting schedule available, it does allow employees to enter the plan on their hire date. The employee census is as follows:

EMPLOYEE	AGE	COVERED COMP	EMPLOYEE DEFERRAL	YEARS IN PLAN
Tyler	57	$150,000	8.67%	10
Tanya	23	$100,000	Not yet participating	
Timmy	37	$80,000	16.25%	10
Tom	31	$76,000	4.00%	5

Tyler established the plan ten years ago to benefit him and his only employee, his son Timmy. Since then Tyler hired his other son, Tom, and his new wife Tanya. Tyler wanted to establish the 401(k) plan to encourage his children to save for their future. He also wanted a vesting schedule to ensure that they would learn the responsibility of sticking to their employment commitments. The family has come to you for recommendations to help them maximize their plan contributions. Since both of his sons have shown commitment over the past years, Tyler is willing to make some alterations to the plan in order to increase the retirement savings for all of them. Which of the following would not be one of your recommendations?

   a. Tyler and Tom should increase their contributions in order to reach the total maximum deferral limit.

   b. Tanya should enter the plan and contribute 20 percent of her salary.

   c. Tom is not 100 percent vested in the employer match, thus he should stay employed at least one more year.

   d. Tyler should consider adding a profit sharing contribution to the plan in order to increase the contributions.

14. Sew What, the best seamstress shop in town, sponsors a 401(k) plan. The plan provides a dollar-for-dollar match for employee contributions up to six percent and has immediate vesting for all contributions. For ADP purposes, the company has not made the top 20 percent election for the determination of who is highly compensated. The company has the following employee information:

Employee	Ownership	Compensation	Elective Deferral	Deferral Percentage
Lois	93%	$201,000	$14,000	6.97%
Frank	5%	$150,000	$14,000	9.33%
Karen	2%	$140,000	$12,600	9.00%
Jeanette	-	$40,000	$4,000	10.00%
Joyce	-	$30,000	-	0.00%
Ronnie	-	$30,000	$1,800	6.00%
Kali	-	$30,000	-	0.00%

Which of the following statements is correct?

   a. Karen is not highly compensated.

   b. The plan passes the ADP test if Joyce and Kali were not eligible.

   c. Joyce and Kali are not considered when calculating the ADP test because they do not contribute.

   d. The top heavy rules require Sew What to make a 3% contribution for Jeanette, Joyce, Ronnie, and Kali.

15. BigCorp, LLC has a 401(k) plan that allows for hardship distributions. Sandra would like to return to school to get a Masters degree. She has $3,000 in her savings account to use, but would like to take a hardship distribution from her 401(k) plan for the maximum amount available. Sandra's program will take two years and cost $7,000 per year. Sandra's 401(k) account balance is $20,000. Sandra has never made any hardship distributions and her elective contributions to the plan total $10,000. How much can Sandra withdraw as a hardship distribution?

   a. $4,000.

   b. $7,000.

   c. $10,000.

   d. $20,000.

16. ABC Company has three employees: Ann, Brenda, and Curtis. Their compensation is $50,000, $150,000, and $200,000 respectively. ABC is considering establishing a straight 10% profit sharing plan or an integrated profit sharing plan using a 10% contribution for base compensation and 15.7% for excess compensation. Which of the following statements are correct?

    a. If the integrated plan is selected, then the total contribution for all employees is $56,524.

    b. The effect of the integrated plan results in an increase in Brenda's contribution of $1,796.

    c. If the integrated plan is selected, the base contribution for all employees is $53,000.

    d. If the integrated plan is selected, Curtis' total contribution is $31,400.

17. JJ is a Marine, who served our country for the last 25 years. He has $250,000 in his US Government Thrift Savings Plan. Which of the following plans is JJ's Thrift Plan most similar to?

    a. Defined benefit plan.

    b. Cash balance plan.

    c. Profit sharing plan.

    d. 401(k) plan.

18. Nex sponsors a DB(k) plan that provides benefits for all employees. Nex adopted the plan four years ago. Kleen, who is age 55 and earns $100,000, has been employed for the last ten years with Nex. Which of the following statements is correct regarding Kleen's benefits under Nex's DB(k) plan?

    a. Kleen will be limited on his deferral to the 401(k) plan because of the required contribution to the DB part of the plan.

    b. If the DB(k) plan provides for a cash balance option, then Kleen should be receiving pay credits of 6% per year.

    c. All benefits provided under the DB(k) plan will be 100 percent vested for Kleen.

    d. Because this plan is a proto-type DB(k) plan, Nex will not have to file a Form 5500.

19. Which of the following vesting schedules may a top-heavy profit sharing plan not use?

    a. 1 to 4 year graduated.

    b. 35% after 1 year, 70% after 2 years, and 100% after 3 years.

    c. 2 to 6 year graduated.

    d. 4 year cliff.

20. Aztec Clay Distributor is a family owned business that is owned by Alice, Bill, Chad and Zion. Alice and Bill are over 50. Zion is not an employee, rather a silent or somewhat silent partner. Alice and Bill are married and Chad is their 25-year-old son who has a degree in Soil Science from Dhaka University in Bangladesh. Aztec sponsors a 401(k) plan. The employee census information is in the chart below.

Employee	Ownership	Salary	Annual Elective Deferral	Account Balance	Status
Alice	30%	$330,000	$20,000	$400,000	Officer
Bill	3%	$210,000	$20,000	$600,000	
Chad	4%	$80,000	$10,000	$150,000	
Dave	0%	$180,000	$15,000	$150,000	Officer
Erin	0%	$140,000	$15,000	$100,000	
Frank	0%	$50,000	$8,000	$50,000	
Ginger	0%	$40,000	$0	$10,000	
Haley	0%	$30,000	$2,000	$30,000	
Irish	0%	$20,000	$1,000	$10,000	
Jen	0%	$20,000	$0	$5,000	
		$1,100,000	$91,000	$1,505,000	

Assuming the company did not elect the exception to the definition of highly compensated employees, the average ADP of the highly compensated employees can be no greater than what percent?

   a. 7.53%.
   b. 8.32%.
   c. 8.65%.
   d. 11.98%.

21. Aztec Clay Distributor is a family owned business that is owned by Alice, Bill, Chad and Zion. Alice and Bill are over 50. Zion is not an employee, rather a silent or somewhat silent partner. Alice and Bill are married and Chad is their 25-year-old son who has a degree in Soil Science from Dhaka University in Bangladesh. Aztec sponsors a 401(k) plan. The employee census information is in the chart below.

Employee	Ownership	Salary	Annual Elective Deferral	Account Balance	Status
Alice	30%	$330,000	$20,000	$400,000	Officer
Bill	3%	$210,000	$20,000	$600,000	
Chad	4%	$80,000	$10,000	$150,000	
Dave	0%	$180,000	$15,000	$150,000	Officer
Erin	0%	$140,000	$15,000	$100,000	
Frank	0%	$50,000	$8,000	$50,000	
Ginger	0%	$40,000	$0	$10,000	
Haley	0%	$30,000	$2,000	$30,000	
Irish	0%	$20,000	$1,000	$10,000	
Jen	0%	$20,000	$0	$5,000	
		$1,100,000	$91,000	$1,505,000	

If Aztec established a profit-sharing plan, what is the most that Aztec could contribute for 2016 to the profit-sharing plan?

    a. $184,000.

    b. $252,250.

    c. $258,750.

    d. $275,000.

22. Sheehan works for Andy Company and is a superior sales guy. His total compensation this year is $600,000. Andy sponsors an integrated profit sharing plan with a base percentage of 5.5% and a maximum excess percentage. It uses the current wage base as the integration level. How much will the company contribute for Sheehan for ?

    a. $14,300.

    b. $22,633.

    c. $29,150.

    d. $53,000.

23. Thibodaux Company sponsors an integrated profit sharing plan with a base percent of 20%. Boudreaux, who is 60 years old, earns $330,000 per year. Assuming the plan uses the 2016 Social Security wage base as the integration level, how much more will Boudreaux receive because the plan is integrated over a plan that contributes a flat 20% of compensation?

    a. $0.

    b. $5,500.

    c. $8,351.

    d. $12,056.

QUICK QUIZ EXPLANATIONS

QUICK QUIZ 5.1
1. False. A profit sharing plan allows all eligible employees to participate in the profits of the company. An eligible employee does not have to be an officer or shareholder to participate in a profit sharing plan.
2. False. A pension plan may not invest more than 10 percent of its assets in employer securities.
3. True.

QUICK QUIZ 5.2
1. False. Permitted disparity is a technique of allocating plan contributions to employees' accounts that will provide higher contributions to those employees whose compensation is in excess of the Social Security wage base (or integration level) for the plan year.
2. True.
3. False. New comparability plans are under great scrutiny by the IRS and the regulations associated with new comparability plans restrict their flexibility.

QUICK QUIZ 5.3
1. False. A profit sharing plan, like other qualified plans, may not require participants to wait more than two years to become eligible.
2. False. Under the PPA 2006, profit sharing plans must use a 3-year cliff vesting schedule or a 2 to 6 year graduated vesting schedule.
3. True.

QUICK QUIZ 5.4
1. False. For tax years after 1996, tax-exempt entities are permitted to establish 401(k) plans.
2. True.
3. True.

QUICK QUIZ 5.5
1. True.
2. False. A 401(k) must generally have two entrance dates per year to meet the requirements of a qualified plan.

QUICK QUIZ 5.6
1. True.
2. True.
3. False. Employee elective deferrals must be deposited and segregated from the employer's assets by the earliest date that is reasonably possible. However, the segregation of the funds must be completed by the 15th day of the month following the deferral from the employee's compensation.
4. True.
5. False. A negative election requires an employee to proactively opt-out of the plan.

QUICK QUIZ EXPLANATIONS

QUICK QUIZ 5.7
1. False. Matching contributions vest on a 3 year cliff or 2 to 6 year graded vesting schedule.
2. True.
3. False. The annual deferral limit of $18,000 for 2016 is the maximum that could be contributed to either account or in combination. A taxpayer cannot defer $18,000 to the pre-tax account and another $18,000 to the Roth account.

QUICK QUIZ 5.8
1. True.
2. True.
3. False. If a CODA fails the ADP test, there are four alternative remedies to bring the plan into compliance: corrective distributions, recharacterization, qualified nonelective contributions (QNEC), or qualified matching contributions (QMC).
4. False. The pre-PPA 2006 safe harbor provisions require that matching contributions or nonelective contributions must be 100% vested to avoid calculating the ADP test.

QUICK QUIZ 5.9
1. False. In addition to the normal distribution options, 401(k) participants may also take distributions for hardships.
2. True.
3. False. Hardship distributions can only be provided if there is an immediate and heavy financial need and the withdrawal is necessary to satisfy the need (i.e., the participant does not have other resources that could be used to satisfy the need).

STOCK BONUS PLANS AND EMPLOYEE STOCK OWNERSHIP PLANS

LEARNING OBJECTIVES

After reading this chapter, you should be able to:
1. Explain the similarities between stock bonus plans and profit sharing plans.
2. Explain the differences between stock bonus plans and profit sharing plans.
3. Understand the differences between a stock bonus plan and an ESOP.
4. Determine whether the advantages of an ESOP are appropriate for a given situation.
5. Explain how the ESOP trustee may have a potential conflict of interest while attempting to execute the trustee's duties.
6. Describe how ESOPs work when adopted by an S corporation.

INTRODUCTION

As discussed in the previous chapter, profit sharing plans allow employers to contribute to a qualified plan on behalf of employees of the organizations. However, a profit sharing plan may not be the best option for an organization or company that has limited cash resources. For example, a company might be unable to contribute large amounts of cash to a profit sharing plan due to internal cash needs. In such an situation, a stock bonus plan or employee stock ownership plan (ESOP) may be a viable short to intermediate term alternative to a profit sharing plan, while still providing the advantages of a qualified plan.

A **stock bonus plan** is a plan established and maintained by an employer to provide benefits similar to those of a profit sharing plan.[1] While contributions by the employer are similar in deductibility to a profit sharing plan, a stock bonus plan is not dependent upon profits. Both contributions to and distributions from a stock bonus plan are generally in the form of employer stock. Thus, a stock bonus plan does not require the corporation to use currently needed cash flow. For purposes of allocating and distributing the stock of the employer, which is to be shared among the employees or their beneficiaries, such a plan is subject to the same basic qualified plan requirements as profit sharing plans.

An Employee Stock Ownership Plan (ESOP) is a qualified plan that invests primarily in "qualifying employer securities," typically shares of stock in the corporation creating the plan.[2] ESOPs were first enacted into federal legislation in 1974 under ERISA. At the time, Congress wanted to give employers an incentive to provide rank-and-file employees an ownership stake in the corporation for which they worked. Consequently, Congress established laws creating stock bonus plans and ESOPs, which provide an incentive to invest primarily in employer securities. This chapter discusses both the stock bonus plan and the ESOP in detail.

---

1. The term "stock bonus plan" is defined in the Treas. Reg. at §1.401-1(b)(1)(iii) as follows: A stock bonus plan is a plan established and maintained by an employer to provide benefits similar to those of a profit-sharing plan, except that the contributions by the employer are not necessarily dependent upon profits and the benefits are distributable in stock of the employer company. For the purpose of allocating and distributing the stock of the employer which is to be shared among his employees or their beneficiaries, such a plan is subject to the same requirements as a profit-sharing plan
2. IRC §1107 (d)(6)(A).

KNOW THE NUMBERS (2016)	
ESOP Account Balance	$1,070,000
Covered Compensation	$265,000

STOCK BONUS PLANS

Stock bonus plans are defined contribution profit sharing plans that allow employers to contribute stock to a qualified plan on behalf of their employees. As with all qualified plans, earnings within a stock bonus plan are tax deferred until the stock, its value in cash, or other securities are distributed from the plan. Because stock bonus plans are not subject to mandatory funding, contributions can and generally are made on a discretionary basis. However, when contributions are made, they must be made to participant's accounts on a nondiscriminatory basis. The contributions cannot discriminate against the **rank-and-file employees** for the benefit of shareholders, officers, and highly compensated employees. Thus, a stock bonus plan is a variation of a profit sharing plan yet has some distinct differences from other profit sharing plans.

Generally, stock bonus plans must satisfy the following requirements:[3]
- Unlike profit sharing plans, stock bonus plan participants must have pass through voting rights on employer stock held by the plan.[4]
- Participants must have the right to demand employer securities on plan distributions.
- Participants must have the right to demand that the employer repurchase the employer's securities if they are not publicly traded (the put option).[5]
- Participants must be able to elect to have distributions begin within one year of normal retirement age, death, or disability, or within five years for other modes of employment termination.[6]
- Distributions must be fully paid within five years of commencement of distributions.[7]

ADVANTAGES AND DISADVANTAGES OF STOCK BONUS PLANS

Stock bonus plans are profit sharing plans for which an employer makes contributions of employer stock on behalf of a participant to a qualified plan as part of the employee's overall compensation package. Similar to profit sharing plans, stock bonus plans are designed to provide benefits to both employers and employees. The fair market value of contributions of employer stock are tax deductible to the employer, which can result in decreased income tax costs for the corporation. The contributions are not required to be fixed in amount, as there is no annual mandatory contribution requirement for stock bonus plans, which allows the corporation flexibility in funding. Stock bonus plans also promote productivity within the corporation because participants, as shareholders, have a vested financial interest in the growth and success of the corporation (although this does not always lead to an increase in stock prices).

---

3. IRC §§401(a)(22) and 401(a)(23).
4. IRC §409(e).
5. IRC §409(h).
6. There are certain expectations. See IRC §409(o).
7. IRC §409(o).

Disadvantages to the Employees

While the advantages of stock bonus plans are attractive, stock bonus plans do have drawbacks. To the employee, there is the risk associated with the non-diversified investment portfolio. The employee earns income from the employer and also has an investment in the stock of the employer. In other words, if the corporation were to fail, the entire value in the employee retirement accounts may be lost as well as the employee's job and source of income (wages).

Disadvantages to the Employer

One disadvantage to the employer is that the ownership and control of the corporation is diminished or "**diluted**" as shares are granted to the employees. This has a greater impact on smaller, closely held corporations.

KEY CONCEPTS

1. List the requirements of a stock bonus plan.

2. What are the advantages and disadvantages of a stock bonus plan?

3. What are the main differences between a stock bonus plan and a profit sharing plan?

4. Why are valuations performed for stock bonus plans?

With stock bonus plans, the required "**repurchase option**" (**put option**) could deplete the cash of the corporation. A repurchase option allows a terminating employee the choice to receive the cash equivalent of the employer's stock if the stock is not readily tradeable on an established market. If the repurchase occurs at an unexpected time (e.g., upon the death of participant), the forced sale of stock back to the corporation may drain the corporation's cash flow as well as result in a costly appraisal of the stock to determine the value to pay the employee-participant's heirs. In such a situation, the strain on the cash flow of the employer may have a negative impact on the corporation as a whole.

FEATURES OF STOCK BONUS PLANS AS COMPARED TO PROFIT SHARING PLANS

As discussed above, stock bonus plans are a particular type of profit sharing plan and have many profit sharing characteristics. The features of stock bonus plans will be discussed in relation to profit sharing plans in order to identify the similarities and differences between the two types of plans.

Contributions and Deductions

As with all qualified plans, stock bonus plans and profit sharing plans must be established by December 31st of the year for which the employer will be contributing to the plan. Meanwhile, contributions can be made to the plan as late as the due date of the income tax return, including permitted extensions.

Contributions to stock bonus plans and profit sharing plans are **discretionary**, but must meet the general profit sharing plan requirement of "**substantial and recurring**." While most contributions to stock bonus plans are tied to the corporation's profitability, there is no requirement that a corporation must contribute to the plan in a year in which it has earnings nor is there a prohibition against contributions to the plan in years in which the corporation has losses.

Like profit sharing plans, stock bonus plans have a deductible contribution limit of 25 percent of covered compensation (limited to $265,000 for 2016) per employee.[8] When stock is contributed, the fair market value of the stock, as determined by a qualified appraiser, is deductible. In some instances, an employer may contribute more than the permitted 25 percent, in which case the employer would deduct the 25 percent and could carry forward the amount which exceeds the 25 percent limit and deduct the excess in a future year. However, the amount carried forward when added to the contribution made for the future year cannot exceed 25 percent, and the employer must pay a 10 percent excise tax on the portion of the contribution that exceeds 25 percent of covered compensation for the current year.[9]

Valuation of Employer Stock in Stock Bonus Plans
An important area of plan administration for a stock bonus plan is the valuation or appraisal of the employer's securities. Valuations are performed to determine the value of the contribution for the corporation's income tax deduction purposes and the corporation's financial statements. Valuations are also completed to periodically inform the participants of the stock's value. The employer will track the value of the contributions and therefore the amount of ordinary income that the employee will have to recognize upon distribution. A valuation also allows the employee to determine the sales price of the stock if the employee is exercising the repurchase option (put option).

For private or closely held corporations, determining the value of securities is often difficult. The law requires valuations of employers' securities and if those securities are not readily tradable on an established securities market, then these valuations must be undertaken by independent appraisers.[10] The appraiser must be an uninterested, independent party. The valuation must be done in good faith and must be based on all factors relevant to determining the securities' fair market value.[11] The valuation therefore involves an assessment of what a willing buyer would pay to a willing seller for the securities or business.[12] These valuations, which can be costly, are used on an annual basis to determine the value of the securities, that, for example, were contributed by the employer for tax deduction purposes or that were subjected to a repurchase option of a departing employee.

QUICK QUIZ 6.1

1. A stock bonus plan is a particular type of profit sharing plan, so they share many characteristics.
   a. True
   b. False

2. A valuation of an employer's securities is performed only at the creation of the stock bonus plan.
   a. True
   b. False

3. A stock bonus plan may require an employee to attain six years of service before considering the employee eligible.
   a. True
   b. False

True, False, False.

8. IRC §404(a)(3).
9. IRC §4972(a).
10. IRC §401 (a)(28)(C).
11. Regulations §54.4975-11(d)(5). See also *Donovan v. Cunningham* 541 ESOPs 246 (S.D. Texas 1982).
12. Revenue Ruling 59-60.

Eligibility

Stock bonus plans are subject to standard eligibility rules discussed in Chapter 3, the same as other qualified plans, including profit sharing plans. The standard eligibility of age 21 and one-year of service generally applies to stock bonus plans. As discussed before, plan sponsors could make the eligibility requirements less restrictive.

Like other qualified plans, stock bonus plans may require a two year waiting period before the employee is eligible. However, if the employer requires a two year waiting period, then all contributions must be 100 percent vested after the two year waiting period.

KEY CONCEPTS

1. Define net unrealized appreciation.

2. What is the advantage to an employee of receiving a stock distribution from a stock bonus plan rather than receive the distribution in cash?

Allocation Methods

The allocation methods for contributions to participants' accounts in stock bonus plans are the same as those for profit sharing plans. The difference is that normally employer stock is contributed to the stock bonus plan rather than cash.

The standard allocation method for a stock bonus plan is to allocate contributions based on a percentage of each employee's compensation. Whenever stock is contributed, the stock must be valued by a qualified appraiser as discussed previously. Cash is generally only contributed when the plan expects cash distribution elections or the plan needs cash to meet its obligation to provide a market for the stock.

The percentage of compensation method is not the only acceptable allocation method for stock bonus plans. The formulas discussed for profit sharing plans based on age and past service also apply to stock bonus plans, as does the new comparability plan based on the employees' respective classifications in the corporation. These methods apply as long as they do not discriminate in favor of highly compensated employees. As discussed in Chapter 5, stock bonus plans are also permitted to use the technique or method of permitted disparity, also known as Social Security Integration, which allocates plan contributions to employees' accounts and provides greater contributions to those employees whose earnings exceed the Social Security wage base.

Vesting

Similar to profit sharing plans, the vesting rules for stock bonus plans are the same as for other qualified plans as discussed in Chapter 3. The standard three-year cliff vesting schedules and the graduated 2 to 6 year vesting schedules for defined contribution plans as required by the Pension Protection Act of 2006 apply unless the employer selects a two year eligibility rule. The plan sponsor may not exceed these vesting requirements yet is always permitted to be more generous if desired.

Portfolio Diversification

Profit sharing plans are generally designed to invest in **diversified investment portfolios**. Consequently, the assets in these plans are not usually invested exclusively in employer stock. Unlike profit sharing plans, stock bonus plans are usually funded with one hundred percent employer stock. Profit sharing plans assist the employee in preparing for retirement through the growth of the individual participant's account with deferred compensation and tax deferral on earnings. As such, these plans are generally well-diversified investment portfolios. In contrast, stock bonus plans are initially "cash free" to the employer as they are predominately funded with the employer's stock in order to provide benefits to employees without the need to use the corporation's cash. The exclusive use of employer stock as contributions results in an undiversified portfolio for the participant.

To the extent that a stock bonus plan is funded with publicly traded stock, the Pension Protection Act of 2006 requires the plan to allow plan participants to diversify their pre-tax deferrals, after-tax contributions, and employer contributions that have been invested in employer securities. Like other defined contribution plans, the plan must offer a choice of at least three investment options, other than employer securities, each of which must be diversified and have materially different risk and return characteristics. This requirement is consistent with that found in ERISA and generally implies that a plan must provide at least one type of stock, bond, and cash fund as investment options. All plan participants must be allowed to diversify the investment of their elective deferrals and after-tax contributions. In addition, plan participants with three or more years of service must be allowed to diversify the investment of other contributions made on their behalf.

PPA 2006 DIVERSIFICATION REQUIREMENTS FOR PUBLIC COMPANIES

EXHIBIT 6.1

	EMPLOYEE CONTRIBUTIONS*		EMPLOYER CONTRIBUTIONS
	Pre-tax Elective Deferrals	After-tax Contributions	
Participant with less than 3 years of service	Immediate right to diversify	Immediate right to diversify	No requirement to diversify
Participant with 3 years or more of service			Immediate right to diversify

Employee contributions typically occur in 401(k) plans and thrift plans, but not in stock bonus plans or ESOPs.

Voting Rights

If a profit sharing plan consists of employer stock, the plan participant generally does not have voting rights in the stock held by the plan. However, participants in a stock bonus plan must have pass through voting rights on employer stock that is held by the plan on their behalf.[13] **"Pass through" voting rights** mean that the voting rights of the stock pass through from the plan all the way down to the participant. In this case, the participant could vote the shares of stock allocated to his stock bonus plan account. There are exceptions for closely held corporations to limit voting to only those matters that are material. Also, unallocated shares are usually voted by the plan trustee. Unallocated shares are those shares in the trust that have not yet been allocated to individual participants.

---

13. IRC §§401(a)(22) and 409(e).

Distributions

Stock bonus plan distributions are generally made in the form of employer stock. The distribution of stock provides additional income tax benefits because there is a deferral of income tax on the stock's appreciated value until the stock is later sold. Although the stock in the stock bonus plan is usually distributed to the employee, the plan may provide the employee with the choice of receiving the cash equivalent of the shares of stock at the time of distribution. However, if a cash equivalent is received, the deferral of income tax on the stock's appreciated value until the stock is sold is lost.

Generally, stock bonus plans do not permit employees to receive in-service withdrawal distributions from the plan except upon termination, hardship, disability, or retirement. However, stock bonus plans may permit, but are not required to allow, in-service withdrawals after a participant attains two years of participation in the plan. Similar to profit sharing plans, employee/participant loans are available from a stock bonus plan if the plan permits and the loans are available in a nondiscriminatory manner. Generally, employers choose not to permit loans from stock bonus plans.

The taxation of a distribution of employer stock or securities from a stock bonus plan depends on whether the distribution is a lump-sum distribution or a partial distribution. If there is a lump-sum distribution, the employee is subject to ordinary income tax in the year of the distribution based on the fair market value of the employer stock at the time of the original contribution. The net unrealized appreciation (NUA) of the stock (i.e., the appreciation of the stock while held in the plan) is not taxed at the time of the lump-sum distribution but rather is taxed as a long-term capital gain when the stock is ultimately sold (discussed below).

On the other hand, if the distribution of the employer stock or securities is made in installments (a partial distribution), the fair market value of all employer securities distributed in the installment distribution attributable to employer contributions will be taxable as ordinary income. This treatment clearly contrasts with the taxation of a lump-sum distribution.[14] The exception to this rule provided in IRC §401(e)(4)(A) is that NUA excluded from gross income does include any amount attributable to employee nondeductible contributions. NUA attributable to employee deferrals are subject to ordinary taxation.

QUICK QUIZ 6.2

1. Participants of a stock bonus plan must have pass through voting rights on the employer stock held by the plan.
   a. True
   b. False

2. The benefits provided to a plan participant under a top-heavy stock bonus plan must vest at least as rapidly as a 3-year cliff or 2 to 6 year graduated vesting schedule.
   a. True
   b. False

3. A principal disadvantage of a stock bonus plan is net unrealized appreciation.
   a. True
   b. False

4. Stock bonus plans may permit plan loans.
   a. True
   b. False

True, True, False, True.

---

14. IRC §402(e)(4)(A).

Distributions may be subject to the 10 percent early withdrawal penalty if the participant is under the age of 59½. Distributions of stock may also be rolled into an IRA account or to another qualified plan that accepts stock and is willing to accept the rollover. Note that if the employer securities are rolled over to another tax-advantaged account, the ability to benefit from the NUA treatment is lost.

Net Unrealized Appreciation (NUA)

One of the principal benefits of stock bonus plans is net unrealized appreciation (NUA) treatment. **Net unrealized appreciation** is the appreciation in the value of employer stock from the time of contribution to the plan until the time that the stock is distributed to the plan participant. The NUA of the stock (i.e., the gain while being held in the plan) is not taxed as ordinary income at the time of the distribution, but rather is taxed as a long-term capital gain when the stock is sold and is reported on Form 4972. There are no holding period requirements to qualify this gain for the preferential long-term capital gains tax treatment. The cost basis of the stock (as provided by the employer) at the date of contribution is taxable as ordinary income at the date of distribution.

> John is 65 years old. Over his career while working at ABC Corporation (a privately held corporation), he received stock contributions of ABC Corporation to his account in the stock bonus plan. ABC's tax deduction was $20,000, or the combined value of contributions of stock valued at the time of contribution. John decides that he will retire, and he no longer wants to assume the risk that ABC Corporation will remain as an ongoing solvent entity; thus, he decides to take a full distribution from the plan and then sells all of his stock for cash. At distribution, John's ABC stock is valued by an independent appraiser at $100,000. Upon distribution of the stock, John has $20,000 of ordinary income representing the total value of the employer's contribution. The remaining $80,000 ($100,000 - $20,000) of NUA will be taxed at the time of the sale as a long-term capital gain.
>
> If John instead sells the stock two years after distribution for $165,000, he will have a basis of $20,000 (the ordinary income recognized at distribution), $80,000 of NUA (long-term capital gain), and $65,000 of long-term capital gain representing the appreciation of the stock since the date of distribution. If the sale occurs before one year and a day, any post distribution appreciation would be taxed as short-term capital gain, but the long-term capital gain on the NUA would not be affected unless the sale was for less than $100,000.
>
> This example not only stresses the tax implications involved, but it also points out that with an investment in ABC Corporation, John assumes the risk that ABC Corporation will continue as a viable entity. If ABC Corporation goes bankrupt or becomes insolvent, John's stock investment could be completely lost or seriously devalued. Thus, investment risk is an important consideration for a participant in a stock bonus plan.

EXAMPLE 6.1

	Value	Comment
FMV of stock when distributed	$100,000	Stock will generally be transferred to a brokerage account.
Value of stock when contributed over career	$20,000	Must be included as ordinary income in the year of distribution.
Net unrealized appreciation (NUA)	$80,000	Treated as LTCG when the stock is sold. The basis of the stock equals the amount picked up as ordinary income in the year of distribution.

If John sells the stock immediately, then he has an $80,000 LTCG.	If John holds the stock and sells two years later for $165,000, then he has a gain of $145,000 consisting of NUA of $80,000 and additional appreciation after distribution of $65,000.

As illustrated, the benefit of NUA treatment is that the deferral of taxation on the stock is treated as a capital gain instead of ordinary income. The employee is taxed at ordinary income rates in the year of distribution only on the value of the securities deducted by the employer at the time of contribution to the plan. The net unrealized appreciation (i.e., the gain of the value of the stock while being held in the plan) is not taxed at the time of distribution but is taxed as a long-term capital gain when the stock is later sold by the participant.[15] In order to receive NUA treatment, the distribution must qualify as a lump-sum distribution. Lump-sum distributions and NUA are discussed in more detail in Chapter 7.

Put Options

Stock bonus plans and ESOPs are required, under the same rules, to provide employees with a "put option" or repurchase option whereby the employer buys back the employer stock distributed at a fair market value. These rules are discussed in greater depth later in this chapter under ESOPs.

---

15. IRC §402(e)(4)(B); see also *Villarroel v. Commissioner*, 1998-247 T.C. Memo (1988), aff'd, 202 F.3d 271 (6th Cir. 2000).

COMPARISON OF STOCK BONUS PLANS TO PROFIT SHARING PLANS*

EXHIBIT
6.2

	Stock Bonus Plans	Profit Sharing Plans
Plan Establishment	December 31	December 31
Date of Contribution	Due date of tax return plus extensions	Due date of tax return plus extensions
Type of Contributions	*Generally stock*	*Generally cash*
Deductible Contribution Limit	25% of covered compensation	25% of covered compensation
Valuation	*Generally needed annually*	*Generally unnecessary*
Eligibility	Same as other Qualified Plans (age 21 and 1 year of service or 2 years with 100% vesting)	Same as other Qualified Plans (age 21 and 1 year of service or 2 years with 100% vesting)
Allocation Method	% of compensation or formula based on age, service of classification	% of compensation or formula based on age, service of classification
Vesting	Same as other Defined Contribution Qualified Plans (3-year cliff or 2 to 6 year graduated vesting)**	Same as other Defined Contribution Qualified Plans (3-year cliff or 2 to 6 year graduated vesting)**
Portfolio Diversification	*No****	*Generally yes*
Voting Rights	*Generally yes*	*Generally no*
Type of Distributions	*Generally in stock*	*Generally in cash*
In-Service Withdrawals	May be allowed after two years	May be allowed after two years
Loans	May be allowed (but not usually)	May be allowed (but not usually)
Taxation of Distributions	*Lump-sum distributions will qualify for NUA treatment. Other distributions are treated as ordinary income.*	*Generally full distribution is ordinary income*

* Differences are highlighted in blue.

**Effective for plan years after 2006 under the Pension Protection Act of 2006.

*** Diversification may be required as a result of the PPA 2006.

EXHIBIT
6.3

FORM 1099-R

☐ VOID ☐ CORRECTED		

PAYER'S name, street address, city or town, state or province, country, and ZIP or foreign postal code	**1** Gross distribution $	OMB No. 1545-0119 **2016** Form **1099-R**	**Distributions From Pensions, Annuities, Retirement or Profit-Sharing Plans, IRAs, Insurance Contracts, etc.**
	2a Taxable amount $		
	2b Taxable amount not determined ☐	Total distribution ☐	**Copy 1**
PAYER'S federal identification number	RECIPIENT'S identification number	**3** Capital gain (included in box 2a) $	**4** Federal income tax withheld $	**For State, City, or Local Tax Department**
RECIPIENT'S name		**5** Employee contributions /Designated Roth contributions or insurance premiums $	**6** Net unrealized appreciation in employer's securities $	
Street address (including apt. no.)		**7** Distribution code(s)	IRA/ SEP/ SIMPLE ☐	**8** Other $ %	
City or town, state or province, country, and ZIP or foreign postal code	**9a** Your percentage of total distribution %	**9b** Total employee contributions $	
10 Amount allocable to IRR within 5 years $	**11** 1st year of desig. Roth contrib.	FATCA filing requirement ☐	**12** State tax withheld $ $	**13** State/Payer's state no.	**14** State distribution $ $
Account number (see instructions)			**15** Local tax withheld $ $	**16** Name of locality	**17** Local distribution $ $

Form **1099-R**   www.irs.gov/form1099r   Department of the Treasury - Internal Revenue Service

EMPLOYEE STOCK OWNERSHIP PLANS

Employee Stock Ownership Plans, referred to as ESOPs, are a special form of stock bonus plans that reward employees with both ownership in the corporation and provide owners with substantial tax advantages. An ESOP is controlled through a trust. The sponsor company receives tax deductions for contributions of stock from the corporation. The ESOP then allocates the stock to separate accounts for the benefit of individual employee-participants.

Employee ownership in the context of ESOPs refers to ownership in the stock of the corporation through an employee benefit plan by most or all of the corporation's employees. ESOPs provide corporate owners with a way to transfer significant ownership interests to their employees while benefiting from favorable tax advantages. One underlying rationale for promoting employee ownership is that the long-term health of the free economy is best served through providing employees with ownership of corporate securities beyond normal salaries and wages. Congress envisioned that ESOPs would function both as "an employee retirement benefit plan and a 'technique of corporate finance' that would encourage employee ownership."[16] Because of these dual purposes, ESOPs are not necessarily designed to guarantee retirement benefits because they place employee retirement assets at greater risk than the usual diversified ERISA qualified plans.[17]

A key characteristic of the ESOP is that the trust may borrow money from a bank or other lender to purchase the employer stock. The corporation generally repays the loan through tax deductible contributions to the ESOP. Both the interest and the principal repayments for the loan are income tax deductible. The ESOP can thus be "leveraged." ESOPs with borrowings are referenced as LESOPs, which stands for "Leveraged" Employee Stock Ownership Plans (discussed below). When used in conjunction with financial and estate planning techniques and tax savings strategies, there can be substantial tax and investment benefits gained from utilization of an ESOP. ESOPs are, as one court wrote, "employee benefit plan(s) designed to invest primarily or when certain safeguards are present, solely in securities issued by the sponsoring corporation."

KEY CONCEPTS

1. What are ESOPs and why are they used?

2. List the parties of a typical leveraged ESOP.

3. List the requirements necessary for the owners of a closely held corporation to qualify for nonrecognition of capital gain at the creation of an ESOP.

4. Discuss three advantages and disadvantages of an ESOP.

To become eligible for these tax advantages, the ESOP must satisfy various rules of the IRC and of ERISA. Like other qualified plans, the ESOP must satisfy applicable rules of employee vesting, participation, eligibility, and coverage. The ESOP must also have a trustee who is charged with a fiduciary duty to handle and maintain the plan in the best interest of plan participants and their beneficiaries.

---

16. ***Martin v. Feilen***, 965 F.2d 660, 664 (8th Cir. 1992), *cert. denied*, 506 U.S. 1054, 113 S.Ct. 979, 122 L.Ed.2d 133 (1993).
17. ***Moench v. Robinson***, 62 F.3d 553, 568 (3rd Cir. 1995) (quoting ***Martin v. Feilen***, 965 F.2d 660, 664).

| EXHIBIT 6.4 | FACTS ABOUT ESOPs |

According to the ESOP Association:[1]
- There were roughly 10,000 ESOPs in the United States covering more than 10 million participants.
- ESOPs controlled about $940 billion in assets at the end of 2011.
- Of these ESOPs, roughly 97 percent were for closely held corporations while about three percent were for publicly traded corporations.
- About 5,000 corporations are now majority employee-owned by the ESOP.
- At least 75% of the ESOPs are or were leveraged.

The ESOP Association, which represents approximately 1,400 ESOP corporations, touts the following information concerning ESOPs:[2]
- Approximately 99 percent of the members of the ESOP Association are private, closely held corporations.
- Approximately two-thirds of the members of the ESOP Association have less than 250 employees, although there are ESOPs in large businesses as well.
- While ESOPs exist in a broad range of industries, roughly 23 percent of the members of the ESOP Association are in manufacturing, followed by 15 percent in construction.
- The ESOP Association's members had, on average, annual sales revenue ranging from 20 million to 50 million.
- Approximately 65 percent of the members of the ESOP Association report that their ESOPs have been in place for at least 10 years.
- Roughly 83 percent of the members of the ESOP Association have corporations that are more than 50 percent owned by the ESOPs.
- Roughly 94 percent of the members of the ESOP Association provide a supplemental benefit plan as well as the ESOP, including 401(k) plans, pension plans, and profit sharing plans.
- Research shows that the implementation of an ESOP results in more information sharing, communications, and involvement in decision making for the employee-owners.
- Roughly 83 percent of the members of the ESOP Association report that motivation and productivity increased as a result of the ESOPs.
- ESOP Association members have, on average, an account balance of $113,318.

1. See www.esopassociation.org and its resource library for more information. The ESOP Association, founded in 1978, is a national association of corporations with employee stock ownership plans and service providers with a professional commitment to employee ownership through ESOPs. The ESOP Association has a library that is informative and provides much information concerning ESOPs. According to its website, the ESOP Association is the leading voice in America for employee ownership through ESOPs, and devotes considerable time to creating and maintaining favorable ESOPs legislation. Further, the ESOP Association is a prime source for educational materials necessary for successful implementation and administration of an ESOP.
2. Source: The ESOP Association, "2015 Company Survey."

THE ESOP TRANSACTION

The corporation, the principal shareholder of the corporation, the ESOP trust, the trustee or trustees, a lender, and employees are all part of the process of establishing an ESOP. Most ESOPs are leveraged because money must be borrowed to purchase the stock from the principal shareholder. In a **leveraged ESOP**, the corporation makes tax deductible contributions to the trust in the form of both principal and interest for the loan. The trust receives these funds and the trust, through a trustee, then repays the acquisition loan from a bank or other lender. The trust purchases shares of the corporate stock from the principal shareholder, and these shares are normally pledged as security for the bank loan. The corporation and generally the principal shareholder (seller) guarantee the loan, and the corporation's assets are pledged as collateral for the loan. Prior to the allocation of the actual shares to the participant's account within the trust, the pledged shares are held in a separate holding account (suspense) and referred to as unallocated.

As the trust repays the bank loan, an appropriate allocation of shares are withdrawn from the holding account and allocated to the account of the individual participant. Once a share of stock has been withdrawn from the holding account, that share may no longer act as pledged collateral for the debt. However, a proportionate amount of the loan was repaid; therefore, there is no need for additional cash or funds from the corporation to maintain the loan. There may, however, be a need for cash if the trust needs or wants to redeem distributed shares.

The following diagram illustrates the various relationships and transactions regarding a leveraged ESOP.

VARIOUS RELATIONSHIPS AND TRANSACTIONS IN A LEVERAGED ESOP

EXHIBIT 6.5

1. An ESOP obtains a loan from a bank or other outside lender. The ESOP signs a promissory note for the money.
2. The employer guarantees the loan on behalf of the ESOP.
3. The ESOP uses the money from the loan to buy stock from existing shareholder (or employer).
4. The stock purchased by the ESOP is held in an ESOP suspense account, and is released for allocation to participant accounts over time as the loan is repaid with funds contributed to the ESOP by the employer. These allocations are in lieu of a cash contribution that could have been made to a retirement plan.
5. The employer contributes funds to the ESOP so that the ESOP can make its annual debt repayment to the bank (or other lender).
6. Employees are entitled to receive distributions of employer stock in kind upon termination or retirement.
7. Employees are entitled to sell back or "put" the stock back to the employer.
8. Shareholders may also be required to guarantee the ESOP loan.

Practical Uses of ESOPs and Nonrecognition of Gain Treatment

Most commonly, an ESOP is used to buy the stock of the retiring or departing owner or owners of a closely held corporation in order to achieve deferral of federal income taxes. The establishment of ESOPs allow owners of closely held businesses to sell all or part of their interest in the corporation and defer recognition of the capital gain. This tax benefit is known as **nonrecognition of gain treatment** and is provided for by §1042 of the Internal Revenue Code.[18] In order to qualify for nonrecognition of gain treatment, the following requirements apply:[19]

1. The ESOP must own at least 30 percent of the corporation's stock immediately after the sale (notice that the controlling interest may remain owned elsewhere, but if this occurs the ESOP share should have been valued using a minority share discount).

2. The seller or sellers must reinvest the proceeds from the sale into qualified replacement securities (defined below) within 12 months after the sale and hold such securities three years.

3. The corporation that establishes the ESOP must have no class of stock outstanding that is tradable on an established securities market.

4. The seller or sellers, relatives of the seller or sellers, and 25 percent shareholders in the corporation are precluded from receiving allocations of stock acquired by the ESOP through the rollover.

5. The ESOP may not sell the stock acquired through the rollover transaction for three years. The requirement, however, will not apply if the corporation is sold. The three-year period is called a "holding" period, which prevents unnecessary, duplicative rollovers by the corporation.

6. The stock sold to the ESOP must be common or convertible preferred stock and must have been owned by the seller for at least three years prior to the sale.

If all of these requirements are satisfied, the sellers (usually former principals of the corporation) may reinvest the proceeds from the sale within 12 months of the sale into qualified replacement securities (securities of domestic corporations as defined below), and carry over their former adjusted basis from the corporation into the qualified replacement securities. As long as the seller retains these replacement securities, there will be no taxable event. If the seller later sells some or all of these replacement securities, the seller will have capital gains or losses determined by the carry over basis. If the seller dies, then the seller's heirs (or estate) are entitled to a new adjusted basis equal to the date of death fair market value, thus avoiding capital gains taxation altogether. The nonrecognition of gain treatment is not available to the seller of an S Corporation that establishes an ESOP because IRC §1042 only allows owners of closely held C Corporations to do so.[20]

For the deferral of capital gain recognition to occur, the reinvestment must be made into qualified replacement securities. **Qualified replacement securities** are securities in a domestic corporation, including stocks, bonds, debentures, or warrants, which receive no more than 25 percent of their income from passive investments. The qualified replacement securities can be in the form of stock in an S Corporation. However, stock of the corporation that issued the employer securities (or a

---

18. IRC §1042.
19. IRC §1042(c)(3); see also Temp. Regulations §1.1042-IT, Q and A-3(c).
20. IRC §1042(c)(1)(A).

corporation that is part of a control group with that corporation) cannot serve as a qualified replacement security.

Advantages and Disadvantages of ESOPs

There are many reasons why the ESOP is the most common type of stock bonus plan. ESOPs benefit the employer-corporation and its participants in various ways. From the corporation's perspective, the ESOP creates a market for the stock of privately held corporations. It is crucial for shareholders to have a market for their stock for financial planning and estate planning issues.

Advantages to the Employer

The shareholders, often owners who will soon retire, may sell shares to the plan, which is a ready and available buyer. Hence, ESOPs are frequently used as estate planning vehicles for closely held corporations and their owners. Without the ESOP, there may not be a market for the privately held corporate stock. Also, the corporation or trust is allowed to borrow money in order to provide contributions resulting in funds being provided immediately to the ESOP, while the employer repays the loan to the ESOP with tax deductible contributions. Not only do these tax deductions save the corporation cash, the cash flow of the corporation is further strengthened because in the ESOP exchange, the trust allocates shares to the employees' accounts while the corporation is paying cash to the bank (in a leveraged ESOP) and deducting such payments for both principal and interest. By providing employees with a stake in the corporation, employers give economic incentives to employees, which increases motivation and improves employee retention.

Advantages to the Employees

From the employees' perspective, the ESOP provides them with a type of retirement vehicle. The ESOP provides them with ownership in the corporation where they work, which tends to improve a worker's attitude, motivation, sense of loyalty, and belonging to the corporation. The employee-participant may also benefit from net unrealized appreciation (NUA) at the time of stock distributions because of favorable capital gains rates and deferred recognition.

Disadvantages to the Employees

There are disadvantages to ESOPs as well. There is an inherent lack of diversification of the individual "investment" portfolio because ESOPs must invest primarily in the stock of the corporation. As a result, an employee-participant's account is susceptible to fluctuations or drastic drops in value because of the corporation's stock. This means that a long-time employee who has received large allocations of the stock has significant nondiversified portfolio risk. This risk can be mitigated somewhat for ESOP participants that are at least 55 years of age and who have completed at least 10 years of participation in the plan. This special diversification treatment is discussed later in this chapter.

Disadvantages to the Employer

From the shareholder's perspective, ESOPs "dilute" ownership in the corporation by reducing the concentration of shares from the sellers to broaden the employees' holdings. Moreover, the repurchase option for stock that is not readily tradable can create cash flow problems and administrative concerns.[21] With the repurchase option, an employee can force the corporation to repurchase the stock originally issued and distributed to the employee-participant. In addition, the

21. See previous section on Repurchase Option.

corporation creating the ESOP has substantial costs in setting up the plan, drafting plan documents, and administering the plan.

Plan administration can also be costly, and the annual appraisals create significant and recurring expenses for closely held corporations. These appraisals are necessary to determine the value of the tax deduction for the employer and to determine the price that an employer or trust would pay for the repurchase of ESOP distributed shares.

Employer-corporations must also be ready to purchase the shares of departing employees, which can further diminish or stretch the cash flow of a corporation. The lender involved with a leveraged ESOP may also place more scrutiny or requirements upon the employer, especially for annual valuations, which add to administrative costs of the plan.

ESOPs can generally use any allocation method permitted by profit sharing plans or stock bonus plans. However, ESOPs cannot be integrated with Social Security. This limitation is somewhat unique as most other qualified plans can be integrated with Social Security.[22]

EXHIBIT 6.6	ADVANTAGES AND DISADVANTAGES OF ESOPS	
	Advantages	**Disadvantages**
Employer	• Creates a market for stock in a private/closely held corporation • Helps retain employees • Improves employee loyalty • Employer-owners may create a diversified portfolio without recognition of capital gain • Corporation can borrow against stock • Corporation can improve the current cash flow of the corporation by taking a tax deduction on stock contributions	• Dilutes ownership • Administrative costs • May strain employer cash flow to meet payout requirements to departing employees at uncertain times • Periodic appraisal costs are expensive • Personal liability concerns for officers or management who also serve as trustees of ESOPs • Creates cash flow uncertainty in the future • Social Security integration is not permitted
Employee	• Acquires ownership in employer corporation • Employees have better perception of or attitude towards employer corporation • Favorable tax treatment on stock distributions (NUA) • Can force employer to repurchase stock at end of employment (put option) • Receives stock as form of compensation	• Employee bears risk of employer's insolvency (nondiversification) • Value of stock subject to appraiser • Stock value subject to fluctuation • Stock not liquid

---

22. Social Security integration is also not available with respect to elective deferrals or matching contributions, such as in a 401(k) plan. Treas. Reg. §1.401(l)-1(a)(4).

VOTING

Generally, ESOP participants have the same voting rights with their allocated shares as other shareholders, including the right to vote the shares and the right to earn dividends. For public ESOP corporations registered with the Securities and Exchange Commission, participants have full voting rights. However, ESOPs of privately held corporations are not required to provide full voting rights for these shares. The law merely requires that participants possess voting rights on major corporate decisions. Such major corporate decisions are considered to be mergers, acquisitions, consolidation, reclassification, liquidation, dissolution, recapitalization, or sale.

The trustee of the ESOP votes the shares on behalf of these participants on regular corporate matters beyond those listed above. For stock in a privately held corporation under these circumstances, the IRC allows the plan to authorize the ESOP trustee to vote the stock as one vote for each participant.[23]

QUICK QUIZ 6.3

1. In a leveraged ESOP, the corporation makes after-tax contributions to a trust on behalf of its employees.
   a. True
   b. False

2. Foreign securities may qualify as qualified replacement securities.
   a. True
   b. False

3. The creation of an ESOP may dilute ownership in the corporation.
   a. True
   b. False

False, False, True.

ESOP trustees must discharge their duties by evaluating the best interests of the beneficiaries in the abstract as beneficiaries, not as directors who may lose control of the corporation nor should they discharge their duties as employees, some of whom may lose their jobs if control of the corporation changes hands.[24] Courts have commented that it is appropriate for trustees to put aside personal judgment in favor of carrying out the wishes of the trust participants.[25] The trust documents concerning an ESOP must be construed in light of ERISA's policies, and trust documents cannot excuse trustees from their fiduciary duties under ERISA.[26]

CONTRIBUTIONS TO ESOPs

ESOPs can provide generous tax benefits. These tax benefits were created to provide an incentive for employers and corporations to implement ESOPs and build work forces comprised of many employee-owners. Contributions to ESOPs are undertaken by the corporation and are made to the trust though the trustee. The corporation contributes cash or stock to the trust so that the trust can buy new or existing shares. The trust also has the option to borrow funds to buy shares while the corporation makes cash contributions to the plan so that the loan can be repaid. While there are significant tax benefits with ESOPs, there are limitations to contributions to an ESOP.[27] Contributions to ESOPs may be in cash or in the form of employer securities. The employer may

---

23. IRC §409(e)(3). See also *Schoenholtz v. Doniger*, 657 F.Supp. 899 (S.D.N.Y. 1987).
24. *Danaher Corp. v. Chicago Pneumatic Tool Co.*, 635 F. Supp. 246, 249-250 (S.D.N.Y. 1986).
25. Id.
26. *Central States, Southeast and Southwest Areas Pension Fund v. Central Transport*, 472 U.S. 559, 568 (1985).

deduct the value of the stock contributed and in the process, increase the corporation's cash profits by the taxes avoided.

Employer contributions to ESOPs are deductible by the employer just like any contribution to a qualified profit sharing plan or stock bonus plan, but contributions are subject to the 25 percent limit of covered compensation.[28] However, if the employer's stock is obtained by virtue of a loan (leveraged ESOP), then the permissible deductions for the employer are increased for the interest on the loan. In other words, the employer is allowed to deduct all interest paid on the loan over and above the 25 percent deduction of total eligible payroll of the plan participants.[29] The interest deduction is unlimited.

EXAMPLE 6.2

If XYZ Corporation contributes 33% of covered compensation to the ESOP for principal and interest on the loan to the ESOP, this entire amount is deductible if 25% was applied to pay principal and 8% was applied to pay for interest payments.

Employers are further allowed tax deductions for dividends paid on stock held by an ESOP under various circumstances. This deduction, which was temporarily expanded under EGTRRA 2001, has now been made permanent under the Pension Protection Act of 2006. Dividends that are paid in cash for stock purchases with an ESOP securities purchase loan are tax deductible by the employer/plan sponsor. Dividends, regardless of whether received outright or reinvested, are taxable as current ordinary income to the employee. Cash dividends on stock purchased with an ESOP securities acquisition loan are included in the 25 percent contribution limit for leveraged ESOPs. Also, employers may take a deduction on dividends applied to loan payments to a leveraged ESOP. Finally, if employees voluntarily reinvest dividends in the corporation's stock held by an ESOP, then these dividends are deductible by the employer.

KEY CONCEPTS

1. Explain the voting rights of ESOP participants of public corporations.

2. Discuss the scenario in which the employer's deduction related to an ESOP may exceed 25% of the total covered compensation.

3. If securities are not readily tradable, how is the value of the security determined for purposes of the ESOP contribution?

DISTRIBUTIONS

Distributions from ESOPs, much like general stock bonus plans, are largely subject to the same restrictions applicable to distributions from any qualified plan. Therefore, the distribution rules for stock bonus plans discussed earlier in this chapter generally apply to ESOPs as well. The exceptions are discussed below. Aside from the general exceptions, distributions before age 59½, death, disability, or retirement are subject to the 10 percent penalty. There is no requirement for an ESOP or stock bonus plan to provide a joint and survivor annuity or a spousal death benefit.

---

27. Effective January 1, 2002, the Economic Growth And Tax Relief Reconciliation Act of 2001 (EGTRRA 2001), IRC §616(c), expanded some tax benefits regarding contributions. Conversely, other areas were limited, including certain allocations to S Corporations. It should also be noted that IRC Section 133 provided banks with a 50 percent exclusion on ESOP loans. However, this section was repealed for loans issued after 1995.
28. IRC §404(a)(3).
29. IRC §404(a)(9)(B).

An ESOP may pay distributions in a lump sum or in installments. By using lump sum distributions, a company accelerates its repurchase obligation, allows current employees who participate to share in potential growth of the company, and protects former employee from absorbing future losses in company value. By using installment distributions, ESOPs are permitted to pay distributions in substantially equal payments over a period not longer than five years.[30] Installments allow former participants to continue ownership in the company while the stock remains in the account of the participant. Installments may exceed five years in the case of a participant with an account balance in excess of $1,070,000 for 2016, five years plus one additional year for each $210,000 for 2016 over $1,070,000 (but not more than five additional years) is allowed.[31]

An ESOP is subject to the minimum distribution requirements of IRC §401(a)(9) (as discussed in Chapter 7). However, plan participants can elect to receive substantial equal periodic payments of their account balance not less than once per year after the participant separates from service. The substantially equal periodic payments must be for a period no longer than five years, unless the participant's account balance is valued at more than $1,070,000 for 2016, in which case the distribution period may be extended one year for each additional $210,000 for 2016 of account value up to a total of ten years. If the participant's separation from service is due to the participant's attainment of the plan's normal retirement age, death, or disability, these substantially equal periodic payments must begin within one year after the participant's separation from service. If the participant's separation is for any other reason, these substantially equal periodic payments must begin within one year after the fifth year after the participant's separation.[32]

These rules simply provide the plan participant with a level of protection from the plan sponsor spreading out distributions over an extended period of time.

Any distribution from an ESOP that is not a lump distribution of the employer securities will not be eligible to receive NUA treatment and will be taxed as ordinary income. These distributions may also be subjected to the 10 percent early withdrawal penalty unless the distribution complies with one of the exceptions detailed in Chapter 7.

---

30. IRC §409(o)(1)(C).
31. IRC §409(o)(1)(C)(ii).
32. IRC §409(o)(1).

EXAMPLE 6.3

Fred retires, at normal retirement age, from his career with Risky Business in 2016. At his retirement, the value of Fred's ESOP is $400,000. Fred may have several options:

1. The plan may allow Fred to take distributions from the plan at his discretion.
2. The plan may allow Fred to roll over the account balance into an IRA rollover account.
3. Fred may leave the assets in his ESOP until he attains the age of 70½, at which time he will be required to begin taking his required minimum distributions.
4. The plan must allow Fred, if he elects, to begin taking annual substantially equal periodic payments in 2017.

In any case, if Fred's distribution is not a lump-sum distribution of his employer's securities, the distribution will be taxed as ordinary income.

Valuation of Employer Stock in ESOPs

Valuation of the employer's securities is an important area of ESOP administration. Valuations are necessary for various reasons, which include:

- When contributions are made to an employee's account, the employer must know the value of the contribution for the corporation's tax deduction purposes.
- When contributions are made to an employee's account, the employee must know the value of the contribution for future NUA calculation.
- If a lender lends money to leverage the ESOP, the lender must know the value of the stock to determine if and how much money to lend to the corporation.
- If an employee exercises the put or repurchase option, the value of the stock must be determined.
- Valuations are needed for financial statements and reports.

Valuations for ESOP transactions should be guided by current appraisals by outside, independent valuation experts. Publicly traded stock is readily valued by looking to the stock's market price, whereas determining the value of a closely held corporation's securities is much more involved and costly. If securities are not readily tradable on an established securities market, then valuations must be undertaken by independent appraisers, who must be uninterested, independent parties.[33] The corporation's lender may also place further requirements on the corporation regarding the valuation of the stock. The valuation must be done in good faith and must be based on all factors relevant to determining the securities' fair market value, resulting in an assessment of what a willing buyer would pay to a willing seller for the securities.[34]

---

33. IRC §401(a)(28)(C).
34. Regulations §54.4975-11(d)(5). See also ***Donovan v. Cunningham*** 541 ESOPs 246 (S.D. Texas 1982).

If a valuation is overstated the corporation may be penalized. Any tax deduction based on these valuations can be lost if the value used is later determined to be overstated. Also, if the securities are purchased by the ESOP for an amount higher than their fair market value, then the corporation may be subject to excise tax.[35] In some extreme cases, the ESOP may be disqualified altogether, losing its status as an ESOP and as a qualified plan. If the trustee is found to have caused the ESOP to buy stock at a price greater than its fair market value, the trustee may be deemed to have violated his fiduciary obligations and can be personally liable to the ESOP participants for the amount of the overpayment.

ERISA requires the ESOP to purchase the stock using an **adequate consideration standard**. Adequate consideration has been defined as fair market value determined in good faith.[36] **Fair market value** in the context of fiduciary breaches in ERISA cases has been defined as "the price that a willing buyer would pay a willing seller, both having reasonable knowledge of the pertinent facts."

QUICK QUIZ 6.4

1. The majority of ESOPs are established by publicly traded corporations.
   a. True
   b. False

2. ESOPs for privately held corporations are not required to provide full voting rights for shares held in the plan.
   a. True
   b. False

3. Employer contributions to an ESOP are tax deductible.
   a. True
   b. False

4. An ESOP is not subject to the minimum distribution rules.
   a. True
   b. False

False, True, True, False.

EXAMPLE 6.4

Matthew has owned a toy train business for 30 years. He wants to retire early. The business is worth approximately $10 million. Matthew cannot find a third-party buyer for his business; thus, he has been advised to consider the establishment of an ESOP. Matthew hires an appraiser, who values the stock at $10 million. A banker agrees that the corporation is worth approximately $10 million, and the bank lends money to Matthew's train business to establish an ESOP. Matthew can, in effect, sell his stock to the ESOP and receive non-recognition of gain treatment if the ESOP holds the stock for more than three years, the ESOP owns more than thirty percent (30%) of the stock, and Matthew purchases qualified replacement property within twelve months of the sale.

In the scenario above, Matthew was able to eliminate his concentrated portfolio and was also able to reduce his business risk in the train corporation by diversifying his portfolio without incurring taxation and related costs. Matthew was also able to align the economic incentives of the employees to that of the business by making employees part owners in the train business. Unfortunately, both Matthew and the corporation will probably be required by the bank to be guarantors of the loan to the trust; thus, Matthew will retain some risk until the loan is repaid.

---

35. Revenue Ruling, 69-494, 1969-2 C.B. 88.
36. 29 U.S.C. §1002 (18)(B).

EXAMPLE 6.5

Assume the same facts as above except that Matthew has an adjusted basis of $300,000 in the corporation, and he sells seventy percent (70%) of his stock in the corporation to the ESOP and uses those funds to obtain a diversified portfolio of common stock by purchasing $1 million of stock in corporations A, B, C, D, E, F, and G ($1 million for each), for a total of $7 million. The basis of the $7 million is $210,000 (70% of $300,000). The qualified replacement property is all stock in domestic corporations. Assume that after the transactions and within applicable time periods, Matthew sells stock A for $1.5 million and sells stock B for $850,000. What is the tax treatment for the sale of A and B?

Matthew will be taxed once he sells the stock. His adjusted basis is his "carry over basis" in the original shares of stock. The basis in stock A is $30,000, 1/7th of 70% of $300,000. With an adjusted basis of $30,000, the first $30,000 is a return of basis. The remaining $1,470,000 is taxed as a long-term capital gain. As for stock B, his adjusted basis again is $30,000, 1/7th of 70% of $300,000. The first $30,000 is a return of basis, while the remaining $820,000 ($850,000 - $30,000) is taxed as a long-term capital gain.

EXAMPLE 6.6

Assume that Matthew bequeaths stock in corporations C, D, and E to Michael, his brother. At the time of Matthew's death, the stock in C, D, and E were worth $2 million each. If Michael inherits and then sells these stocks, what would his basis be?

With capital assets, there is a "step to fair market value" or an adjustment to fair market value of the adjusted basis at the time of death. The "step up" in this case occurs at death, and Matthew's original adjusted basis $300,000 is not taken into account. Therefore, Michael's (the heir of the stock) basis is $2 million dollars for each stock C, D, and E.

DIVERSIFICATION ISSUES

ESOPs are permitted to hold 100 percent of the corporate stock in the trust. Most, if not all, of the stock in the ESOP trust is stock in the corporation where the employee-participant works. If the corporation files for bankruptcy or becomes insolvent, then the employee-participant will likely lose his entire investment. Employees with corporate stock in ESOPs are prohibited from selling their shares to diversify their holdings while employed unless they meet certain requirements. Under the IRC, qualified participants may force diversification of their holdings if they are a **qualified participant** during the **qualified election period**.

Qualified participant - the term "qualified participant" means any employee who has completed at least 10 years of participation under the plan and has attained age 55.

Qualified election period - the term "qualified election period" means the 6-plan-year period beginning with the first plan year in which the individual first became a qualified participant.

If the participant meets these qualification requirements, the ESOP must provide the participant with either the opportunity to receive a distribution from the ESOP or alternative investment options for a percentage of his account. The qualified participant must be offered a diversification election within 90 days after the close of each plan year beginning with the year after the employee becomes qualified.[37] The participant may elect to diversify up to 25 percent of the account balance into non-employer stock at this time. The election to diversify is cumulative; therefore, if an election is made to diversify 10 percent of the assets in the first eligible year, an election could be made to diversify an additional 15 percent of the account balance the following year. The final election year is the last year of the 6-plan-year period. In the final election year, the cumulative diversifiable percentage is increased to 50 percent.[38]

The plan documents may satisfy the requirements of diversification of investments if the plan documents offer at least three investment options (consistent with regulations prescribed under the Internal Revenue Code, e.g., a cash fund, a bond fund, and a stock fund) to each participant making a diversification election. Within 90 days after the period during which the election was chosen, the plan must invest the portion of the participant's account covered by the election.[39]

Kerstin is a participant in Smith Corporation's ESOP. Kerstin has been with the company for 20 years. Kerstin turns 55 this year. The ESOP must allow Kerstin to diversify up to 25% of her account balance for the current year. Assume she has the plan diversify 15% for the current year, next year she could diversify the remaining 10% allowed for a total of 25%.

EXAMPLE 6.7

Ben has 10 years of participation in the Blackrock Corporation ESOP and turns age 55 in November of the 2016 plan year. The ESOP uses a calendar year plan. During the 90-day period beginning on January 1, 2017, and ending on March 31, 2017, Ben may direct the trustee to diversify up to 25% of his account balance. If he elects to diversify the 25% maximum amount, then he could only elect to diversify amounts attributable to increases (from investment gains or additional contributions) in his account balance during the 2018, 2019, 2020 and 2021 election periods. From January 1, 2022, to March 31, 2022, Ben must be given the opportunity to diversify up to a cumulative 50% of his account balance at the end of the 2021 plan year.

EXAMPLE 6.8

If Ben did not elect to diversify any portion of the ESOP account balance during the 2017 election period, a similar election would be available during the 2018, 2019, 2020 and 2021 election periods. In each year, he could elect to diversify the portion of his account balance that, when aggregated with prior amounts for which diversification was elected, did not exceed 25% of the account balance at the end of that year. If Ben did not elect any diversification during the 2017 - 2021 election periods, a final election would be available in 2022 (the election period following the plan year in which he reaches age 60) to diversify as much as 50% of his account balance.

---

37. IRC §401(a)(28)(B)(i).
38. IRC §401(a)(28).
39. IRC §401(a)(28)(B)(ii).

Although the Pension Protection Act of 2006 mandates certain investment diversification requirements for defined contribution plans (for plan years beginning after 2006), the new diversification requirements do not apply to an ESOP if:

1. there are no contributions to the ESOP (or earnings thereunder) that are subject to the special nondiscrimination tests that apply to elective deferrals, employee after-tax contributions, and matching contributions; and
2. the ESOP is a separate plan from any other qualified plan of the employer.

Therefore, while many ESOPs will qualify for the above exception and will thus only be subject to the general ESOP diversification requirements discussed above, ESOPs that provide for elective deferrals will need to comply with the new diversification requirements. The new diversification requirements, which also affect defined contribution pension plans, are discussed in greater depth in Chapter 4.

PUT OPTIONS

Once a plan meets the distribution requirements and a participant is entitled to a distribution from the plan, the participant has the right to demand that the benefits be distributed in the form of employer securities. If the employer securities are not readily tradable on an established market, the participant has the right to require that the employer repurchase the employer securities under a fair market valuation formula. This is referred to as a "put option" or "repurchase option" under ESOPs. This also applies equally with stock bonus plans.

> **KEY CONCEPTS**
>
> 1. Under what circumstances can an ESOP participant require the employer to diversify the participant's holdings?
>
> 2. When must a closely held corporation provide a put option to the participants of an ESOP?
>
> 3. Explain the inherent conflict of interest within an ESOP.
>
> 4. Discuss the impact of an S Corporation ESOP participant demanding a stock distribution.

The put or repurchase option is a substantial benefit to an employee-participant of an ESOP. A closely held or private corporation that sponsors an ESOP must provide for a "put option" on corporate stock that is distributed to employee-participants.[40] The rank-and-file employees are protected with the put option because the employee may force the corporation to "buy back" the stock at the fair market value when there otherwise would be no market for the stock. If no put option is provided, then the corporation could choose not to purchase the departing employee's stock, leaving the employee with stock that cannot be sold or liquidated. Indeed, this rule applies to closely held or private corporations because the inherent nature of closely held or private corporations is that there is no readily established securities market for the stock. ESOPs may offer the right of first refusal to the corporation to buy back the stock from participants to prevent the stock from being owned and controlled by outside entities. At a minimum, the put option must be available during two time periods, one for no less than sixty days immediately following the distribution and the second, if the put option is not exercised within such 60-day period, for an additional period of at least 60 days in the following plan year.[41]

---

40. IRC §409(h).
41. IRC §409(h)(4).

If a corporation is forced to repurchase the stock that was distributed to the employee as part of a total distribution,[42] then the corporation's repurchasing of that stock under a fair valuation formula[43] is satisfied if the corporation pays the participant in substantial equal periodic payments over a period beginning no later than 30 days after the exercise of the put option. However, this periodic payment must not be paid less frequently than annually and must be completed within five years.[44] For periodic repayments, reasonable interests and adequate security must be given.[45] If a put option is exercised after an installment distribution of the employer stock, then the employer must repurchase the stock within 30 days to fulfill the put option.[46]

> Michael, an employee of KAC corporation, receives a stock distribution of ten shares of stock in KAC corporation on October 10, 2016 as a participant of an ESOP. KAC is a closely held corporation. If Michael exercises his put option ninety days after distribution, is KAC corporation required to honor his put option?
>
> The answer is initially no, but ultimately yes. Michael must exercise his put option within 60 days following the distribution according to IRC §409(h)(4); however, IRC §409(h)(4) also provides an additional 60 day period in the following plan year, which would start on January 1, 2017 and continue through February 28, 2017, and thus Michael's exercise of his put option would be timely under IRC §409(h)(4) with respect to the additional 60 days within the following taxable year of the plan.

EXAMPLE 6.9

---

42. Total distribution is defined as the distribution within one tax year of the balance of the recipient's account. IRC §409(h)(5).
43. IRC §409(h)(1)(B).
44. IRC §409(h)(5), 409(h)(5)(A) and 409(h)(5)(B).
45. IRC §409(h)(5)(B).
46. IRC §409(h)(6).

Case Study 6.1

The case of **Roth v. Sawyer-Cleaton Lumber Co.**,[1] dealt with the ESOP trustees' decisions concerning put options. Roth was a former employee of Sawyer-Cleaton, a closely held corporation engaged in lumber sales. Under the corporation's ESOP plan documents, each participant had one account consisting of corporation stock and another consisting of other investments, and participants could exercise a put option on stock issued. At the time of Roth's retirement in 1988, Roth chose to exercise his put option. The stock sale was accomplished through a promissory note and stock pledge agreement. The Plan obligated itself to make payments to Roth over ten years with Roth retaining a security interest in his stock under the stock pledge agreement. Roth received partial payment of the sums due under the promissory note, but the corporation began to experience financial troubles. In 1990, the corporation terminated its business operations, and the Plan defaulted on payments due under the promissory note.

By 1991, the corporation was forced into Chapter 7 bankruptcy and Roth's stock and security became worthless.[2] Roth sued the ESOP and its trustees, claiming breach of fiduciary duty because of the failure to adequately secure notes given from the Plan and the assumption of the notes by the Plan. The court ultimately concluded that Roth's loss caused by the trustees' decision to secure the plaintiff's promissory note with corporation stock and to make the ESOP the obligated party on the plaintiff's notes. Therefore, the trustees in that case could be liable for breach of fiduciary duty.[3]

1. *Roth v. Sawyer-Cleaton Lumber Co.*, 61 F.3d 599 (8th Cir. 1995).
2. *Roth*, 61 F.3d 599, 601.
3. *Id*. at 605.

THE ESOP TRUSTEE AND "INHERENT" CONFLICTS

The ESOP is created by written plan documents, which are responsible for the establishment of the trust. The plan sponsor establishes the plan and the trust, and in some cases the trust borrows from a bank or other type of lender. The tax deductible contributions are paid to the trust, and in some cases the trust repays funds to the bank or lender. Under this complicated set of transactions, the trust must use the loan proceeds to acquire the employer stock. The trust is administered by the trustee, who, depending on the specific plan and the documents creating it, is an individual, a group of individuals, committee, or entity.[47] The trustee holds funds "in trust" for the benefit of employees, participants, and their beneficiaries. The trustee purchases employer securities, deals with the corporation, interacts with the bank or lender, and keeps the employee-participants apprised of the status and value of their accounts. In addition to all of these duties, the ESOP

47. Interestingly, the corporation may have its own ESOP committee that is part of the corporation and not the ESOP, and the ESOP committee could have been charged with establishing and drafting the documents that formed the ESOP and its trustee.

trustee must strive to preserve the ESOP's fundamental goal of investing plan assets into employer securities. The trustee is held to the standard of a fiduciary.

There are times where the interests of the employees, the interests of the corporation, and the interests of the management of the corporation are different or even in conflict. Often, the trustee is forced to navigate these complicated and perplexing issues and bear the brunt of criticism or claims. There has been much litigation over these issues in the case law.[48] Occasionally, individuals serve in a dual capacity concerning the ESOP, both as trustees of the ESOP and as officers, directors, or employees of the corporation. The corporation is the plan sponsor and a potential conflict of interest can arise. Here, as detailed in *Shoen v. Americo, 885 F.Supp. 1332*, the ideal course of action for the trustee could be that "trustees of an [ESOP] must discharge their duties by evaluating the best interest of the beneficiaries in the abstract as beneficiaries, not as directors who may lose control of the corporation nor as employees, some of whom may lose their jobs if control of the corporation changes hands."[49] The courts have generally concluded that if the conflict of interest is so great that it is virtually impossible for the fiduciary to discharge the duties with "an eye to the beneficiaries' interests," then the preferred course of action for a fiduciary of a plan holding or acquiring the stock of a target, who is also an officer, director, or employee of a party in interest seeking to acquire or retain control of the target, is to resign and clear the way for the appointment of a genuinely neutral trustee to manage the assets involved in the control contest.[50]

There are cases in which the conflict of interest, although substantial, is not so great as to require the trustee's resignation. The question in these cases becomes whether the fiduciary engaged in an intensive and independent investigation of alternatives to insure that the action taken was in the shareholders' best interests. One element of this inquiry is the extent to which the use of the trust's assets track the best interest of another party. The bottom line is, considering the duty imposed on the fiduciary under these circumstances, trustees must avoid placing themselves in a position where their acts as officers or directors of the corporation will prevent their functioning with the complete loyalty to participants demanded of them as trustees of the pension plan.[51] For instance, ESOP trustees will probably be found to have breached their fiduciary duties if they form a separate corporation designed to compete with the corporation where they are an ESOP trustee.[52]

The court in the *Shoen* decision also noted a second problem that is common in litigation concerning control of the corporation as it relates to the trustee's duty to monitor communications to participants. ESOPs, the court acknowledged in *Shoen*, typically contain provisions for "pass through" voting by the participants to qualify for favorable tax treatment under IRC §409. Basically each participant can direct the ESOP trustees on how to vote the shares allocated to the participant's individual account in the ESOP if it is a closely held corporation not concerning major corporate decisions. The court in *Shoen* explained that the contesting parties desired to communicate quickly and frequently with the participants, and in such a situation, according to the Department of Labor, the trustee's fiduciary duty mandates that the trustee insure that

48. See, for example, *Shoen v. Americo*, 885 F.Supp. 1332, 1348 (D. Nev. 1994); *Chas v. Archer*, 827 F.Supp. 159, 169 (W.D.N.Y. 1993).
49. *Central Trust Corporation, N.A. v. American Avents Corp.*, 771 F.Supp. 871, 874-875 (S.D. Ohio 1989).
50. *Danaher Corp. v. Chicago Pneumatic Tool Co.*, 635 F. Supp. 246, 250 (S.D.N.Y. 1986) (quoting *Leigh v. Engle*, 727 F.2d 113, 122 (7th Cir. 1984).
51. *Shoen*, 885 F.Supp. at 1348; *Donovan v. Bierwirth*, 680 F.2d 263, 271 (2nd Cir. 1982).
52. See *Neyer, Tisco & Hindo, Ltd. v. Russell*, 1993 WL 52552 (E.D. Pa. 1993).

necessary information is given to participants, that misleading or false information is not provided to participants, and that participants render an independent decision free from duress or pressure from their employer as to how to vote.[53] The court also indicated that ESOPs have been known to be established to serve as anti-takeover devices, with the theory being that the ESOP will own a significant amount of the corporation's stock and will, because the voting of that stock is directed by the corporation's employees through the "pass through" framework, be friendlier in a contest of control to the incumbent management than to an outside, hostile force or entity.[54]

For an investment advisor to be deemed a "fiduciary" under ERISA's "renders investment advice" definition, the investment advisor must render advice pursuant to an agreement, be paid for such advice, and have influence approaching control over benefit plan's investment decisions.[55] The trustee must also be prudent. ERISA's "prudence" requirement commands a fiduciary to act "with the care, skill, prudence, and diligence under circumstances then prevailing that a prudent man acting in a like capacity and familiar with such matters would use in the conduct of an enterprise of a like character and with like aims."[56]

Case Study 6.2

In *Kuper v. Iovenko*,[1] the plaintiffs filed claims under ERISA for breach of fiduciary duty against the ESOP trustees and administrators. The plaintiffs were employees of the Emery Division of Quantum Chemical Corp. These employees were participants in the corporation's ESOP. Quantum entered into an agreement to sell its Emery Division to Henkel Corporation. Henkel Corporation, in the meantime, agreed to employ existing employees of Emery Division under comparable terms and to accept the trust-to-trust transfer of the ESOP assets of those employees who continued employment with Henkel Corporation following the sale. Although the sale was effective on April 17, 1989, the trust-to-trust transfer of ESOP assets was not completed until roughly a year and a half later. During this 18-month period, Quantum's stock declined in value from more than $50 per share to approximately $10 per share. Plaintiffs contended that Quantum's acknowledged failure to consider diversifying or liquidating the ESOP constituted a breach of fiduciary duty owed to the plan and its participants.

1. *Kuper v. Iovenko*, 66 F.3d 1447 (6th Cir.1995).

---

53. *Shoen*, 885 F.Supp. at 1349.

Case Study 6.2 Continued

Finally, the United States Sixth Circuit conducted a balancing act of the competing concerns. After this delicate balancing of varying interests, the Court held that an ESOP fiduciary's decision to continue investing in employer securities is reviewed for abuse of discretion. This balancing act is done with the purpose of ERISA on the one hand and the nature of ESOPs on the other. In this scenario, the courts may presume that a fiduciary's decision to remain invested in employer securities was reasonable. A plaintiff may rebut this presumption of reasonableness by showing that a prudent ESOP fiduciary acting under similar circumstances would have made a different investment decision.[1]

In defending the case, the defendants in **Kuper** asserted that the terms of the ESOP did not give them discretion to diversify or to liquidate the ESOP funds. The United States Sixth Circuit Court of Appeals discussed the duties of ERISA fiduciaries in general and the exemptions from those duties for ESOP fiduciaries.[2] Fiduciary duties under ERISA, the court explained, have three components:

- the duty of loyalty, which requires the fiduciary to make all decisions regarding an ERISA plan "with an eye single to the interests of the participants and beneficiaries;"[3]
- the "prudent man" obligation, which requires the fiduciary to act as a prudent person would act in a similar situation or under similar circumstances; and
- the exclusive purpose obligation, which requires the fiduciary to act for the exclusive purpose of providing benefits to plan beneficiaries.[4]

The United States Sixth Circuit reasoned that an ESOP fiduciary is exempt from the duty to diversify investments and cannot be held liable for failing to diversify investments even if diversification would be prudent under the terms of a non-ESOP plan. These statutory exemptions, however, do not relieve a fiduciary from the general fiduciary responsibilities enumerated above.[5] "Thus, ESOP fiduciaries must, then, wear two hats and are expected to administer ESOP investments consistent with the provisions of both a specific employee benefits plan and ERISA... These competing concerns make it more difficult to delineate the responsibilities of ESOP trustees."[6]

1. See also *Keach v. United States Trust Co., N.A.*, 222 F.Supp.2d 1224 (C.D.Ill. Dec. 30, 2002), 2002 WL 31887909.
2. **Kuper v. Iovenko**, 66 F.3d 1447, 1458 (6th Cir.1995).
3. **Kuper**, 66 F.3d at 1458.
4. *Id.*
5. *Id.* (citing **Martin v. Feilen**, 965 F.2d 660, 665 (8th Cir.1992)).
6. *Id.*

---

54. *Id.* at 1355 n.35.
55. ERISA, 29 U.S.C.A. §1002(21)(A)(ii).
56. 29 U.S.C. §1104(a)(1)(B).

Case Study 6.3

In some situations, an ESOP trustee may be deemed to have been required to obtain advice from a separate independent party. In **Leigh v. Eagle**,[1] plan administrators played a role in having the plan they directed to invest, along with corporations they controlled, into the stock of corporations that the plan administrators, i.e., fiduciaries, were attempting to acquire. The plan administrators did not perform an independent, diligent investigation into the investment options available to the trust. Nor did these fiduciaries seek out independent advice from separate third parties concerning investment options. Even though the trust did not lose money and the trust did not decrease in value based on the actions of these fiduciaries, the court found that the fiduciaries nonetheless breached their duty by failing to seek out independent advice or embark on an independent, diligent investigation into investment options available to the trust.

1. **Leigh v. Eagle**, 727 F.2d 113, 129 (7th Cir. 1984).

Case Study 6.4

In **Wright v. Oregon Metallurgical Corp.**,[1] an Oregon District Court was asked to evaluate an ESOP trustee's fiduciary obligations. The fiduciary duties in that case arose with the creation of an ESOP designed to finance the leveraged buyout of the owner's shares. The Court explained that under ERISA, a fiduciary is required to discharge his duties:
* "Solely in the interest of the participants and beneficiaries;" and
* with the exclusive purpose of providing benefits to participants and their beneficiaries and defraying reasonable expenses of administering the plan [the exclusive purpose requirement];
* with the care, skill, prudence, and diligence under circumstances then prevailing that a prudent man acting in a like capacity and familiar with such matters would use in the conduct of an enterprise of a like character and with like aims [the prudence requirement];
* by diversifying the investments of the plan in order to minimize the risk of large losses, unless under the circumstances it is clearly prudent not to do so [the diversification requirement]; and
* in accordance with the documents and instruments governing the plan insofar as such documents and instruments are consistent with the provisions of ERISA.

1. **Wright v. Oregon Metallurgical Corp.**, 222 F. Supp. 2d 1224, 28 Employee Benefits Cas. 2006 (D. Oregon, Aug. 6, 2002).

The law and jurisprudence relating to trustees shows that the ESOP trustee must strive to preserve the ESOP's fundamental goal of investing plan assets into employer securities, all the while being held to the standard of a fiduciary while purchasing employer securities, dealing with the corporation, interacting with the bank or lender, and keeping employee-participants updated as to the value of their accounts and status of the ESOP as a whole.

S Corporations' Role as an Owner of ESOPs

IRC §1361 was amended in 1996 by the Small Business Job Protection Act, which allowed qualified plan trusts and §501(c)(3) organizations to be shareholders of S Corporations. Therefore, S Corporations may establish ESOPs, and ESOPs are permitted to own the stock of an S Corporation.[57] **S Corporations** are generally small corporations that:

- have no more than 100 shareholders,
- have shareholders that are individuals, and[58]
- have only one class of stock.

A significant change in the law occurred when an ESOP maintained by an S Corporation was treated as not violating the Code's qualification requirements nor as engaging in a prohibited transaction. In accordance with plan documentation, distributions of S Corporation stock that constitute qualifying employer securities held by the ESOP may be used to make interest and principal payments on loans utilized to acquire securities.

At first, it would appear that the 100 shareholder limitation would create an issue with respect to the number of participants in the ESOP. Nonetheless, the participants in the ESOP are not counted towards the 100 shareholder limit for an S Corporation. Instead, the ESOP is deemed to be only one shareholder.

> Matthew, Patrick, Michael, and American ESOP all hold shares in the same S Corporation. American ESOP has seven employee-participants in its ESOP. Matthew, Patrick and Michael are not employee-participants of American ESOP. Based on this factual scenario, how many shareholders are there of the S Corporation?
>
> The answer is four. Matthew, Patrick, and Michael count as three shareholders and American ESOP is considered to be one shareholder. American ESOP is not deemed to be seven shareholders because the employee-participants are not counted towards the aggregate number of shareholders in the S Corporation.

EXAMPLE 6.10

The Taxpayer Relief Act of 1997 also added several beneficial changes to the way ESOPs and S Corporations are treated, including an amendment to §409(h)(2) of the IRC. This amendment allowed ESOPs the power to prevent participants from demanding stock distributions. Otherwise, a participant could terminate a corporation's S Corporation status by demanding a stock distribution and then placing that stock in an IRA, which is not permitted to hold stock in an S Corporation.[59] This law was somewhat modified concerning banks that are S Corporations. Section 1361 of the Internal Revenue Code now provides that an IRA or Roth IRA may be a

---

57. IRC §1361.
58. The shareholders can be individuals, an estate, some trusts, a qualified retirement plan, or other qualified entities, but generally must be an individual. Also, a nonresident alien cannot serve as a shareholder of an S Corporation.
59. IRC §409(h)(2).

shareholder of a bank that is an S Corporation, but only to the extent of bank stock held by the IRA as of the date of enactment of the provision, which is October 22, 2004.[60] With respect to dividends, the IRC prohibits S Corporations from deducting dividends paid from employer securities that are held by ESOPs.[61]

The income of an S Corporation passes through to the ESOP, and because an ESOP is tax exempt, no tax is paid on the income until it is distributed to the ESOP participant. ESOPs are advantageous in S Corporations to the extent that, among the S Corporation owners, the ESOP is not required to pay federal income taxes on its profits. In sum, it is important to note in the financial planning and estate planning process that ESOPs used in conjunction with S corporations can provide significant financial benefits to owners and employees. The same is likewise true for stock bonus plans.

Ultimately, the attractiveness of flow-through income from an S corporation avoiding taxation in an ESOP until distributed was too much for some taxpayers and resulted in significant abuse during the late 1990s. As a result, Congress added IRC §409(p) in 2001, entitled Prohibited Allocations of Securities in an S corporation, which is designed to limit a concentration of the benefits of an ESOP to a small number of persons.

The general rule under this section is that no allocations of stock within the ESOP can accrue to a disqualified person in a nonallocation year. Below are the definitions of disqualified persons and a nonallocation year.

Disqualified persons - any person who:
1. owns with other family members 20 percent or more of the stock of the company, or
2. in the case of someone without other family ownership, owns 10 percent or more of the stock of the company.

Nonallocation year[62] - any plan year of an employee stock ownership plan that holds employer securities consisting of stock in an S corporation, and disqualified persons own at least 50 percent of the number of shares of stock in the S corporation.

In effect, the owners of a closely held S corporation are prohibited from benefiting under an ESOP arrangement when there is a significant concentration of ownership. However, these rules should not be considered as a reason to not consider an ESOP for an S corporation. On the contrary, Congress purposely changed the Internal Revenue Code to allow S corporations to benefit from ESOP arrangements. These rules that were put in place in 2001 were intended to minimize the abusive transactions involving ESOPs and S corporations.

---

60. IRC §1361(c)(2)(A)(vi).
61. IRC §404(k)(1).
62. IRC §409(p)(3)(A).

Case Study 6.5

Ries Enterprises, Inc. v. Commissioner, U.S. Tax Court, Dkt. No. 9941-11, TC Memo. 2014-14 (January 27, 2014).

John Ries ("Ries") incorporated the subject company ("Petitioner") in 2002 to engage in the rental and leasing business. In the same year, Petitioner elected to be treated as an S corporation. With this election, in 2002 Petitioner filed a Form 1120S, U.S. Income Tax Return for an S Corporation, and did not pay federal income tax. Petitioner had two classes of stock outstanding at the time it elected to be treated as an S corporation.

In its ruling, the Tax Court found that, for purposes of Section 409(p), 2002 was a "nonallocation" year. A nonallocation year, the Tax Court reasoned, includes any plan year of an ESOP holding shares of an S corporation where a disqualified person owns at least 50 percent of the S corporation's outstanding stock. See Ries Enterprises, TC Memo Ruling, at p. 13 (citing Section 409(p)(3)(A)) et seq. A taxpayer is treated as owning the shares that his or her spouse owns. Id. (citing Section 409(p)(3)(B). A taxpayer is also treated as owning deemed-owned shares. A Trust held 80 percent of Petitioner's stock during 2002, and Mr. Ries and his wife owned the remaining 20 percent. Mr. Ries, a disqualified person, was therefore treated as owning all of Petitioner's stock for 2002. Id. at 13-14 (citing Section 409(p)(3)).

Based on the foregoing, the court ruled that the plan made an impermissible allocation of Petitioner's stock in 2002, thereby violating Section 409(p). In short, the S corporation's sole owner was a disqualified person in an nonallocation year, and hence the prohibited transaction tax applied.

SUMMARY

Stock bonus plans provide benefits similar to those of profit sharing plans, except that benefits are normally distributed in the form of employer securities. ESOPs are the most common type of stock bonus plans. An ESOP can be a very powerful tool for closely held businesses. ESOPs provide tax benefits and satisfy the employer's goals of having motivated, loyal, and long-term employees. Meanwhile, the employees are provided with value for services rendered and are able to accumulate assets that are provided over time towards retirement. Employees also become part owners of a corporation in which they work, which should increase their productivity, efficiency, and motivations. A key ingredient of the ESOP is that the corporation has the ability to borrow (leverage) to purchase the employer stock.

The leveraging aspect of ESOPs, along with the tax deductibility of the payments, make ESOPs a very attractive tool in the financial planning and estate planning areas. On the other hand, because the investments of ESOPs are primarily in employer securities, it is a highly non-diversified and risky investment depending on the strength, standing, and goodwill of the corporation as an on going entity. If the corporation were to fail, the ESOP and the accounts of the individual employee-participants may be rendered worthless. Nonetheless, depending on each individual situation, financial planning advice and estate planning advice must be given with these advantages and disadvantages in mind. The ESOP trustees may be the ones named in subsequent lawsuits if ESOPs fail, or the businesses with which they are affiliated fail.

Stock bonus plans and ESOPs are primarily used to avoid putting cash into a qualified plan while a corporation is growing and needs the cash for growth. The problem with these plans is that eventually cash must be contributed to diversify the 55-year olds, those terminating participants, and in the case of a closely held corporation to provide a market for those retirees or plan participants who wish to sell their shares. It is also important to remember that stock bonus plans and ESOPs are "pay me now or pay me later" qualified plans and as the employer stock becomes more valuable, the plan will need more and more cash to redeem any outstanding shares. Sponsors considering adopting a stock bonus or ESOP plan should carefully consider not only the initial tax deduction and cash flow impact but the ultimate necessity to fund the plan with sufficient cash to redeem shares under the put option and diversify the investment portfolios for those participants age 55 or older.

QUICK QUIZ 6.5

1. The put option protects the rank-and-file employees.
   a. True
   b. False

2. The trustee of an ESOP must act in the best interest of the plan participants and beneficiaries.
   a. True
   b. False

3. An S Corporation cannot establish an ESOP.
   a. True
   b. False

True, True, False.

COMPARISON OF STOCK BONUS PLANS TO ESOPS

EXHIBIT
6.7

	Stock Bonus Plans	ESOPs
Plan Establishment	December 31	December 31
Date of Contribution	Due date of tax return plus extensions	Due date of tax return plus extensions
Type of Contributions	Generally stock	Generally stock
Deductible Contribution Limit	*25% of covered compensation*	*25% of covered compensation plus interest paid on loan*
Valuation	Generally needed	Generally needed plus dividends (in certain circumstances)
Eligibility	Same as other Qualified Plans (21 and 1 year of service or 2 years with 100% vesting)	Same as other Qualified Plans (21 and 1 year of service or 2 years with 100% vesting)
Allocation Method	% of compensation or formula based on age, service of classification	% of compensation or formula based on age, service of classification
Integration with Social Security	*Yes*	*No*
Vesting	Same as other Defined Contribution Qualified Plans (3-year cliff or 2 to 6 year graduated vesting)*	Same as other Defined Contribution Qualified Plans (3-year cliff or 2 to 6 year graduated vesting)*
Portfolio Diversification	*No**	Yes, up to 25% (or 50% in final year) if at least 55 years old and 10 years of participation
Voting Rights	Generally yes	Generally yes
Distributions	Generally stock	Generally stock
In-Service Withdrawals	May be allowed after two years of participation	May be allowed after two years of participation
Loans	May be allowed (but not usually)	May be allowed (but not usually)
Taxation of Distributions	Ordinary income with NUA treatment available	Ordinary income with NUA treatment available

Note: The differences between Stock Bonus Plans and ESOPs are highlighted in blue.

Effective for plan years after 2006 under the Pension Protection Act of 2006.

*** Diversification may be required under PPA 2006 for stock bonus plans of publicly traded companies.*

KEY TERMS

ADEQUATE CONSIDERATION STANDARD - Fair market value determined in good faith.

DILUTION - The reduction in the monetary value or voting power of an owner's stock as a result of contributions to stock bonus plans and ESOPs.

DISCRETIONARY - The choice for a plan sponsor of a profit sharing plan as to the amount and frequency of a contribution.

DISQUALIFIED PERSONS - any person who owns with other family members 20 percent or more of the stock of the company, or in the case of someone without other family ownership, owns 10 percent or more of the stock of the company.

DIVERSIFIED INVESTMENT PORTFOLIOS - An investment portfolio invested in a broad range of investment classes to reduce investment risk.

EMPLOYEE STOCK OWNERSHIP PLAN (ESOP) - A qualified profit sharing plan that utilizes employer contributions to the plan to purchase the stock of the employer's company and allocates the ownership to the plan participants.

FAIR MARKET VALUE - The price that a willing buyer would pay a willing seller, both having reasonable knowledge of the pertinent facts and neither under duress.

LEVERAGED ESOP - An ESOP that borrows the funds necessary to purchase the employer's stock. The interest and principal repayments on the loan are tax deductible for the employer.

NET UNREALIZED APPRECIATION (NUA) - The appreciation in the value of employer stock after the date of contribution to the plan until the date of distribution.

NONALLOCATION YEAR - Any plan year of an employee stock ownership plan that holds employer securities consisting of stock in an S corporation, and disqualified persons own at least 50 percent of the number of shares of stock in the S corporation.

NONRECOGNITION OF GAIN TREATMENT - A delay in the recognition of gain available to owners of a company that sell company stock to an ESOP. The transaction must meet the stated requirements of the IRC and the owner must reinvest the proceeds from the sale within 12 months of the sale into qualified domestic replacement securities.

PASS THROUGH VOTING RIGHTS - The voting rights of the stock pass through from the ESOP or the stock bonus plan to the participant.

KEY TERMS

QUALIFIED PARTICIPANT - The term "qualified participant" means any employee who has completed at least 10 years of participation under the plan and has attained age 55.

QUALIFIED ELECTION PERIOD - The term "qualified election period" means the 6-plan-year period beginning with the first plan year in which the individual first became a qualified participant.

QUALIFIED REPLACEMENT SECURITIES - Securities in a domestic corporation, including stocks, bonds, debentures, or warrants, which receive no more than 25% of their income from passive investments.

RANK-AND-FILE EMPLOYEES - The non-key, non-highly compensated employees.

REPURCHASE OPTION (PUT OPTION) - An option that allows a terminating employee to receive in cash the fair market value of the employer's stock within a stock bonus plan or ESOP if the employer stock is not readily tradeable on an established market. An option to sell to the employer.

S CORPORATIONS - Small corporations taxed as pass-through entities that cannot have more than 100 individual shareholders and have only one class of stock.

STOCK BONUS PLAN - A qualified profit sharing plan funded solely with employer stock.

SUBSTANTIAL AND RECURRING - IRC standard defining the frequency requirement of contributions by employers to profit sharing plans.

DISCUSSION QUESTIONS

1.   List the required characteristics of a stock bonus plan.

2.   List advantages and disadvantages of stock bonus plans.

3.   List at least three distinctions between profit sharing plans and stock bonus plans.

4.   Why are valuations of the employer's securities completed each year for the plan sponsor of a stock bonus plan?

5.   What are the eligibility requirements for stock bonus plans?

6.   Describe the standard method of allocating contributions to a stock bonus plan.

7.   Explain the stock voting rights of stock bonus plan participants.

8.   Define net unrealized appreciation and discuss the tax advantages related to it.

9.   Define ESOPs and discuss when they are used.

10. Discuss how the leveraged ESOP works.

11. For the owner of a closely held business to qualify for the nonrecognition of capital gain treatment certain requirements must be met. List these requirements.

12. Define qualified replacement securities.

13. List several advantages of an ESOP.

14. List several disadvantages of an ESOP.

15. Describe the voting rights of ESOP participants.

16. Discuss the limitations on contributions to ESOPs.

17. What are the requirements necessary for an employee to force diversification of his holdings in the ESOP?

18. Describe the requirements of the "put option" for an ESOP.

19. Discuss how the changes created by the Taxpayer Relief Act of 1997 with regard to ESOPs impact S Corporations.

MULTIPLE CHOICE PROBLEMS

1. Which of the following are requirements for a qualified stock bonus plan?

   1. Participants must have pass through voting rights for stock held by the plan.
   2. Participants must have the right to demand employer securities at a distribution, even if the plan sponsor is a closely held corporation.

   a. 1 only.
   b. 2 only.
   c. Both 1 and 2.
   d. Neither 1 nor 2.

2. Mike, age 60, is a participant in the stock bonus plan of Tantalus, Inc., a closely held corporation. Mike received contributions in shares to the stock bonus plan and Tantalus, Inc. took income tax deductions as follows:

Year	# of Shares	Value per Share (At Time of Contribution)
2011	100	$10
2012	125	$12
2013	150	$13
2014	200	$15
2016	400	$18

   Mike terminates employment and takes a distribution from the plan of 975 shares of Tantalus, Inc., having a fair value of $19,500. What are Mike's tax consequences?

   a. There are no immediate tax consequences because he has not sold the stock.
   b. Mike has ordinary income of $14,650 at distribution.
   c. Mike has net unrealized appreciation of $19,500 at distribution.
   d. Mike has ordinary income of $19,500 at distribution.

3. Cavin sells stock several years after he received it as a distribution from a qualified stock bonus plan. When the stock was distributed, he had a net unrealized appreciation of $7,500. Cavin also had ordinary income from the distribution of $29,000. The fair market value of the stock and the sales price at the time of sale was $81,000. How much of the sale price will be subject to long-term capital gain treatment?

   a. $7,500.
   b. $44,500.
   c. $52,000.
   d. $73,500.

4. Davin sells stock six months after he received it as a distribution from a qualified stock bonus plan. When the stock was distributed, he had a net unrealized appreciation of $7,500. He also had ordinary income from the distribution of $29,000. The fair value of the stock at the time of sale was $81,000. How much of the sale price will be subject to long-term capital gain treatment?

    a. $7,500.
    b. $44,500.
    c. $52,000.
    d. $73,500.

5. Which of the following are costs of a stock bonus plan?

    1. Periodic appraisal costs.
    2. Periodic actuarial costs.

        a. 1 only.
        b. 2 only.
        c. Both 1 and 2.
        d. Neither 1 nor 2.

6. Patrick and Kevin own Irisha Corporation and plan to retire. They would like to leave their assets to their children; therefore, they transfer 70 percent of the stock to a trust for the benefit of their 10 children pro rata. Patrick and Kevin then plan to sell the remaining Irisha shares to a qualified ESOP plan. Which of the following is correct?

    1. The stock transfer to the ESOP is not a 50 percent transfer and therefore will not qualify for nonrecognition of capital gains.
    2. Any transfer to an ESOP of less than 50 percent ownership may be subject to a minority discount on valuation.

        a. 1 only.
        b. 2 only.
        c. Both 1 and 2.
        d. Neither 1 nor 2.

7. BJ owns NOCTM, Inc. and sells 100 percent of the corporate stock (all outstanding stock) on January 1, 2016 to an ESOP for $5,000,000. His adjusted basis in the stock was $2,400,000. Which of the following is correct?

    1. If BJ reinvests the $5,000,000 in qualified domestic securities within 18 months, he has a carryover basis of $2,400,000 in the qualified domestic security portfolio and no current capital gain.

    2. BJ has a long-term capital gain of $2,600,000 reduced by the 20 percent small business credit; therefore, his gain is $2,080,000 if he does not reinvest in qualified domestic securities within 18 months.

      a. 1 only.

      b. 2 only.

      c. Both 1 and 2.

      d. Neither 1 nor 2.

8. One of the disadvantages of an ESOP is that the stock is an undiversified investment portfolio. Which of the following is correct?

    1. An employee, age 55 or older, who has completed 10 years of participation in an ESOP may require that 100 percent of the account balance be diversified.

    2. An employee who receives corporate stock as a distribution from an ESOP may enjoy net unrealized appreciation treatment at the time of distribution.

      a. 1 only.

      b. 2 only.

      c. Both 1 and 2.

      d. Neither 1 nor 2.

9. Taylor, age 65, retires from Tickle Tile corporation and receives 25,000 shares of Tickle Tile stock with a fair market value of $500,000 in 2016. Taylor recognized $48,000 of ordinary income upon the distribution. What is Taylor's NUA immediately after the distribution?

      a. $48,000.

      b. $348,000.

      c. $452,000.

      d. $500,000.

10. Meb, the owner of Meb's Hardware, is considering establishing a stock bonus plan. She recently talked with her advisor, Don T. Know. Don T. Know never studied when he took his certificate program, therefore he gave Meb incorrect information about stock bonus plans. Which of the following statements given to Meb was correct?

    a.   Meb can establish a stock bonus plan for the previous year anytime before the due date (plus extensions) of Meb's Hardware's tax return.

    b.   When the employee's of Meb's Hardware receive distributions of stock from the stock bonus plan, they will receive capital gain treatment on the distribution equal to the value of the stock as contributed by Meb's Hardware.

    c.   A valuation of the stock of Meb's Hardware is required when the stock bonus plan is established, but subsequent valuations are unnecessary.

    d.   Meb can require the employees to be age 21 and employed for two years before becoming eligible for the stock bonus plan.

11. Sam is a participant in RFK, Inc.'s ESOP. Sam has been a participant in the plan for eight years, and her account balance in the plan is $1,000,000 and is completely funded with employer securities. The plan defines the normal retirement age as 65 years old. Sam is 64 years old this year and would like to retire. Her advisor mentioned that she should have a more diversified portfolio. What, if anything, can she do to diversify her portfolio?

    a.   The only way Sam can diversify her portfolio is to take a distribution of the employer stock from the ESOP and reinvest the value in a diversified portfolio.

    b.   Sam can require the ESOP to diversify her up to 25 percent of her portfolio.

    c.   Since Sam is in the final election year she can require the ESOP to diversify 50 percent of her portfolio.

    d.   Sam can diversify 10 percent each year until the portfolio is completely diversified.

12. Rustin recently retired from Fox, Inc., a national plastics supplier. When Rustin retired his stock bonus plan had 10,000 shares of Fox, Inc. stock. Fox, Inc. took deductions equal to $20 per share for the contributions made on Rustin's behalf. At retirement, Rustin took a lump-sum distribution of the employer stock. The fair market value of the stock at distribution was $35 per share. Six months after distribution, Rustin sold the stock for $40 per share. What amount was subject to ordinary income tax on Rustin's tax return at the date Fox, Inc. contributed the stock to the plan?

    a. $0.

    b. $200,000.

    c. $350,000.

    d. $400,000.

13. Assume the same facts presented in question 12. What amount was subject to ordinary income on Rustin's tax return at the date the stock was distributed?

    a. $0.

    b. $200,000.

    c. $350,000.

    d. $400,000.

14. Assume the same facts presented in question 12. How much gain was Rustin subject to at the date the stock was distributed?

    a. $0.

    b. $50,000 short-term capital gain.

    c. $200,000 long-term capital gain.

    d. $150,000 long-term capital gain and $5,000 short-term capital gain.

    e. $400,000 long-term capital gain.

15. Assume the same facts presented in question 12. Which of the following gain was Rustin subject to at the date the stock was sold?

    a. $0.

    b. $50,000 short-term capital gain.

    c. $200,000 long-term capital gain.

    d. $150,000 long-term capital gain and $50,000 short-term capital gain.

    e. $400,000 long-term capital gain.

16. To qualify for nonrecognition of gain treatment, the following requirements apply:

    a. The ESOP must own at least 30% of the corporation's stock immediately after the sale.

    b. The corporation that establishes the ESOP must have no class of stock outstanding that is tradable on an established securities market.

    c. The seller and 25% shareholders in the corporation are precluded from receiving allocations of stock acquired by the ESOP through the rollover.

    d. The stock sold to the ESOP must be common or convertible preferred stock and must have owned by the seller for at least 3 years prior to the sale.

    e. All of the above.

17. Which phrase best completes the following sentence: "A repurchase option allows a terminating employee the choice to receive the cash equivalent of the employer's stock if the stock is _____."

    a. Convertible.

    b. Tradeable.

    c. Not readily tradeable.

    d. Not readily tradeable on an established market.

18. Which of the following are false as to ESOPs?

    1. An ESOP is controlled through a trust.

    2. ESOPs provide corporate owners with a way to transfer ownership interests to their employees.

    3. The trust of an ESOP is prohibited from borrowing money from a bank to purchase the employer stock.

        a. 3 only.

        b. 1 and 2.

        c. 2 and 3.

        d. None of the above.

19. The following definition applies to which of the following terms: "the corporation makes tax deductible contributions to a trust in the form of both principal and interest for the loan."

    a. A stock bonus plan.

    b. An ESOP.

    c. A leveraged ESOP.

    d. A S corp ESOP.

20. ESOP distributions can be made in installments:

    1. No longer than 5 years under any scenario.

    2. No longer than 5 years unless the account balance exceeds $1,070,000 for 2016, in which case an additional year is allowed for each $210,000 (2016) over $1,070,000 but not more than 5 additional years.

    3. In substantially equal payments.

        a. 3 only.

        b. 1 and 3.

        c. 2 and 3.

        d. All of the above.

21. Baily is 56 years old and obtained ten years of participation in the Blackwater ESOP in Year 1. Assume she elects to diversify 20% of her account balance, which was $100,000, during the 90-day period following Year 1. Which of the following is correct?

    a. If the account value at the end of Year 3 was $150,000, Baily could diversify $37,500 during the 90-day period following Year 3.

    b. Baily can diversify an additional $5,000 anytime before the final year of the election period.

    c. Baily can diversify an additional 5% anytime before the final year of the election period.

    d. During the 90-day period following Year 6, Baily could diversify up to $100,000, on a cumulative basis with prior diversification amounts, assuming her plan balance was $200,000 at the end of Year 6.

QUICK QUIZ EXPLANATIONS

QUICK QUIZ 6.1
1. True.
2. False. A valuation of an employer's securities must generally be performed annually in order to determine the employer's tax deduction and for the purposes of the employer's financial statements.
3. False. Stock bonus plans are subject to the same eligibility rules as other qualified plans. Therefore, the standard eligibility criteria of age 21 and one year of service applies to stock bonus plans.

QUICK QUIZ 6.2
1. True.
2. True.
3. False. Net unrealized appreciation treatment is one of the principal benefits of stock bonus plans. The NUA of the stock is not taxed as ordinary income at the time of distribution, but rather is taxed as a capital gain when the stock is sold.
4. True.

QUICK QUIZ 6.3
1. False. In a leveraged ESPOP, the corporation makes tax deductible contributions to the trust in the form of both principal and interest for the loan that has been used to finance the purchase of stock for the benefit of participants/employees.
2. False. Qualified replacement securities are securities in a domestic corporation, including stocks, bonds, debentures, or warrants.
3. True.

QUICK QUIZ 6.4
1. False. The majority of ESOPs are established by closely held corporations in order to help create a market for the corporation's stock.
2. True.
3. True.
4. False. An ESOP is subject to the minimum distribution requirements of IRC §401(a)(9).

QUICK QUIZ 6.5
1. True.
2. True.
3. False. Under IRC §1361, S Corporations are allowed to establish ESOPs.

DISTRIBUTIONS FROM QUALIFIED PLANS

LEARNING OBJECTIVES

After reading this chapter, you should be able to:
1. Explain the distribution options available to participants from qualified plans.
2. Understand the differences among QJSAs, QPSA and QOSAs.
3. Understand how distributions from qualified plans are taxed and the exceptions to the general rule.
4. Describe the rules regarding rollovers, including rollovers attributable to Roth IRAs and Roth accounts.
5. Calculate the taxable portion of a distribution that partially consists of after-tax contributions or other basis.
6. Discuss the rules surrounding loans from qualified plans.
7. Understand the additional 10 percent penalty on distributions from qualified plans and the exceptions to the penalty.
8. Understand and calculate minimum distributions for participants and beneficiaries.
9. Understand the creditor issues surrounding inherited IRAs and how to plan for the issue.

INTRODUCTION

This chapter focuses on distributions from qualified plans and, as discussed in previous chapters, the relationship between the government, the participant, and the plan sponsor (employer). The government allows the participant and/or the plan sponsor to deposit pretax funds into an account that will grow tax-free until distribution to the participant (or the participant's beneficiaries), at which time the funds will be subject to income tax.[1]

To receive the tax-free growth of the assets within the plan, the plan participant must follow precise rules and requirements regarding distributions from the plan. This chapter covers the requirements, benefits, stipulations, and consequences of taking distributions for retirement, as well as the impact of taking distributions prior to retirement or not using the funds during retirement.

While this chapter focuses on distributions from qualified plans, distributions from other tax-advantaged accounts, such as IRAs, SIMPLEs, 403(b) plans, and 457 plans will be discussed in Chapters 9 and 10.

DISTRIBUTION OPTIONS

Distributions are disbursements of assets from a qualified plan with no intention by the participant of returning the assets to the plan. Distributions include in-service withdrawals, payments made upon termination or retirement, and may also include certain distributions related to qualified domestic relations orders. Loans taken from a qualified plan are not distributions unless the loan is not repaid and the transaction is deemed a distribution (discussed below).

---

1. Elective deferrals to Roth accounts and contributions to thrift savings plans may be made on an after-tax basis. Roth contributions and earnings generally grow tax-free and qualified distributions are tax free.

A qualified plan may, by law, offer a wide range of distribution options, but each plan document establishes the options actually available to the participants of a particular plan. Generally, qualified plans offer a variety of distribution options including a lump-sum distribution, a rollover distribution, a single life annuity, or a joint life annuity option. The plan may also offer in-service distributions and hardship withdrawals before retirement (discussed below).

EXHIBIT 7.1

DISTRIBUTION OPTIONS

- Annuities
- Lump-sum distributions
- Rollovers
- In-service withdrawals
- Non-repaid loans

PENSION PLANS

Pension plans are generally not permitted to offer in-service withdrawals to participants unless the participant is participating in a phased-in retirement.[2] (Note that in-service withdrawals could be made once the participant reaches retirement age, but because of the continued accrual of benefits, plans do not often permit such withdrawals). Thus, distributions from pension plans are normally made because of the participant's termination of employment, early retirement, normal retirement, disability, or death.

KEY CONCEPTS

1. What are the distribution options for pension plans?

2. What are the distribution options for profit sharing plans?

Early Termination

A participant who terminates employment before normal retirement age may have up to three options:

1. receive a lump-sum distribution of the qualified plan assets,
2. roll the assets over to an IRA or other qualified plan, or
3. leave the funds in the pension plan.

However, these options depend on the plan document. Many pension plans do not have lump-sum options.

---

2. Under the Pension Protection Act of 2006, pension plans may offer in-service withdrawals to employees who are age 62 or older. This type of distribution, also known as phased retirement, is intended to enable older workers to become part-time employees and receive benefits to maintain their current earnings level. This provision is effective for plan years beginning after 2006.

If the participant's vested account balance is less than $5,000, then the law permits, but does not require, the plan to distribute the balance to the participant if the participant does not make a timely election. This situation is called a forced payout. Before March 28, 2005, a plan could simply distribute the account balance and still meet its fiduciary duty. However, the Department of Labor issued final regulations that changed the responsibilities of plan administrators with regards to forced payouts. Section 2550.404a-2 of the Department of Labor regulations now require that forced payouts between $1,000 and $5,000 be directly rolled to an IRA if the participant has not made a timely election and the plan requires a forced payout. A forced payout for amounts less than $1,000 are not affected by this change.

Normal Retirement

At the participant's normal retirement age, a pension plan will typically distribute retirement benefits through an annuity payable for the remainder of the participant's life. The plan may also provide for a lump-sum distribution option that pays the participant an amount equal to the present value of the annuity. Under PPA 2006, the interest rate to be used in determining the value of lump-sum distributions from defined benefit plans after 2006 is based on the corporate bond yield curve of investment-grade corporate bonds of varying maturities.[3] While the plan document dictates the distribution options available to the participant, a single life annuity is generally the automatic form of benefit for a single participant. However, married individuals must be offered a qualified joint and survivor annuity (QJSA). Other annuity options may include term certain features, which ensure that payments will continue even after death, for the number of years specified as the term certain. Regardless of the form, distributions from qualified pension plans are generally characterized as ordinary income for income tax purposes.

QUICK QUIZ 7.1

1. Pension plans generally provide a lump-sum distribution.
   a. True
   b. False

2. A qualified joint and survivor annuity and qualified pre-retirement survivor annuity are required for pension plans.
   a. True
   b. False

3. Profit sharing plans may allow for inservice withdrawals.
   a. True
   b. False

False, True, True.

---

3. Prior to the Pension Protection Act of 2006, the interest rate used to determine the present value of the annuity was generally the 30-year Treasury security rate for the month before the date of distribution.

Qualified Joint and Survivor Annuity (QJSA)

A **Qualified Joint and Survivor Annuity (QJSA)** must be provided, but can be waived, to married participants of a pension plan and must also be provided to married participants of profit sharing plans unless the plan meets the following criteria:

1. The plan provides that the participant's nonforfeitable accrued benefit is payable in full, upon the participant's death, to the participant's surviving spouse (unless the participant elects, with spousal consent, that such benefit be provided instead to a designated beneficiary).

2. The participant does not elect the payment of benefits in the form of a life annuity.

In order to meet the first requirement, two additional requirements must be met. First, the benefit must be available to the surviving spouse within a reasonable time after the participant's death. A "reasonable time" is defined by the IRC to mean within the 90-day period following the date of death. Longer periods may be deemed a reasonable time based on the particular facts and circumstances. Second, the benefit payable to the surviving spouse must be adjusted for gains or losses occurring after the participant's death in accordance with plan rules governing the adjustment of account balances for other plan distributions.[4]

The QJSA pays a benefit to the participant and spouse as long as either lives. At the death of the first spouse, the surviving spouse's annuity payments can range from 50 percent to 100 percent of the joint life benefit, depending on the plan provisions and the participant election. Because the annuity is paid as long as either spouse is living, the QJSA is actuarially reduced compared to an annuity payment that would have been derived using the participants' single life expectancy. The reduction is to actuarially compensate for the continuing payments to the surviving spouse after the first spouse's death. The nonparticipant spouse beneficiary may choose to waive his right to a QJSA by executing a notarized or otherwise official waiver of benefits. The waiver may be made during the 90-day period beginning 90 days before the annuity start date.

---

4. Treas. Reg. §1.401(a)-20 Q-A #3.

EXHIBIT
7.2

SAMPLE WAIVER OF QUALIFIED JOINT AND SURVIVOR ANNUITY

Participant Information	Employer Plan Name: _____ Full Name of Participant: _____ Social Security Number: ___ - __ - ____ Daytime Phone Number: (___)___ - ____
Participant's Authorized Signature	I have made an election for distribution of benefits in a form other than a Qualified Joint and Survivor Annuity. The plan administrator has provided me with a written explanation of the effect of this election, my right to waive the joint and survivor payment form and the financial effect of selecting an alternate payment form. I understand that this election is revocable up until the beginning distribution date, and anytime thereafter for assets that are not yet distributed. I hereby waive the distribution of plan benefits in the form of a Qualified Joint and Survivor Annuity ("QJSA"). I hereby waive the QJSA 30-day notice period under Internal Revenue Code sections 401(a)(11) and 417(a)(7). _____ **Signature of Spouse of Participant** **Date**
Consent of Spouse	I, _____[insert your name], am the spouse of _____ [insert name of Participant]. I understand that I have the right to have my spouse's Employer's Plan pay my spouse's retirement benefits in the form of a Qualified Joint Survivor Annuity ("QJSA"), and I agree to waive that right. I understand that by signing this agreement, I may receive less money than I would have received under the QJSA payment form and I may receive nothing after my spouse dies depending on the payment form that my spouse chooses. I understand that by signing this waiver, my spouse can choose any retirement benefit form that is allowed by the Plan without telling me and without getting my agreement. I also understand that my spouse can change the retirement benefit form selected at any time without telling me and without getting my agreement. I understand that I can limit my spouse's choice to a particular retirement benefit form and that I am waiving that right. I understand that I do not have to sign this agreement. I am signing voluntarily. I understand that if I do not sign this agreement, then my spouse and I will receive payments from the plan in the form of a QJSA. I hereby consent to my spouse's waiver of the QJSA 30-day notice period under Internal Revenue Code sections 401(a)(11) and 417(a)(7). I have executed this consent this _____ day of _____, 20_____, which is no more than 90 days from the beginning payment date requested by my spouse. _____ **Signature of Spouse of Participant**
Witnessed By: Employer's Plan Representative OR Notary Public	Signature of Spouse witnessed this _____day of _____ , 20 _____. _____ **Employer's Plan Representative** Subscribed and sworn to before me this _____day of _____, 20 _____. _____ My commission expires _____ **Notary Public** **(SEAL)**

Qualified Pre-Retirement Survivor Annuity (QPSA)

A **qualified pre-retirement survivor annuity (QPSA)** must also be provided to married participants of a pension plan or a profit sharing plan utilizing the same criteria as discussed above.[5] A QPSA provides a benefit to the surviving spouse if the participant dies before attaining normal retirement age. A QPSA is essentially a term insurance policy paid for by a reduction in the ultimate pension plan retirement benefit that the participant would have received from the plan at normal retirement age.

The nonparticipant spouse is offered the QPSA and may choose whether to accept or waive the option. The QPSA may be waived by the nonparticipant spouse via a written notarized waiver. (In some cases, the signature can be witnessed by a plan official instead of being notarized.) The waiver may be made beginning the first day of the plan year in which the participant attains age 35 until the day the participant dies.[6] In addition, the waiver can be revoked at any time during this period. Since any waiver is generally executed when the participant is age 35, this waiver or acceptance decision is critical, as it may impact the family's overall future financial plan. Advisors should carefully review the couple's life insurance situation before making a determination as to whether they should waive the QPSA. Assuming the QPSA is elected and the surviving spouse receives the benefit, there is no adjusted basis in the benefit. Thus, the full value of distribution under the QPSA is subject to ordinary income tax in addition to estate tax.

QPSA BENEFIT COMPARISON

EXHIBIT 7.3

The difference between the two lines is the premium cost of life insurance associated with the QPSA.

---

5. IRC §401(a)(11).
6. IRC §417(a)(6)(B).

EXHIBIT
7.4

PENSION PLAN NORMAL RETIREMENT AGE DISTRIBUTION OPTIONS

- Qualified Joint and Survivor Annuity (QJSA)
- Single Life Annuity if QJSA is waived or no spouse
- Lump-Sum

EXHIBIT
7.5

CHARACTERISTICS OF AN EFFECTIVE WAIVER QPSA OR QJSA BENEFITS

- In writing
- Clearly indicates that the QPSA or QJSA will be waived and the consequences of the waiver
- Signed by the nonparticipant spouse
- Notarized or witnessed by a plan official

PPA 2006 amends IRC §417 that requires a plan subject to the annuity requirement under IRC §401(a)(11) to offer a **qualified optional survivor annuity (QOSA)** to a plan participant who has waived the QJSA. A QOSA is an annuity for the life of a participant with a survivor annuity for the life of the participant's spouse that is equal to a specified applicable percentage of the amount of the annuity that is payable during the joint lives of the participant and the spouse (and that is actuarially equivalent to a single life annuity for the life of the participant). Written explanation of the terms and conditions of the QOSA must be provided to participants.

The level of the spouse survivor annuity under the QOSA depends on a plan's level of spouse survivor annuity under the QJSA. For the married participant under a plan, if the QJSA provides a survivor annuity for the life of the participant's spouse that is less than 75 percent of the amount of the annuity that is payable during the joint lives of the participant and the participant's spouse, then the QOSA must provide a spouse survivor annuity of 75 percent. In the same situation, if the QJSA provides a survivor annuity for the life of the participant's spouse that is greater than or equal to 75 percent of the amount of the annuity that is payable during the joint lives of the participant and the participant's spouse, the QOSA must provide a spouse survivor annuity of 50 percent.[7]

QJSA vs. QOSA	
QJSA Participant / Survivor Nonparticipant Spouse	QOSA Participant / Survivor Nonparticipant Spouse
If 100% / < 75%	then, 100% / 75%
If 100% / ≥ 75%	then, 100% / 50%

The QOSA must be actuarially equivalent to a single annuity for the life of a participant, and applies to distributions for annuity start dates in plan years beginning after December 31, 2007. A plan amendment pursuant to statutory provisions can be delayed until the last day of the first plan year beginning on or after January 1, 2009. A plan amendment is not required if the plan currently provides an optional joint and survivor annuity that meets the QOSA requirements. Further information on this topic is available in IRS Notice 2008-30.

---

7. IRC §417(g).

Rollover

A distribution from a pension plan may be rolled over into another qualified plan or an IRA provided the participant is not required to begin taking the required minimum distributions. If the assets are rolled over, the participant defers recognition of ordinary income until the assets are distributed from the rollover account. However, in certain situations when a distribution is taken as a lump-sum distribution, the recipient may receive favorable tax treatment on the distribution (Net Unrealized Appreciation (NUA), 10-year forward averaging, and/or pre-74 capital gain treatment) as discussed below. These favorable tax treatments will be lost if the distribution is rolled over to an IRA or to a plan that is not a qualified plan.

PROFIT SHARING PLANS

Profit sharing plans generally provide participants with a distribution of the plan's assets at the participant's termination. At termination, the participant may be able to take a lump-sum distribution taxed as ordinary taxable income, annuitize the value of the account (if the plan document permits), or roll the assets over into a rollover qualified plan or IRA to continue the deferral of the income tax depending on the options available. In contrast to pension plans, profit sharing plans are not required to offer survivor benefits if the plan does not pay the participant in the form of a life annuity benefit and the participant's nonforfeitable accrued benefit is payable to the surviving spouse upon the participant's death. (See discussion in QJSA above.) Profit sharing plans also differ from pension plans because profit sharing plans may allow for in-service withdrawals for participants of any age (plan dependent) and most 401(k) plans generally allow plan loans to participants in the plan document.

TAXATION OF DISTRIBUTIONS

Distributions from qualified retirement plans are generally subject to ordinary income tax because the plans usually contain both contributions and earnings that have never been subjected to income tax. The contributions to the plan were effectively wages that would have been taxed at ordinary income tax rates had they been paid directly to the participant. These contributions have not yet been subjected to income tax because the benefits were held in a qualified plan. Therefore, when the plan assets are distributed, they are included in the participant's income and are taxed as ordinary income at the value upon distribution.

Just as the government requires an employer to withhold a specific amount of tax from an employee's wages to ensure that the government receives the income tax, a distribution from a qualified retirement plan is also subject to income tax withholding requirements. Generally, the plan custodian is required to withhold a mandatory 20 percent from most non-periodic distributions (any payment that is not part of an annuity) made to the participant (the 20 percent withholding requirement does not apply to hardship distributions or loans).[8] If income tax is not withheld or insufficient income tax is withheld, the recipient may be required to make estimated tax payments or otherwise be subject to penalties for insufficient withholdings or estimated tax payments. This withholding requirement only pertains to qualified plans and not to distributions from IRAs.

---

8. IRC §§3405(c) and 402(c)(4).

ROLLOVERS

Even when the participant has the option of taking a lump-sum distribution, the participant is not required to withdraw the account balance. Instead, the participant may elect to **rollover** or transfer the balance of the account into another tax-advantaged qualified plan or an IRA account to continue to defer the recognition of income taxes until the ultimate distribution of the assets from the new plan. Generally, a participant will elect to rollover an account balance when the participant has terminated employment but would like to continue to benefit from the tax-deferred growth of the assets and plan for retirement. A participant may also elect a rollover to increase his investment choices or to have more control over the plan assets. It is important to note that the rules regarding rollovers have been significantly broadened over the years,[9] including the expanded rules for 403(b) and 457 plans as discussed in Chapter 10.

The decision to rollover qualified plan assets into an IRA should be considered carefully. Once the assets are deposited into the IRA, the assets will continue to benefit from the tax-deferred growth until a distribution is taken from the IRA account. However, any assets deposited into the IRA lose the ERISA alienation protection,[10] the benefit of **10-year forward averaging**, the benefit of **pre-1974 capital gain treatment**, and the benefit of **net unrealized appreciation** (NUA). The opportunity to benefit from 10-year forward averaging, pre-1974 capital gain treatment, and net unrealized appreciation does not exist for distributions from IRAs. All of these topics are discussed in detail below.

There are two primary reasons that funds rolled over to an IRA from a qualified plan should be segregated from other IRA assets. The first reason is that funds that are rolled from a qualified plan can later be rolled over into another qualified plan, assuming the receiving plan permits such contributions. While funds from a traditional IRA can also be rolled over, not all plans permit such rollovers. Secondly, it appears that rollovers, unlike traditional IRAs, are fully protected under bankruptcy law and therefore rollover funds should be segregated to maintain this protection.[11] Accounts that hold rollover funds are often referred to as IRA rollover accounts or **Conduit IRAs**, as they provide a conduit to another qualified plan.

---

9. Both EGTRRA 2001 and PPA 2006 provided more flexibility to move qualified and tax deferred funds from one plan to another.
10. Although assets rolled over into an IRA lose ERISA protection, as a result of the Bankruptcy Abuse Prevention and Consumer Protection Act (BAPCPA 2005), rollover IRAs are fully protected. In addition, assets in IRAs are protected up to $1 million (indexed) under federal bankruptcy laws (11USC §522). Therefore, the loss of ERISA protection is not as significant as it was before the BAPCPA 2005.
11. 11 USC 522(n).

THE COST OF A ROLLOVER FROM A QUALIFIED PLAN TO AN IRA

EXHIBIT
7.6

- Lose ERISA anti-alienation protection (but not protection under federal bankruptcy laws)
- Lose potential 10-year forward averaging
- Lose potential Net Unrealized Appreciation (NUA)
- Lose potential pre-1974 capital gain treatment

Rollovers may be accomplished in one of the two following ways:
1. Direct rollover
2. Indirect rollover

Direct Rollover

A **direct rollover** occurs when the plan trustee distributes the account balance directly to the trustee of the recipient account. A direct rollover is usually completed with a wire transfer from the old custodian to the new custodian or a check is issued from the old custodian negotiable only by the custodian of the new account. All qualified plans must provide for the availability of direct rollovers of certain distributions. If the participant elects a direct rollover, then the original plan custodian is not required to withhold 20 percent of the distribution for federal income tax.

Under the Pension Protection Act of 2006, direct rollovers from qualified plans to Roth IRAs are allowed after 2007. Under previous law, a rollover from a qualified plan to a Roth IRA generally required the use of a conduit traditional IRA. Exhibit 7.9 provides a great summary of permissible rollovers.

EXHIBIT
7.7

DIRECT VS INDIRECT ROLLOVERS

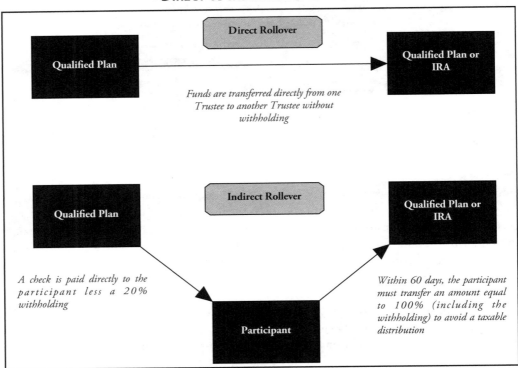

Indirect Rollover

The second method of completing a rollover is indirectly through a distribution to the participant with a subsequent transfer by the participant to another account. In this instance the original custodian issues a check to the participant in the amount of the full account balance reduced by the 20 percent mandatory withholding allowance. In order to complete the rollover, the participant must then reinvest the full original account balance of the qualified plan (including the 20 percent mandatory withholding) within 60 days of the original distribution into the new qualified plan or IRA. The 60-day clock starts with the participant's constructive receipt of the distribution (usually upon receipt of the check). The PPA 2006 makes permanent EGTRRA rules giving the IRS authority to extend the 60-day rollover period when a person's failure to comply is due to events beyond the reasonable control of that person.

In determining whether to grant such a waiver, the IRS will consider all relevant facts and circumstances, including:
- errors committed by a financial institution,
- inability to complete a rollover due to death, disability, hospitalization, incarceration, restrictions imposed by a foreign country or postal error,
- the use of the amount distributed (for example, in the case of payment by check, whether the check was cashed), and
- the time elapsed since the distribution occurred.[12]

---

12. Revenue Procedure 2003-16.

WAIVER OF 60-DAY ROLLOVER REQUIREMENT

EXHIBIT
7.8

In *PLR 201143027*, the IRS waived the 60-day rollover requirement due to an error by the taxpayer's financial advisor. The financial advisor acknowledged that he misunderstood the taxpayer and deposited the rollover amount into a taxable account instead of a self-directed IRA.

In *PLR 201143029*, the IRS waived the 60-day rollover requirement when funds were transferred to a financial institution that was involved in a plan to defraud investors in a Ponzi scheme. The criminal charges were upheld and the president of the financial institution pled guilty and was convicted in a U.S. District Court on charges of securities and mail fraud.

In *PLR 201143031*, the IRS waived the 60-day rollover requirement due to a failure to comply with the requirement as a result of the taxpayer's diminished mental capacity. The taxpayer represented that he has limited memory retention and moderate dementia, which caused problems with his judgment, and that he did not understand the implications of the withdrawal from his IRA.

In *Blake Sime Atkin and Susan M. Atkin v. Commissioner, T.C. Memo. 2008-93, 95 T.C.M. 1364, (Apr. 10, 2008)*, the Tax Court held that the taxpayer was liable for income tax, the 10 percent early withdrawal penalty and accuracy related penalties for failing to rollover funds from a SEP IRA within the permitted 60-day period.

Facts:
- Mr. Atkin (age 45) received a distribution in 2002 of $25,000 from his SEP IRA and deposited it into his law firm operating account.
- Within 60 days, he instructed his bookkeeper to send a check in the amount of $25,000 to his broker (Mr. Barben), who never received the funds.
- The Atkins did not report the original distribution on their tax return.
- In 2006, Mr. Atkin segregated the $25,000 into a separate taxable account.

Findings:
- The Atkins argued against the accuracy related penalty. The court wrote, "We disagree and find that petitioners failed to exercise due care or to act as a reasonable person would under the circumstances. Petitioners were allegedly unaware that the $25,000 check was not cashed until respondent brought it to their attention after years had passed. Petitioners never received monthly statements from the IRA and never followed up with Mr. Barben to make sure that he had opened the IRA. Further, Mr. Atkin should have been aware that his law firm's operating account had $25,000 more than he thought it should have. After Mr. Atkin told his bookkeeper to write a check to open an IRA, he took no steps to follow up in over 2 years."
- The court found the Atkins responsible for the income tax, early withdrawal penalty and the accuracy related penalty.
- The court also noted that the Atkins failed to apply to the Secretary for a waiver.

One of the problems with the **indirect rollover** method is that the distribution is subject to the mandatory withholding of 20 percent, but 100 percent of the account balance must be deposited in the new qualified plan or IRA within 60 days of the date of distribution. Thus, the participant must utilize funds from other sources in the amount of the 20 percent withheld and deposit 100 percent of the distribution amount into the rollover account.

Kristi, age 28, took a distribution from her 401(k) plan of her entire account balance of $85,000. She intended to rollover the $85,000 to an IRA at a brokerage company, but decided to receive the check herself rather than have the custodian do a direct trustee to trustee rollover. The custodian of the 401(k) plan withheld 20% of the account balance ($17,000) (as required by law) and sent Kristi a check in the amount of $68,000. In order to avoid having to recognize any taxable income, Kristi must open the IRA and deposit $85,000 (not $68,000) within 60 days of receiving the $68,000 check. Kristi will then receive a tax refund of the $17,000 withheld when she files her federal income tax return. To avoid the 20% withholding requirement, Kristi could have initiated a direct rollover from the 401(k) to her new IRA.

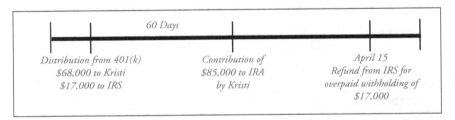

Indirect rollovers usually occur due to poor planning or because the account owner wants to use the funds during the 60-day period. To prevent potential abuse, the IRS only permits an individual to have one indirect rollover from an IRA per year.[13] This limit previously applied on an individual account basis. However, that is no longer the case. As of January 1, 2015, individuals are only permitted one annual 60-day rollover from any of the individual's IRAs. This change is a significant departure from the previous interpretation of this rule. The one year waiting period does not apply to indirect rollovers from qualified plans to IRAs. There can also be an unlimited number of direct rollovers during the year.

13. Proposed Regulation §1.408-4(b)(4)(ii) and IRS Publication 590, Individual Retirement Arrangements (IRAs), provided that this limitation is applied on an IRA-by-IRA basis. However, a recent Tax Court opinion, Bobrow v. Commissioner, T.C. Memo. 2014-21, held that the limitation applies on an aggregate basis, meaning that an individual could not make an IRA-to-IRA rollover if he or she had made such a rollover involving any of the individual's IRAs in the preceding 1-year period. In Announcement 2014-32, the IRS made clear that the new interpretation will apply beginning Jan. 1, 2015, and said that a distribution from an IRA received during 2014 and properly rolled over (normally within 60 days) to another IRA, will have no impact on any distributions and rollovers during 2015 involving any other IRAs owned by the same individual. This will give IRA owners a fresh start in 2015 when applying the one-per-year rollover limit to multiple IRAs.

Kelly, who is 42 years old, has five IRAs. On January 25th of Year 1, she takes a distribution of $45,000 from IRA 1. On March 20th, she deposits the $45,000 into IRA 4. Based on her actions, she has made use of the 60-day rollover rule. There is no tax impact to this scenario. On December 15th of the same year, Kelly takes a distribution of $25,000 from IRA 3. She rolls over the funds on February 2nd of Year 2. In this case, Kelly has violated the one indirect IRA rollover per year rule. As a result, Kelly has made a taxable distribution from IRA 3 in the amount of $25,000. The $25,000 is taxable in Year 1 and will likely be subject to the 10% early withdrawal penalty. In addition, she has made an impermissible IRA contribution, which will need to be removed from the IRA.

EXAMPLE 7.2

Cindy, who is 42 years old, has five IRAs. On January 12th, she converts IRA 2, which is a traditional IRA, into a Roth IRA. On March 25th, she takes a distribution of $20,000 from IRA 1. On May 20th, she rolls over the $20,000 into IRA 4. She has made use of the 60-day rollover rule. The conversion is subject to income tax. However, there is no tax impact to the rollover.

EXAMPLE 7.3

Planning for a Rollover

As mentioned above, plan sponsors are required to offer the participant the choice of a direct rollover at the time of the distribution, but qualified plans are not required to accept rollovers from other qualified plans or IRAs. Thus, without proper planning, an individual who takes a distribution from a qualified plan with the intention of completing an indirect rollover into another qualified plan may fail to meet the 60 day requirement if their new qualified plan does not accept rollovers from other plans. Qualified plans are required to provide participants with a written explanation of the distribution options, the mandatory withholding rules, and any other rules relating to the taxation of distributions. Additionally, any necessary spousal waivers must be secured in advance of any distribution.

Neither direct nor indirect rollovers may consist of any distribution from a qualified plan that is one of a series of substantially equal periodic payments (not less frequently than annually) made for the life of the participant, the joint lives of the participant and the participant's designated beneficiary, or for a period of 10 years or more. In addition, any distribution on account of a required minimum distribution (discussed below), a substantially equal periodic payments election under IRC §72(t), and hardship withdrawals may not be rolled over into another qualified plan or IRA.

EXHIBIT 7.9

SUMMARY OF ALLOWABLE ROLLOVERS

				ROLL TO				
		Traditional IRA	**SEP-IRA**	**SIMPLE IRA**	**Roth IRA**	**Government 457(b)**	**403(b)**	**Qualified Plan**	**Designated Roth Account 401(k), 403(b), 457(b)**
ROLL FROM	**Traditional IRA**	Yes	Yes	No	Yes, must include in income.	Yes, must have separate accounts.	Yes	Yes	No
	SEP-IRA	Yes	Yes	No	Yes, must include in income.	Yes, must have separate accounts.	Yes	Yes	No
	SIMPLE IRA	Yes, after 2 years.	Yes, after 2 years.	Yes	Yes, after 2 years. Must include in income.	Yes, after 2 years. Must have separate accounts.	Yes, after 2 years.	Yes, after 2 years.	No
	Roth IRA	No	No	No	Yes	No	No	No	No
	Government 457(b)	Yes	Yes	No	Yes. Must include in income.	Yes	Yes	Yes	Yes as in plan rollover. Must include in income.
	403(b)	Yes	Yes	No	Yes. Must include in income.	Yes, must have separate accounts.	Yes	Yes	Yes as in plan rollover. Must include in income.
	Qualified Plan	Yes	Yes	No	Yes. Must include in income.	Yes, must have separate accounts.	Yes	Yes	Yes as in plan rollover. Must include in income.
	Designated Roth Account 401(k), 403(b), 457(b)	No	No	No	Yes	No	No	No	Yes, if a direct trustee to trustee transfer.

After-Tax Contributions

If a qualified plan consists of employee after-tax contributions, these contributions may be rolled over into another qualified plan that accepts after-tax dollars or into a traditional IRA. In the case of a rollover of after-tax contributions from one qualified plan to another qualified plan, the rollover can only be accomplished through a direct rollover. A qualified plan is not permitted to accept rollovers of after-tax contributions unless the plan provides separate accounting for such contributions and the applicable earnings on those contributions. Conversely, after-tax contributions are not permitted to be rolled over from an IRA into a qualified plan.[14]

IRS Notice 2014-54 provides rules for allocating pretax and after-tax amounts among disbursements that are made to multiple destinations from a qualified plan. For example, a retiree who has pre-tax and after-tax funds in a 401(k) plan may want to rollover the pre-tax portion to a traditional IRA and the after-tax funds to a Roth IRA. The IRS, in Notice 2014-35, finally acquiesced to this type of arrangement. Following are two general rules to keep in mind:

- Each distribution from a retirement plan will include a pro-rata share of both after-tax and pretax amounts.
- Under IRC §402(c)(2), a rollover first consists of the pre-tax amount.

> **EXAMPLE 7.4**
>
> Bob participates in a qualified plan that does not contain a designated Roth account. Bob's $250,000 account balance consists of $200,000 of pretax amounts and $50,000 of after-tax amounts. Bob separates from service and is entitled to, and requests, a distribution of $100,000.
>
> The pretax amount with respect to the distribution is $80,000 ($100,000 x $200,000/$250,000). Bob specifies that $70,000 is to be directly rolled over to the qualified plan maintained by his new employer and that $30,000 is to be paid to Bob. Because the pretax amount exceeds the amount directly rolled over, the amount directly rolled over to the new plan consists entirely of pretax amounts.
>
> The amount paid to Bob (prior to application of withholding) consists of $10,000 in pretax amounts and $20,000 in after-tax amounts. Prior to the 60th day after the distribution, Bob chooses to roll over $12,000 to an IRA. Because the amount rolled over in the 60-day rollover exceeds the remaining pretax amounts, the amount rolled over to the IRA consists of $10,000 of pretax amounts and $2,000 of after-tax amounts.

> **EXAMPLE 7.5**
>
> Assume the same facts as in the previous example, except that Bob chooses to make a direct rollover of $80,000 to a traditional IRA and $20,000 to a Roth IRA.
>
> Bob is permitted to allocate the $80,000 that consists entirely of pretax amounts to the traditional IRA so that the $20,000 rolled over to the Roth IRA consists entirely of after-tax amounts.

---

14. IRC §408(d)(3)(C).

Rollovers to Roth IRAs and Roth Accounts

Roth IRAs continue to be a hot topic, although they have been around since their creation by the Taxpayer Relief Act of 1997. The enthusiasm is largely driven by the fact that qualified distributions from Roth IRAs and Roth accounts are not subject to income taxation or penalties.

Today, taxpayers have several options to fund Roth-type vehicles: They can contribute to Roth IRAs assuming they meet the AGI limits and can defer compensation into a Roth account assuming that it is an option provided by their employer's 401(k), 403(b) or 457 plan (the only plans that permit Roth accounts). In addition, taxpayers have several options available to convert pre-tax money, such as in a qualified plan or traditional IRA, to Roth money. This section discusses benefits and implications of converting pre-tax retirement funds as well as the available conversion options.

History of Roth IRAs and Accounts	
1997	Roth IRA created by Taxpayer Relief Act of 1997.
2001	Economic Growth and Tax Relief Reconciliation Act of 2001 (EGTRRA) created Roth Accounts for 401(k) plans and 403(b) plans effective in 2006.
2005	The Tax Increase Prevention and Reconciliation Act of 2005 eliminated the AGI limit of $100,000 for conversions effective after 2009.
2006	Pension Protection Act 2006 provided for direct rollovers from qualified plans to Roth IRAs.
2010	The Small Business Jobs and Credit Act of 2010 provided for Roth accounts in governmental 457(b) plans and provided for in-plan Roth Rollovers.
2012	The American Taxpayer Relief Act of 2012 added IRC Section 402A(c)(4)(E), which permits transfers of any amounts not otherwise distributable under the qualified plan to a designated Roth account for the benefit of the individual.
2013	The IRS issued Notice 2013-74, which provides guidance on the funds that can be rolled over to a designated Roth account within the same qualified plan. For the most part, any funds that are vested can be rolled over to a designated Roth account.
2014	The IRS issued Notice 2014-54, which provides rules for allocating pretax and after-tax amounts among disbursements that are made to multiple destinations from a qualified plan. These rules provide authority for allocating the pre-tax portion of a rollover from a qualified plan to a traditional IRA and allocating the after-tax portion to a Roth IRA.

Benefits and Implications of a Roth Conversion

There are two basic types of "conversions" that permit a taxpayer to change pre-tax retirement funds into Roth funds:

1. A qualified rollover contribution[15] (we will use the word conversion for short),[16] which generally means transferring assets from a traditional IRA or qualified plan to a Roth IRA.
2. An in-plan Roth rollover, whereby pre-tax funds in a qualified plan are converted or rolled over into a Roth account in a 401(k) plan, 403(b) plan, or governmental 457 plan.

While there are differences between the two, effectively they accomplish the same objective and both types have several advantages and implications. It is important to understand that when funds are converted, it requires that the pre-tax conversion amount be included into taxable income in the year of conversion. To the extent there is after-tax funds in the account that is being converted, these funds are not subject to taxation.

Benefits of Conversion

The benefits of conversion include the possibility of:

- tax reduction/tax diversification,
- tax-deferred funds transfer,
- minimum distribution avoidance, and
- possible estate tax reduction.

Tax Reduction / Tax Diversification: It may be possible for a taxpayer to reduce the total tax on retirement plan assets in certain situations through a Roth type conversion. The easiest case to make is for those taxpayers who are in a relatively low tax bracket today but expect to be in a higher bracket in the future. A conversion under this scenario results in the taxpayer paying income tax today at a lower rate than if the funds were deferred until the future. However, it is not always possible to know the income tax rates in the future, which could be higher or lower. In addition, the funds within the Roth could be deferred until the next generation, who might be paying income tax at a higher rate (prime earning years) or at a lower rate. Converting provides possible total tax reduction, but certainly provides for tax diversification.

Funds distributed from a Roth IRA or Roth account during retirement will generally not be subject to income tax or penalties.[17] The conversion effectively reduces the income during retirement that would have been subject to income tax if the funds were distributed from a traditional IRA or qualified plan. This reduction may also reduce the overall tax rate on other retirement income sources, such as deferred compensation or Social Security.

Earnings on investments held in a taxable account are taxable in the year earned, while earnings on investments held in an IRA are only taxable when distributed. Earnings within a Roth IRA or Roth account will never be taxed assuming a qualified distribution.[18] This benefit actually offsets the potential risk of paying tax today at a higher rate than during retirement.

---

15. The PPA 2006 expanded the definition of a qualified rollover contribution, which is defined in IRC §408A(e), to include qualified plans, annuities and 457 plan amounts.
16. Technically, conversions are transfers from a traditional IRA to a Roth IRA, however, the term is being used for simplicity.
17. Generally after age 59½.
18. A qualified distribution will generally occur after five years and after attainment of age 59½ - see Exhibit 7.14 for the differences between Roth IRAs and Roth Accounts.

For taxpayers who have net operating loss (NOL) carryforward amounts, Roth conversions can be accomplished with no direct tax cost. This strategy is helpful since it accomplishes the objective of conversion with little or no income tax cost. In addition, it may be helpful to the individual to use up the remaining NOL, which can only be carried forward for 20 years.

Tax-Deferred Funds Transfer: Assets in a traditional IRA or qualified plan are tax deferred, meaning that the funds will be subject to tax when distributed. Therefore, the deferred assets have a corresponding liability attached, which is the future tax that will be paid. By converting and paying tax with assets outside of an IRA or qualified plan, a taxpayer ends up with a Roth account that has no future tax liability. Effectively, the taxpayer has shifted funds to a tax exempt account.

Assume Jordan has $100 in a traditional IRA and her effective tax rate is 30 percent. Prior to the conversion, the IRA is worth $70 after tax. After the conversion, the Roth IRA is worth $100 after-tax, since all distributions will be tax-free. In effect, there has been a transfer or shift to the Roth account of $30.

Minimum Distribution Avoidance: Traditional IRAs and qualified plans are subject to minimum distributions, which are discussed in depth later in this chapter and require that distributions occur after attainment of age 70½. However, Roth IRAs are not subject to minimum distributions. Minimum distributions force taxpayers to take distributions so that the government can generate tax revenue. Roth IRAs do not have this same requirement until after the owner dies. Minimum distributions are not required for Roth IRAs, but are required for Roth accounts.

Estate Tax Reduction: As discussed above, tax deferred assets have an inherent liability representing the tax that must ultimately be paid on the tax deferred funds. Converting these tax-deferred funds into Roth funds requires that tax be paid in the year of conversion. This payment of tax reduces the assets that will be included in the taxpayer's gross estate at death resulting in potentially lower estate tax.[19] Clearly with the increased lifetime exemption that is currently in place, this benefit is only applicable to high net worth individuals.

Consequences and Implications

As mentioned above, Roth conversions and in-plan Roth rollovers both require that the taxpayer include the conversion amount into taxable income in the year of conversion. The converted amount is reported on Form 1040 and will result in higher income taxes. In addition, it may cause the taxpayer's income to increase such that deductions and exemptions are phased out or credits are lost. Because the tax liability is accelerated, the taxpayer is out of pocket these funds. In addition, there is the risk that tax rates will be lower in the future, which could greatly reduce the benefits of the conversion.

There is a clear monetary advantage to converting if it can be accomplished at a current tax rate that is lower than future tax rates. Therefore, taxpayers should consider converting over time when the value of the pre-tax assets is low, such as on market drops or corrections, and in years that taxable income is low. This strategy is helpful in minimizing the tax attributable to conversions.

---

19. There is an itemized deduction under IRC §691(c) that allows heirs to deduct estate tax attributable to income in respect of a decedent (IRD) included in the gross estate. This deduction is intended to reconcile the inherent liability attributable to tax deferred funds, but does not do so perfectly.

Recharacterizing Roth Conversions

While not available to in-plan Roth rollovers, taxpayers are permitted to recharacterize Roth conversions, which can help manage the inherent tax implications. This option is extremely helpful when a traditional IRA is converted and the market value of the assets drops due to changes is the value of underlying investments. In such a case, the taxpayer can effectively click the "undo" button and recharacterize the funds as pre-tax funds. Taxpayers have the ability to recharacterize a Roth conversion up to the due date of the income tax return, including extensions.[20] Taxpayers can also consider converting a traditional IRA to multiple Roth IRAs. This technique may allow the taxpayer to reduce tax on the conversion if the value of one of the Roth IRAs decreases. See Exhibits 7.12 and 7.13.

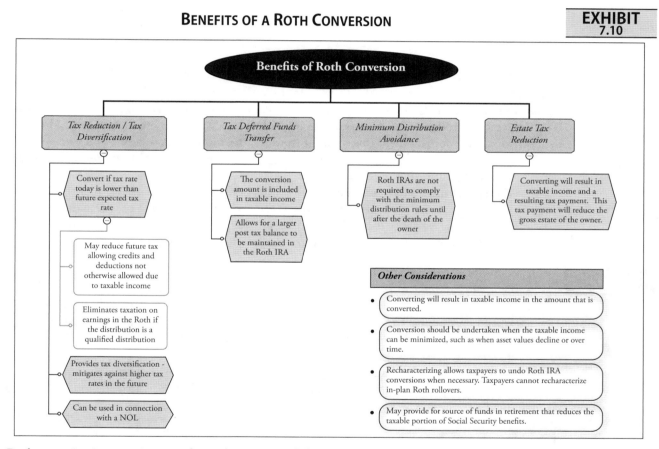

BENEFITS OF A ROTH CONVERSION

EXHIBIT 7.10

Recharacterization requires notifying the trustee of the Roth IRA that the taxpayer has elected to treat the contribution as having been made to a traditional IRA and not the Roth IRA. The original Roth conversion will likely trigger a Form 1099R with the converted amount, which should not be reported as taxable income on Form 1040. However, it is possible that a recharacterization and subsequent reporting of the transfer as non-taxable will trigger a letter from the IRS inquiring about the transaction. Such an inquiry is easily handled by explaining the recharacterization.

---

20. Treas. Reg. §1.408A-5, Q-6.

EXAMPLE 7.7

In May 2016, Colin converts $100,000 in his traditional IRA to a Roth IRA. The value of the assets in the Roth IRA drops by 40 percent due to a significant decline in the stock market that occurs in October 2016. The Roth conversion results in Colin incurring $100,000 of taxable income, when he could have waited and converted only $60,000 (after the 40 percent drop). Accordingly, prior to the due date (plus extensions) for filing his Federal income tax return for 2016, Colin decides to recharacterize the conversion contribution. He instructs the trustee of the Roth IRA to transfer in a trustee-to-trustee transfer the amount of the contribution, plus net income, to the trustee of a new traditional IRA. Colin notifies the trustee of the Roth IRA and the trustee of the traditional IRA that he is recharacterizing his IRA contribution. On his Federal income tax return for 2016, he treats the original amount of the conversion as having been contributed to the traditional IRA and not the Roth IRA. As a result, for Federal tax purposes, the contribution is treated as having been made to the traditional IRA and not to the Roth IRA.

A question that certainly arises after a recharacterization is whether the same funds can be subsequently converted to another Roth IRA. In other words, can an individual convert funds from a traditional IRA to a Roth IRA, recharacterize, and subsequently convert back to another Roth IRA. The answer to this question is yes. The individual can "reconvert" to a Roth IRA. However, the individual may not reconvert that amount from the traditional IRA to a Roth IRA before:

1. The beginning of the taxable year following the taxable year in which the amount was converted to a Roth IRA or, if later,
2. The end of the 30-day period beginning on the day on which the IRA owner transfers the amount from the Roth IRA back to a traditional IRA by means of a recharacterization (regardless of whether the recharacterization occurs during the taxable year in which the amount was converted to a Roth IRA or the following taxable year).

EXAMPLE 7.8

Assume the same facts as the above example. Colin converts his traditional IRA, then subsequently recharacterizes in November 2016. He could reconvert the funds to a Roth IRA in 2017 under these facts. If he had waited until sometime in 2017 to recharacterize, then he would have to wait an additional 30 days. However, he cannot recharacterize beyond the due date, including extensions, of his 2016 federal income tax return.

The ability to recharacterize and reconvert, along with the ability to convert over time provides taxpayers with an opportunity to take advantage of the benefits of Roth IRAs while minimizing the tax attributable to the conversion.

Timetable for Roth IRA Conversion / Recharacterization / Re-Conversion

EXHIBIT 7.11

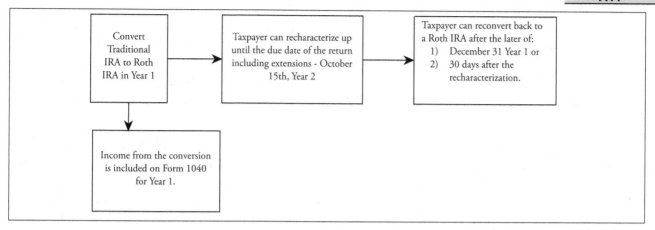

Converting Traditional IRA to Roth IRA

EXHIBIT 7.12

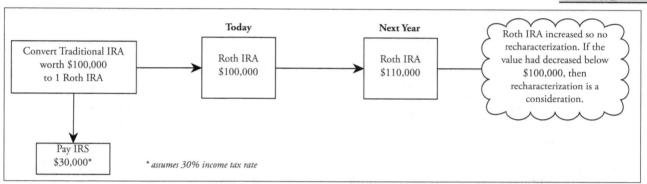

Converting Traditional IRA to 3 Roth IRAs Based on Asset Class

EXHIBIT 7.13

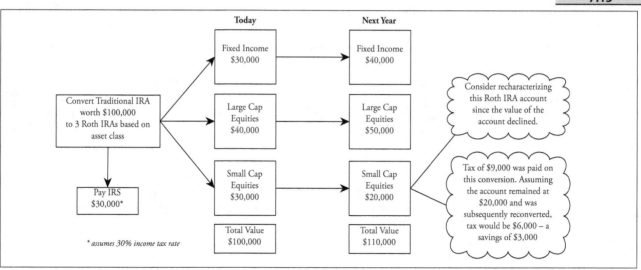

In-Plan Roth Rollover

The Small Business Jobs Act (SBJA) of 2010 signed by the President on September 27, 2010 made several important changes to the Internal Revenue Code dealing with elective deferrals in Roth accounts. SBJA 2010 added IRC §402A(c)(4) to the Code to permit plans that include a qualified Roth contribution program to allow individuals to roll over amounts from their accounts to their designated Roth accounts in the plan.[21] This option, which can be accomplished as a direct rollover or as an indirect rollover, is akin to converting funds in a traditional IRA to a Roth IRA. In addition, SBJA 2010 permits governmental 457(b) plans to include designated Roth accounts for years after 2010.

An "in-plan Roth rollover" is a distribution from an individual's plan account, other than a designated Roth account, that is rolled over to the individual's designated Roth account in the same plan, pursuant to new IRC §402A(c)(4).[22] The rollover may be accomplished by a direct rollover or by a distribution of funds to the individual who then rolls over the funds into the individual's designated Roth account in the plan within 60 days. An in-plan Roth rollover is generally not considered a distribution from the plan, but will result in the individual being taxed on the amount of the rollover.

In-plan Roth rollovers are a great option for individuals who are interested in converting pre-tax funds to Roth status. Before this law, taxpayers could only convert pre-tax funds in a qualified plan to a Roth IRA by distributing the funds from the qualified plan. Distributions from qualified plans lose the benefits available to ERISA funds and resulted in what the industry calls "leakage" or the transfer of assets from the employer plans to IRAs. The new law protects against leakage by allowing employees the ability to have in-plan Roth rollovers and employers to restrict in-service withdrawals solely to Roth rollovers. In addition, this law is a revenue accelerator for the federal government and is expected to generate over $5 billion over a ten-year period.

Amounts Eligible for In-Plan Roth Rollovers[23] (Old Rules)

IRS Notice 2010-84 provides that any vested amount held in a plan account for a plan participant (other than an amount held in a designated Roth account) is eligible for an in-plan Roth rollover to a designated Roth account in the same plan. Prior to the enactment of IRC §402A(c)(4)(E), an amount was not eligible for an in-plan Roth rollover unless it satisfied the rules for distribution under the Code and was an eligible rollover distribution as defined in §402(c)(4).[24] Thus, in the case of a 401(k) plan participant who has not had a severance from employment, an in-plan Roth rollover from the participant's pre-tax elective deferral account was permitted to be made only if the participant had reached age 59½, had died or became disabled, or received a qualified reservist distribution as defined in IRC §72(t)(2)(G)(iii).[25]

---

21. Effective for distributions made after September 27, 2010.
22. After September 27, 2010.
23. Notice 2013-74 modifies Notice 2010-84 based on the changes provided in IRC Section 402A(c)(4)(E).
24. Generally, an eligible rollover distribution is a distribution that is not a required minimum distribution, a corrective distribution of excess contributions or deferrals, a hardship distribution, a loan treated as a distribution, a distribution that is one of a series of substantially equal payments made at least annually over a lifetime or 10 years, dividends on employer securities, or the cost of life insurance coverage.
25. See Rev. Rul. 2004-12, 2004-1 C.B. 478, for a discussion of the various distribution timing restrictions applicable to amounts held in a plan.

Rollover contributions, after-tax contributions, employer profit sharing contributions and employee deferrals continue to be eligible rollover amounts.

> DD worked for Big Co for many years and accumulated a sizeable balance in her retirement plan that was subsequently rolled into the qualified plan of Small Co, her current employer. Small Co sponsors a 401(k) plan with a Roth account. If permitted by the plan, DD can convert the pre-tax rollover to the Roth account via an in-plan Roth rollover election. Assuming that the amount rolled over to the Roth account was $100,000, she would have taxable income of $100,000 in the year of the in-plan Roth rollover. The $100,000 is not subject to any penalties, regardless of her age. In addition, she would not have the ability to change her mind or recharacterize the $100,000. However, all qualified distributions from this account will be tax-free.

EXAMPLE 7.9

The taxable amount of a distribution that an individual rolls over in an in-plan Roth rollover is includible in gross income in the taxable year in which the distribution occurs. However, the rollover amount is not subject to the 10 percent early withdrawal amount.

IRC Section 402A(c)(4)(E) - More Liberal In-Plan Roth Rollover Options (New Rules)

The American Taxpayer Relief Act of 2012 added IRC Section 402A(c)(4)(E), which permits transfers of any amounts not otherwise distributable under the qualified plan to a designated Roth account for the benefit of the individual. It appears that Congress felt that the rules that were in place were to restrictive and it wanted to permit more individuals to take advantage of the ability to convert pre-tax funds into Roth funds within a designated Roth account.[26]

Notice 2013-74 clarifies the rules for in-plan Roth rollovers after ATRA 2012:
* To be eligible for an in-plan Roth rollover, an amount must be vested.
* Amounts no longer have to be distributable to be rolled over. The following can now be rolled over without regard to whether they satisfy the conditions for distribution:
    * Elective deferrals in § 401(k) plans and § 403(b) plans;
    * Matching contributions and nonelective contributions, including qualified matching contributions and qualified nonelective contributions described in § 1.401(k)-6; and
    * Annual deferrals made to governmental § 457(b) plans.
    * Note: The federal government's Thrift Savings Plan is treated as a § 401(k) plan for this purpose.

Based on this IRS Notice and the law, most vested amounts within an eligible plan can be rolled over as an in-plan Roth rollover to a Roth Account.

Taxation Rules Applicable to a Distribution from a Designated Roth Account that is Rolled Over.[27]

A distribution from a Roth account is permitted to be rolled over into another designated Roth account or a Roth IRA without inclusion into gross income. Rollovers from a Roth account to another Roth account must generally be accomplished through a direct rollover (i.e., not using the 60-day rollover).[28]

---

26. Note that the result of more in-plan Roth rollovers is an acceleration of tax revenue.
27. Treas. Reg. §1.402A-1.

If a distribution from a designated Roth account is made to an employee, the employee would still be able to rollover the entire amount (or any portion thereof) into a Roth IRA within 60-days.

If less than 100 percent of a distribution is rolled over from a Roth Account and it is not a qualified distribution, then the part that is rolled over is deemed to consist first of the portion of the distribution that is attributable to income under section IRC §72(e)(8). This treatment is a benefit to the taxpayer as the taxable portion is rolled over first.

If an employee receives a distribution from a designated Roth account, the portion of the distribution that would be includible in gross income is permitted to be rolled over into a designated Roth account under another plan. The employee's period of participation under the distributing plan is not carried over to the recipient plan for purposes of satisfying the 5-taxable-year period of participation requirement under the recipient plan. Generally, the taxable year in which the recipient plan accepts such rollover contribution is the taxable year that begins the participant's new 5-taxable-year period of participation. However, if the participant is rolling over to a plan in which the participant already has a pre-existing designated Roth account with a longer period of participation, the starting date of the recipient account is used to measure the participant's 5-taxable-year period of participation.

EXAMPLE 7.10

Employee B receives a $14,000 eligible rollover distribution that is not a qualified distribution from B's designated Roth account, consisting of $11,000 of investment in the contract and $3,000 of income. Within 60 days of receipt, Employee B rolls over $7,000 of the distribution into a Roth IRA. The $7,000 is deemed to consist of $3,000 of income and $4,000 of investment in the contract. Because the only portion of the distribution that could be includible in gross income (the income) is rolled over, none of the distribution is includible in Employee B's gross income.

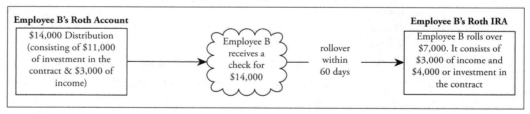

Rolling Over Funds from Inherited IRAs and Qualified Plans to a Roth IRA or Roth Account
There are several recent changes to the law that permit inherited IRAs or qualified plans to be rolled over to a Roth IRA or account. With the PPA 2006 expansion of the term, qualified rollover contribution, inherited assets in a qualified plan can now be rolled directly to a Roth IRA by the beneficiary.[29] While the beneficiary will be required to include the conversion amount into taxable income and will be responsible for taking minimum distributions from the account, it may be a

---

28. If a distribution from a designated Roth account is rolled over to another designated Roth account in a direct rollover, the amount of the rollover contribution allocated to investment in the contract in the recipient designated Roth account is the amount that would not have been includible in gross if the distribution had not been rolled over. Thus, if an amount that is a qualified distribution is rolled over, the entire amount of the rollover contribution is allocated to investment in the contract. If the entire account balance of a designated Roth account is rolled over to another designated Roth account in a direct rollover, and, at the time of the distribution, the investment in the contract exceeds the balance in the designated Roth account, the investment in the contract in the distributing plan is included in the investment in the contract of the recipient plan.

29. See IRS Notices 2008-30 and 2009-75.

strategy that should be considered. However, the considerations regarding minimizing tax during the conversion still apply.

In addition, an in-plan Roth rollover can be elected by a beneficiary if he is a surviving spouse, but cannot be elected by a non-spouse beneficiary. In addition, an inherited IRA from a spouse can be converted to a Roth IRA.[30]

CHARACTERISTICS OF ROTH IRAS AND ROTH ACCOUNTS

EXHIBIT 7.14

Characteristic	Roth IRA	Roth Account
Participation	Anyone with earned income under limit.	Anyone who is a participant in a 401(k), 403(b) or 457 plan that permits Roth contributions.
Contribution limits	IRA Annual limit - for 2016, $5,500 plus $1,000 catch up if age 50 or older. Subject to AGI limit: Single ($61,000-$71,000); MFJ ($184,000-$194,000)	Deferral limit - for 2016, $18,000 plus $6,000 if age 50 or older. No AGI limits.
Recharacterization permitted	Yes - permitted[1]	No - not permitted. Once the rollover takes place, it cannot be undone.
Minimum distributions	Only after death of participant	Yes - required
Requirements for qualified distribution	5 years & on account of death, disability, age 59 ½ or first time home purchase (up to $10,000).	5 years & on account of death, disability or age 59½.
Tax for nonqualified distributions (early distributions penalties may apply to part of the distribution)	Nonqualified distributions are distributed in order: contributions (basis), conversions (basis), then earnings (taxable).	Nonqualified distributions are prorated between Roth contributions (basis) and earnings (taxable).
5 year holding period for qualified distributions	Begins Jan 1 of the year for which a contribution is made to any Roth IRA.	Each Roth account has a separate beginning date, which starts Jan. 1 of the year for which a contribution if first made.
Loans	Not permitted	Allowed if provided for in the plan document.
Withdrawals	Withdrawals can occur anytime - nonqualified distribution may be subject to tax and penalty.	Withdrawals are only allowed if permitted by the plan. Nonqualified distribution may be subject to tax and penalty.
Beneficiary	Anyone	Anyone, but for a nonspouse beneficiary, spouse must consent.
Conversion from a Qualified plan to:	Permitted - no income limitations	Permitted as an in-plan Roth rollover
Conversion from a traditional IRA to:	Permitted - no income limitations	Not permitted

1. The taxpayer can "reconvert" the later of: (1) the beginning of the following year after conversion, or (2) 30 days after the recharacterization.

---

30. See IRS Notice 2010-84.

ADJUSTED BASIS

A participant will have an **adjusted basis** in distributions received from a qualified plan if either of the following have occurred:

- the participant made after-tax contributions to a contributory qualified plan, or
- the participant was taxed on the premiums for life insurance held in the qualified plan.

When a plan participant contributes after-tax funds to a qualified plan, the participant will have an adjusted basis in the qualified plan equal to the amount of after-tax funds contributed to the plan during participation. Distributions from qualified plans that have an adjusted basis will be partially treated as a nontaxable return of basis while the remaining portion of the distribution will be taxed as ordinary income. The calculation will vary depending upon whether a distribution is taken as an annuity or lump-sum. Lump-sum distributions are discussed in a later section.

Annuity Payments

Amounts distributed as an annuity are taxable to the participant of a qualified plan in the year in which the annuity payments are received. Each annuity payment is considered a partially tax-free return of adjusted basis and partially ordinary income using an inclusion/exclusion ratio. The numerator for the exclusion ratio is the cost basis in the annuity, and the denominator of the exclusion ratio is the total of the expected benefit that will be payable from the annuity.

$$\frac{\text{Cost Basis in the Annuity}}{\text{Total Expected Benefit}} = \text{Exclusion Ratio}$$

Kim is a participant in a qualified plan from which she is to receive annuity payments of $3,000 per month for an expected period of 20 years. Kim has an adjusted basis in the qualified plan in the amount of $180,000. How much of each annuity distribution to Kim is subject to ordinary income?

$$\frac{\text{Cost Basis in the Annuity}}{\text{Total Expected Benefit}} = \text{Exclusion Ratio}$$

$$\frac{\$180,000}{\$3,000 \times 20 \text{ years} \times 12 \text{ months}} = \text{Exclusion Ratio}$$

$$\frac{\$180,000}{\$720,000} = 25\% \text{ Exclusion Ratio}$$

$3,000 x 25% = $750 of each monthly payment is return of adjusted basis.

$3,000 - $750 = $2,250 of each monthly payment is subject to ordinary income tax.

Once the participant has recovered the entire cost basis of the annuity, all future monthly payments will be fully taxed.[31] In the event that the participant dies before recovering all of the cost basis, a deduction (miscellaneous itemized deduction not subject to two percent) will be available on the participant's final income tax return for the unrecovered investment.[32] Distributions that are not lump-sum and are not part of an annuity are taxed pro rata to the account balance in comparison to the pre-taxed portion.

---

31. IRC §72(b)(2).
32. IRC §72(b)(3).

Lump-Sum Distributions

Participants may take a full distribution, often called a lump-sum distribution, from a plan upon termination of employment. Any after-tax contributions will simply offset the taxable distribution. Lump-sum distributions are discussed in detail below.

LUMP-SUM DISTRIBUTIONS

Lump-sum distributions from a qualified pension or profit sharing plan may receive special income tax treatment. A lump-sum distribution must meet the following four requirements, as outlined in Part I of Form 4972:

1. the distribution must represent the employee's entire accrued benefit in the case of a pension plan or the full account balance in the case of a defined contribution plan.
2. a distribution of the balance of a participant's entire accrued benefit or account balance must be made within one taxable year.
3. the distribution must be on account of either the participant's death, attainment of age 59½, separation from service (does not apply to self-employed individuals in the plan), or disability.[33]
4. the employee must have participated in the plan for at least five taxable years prior to the tax year of distribution (waived if the distribution is on account of death).

The taxpayer must elect lump-sum distribution treatment by attaching Form 4972 to the taxpayer's federal income tax return. This must be filed by the participant, or (in the case of the participant's death) by his estate within one year of receipt of the distribution.

All of the four requirements must be met in order for the distribution to qualify as a lump-sum distribution and therefore qualify for any of the special tax treatments described below.

Distributions from qualified plans are generally taxed as ordinary income, but when a distribution is considered a lump-sum distribution, the distribution may qualify for one of the following special tax treatments:

- 10-year forward averaging.
- Pre-1974 capital gain treatment.
- Net Unrealized Appreciation (NUA).

However, simply because a distribution may qualify for one of the following special tax treatments does not mean that it is the best choice for the individual receiving the distribution. In many cases, the best choice may be to rollover the distribution into an IRA and defer taxation. However, it is always important to evaluate the options that are available.

---

33. IRC §402(e)(4)(D)(i).

EXHIBIT 7.15

FORM 4972

Form **4972**		**Tax on Lump-Sum Distributions**	OMB No. 1545-0193
		(From Qualified Plans of Participants Born Before January 2, 1936)	20**15**
Department of the Treasury Internal Revenue Service (99)		▶ Information about Form 4972 and its instructions is available at *www.irs.gov/form4972*. ▶ Attach to Form 1040, Form 1040NR, or Form 1041.	Attachment Sequence No. **28**

Name of recipient of distribution | Identifying number

Part I	Complete this part to see if you can use Form 4972			Yes	No
1	Was this a distribution of a plan participant's entire balance (excluding deductible voluntary employee contributions and certain forfeited amounts) from all of an employer's qualified plans of one kind (for example, pension, profit-sharing, or stock bonus)? If "No," **do not** use this form		1		
2	Did you roll over any part of the distribution? If "Yes," **do not** use this form		2		
3	Was this distribution paid to you as a beneficiary of a plan participant who was born before January 2, 1936?		3		
4	Were you **(a)** a plan participant who received this distribution, **(b)** born before January 2, 1936, **and (c)** a participant in the plan for at least 5 years before the year of the distribution?		4		
	If you answered "No" to both questions 3 **and** 4, **do not** use this form.				
5a	Did you use Form 4972 after 1986 for a previous distribution from your own plan? If "Yes," **do not** use this form for a 2015 distribution from your own plan		5a		
b	If you are receiving this distribution as a beneficiary of a plan participant who died, did you use Form 4972 for a previous distribution received as a beneficiary of that participant after 1986? If "Yes," **do not** use this form for this distribution		5b		

Part II	Complete this part to choose the 20% capital gain election (see instructions)		
6	Capital gain part from Form 1099-R, box 3	6	
7	Multiply line 6 by 20% (.20) . . . . ▶	7	
	If you also choose to use Part III, go to line 8. Otherwise, include the amount from line 7 in the total on Form 1040, line 44; Form 1040NR, line 42; or Form 1041, Schedule G, line 1b.		

Part III	Complete this part to choose the 10-year tax option (see instructions)				
8	If you completed Part II, enter the amount from Form 1099-R, box 2a minus box 3. If you did not complete Part II, enter the amount from box 2a. Multiple recipients (and recipients who elect to include NUA in taxable income) see instructions			8	
9	Death benefit exclusion for a beneficiary of a plan participant who died before August 21, 1996 .			9	
10	Total taxable amount. Subtract line 9 from line 8			10	
11	Current actuarial value of annuity from Form 1099-R, box 8. If none, enter -0-			11	
12	Adjusted total taxable amount. Add lines 10 and 11. If this amount is $70,000 or more, **skip** lines 13 through 16, enter this amount on line 17, and go to line 18			12	
13	Multiply line 12 by 50% (.50), but **do not** enter more than $10,000 . .	13			
14	Subtract $20,000 from line 12. If line 12 is $20,000 or less, enter -0-	14			
15	Multiply line 14 by 20% (.20)	15			
16	Minimum distribution allowance. Subtract line 15 from line 13			16	
17	Subtract line 16 from line 12			17	
18	Federal estate tax attributable to lump-sum distribution			18	
19	Subtract line 18 from line 17. If line 11 is zero, **skip** lines 20 through 22 and go to line 23 . . .			19	
20	Divide line 11 by line 12 and enter the result as a decimal (rounded to at least three places)	20	.		
21	Multiply line 16 by the decimal on line 20	21			
22	Subtract line 21 from line 11	22			
23	Multiply line 19 by 10% (.10)			23	
24	Tax on amount on line 23. Use the Tax Rate Schedule in the instructions			24	
25	Multiply line 24 by ten (10). If line 11 is zero, **skip** lines 26 through 28, enter this amount on line 29, and go to line 30			25	
26	Multiply line 22 by 10% (.10)	26			
27	Tax on amount on line 26. Use the Tax Rate Schedule in the instructions	27			
28	Multiply line 27 by ten (10)			28	
29	Subtract line 28 from line 25. Multiple recipients see instructions . . . . . . ▶			29	
30	**Tax on lump-sum distribution.** Add lines 7 and 29. Also include this amount in the total on Form 1040, line 44; Form 1040NR, line 42; or Form 1041, Schedule G, line 1b . . . . . . ▶			30	

For Paperwork Reduction Act Notice, see instructions. | Cat. No. 13187U | Form **4972** (2015)

SPECIAL TAX TREATMENT

EXHIBIT
7.16

- 10-year forward averaging
- Pre-1974 capital gains treatment
- NUA treatment

10-Year Forward Averaging

A participant born prior to January 2, 1936 may be eligible for 10-year forward averaging when taking a lump-sum distribution from a qualified plan. Contrary to its title, 10-year forward averaging does not allow the taxpayer to pay the income tax attributable to the lump-sum distribution over a 10-year period, but it still may lower the current income tax attributable to the lump-sum distribution. Because the income tax system incorporates graduated tax rate schedules, any large or relatively large distribution will cause the taxpayer to pay tax at higher rates because the entire distribution is included as ordinary income. If the distribution were large enough, it could cause a taxpayer to move from the lowest tax bracket through all of the rates up to the top tax bracket. This result is often referred to as "bracket creep" since this type of distribution will cause the taxpayer to pay various rates of tax on different parts of the distribution. 10-year forward averaging is designed to mitigate the negative impact attributable to a move to a higher income tax bracket because of a lump-sum distribution.

Under 10-year forward averaging, the income tax due on a lump-sum distribution is calculated by dividing the taxable portion of the lump-sum distribution by 10 and then applying the 1986 individual income tax rates (see Exhibit 7.15) to the result (one-tenth of the total taxable distribution). This result is then multiplied by 10 to determine the total income tax due on the distribution.

Because the 1986 individual income tax rates are used in the calculation and not the tax rates for the year of distribution, consideration must be given to both current rates and the 1986 rates. There has been a declining trend in income tax rates over the last 30 years, which has reduced the benefits of 10-year forward averaging. 10-year averaging does not allow the tax to be paid over various years; rather, the tax is paid in the year of the lump-sum distribution. The following exhibit illustrates the 10-year forward averaging calculation.

EXHIBIT 7.17

CALCULATION OF 10-YEAR FORWARD AVERAGING

Step		Notes
1	**Lump-Sum distribution**	
2	Less employee's contributions that were previously taxed and the cost of insurance	This includes participant's after-tax contributions to a qualified plan, PS-58 costs (resulting from life insurance within a qualified plan), and certain loans from qualified plans that are treated as taxable distributions.
3	Less minimum distribution allowance (only applicable to small lump-sum distributions less than $70,000)	The minimum distribution allowance is the lesser of: 1. $10,000 or 2. one-half of the adjusted total taxable amount of the lump-sum distribution for the taxable year, reduced (but not below zero) by 20 percent of the excess (if any) of the adjusted total taxable amount over $20,000.
4	**Equals taxable amount of distribution**	
5	Divide the taxable amount by 10	
6	Determine the tax on the result determined in Step 5	Tax is calculated by using 1986 income tax rates.
7	Multiply the result of Step 6 by 10	Result is tax attributable to distribution.
8	Pay the tax from Step 7	The tax is paid in one payment.

EXHIBIT 7.18

1986 INCOME TAX RATE TABLE FOR TEN-YEAR AVERAGING CALCULATION

Over -	But Not Over --	The Tax Is	Amount Over --
-0-	1,190	11%	0
1,190	2,270	130.90 + 12%	1,190
2,270	4,530	260.50 + 14%	2,270
4,530	6,690	576.90 + 15%	4,530
6,690	9,170	900.90 + 16%	6,690
9,170	11,440	1,297.70 + 18%	9,170
11,440	13,710	1,706.30 + 20%	11,440
13,710	17,160	2,160.30 + 23%	13,710
17,160	22,880	2,953.80 + 26%	17,160
22,880	28,600	4,441.00 + 30%	22,880
28,600	34,320	6,157.00 + 34%	28,600
34,320	42,300	8,101.80 + 38%	34,320
42,300	57,190	11,134.20 + 42%	42,300
57,190	85,790	17,388.00 + 48%	57,190
85,790	....	31,116.00 + 50%	85,790

Kerstin is covered under a noncontributory qualified plan She has never made any contributions to the plan; all contributions were pretax employer contributions. She was born before 1936 and takes a lump-sum distribution that qualifies for 10-year forward averaging. How much income tax will she pay utilizing 10-year forward averaging if her account balance is $100,000 at the time of the distribution?

EXAMPLE 7.12

Lump-sum distribution	$100,000.00
Less minimum distribution allowance	0.00*
Taxable portion of distribution	$100,000.00
One tenth of taxable portion	$10,000.00
Tax on one tenth of distribution	$1,447.10 10-year forward averaging rate table (1986 Tax Rates)
Tax due on distribution ($1,447.10 x 10)	$14,471.00 Ten times the amount previously calculated

* The lesser of $10,000 or $50,000 (50,000 = 0.5 x $100,000) is $10,000.
The $10,000 is reduced by $16,000 (16,000 = 20% x ($100,000 - $20,000)), but not below zero.
Therefore, the minimum distribution allowance is zero.

Before electing 10-year averaging, a lump-sum distribution recipient should evaluate the tax that would be paid under the current ordinary income tax rates versus the 10-year forward averaging rates. In addition, prior to electing a lump-sum distribution, the participant might want to consider the long-run strategy of rolling the account balance into an IRA, deferring tax, and taking minimum distributions when required.

2016 Unmarried Individuals Income Tax Rates

EXHIBIT 7.19

If taxable income is over--	But not over--	The tax is:
$0	$9,275	10% of the amount over $0
$9,275	$37,650	$927.50 plus 15% of the amount over $9,275
$37,650	$91,150	$5,183.75 plus 25% of the amount over $37,650
$91,150	$190,150	$18,558.75 plus 28% of the amount over $91,150
$190,150	$413,350	$46,278.75 plus 33% of the amount over $190,150
$413,350	$415,050	$119,934.75 plus 35% of the amount over $413,350
$415,050	no limit	$120,529.75 plus 39.6% of the amount over $415,050

EXHIBIT
7.20

2016 MARRIED FILING JOINTLY INCOME TAX RATES

If taxable income is over--	But not over--	The tax is:
$0	$18,550	10% of the amount over $0
$18,550	$75,300	$1,855 plus 15% of the amount over $18,550
$75,300	$151,900	$10,367.50 plus 25% of the amount over $75,300
$151,900	$231,450	$29,517.50 plus 28% of the amount over $151,900
$231,450	$413,350	$51,791.50 plus 33% of the amount over $231,450
$413,350	$466,950	$111,818.50 plus 35% of the amount over $413,350
$466,950	no limit	$130,578.50 plus 39.6% of the amount over $466,950

EXAMPLE
7.13

Joe Bob, a single taxpayer, takes a $600,000 lump-sum distribution from CR Inc. qualified plan. Joe Bob did not make any contributions and the plan did not contain any insurance. How much is Joe Bob's tax if he elects 10-year forward averaging?

Line 1	Lump-Sum Distribution	$600,000	
Line 2	Less: Employee Contributions	0	
Line 3	Less: MD Allowance	0	
Line 4	Equals taxable amount of distribution	$600,000	
Line 5	Divide the taxable amount by 10	$60,000	
Line 6	Tax on Line 5	$18,736.80	($17,388 + 0.48($2,810))
Line 7	Multiply the result of Step 6 by 10	$187,368.00	
Line 8	Pay the tax from Step 7	$187,368.00	(31.228%)

EXAMPLE
7.14

Assume the same facts as above, except Joe Bob does not elect 10-year averaging. The tax is now $193,769.95.

Line 1	Lump-Sum Distribution	$600,000.00	
Line 2	Tax on Line 1	$193,769.95	
Line 3	Pay the tax from Line 2	$193,769.95	(32.29%)

Notice that in this instance it is in Joe Bob's best interest to elect 10-year averaging because he will pay less tax. However, this is only in the case of taking a full distribution. His other option is to continue to defer taxation on the funds, which is likely to be his best choice.

If Joe Bob was married then the tax would be:

Line 1	Lump-Sum Distribution	$600,000.00	
Line 2	Tax on Line 1	$183,266.30	
Line 3	Pay the Tax from Line 2	$183,266.30	(30.54%)

If Joe Bob was married, then not electing the 10-year averaging would be best because he would pay less tax. Again, Bob will likely be better off deferring tax on these funds by not taking a full distribution. In addition, he preserves the creditor protection on the funds while they remain in a qualified plan.

Pre-1974 Capital Gain Treatment

Participants born prior to January 2, 1936 are also eligible to treat the portion of a lump-sum distribution attributable to pre-1974 participation in a qualified plan as a long-term capital gain (taxable at 20 percent, not eligible for special 15 percent capital gains rate).[34] To calculate the portion that will be considered long-term capital gain, the total lump-sum distribution is multiplied by the ratio of the participant's number of months of pre-1974 participation in the qualified plan to the total number of months of the participant's plan participation. The portion remaining of the lump-sum distribution is eligible for ten-year forward averaging, or is otherwise taxed as ordinary income.

$$\text{Long-term capital gain portion} = \frac{\text{Months of pre-1974 participation}}{\text{Total months of participation}} \times \text{Taxable distribution}$$

EXAMPLE 7.15

Josh is covered under a noncontributory qualified plan. He has never made any contributions to the plan; all contributions have been pretax employer contributions. He was born before 1936 and qualifies for pre-1974 capital gain treatment. He has been in the plan since 1968 and is taking a lump-sum distribution of $1,000,000 in 2016. What portion of the distribution from the qualified plan qualifies for capital gain treatment?

$$\text{Long-term capital gain portion} = \frac{6 \text{ years } (1974\text{-}1968) \times 12 \text{ months}}{48 \text{ years } (2016\text{-}1968) \times 12 \text{ months}} \times \$1,000,000$$

$$\text{Long-term capital gain portion} = \frac{72 \text{ months}}{576 \text{ months}} \times \$1,000,000$$

$$\text{Long-term capital gain portion} = \$125,000$$

The remaining $875,000 ($1,000,000 - $125,000) is taxed at ordinary income tax rates or may be eligible for 10-year forward averaging.

---

34. Section 1122(h)(3) of the Tax Reform Act of 1986, PL 99-514 as amended by PL 100-647(1988).

Net Unrealized Appreciation (NUA)[35]

Taxpayers who receive a lump-sum distribution of employer securities (such as stock) may receive special tax treatment on the distribution. This tax treatment consists of favorable capital gain treatment instead of ordinary income tax treatment on the NUA portion of the distribution as well as deferral of recognition of the gain on the NUA portion until the distributed employer securities are sold. Although this treatment certainly applies to lump-sum distributions of employer securities from any qualified plan, it is most likely to occur from a stock bonus plan or ESOP.

Employer securities generally include stocks, bonds, and debentures of the employer corporation as well as securities of a parent company or subsidiary. However, distributions generally consist of employer stock.

Net unrealized appreciation (NUA) is defined as the excess of the fair market value of the employer securities at the date of the lump-sum distribution over the cost of the employer securities at the date the securities were contributed to the qualified plan.

	Fair Market Value at Date of Distribution
-	Value of Securities at the Date of the Employer Contribution
=	Net Unrealized Appreciation

The portion of the lump-sum distribution attributable to the cost of the employer securities (the value of the employer's tax deduction) will be taxable as ordinary income (eligible for 10-year forward averaging if the participant was born before January 2, 1936) to the participant in the year of the distribution and this value is considered the participant's adjusted basis in the employer securities. At the date of the subsequent sale of the employer securities, the participant will be required to recognize the long-term capital gain deferred since the date of the distribution. Any subsequent gain after the distribution date will be treated as either short-term capital gain or long-term capital gain based on the holding period beginning at the date of the distribution. If at the date of the subsequent sale the value of the employer securities has decreased since the date of the initial distribution, the participant will decrease the recognition of the deferred long-term capital gain to an amount equal to the differences between the fair market value of the stock at the date of the subsequent sale and the adjusted basis of the securities.

---

35. IRC §1402(e)(4).

ILLUSTRATION OF NET UNREALIZED APPRECIATION

EXHIBIT
7.21

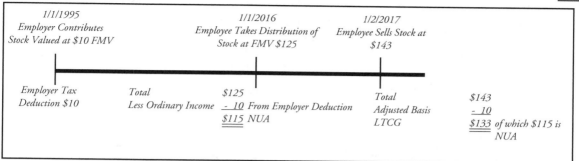

Cody received a lump-sum distribution of his employer's stock from his qualified plan. The lump-sum distribution consisted of 1,000 shares of the employer's stock valued at $2,000,000 as of the date of the distribution. The value of the stock at the date the employer contributed the stock to the plan was $500,000. When Cody receives the $2,000,000 lump-sum distribution of the employer stock, $500,000 of the distribution will be taxed as ordinary income in the year of the lump-sum distribution. The remaining gain of $1,500,000 will not be recognized until the employer stock is sold. At the date the employer stock is sold, Cody's adjusted basis in the stock will be $500,000, the amount taxed as ordinary income in the year of distribution. If he subsequently sells the stock for any amount greater than $500 per share, then Cody will have a capital gain. The first $1,500,000 of gain will be taxable as long-term capital gain and any gain in excess will be short or long-term capital gain depending on the holding period after the distribution date. Thus, if he sold it at the date of distribution for $2,000,000 then he would have a long-term capital gain of $1,500,000, the NUA.

Assume, utilizing the facts above, that Cody sells the stock two years after the distribution date for $2,120 per share. What would be the tax consequences?

$2,120,000	Sales price ($2,120 x 1,000 shares)
$500,000	Adjusted basis (taxed as ordinary income in the year of distribution)
$1,620,000	Long-term capital gain (NUA ($1,500,000) and subsequent long-term capital gain ($120,000))

If Cody had held the stock for less than one year and one day (the long-term holding period requirement), the tax consequences would be different and as follows:

$2,120,000	Sales price ($2,120 x 1,000 shares)
$500,000	Adjusted basis (taxed as ordinary income in the year of distribution)
$1,620,000	Total capital gain
$1,500,000	Long-term capital gain (NUA)
$120,000	Short-term capital gain on sale held less than 1 year and 1 day

There are several issues involved in this type of transaction. First, the participant must qualify for lump-sum distribution treatment. Second, the NUA portion must be relatively high in comparison to the cost basis portion; otherwise, the recipient may be paying too much immediate ordinary income tax for the benefit of future long-term capital gain treatment. The next issue concerns whether the stock is to be held by the recipient. If so, then the investment risks of holding a large concentration of a single security must be considered. Finally, cash flow considerations must be evaluated to determine the impact of holding the securities versus selling the securities. Note: The amount of the distribution subject to ordinary income tax is also subject to a penalty if there is no exception in the Code. A penalty would apply if a taxpayer received a lump-sum distribution, was under the age of 59½ and did not qualify for an exception.

In the event that this type of transaction does not make economic sense for a participant, the assets in the qualified plan can be rolled over into an IRA. However, if these assets are rolled into an IRA, the benefits of NUA are lost because distributions from IRAs are always characterized as ordinary income.[36] The loss of the special tax treatment may not be that important if the NUA portion is relatively small compared to the ordinary income element, and the rollover allows for the continued deferral of income tax.

Inherited Securities with NUA Resulting from a Qualified Plan Distribution

Stock that was part of a distribution from a qualified plan may be transferred upon the death of the participant to a beneficiary or heir. The question arises, "How should this stock be treated by the beneficiary for tax purposes?" There are two competing concepts in the IRC that must be considered. First is the concept of adjustment to FMV at the date of death. If this rule is applied, the stock, which is a capital asset, would simply have the same adjusted basis to the heir as the fair market value reported for estate tax purposes. The second concept is that of income in respect to a decedent, which is income earned at death yet not recognized for tax purposes prior to death. Such income will not receive an adjustment to FMV at date of death. For example, the adjusted basis of assets in a qualified plan or IRA are not adjusted to fair market value as a result of the death of the owner.

The appropriate tax treatment is a fair application of the competing concepts. The inherited stock will receive an adjustment of basis to FMV at date of death less any unrecognized NUA. The tax will be paid when the assets are disposed of by the heirs.

Assume the same facts from Example 7.12, except that Cody dies shortly after the lump-sum distribution. At his death, the total value of the stock is $2,750,000. There is still $1,500,000 of NUA that has not been taxed. Cody's heirs would generally receive stock with a new adjusted basis equal to the fair market value at the date of death (a step to the fair market value). However, when received as part of a lump-sum distribution of employer securities, the heirs' adjusted basis in the stock is equal to the fair market value of the stock at the date of death less the NUA. Therefore in this example, Cody's heirs will have an adjusted basis in the stock of $1,250,000 ($2,750,000 - $1,500,000).

---

36. The only exception to ordinary income in an IRA is basis.

QUALIFIED DOMESTIC RELATIONS ORDER

ERISA generally prevents a participant's qualified plan assets from being assigned or alienated in favor of a third party. However, a spouse or former spouse may be entitled to a portion of a participant's qualified plan benefits. An exception to the ERISA anti-alienation rules has been made if the assignment or alienation is at the direction of a **Qualified Domestic Relations Order (QDRO)**.

A QDRO is an order, judgment, or decree pursuant to a state domestic relations law that creates or recognizes the right of a third party alternate payee (nonparticipant) to receive benefits from a qualified plan. QDROs can be used for the provision of child support, alimony, or marital property rights to a spouse, former spouse, child, or other dependent of a participant. A QDRO can be issued by a judge or state agency that has the authority to issue orders, judgments, or decrees.

Although there is not a particular form that must be followed, a QDRO must specify the name and last known mailing address of the participant and the name and mailing address of each third party alternate payee covered by the order. It must also specify the amount or percentage of the participant's benefits to be paid by the plan to each third party alternate payee or the manner in which the amount or percentage is to be determined, the number of payments or period to which such order applies, and each plan to which the QDRO applies. A QDRO can give the third party payee all or part of the retirement benefits. The QDRO cannot, however, provide for any distribution mechanism or benefit not allowed by the retirement plan itself.

The administrator of the qualified plan is responsible for determining whether a domestic relations order is qualified. Therefore, the plan document must establish reasonable procedures to determine the qualified status. Administrators are required to notify participants and alternate payees when they receive a domestic relations order and to furnish a copy of the

QUICK QUIZ 7.2

1. Rollovers can consist of distributions of any kind including those from a qualified plan that are part of a series of substantially equal periodic payments.
   a. True
   b. False

2. Distributions from qualified plans are always treated as ordinary income.
   a. True
   b. False

3. QDROs allow retirement benefits to be distributed to a payee spouse without triggering a tax consequence.
   a. True
   b. False

False, False, False.

plan's procedures for determining the qualified status of such orders. Once the administrator determines the plan is qualified, the administrator must follow the plan's procedures for making QDRO distributions.

QDROs are often used either to provide support payments to the alternate payee or to divide marital property pursuant to divorce. There are two basic approaches that may be used to divide the benefit depending on the reason the QDRO is being used. One approach, often called the "**shared payment approach**," splits the actual benefit payments made between the participant and the alternate payee. Thus, each payment that would be made to the participant under the plan is split such that the alternate payee receives part of the payment and the participant receives the remaining portion of the payment. Under this approach, the alternate payee will not receive any payments unless the participant receives a payment or is already in pay status. This approach is often used when a participant has already begun to receive a stream of payments from the plan, usually at retirement, such as a life annuity.

After many years of marriage, Paul and Lucy filed for divorce. Paul has a qualified retirement plan from his previous employer. He currently receives $800 per month in retirement benefits. Assume the qualified plan allows for a shared payment approach for QDRO distributions. If Paul and Lucy's QDRO allocated 50% of the benefit to be paid to each, then each month Paul will receive $400 and Lucy will receive $400.

The second approach, often called the "**separate interest approach**," divides the participant's retirement benefit into two separate portions. Depending on the plan document, this may give the alternate payee the right to receive a lump-sum distribution equal to the present value of the account balance or a separate right to receive their portion of the retirement benefit payable at a later time similar to that of the participant. This approach is often used when the retirement plan is being divided pursuant to divorce but before the participant retires.

EXAMPLE 7.19

After several years of marriage, Steven and Jeanette have filed for divorce. Steven has a qualified retirement plan through his current employer with an account balance of $100,000. Assume the qualified plan allows for a separate interest approach for QDRO distributions. The plan states that if a QDRO is issued, then the QDRO must provide for a lump-sum distribution of a percentage of the account balance to the nonparticipant as ordered by the court. If Steven and Jeanette's QDRO states that Jeanette is to receive 40% of the account balance, then a lump distribution will be made by the plan to Jeanette in the amount of $40,000.

Note: The plan document, and not the court, determines how the retirement plan will satisfy QDROs (i.e., split account, payout the present value). As long as the QDRO complies with the plan document, the participant and the alternate payee can agree to the approach utilized.

EXAMPLE 7.20

After several years of marriage, Chris and Jenn filed for divorce. Jenn has a qualified retirement plan through her current employer. Assume the qualified plan allows for a separate interest approach for QDRO distributions. The qualified plan documents provide that if a QDRO is issued, then the QDRO can provide for any one of the following:

- A lump-sum distribution to the alternate payee of the present value of the estimated future benefit.
- A lump-sum distribution of a percentage of the account balance.
- A separation of the account balance where a percentage of the account is allocated to each party and is maintained by the plan provider for each party payable when the participant reaches retirement age regardless of whether the participant actually retires.

Chris and Jenn's QDRO can utilize any one of these three methods to separate the plan interest.

A distribution pursuant to a QDRO will not be considered a taxable distribution to the third party alternate payee as long as the assets are deposited into the recipient's IRA or qualified plan. If a distribution pursuant to a QDRO is not deposited in an IRA or other qualified plan, the third party alternate payee will be subjected to tax at ordinary income tax rates on the value of the distribution. However, the distribution is not subject to the 10 percent early withdrawal penalty if it is not deposited into the recipient's IRA or qualified plan, as this is one of the exceptions to the 10 percent penalty.[37]

<table>
<tr><td align="center">**SAMPLE QDRO**</td><td>**EXHIBIT**
7.22</td></tr>
</table>

QUALIFIED DOMESTIC RELATIONS ORDER
PAUL AND LUCY SMITH

Parties

The Participant is Paul Smith. The Participant's address is 123 Blueberry Lane, Any City, All States, 12345. The Participant's Social Security number is 123-45-6789.

The Alternate Payee is Lucy Smith. The Alternate Payee's address is 987 Strawberry Lane, Any City, All States, 12345. The Alternate Payee's Social Security number is 987-65-4321. The Alternate Payee is the former spouse of the Participant.

Plan

This order applies to benefits under the ABC Retirement Plan, herein called the Plan.

Amount of Benefits to be Paid to Alternate Payee

The Alternate Payee shall receive 50% of each benefit payment made from the Plan.

Form and Commencement of Payment to Alternate Payee

The Alternate Payee shall receive payments from the Plan of the benefits assigned to the Alternate Payee under this Order (including payments attributable to the period in which the issue of whether this Order is a qualified domestic relations order is being determined) commencing as soon as practicable after this Order has been determined to be a qualified domestic relations order or, if later, on the date the Participant commences receiving benefit payments from the Plan. Payment to the Alternate Payee shall cease on the earlier of: Alternate Payee's remarriage, or the date that payments from the Plan with respect to the Participant cease.

---

37. IRC §72(t)(2)(C).

EXHIBIT
7.23

QUALIFIED DOMESTIC RELATION ORDER

A "qualified domestic relations order" (QDRO) is:
- A domestic relations order
- That creates or recognizes the existence of an "alternate payee's" right to receive, or assigns to an alternate payee the right to receive, all or a portion of the benefits payable with respect to a participant under a retirement plan, and contains specific information and does not require the plan to do specific things as follows.

QDROs must contain the following information:[1]
- The name and last known mailing address of the participant and each alternate payee;
- The name of each plan to which the order applies;
- The dollar amount or percentage (or the method of determining the amount or percentage) of the benefit to be paid to the alternate payee, and
- The number of payments or time period to which the order applies.

QDRO must <u>not</u> contain: [2]
- The order must not require a plan to provide an alternate payee or participant with any type or form of benefit, or any option, not otherwise provided under the plan,
- The order must not require a plan to provide for increased benefits (determined on the basis of actuarial value),
- The order must not require a plan to pay benefits to an alternate payee that are required to be paid to another alternate payee under another order previously determined to be a QDRO, and
- The order must not require a plan to pay benefits to an alternate payee in the form of a qualified joint and survivor annuity for the lives of the alternate payee and his or her subsequent spouse.

1. ERISA §206(d)(3)(C)(i)-(iv); IRC §414(p)(2)(A)-(D).
2. ERISA §§206(d)(3)(D)(i)-(iii), 206(d)(3)(E)(i)(III); IRC §§414(p)(3)(A)-(C), 414(p)(4)(A)(iii).

PLAN LOANS

Although distributions of qualified plan assets to participants are generally not permitted until retirement or termination, qualified plans are permitted, but not required, to provide loans from the plan to participants. A loan must be evidenced by a legally enforceable agreement, which complies with the requirements in the IRC.

Loans are utilized typically to increase plan participation and help the plan pass its nondiscrimination testing. **Plan loans** must be made available to all participants and beneficiaries on an effectively equal basis, must be limited in amount,

KEY CONCEPTS

1. What is the maximum amount a participant can borrow from a 401(k) plan?

2. When must loans from a 401(k) plan be repaid?

3. Discuss the impact of plan termination on plan loans.

must be repaid within a certain time period, must bear a reasonable rate of interest, must be adequately secured, and the administrator must maintain proper accounting for the loans. Although any qualified plan could establish a loan provision, loan provisions are common only in cash or deferred arrangement (**CODA**) type plans such as 401(k) and 403(b) plans. Loans are prohibited on other tax-sheltered retirement savings vehicles, such as IRAs, SEPs, and SIMPLEs (discussed later).

Amount of Loan

Loans from qualified plans may not exceed the lesser of $50,000 (subject to a reduction) or one-half of the fair market value of the participant's vested accrued benefit under the plan. However, where a participant's vested accrued benefit is less than $20,000, the available plan loan is limited to the lesser of the vested accrued benefit or $10,000. Consider the examples (A - F) in the following table:

	Vested Accrued Benefit	Maximum Permissible Loan
A	$1,000,000	$50,000
B	$120,000	$50,000
C	$80,000	$40,000
D	$24,000	$12,000
E	$18,000	$10,000
F	$9,000	$9,000

Reduction of $50,000 limit: If the participant had an outstanding loan balance within the previous twelve months, the otherwise maximum permissible loan is reduced by the highest outstanding loan balance during the twelve month period ending the day prior to when the current loan is made.

Pat has $125,000 in vested plan benefits. He borrowed $40,000 on January 1, 2016 from his 401(k) plan and repaid $25,000 on August 14, 2016. On December 31, 2016, Pat's maximum permissible loan from the plan would be $10,000. Pat is subjected to this limitation because his highest outstanding balance within twelve months of December 30, 2016 (the day before the date of the calculation) is $40,000. The otherwise maximum permissible loan amount of $50,000 must be reduced by $40,000 to determine the ultimate maximum loan amount available of $10,000.

EXAMPLE
7.21

If instead, Pat calculated his maximum permissible loan on August 16, 2017, he could borrow $35,000 because of the previous repayment. This is calculated by reducing the maximum loan of $50,000 by the highest outstanding loan balance within the prior twelve months of $15,000 ($40,000 - $25,000).

Luka has a vested account balance in his employer-sponsored qualified profit sharing plan of $90,000. Luka had an outstanding loan balance within the prior 12 months of $30,000 that has been reduced to $15,000. What is the maximum loan Luka could take from this qualified plan, assuming the plan permitted loans?

The maximum loan an individual can take is the lesser of $50,000 or 50% of their vested account balance. The $50,000 maximum is reduced by the highest outstanding balance within 12 months of $30,000. This reduction nets to $20,000. Luka's vested amount is $90,000. Half of this amount is $45,000. However, since Luka has an outstanding loan balance of $15,000, the maximum loan available is the lesser of $20,000 or $30,000 ($45,000 minus $15,000).

For purposes of the loan calculation, all plans under the same employer are treated as one for the employer.

Repayment of Loans

Loans from qualified plans are usually repaid through payroll deductions and must generally be repaid within five years from the date the loan commences; otherwise, the loan is treated as a distribution as of the date of the original loan. Loans treated as a distribution will be treated in the same manner as any other distribution from a qualified plan and will be subject to ordinary income tax and potentially the early withdrawal penalty of 10 percent if the participant fails to meet one of the exceptions (discussed below).

The five-year repayment rule does not apply to loans that are used for the purchase of a principal residence. In such a case, the IRC provides that the loan must be repaid over "a reasonable time" determined at the time of the loan. Presumably, the repayment of loans for purposes of a purchase of a personal residence could be over 30 years (the life of the mortgage), but 10 years is a typical maximum repayment period. As each plan may have different loan provisions, it is important to determine the provisions that are provided in the plan document and determine the policies from the loan administrator.

**QUICK QUIZ
7.3**

1. Loans from qualified plans can never exceed 50% of the participant's vested account balance.
   a. True
   b. False

2. Loans from qualified plans must always be repaid within five years.
   a. True
   b. False

3. The law requires loans from qualified plans to be repaid upon the participant's termination of employment from the plan sponsor.
   a. True
   b. False

False, False, False.

Loans are not only required to be repaid within a specific period of time, but are also required to be repaid in a specific manner over the repayment period. Substantially level amortization of the loan is required over the term of the loan.[38] Loan repayments must be level over the repayment period and must be made at least quarterly. In other words, the loan cannot be repaid in full with a payment (or payments) at the end of the five-year period. Generally employers require that loans be

---

38. IRC §72(p)(2)(C).

repaid only through payroll and if not repaid before termination, the loan may be treated as a distribution.

Kim has a vested accrued benefit of $200,000 and receives $70,000 to be repaid in level quarterly installments over five years. Kim has a deemed distribution of $20,000 (the excess of $70,000 over $50,000) at the time of the loan because the loan exceeds the $50,000 maximum permissible loan limit. The remaining $50,000 loan is not a deemed distribution.

EXAMPLE 7.23

Ginger has a vested accrued benefit of $30,000 and borrows $20,000 from her plan as a loan repayable in level monthly installments over five years. Ginger's maximum permissible loan is $15,000 (50% of $30,000), so her loan is $5,000 more than permissible. In this case, Ginger has a deemed distribution of $5,000 at the date of the loan. The remaining $15,000 is a permissible loan and would not be a deemed distribution. The $5,000 will be taxed as ordinary income and potentially subject to a 10% early withdrawal penalty unless Ginger meets one of the exceptions.

EXAMPLE 7.24

Cindy has a vested accrued benefit of $100,000, and she takes a $50,000 loan. The loan is repayable in level quarterly installments over seven years, and Cindy is using the proceeds to buy a new car. Because the repayment period of the loan exceeds the maximum term of five years, Cindy has a deemed distribution of $50,000 at the date the loan is made. The $50,000 will be taxed as ordinary income and potentially subject to a 10% early withdrawal penalty unless Cindy meets one of the exceptions.

EXAMPLE 7.25

Interest on Loans

When a loan is made, securities are sold and funds are removed from the participant's account. This loan amount must be paid back to the participant's account using a level amortization that includes interest. The interest charged on the loan must be at a commercially reasonable rate of interest. It should be noted that the interest is paid to the participant's account and it is paid with after-tax dollars from the participant.

Because the loan interest is paid back with after-tax dollars, those dollars will be taxed twice. The first taxation is when the participant earns the funds. Then the after-tax dollars are paid to the plan. However, these contributions do not create basis inside the qualified plan and will be taxable upon distribution.

EXHIBIT
7.24

LOAN SUMMARY

- Qualified plans may permit loans up to the lesser of one-half of the vested plan accrued benefit up to $50,000.
- If the vested accrued benefit is less than or equal to $20,000, then a loan is permitted up to the lesser of $10,000 or the vested accrued benefit.
- Reduce maximum loan of $50,000 by maximum outstanding loan within the past year.
- Loans are usually associated with 401(k) and 403(b) plans.
- Loans must generally be repaid within five years with an exception for loans associated with the purchase of personal residences, which must be reasonable and could be as long as 30 years.
- Loan interest must be at a commercially reasonable rate and is paid back to the participant's account.

Impact of Loans When an Employee is Terminated

Most plan documents require that loans be repaid upon termination of employment; however, this is not a requirement under the law. Loan repayments are generally accommodated through payroll deduction, which, of course, is unavailable after termination occurs. If a participant fails to repay a loan from a qualified plan before termination, the employer will generally declare the unpaid portion a deemed distribution, which will be subject to ordinary income tax and possibly the 10 percent early withdrawal penalty.

However, plans may provide that the outstanding loan balance reduce the amount of a direct rollover distribution. The examples that follow illustrate this available option.

In 2016, Alina has a vested account balance of $10,000 in Plan Y, of which $3,000 is invested in a plan loan to Alina that is secured by the remainder of her vested account balance. Upon termination of employment in 2016, Alina, who is under the age of 70½, elects a direct rollover distribution of her entire account balance of Plan Y, and the outstanding plan loan is offset against the distributable account balance.

Plan Y must pay $7,000 ($10,000 - $3,000) directly to the eligible retirement plan chosen by Alina in the direct rollover. When Alina's account balance was offset by the amount of the $3,000 unpaid loan balance, Alina received a plan loan offset amount (equivalent to $3,000), an eligible rollover distribution. Alina must roll over $3,000 to an eligible retirement plan within a 60-day period, or else the $3,000 distribution will be treated as any other distribution from a qualified plan, subject to ordinary income tax and possibly early withdrawal penalty.[39]

---

39. IRC §402(c)(3).

Assume the same facts as in the previous example except that the terms governing the plan loan to Alina provide that upon termination of employment, Alina's account balance is automatically offset by the amount of any unpaid loan balance to repay the loan. Alina terminates employment but does not request a distribution from Plan Y. Nevertheless, pursuant to the terms governing the plan loan, Alina's account balance is automatically offset by the amount of the $3,000 unpaid loan balance.

EXAMPLE 7.27

The $3,000 plan loan offset amount attributable to the plan loan in this example is treated in the same manner as the $3,000 plan loan offset amount in the prior example. Alina will have ordinary income and possible early withdrawal penalty.

Assume the same facts as in the previous example except that instead of providing for an automatic offset upon termination of employment to repay the plan loan, the terms governing the plan loan require full repayment of the loan by Alina within 30 days of termination of employment. Alina terminates employment, does not elect a distribution from Plan Y, and also fails to repay the plan loan within 30 days. The administrator of Plan Y declares the plan loan to Alina in default and executes on the loan by offsetting Alina's account balance by the amount of the $3,000 unpaid loan balance.

EXAMPLE 7.28

The $3,000 plan loan offset amount attributable to the plan loan in this example is treated in the same manner as the $3,000 plan loan offset amount in the previous two examples. The result in this example is the same even though the plan administrator treats the loan as in default before offsetting Alina's accrued benefit by the amount of the unpaid loan.

Again assume the same facts as the previous example except that Alina elects to receive the distribution of the account balance that remains after the $3,000 offset to repay the plan loan instead of electing a direct rollover of the remaining account balance.

EXAMPLE 7.29

In this case, the taxable amount of the distribution to Alina is $10,000, not $3,000. Because the amount of the $3,000 offset attributable to the loan is included in determining the amount that equals 20 percent of the eligible rollover distribution received by Alina, withholding in the amount of $2,000 (20 percent of $10,000) is required. The $2,000 is required to be withheld from the $7,000 to be distributed to Alina in cash so that Alina actually receives a check for $5,000.

Alina would still be entitled to roll over the entire $10,000 within the 60-day period and to avoid applicable income tax and penalties.

Alina's Vested Account Balance = $10,000			
Loan = $3,000			
Terminates and Rolls Over	**Terminates and Does Not Rollover**	**Terminates and Required Repayment within 30 Days**	**Terminates Takes Distribution of Vested Account Balance**
Alina must rollover $3,000 to an eligible retirement plan within a 60-day period (30-day period in the third example) of the termination, or the $3,000 will be subjected to ordinary income tax and possibly the 10 percent early withdrawal penalty.			Alina receives a distribution in the amount of $5,000, $10,000 less withholding and less the outstanding loan. To avoid taxation on the full $10,000, Alina must contribute $10,000 to a new retirement plan or IRA within a 60-day period.

EXAMPLE 7.30

Fred, age 40, has an account balance in Plan Z, a qualified profit sharing plan that includes a CODA. Plan Z does not permit after-tax employee contributions. In 2016, Fred receives a loan from Plan Z. In 2018, Fred stops repayment, and is therefore taxed on a deemed distribution equal to the amount of the unpaid loan balance. The deemed distribution is not an eligible rollover distribution because Fred has not separated from service or experienced any other event that permits the distribution of the elective contributions that secure the loan. Plan Z is prohibited from executing on the loan. Accordingly, Fred's account balance is not offset by the amount of the unpaid loan balance at the time Fred stops repayment on the loan. Thus, there is no distribution of an offset amount that is an eligible rollover distribution in 2018. The deemed distribution is also subject to the 10% early withdrawal penalty.

EXHIBIT 7.25

LOAN SUMMARY FOR FAILURE TO REPAY LOAN OR TERMINATION OF EMPLOYMENT

- Many qualified plans treat an outstanding loan as a distribution from the plan and issue the participant a Form 1099R (distributions from a retirement plan). The participant will then report this distribution as ordinary income, and it may be subject to the 10% early withdrawal penalty if the participant does not meet one of the exceptions.

- A qualified plan may provide that the employee has a certain period of time to repay the loan after termination, or it will otherwise treat the loan as a distribution.

- Finally, qualified plans may provide that the loan is simply an offset of the distribution, and this offset can either be treated as a taxable distribution or may be rolled over by the participant to another qualified plan.

DISTRIBUTIONS PRIOR TO 59½

In some cases, individuals may want or need to take distributions from a qualified plan before their retirement. To discourage taxpayers from using the funds before retirement, taxable distributions before the age of 59½ will generally be subject to a 10 percent early withdrawal penalty. Most plans also limit the ability of participants to take early distributions from a qualified plan except in the case of the participant's termination, death, or retirement. However, some plans may permit rollovers and substantially equal periodic payments as distributions

KEY CONCEPTS

1. What is the penalty for taking distributions from a qualified plan before the participant attains the age of 59½?

2. List the exceptions to the early withdrawal penalty.

before the age of 59½. Although not common, profit sharing plans may permit in-service distributions from the plan after the participant has participated in the plan for at least two years. This provision may be included in a plan to encourage plan participation within a company by alleviating the employees' fear of not being able to access the funds.

EARLY WITHDRAWAL PENALTY

In any case, a distribution prior to the participant attaining the age of 59½ may be subjected to a 10 percent **early withdrawal penalty** unless the distribution is on account of one of several exceptions.[40] All of the exceptions coincide with the government's intention that participants use the plan assets for their retirement, but in circumstances like death and disability, it makes sense to allow the participant (or the participant's beneficiaries) to withdraw the assets prior to their scheduled retirement.

The general rule under IRC §72(t) is that any distribution from a qualified plan (or IRA) that is taxable will result in an additional tax of 10 percent applied to the amount that is includable in gross income.

Kris, who is 40 years old, takes a distribution from his IRA to purchase a new ski boat. The distribution is in the amount of $10,000. However, 20 percent of the distribution is not taxable because it is deemed a return of basis, which is from Kris making non-deductible IRA contributions in prior years. In this case, Kris will have ordinary income of $8,000 and the 10 percent early withdrawal penalty will be applied to the $8,000 taxable amount. Therefore, the penalty is $800.

EXAMPLE 7.31

---

40. With SIMPLE plans, the early withdrawal penalty is increased to 25% if the withdrawal occurs within the first two years of plan participation.

Exceptions to the 10 Percent Early Withdrawal Penalty

As mentioned above, the general rule of a 10 percent early withdrawal penalty will apply unless there is a valid exception. These exceptions are discussed below:

EXHIBIT
7.26

SUMMARY OF 10 PERCENT PENALTY EXCEPTIONS

Exceptions to 10% Early Withdrawal Penalty
• Attainment of age 59½
• Death
• Disability
• Substantially equal periodic payments (§72(t))
• Separated from service after attainment of age 55
• Dividends paid from an ESOP
• IRS tax levy on a plan
• Medical expenses that exceed 10 percent of AGI
• Qualified Domestic Relations Order (QDRO)
• Individuals called to active duty
• Qualified public safety employee who separates from service after age 50

Age 59½

Any distribution from a qualified plan that is made on or after the date on which the employee attains age 59½ is not subject to the 10 percent penalty. This exception is intended to encourage individuals to save for their retirement and not use the funds before such time.

Death

Any distribution made to a beneficiary (or to the estate of the employee) on or after the death of the employee is not subject to the 10 percent penalty. Therefore, any inherited qualified plan interest can be distributed without regard to the age of the beneficiary and avoid the 10 percent penalty.

Disability

The 10 percent penalty will not apply in case of a participant's disability. An individual is considered to be disabled if he is unable to engage in any substantial gainful activity by reason of any medically determinable physical or mental impairment which can be expected to result in death or to be of long-continued and indefinite duration. An individual must be able to furnish proof of the disability in such form and manner as the Secretary may require.[41] Whether or not impairment in a particular case constitutes a disability is to be determined with reference to all the facts in the case.

41. IRC §72(m)(7).

The Treasury regulations provide the following list of impairments that are generally considered to prevent substantial gainful activity:[42]

1. Loss of use of two limbs;
2. Certain progressive diseases which have resulted in the physical loss or atrophy of a limb, such as diabetes, multiple sclerosis, or Buergers disease;
3. Diseases of the heart, lungs, or blood vessels which have resulted in major loss of heart or lung reserve as evidenced by X-ray, electrocardiogram, or other objective findings, so that despite medical treatment breathlessness, pain, or fatigue is produced on slight exertion, such as walking several blocks, using public transportation, or doing small chores;
4. Cancer which is inoperable and progressive;
5. Damage to the brain or brain abnormality which has resulted in severe loss of judgment, intellect, orientation, or memory;
6. Mental diseases (e.g., psychosis or severe psychoneurosis) requiring continued institution-alization or constant supervision of the individual;
7. Loss or diminution of vision to the extent that the affected individual has a central visual acuity of no better than 20/200 in the better eye after best correction, or has a limitation in the fields of vision such that the widest diameter of the visual fields subtends an angle no greater than 20 degrees;
8. Permanent and total loss of speech; and
9. Total deafness uncorrectible by a hearing aid.

The regulations go on to state that one or more of the impairments listed above will not automatically permit a finding that the individual is disabled. The impairment must be evaluated in terms of whether it does in fact prevent the individual from engaging in customary or any comparable substantial gainful activity.

---

42. Treas. Reg. §1.72-17A.

EXHIBIT
7.27

FORM 5329

Form **5329**	**Additional Taxes on Qualified Plans (Including IRAs) and Other Tax-Favored Accounts**	OMB No. 1545-0074
	▶ **Attach to Form 1040 or Form 1040NR.**	20**15**
Department of the Treasury Internal Revenue Service (99)	▶ **Information about Form 5329 and its separate instructions is at** *www.irs.gov/form5329.*	Attachment Sequence No. **29**

Name of individual subject to additional tax. If married filing jointly, see instructions.　　　　　　Your social security number

Fill in Your Address Only If You Are Filing This Form by Itself and Not With Your Tax Return ▶

Home address (number and street), or P.O. box if mail is not delivered to your home　　　Apt. no.

City, town or post office, state, and ZIP code. If you have a foreign address, also complete the spaces below (see instructions).

If this is an amended return, check here ▶ ☐

Foreign country name　　　Foreign province/state/county　　　Foreign postal code

If you **only** owe the additional 10% tax on early distributions, you may be able to report this tax directly on Form 1040, line 59, or Form 1040NR, line 57, without filing Form 5329. See the instructions for Form 1040, line 59, or for Form 1040NR, line 57.

	Part I	**Additional Tax on Early Distributions.** Complete this part if you took a taxable distribution before you reached age 59½ from a qualified retirement plan (including an IRA) or modified endowment contract (unless you are reporting this tax directly on Form 1040 or Form 1040NR—see above). You may also have to complete this part to indicate that you qualify for an exception to the additional tax on early distributions or for certain Roth IRA distributions (see instructions).		
1	Early distributions included in income. For Roth IRA distributions, see instructions	**1**		
2	Early distributions included on line 1 that are not subject to the additional tax (see instructions). Enter the appropriate exception number from the instructions: _____	**2**		
3	Amount subject to additional tax. Subtract line 2 from line 1	**3**		
4	**Additional tax.** Enter 10% (.10) of line 3. Include this amount on Form 1040, line 59, or Form 1040NR, line 57 .	**4**		
	Caution: *If any part of the amount on line 3 was a distribution from a SIMPLE IRA, you may have to include 25% of that amount on line 4 instead of 10% (see instructions).*			

	Part II	**Additional Tax on Certain Distributions From Education Accounts and ABLE Accounts.** Complete this part if you included an amount in income, on Form 1040 or Form 1040NR, line 21, from a Coverdell education savings account (ESA), a qualified tuition program (QTP), or an ABLE account.		
5	Distributions included in income from a Coverdell ESA, a QTP, or an ABLE account	**5**		
6	Distributions included on line 5 that are not subject to the additional tax (see instructions) . . .	**6**		
7	Amount subject to additional tax. Subtract line 6 from line 5	**7**		
8	**Additional tax.** Enter 10% (.10) of line 7. Include this amount on Form 1040, line 59, or Form 1040NR, line 57	**8**		

	Part III	**Additional Tax on Excess Contributions to Traditional IRAs.** Complete this part if you contributed more to your traditional IRAs for 2015 than is allowable or you had an amount on line 17 of your 2014 Form 5329.			
9	Enter your excess contributions from line 16 of your 2014 Form 5329 (see instructions). If zero, go to line 15		**9**		
10	If your traditional IRA contributions for 2015 are less than your maximum allowable contribution, see instructions. Otherwise, enter -0-	**10**			
11	2015 traditional IRA distributions included in income (see instructions) .	**11**			
12	2015 distributions of prior year excess contributions (see instructions) .	**12**			
13	Add lines 10, 11, and 12		**13**		
14	Prior year excess contributions. Subtract line 13 from line 9. If zero or less, enter -0-		**14**		
15	Excess contributions for 2015 (see instructions)		**15**		
16	Total excess contributions. Add lines 14 and 15		**16**		
17	**Additional tax.** Enter 6% (.06) of the **smaller** of line 16 **or** the value of your traditional IRAs on December 31, 2015 (including 2015 contributions made in 2016). Include this amount on Form 1040, line 59, or Form 1040NR, line 57 .		**17**		

	Part IV	**Additional Tax on Excess Contributions to Roth IRAs.** Complete this part if you contributed more to your Roth IRAs for 2015 than is allowable or you had an amount on line 25 of your 2014 Form 5329.			
18	Enter your excess contributions from line 24 of your 2014 Form 5329 (see instructions). If zero, go to line 23		**18**		
19	If your Roth IRA contributions for 2015 are less than your maximum allowable contribution, see instructions. Otherwise, enter -0-	**19**			
20	2015 distributions from your Roth IRAs (see instructions)	**20**			
21	Add lines 19 and 20		**21**		
22	Prior year excess contributions. Subtract line 21 from line 18. If zero or less, enter -0-		**22**		
23	Excess contributions for 2015 (see instructions)		**23**		
24	Total excess contributions. Add lines 22 and 23		**24**		
25	**Additional tax.** Enter 6% (.06) of the **smaller** of line 24 **or** the value of your Roth IRAs on December 31, 2015 (including 2015 contributions made in 2016). Include this amount on Form 1040, line 59, or Form 1040NR, line 57		**25**		

For Privacy Act and Paperwork Reduction Act Notice, see your tax return instructions.　　　Cat. No. 13329Q　　　Form **5329** (2015)

FORM 5329 CONTINUED

Form 5329 (2015)   Page **2**

Part V   **Additional Tax on Excess Contributions to Coverdell ESAs.** Complete this part if the contributions to your Coverdell ESAs for 2015 were more than is allowable or you had an amount on line 33 of your 2014 Form 5329.

26	Enter the excess contributions from line 32 of your 2014 Form 5329 (see instructions). If zero, go to line 31	**26**	
27	If the contributions to your Coverdell ESAs for 2015 were less than the maximum allowable contribution, see instructions. Otherwise, enter -0-	**27**	
28	2015 distributions from your Coverdell ESAs (see instructions)	**28**	
29	Add lines 27 and 28	**29**	
30	Prior year excess contributions. Subtract line 29 from line 26. If zero or less, enter -0-	**30**	
31	Excess contributions for 2015 (see instructions)	**31**	
32	Total excess contributions. Add lines 30 and 31	**32**	
33	**Additional tax.** Enter 6% (.06) of the **smaller** of line 32 **or** the value of your Coverdell ESAs on December 31, 2015 (including 2015 contributions made in 2016). Include this amount on Form 1040, line 59, or Form 1040NR, line 57	**33**	

Part VI   **Additional Tax on Excess Contributions to Archer MSAs.** Complete this part if you or your employer contributed more to your Archer MSAs for 2015 than is allowable or you had an amount on line 41 of your 2014 Form 5329.

34	Enter the excess contributions from line 40 of your 2014 Form 5329 (see instructions). If zero, go to line 39	**34**	
35	If the contributions to your Archer MSAs for 2015 are less than the maximum allowable contribution, see instructions. Otherwise, enter -0-	**35**	
36	2015 distributions from your Archer MSAs from Form 8853, line 8	**36**	
37	Add lines 35 and 36	**37**	
38	Prior year excess contributions. Subtract line 37 from line 34. If zero or less, enter -0-	**38**	
39	Excess contributions for 2015 (see instructions)	**39**	
40	Total excess contributions. Add lines 38 and 39	**40**	
41	**Additional tax.** Enter 6% (.06) of the **smaller** of line 40 **or** the value of your Archer MSAs on December 31, 2015 (including 2015 contributions made in 2016). Include this amount on Form 1040, line 59, or Form 1040NR, line 57	**41**	

Part VII   **Additional Tax on Excess Contributions to Health Savings Accounts (HSAs).** Complete this part if you, someone on your behalf, or your employer contributed more to your HSAs for 2015 than is allowable or you had an amount on line 49 of your 2014 Form 5329.

42	Enter the excess contributions from line 48 of your 2014 Form 5329. If zero, go to line 47	**42**	
43	If the contributions to your HSAs for 2015 are less than the maximum allowable contribution, see instructions. Otherwise, enter -0-	**43**	
44	2015 distributions from your HSAs from Form 8889, line 16	**44**	
45	Add lines 43 and 44	**45**	
46	Prior year excess contributions. Subtract line 45 from line 42. If zero or less, enter -0-	**46**	
47	Excess contributions for 2015 (see instructions)	**47**	
48	Total excess contributions. Add lines 46 and 47	**48**	
49	**Additional tax.** Enter 6% (.06) of the **smaller** of line 48 **or** the value of your HSAs on December 31, 2015 (including 2015 contributions made in 2016). Include this amount on Form 1040, line 59, or Form 1040NR, line 57	**49**	

Part VIII   **Additional Tax on Excess Contributions to an ABLE Account.** Complete this part if contributions to your ABLE account for 2015 were more than is allowable.

| 50 | Excess contributions for 2015 (see instructions) | **50** | |
| 51 | **Additional tax.** Enter 6% (.06) of the **smaller** of line 50 **or** the value of your ABLE account on December 31, 2015. Include this amount on Form 1040, line 59, or Form 1040NR, line 57 | **51** | |

Part IX   **Additional Tax on Excess Accumulation in Qualified Retirement Plans (Including IRAs).** Complete this part if you did not receive the minimum required distribution from your qualified retirement plan.

52	Minimum required distribution for 2015 (see instructions)	**52**	
53	Amount actually distributed to you in 2015	**53**	
54	Subtract line 53 from line 52. If zero or less, enter -0-	**54**	
55	**Additional tax.** Enter 50% (.50) of line 54. Include this amount on Form 1040, line 59, or Form 1040NR, line 57	**55**	

Sign Here Only If You Are Filing This Form by Itself and Not With Your Tax Return

Under penalties of perjury, I declare that I have examined this form, including accompanying attachments, and to the best of my knowledge and belief, it is true, correct, and complete. Declaration of preparer (other than taxpayer) is based on all information of which preparer has any knowledge.

▶ _____   ▶ _____
     Your signature   Date

Paid Preparer Use Only	Print/Type preparer's name	Preparer's signature	Date	Check ☐ if self-employed	PTIN
	Firm's name ▶		Firm's EIN ▶		
	Firm's address ▶		Phone no.		

Form **5329** (2015)

Substantially Equal Periodic Payments

If the distribution is part of a series of substantially equal periodic payments, also called Section 72(t) distributions, (made at least annually for the life or life expectancy of the participant or the joint lives or joint life expectancies of the participant and his designated beneficiary), the payments will not be subjected to the 10 percent early withdrawal penalty. The payments must begin after the participant has separated from service, and to be considered substantially equal periodic payments, the payments must be made in any one of the following three ways: [43]

1. **Required Minimum Distribution Method.**

   The payments are calculated in the same manner as required under minimum distribution rules (discussed below). Note that payments are recalculated annually.

2. **Fixed Amortization Method.**

   The payment is calculated over the participant's life expectancy if single, or the joint life expectancy if married, and the interest rate is reasonable (not to exceed 120% of the federal midterm rate). This method creates a series of installment payments that remain the same in subsequent years.

3. **Fixed Annuitization Method.**

   The participant takes distributions of the account over a number of years determined by dividing the account balance by an annuity factor using a reasonable interest rate and mortality table. Under this method, the payment does not change in future years.

EXAMPLE 7.32

Mr. B, age 50, would like to explore his distribution options under IRC §72(t) rules. His account balance is $400,000.[44]

Option 1 - Required Minimum Distribution Method

Assume the required minimum distribution factor was 34.2 years.[45]

$$\frac{\$400,000}{34.2} = \$11,695.91 \text{ per year (1st year)}$$

Option 2 - Fixed Amortization Method

Assume the interest rate is 2.0%, and the single life expectancy is 34.2 years.[46] The annual distribution amount is calculated by amortizing the account balance of $400,000 over Mr. B's single life expectancy (34.2 years) at an interest rate of 2.0%. If an end-of-the year payment is calculated, then the annual distribution amount is $16,260.57.[47]

---

43. These three methods are set forth in Notice 89-25 as modified by Rev. Ruling 2002-62. An alternate method may be used, but must be approved through the use of a private letter ruling.
44. This example is derived from "Retirement Plan FAQs Regarding Rev. Ruling 2002-62," available at http://www.irs.gov/retirement/article/0,id=103045,00.html#7.
45. The factor is determined by the "Single Life Table" in Reg. §1.401(a)(9) - 9.
46. The interest rate is 120% of the applicable midterm rate. The interest rate in this example is provided for illustration purposes.
47. When comparing these three methods, it is easiest to use one of the many 72(t) calculators available online, such as the calculator provided Bankrate.com (available at http://www.bankrate.com/brm/calculators/retirement/72t_distribution_calculator.asp).

Option 3 -Fixed Annuitization Method

Under this method, the annual distribution amount is equal to the account balance of $400,000 divided by the cost of an annuity factor that would provide one dollar per year over Mr. B's life, beginning at age 50. The age 50 annuity factor (24.683) is calculated based on the mortality table in Appendix B of Revenue Ruling 2002-62 and an interest rate of 2.0%. Such calculations would normally be made by an actuary.

$$\frac{\$400,000}{24.683} = \$16,205.49$$

Notice that Options 2 and 3 provide a larger payment than Option 1. For example, a person may want the larger payment to help finance a new business venture. The participant can choose any of the methods.

In the case above, Mr. B may choose Option 1 if he needs some current income but does not want to significantly deplete his account balance. Recall that he must continue to withdraw until he is 59½. Mr. B could choose Option 2 or 3, which provide larger payments, if, for example, he were starting a new business and needed the extra cash flow, or expected that business losses from a flow-through entity would shelter part of the distributions.

SUMMARY OF 72(t) DISTRIBUTIONS*			
	RMD Method	Fixed Amortization Method	Fixed Annuitization Method
Annual Payment	$11,695.91	$16,260.57	$16,205.49

* Based on an individual at age 50 with an account balance of $400,000, an expected interest rate of 2.0%, and a life expectancy of 34.2 years.

The payment calculated under one of the methods determined above must continue exactly as calculated for the later of five years from the date of the first payment or the participant attaining the age of 59½.[48] If the payments change in any way, the participant will be considered to have made a distribution equal to the full account balance of the qualified plan in the first year of the substantially equal periodic payments. The addition of this amount to the participant's taxable income will also subject the participant to an early withdrawal penalty as well as penalties and interest for the years passed since the first year of the distribution.

---

48. Rev. Ruling 2002-62: Permits a participant a one-time election to change from the 2nd or 3rd method to the 1st (RMD) method.

Case Study 7.1

In *Gregory T. and Kim D. Benz v. Commissioner., U.S. Tax Court, 132 T.C. No. 15, (May 11, 2009)*, the Tax Court held that a distribution from an IRA for qualified higher education expenses is not an impermissible modification of a series of substantially equal periodic payments.

Facts:
- In 2002, Petitioner's wife elected to receive a series of substantially equal periodic payments from her IRA that qualified for a statutory exception to the 10 percent early withdrawal penalty.
- IRC §72(t)(4) provides that a modification of a series of periodic payments within the first 5 years (other than by reason of the employee's death or disability) or before age 59½ will be subject to the 10 percent penalty. It also results in all payments under the substantially equal periodic payment exception to be subject to the 10 percent penalty.
- In 2004, Petitioners wife received additional distributions to pay for qualified higher education costs for her son.
- Petitioners reported all distributions on their Form 1040 as taxable, but not subject to the 10 percent penalty.

Issues:
- The sole issue for decision is whether a distribution for qualified higher education expenses is an impermissible modification of a series of substantially equal periodic payments.

Arguments:
- The IRS argues that an employee who elects a series of substantially equal periodic payments is not allowed any further distributions within the first 5 years of the election irrespective of whether the distribution would qualify for another statutory exception to the §72(t) tax unless the employee dies or becomes disabled.
- Petitioners argue that a distribution used for a purpose that qualifies for a statutory exception is not a modification of a series of substantially equal periodic payments that triggers the recapture tax under §72(t)(4).
- In *Arnold v. Commissioner*, 111 T.C. 250, 255-256 (1998), the Court held that an additional distribution that did not qualify for a statutory exception was an impermissible modification to a series of substantially equal periodic payments.

Findings:
- The court held that a distribution for qualified higher education expenses is not a modification of a series of substantially equal periodic payments.
- It considered the *Arnold v. Commissioner* case, but also considered the language in the IRC that allows for multiple exceptions to the 10 percent penalty.
- The court noted that the legislative purpose of the 10-percent additional tax is that premature distributions from IRAs frustrate the intention of saving for retirement, and §72(t) discourages this from happening." This legislative purpose is not frustrated where an employee receives distributions for more than one of the purposes that Congress has recognized as deserving special treatment.

Revenue Ruling 2002-62 allows a taxpayer to make a one-time irrevocable switch from the fixed amortization or fixed annuitization methods to the required minimum distribution method. If the switch is made then the required minimum distribution method must be used for all subsequent years. The change would be useful in cases where the value of the account had declined substantially and the taxpayer wanted to reduce the required annual payments for future years.

Once the distribution under §72(t) has been elected, the rules must be followed precisely to avoid being subject to the 10 percent penalty. If a mistake is made, the results are often irreversible and costly including unnecessary tax and penalties. Errors typically will disqualify all prior year distributions under §72(t), subjecting them to the 10 percent penalty and interest. Revenue Ruling 2002-62 states that additional contributions cannot be made to the account (other than investment gains) nor can amounts from the plan be rolled over tax-free into another account without subjecting the account to the 10 percent penalty.

From a planning perspective, taxpayers can separate retirement accounts to control the amount of the substantial equal payments. Taxpayers do not have to take these payments on the entire combined balance of all IRAs. This flexibility allows taxpayers to increase the distributions over time and Revenue Ruling 2002-62 allows them to decrease it one time.

QUICK QUIZ 7.4

1. Distributions before a participant attains the age of 59½ will generally be subject to a 10 percent penalty.
   a. True
   b. False

2. If the participants are already separated from service due to retirement and they wait until they attain age 55 to begin distributions, then they will not be subject to the 10 percent penalty.
   a. True
   b. False

True, False.

Separated From Service After Attainment of Age 55

A distribution to an employee from a qualified plan will avoid the 10 percent early withdrawal penalty if it is made after the employee has separated from service for the employer maintaining the plan and such separation from service occurred during or after the calendar year in which the employee attained age 55.[49]

This exception may be extremely helpful to those employees who take an early retirement package and need funds from their retirement plan prior to receiving Social Security benefits. It is important to note that this exception is only applicable to distributions from qualified plans and is not available to distributions from IRAs.

It should be noted that this exception will not apply if an individual separates from service before age 55 and defers distributions until after the attainment of age 55. In other words, the employee must turn age 55 (or older) within the year of separation of service.

49. IRC §72(t)(2)(A)(v) and IRS Notice 87-13.

Dividends Paid from an ESOP

The government provides an exception to the 10 percent early withdrawal penalty if the distributions are dividends paid within 90 days of the plan year end from an ESOP.

IRS Tax Levy on the Plan

If the distribution is made to pay certain unpaid income taxes because of a tax levy on the plan, the distribution will not be subject to the 10 percent penalty.

Case Study 7.2

In **Francisco A. Murillo v. Commissioner, (1998-13 Tax Court Memo Ruling, 75 TCM 1564)**, the tax court found that a forfeited IRA account for the purpose of a tax levy is not subject to the 10 percent penalty.

Mr. Murillo was indicted with: (1) Conspiracy to structure cash deposits into bank accounts in the New York area for the purpose of avoiding Federal currency transaction reporting requirements; (2) 22 substantive structuring counts relating to approximately $1,026,855 in U.S. currency deposited into various bank accounts during the period January 19, 1988, through August 23, 1989; and (3) 10 counts alleging violations of customs reporting requirements.

In contrast to the Murillo case above, the Tax Court found in **James A. and Linda A. Willhite v. Commissioner**, T.C. Memo. 2009-263, 98 T.C.M. 470 that the petitioner was liable for the 10 percent penalty because he received the distribution before receiving the notice to levy from the IRS.

The conclusion can be drawn that this exception should only apply in the event that a taxpayer receives a distribution directly as a result of an IRS levy.

Medical Expenses in Excess of 10 Percent of AGI

There is no 10 percent penalty if the distribution is made to the participant for certain medical expenses paid during the year greater than 10 percent of the participant's adjusted gross income (whether the person itemizes or not). Naturally, these expenses cannot be reimbursed by a health care provider or employer.

It should be noted that ATRA 2012 increased the hurdle rate for medical expenses from 7.5 percent to 10 percent, which has impacted this exception. Also, in the case of any taxable year beginning after December 31, 2012, and ending before January 1, 2017, a taxpayer who has attained age 65 before the close of such taxable year, can use 7.5 percent in lieu of 10 percent.

Qualified Domestic Relations Orders (QDRO)

Distributions to an alternate payee pursuant to a QDRO are not subject to the 10 percent early withdrawal penalty. The QDRO must relate to child support, alimony payments, or marital property rights to a spouse, former spouse, child, or other dependent. In addition the QDRO must specify:[50]

- The name and the last known mailing address (if any) of the participant and the name and mailing address of each alternate payee covered by the order,
- The amount or percentage of the participant's benefits to be paid by the plan to each such alternate payee, or the manner in which such amount or percentage is to be determined,
- The number of payments or period to which such order applies, and
- Each plan to which the order applies.

In addition the order cannot require the plan to pay in a manner not provided for in the plan document nor can it provide that the plan provide higher benefits than are due to the participant.

Individuals Called to Active Duty

IRC §72(t)(2)(G) provides that distributions from an IRA or attributable to deferrals by anyone called to active duty for a period in excess of 179 days or for an indefinite period are not subject to the 10 percent penalty. This exception applies for individuals ordered to active duty after September 11, 2001.

This exception also provides these active duty personnel an opportunity to repay the distribution back to the IRA or plan within two years after the end of the active duty period. However, this contribution cannot be deducted.

Distributions to Qualified Public Safety Employees in Governmental Plans

Under the Pension Protection Act of 2006, the 10 percent early withdrawal tax does not apply to distributions from a governmental defined benefit pension plan paid to a qualified public safety employee who separates from service after age 50. A qualified public safety employee is an employee of a State or political subdivision of a State if the employee provides police protection, fire fighting services, or emergency medical services for any area within the jurisdiction of such State or political subdivision. This provision is effective as of August 17, 2006.

---

50. IRC §414(p).

EXHIBIT	SUMMARY OF **10** PERCENT PENALTY EXCEPTIONS FOR QUALIFIED PLANS
7.28	

- Distribution is made after the participant is age 59½.
- Distribution is made on account of death of the participant.
- Distribution is made on account of disability of the participant.
- Distribution is part of a series of substantially equal periodic payments made at least annually for the life or life expectancy of the participant or the joint lives or joint life expectancies of the participant and his designated beneficiary (§72(t)).
- Distribution is made after separation from service after the participant attains age 55.
- Distributions are dividends paid within 90 days of the plan year from an ESOP.
- Distribution is made to pay certain unpaid income taxes because of a tax levy on the plan.
- Distributions made to the participant for certain medical expenses paid during the year greater than 10 percent of adjusted gross income.
- Distributions pursuant to a Qualified Domestic Relations Order (QDRO).
- Individuals called to active duty.
- Distributions to qualified public safety employees in governmental plans.

Other exceptions to the 10 percent early withdrawal penalty are plan rollovers and plan loans. As discussed previously, these withdrawals receive preferential treatment. In addition, other exceptions discussed in Chapter 9 apply specifically to IRAs.

SUMMARY OF EXCEPTIONS FOR QUALIFIED PLANS AND IRAs

EXHIBIT
7.29

Exception to 10% Penalty	Qualified Plan	IRA	IRC §(s)
After participant/IRA owner reaches age 59	Yes	Yes	72(t)(2)(A)(i)
After death of the participant/IRA owner	Yes	Yes	72(t)(2)(A)(ii)
Total and permanent disability of the participant/IRA owner	Yes	Yes	72(t)(2)(A)(iii)
Series of substantially equal payments	Yes	Yes	72(t)(2)(A)(iv)
Separation from service during or after year employee reaches age 55 (age 50 for public safety employees)	Yes	No	72(t)(2)(A)(v) and 72(t)(10)
Dividend pass through from an ESOP	Yes	N/A	72(t)(2)(A)(vi)
Because of an IRS levy of the plan	Yes	Yes	72(t)(2)(A)(vii)
Amount of your unreimbursed medical expenses (>10% AGI)	Yes	Yes	72(t)(2)(B)
To an alternate payee under a Qualified Domestic Relations Order	Yes	No	72(t)(2)(C)
Payment of health insurance premiums paid while unemployed	No	Yes	72(t)(2)(D)
Qualified higher education expenses	No	Yes	72(t)(2)(E)
Qualified first-time homebuyers up to $10,000	No	Yes	72(t)(2)(F)
Certain distributions to qualified military reservists called to active duty	Yes	Yes	72(t)(2)(G)
Corrective distributions	Yes	No	401(k)(8)(D), 401(m)(7), and 402(g)(2)(C)
Rollovers	Yes	Yes	402(c), 403(a)(4), 403(b)(8), 408(d)(3) and 408A(d)(3)(A)
Governmental 457(b) distributions are not subject to the 10% additional tax except for distributions attributable to rollovers from another type of plan or IRA.			

MINIMUM DISTRIBUTIONS

Assets in qualified plans and other tax-advantaged plans enjoy tax-deferred growth. However, this favorable tax treatment is for the purpose of encouraging individuals to save for retirement. The IRC has established age 70½ as the maximum deferral age before distributions must begin. Once a taxpayer attains the age of 70½, the minimum distribution rules must be complied with by the taxpayer. The minimum distribution rules require individuals to begin taking minimum distributions when the participant attains the age of 70½. If the funds are not distributed by the required date, a 50 percent excise tax will be levied on the participant for failure to take the **required minimum distribution (RMD)**. The penalty is calculated on the amount equal to the RMD less any distribution that was taken, but the result cannot be less than zero. It is important to note that the minimum distribution is in fact a minimum amount. Distributions in excess of the minimum distribution can certainly be taken by the participant or owner.

Minimum distributions apply to assets in a qualified plan, IRA, 403(b), SEP, SIMPLE, or 457 plan. While minimum distribution rules do not apply to Roth IRAs, they do apply to Roth accounts in a 401(k) or 403(b) plan.[51]

> ### KEY CONCEPTS
>
> 1. When must minimum distributions begin?
>
> 2. How is the minimum distribution calculated?
>
> 3. What effect does death of the participant have on minimum distributions?

The first distribution must be taken by April 1 of the year following the year the participant attains the age of 70½. However, for each year thereafter, the RMD must be taken before December 31 of the tax year. The special first year option allows a participant to delay the first payment until April 1 following the year in which the participant turns 70½. However, such a delay only applies to the first distribution and could cause a bunching of income in the year after the participant attains the age of 70½. If the participant delays taking the first RMD until April 1 of the year following the attainment of age 70½, the second RMD must still be taken by December 31 of that same year.

EXAMPLE 7.33

Paul turned 70½ in March of this year. He was a participant in a qualified plan with his previous employer but has not received any distributions since retirement. Since Paul turned 70½ this year, he will have to take the RMD from his retirement plan for this year. The last date he can take his distribution for this year without incurring a minimum distribution penalty is April 1 of next year. The last date he can withdraw his distribution for next year is December 31 of next year.[52]

---

51. Minimum distribution rules also apply to inherited Roth IRAs.
52. Because Paul is already 70½, he will have to take a minimum distribution before he rolls over the balance to an IRA because he is in what is called "a distribution year."

Case Study 7.3

In the case of ***Lee v. California Butchers' Pension Trust Fund***,[1] Lee (the pensioner) who retired at age 73 brought an action against pension trust fund ("Fund"), claiming that the Fund violated, among other things, ERISA by underpaying his pension. The United States Ninth Circuit Court of Appeals concluded that the Fund improperly denied increased benefits to the pensioner.

Lee worked at Safeway as a butcher for 30 years. He retired in 1992 at age 73. The dispute in this case dealt with the amount of money that Mr. Lee was entitled to be paid every month in his pension. He wanted to be paid as though he had worked 30 years and retired in 1992. The Fund insisted on paying him as though he had retired in 1990 instead of 1992, and then started working again. The effect of the Fund decision was to pay Mr. Lee $815.50 per month instead of $1,498.20. The Internal Revenue Code requires pension plans to begin paying people their pensions after they attain age 70½ whether they keep working or not. Thus, the plan started paying Lee his pension in 1990 because he had reached age 70½.

A collective bargaining agreement increased pensions for people who retired beginning in 1992. When the 1992 increases came into effect, Lee obviously wanted them calculated on all his years of service. However, the Fund did not pay him on the basis that he had worked almost 30 years. Instead, it just applied the higher amounts to his two years of service following the 1990 beginning date of his distributions, as though he had only worked as a butcher covered by the plan for two years, resulting in his obtaining the pre-1992 calculation applied to almost all his years of work, and the post-1992 calculation only on his post-age-70½ work. Lee's lawyer initiated correspondence with the Fund about the calculation in December of 1991. After repeated inquiry, Lee's lawyer was told that the plan deemed him to have retired April 1, 1990.

Lee filed suit, claiming that the Fund discriminated against him based on his age (i.e., that he had turned 70½ before the 1992 increase) and violated the plan provisions because the tax provision just meant that Lee had to start drawing his pension so he would start paying income tax on the money, not that he had to retire at age 70½. Because Lee was not required to retire at age 70½ and had not in fact retired, he could not be "deemed" to have retired. The Fund argued that it correctly denied Lee's claim because the Internal Revenue Code required them to distribute his entire interest at age 70½. Congress amended the Internal Revenue Code in 1986 to require pension plans to begin distributing benefits when the pensioner reaches age 70½.[2]

---

1. ***Lee v. California Butchers' Pension Trust Fund***, 154 F.3d 1075 (9th Cir. 1998).
2. See IRC §401(a)(9)(A)(ii) (1990).

The Fund read this to mean that a person must be treated as having retired at age 70½ and referred to such an employee's status as "legally retired" and distinguished it from "physically retired." The Court disagreed with the Fund and ruled in Lee's favor, explaining that there were no words in the statute or plan to support what the trustees did. Lee was not "legally" or "physically" retired in 1990; rather, he was indeed working at Safeway as a butcher. IRC §401(a)(9) limited use of pension funds as tax shelters beyond age 70½, but did not say a word about requiring people to quit working or authorizing plans to deprive them of increases and accruals following age 70½ when they are still working. The Court concluded that the law did not require the employee to be retired, just that his money be "distributed," beginning by the specified date. As no possible reading of the plan language could "deem" Lee to have retired in 1990, under the plan, Lee was to be "deemed retired" after he quit working in 1992, at which time he was entitled to the increased benefits available to all employees who stopped working after January 1, 1992. The Fund's denial of the increase to Lee was therefore considered to be an abuse of discretion.

An exception to the general RMD for qualified plans exists if a participant is still employed by the plan sponsor of a qualified plan upon attainment of age 70½. A participant that is still employed by the plan sponsor of the qualified plan does not have to begin taking RMD until April 1 of the year after the participant terminates employment with the plan sponsor. The exception is not available for any participant that owns more than five percent of the ownership of the plan sponsor in the year the participant reaches the age of 70½. In addition, if the participant is a more than five percent owner and begins taking the RMD, he cannot discontinue taking the distributions should he no longer own greater than five percent of the company at some future date. However, while the law permits the delay, a qualified plan may require all individuals, even those participants that have continued employment past the age of 70½, to take RMD at 70½; the discretion is given to the plan's sponsor.

EXHIBIT 7.30	REQUIRED MINIMUM DISTRIBUTIONS

- Must begin by April 1 of the year after the participant attains the age of 70½.
- Unless the participant is still employed by the plan sponsor, then the RMD must be taken by April 1 of the year after the participant terminates service with the plan sponsor. Exception: Does not apply for a more than 5 percent owner of the plan sponsor.

Mary, age 74, works at the local grocery store. She is a participant in the grocer's profit sharing plan but has not begun taking RMD. If Mary terminates employment in August 1 of this year, she must take her first RMD by April 1 of next year.

EXAMPLE 7.34

MINIMUM DISTRIBUTION SUMMARY

EXHIBIT 7.31

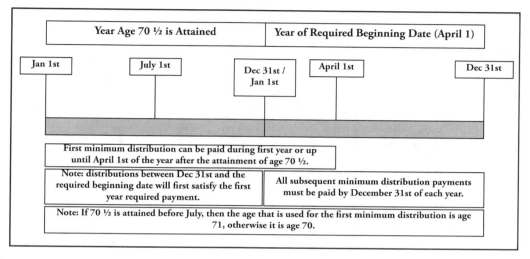

| Year Age 70 ½ is Attained | Year of Required Beginning Date (April 1) |

Jan 1st   July 1st   Dec 31st / Jan 1st   April 1st   Dec 31st

First minimum distribution can be paid during first year or up until April 1st of the year after the attainment of age 70 ½.

Note: distributions between Dec 31st and the required beginning date will first satisfy the first year required payment.

All subsequent minimum distribution payments must be paid by December 31st of each year.

Note: If 70 ½ is attained before July, then the age that is used for the first minimum distribution is age 71, otherwise it is age 70.

CALCULATING THE REQUIRED MINIMUM DISTRIBUTION

The required minimum distribution (RMD) is determined each year by dividing the account balance as of the close of business on December 31 of the year preceding the distribution year by the distribution period determined according to participant's age as of December 31 of the distribution year in the uniform lifetime table (See Exhibit 7.27).[53]

$$\text{Minimum Distribution} = \frac{\text{Value of the plan asset at the end of the prior year}}{\text{Life Expectancy Factor}^{54}}$$

Assume Paul's account balance at December 31, 2015 was $400,000, and he is 71 by December 31, 2016. He, therefore, uses a distribution period from the uniform lifetime table of 26.5 and will need to take a distribution for 2016 of $15,094.34 by April 1, 2017. If he delays until April 1, 2017, he must also take a distribution for 2017 by December 31, 2017.

EXAMPLE 7.35

$$\frac{\$400,000}{26.5} = \$15,094.34$$

53. Treas. Reg. §1.401(a)(9)-9. In the past, the above calculation permitted an exception. An alternate calculation was used for the second year of RMD when the first RMD was not taken until the subsequent tax year. In this case, to calculate the RMD for the second year, the plan account balance at the end of the preceding year was reduced by the first year's RMD that had not been taken at that time. This adjustment only applied to the second distribution, and it was to the taxpayer's benefit. When the revised regulations were promulgated (Treas. Reg §1.401(a)(9)-5, A-3(c)) this exception was not part of the revised regulations, thus requiring all distributions to be calculated the same regardless of whether the first distribution was delayed until the second year.

54. The life expectancy factor is determined based on the age at the end of the year for which minimum distributions are being determined.

Assume Paul's account balance at December 31, 2016 was $480,000, and he took his 2016 distribution in April of 2017. He will need to take $18,750 by December 31, 2017 for 2017, in addition to his April 1, 2017 distribution ($15,094.34). Note that when two distributions are combined in one year, it can cause the recipient to move up in the progressive tax brackets due to the stacking of two payments.

$$\frac{\$480,000}{25.6} = \$18,750$$

EXAMPLE 7.36

Kendal attained the age of 70½ in October 2016. He retired several years ago but has not taken any distributions yet. His account balance on December 31, 2015 was $100,000, and his balance on December 31, 2016 was $110,000. The first year for which Kendal must take a minimum distribution is 2016 (although he may wait until April 1, 2017 to actually take the first distribution). To calculate the 2016 distribution, determine the factor from the uniform lifetime table based on his age at December 31, 2016 (70). The distribution period is 27.4. Utilizing the end of the prior year's account balance of $100,000, Kendal's required minimum distribution for 2016 is $3,649.64.

$$\frac{\$100,000}{27.4} = \$3,649.64$$

For 2017, the distribution will be $4,150.94. Each year after that, the end of the prior year account balance and the age related distribution period at current year end will be used to determine the RMD.

$$\frac{\$110,000}{26.5} = \$4,150.94$$

EXAMPLE 7.37

John is 70½ on October 15, 2016. John's year-end account balance for 2015, 2016, 2017, and 2018 are $300,000, $360,000, $420,000, and $502,000 respectively. Calculate John's minimum distribution for years 2015, 2016, 2017, 2018, and 2019. (See the Uniform Lifetime Table, Exhibit 7.32).

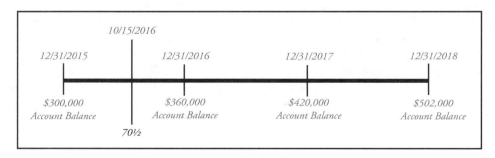

Minimum distribution calculation for 2015:

There is no minimum distribution required for 2015 because John is not yet 70½.

Minimum distribution calculation for 2016:

$$\frac{\$300,000}{27.4} = \$10,948.91$$

Minimum distribution calculation for 2017:

$$\frac{\$360,000}{26.5} = \$13,584.91$$

Minimum distribution calculation for 2018:

$$\frac{\$420,000}{25.6} = \$16,406.25$$

Minimum distribution calculation for 2019:

$$\frac{\$502,000}{24.7} = \$20,323.89$$

UNIFORM LIFETIME TABLE USED BY PARTICIPANTS

EXHIBIT
7.32

Age of Employee	Distribution Period	Age of Employee	Distribution Period
70	27.4	93	9.6
71	26.5	94	9.1
72	25.6	95	8.6
73	24.7	96	8.1
74	23.8	97	7.6
75	22.9	98	7.1
76	22.0	99	6.7
77	21.2	100	6.3
78	20.3	101	5.9
79	19.5	102	5.5
80	18.7	103	5.2
81	17.9	104	4.9
82	17.1	105	4.5
83	16.3	106	4.2
84	15.5	107	3.9
85	14.8	108	3.7
86	14.1	109	3.4
87	13.4	110	3.1
88	12.7	111	2.9
89	12.0	112	2.6
90	11.4	113	2.4
91	10.8	114	2.1
92	10.2	115 and over	1.9

When calculating the RMD for the plan participant, always use the **uniform lifetime table**, which accounts for the age of the account holder and one other person who is 10 years younger. One exception to this rule occurs when the participant's sole designated beneficiary is the participant's spouse and that spouse is more than 10 years younger than the participant. In that case, use the **joint life expectancy table** to calculate the RMD. Utilizing the joint life expectancy tables will result in a longer life expectancy and decrease the RMD. An excerpt of the joint life expectancy chart is provided below. The complete chart can be found at Treas. Reg. §1.401(a)(9)-9, and in IRS Publication 590.

EXAMPLE 7.38

Assume the same facts as Example 7.32 except that Kendal is married, and his wife Julie, age 69 at December 31, 2016, is the sole beneficiary. The minimum distribution will be calculated exactly as it was previously because Julie is not more than 10 years younger than Kendal.

EXAMPLE 7.39

Now, assume the same facts as the above example except that Kendal is married, and his wife Julie, age 39 at December 31, 2016, is the sole beneficiary. Now the joint and survivor tables are used to determine the life expectancy because Julie is more than 10 years younger than Kendal. Their joint life expectancy is 44.9 (age 70 and 39). Under this scenario, Kendal's RMD will be $2,227.17 ($100,000/44.9).

EXAMPLE 7.40

Assume the same facts as the above example except that Kendal's daughter Jaime, age 22 on December 31, 2016, is the sole beneficiary. In this case, the uniform table is used to determine the distribution period. Therefore, the RMD is the same as the first example ($100,000/27.4 = $3,649.64).

EXCERPT FROM THE JOINT AND LAST SURVIVOR TABLE (USED BY PARTICIPANTS WITH SPOUSES MORE THAN 10 YEARS YOUNGER THAN THE PARTICIPANT)

EXHIBIT
7.33

Ages	30	31	32	33	34	35	36	37	38	39
30	60.2	59.7	59.2	58.8	58.4	58.0	57.6	57.3	57.0	56.7
31	59.7	59.2	58.7	58.2	57.8	57.4	57.0	56.6	56.3	56.0
32	59.2	58.7	58.2	57.7	57.2	56.8	56.4	56.0	55.6	55.3
33	58.8	58.2	57.7	57.2	56.7	56.2	55.8	55.4	55.0	54.7
34	58.4	57.8	57.2	56.7	56.2	55.7	55.3	54.8	54.4	54.0
35	58.0	57.4	56.8	56.2	55.7	55.2	54.7	54.3	53.8	53.4
36	57.6	57.0	56.4	55.8	55.3	54.7	54.2	53.7	53.3	52.8
37	57.3	56.6	56.0	55.4	54.8	54.3	53.7	53.2	52.7	52.3
38	57.0	56.3	55.6	55.0	54.4	53.8	53.3	52.7	52.2	51.7
39	56.7	56.0	55.3	54.7	54.0	53.4	52.8	52.3	51.7	51.2
40	56.4	55.7	55.0	54.3	53.7	53.0	52.4	51.8	51.3	50.8
41	56.1	55.4	54.7	54.0	53.3	52.7	52.0	51.4	50.9	50.3
42	55.9	55.2	54.4	53.7	53.0	52.3	51.7	51.1	50.4	49.9
43	55.7	54.9	54.2	53.4	52.7	52.0	51.3	50.7	50.1	49.5
44	55.5	54.7	53.9	53.2	52.4	51.7	51.0	50.4	49.7	49.1
45	55.3	54.5	53.7	52.9	52.2	51.5	50.7	50.0	49.4	48.7
46	55.1	54.3	53.5	52.7	52.0	51.2	50.5	49.8	49.1	48.4
47	55.0	54.1	53.3	52.5	51.7	51.0	50.2	49.5	48.8	48.1
48	54.8	54.0	53.2	52.3	51.5	50.8	50.0	49.2	48.5	47.8
49	54.7	53.8	53.0	52.2	51.4	50.6	49.8	49.0	48.2	47.5
50	54.6	53.7	52.9	52.0	51.2	50.4	49.6	48.8	48.0	47.3
51	54.5	53.6	52.7	51.9	51.0	50.2	49.4	48.6	47.8	47.0
52	54.4	53.5	52.6	51.7	50.9	50.0	49.2	48.4	47.6	46.8
53	54.3	53.4	52.5	51.6	50.8	49.9	49.1	48.2	47.4	46.6
54	54.2	53.3	52.4	51.5	50.6	49.8	48.9	48.1	47.2	46.4
55	54.1	53.2	52.3	51.4	50.5	49.7	48.8	47.9	47.1	46.3
56	54.0	53.1	52.2	51.3	50.4	49.5	48.7	47.8	47.0	46.1
57	54.0	53.0	52.1	51.2	50.3	49.4	48.6	47.7	46.8	46.0
58	53.9	53.0	52.1	51.2	50.3	49.4	48.5	47.6	46.7	45.8
59	53.8	52.9	52.0	51.1	50.2	49.3	48.4	47.5	46.6	45.7
60	53.8	52.9	51.9	51.0	50.1	49.2	48.3	47.4	46.5	45.6
61	53.8	52.8	51.9	51.0	50.0	49.1	48.2	47.3	46.4	45.5
62	53.7	52.8	51.8	50.9	50.0	49.1	48.1	47.2	46.3	45.4
63	53.7	52.7	51.8	50.9	49.9	49.0	48.1	47.2	46.3	45.3
64	53.6	52.7	51.8	50.8	49.9	48.9	48.0	47.1	46.2	45.3
65	53.6	52.7	51.7	50.8	49.8	48.9	48.0	47.0	46.1	45.2
66	53.6	52.6	51.7	50.7	49.8	48.9	47.9	47.0	46.1	45.1
67	53.6	52.6	51.7	50.7	49.8	48.8	47.9	46.9	46.0	45.1
68	53.5	52.6	51.6	50.7	49.7	48.8	47.8	46.9	46.0	45.0
69	53.5	52.6	51.6	50.6	49.7	48.7	47.8	46.9	45.9	45.0
70	53.5	52.5	51.6	50.6	49.7	48.7	47.8	46.8	45.9	44.9
71	53.5	52.5	51.6	50.6	49.6	48.7	47.7	46.8	45.9	44.9
72	53.5	52.5	51.5	50.6	49.6	48.7	47.7	46.8	45.8	44.9
73	53.4	52.5	51.5	50.6	49.6	48.6	47.7	46.7	45.8	44.8
74	53.4	52.5	51.5	50.5	49.6	48.6	47.7	46.7	45.8	44.8
75	53.4	52.5	51.5	50.5	49.6	48.6	47.7	46.7	45.7	44.8
76	53.4	52.4	51.5	50.5	49.6	48.6	47.6	46.7	45.7	44.8
77	53.4	52.4	51.5	50.5	49.5	48.6	47.6	46.7	45.7	44.8
78	53.4	52.4	51.5	50.5	49.5	48.6	47.6	46.6	45.7	44.7
79	53.4	52.4	51.5	50.5	49.5	48.6	47.6	46.6	45.7	44.7

EXCERPT FROM THE JOINT AND LAST SURVIVOR TABLE (CONTINUED)

Ages	40	41	42	43	44	45	46	47	48	49
40	50.2	49.8	49.3	48.9	48.5	48.1	47.7	47.4	47.1	46.8
41	49.8	49.3	48.8	48.3	47.9	47.5	47.1	46.7	46.4	46.1
42	49.3	48.8	48.3	47.8	47.3	46.9	46.5	46.1	45.8	45.4
43	48.9	48.3	47.8	47.3	46.8	46.3	45.9	45.5	45.1	44.8
44	48.5	47.9	47.3	46.8	46.3	45.8	45.4	44.9	44.5	44.2
45	48.1	47.5	46.9	46.3	45.8	45.3	44.8	44.4	44.0	43.6
46	47.7	47.1	46.5	45.9	45.4	44.8	44.3	43.9	43.4	43.0
47	47.4	46.7	46.1	45.5	44.9	44.4	43.9	43.4	42.9	42.4
48	47.1	46.4	45.8	45.1	44.5	44.0	43.4	42.9	42.4	41.9
49	46.8	46.1	45.4	44.8	44.2	43.6	43.0	42.4	41.9	41.4
50	46.5	45.8	45.1	44.4	43.8	43.2	42.6	42.0	41.5	40.9
51	46.3	45.5	44.8	44.1	43.5	42.8	42.2	41.6	41.0	40.5
52	46.0	45.3	44.6	43.8	43.2	42.5	41.8	41.2	40.6	40.1
53	45.8	45.1	44.3	43.6	42.9	42.2	41.5	40.9	40.3	39.7
54	45.6	44.8	44.1	43.3	42.6	41.9	41.2	40.5	39.9	39.3
55	45.5	44.7	43.9	43.1	42.4	41.6	40.9	40.2	39.6	38.9
56	45.3	44.5	43.7	42.9	42.1	41.4	40.7	40.0	39.3	38.6
57	45.1	44.3	43.5	42.7	41.9	41.2	40.4	39.7	39.0	38.3
58	45.0	44.2	43.3	42.5	41.7	40.9	40.2	39.4	38.7	38.0
59	44.9	44.0	43.2	42.4	41.5	40.7	40.0	39.2	38.5	37.8
60	44.7	43.9	43.0	42.2	41.4	40.6	39.8	39.0	38.2	37.5
61	44.6	43.8	42.9	42.1	41.2	40.4	39.6	38.8	38.0	37.3
62	44.5	43.7	42.8	41.9	41.1	40.3	39.4	38.6	37.8	37.1
63	44.5	43.6	42.7	41.8	41.0	40.1	39.3	38.5	37.7	36.9
64	44.4	43.5	42.6	41.7	40.8	40.0	39.2	38.3	37.5	36.7
65	44.3	43.4	42.5	41.6	40.7	39.9	39.0	38.2	37.4	36.6
66	44.2	43.3	42.4	41.5	40.6	39.8	38.9	38.1	37.2	36.4
67	44.2	43.3	42.3	41.4	40.6	39.7	38.8	38.0	37.1	36.3
68	44.1	43.2	42.3	41.4	40.5	39.6	38.7	37.9	37.0	36.2
69	44.1	43.1	42.2	41.3	40.4	39.5	38.6	37.8	36.9	36.0
70	44.0	43.1	42.2	41.3	40.3	39.4	38.6	37.7	36.8	35.9
71	44.0	43.0	42.1	41.2	40.3	39.4	38.5	37.6	36.7	35.9
72	43.9	43.0	42.1	41.1	40.2	39.3	38.4	37.5	36.6	35.8
73	43.9	43.0	42.0	41.1	40.2	39.3	38.4	37.5	36.6	35.7
74	43.9	42.9	42.0	41.1	40.1	39.2	38.3	37.4	36.5	35.6
75	43.8	42.9	42.0	41.0	40.1	39.2	38.3	37.4	36.5	35.6
76	43.8	42.9	41.9	41.0	40.1	39.1	38.2	37.3	36.4	35.5
77	43.8	42.9	41.9	41.0	40.0	39.1	38.2	37.3	36.4	35.5
78	43.8	42.8	41.9	40.9	40.0	39.1	38.2	37.2	36.3	35.4
79	43.8	42.8	41.9	40.9	40.0	39.1	38.1	37.2	36.3	35.4
80	43.7	42.8	41.8	40.9	40.0	39.0	38.1	37.2	36.3	35.4
81	43.7	42.8	41.8	40.9	39.9	39.0	38.1	37.2	36.2	35.3
82	43.7	42.8	41.8	40.9	39.9	39.0	38.1	37.1	36.2	35.3
83	43.7	42.8	41.8	40.9	39.9	39.0	38.0	37.1	36.2	35.3
84	43.7	42.7	41.8	40.8	39.9	39.0	38.0	37.1	36.2	35.3
85	43.7	42.7	41.8	40.8	39.9	38.9	38.0	37.1	36.2	35.2
86	43.7	42.7	41.8	40.8	39.9	38.9	38.0	37.1	36.1	35.2
87	43.7	42.7	41.8	40.8	39.9	38.9	38.0	37.0	36.1	35.2
88	43.7	42.7	41.8	40.8	39.9	38.9	38.0	37.0	36.1	35.2
89	43.7	42.7	41.7	40.8	39.8	38.9	38.0	37.0	36.1	35.2

Effect of Multiple Qualified Plans or IRAs

As discussed, upon reaching age 70½, taxpayers are required to begin taking minimum distributions. However, it is important to understand that a minimum distribution must be taken from each qualified plan in which the taxpayer has an account balance. Therefore, if the taxpayer had three qualified plans resulting from previous jobs, then three minimum distributions would have to be taken.

Many taxpayers have multiple IRAs; however, taxpayers are permitted to combine the value of all of their IRAs in determining the required minimum distribution. In addition, the amount distributed for purposes of complying with the minimum distribution rules can be taken from one IRA or multiple IRAs depending on the wishes of the taxpayer.[55]

Qualifying Longevity Annuity Contract

The Treasury issued proposed regulations (1.401(a)(9)-6) defining qualifying longevity annuity contracts (QLAC). A QLAC is an annuity contract (that is not a variable annuity, equity-indexed contract, or similar contract) that is purchased from an insurance company for an employee states that it is intended to be a QLAC and that satisfies each of the several requirements.

Distributions from the annuity must begin no later than the specified annuity starting date nor after the owner turns age 85. Premiums for the QLAC cannot exceed the lesser of $125,000 (as adjusted for inflation) or 25 percent of the employee's account balance under the plan.

If the QLAC satisfies these rules (and others), the value of the contracts is not considered for purposes of minimum distributions.

EFFECT OF PARTICIPANT'S DEATH ON MINIMUM DISTRIBUTIONS

Minimum distributions are still required to be taken even after a participant dies. An important distinction is made depending on whether the participant died before or after beginning minimum distributions. In either case, in the year of the participant's death, the RMD is calculated as if the participant has not died.

Note that the beneficiary of a qualified plan may withdraw all of the assets of the qualified plan after the death of the participant with no penalty. Recall that the 10 percent early withdrawal penalty does not apply to distributions taken after death. The RMD rules only apply when the beneficiary wants to delay withdrawing the assets of the qualified plan.

Death after Beginning of Minimum Distributions

If the participant dies after beginning to take minimum distributions, then the calculation of subsequent minimum distributions uses the designated beneficiary's single life expectancy factor as determined on the last day of the year following the year of the participant's death. This life expectancy factor is reduced by one in each succeeding year to determine the required distribution amount.

Qualified plans may disregard any beneficiary eliminated by an effective disclaimer or distribution of the benefit during the period between the participant's death and December 31 of the following

---

55. Treas. Reg. §1.408-8, Q-9.

year. If there is more than one designated beneficiary, the beneficiary with the shortest life expectancy (usually the oldest beneficiary) is used as the measuring life, but the plan may also be divided into a separate account for each beneficiary to utilize the life expectancy of each beneficiary for the calculation of the required minimum distribution.[56]

If a trust is named as the beneficiary, the beneficiaries of the trust will be treated as the designated beneficiaries provided:

- the trust is valid under state law;
- the trust is irrevocable or will become so upon the participant's death (e.g., inter vivos trust);
- the trust beneficiaries are identifiable from the trust instrument; and
- appropriate documentation has been provided to the plan administrator.

Spouse Beneficiary

If the surviving spouse is a beneficiary of the plan, then the surviving spouse can receive distributions over his remaining single-life expectancy (see Exhibit 7.35), recalculated each year based on the single life expectancy table. Distributions must begin, however, in the year following the year of the participant's death. Alternatively, if the surviving spouse is the sole beneficiary, the surviving spouse may rollover the plan balance to his own account and wait until he attains age 70½ to begin taking minimum distributions utilizing the uniform life table for his own life expectancy at that point.

There are a number of reasons why a surviving spouse would choose to either leave the deceased spouse owner's account intact or, alternatively, roll the account over to the surviving spouse's name. If the account remains in the decedent's name, it will be retitled after death "Mr. John Doe Plan for the Benefit of Mrs. Jane Doe." If rolled over and put into spouse's name, the title of the account will be Mrs. Jane Doe, IRA. If placed in the surviving spouse's own name, then the surviving spouse can name the beneficiary. If left intact as a qualified plan, the ERISA protection remains. If rolled over to an IRA, ERISA protection is lost, but creditor protection is provided up to certain limits under the BAPCPA 2005.

In the case of a spouse who is much younger than the decedent owner, leaving the account intact if distributions have begun will assure continuing cash flows. If a surviving spouse needs the money, this approach would provide penalty-free funds because the surviving spouse would otherwise have to wait until retirement to collect the funds (penalty-free) if the assets are rolled over into the surviving spouse's name. Keep in mind that the spouse is not limited to taking just the minimum distributions. Alternatively, if the surviving spouse is older than the owner, leaving the account intact will allow the surviving spouse to stretch out the distributions. In the case of a surviving spouse who is younger than the decedent and does not need the cash flow, rolling the account over to the surviving spouse's name allows for continual deferral and the designation of a new beneficiary; thus, creating the opportunity to stretch out the minimum distributions far into the future.

---

56. See Treas. Reg. §1.401(a)(9)-8 for more information on establishing separate accounts.

EXAMPLE
7.41

Louise, age 72, had been taking minimum distributions from her qualified plan for the past two years. Louise died this year, the sole beneficiary of her qualified plan was her husband, Harry, age 68. The RMD for this year will be calculated based on the uniform life table and Louise's age at the end of this year. After that RMD is taken, Harry can choose to either roll Louise's qualified plan balance into an IRA for himself and wait until he is 70½ to begin taking the required minimum distributions, or Harry may begin taking minimum distributions based on his life expectancy as calculated by the single life expectancy table in the year after Louise's death.

Assuming the following account balances and information:

Date	Account Balance	Louise's Age	Harry's Age
12/31 of Year 1 (Before Death)	$400,000	72	68
12/31 of Year 2 (Death)	$425,000	Year of Death	69
12/31 of Year 3 (After Death)	$490,000	-	70

The RMD for Year 2, the year in which Louise died, is based on Louise's life expectancy utilizing the uniform life table for this year and the account balance at the end of the previous year as follows:

$$\frac{\$400,000}{24.7 \text{ (at age 73)}} = \$16,194.33$$

For Year 3, Harry could roll the remaining plan balance to an IRA for himself, take a full taxable distribution of the account balance, or, alternatively, he may begin taking RMD over his life expectancy as determined by the single life expectancy table as follows:

$$\frac{\$425,000}{17.0 \text{ (at age 70)}} = \$25,000.00$$

For Year 4, Harry's RMD would be calculated using the recalculated single life expectancy as follows:

$$\frac{\$490,000}{16.3 \text{ (at age 71)}} = \$30,061.35$$

Nonspouse Beneficiary

If the beneficiary is someone other than the participant's surviving spouse, then the distribution period is the remaining single, non-recalculated life expectancy of the designated beneficiary. If the beneficiary is significantly younger than the decedent, the minimum distribution rules permit the beneficiary to "stretch out" the distributions taken. If more than one nonspouse beneficiary exists, the shortest life expectancy of the beneficiaries is used. As always in the year of the participant's death, the RMD is calculated based on the participant's life expectancy (Uniform Lifetime table). Subsequently, however, the life expectancy for the nonspouse beneficiary is calculated using the age of the designated beneficiary in the year following the year of the participant's death (Single Life Expectancy for Beneficiaries table Exhibit 7.34). In subsequent years, the beneficiary's life expectancy is not recalculated. Instead, the life expectancy factor for the first year is reduced by one for each subsequent year.

EXHIBIT
7.34

SINGLE LIFE EXPECTANCY USED BY BENEFICIARIES

Age	Life Expectancy	Age	Life Expectancy	Age	Life Expectancy	Age	Life Expectancy
0	82.4	28	55.3	56	28.7	84	8.1
1	81.6	29	54.3	57	27.9	85	7.6
2	80.6	30	53.3	58	27.0	86	7.1
3	79.7	31	52.4	59	26.1	87	6.7
4	78.7	32	51.4	60	25.2	88	6.3
5	77.7	33	50.4	61	24.4	89	5.9
6	76.7	34	49.4	62	23.5	90	5.5
7	75.8	35	48.5	63	22.7	91	5.2
8	74.8	36	47.5	64	21.8	92	4.9
9	73.8	37	46.5	65	21.0	93	4.6
10	72.8	38	45.6	66	20.2	94	4.3
11	71.8	39	44.6	67	19.4	95	4.1
12	70.8	40	43.6	68	18.6	96	3.8
13	69.9	41	42.7	69	17.8	97	3.6
14	68.9	42	41.7	70	17.0	98	3.4
15	67.9	43	40.7	71	16.3	99	3.1
16	66.9	44	39.8	72	15.5	100	2.9
17	66.0	45	38.8	73	14.8	101	2.7
18	65.0	46	37.9	74	14.1	102	2.5
19	64.0	47	37.0	75	13.4	103	2.3
20	63.0	48	36.0	76	12.7	104	2.1
21	62.1	49	35.1	77	12.1	105	1.9
22	61.1	50	34.2	78	11.4	106	1.7
23	60.1	51	33.3	79	10.8	107	1.5
24	59.1	52	32.3	80	10.2	108	1.4
25	58.2	53	31.4	81	9.7	109	1.2
26	57.2	54	30.5	82	9.1	110	1.1
27	56.2	55	29.6	83	8.6	111+	1.0

EXAMPLE
7.42

Cheryl dies in August 2016 at the age of 73. The beneficiary of her qualified plan is her daughter, Elizabeth, who was 42 when Cheryl died. Assuming the facts below, calculate the RMD for 2016, 2017, and 2018.

Date	Account Balance	Cheryl's Age	Elizabeth's Age
12/31/2015	$100,000	73	42
12/31/2016	$95,000	-	43
12/31/2017	$87,000	-	44

For 2016, the RMD is calculated utilizing the uniform life table life expectancy based on the age Cheryl would have been at 12/31/2016 and the account balance at 12/31/2015.

$$\frac{\$100,000}{23.8 \text{ (at age 74)}} = \$4,201.68$$

For 2017, the RMD is calculated based on Elizabeth's life expectancy utilizing the single life expectancy table for Elizabeth's age at 12/31/2017 and the plan account balance at 12/31/2016.

$$\frac{\$95,000}{39.8 \text{ (at age 44)}} = \$2,386.93$$

For 2018, the RMD is calculated utilizing the account balance at 12/31/2017 and Elizabeth's life expectancy as calculated in the prior year reduced by one.

$$\frac{\$87,000}{39.8 - 1 \text{ (at age 45)}} = \$2,242.27$$

The RMD calculations for all subsequent years would continue to reduce Elizabeth's life expectancy calculated in 2017 by one for each year after 2017. The life expectancy would not be recalculated. In this example, Elizabeth can withdraw all of the account balance after Cheryl's death as a lump-sum or in payments larger than the RMD, but in no case would Elizabeth be able to withdraw less than the RMD in any year.

Under the Pension Protection Act of 2006, the benefits of a nonspouse beneficiary may be transferred directly into an IRA. The IRA is treated as an inherited IRA of the nonspouse beneficiary. Thus, distributions from the inherited IRA are subject to the normal distribution rules applicable to beneficiaries. This provision applies to amounts payable to a beneficiary under a qualified retirement plan, 457 plan, or tax-sheltered annuity and is effective for tax years after 2006.

No Beneficiary

If no beneficiary has been named by December 31 of the year following the owner's death (or the beneficiary is the decedent's estate or a charity), then distributions must continue over the remaining distribution period of the deceased owner. The remaining distribution period is reduced by one each year.

Robin began taking the RMD from her profit sharing plan in 2016. In 2018, Robin died after suffering a heart attack. She had not named a beneficiary of her profit sharing plan at the time of her death. Robin's estate may choose to take a full distribution of Robin's profit sharing plan account balance or, alternatively, may choose to defer distributions from the plan to the RMD. In the year of Robin's death, the RMD would be calculated as if Robin had not died. In the year after Robin's death, the RMD would be calculated based on the account balance at the end of the prior year, and Robin's life expectancy is calculated in the year of her death from the uniform life table reduced by one.

Death Before Required Beginning Date

If the participant dies before the required beginning date (before minimum distributions have begun), then the minimum distribution rules will depend on the designated beneficiary.

Spouse Beneficiary

If the surviving spouse is the beneficiary of the plan, the surviving spouse can receive distributions over his remaining single-life expectancy, recalculated each year under the **single life expectancy table**.[57] Distributions must begin in the year in which the owner would have attained age 70½. Alternatively, if the surviving spouse is the sole beneficiary, the surviving spouse can roll the plan balance over and wait until he attains age 70½ to begin taking minimum distributions. The surviving spouse can also elect to distribute the entire account balance within five years after the year of the owner's death.

Matthew died at the age of 37 in 2016. His wife, Sara, was the sole beneficiary of his profit sharing plan. Since Matthew had not begun taking RMD before his death, Sara has four options in relation to Matthew's profit sharing plan.

1. Sara may withdraw Matthew's entire account balance immediately.
2. Sara may choose to leave the assets in the plan, but she must take a distribution of the account balance before the end of the fifth year after Matthew's death.
3. Sara may choose to roll the account balance to an IRA for her benefit. In this case, the RMD would begin when Sara attained the age of 70½ and would be based on Sara's life expectancy as determined by the uniform life expectancy table. In addition, she could not take a distribution until age 59½ without having the 10 percent early withdrawal penalty apply.
4. Sara may elect to take distributions from the plan based on her recalculated life expectancy (single life expectancy table) each year. Sara may choose to begin the distribution immediately or wait until Matthew would have been 70½.

---

57. IRC §401(a)(9)(B)(iv)(II) and Treas. Reg. §1.401(a)(9)-5 Q&A-5(c)(1) and (2).

Nonspouse Beneficiary

If the beneficiary is someone other than the surviving spouse, then the beneficiary has two options. The first distribution period option is the remaining single, non-recalculated life expectancy of the designated beneficiary. Life expectancy is calculated using the age of the designated beneficiary in the year following the year of the employee's death, reduced by one for each subsequent year. Alternatively, the beneficiary can elect to distribute the entire account balance within five years after the year of the owner's death.

In this case, the RMD is calculated in the same manner as discussed above (distributions after RMD had begun), except that the beneficiary may choose to leave assets in the account and not take distributions from the plan until the fifth year after the participant's death. In the fifth year, however, the beneficiary must take a distribution of the entire account balance. The beneficiary cannot start taking distributions over their life expectancies at that time. The 5-year rule allows the beneficiary to forego taking distributions for the four years after the death of the participants; whereas, in all other cases, the beneficiary must take at least the annual minimum distributions calculated based on his non-recalculated single life expectancy.

QUICK QUIZ 7.5

1. The first minimum distribution must always be taken no later than April 15 of the year following the year the participant attains the age of 70½.
   a. True
   b. False

2. Designated beneficiaries for minimum distributions are determined on the last day of the year following the year of the participant's death.
   a. True
   b. False

3. With regard to minimum distributions, a surviving spouse receives more favorable options than any other type of beneficiary in the event of the owner's death.
   a. True
   b. False

False, True, True.

No Beneficiary

If no beneficiary has been named by December 31 of the year following the owner's death (or the beneficiary is the decedent's estate or charity), the account must be fully distributed before the end of the fifth year following the year of death. The account balance may be distributed anytime before the end of the fifth year but may never extend beyond.

EXHIBIT
7.35

DEATH OF PARTICIPANT SUMMARY

	OPTIONS AFTER MINIMUM DISTRIBUTIONS BEGIN*
Spouse Beneficiary	1. Spouse can receive distributions over the surviving spouse's remaining single life expectancy as <u>recalculated</u> using the single life table. 2. Rollover plan balance to an IRA in surviving spouse's name and delay distributions until spouse is 70½.
Nonspouse Beneficiary	1. Distribution period is the longer of the remaining single life expectancy (not recalculated) of the designated beneficiary (reduced by one year) or the remaining life expectancy of the participant. 2. Rollover plan balance to an IRA in the name of the deceased IRA owner for the benefit of the beneficiary and distribute over the longer of the remaining single life expectancy of the beneficiary or the remaining life expectancy of the participant (not recalculated).
No Beneficiary	1. Distributions must continue over the remaining distribution period of the deceased owner (uniform life table). The decedent's remaining distribution period is reduced by one each year.
	OPTIONS BEFORE MINIMUM DISTRIBUTIONS BEGIN*
Spouse Beneficiary	1. Distribution over surviving spouse's remaining single life expectancy as <u>recalculated</u> using single life expectancy table beginning when the participant would have turned 70½. 2. Distribute participant's account within 5 years. 3. Roll plan assets to an IRA in surviving spouse's name and wait until surviving spouse is 70½ to begin RMD.
Nonspouse Beneficiary	1. Distribute participant's account within 5 years. 2. Remaining single life expectancy (not recalculated) of designated beneficiary (reduced by one year). 3. Roll plan assets to an IRA in the name of the deceased IRA owner for the benefit of the beneficiary and then distribute within 5 years or over the remaining single life expectancy of the beneficiary (not recalculated). (PPA 2006)
No Beneficiary	1. Distribute participant's account within 5 years.

* In all cases, the beneficiary can take more than the minimum distribution.

STRETCH IRAS

Stretch IRAs have been a topic in estate and financial planning for years, if not decades. The concept of a stretch IRA is to minimize distributions from the IRA so that tax deferred assets can grow as much as possible unimpaired from income tax. This minimization strategy occurs not only during the life of the owner (or participant), but also during the life of the beneficiary. For the taxpayer attempting to "stretch out" an IRA for the longest period of time, it is important to select the most appropriate beneficiary.

As discussed in this chapter, taxpayers are required to take distributions from their retirement accounts after age 70½ and beneficiaries are required to take distributions from inherited IRAs. Each time a distribution is taken from a traditional IRA, it is subject to ordinary income tax. Distributions from a Roth IRA or Roth Account are not subject to income tax, but the earnings on the funds distributed from the Roth IRA or Account will be taxable. These required distributions reduce the value of the IRA over time. Thus, the objective of "stretching" is to reduce these distributions as much as possible.

KEY CONCEPTS

1. What is the concept of stretch IRAs?

2. What type of beneficiary is best for stretching IRAs?

3. Why should Roth IRAs be stretched when distributions are generally not taxable?

Accomplishing the objective of reducing required distributions after the death of the participant is best achieved by choosing a very young beneficiary. Beneficiaries taking minimum distributions use the single-life table. Consider the required distribution from an inherited IRA for a 45 year-old compared to a 10 year-old. The life expectancy factor for a 45 year-old is 38.8, which results in a required distribution of 2.57 percent of the account value. The life expectancy factor for a 10 year-old is 72.8, which results in a required distribution of 1.37 percent of the account value. While the difference between the two distributions does not seem significant, it makes a significant difference, especially over time. For example, after ten years, the life expectancy factor for a 55 year-old is 29.6, which results in a required distribution of 3.38 percent of the account value. The life expectancy factor for a 20 year-old is 63.0, which results in a required distribution of 1.59 percent of the account value.

> This example compares the balances of an inherited IRA valued at $100,000 left to a 45 year old and one that is left to a 10 year old. Minimum distributions will be taken at the end of each year based on the required distribution. These distributions will be reduced by a tax rate of 30 percent and will accumulate in a taxable account. Both the IRA and the taxable account will earn a rate of return of 9 percent on account balances, but the earnings within the taxable account are subject to a 30 percent income tax rate. The following table depicts the account value after 20, 40, and 60 years:

EXAMPLE 7.45

	45 YEAR-OLD			10 YEAR-OLD		
Year	Traditional IRA Balance	Value of Distributions in a Taxable Account	Total Value of IRA & Taxable Account	Traditional IRA Balance	Value of Distributions in a Taxable Account	Total Value of IRA & Taxable Account
0	$100,000	$0	$100,000	$100,000	$0	$100,000
20	$308,897	$166,240	$475,137	$447,769	$89,951	$537,720
40	$362,667	$1,313,048	$1,675,714	$1,621,358	$800,667	$2,422,025
60	$4,367	$5,457,149	$5,461,516	$4,153,932	$5,460,044	$9,613,976

The value of the two accounts for the 10 year-old beneficiary is significantly greater than the value of the accounts for the 45 year-old.[58] This increased value illustrates the value of "stretching" the IRA. The two graphs illustrate the account balances in the IRAs.

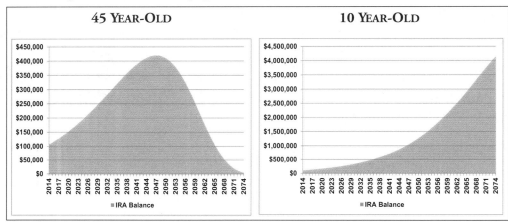

The table below uses the same assumptions as above, except that it assumes that the accounts are Roth IRAs, which reduces income taxes paid by the beneficiaries and results in larger account balances.

	45 YEAR-OLD			10 YEAR-OLD		
Year	Roth IRA Balance	Value of Distributions in a Taxable Account	Total Value of IRA & Taxable Account	Roth IRA Balance	Value of Distributions in a Taxable Account	Total Value of IRA & Taxable Account
0	$100,000	$0	$100,000	$100,000	$0	$100,000
20	$308,897	$237,485	$546,382	$447,769	$128,502	$576,271
40	$362,667	$1,875,782	$2,238,449	$1,621,358	$1,143,810	$2,765,168
60	$4,367	$7,795,927	$7,800,295	$4,153,932	$7,800,063	$11,953,995

The table depicting the account values with the Roth IRA helps to explain the value of converting today a traditional IRA to a Roth IRA. This benefit holds even when the income tax that would have been used to pay the tax on the conversion is incorporated into the comparison.

---

58. The IRA account assets are pre-tax. However, even adjusting for the tax owed on these funds, the value of the accounts for the 10 year-old are significantly higher.

The example above illustrates the power of stretching an IRA and why it has been a topic with planners for years. It should be noted that "stretch IRAs" is also a topic in Congress and there have been proposals by members of Congress and a proposal in President Obama's budget to limit the distribution period for inherited IRAs to five years. However, for now, there does not appear to be much chance that "stretch IRAs" will go away in the near term.

PLANNING FOR QUALIFIED PLANS AND IRA BENEFICIARIES

CREDITOR PROTECTION

One of the benefits of qualified plans and IRAs is that the funds are protected from creditors. It is important to keep in mind that no one anticipates having creditor problems, so proactively accumulating wealth in these vehicles is wise. Remember that the US Bankruptcy code, as a result of the Bankruptcy Abuse Prevention and Consumer Protection Act, provides for the following exemptions related to retirement plans:

1. All ERISA type retirement plans and rollovers from them to IRAs are exempt for an unlimited amount.
2. SEP and SIMPLE IRAs are exempt up to an unlimited amount.
3. Traditional and Roth IRAs are exempt up to $1,000,000, which is periodically adjusted for inflation.

IRAs and qualified plans are also beneficial in terms of deferring taxation and planning is often done to "stretch" these accounts far into the future to the next generation. The question arises as to how an inherited IRA is treated in terms of creditor protection.

The issue of inherited IRAs being part of bankrupt estates is becoming more prevalent since there are more assets in IRAs today and bankruptcy filings have increased as a result of the economic troubles over the last several years. Several court cases over the last several years have ruled on this issue inconsistently.

While the trend in the court cases appeared to be heading toward affording creditor protection for inherited IRAs under the federal bankruptcy laws, the question has been answered by the U.S. Supreme Court in the Clark v. Rameker case in 2014.

In Clark *v.* Rameker, the Supreme Court ruled that the funds in an inherited IRA are not protected from creditors and that the funds are part of the bankruptcy estate assets. The court stated that the Bankruptcy Code makes clear that funds held in inherited IRAs are not "retirement funds" within the meaning of §522(b)(3)(C)'s bankruptcy exemption. The court went on to say in the opinion that there are three legal characteristics of inherited IRAs that lead to the conclusion that funds held in such accounts are not objectively set aside for the purpose of retirement.

- First, the holder of an inherited IRA may never invest additional money in the account. 26 U. S. C. §219(d)(4). Inherited IRAs are thus unlike traditional and Roth IRAs, both of which are quintessential "retirement funds." For where inherited IRAs categorically prohibit contributions, the entire purpose of traditional and Roth IRAs is to provide tax incentives for account holders to contribute regularly and over time to their retirement savings.

- Second, holders of inherited IRAs are required to withdraw money from such accounts, no matter how many years they may be from retirement. Under the Tax Code, the beneficiary of an inherited IRA must either withdrawal of the funds in the IRA within five years after the year of the owner's death or take minimum annual distributions every year. That the tax rules governing inherited IRAs routinely lead to their diminution over time, regardless of their holders' proximity to retirement, is hardly a feature one would expect of an account set aside for retirement.
- Finally, the holder of an inherited IRA may withdraw the entire balance of the account at any time—and for any purpose—without penalty. Whereas a withdrawal from a traditional or Roth IRA prior to the age of 59½ triggers a 10 percent tax penalty subject to narrow exceptions—a rule that encourages individuals to leave such funds untouched until retirement age—there is no similar limit on the holder of an inherited IRA. Funds held in inherited IRAs accordingly constitute "a pot of money that can be freely used for current consumption," not funds objectively set aside for one's retirement.

The court went on to say the following:
- As a general matter, those provisions [in the bankruptcy code] effectuate a careful balance between the interests of creditors and debtors. On the one hand, we have noted that "every asset the Code permits a debtor to withdraw from the estate is an asset that is not available to creditors." On the other hand, exemptions serve the important purpose of "protect[ing] the debtor's essential needs."
- Allowing debtors to protect funds held in traditional and Roth IRAs comports with this purpose by helping to ensure that debtors will be able to meet their basic needs during their retirement years. At the same time, the legal limitations on traditional and Roth IRAs ensure that debtors who hold such accounts (but who have not yet reached retirement age) do not enjoy a cash windfall by virtue of the exemption—such debtors are instead required to wait until age 59½ before they may withdraw the funds penalty-free.
- The same cannot be said of an inherited IRA. For if an individual is allowed to exempt an inherited IRA from her bankruptcy estate, nothing about the inherited IRA's legal characteristics would prevent (or even discourage) the individual from using the entire balance of the account on a vacation home or sports car immediately after her bankruptcy proceedings are complete. Allowing that kind of exemption would convert the Bankruptcy Code's purposes of preserving debtors' ability to meet their basic needs and ensuring that they have a "fresh start," *Rousey*, 544 U. S., at 325, into a "free pass." We decline to read the retirement funds provision in that manner.

With this ruling, the Court has resolved the conflict between the Seventh Circuit's ruling and the Fifth Circuit's decision in Chilton. Inherited IRAs are NOT protected under 11 U. S. C. §522(b)(3)(C).

However, debtors may find protection under state bankruptcy statutes. For example, Texas enacted SB 181061 in 2011, which affords the same level of creditor protection to inherited IRAs as to traditional IRAs.

CONTROLLING AND PROTECTING INHERITED IRAS

As of September 2015, assets in individual retirement accounts (IRAs) totaled $7.3 trillion and was the largest component of the almost $25 trillion in retirement assets in the United States.[59] For many Americans, IRAs are a significantly large portion of their net worth. In some cases, IRAs may contain substantial balances and should be part of an overall financial and estate plan.

There are two significant risks that are associated with inherited IRAs. These risks include the depletion of the IRA assets by the beneficiary and the creditor risk associated with inherited IRAs.

As discussed above, one of the benefits of an IRA is the ability to stretch out the distributions over the life of two individuals (the owner and the beneficiary). This stretching of the IRA allows for larger tax-deferred growth. However, beneficiaries of IRAs have full control over the IRA assets and can take out more than the required minimum distributions or even liquidate the IRA. Taking larger than required distributions is very common and is often in conflict with the wishes of the IRA owner, who is now deceased. There is no mechanism to prevent a beneficiary from simply taking the money out of a traditional custodial IRA.

The second risk applies to nonspousal IRAs who have immediate or potential creditor problems and was discussed above. There are two possible solutions to the above risks: the trusteed IRA and the "See Through" Trust as a beneficiary to the IRA.

To understand how to resolve the above issues, it is important to realize how IRAs are set up. IRAs may be structured as a custodial IRA (under IRC Section 408(h)) or as a trusteed IRA (under IRC Section 408(a)). Custodial IRAs, which are most common today, can be set up with a see-through trust as a beneficiary. This type of arrangement creates a trust between the IRA and the beneficiary and resolves both of the above issues. The other alternative is to create a Trusteed IRA, which is effectively an IRA within a trust. Both of these alternatives resolve the two risks discussed above.

QUICK QUIZ 7.6

1. A stretch IRA requires that a beneficiary set up a special type of account after the death of the account owner.
    a. True
    b. False

2. Stretch IRAs are best accomplished by choosing young beneficiaries?
    a. True
    b. False

3. Leaving an IRA to a spouse could be a better way to stretch an IRA than leaving it to a child?
    a. True
    b. False

False, True, True.

---

59. ICI.org

TRUSTEED IRAs

Trusteed IRAs, which can be either traditional or Roth IRAs, are trusts established within the United States. They are IRAs and trusts, and therefore, have the same advantages of IRAs, including creditor protection and tax deferral while the owner is alive, and the same advantages of trusts. The structure of the trust allows for the unique advantage of being able to control the distributions from the IRA after the owner dies, which provides creditor protection and reduces the likelihood of the assets being prematurely consumed.

When established, trusteed IRAs are structured to make pre-defined payments to beneficiaries. These amounts might be limited to:
1. The required minimum distribution,
2. The required minimum distribution plus additional amounts under an ascertainable standard for the benefit of the beneficiaries (generally for health, education, maintenance, or support), or
3. The greater of income or the required minimum distribution.

In addition to controlling the distributions to beneficiaries, a trusteed IRA can be set up to control who receives the funds after the death of the primary beneficiary. Typically, the beneficiary of an inherited custodial IRA will choose the person to receive the assets after he or she dies.

Trusteed IRAs are established with an institutional trustee who will generally manage the trust and often the assets of the IRA. Trusteed IRAs are more expensive than custodial assets, but less expensive than a See-Through trust. There is often a 100 to 150 basis point fee as well as an asset minimum (generally $500,000 to $1 million).

"SEE-THROUGH" TRUST

Owners of IRAs can name a see-through trust as a beneficiary. A see-through trust is a stand-alone trust used as a beneficiary of a retirement (IRA) account. The IRS has four minimum distribution trust rules that must be followed in naming a trust as the beneficiary of an IRA.
- The trust must be valid under state law.
- The trust is irrevocable or will by its terms, become irrevocable upon the death of the IRA owner.
- The beneficiaries of the trust are identifiable.
- A copy of the trust documents must be provided to the IRA custodian by October 31 of the year immediately following the year in which the IRA owner died.

A see-through trust allows the custodian to determine the required minimum distribution (RMDs) by looking through the trust to the life expectancies of the trust beneficiaries. The trust can have the strongest spendthrift provisions permitted by law. The trustee can be empowered to direct the custodian's investments and direct the custodian to distribute more but not less than the RMDs at the trustee's discretion.

SEE-THROUGH TRUST

EXHIBIT
7.36

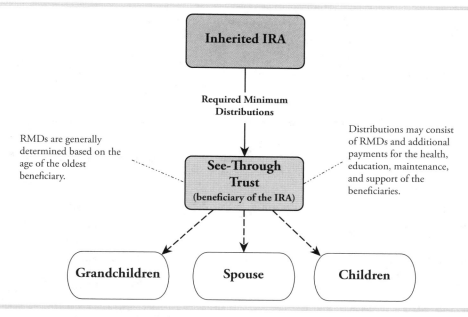

RMDs are generally determined based on the age of the oldest beneficiary.

Distributions may consist of RMDs and additional payments for the health, education, maintenance, and support of the beneficiaries.

QUICK QUIZ 7.7

1. Inherited IRAs are protected in bankruptcy because they are IRAs.
   a. True
   b. False

2. Trusteed IRAs allow IRA owners to control how distributions from the IRA will be paid out and to whom the assets will pass to after the death of the primary beneficiary.
   a. True
   b. False

3. See-through trusts are the same as trusteed IRAs.
   a. True
   b. False

The see-through trust can be either a conduit trust (distribution by custodian is exactly distributed by trustee to beneficiary) or an accumulation trust. The accumulation trust is much more complex and requires specialized tax knowledge to properly draft. The accumulation trust is especially useful if the IRA is a Roth IRA and deferral and growth are objective as well as creditor protection. An accumulation trust can also be used as a special needs trust. However, it is important to keep in mind that the tax brackets for trusts are massively compressed with income above $12,400 taxed at 39.6 percent.

KEY TERMS

ADJUSTED BASIS - The portion of a distribution that is not subject to income tax. Usually, the return of after-tax contributions or nondeductible contributions.

CODA (CASH OR DEFERRED ARRANGEMENT) - Permits an employee to defer a portion of their salary on a pretax basis to a qualified plan or receive the salary as current taxable income.

CONDUIT IRAS - Accounts that hold rollover funds are often referred to as IRA rollover accounts.

DIRECT ROLLOVER - Occurs when the plan trustee distributes the account balance directly to the trustee of the recipient account.

EARLY WITHDRAWAL PENALTY - A 10 percent penalty on distributions made before the participant attains the age of 59½ (exceptions apply).

FIXED AMORTIZATION METHOD - The payment is calculated over the participant's life expectancy if single, or the joint life expectancy if married, and the interest rate is reasonable.

FIXED ANNUITIZATION METHOD - The participant takes distributions of the account over a number of years determined by dividing the account balance by an annuity factor using a reasonable interest rate and mortality table.

INDIRECT ROLLOVER - A distribution to the participant with a subsequent transfer to another qualified account (or IRA).

JOINT LIFE EXPECTANCY TABLE - The life expectancy table used to determine a participant's RMD when the participant's sole designated beneficiary is the participant's spouse and that spouse is more than 10 years younger than the participant.

LUMP-SUM DISTRIBUTIONS - A complete distribution of a participant's account balance within one taxable year on account of death, disability, attainment of age 59½, or separation from service. Some lump-sum distributions from qualified plans are eligible for special taxation options.

NET UNREALIZED APPRECIATION (NUA) - A special taxation treatment for a lump-sum distribution from a qualified plan that treats part of the distribution as capital gain.

PLAN LOANS - Loans from a qualified plan made available to all participants on an effectively equal basis that are limited in amount (no greater than $50,000 or half of the vested account balance), are repaid within a certain time period (usually five years), bear a reasonable rate of interest, are adequately secured, and require the administrator to maintain a proper accounting.

PRE-1974 CAPITAL GAIN TREATMENT - A special taxation treatment for lump-sum distributions from qualified plans that treats the distribution attributable to pre-1974 participation in the plan as long-term capital gain.

KEY TERMS

QUALIFIED DOMESTIC RELATIONS ORDER (QDRO) - A court order related to divorce, property settlement, or child support that can divide a participant's interest in a qualified plan.

QUALIFIED JOINT AND SURVIVOR ANNUITY (QJSA) - The QJSA pays a benefit to the participant and spouse as long as either lives; although, at the death of the first spouse, the annuity may be reduced.

QUALIFIED OPTIONAL SURVIVOR ANNUITY (QOSA) - An annuity for the life of a participant with a survivor annuity for the life of the participant's spouse that is equal to a specified applicable percentage of the amount of the annuity that is payable during the joint lives of the participant and the spouse (and that is actuarially equivalent to a single life annuity for the life of the participant).

QUALIFIED PRE-RETIREMENT SURVIVOR ANNUITY (QPSA) - Provides a benefit to the surviving spouse if the participant dies before attaining normal retirement age.

REQUIRED MINIMUM DISTRIBUTION (RMD) - A minimum amount that must be withdrawn from a qualified plan (or IRA) each year after the participant attains the age of 70½. The amount is calculated using either the uniform distribution table, the single life expectancy table, or the joint life expectancy tables.

REQUIRED MINIMUM DISTRIBUTION METHOD - The payment is calculated in the same manner as required under minimum distribution rules. Note that payments are recalculated annually.

ROLLOVER - To elect to transfer funds from one tax-advantaged account to another tax-advantaged account to continue to defer the recognition of income taxes until the ultimate distribution of the assets.

SEPARATE INTEREST APPROACH - Divides the participant's retirement benefit into two separate portions: one for the alternate payee and one for the participant.

SINGLE LIFE EXPECTANCY TABLE - Tables used to calculate the required minimum distribution for beneficiaries.

SHARED PAYMENT APPROACH - Splits the actual benefit payments made between the participant and the alternate payee.

SEE-THROUGH TRUST – A trust that is the beneficiary of a custodial IRA. It provides for more control over distribution of IRA assets after the owner's death, as well as providing increased creditor protection for the beneficiaries of the trust.

TRUSTEED IRA – A trust established within the United States that holds IRA assets, which is an alternative to a custodial IRA. It allows for ultimate control over the distribution of the IRA assets by the owner after his or her death and provides creditor protection for the beneficiaries.

KEY TERMS

10-YEAR FORWARD AVERAGING - A method of income tax calculation for certain lump-sum distribution from qualified plans that divides the taxable portion of the lump-sum distribution by 10 and applies the result to the 1986 individual income tax rates. The resulting calculation is then multiplied by 10 to determine the total income tax due on the distribution.

UNIFORM LIFETIME TABLE - A table used to calculate the RMD for the plan participant unless the participant's sole designated beneficiary is the participant's spouse and that spouse is more than 10 years younger than the participant.

DISCUSSION QUESTIONS

1. Describe the distribution options for pension plans.

2. Describe the distribution options for profit sharing plans.

3. Describe rollovers and when and how they are used.

4. Discuss the circumstances that will result in a qualified retirement plan participant having adjusted basis in plan assets.

5. List the three special options available for lump-sum distributions from a qualified plan.

6. Describe qualified plan loans and their limitations.

7. How are Qualified Domestic Relations Orders (QDRO) treated with regards to qualified retirement plans?

8. Discuss the penalty for distributions from a qualified plan before 59½.

9. Explain when minimum distributions must begin.

MULTIPLE CHOICE PROBLEMS

1. Which of the following distributions from a qualified plan would not be subject to the 10 percent early withdrawal penalty, assuming the participant has not attained age 59½?

    1. A distribution made to a spouse under a Qualified Domestic Relations Order (QDRO).
    2. A distribution from a qualified plan used to pay the private health insurance premiums of a current employee of Clinical Trials Company.
    3. A distribution to pay for costs of higher education.
    4. A distribution made immediately after separation from service at age 57.

        a. 1 and 2.
        b. 1 and 3.
        c. 1 and 4.
        d. 2 and 3.

2. Ginger, who is 75 years old, requested from the IRS a waiver of the 60-day rollover requirement. She indicated that she provided written instructions to her financial advisor that she wanted to take a distribution from her IRA and roll it over into a new IRA. Her financial advisor inadvertently moved the funds into a taxable account. Ginger did not make the request of the IRS until five years after the mistake was made. Will the IRS permit the waiver?

    a. No. The IRS never waives this requirement, except under the most extreme of circumstances.
    b. Yes. The mistake was the fault of the financial advisor and the IRS regularly grants waivers in these circumstances.
    c. No. Ginger waited beyond the one-year period for filing such a request.
    d. No. Ginger waited an unreasonable amount of time before filing the request.

3. MaryAnn, who is 75 years old, requested from the IRS a waiver of the 60-day rollover requirement. She indicated that she provided written instructions to her financial advisor that she wanted to take a distribution from her IRA and roll it over into a new IRA. Her financial advisor inadvertently moved the funds into a taxable account. MaryAnn did not make the request of the IRS until six months after the mistake was made. Will the IRS permit the waiver?

    a. No. The IRS never waives this requirement, except under the most extreme of circumstances.
    b. Yes. The mistake was the fault of the financial advisor and the IRS regularly grants waivers in these circumstances.
    c. No. MaryAnn waited beyond 90-days for filing such a request.
    d. No. MaryAnn waited an unreasonable amount of time before filing the request.

4. Laura, age 43, has several retirement accounts and wants to know what accounts can be rolled over to other accounts. Which of the following statements regarding rollovers is not correct?

   a. She could take a distribution from her SEP IRA and roll it over to a qualified plan without incurring a 20% withholding.

   b. She could rollover her government 457(b) plan to her new employer's qualified plan.

   c. She could rollover the funds from her old employer's qualified plan to her new employer, who sponsors a 401(k) plan with a Roth account, and be able convert the funds in an in-plan Roth rollover.

   d. She could rollover her traditional IRA to her SIMPLE IRA.

5. Which of the following are benefits of converting assets in a qualified plan to a Roth account through an in-plan Roth rollover?

   1. The conversion may result in a reduction in income tax in future years.

   2. The conversion will result in increasing after-tax deferred assets and reducing the gross estate.

   3. The conversion will eliminate the need for minimum distributions during the life of the participant.

   a. 1 and 2.

   b. 2 and 3.

   c. 1 and 3.

   d. 1, 2 and 3.

6. In May 2016, Seth converts $100,000 in his traditional IRA to a Roth IRA. The value of the assets in the Roth IRA drops by 40 percent due to a significant decline in the stock market that occurs in October 2016. The Roth conversion results in Seth incurring $100,000 of taxable income, when he could have waited and converted only $60,000 (after the 40 percent drop). Which of the following statements is correct?

   a. Seth cannot recharacterize the conversion, but he will have a larger after-tax basis, which could be helpful in the event of a nonqualified distribution.

   b. Seth can recharacterize as long as it is done within six months from the date of the conversion.

   c. Seth can recharacterize after December 31, 2016.

   d. Seth cannot recharacterize, but can take a deduction on Schedule D for the loss when he files his form 1040.

7. In June 2016, Cody converts $100,000 in his 401(k) plan to a Roth account through a in-plan Roth rollover. The value of the assets in the Roth account drops by 40 percent due to a significant decline in the stock market that occurs in August 2016. The in-plan Roth rollover results in Cody incurring $100,000 of taxable income, when he could have waited and converted only $60,000 (after the 40 percent drop). Which of the following statements is correct?

    a. Cody cannot recharacterize the conversion, but he will have a larger after-tax basis, which could be helpful in the event of a nonqualified distribution.

    b. Cody can recharacterize as long as it is done within six months from the conversion.

    c. Cody can recharacterize after December 31, 2016.

    d. Cody cannot recharacterize, but can take a deduction on Schedule D for the loss when he files his Form 1040.

8. Reese has assets both in her Roth IRA and in her Roth account that is part of her employer's 403(b) plan. However, she is not sure about the differences between the two types of accounts. Which of the following statements would you tell her is correct?

    a. Both Roth IRAs and Roth accounts have a five-year holding period requirement, but the establishment of the first Roth IRA or Roth account starts the five-year holding period for all Roth IRAs and Roth accounts.

    b. Both Roth IRAs and Roth accounts have the same rules regarding the definition of a qualified distribution.

    c. The minimum distribution rules for Roth IRAs and Roth accounts are the same.

    d. The nature of the income received by beneficiaries in a qualified distribution is the same for distributions from both Roth IRAs and Roth accounts.

9. Bobby Brown would not listen to his financial advisor and decided to rollover his qualified plan assets to a traditional IRA. Which of the following is correct?

    a. Bobby is entitled to the same alternative tax options in an IRA that are available in a qualified plan.

    b. Bobby has the same or more investment options in his IRA as compared to his qualified plan.

    c. Bobby can now convert the funds to a Roth IRA, where before he could not.

    d. Bobby has lost some of his creditor protection by moving the funds from a qualified plan to an IRA.

10. Gerry is 70½ on April 1 of the current year and must receive a minimum distribution from his qualified plan. The account balance had a value of $423,598 at the end of last year. The distribution period for a 70 year old is 27.4, and for a 71 year old it is 26.5. If Gerry takes a $15,000 distribution next April 1st, what is the amount of the minimum distribution tax penalty associated with his first year's distribution?

    a. $0.

    b. $230.

    c. $492.

    d. $985.

11. Josh recently died at the age of 63, leaving a qualified plan account with a balance of $1,000,000. Josh was married to Kay, age 53, who is the designated beneficiary of the qualified plan. Which of the following is correct?

    a. Kay must distribute the entire account balance within five years of Josh's death.

    b. Kay must begin taking distributions over Josh's remaining single-life expectancy.

    c. Any distribution from the plan to Kay will be subject to a 10 percent early withdrawal penalty until she is 59½.

    d. Kay can receive annual distributions over her remaining single-life expectancy, recalculated each year.

12. Andrea recently died at age 77, leaving behind a qualified plan worth $200,000. Andrea began taking minimum distributions from the account after attaining age 70½ and correctly reported the minimum distributions on her federal income tax returns. Before her death, Andrea named her granddaughter, Reese age 22, as the designated beneficiary of the account. Now that Andrea has died, Reese has come to you for advice with respect to the account. Which of the following is correct?

    a. Reese must distribute the entire account balance within five years of Andrea's death.

    b. In the year following Andrea's death, Reese may begin taking distributions from the account based on Reese's remaining life expectancy, recalculated each year.

    c. In the year following Andrea's death, Reese must begin taking distributions over Andrea's remaining single-life expectancy.

    d. Reese can roll the account over to an IRA and name a new beneficiary.

13. The early distribution penalty of 10 percent does not apply to qualified plan distributions:

    1. Made after attainment of the age of 55 and separation from service.

    2. Made for the purpose of paying qualified higher education costs.

    3. Paid to a designated beneficiary after the death of the account owner who had not begun receiving minimum distributions.

      a. 1 only.

      b. 1 and 3.

      c. 2 and 3.

      d. 1, 2, and 3.

14. Which of the following statements is/are correct regarding the early distribution 10 percent penalty tax from a qualified plan?

    1. Retirement at age 55 or older exempts the distributions from the early withdrawal penalty tax.

    2. Distributions used to pay medical expenses in excess of the 10% of AGI for a tax filer who itemizes are exempt from the early withdrawal penalty.

    3. Distributions that are part of a series of equal periodic payments paid over the life or life expectancy of the participant are exempt from the early withdrawal penalty.

      a. 3 only.

      b. 1 and 3.

      c. 2 and 3.

      d. 1, 2, and 3.

15. Steve, age 69, is an employee of X2, Inc. He plans to work until age 75. He currently contributes 6 percent of his pay to his 401(k) plan, and his employer matches with 3 percent. Which one of the following statements is true?

      a. Steve is required to take minimum distributions from his 401(k) plan beginning April 1 of the year after he attains age 70½.

      b. Steve is required to take minimum distributions from his 401(k) plan beginning April 1 of the year after he retires.

      c. Steve is required to take minimum distributions from his Traditional IRA beginning April 1 of the year after he retires.

      d. Steve cannot contribute to his 401(k) plan after age 70½ in any case.

16. Jose Sequential, age 70½ in October of this year, worked for several companies over his lifetime. He has worked for the following companies (A-E) and still has the following qualified plan account balances at those companies.

Company	Jose's Account Balance
A	$250,000
B	$350,000
C	$150,000
D	$350,000
E	$200,000

Jose is currently employed with Company E. What, if any, is his required minimum distribution for the current year from all plans? Life expectancy tables are 27.4 for age 70 and 26.5 for age 71.

    a. $0.

    b. $40,146.

    c. $41,509.

    d. $47,445.

17. Tom, age 39, is an employee of Star, Inc., which has a profit sharing plan with a CODA feature. His total account balance is $412,000, $82,000 of which represents employee elective deferrals and earnings on those deferrals. The balance is profit sharing contributions made by the employer and earnings on those contributions. Tom is 100 percent vested. Which of the following statements is/are correct?

    1. Tom may take a loan from the plan, but the maximum loan is $41,000 and the normal repayment period will be 5 years.

    2. If Tom takes a distribution (plan permitting) to pay health care premiums (no coverage by employer) he will be subject to income tax, but not the 10% penalty.

    a. 1 only.

    b. 2 only.

    c. Both 1 and 2.

    d. Neither 1 nor 2.

18. On January 5, Cindy, age 39, withdrew $42,000 from her qualified plan. Cindy had an account balance of $180,000 and an adjusted basis in the account of $30,000. Calculate any early withdrawal penalty.

    a. $0.

    b. $1,200.

    c. $3,500.

    d. $4,200.

19. Brenda, age 53 and a recent widow, is deciding between taking a lump-sum distribution from her husband's pension plan of $263,500 now or selecting a life annuity starting when she is age 65 (life expectancy at 65 is 21 years) of $2,479 per month. Current 30-year treasuries are yielding 6 percent annually. Which of the statements below are true?

   1. If she takes the lump-sum distribution, she will receive $263,500 in cash now and be able to reinvest for 34 years, creating an annuity of $4,570 per month.

   2. If she takes the lump-sum distribution she will be subject to the 10% early withdrawal penalty.

       a. 1 only.

       b. 2 only.

       c. Both 1 and 2.

       d. Neither 1 nor 2.

20. Nancy, age 70 on February 2, 2016, had the following account balances in a qualified retirement plan.

12/31/2015	$500,000
12/31/2016	$478,000
12/31/2017	$519,000
12/31/2018	$600,000

    Assuming that Nancy is retired and has never taken a distribution prior to 2017, what is the total amount of minimum distribution required in 2017? Life expectancy factors according to the uniform life table are 27.4 for a 70 year old and 26.5 for a 71 year old.

       a. $18,038.

       b. $18,248.

       c. $35,597.

       d. $36,286.

21. Which of the following is/are elements of an effective waiver for a pre-retirement survivor annuity?

    1. Both spouses must sign the waiver.

    2. The waiver must be notarized or signed by a plan official.

    3. The waiver must indicate that the person(s) waiving understand the consequences of the waiver.

       a. 2 only.

       b. 1 and 3.

       c. 2 and 3.

       d. 1, 2, and 3.

22. Which of the following is true regarding QDROs?

   a. The court determines how the retirement plan will satisfy the QDRO. (i.e. split accounts, separate interest).

   b. In order for a QDRO to be valid, the order must be filed on Form 2932-QDRO provided by ERISA.

   c. All QDRO distributions are charged a 10% early withdrawal penalty.

   d. A QDRO distribution is not considered a taxable distribution if the distribution is deposited into the recipient's qualified plan.

23. Pander's Box, a shop that specializes in custom trinket and storage boxes, has a 401(k) plan. The plan allows plan loans up to the legal limit allowed by law and they may be repaid under the most generous repayment schedule available by law. The plan has the following employee information:

EMPLOYEE	401(k) BALANCE	OUTSTANDING LOAN
Karen	$400,000	$0
Teddy	$250,000	$30,000
Josh	$75,000	$0
Justin	$15,000	$0

   Which of the following statements is correct?

   a. If Teddy quit today, state law requires that he repay the loan within five days.

   b. The maximum Karen can borrow from her account is $200,000.

   c. The maximum Justin can borrow from his account is $10,000.

   d. If Josh wanted to borrow money from his plan for the purchase of a personal residence, he would have to pay the loan back within five years.

24. One approach that is used in some domestic relations orders is to "split" the actual benefit payments made with respect to a participant under the plan to give the alternate payee part of each payment. Under this approach, the alternate payee will not receive any payments unless the participant receives a payment or is already in pay status. This approach is often used when a support order is being drafted after a participant has already begun to receive a stream of payments from the plan (such as a life annuity). This approach to dividing retirement benefits is often called what?

   a. The separate interest approach.

   b. The split payment approach.

   c. The shared payment approach.

   d. The divided annuity approach.

25. Roger and Robin were happily married until Roger fell in love with Sam. As a result, Roger and Robin have agreed they need to get a divorce. As part of the process, the court has provided a domestic relations order that calls for Robin's profit-sharing plan to be divided into equal portions such that Roger will have his own account with half of the value of the retirement account. What type of approach has been taken?

    a. The separate interest approach.

    b. The split payment approach.

    c. The shared payment approach.

    d. The divided account approach.

26. Decatur 401(k) Plan maintains a loan program for its participants. The plan has 50 participants, three of whom had participant loans. Decatur conducted a year-end review of its loan program and found the following:

- Bob received a loan from the plan one year ago for $60,000 over a five-year term, amortized monthly using a reasonable interest rate. Bob timely made the required payments. Bob's vested account balance is $180,000.
- Sandi received a loan of $10,000 to help her mother move to Florida this year, amortized over 72 months. Payments are timely and the interest rate is reasonable.

Which of the following individuals have loans that do not comply with the IRC?

    a. Bob.

    b. Sandi.

    c. Both Bob and Sandi.

    d. Neither Bob nor Sandi.

27. Jim, a participant in the Zappa retirement plan, has requested a second plan loan. Jim's vested account balance is $80,000. He borrowed $27,000 eight months ago and still owes $18,000 on that loan. How much can he borrow as a second loan?

    a. $13,000.

    b. $22,000.

    c. $23,000.

    d. $31,000.

28. Tim, a participant in the Zappa retirement plan, has requested a second plan loan. Tim's vested account balance is $70,000. He borrowed $30,000 ten months ago and still owes $20,000 on that loan. Could he increase his maximum permissible loan if he repaid the outstanding loan before taking the new loan?

    a. No. Paying off the loan will not increase an available loan.

    b. Yes. Paying off the loan will increase the loan available by $15,000.

    c. Yes. Paying off the loan will increase the loan available by $5,000.

    d. No. He is not permitted to pay off the loan.

QUICK QUIZ EXPLANATIONS

QUICK QUIZ 7.1
1. False. Pension plans typically distribute retirement benefits through an annuity payable for the remainder of the participant's life. The plan may provide for a lump-sum distribution option.
2. True.
3. True.

QUICK QUIZ 7.2
1. False. Neither direct nor indirect rollovers may consist of any distribution from a qualified plan that is one of a series of substantially equal periodic payments. In addition, distributions on account of a required minimum distribution and hardship withdrawals may not be rolled over into another qualified plan or IRA.
2. False. Distributions from qualified plans are generally taxed as ordinary income, but when a distribution is considered a lump-sum distribution, the distribution may qualify for 10-year forward averaging, pre-1974 capital gain treatment, or Net Unrealized Appreciation (NUA).
3. False. A distribution pursuant to a QDRO that is not deposited into an IRA or other qualified plan will be subjected to tax at ordinary income rates on the distribution.

QUICK QUIZ 7.3
1. False. If the vested accrued benefit is less than or equal to $20,000, then a loan is permitted up to the lesser of $10,000 or the vested accrued benefit. Therefore, if an individual had an account balance of $17,000 with a vested accrued benefit of $15,000, he would be eligible for a loan of $10,000, which is greater than 50 percent of the account balance.
2. False. Although loans from qualified plans must generally be repaid within five years, the five-year repayment rule does not apply to loans that are used for the purchase of a principal residence.
3. False. Most plan documents require that loans be repaid upon termination of employment; however, this is not a requirement under the law.

QUICK QUIZ 7.4
1. True.
2. False. The 10 percent penalty exception applies if the participant separates from service after age 55. There is no exception for situations where the participant separates from service before age 55, but waits until age 55 to receive distributions.

QUICK QUIZ 7.5
1. False. The first minimum distribution must be made by April 1 of the year after the year in which the participant attains the age of 70½ unless the participant is still employed by the plan sponsor, in which case the first minimum distribution must be taken by April 1 of the year after the participant terminates service with the plan sponsor.
2. True.
3. True.

QUICK QUIZ EXPLANATIONS

QUICK QUIZ 7.6

1. False. A stretch IRA is the concept of minimizing distributions from an IRA such that the assets grow unimpaired from income tax for as long as possible.
2. True.
3. True.

QUICK QUIZ 7.7

1. False. The Supreme Court ruled in Clark v. Ramaker that inherited IRAs are not retirement plans and therefore, are subject to claims of creditors in bankruptcy.
2. True.
3. False. A see-through trust is a beneficiary of a custodial IRA, whereas a trusteed IRA is the IRA itself, as well as being a trust.

CHAPTER

8

INSTALLATION, ADMINISTRATION, AND TERMINATION OF QUALIFIED PLANS

LEARNING OBJECTIVES

After reading this chapter, you should be able to:
1. Use the plan selection process to identify the best plans for a business to adopt.
2. Understand the requirements for establishing a qualified plan.
3. Describe the documents that must be provided to employees and other interested parties related to qualified plans.
4. Compare the investment options available to a plan sponsor.
5. Determine the requirements for a self-employed plan participant.
6. Discuss prohibited transactions and the penalties for engaging in such a transaction.
7. Understand the various Form 5500 filing requirements for qualified plans.
8. Calculate the maximum contribution for a self-employed plan participant.
9. Identify the types of qualified plan terminations.
10. Determine the implications for assets reverting back to the plan sponsor upon plan termination.

INTRODUCTION

In today's economic environment, retirement plans are an essential component of the overall compensation package of an employer and are designed to attract, retain, and reward talented employees. The selection of an appropriate qualified plan can be both time-consuming and expensive. Depending on the plan selected, numerous initial and continuing requirements must be met to ensure that the plan retains its qualified, and thus tax-advantaged, status. Once a plan is established, annual testing, yearly contributions, and yearly filings may also be required. Special rules also apply to plan amendments and terminations of qualified plans when needed. This chapter will discuss plan selection, installation, administration, and amending and terminating a qualified plan.

QUALIFIED PLAN SELECTION

Selecting a qualified plan begins with the consideration of a number of relevant issues including business, financial, and sometimes personal goals. Other issues that impact plan selection are the employee census, employee turnover, funding requirements, philosophy about employee savings, and the cost to adopt, implement, and maintain the plan. The retirement plan decision-makers in a small company are usually the owners, while executive management and human resources management usually make the decisions for a large company. Decision-makers are often assisted in plan selection by qualified plan experts who help the decision-makers consider the many factors at issue when selecting a plan. For large companies, the decisions are usually based on the business objectives of the company, but for small or closely held businesses, plan choice is often based on both the owner's business and personal objectives.

BUSINESS OBJECTIVES

The first step in plan selection is to determine the business objectives for establishing a qualified plan. Although they can vary, the typical objectives of a large company include being competitive in the labor market by offering a qualified plan that fits within an overall compensation package. For a smaller company, the ability to assist the small business owner with tax-deferred savings is frequently a primary personal objective. Other common reasons companies establish qualified plans are to attract, reward, and retain employees, assist employees in saving for retirement, or simply to benefit the employees through the adoption of a tax-advantaged plan.

KEY CONCEPTS ✓

1. What business and personal issues should be considered when making a qualified plan selection?

2. What is an employee census and why is it important?

3. What are the general characteristics of qualified plans?

STEPS IN QUALIFIED RETIREMENT PLAN SELECTION

EXHIBIT 8.1

Concept Summary

1. Establish the objectives for the plan (Sample Objectives).
   - To benefit owners of a small businesses
   - To benefit all employees
   - To benefit select employees
   - To attract, retain, or reward employees
   - To encourage early retirement
   - To provide a tax-advantaged benefit
2. Prepare an employee census to identify the beneficiaries of various plans and the financial impact of alternative plans on the employer sponsor.
3. Identify the types of plans that can meet both the qualitative and quantitative objectives.
4. Assess each plan's financial characteristics:
   - Contribution costs
   - Costs of administration
   - Flexibility of contributions
   - Burden of investment risks
   - Necessity of mandatory funding
5. Select plan.

EMPLOYEE CENSUS

An important first step to consider when selecting a qualified plan is to prepare an employee census. If the primary goal of having a plan is to simply provide a savings vehicle such as a 401(k) plan, the **employee census** may not be important. However, if the purpose of the plan is to benefit the small business owner, the employee census is essential. The census will identify each employee, their age, compensation, number of years of employment, and any ownership interest. Each element of the census is important to consider because plans can be structured to benefit highly compensated employees, nonhighly compensated employees, older or younger employees, employees who have a certain length of service, a group of employees, or some mix of these employees. The census helps to identify which employees will benefit (and to what extent) from using various possible types of plans. In addition to a current census, a review of employee turnover is essential to plan selection because such a review can help determine the appropriate vesting schedules and how to deal with forfeitures resulting from employee termination.

EXAMPLE 8.1

SAMPLE EMPLOYEE CENSUS				
Employee	**Age**	**Compensation**	**Ownership Interest**	**Length of Service**
Alex	30	$200,000	100%	10 Years
Becky	35	$35,000	0	5 Years
Cameron	30	$30,000	0	1 Year
Derrick	30	$30,000	0	1 Year
Total		**$295,000**	**100%**	
Expected Turnover 0 for Alex and Becky and by year 3 for Cameron and Derrick.				

Consider the Sample Employee Census above. Suppose Alex (the owner) wanted to establish a plan to benefit all employees who would save for their own retirement. He should consider a 401(k) plan with an employer match of up to 3% of covered compensation. Alex could simply reduce future compensation raises by 3% and thus have a net zero cost of funding the plan. The 401(k) employer match is also discretionary, leaving the sponsor with cash flow flexibility.

Suppose an additional objective was to benefit only those who are employed by the company for at least three years. Because the plan utilizes an employer match, the longest cliff vesting schedules Alex could use is a 3-year cliff vesting schedule. This would still only require Alex to provide a vested match to those employees who remained employed for three years.

If Alex was much older than Becky, Cameron, and Derrick, he might consider using an age-weighted profit sharing plan, so that most of the contributions and benefits would be contributed to the plan on his behalf.

An employee census is an essential tool in determining which employees will benefit and how much they will benefit using various plans. The employee census is then used to help select the best plan to accomplish the goals of the company and its owners.

CASH FLOW CONSIDERATIONS

The decision maker should always consider the company's financial stability and the predictability of its cash flows prior to plan selection. The company's cash flows dictate how committed the company can be with regard to mandatory contributions, such as those required for pension plans. For example, if cash flows fluctuate widely from year to year, it is probably not prudent to adopt a pension plan because of the **mandatory funding requirement**. In the case of fluctuating cash flows, it is more prudent to select some type of qualified profit sharing plan because profit sharing plans have **discretionary contributions** each year. However, if cash flows are stable and predictable, then the company may want to consider either pension or profit sharing plans.

ADMINISTRATION COSTS

When a company implements a qualified plan, there are numerous costs associated with adopting and administering the plan. Establishing a plan generally requires an advisor or retirement plan expert to assist the company in selecting and adopting the plan. In addition, once the plan has been adopted, the company must pay for the actual funding of the plan if the plan includes employer contributions. If the plan is large and has many participants, the sponsor may need to hire employees to administer the plan during the year and file the necessary compliance forms or outsource this function to an outside vendor such as a **third party administrator** (TPA).

QUICK QUIZ 8.1

1. Plan selection should only focus on the needs of the company and should never focus on the needs of the small business owner as this would be a conflict of interest.
   a. True
   b. False

2. While an employee census is generally essential, it may not be critical if the only objective is to provide a savings vehicle.
   a. True
   b. False

3. An employer with fluctuating cash flows will generally choose a pension plan.
   a. True
   b. False

False, True, False.

A company's ability to afford such costs impacts the type of plan chosen. For example, profit sharing plans are often very easy to set up with many prototype plans available, have discretionary contributions and minimal annual testing; therefore, they are relatively inexpensive to establish and maintain. Adding a 401(k) feature (**CODA**) to a profit sharing plan increases the cost slightly because of the annual **ADP** and **ACP** testing (as discussed in Chapter 5) and the matching contributions. The testing and its associated cost could be avoided by adopting a safe harbor 401(k) plan, which does not require certain nondiscrimination tests (such as ADP and ACP testing).

Stock bonus plans and ESOPs often require annual valuations of the stock of the business by a valuation expert, making the administration of this type of plan more expensive than a simple profit sharing plan. Defined benefit plans require PBGC insurance premiums, and actuaries are needed annually to determine plan contributions, making the defined benefit plan potentially the most expensive plan to adopt. Large companies may be able to absorb the substantial costs associated with a defined benefit plan, while small companies may be more sensitive to controlling plan costs. However, today there is a trend for large companies to convert defined benefit plans to cash balance pension plans in an attempt to reduce certain costs and for newer companies to avoid defined benefit plans altogether. This illustrates the need for consideration to be given to plan costs for adoption and administration during plan selection.

EXHIBIT 8.2	COMMON PLAN ADMINISTRATION COSTS

- Consultation and plan set-up/implementation expenses
- Funding
- Recordkeeping
- Administration
- Nondiscrimination Testing
- Reporting/Disclosure to Participants (including statements and summary annual reports)
- IRS/Department of Labor Reporting (Form 5500)
- Fiduciary Duties (such as fulfilling ERISA §404(c) requirements with education programs and enrollment meetings)

EXHIBIT 8.3	TPA OR BUNDLED PROVIDERS' FUNCTIONS

- Trustee Duties
- Recordkeeping
- Administration
- Investment Management
- Reporting and Disclosure

OWNER'S BUSINESS AND PERSONAL OBJECTIVES

If the company is a small or closely held company, then the owner's personal and business objectives are critical in plan selection. Small business owners typically want to reduce their current taxes and save for their own financial future. For example, key owners of small companies generally want a majority of plan benefits for themselves and less for the rank-and-file employees, especially those who do not stay with the employer for a long period. The owners may select a plan that will meet this need or use various techniques to modify the plan to primarily benefit owners and/or key employees. Since these are the decision-makers that advisors will be working with, it is important to understand and try to achieve their goals.

QUALIFIED PLAN SUMMARY OF CHARACTERISTICS

EXHIBIT
8.4

Qualified Plan	Who Generally Contributes	Mandatory Funding	Investment Risk	Company Stock %[1]	Permits Soc. Sec. Integration	Required Expert	Who is Generally Favored?[2]	QJSA / QOSA/ QPSA[3]
PENSION PLANS								
Defined Benefit Pension Plan	ER	Yes	ER	≤ 10%	Yes	Actuary and Pension Expert	Older Age Entrants	Yes
Cash Balance Pension Plan	ER	Yes	ER	≤ 10%	Yes	Actuary and Pension Expert	Younger Persons	Yes
Target Benefit Pension Plan	ER	Yes	EE	≤ 10%	Yes	Actuary once and Pension Expert	Older Age Entrants	Yes
Money Purchase Pension Plan	ER	Yes	EE	≤ 10%	Yes	None[4]	Younger Persons	Yes
PROFIT SHARING PLANS								
Profit Sharing Plan	ER	No	EE	≤ 100%	Yes	None[2]	Highly Compensated and Younger Persons	No
Stock Bonus Plan	ER	No	EE	≤ 100%	Yes	Valuation Specialist and Pension Expert	Highly Compensated and Long Length of Service	No
ESOP	ER	No	EE	≤ 100%	No	Valuation Specialist and Pension Expert	Highly Compensated and Long Length of Service	No
401(k) Plan/ 401(k) Roth Account	EE and ER	No[5]	EE	≤ 100%	No[6]	Pension Expert	Savers and Younger Persons	No
Thrift Plan	EE	No	EE	≤ 100%	Yes	Pension Expert	Savers and Younger Persons	No
Age-Based Profit Sharing Plan	ER	No	EE	≤ 100%	Yes	Pension Expert	Older Highly Compensated	No
New Comparability Plan	ER	No	EE	≤ 100%	Yes	Pension Expert	Owners	No

EE = Employee, ER = Employer

1. Note that as a result of PPA 2006, certain defined contribution plans holding publicly traded employer securities are subject to new diversification requirements, which requires that employees be permitted to diversify 100% of their contributions and 100% of employer contributions after 3 years. See Chapter 3 for more detail.
2. Where younger persons are favored, it is because they benefit from a greater number of compounding periods. However, through cross-testing and other methods, most plans can be structured to benefit the owners and highly compensated employees.
3. Qualified Joint and Survivor Annuity/Qualified Pre-Survivor Annuity.
4. Many prototype plans are available.
5. 401(k) plans may have mandatory funding if there is a matching contribution for a safe harbor plan.
6. If a CODA feature is a part of the profit sharing plan then, the profit sharing plan can be integrated, but not the CODA portion.

PLAN SELECTION APPLICATION

After evaluating each of the above issues, a financial advisor/pension expert can assist the owner or key decision maker in determining which plan suits the owner and the company's needs. The following exhibit summarizes some of the important issues to consider in plan selection.

The following examples demonstrate the plan selection process.

Assume Alex owns a small company with the following employee census information:

EMPLOYEE CENSUS				
Employee	**Age**	**Compensation**	**Ownership**	**Length of Service**
Alex	30	$200,000	100%	10 Years
Becky	35	$35,000	0	5 Years
Cameron	30	$30,000	0	1 Year
Derrick	30	$30,000	0	1 Year
Total		**$295,000**	**100%**	

Assuming the company has sufficient cash flow to fund a plan, the most obvious plan recommendation would be a profit sharing plan. The plan could be integrated with Social Security, thus providing Alex an even greater share of the contributions than a nonintegrated plan. A profit sharing plan would allow a contribution of up to 25% of covered compensation and would help maximize contributions to Alex.

The profit sharing plan could also include a CODA (401(k)) feature if Alex wanted the employees to contribute to the plan. The CODA feature would allow employees to make elective deferrals into the plan. The company could then match employee contributions to encourage employee participation.

Assume instead that Alex is 51 years old and wants to maximize contributions for his own benefit. Since, in this case, Alex is significantly older than the other employees, a defined benefit plan or age-weighted profit sharing plan may be more appropriate than a straight profit sharing plan or an integrated profit sharing plan. Either of these plans would allow for higher contributions on behalf of Alex because of his age. In choosing between a defined benefit and an age-weighted profit sharing plan, Alex is choosing between mandatory funding for the defined benefit plan and discretionary funding for the age-based plan. Also, the costs of maintaining the plans will be quite different because a defined benefit plan requires annual actuarial determinations and a profit sharing plan does not utilize actuaries. Alex will have to compare the advantages and disadvantages of each of the plans in making his decision.

Edward and Fran each own 50% of a small company with the following employee census.

EXAMPLE
8.3

EMPLOYEE CENSUS				
Employee	**Age**	**Compensation**	**Ownership**	**Length of Service**
Edward	55	$300,000	50%	10 Years
Fran	30	$300,000	50%	10 Years
Gerry	35	$30,000	0	1 Year
Harriet	30	$30,000	0	1 Year
Total		**$660,000**	**100%**	

The age difference between Edward and Fran (owners) makes the plan selection slightly more challenging. An age-weighted plan would be beneficial for Edward. However, because Fran is much younger than Edward, such a plan would not equally benefit Fran. Assuming they both wanted to benefit equally and did not want to consider a defined benefit plan, a 401(k) plan would be most appropriate because it would allow them to each receive the maximum contribution up to the annual additions limit ($53,000 for 2016). In addition, the plan could be integrated with Social Security to provide higher benefits for the highly compensated employees, Edward and Fran.

ASSUMPTIONS: WAGE BASE $118,500, BASE RATE 6.00%, 401(k) LIMIT $18,000					
	Edward	**Fran**	**Gerry**	**Harriet**	**Total**
Compensation	$265,000	$265,000	$30,000	$30,000	$590,000
401(k) Deferral	$18,000	$18,000	$10,000	-	$46,000
401(k) Match at 4%	$10,600	$10,600	$1,200	-	$22,400
Integrated Profit Sharing Contribution					
Base	$7,110	$7,110	$1,800	$1,800	$17,820
Excess	$17,141	$17,141	-	-	$34,281
Total	$24,251	$24,251	$1,800	$1,800	$52,101
Total	**$52,851**	**$52,851**	**$13,000**	**$1,800**	**$120,501**
% of Total	**43.9%**	**43.9%**	**10.8%**	**1.5%**	**100%**
Analysis					
Integration Benefit	$8,351	$8,351	-	-	$16,701
Percentage - Total	19.9%	19.9%	43.3%	6.0%	
Percentage - Employee	6.8%	6.8%	33.3%	0.0%	
Percentage - Employer	13.2%	13.2%	10.0%	6.0%	
Total ER Contribution	**$34,851**	**$34,851**	**$3,000**	**$1,800**	**$74,501**
% of Total	**46.8%**	**46.8%**	**4.0%**	**2.4%**	**100%**

The chart above illustrates a safe harbor integrated 401(k) plan. Edward and Fran are almost able to reach their IRC Section 415(c) limit of $53,000 (2016). In addition, Edward could defer even more for his catch up contribution because he is over the age of 50.

The plan requires a 4 percent match, which is available to all employees deferring into the plan. Notice that Gerry receives a matching contribution, while Harriet does not. In addition, the plan provides for an integrated profit-sharing plan contribution. The base percentage of 6 percent has been selected to allow the owners to almost reach their annual additions limit. Notice that the owners are the only two that enjoy the excess benefit. Also notice that 93 to 94 percent of the benefit of the employer contribution is going to the owners.

As an alternative, a new comparability plan would permit them to create classes of employees such that higher contributions were allocated to the owner group and lower contributions were allocated to the rank-and-file group. New comparability plans are discussed in more detail in Chapter 5.

If they were open to considering a defined benefit plan or cash balance plan, Edward and Fran could likely increase the amounts contributed on their behalf significantly without much additional contribution for the other employees.

Irene has been the owner of Irene's Pet Shop for 10 years. She decided to establish a retirement plan for her corporation. She has come to you and indicated that she wants to make all initial contributions to the plan using company stock. She may also want to integrate the plan with Social Security.

Either a qualified profit sharing or stock bonus plan would be an appropriate plan for Irene since she wants to use 100% company stock for the initial and subsequent contributions. Both plans also allow integration with Social Security.

TAXONOMY OF PLAN SELECTION

EXHIBIT
8.5

1. Assume that the sponsor company wants a qualified plan. The sponsor must be willing to comply with the qualified plan requirements, including:
    - Nondiscrimination and broad coverage
    - Eligibility rules
    - Coverage rules
    - Reporting rules
    - Testing rules
    - Disclosure rules
    - Vesting rules
2. Prepare an employee census
3. Determine if (A) mandatory or (B) discretionary funding is appropriate
    A. Mandatory funding:
        - Determine whether investment risk will be borne by the employer or the employee:
            - Employer: Either defined benefit pension plan or cash balance pension plan
                - If the plan favors older age entrants - defined benefit pension plan
                - If the plan favors younger age entrants - cash balance pension plan
            - Employee: Either target benefit pension plan or money purchase pension plan
                - If the employer is willing to endure larger establishment costs - target benefit pension plan
                - If the employer wants low establishment costs - money purchase pension plan
        a. Discretionary funding:
        - If employee contributions to the qualified plan are desired (self reliance - contributory):
            - Pretax: 401(k) Plan
            - After-tax: Thrift Plan/401(k) Roth
        - If only the employer contributes to the qualified plan (noncontributory):
            - Contributions of company stock: profit sharing plan, stock bonus plan, ESOP
            - Test benefits for discrimination rather than contributions (cross-test): Age-based profit sharing plan, new comparability plan
        - If the employer wants low initial costs - profit sharing plan
        - If the employer is willing to pay additional costs - stock bonus plan, ESOP, age-based profit sharing plan, or new comparability plan
        - If the employer wants integration - profit sharing plan or stock bonus plan

EXHIBIT
8.6

PLAN SELECTION FLOW CHART

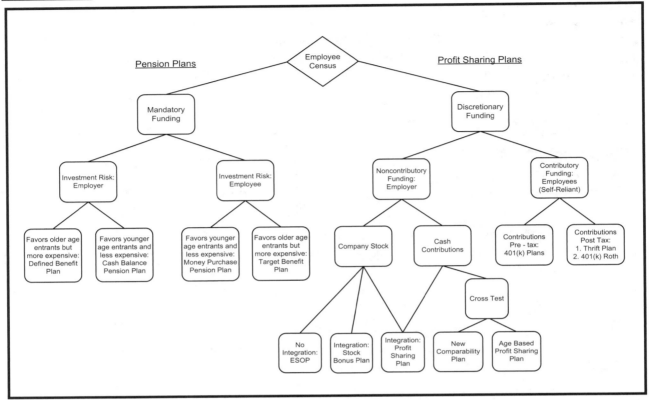

ESTABLISHING A QUALIFIED PLAN

The employer-sponsor is responsible for setting up and maintaining the qualified plan. There are several steps involved in establishing a qualified plan. First, the employer must select and adopt the appropriate plan. Next, the employer must communicate the plan to employees and establish a procedure for funding and administering the plan. Remember that the employer (owner) does not necessarily need to have employees other than himself to establish a qualified plan. A self-employed person who has no other employees can establish a qualified plan.

KEY CONCEPTS

1. What are the requirements for establishing a qualified plan?

2. How and when should employees be notified when a qualified plan is established?

3. Who may manage the qualified plan assets?

ADOPTING A WRITTEN PLAN

A qualified plan must be detailed in a written plan that is adopted by the company. To take an income tax deduction for contributions for a particular tax year, the plan must be adopted by the last day of that particular tax year. In some cases, the company may elect for the plan to have a different tax year than the company.

> If a company is on a calendar year basis, then the plan must be adopted by December 31 of the year in which the deduction is desired. If, instead, the company is on a fiscal year ending August 31, then the plan should be adopted by August 31.

EXAMPLE 8.5

The company can individually design the plan using an **ERISA attorney** (expensive), or the company can use an IRS-approved master or prototype plan (very inexpensive). Once adopted, information about the plan must be communicated in writing to the employees as detailed below.

Master or Prototype Plans

The majority of qualified plans follow standard forms called master or prototype plans. These plans have been pre-approved by the IRS and are available for employers to simply adopt. **Master plans** provide a single trust or custodial account that is jointly used by all adopting employers. **Prototype plans** allow each employer to establish their own separate trust or custodial account. IRS approved master or prototype plans can often be obtained from banks, trade or professional organizations, insurance companies, investment houses, or mutual funds. These organizations will assist the employer by offering them a basic plan and trust document. They will also use an adoption agreement, so that the employer can elect, by checking the box, various options such as participation requirements, vesting schedules, contribution limits, investment options, and conditions for withdrawals.

Individually Designed Plans

If the company has specific needs that are not addressed in a master or prototype plan, or if they so choose, the company can have their own individually drafted plan. However, in order to be considered a qualified plan, the plan must be permanent and for the exclusive benefit of the employees and their beneficiaries. The adopted plan should detail the procedure for amending and identify who can amend the plan should it be necessary.

Individually designed plans are less common because of the cost to design and draft and because of the wide availability of prototype plans. While advance IRS approval is not required to adopt an individually drafted plan, approval can and usually is sought from the IRS. This approval is accomplished by requesting a determination letter and paying the required fee. Creating an individually designed plan usually requires the services of an ERISA attorney, making the plan much more expensive than prototype plans.

| EXHIBIT 8.7 | TYPES OF PLANS |

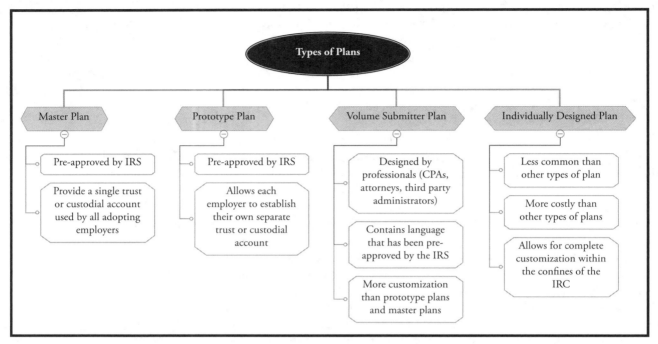

Volume Submitter Plan

A volume submitter plan falls in between a prototype plan and an individually designed plan. It is a plan that is designed by a professional, such as an attorney, CPA or third party administrator, which contains language that has been pre-approved by the IRS. This type of plan allows for more customization than a standard prototype plan, but is generally much less costly than an individualized plan.

Determination Letters

Determination letters may be used when a retirement plan is adopted, amended, or terminated. They may be filed in advance of the plan being adopted or immediately thereafter, usually by filing Form 5300. While they are not required in any of these circumstances, they are useful to the plan sponsor because they allow the plan sponsor to rely on the response from the IRS. If the IRS has any issues with the plan design, the plan can be amended immediately to ensure compliance.

Determination letters are usually accompanied by the appropriate fee. The fee is based on the type of transaction involved. Some small employers may be exempt from paying the fee if they meet certain criteria. The fee is determined on IRS Form 8717.

Determination letters are generally narrow in scope and address particular issues. For example, a favorable determination letter may be received that indicates that the plan meets the qualified plan rules, but the determination letter may or may not verify that certain types of contributions to the plan are income tax deductible. Just because a plan receives a favorable determination letter does not mean that it cannot lose its qualified status if it does not continue to comply with provisions of the plan document as well as with the IRC and ERISA. It is critical to understand that the sponsor must follow the provisions established in the plan document. It is also equally important that a plan be amended to reflect current law so that it continues to comply and does not risk losing its qualified status.

FORM 8717: USER FEE FOR EMPLOYEE PLAN DETERMINATION LETTER REQUESTED

EXHIBIT 8.8

Form **8717** (Rev. August 2014) Department of the Treasury Internal Revenue Service	**User Fee for Employee Plan Determination Letter Request** ▶ Attach to determination letter application. ▶ For the latest information about this form, go to *www.irs.gov/form8717*.	For IRS Use Only	OMB No. 1545–1772 Amount paid _____

1 Name of plan sponsor (employer if single-employer plan)

2 Sponsor's employer identification number	**3** Plan number	**4** Plan name

Caution. *If you qualify for the exemption from user fees for small business employers, complete only the certification below (see the instructions on page 2 for details). For all other applications, leave the certification blank and check the appropriate box in column B of line 5.*

Certification

I certify that the application for a determination letter on the qualified status of the plan listed above meets the conditions for exemption from user fees described in section 7528(b)(2)(B) of the Internal Revenue Code.

Sign Here ▶ _____ Date ▶ _____

Type or print name and title ▶ _____

		Fee Schedule	
Form Submitted		**A**	**B** no Demo 5 and no Demo 6:
5a	**Form 5300:**		☐ $ 2,500
b	**Form 5307:**		☐ $ 500
c	**Form 5310:**		☐ $ 2,000
d			
e	Multiple employer plans (**Form 5300**):		
	(1) 2 to 10 Forms 5300 submitted		☐ **(1)** $ 3,000
	(2) 11 to 99 Forms 5300 submitted		☐ **(2)** $ 3,000
	(3) 100 to 499 Forms 5300 submitted		☐ **(3)** $ 15,000
	(4) Over 499 Forms 5300 submitted		☐ **(4)** $ 15,000
f	Multiple employer plans (**Form 5310**):		
	(1) 2 to 10 employers maintaining the plan		☐ **(1)** $ 3,000
	(2) 11 to 99 employers maintaining the plan		☐ **(2)** $ 3,000
	(3) 100 to 499 employers maintaining the plan		☐ **(3)** $ 15,000
	(4) Over 499 employers maintaining the plan		☐ **(4)** $ 15,000
g	Reserved		
	(1a)		
	(1b)		
	(2a)		
	(2b)		
	(3)		
	(4)		
h	Reserved		
	(1a)		
	(1b)		
	(2)		
	(3)		
	(4a)		
	(4b)		
	(5)		
	(6)		
	(7)		
i	Form 5316 (Group trusts)		☐ $ 1,000

Attach Check or Money Order Here

Cat. No. 64727O   Form **8717** (Rev. 8-2014)

EXHIBIT 8.9

SAMPLE PLAN ADOPTION AGREEMENT

Sample Plan Adoption Agreement
401(k) Plan

Employer Information

Name: _____   Telephone: _____
Address: _____   EIN: _____
_____   Plan Administrator: _____

Plan Information

Name of Plan: _____

Plan Number: _____   Plan Year: ❏ Calendar year   ❏ Fiscal year ending

Effective Date: ❏ January 1, _____; or ❏ _____ (For initial plan year enter a date between January 1 and October 1.)
   ❏ This is a restatement of a prior plan known as:
   The restated effective date of the plan is:

Coverage Information

The eligibility requirements for participation in the Plan will be:

1. Eligibility Service Requirement (check one)
   ❏   No eligibility service requirement.
   ❏   Six months of employment. (If this option is selected, an Employee will not be required to complete any specified number of
        Hours of Service in the six-month period.)
   ❏   One year of service.

2. Age Requirement
   ❏   No minimum age requirement
   ❏   _____ Years (cannot be more than 21).

The requirements listed above are (check one):
   ❏   Applicable to all Employees.
   ❏   Applicable to all Employees except those Employees employed on the Effective Date. Such Employees will participate immediately.
        All other Employees will need to satisfy the requirements listed above.

Employer Contribution Information

The Employer shall contribute on behalf of each Participant for each Plan Year in accordance with one of the following as indicated in the
Summary Plan Description:
   ❏   Matching Contributions in the amount of the Participant's Elective Deferral up to 4%.
   ❏   Nonelective Contribution of 3% of each Participant's Compensation.

Vesting Information

A participant's vested interest in his or her Employer Contribution Account will be:
   ❏   100% immediately vested at all times.
   ❏   100% vested after _____ Years of Service (not to exceed 3 years). A Participant will be 0% vested prior to completing this period.
   ❏

Years of Service	Vested Percentage
1	0%
2	20%
3	40%
4	60%
5	80%
6	100%

Signatures

Employer: _____   Trustee (optional): _____
By (Authorized Signature): _____   By (Authorized Signature): _____
Date: _____   Date: _____

NOTIFYING ELIGIBLE EMPLOYEES

Information regarding the qualified plan must be distributed to employees who might be eligible for the plan. In addition, the information must be furnished to the ineligible employees working at the same facility. This information helps to inform the employee of his rights under ERISA and the qualified retirement plan.

Before the IRS can issue a determination letter on the qualified status of a retirement plan, the employer must provide the IRS with satisfactory evidence that it has notified the persons who qualify as interested parties. **Interested parties** with regard to notification are present employees who are eligible to participate in the plan and present employees who are not eligible for the plan but whose principal place of employment is the same as the principal place of employment of any employee who is eligible to participate.

> Loupili company wants to establish a qualified retirement plan that requires one year of service to participate. Loupili has two offices, one on the north side of town called the North office and one on the south side of town called the South office. The North office has 32 employees, and the South office has 10 employees. The North office has been operational for several years, and half of its employees are eligible to participate in the qualified retirement plan. The South office was recently opened, and none of the employees have met the service requirement to be eligible. Loupili must notify all of the employees in the North office because some of them are eligible and the others work in the same office as eligible individuals. The employees in the South office do not need to be notified at this time because none of them are eligible for the plan.

EXAMPLE 8.6

Proper advance notice can be made in person, via e-mail or mail, or by posting a notice in a location generally used for posting notices to employees. If notification is made to the eligible employees in person or by posting, then the notice must be given between seven and 21 days before the determination application is mailed to the IRS. If the notice is mailed to the eligible employees, then it must be mailed at least ten days before, but not more than 24 days before, the determination application is mailed to the IRS.[1] Below is a sample form taken from Revenue Procedure 2011-6 that can be used to notify employees.

---

1. Rev. Proc. 2011-6.

EXHIBIT
8.10

SAMPLE NOTICE TO INTERESTED PARTIES

1. Notice To:_____[describe class or classes of interested parties]

An application is to be made to the Internal Revenue Service for an advance determination on the qualification of the following employee pension benefit plan:

2. _____
        (name of plan)

3. _____
        (plan number)

4. _____
        (name and address of applicant)

5. _____
        (applicant EIN)

6. _____
        (name and address of plan administrator)

7. The application will be filed on _____ for an advance determination as to whether the plan meets the qualification requirements of § 401 or 403(a) of the Internal Revenue Code of 1986, with respect to the plan's _____ [initial qualification, amendment, termination, or partial termination]. The application will be filed with:

      EP Determinations
      Internal Revenue Service
      P.O. Box 12192
      Covington, KY 41012-0192

8. The employees eligible to participate under the plan are: _____

9. The Internal Revenue Service _____[has/has not] previously issued a determination letter with respect to the qualification of this plan.

RIGHTS OF INTERESTED PARTIES

10. You have the right to submit to EP Determinations, at the above address, either individually or jointly with other interested parties, your comments as to whether this plan meets the qualification requirements of the Internal Revenue Code.

    You may instead, individually or jointly with other interested parties, request the Department of Labor to submit, on your behalf, comments to EP Determinations regarding qualification of the plan. If the Department declines to comment on all or some of the matters you raise, you may, individually, or jointly if your request was made to the Department jointly, submit your comments on these matters directly to EP Determinations.

REQUESTS FOR COMMENTS BY THE DEPARTMENT OF LABOR

11. The Department of Labor may not comment on behalf of interested parties unless requested to do so by the lessor of 10 employees or 10 percent of the employees who qualify as interested parties. The number of persons needed for the Department to comment with respect to this plan is _____. If you request the Department to comment, your request must be in writing and must specify the matters upon which comments are requested, and must also include:

    (1) the information contained in items 2 through 5 of this Notice; and

    (2) the number of persons needed for the Department to comment.

A request to the Department to comment should be addressed as follows:

> Deputy Assistant Secretary
> Employee Benefits Security Administration
> ATTN: 3001 Comment Request
> U.S. Department of Labor,
> 200 Constitution Avenue, N.W.
> Washington, D.C. 20210

COMMENTS TO THE INTERNAL REVENUE SERVICE

12. Comments submitted by you to EP Determinations must be in writing and received by them by _____. However, if there are matters that you request the Department of Labor to comment upon on your behalf, and the Department declines, you may submit comments on these matters to EP Determinations to be received by them within 15 days from the time the Department notifies you that it will not comment on a particular matter, or by _____, whichever is later, but not after _____. A request to the Department to comment on your behalf must be received by it by _____ if you wish to preserve your right to comment on a matter upon which the Department declines to comment, or by_____ if you wish to waive that right.

ADDITIONAL INFORMATION

13. Detailed instructions regarding the requirements for notification of interested parties may be found in sections 17 and 18 of Rev. Proc. 2011–6. Additional information concerning this application (including, where applicable, an updated copy of the plan and related trust; the application for determination; any additional documents dealing with the application that have submitted to the Service; and copies of section 17 of Rev . Proc. 2011–6 are available at _____ during the hours of _____ for inspection and copying. (There is a nominal charge for copying and/or mailing.)

The employer is required to provide, free of charge, a summary of the details of the qualified retirement plan, called a **Summary Plan Description**,[2] to employees, participants, and beneficiaries under pay status (receiving benefits). The summary must be furnished within 90 days after the person becomes a participant, or first receives benefits as a beneficiary, or within 120 days after the plan is established under ERISA. The Summary Plan Description explains in plain language what the plan provides and how it operates. It provides information on when an employee can begin to participate in the plan, how service and benefits are calculated, when benefits become vested, when and in what form benefits are paid, and how to file a claim for benefits. The Summary Plan Description is needed because the plan document is lengthy and has substantial legal jargon that many employees may not understand. The Summary Plan Description must be re-issued every 10 years (the interval decreases to five years if the plan was amended).

The employer should ensure that the Summary Plan Description accurately reflects what is included in the actual plan to avoid potential liability. Many employers use disclaimers in the Summary Plan Description that state that in the event that the Summary Plan Description is different than the plan document, the plan document controls the provisions of the qualified plan. This strategy has been effective for some companies in the past; however, it has and will continue to be a source of litigation until it is legislatively decided.

The employer is also required to provide the plan participants notices of any plan amendments or changes. This notice can be provided either through a revised Summary Plan Description or in a separate document, called a **Summary of Material Modifications**. This document must be given to participants free of charge within 210 days after the end of the plan year in which a change is adopted and applies when there are substantive changes in the plan.

---

2. ERISA §1022.

In addition to the Summary Plan Description, the employer must automatically provide the participants, free of charge, a copy of the plan's Summary Annual Report each year. The Summary Annual Report is a summary of the annual financial report that the plan files with the Department of Labor each year (Form 5500 discussed later in this chapter). Participants may also ask the plan administrator for a copy of the plan's annual report in its entirety if they wish to learn more about the plan.

<table>
<tr><td>

EXHIBIT
8.11

</td><td>

SAMPLE SUMMARY ANNUAL REPORT

</td></tr>
</table>

Summary Annual Report
ABC Company Defined Contribution Retirement Plan

This is a summary of the annual report for the **ABC Company Defined Contribution Retirement Plan** EIN XX-XXXXXXX, for the period January 1, 2014 through December 31, 2014. The annual report has been filed with the Pension and Welfare Benefits Administration, U.S. Department of Labor, as required under the Employee Retirement Income Security Act of 1974 (ERISA).

Basic Financial Statement

Benefits under the plan are provided by trust and insurance. Plan expenses were $XX,XXX,XXX. These expenses included $XX,XXX,XXX in administrative expenses and $XX,XXX,XXX in benefits paid to participants and beneficiaries. A total of XX,XXX persons were participants in or beneficiaries of the plan at the end of the plan year, although not all of these persons had yet earned the right to receive benefits.

The value of the plan assets, after subtracting liabilities of the plan was $XXX,XXX,XXX as of December 31, 20 0, compared to $XXX,XXX,XXX as of January 1, 20 0. During the plan year, the plan experienced a decrease in its net assets of $XX,XXX,XXX.

This decrease included unrealized depreciation in the value of plan assets; that is, the difference between the value of the plan's assets at the end of the year and the value of those assets at the beginning of the year. The plan had a total negative income of $X,XXX,XXX, including employer contributions of $X,XXX,XXX, realized losses of $X,XXX,XXX from the sale of assets, and negative net earnings from investments of $X,XXX,XXX (which includes unrealized losses on assets).

Minimum Funding Standards

Enough money was contributed to the plan to keep it funded in accordance with the minimum funding standards of ERISA.

Your Rights To Additional Information

You have the right to receive a copy of the full annual report, or any part thereof, on request. The following items are included in the report:
1. an accountant's report;
2. assets held for investment;
3. financial information; and
4. insurance information.

To obtain a copy of the full annual report, or any part thereof, write or call ABC Company, 123 Lovers Lane, Anytown, USA, telephone number (555) 555-2004. The charge to cover copying will be 25 cents per page or any part thereof.

You also have the right to receive from the plan administrator, on request and at no charge, a statement of the assets and liabilities of the plan and accompanying notes, or a statement of income and expenses of the plan and accompanying notes, or both. If you request a copy of the full annual report from the plan administrator, these two statements and accompanying notes will be included as part of that report. The charge to cover copying costs given above does not include a charge for the copying of these portions of the report because these portions are furnished without charge.

You also have the legally protected right to examine the annual report at ABC Company, 123 Lovers Lane, Anytown, USA, telephone number (555) 555-2004 and at the U.S. Department of Labor in Washington, D.C., or to obtain a copy from the U.S. Department of Labor upon payment of copying costs. Requests to the Department should be addressed to: Public Disclosure Room, Pension and Welfare Benefit Administration, Department of Labor, 200 Constitution Avenue, N.W., Washington, D.C. 20210.

SOURCES OF PLAN INFORMATION[3]

EXHIBIT
8.12

Document	Type of Information	To Whom	When
Summary Plan Description (SPD):	Primary vehicle for informing participants and beneficiaries about their plan and how it operates. Must be written for average participant and be sufficiently comprehensive to apprise covered persons of their benefits, rights, and obligations under the plan. Must accurately reflect the plan's contents as of the date not earlier than 120 days prior to the date the SPD is disclosed. See 29 CFR §§2520.102-2 and 2520.102-3 for style, format, and content requirements.	Participants and those pension plan beneficiaries receiving benefits. (Also see "Plan Documents" below for persons with the right to obtain SPD upon request). See 29 CFR §2520.102-2(c) for provisions on foreign language assistance when a certain portion of plan participants are literate only in the same non-English language.	Automatically to participants within 90 days of becoming covered by the plan and to pension plan beneficiaries within 90 days after first receiving benefits. However, a plan has 120 days after becoming subject to ERISA to distribute the SPD. Updated SPD must be furnished every 5 years if changes made to SPD information or plan is amended. Otherwise must be furnished every 10 years. See 29 CFR §2520.104b-2.
Summary of Material Modification (SMM)	Describes material modifications to a plan and changes in the information required to be in the SPD. Distribution of updated SPD satisfies this requirement. See 29 CFR §2520.104b-3.	Participants and those pension plan beneficiaries receiving benefits. (Also see "Plan Documents" below for persons with the right to obtain SMM upon request).	Automatically to participants and pension plan beneficiaries receiving benefits; not later than 210 days after the end of the plan year in which the change is adopted.
Summary Annual Report (SAR)	Narrative summary of the Form 5500. See 29 CFR §2520.104b-10(d) for prescribed format.	Participants and those pension plan beneficiaries receiving benefits. For plan years beginning after December 31, 2007, the SAR is no longer required for defined benefit pension plans, which now instead provide the annual funding notice (see below).	Automatically to participants and pension plan beneficiaries receiving benefits within 9 months after end of plan year, or 2 months after due date for filing Form 5500 (with approved extension).
Plan Documents	The plan administrator must furnish copies of certain documents upon written request and must have copies available for examination. The documents include the latest updated SPD, latest Form 5500, trust agreement, and other instruments under which the plan is established or operated.	Participants and beneficiaries. Also see 29 CFR §2520.104a-8 regarding the Department's authority to request documents.	Copies must be furnished no later than 30 days after a written request. Plan administrator must make copies available at its principal office and certain other locations as specified in 29 CFR §2520.104b-1(b).

3. Reporting and Disclosure Guide for Employee Benefit Plans, U.S. Department of Labor, September 2014.

Document	Type of Information	To Whom	When
Periodic Pension Benefit Statement	Content of statements varies depending on the type of plan. In general, all statements must indicate total benefits and total nonforfeitable pension benefits, if any, which have accrued, or earliest date on which benefits become nonforfeitable. Benefit statements for an individual account plan must also provide the value of each investment to which assets in the individual account have been allocated.	Participants and beneficiaries.	In general, at least once each quarter for individual account plans that permit participants to direct their investments; at least once each year, in the case of individual account plans that do not permit participants to direct their investments; and at least once every three years in the case of defined benefit plans or, in the alternative, defined benefit plans can satisfy this requirement if at least once each year the administrator provides notice of the availability of the pension benefit statement and the ways to obtain such statement. In addition, the plan administrator must furnish a benefit statement to a participant or beneficiary upon written request, limited to one request during any 12-month period.
§404(c) Plan Disclosures	Investment-related and certain other disclosures for participant-directed individual account plans described in 29 CFR §2550.404c-1, including blackout notice for participant-directed individual account plans described in ERISA §404(c)(1)(A)(ii), as described below.	Participants or beneficiaries, as applicable.	Certain information should be furnished to participants or beneficiaries before the time when investment instructions are to be made; certain information must be furnished upon request.
Notice of Blackout Period for Individual Account Plans	Notification of any period of more than 3 consecutive business days when there is a temporary suspension, limitation or restriction under an individual account plan on directing or diversifying plan assets, obtaining loans, or obtaining distributions.	Participants and beneficiaries of individual account plans affected by such blackout periods and issuers of affected employer securities held by the plan.	Generally at least 30 days but not more than 60 days advance notice. See ERISA §101(i) and 29 CFR §2520.101-3 for further information on the notice requirement.

http://www.dol.gov/ebsa/pdf/rdguide.pdf

QUALIFIED TRUST

The assets of the qualified plan must be placed in a qualified trust or a custodial account.[4] IRC §401(a) describes the specific requirements for a qualified trust. Generally, a **qualified trust** is a trust established or organized in the United States that is maintained by an employer for the exclusive benefit of the employer's employees. The trust must distribute assets to employees and not discriminate against certain employees. **Custodial Accounts** are generally maintained by a bank or other financial institution.

401(a) SUMMARY OF QUALIFIED TRUST[5]

EXHIBIT 8.13

- The trust must be established or organized in the United States and maintained at all times as a domestic trust in the United States.
- The trust must be part of a pension, profit-sharing, or stock bonus plan established by an employer for the exclusive benefit of his employees or their beneficiaries.
- The trust must be formed for the purpose of distributing to the employees or their beneficiaries the corpus and income of the fund accumulated by the trust in accordance with the plan.
- It must be impossible under the trust instrument at any time before the satisfaction of all liabilities with respect to employees and their beneficiaries under the trust, for any part of the corpus or income to be used for, or diverted to, purposes other than for the exclusive benefit of the employees or their beneficiaries.
- The trust must be part of a plan that benefits prescribed percentages of the employees or which benefits such employees as qualify under a classification set up by the employer and found by the Commissioner of the IRS not to be discriminatory in favor of certain specified classes of employees.
- The trust must be part of a plan under which contributions or benefits do not discriminate in favor of certain specified classes of employees.
- The trust must be part of a plan that provides certain nonforfeitable rights.
- If the trust forms part of a pension plan, the plan must provide that forfeitures must not be applied to increase the benefits any employee would receive under such plan.
- The trust must, if the plan benefits any self-employed individual who is an owner-employee, satisfy the additional requirements for qualification.

INVESTING PLAN ASSETS

Investing plan assets is a critical element of overall plan management. Plan assets will either be managed by the plan sponsor (or an asset management firm hired by the plan sponsor) or individually by the plan participants. In many cases, the type of plan and who retains the investment risk will dictate whether the plan assets are managed by the plan sponsor or self-directed by the plan participants. Defined benefit plan sponsors are responsible for funding a determined retirement benefit for plan participants based upon a specific formula and therefore retain the investment risk. As a result, the sponsor will generally hire an outside asset management firm to

4. IRC §401(a).
5. IRC §401(a) summarized.

invest the plan assets in such a way as to fund the pension liabilities over time. Cash balance pension plans function in a similar manner to defined benefit plans, and the assets are generally managed in a similar function.

Defined contribution plan participants bear the investment risk for the assets in their accounts. Despite this, plan sponsors may choose to manage the plan assets or hire an outside asset management firm to manage the assets for the plan participants.

Plan sponsors are generally considered fiduciaries of qualified plans. Being classified as a fiduciary requires a certain level of responsibility and prudence. Employers and plan sponsors have attempted to shift some or all of the fiduciary responsibility from the sponsor to the employees following the guidelines under ERISA §404(c).[6]

Even when plan sponsors choose to shift the management responsibility of the investment assets to the plan participants, the plan sponsor still retains certain responsibilities over the choices and alternative investments available to the participants.

Retirement plan sponsors must provide a broad range of investment choices for participants to manage their retirement assets. A plan must offer a broad range of investment alternatives (at least three) that are sufficient to provide participants or beneficiaries with a reasonable opportunity to materially affect the potential return on amounts in his individual account. Generally, a plan will provide at least one stock investment option, one bond investment option, and one cash or money market type investment option. This combination of security options allows an investor to create relatively efficient portfolios by allocating different amounts to the three funds.

The plan must therefore provide the participants with at least three alternatives to invest in within the retirement plan. These alternatives must meet the following criteria:
- be diversified,
- have materially different risk and return characteristics, which in the aggregate enable the participant or beneficiary to achieve a portfolio with aggregate risk and return characteristics at any point within the range normally appropriate (efficient frontier) for the participant or beneficiary, and

---

6. 29 USC §1104(c)(1)(A)(ii) provides that: no person who is otherwise a fiduciary shall be liable under this part for any loss, or by reason of any breach, which results from such participant's or beneficiary's exercise of control, except that this clause shall not apply in connection with such participant or beneficiary for any blackout period during which the ability of such participant or beneficiary to direct the investment of the assets in his account is suspended by a plan sponsor or fiduciary.

- each alternative, when combined with investments in the other alternatives tends to minimize through diversification the overall risk of a participant's or beneficiary's portfolio.

IRS regulations, directing the types of investments that should be included in a retirement plan, are consistent with concepts and notions that competent advisors use in advising clients regarding investing, diversification, and the balance between increasing returns and reducing risk within a portfolio.

ADMINISTRATION

Qualified retirement plans require ongoing administration and maintenance. Informational compliance tax returns, such as IRS Form 5500, must be filed annually. The allocation of contributions to employees' accounts or determination of accrued benefits must also be completed at least annually. Other administrative duties include annual testing to comply with IRS regulations and amending the plan document for tax law changes. Besides performing the administrative duties, the plan sponsor frequently retains and is responsible for an investment adviser to assure that plan assets are managed for the sole benefit of participants and their beneficiaries. The plan sponsor may outsource each of these tasks to a third party administrator or other provider.

KEY CONCEPTS

1. What are the minimum funding requirements for qualified plans, and when may contributions be deducted by the employer?

2. How are forfeitures treated in qualified plans?

3. What transactions are prohibited for a qualified plan?

4. What regulatory bodies and filing requirements are involved with the operation of a qualified plan?

OPERATING THE PLAN

Covering Eligible Employees

Recall from Chapter 3 that a qualified retirement plan must benefit a broad range of rank-and-file employees, not just the highly compensated or key employees. The company can establish age and service requirements (within the guidelines prescribed by the IRC) in order to control the number of individuals eligible to be in the plan. In addition, qualified plans require annual coverage testing to ensure that the rank-and-file employees (nonhighly compensated and nonkey) are sufficiently covered. Recall from Chapter 5 that some 401(k) plans have an "automatic enrollment" or "negative election" feature. These features help to increase coverage of nonhighly compensated employees. Refer to Chapter 3 for more specific information on the coverage rules and Chapters 3 through 6 for detailed information on each plan's specific annual testing requirements.

Making Appropriate Contributions
Minimum Funding Requirement

In general, sponsors of money purchase pension plans, cash balance pension plans, defined benefit pension plans, and target benefit pension plans must contribute enough money into the plan to satisfy the minimum funding requirements as determined by an actuary for each year.

EXAMPLE 8.7

Loopili Corporation has a money purchase pension plan for which they contribute two percent of covered compensation each year. Loopili has four employees that each make $20,000. By the required contribution date (tax return due date plus extensions) Loopili must contribute $1,600 to the plan ($20,000 x 4 employees x 2%).

Determining the amount needed to satisfy the minimum funding standard for a defined benefit plan is complicated. The amount is based on what should be contributed under the plan formula using actuarial assumptions and formulas. Actuaries work with the plan sponsor to determine the minimum funding for a defined benefit plan. The actuarial assumptions will take into account factors such as life expectancy, likelihood of early retirement, mortality rates, inflation rates, investment return rates, and the expected rate of forfeitures.

Defined benefit plans must make quarterly installment payments of the required contributions. If installment payments are not made on time, then the company must pay interest on any underpayment for the period of the underpayment. The installment payment due dates are 15 days after the end of each quarter. For a calendar-year plan, the installment payments are due April 15, July 15, October 15, and January 15 (of the following year). Each quarterly installment payment must be 25 percent of the required annual payment.

Contributions in General

A qualified plan is generally funded by employer contributions (often called a noncontributory plan because employees do not contribute to the plan), but employees participating in the plan may also be permitted to make contributions (a contributory plan). As explained earlier, one of the benefits of qualified plans is that the employer is allowed to take a deduction in the year of contribution, but the employee does not have to include the income as taxable income in that year. The deductibility of these contributions in effect reduces the overall cost to the employer of the qualified plan.

A company can make deductible contributions for a tax year up to the due date of their tax return (plus extensions) for the year of contribution. A promissory note made out to the plan for contributions is a prohibited transaction and is not a payment that qualifies for an income tax deduction.

While the employer generally applies contributions in the year in which they are paid, the employer may apply the payment to the previous year if all the following requirements are met:

1. The contributions are made by the due date of the tax return for the previous year (plus extensions).
2. The plan was established by the end of the previous year (the plan year).
3. The plan treats the contributions as though it had received them on the last day of the previous year.
4. The company specifies in writing to the plan administrator or trustee that the contributions apply to the previous year, or the company takes a deduction for the amount of the contributions on the tax return for the previous year.

Self-employed individuals can make contributions on behalf of themselves only if they have positive net earnings (compensation) from self-employment in the trade or business for which the plan was established. The net earnings must be from the self-employed individual's personal services and not from investments. A self-employed individual cannot make a contribution for himself in a year in which he has a loss, but he can still make contributions for other employees based on the employees' compensation.

There are certain limits on the contributions and other annual additions a company can make each year on behalf of plan participants (discussed in Chapter 3). There are also limits on the deductible amount of plan contributions. The limits differ depending on whether the plan is a defined contribution plan or a defined benefit plan.

For 2016, the annual benefit for a defined benefit plan participant cannot exceed the lesser of 100 percent of the participant's average compensation for his highest three consecutive calendar years or $210,000. For 2016, a defined contribution plan's annual contributions and other additions (excluding the earnings of the plan assets) to a participant account cannot exceed the lesser of 100 percent of the participant's compensation or $53,000. Catch-up contributions for those participants age 50 and over are not subject to the annual defined contribution limit and thus can be in addition to these limits.

In the event that more money is contributed to a defined contribution plan than is allowed under the limits above, the excess amount is called the excess annual addition. A plan can correct excess annual additions if the excess was caused by a reasonable error in estimating a participant's compensation, determining the elective deferrals permitted, or because of forfeitures allocated to participants' accounts. To do so, the plan can allocate the excess to other participants in the plan to the extent of their unused limits for the year. If these limits are exceeded, they can hold the excess in a separate account and allocate it to participants' accounts in later years before making any contributions for that year, or they can return employee after-tax contributions or elective deferrals. Returning employee after-tax contributions or distributing of elective deferrals to correct excess annual additions is considered a corrective distribution rather than a distribution of accrued benefits. The penalties for early distributions and excess distributions do not apply.

CORRECTING EXCESS ANNUAL ADDITIONS

EXHIBIT 8.14

- Allocate the excess annual additions to other plan participants.
- Hold excess annual additions in a separate account and allocate in future years.
- Make corrective distributions.

Participants may be permitted to make nondeductible contributions to a plan in addition to the employer's contributions. Even though these employee contributions are not deductible, the earnings will accrue tax-free until distributed in later years. These contributions must satisfy certain nondiscrimination tests.

Taking Deductions
Employer Deduction

The employer can usually deduct, subject to certain limitations, contributions made to a qualified plan, including those made for their own retirement. The contributions (and the attributable earnings and gains) are generally not taxed to the employee until distributed by the plan. The deduction limit for contributions to a qualified plan depends on the type of plan.

The deduction for contributions to a defined contribution plan cannot exceed 25 percent of the covered compensation paid or accrued during the year to eligible employees participating in the plan. If the individual is self-employed, he must reduce this limit in figuring the deduction for contributions made to his own account. Recall that the maximum compensation that can be taken into account when calculating plan funding for each employee is the covered compensation limit, $265,000 for 2016.

The deduction for contributions to a defined benefit plan is based on actuarial assumptions and computations. Consequently, an actuary must calculate the appropriate amount of mandatory funding.

Deduction Limit for Self-Employed Individuals (Keogh Plans)

Sole proprietors who file a Schedule C, partners of a partnership, and members of an LLC taxed as a partnership are generally treated as self-employed individuals for tax purposes. In contrast, owners of C-corporations and S-corporations may also be employees of those entities. While self-employed individuals may adopt basically any qualified plan (generally not a stock bonus plan or an ESOP since there is no stock involved with sole proprietorships, partnerships, or LLCs), the plan they choose to adopt will be referred to as a **Keogh plan**. A Keogh plan is simply a qualified plan for a self-employed person. An important distinction of Keogh plans is the reduced contribution that can be made on behalf of the self-employed individual. The employees of a firm that maintains a Keogh plan will generally be treated in the same manner as if the plan was not a Keogh plan. Employees will generally receive a benefit based on their W-2 income. The reason for the distinction is that self-employed individuals do not receive a form W-2 and will instead file a Schedule C or receive a schedule K-1, which details the owner's earnings.

There is a special computation needed to calculate the maximum contribution and tax deduction for a Keogh plan on behalf of self-employed individuals. Since self-employed individuals do not have W-2s, the IRC uses the term "earned income" to denote the amount of compensation that is earned and can be considered by the self-employed individual.

Earned income is defined as net earnings from self-employment less one-half of self-employment tax less the deduction for contributions to the qualified plan on behalf of the self employed person. Through this process, the IRC attempts to treat self-employed individuals as if they were corporations instead of self-employed. Both employers and employees each pay one-half of self-employment taxes; however, in the case of self-employed individuals, they are required to pay both halves. If the company was a corporation, then it would deduct one half of the self employment taxes paid on behalf of the individual in arriving at net income. Therefore, earned income for self-employed individuals is the self-employment income reduced by one-half of self-employment tax. Similarly, a corporation would deduct the contribution made to a qualified retirement plan in arriving at net income. Therefore, calculating earned income for a self-employed individual also requires a reduction for the amount of the contribution to the Keogh plan.

Recall from Chapter 4 that the two primary parts of the Social Security system are OASDI (Old Age Survivor Disability Insurance) and Medicare. Both employers and employees contribute to the system through FICA payments that consist of 6.2 percent for OASDI and 1.45 percent for Medicare. The OASDI portion of 6.2 percent applies to income up to the Social Security wage base ($118,500 for 2016) while the Medicare portion applies to all income with no limit.

The deduction for the self-employed person's contributions and net earnings is interrelated and depends on each other. For this reason, the self-employed person must determine the deduction for their own contributions by using simultaneous equations or a circular calculation or by using the simpler method described below that adjusts the plan contribution rate for the self-employed person.

To calculate the self-employed individual's 2016 contribution to the Keogh plan, utilize the following formulas:

1. Calculate the self-employed individual's contribution rate:

$$\text{Self-Employed Contribution Rate} = \left(\frac{\text{Contribution Rate to Other Participants}}{1 + \text{Contribution Rate to Other Participants}} \right)$$

2. Calculate Self-Employment Tax:

    Net Self-Employment Income
    Times: 92.35%
    Net Earnings subject to Self Employment Tax
    Times: 15.3% up to $118,500 + 2.9% over $118,500
    Equals: Self-Employment Tax

3. Calculate the self employed individual's contribution:

    Net Self-Employment Income
    Less: ½ of Self-Employment Taxes
    Equals: Adjusted Net Self-Employment Income (Earned Income)
    Times: Self-Employed Contribution Rate
    Equals: Self-Employed Individual's Qualified Plan Contribution

EXAMPLE 8.8

Jack has Schedule C net income of $200,000 and wants to know the maximum amount he can contribute to a Keogh profit sharing plan. In this instance Jack can contribute $37,995 to the plan for 2016. The contribution is calculated as follows:

1. Calculate the self employed individual's contribution rate:

$$\text{Self-Employed Contribution Rate} = \left(\frac{25\%}{1 + 25\%} \right)$$

Self-Employed Contribution Rate = 20%

2. Calculate Self-Employment Tax:

$200,000	Net Self-Employment Income
x 0.9235	Times: 92.35%
$184,700	**Net Earnings subject to Self-Employment Tax**
x 15.3%/2.9%	Times: 15.3% up to $118,500 + 2.9% over $118,500 ($66,200)
$20,050.30	**Equals: Self-Employment Tax ($18,130.50 + $1,919.80)**

3. Calculate the self-employed individual's contribution:

$200,000	Net Self-Employment Income
$10,025	Less: ½ of Self-Employment Taxes (50% x $20,050.30)
$189,975	**Equals: Adjusted Net Self-Employment Income**
x 0.20	Times: Self-Employed Contribution Rate
$37,995	**Equals: Self-Employed Individual's Qualified Plan Contribution**

Check figure:

$$\frac{\$37,995}{\$189,975 - \$37,995} = 25\%$$

When solving the Keogh contribution calculation, it is important to understand that while 25 percent is the limit for employee compensation, the self-employed individual maximum is 25 percent of the self-employed individual's earned income. The 25 percent of earned income effectively translates to 20 percent of net self-employed income less one-half of self employment tax. The reason is because the self-employed individual is responsible for the employer's share of self-employment taxes, and the self-employed individual's ultimate compensation is relative to the retirement contribution made on his behalf.

Thus, in the example above, Jack's earned income is calculated as follows:

EXAMPLE
8.9

$200,000	Schedule C net income
- $10,025	Less: ½ self-employment taxes
- $37,995	Less: Keogh contribution
$151,980	Earned income
x 0.25	Times: 25% to determine Keogh contribution
$37,995	**Total Keogh contribution**

Notice that the maximum Keogh contribution is exactly 25% of the earned income.

If the contribution rate for other employees is less than 25 percent, then the rate used is calculated in the same manner as discussed above.

Contribution Rate	Self-Employed Contribution Rate
5.0%	4.7619%
10.0%	9.0909%
15.0%	13.0435%
20.0%	16.6667%
25.0%	20.0000%

EXHIBIT
8.15

FORM 1040 SCHEDULE SE

SCHEDULE SE
(Form 1040)

Department of the Treasury
Internal Revenue Service (99)

Self-Employment Tax

▶ Information about Schedule SE and its separate instructions is at *www.irs.gov/schedulese*.
▶ **Attach to Form 1040 or Form 1040NR.**

OMB No. 1545-0074

20**15**

Attachment
Sequence No. **17**

Name of person with **self-employment** income (as shown on Form 1040 or Form 1040NR)

Social security number of person
with **self-employment** income ▶

Before you begin: To determine if you must file Schedule SE, see the instructions.

May I Use Short Schedule SE or Must I Use Long Schedule SE?

Note. Use this flowchart **only if** you must file Schedule SE. If unsure, see *Who Must File Schedule SE* in the instructions.

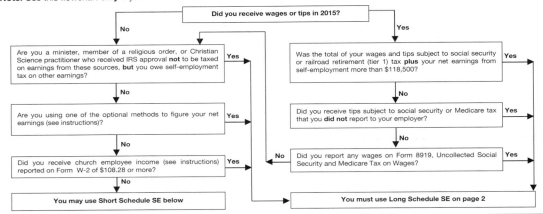

Section A—Short Schedule SE. Caution. Read above to see if you can use Short Schedule SE.

1a	Net farm profit or (loss) from Schedule F, line 34, and farm partnerships, Schedule K-1 (Form 1065), box 14, code A	**1a**	
b	If you received social security retirement or disability benefits, enter the amount of Conservation Reserve Program payments included on Schedule F, line 4b, or listed on Schedule K-1 (Form 1065), box 20, code Z	**1b**	( )
2	Net profit or (loss) from Schedule C, line 31; Schedule C-EZ, line 3; Schedule K-1 (Form 1065), box 14, code A (other than farming); and Schedule K-1 (Form 1065-B), box 9, code J1. Ministers and members of religious orders, see instructions for types of income to report on this line. See instructions for other income to report	**2**	
3	Combine lines 1a, 1b, and 2	**3**	
4	Multiply line 3 by 92.35% (.9235). If less than $400, you do not owe self-employment tax; **do not** file this schedule unless you have an amount on line 1b . . . . ▶	**4**	
	Note. If line 4 is less than $400 due to Conservation Reserve Program payments on line 1b, see instructions.		
5	**Self-employment tax.** If the amount on line 4 is:		
	• $118,500 or less, multiply line 4 by 15.3% (.153). Enter the result here and on **Form 1040, line 57,** or **Form 1040NR, line 55**		
	• More than $118,500, multiply line 4 by 2.9% (.029). Then, add $14,694 to the result. Enter the total here and on **Form 1040, line 57,** or **Form 1040NR, line 55**	**5**	
6	**Deduction for one-half of self-employment tax.** Multiply line 5 by 50% (.50). Enter the result here and on **Form 1040, line 27,** or **Form 1040NR, line 27**	**6**	

For Paperwork Reduction Act Notice, see your tax return instructions.   Cat. No. 11358Z   Schedule SE (Form 1040) 2015

FORM 1040 SCHEDULE SE CONTINUED

Name of person with **self-employment** income (as shown on Form 1040 or Form 1040NR)	Social security number of person with **self-employment** income ▶

Section B—Long Schedule SE

Part I   Self-Employment Tax

Note. If your only income subject to self-employment tax is **church employee income,** see instructions. Also see instructions for the definition of church employee income.

A   If you are a minister, member of a religious order, or Christian Science practitioner **and** you filed Form 4361, but you had $400 or more of **other** net earnings from self-employment, check here and continue with Part I . . . . . . ▶ ☐

1a   Net farm profit or (loss) from Schedule F, line 34, and farm partnerships, Schedule K-1 (Form 1065), box 14, code A. **Note.** Skip lines 1a and 1b if you use the farm optional method (see instructions)   **| 1a |**

b   If you received social security retirement or disability benefits, enter the amount of Conservation Reserve Program payments included on Schedule F, line 4b, or listed on Schedule K-1 (Form 1065), box 20, code Z   **| 1b | (|) |**

2   Net profit or (loss) from Schedule C, line 31; Schedule C-EZ, line 3; Schedule K-1 (Form 1065), box 14, code A (other than farming); and Schedule K-1 (Form 1065-B), box 9, code J1. Ministers and members of religious orders, see instructions for types of income to report on this line. See instructions for other income to report. **Note.** Skip this line if you use the nonfarm optional method (see instructions) . . . . **| 2 |**

3   Combine lines 1a, 1b, and 2 . . . . **| 3 |**

4a   If line 3 is more than zero, multiply line 3 by 92.35% (.9235). Otherwise, enter amount from line 3   **| 4a |**
    Note. If line 4a is less than $400 due to Conservation Reserve Program payments on line 1b, see instructions.

b   If you elect one or both of the optional methods, enter the total of lines 15 and 17 here . . **| 4b |**

c   Combine lines 4a and 4b. If less than $400, **stop;** you do not owe self-employment tax.
    Exception. If less than $400 and you had **church employee income,** enter -0- and continue ▶ **| 4c |**

5a   Enter your **church employee income** from Form W-2. See instructions for definition of church employee income . . . **| 5a |**

b   Multiply line 5a by 92.35% (.9235). If less than $100, enter -0- . . . . **| 5b |**

6   Add lines 4c and 5b . . . . **| 6 |**

7   Maximum amount of combined wages and self-employment earnings subject to social security tax or the 6.2% portion of the 7.65% railroad retirement (tier 1) tax for 2015 . . . . . . **| 7 | 118,500 | 00 |**

8a   Total social security wages and tips (total of boxes 3 and 7 on Form(s) W-2) and railroad retirement (tier 1) compensation. If $118,500 or more, skip lines 8b through 10, and go to line 11 **| 8a |**

b   Unreported tips subject to social security tax (from Form 4137, line 10) **| 8b |**

c   Wages subject to social security tax (from Form 8919, line 10) **| 8c |**

d   Add lines 8a, 8b, and 8c . . . . **| 8d |**

9   Subtract line 8d from line 7. If zero or less, enter -0- here and on line 10 and go to line 11 . ▶ **| 9 |**

10   Multiply the **smaller** of line 6 or line 9 by 12.4% (.124) . . . . **| 10 |**

11   Multiply line 6 by 2.9% (.029) . . . . **| 11 |**

12   **Self-employment tax.** Add lines 10 and 11. Enter here and on **Form 1040, line 57,** or **Form 1040NR, line 55** **| 12 |**

13   Deduction for one-half of self-employment tax.
    Multiply line 12 by 50% (.50). Enter the result here and on **Form 1040, line 27,** or **Form 1040NR, line 27** . . . . **| 13 |**

Part II   Optional Methods To Figure Net Earnings   (see instructions)

Farm Optional Method. You may use this method **only** if **(a)** your gross farm income[1] was not more than $7,320, **or (b)** your net farm profits[2] were less than $5,284.

14   Maximum income for optional methods . . . . **| 14 | 4,880 | 00 |**

15   Enter the **smaller** of: two-thirds (²/₃) of gross farm income[1] (not less than zero) **or** $4,880. Also include this amount on line 4b above . . . . **| 15 |**

Nonfarm Optional Method. You may use this method **only** if **(a)** your net nonfarm profits[3] were less than $5,284 and also less than 72.189% of your gross nonfarm income,[4] **and (b)** you had net earnings from self-employment of at least $400 in 2 of the prior 3 years. **Caution.** You may use this method no more than five times.

16   Subtract line 15 from line 14 . . . . **| 16 |**

17   Enter the **smaller** of: two-thirds (²/₃) of gross nonfarm income[4] (not less than zero) **or** the amount on line 16. Also include this amount on line 4b above . . . . **| 17 |**

[1] From Sch. F, line 9, and Sch. K-1 (Form 1065), box 14, code B.
[2] From Sch. F, line 34, and Sch. K-1 (Form 1065), box 14, code A—minus the amount you would have entered on line 1b had you not used the optional method.

[3] From Sch. C, line 31; Sch. C-EZ, line 3; Sch. K-1 (Form 1065), box 14, code A; and Sch. K-1 (Form 1065-B), box 9, code J1.
[4] From Sch. C, line 7; Sch. C-EZ, line 1; Sch. K-1 (Form 1065), box 14, code C; and Sch. K-1 (Form 1065-B), box 9, code J2.

Schedule SE (Form 1040) 2015

EXAMPLE 8.10

Robbins Co., a sole proprietorship, employs B, C, D, and E as well as the sole proprietor, A, who files a Schedule C for his business.

	Compensation	Contributions
A*	$150,000	See note below
B	$100,000	$15,000
C	$80,000	$12,000
D	$50,000	$7,500
E	$20,000	$3,000

*A's compensation is Schedule C net income

Robbins maintains a Keogh profit plan with a 15% contribution to each employee (not the owner). In spite of the fact that each employee receives exactly 15%, A is limited to receiving 13.0435% (0.15/1.15) of $150,000 less one-half of the self-employment taxes due on his earnings.

$150,000	Schedule C net income
- $6,000	Less: ½ self-employment taxes ($12,000 assumed for ease of calculation)
$144,000	Self-employment income
x 0.130435	Contribution rate (0.15/1.15)
$18,782.64	**Contribution on behalf of A ***

* Rounding was not utilized when applying the contribution rate (0.130434783).

The special calculation is required because Schedule C net income is presumed to include the qualified plan contribution and because one-half of the self-employment taxes are deductible for self-employed persons after the calculation of the Schedule C net income. For all of the other employees, their contribution is calculated based upon 15% of their compensation.

Where To Deduct Contributions

Deductions for contributions to qualified plans made for employee-participants are taken on the employer's tax return. For example, sole proprietors deduct contributions on Form 1040, either Schedule C (Profit or Loss From Business) or Schedule F (Profit or Loss From Farming). Partnerships and most LLCs deduct contributions on Form 1065 (U.S. Return of Partnership Income Tax Return), Form 1120-A (U.S. Corporation Short-Form Income Tax Return), or Form 1120S (U.S. Income Tax Return for an S Corporation). Sole proprietors and partners deduct contributions for themselves on Form 1040, line 28. If the self-employed person is a partner, then contributions for that partner from the partnership are shown on Form 1065, Schedule K-1 (Partner's Share of Income, Credits, Deductions, etc.).

ADJUSTED GROSS INCOME SECTION OF FORM 1040

EXHIBIT 8.16

Adjusted Gross Income	23	Educator expenses	23	
	24	Certain business expenses of reservists, performing artists, and fee-basis government officials. Attach Form 2106 or 2106-EZ	24	
	25	Health savings account deduction. Attach Form 8889	25	
	26	Moving expenses. Attach Form 3903	26	
	27	Deductible part of self-employment tax. Attach Schedule SE	27	
	28	Self-employed SEP, SIMPLE, and qualified plans	28	
	29	Self-employed health insurance deduction	29	
	30	Penalty on early withdrawal of savings	30	
	31a	Alimony paid **b** Recipient's SSN ▶	31a	
	32	IRA deduction	32	
	33	Student loan interest deduction	33	
	34	Tuition and fees. Attach Form 8917	34	
	35	Domestic production activities deduction. Attach Form 8903	35	
	36	Add lines 23 through 35	36	
	37	Subtract line 36 from line 22. This is your **adjusted gross income** ▶	37	

Carryover of Excess Contributions

If the employer contributes more to the qualified plan than the permitted deduction for the year, the excess contribution can be carried over and deducted in future years, combined with, or in lieu of, contributions for those years. The combined deduction in a later year is limited to 25 percent of the participating employees' compensation for that year. This percentage limit must be reduced to figure the maximum deduction for contributions made for the self-employed individual.

The amount that can be carried over and deducted may be subject to an excise tax. If the employer contributes more than the deductible amount to a retirement plan, the employer has made a nondeductible contribution and may be liable for an excise tax. In general, a 10 percent excise tax applies to nondeductible excess contributions made to qualified pension and profit sharing plans.

The 10 percent excise tax does not apply to any contribution made for a self-employed individual to meet the minimum funding requirements in a defined benefit plan. Even if that contribution is more than the earned income from the trade or business for which the plan is set up, the difference is not subject to this excise tax.

If the employer maintains a defined benefit plan, the following exceptions may enable them to avoid the 10 percent penalty on certain nondeductible contributions. If contributions to one or more defined contribution plans are not deductible only because they are more than the combined plan deduction limit, the 10 percent excise tax does not apply to the extent the difference is not more than the greater of six percent of the participants' compensation (including elective deferrals) for the year or the sum of employer matching contributions and the elective deferrals to a 401(k) plan. [7]

In figuring the 10 percent excise tax, the employer can choose not to take into account as nondeductible contributions for any year contributions to a defined benefit plan that are not more than the full funding limit figured without considering the current liability limit. The employer applies the overall limits on deductible contributions first to contributions to defined contribution plans and then to contributions to defined benefit plans. If the employer uses this exception, the employer cannot also use the exception discussed above regarding contributions to one or more defined contribution plans.

---

7. See Chapter 3 for more information on combined limits for defined contribution plans and defined benefit plans.

Forfeitures

Generally, **forfeitures** occur when employees terminate employment. In the event that there are forfeitures from a defined contribution plan, the forfeited amounts can be used to either reduce the employer's contributions under the plan or can be reallocated to the remaining plan participants. Employers often anticipate the effect of forfeitures on remaining plan participants in determining the costs of a qualified plan.

Loopili Corporation recently established a profit sharing plan that requires three years of service before obtaining a vested right to benefits under the plan. Lucy, one of the company's employees, resigned from her position after two years of service and has an unvested account balance of $8,000. Loopili Corporation may reduce its next contribution to the plan by $8,000 or reallocate the $8,000 to the remaining participants.

Defined benefit plans are required to use forfeitures to reduce plan costs. Forfeitures cannot be allocated to the participant's accounts because participants of defined benefit plans do not have individual accounts. Contributions to defined benefit plans are made yearly to keep the plan actuarially on target to pay the expected required benefits. If the plan is over-funded one year, then the company pays less in the subsequent year. The over-funded amount is not returned to the employer until all claims from the plan have been paid, and the plan document allows the plan to distribute the assets to the employer.

Assume for this example Loopili Corporation established a defined benefit plan in favor of its employees based on years of service. Last year the plan assets were $1,000,000, and the actuary estimated that the plan assets needs to be $1,200,000 to fund the required benefits. The company contributes the necessary $200,000 bringing the account balance to $1,200,000 for the current year. During the year, Andy, a long time employee, died prematurely. At the end of the year the actuary estimates that the plan only needs $1,180,000 to fund the needed benefits. The company is not able to take back the excess $20,000. That amount will stay in the plan and reduce contributions in future years.

TREATMENT OF FORFEITURES FROM TERMINATIONS

EXHIBIT
8.17

Defined Benefit Plans	Defined Contribution Plans
• Forfeitures may reduce plan costs	• Forfeitures may reduce plan costs or • Allocate forfeitures to remaining participants

PROHIBITED TRANSACTIONS

Prohibited transactions are transactions between the plan and a disqualified person that are prohibited by law. The prohibited transaction rules usually pertain to related party activities and are imposed to address potential conflicts with parties-in-interest. If a disqualified person takes part in a prohibited transaction, that disqualified person will be subject to a tax as discussed below.

DEFINITION OF DISQUALIFIED PERSON

EXHIBIT
8.18

A disqualified person is any of the following:
1. A fiduciary of the plan.
2. A person providing services to the plan.
3. An employer, any of whose employees are covered by the plan.
4. An employee organization, any of whose members are covered by the plan.
5. Any direct or indirect owner of 50% or more of any of the following:
    - The combined voting power of all classes of stock entitled to vote, or the total value of shares of all classes of stock of a corporation that is an employer or employee organization described in (3) or (4).
    - The capital interest or profits interest of a partnership that is an employer or employee organization described in (3) or (4).
    - The beneficial interest of a trust or unincorporated enterprise that is an employer or an employee organization described in (3) or (4).
6. A member of the family of any individual described in (1), (2), (3), or (5). (A member of a family is the spouse, ancestor, lineal descendant, or any spouse of a lineal descendant.)
7. A corporation, partnership, trust, or estate of which (or in which) any direct or indirect owner described in (1) through (5) holds 50% or more of any of the following:
    - The combined voting power of all classes of stock entitled to vote or the total value of shares of all classes of stock of a corporation.
    - The capital interest or profits interest of a partnership.
    - The beneficial interest of a trust or estate.
8. An officer, director (or an individual having powers or responsibilities similar to those of officers or directors), a 10% or more shareholder, or highly compensated employee (earning 10% or more of the yearly wages of an employer) of a person described in (3), (4), (5), or (7).
9. A 10% or more (in capital or profits) partner or joint venture of a person described in (3), (4), (5), or (7).
10. Any disqualified person, as described in (1) through (9) above, who is a disqualified person with respect to any plan to which a §501(c)(22) trust is permitted to make payments under §4223 of ERISA.

Prohibited transactions generally include actions by a disqualified person that potentially could have adverse consequences to the plan or participants. A transfer of plan income or assets to, use of them by, or for the benefit of a disqualified person is a prohibited transaction. A prohibited transaction is also any act of a fiduciary that uses plan income or assets in his own interest. The receipt of consideration by a fiduciary for his own account from any party dealing with the plan in a transaction that involves plan income or assets is prohibited. Selling, exchanging with, or leasing property, as well as lending money or extending credit to a disqualified person by the plan is prohibited.

PROHIBITED TRANSACTIONS

A fiduciary with respect to a plan shall not cause the plan to engage in a transaction, if the fiduciary knows or should know that such transaction constitutes a direct or indirect-
- sale or exchange, or leasing, of any property between the plan and a party in interest;
- lending of money or other extension of credit between the plan and a party in interest;
- furnishing of goods, services, or facilities between the plan and a party in interest;
- transfer to, or use by or for the benefit of a party in interest, of any assets of the plan; or
- acquisition, on behalf of the plan, of any employer security or employer real property in violation of ERISA §1107 (a).

Certain transactions are exempt from being treated as prohibited transactions. For example, a prohibited transaction does not take place if a disqualified person receives any benefit that they are entitled as a plan participant or beneficiary. However, the benefit must be figured and paid under the same terms as for all other participants and beneficiaries.

In the past, ERISA fiduciary standards and prohibited transaction rules often discouraged employers from furnishing investment advice and information to plan participants. The Pension Protection Act of 2006 created a new exception to the prohibited transactions rule permitting plan fiduciaries to be compensated for giving participants investment advice through an eligible investment advice arrangement, subject to rules intended to limit the possibility of abuse.[8] For employer-sponsored plans subject to ERISA, a fiduciary that is a registered investment company, bank, insurance company or registered broker-dealer is engaged in an eligible investment advice arrangement if either: (1) its fee does not vary depending on the investment choices that participants make, or (2) its recommendations are based on a computer model certified by an independent third party. Under either approach, the PPA 2006 requires several safeguards, including an annual audit of the arrangement. If these requirements are met, the following are exempt from prohibited transaction treatment: (1) the provision of investment advice; (2) an investment transaction (e.g., sale of a security); and (3) the direct or indirect receipt of fees or other compensation in connection with the provision of the advice or an investment transaction pursuant to the advice. This exemption is available for advice provided after December 31, 2006.

8. IRC §4975(f)(8).

The initial penalty on a prohibited transaction is a 15 percent excise tax on the amount involved for each year (or part of year) in the taxable period. Under the PPA 2006, no excise tax will be assessed if the transaction is corrected within 14 days of the date the disqualified person (or other person knowingly participating in the transaction) discovers, or reasonably should have discovered, the transaction was a prohibited transaction. If the transaction is not corrected within the taxable period, an additional tax of 100 percent of the amount involved is imposed.

The term "correct" means, with respect to a transaction:
- to undo the transaction to the extent possible and in any case to make good to the plan or affected account any losses resulting from the transaction; and
- to restore to the plan or affected account any profits made through the use of assets of the plan.

Both taxes (the 15 percent tax and the 100 percent tax) are payable by any disqualified person who participated in the transaction (other than a fiduciary acting only as such). If more than one person takes part in the transaction, each person can be jointly and severally liable for the entire tax. The amount involved in a prohibited transaction is the fair market value of any property received or given. If services are performed, the amount involved is any excess compensation given or received.

The taxable period starts on the transaction date and ends on the earliest of the following days:
- The day the IRS mails a notice of deficiency for the tax.
- The day the IRS assesses the tax.
- The day the correction of the transaction is completed.
- Payment of the 15 percent tax with Form 5330.

If a disqualified person participates in a prohibited transaction, that person can avoid the 100 percent tax by correcting the transaction as soon as possible. Correcting the transaction means rectifying it to the fullest extent without putting the plan in a worse financial position than if the fiduciary had originally acted under the highest fiduciary standards.

EXAMPLE 8.13

Ortez Inc. sponsors a 401(k) plan that allows participant contributions. The company pays its employees and withholds the contributions on a bi-weekly basis. The plan does not allow participants to direct their investments. The plan fiduciary invests the plan assets in a diversified portfolio of investments. Assume employee contributions were not deposited into the plan for the first pay period of the year. Therefore, the participant contributions that normally would have been deposited remained in Ortez Inc.'s general assets. Since the employer was able to use the money that belonged to the participants, they engaged in a prohibited transaction (the use of assets for the benefit of a disqualified person - the employer). Ortez Inc. realized the error a month later. To avoid the 100% penalty, Ortez Inc. must not only deposit the employee contributions into the participant's account, but they must also deposit additional funds to compensate for the earnings on the contribution the participants did not receive (the amount required is determined using the IRC §6621 rate compared to the plan's earning rate).[9]

---

9. http://www.dol.gov/ebsa/faqs/faq_vfcp.html.

If the prohibited transaction is not corrected during the taxable period, the disqualified person usually has an additional 90 days after the day the IRS mails a notice of deficiency for the 100 percent tax to correct the transaction. This correction period (the taxable period plus the 90 days) can be extended if the IRS grants reasonable time needed to correct the transaction or the disqualified person petitions the Tax Court. If the disqualified person corrects the transaction within this period, the IRS will abate, credit, or refund the 100 percent tax.

ERISA AND FILING REQUIREMENTS

ERISA

The **Employee Retirement Income Security Act of 1974** (ERISA) places several burdens on retirement plan administration. One of the key obligations ERISA imposes is that of fiduciary responsibility. While several people may be imposed with the fiduciary duty, the duty is generally imposed on those individuals that have authority over the plan's management, administration, or disposition of the plan's assets. The duty is also imposed on individuals that render investment advice on the plan's assets for a fee. Plan fiduciaries may include plan administrators, plan trustees, and members of the plan's investment committee.

Things a Fiduciary Must Do

First, the **fiduciary**[10] must exercise the care, skill, and diligence of a prudent person acting solely in the interest of plan participants and their beneficiaries. Second, the fiduciary also has an obligation to diversify the plan's assets to reduce the risk of loss. Third, the fiduciary must also act in accordance with the plan's provisions and must refrain from acts forbidden under the law. Effectively, the fiduciary must "do the right thing" and not violate the provisions of the plan or the laws.

Things a Fiduciary Must Not Do

Fiduciaries are prohibited from engaging in certain activities. First, they may not be paid for their services if they are already receiving full-time pay from an employer or union whose employees or members are participants. Second, they cannot act in any transaction involving the plan on behalf of a party whose interests are adverse to those of the plan, its participants, or beneficiaries. Third, they may not receive any consideration for their own personal account from any party dealing with the plan in connection with a transaction involving the assets of the plan. Fourth, they may not cause a plan to engage in certain transactions with parties in interest. Fifth, they may not permit more than 10 percent of a pension plan's assets to be invested in employer securities.

If a plan fiduciary does not exercise the necessary care, skill, and diligence of a prudent person or engages in prohibited transactions, the fiduciary may be held personally liable for any losses the plan suffers. The plan fiduciary may also be required to remit to the plan any profits earned through improper use of the assets. In some instances, a court may relieve a fiduciary of his services to the plan due to fiduciary misconduct.

---

10. 29 USC §1104.

Periodic Pension Benefit Statements

As a result of the Pension Protection Act of 2006, the administrator of a defined contribution plan is required (beginning in 2007) to provide a benefit statement:

1. to a participant or beneficiary who has the right to direct the investment of assets in his account, at least quarterly,
2. to any other participant or other beneficiary who has his own account under the plan, at least annually, and
3. to other beneficiaries, upon written request, but limited to one request during any 12-month period.

A benefit statement provided with respect to a defined contribution plan must include the value of each investment to which assets in the individual's account are allocated, including the value of any assets held in the form of employer securities.

Also as a result of the Pension Protection Act of 2006, the administrator of a defined benefit plan is required either:

1. to furnish a benefit statement at least once every three years to each participant who has a vested accrued benefit under the plan and who is employed by the employer at the time the benefit statements are furnished to participants; or
2. to furnish at least annually to each participant notice of the availability of a benefit statement and the manner in which a participant can obtain it.

The administrator of a defined benefit pension plan is also required to furnish a benefit statement to a participant or beneficiary upon written request, limited to one request during any 12-month period.

For both a defined contribution plan and a defined benefit plan, a benefit statement must be written in a manner calculated to be understood by the average plan participant.

Department of Labor

The **Department of Labor** administers and enforces more than 180 federal laws covering many workplace activities for about 10 million employers and 125 million workers. The Employee Benefits Security Administration (EBSA), an agency of the Department of Labor, oversees plan administration, primarily focusing on being an advocate for the employee. Applicable to this text, the Department of Labor is charged with enforcing the rules governing the conduct of plan managers, investment of plan assets, reporting and disclosure of plan information, enforcement of the fiduciary provisions of the law, and workers' benefit rights as regulated by ERISA.

Pension Benefit Guaranty Corporation

Recall from Chapter 4 that the **Pension Benefit Guaranty Corporation** was established in 1974 when President Gerald R. Ford signed ERISA into law. The PBGC, just as its name implies, acts to guarantee pension benefits. It is a federal corporation that acts as an insurance provider to maintain the benefits promised to employees by their defined benefit pension plans. The plan sponsors of defined benefit and cash balance pensions plans pay premiums for the insurance coverage, but the PBGC only provides plan participants with a limited benefit in the case of the plan completely or partially terminating with an unfunded or underfunded liability.

The PBGC does not cover defined contribution plans, nor does it cover defined benefit pension plans of professional services corporations with 25 or fewer participants. The PBGC does cover all other defined benefit plans at a cost to the plan sponsor of $64 (2016) per plan participant per year and $30 (2016) per $1,000 of plan underfunding for the year.

Reporting Requirements

The employer generally must file an annual report with the Department of Labor. Generally, this is accomplished by filing Form 5500, which is primarily an informational return. Some employers are allowed to file an abbreviated form called Form 5500-EZ, and other organizations are exempt from filing altogether. If a report is due, then it must be filed with the Department of Labor by the last day of the 7th month after the plan year end. The Department of Labor will then provide the necessary information to the IRS and PBGC. In addition, the Pension Protection Act of 2006 requires any PBGC-insured plans to provide participants, the PBGC, and any union that represents employees covered by the plan with an annual funding notice beginning in 2008. The notice must include information about the plan's funded status and the allocation of its assets. The PPA 2006 further requires that certain Form 5500 information be made available on the Internet and on the employer's intranet (if applicable) beginning in 2008. Below is a discussion of Form 5500.

QUICK QUIZ 8.3

1. Defined benefit plans must make quarterly installment payments of the required contributions.
   a. True
   b. False

2. Defined benefit plans may use forfeitures to reduce plan costs or reallocate them to plan participants.
   a. True
   b. False

3. If a prohibited transaction occurs in a qualified plan, a 100% penalty may be assessed if not timely corrected.
   a. True
   b. False

True, False, True.

Form 5500–EZ

Form 5500–EZ is used if the plan only provides benefits for the employer, the employer and their spouse, or one or more partners and their spouses. A plan that benefits employees other than an owner, spouse, partner or partner's spouse cannot use Form 5500-EZ. Form 5500-EZ can be used for defined benefit plans and defined contribution plans, but not for ESOPs. A plan that covers a business that is a member of an affiliated service group, a controlled group of corporations, or a group of businesses under common control, or a plan that covers a business that leases employees cannot file a Form 5500-EZ.

Form 5500-SF

The Form 5500-SF, Short Form Annual Return/Report of Small Employee Benefit Plan, is a simplified annual reporting form for use by certain small pension and welfare benefit plans. To be eligible to use Form 5500-SF, the plan must:
- be a small plan (i.e., generally have fewer than 100 participants at the beginning of the plan year),
- meet the conditions for being exempt from the requirement that the plan's books and records be audited by an independent qualified public accountant (IQPA),

- have 100% of its assets invested in certain secure investments with a readily determinable fair value, such as mutual fund shares, investment contracts with insurance companies and banks valued at least annually, publicly traded securities held by a registered broker dealer, cash and cash equivalents,
- hold no employer securities (ESOPs not permitted), and
- not be a multi-employer plan.

Form 5500

All other employers, unless exempt from filing, must file a Form 5500. Form 5500 contains the basic identifying information of the plan. For small plans with fewer than 100 participants at the beginning of the year that do not qualify to file Form 5500-SF, they must file 5500, but do not have to file as many schedules as larger plans with 100 or more participants. As detailed in Exhibit 8.20, there are several schedules that may also have to be completed depending on the type and nature of the plan.

Exemption from Filing Form 5500

Form 5500–EZ and Form 5500 are not required if the employer has only a one-participant plan that had total plan assets of $250,000 or less for a plan year.

New Annual Reporting Requirements for Code Section 403(b) Plans

The Department of Labor (DOL) repealed, starting with the 2009 annual return/report, the special limited financial reporting rules that applied to Code §403(b) plans. Thus, beginning with the 2009 plan year, administrators of 403(b) plans subject to Title I of ERISA, like administrators of 401(k) plans, must file financial and other compliance information about the plans annually with the government on a Form 5500 or Form 5500-SF. Large 403(b) plans (generally those with 100 or more participants) also must include a report of an independent qualified public accountant (IQPA) with their Form 5500. The IRS has a new website for administrators of 403(b) plans: http://www.dol.gov/ebsa/403b.html.

EXHIBIT
8.20

SUMMARY OF FORM 5500

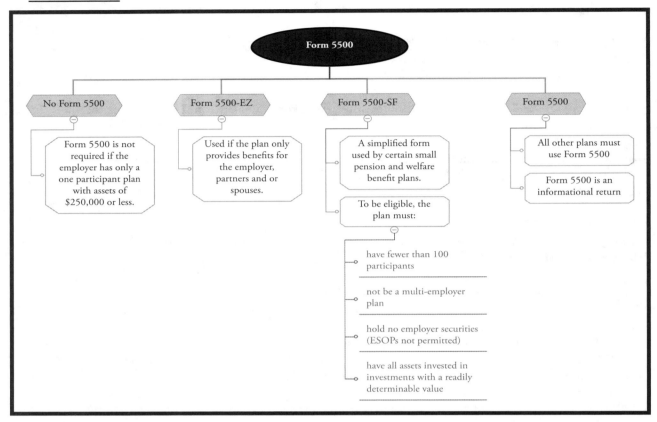

EFAST2 Processing System

Effective January 1, 2010, all pension and welfare plans that are required to submit an annual return/report under Title I of ERISA (Form 5500 or Form 5500-SF) must do so electronically for all plan years using the new EFAST2 Processing System.[11] The Form 5500-EZ cannot be submitted electronically and must be filed using paper based forms.

11. See https://www.efast.dol.gov/welcome.html.

QUICK REFERENCE CHART FOR FORM 5500

EXHIBIT
8.21

	LARGE PENSION PLAN[1]	SMALL PENSION PLAN[1]
Form 5500	Must complete.	Must complete.
Schedule A (Insurance Information)	Must complete if plan has insurance contracts for benefits or investments.	Must complete if plan has insurance contracts for benefits or investments.
Schedule C (Service Provider Information)	Must complete if service provider was paid $5,000 or more and/or an accountant or actuary was terminated.	Not required.
Schedule D (DFE/Participating Plan Info.)	Must complete Part I if plan participated in a CCT, PSA, MTIA, or 103-12 IE.	Must complete Part I if plan participated in a CCT, PSA, MTIA, or 103-12 IE.
Schedule G (Financial Transaction Schedules)	Must complete if Schedule H, line 4b, 4c, or 4d is "Yes."[2]	Not required.
Schedule H (Financial Information)	Must complete.[2]	Not required.
Schedule I (Financial Information - Small Plan)	Not required.	Must complete.
Schedule MB (Actuarial Information)	Must complete if multiemployer defined benefit plan or money purchase plan subject to minimum funding standards.[3]	Must complete if multiemployer defined benefit plan or money purchase plan subject to minimum funding standards.
Schedule R (Retirement Plan Information)	Must complete.[4]	Must complete.[4]
Schedule SB (Actuarial Information)	Must complete if single-employer or multi-employer defined benefit plan, including an eligible combined plan and subject to minimum funding standards.	Must complete if single-employer or multi-employer defined benefit plan, including an eligible combined plan and subject to minimum funding standards.
Accountant's Report	Must attach.	Not required unless Schedule I, line 4k, is checked "No."

1. This chart provides only general guidance. Not all rules and requirements are reflected. A large plan is defined as a plan that covered 100 or more participants as of the beginning of the plan year. A small plan is a plan that covered fewer than 100 participants as of the beginning of the plan year.
2. Schedules of assets and reportable (5%) transactions also must be filed with the Form 5500 if Schedule H, line 4i or 4j is "Yes," but use of printed form not required.
3. Money purchase defined contribution plans that are amortizing a funding waiver are required to complete lines 3, 9, and 10 of the Schedule MB in accordance with the instructions. Also see instructions for line 5 of Schedule R and line 12a of Form 5500-SF.
4. A pension plan is exempt from filing Schedule R if all of the following four conditions are met:
    The plan is not a defined benefit plan or otherwise subject to the minimum funding standards of Code §412 or ERISA §302.
    No in-kind distributions reportable on line 1 of Schedule R were distributed during the plan year.
    No benefits were distributed during the plan year that are reportable on Form 1099-R using an EIN other than that of the plan sponsor or plan administrator.
    In the case of a plan that is not a profit sharing, ESOP, or stock bonus plan, no plan benefits were distributed during the plan year in the form of a single sum distribution.

EXHIBIT
8.22

FORM 5500

| **Form 5500** Department of the Treasury Internal Revenue Service

Department of Labor Employee Benefits Security Administration

Pension Benefit Guaranty Corporation | **Annual Return/Report of Employee Benefit Plan**
This form is required to be filed for employee benefit plans under sections 104 and 4065 of the Employee Retirement Income Security Act of 1974 (ERISA) and sections 6047(e), 6057(b), and 6058(a) of the Internal Revenue Code (the Code).

▶ **Complete all entries in accordance with the instructions to the Form 5500.** | OMB Nos. 1210-0110
1210-0089

2015

This Form is Open to Public Inspection |

Part I   **Annual Report Identification Information**

For calendar plan year 2015 or fiscal plan year beginning   and ending

A This return/report is for: ☐ a multiemployer plan;   ☐ a multiple-employer plan (Filers checking this box must attach a list of participating employer information in accordance with the form instructions); or

       ☐ a single-employer plan;   ☐ a DFE (specify) ____

B This return/report is: ☐ the first return/report;   ☐ the final return/report;

       ☐ an amended return/report;   ☐ a short plan year return/report (less than 12 months).

C If the plan is a collectively-bargained plan, check here. . . . . ▶ ☐

D Check box if filing under: ☐ Form 5558;   ☐ automatic extension;   ☐ the DFVC program;

       ☐ special extension (enter description)

Part II   **Basic Plan Information**—enter all requested information

1a Name of plan	**1b** Three-digit plan number (PN) ▶
	1c Effective date of plan
2a Plan sponsor's name (employer, if for a single-employer plan) Mailing address (include room, apt., suite no. and street, or P.O. Box) City or town, state or province, country, and ZIP or foreign postal code (if foreign, see instructions)	**2b** Employer Identification Number (EIN)
	2c Plan Sponsor's telephone number
	2d Business code (see instructions)

Caution: A penalty for the late or incomplete filing of this return/report will be assessed unless reasonable cause is established.

Under penalties of perjury and other penalties set forth in the instructions, I declare that I have examined this return/report, including accompanying schedules, statements and attachments, as well as the electronic version of this return/report, and to the best of my knowledge and belief, it is true, correct, and complete.

SIGN HERE			
	Signature of plan administrator	Date	Enter name of individual signing as plan administrator
SIGN HERE			
	Signature of employer/plan sponsor	Date	Enter name of individual signing as employer or plan sponsor
SIGN HERE			
	Signature of DFE	Date	Enter name of individual signing as DFE

Preparer's name (including firm name, if applicable) and address (include room or suite number)	Preparer's telephone number

For Paperwork Reduction Act Notice and OMB Control Numbers, see the instructions for Form 5500.   Form 5500 (2015)
v. 150123

FORM 5500 CONTINUED

Form 5500 (2015)   Page **2**

3a Plan administrator's name and address ☐ Same as Plan Sponsor

3b Administrator's EIN

3c Administrator's telephone number

4 If the name and/or EIN of the plan sponsor has changed since the last return/report filed for this plan, enter the name, EIN and the plan number from the last return/report:

a Sponsor's name

4b EIN

4c PN

5 Total number of participants at the beginning of the plan year — **5**

6 Number of participants as of the end of the plan year unless otherwise stated (welfare plans complete only lines **6a(1)**, **6a(2)**, **6b**, **6c**, and **6d**).

a(1) Total number of active participants at the beginning of the plan year.................................... **6a(1)**

a(2) Total number of active participants at the end of the plan year .... **6a(2)**

b Retired or separated participants receiving benefits... **6b**

c Other retired or separated participants entitled to future benefits.. **6c**

d Subtotal. Add lines **6a(2)**, **6b**, and **6c**. **6d**

e Deceased participants whose beneficiaries are receiving or are entitled to receive benefits............ **6e**

f Total. Add lines **6d** and **6e**.. **6f**

g Number of participants with account balances as of the end of the plan year (only defined contribution plans complete this item).. **6g**

h Number of participants that terminated employment during the plan year with accrued benefits that were less than 100% vested **6h**

7 Enter the total number of employers obligated to contribute to the plan (only multiemployer plans complete this item) **7**

8a If the plan provides pension benefits, enter the applicable pension feature codes from the List of Plan Characteristics Codes in the instructions:

b If the plan provides welfare benefits, enter the applicable welfare feature codes from the List of Plan Characteristics Codes in the instructions:

9a Plan funding arrangement (check all that apply)
(1) ☐ Insurance
(2) ☐ Code section 412(e)(3) insurance contracts
(3) ☐ Trust
(4) ☐ General assets of the sponsor

9b Plan benefit arrangement (check all that apply)
(1) ☐ Insurance
(2) ☐ Code section 412(e)(3) insurance contracts
(3) ☐ Trust
(4) ☐ General assets of the sponsor

10 Check all applicable boxes in 10a and 10b to indicate which schedules are attached, and, where indicated, enter the number attached. (See instructions)

a Pension Schedules
(1) ☐ **R** (Retirement Plan Information)
(2) ☐ **MB** (Multiemployer Defined Benefit Plan and Certain Money Purchase Plan Actuarial Information) - signed by the plan actuary
(3) ☐ **SB** (Single-Employer Defined Benefit Plan Actuarial Information) - signed by the plan actuary

b General Schedules
(1) ☐ **H** (Financial Information)
(2) ☐ **I** (Financial Information – Small Plan)
(3) ___ **A** (Insurance Information)
(4) ☐ **C** (Service Provider Information)
(5) ☐ **D** (DFE/Participating Plan Information)
(6) ☐ **G** (Financial Transaction Schedules)

AMENDING AND TERMINATING A QUALIFIED PLAN

Just as adopting a qualified plan often makes good business sense, terminating or changing a qualified plan may also make good business sense. Employers may (and should) reserve the right to change or terminate the plan and to discontinue contributions within the plan document. There are many reasons for changing provisions of a qualified plan. Changes (amendments) are often used to solve original defects in the plan document, maximize benefits to key employees, or comply with a new tax law requirement. In addition, there are other reasons for

terminating a qualified plan. Terminations often occur when a law change occurs that makes one type of plan less advantageous than it was previously, the company can no longer financially maintain the plan, or the company realizes the plan no longer meets the needs of the employees or the company.

REASONS TO AMEND OR TERMINATE A PLAN

Qualified plans, especially for small employers, are often changed to maximize the provision of benefits to key employees. Some plans allow forfeitures to be reallocated to other plan participant's or may be used to reduce plan costs. Small business owners frequently change this election based on the benefits they are able to receive from the plan. For example, consider an owner who has compensation of $100,000 when the plan is first established. Due to the amount of his compensation, the owner is unable to receive the maximum contribution allowed for the year ($53,000 for 2016); therefore, the logical choice would be to allow forfeitures to be reallocated to remaining participants, so that his contributions can be increased by the other's forfeitures. In later years, when his compensation is $400,000 and he is able to receive the maximum contribution, it no longer makes sense from his perspective to allow reallocation of forfeitures. Since he has already reached his annual additions limit, the reallocated forfeitures could not be used to increase his account. In such an instance, he may amend the plan to require that forfeitures only reduce future plan costs.

Another reason a plan may be changed or terminated is that a law change may make an entire plan or plan provision obsolete. For example, before the Economic Growth and Tax Relief and Reconciliation Act of 2001 (EGTRRA 2001) was enacted, the contribution limit for a profit sharing plan was 15 percent of employer compensation. An extra 10 percent was available for employers to increase their total contribution through the adoption of pension plans (namely money purchase pension plans). To do this, many employers selected what is referred to as a **Tandem Plan** (typically combined a 10 percent money purchase pension plan with a 15 percent profit sharing plan so that owners would be able to receive the maximum contribution each year into their qualified plan), while only exposing themselves to a 10 percent mandatory contribution. When EGTRRA 2001 passed, it increased the contribution limit for profit sharing plans to 25 percent, which virtually made Tandem Plans obsolete. The reason is simple. Recall the money purchase pension plan requires a mandatory fixed contribution each year, while the profit sharing plan allows the employer the discretion to determine the contribution percentage each year. With the profit sharing plan able to reach the maximum limit of 25 percent, it becomes unnecessary for the employer to take the risk involved with the fixed contribution of the money purchase pension plan. Therefore, many plans were amended so that the money purchase pension plan was terminated and the plan remaining consisted solely of a profit sharing plan.

A qualified plan may also be terminated when the employer finds that they can no longer financially support the plan they have in place. Sometimes the decision is made by the employer, while other times the decision is made by the PBGC. The employer will frequently reach out for debt relief when it has filed for bankruptcy (Chapter 7) or reorganization (Chapter 11). The PBGC also has the right to step in to terminate a plan if the plan is under-funded and the PBGC feels that it needs to protect its risk that the plan will go under.

A plan may also be terminated simply because the employer finds that the plan is not meeting the needs of the employees or the company. Sometimes the plan benefits are so small that the cost of administering the plan is prohibitive. The employer may realize that a simple increase in compensation for the employees will satisfy the same goodwill as a qualified plan and at a lower cost.

AMENDING OR TERMINATING A QUALIFIED PLAN

EXHIBIT
8.23

- To maximize benefits for key employees
- Law changes
- Employer is unable to support
- Benefits were not sufficient

AMENDING A QUALIFIED PLAN

Plan changes are very common due to tax law changes, business changes, or to solve a defect in the plan. Changes are often easily implemented by amending the plan document. When the plan document is amended, the administrator must also revise the Summary Plan Description. The employer is also required to provide the plan participants notices of any plan amendments or changes. Notice can be made either through a revised Summary Plan Description or in a separate document called a Summary of Material Modifications. This document must also be provided to participants free of charge within 210 days after the end of the plan year in which a change is adopted.

TERMINATING A QUALIFIED PLAN

When a qualified plan is terminated, and presuming that sufficient funds are available, all of the participants in the plan become fully vested in their benefits as of the date of termination.[12] Sponsors that terminate a qualified plan must discontinue all contributions and benefit accruals and must distribute all plan assets within a reasonable period of time after the termination of the plan. The method of obtaining a termination and the requirements that need to be met are different for defined-benefit plans and defined-contribution plans.

---

12. Treas. Reg. 1.411(d)-2(a)(1).

Permanency Requirement

Although qualified plans are required to be permanent, permanency does not necessarily require that the plan never terminate or continue in existence forever. Permanency in this context just means that the plan must not be established as a temporary program. The goal behind the "permanency" requirement is to dissuade owners from creating plans that will only benefit the owners and key employees and then having the plan vanish before benefits can be accrued by rank-and-file employees. Unfortunately, the abandonment of the plan for any reason other than business necessity within the first few years after it is established will be evidence that the plan was not a bona fide program for the exclusive benefit of employees. This is especially true when a pension plan is abandoned soon after pensions have been fully funded for officers or shareholders. The permanency of the plan is indicated by all of the surrounding facts and circumstances, including the likelihood of the employer's ability to continue contributions as provided under the plan.

Defined Benefit Plan Terminations

Because the PBGC is responsible for under-funded defined benefit plans, there are more requirements for terminating a defined benefit plan than for a defined contribution plan. Title IV of ERISA requires that a defined benefit plan terminate under a standard, distress, or involuntary termination. See Example 8.14.

Standard Termination

A **standard termination** is voluntary and may occur when the employer has sufficient assets to pay all benefits (liabilities) at the time of final distribution. To terminate a defined benefit plan this way, the administrator must first notify all affected parties between 60 and 90 days before the proposed termination date.

An affected party is:
1. a plan participant,
2. a beneficiary of a deceased participant or an alternate payee under a qualified domestic relations order, and
3. any employee organization representing plan participants.

The termination date can be any date selected by the administrator, including a weekend or holiday. The administrator must then notify the PBGC. The PBGC must approve the termination because it will be liable should the organization not be able to pay the intended debts. Assuming the plan has met the PBGC requirements, then the date of termination will generally be the date proposed by the administrator in the notice of intent to terminate.

Distress Termination

A **distress termination** is voluntary and occurs when the employer is in financial difficulty and is unable to continue with the plan financially. Generally a distress termination occurs when the company is in liquidation, in bankruptcy (Chapter 7), or has filed for reorganization (Chapter 11). It can also occur when the company can no longer pay debts or the pension costs are simply unreasonable. The administrator must also notify the affected parties and the PBGC, as discussed above.

US Airways is an example of a company that decided it could no longer fund the plan it had in place. In 2003, US Airways filed for Chapter 11 bankruptcy and requested that the bankruptcy court allow them to terminate the pension plan they had in place for the pilots. At the time, the plan was underfunded by approximately $2.5 billion dollars, and the company claimed that fulfilling this obligation would prevent them from successfully reorganizing and emerging from bankruptcy. The court allowed the termination and left the company free to establish a more conservative defined contribution plan. The impact was that the PBGC took over the plan and only protected benefits up to the 2003 PBGC limit, approximately $43,000 (2004 benefits were approximately $44,000). Many pilots saw their benefits reduced from as much as $144,000 annually to approximately $19,000 annually for those age 55, due to the PBGC limit and the actuarial reduction from normal retirement age of 65 to 55. Note that the 2016 maximum annual benefit for retirement for PBGC purposes at age 65 is $60,136.

Involuntary Termination

An **involuntary termination** may be initiated by the PBGC for a plan that is unable to pay benefits from the plan in order to limit the amount of exposure to the PBGC. The PBGC may terminate a pension plan, even if a company has not filed to terminate a plan on its own initiative, if:

- the plan has not met the minimum funding requirements;
- the plan cannot pay current benefits when due;
- a lump-sum payment has been made to a participant who is a substantial owner of the sponsoring company; or
- the loss to PBGC is expected to increase unreasonably if the plan is not terminated.[13]

The PBGC must terminate a plan if assets are unavailable to pay benefits currently due. Under the Pension Protection Act of 2006, the plan sponsor or plan administrator of a plan that has received notice from the PBGC of a determination that the plan should be involuntarily terminated is required to provide an affected party with any information provided to the PBGC in connection with the plan termination.

---

13. www.pbgc.gov.

Case Study 8.1

A request for a distress termination was made in the Chapter 11 bankruptcy reorganization in *In re Diversified Industries, Inc.*[1] The Chapter 11 debtor-employer filed a motion with the Bankruptcy Court for authorization to file a notice of intent with Pension Benefit Guaranty Corporation ("PBGC") to terminate five defined benefit plans. The facts showed that the plans were underfunded. The total unpaid minimum contributions for all of these plans as of December 31, 1992 was $2,841,000. The Debtor gave notice of its intent to seek termination of all pension plans. Since there were no objections to the termination of four of these plans, the Court granted authorization and the Debtor initiated the process with PBGC to terminate those four. The benefits for all the participants in those four plans were fully guaranteed by PBGC. The Debtor elected to seek authorization from the PBGC to terminate the remaining plan ("the Plan") pursuant to ERISA's distress termination procedure.

The Plan provided substantial pension benefits for Mr. Ben Fixman and certain other present and former members of the Debtor's senior management team, but a large portion of these benefits were not guaranteed by the PBGC. It was uncontested that if the senior management pension plans were terminated, Mr. Fixman would lose a greater sum than any other employee. Mr. Fixman's pension plan provided him with an annual payment of approximately $136,000. If the Plan were to be terminated, his annual pension would drop to approximately $27,000, the maximum payment that PBGC insured. Mr. Fixman filed an objection to the Debtor's motion, claiming in part that the Debtor was required under ERISA to have the Bankruptcy Court determine whether the Plan could be terminated.

The Bankruptcy Court concluded that due to the Plan's insolvency, the only method of termination was by means of distress termination, which required the plan administrator to provide 60 days' advance notice of intent to terminate to the affected parties, to submit to the PBGC various information as required by ERISA, and to submit information for the PBGC to determine whether the distress criteria had been met.[2] Before submitting the request to terminate the Plan to the PBGC, the Bankruptcy Court explained that the Debtor must satisfy a "business judgment" test and show that the decision is a reasonable exercise of its business judgment. At a hearing, the Debtor proved that it was in its best interest to seek termination of the Plan because, unless the Plan was terminated, the Debtor and its subsidiaries would be unable to pay their debts when due, resulting in the Debtor being unable to continue in business outside the Chapter 11 reorganization process. Accordingly, the court ordered that the Debtor submit the appropriate notices under ERISA to the PBGC to institute the proceedings at that agency to terminate the Plan.

---

1. In *re Diversified Industries, Inc.*, 166 B.R. 141 (Bkrtcy. E.D. Mo. 1993).
2. Employee Retirement Income Security Act of 1974, §4041(c); 29 U.S.C.A. §1341(c).

Defined Contribution Plan Terminations

Compared to defined benefit plans, terminating a defined contribution plan is relatively easy. Defined contribution plans are already funded and not subject to PBGC. Essentially, all the employer must do to terminate the plan is pass a corporate resolution to do so. At that point, any final promised contributions must be completed and the assets must be distributed from the plan.

Partial Terminations

In some instances, a plan, by operation of law, will experience a partial termination. This can occur when the employer changes the plan so that it is very adverse to the employees, or there is a significant severance of employees covered by the plan (i.e., a layoff). A partial termination is decided on a facts and circumstances test; therefore, companies who plan to make decisions that will affect a large number of employees should consider how their actions will affect their qualified plans. Similar to a full termination, the benefits of the plan participants will be 100 percent vested in the event there is a partial termination.

PLAN FREEZE

In some cases, an employer may find that they no longer want to contribute to a plan but do not want to fully terminate the plan. This can be accomplished by freezing the plan (**plan freeze**). For defined contribution plans, a freeze simply means that the employer will no longer make any contributions. For a defined benefit plan, participants will no longer accrue additional benefits but the plan sponsor must maintain the previously accrued benefits. The plan will continue to benefit from the tax deferral on the plan's earnings until the plan distributes its assets according to the plan document.

QUICK QUIZ 8.4

1. Qualified plans are often amended to maximize benefits to key employees.
   a. True
   b. False

2. Qualified plan amendments are difficult and require approval by ERISA.
   a. True
   b. False

3. Qualified plans may never terminate without losing their qualified status retroactively to inception.
   a. True
   b. False

True, False, False.

TAX ON REVERSION OF QUALIFIED PLAN ASSETS TO EMPLOYER[14]

While plan sponsors are prohibited under ERISA from withdrawing assets from a qualified plan, they can recoup assets in the plan that exceed the liabilities and obligations provided for under the plan upon plan termination. There is a 20 percent excise tax on any amount of assets that revert back to the employer from a qualified plan. If certain requirements are not met, then the excise tax is increased to 50 percent of the reversionary amount. These requirements include:

- the employer establishes a qualified replacement plan, or
- provides for specific benefit increases.

This 50 percent excise tax does not apply in the event that the plan sponsor is in bankruptcy. It should be evident that it is unlikely that assets will revert back to the employer in or out of bankruptcy and it is costly when it occurs.

---

14. IRC §4980.

KEY TERMS

ACTUAL CONTRIBUTION PERCENTAGE TEST (ACP) - A nondiscrimination test that limits the sum of employee after-tax contributions for the highly compensated employees (HC) based on the sum of employee after-tax contributions for the non- highly compensated employees (NHC). The test also includes employer matching contributions.

ACTUAL DEFERRAL PERCENTAGE TEST (ADP) - A nondiscrimination test that limits employee elective deferrals for the HC based on the elective deferrals of the NHC.

CASH OR DEFERRED ARRANGEMENT (CODA) - Permits an employee to defer a portion of their salary on a pretax basis to a qualified plan or receive the salary as current taxable income.

CUSTODIAL ACCOUNTS - Accounts generally maintained by a bank or other financial institution for the benefit of participants.

DEPARTMENT OF LABOR - Governmental department charged with enforcing the rules governing the conduct of plan managers, investment of plan assets, reporting and disclosure of plan information, enforcement of the fiduciary provisions of the law, and workers' benefit rights as regulated by ERISA.

DETERMINATION LETTER - A request filed with the IRS requesting a determination on a particular topic. In the case of a retirement plan, they are used when a plan is adopted, amended, or terminated to assure the plan sponsor that the qualified plan complies with applicable provisions.

DISCRETIONARY CONTRIBUTIONS - Allows an employer to decide each year whether to make a matching or nonelection contribution and then inform the plan participants.

DISTRESS TERMINATION - Termination that occurs when the employer is in financial difficulty and is unable to continue with a defined benefit plan.

EMPLOYEE CENSUS - A matrix of information that is used in plan selection and identifies each employee, their age, compensation, number of years of employment, and any ownership interest in the plan sponsor.

EMPLOYEE RETIREMENT INCOME AND SECURITY ACT (ERISA) - Legislation enacted by Congress in 1974 as a result of various abuses by plan sponsors to provide protection for an employee's retirement assets, both from creditors and from plan sponsors.

ERISA ATTORNEY - An attorney who specializes in ERISA law.

FIDUCIARY - An individual that has a special relationship of trust, confidence, and responsibility in certain financial obligations.

KEY TERMS

FORFEITURES - The percentage or amount of a participant's accrued benefit that was not vested to the employee at the employee's termination from the plan sponsor. The forfeited amount stays in the plan and may be allocated to the other plan participants (defined contribution plan) or reduce future plan costs (defined contribution plan or defined benefit plan).

INTERESTED PARTIES - Present employees who are eligible to participate in the plan and present employees who are not eligible for the plan but whose principal place of employment is the same as the principal place of employment of any employee who is eligible to participate.

INVOLUNTARY TERMINATION - Termination initiated by the PBGC for a defined benefit plan that is unable to pay benefits from the plan.

KEOGH PLAN - A qualified plan for a self-employed individual.

MANDATORY FUNDING REQUIREMENT - An amount or percentage that must be contributed to a qualified pension plan by the employer each plan year.

MASTER PLAN - Provides a single trust or custodial account that is jointly used by all adopting employers.

PENSION BENEFIT GUARANTY CORPORATION (PBGC) - Established in 1974 when President Gerald R. Ford signed the Employee Retirement Income Security Act (ERISA) into law. The PBGC guarantees qualified pension benefits. It is a federal corporation that acts as an insurance provider to maintain the benefits promised to employees by their defined benefit pension plans.

PLAN FREEZE - Employer will no longer make any contributions to the plan, but does not want to fully terminate the plan.

PROHIBITED TRANSACTIONS - Transactions between the plan and a disqualified person that are prohibited by law.

PROTOTYPE PLAN - A prepackaged plan that allows the sponsor to use a check the box approach to plan choices.

QUALIFIED TRUST - A trust established or organized in the U.S. that is maintained by the employer for the exclusive benefit of employees.

STANDARD TERMINATION - Termination in which the employer has sufficient assets to pay all benefits (liabilities) at the time of final distribution.

SUMMARY OF MATERIAL MODIFICATIONS - Document that provides in plain language the modifications made to a qualified plan.

KEY TERMS

SUMMARY PLAN DESCRIPTION - Document that explains in plain language the details of a retirement plan and how it operates. It provides information on when an employee can begin to participate in the plan, how service and benefits are calculated, when benefits become vested, when and in what form benefits are paid, and how to file a claim for benefits.

TANDEM PLAN - A 10% money purchase pension plan combined with a 15% profit sharing plan. These were popular prior to TRA 2001.

THIRD PARTY ADMINISTRATOR - An organization unrelated to the plan sponsor who is paid to administer the plan sponsor's qualified or other retirement plan.

VOLUME SUBMITTER PLAN - A plan that is designed by a professional, such as an attorney, CPA or third party administrator, which contains language that has been pre-approved by the IRS. This type of plan allows for more customization than a standard prototype plan, but is generally much less costly than an individualized plan.

DISCUSSION QUESTIONS

1. Describe the business and personal issues that should be considered when making a qualified plan selection.

2. What is an employee census and why is it important?

3. Explain the steps involved in adopting a qualified plan.

4. How and when should employees be notified when a qualified plan is established?

5. What are the minimum funding requirements for qualified plans?

6. When may contributions to a qualified plan be deducted by the employer?

7. Explain how forfeitures are treated in qualified plans.

8. List the transactions that are prohibited in a qualified plan and the exceptions.

9. Describe the regulatory bodies, other than the IRS, and filing requirements involved with the operation of a qualified plan.

10. Under what circumstances would a qualified plan be amended or terminated?

11. Describe how a qualified plan is amended.

12. Describe how a qualified plan is terminated.

13. List and describe the three types of terminations.

14. Describe under what conditions assets from a qualified plan can revert to the employer.

MULTIPLE CHOICE PROBLEMS

1. Generally, which of the following are contributory plans?

    a. 401(k) and money purchase pension plans.
    b. 401(k) and thrift plans.
    c. Thrift plans and ESOPs.
    d. Money purchase pension plans and profit sharing plans.

2. Which of the following generally contribute to defined benefit plans, profit sharing plans, and money purchase pension plans?

    a. Employees only.
    b. Employer only.
    c. Both employer and employees.
    d. Employer, employees, and government.

3. Who generally makes elective deferrals to a 401(k) plan?

    a. Employees only.
    b. Employer only.
    c. Employees and employer.
    d. Employees, employers, and forfeitures.

4. Plans that require mandatory funding are generally funded by?

    a. The employee.
    b. The employer.
    c. The employee and the employer.
    d. For PBGC insured plans, the employee and the employer.

5. Employees generally contribute to which of the following plans?

    1. 401(k) plans.
    2. Thrift plans.
    3. Cash balance pension plans.
    4. Defined benefit pension plans.

    a. 1 and 2.
    b. 1 and 4.
    c. 2 and 3.
    d. 3 and 4.

6. Which of the following qualified plans require mandatory funding?

    1. Defined benefit pension plans.

    2. 401(k) plans with an employer match organized as a profit sharing plan.

    3. Cash balance pension plans.

    4. Money purchase pension plans.

        a. 1 and 3.

        b. 1, 2, and 3.

        c. 1, 3, and 4.

        d. 1, 2, 3, and 4.

7. Company A has been capitalized by MJBJ Vulture Capital, a venture capital company. Company A's cash flows are expected to fluctuate significantly from year to year, due to phenomenal growth. They expect to go public within three years. Which of the following would be the best qualified plan for them to consider adopting?

        a. Profit sharing plan.

        b. New comparability plan.

        c. 401(k) plan with a match.

        d. Stock bonus plan.

8. Investment portfolio risk is generally borne by the participant/employee in all of the listed qualified plans, except:

    1. Defined benefit pension plan.

    2. Cash balance pension plan.

    3. 401(k) plan.

    4. Profit sharing plan.

        a. 1 and 2.

        b. 2 and 3.

        c. 3 and 4.

        d. 1, 3, and 4.

9. The target benefit pension plan and the money purchase pension plan provide some employee/participant investment diversification protections by limiting the investment amount in employer stock to less than or equal to:

        a. 5%.

        b. 10%.

        c. 20%.

        d. 100%.

10. Qualified retirement plans that permit the employer unlimited investment in sponsor company stock are:

    1. 401(k) plans.

    2. Stock bonus plans.

    3. Profit sharing plans.

    4. ESOPs.

        a. 3 only.

        b. 4 only.

        c. 3 and 4.

        d. 1, 2, 3, and 4.

11. Generally, older age entrants are favored in which of the following plans?

    1. Defined benefit pension plans.

    2. Cash balance pension plans.

    3. Target benefit pension plans.

    4. Money purchase pension plans.

        a. 1 and 2.

        b. 1 and 3.

        c. 2 and 3.

        d. 4 only.

12. A distress termination of a qualified retirement plan occurs when:

    1. The PBGC initiates a termination because the plan was determined to be unable to pay benefits from the plan.

    2. An employer is in financial difficulty and is unable to continue with the plan financially. Generally, this occurs when the company has filed for bankruptcy, either Chapter 7 liquidation or Chapter 11 reorganization.

    3. The employer has sufficient assets to pay all benefits vested at the time, but is distressed about it.

    4. When the PBGC notifies the employer that it wishes to change the plan due to the increasing unfunded risk.

        a. 2 only.

        b. 1 and 2.

        c. 1, 2, and 3.

        d. 1, 2, and 4.

13. Marie, the sole shareholder in Marie's Pastries, is contemplating establishing a qualified plan. The corporation's employee census is as follows:

MARIE'S PASTRIES EMPLOYEE CENSUS				
Employee	Age	Compensation	Ownership	Length of Service
Marie	55	$200,000	100%	30 Years
Cheryl	38	$45,000	0	20 Years
Jeff	42	$28,000	0	14 Years
Ruby	34	$24,000	0	11 Years
Total		$297,000	100%	
The company experiences very low turnover.				

Marie, a long-time widow, has always treated the employees like her family and the company has experienced very low turnover. She would like to use the retirement plan to assist her in transferring ownership interest to the employees as she is ready to retire. She has a strong preference for avoiding and deferring taxes. She is opposed to mandatory funding and indifferent to integration. Which plan would be appropriate for Marie?

    a. Stock bonus plan.

    b. Money purchase pension plan.

    c. Defined benefit plan.

    d. Employee stock ownership plan.

14. Westgate Inc., recently adopted a profit sharing plan. Westgate has two offices, the North Westgate office and the South Westgate office. There are 10 employees in the North Westgate office, 5 of which are eligible for the plan; and 15 employees in the South Westgate office that are all eligible for the plan. Which of the following statements is true?

    a. If Westgate decides to notify the employees about the plan via mail, the letters must be mailed at least 30 days before mailing the determination letter to the IRS.

    b. A Summary Plan Description must be furnished to each participant within 120 days of plan establishment.

    c. If Westgate adopted a prototype plan then they will use a single trust or custodial account that has been adopted by all employers using that prototype plan.

    d. Westgate only needs to notify the employees that are eligible for the plan that the company has adopted a qualified plan.

15. Tracy, age 46, is a self-employed financial planner and has Schedule C income from self-employment of $56,000. He has failed to save for retirement until now. Therefore, he would like to make the maximum contribution to his profit sharing plan. How much can he contribute to his profit sharing plan account for 2016?

    a. $9,464.

    b. $10,409.

    c. $11,200.

    d. $14,000.

16. Which of the following statements are correct regarding assets reverting back to the sponsor or a qualified plan?

    1. Under a merger, assets from a qualified plan can revert back to the plan sponsor without regard to the relationship between the value of the plan assets compared to the value of the obligations under the plan.

    2. Any reversion of plan assets will always be subject to a 20 percent penalty.

        a. 1 only.

        b. 2 only.

        c. Both 1 and 2.

        d. Neither 1 nor 2.

17. Beth Ann, age 55, is an attorney who is self employed. Her assistant, Buffy, has worked with her for five years. Beth Ann is establishing a SEP for this year and is willing to make a contribution of 10 percent of Buffy's salary to the SEP. If Beth Ann earns $90,000 after paying Buffy, her expenses, and the contribution to Buffy's SEP, what is the most that she can contribute to the SEP on her behalf for 2016?

    a. $7,026.

    b. $7,604.

    c. $8,182.

    d. $16,728.

18. Steve is self-employed as a marketing consultant. He works primarily with start-up internet companies helping to develop corporate brand programs. Several years ago, he established a 401(k) profit-sharing plan and has accumulated $385,000 in the plan. Which of the following forms should he file to meet his compliance requirements?

    a. Form 5500 EZ.

    b. Form 5500 SF.

    c. Form 5500.

    d. He does not need to file a Form 5500 of any type.

QUICK QUIZ EXPLANATIONS

QUICK QUIZ 8.1

1. False. With a small business, the plan selection process must focus on both the needs of the company and the needs of the small business owner. Meeting the owner's needs as well as the company's needs is critical to establishing a successful retirement plan.
2. True.
3. False. An employer with fluctuating cash flows would be more likely to choose some type of qualified profit sharing plan that has discretionary contributions each year rather than a pension plan that has mandatory funding requirements.

QUICK QUIZ 8.2

1. False. To take an income tax deduction for contributions for a particular tax year, the plan must be adopted by the last day of that particular tax year.
2. True.
3. False. Even when plan sponsors choose to shift the management responsibility of the investment assets to the plan participants, the plan sponsor still retains certain responsibilities over the choices and alternative investments available to the participants.

QUICK QUIZ 8.3

1. True.
2. False. Defined benefit plans may only use forfeitures to reduce plan costs.
3. True.

QUICK QUIZ 8.4

1. True.
2. False. Plan changes are very common due to tax law changes, business changes, or to solve a defect in the plan. Changes are often easily implemented by amending the plan document. When the plan document is amended, the administrator must also revise the Summary Plan Description.
3. False. Termination of a qualified plan does not necessarily mean that the plan retroactively loses its qualified status.

CHAPTER

9

IRAS AND SEPS

LEARNING OBJECTIVES

After reading this chapter, you should be able to:

1. Contrast the characteristics of IRAs with qualified plans.
2. Explain the impact of compounding on the ending value of an IRA account after years of continuous funding.
3. Describe the funding limits for traditional and Roth IRAs.
4. Describe the impact of converting funds in a traditional IRA or qualified plan to a Roth IRA.
5. Determine the deductibility of contributions to a traditional IRA including taking into consideration the characterization of active participant status.
6. Calculate the penalties associated with overfunding traditional and Roth IRAs.
7. Understand the importance of Form 8606.
8. Describe the nature of the taxation of distributions from traditional and Roth IRAs.
9. Understand the exceptions to the 10 percent early withdrawal penalty that apply exclusively to IRAs.
10. Explain the types of investments that are permitted to be held within an IRA.
11. Contrast the features of *my*RA with that of traditional and Roth IRAs.
12. Explain the advantages of *my*RA over other methods of saving for retirement.
13. Describe the advantages and rules associated with Simplified Employee Pensions (SEPs).

INTRODUCTION

IRAs, SEPs, SARSEPs, SIMPLEs, and tax sheltered annuities (403(b) plans) are not qualified plans, do not meet the requirements under IRC §401(a), and are not entitled to the same benefits as qualified plans. They are referred to as "other tax-advantaged plans" to indicate that, while not qualified plans, they have many of the same benefits and features as qualified plans. While all of these plans have many of the benefits of qualified plans, they also have certain advantages over qualified plans. Similar to qualified plans, tax-advantaged plans are all tax deferred, meaning that earnings within the trust or plan are not taxed until a distribution occurs. In addition, all of these tax-advantaged plans provide for sheltering of current income from taxation.

However, IRAs, SEPs, and SIMPLEs have many key differences from qualified plans. First, IRAs, SEPs, and SIMPLEs are not subject to the same federal reporting requirements as qualified plans. Second, lump-sum distribution options such as NUA, pre-74 capital gain treatment, and 10-year forward averaging are not permitted for distributions from IRAs, SEPs, SIMPLEs, or 403(b) plans. Third, these plans also do not have the same non-alienation of benefits protection found under ERISA. Fourth, these plans, with the exception of the 403(b) plan, are not permitted to offer loans to participants. Fifth, whereas qualified plans typically have specific vesting schedules for contributions made by the employer on behalf of the employee, other tax-advantaged plans always provide for 100 percent vesting, with the exception of some employer contributions to 403(b) plans.

This chapter discusses the rules surrounding Traditional IRAs, IRA annuities, Roth IRAs, SEPs, and SARSEPs. SIMPLE plans, 403(b) plans, and 457 plans are discussed in the following chapter.

CHARACTERISTICS OF QUALIFIED PLANS AND OTHER TAX-EXEMPT PLANS

EXHIBIT 9.1

Characteristic	Qualified Plans	IRAs	SEP IRAs	SIMPLE IRAs**	403(b) Plans
Provides for tax deferral for deposits and savings	✓	✓	✓	✓	✓
Provides shelter for current income	✓	✓	✓	✓	✓
Annual reporting – Form 5500	✓	✗	✗	✗	Maybe***
Vesting required	✓	✗	✗	✗	Maybe
Loans are permitted	✓	✗	✗	✗	✓
Protection under ERISA	✓	✗****	✗****	✗****	Maybe*
10-year averaging permitted	✓	✗	✗	✗	✗
Pre-74 capital gain treatment	✓	✗	✗	✗	✗
Distributions eligible for NUA	✓	✗	✗	✗	✗

*Many 403(b) plans provide for ERISA protection; however, some do not.
** There are very few, if any, SIMPLE 401(k)s.
***Employer maintained 403(b) plans must file Form 5500.
**** Although federal bankruptcy protection is available under the Bankruptcy Abuse Prevention and Consumer Protection Act of 2005.

✓ YES ✗ NO

KNOW THE NUMBERS (2016)

	Traditional IRA	Roth IRA	SEP	SARSEP
Contribution Limit	$5,500	$5,500	25% or $53,000	$18,000
Catch-Up (Over age 50)	$1,000	$1,000	N/A	$6,000
Contribution Phaseout 2016	N/A	Single: $117,000 – $132,000 MFJ: $184,000 – $194,000 MFS: $0,000 – $10,000	N/A	N/A
Deduction Phaseouts 2016	Not an Active Participant: No Limit Active Participant: Single: $61,000 – $71,000 MFJ: $98,000 – $118,000 One Spouse is an Active Participant: $184,000 – $194,000	N/A	N/A	N/A
Provide to Employee With	N/A	N/A	Compensation > $600	N/A

INDIVIDUAL RETIREMENT ACCOUNT

The Individual Retirement Account (IRA) has been available since 1974. The amount that could be contributed on a tax-deferred basis per person per year was once limited to $1,500, but that has now been increased to $5,500 for 2016 with an additional deferral of $1,000 for 2016 for persons age 50 or older. The rules regarding deductibility have also changed as will be explained in this chapter. The IRA has great potential as an accumulation device for retirement when started early and funded annually. Consider an individual who makes annual year-end

deposits of $5,500 in a mutual fund earning a 10 percent return each year for 40 years (age 25-65).[1] The future accumulated balance of the account at age 65 is $2,434,259 even though the individual only deposited a total of $220,000. The compound growth potential of such accounts often makes the tax deductibility of the contribution a less significant issue than the accumulation, as illustrated in the graph below.

There are two general types of **individual retirement accounts** (IRAs) under present law: traditional IRAs, to which both deductible and nondeductible contributions may be made, and Roth IRAs, to which only nondeductible contributions may be made.[2] Many of the rules relating to traditional IRAs and Roth IRAs are the same and will be discussed together under traditional IRAs. The differences between the types of IRAs are discussed later in this chapter.

TRADITIONAL IRAS

Traditional IRAs have been available for many years and as the limits on both contributions and deductions have increased, these retirement vehicles remain an important part of retirement planning for individuals. IRAs take one of two forms, an individual retirement account or an **individual retirement annuity**. An IRA account can hold a wide variety of investments and can be

---

1. IRC §408.
2. This chapter does not consider Coverdell IRAs (formerly known as Education IRAs).

held by a wide variety of **custodians** (e.g., brokerage, bank, mutual fund, etc.). An IRA annuity is usually held by an insurance company as custodian. As a result of the increased contribution limits established under EGTRRA 2001, and made permanent by PPA 2006, IRAs have become a more significant part of planning for retirement.

History of IRAs[3]

EXHIBIT
9.2

Individual retirement accounts were introduced in 1974 with the enactment of the Employee Retirement Income Security Act (ERISA). As the Congress originally conceived the accounts, participants could contribute up to $1,500 a year and reduce their taxable income by the amount of their contributions. Initially, ERISA restricted IRAs to workers who were not covered by a qualified employment-based retirement plan. But the 1981 Economic Recovery Tax Act allowed all taxpayers under the age of 70½ to contribute to an IRA, regardless of their coverage under a qualified plan. It also raised the maximum annual contribution to $2,000 and allowed participants to contribute $250 on behalf of a nonworking spouse. The Tax Reform Act of 1986 reversed the trend toward expanded participation by phasing out the deduction for IRA contributions among higher-earning workers who are covered by an employment-based retirement plan themselves or who have a covered spouse.

In the 1990s, the Congress raised some of the limits it had previously placed on IRA contributions and also created the Roth IRA - a new type of account that features non-deductible contributions and tax-exempt withdrawals. The Small Business Job Protection Act of 1996 raised the limit on contributions on behalf of nonworking spouses from $250 to $2,000. Further changes came in the Taxpayer Relief Act of 1997. In addition to creating Roth IRAs, it increased the income threshold above which deductible contributions are phased out and distinguished between taxpayers who are covered by an employment-based plan and those who are not but whose spouses are covered. The income thresholds for the latter category of taxpayers are now higher than those for the former, which allows more people who are not covered by an employer's retirement plan to make tax-deductible contributions.

Additional changes to IRAs resulted from the Economic Growth and Tax Relief Reconciliation Act of 2001 (EGTRRA). The law raised the limit on contributions beginning in 2002 and allowed "catch-up" contributions by people ages 50 and above. It also provided a nonrefundable credit for certain contributions to an IRA or a 401(k)-type plan.

Contribution Limits

Prior to EGTRRA 2001, contributions to a traditional IRA were limited each year to the lesser of $2,000 or earned income. EGTRRA 2001, however, increased the maximum contribution over several years. As a result, individuals could contribute a maximum of $3,000 or earned income in 2004, $4,000 or earned income in 2005-2007, and $5,000 or earned income in 2008. Beginning in 2009, the $5,000 contribution limit is subject to adjustment for inflation (the contribution limit

---

3. http://www.cbo.gov/OnlineTaxGuide/Page_2A.htm. Note: Link is no longer active.

is $5,500 for 2016).[4] In addition, individuals who have attained the age of 50 before the end of the current taxable year are also eligible to make catch-up contributions, thereby further increasing the annual IRA contribution limit. These contribution limits, which are combined for both traditional and Roth IRAs, are summarized in the following chart. Note that the catch-up contribution is not adjusted for inflation.

CONTRIBUTION LIMIT FOR IRAS (TRADITIONAL & ROTH)

Year	Annual Limit	Catch-Up Limit (for those over age 50)	Maximum Contribution
2016	$5,500	$1,000	$6,500

The following chart and graph depict the accumulation over time in an IRA assuming a $5,500 contribution was made to the account at the beginning of each year and without considering the availability of the catch-up contribution and the increase in the limits. Notice that after ten years, $55,000 of deposits have accumulated to $96,421 assuming a 10 percent rate of return. After thirty years, $995,189 has accumulated assuming a 10 percent rate of return.

Years	Amount Deposited	8% Return	10% Return	12% Return
1-5	$27,500	$34,848	$36,936	$39,134
1-10	$55,000	$86,050	$96,421	$108,100
1-15	$82,500	$161,284	$192,224	$229,643
1-20	$110,000	$271,826	$346,514	$443,843
1-25	$137,500	$434,249	$595,000	$821,337
1-30	$165,000	$672,902	$995,189	$1,486,609

---

4. IRC §219(b)(5)(D).

A straight deposit equal to $5,500 per year assuming contributions are made at the end of each year at various earning rates for 30 and 40 years are:

EXAMPLE 9.2

Years (N)	Rate (i)	Annual PMT	Amount Deposited	FV
30	8%	$5,500	$165,000	$623,057.66
30	10%	$5,500	$165,000	$904,717.12
30	12%	$5,500	$165,000	$1,327,329.76
40	8%	$5,500	$220,000	$1,424,810.85
40	10%	$5,500	$220,000	$2,434,259.06
40	12%	$5,500	$220,000	$4,219,002.81

Earned Income - Individual IRA

The annual contributions to an IRA are limited to the lesser of an individual's earned income or the annual limit in effect. **Earned income** includes any type of compensation where the individual has performed some level of services for an employer or is considered self-employed. Compensation includes earnings for W-2 employees or those individuals who are self-employed, whether they operate a sole proprietorship, partnership, or an LLC taxed as a sole proprietorship or partnership. Earned income also includes alimony received by the taxpayer. For federal income tax purposes, **alimony** is deductible by the payor and is includible as earned income by the recipient. Exhibit 9.4 provides a list of earned income and a separate list of what is not earned income.

In Letter Ruling 9202003, the IRS ruled that hogs transferred from a husband to his wife (a bona fide employee) did in fact constitute compensation (earned income) and could be used as the basis for contributions to an IRA.

EXAMPLE 9.3

Earned Income - Spousal IRA

Individuals who do not have any earned income may still be eligible to establish an IRA if their spouse has sufficient earned income. An IRA for a spouse who has no earned income is generally referred to as a spousal IRA and can be established provided the other spouse has sufficient earned income. The necessary level of earned income is equal to the total amount that is to be contributed to both IRAs. **Spousal IRAs** can be established up to the contribution limit for the year in question ($5,500 for 2016). The catch-up contribution is also available for those individuals age 50 and over.

Jack, age 48, and Sydney, age 43, have been married for 20 years and are currently retired. Although Jack is unemployed, Sydney earns $11,000 from her part-time work at the local market during 2016. Because Sydney has income of $11,000, both Jack and Sydney can contribute up to $5,500 to each of their IRAs in 2016.

EXAMPLE 9.4

Jeff, age 54, and Brit, age 52, have been married for 20 years and are planning to retire in six years. Although Jeff is currently unemployed, Brit earns $38,000 from her work at the local school. Brit's income of $38,000 would allow each of them to contribute up to $5,500 to each of their IRAs during 2016. In addition, each of them can contribute an extra $1,000 for 2016 as a catch-up contribution because they are both over age 50.

EXAMPLE 9.5

EXHIBIT
9.4

EXAMPLES OF EARNED INCOME AND WHAT IS NOT EARNED INCOME

Earned Income:
• W-2 income
• Schedule C net income
• K-1 income from a partnership (or an LLC taxed as a partnership) where the partner is a material participant
• Alimony

Not Earned Income:
• Earnings and profits from property, such as rental income, interest income, and dividend income
• Capital gains
• Pension and annuity income
• Deferred compensation received (compensation payments postponed from a past year)
• Income from a partnership for which you do not provide services that are a material income producing factor
• Any amounts excluded from income, such as foreign income and housing costs
• Unemployment benefits
• Investment returns as a limited partner in a partnership
• Income flowing from an S-corporation via Schedule K-1
• Social Security benefits
• Workers' compensation

Case Study 9.1

In *Gary H. and L. Marianne Bell v. Commissioner, T.C. Summary Opinion 2006-146*, the court ruled against the Bells when they attempted to take a deduction for an IRA contribution based on income from a defined contribution plan.

Earned Income - Attainment of 70½

Contributions to a traditional IRA are not permitted in the year or any years after the year in which an individual attains age 70½.[5] This limitation for traditional IRAs does not apply to Roth IRAs. Individuals who have sufficient earned income may continue to contribute to a Roth IRA after the attainment of age 70½.

Billy and Alice have been married for many years. Although Billy is currently retired, he has a part-time position at the local superstore earning $13,000 each year. Billy turned 70 on March 8th of 2016. Alice is 40 and is a stay-home mom. Because Billy will attain the age of 70½ during the current year, he is not permitted to contribute to a traditional IRA. However, Alice may contribute $5,500 for 2016 to a spousal IRA (either traditional or Roth), and Billy can contribute $5,500 to a Roth IRA (with the availability of a $1,000 catch-up contribution).

---

5.   IRC §219(d)(1).

Excess Contributions

Contributions that exceed the limits discussed above ($5,500 for 2016) are subject to an excise tax penalty of six percent. This penalty is charged each year that the excess contribution remains in the IRA.[6] The taxpayer can avoid the excise penalty on excess contributions by withdrawing the excess contribution and the earnings attributable to the excess contributions by the due date (excluding extensions) of the federal income tax return (April 15th for calendar year taxpayers). These excess contributions rules and the penalty apply to both traditional and Roth IRAs.

> In 2016, Sara, age 32, contributed $6,000 to her IRA. She made an excess contribution of $500 that will be subject to a six percent penalty if she does not withdraw the excess contribution and any related earnings by April 15, 2017.

EXAMPLE 9.7

> In 2016, Sara, age 32, contributed $4,500 to her traditional IRA and $1,500 to her Roth IRA. She has made an excess contribution of $500. She can avoid the six percent penalty by withdrawing the excess contribution and any related earnings from either the IRA or the Roth IRA account (or both) by April 15, 2017.

EXAMPLE 9.8

The calculation of earnings attributable to the excess IRA contribution is based on a prorated portion of the earnings accrued by the IRA while the excess contribution remained in the IRA.

Timing of Contributions to IRAs

As discussed in Chapter 8, contributions to qualified plans can be made as late as the due date of the tax return including extensions. For most entities with a calendar year end, the final date a contribution can be made to a qualified plan is September 15th. For self-employed individuals, the final date a contribution can be made to a qualified plan is October 15th. However, for IRAs, contributions must be made to both traditional and Roth IRA accounts by the due date of the individual federal income tax return without considering extensions. For most taxpayers, this due date is April 15th of the year following the tax year end.

Finally, with the exception of rollover contributions from other IRAs, a contribution to a traditional IRA or Roth IRA must be made in cash.[7] No other type of asset may be contributed to an IRA.

Deductibility of IRA Contributions

Provided an individual has sufficient earned income, the individual may contribute the maximum amount

QUICK QUIZ 9.1

1. A 55-year old individual can contribute a maximum of $5,500 to an IRA in 2016.
   a. True
   b. False

2. Annual contributions to an IRA are limited to the lesser of a single individual's earned income or the annual limit in effect.
   a. True
   b. False

3. Persons who do not have any earned income may not contribute to an IRA.
   a. True
   b. False

False, True, False.

---

6. IRC §4973.
7. IRC §408(a)(1).

to a traditional IRA on an annual basis. However, the deductibility of the traditional IRA contribution on an individual's federal income tax return is dependent on several factors, including coverage or participation in a qualified plan or other retirement plan, which is referred to as whether the individual is an **active participant**, and the amount of the individual's **adjusted gross income** (AGI). If the individual and spouse (if any) are not active participants in a qualified plan or retirement plan (defined later), they may contribute to a deductible IRA to the lesser of the IRA contribution limit or earned income. Even if the individual or their spouse is an active participant, they still may be able to contribute to a deductible IRA if the AGI of the taxpayer (and spouse, if any) is below certain threshold limits as discussed below.

Not Active Participants of Qualified or Other Retirement Plan

An individual who is not an active participant does not have an income limitation for purposes of deducting his IRA contributions. Therefore, if an individual earns a substantial amount of income (e.g., $1,000,000) and is not an active participant, then the individual may fully deduct a contribution (within the contribution limit) to his traditional IRA account.

EXHIBIT 9.5

WHO CAN DEDUCT CONTRIBUTIONS TO A TRADITIONAL IRA

Taxpayer is not an active participant	Taxpayer(s) is an active participant		One spouse is an active participant, the other is not
No AGI Limit	Single	**AGI Phaseout** $61,000 – $71,000 (2016)	The spouse who is not an active participant may have a deductible traditional IRA contribution as long as their joint AGI does not exceed $194,000. The deductible IRA contribution is phased out between $184,000 and $194,000 for 2016.
	MFJ	**AGI Phaseout** $98,000 – $118,000 (2016)	

Active Participants of Qualified or Other Retirement Plans

For individuals or married couples filing jointly who are considered active participants (defined below) of a qualified plan or other retirement plan, there is an income test to determine the deductibility of IRA contributions. If the taxpayer's AGI is greater than the upper limit of the phaseout, no deduction is permitted. If the taxpayer's AGI is less than the lower limit of the phaseout, then a full deduction is permitted. If the taxpayer's AGI is between the limits, then the deduction is ratably phased out.

Married couples filing separately are effectively phased out between an AGI of $0 and $10,000. Individuals falling within these phaseout ranges must calculate the deductible amount of the contribution utilizing the calculation discussed below.

As illustrated in Exhibit 9.5, simply because one spouse is covered by a qualified plan does not prohibit the other spouse from deducting a contribution to a traditional IRA. However, this ability to deduct the contribution is phased out for married individuals with AGI beginning at $184,000 and is completely phased out for AGI at or above $194,000.

Calculation of IRA Deduction – Subject to Phaseout

An individual who is an active participant in a retirement plan and has an AGI within the **phaseout** range will have a reduced maximum deductible IRA contribution. The deduction limit ($5,500 for 2016) will be reduced based on a proportion equal to the amount by which the individual's AGI exceeds the lower limit of the phaseout range divided by $10,000 (or $20,000 in the case of a joint return for a taxable year beginning after December 31, 2006). The calculation of this reduction in the IRA deductibility limit is as follows:[8]

$$\text{Reduction} = \text{Contribution Limit}^{**} \times \frac{\text{AGI} - \text{Lower Limit}}{\$10,000^*}$$

* $20,000 for joint returns after December 31, 2006
** Including catch-up contribution

Consider the following examples:

> Fred is single, age 38, and an active participant in his employer's qualified retirement plan. His AGI for 2016 is $62,000, and he makes the maximum contribution to his traditional IRA.
>
> $$\text{Reduction} = \$5,500 \times \frac{\$62,000 - \$61,000}{\$10,000} = \$550$$
>
> Thus, Fred's traditional IRA deduction for 2016 is reduced by $550 to $4,950 ($5,500 - $550).

EXAMPLE 9.9

> Assume the same facts as above except that Fred is over the age of 50 and is eligible for the catch-up contribution of $1,000. In this case, the traditional IRA deduction is reduced by $650.
>
> $$\text{Reduction} = \$6,500 \times \frac{\$62,000 - \$61,000}{\$10,000} = \$650$$
>
> Thus, Fred's traditional IRA deduction for 2016 is reduced to $5,850 ($6,500 - $650). Notice that the portion that is phased out represents 10 percent of the allowable contribution. Therefore, with the additional $1,000 contribution, only 90 percent or $900 will be deductible ($4,950 + $900 = $5,850).

EXAMPLE 9.10

> Rob, age 32, and Sara, age 31, are married and are active participants in qualified plans. They file a joint return and have AGI of $102,000 for 2016. Both Rob and Sara make the maximum contribution to their respective traditional IRAs in 2016.
>
> $$\text{Reduction} = \$5,500 \times \frac{\$102,000 - \$98,000}{20,000} = \$1,100$$
>
> Thus, Rob and Sara can each deduct $4,400 ($5,500 - $1,100).

EXAMPLE 9.11

---

8. IRC §219(g)(2)(A).

EXAMPLE 9.12

Nick and Kim are married and file jointly. Kim is an attorney who earns $130,000 per year and is an active participant in the firm's qualified plan. She also has portfolio income of $15,000 per year. Nick is unemployed and goes to the bar every day and plays Gin Rummy. Can Nick make a contribution to a traditional IRA, and is it deductible? Yes. Nick can contribute because together Kim and Nick have sufficient earned income and the contribution is deductible because their joint AGI for 2016 is less than $184,000. Therefore, Nick can make the maximum contribution (subject to his age) to the IRA for the current year and fully deduct it.

Where is the Traditional IRA Deduction Taken

The deduction for contributions to traditional IRAs is a deduction for AGI. The deduction is listed on line 32 of the individual's Form 1040.

EXHIBIT 9.6

ADJUSTED GROSS INCOME SECTION OF FORM 1040

Adjusted Gross Income	23	Educator expenses	23		
	24	Certain business expenses of reservists, performing artists, and fee-basis government officials. Attach Form 2106 or 2106-EZ	24		
	25	Health savings account deduction. Attach Form 8889	25		
	26	Moving expenses. Attach Form 3903	26		
	27	Deductible part of self-employment tax. Attach Schedule SE	27		
	28	Self-employed SEP, SIMPLE, and qualified plans	28		
	29	Self-employed health insurance deduction	29		
	30	Penalty on early withdrawal of savings	30		
	31a	Alimony paid b Recipient's SSN ▶	31a		
→	32	IRA deduction	32		
	33	Student loan interest deduction	33		
	34	Tuition and fees. Attach Form 8917	34		
	35	Domestic production activities deduction. Attach Form 8903	35		
	36	Add lines 23 through 35		36	
	37	Subtract line 36 from line 22. This is your adjusted gross income	▶	37	

Active Participant Status

As discussed above, the deductibility of traditional IRA contributions may be reduced if the taxpayer is an active participant in a retirement plan for the year of contribution to the traditional IRA. An active participant is an employee who has benefitted under one of the following plans through a contribution or an accrued benefit:[9]

- qualified plan
- annuity plan
- tax sheltered annuity (403(b) plan)
- certain government plans[10]
- simplified employee pension plans (SEPs)
- simple retirement accounts (SIMPLEs)

Active participant status for an employee depends on the type of retirement plan. For a defined benefit plan, an individual who is not excluded under the eligibility provisions of the plan is considered to be an active participant in the plan, regardless of whether such individual has elected to decline participation in the plan, has failed to make a mandatory contribution specified under the plan, or has failed to perform the minimum service required to accrue a benefit under the

---

9. IRC §219(g)(5).
10. Does not include 457 plans – IRC §219(g)(5). In addition, certain armed forces reserve members and volunteer firefighters may not be considered active participants.

plan.[11] For example, when a participant completes an additional year of service in a defined benefit plan that calculates the benefit based on years of service, then, the participant has accrued additional benefits in that year.

An individual is an active participant in a money purchase pension plan or target benefit pension plan if the employer is required to make a contribution on behalf of that employee. Since these plans must comply with mandatory funding requirements, most employees who are eligible for such plans and are covered will be active participants.

Because contributions to profit sharing plans (and stock bonus plans) are discretionary from the employer, the determination of active participant status is dependent on whether the participant receives a contribution for the year. Remember the contribution may come from the employer, employee, or from a plan forfeiture allocation. Also, qualified nonelective contributions, as well as qualified matching contributions, will qualify as a contribution to the plan for the year. Any of these contributions will cause an individual to be classified as an active participant for the year for which the contribution was made. An employee is considered an active participant even if the contributions to the account are completely forfeitable. In other words, even if the employee is not vested in any benefit, he will still be considered an active participant if he receives a contribution to his account for the current year.

> ### KEY CONCEPTS
>
> 1. What is the penalty for excess contributions to an IRA?
>
> 2. List the factors that affect the deductibility of IRA contributions on an individual's federal tax return.
>
> 3. What are the required minimum distribution rules for IRAs?

As previously discussed, contributions to traditional IRAs are required to be made by April 15th for the previous year, while contributions to qualified plans can be made as late as the due date of the company's income tax return including extensions. With a profit sharing plan, an individual may not know whether or not he will be an active participant for a particular year until after he is required to make the contribution to the IRA account. Because of the timing difference, certain provisions permit such qualified plan contributions to be considered for the following year for purposes of traditional IRA deductibility.[12]

> **EXAMPLE 9.13**
>
> George is employed by Hone Company, which sponsors a profit-sharing plan. The plan was established in 2001. Hone decides in August of 2017 to make a contribution to the plan for the year 2016. Since Hone made the contribution in 2017, George would be considered an active participant for the year 2017, not 2016. However, if a contribution was made for George in 2016, then George would be an active participant for 2016.

As discussed, an employee who makes an employee elective deferral contribution to a plan, such as a 401(k) plan, is considered an active participant for the current year. However, just because an employee is eligible to defer a portion of his salary into a 401(k) plan does not automatically make the employee an active participant for the current year (e.g., the employee does not defer).[13]

---

11. Internal Revenue Bulletin 1987-5, Notice 87-16.
12. Treas. Reg. §1.219-2.
13. Treas. Reg. §1.219-2(e).

For spouses filing jointly, the active participation status of one spouse does not constitute active participant status of the other spouse.[14] If only one spouse is an active participant, then the spouse that is not an active participant may make a deductible IRA contribution as long as the couple's joint income (adjusted gross income) does not exceed $194,000 (the ability to take a deduction phases out from $184,000 to $194,000).

EXAMPLE 9.14

Bob's employer sponsors a money purchase pension plan with a contribution level of seven percent of compensation. Bob meets the eligibility requirements. Therefore, Bob is an active participant for purposes of IRA deductibility.

EXAMPLE 9.15

Joe is a participant of his company's profit sharing plan. However, the company had a bad year and did not make a contribution to the profit sharing plan, and no employees terminated employment with non-vested benefits during the current year. Joe is not an active participant in the plan because he did not receive any employer contribution or any forfeiture allocation.

EXAMPLE 9.16

Deanna is employed with Kensington Company where she is eligible to defer up to 80 percent of her salary into the 401(k) plan. Deanna does not defer anything in her 401(k) plan, nor does she receive a contribution by the employer or a forfeiture allocation. Deanna is not an active participant for purposes of IRA deductibility for that year.[15]

EXAMPLE 9.17

Deanna, who is a non-highly compensated employee, is employed with Kensington Company where she is eligible to defer up to 80 percent of her salary into the 401(k) plan. Deanna does not defer anything in her 401(k) plan, nor does she receive a forfeiture allocation. However, Deanna does receive a small contribution from the employer in the form of a qualified nonelective contribution.[16] Deanna is considered an active participant for purposes of IRA deductibility.

EXAMPLE 9.18

Aaron and Stacey are married and file a joint income tax return. Their joint AGI in 2016 is $145,000. Stacey is a dentist who earns a salary of $100,000 per year, and she defers the maximum to her 401(k) plan. Aaron is a personal trainer earning $45,000 in fees per year. He files a Schedule C with his federal income tax return. Stacey is an active participant in a qualified plan, but Aaron is not. Although he should probably establish a Keogh plan for his self-employment income, he is not currently an active participant. Because their joint AGI is less than $184,000 and he is not an active participant in a qualified plan, Aaron can make a fully deductible traditional IRA contribution. Stacey could make a non-deductible IRA contribution or a contribution to a Roth IRA.

---

14. IRC §219(g)(7).
15. However, Deanna is considered covered for purposes of the coverage rules.
16. Qualified nonelective contributions (QNECs) are contributions made to non-highly compensated employees so that the plan sponsor meets the ADP requirements.

Non-Deductible IRA Contributions

Although one of the advantages of an IRA contribution is that it is often income tax deductible for AGI, contributions to an IRA can be non-deductible.[17] Generally, taxpayers make non-deductible contributions to traditional IRAs if they are active participants in a qualified plan and their income exceeds the phaseout limits. However, any taxpayer can make a non-deductible contribution as long as they have earned income. These non-deductible contributions receive the benefit of the deferral of income tax on the current earnings within the IRA.

When an individual makes a non-deductible contribution to an IRA, the individual has an adjusted basis in the IRA. Withdrawals from the IRA will consist partially of account earnings that have not been subject to income tax and partially of return of adjusted basis for which the individual has already paid income tax.

Individuals who have non-deductible IRA contributions should file Form 8606 with their federal income tax return. This form should be filed each year to track the adjusted basis of an individual's IRA account (see lines 1 and 2 on Form 8606).

According to the form instructions, if you are required to file Form 8606 to report a nondeductible contribution to a traditional IRA, but do not do so, you must pay a $50 penalty. Overstating nondeductible contributions will result in a $100 penalty.[18]

---

17. IRC §408(o)(2)(B)(ii).
18. Instructions to Form 8606.

EXHIBIT 9.7

FORM 8606

Form **8606**	**Nondeductible IRAs**	OMB No. 1545-0074
Department of the Treasury Internal Revenue Service (99)	▶ Information about Form 8606 and its separate instructions is at *www.irs.gov/form8606*. ▶ Attach to Form 1040, Form 1040A, or Form 1040NR.	20**15** Attachment Sequence No. **48**

Name. If married, file a separate form for each spouse required to file Form 8606. See instructions. **Your social security number**

Fill in Your Address Only If You Are Filing This Form by Itself and Not With Your Tax Return ▶

Home address (number and street, or P.O. box if mail is not delivered to your home) | Apt. no.

City, town or post office, state, and ZIP code. If you have a foreign address, also complete the spaces below.

Foreign country name | Foreign province/state/county | Foreign postal code

Part I   **Nondeductible Contributions to Traditional IRAs and Distributions From Traditional, SEP, and SIMPLE IRAs**

Complete this part only if one or more of the following apply.

- You made nondeductible contributions to a traditional IRA for 2015.
- You took distributions from a traditional, SEP, or SIMPLE IRA in 2015 **and** you made nondeductible contributions to a traditional IRA in 2015 or an earlier year. For this purpose, a distribution does not include a rollover, one-time distribution to fund an HSA, conversion, recharacterization, or return of certain contributions.
- You converted part, but not all, of your traditional, SEP, and SIMPLE IRAs to Roth IRAs in 2015 (excluding any portion you recharacterized) **and** you made nondeductible contributions to a traditional IRA in 2015 or an earlier year.

1	Enter your nondeductible contributions to traditional IRAs for 2015, including those made for 2015 from January 1, 2016, through April 18, 2016 (see instructions)	**1**	
2	Enter your total basis in traditional IRAs (see instructions)	**2**	
3	Add lines 1 and 2	**3**	
	In 2015, did you take a distribution from traditional, SEP, or SIMPLE IRAs, or make a Roth IRA conversion? **No** ──▶ Enter the amount from line 3 on line 14. Do not complete the rest of Part I. **Yes** ──▶ Go to line 4.		
4	Enter those contributions included on line 1 that were made from January 1, 2016, through April 18, 2016	**4**	
5	Subtract line 4 from line 3	**5**	
6	Enter the value of **all** your traditional, SEP, and SIMPLE IRAs as of December 31, 2015, plus any outstanding rollovers (see instructions) . .	**6**	
7	Enter your distributions from traditional, SEP, and SIMPLE IRAs in 2015. **Do not** include rollovers, a one-time distribution to fund an HSA, conversions to a Roth IRA, certain returned contributions, or recharacterizations of traditional IRA contributions (see instructions) .	**7**	
8	Enter the net amount you converted from traditional, SEP, and SIMPLE IRAs to Roth IRAs in 2015. **Do not** include amounts converted that you later recharacterized (see instructions). Also enter this amount on line 16 .	**8**	
9	Add lines 6, 7, and 8 . . . . **9**		
10	Divide line 5 by line 9. Enter the result as a decimal rounded to at least 3 places. If the result is 1.000 or more, enter "1.000"	**10** × .	
11	Multiply line 8 by line 10. This is the nontaxable portion of the amount you converted to Roth IRAs. Also enter this amount on line 17 . . .	**11**	
12	Multiply line 7 by line 10. This is the nontaxable portion of your distributions that you did not convert to a Roth IRA	**12**	
13	Add lines 11 and 12. This is the nontaxable portion of all your distributions	**13**	
14	Subtract line 13 from line 3. This is **your total basis in traditional IRAs for 2015 and earlier years**	**14**	
15	**Taxable amount.** Subtract line 12 from line 7. If more than zero, also include this amount on Form 1040, line 15b; Form 1040A, line 11b; or Form 1040NR, line 16b	**15**	
	Note. You may be subject to an additional 10% tax on the amount on line 15 if you were under age 59½ at the time of the distribution (see instructions).		

For Privacy Act and Paperwork Reduction Act Notice, see separate instructions.   Cat. No. 63966F   Form **8606** (2015)

FORM 8606 CONTINUED

Part II   **2015 Conversions From Traditional, SEP, or SIMPLE IRAs to Roth IRAs**

Complete this part if you converted part or all of your traditional, SEP, and SIMPLE IRAs to a Roth IRA in 2015 (excluding any portion you recharacterized).

16	If you completed Part I, enter the amount from line 8. Otherwise, enter the net amount you converted from traditional, SEP, and SIMPLE IRAs to Roth IRAs in 2015. **Do not** include amounts you later recharacterized back to traditional, SEP, or SIMPLE IRAs in 2015 or 2016 (see instructions)	**16**	
17	If you completed Part I, enter the amount from line 11. Otherwise, enter your basis in the amount on line 16 (see instructions)	**17**	
18	**Taxable amount.** Subtract line 17 from line 16. If more than zero, also include this amount on Form 1040, line 15b; Form 1040A, line 11b; or Form 1040NR, line 16b	**18**	

Part III   **Distributions From Roth IRAs**

Complete this part only if you took a distribution from a Roth IRA in 2015. For this purpose, a distribution does not include a rollover, one-time distribution to fund an HSA, recharacterization, or return of certain contributions (see instructions).

19	Enter your total nonqualified distributions from Roth IRAs in 2015, including any qualified first-time homebuyer distributions (see instructions)	**19**	
20	Qualified first-time homebuyer expenses (see instructions). **Do not** enter more than $10,000 . .	**20**	
21	Subtract line 20 from line 19. If zero or less, enter -0-	**21**	
22	Enter your basis in Roth IRA contributions (see instructions). If line 21 is zero, **stop here**	**22**	
23	Subtract line 22 from line 21. If zero or less, enter -0- and skip lines 24 and 25. If more than zero, you may be subject to an additional tax (see instructions)	**23**	
24	Enter your basis in conversions from traditional, SEP, and SIMPLE IRAs and rollovers from qualified retirement plans to a Roth IRA (see instructions)	**24**	
25	**Taxable amount.** Subtract line 24 from line 23. If more than zero, also include this amount on Form 1040, line 15b; Form 1040A, line 11b; or Form 1040NR, line 16b	**25**	

Sign Here Only If You Are Filing This Form by Itself and Not With Your Tax Return	Under penalties of perjury, I declare that I have examined this form, including accompanying attachments, and to the best of my knowledge and belief, it is true, correct, and complete. Declaration of preparer (other than taxpayer) is based on all information of which preparer has any knowledge.			
	▶ Your signature		▶ Date	
Paid Preparer Use Only	Print/Type preparer's name	Preparer's signature	Date	Check ☐ if self-employed PTIN
	Firm's name ▶			Firm's EIN ▶
	Firm's address ▶			Phone no.

Form **8606** (2015)

Saver's Credit (Retirement Savings Contribution Credit)

The **retirement savings contributions credit** is intended to encourage lower-income taxpayers to save for retirement. The rate used in calculating the credit is reduced as modified adjusted gross income (MAGI) increases, until the rate reaches zero percent at MAGI of $61,500 on a joint return for 2016, $46,125 for a head of household for 2016, and $30,750 in all other cases for 2016. For purposes of this credit, MAGI is defined in IRS Publication 590 as adjusted gross income less any exclusion or deduction claimed for the year for foreign earned income, foreign housing costs, income for bona fide residents of American Samoa, or income from Puerto Rico.

The retirement savings contributions credit is available to an eligible individual who makes qualified retirement savings contributions of up to $2,000 for a tax year. An eligible individual is a person who is 18 or older at the end of the tax year if that person is not allowed to be claimed as a dependent of another person for the year and is not considered to be a full-time student.

The amount of the credit is determined by multiplying a taxpayer's qualified retirement savings contributions (after the reduction for certain distributions) by the applicable percentage from Exhibit 9.8.

EXHIBIT 9.8

APPLICABLE PERCENTAGE FOR QUALIFIED RETIREMENT SAVINGS CONTRIBUTIONS CREDIT (2016)

Joint Return Modified AGI		Head of a Household Modified AGI		All Other Cases Modified AGI		Applicable Percentage
Over	Not over	Over	Not over	Over	Not over	
$0	$37,000	$0	$27,750	$0	$18,500	50%
37,000	40,000	27,750	30,000	18,500	20,000	20%
40,000	61,500	30,000	46,125	20,000	30,750	10%
61,500	--	46,125	--	30,750	--	0%

The maximum credit is $1,000 per person each year, or $2,000 on a joint return. Any credit that cannot be used in the current year is lost.

EXAMPLE 9.19

Kiley contributed $4,000 to her Roth IRA for 2016. She had MAGI of $15,000 for 2016 and used the single filing status. She has never taken a distribution from a retirement plan. Her maximum credit for 2016 is $1,000 ($2,000 x 50%).

Assume the same facts as above, except that Kiley contributes $5,000 to her Roth IRA for 2016. Also assume that her MAGI was $19,000 for 2016, then her maximum credit is $400 ($2,000 x 20%).

Reese, who works at a retail store, is married and earned $30,000 in 2016. Reese's husband was unemployed in 2016 and did not have any earnings. Reese contributed $1,000 to her IRA in 2016. After deducting her IRA contribution, the adjusted gross income shown on her joint return is $29,000. Reese may claim a 50% credit, $500, for her $1,000 IRA contribution.

EXAMPLE 9.20

Seth, who is an architect, is married and earned $39,000 in 2016. Seth's wife, Morgan, is an actress, but did not have any earnings in 2016. Seth, who is concerned about their retirement, contributed $2,000 to each of their Roth IRAs in 2016. The adjusted gross income shown on their joint return is $39,000. Seth and Morgan may claim a 20% credit, $800 (20% up to $4,000), for their contributions to the Roth IRAs.

EXAMPLE 9.21

If Seth would have established traditional IRAs for Morgan and himself, then he would have reduced his AGI to $35,000 ($39,000 - $4,000) and therefore would have had a credit of 50% of $4,000 or $2,000.

Distributions from Traditional IRAs

Generally, distributions from traditional IRAs are taxed as ordinary income. The one exception is for distributions consisting of a combination of tax-deferred earnings and the return of adjusted basis that results from either non-deductible IRA contributions or rollovers of contributions from qualified plan balances that included after-tax contributions (such as thrift plans). In such cases, each distribution will consist of a combination of return of **adjusted basis** (AB) and ordinary income. The ratio of return of AB is equal to the ratio of the total AB of the account before the withdrawal to the fair market value of the total account balance. The calculation will be made each year on Form 8606 (see Part 1).

$$\text{Ratio of AB} = \frac{\text{AB before withdrawal}}{\text{FMV of account at withdrawal}}$$

Andy has a traditional IRA with an account balance of $100,000. Over the years, he made after-tax contributions of $25,000, and the remaining $75,000 is attributable to pretax contributions and earnings. Therefore, Andy has an adjusted basis of $25,000, the total amount contributed after tax. When Andy begins receiving distributions, the distribution will be partially a return of basis and partially ordinary income. The ratio is calculated by dividing the AB over the fair market value ($25,000/$100,000 = ¼). Thus, if Andy took a $10,000 distribution then ¼ ($2,500) would be a return of basis and ¾ ($7,500) would be ordinary income.

EXAMPLE 9.22

Required Minimum Distributions

Traditional IRA distributions can be taken at anytime, but the **required minimum distribution** (RMD) rules require that the distributions must (except Roth IRAs) begin by April 1st of the year following the year in which the owner attains the age of 70½.[19] The minimum distribution rules require that traditional IRA owners begin receiving distributions from their accounts based on the same factors as discussed in Chapter 7 for qualified plans. These rules prohibit a taxpayer from continuing to indefinitely accrue tax-deferred earnings within their traditional IRA. Required distributions that are not taken are subject to a 50 percent excise tax.

The 10 Percent Penalty and its Exceptions for Early Withdrawals

By allowing deductions for traditional IRA contributions and by allowing balances in IRAs (both traditional and Roth) to grow on a tax-deferred basis, the government forfeits current income (tax revenue) to encourage taxpayers to save for retirement in their IRAs. The government also encourages taxpayers to leave funds in their traditional and Roth IRAs until retirement by imposing a 10 percent premature withdrawal penalty on taxable distributions prior to age 59½. Therefore, traditional and Roth IRA distributions before the age of 59½ will generally be subject to the 10 percent penalty unless a specific exception applies. Exhibit 9.9 summarizes the exceptions to the 10 percent withdrawal penalty for distributions from IRAs and qualified plans.

QUICK QUIZ 9.2

1. IRA contributions that exceed the contribution limits are subject to an excise tax of 6 percent.
   a. True
   b. False

2. Individuals who are active participants in a qualified retirement plan or SEP may be subject to a reduced maximum deductible IRA contribution.
   a. True
   b. False

3. Lump-sum IRA distributions may be taken at any time without being subject to penalty.
   a. True
   b. False

True, True, False.

---

19. The minimum distribution rules do not apply to Roth IRAs.

SUMMARY OF 10 PERCENT PENALTY EXCEPTIONS

EXHIBIT
9.9

Applies to Distributions from:	Exception to 10% Early Withdrawal Penalty
Both Qualified Plans & IRAs	• Death • Attainment of age 59½ • Disability • Substantially equal periodic payments (§72(t)) • Medical expenses that exceed 10% of AGI • Rollover • Because of an IRS tax levy • Certain distributions to qualified military reservists called to active duty
Only Qualified Plans	• Qualified Domestic Relations Order (QDRO) • Attainment of age 55 and separation from service • Public safety employee who separates from service after age 50 • Dividend pass through from an ESOP
Only IRAs	• Higher education expenses • First time home purchase (up to $10,000) • Payment of health insurance premiums by unemployed

The 10 percent penalty does not apply if a distribution is received after the owner attains the age of 59½, by a beneficiary after the account owner's death, because of the account owner's disability, for medical expenses in excess of 10 percent of the participant's AGI, if the distribution is part of a series of substantially equal periodic payments, because of an IRS tax levy, or received by a qualified military reservist. Taxpayers age 65 or older can substitute a 7.5 percent limit for the 10 percent limit. The final exceptions from the 10 percent penalty apply only for withdrawals from IRAs (not qualified plans) for higher education expenses, for acquisition costs of a first home (up to $10,000), and for health insurance premiums paid by the unemployed.

Higher Education Expenses

The education expense exception is for higher education expenses (post-secondary educational institutions) for the benefit of the taxpayer, taxpayer's spouse, child, or grandchild at an eligible educational institution. Qualified expenses include tuition, fees, books, supplies. Room and board will also be included if the student is at least half time.[20]

First Time Home Purchase

The first time home purchase exception applies up to a lifetime maximum of $10,000 for the acquisition of a home for the taxpayer, taxpayer's spouse, child, grandchild, or ancestor of such taxpayer or taxpayer's spouse. A first time home buyer is defined as an individual (and if married, such individual's spouse) that had no present ownership interest in a principal residence during the 2-year period ending on the date of acquisition of the principal residence to which the exception applies.[21]

20. IRC §529(e)(3).
21. IRC §72(t)(8)(D)(i)(I).

Health Insurance Premiums

The payment of health insurance premiums by an unemployed individual is not subject to the 10 percent penalty. The individual must have received unemployment compensation for 12 consecutive weeks under any federal or state unemployment compensation law.[22] The exception no longer applies when the individual has regained employment and has been employed for 60 days.

IRA ANNUITY VS. IRA ACCOUNTS

An individual retirement annuity is different than a traditional IRA because it is an annuity contract or endowment contract issued by an insurance company. However, an IRA annuity must meet certain similar requirements regarding transferability, nonforfeitability, premiums, and distributions.

Transferability and Nonforfeitability

An IRA annuity is not transferable by the owner and the benefits must not be forfeitable. The proceeds from an IRA annuity must be received by the owner or by a beneficiary of the contract. Similar to traditional IRAs, these IRA annuities cannot be pledged as collateral nor can loans be taken from the contract.

> ## KEY CONCEPTS
>
> 1. What is the difference between a traditional IRA and an individual retirement annuity?
>
> 2. How does a Roth IRA differ from a traditional IRA?
>
> 3. What are the income limits for Roth IRA contributions?
>
> 4. How can qualified plan assets be converted to a Roth IRA?
>
> 5. What are the requirements for a distribution from a Roth IRA to be classified as a qualified distribution?

Premiums

The annual premiums for an IRA annuity may not exceed $5,500 for 2016. The premiums for the IRA annuity cannot be fixed. In the event that premium payments cease, the owner must be given the right to receive a paid up annuity and the owner of the annuity must also be allowed to forego payment of the annuity premium.

Distributions

The distribution rules for IRA annuities are the same as for traditional IRAs. This includes the required minimum distribution beginning April 1st of the year following the year the owner attains the age of 70½ and the 10 percent penalty for distributions before age 59½.

ROTH IRAS

Roth IRAs were created by the Taxpayer Relief Act of 1997. Roth IRAs are very attractive because, although the contributions to a Roth IRA are not deductible, qualified distributions (defined below) from Roth IRA accounts consist solely of tax-free income. In other words, the tax-deferred earnings may be distributed without ever being subjected to income tax. Additionally, Roth IRAs may be funded after the owner attains the age of 70½ and are not subject to the required minimum distribution rules during the owner's life.

---

22. IRC §72(t)(2)(D)(i).

Roth IRAs and traditional IRAs share many of the same features and characteristics. The same contribution limitations that apply to traditional IRAs also apply to Roth IRAs, and this limit is an aggregate limit that includes contributions to both types of IRAs. Roth IRAs and traditional IRAs also share the prohibited transaction rules (as discussed below), the permitted investment rules, and the definition of earned income.

SIMILARITIES AND DIFFERENCES OF TRADITIONAL VS. ROTH IRAs

EXHIBIT 9.10

	Traditional IRA	Roth IRA
Earned Income	✓	✓
Contributions	Contributions **cannot** be made beyond 70½	Contributions **can** be made beyond 70½
Deductions	✓	N/A
Investment Choices	✓	✓
Minimum Distribution Rules	During life and after death	Only after death
Prohibited Transactions	✓	✓
Distributions	**Usually taxable**	**Usually tax free**

✓ = *same*

Taxpayers can fund Roth IRAs by either making cash contributions or by converting traditional IRAs or qualified plan balances into Roth IRAs.[23] When funding a Roth IRA, dollar limitations prevent contributions beyond certain income levels. As a result, high income and high net worth taxpayers generally cannot establish or fund Roth IRAs. However, they may be able to fund Roth accounts in 401(k) plans, 403(b) plans or 457 plans.

Contributions

Both Roth IRAs and traditional IRAs share an annual single contribution limit and use the same definition for earned income. However, taxpayers may only contribute to a Roth IRA if they fall within the prescribed income limits. For single individuals, the 2016 limit, based on AGI, ranges from $117,000 to $132,000. If a single taxpayer's adjusted gross income is below $117,000, then a full contribution can be made to a Roth IRA. If the taxpayer's AGI exceeds $132,000, then the taxpayer may not contribute to a Roth IRA. If the taxpayer's AGI falls between the limits, then the contribution is limited based on a phaseout calculation. For married taxpayers filing jointly, the AGI limit ranges from $184,000 to $194,000 (for 2016), so a couple (both below the age of 50) filing jointly could contribute $11,000 to their Roth IRAs for the year 2016 if their income is below $184,000.

---

23. With the changes of the PPA 2006, qualified plans can be converted directly to Roth IRAs after December 31, 2007.

EXHIBIT
9.11

FUNDING ROTH IRAS (2016 AGI LIMITS)

	Contribution AGI Phaseout Limit ($)
Single	$117,000 – $132,000
Married Filing Jointly	$184,000 – $194,000
Married Filing Separate	$0,000 – $10,000

* Under TIPRA 2005, the Conversion AGI Limit was eliminated for tax years after 2009.

Roth Accounts

The TRA 2001 created what is referred to as Roth accounts. These accounts permit employees to defer current income (on an after-tax basis) into the account with qualifying distributions being free from income tax. Today, Roth accounts are permitted in 401(k) plans, 403(b) plans, and 457 plans. This topic is discussed in more detail in Chapter 5.

Conversions

Both qualified plan balances and traditional IRAs can be converted to a Roth IRA. By converting a traditional IRA to a Roth IRA, a taxpayer hopes to receive distributions that are completely income tax-free. However, at the time of the conversion, the taxpayer must include the value of the **conversion** amount in their taxable income. Therefore, the taxpayer is making the choice to forego funds (those used to pay the tax) by paying tax today to save tax in the future. Generally, this is an effective strategy when the person converting to the Roth has lower current income tax rates than their future expected income-tax rates.

For tax years before 2010, taxpayers were permitted to convert traditional IRAs to Roth IRAs only if their AGI was less than or equal to $100,000. This same dollar limitation applied to single taxpayers and married taxpayers filing jointly and did not include the conversion amount in the calculation of AGI. Married taxpayers filing separate returns were not eligible to convert a traditional IRA to a Roth IRA.

The Tax Increase Prevention and Reconciliation Act of 2005 (TIPRA 2005) was signed into law on May 17, 2006. Under TIPRA 2005, the $100,000 adjusted gross income ceiling for converting a traditional IRA to a Roth IRA is eliminated for tax years after 2009. Qualified plan balances can also be directly converted into a Roth IRA without regard to the level of income of the taxpayer. Therefore, today, even high-income taxpayers can choose to convert IRAs or qualified plan balances to Roth IRAs. Whether or not taxpayers with higher income levels will choose to convert their IRAs will depend on many factors, including current marginal tax rates and future expected tax rates.

Recharacterized Contributions

IRA owners may **recharacterize** certain **contributions**[24] made to one type of IRA as made to a different type of IRA for a taxable year. For example, this may occur if a contribution is made to a traditional IRA, and the owner subsequently decides that it is better to contribute the funds to a Roth IRA. The individual can transfer the contribution (or a portion of the contribution) and its

---

24. Treas. Reg. §1.408A.

attributable earnings in a trustee-to-trustee transfer from the trustee of the FIRST IRA to the trustee of the Roth IRA (the SECOND IRA), and the individual can elect to treat the contribution as having been made to the SECOND IRA, instead of to the FIRST IRA, for federal income tax purposes.

These types of recharacterizations must be made by the due date of the individual's tax return (including extensions). However, the IRS has made exceptions in certain cases.

Andrea contributes $5,500 to her traditional IRA for 2016. Prior to the due date (plus extensions) for filing her federal income tax return, she decides that she would prefer to contribute to a Roth IRA instead. Andrea instructs the trustee of the traditional IRA to transfer in a trustee-to-trustee transfer the amount of the contribution, plus attributable earnings, to the trustee of a Roth IRA. She notifies the trustee of the traditional IRA and the trustee of the Roth IRA that she is recharacterizing the $5,500 contribution. On her federal income tax return, Andrea treats the $5,500 as having been contributed to the Roth IRA and not the traditional IRA.

EXAMPLE 9.23

Contributions to Roth IRAs can also be recharacterized as traditional IRA contributions. This type of recharacterization might apply in the event that a taxpayer made a contribution to a Roth IRA because he anticipated meeting the income limitations and later realized that his income exceeded the income limits.

Kristi, who is single, contributes $5,500 to her Roth IRA for 2016. However, she receives a significantly larger bonus because of her hard work and dedication to the firm. This unusually large bonus causes her income to exceed $132,000 (the 2016 income limit for contributions to Roth IRAs). As a result, she recharacterizes the contribution to the Roth IRA as a contribution to her traditional IRA. If Kristi is not an active participant, she can deduct this contribution on her federal tax return. However, if she is an active participant, then she would effectively be making an after-tax contribution to her traditional IRA and would be required to file Form 8606.

EXAMPLE 9.24

As discussed in Chapter 7, Conversions from a traditional IRA or qualified plan to a Roth IRA can also be recharacterized.[25] If a taxpayer converted a traditional IRA and the value of the account subsequently dropped, the taxpayer could recharacterize the conversion. This option would likely reduce the taxpayer's tax attributable to the conversion.

Distributions

Distributions from IRAs and other retirement plans are generally treated as ordinary income. However, distributions from Roth IRAs are designed to be tax-free in retirement. A distribution from a Roth IRA is not included in the owner's gross income and is not subject to the 10 percent early withdrawal penalty if it is a "**qualified distribution**." Distributions that do not meet the definition of a qualified distribution may be subject to income tax and the early withdrawal penalty.

Qualified Distributions

A qualified distribution is a distribution from a Roth IRA that satisfies both of the following tests:

1. The distribution must be made after a five-taxable-year period (which begins January 1st of the taxable year for which the first regular contribution is made to any Roth IRA of the individual or, if earlier, January 1st of the taxable year in which the first conversion contribution is made to any Roth IRA of the individual), **AND**

2. The distribution satisfies one of the following four requirements:
   - made on or after the date on which the owner attains the age 59½,
   - made to a beneficiary or estate of the owner on or after the date of the owner's death,
   - is attributable to the owner being disabled, or
   - for first time home purchase (lifetime cap of $10,000 for first time homebuyers includes taxpayer, spouse, child, or grandchild who has not owned a house for at least 2 years).

25. Recall that in-plan Roth rollovers cannot be recharacterized.

On July 5, 2016, Tom Hall established a Roth IRA for year 2016 with a $1,200 contribution. Since this was his first contribution to a Roth IRA, his five-year period begins on January 1, 2016.

On February 16, 2017, Mary made an initial contribution of $900 to a Roth IRA. She made the contribution for the 2016 tax year (recall that a taxpayer can make contributions until April 15 of the following year to a traditional or Roth IRA for the prior tax year). Mary's five-year period begins on January 1, 2016 even though she made her initial contribution in 2017 because the contribution was for the 2016 tax year.

Colin decides that he wants a sailboat as a present for his 60th birthday. He decides to liquidate his Roth IRA to make the purchase. His first contribution to a Roth IRA was in 2001. Since he established the Roth IRA more than five years before the distribution and he is over the age of 59½, the distribution is a qualified distribution and is not subject to income tax or penalty.

The five-taxable-year period is not re-determined when the owner of a Roth IRA dies. Thus, the beneficiary of the Roth IRA would need to wait until the end of the original five-taxable-year period for the distribution to be a qualified distribution. Prior to the end of the five-year period, minimum distributions could be taken from the contribution and conversion layers without tax or penalty.

Jay first contributes to a Roth IRA three years ago. He also converted a traditional IRA to his Roth IRA last year. Unfortunately, a meat truck accidently tips over and crushes him to death. His son inherits the IRA and needs to begin taking minimum distributions. Although the distribution is on account of the death of the owner, it is not a qualified distribution because the five-year period has not elapsed. Therefore, he will need to take distributions from the inherited Roth IRA from the contribution and conversion layers to avoid income tax until the five-year period is met.

Nonqualified Distributions

Any amount distributed from an individual's Roth IRA that is not a qualified distribution is treated as made in the following order (determined as of the end of a taxable year and exhausting each category before moving to the following category):
1. from regular contributions (i.e., the $5,500 for 2016 annual contributions),
2. from conversion contributions on a first-in-first-out basis, and then
3. from earnings.

In the event a distribution is not a qualified distribution, the first layer will be return of adjusted basis (from after-tax contributions), followed by post-tax conversion contributions. Since these contributions have already been taxed there will be no income tax consequences (although there may be a penalty). The final layer consists of the tax-deferred earnings on contributions and conversions within the Roth IRA, which will be subject to tax and penalty if the distribution is not a qualified distribution.

Distributions will generally not be taxable to the extent that total distributions do not exceed total contributions and conversions. However, if an individual takes a distribution that is not a qualified distribution and the amount of the distribution is neither contributed to another Roth IRA in a qualified rollover contribution nor constitutes a corrective distribution, part of the distribution may be includible in the individual's gross income. The amount included in the owner's gross income is the amount by which the total of all distributions (qualified or not) taken through the years exceeds the amount of all contributions and conversions to all of the individual's Roth IRAs.

EXHIBIT 9.12

ROTH IRA DISTRIBUTIONS

10 Percent Early Withdrawal Penalty

The 10 percent early withdrawal penalty will generally apply to any portion of a distribution from a Roth IRA that is includible in gross income (such as distributions that consist of earnings within the Roth IRA). The penalty also applies to a nonqualified distribution, even if it is not includible in gross income, to the extent it is allocable to a conversion contribution if the distribution is made within the five-taxable-year period beginning with the first day of the individual's taxable year in which the conversion contribution was made.

It is important to note that although a nonqualified distribution may be subject to the 10 percent penalty based on the Roth IRA rules, the penalty may be avoided if the distribution falls within one of the exceptions for IRAs discussed earlier in this chapter.

For example, a distribution could avoid the 10 percent penalty if the proceeds were used for qualified higher education expenses or to pay for certain medical costs. The following table summarizes the treatment from the standpoint of taxation and penalties of distributions from a Roth IRA to the extent the distribution is not a qualified distribution.

SUMMARY OF NONQUALIFIED ROTH IRA DISTRIBUTIONS

EXHIBIT 9.13

	Subject to Taxation?	Subject to 10% Penalty?
Contributions	No	No
Conversions	No	Yes Within five years of conversion*
Earnings	Yes	Yes*

Penalty will not apply if the distribution falls within the exceptions listed above.

Joyce, age 45, contributed a total of $10,000 to her Roth IRA beginning six years ago. She also converted a traditional IRA with a balance of $25,000 to a Roth IRA two years ago. Her current account balance in both Roth IRAs is $43,000. If she receives a complete distribution from both of these Roth IRAs and uses the proceeds to pay for her son's college tuition, then the distribution will have the following tax treatment:

EXAMPLE 9.29

The distribution does not meet both of the requirements of a qualified distribution. Therefore, the earnings portion of the distribution ($8,000) is subject to ordinary income tax, but none of the distribution will be subject to the 10 percent early withdrawal penalty. The penalty does not apply because the proceeds are being used for qualified higher education expenses, one of the exceptions to the 10 percent early withdrawal penalty.

Assume the same facts as above, except that Joyce took the distribution from her Roth IRAs to be used as a down payment on her son's new Porsche sports car. The distribution will have the following tax treatment:

EXAMPLE 9.30

The distribution does not meet both of the requirements of a qualified distribution. Therefore, the earnings portion of the distribution ($8,000) is subject to ordinary income tax. In addition, the 10 percent early withdrawal penalty applies to the conversion portion of the distribution because she has converted from a traditional IRA to a Roth IRA within the last five years. The $8,000 of earnings that is considered taxable income is also subject to the 10 percent early withdrawal penalty and the $25,000 conversion is subject to the 10 percent penalty but is not taxable.

If Joyce was over the age of 59½, then the distribution would have been a qualified distribution and none of the distribution would be subject to ordinary income tax or penalty. The year of the conversion is only a factor when the distribution is not a qualified distribution. In this case, the Roth IRA was established six years ago, and Joyce was over 59½, thus the distribution was a qualified distribution.

EXAMPLE 9.31

Brad is 61 years old and first contributed to a Roth IRA three years ago. His contributions to the Roth IRA total $6,000. In addition, Brad converted his traditional IRA to a Roth IRA last year. The conversion was in the amount of $20,000. If Brad takes a $35,000 distribution from the Roth IRA, it will have the following tax treatment:

The distribution has not met the five-year requirement to be a qualified distribution. Therefore, the portion of the distribution that consists of earnings ($9,000) is subject to ordinary income tax, but none of the distribution will be subject to the 10 percent early withdrawal penalty. The penalty does not apply because Brad is over the age of 59½, one of the exceptions to the 10 percent early withdrawal penalty.

COMPARING ROTH IRAS TO TRADITIONAL IRAS

Two important distinctions when comparing Roth IRAs to traditional IRAs are:
1. unlike traditional IRAs, an individual can make a contribution to a Roth IRA after the age of 70½; and
2. the required minimum distribution rules do not apply to Roth IRAs during the life of the original account owner, but, like traditional IRAs, do apply to the beneficiaries.

OTHER IRA ISSUES

Investments

Individuals have a plethora of options regarding the investment choices for assets purchased or held in an IRA. Investments in cash, stocks, bonds, and even options are permitted. However, custodians often limit IRA owners from investing in certain option contracts, especially naked options, within an IRA.

Although there is great freedom of investment choices, certain types of investments are prohibited. Life insurance and collectibles[26] are not allowed to be held within an IRA. If either life insurance or collectibles are purchased within an IRA, the value of the purchase is treated as a distribution from the IRA account and is subject to tax and/or penalty.

KEY CONCEPTS

1. What are the limitations on the types of investments that can be held in an IRA?
2. What are the rollover rules for transferring balances from a qualified plan to an IRA?
3. What are the distribution rules for an IRA?
4. What transactions are considered prohibited for an IRA?

Collectibles include all of the following:[27]
- any work of art
- any rug or antique
- any metal or gem
- any stamp or coin
- any alcoholic beverage

An exception to the collectibles rule exists for certain coins and bullion. U.S. gold, silver, and platinum minted coins, such as American Gold, Silver, and Platinum Eagle coins, are permitted to

---

26. IRC §408(a)(3).
27. IRC §408(m).

be held in an IRA account. However, coins of most foreign countries, such as South African Krugerrands, are considered collectibles and are therefore not permissible investments for an IRA. In addition, investments in gold, silver, platinum, or palladium bullion are permitted.

Tax-Free Distributions for Charitable Purposes

First introduced under the Pension Protection Act of 2006, qualified charitable distributions[28] from a traditional or Roth IRA may be excluded from gross income for years 2007 through 2014. The Protecting Americans from Tax Hikes Act of 2015 (PATH 2015) makes this provision permanent for years 2015 and beyond. The exclusion may not exceed $100,000 per taxpayer per tax year. A qualified charitable distribution is any distribution from an IRA directly by the IRA trustee to a charitable organization. Qualified charitable distributions are taken into account for purposes of the minimum distribution rules applicable to traditional IRAs to the same extent the distribution would have been taken into account under such rules had the distribution not been directly distributed under this provision. Distributions are eligible for this exclusion only if made on or after the date the IRA owner attains age 70½.

This provision is extremely helpful for those taxpayers with charitable intent. Without this law change, a taxpayer would take a distribution from his IRA, which would be subject to ordinary income, and then contribute that amount to charity. Although the taxpayer might be able to take a charitable deduction, that deduction is "below-the-line" and subject to phase-out limits, and does not completely offset the inclusion into income. The old rules actually result in a cost to the taxpayer who gives away funds from his IRAs. This exclusion makes it easier and tax-free, thus benefiting both charities and taxpayers.

IRA Rollovers

There are a variety of rollover rules that facilitate taxpayers transferring their retirement balances from one type of plan or account to another. These rules address transfers from qualified plans and from IRAs. EGTRRA 2001 greatly enhanced the portability and flexibility of transferring retirement funds.

---

28. IRC §408(d)(8).

EXHIBIT
9.14

SUMMARY OF ALLOWABLE ROLLOVERS

	ROLL TO							
	Traditional IRA	SEP-IRA	SIMPLE IRA	Roth IRA	Government 457(b)	403(b)	Qualified Plan	Designated Roth Account 401(k), 403(b), 457(b)
Traditional IRA	Yes	Yes	No	Yes, must include in income.	Yes, must have separate accounts.	Yes	Yes	No
SEP-IRA	Yes	Yes	No	Yes, must include in income.	Yes, must have separate accounts.	Yes	Yes	No
SIMPLE IRA	Yes, after 2 years.	Yes, after 2 years.	Yes	Yes, after 2 years. Must include in income.	Yes, after 2 years. Must have separate accounts.	Yes, after 2 years.	Yes, after 2 years.	No
Roth IRA	No	No	No	Yes	No	No	No	No
Government 457(b)	Yes	Yes	No	Yes. Must include in income.	Yes	Yes	Yes	Yes as in plan rollover. Must include in income.
403(b)	Yes	Yes	No	Yes. Must include in income.	Yes, must have separate accounts.	Yes	Yes	Yes as in plan rollover. Must include in income.
Qualified Plan	Yes	Yes	No	Yes. Must include in income.	Yes, must have separate accounts.	Yes	Yes	Yes as in plan rollover. Must include in income.
Designated Roth Account 401(k), 403(b), 457(b)	No	No	No	Yes	No	No	No	Yes, if a direct trustee to trustee transfer.

Distributions from Qualified Plans

When an individual terminates employment with the plan sponsor of a qualified plan, the individual may roll the qualified plan balance over into an IRA. Typically, an IRA that holds funds that have been transferred from a qualified plan is referred to as a "conduit" IRA or an IRA rollover account. The funds in such a conduit IRA are allowed to be rolled back into another qualified plan, assuming the new plan permits such rollovers.

> Craig leaves his employer, Planet Source, where he was a participant in a qualified plan. Craig can rollover his balance in his qualified plan into an IRA, which is generally referred to as a conduit IRA. Once Craig finds a new employer, he can rollover the funds in the conduit IRA into the new qualified plan (assuming that the plan permits such a rollover contribution). Alternatively, Craig could maintain the conduit IRA until he turns age 70½, at which point he would be required to begin taking minimum distributions.

EXAMPLE 9.32

It is important to consider the assets that are being transferred from the qualified plan to the IRA. If assets that are not permitted to be held in an IRA, although allowed in a qualified plan, are rolled into an IRA, then there may be a deemed distribution that will be subject to taxable income and possibly the 10 percent premature withdrawal penalty. For example, life insurance can be held in a qualified plan but not in an IRA.

If a participant in a qualified plan wishes to convert to a Roth IRA through a rollover, it is no longer necessary that the participant first roll the qualified plan proceeds into a traditional IRA and then to the Roth IRA. As of 2008, a participant can roll directly from a qualified plan to a Roth IRA.[29] However, the rolled over amount will be includible in taxable income.

Many taxpayers and advisors often leave funds in a conduit IRA and never roll the funds over to another qualified plan because there are few real benefits (other than creditor protection) to having funds in a qualified plan versus having funds in an IRA. The following exhibit identifies some of the benefits of a qualified plan versus an IRA.

---

29. Under the PPA 2006, direct rollovers from qualified plans to Roth IRAs are allowed after 2007. Under previous law, a rollover from a qualified plan to a Roth IRA generally required the use of a conduit traditional IRA.

EXHIBIT
9.15

COMPARISON OF BENEFITS FOR QUALIFIED PLANS VS. IRAS

Benefits	Qualified Plan	IRA
Ten-year forward averaging and pre-1974 capital gain treatment permitted?	Yes, if participant is born prior to 1/2/36	No
Loans may be permitted?	Yes, if plan permits loans	No
Assets are protected from creditors (ERISA or state law)?	Yes, ERISA	Yes, under the federal bankruptcy laws.*
Assets can be invested in life insurance?	Yes	No
Participants/owners have complete discretion of investment decisions?	Generally No	Yes
60 day rollover?	No	Yes

Except inherited IRAs may not be protected from creditors in bankruptcy. (See Chapter 7)

As discussed in Chapter 7, although 10-year forward averaging and capital gain treatment for pre-1974 participation is available for lump-sum distributions from a qualified plan, it is only available for those taxpayers born prior to January 2, 1936. Thus, the number of taxpayers who would qualify for **10-year forward averaging** or **pre-1974 capital gain treatment** is minimal. One advantage of a qualified plan is that participants may be able to withdraw a portion of the plan balance as a loan. However, the plan must provide for this feature and many plans do not permit loans. Although IRAs do not allow for loans, they do permit a rollover of 60 days that can, in effect, be a short-term loan (see discussion below). One of the most advantageous features of a qualified plan is the creditor protection that is provided by ERISA. This type of protection is not available to IRAs, however federal bankruptcy law now protects certain IRA accounts.[30]

Employee after-tax contributions from a qualified plan may be rolled over into another qualified plan or a traditional IRA for years after December 31, 2001. In the case of a rollover from a qualified plan to another qualified plan, the rollover is permitted only through a direct transfer. In addition, a qualified plan is not permitted to accept rollovers of after-tax contributions unless the plan provides separate accounting for such contributions and earnings. After-tax contributions, including nondeductible contributions to an IRA, are not permitted to be rolled over from an IRA into a qualified plan or 403(b) plan.

60-day Period

Taxpayers have the ability to take a distribution from an IRA at any time. However, distributions from IRAs will generally be taxed as ordinary income and may be subject to the 10 percent early withdrawal penalty if the distribution is not rolled back into another IRA within 60 days from the original distribution. (Although, the IRS may waive the 60-day requirement in the event the delay is caused by casualty, disaster, or other events beyond the taxpayers control.) This rule permits taxpayers to receive a distribution, make use of the funds for a period of 60 days, and then redeposit the funds into an IRA without any tax consequences. The PPA 2006 makes permanent EGTRRA rules giving the IRS authority to extend the 60-day rollover period when a person's

---

30. Bankruptcy Abuse Prevention and Consumer Protection Act of 2005.

failure to comply is due to events beyond the reasonable control of that person. There are many examples of the IRS waiving or extending the 60-day period. The following example from a private letter ruling illustrates this point.

EXAMPLE
9.33

IRS Letter Ruling 200925047 (Mar. 26, 2009)

Taxpayer A, asserts that on Date 3, Taxpayer A received a distribution of Amount L from Plan X. Taxpayer A asserts that her failure to accomplish a rollover of Amount L within the 60 day period prescribed by section 402(c)(3)(A) of the Code was due to the failure of her tax service provider, Attorney V, to provide correct advice regarding the distribution of Amount L from Plan X.

On Date 1, Taxpayer A's husband, Decedent D, died having designated Taxpayer A as the beneficiary of his account balance in Plan X, a plan intended to be qualified under Section 401(a) of the Internal Revenue Code. In addition to her husband's sudden and unexpected death at age 55, Taxpayer A had lost her father and uncle earlier in the year. After her husband's death, Taxpayer A began exhibiting signs of depression such as sleeplessness, extreme weight loss, and potentially dangerous lapses of concentration due to her grief.

During this period on Date 2, three months after Decedent D's death, Plan X distributed a check in Amount M, (Amount L minus tax withholding) which Taxpayer A deposited in a money market account for safe keeping. Taxpayer A sought professional treatment for anxiety and depression during the 60 day period after the distribution of Amount L from Plan X. Taxpayer A was prescribed drugs to alleviate depression and anxiety. Taxpayer A has submitted documentation from health care providers Dr. L, Health Care Provider O, Instructor C, and Individual K attesting to Taxpayer A's depression and out of character behavior during the 60-day rollover period.

Decedent D and Taxpayer A retained Attorney V to prepare their wills. Attorney V took control of Decedent D's estate tax planning from Taxpayer A after Decedent D's death and was in charge of Decedent D's estate inventory both before and after the Date 2 distribution from Plan X and throughout the following 60-day rollover period. In Fact, the distribution of Amount M was included as an asset on the Estate Inventory filed with the Probate Court of the county of Decedent D's last residence. Before the end of the 60-day rollover period Taxpayer A was assured by Attorney V that she would have no income tax liabilities as a result of Taxpayer A's inheritance of assets from Decedent D.

Taxpayer A submits that during the depression treatment period which included all of the 60-day rollover period, she relied on Attorney V to handle the financial affairs of Decedent D and Attorney V failed to timely inform Taxpayer A of the availability of a rollover option for Amount L from Plan X and failed to properly advise her and to properly manage the distribution of Amount L until after the 60-day period for a rollover to an IRA had expired. Taxpayer A was notified of her lost opportunity for a rollover of the Amount L Plan X distribution by Certified Financial Planner M after the expiration of the 60-day rollover period who advised Taxpayer A to write the Internal Revenue Service for a 60-day rollover waiver request.

> Based on the above information, the Service waived the 60-day rollover period found in section 402(c)(3)(A). As a result Taxpayer A is granted a period of 60 days from the issuance of this ruling letter to contribute Amount L, or any portion thereof, to an IRA.

Generally, if the taxpayer makes a tax-free rollover of any part of a distribution from a traditional IRA they cannot make another tax-free rollover from that same IRA or any other of their IRAs within a one-year period. The one-year period begins on the date the taxpayer received the IRA distribution, not on the date they rolled it back into an IRA.[31]

> Kole has two traditional IRAs: IRA-1 and IRA-2. Kole makes a tax-free rollover of a distribution from IRA-1 into a new traditional IRA (IRA-3). Kole cannot within 1 year of the distribution from IRA-1, make a tax-free rollover of any distribution from any of his IRAs into another traditional IRA.

Rollover to Qualified Plans

In the past, only funds held in a conduit IRA could be rolled back into a qualified plan. However, distributions after December 31, 2001 from an IRA are now permitted to be rolled over into a qualified plan, §403(b) annuity, or governmental §457 plan. Although it is now permissible to roll an IRA balance into a qualified plan, 403(b), or 457 plan, these plans are not required to accept such rollovers.

Lump-sum distributions from qualified plans may receive special tax treatment, including pre-74 capital gains treatment and 10-year forward averaging. However, a distribution from a qualified plan is not eligible for capital gains or averaging treatment if there was a rollover to the plan that would not have been permitted under present law. Thus, in order to preserve capital gains and averaging treatment for a qualified plan distribution that is rolled over, the rollover would have to be made to a conduit IRA and then rolled back into a qualified plan. In effect, the IRS does not permit taxpayers to receive special tax treatment on funds held in an IRA that would never have qualified for special tax treatment.

ERISA Protection vs. State Law Protection

As discussed in Chapter 3, qualified plans are protected by ERISA, which provides that a participant's accounts and benefits under the plan may not be alienated or assigned.[32] However, IRAs are not afforded this same protection because IRAs are not exempt from creditor's claims under ERISA.

---

31. IRC Section 408(d)(3)(A)(i) provides generally that any amount distributed from an IRA will not be included in the gross income of the distributee to the extent the amount is paid into an IRA for the benefit of the distributee no later than 60 days after the distributee receives the distribution. This type of rollover is generally referred to as an indirect rollover. Section 408(d)(3)(B) provides that an individual is permitted to make only one rollover described in the preceding sentence in any 1-year period. Previously, Proposed Regulation § 1.408-4(b)(4)(ii) and IRS Publication 590, Individual Retirement Arrangements (IRAs), provided that this limitation is applied on an IRA-by-IRA basis. However, a recent Tax Court opinion, Bobrow v. Commissioner, T.C. Memo. 2014-2, held that the limitation applies on an aggregate basis, meaning that an individual could not make an IRA-to-IRA rollover if he or she had made such a rollover involving any of the individual's IRAs in the preceding 1-year period. In Announcement 2014-32, the IRS made clear that it will follow the Tax Court's opinion and the new interpretation will apply beginning Jan. 1, 2015. Although an eligible IRA distribution received on or after Jan. 1, 2015 and properly rolled over to another IRA will still get tax-free treatment, subsequent distributions from any of the individual's IRAs (including traditional and Roth IRAs) received within one year after that distribution will not get tax-free rollover treatment.
32. ERISA § 206(d).

Case Study 9.2

Lawrence F. Peek And Sara L. Peek, and Darrell G. Fleck And Kimberly J. Fleck (Taxpayers) vs. Commissioner of the Internal Revenue Service (IRS)

In 2001 Taxpayers established new traditional IRAs. Taxpayers formed FP Corp. and directed their new IRAs to use rolled-over cash to purchase 100% of FP Corp.'s newly issued stock. Taxpayers used FP Corp. to acquire the assets of AFS Corp. Taxpayers personally guaranteed loans of FP Corp. that arose out of the asset purchase. In 2003 and 2004 Taxpayers undertook to roll over the FP Corp. stock from their traditional IRAs to Roth IRAs, including in Taxpayers' income the value of the stock rolled over in those years. In 2006 after the FP Corp. stock had significantly appreciated in value, Taxpayers directed their Roth IRAs to sell all of the FP stock. Taxpayers' personal guaranties on the loans of FP Corp. persisted up to the stock sale in 2006. IRS contends that Taxpayers' personal guaranties of the FP Corp. loan were prohibited transactions, and, as a result, the gains realized in 2006 and 2007 from the 2006 sales of FP stock should be included in Taxpayers' income.

The Tax Court Held:

- Each of Taxpayers personal guaranties of the FP Corp. loan was an indirect extension of credit to the IRAs, which is a prohibited transaction; and under IRC Section 408(e), the accounts that held the FP Corp. stock ceased to be IRAs.
- The gains realized on the sale of the FP Corp. stock are included in Taxpayers' income.
- Taxpayers are liable for the accuracy-related penalty under IRC Section 6662.

Since the Court held that the loan guaranties were prohibited transactions, it did not need to address nor did it address two other issues that appear problematic for the Taxpayers:

- FP Company made payments of wages to Mr. Fleck and Mr. Peek, which the IRS contends were prohibited transactions under section 4975(c)(1)(D).
- FP Company made payments of rent to an entity owned by Mrs. Fleck and Mrs. Peek, which the IRS contends were prohibited transactions under section 4975(c)(1)(E).

The Supreme Court ruled on April 4, 2005 that IRAs can be exempt property in a bankruptcy proceeding. Although providing some protection where there was none previously, the ruling does not provide blanket protection for IRAs.

Case Study 9.3

Rousey Et Ux v. Jacoway: Several years after petitioners deposited distributions from their pension plans into Individual Retirement Accounts (IRAs), the Rouseys filed a joint petition under Chapter 7 of the Bankruptcy Code. They sought to shield portions of their IRAs from their creditors by claiming them as exempt from the bankruptcy estate under 11 U. S. C. §522(d)(10)(E), which provides, inter alia, that a debtor may withdraw from the estate his "right to receive . . . a payment under a stock bonus, pension, profit sharing, annuity, or similar plan or contract on account of . . . age." Respondent Jacoway, the Bankruptcy Trustee, objected to the Rouseys' exemption and moved for turnover of the IRAs to her. The Bankruptcy Court sustained her objection and granted her motion, and the Bankruptcy Appellate Panel (BAP) agreed. The Eighth Circuit affirmed, concluding that, even if the Rouseys' IRAs were "similar plans or contracts" to the plans specified in §522(d)(10)(E), their IRAs gave them no right to receive payment "on account of age," but were instead savings accounts readily accessible at any time for any purpose.

However, the Supreme Court held that the Rouseys can exempt IRA assets from the bankruptcy estate because the IRAs fulfill both of the §522(d)(10)(E) requirements at issue here—they confer a right to receive payment on account of age and they are similar plans or contracts to those enumerated in §522(d)(10)(E).

However, as a result of the Bankruptcy Abuse Prevention and Consumer Protection Act of 2005 (BAPCPA 2005), IRAs are now afforded similar protection to qualified plans under Federal Bankruptcy law. The Act clarifies that retirement accounts that are exempt from tax under the Internal Revenue Code are also exempt from the debtor's estate. The aggregate value of the assets in a traditional IRA or a Roth IRA that may qualify for this exemption cannot exceed $1 million for an individual debtor.[33] However, the assets subject to the $1 million cap do not include amounts attributable to rollover contributions or earnings on these amounts. This exemption is generally available to all debtors, regardless of whether they choose the federal bankruptcy exemptions or the exemptions available under the laws of their state. Despite this expanded protection for IRAs, consideration should still be given to all of the facts and circumstances surrounding a rollover from a qualified plan to an IRA since IRAs are still not provided the same anti-alienation protection provided under ERISA.[34] Note that inherited IRAs with a nonspouse beneficiary may not be protected in bankruptcy. Additional information on inherited IRAs with a nonspouse beneficiary is available in Chapter 7.

---

33. This amount is periodically indexed.
34. Bankruptcy Abuse Prevention and Consumer Protection Act of 2005 (BAPCPA 2005), §224.

Case Study 9.4

The *In re Dubroff*[1] case involved Dubroff, a Chapter 7 debtor, who claimed an exemption under New York law for the entire value of his IRA.[2] The creditors and bankruptcy trustee objected. Ultimately, the United States Second Circuit Court of Appeals held that the debtor could claim exemption for his IRA pursuant to a New York bankruptcy exemption statute. The Court reasoned that the Chapter 7 debtor could claim the exemption for his IRA under the New York bankruptcy exemption statute that exempted pension plans that qualify as an IRA under Internal Revenue Code and make payment on account of age. A subsequent statutory amendment to the New York law also explicitly exempted IRAs from satisfaction of money judgments. This case illustrates the importance of an IRA plan complying with all requirements of the Internal Revenue Code because, if such requirements are not met, the state protection afforded IRA assets of being free from seizure to satisfy money judgments or creditors in bankruptcy may otherwise be lost.

1. *In re Dubroff*, 119 F.3d 75 (2nd Cir. 1997).
2. Under Chapter 7 of the United States Bankruptcy Code, 11 U.S.C. §§101-1330, the debtor claimed an exemption under N.Y. Debt. & Cred. Law §282(2)(e) for the entire value of his IRA, which amounted to $43,974.

Prohibited Transactions

There are certain transactions that an owner or beneficiary is not permitted to engage in with an IRA. An IRA loses its tax exemption when the account ceases to be an IRA by reason of a **prohibited transaction**. If an individual or beneficiary of an IRA engages in any of the following transactions, then the account will cease to be an IRA as of the first day of the current taxable year:[35]

- selling, exchanging, or leasing of any property to an IRA,
- lending money to an IRA,
- receiving unreasonable compensation for managing an IRA,
- pledging an IRA as security for a loan,
- borrowing money from an IRA, or
- buying property for personal use (present or future) with IRA funds.

In the event that a prohibited transaction has occurred, the account ceases to be an IRA as of the beginning of the year and the entire balance in the IRA is treated as having been distributed.[36] In this case, the taxpayer will be subject to ordinary income tax on the entire balance and will also be subject to the 10 percent early withdrawal penalty if not otherwise exempted, as discussed above.

---

35. IRC §408(e)(2).
36. IRC §408(e)(2)(B).

A similar rule applies to an IRA annuity. If an individual borrows money against an IRA annuity contract, the individual must include the fair market value of the annuity contract as of the first day of the tax year in his gross income. The distribution may also be subject to the 10 percent early withdrawal penalty.

Transfers Incident to Divorce

If an interest in an IRA is transferred from a spouse or former spouse (transferor) to an individual (transferee) by reason of divorce, **qualified domestic relations order (QDRO)**, separate maintenance decree, or a written document related to such a decree, starting from the date of the transfer, the interest in the IRA is treated as the individual's (transferee's) IRA.[37]

However, if an owner receives a distribution from an IRA and subsequently transfers the distributed funds to the other spouse pursuant to a divorce decree, the distribution is subject to ordinary income tax and, potentially, a 10 percent early withdrawal penalty.

If an individual is required to transfer some or all of the assets of his traditional IRA to a spouse or former spouse, there are two commonly used methods to make the transfer. The individual can instruct the custodian to simply change the name on the account to the name of the spouse or former spouse, or one spouse can direct the trustee of his IRA to transfer the funds directly to the trustee of the other spouse's IRA.

myRA | my RETIREMENT ACCOUNT

As discussed in Chapter 1, there is ample evidence that suggests Americans are not adequately prepared for retirement in terms of savings rate or accumulated savings. In addition, there is not enough access to company sponsored retirement plans for employees of smaller companies and participation rates in plans should be higher.

In an attempt to help resolve this issue, President Obama, in the State of the Union speech on January 28, 2014, announced the creation of a new type of retirement plan that allows individuals a way to begin saving for retirement. The plan, called **myRA**, is an attempt to provide access to a retirement account for those who do not have access at work.

---

37. IRC §408(d)(6).

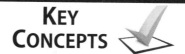

The U.S. Department of the Treasury developed *my*RA (my Retirement Account) as a new type of Roth IRA with an investment fund that is backed by the United States Treasury and the account carries no risk of losing money. The fund is a government securities fund for federal employees.[38]

CONTRIBUTIONS

The annual limit for *my*RA account is the same as for IRAs, up to $5,500 per year (or $6,500 per year for individuals who will be 50 years of age or older at the end of the year). However, there is no minimum and contributions are made through direct deposit from the employer. The *my*RA account can have a maximum balance of $15,000 or a lower balance for up to 30 years, When either of these limits is reached, savings must be rolled over (transferred) into a private-sector Roth IRA. A rollover to the private sector allows savings to continue beyond the *my*RA starter savings account. Savers can choose to roll over their account balance into a private-sector Roth IRA at any time.

Contributions can be continued with a new employer, as long as direct deposit is offered from the employer. However, the overall annual IRA limit applies from all sources, including *my*RA. For example, if a saver fully funded her *my*RA, then she could not also fund a traditional or Roth IRA.

DISTRIBUTIONS

The distribution rules are identical to those for Roth IRAs. Qualified distributions will be tax-free and penalty-free. Distributions that are not qualified will be taxed in the same manner as non-qualified distributions from Roth IRAs.

BENEFITS OF myRA

The primary benefit of this plan is that it allows employees to set up a retirement plan with minimal assistance from the employer. The plan is designed to have minimal employer involvement and does not require an employer to sponsor a plan or establish a plan. The only employer requirement is that direct deposit must be offered. All other retirement plans offered through an employer require more employer participation. The structure of this program is similar to payroll deduction IRAs.

KEY CONCEPTS

1. What is a *my*RA account?

2. How is a *my*RA account similar to an IRA?

3. What is one of the primary benefits of a *my*RA account?

4. What are the limits for a *my*RA account?

QUICK QUIZ 9.5

1. One of the drawbacks of a *my*RA account is that it requires an employer to set up an account for the employee.
   a. True
   b. False

2. The contribution limits for a myRA account are the same as a traditional or Roth IRA.
   a. True
   b. False

3. One of the advantages of a myRA account is the ability to purchase individual securities within the account.
   a. True
   b. False

False, True, False.

---

38. https://myra.treasury.gov/

Another important benefit of this account is that it allows employees to save through payroll deduction. This feature is important because it allows employees to save before receiving the funds. This account also benefits from the same attributes of Roth IRAs, including taxed deferred earnings, potential tax-free distributions and protections from creditors.

SIMPLIFIED EMPLOYEE PENSION (SEPS)

A **simplified employee pension (SEP)** is a practical retirement plan alternative to a qualified plan that can be used by small businesses and sole proprietors. SEPs are easier to establish than qualified plans and have practically no filing requirements. Because SEPs use IRAs as the receptacle for contributions, there is no trust accounting for the plan sponsor. In addition, SEPs have similar characteristics to profit sharing plans in terms of funding limits.

Because a SEP is not a qualified plan, it has some unique rules compared to the rules for qualified plans. For example, SEPs have more liberal participation requirements than qualified plans, have a later establishment date, and have different contribution, distribution, and vesting rules.

KEY CONCEPTS

1. List the coverage requirements for an employee to participate in a SEP.

2. How does an employer establish a SEP?

3. When is the latest date that an employer can establish a SEP?

4. Identify the contribution rules for SEPs.

5. When may an employee withdraw funds from his SEP?

PARTICIPATION

Employers that sponsor SEPs must provide benefits to almost all employees. The requirements for coverage include the following:
- Attainment of age 21 or older
- Performance of services for three of the last five years
- Received compensation of at least $600 during the year

The participation rules for SEPs mean that an employer must cover all employees who are 21 years of age, have worked for the company for a period of three years or more, and have earned more than $600 during the current year. Based on this definition, even part-time employees must be covered. However, the three-year requirement allows the employer to exclude anyone who has not worked for at least three years. Therefore, if a company has high employee turnover, a SEP may be used to exclude employees who do not remain employed for a period of at least three years.

It is important to note that contributions must be made on behalf of all employees who meet the participation rules during the calendar year whether or not they are still employed as of the end of the year and whether or not they are still alive. For example, an employee who resigned in March and earned more than $600 would be entitled to a contribution based on the employee's earnings through his termination date.

In addition, those employees over the age of 70½ who meet the eligibility rules must also receive an employer contribution to their SEP.

As with qualified plans, the employer may impose less restrictive participation requirements for its employees than those discussed above but not more restrictive requirements.

Employees can also be excluded from participation in a SEP if they are members of either of the following groups:
- Employees covered by a union agreement if their retirement benefits were bargained for in good faith by their union and their employer.
- Nonresident alien employees who have no U.S. source earned income from their employer.

ESTABLISHMENT OF A SEP

SEPs can be established, as well as funded, for a plan year as late as the due date of the federal income tax return including extensions. Therefore, SEPs can be established for the following entities as late as the date indicated below:

Entity	Due date of return	Final extension
Sole proprietorship (Schedule C)	April 15th	October 15th
Partnership (Form 1065)	April 15th	September 15th
Corporation (Form 1120)	March 15th	September 15th
S-Corporation (Form 1120S)	March 15th	September 15th

The ability to establish a SEP as late as ten months after the tax-year end is a significant advantage over qualified plans. Recall from Chapter 8 that qualified plans must be established by December 31st of the plan year. This establishment feature allows an advisor to recommend establishing a retirement plan and implementing it for the previous year.

To establish a SEP, the employer must complete three basic steps:
1. A formal written agreement to provide benefits to all eligible employees must be executed.
2. All eligible employees must be given notice about the SEP.
3. A SEP-IRA (the receptacle account) must be set up for each eligible employee.

The standard method of complying with the first requirement is to adopt the IRS model SEP using Form 5305-SEP (See Exhibit 9.16). Using Form 5305-SEP allows the plan to be established without IRS approval or a determination letter, and the form does not have to be filed with the IRS or the Department of Labor. The plan sponsor should keep the original form. Most financial service companies, including banks, mutual funds, brokerage houses, and insurance companies, have prototype SEP documents that can be used by employers.

EXHIBIT 9.16

FORM 5305-SEP[39]

Form **5305-SEP** (Rev. December 2004) Department of the Treasury Internal Revenue Service	**Simplified Employee Pension—Individual Retirement Accounts Contribution Agreement** (Under section 408(k) of the Internal Revenue Code)	OMB No. 1545-0499 **Do not** file with the Internal Revenue Service

_____ makes the following agreement under section 408(k) of the
(Name of employer)   Internal Revenue Code and the instructions to this form.

Article I—Eligibility Requirements (check applicable boxes—see instructions)

The employer agrees to provide discretionary contributions in each calendar year to the individual retirement account or individual retirement annuity (IRA) of all employees who are at least _____ years old (not to exceed 21 years old) and have performed services for the employer in at least _____ years (not to exceed 3 years) of the immediately preceding 5 years. This simplified employee pension (SEP) ☐ includes ☐ **does not** include employees covered under a collective bargaining agreement, ☐ includes ☐ **does not** include certain nonresident aliens, and ☐ includes ☐ **does not** include employees whose total compensation during the year is less than $450*.

Article II—SEP Requirements (see instructions)

The employer agrees that contributions made on behalf of each eligible employee will be:

A. Based only on the first $205,000* of compensation.
B. The same percentage of compensation for every employee.
C. Limited annually to the smaller of $41,000* or 25% of compensation.
D. Paid to the employee's IRA trustee, custodian, or insurance company (for an annuity contract).

_____   _____
Employer's signature and date   Name and title

Most recent version available at time of printing.

According to the IRS, Form 5305-SEP cannot be used in the following situations:

- The employer currently maintains another qualified retirement plan. However, this does not prevent the employer from sponsoring a SEP.
- If IRAs have not been established for any eligible employees.
- If the employer is a member of any of the following groups (unless all eligible employees of all the members of these groups, trades, or businesses participate in the SEP):
  - An affiliated group described in §414(m),
  - A controlled group of corporations described in §414(b),
  - Trades or businesses under common control described in §414(c), or
  - The employer does not pay the cost of the SEP contributions.

The employer must provide eligible employees with a copy of Form 5305-SEP, its instructions, and other information. This notification is a key element in establishing a SEP and is consistent with the establishment of qualified plans. Employees must be given notice of their rights relating to the employer's retirement plan.

39. The Form 5305-SEP is current. The numbers in the form with an asterisk are indexed.

CONTRIBUTIONS

Similar to profit sharing plans, employer contributions to SEPs are discretionary from year to year. Because of the discretionary nature of the contributions, SEPs are often used by small businesses that cannot or do not wish to commit to a mandatory contribution every year. However, in years that a contribution is made to a SEP, a contribution must be made for all employees eligible during the year, whether or not they are employed or alive as of the end of the year.

Contributions to SEPs are made by the employer and must be made to employees' IRA accounts based on a written formula that does not discriminate in favor of highly compensated employees. However, contributions to SEPs may be integrated with Social Security (permitted disparity). The contribution, subject to the limits discussed below, made for the employee is excluded from the employee's gross income and not subject to FICA or FUTA.

The limit for contributions to a SEP is the lesser of 25 percent of an employee's compensation or $53,000[40] for 2016. As with qualified plans, no more than $265,000 of compensation for 2016 can be considered for purposes of contributions to a SEP. Therefore, the maximum contribution for any employee in year 2016 is $53,000. It is important to understand that an employee might receive more than 25 percent of his compensation in a qualified plan through integration or cross-testing, but an employee cannot receive more than 25 percent of his compensation in a SEP.

For self-employed individuals, the 25 percent limit converts to 20 percent (0.25 ÷ 1.25) of net self-employment income. Recall that the 25 percent limit for self-employed individuals is based on earned income, not total income.[41]

Contributions to a SEP are included under IRC §415(c) for purposes of determining the annual contributions limit under IRC §415(c). Therefore, if the employer maintains a defined contribution qualified plan in addition to a SEP, both the SEP contribution and the qualified plan contribution are added together to determine whether or not the annual contributions limit ($53,000 for 2016) has been violated.

If the employer maintains a profit sharing plan in addition to a SEP, then contributions to the SEP reduce the 25 percent limit of the profit-sharing plan. In other words, the maximum that could be

QUICK QUIZ 9.6

1. Requirements for coverage in a SEP include an employee's performance of service for three of the last five years.
   a. True
   b. False

2. Part-time employees are exempt from being included in a SEP.
   a. True
   b. False

3. Employer contributions to SEPs are discretionary and do not have to be made each year.
   a. True
   b. False

4. Employer contributions to a SEP are 100% vested.
   a. True
   b. False

True, False, True, True.

---

40. IRC §§402(h)(2) and 408(j).
41. See Chapter 8 for more information on contribution for self-employed taxpayers.

contributed to a SEP and a profit-sharing plan in total cannot exceed 25 percent of total covered compensation.

Excess contributions are contributions in excess of the 25 percent or $53,000 limit for 2016. These excess contributions cannot be deducted in the current year but may be carried forward and deducted in a future year. However, excess contributions are generally subject to a 10 percent excise tax. This treatment is the same as with qualified plans.

DEDUCTIONS

Contributions to a SEP are deductible for the employer and excludable for the employees up to the limits discussed above. The employer's deduction for contributions to a SEP is generally claimed on the following forms:

Entity	Where to Deduct Contribution
Unincorporated business	Schedule C or Schedule F of Form 1040
Partnership	Form 1065
Corporation	Form 1120
S-Corporation	Form 1120S

The employer's deduction for contributions to a SEP is claimed on line 28 of Form 1040 if self-employed. This includes both sole proprietors and partners. Partnerships must distribute Schedule K-1 to all of its partners and passes its deduction for contributions to a SEP to the partner by way of Schedule K-1.

<table>
<tr><td>EXHIBIT
9.17</td><td colspan="2" align="center">ADJUSTED GROSS INCOME SECTION OF FORM 1040</td></tr>
</table>

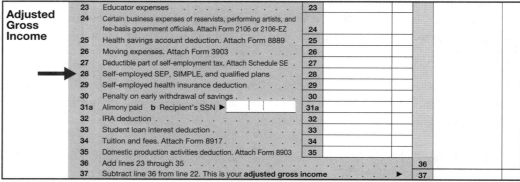

The deduction for contributions made to a SEP on behalf of the employer will be deducted on the tax return for corporations and S-corporations as with the deduction for contributions made on behalf of the employees.

VESTING AND WITHDRAWALS

Contributions for a SEP are made to IRA accounts on behalf of employees. As a result, there is no vesting for employer contributions. Once the contribution is made to an employee's SEP-IRA, the funds within that account immediately belong to the employee.

Further, employees are able to withdraw funds in any amount from their SEP-IRA because of the nature of the account – that is, because it is an IRA. This ability to withdraw funds is available at all times, including while the employee is still employed. However, if the employee does receive a distribution from the SEP-IRA, the distribution will be subject to ordinary income tax and may be subject to the early withdrawal penalty unless the distribution qualifies for any of the exceptions to the 10 percent early withdrawal penalty as discussed earlier for IRAs and Roth IRAs.

Note that contributions to SEPs are made to traditional IRA accounts and cannot be made to Roth IRA accounts.

SALARY REDUCTION SIMPLIFIED EMPLOYEE PENSION (SARSEPS)

Although SIMPLE plans were introduced by Congress to replace **SARSEPs**, which are not permitted to be established for years after 1996, many of the SARSEPs in existence prior to 1997 are still in operation. SARSEPs allow employees to elect to defer a portion of their current salary into a SEP-IRA in a similar fashion to 401(k) plans. In fact, the SARSEP deferral limit is the same as 401(k) plans. However, the SARSEP was very easy to establish and had minimal reporting and testing requirements.

To establish a SARSEP, an employer had to meet the following provisions:

- At least 50 percent of the employees eligible to participate must choose to defer a portion of their salary.
- The employer had to have no more than 25 eligible employees.
- The elective deferrals of the highly compensated employees had to meet the SARSEP ADP test (discussion follows).

> **KEY CONCEPTS**
>
> 1. What provisions were required in order for an employer to establish a SARSEP?
>
> 2. How do elective deferrals into a SARSEP work with other salary deferral type plans?

SARSEP ADP TEST

Under this test, the amount deferred each year by each eligible highly compensated employee as a percentage of pay (the deferral percentage) cannot be more than 125 percent of the average deferral percentage (ADP) of all nonhighly compensated employees eligible to participate.[42]

The deferral percentage equals:

$$ADP = \text{Elective employee deferral} \div \text{Employee's compensation}$$

---

42. The ADP test for 401(k) plans consists of three separate tests, one of which is the 125 percent test.

EXAMPLE
9.35

Consider the following example for Affable Company:

Employee	Ownership	Compensation	Elective Deferral	ADP
A	60%	$200,000	$11,000	5.50%
B	30%	$140,000	$9,800	7.00%
C	5%	$85,000	$3,400	4.00%
D	3%	$80,000	$5,000	6.25%
E	2%	$50,000	$2,500	5.00%
F	-	$40,000	$2,000	5.00%

Employees A and B are the only highly compensated employees. Their actual deferral percentage equals 6.25 percent [(5.50 + 7.00) ÷ 2]. The other four employees are non-highly compensated and have an actual deferral percentage of 5.06 percent [(4.00 + 6.25 + 5.00 + 5.00) ÷ 4]. The plan meets the ADP test because the ADP of the HCs is less than 1.25 times the ADP of the NHCs. The ADP of the NHCs times 1.25 equals 6.33, whereas the ADP for the HCs equals 6.25 percent.

ELECTIVE DEFERRAL LIMIT

An employee cannot defer more than $18,000 for 2016 of their compensation into a SARSEP. However, those taxpayers who have attained the age of 50 by the end of the tax year may make additional catch-up contributions as detailed in the chart that follows.

EXHIBIT
9.18

SUMMARY OF ELECTIVE DEFERRAL LIMITS (2016)

SARSEPs, 401(k) PLANS, 403(b) PLANS, 457 PLANS		ROTH 401(k) PLANS		SIMPLE PLANS	
Annual Deferral Limit	Catch-Up Contributions	Annual Deferral Limit	Catch-Up Contributions	Annual Deferral Limit	Catch-Up Contributions
$18,000	$6,000	$18,000	$6,000	$12,500	$3,000

It is important to note that the $18,000 deferral limit for 2016 applies to the aggregate elective deferrals the employee makes for the year to a SARSEP and any of the following plans:
- Cash or deferred arrangement (401(k) plan)
- Salary reduction arrangement under a tax-sheltered annuity plan (403(b) plan)
- SIMPLE IRA plan

This rule prevents an employee of a company who defers the maximum into his employer's 401(k) plan from also deferring salary from another source into one of the above plans. However, other income sources may be eligible to be considered for some other type of qualified plan arrangement or simplified employee pension.

If the employer makes nonelective contributions to the SARSEP, the combined employee and employer contributions cannot exceed the lesser of 25 percent of the employee's compensation or $53,000 for 2016.

EXCESS DEFERRALS

Excess deferrals in a SARSEP are elective contributions made by highly compensated employees that violate the SARSEP ADP test. The highly compensated employees must be given notice within 2½ months after the end of the plan year of their excess contributions. These deferral contributions must then be removed from the SARSEP. If the employer does not inform the highly compensated employees, then the employer must pay a 10 percent excise tax on the excess portion.

QUICK QUIZ 9.7

1. To establish a SARSEP, an employer had to have a minimum of 25 employees.
   a. True
   b. False

2. An employee, age 40, cannot defer more than $18,000 for 2016 of their compensation into a SARSEP in a single year.
   a. True
   b. False

False, True.

KEY TERMS

ACTIVE PARTICIPANT - Individuals who participate in a qualified plan under IRC 401(a), a 403(b) plan, a government retirement plan, a SEP, or a SIMPLE. Participating means receiving a benefit under the plan.

ADJUSTED BASIS (AB) - The portion of a distribution that is not subject to income tax. Usually, the return of after-tax contributions or nondeductible contributions.

ADJUSTED GROSS INCOME (AGI) - A tax return amount that includes an individual's income less certain deductions, known as "above-the-line" deductions. AGI is calculated before subtracting the standard or itemized deductions and the personal and dependency exemptions. The calculated AGI affects the deductibility of traditional IRA contributions and the ability to make Roth IRA contributions.

ALIMONY - Support payments from one ex-spouse to the other. Alimony received is considered earned income for purposes of making IRA contributions.

CONTRIBUTIONS - Payments to an IRA.

CONVERSION - When a traditional IRA is converted to a Roth IRA. At the date of conversion, an individual includes the fair market value of the traditional IRA into the individual's adjusted gross income.

CUSTODIANS - Brokerage company, bank, or mutual fund company that holds an individual's IRA.

EARNED INCOME - Any type of compensation where the individual has performed some level of service for an employer or is considered self-employed, plus alimony received.

INDIVIDUAL RETIREMENT ACCOUNT (IRA) - Two general types under present law: traditional IRAs, to which both deductible and nondeductible contributions may be made, and Roth IRAs, to which only nondeductible contributions may be made.

INDIVIDUAL RETIREMENT ANNUITY - An annuity contract or endowment contract issued by an insurance company that follows many of the same rules for deductibility of premium payments and the limits for premium payments as a traditional IRA.

MYRA (MY RETIREMENT ACCOUNT) - A new type of Roth IRA with an investment fund that is backed by the United States Treasury and the account carries no risk of losing money.

PHASEOUT - The AGI range that will affect the deductibility of IRA contributions and an individual's ability to make contributions to a Roth IRA.

PRE-1974 CAPITAL GAIN TREATMENT - A special taxation treatment for lump-sum distributions from qualified plans that treat the distribution attributable to pre-1974 participation in the plan as long-term capital gain.

KEY TERMS

PROHIBITED TRANSACTIONS - Transactions that an owner or beneficiary is not permitted to engage in with an IRA.

QUALIFIED DISTRIBUTION - A distribution from a Roth IRA that is made after a five-taxable-year period and on account of the account owner's death, disability, attainment of age 59½, or first-time home purchase.

QUALIFIED DOMESTIC RELATIONS ORDER (QDRO) - A court order related to divorce, property settlement, or child support that can divide a participant's interest in a qualified plan.

RECHARACTERIZE - Transferring a contribution and its attributable earnings from a traditional IRA to a Roth IRA or vice versa. The recharacterization must occur by the tax return filing date including extensions for the year of the recharacterization.

REQUIRED MINIMUM DISTRIBUTION (RMD) - A minimum amount that must be withdrawn from a qualified plan each year after the participant attains the age of 70½. The amount is calculated using either the uniform distribution table, the single life expectancy table, or the joint life expectancy tables.

ROTH IRA - An IRA created by the Taxpayer Relief Act of 1997. Contributions to a Roth IRA are nondeductible and qualified distributions are excluded from an individual's taxable income.

SARSEP - Salary Reduction Simplified Employee Pension. A plan that can no longer be established but allowed employees to elect to defer a portion of their current salary into a SEP-IRA in a similar fashion to a 401(k) plan.

SAVERS CREDIT (RETIREMENT SAVINGS CONTRIBUTIONS CREDIT) - A tax credit for making eligible contributions to an IRA or employer-sponsored retirement plan.

SIMPLIFIED EMPLOYEE PENSION (SEP) - A practical retirement plan alternative to a qualified plan that can be used by small businesses and sole proprietors. It follows many of the same limits as qualified plans but may require the employer to cover more employees.

SPOUSAL IRA - An IRA created on behalf of a spouse who does not have the necessary earned income to make a contribution to an IRA of their own but can borrow earned income from their spouse.

10-YEAR FORWARD AVERAGING - A method of income tax calculation for certain lump-sum distribution from qualified plans that divides the taxable portion of the lump-sum distribution by 10 and applies the result to the 1986 individual income tax rates. The resulting calculation is then multiplied by 10 to determine the total income tax due on the distribution.

TRADITIONAL IRA - An IRA that may accept deductible and nondeductible contributions and whose assets grow tax-deferred until distribution.

DISCUSSION QUESTIONS

1. What is the limit on contributions to an IRA for 2016?

2. List items of income that are considered earned income for purposes of IRA contributions.

3. What is a spousal IRA?

4. Why is age 70½ significant to traditional IRA contributions?

5. How are excess contributions to an IRA penalized?

6. Discuss the ability to deduct a contribution made to a traditional IRA given a person who is not covered by a qualified retirement plan.

7. Discuss the ability to deduct a contribution made to a traditional IRA when an employee is covered by a qualified retirement plan.

8. Discuss the ability to deduct a contribution made to a traditional IRA given an employee covered by a qualified retirement plan who has a spouse who is not covered by a qualified retirement plan.

9. Define active participant status for purposes of deducting IRA contributions.

10. What are the minimum distribution rules for traditional IRAs?

11. When is the early withdrawal penalty applicable to traditional IRAs?

12. How do individual retirement annuities differ from a traditional IRA account?

13. Compare and contrast a traditional IRA to a Roth IRA.

14. How does the definition of earned income for a Roth IRA compare with the definition of earned income for a traditional IRA?

15. Identify the 2016 AGI income limits for contributions to a Roth IRA.

16. What are the income limits for converting a traditional IRA to a Roth IRA?

17. How can the assets of a qualified plan be converted into a Roth IRA?

18. What is a "qualified distribution" from a Roth IRA?

19. How is a nonqualified distribution from a Roth IRA taxed?

20. What are the minimum distribution rules relating to Roth IRAs?

21. What types of investments may be held in an IRA and what investments are specifically prohibited from being held in an IRA?

22. What types of coins are permitted IRA investments?

23. Discuss the impact of violating the prohibited transaction rules of an IRA.

24. What are the SEP coverage requirements?

25. What employees may be excluded from participation in a SEP?

26. What is the 2016 contribution limit for a SEP?

27. How and when is a SEP established?

28. What vesting options are available for a SEP?

29. Compare and contrast a SEP and a profit sharing plan.

30. How are the elective deferrals into a SARSEP considered in relation to other salary deferral type plans?

MULTIPLE CHOICE PROBLEMS

1. Which statements are generally correct regarding penalties associated with IRA accounts?

    1. Distributions made prior to 59½ are subject to the 10% premature distribution penalty.
    2. There is a 50% excise tax on a required minimum distribution not made by <u>April 1</u> of the year following the year in which age 70½ is attained.

    a. 1 only.
    b. 2 only.
    c. Both 1 and 2.
    d. Neither 1 nor 2.

2. David took a lump-sum distribution from his employer's qualified plan at age 56 when he terminated his service. He rolled over his distribution using a direct rollover to an IRA. Assuming David has met 10-year forward averaging requirements, which of the following is/are correct regarding tax treatment of the transaction?

    1. If at age 59 he distributes the IRA, he benefits from 10-year forward averaging.
    2. If he rolls the entire IRA to a new employer's qualified plan, he may be eligible for forward averaging treatment in the future.
    3. If he rolls over a portion of the IRA to a new employer's qualified plan, he may preserve any eligibility for forward averaging on that portion that was rolled over.
    4. If David immediately withdraws the entire amount from his IRA, he may benefit from 10-year forward averaging.

    a. 2 only.
    b. 2 and 3.
    c. 2, 3, and 4.
    d. 1, 2, 3, and 4.

3. Robin and Robbie, both age 45, are married and filed a joint return for 2016. Robbie earned a salary of $90,000 in 2016 and is covered by his employer's 401(k) plan. Robbie and Robin earned interest of $30,000 in 2016 from a joint savings account. Robin is not employed, and the couple had no other income. On April 15, 2017, Robbie contributed $5,500 to an IRA for himself and $5,500 to an IRA for Robin. The maximum allowable IRA deduction on the 2016 joint return is:

    a. $0.
    b. $4,500.
    c. $5,500.
    d. $11,000.

4. Amy, divorced and age 55, received taxable alimony of $50,000 in 2016. In addition, she received $1,800 in earnings from a part-time job. Amy is not covered by a qualified plan. What was the maximum deductible IRA contribution that Amy could have made for 2016?

   a. $1,800.

   b. $2,800.

   c. $5,500.

   d. $6,500.

5. Which of the following statements is not correct about Form 8606?

   a. The form tracks basis for contributions and conversions to Roth IRAs.

   b. The form tracks in-plan Roth rollovers.

   c. The form is used for distributions from Roth IRAs.

   d. The form tracks basis for nondeductible traditional IRAs.

6. For the year 2016, Katy (age 35) and Stefen (age 38), a married couple, reported the following items of income:

	Katy	Stefen	Total
Wages	$50,000	--	$50,000
Dividend income	$2,000	$1,200	$3,200
Cash won from lottery		$500	$500
	$52,000	$1,700	$53,700

   Katy is covered by a qualified plan. Stefen does not work, he makes wine and drinks all day. Assuming a joint return was filed for 2016, what is the maximum tax deductible amount that they can contribute to their IRAs?

   a. $2,500.

   b. $5,500.

   c. $7,500.

   d. $11,000.

7. Which of the following cannot be held in an IRA account as an investment?

   a. A U.S. gold coin.

   b. Option contracts (calls).

   c. Variable life insurance.

   d. Municipal bonds.

8. Phillip, who is currently age 52, made his only contribution to his Roth IRA in 2016 in the amount of $5,500. If he were to receive a total distribution of $11,000 from his Roth IRA in the year 2021 to purchase a new car, how would he be taxed?

   a. Since Phillip waited five years, the distribution will be classified as a "qualified distribution" and will therefore not be taxable or subject to the 10% early distribution penalty.

   b. Since Phillip waited five years, the distribution will be classified as a "qualified distribution" and will therefore not be taxable but will be subject to the 10% early distribution penalty.

   c. Although Phillip waited five years, the distribution will not be classified as a "qualified distribution" and will therefore be taxable and will be subject to the 10% early distribution penalty.

   d. Although Phillip waited five years, the distribution will not be classified as a "qualified distribution" and will therefore be taxable to the extent of earnings and will be subject to the 10% early distribution penalty on the amount that is taxable.

9. Jim, who is age 39, converts a $74,500 Traditional IRA to a Roth IRA in 2016. Jim's adjusted basis in the Traditional IRA is $10,000. He also makes a contribution of $5,500 to a Roth IRA in 2016 for the tax year 2016. If Jim takes a $4,000 distribution from his Roth IRA in 2017 when the account is worth $100,000, how much total federal income tax, including penalties, is due as a result of the distribution assuming his 2017 federal income tax rate is 28 percent?

   a. $0.
   b. $224.
   c. $800.
   d. $1,120.

10. Jack and Jill, both age 43, are married, made $20,000 each, and file a joint tax return. Jill has made a $5,500 contribution to her Traditional IRA account and has made a contribution of $2,000 to a Coverdell Education Savings Account for 2016. What is the most that can be contributed to a Roth IRA for Jack for 2016?

   a. $0.
   b. $2,000.
   c. $5,500.
   d. $11,000.

11. Ah and Ha, both age 33, are married, not covered by a qualified plan, and file a joint tax return. They have AGI of $164,000. Ah's mother contributed $2,000 to a Coverdell Education Savings Account for each of their two children. What is the most that Ah and Ha can contribute in total together to a Traditional IRA for 2016?

    a. $0.

    b. $1,000.

    c. $5,500.

    d. $11,000.

12. What is the first year in which a single taxpayer, age 54 in 2016, could receive a qualified distribution from a Roth IRA if he made his first $3,500 contribution to the Roth IRA on April 1, 2017, for the tax year 2016?

    a. 2019.

    b. 2020.

    c. 2021.

    d. 2022.

13. Kathy (age 55) is single, recently divorced, and has received the following items of income this year:

Pension annuity income from QDRO	$21,000
Interest and dividends	$5,000
Alimony	$1,000
W-2 Income	$1,200

What is the most that Kathy can contribute to a Roth IRA for 2016?

    a. $1,200.

    b. $2,200.

    c. $5,500.

    d. $6,500.

14. Which of the following statements is/are correct regarding SEP contributions made by an employer?

    1.   Contributions are subject to FICA and FUTA.

    2.   Contributions are currently excludable from employee-participant's gross income.

    3.   Contributions are capped at $18,000 for 2016.

       a.   1 only.

       b.   2 only.

       c.   1 and 2.

       d.   1, 2, and 3.

15. For 2016, what is the maximum amount that can be contributed to a SEP?

       a. $10,000.

       b. $18,000.

       c. $18,000.

       d. $53,000.

16. A SEP is not a qualified plan and is not subject to all of the qualified plan rules. However, it is subject to many of the same rules. Which of the following are true statements?

    1.   SEPs and qualified plans have the same funding deadlines.

    2.   The contribution limit for SEPs and qualified plans (defined contribution) is $53,000 for the year 2016.

    3.   SEPs and qualified plans have the same ERISA protection from creditors.

    4.   SEPs and qualified plans have different nondiscriminatory and top-heavy rules.

       a.   1 only.

       b.   1 and 2.

       c.   2 and 4.

       d.   1, 2, 3, and 4.

17. Mary, age 50, has an IRA with an account balance of $165,000. Mary has recently been diagnosed with an unusual disease that will require treatment costing $50,000, which she will have to pay personally. Mary's AGI will be $100,000 this year. Which of the following statements are true?

    1.   Mary can immediately borrow up to $50,000 from her account and repay within five years.

    2.   Mary can distribute $50,000 subject to income tax but not subject to the 10% penalty because it will be used to pay medical expenses.

       a.   1 only.

       b.   2 only.

       c.   Both 1 and 2.

       d.   Neither 1 nor 2.

18. Delores, age 62, single, and retired, receives a defined benefit pension annuity of $1,200 per month from Bertancinni Corporation. She is currently working part time for Deanna's Interior Design and will be paid $18,000 this year (2016). Deanna's Interior has a 401(k) plan, but Delores has made no contribution to the plan and neither will Deanna this year. Can Delores contribute to a traditional IRA or a Roth IRA for the year and what is the maximum contribution?

    a. $5,500 to a traditional IRA or $5,500 to a Roth IRA.

    b. $0 to a traditional IRA or $5,500 to a Roth IRA.

    c. $6,500 to a traditional IRA or $0 to a Roth IRA.

    d. $6,500 to a traditional IRA or $6,500 to a Roth IRA.

19. Which of the following people can make a deductible contribution to a traditional IRA for 2016?

	Person	AGI	Covered by Qualified Plan	Marital Status
1.	Dianne	$90,000	Yes	Married
2.	Joy	$50,000	Yes	Single
3.	Kim	$280,000	No	Married
4.	Loretta	$75,000	Yes	Single

    a. None.

    b. 1, 2, and 3.

    c. 1, 2, and 4.

    d. 1, 2, 3, and 4.

20. The early distribution penalty of 10 percent does not apply to IRA distributions:

    1. Made after attainment of the age of 55 and separated from service.

    2. Made for the purpose of paying qualified higher education costs.

    3. Paid to a designated beneficiary after the death of the account owner who had not begun receiving minimum distributions.

        a. 1 only.

        b. 1 and 3.

        c. 2 and 3.

        d. 1, 2, and 3.

21. Nick, who is age 45, operates a landscaping business and is self-employed. He has an assistant, Louis, who has worked with him for five years. Nick is establishing a SEP for 2016 and is willing to make a contribution of 25 percent of Louis's salary to the SEP. If Nick earns $100,000 after paying Louis, his expenses, and the contribution to Louis's SEP, what is the most that he can contribute to the SEP for himself?

    a. $18,587.

    b. $20,000.

    c. $23,234.

    d. $25,000.

22. Roger converted all $100,000 in his traditional IRA to his Roth IRA on December 1, 2012. His Form 8606 from prior years shows that $20,000 of the amount converted is his basis. Roger included $80,000 ($100,000 - $20,000) in his gross income on his Form 1040 for the year. On April 5th, 2016, Roger made a regular contribution of $5,000 to a Roth IRA for the 2015 year. Roger took a $10,000 distribution from his Roth IRA on July 31st of 2016 to purchase a ticket for a trip on a cruise ship for his 61st birthday present to himself. How is the distribution taxed if the value of the account just before the distribution equals $120,000?

    a. The distribution is tax free and penalty free.

    b. The distribution is not subject to tax, but he will have to pay a penalty of $500.

    c. $1,250 of the distribution is taxable but there is no penalty.

    d. $1,250 of the distribution is taxable and there is a penalty of $500.

23. Mr. Reid was very active and loved to go skiing. Unfortunately, he was prone to skiing though the trees and did not believe in helmets. In March of 2016, he skied into a large pine tree that abruptly ended his life. At that time, his Roth IRA contained regular contributions of $10,000, first made in 2014, a conversion contribution of $40,000 that was made in 2013, and earnings of $10,000. He never made any distributions from his IRA. When he established this Roth IRA (his first) in 2013, he named each of his two children, Bill and Phil, as equal beneficiaries. Each child will receive one-half of each type of contribution and one-half of the earnings. Which of the following is true regarding a distribution after Mr. Reid. dies?

    a. If Bill immediately takes out all $30,000 from the Roth IRA, the entire distribution will be characterized as ordinary income.

    b. If Phil immediately takes out all $30,000 from the Roth IRA, the entire distribution will not be taxable because it is a qualified distribution from a Roth IRA.

    c. If Bill immediately takes out all $30,000 from the Roth IRA, $5,000 of the distribution will be characterized as ordinary income, but he will not have to pay a penalty.

    d. If Phil immediately takes out all $30,000 from the Roth IRA, he will have a penalty of $2,500, in addition to paying income tax on the earnings.

QUICK QUIZ EXPLANATIONS

QUICK QUIZ 9.1
1. False. A 55-year old individual can contribute the maximum amount plus an additional deferral for persons age 50 or older.
2. True.
3. False. Individuals who do not have any earned income may still be eligible to establish an IRA if their spouse has sufficient earned income.

QUICK QUIZ 9.2
1. True.
2. True.
3. False. Generally, distributions from traditional IRAs are taxed as ordinary income. In addition, the government encourages taxpayers to leave funds in their IRAs until retirement by imposing a 10 percent premature withdrawal penalty for distributions prior to age 59½.

QUICK QUIZ 9.3
1. True.
2. False. Roth IRAs may be funded after the account owner attains age 70½.
3. True.
4. True.

QUICK QUIZ 9.4
1. False. Collectibles are not a permitted investment for IRAs.
2. True.
3. False. IRAs are not exempt from creditor's claims as a result of ERISA. However, IRA account balances up to $1 million (indexed) are protected from creditors under federal bankruptcy law as a result of the Bankruptcy Abuse Prevention and Consumer Protection Act of 2005.
4. True.

QUICK QUIZ 9.5
1. False. The only requirement for an employer is that the employer offer direct deposit
2. True.
3. False. All funds in these accounts are invested in a fixed income fund that consists of government securities.

QUICK QUIZ 9.6
1. True.
2. False. Part-time employees must be covered by a SEP as long as they have attained the age of 21, performed services for three of the last five years, and have received compensation of at least $600 during the year.
3. True.
4. True.

QUICK QUIZ 9.7
1. False. An employer may not establish a SARSEP if he has more than 25 employees.
2. True.

10

SIMPLE, 403(b), AND 457 PLANS

LEARNING OBJECTIVES

After reading this chapter, you should be able to:

1. Identify other tax-advantaged plans.
2. Compare and contrast qualified plans with other tax-advantaged plans.
3. Explain how SIMPLEs work and when they should be considered.
4. Understand the similarities and differences between 403(b) plans and 401(k) plans.
5. Describe how the deferral limits for SIMPLEs, SARSEPs, 401(k) plans and 403(b) plans work together.
6. Differentiate between private and public eligible 457 plans as well as ineligible 457 plans.

INTRODUCTION

A company may wish to establish a retirement plan but may be unable or unwilling to incur the costs associated with a qualified plan. The IRC provides for "other tax-advantaged plans" that provide favorable tax treatment but are not qualified plans. These plans are often easier and less costly to administer. This chapter discusses in detail three of these "other tax-advantaged plans," SIMPLEs, 403(b)s, and 457 plans.

SIMPLEs (Savings Incentive Match Plans for Employees) provide incentives to "small employers" (100 or fewer employees)[1] to adopt retirement plans for employees with less administrative costs and fewer set-up procedures than qualified plans and no annual filing requirements. SIMPLEs were created by the American Jobs Creation Act of 1996.[2]

Section 403(b) plans, also called "Tax Sheltered Annuities" (TSAs) or "Tax-Deferred Annuities" (TDAs), are plans available to certain non-profit organizations and to employees of public educational systems. The limits for employee elective deferral contributions to 403(b) plans were increased and catch-up provisions for those persons over 50 years old were added, allowing for employee elective deferrals equal to that of 401(k) plans.

Section 457 plans resemble deferred compensation plans that allow certain employees of state and local governments and of nongovernmental tax-exempt entities the ability to defer compensation free from current income taxation. These employee deferral contributions to 457 plans are separate and not combined with other deferral contributions to retirement plans such as SARSEPs, 401(k)s, SIMPLEs, or 403(b)s for purposes of overall contribution limits.

---

1. IRC §408(p).
2. Pub.L.No.104-188, 110 Stat.1755 (1996) (Codified at IRC §408(p)(2001)).

	KNOW THE NUMBERS (2016)			
SIMPLEs	Total Elective Contribution $12,500		Catch-Up > 50 $3,000	
403(b) Plans	Annual Deferral Limit $18,000		Catch-Up > 50 $6,000	
457 Plans	Annual Deferral Limit $18,000	Catch-Up > 50 $6,000		Final 3-Year Catch -Up $18,000

SIMPLES

Savings Incentive Match Plans for Employees, referred to as "**SIMPLEs**," are retirement plans for small employers. Many smaller employers are reluctant to set up qualified retirement plans because of the complicated rules and administrative costs that accompany qualified plans. SIMPLEs, however, are both easy to establish and maintain and provide an incentive to small employers to adopt retirement plans because they possess tax advantages similar to qualified plans. In addition, SIMPLE plans are attractive to employers because they are not required to meet all of the nondiscrimination rules applicable to qualified retirement plans and they do not have the burdensome annual filing requirements.

A SIMPLE allows employees to make elective deferral contributions similar to a 401(k) plan. The employer/sponsor is required to match employee elective deferral contributions made by employees or, alternatively, to make nonelective contributions for all employees who are eligible. The employer and employee enter into a written agreement that directs the employer to make employee elective deferral contributions to the accounts of eligible employees in exchange for a salary reduction.

> Karli makes an election to reduce her salary from $50,000 to $45,000 and have her employer deposit the $5,000 into a SIMPLE IRA. The employer will also match the employee's contribution up to 3% of salary ($50,000 x 0.03 = $1,500) into the SIMPLE IRA.

EXAMPLE 10.1

A SUMMARY OF THE CHARACTERISTICS OF SIMPLEs

EXHIBIT 10.1

- Employer establishes SIMPLE plan.
- Employer contracts with employee to have salary reduction.
- Employer withholds employee deferral over the course of a year.
- Employee elective deferrals are not subject to income tax but are subject to payroll tax.
- Employer deposits match on a regular basis tax deferred without payroll tax.
- Earnings grow tax deferred on all contributions.

TYPES OF SIMPLES

When establishing a SIMPLE, the sponsor company has two choices in determining the vehicle used to hold the assets of the plan. A company may choose either an IRA or 401(k) for the plan. Therefore, a sponsor company may establish the SIMPLE as either a SIMPLE IRA plan or a SIMPLE 401(k) plan. In most instances, the company will establish a SIMPLE IRA because there are fewer administrative burdens than for SIMPLE 401(k) plans. SIMPLE 401(k) plans are very rare in practice.

> ### KEY CONCEPTS ✔
>
> 1. What are SIMPLE plans?
> 2. What types of SIMPLE plans are available?
> 3. List the requirements to establish a SIMPLE plan.

The SIMPLE IRA

A **SIMPLE IRA** is a SIMPLE plan that utilizes an IRA account as the funding vehicle of the plan. The SIMPLE IRA is established utilizing an individual retirement account (or an individual retirement annuity). The plan is established by the employer via a written plan that allows each employee to choose between directing the employer to make contributions to the SIMPLE IRA plan or allowing the employee to receive such payments directly in cash (a CODA feature) as compensation. SIMPLE IRAs require the employer to either match the employee contributions of those that participate or provide nonelective contributions to all employees who are eligible. All contributions made under a SIMPLE IRA must be paid to a SIMPLE IRA, not to any other type of IRA. SIMPLE IRA plans can be established by for-profit entities, tax-exempt employers, and governmental entities.

The SIMPLE 401(k)

A **SIMPLE 401(k)** is a SIMPLE plan that utilizes a 401(k) plan as the funding vehicle of the plan. Unlike the SIMPLE IRA, plan loans are permitted with a SIMPLE 401(k). SIMPLE 401(k) plans must be maintained by an eligible employer and satisfy contribution requirements, eligibility requirements, and vesting requirements. A SIMPLE 401(k) plan must be maintained on a calendar year basis and not a fiscal year basis. An employer may adopt a SIMPLE 401(k) plan if it has 100 or fewer employees. A SIMPLE 401(k) is not subject to nondiscrimination requirements or top-heavy restrictions if it meets certain contribution and other requirements that are discussed in this chapter, but the administrative requirements are greater as compared to a SIMPLE IRA.

ESTABLISHING A SIMPLE

A SIMPLE IRA plan can be maintained only on a calendar year basis. As such, plan contributions to the SIMPLE IRA, as well as the eligibility of employers who establish the SIMPLE IRA, are determined on a calendar year basis.[3]

SIMPLEs are designed for the small employer. A SIMPLE is very easy to establish and maintain as it has minor administrative costs and does not have any annual filing requirements. There are definite advantages for SIMPLEs compared to qualified plans. As discussed throughout this book, qualified plans have significant administrative costs and burdensome rules and requirements.

---

3. IRC §408(p)(6)(C).

Who Can Establish a SIMPLE?

SIMPLE plans can only be established for companies who employ 100 or fewer employees who earned at least $5,000 of compensation from the employer for the preceding calendar year. The employer can be a C corporation, partnership, S corporation, limited liability company, sole proprietorship, tax-exempt entity, or governmental entity. Whether the employees are eligible to participate in the SIMPLE or not, all employees who earned $5,000 or more in the previous year that are employed at any time during the calendar year are taken into consideration for purposes of counting the 100 employee limitation. Accordingly, even employees that can be excluded, such as nonresident aliens or those employees who do not meet the plan's minimum eligibility requirements, must all be considered in the 100 employee limitation to avoid a company that truly has more than 100 employees being eligible to establish a SIMPLE. Leased employees or self-employed individuals who received earned income from the employer in the preceding calendar year are also included in the calculation for the 100 employee limitation rule.[4]

> Z-Mart Corporation employed 150 employees in 2016, 115 of whom were nonresident aliens. For calendar year 2017, the company would only have 35 employees eligible to participate in the year 2017, but Z-Mart Corporation may not establish a SIMPLE IRA plan in calendar year 2016 because the company employed 150 employees (though 115 of them were nonresident aliens). The company had fewer than 100 eligible participants, but for purposes of the 100 employee limitation, nonresident aliens must be considered for the preceding calendar year in the calculation of the eligibility of the company as a whole.

EXAMPLE
10.2

ENTITIES THAT CAN ESTABLISH SIMPLE PLANS

EXHIBIT
10.2

C Corporations
S Corporations
Limited Liability Companies (LLC)
Partnerships
Proprietorships
Government Entities

---

4. IRC §408(p)(2)(C)(i)(I).

Two-Year Grace Period for Employers Who Cease to Comply with 100 Employee Limit

If an employer meets the 100 employee limitation in a given year, then the employer will have a two year "**grace period**" where the employer can exceed the limitation without losing eligibility to maintain the SIMPLE. In other words, if an employer in a calendar year satisfies the 100 employee limitation, that employer is treated as if it satisfied the 100 employee limitation for two calendar years immediately after the calendar year for which it last satisfied the 100 employee limitation.[5]

However, if the employer undergoes an acquisition, disposition, or other similar transaction, the employer will retain eligibility (i.e., not deemed as exceeding the 100 employee limitation) for the year of the transaction plus the two subsequent years, only if both of the following two rules are met:

1. the plan coverage has not significantly changed during the grace period, and
2. the SIMPLE plan would have continued to qualify after the transaction if the employer had remained as a separate employer.[6]

If, at any time within the two years, the employer does not meet the requirements listed above, neither the employer nor the employee will be permitted to make contributions to the plan.

Other Plans Not Allowed

An employer may not establish a SIMPLE if the employer contributes to a defined contribution plan for its employees during the year, if its employees accrue a benefit from a defined benefit plan during the year, or if the employer contributes to a SEP or 403(b) plan during the year.[7]

If an employer maintains another qualified plan solely to benefit union employees whose retirement benefits were the subject of good faith bargaining, the employer can make contributions to a SIMPLE plan. All the eligibility and contribution rules will apply and the SIMPLE must exclude those union employees.

How is a SIMPLE Established?

SIMPLEs are easy to establish and maintain in comparison to other types of qualified retirement plans. There are few administrative costs associated with the SIMPLE plan because there are no annual filing requirements. At the inception, an employer files **Form 5304-SIMPLE** or **Form 5305-SIMPLE** to establish a SIMPLE IRA plan. These are model SIMPLE plan documents. Form 5304 applies to employers who allow plan participants to select the financial institution that will

---

5. IRC §408(p)(2)(C)(i)(II).
6. IRC §408(p)(4), §408(p)(10).
7. IRC §408(p)(2)(D).

receive their contributions while Form 5305 (revised March 2012) applies to those SIMPLEs that require initial contributions to be deposited at a designated financial institution. As a further illustration of the relaxed administrative rules and required paperwork, Forms 5304-SIMPLE and 5305-SIMPLE by themselves: (1) satisfy employer notification requirements for SIMPLEs, (2) maintain the SIMPLE plan records, and (3) establish proof that the employer set up a SIMPLE plan for its employees.

An employer can establish a SIMPLE IRA plan any time between January 1 and October 1 of the year in which it wants the plan to begin unless the employer or one of its predecessors previously maintained a SIMPLE IRA plan. If the employer previously maintained a SIMPLE IRA plan, then the employer must establish the SIMPLE IRA by January 1 of the year in which it wants the plan to begin. New employers who begin business after October 1 of the year may establish a SIMPLE IRA after October 1 if the SIMPLE is established as soon as administratively feasible.

KEY CONCEPTS

1. Identify the characteristics of a SIMPLE IRA.

2. Identify the characteristics of a SIMPLE 401(k) plan.

In any case, the employer must provide the participants with a 60-day period of time during which they can make their deferral elections. This 60-day period must occur every plan year between November 2 and December 31. If a plan is established during the year, or an employee becomes eligible during the year, the participant's 60-day election period must include the date of eligibility.

EXHIBIT 10.3

FORM 5304-SIMPLE

Form **5304-SIMPLE** (Rev. March 2012) Department of the Treasury Internal Revenue Service	**Savings Incentive Match Plan for Employees of Small Employers (SIMPLE)—Not for Use With a Designated Financial Institution**	OMB No. 1545-1502 **Do not** file with the Internal Revenue Service

_____ establishes the following SIMPLE

       Name of Employer

IRA plan under section 408(p) of the Internal Revenue Code and pursuant to the instructions contained in this form. _____

Article I—Employee Eligibility Requirements *(complete applicable box(es) and blanks—see instructions)*

1   **General Eligibility Requirements.** The Employer agrees to permit salary reduction contributions to be made in each calendar year to the SIMPLE IRA established by each employee who meets the following requirements (select either 1a or 1b):

a   ☐ **Full Eligibility.** All employees are eligible.

b   ☐ **Limited Eligibility.** Eligibility is limited to employees who are described in both (i) and (ii) below:

    (i)   **Current compensation.** Employees who are reasonably expected to receive at least $ _____ in compensation (not to exceed $5,000) for the calendar year.

    (ii)   **Prior compensation.** Employees who have received at least $ _____ in compensation (not to exceed $5,000) during any _____ calendar year(s) (insert 0, 1, or 2) preceding the calendar year.

2   **Excludable Employees.**

     ☐ The Employer elects to exclude employees covered under a collective bargaining agreement for which retirement benefits were the subject of good faith bargaining. *Note: This box is deemed checked if the Employer maintains a qualified plan covering only such employees.*

Article II—Salary Reduction Agreements *(complete the box and blank, if applicable—see instructions)*

1   **Salary Reduction Election.** An eligible employee may make an election to have his or her compensation for each pay period reduced. The total amount of the reduction in the employee's compensation for a calendar year cannot exceed the applicable amount for that year.

2   **Timing of Salary Reduction Elections**

a   For a calendar year, an eligible employee may make or modify a salary reduction election during the 60-day period immediately preceding January 1 of that year. However, for the year in which the employee becomes eligible to make salary reduction contributions, the period during which the employee may make or modify the election is a 60-day period that includes either the date the employee becomes eligible or the day before.

b   In addition to the election periods in 2a, eligible employees may make salary reduction elections or modify prior elections _____ , _____ . If the Employer chooses this option, insert a period or periods (for example, semi-annually, quarterly, monthly, or daily) that will apply uniformly to all eligible employees.

c   No salary reduction election may apply to compensation that an employee received, or had a right to immediately receive, before execution of the salary reduction election.

d   An employee may terminate a salary reduction election at any time during the calendar year. ☐ If this box is checked, an employee who terminates a salary reduction election not in accordance with 2b may not resume salary reduction contributions during the calendar year.

Article III—Contributions *(complete the blank, if applicable—see instructions)*

1   **Salary Reduction Contributions.** The amount by which the employee agrees to reduce his or her compensation will be contributed by the Employer to the employee's SIMPLE IRA.

2a   **Matching Contributions**

    (i)   For each calendar year, the Employer will contribute a matching contribution to each eligible employee's SIMPLE IRA equal to the employee's salary reduction contributions up to a limit of 3% of the employee's compensation for the calendar year.

    (ii)   The Employer may reduce the 3% limit for the calendar year in (i) only if:

      (1) The limit is not reduced below 1%; **(2)** The limit is not reduced for more than 2 calendar years during the 5-year period ending with the calendar year the reduction is effective; and **(3)** Each employee is notified of the reduced limit within a reasonable period of time before the employees' 60-day election period for the calendar year (described in Article II, item 2a).

b   **Nonelective Contributions**

    (i)   For any calendar year, instead of making matching contributions, the Employer may make nonelective contributions equal to 2% of compensation for the calendar year to the SIMPLE IRA of each eligible employee who has at least $ _____ , (not more than $5,000) in compensation for the calendar year. No more than $250,000* in compensation can be taken into account in determining the nonelective contribution for each eligible employee.

    (ii)   For any calendar year, the Employer may make 2% nonelective contributions instead of matching contributions only if:

      (1) Each eligible employee is notified that a 2% nonelective contribution will be made instead of a matching contribution; and

      (2) This notification is provided within a reasonable period of time before the employees' 60-day election period for the calendar year (described in Article II, item 2a).

3   **Time and Manner of Contributions**

a   The Employer will make the salary reduction contributions (described in 1 above) for each eligible employee to the SIMPLE IRA established at the financial institution selected by that employee no later than 30 days after the end of the month in which the money is withheld from the employee's pay. See instructions.

b   The Employer will make the matching or nonelective contributions (described in 2a and 2b above) for each eligible employee to the SIMPLE IRA established at the financial institution selected by that employee no later than the due date for filing the Employer's tax return, including extensions, for the taxable year that includes the last day of the calendar year for which the contributions are made.

---

* This is the amount for 2012. For later years, the limit may be increased for cost-of-living adjustments. The IRS announces the increase, if any, in a news release, in the *Internal Revenue Bulletin*, and on the IRS's internet website at **IRS.gov.**

For Paperwork Reduction Act Notice, see the instructions.   Cat. No. 23377W   Form **5304-SIMPLE** (Rev. 3-2012)

FORM 5304-SIMPLE CONTINUED

Form 5304-SIMPLE (Rev. 3-2012)

Article IV—Other Requirements and Provisions

1   **Contributions in General.** The Employer will make no contributions to the SIMPLE IRAs other than salary reduction contributions (described in Article III, item 1) and matching or nonelective contributions (described in Article III, items 2a and 2b).

2   **Vesting Requirements.** All contributions made under this SIMPLE IRA plan are fully vested and nonforfeitable.

3   **No Withdrawal Restrictions.** The Employer may not require the employee to retain any portion of the contributions in his or her SIMPLE IRA or otherwise impose any withdrawal restrictions.

4   **Selection of IRA Trustee.** The Employer must permit each eligible employee to select the financial institution that will serve as the trustee, custodian, or issuer of the SIMPLE IRA to which the Employer will make all contributions on behalf of that employee.

5   **Amendments To This SIMPLE IRA Plan.** This SIMPLE IRA plan may not be amended except to modify the entries inserted in the blanks or boxes provided in Articles I, II, III, VI, and VII.

6   **Effects Of Withdrawals and Rollovers**

a   An amount withdrawn from the SIMPLE IRA is generally includible in gross income. However, a SIMPLE IRA balance may be rolled over or transferred on a tax-free basis to another IRA designed solely to hold funds under a SIMPLE IRA plan. In addition, an individual may roll over or transfer his or her SIMPLE IRA balance to any IRA or eligible retirement plan after a 2-year period has expired since the individual first participated in any SIMPLE IRA plan of the Employer. Any rollover or transfer must comply with the requirements under section 408.

b   If an individual withdraws an amount from a SIMPLE IRA during the 2-year period beginning when the individual first participated in any SIMPLE IRA plan of the Employer and the amount is subject to the additional tax on early distributions under section 72(t), this additional tax is increased from 10% to 25%.

Article V—Definitions

1   **Compensation**

a   **General Definition of Compensation.** Compensation means the sum of the wages, tips, and other compensation from the Employer subject to federal income tax withholding (as described in section 6051(a)(3)), the amounts paid for domestic service in a private home, local college club, or local chapter of a college fraternity or sorority, and the employee's salary reduction contributions made under this plan, and, if applicable, elective deferrals under a section 401(k) plan, a SARSEP, or a section 403(b) annuity contract and compensation deferred under a section 457 plan required to be reported by the Employer on Form W-2 (as described in section 6051(a)(8)).

b   **Compensation for Self-Employed Individuals.** For self-employed individuals, compensation means the net earnings from self-employment determined under section 1402(a), without regard to section 1402(c)(6), prior to subtracting any contributions made pursuant to this plan on behalf of the individual.

2   **Employee.** Employee means a common-law employee of the Employer. The term employee also includes a self-employed individual and a leased employee described in section 414(n) but does not include a nonresident alien who received no earned income from the Employer that constitutes income from sources within the United States.

3   **Eligible Employee.** An eligible employee means an employee who satisfies the conditions in Article I, item 1 and is not excluded under Article I, item 2.

4   **SIMPLE IRA.** A SIMPLE IRA is an individual retirement account described in section 408(a), or an individual retirement annuity described in section 408(b), to which the only contributions that can be made are contributions under a SIMPLE IRA plan and rollovers or transfers from another SIMPLE IRA.

Article VI—Procedures for Withdrawals *(The Employer will provide each employee with the procedures for withdrawals of contributions received by the financial institution selected by that employee, and that financial institution's name and address (by attaching that information or inserting it in the space below) unless: (1) that financial institution's procedures are unavailable, or (2) that financial institution provides the procedures directly to the employee. See **Employee Notification** in the instructions.)*

Article VII—Effective Date

This SIMPLE IRA plan is effective _____ . See instructions.

*   *   *   *   *

_____   By: Signature _____   Date _____
Name of Employer

_____   Name and title _____
Address of Employer

Form **5304-SIMPLE** (Rev. 3-2012)

FORM 5304-SIMPLE CONTINUED

Model Notification to Eligible Employees

I.   Opportunity to Participate in the SIMPLE IRA Plan

You are eligible to make salary reduction contributions to the _____ SIMPLE IRA plan. This notice and the attached summary description provide you with information that you should consider before you decide whether to start, continue, or change your salary reduction agreement.

II.   Employer Contribution Election

For the _____ calendar year, the Employer elects to contribute to your SIMPLE IRA *(employer must select either (1), (2), or (3)):*

☐ **(1)** A matching contribution equal to your salary reduction contributions up to a limit of 3% of your compensation for the year;

☐ **(2)** A matching contribution equal to your salary reduction contributions up to a limit of _____ % *(employer must insert a number from 1 to 3 and is subject to certain restrictions)* of your compensation for the year; or

☐ **(3)** A nonelective contribution equal to 2% of your compensation for the year (limited to compensation of $250,000*) if you are an employee who *makes at least $* _____ *(employer must insert an amount that is $5,000 or less)* in compensation for the year.

III.   Administrative Procedures

To start or change your salary reduction contributions, you must complete the salary reduction agreement and return it to
_____ (employer should designate a place or
individual by _____ *(employer should insert a date that is not less than 60 days after notice is given).*

IV.   Employee Selection of Financial Institution

You must select the financial institution that will serve as the trustee, custodian, or issuer of your SIMPLE IRA and notify your Employer of your selection.

Model Salary Reduction Agreement

I.   Salary Reduction Election

Subject to the requirements of the SIMPLE IRA plan of _____ *(name of
employer)* I authorize _____ % or $ _____ (which equals _____ % of my current rate of pay) to be withheld from my pay for each pay period and contributed to my SIMPLE IRA as a salary reduction contribution.

II.   Maximum Salary Reduction

I understand that the total amount of my salary reduction contributions in any calendar year cannot exceed the applicable amount for that year. See instructions.

III.   Date Salary Reduction Begins

I understand that my salary reduction contributions will start as soon as permitted under the SIMPLE IRA plan and as soon as administratively feasible or, if later, _____ . *(Fill in the date you want the salary reduction contributions to begin. The date must be after you sign this agreement.)*

IV.   Employee Selection of Financial Institution

I select the following financial institution to serve as the trustee, custodian, or issuer of my SIMPLE IRA.

_____
Name of financial institution

_____
Address of financial institution

_____
SIMPLE IRA account name and number

I understand that I must establish a SIMPLE IRA to receive any contributions made on my behalf under this SIMPLE IRA plan. If the information regarding my SIMPLE IRA is incomplete when I first submit my salary reduction agreement, I realize that it must be completed by the date contributions must be made under the SIMPLE IRA plan. If I fail to update my agreement to provide this information by that date, I understand that my Employer may select a financial institution for my SIMPLE IRA.

V.   Duration of Election

This salary reduction agreement replaces any earlier agreement and will remain in effect as long as I remain an eligible employee under the SIMPLE IRA plan or until I provide my Employer with a request to end my salary reduction contributions or provide a new salary reduction agreement as permitted under this SIMPLE IRA plan.

Signature of employee _____ Date _____

* This is the amount for 2012. For later years, the limit may be increased for cost-of-living adjustments. The IRS announces the increase, if any, in a news release, in the Internal Revenue Bulletin, and on the IRS website at **IRS.gov.**

Form **5304-SIMPLE** (Rev. 3-2012)

FORM 5305-SIMPLE

EXHIBIT
10.4

Form **5305-SIMPLE** (Rev. March 2012) Department of the Treasury Internal Revenue Service	**Savings Incentive Match Plan for Employees of Small Employers (SIMPLE)— for Use With a Designated Financial Institution**	OMB No. 1545-1502 **Do not** file with the Internal Revenue Service

_____ establishes the following SIMPLE
Name of Employer

IRA plan under section 408(p) of the Internal Revenue Code and pursuant to the instructions contained in this form.

Article I—Employee Eligibility Requirements (complete applicable box(es) and blanks—see instructions)

1   **General Eligibility Requirements.** The Employer agrees to permit salary reduction contributions to be made in each calendar year to the SIMPLE individual retirement account or annuity established at the designated financial institution (SIMPLE IRA) for each employee who meets the following requirements (select either 1a or 1b):

a   ☐   **Full Eligibility.** All employees are eligible.

b   ☐   **Limited Eligibility.** Eligibility is limited to employees who are described in both (i) and (ii) below:

    (i)   **Current compensation.** Employees who are reasonably expected to receive at least $ _____ in compensation (not to exceed $5,000) for calendar year.

    (ii)   **Prior compensation.** Employees who have received at least $ _____ in compensation (not to exceed $5,000) during any _____ calendar year(s) (insert 0, 1, or 2) preceding the calendar year.

2   **Excludable Employees**

    ☐   The Employer elects to exclude employees covered under a collective bargaining agreement for which retirement benefits were the subject of good faith bargaining. **Note:** _This box is deemed checked if the Employer maintains a qualified plan covering only such employees._

Article II—Salary Reduction Agreements (complete the box and blank, if applicable—see instructions)

1   **Salary Reduction Election.** An eligible employee may make an election to have his or her compensation for each pay period reduced. The total amount of the reduction in the employee's compensation for a calendar year cannot exceed the applicable amount for that year. See instructions.

2   **Timing of Salary Reduction Elections**

a   For a calendar year, an eligible employee may make or modify a salary reduction election during the 60-day period immediately preceding January 1 of that year. However, for the year in which the employee becomes eligible to make salary reduction contributions, the period during which the employee may make or modify the election is a 60-day period that includes either the date the employee becomes eligible or the day before.

b   In addition to the election periods in 2a, eligible employees may make salary reduction elections or modify prior elections _____ . If the Employer chooses this option, insert a period or periods (e.g., semi-annually, quarterly, monthly, or daily) that will apply uniformly to all eligible employees.

c   No salary reduction election may apply to compensation that an employee received, or had a right to immediately receive, before execution of the salary reduction election.

d   An employee may terminate a salary reduction election at any time during the calendar year. ☐ If this box is checked, an employee who terminates a salary reduction election not in accordance with 2b may not resume salary reduction contributions during the calendar year.

Article III—Contributions (complete the blank, if applicable—see instructions)

1   **Salary Reduction Contributions.** The amount by which the employee agrees to reduce his or her compensation will be contributed by the Employer to the employee's SIMPLE IRA.

2 a   **Matching Contributions**

    (i)   For each calendar year, the Employer will contribute a matching contribution to each eligible employee's SIMPLE IRA equal to the employee's salary reduction contributions up to a limit of 3% of the employee's compensation for the calendar year.

    (ii)   The Employer may reduce the 3% limit for the calendar year in (i) only if:

      (1) The limit is not reduced below 1%; **(2)** The limit is not reduced for more than 2 calendar years during the 5-year period ending with the calendar year the reduction is effective; and **(3)** Each employee is notified of the reduced limit within a reasonable period of time before the employees' 60-day election period for the calendar year (described in Article II, item 2a).

b   **Nonelective Contributions**

    (i)   For any calendar year, instead of making matching contributions, the Employer may make nonelective contributions equal to 2% of compensation for the calendar year to the SIMPLE IRA of each eligible employee who has at least $ _____ (not more than $5,000) in compensation for the calendar year. No more than $250,000* in compensation can be taken into account in determining the nonelective contribution for each eligible employee.

    (ii)   For any calendar year, the Employer may make 2% nonelective contributions instead of matching contributions only if:

      (1) Each eligible employee is notified that a 2% nonelective contribution will be made instead of a matching contribution; and

      (2) This notification is provided within a reasonable period of time before the employees' 60-day election period for the calendar year (described in Article II, item 2a).

3   **Time and Manner of Contributions**

a   The Employer will make the salary reduction contributions (described in 1 above) to the designated financial institution for the IRAs established under this SIMPLE IRA plan no later than 30 days after the end of the month in which the money is withheld from the employee's pay. See instructions.

b   The Employer will make the matching or nonelective contributions (described in 2a and 2b above) to the designated financial institution for the IRAs established under this SIMPLE IRA plan no later than the due date for filing the Employer's tax return, including extensions, for the taxable year that includes the last day of the calendar year for which the contributions are made.

* _This is the amount for 2012. For later years, the limit may be increased for cost-of-living adjustments. The IRS announces the increase, if any, in a news release, in the Internal Revenue Bulletin, and on the IRS's internet website at **IRS.gov.**_

For Paperwork Reduction Act Notice, see instructions.   Cat. No. 23063F   Form **5305-SIMPLE** (Rev. 3-2012)

Form 5305-SIMPLE Continued

Article IV—Other Requirements and Provisions

1 **Contributions in General.** The Employer will make no contributions to the SIMPLE IRAs other than salary reduction contributions (described in Article III, item 1) and matching or nonelective contributions (described in Article III, items 2a and 2b).

2 **Vesting Requirements.** All contributions made under this SIMPLE IRA plan are fully vested and nonforfeitable.

3 **No Withdrawal Restrictions.** The Employer may not require the employee to retain any portion of the contributions in his or her SIMPLE IRA or otherwise impose any withdrawal restrictions.

4 **No Cost Or Penalty For Transfers.** The Employer will not impose any cost or penalty on a participant for the transfer of the participant's SIMPLE IRA balance to another IRA.

5 **Amendments To This SIMPLE IRA Plan.** This SIMPLE IRA plan may not be amended except to modify the entries inserted in the blanks or boxes provided in Articles I, II, III, VI, and VII.

6 **Effects Of Withdrawals and Rollovers**

a An amount withdrawn from the SIMPLE IRA is generally includible in gross income. However, a SIMPLE IRA balance may be rolled over or transferred on a tax-free basis to another IRA designed solely to hold funds under a SIMPLE IRA plan. In addition, an individual may roll over or transfer his or her SIMPLE IRA balance to any IRA or eligible retirement plan after a 2-year period has expired since the individual first participated in any SIMPLE IRA plan of the Employer. Any rollover or transfer must comply with the requirements of section 408.

b If an individual withdraws an amount from a SIMPLE IRA during the 2-year period beginning when the individual first participated in any SIMPLE IRA plan of the Employer and the amount is subject to the additional tax on early distributions under section 72(t), this additional tax is increased from 10% to 25%.

Article V—Definitions

1 **Compensation**

a **General Definition of Compensation.** Compensation means the sum of wages, tips, and other compensation from the Employer subject to federal income tax withholding (as described in section 6051(a)(3)), the amounts paid for domestic service in a private home, local college club, or local chapter of a college fraternity or sorority, and the employee's salary reduction contributions made under this plan, and, if applicable, elective deferrals under a section 401(k) plan, a SARSEP, or a section 403(b) annuity contract and compensation deferred under a section 457 plan required to be reported by the Employer on Form W-2 (as described in section 6051(a)(8)).

b **Compensation for Self-Employed Individuals.** For self-employed individuals, compensation means the net earnings from self-employment determined under section 1402(a), without regard to section 1402(c)(6), prior to subtracting any contributions made pursuant to this plan on behalf of the individual.

2 **Employee.** Employee means a common-law employee of the Employer. The term employee also includes a self-employed individual and a leased employee described in section 414(n) but does not include a nonresident alien who received no earned income from the Employer that constitutes income from sources within the United States.

3 **Eligible Employee.** An eligible employee means an employee who satisfies the conditions in Article I, item 1 and is not excluded under Article I, item 2.

4 **Designated Financial Institution.** A designated financial institution is a trustee, custodian, or insurance company (that issues annuity contracts) for the SIMPLE IRA plan that receives all contributions made pursuant to the SIMPLE IRA plan and deposits those contributions to the SIMPLE IRA of each eligible employee.

Article VI—Procedures for Withdrawals and Transfers *(The designated financial institution will provide the instructions (to be attached or inserted in the space below) on the procedures for withdrawals of contributions by employees.)*

Article VII—Effective Date

This SIMPLE IRA plan is effective _____ . See instructions.

*   *   *   *   *

Name of Employer   By: Signature   Date

Address of Employer   Name and title

The undersigned agrees to serve as designated financial institution, receiving all contributions made pursuant to this SIMPLE IRA plan and depositing those contributions to the SIMPLE IRA of each eligible employee as soon as practicable. Upon the request of any participant, the undersigned also agrees to transfer the participant's balance in a SIMPLE IRA established under this SIMPLE IRA plan to another IRA without cost or penalty to the participant.

Name of designated financial institution   By: Signature   Date

Address   Name and title

Form **5305-SIMPLE** (Rev. 3-2012)

FORM 5305-SIMPLE CONTINUED

Model Notification to Eligible Employees

I. Opportunity to Participate in the SIMPLE IRA Plan

You are eligible to make salary reduction contributions to the _____ SIMPLE IRA plan. This notice and the attached summary description provide you with information that you should consider before you decide whether to start, continue, or change your salary reduction agreement.

II. Employer Contribution Election

For the _____ calendar year, the Employer elects to contribute to your SIMPLE IRA *(employer must select either (1), (2), or (3)):*

☐ **(1)** A matching contribution equal to your salary reduction contributions up to a limit of 3% of your compensation for the year;

☐ **(2)** A matching contribution equal to your salary reduction contributions up to a limit of _____ % *(employer must insert a number from 1 to 3 and is subject to certain restrictions)* of your compensation for the year; or

☐ **(3)** A nonelective contribution equal to 2% of your compensation for the year (limited to compensation of $250,000*) if you are an employee who makes at least $ _____ *(employer must insert an amount that is $5,000 or less)* in compensation for the year.

III. Administrative Procedures

To start or change your salary reduction contributions, you must complete the salary reduction agreement and return it to _____ *(employer should designate a place or individual)* by _____ *(employer should insert a date that is not less than 60 days after notice is given)*.

Model Salary Reduction Agreement

I. Salary Reduction Election

Subject to the requirements of the SIMPLE IRA plan of _____ *(name of employer)* I authorize _____ % or $ _____ (which equals _____ % of my current rate of pay) to be withheld from my pay for each pay period and contributed to my SIMPLE IRA as a salary reduction contribution.

II. Maximum Salary Reduction

I understand that the total amount of my salary reduction contributions in any calendar year cannot exceed the applicable amount for that year. See instructions.

III. Date Salary Reduction Begins

I understand that my salary reduction contributions will start as soon as permitted under the SIMPLE IRA plan and as soon as administratively feasible or, if later, _____ . *(Fill in the date you want the salary reduction contributions to begin. The date must be after you sign this agreement.)*

IV. Duration of Election

This salary reduction agreement replaces any earlier agreement and will remain in effect as long as I remain an eligible employee under the SIMPLE IRA plan or until I provide my Employer with a request to end my salary reduction contributions or provide a new salary reduction agreement as permitted under this SIMPLE IRA plan.

Signature of employee _____   Date _____

* This is the amount for 2012. For later years, the limit may be increased for cost-of-living adjustments. The IRS announces the increase, if any, in a news release, in the Internal Revenue Bulletin, and on the IRS website at **IRS.gov.**

Form **5305-SIMPLE** (Rev. 3-2012)

Eligibility

To be eligible for a SIMPLE, an employer cannot have more than 100 employees and all employees considered eligible must benefit from the SIMPLE. Eligible employees are those employees who earned at least $5,000 in compensation from the employer during any two preceding calendar years and who are reasonably expected to earn at least $5,000 in compensation during the current calendar year.[8] Employers have the option to choose less restrictive eligibility requirements. Air pilots, nonresident aliens, and union employees whose retirement benefits were the subject of good faith bargaining may be excluded from the eligibility requirements of a SIMPLE IRA plan by the employer.

The employer and employee eligibility for a SIMPLE is determined based on the calendar year, January 1 to December 31. A SIMPLE plan cannot use any other fiscal years (other than those that mimic calendar years) to determine eligibility requirements.

EXHIBIT 10.5	ELIGIBILITY CHARACTERISTICS

- Employees who earned $5,000 during any two preceding calendar years.
- Employees who are expected to earn $5,000 during the current calendar year.

Vesting

All employer contributions to SIMPLE IRA accounts on behalf of employees and the related earnings are fully (100%) and immediately vested and cannot be forfeited by the employee.[9] All contributions under the SIMPLE 401(k) plan are likewise fully and immediately vested.

SIMPLE IRAs

Employee Elective Deferral Contributions

With the exception of certain rollover contributions, the only contributions that may be made under a SIMPLE IRA plan are the employee's elective deferral contributions and the required employer matching contributions or nonelective contributions.[10] Similar to other cash or deferred arrangement (CODA) type plans, rather than have funds paid directly in cash to the employee through payroll, an employee's elective deferral contribution or salary reduction contribution is made to the employee's SIMPLE IRA account.

The SIMPLE IRA permits employees to defer a percentage or a dollar amount of their compensation for the year. Within 60 days prior to the beginning of the plan year, the employee elects the amount to defer under the plan. The employer is not allowed to place any restriction on the employee's elective deferral unless the annual limit on the salary reduction amount is reached, $12,500 for 2016.[11]

---

8. IRC §408(p)(4).
9. IRC §408(p)(3).
10. IRC §408(p)(2)(A), § 408(p)(2)(A)(iii).
11. IRC §408(p)(2)(A)(ii).

SIMPLE Characteristics

EXHIBIT
10.6

- Employee elective deferral (optional)
- Employer match (or nonelective contribution)
- 100% vesting in all contributions and earnings
- Employer must have ≤ 100 employees

Annual Limit on Employee Elective Contributions for SIMPLE IRAs

Employees may make annual elective deferrals to a SIMPLE IRA plan for 2016 and thereafter, in the amount of $12,500 adjusted for inflation.

Year	Total Elective Contribution	Catch-Up
2016	$12,500	$3,000

The $12,500 limitation is adjusted for inflation in increments of $500 (the inflation adjustment is rounded downward to the nearest $500). The base period for calculating the inflation adjustment is the calendar quarter beginning July 1, 2004.[12]

Salary Reduction Catch-up Contributions for SIMPLE IRAs

For employees who have attained the age of 50 by the end of the calendar year and if there are no other elective contributions that can be made for them during the calendar year, such employees are permitted to make additional elective contributions, also known as "catch-up contributions," to the plan for that calendar year. The maximum catch-up contribution for such an eligible employee for the calendar year is the lesser of:

- the catch-up contribution limit of $3,000 for 2016,[13] or
- the employee's compensation for the year reduced by all of the employee's other elective deferrals for the year to other SIMPLEs, or 401(k) plans, SEPs, and 403(b) plans.

> In July of 2016, Joseph, age 54, began working for Knowledger Contributions, which sponsors a SIMPLE. Between July and December of 2016, Joseph earns $14,000. He defers $12,500 to the SIMPLE. Therefore, he can only defer an additional $1,500 ($14,000 - $12,500) to the SIMPLE under the catch-up provision because of his compensation reduced by the elective deferral.

EXAMPLE
10.3

---

12. IRC §408(p)(2)(A)(ii), as amended by EGTRRA 2001, §611(f)(1); §408(p)(2)(E), as amended by EGTRRA 2001, §611(f)(2); EGTRRA 2001, §611(i)(1).

13. After the 2006 calendar year, the $2,500 limitation was adjusted for inflation in increments of $500, and the base period for calculating the inflation adjustment was the calendar quarter starting July 1, 2005. IRC §414(v), as amended by EGTRRA, 2001, §631(a).

Employer Contributions

An employer who sponsors a SIMPLE IRA is required to make either matching contributions to those employees who make elective deferrals or, alternatively, to make nonelective contributions to all eligible employees.

Employer Matching Contributions

If the employer elects to make matching contributions, the employer is generally required to match the employee's elective deferral contributions on a dollar-for-dollar matching basis up to three percent of the compensation of the employee (without regard to the covered compensation limit) for the entire calendar year.[14]

The employer may reduce the three percent matching contribution requirement for a calendar year, but only under all of the following circumstances:[15]

- the limit is reduced to no less than one percent,
- the limit is not reduced for more than two years out of the five year period that ends with (and includes) the year for which the election is effective, and
- employees are notified of the reduced limit within a reasonable period of time before the sixty day election period for a salary reduction agreement.

This only applies to SIMPLE IRAs and hence is not available for SIMPLE 401(k)s.[16]

An employer normally must match each employee's elective deferral contribution dollar-for-dollar up to 3% of the employee's compensation. Michael is employed by Thomas Co. in 2016. Michael earned $30,000 and elected to defer 10% of his salary. Thomas was self-employed and his net earnings were $300,000. Thomas elects to defer 3% of his earnings to his SIMPLE IRA. Thomas Company makes a 3% matching contribution. The total contribution to Michael's SIMPLE IRA for 2016 is $3,900 as calculated below. Notice that the match for Thomas is not limited to 3% of $265,000 (the covered compensation limit for qualified plans). The limit is $9,000 (3% of $300,000).

Michael's elective deferral contribution ($30,000 x 10%)	$3,000
Matching contribution by Thomas Co. ($30,000 x 3%)	$900
2016 Total SIMPLE IRA Contribution	**$3,900**

Using the same facts as above, the total contribution for 2016 to Thomas's SIMPLE IRA is $18,000 as calculated below:

Thomas's elective deferral contribution ($300,000 x 3%)	$9,000
Matching contribution by Thomas Co. ($300,000 x 3%)	$9,000
2016 Total SIMPLE IRA Contribution	**$18,000**

---

14. IRC §408(p)(2)(A)(iii).
15. IRC §408(p)(2)(C)(ii).
16. IRC §401(k)(11)(B)(i).

Nonelective Contributions by Employer

The alternative for the employer who chooses not to match employee elective deferrals is to make nonelective contributions for all eligible employees. If the employer chooses to make **nonelective contributions**, then the employer must contribute two percent of each eligible employee's compensation (up to the covered compensation limit of $265,000 for 2016) to the SIMPLE IRA. The contribution must be made for all eligible employees who earn at least $5,000 from the employer for the year, or less if elected by the employer. If the employer decides to make nonelective contributions, the employer is required to make those nonelective contributions whether or not the employee chooses to make any elective deferral contributions. The employees must be notified within a reasonable time period before the 60 day election period of the employer's choice of the two percent nonelective contribution method or the matching contribution.

Matthew, an employee of Kathleen's Company, earned $40,000 in 2016 and agreed to make elective deferral contributions of 9% of his salary to his SIMPLE IRA. Kathleen earned $60,000 net self-employment income and chose to make elective deferral contributions of 10% of her earnings. Kathleen's Company, as the employer, made a nonelective contribution of 2% to each eligible employee. The total contribution to Matthew's SIMPLE IRA for 2016 is $4,400 as calculated below.

EXAMPLE
10.5

Matthew's elective deferral contribution ($40,000 x 0.09)	$3,600
Nonelective contribution by Kathleen Co. ($40,000 x 0.02)	$800
2016 Total Contribution for Matthew	**$4,400**

Using the same facts as above, the total contribution to Kathleen's SIMPLE IRA for 2016 is $7,200 as calculated below.

Kathleen's elective deferral contribution ($60,000 x 0.10)	$6,000
Nonelective contribution by Kathleen Co. ($60,000 x 0.02)	$1,200
2016 Total Contribution for Kathleen	**$7,200**

Taxation of Contributions

SIMPLE IRA contributions are contemporaneously tax deductible for the small employer. The deductible amount includes the employee elective deferral contributions (as compensation) and any employer match or nonelective contribution. The contributions to a SIMPLE IRA are not subject to a limitation based on a percentage of compensation, but the employee's elective deferral is limited to $12,500 for 2016.

Employer Contributions	Employee Elective Deferrals
• 3% match, or • 2% nonelective contribution for all eligible employees	• % or $ contribution up to $12,500 plus $3,000 for over age 50 for 2016

Employers are allowed to deduct contributions for the taxable year only if the contributions are made on or before the date that the employer's tax return is due. The elective contributions of the employee that are being made into the SIMPLE IRA account must be contributed by the employer no later than 30 days following the last day of the month of the contributions. [17] The employer must also make any matching contributions or nonelective contributions by the date that its tax return is due for that tax year, including extensions.

Employee elective deferral contributions and employer contributions made to SIMPLE IRAs are excluded from an employee's taxable income and are not subject to federal income tax withholding. An employee's elective deferral contributions are, however, subject to payroll taxes (OASDI and Medicare), but the employer matching or nonelective contributions made to SIMPLE IRA accounts are not subject to payroll tax (OASDI and Medicare).

Withdrawals and Distributions

Distributions from a SIMPLE IRA plan are includible as ordinary income in the individual employee's taxable income in the year in which they are withdrawn. SIMPLE IRA plan distributions are taxed in the same manner as distributions from a traditional IRA. As a general rule, trustee-to-trustee transfers (direct), and rollovers of SIMPLE IRAs are not taxable distributions. SIMPLE distributions may be subjected to an early withdrawal penalty of 10 percent if received prior to age 59½. The exclusions from the 10 percent penalty for SIMPLE IRAs are the same as described in Chapter 9 for IRAs.

A distribution or transfer made from a SIMPLE IRA during the first two years of an employee's participation in the SIMPLE must be contributed to another SIMPLE IRA to avoid taxation and penalty. After the two year participation period, a SIMPLE IRA can be transferred or rolled over tax-free to:
- an IRA other than a SIMPLE IRA,
- a qualified plan,
- a 403(b) account or tax sheltered annuity, or
- a deferred compensation plan of a State or local government (457 plan).

---

17. IRC §408(p)(5)(B).

If a distribution is taken from a SIMPLE IRA plan during the first two years of an employee's participation in the plan and if the distribution is subject to the early withdrawal penalty, the penalty tax increases from 10 percent to 25 percent. If the distribution is made on account of a penalty exclusion (as described in Chapter 9), then the 25 percent penalty tax will not apply.[18] After the employee's first two years of plan participation, the 10 percent penalty for early withdrawal will apply if the distribution is not because of a penalty excluded reason.

SIMPLE 401(k) PLANS

A SIMPLE 401(k) plan is a qualified plan and must generally satisfy the same requirements as 401(k) plans and SIMPLE IRA plans. The differences between SIMPLE 401(k)s and SIMPLE IRAs or between SIMPLE 401(k)s and 401(k)s are discussed below, along with other attributes of SIMPLE 401(k)s.

Under a SIMPLE 401(k) plan, an employee may choose to reduce his salary in return for "salary reduction contributions" or deferrals to a SIMPLE 401(k) account. This salary reduction contribution is expressly stated as a percentage of the employee's compensation but may not exceed $12,500 for 2016. The employer may, but is not required to, permit certain employees to use the catch-up feature, under which employees age 50 and over may defer a contribution of up to $3,000 for 2016.

The rules concerning contributions for employers to regular 401(k) plans, discussed in Chapter 5, also apply to SIMPLE 401(k)s. The limitation of $12,500 for 2016 or employee elective deferral contributions to the SIMPLE IRA plans (discussed above) also apply to the SIMPLE 401(k)s.

A participant of a SIMPLE 401(k) may take a loan (plan permitting) from a SIMPLE 401(k), unlike a participant of a SIMPLE IRA. The amount of the loan is subject to the same restrictions, discussed in Chapter 7, as loans from qualified plans.

Employers who sponsor SIMPLE 401(k) plans must make either: (1) a matching contribution, or (2) a nonelective contribution to the plan. An employer is required to match the elective deferral contribution of the employee on a dollar-for-dollar basis up to three percent of the employee's compensation for the calendar year.[19] In contrast to a SIMPLE IRA plan, the employer does not have the available option of reducing matching contributions to less than three percent of the compensation of each employee.

---

18. IRC §72(t)(6).
19. IRC §401(k)(11)(B)(i)(II).

As an alternative to matching elective deferral contributions, an employer that has established a SIMPLE 401(k) plan may elect to provide nonelective contributions of two percent of each eligible employee's compensation. The nonelective contributions of the employer are required to be made for each eligible employee, regardless of whether that employee elects to make any salary reduction deferral contributions. Under these circumstances, the employer is permitted, but is not required, to limit nonelective contributions to only those eligible employees (those employees who meet the eligibility rules).[20]

No other contribution may be made to the trust comprising the SIMPLE 401(k) account. No contributions can be made nor may benefits accrue for services during the year pursuant to any other qualified retirement plan of the employer for any employee participating in the SIMPLE 401(k) plan. The ADP test, ACP test, and top-heavy rules, explained in prior chapters, do not apply to SIMPLE 401(k)s because they are essentially safe harbor plans. Furthermore, annual filings of the Form 5500 are not required for SIMPLE 401(k) plans. Once again, though, there are few SIMPLE 401(k) plans that have been established.

QUICK QUIZ 10.2

1. Employers who sponsor a SIMPLE IRA must make either matching contributions or nonelective contributions.
   a. True
   b. False

2. Distributions from SIMPLE IRAs are generally taxed like traditional IRAs.
   a. True
   b. False

3. Employers that sponsor SIMPLE 401(k) plans must allow for catch-up contributions for participants over 50.
   a. True
   b. False

True, True, False.

CONCLUSION

SIMPLEs are retirement plans for small employers, and like their name implies, are very easy to establish and maintain, have less administrative costs than other retirement plans, and do not have any annual filing requirements. As discussed, SIMPLEs can take the form of a SIMPLE IRA or SIMPLE 401(k), both of which essentially share the same rules. In practice, most employers chose the SIMPLE IRA instead of the SIMPLE 401(k). Although the 401(k) version has loans as an available option, it also has greater administrative requirements.

---

20. IRC §401(k)(11)(B)(ii).

Concept Summary - SIMPLE Plans

EXHIBIT
10.7

SIMPLE	Savings Incentive Match Plan for Employees
Application	Small employers (limit of 100 employees with compensation > $5,000)
Style	Self-reliant employee elective deferral contributions and employer match
Type	Could be SIMPLE 401(k), but almost all are SIMPLE IRAs
Established By What Date	Generally, October 1 of year the plan starts
Characteristics	No annual filing requirement, minor costs No other retirement plans are permitted
Employee Elective Deferral Contribution Limit	Lesser of $12,500 for 2016 salary reduction or 100% salary
Catch-Up Contribution for Age 50	Yes, $3,000 for 2016
Available Employer Contributions	Dollar-for-dollar match up to the lesser of 3% of compensation (without regard to covered compensation limit) or $12,500 <u>or</u> 2% of compensation (up to covered compensation limit of $265,000 for 2016) nonelective contribution for each eligible employee regardless of deferral
Penalties for In-Service Withdrawals	For SIMPLE IRA, 25% if within first 2 years, unless penalty exception applies; 10% after 2 years unless penalty exception applies. For SIMPLE 401(k), the penalty is 10% unless penalty exception applies.
Loans Permitted	No - SIMPLE IRA; Yes - SIMPLE 401(k)
In-Service Withdrawals	Yes, subject to income and penalties

EXHIBIT 10.8

SIMPLE IRA, SIMPLE 401(k), AND 401(k) PLAN COMPARISON

	SIMPLE IRA	SIMPLE 401(k)	401(k) Plans
Application	Small employers (limit of 100 employee's with compensation > $5,000)	Same as SIMPLE IRA	Most employers
Style	Self-reliant employee elective deferral contributions and employer match		
Established By What Date	Generally, October 1 of the year the plan starts	Same as SIMPLE IRA	By 12/31 of year before
Ability to have Other Plans	Must not have another retirement plan	Same as SIMPLE IRA	There may be other plans
Filings and Costs	No annual filing requirement, minor costs	Same as 401(k) Plan	Annual filing required and administrative costs
Annual Testing	None required if meet contribution requirements	None required if meet contribution requirements	Required
Vesting	All contributions are fully vested	All contributions are fully vested	Vesting schedules allowed
Employee Elective Deferral Contribution Limit	$12,500 for 2016	Same as SIMPLE IRA	$18,000 for 2016
Catch-Up Contribution for Age 50 and over	$3,000 for 2016	Same as SIMPLE IRA	$6,000 for 2016
Employer Contribution	The employer must generally make: • A dollar-for-dollar match up to 3% of pay or • A 2% nonelective contribution for each eligible employee.	Same as SIMPLE IRA except for the employer-match cannot be reduced to as low as 1% for no more than 2 out of 5 years, including the year of election.	Employer may contribute
Loans Permitted	No	Same as 401(k) Plan	Yes
In-Service Withdrawals	Permitted, but 10% penalty if under age 59½ (unless penalty exception applies). If withdrawals are made within the first two years of participation, the 10% additional tax is increased to 25% (unless penalty exception applies).	Same as 401(k) Plan	Permitted, but possible 10% penalty if under age 59½ (unless penalty exception applies)

403(b) PLANS OR TAX SHELTERED ANNUITIES (TSAs)

Under §403(b) of the IRC, plans called **tax sheltered or deferred annuities**, or "**403(b) plans**," are available to the employees of certain qualified nonprofit organizations, public educational systems, cooperative hospital service organizations, and to certain ministers. The employee elective deferral contributions limits of 403(b) plans, along with the catch-up provisions, allow for the deferral of significant amounts for those employees who are age 50 or older.

DEFINITION OF A 403(b) PLAN

A 403(b) plan is a retirement plan for certain employees of public schools, certain ministers, and employees of various tax-exempt organizations. It is a tax-sheltered retirement plan, but not a qualified plan. The 403(b) plan is established by the employer and the employee has an individual account earmarked as his or her 403(b) plan account. Many consider 403(b) plans of nonprofit entities to be the counterpart to the 401(k) plans of for-profit entities. Sometimes, 403(b) plans are termed "401(k) plans for nonprofits." Though not considered qualified plans, many 403(b) plans offer similar attributes as qualified defined contribution plans. There are two basic types of 403(b) plans. The first type is a salary reduction plan,

KEY CONCEPTS

1. What are 403(b) plans?
2. When does ERISA apply to 403(b) plans?
3. Who is eligible for a 403(b) plan?
4. What rules are applicable to employee contributions to 403(b) plans?

which only accepts employee deferrals. This is the most common type of plan. The second type of plan is an employer-funded plan, which accepts employee and employer contributions. This type of 403(b) plan is less common.

Entities that can Establish 403(b) Plans

Only employers may set up 403(b) accounts. Individuals cannot establish 403(b) accounts on their own. Interestingly, however, self-employed ministers (discussed briefly below) are considered both employees and employers, and thus are able to contribute to a retirement 403(b) income account for their own benefit. Generally, employers that are eligible to establish 403(b) plans are nonprofit religious, charitable, scientific, educational, and other public interest organizations such as private schools, colleges, universities, and teaching hospitals.

Technically, the two types of entities that can establish 403(b) plans are:
1. Tax-exempt organizations under IRC §501(c)(3), or
2. Public schools or public educational organizations.

Section 501(c)(3) Organizations

Section 501(c)(3) organizations are nonprofit tax-exempt organizations that are established under IRC §501(c)(3) of the Internal Revenue Code. Section 501(c)(3) organizations are nonprofit entities such as corporations, community chests, funds, or foundations. They are organized exclusively (1) for religious, charitable, scientific, literary, or educational purposes, (2) to foster amateur sports competition nationally or internationally, unless any of their activities involve providing athletic equipment or facilities, or (3) to prevent cruelty to children or animals. Net earnings of the organization may not inure to the benefit of private shareholders. Further, no lobbying activities (other than by public charities) can comprise a substantial part of the organization's activities, nor can the organization participate in any political campaign for any candidate for public office.[21]

Public Schools or Public Educational Organizations

In general, public schools can establish 403(b) plans, and most often the public educational system of a state or community will establish a 403(b) plan. A public educational system is an organization run by a state, political subdivision, or agency that maintains a faculty and curriculum and has regularly enrolled students in attendance where educational activities are conducted.[22]

ERISA APPLICABILITY

The issue of whether ERISA applies to a 403(b) plan is important. If ERISA applies, then the plan requirements change. ERISA applies if the 403(b) plan is considered to be an "employee benefit pension plan." An employee benefit pension plan is defined as any plan, fund, or program established or maintained by an employer that provides retirement income to employees or defers income of employees for periods until termination of employment or beyond. Governmental TSAs and church-related TSAs are not subject to ERISA, but plans of §501(c)(3) organizations may be subject to ERISA unless employer involvement is so minimal that it falls short of the requirement that a plan be sponsored by an employer (as discussed below).

It is very common for a 403(b) plan to be a part of an overall pension or retirement plan. The 403(b) portion may be referred to as the supplemental retirement plan. If this is the case, then the plan is subject to ERISA requirements.

Generally 403(b) plans are not subject to ERISA rules if the following are true:
- employee participation is voluntary,
- there are no employer contributions,
- employee has solely enforceable rights under the plan,
- employer's involvement is limited in scope, and
- sponsored by a government or religious institution.

Suppose Loyola University had a retirement plan that required employees to contribute 3.5 percent of their salary to the plan and the university contributed eight percent to the plan. Loyola also maintained a 403(b) plan that allowed employees to choose elective deferrals up to the maximum provided by the law. In this case, Loyola's 403(b) plan would be subject to ERISA requirements because it is maintained as an "employer benefit pension plan."

If a 403(b) plan only provides for salary reduction agreements, then the plan is not considered to be established or maintained by the employer and ERISA is inapplicable. If ERISA applies, nonelective deferral contributions must satisfy nondiscrimination requirements, matching contributions must satisfy the ACP test, and the plan is subject to pre-retirement joint and survivor annuity elections and joint and survivor elections at retirement as distribution requirements.

21. IRC §501(c)(3).
22. IRC §403(b)(1)(A)(ii).

To illustrate this point, consider the scenario of a 403(b) plan that only provides for elective deferrals (i.e., salary reduction contributions). In such a case, only one nondiscrimination requirement will apply: If one employee has the right to elect to have the employer make salary reduction contributions under a salary reduction agreement, then all employees must be permitted to elect salary deferral contributions. If, however, the plan contains employer contributions beyond salary reduction contributions, then contributions to the 403(b) plan are subject to the general nondiscrimination rules applicable to qualified retirement plans and may not discriminate in favor of the HCE.

Employee deferrals to a 403(b) plan are not subject to the actual deferral percentage (ADP) test discussed in Chapter 5. However, a 403(b) plan must generally allow all eligible employees to make elective deferrals to the plan under what is referred to as the universal availability rule. Under this rule, if an employer permits one employee to defer salary by contributing it to a 403(b) plan, the employer must extend this offer to all employees with the following exceptions:

- employees who will contribute $200 or less annually,
- employees who participate in a 401(k) or 457(b) plan or in another 403(b) plan of the employer,
- nonresident aliens,
- employees who normally work less than 20 hours per week, and
- students who are enrolled and regularly attending classes at such school, college, or university.

ELIGIBILITY

Eligible employees can participate in a 403(b) plan sponsored through an employer. 403(b) plans with immediate vesting may require a maximum waiting period of two years and the attainment of age 21, or one year and the attainment of age 26 (educational institutions only). Plans that do not offer immediate vesting may not have a waiting period longer than one year and the attainment of age 21. The following are considered eligible employees (who must meet the age and service requirements) to participate in a 403(b) plan:

1. Employees of tax-exempt organizations as defined under IRC §501(c)(3).
2. Employees who are involved in the day-to-day operations of a public school or public school system.
3. Employees of cooperative hospital service organizations.[23]
4. Ministers who meet one of the following criteria:
    - Ministers that are employed by §501(c)(3) organizations (discussed above).
    - Ministers that are self-employed. A self-employed minister is deemed as employed by a tax-exempt organization that is a qualified employer.
    - Ministers who are employed by organizations that are not §501(c)(3) organizations and function as ministers in their day-to-day responsibilities with their employer.

Self-employed ministers must report total contributions to 403(b) accounts as a tax deduction on their tax returns.

---

23. Cooperative hospital service organizations are codified in IRC §501(e). They are deemed to be §501(c)(3) organizations, and thus are allowed to form a 403(b) plan for employees.

Notes on Employees

When the term "employee" is used in discussing these rules, an employer-employee relationship must exist to allow the employee to be eligible to participate. The individual must be an employee, not an independent contractor. There are many IRS guidelines for characterizing someone as an employee or independent contractor based on the relationship between the individual and the company. Some emphasis is placed on the amount of control, direction, and supervision that the employer has over the individual.

Case Study 10.1

In **Azad v U.S.,**[1] a radiologist was on salary at a hospital. The radiologist's work at the hospital was not supervised nor was it directed by the hospital. The Court concluded that the radiologist was not an employee as defined by the IRC, and was not permitted to exclude from his gross income those amounts contributed to an annuity contract by the employer.

1. **Azad v. U.S.**, 277 F. Supp. 258 (D.C. Minn. 1966), aff'd, 388 F.2d 74 (8th Cir. 1968).

EMPLOYEE CONTRIBUTIONS

Employees' elective deferral contributions to 403(b) accounts are very similar to employee elective deferral contributions to 401(k) plans, SARSEPs, and 457 plans. While a 403(b) plan is established by the employer, the employee has an individual 403(b) account for his own benefit. Only the employer is allowed to make contributions to the 403(b) account on behalf of the employee (usually through employee salary reduction), but some plans may also allow employees to make after-tax contributions similar to a thrift plan.

The following contributions are permissible contributions (but are not required) for 403(b) accounts:

- employee elective deferrals
- nonelective contributions
- after-tax contributions
- any combination of the above

With employee "elective deferrals," contributions can be made under a salary reduction agreement where the employee agrees that the employer will withhold money from the employee's paycheck so that these funds can be contributed directly into the 403(b) account for the benefit of the employee. The employee is not subject to income tax on the contribution until the funds are withdrawn from the 403(b) account by the employee. However, the elective deferral amounts are subject to payroll taxes exactly as are 401(k) elective deferrals. For 2016, an employee can electively defer no more than $18,000, subject to catch-up provisions discussed later in this chapter. Deferrals can also be made to a Roth account if it is part of the 403(b) plan, but these deferrals consist of after-tax contributions.

Unlike employee elective deferrals, "nonelective contributions" are not made under a salary reduction agreement. Instead, nonelective contributions are matching contributions, mandatory contributions from the employer, or even discretionary contributions by the employer. Again, the employee does not pay taxes on these contributions until withdrawn by the employee from the account.

Finally, an employee may contribute after-tax or non-deductible funds to a 403(b) account. Although after-tax contributions to 403(b) accounts are allowed, they are unusual in practice, other than to Roth accounts, discussed below. Unlike the elective deferral and nonelective contributions, however, the amounts contributed in after-tax contributions are not excluded from the income of the employee and will therefore create an adjusted basis in the 403(b) account. When the participant takes a withdrawal from such an account, some of the funds will be return of capital and, therefore, nontaxable.

Limits on Elective Deferrals

An elective deferral is basically an employee's contribution to an employee's account through a voluntary salary reduction agreement. While technically only employers can actually make contributions into the 403(b) accounts on behalf of the employees, employees voluntarily elect or decide to reduce their salary by a certain amount, and that forgone amount is contributed by the employer for the benefit of the employees into the 403(b) account. Commonly, this is referred to as a cash or deferred arrangement (CODA) because the employee has the choice of receiving the funds in cash or deferring the income. Therefore, the employee is directing the employer to place these deferral amounts into this account on his behalf.

During a given year, an employee may enter into more than one salary reduction agreement. If elective deferrals are made to more than one 403(b) account for a given employee (irrespective of whether the contributions were made by the same employer) in the same year, then there must be a summary of all such elective deferrals to determine if the aggregate amount exceeds the employee's limit for that year, $18,000 for 2016. If elective deferrals are made to other retirement plans on behalf of the employee, then the limit on elective deferrals applies to the total, aggregate amount. Other accounts that are included in the aggregate total are 401(k) plans, SIMPLEs, SARSEPs, and all 403(b) plans.[24] If an amount contributed exceeds the limit, the employee must include the excess in gross income on his tax return for the year contributed.

403(b) ANNUAL ELECTIVE DEFERRALS LIMITS*

EXHIBIT 10.9

Year	Annual Deferral Limit	Catch-Up Contributions **	Total Deferral
2016	$18,000	$6,000	$24,000

The same limits apply to SARSEPs, 401(k) plans, and 457 plans.
*** Age 50 or older*

The limit on elective deferrals for 2016 that can be contributed to a 403(b) account through a salary reduction agreement is $18,000. There are certain exceptions to the general limit of $18,000 for 2016 for contributions to 403(b) plans. Those age 50 and over, and those with at least 15 years of service to the employer can make additional, or catch-up, contributions.

---

24. Also included are §501(c)(18) plans and trusts established prior to June 25, 1959.

Catch-Up Contributions

Age 50 Catch-Up Provisions

There are "catch-up" provisions for certain employees participating in a 403(b) plan. In addition to the contribution limits to a 403(b) plan, employees age 50 and over at the end of the year may make additional contributions under the catch-up provisions of IRC §403(b). An employee is eligible to make catch-up contributions if the employee has reached age 50 by the end of the year, and the maximum amount of elective deferrals that can be made to the employee's account have been satisfied for the year. If these two elements exist, then the total amount of "catch-up contributions" for the employee age 50 and over would be the lesser of $6,000 for 2016, or includable compensation (explained below) subtracted by other elective deferrals for the year. When determining what catch-up contributions are allowable under 403(b), all catch-up contributions made by the employer on behalf of the employee must be combined, and these amounts include contributions made to qualified retirement plans, 401(k) plans, 403(b) plans, SEPs, and SIMPLEs.

"15-Year Rule" Exception

There is a special catch-up rule, in addition to the $6,000 catch-up for participants age 50 and over, that applies only for 403(b) plans for employees who have at least 15 years of service with a public school system, hospital, home health service agency, health and welfare service agency, church, or convention or association of churches (or associated organization).[25] Note that the 15 years of service are not required to be consecutive. If an employee has worked for 15 years with an organization that qualifies for eligibility under a 403(b) plan, then the limit of elective deferrals to the 403(b) account is increased by the lesser of the following:

- $3,000,
- $15,000, reduced by increases to the general limit that were allowed in previous years due to the **15-year rule**, or
- $5,000 times the number of years of service for the organization by the employee, subtracted from the total elective deferrals made by the employer on behalf of the employee for earlier years.

If an employee qualifies for the 15-year rule, the maximum elective deferrals for the 403(b) plan for the plan year may be as high as $27,000 for 2016 ($18,000 maximum deferral plus $3,000 from the 15-year rule plus $6,000 for the 50 and over catch-up rule).

Employee	Age	Years of Service	Maximum Deferral
A	25	2	$18,000
B	52	3	$24,000
C	52	16	$27,000

Roth Contributions (Roth Accounts)

403(b) plans, along with and 401(k) plans and 457(b) plans, may allow employees to make contributions to Roth accounts. These contributions are not excludable from the employee's gross income. Instead, these contributions will consist of after-tax dollars, just like contributions to Roth IRAs. Distributions attributable to these Roth contributions will be non-taxable and will not be

---

25. IRS Publication 571.

subject to penalties if the distribution is a qualifying distribution. The qualifying distribution rules are discussed in Chapter 7 and are virtually the same as those for distributions from Roth IRAs as discussed in Chapter 9. Plans that establish Roth accounts are required to maintain separate accounts and maintain separate records for these Roth contributions and earnings allocable to the contributions.

These Roth contributions provide a great opportunity for employees to save for retirement. Although the contributions are not pretax, all qualifying distributions will be tax-free and penalty free. The contribution limit for Roth accounts in 2016 is $18,000, significantly higher than the limits for contributions to Roth IRAs. In addition, catch-up contributions can be directed to the Roth account, as well as the traditional account. Contributions to Roth IRAs are also limited based on annual income, but Roth accounts within 403(b) plans do not have such income limitations. Therefore, a highly compensated employee would be able to fund a Roth only through a Roth account, not a Roth IRA.

As discussed in Chapter 7, The Small Business Jobs Act (SBJA) of 2010 made several important changes to the Internal Revenue Code dealing with elective deferrals in Roth accounts. SBJA 2010 added IRC §402A(c)(4) to the Code to permit plans that include a qualified Roth contribution program to allow individuals to roll over amounts from their accounts to their designated Roth accounts in the plan.[26] This option, which can be accomplished as a direct rollover or as an indirect rollover, is akin to converting funds in a traditional IRA to a Roth IRA. In addition, SBJA 2010 permits governmental 457(b) plans to include designated Roth accounts for years after 2010.

An "in-plan Roth rollover" is a distribution[27] from an individual's plan account, other than a designated Roth account, that is rolled over to the individual's designated Roth account in the same plan, pursuant to new IRC §402A(c)(4). An in-plan Roth rollover is generally not considered a distribution from the plan, but will result in the individual being taxed on the amount of the rollover. The American Taxpayer Relief Act of 2012 expanded the amounts that are permitted to be rolled over in an in-plan Roth rollover.

EMPLOYER CONTRIBUTIONS

Nonelective contributions are matching contributions, mandatory contributions, or even discretionary contributions from the employer. Employer matching contributions are based on the employee's deferral, and the employer may make other contributions without regard to the employee's elective deferral. Unlike employee elective deferrals, nonelective contributions are not made under a salary

QUICK QUIZ 10.3

1. Employers or individuals can establish a 403(b) plan.
   a. True
   b. False

2. 403(b) plans may be covered under ERISA.
   a. True
   b. False

3. Additional catch-up contributions to a 403(b) plan may be after-tax contributions from the employee.
   a. True
   b. False

False, True, False.

---

26. Effective for distributions made after September 27, 2010.
27. After September 27, 2010.

reduction agreement. As discussed earlier, the nonelective employer contributions (other than salary reduction contributions) to the 403(b) account subject the plan to ERISA.

The Limit on Annual Additions

There is a limit on "annual additions" or amounts added to an account over the course of a year for an employee in a 403(b) plan to comply with IRC §415(c). The limitation applies to an aggregate of all contributions. The total contributions are comprised of elective deferrals, nonelective contributions, and after-tax contributions. The maximum for 2016 is the lesser of $53,000, or 100 percent of the employee's covered compensation for the employee's most recent year of service. If an employee contributed to more than one 403(b) account, all employer contributions to the accounts must be combined when determining if they exceed acceptable limits.

Includable Compensation for the Most Recent Year of Service

The definition of **includable compensation** for the most recent year of service is that amount of taxable wages and benefits that are received by the employee from the employer. When figuring includable compensation for the most recent year of service, it could be that the most recent year of service is not the same as the employer's most recent annual work period. In such a case, the most recent year of service is determined by calculating the previous full year of service for the employee's position.

A full year of service is equal to full time employment for the annual work period of the employer. For instance, if an employee worked the last four months of 2016 and the next nine months of 2017, then the most recent year of service would have been the first nine months of 2017 and the last three months of 2016, totaling the most previous 12-month period of work.

Once the most recent year of service has been identified, the next step is to quantify the includable compensation earned during that full year of service. Includable compensation is the total of income and benefits received from an employer maintaining a 403(b) account and the amount included in the income of the employee. The following amounts are considered as includible compensation:

- elective deferrals
- amounts contributed by an employer under a Cafeteria Plan
- amounts contributed under an eligible Section 457 nonqualified deferred compensation plan
- wages, salaries, and fees for personal services earned with the employer maintaining the 403(b) account
- income excluded under the Foreign Earned Income exclusion
- qualified transportation or fringe benefits

Meanwhile, the following items are not considered includible compensation:
- the employer's contributions to the employee's 403(b) account
- compensation earned while the employee was not eligible
- the employer's contributions to a qualified plan on behalf of the employee that are excluded from income
- the cost of incidental life insurance

VESTING

403(b) plans will often provide for full and immediate vesting on all amounts contributed to the plan. Employee contributions are always fully vested. However, employers that make contributions to a 403(b) plan must make a choice about whether to impose a vesting schedule or not. If the employer chooses to include vesting, it must be consistent with the requirements for 401(k) plans and other defined contribution plans. These vesting requirements permit an employer to choose between the 3-year cliff and the 2-6 graduated methods.

Final regulations under IRC §403(b) were published on July 26, 2007 and generally became effective January 1, 2009. One of the requirements of these regulations is that sponsors of 403(b) plans are required to maintain a written plan.

The IRS published model plan language that may be used by public schools either to adopt a written plan or amend a plan to reflect the requirements of IRC §403(b) and the regulations. Interestingly, the language for the prototype 403(b) plan provides for full and immediate vesting on all amounts. Even though this language is in the prototype plans, employers are still permitted to include vesting on employer contributions.

KEY CONCEPTS

1. What are the available investment choices for 403(b) plans?

2. How are loans and distributions from a 403(b) plan taxed?

3. What rollover, distribution, and minimum distribution rules apply to 403(b) plans?

INVESTMENT CHOICES AND LIMITATIONS

Funds within a 403(b) account can only be invested in either insurance annuity contracts or mutual funds. Specifically, individual accounts in 403(b) plans must be one of the following forms:
- A contract provided through an insurance company called an annuity contract;
- An account invested in mutual funds only, which is referred to as a custodial account; or
- An account for church employees that is a retirement income account, which invests in either annuities or mutual funds.

Annuity Contracts

"**Annuity contracts**" are not specifically defined in the Internal Revenue Code. An annuity contract must be purchased for the employee from an insurance company and may give a fixed benefit or a variable benefit depending on the performance of the investment.[28] Any contract or certificate that is transferable to a person other than a trustee is not an annuity contract.

---

28. Treasury Regulation §1.403(b)-1(c)(3).

LOANS

While in-service withdrawal distributions to employees are generally not permitted until retirement or termination, ERISA plans are permitted to make loans to plan participants. Loans to 403(b) employee-participants are allowed and are subject to the same limitations and requirements applicable to loans from qualified retirement plans (e.g., 401(k) plan). Although any qualified plan may establish a loan provision, they are generally found only in 401(k) plans and 403(b) plans. As discussed fully in Chapter 7, plan loans must be made available to all participants and beneficiaries on an effectively equal basis, must be limited in amount, must be repaid within a certain time period, must bear a reasonable rate of interest, must be adequately secured, and the administrator must maintain proper accounting for the loans.

When an employee is terminated or if the TSA is terminated, then any outstanding loan will be affected. Loan repayments are generally accomplished through payroll deduction, which of course is unavailable after employee termination occurs. If an employee fails to repay a loan from a qualified plan upon termination, the employer will generally declare the unpaid portion a deemed distribution, which will be subject to ordinary income tax and possibly an early withdrawal penalty of 10 percent if under the age of 59½. However, plans may provide alternatives such as reducing the amount of a direct rollover distribution and providing the employee a certain period of time to repay the loan before it will be treated as a distribution.

DISTRIBUTIONS

Because 403(b) plans fall within the ERISA plan area, they follow many of the same rules regarding distributions applicable to other qualified plans. Generally, distributions can be paid from a 403(b) account only after the following events:

- the employee turns age 59½,
- the employee is separated from service,
- the employee dies,
- the employee becomes disabled, or
- for salary reduction contributions, the employee endures a severe hardship.[29]

---

29. IRC §403(b)(11).

These restrictions apply only to contributions from salary reduction agreements. Nonelective deferral contributions have no such restrictions upon distribution. However, if distributions attributable to salary reduction contributions or nonelective deferrals occur before the employee turns 59½, then a 10 percent penalty for early withdrawal may apply.

Hardship distributions are permitted in 403(b) plans. Therefore, the hardship rules discussed in Chapter 5 for CODAs can be used for guidance. Hardship distributions from TSAs cannot be rolled over to an IRA and are not subject to the 20 percent income tax withholding rules as discussed in Chapter 7.

ROLLOVERS TO AND FROM 403(b) PLANS

Employee-participants can generally roll over tax-free all or any part of a distribution from a 403(b) plan to a qualified plan, a traditional IRA, or to another 403(b) retirement plan. 403(b) distributions can also be rolled into a Roth IRA after December 31, 2007.[30] Any rollover that is not a direct trustee-to-trustee rollover will be subject to mandatory 20 percent withholding and 100 percent of the distribution must be deposited into the new account by the 60th day following the day on which the employee receives the distribution.

Hardship Exception to Rollover Rules

The IRS may waive the 60-day rollover period if the participant's failure to waive such requirement would be against equity or good conscience, including cases of casualty, disaster, or other events beyond the reasonable control of the individual. To obtain a hardship exception, the participant must apply to the IRS for a waiver of the 60-day rollover requirement. In its determination as to the grant of a waiver, the IRS will consider all relevant facts and circumstances, including:
- whether errors were made by the financial institution facilitating the rollover,
- whether the participant was unable to complete the rollover due to death, disability, hospitalization, incarceration, restrictions imposed by a foreign country or postal error,
- whether the participant used the amount distributed, and
- the time passed since the date of distribution.

There are many exceptions granted by the IRS as a result of "errors" or poor advice or execution made at least in part by a financial institution. In these instances where there is an error, the IRS will waive or extend the 60-day rule.

MINIMUM DISTRIBUTION REQUIREMENTS

403(b) plans are subject to the same minimum distribution requirements applicable to IRAs and qualified plans, which require that an individual begin taking withdrawals from the plan by April 1st of the year after the participant attains the age of 70½. These rules include the latest time that distributions from 403(b) plans may begin and the minimum amount that may be distributed from the 403(b) plan, which are similar to the rules for IRAs and for qualified retirement plans. For a more complete explanation of the minimum distribution requirements, see Chapter 7.

Excess Employer Contributions

If a distribution from a 403(b) plan consists of income that was previously included in income as an excess employer contribution, then that portion of the transfer is not eligible as a rollover

---

30. Pension Protection Act of 2006. See Chapter 9 for more detail.

distribution to an IRA. This transfer does not affect the rollover treatment of the eligible portion of the transferred amounts; however, the ineligible portion is subject to the traditional IRA contribution limits and may create an excess IRA contribution subject to a six percent excise tax. Chapter 9 discusses the traditional IRA contribution limits and the six percent excise tax.

TAXATION OF 403(b) DISTRIBUTIONS

The tax rules that apply to 403(b) distributions are basically the same tax rules that apply to distributions from other qualified retirement plans and IRAs. In most instances, the distributions from 403(b) accounts received by participants are taxable as ordinary income in the year received; however, the employee-participant's return of adjusted basis is not subject to tax. This basis includes the employee's voluntary after-tax contributions, life insurance protection costs, employer contributions previously includible in the employee's income, and loans to the employee secured by the TSA that were deemed as taxable distributions.

QUALIFIED JOINT AND SURVIVOR ANNUITY

As discussed in Chapter 7, a **qualified joint and survivor annuity (QJSA)** is an immediate annuity for the life of the participant coupled with an annuity for the surviving spouse of the participant for the remainder of the spouse's life. The survivor annuity may not be less than 50 percent, nor more than 100 percent, of the payable amount of the annuity during the lifetime of the participant and spouse. While the

**QUICK QUIZ
10.4**

1. For 403(b) plans the "most recent year of service" is always based on a calendar year of service.
   a. True
   b. False

2. Funds within a 403(b) plan may only be invested in either annuity contracts or mutual funds.
   a. True
   b. False

3. 403(b) plans generally provide for 100% immediate vesting of contributions.
   a. True
   b. False

False, True, True.

IRC does not specifically provide that QJSA apply to 403(b) plans, the QJSA requirements control whether ERISA is applicable to the 403(b) plan. Recall that ERISA will apply if the 403(b) plan is an employee benefit pension plan or provides employer contributions beyond salary deferrals. If ERISA does apply to the 403(b) plan, then the QJSA requirements will generally apply.

THE BENEFITS OF 403(b) PLANS AND CONTRIBUTING TO 403(b) PLANS

There are some significant benefits to making employee elective deferral contributions to 403(b) plans. First, the employee does not pay income taxes on the contributions to the plan. This, of course, does not apply to any after-tax contribution but does apply to the elective deferral and the nonelective contributions from the employer. The employee only pays taxes on allowable contributions once withdrawals from the plan are taken. Second, earnings and gains on the amounts placed in a 403(b) account are not subjected to income tax until withdrawn by the employee. Third, the benefits are similar to those in 401(k) plans (as discussed in Chapter 5) and other retirement vehicles because the employees have tax-deferred benefits of growth over time, along with a vehicle where an employer may match benefits and may provide for other incidental contributions for an employee's benefit.

SIMILARITIES AND DIFFERENCES BETWEEN 401(k) PLANS AND 403(b) PLANS

403(b) plans for nonprofit organizations are similar to the 401(k) plans used by for-profit businesses. Like 401(k) plans, 403(b) plans allow employees to defer a portion of their salary. The funds accumulate and grow over time and are not subjected to income taxation by federal or state governments until distributed to the employee.

The tax advantages associated with 401(k) qualified defined-contribution plans are the same as those for 403(b) plans, namely that allowable contributions and the earnings of these contributions are not subject to federal income taxation until withdrawn. The amount of contributions to 401(k) plans and to 403(b) plans may consist of employee elective deferrals, employer contributions, and after-tax employee contributions. 403(b) plans may provide for employer matching contributions, much like 401(k) plans. Participants in a 403(b) plans have the same contribution limits each year as 401(k) plan participants, and the early withdrawal rules are basically the same for both types of plans.

Obviously, there are differences between the two types of plans. However, with the changes to the Code over the last twenty years, the differences between 401(k) plans and 403(b) plans are rather limited. Some of the differences are investment choices and the additional catch-up rules for 403(b) plans.

| EXHIBIT 10.10 | CONCEPT SUMMARY - 403(b) PLANS |

Application	Not-For-Profit institution (large universities)
Style	Self reliance plans; employee only contributions
Subject to ERISA	Maybe (if organized as a qualified plan)
Established By What Date	End of year
Characteristics	Self-reliant savings plan
Elective Deferral Contribution Limit	$18,000 + $6,000 catch-up contribution (2016)
Available Contribution	$53,000 for 2016 or 100% of compensation including elective deferrals
Additional After-Tax Contributions Permitted	Permissible by plan document
Investment Risk	Employee has investment choices and risks
Investment Alternatives	Limited to Insurance Annuities and Mutual Funds
Penalties	10% early withdrawal (if applicable)
Loans Permitted	Yes (regular qualified plan rules on loans if plan permits)
Rollovers	Yes, to IRA, qualified plan, or other 403(b)*
ERISA Protected	Yes, if ERISA plan. ERISA not applicable if governmental or church TSA.
In-Service Withdrawals	Generally no, except hardships, which are plan specific
Vesting	100% for all employee contributions. Employer contributions may be subject to standard vesting (post PPA 2006).

* Rollovers to Roth IRAs are permitted after December 31, 2007.

457 PLANS

Under §457 of the Internal Revenue Code, employees of state and local governments and of nongovernmental tax-exempt entities may participate in tax-free deferred compensation plans to aid employees in saving for retirement. Employee elective deferrals into a **457 plan** do not count against deferrals into 401(k) or 403(b) plans.

DEFINITION OF A 457 PLAN

Section 457 of the Internal Revenue Code allows employees of state and local governments and employees of tax-exempt nongovernmental entities to save tax-deferred compensation for retirement. 457 plans work in many ways like 401(k) and 403(b) plans. Employees contribute a portion of their salary through a payroll reduction. The annual amount that an employee may contribute is limited (except for ineligible 457(f) plans explained below), and employee elective deferral contributions are not includible in an employee's gross income in the year earned but are deferred until paid out or made available to the employee. 457 plans are not "qualified plans" and, thus, are not subject to many of the eligibility standards of IRC 401(a), including such requirements as nondiscrimination, minimum participation, and funding and vesting standards. A 457 plan is a "nonqualified" deferred compensation plan.[31]

31. *Rheal v. Commissioner*, T.C. Memo 1989 - 525.

There are three types of 457 plans: (1) eligible governmental plans under IRC §457(b), (2) eligible tax-exempt plans under IRC §457(b), and (3) "ineligible plans" under IRC §457(f). The following exhibit illustrates how these three types of 457 plans are related.

RELATIONSHIP BETWEEN 457 PLANS

EXHIBIT
10.11

Plans that are "eligible" under **457(b)** allow employees of sponsoring organizations to defer income taxation on savings for retirement into future years. Plans that are "ineligible," found under **§457(f)**, may trigger different tax treatment under §457(f). The main distinction between eligible plans (457(b) plans) and ineligible plans (457(f) plans) is that ineligible plans provide for greater deferral of funds. Most of this section on 457 plans will address rules applicable to 457(b) plans. Ineligible plans and their differences compared to 457(b) plans will be addressed later in the chapter.

ENTITIES THAT CAN ESTABLISH 457(b) PLANS

457(b) plans may only be formed and maintained by employers that are "eligible" as defined under §457.[32] The term eligible employer is defined as a State, a political subdivision of a State, or any agency or instrumentality of a State or political subdivision of a State, and any other organization other than a governmental unit that is exempt from tax.[33] These tax-exempt organizations include trade associations, religious organizations, private hospitals, rural electric cooperatives, farmers' cooperatives, private schools and foundations, labor unions, and charitable organizations. Churches[34] and qualified church-controlled organizations[35] are not considered eligible employers under §457.[36]

---

32. IRC §457(e)(1).
33. IRC §457(e)(1)(A)(B).
34. IRC §3121(w)(3)(A).
35. IRC §3121(w)(3)(B).
36. Note that while churches and qualified church-controlled organizations may not establish 457 plans, tax-exempt church-related entities such as schools and hospitals may still be eligible employers for 457 plans.

ERISA Applicability

457(b) plans sponsored by governmental employers are also called "public 457(b) plans." 457(b) plans for tax-exempt employers are called "private 457(b) plans." Public 457(b) plans are required to be funded through a trust holding all assets and income for the exclusive benefit of plan participants and their beneficiaries.[37] Under private 457(b) plans for tax-exempt employers, ERISA limits participation to a select group of highly compensated employees or management. Private 457(b) plans are offered only to HC employees or top management because funds in the plan are not placed in trust. The private 457(b) plan is "unfunded" and remains vulnerable to the employer's creditors. This poses a potential conflict between ERISA and §457. As a general matter, ERISA requires that private retirement plans be funded through a trust or annuity contract, yet private 457(b) plans must not be funded to receive tax benefits. Nonetheless, this conflict is avoided if the tax-exempt organization under a private 457(b) plan limits participation to HC employees or top management, as the tax-exempt employer would be exempt from ERISA under those circumstances.

An employer does not have to make public 457(b) plans available to all employees but can selectively choose which employees may participate in the plan.

Eligibility

Participants in 457(b) plans must enter into a salary reduction agreement prior to the first day of the month in which compensation will be deferred. New employees may be allowed to defer compensation during the calendar month that the employee starts if he completed a salary reduction agreement before his first day of work. A 457 plan may not accept after-tax contributions from the employee.

Any contributions made by the employer are not vested immediately. 457(b) plans follow the cliff vesting system explained in Chapter 3. However, for ineligible 457(f) plans, the employer agrees to pay the participant a certain amount of money after a specified period of employment, at which time the employee is no longer at "substantial risk of forfeiture" of the funds (discussed below).

---

37. IRC §457(g).

Case Study 10.3

The case of ***In re Leadbetter***[1] dealt with the requirement that funds in a 457 plan remain solely the property and rights of the employer until, of course, such funds are made available to the participant or other beneficiary. While the funds are under the employer's control, they are subject to the claims of the employer's general creditors.

In this bankruptcy appeal, the state of Ohio refused to relinquish deferred compensation held on behalf of the debtor, Walter C. Leadbetter ("Leadbetter") in the Ohio Public Employees Deferred Compensation Program ("Ohio Program"), which was a 457 plan of deferred compensation for state employees. The state of Ohio administered the Ohio Program for state employees. The Ohio Program qualified for tax-deferred status under §457, allowing compensation to be placed in a deferred compensation plan, free from federal income tax until withdrawn from the plan by the employee. Leadbetter, a state employee, agreed to the terms of the program and began deferring compensation into the Ohio Program, and subsequently, Leadbetter filed a voluntary petition for bankruptcy.

During the bankruptcy proceeding, the trustee for the bankruptcy estate discovered over $3,500 in deferred compensation held by the Ohio Program. The trustee sought turnover of those funds to the bankruptcy estate. The Ohio Program objected, arguing that including the deferred compensation in the bankruptcy estate would violate §457(b)(6)'s requirement that the funds remain solely the property of the employer.

Section 457 specifically requires as a condition of tax-deferred status that the funds "remain (until made available to the participant or other beneficiary) solely the property and rights of the employer ... subject only to the claims of the employer's general creditors."[2] Accordingly, the key question before the Court was whether §457(b)(6)'s requirement that the funds remain "solely" the property of the employer prevented the funds from being placed into the bankruptcy estate. The Ohio Program argued that §457(b)(6)'s requirement that the deferred compensation remain "solely" the property of the employer allowed exclusion of the funds from the bankruptcy estate.

The Court disagreed. Under the Ohio Program, an employee can readily surmise that any participant in the 457 plan has an expectancy of a return of investment at some future date as a result of the very purpose of the 457 plan. The Court also reasoned that under §457, a requirement for deferential tax status is that the plan not be a trust.[3] Furthermore, the plan document expressly stated that it did not create a trust and that participants are general creditors, not beneficiaries.

---

1. ***In re Leadbetter***, 992 F.2d 1216, 1993 WL 141068 (6th Cir. 1993).
2. IRC §457(b)(6).
3. See ***Foil v. Commissioner***, 920 F.2d 1196, 1209 (5th Cir.1990) (funds placed in a retirement plan did not qualify for the deferred taxation of §457 because "the funds held in the [retirement] trust belong(ed) to the members as beneficiaries, and [were] not the sole property of the State").

EMPLOYEE CONTRIBUTIONS

Limits

457(b) plans generally operate with employees deferring compensation on a pretax basis through salary reduction agreements with their employer. However, as a result of The Small Business Jobs Act (SBJA) of 2010, governmental 457(b) plans can establish Roth accounts. The deferral amount, instead of being paid as income to the employee, is paid directly to the 457 plan. The annual amount deferred by an employee for an eligible 457(b) plan must not exceed the lesser of 100 percent of the employee's compensation or of the applicable dollar limit for the given calendar year. Stated differently, employees are able to contribute up to the lesser of the following amounts:

- the employee elective deferral of $18,000 for 2016, or
- up to 100 percent of includible compensation, but this amount must be less than the employee elective deferral limit.

Age 50 Catch-Up Contributions for Governmental 457(b) Plans

Section 457(b) permits governmental entities to allow for catch-up contributions for employees age 50 and over. Employees age 50 or over may contribute an additional $6,000 above the elective deferral limit of $18,000 for 2016. Thereafter, the catch-up amount will be increased for cost-of-living adjustments in increments of $500. This catch-up benefit is available only for eligible governmental (public) 457(b) plans.[38] The age 50 catch-up is not available to employees of eligible tax-exempt (private) 457(b) plans.

EXHIBIT 10.12

APPLICABLE ELECTIVE DEFERRAL LIMITS AND CATCH-UP AMOUNTS

Year	Employee Elective Deferral Limit	Catch-Up Amounts (Age 50 or Over)
2016	$18,000	$6,000

---

38. IRC §414(v).

Special "Final 3-Year" Additional Catch-Up Provision

457(b) plans may also have a special catch-up option that is termed the **"final 3-year" catch-up provision**. It applies to both public and private 457(b) plans. It is designed for employees approaching retirement that have not contributed the maximum amount to a 457 plan in previous years. It effectively doubles the employee deferral limit of IRC §402(g), but is limited to prior year employee deferrals not taken. It allows these employees to make up for previously missed contributions as follows: Three years prior to normal retirement age (as defined by the plan) an employee may contribute an additional amount equal to the elective deferral limit, which for 2016 is $18,000. Thus, an employee with adequate compensation could defer $18,000 under the regular deferral limitation and $18,000 as catch-up for a total of $36,000 in 2016. The limits are listed as follows:

MAXIMUM EMPLOYEE ELECTIVE DEFERRAL LIMITS WITH THE "FINAL 3-YEAR" CATCH-UP   **EXHIBIT 10.13**

Year	Normal Deferral	Catch-up Deferral	Total Deferral in the Final 3-Years
2016	$18,000	$18,000	$36,000

This "final 3-year" catch-up option is further limited to prior unused maximum deferral amounts. The catch-up deferral is limited to any unused deferral in the plan.

 EXAMPLE 10.7

Robby has worked for New York City for the last 20 years. He deferred $10,000 into his 457(b) plan for 2013. His normal retirement age, as defined under New York City's 457(b) plan, will be at the end of 2016. Robby has a prior unused maximum deferral amount of $37,000 as of December 31, 2013. How much can Robby contribute as his final three-year catch-up contributions and when?

Robby can contribute "final 3-year" catch-up contributions of up to $17,500 in 2014, up to $18,000 in 2015, and up to $1,500 in 2016. He is limited to $1,500 in 2016 because his prior unused maximum deferral amount of $37,000 has been exhausted ($37,000 - $17,500 - $18,000 - $1,500 = 0). Notice, during the three years prior to his normal retirement age, Robby could also defer up to the regular elective deferral contribution limits.

Employers that sponsor 457 plans are not required to offer the "final 3-year" catch-up option. Furthermore, participants who utilize the "final 3-year" catch-up cannot simultaneously use the age 50 or older catch-up provisions.

The final 3-year catch-up provision is limited to the prior unused deferrals and cannot be combined with the greater than age 50 catch-up provision. In the case in which a participant cannot make use of the 3-year catch up provision, the greater than 50 option is still available.

EMPLOYER CONTRIBUTIONS

As with other retirement plans, an employer may make matching contributions or nonelective deferrals into the 457 plan. Interestingly, the 457(b) contribution limit of $18,000 for 2016 includes both employee contributions and employer matching contributions. This is a significant difference between 457(b) plans and 401(k) or 403(b) plans. As a result, matching contributions by employers in 457 plans are very infrequent compared to those for 401(k) or 403(b) plans. Many 457 plans do not offer a matching contribution at all.

NO INTEGRATION WITH OTHER SALARY DEFERRAL PLANS

A vital and substantial benefit of contributing to a 457 plan is that the contributions to the 457 plan are not aggregated or combined with contributions to other tax-deferred retirement plans. An employee may contribute the maximum amount to a 401(k) plan, 403(b) plan, SARSEP, or SIMPLE IRA, in addition to the deferral limits for 457(b)s. This means that an employee could contribute up to $18,000 for 2016 to a 457(b) plan and up to $18,000 for 2016 to another 403(b) or 401(k) plan if available. Beginning in 2002, the law separated the 457(b) deferral limit from the limit on other retirement plans, resulting in a boost in popularity of the 457 plan.

QUICK QUIZ 10.5

1. Churches may establish 457 plans.
   a. True
   b. False

2. A 457 plan may accept after-tax contributions from employees.
   a. True
   b. False

3. The 457 deferral limit for 2016 is $18,000.
   a. True
   b. False

4. 457 plans have a special final three year catch-up provision that allows employees to contribute up to 100% of their compensation in the last three years.
   a. True
   b. False

False, False, True, False.

EXHIBIT 10.14

SUMMARY OF CONTRIBUTION LIMITS

	457 Contribution	403(b)/401(k)/SARSEP Contribution	Aggregate Total for the Year
2016	$18,000	$18,000	$36,000

EXAMPLE 10.8

Mike, age 35, works for the State of California and earns a salary of $50,000. The State of California offers a 403(b) and a 457(b) plan to its employees. What is the maximum amount that Mike can defer into both plans in 2016? The answer is $36,000, $18,000 into the 457(b) plan and another $18,000 into the 403(b) plan.

> Kathryn, age 64, works for Florida Atlantic University, which offers a 403(b) plan and a 457 plan. Kathryn could defer the following amounts:
>
> - $18,000 as salary deferral into the 403(b) plan
> - $18,000 as salary deferral into the 457(b) plan
> - $6,000 as a catch-up contribution into the 403(b) plan
> - $6,000 as a catch-up contribution into the 457(b) plan
>
> In addition, she could potentially defer up to $3,000 more into the 403(b) plan if she met the requirements and could double her deferral into the 457(b) plan in lieu of the greater than age 50 catch-up contribution if she had prior unused deferral amounts.

DISTRIBUTIONS

Public (governmental) 457(b) plans must maintain and keep all plan assets and income in trust or custodial accounts or annuity contracts for the exclusive benefit of their participants and beneficiaries. 457(b) distributions must be included as ordinary income in the calendar year in which the distributions are made. A distinct advantage of a public 457(b) plan is that the age 59½ withdrawal rule does not apply. Basically, there is no 10 percent penalty for early withdrawal at retirement or upon termination of employment for participants in public 457(b) plans.

However, private 457(b) plans are still subject to a 10 percent penalty for early withdrawal prior to age 59½, unless the employee has terminated employment or is faced with an unforeseeable emergency. When the participant is faced with an "unforeseeable emergency,"[39] such as an unexpected injury or illness, accident, or severe financial hardship, the participant's rights to early withdrawal are subject to the rules specified in the actual plan of the employer.

Similar to the new regulations for 403(b) plans, an employer creating and maintaining a 457(b) plan must establish a plan document that details the rules of the plan. As discussed, public 457(b) plans are more flexible than private 457(b)s concerning distributions. Withdrawals from a 457(b) plan must begin by age 70½ and comply with the minimum distribution rules under IRC Section 401(a)(9).[40]

ROLLOVERS

The rules for rollovers from 457(b) plans are the same as those that apply to rollovers from qualified plans. The important distinction is whether the 457 plan is a public (governmental) 457(b) plan. Public 457(b) plans allow funds to be rolled over into a new employer's 403(b), 401(k), or 457(b) plan if that plan accepts such transfers. Otherwise, the assets can be rolled into an IRA. However, 457(b) plans for nongovernmental tax-exempt entities may allow funds only to be rolled over from the 457(b) plan into another tax-exempt organization's 457(b) plan if the plan accepts such transfers. However, these funds cannot be rolled into an IRA or any another type of employer-sponsored retirement plan.

---

39. IRC §457(d)(1)(A)(iii).
40. IRC §457(d)(2).

BENEFITS AND DISADVANTAGES OF A SECTION 457 PLANS

Pre-tax deferrals into a 457 plan reduce current taxable income. They allow the participant to save on a tax-deferred basis for retirement. The contributions and earnings are able to grow tax deferred. The participant has the ability to contribute to a 457(b) plan, in addition to a 403(b) or a 401(k) plan, depending on whether or not it is offered by the employer. The 457(b) plan also provides "portability" for the participant. Offering portability allows the employee-participant to rollover savings to another public sector employer's 457 plan, if applicable. In other words, a public 457(b) plan may rollover funds into a new employer's 457(b) plan, or even a 401(k) or 403(b) plan, if the plan accepts such transfers. Such funds can also be rolled into an IRA.

QUICK QUIZ 10.6

1. For 2016 an employer can contribute an additional $18,000 to a 457 plan in addition to the employee deferral contribution of $18,000.
   a. True
   b. False

2. Distributions from a 457 plan may be subject to the 10% penalty for early withdrawal prior to age 59½.
   a. True
   b. False

False, True.

In addition, as a result of The Small Business Jobs Act (SBJA) of 2010, governmental 457(b) plans can establish Roth accounts that permit employees to save on an after-tax basis with qualifying distributions being free of tax and penalties. The SBJA also provides for in-plan Roth rollovers, which are discussed in detail in Chapter 7.

One significant drawback to a non-governmental tax-exempt organization offering a 457 plan is that there is a lack of creditor protection concerning the plan assets. A public 457(b) plan for governmental entities requires funds to be placed in a trust for the exclusive benefit of the participant and beneficiaries. However, there is no such requirement for private 457(b) plans for non-governmental, tax-exempt organizations, and therefore private 457(b) plan assets are available to the employer's creditors and the employee may lose access to the funds. This is one very important distinction that should be considered in the financial planning process.

SECTION 457(f) "INELIGIBLE" PLANS

Ineligible plans, under IRC §457(f), are nonqualified deferred compensation plans for state and local governmental employers and for tax-exempt employers. These ineligible plans are also called "top-hat" plans. Only highly compensated employees or top management may participate in a 457(f) plan. Ineligible plans are those plans under §457 that fail to meet one or more requirements of the "eligible plan." 457(f) plans are frequently intentionally ineligible while some are unintentionally ineligible. With ineligible plans under 457(f), there is no limit on the amount of deferral because 457(f) plans are effectively deferred compensation plans.

However, the amounts contributed to 457(f) plans are subject to a "substantial risk of forfeiture." This means that the participant is considered to be a general unsecured creditor of the plan sponsor or employer. The substantial risk of forfeiture is conditioned upon (1) the unsecured status of the employee, and (2) the employee's future performance of substantial services for the employer. The employer agrees to pay the participant a certain amount of money after a specified period of employment, at which time the employee is no longer at "substantial risk of forfeiture" of the funds.

Taxation of funds in an ineligible plan occurs when there is no risk of forfeiture. Amounts may therefore be taxable prior to the actual payment or distribution to the participant. The amounts that are taxable prior to actual payment are included in the gross income of the participant in the first year that the deferral amount is not subject to a substantial risk of forfeiture. The typical deferred compensation arrangement for ineligible 457(f) plans is for presidents, CEOs, and coaches.

> In 2016, X, a tax-exempt entity, agrees to pay deferred compensation to employee D. The amount payable is $100,000 to be paid 10 years later in 2026. The commitment to make the $100,000 payment is not subject to a substantial risk of forfeiture. In 2016, the present value of the $100,000 is $50,000. In 2026, X pays D the $100,000 that is due.
>
> In this example, D has income of $50,000 in 2016.[41] In 2026, D has income of $50,000, the remaining income from the 2016 commitment. If there was a substantial risk of forfeiture, then there is no tax consequence until the payment is made in 2026.

Disadvantages to 457(f) Plans

If the participant terminates employment before the stated payment period, the participant may forfeit all of the 457(f) plan funds. Also, because the funds in the plan remain the employer's property until vested, the employee-participant may lose all the 457(f) account and the funds if the employer goes bankrupt. Also, even though a distribution may not occur, the participant may be taxed on the value of the plan once the funds vest in the participant or are no longer subject to substantial risk of forfeiture.

457(f) plans essentially provide special benefits to executives or individuals that companies or universities want to retain. For instance, in the highly competitive world of college sports, many schools with winning coaches desire to provide such coaches with an incentive to stay through use of 457(f) plans. The college is able to contribute any amount, as there are no limits. As the assets are retained by the employer until paid to the employee, the 457(f) plan creates a tax shelter for the executive or coach. It is protected from claims against the executive or coach, but not from the creditors of the organization.

In conclusion, 457 plans allow employees of tax-exempt organizations and of governments to defer compensation into retirement savings plans. Public 457(b) plans hold funds in trust and are available to all employees while private 457(b) plans are not funded and are available only to high compensated employees or upper management. Salary deferrals into 457(b) plans are not aggregated or combined with salary deferrals to other retirement plans such as 401(k) and 403(b) plans. 457(f) plans are ineligible but allow for an unlimited amount of contributions to the plan. Nonetheless, the participant's funds in a 457(f) plan are subject to a substantial risk of forfeiture.

---

41. Treas. Reg. §1.457-11.

EXHIBIT
10.15

457 PLAN COMPARISON

	Public 457(b) Plans	Private 457(b) Plans	457(f) Plans
Eligible/Ineligible	Eligible	Eligible	Ineligible
Employer/Sponsors	Governmental Entities	Tax-Exempt Organizations under 501(c)	Governmental Entities (Rare) & Tax-Exempt Entities under 501(c)
Assets in Plan	Protected by Trust	Not Protected by Trust; Available to Employer's Creditors	Not Protected by Trust; Available to Employer's Creditors
Elective Deferral Contribution Limits	2016 - $18,000	2016 - $18,000	No Limit
Employees that Participate	Rank and File Employees and Key Management	Key Management and HCs for Tax Exempt Organizations; All Employees if Church-Related Organization	Key Management and HCs
Pretax Contribution	Yes	Yes	Yes
Roth Account Contributions	Yes	No	No
Funds Grow Tax Deferred	Yes	Yes	Yes
Age 50 and Over Catch-Up Provisions	Yes	No	No
3-Year Catch-Up Provisions	Yes 2016 - $18,000	Yes 2016 - $18,000	No
Rollovers	Permitted to 401(k), 403(b), 457(b), or IRA plans*	Not Permitted Unless Rolled Into Another 457(b)	Not Permitted
In-Plan Roth Rollover	Yes	N/A - No Roth Accounts	N/A - No Roth Accounts
10% Penalty for Early Withdrawal	Does not apply to early withdrawal at retirement or upon termination of employment	Yes, unless the employee has terminated employment or is facing an unforeseeable emergency	Not Applicable

Rollovers to Roth IRAs are permitted after December 31, 2007.

CONCEPT SUMMARY - 457 PLANS

EXHIBIT
10.16

Type of Plan	Nonqualified Deferred Compensation Plan
Application	Employees of state and local government, tax-exempt governmental agencies, and 501 entities
Style	Self-reliant, employee elective tax-deferred savings
Qualified Plan	No
Established By What Date	End of year
Characteristics	Deferred compensation plan
Elective Deferral Contribution Limit	Lesser of $18,000 for 2016 or 100% of compensation + $6,000 catch-up for 2016 for age 50 or older (catch-up for public only)
Available Employer Contribution	Permitted, but generally very unusual
Additional After-Tax Contributions Permitted	No
Investment Risk	Employee selects investments and bears risk
Investment Alternatives	Broad
Penalties	Generally not applicable
Loans Permitted	No
Rollovers	• Public 457(b) plans may be rolled over to 457, 403(b), 401(k), or IRA plans permitting. • Private 457(b) plans can only be rolled to other 457(b) plans. 457(f) plans cannot be rolled over. • In-plan Roth rollovers are now permitted for government 457(b) plans.
ERISA Protected	No
In-Service Withdrawals	Yes

KEY TERMS

ANNUITY CONTRACTS - While the contracts are not specifically defined in the Internal Revenue Code, an annuity contract must be purchased for the employee from an insurance company and may give a fixed benefit or a variable benefit depending on the performance of the investment. Any contract or certificate that is transferable to a person other than a trustee is not an annuity contract.

15-YEAR RULE - A special catch-up provision for 403(b) plan participants that have worked for the plan sponsor for 15 years. The catch-up allows them to defer up to an additional $15,000, however, no more than $3,000 per year.

FINAL 3-YEAR CATCH-UP PROVISION - A special catch-up provision for public and private 457(b) plans that allows an individual to defer an additional $18,000 for 2016 to the plan in their final three years before the plan's normal retirement age.

501(c)(3) ORGANIZATIONS - Nonprofit tax-exempt organizations that are established under IRC §501(c)(3) of the Internal Revenue Code.

FORM 5304-SIMPLE - The IRS form used to establish a SIMPLE IRA plan when the employees choose the financial institution.

FORM 5305-SIMPLE - The IRS form used to establish a SIMPLE IRA plan when the employer chooses the financial institution.

457 PLAN - A nonqualified deferred compensation plan for employees of state and local government and tax-exempt entities.

457(b) PLANS - 457(b) plans for governmental and tax-exempt organizations under 501(c) that allow employees to defer income taxation on savings for retirement into future years. Eligible plans are available to most of an employer's employees.

457(f) PLANS - 457(f) plans are comparable to traditional deferred compensation plans for employees of governmental entities and tax-exempt entities under 501(c)(3). Ineligible plans are only available to highly compensated and management employees.

GRACE PERIOD - If an employer meets the 100 employee limitation in a given year, then the employer will have a two year "grace period" when the employer can exceed the limitation without losing eligibility to maintain the SIMPLE.

INCLUDIBLE COMPENSATION - An employee's taxable wages and benefits for the most recent year of service.

NONELECTIVE CONTRIBUTIONS - Contributions to a qualified plan on behalf of all eligible employees.

KEY TERMS

QUALIFIED JOINT AND SURVIVOR ANNUITY (QJSA) - The QJSA pays a benefit to the participant and spouse as long as either lives; although, at the death of the first spouse, the annuity may be reduced.

SAVINGS INCENTIVE MATCH PLANS FOR EMPLOYEES (SIMPLEs) - Retirement plans for small employers with 100 or fewer employees who earn more than $5,000 in a year. SIMPLEs may be established as SIMPLE 401(k) plans or SIMPLE IRAs.

SIMPLE 401(k) - A SIMPLE plan that utilizes a 401(k) plan as the funding vehicle of the plan.

SIMPLE IRA - A SIMPLE plan that utilizes an IRA account as the funding vehicle of the plan.

TAX SHELTERED OR DEFERRED ANNUITIES (403(b) PLANS) - Retirement plans for certain qualified nonprofit organizations or employees of public educational systems – similar to 401(k) plans, but for nonprofit organizations.

DISCUSSION QUESTIONS

1.   Describe SIMPLE plans.

2.   List and define the different types of SIMPLE plans.

3.   What are the rules for establishing a SIMPLE plan?

4.   Identify the characteristics of SIMPLE IRAs.

5.   Identify the characteristics of SIMPLE 401(k) plans.

6.   Describe 403(b) plans.

7.   When does ERISA apply to a 403(b) plan?

8.   Who is eligible to establish a 403(b) plan?

9.   What are the applicable rules regarding employee contributions to 403(b) plans?

10.   What are the applicable rules regarding employer contributions to 403(b) plans?

11.   What investment options are available for 403(b) plans?

12.   How are distributions from 403(b) plans taxed?

13.   What are the rollover, distribution, and minimum distribution rules applicable to 403(b) plans?

14.   What are 457 plans and what entities may establish them?

15.   Who is eligible to establish a 457 plan?

16.   What are the applicable rules regarding employee contributions to 457 plans?

17.   What are the applicable rules regarding employer contributions to 457 plans?

18.   How does a participant's salary deferral to a 457 plan affect his contributions to a qualified plan?

19.   How are distributions from a 457 plan taxed?

20.   What are the benefits and disadvantages of a 457 plan?

21.   What are §457(f) plans and how are the distributions taxed?

MULTIPLE CHOICE PROBLEMS

1. Kim Cat, age 42, earns $300,000 annually as an employee for CTM, Inc. Her employer sponsors a SIMPLE retirement plan and matches all employee contributions made to the plan dollar-for-dollar up to 3% of covered compensation. What is the maximum contribution (employer and employee) that can be made to Kim's SIMPLE account in 2016?

    a. $20,450.

    b. $21,500.

    c. $25,000.

    d. $28,000.

2. Taylor, age 25, works for Swim America. Swim America adopted a SIMPLE plan 6 months ago. Taylor made an elective deferral contribution to the plan of $8,000, and Swim America made a matching contribution of $2,400. Which of the following statements is/are correct?

    1. Taylor can withdraw his entire account balance without terminating employment.
    2. Taylor can roll his SIMPLE IRA into his Traditional IRA.
    3. Taylor will be subject to ordinary income taxes on withdrawals from the SIMPLE.
    4. Taylor may be subject to a 25% early withdrawal penalty on amounts withdrawn from the SIMPLE.

    a. 1 and 2.

    b. 1 and 3.

    c. 2, 3, and 4.

    d. 1, 3, and 4.

3. Which of the following is/are correct regarding SIMPLE plans?

    1. A SIMPLE plan does not require annual testing.
    2. A SIMPLE IRA must follow a 3-year cliff vesting schedule if the plan is top-heavy.
    3. A 25% early withdrawal penalty may apply to distributions taken within the first two years of participation in a SIMPLE plan.
    4. The maximum elective deferral contribution to a SIMPLE 401(k) plan is $18,000 for 2016 and $24,000 for 2016 for an employee who has attained the age of 50.

    a. 3 only.

    b. 1 and 3.

    c. 1, 2, and 3.

    d. 2, 3, and 4.

4. All of the following statements is/are correct regarding tax-sheltered annuities (403(b) plans) except?

    1. The non-age-based catch-up provision is available to employees of all 501(c)(3) organization employers that sponsor a TSA.

    2. Active employees who take withdrawals from TSAs prior to 59½ are subject to a 10% penalty tax.

    3. TSAs are available to all employees of 501(c)(3) organizations who adopt such a plan.

    4. If an employee has had at least 15 years of service with an eligible employer, an additional catch-up contribution may be allowed.

        a. 1 only.

        b. 1 and 2.

        c. 1, 2, and 3.

        d. 2, 3, and 4.

5. Which of the following statements is/are correct regarding TSAs and 457 deferred compensation plans?

    1. Both plans require contracts between an employer and an employee.

    2. Participation in either a TSA or a 457 plan will cause an individual to be considered an "active participant" for purposes of phasing out the deductibility of Traditional IRA contributions.

    3. Both plans allow 10-year forward averaging tax treatment for lump-sum distributions.

    4. Both plans must meet minimum distribution requirements that apply to qualified plans.

        a. 1 only.

        b. 1 and 4.

        c. 2, 3, and 4.

        d. 1, 2, and 4.

6. What is the maximum employee elective deferral contribution (salary reduction) for an employee who is 45 years old under a 403(b) plan in 2016?

        a. $12,500.

        b. $15,500.

        c. $18,000.

        d. $24,000.

7. Which of the following are permitted investments in a 403(b) TSA (TDA) plan?

    1. An annuity contract from an insurance company.

    2. An international gold stock mutual fund.

    3. A self-directed brokerage account consisting solely of U.S. stocks, bonds and mutual funds.

        a. 1 only.

        b. 2 only.

        c. 1 and 2.

        d. 1, 2, and 3.

8. Which of the following characteristics accurately describes a 403(b) plan?

    1. A self-reliant employee elective deferral plan.

    2. The retirement benefit is dependent on the investment results.

    3. The plan generally permits loans.

        a. 1 only.

        b. 2 only.

        c. 1 and 2.

        d. 1, 2, and 3.

9. Which of the following statements is/are correct regarding 403(b) plans?

    1. 403(b) plans are eligible for rollover treatment to IRAs, qualified plans, and other 403(b) plans.

    2. Investments in stocks, bonds, and money markets are available.

    3. Assets in a 403(b) plan are generally 100% vested.

        a. 1 only.

        b. 2 only.

        c. 1 and 3.

        d. 1, 2, and 3.

10. Which of the following types of 457 plans permit employees to defer recognition of income without a risk of forfeiture?

    1. Public 457(b) plans.

    2. 457(f) plans.

    3. Private 457(b) plans.

        a. 1 only.

        b. 2 only.

        c. 1 and 3.

        d. 1, 2, and 3.

11. What is the maximum elective deferral contribution to an eligible governmental 457(b) plan for 2016?

    a. $12,500.

    b. $13,000.

    c. $18,000.

    d. $24,000.

12. What is the maximum catch-up contribution for 2016 under the 457(b) plan "Final 3-Year" rule?

    a. $3,000.

    b. $6,000.

    c. $18,000.

    d. $36,000.

13. James, age 58, has compensation of $150,000 and wants to defer the maximum to his public 457(b) plan. The normal retirement age for his plan is age 60. How much can he defer in 2016 if he has an unused deferral of $60,000 from age 40 to age 49?

    a. $18,000.

    b. $24,000.

    c. $36,000.

    d. $42,000.

14. Henry Hobbs, age 57, has compensation of $72,000. The normal retirement age for his 457(b) plan is age 62. Henry has unused deferrals totaling $22,500 as of January 1, 2016. How much can Henry defer into his 457(b) public plan for the current year?

    a. $18,000.

    b. $24,000.

    c. $36,000.

    d. $42,000.

15. Ben Reynolds, age 63 in 2016, is planning for retirement at normal retirement age of 65 from the Salt Lake City coroner's office, which has a 457(b) plan. Ben has an unused deferral amount of $9,000. Ben has compensation of $128,000 per year as a mortician/autopsy specialist. Ben wants to know the maximum amount he can defer in 2016 in the 457(b) plan.

    a. $18,000.

    b. $24,000.

    c. $27,000.

    d. $36,000.

16. Which of the following plans permit employers to match employee elective deferral contributions or make nonelective contributions?

   1. 457(b) plan.
   2. 401(k) plan.
   3. 403(b) plan.

      a. 2 only.
      b. 3 only.
      c. 2 and 3.
      d. 1, 2, and 3.

17. Roger has a small convenience store with three employees. Each of the employees earns $10 per hour and they each work approximately 1,500 hours per year. His business is very successful. He recently considered adopting a defined benefit plan, but felt it was too expensive. He looked into a 401(k) plan, but thought it was too complicated. Finally, a few of his friends recommended a SIMPLE plan and told him about the basics of the plan. Which of the following statements from his friends is the most incorrect?

      a. SIMPLEs can be established by most small businesses but cannot be established if the business has more than 500 employees.
      b. SIMPLEs can be established by an employer that previously had a qualified plan.
      c. SIMPLEs consider employees who are age 21 or older and who earn over $5,000 and are expected to earn at least $5,000 eligible for the plan.
      d. Employers that sponsor SIMPLEs must provide a matching contribution to employees who defer money into the SIMPLE.

18. Roger has a small convenience store with three employees. Each of the employees earns $10 per hour and they each work approximately 1,500 hours per year. His business is very successful. He recently considered adopting a defined benefit plan, but felt it was too expensive. He looked into a 401(k) plan, but thought it was too complicated. Finally, a few of his friends recommended a SIMPLE plan and told him about the basics of the plan. Which of the following statements from his friends is the most correct?

      a. If Roger's salary is $500,000 and the SIMPLE used a match, then his match would generally equal $12,500.
      b. If Roger established a SIMPLE, he would have to select between graduated and cliff vesting.
      c. If Roger established a SIMPLE using a non-elective contribution, then the other employees would each receive a contribution of $450.
      d. Considering the size of his business, he cannot establish a SIMPLE 401(k).

19. Dr. Means has taught accounting at FAU for the last 30 years and is expected to retire next year, at age 65. FAU sponsors a 403(b) plan and a 457(b) governmental plan. She has been diligent and has always contributed the maximum amounts to each of the plans. If her salary is $100,000, how much can she contribute in total to both plans in 2016?

    a. $24,000.

    b. $48,000.

    c. $60,000.

    d. $63,000.

20. Dr. Wood has taught accounting at FSU (Florida Sate University) for the last 30 years and is expected to retire in a few years, at age 65. FSU sponsors a 403(b) plan and a 457(b) governmental plan. Both plans have Roth accounts available. She has been diligent and always contributed the maximum amounts to the traditional accounts in each of the plans. She is also a partner in an equipment business that has lost money the last several years and she has a net operating loss carry forward. Which of the following statements is true?

    a. Dr. Wood is able to rollover amounts in the traditional deferral account for the 457 plan into the Roth account without terminating employment.

    b. Dr. Wood may receive forfeiture allocations to the Roth account in the 457 plan from employees terminating before full vesting.

    c. The investment options available for both plans includes mutual funds, annuities and individual securities.

    d. The assets in the 403(b) plan are protected in a trust, but that is not the case with the funds in the 457 plan.

21. Which of the following are correct?

    1. SIMPLEs provide incentives to small employers to adopt retirement plans for employees with less administrative costs and fewer set-up procedures than qualified plans.

    2. SIMPLE IRAs can permit loans to employees.

    3. SIMPLE IRAs require the employer either to match the employee contributions of those who participate or to provide nonelective contributions to all eligible employees.

        a. 3 only.

        b. 1 and 2.

        c. 1 and 3.

        d. All of the above.

22. An employer may reduce the three percent matching contribution requirement for a calendar year in a SIMPLE, IRA, but only under which of the following circumstances?

    1. The limit is reduced to no less than one percent.

    2. The limit is not reduced for more than two years out of the five year period that ends with (and includes) the year for which the election is effective.

    3. Employees are notified of the reduced limit within a reasonable period of time before the 60 day election period for a salary reduction agreement.

        a. 1 and 2.

        b. 1 and 3.

        c. 2 and 3.

        d. All of the above must be present.

        e. None of the above must be present.

23. Which term or phrase best completes the following sentence: "Employee contributions in 403(b) plans are _____."

        a. Never matched.

        b. Never fully vested.

        c. Always fully vested.

        d. Vested based on age and years of service.

24. Distributions may be paid from a 403(b) account after:

        a. Employee death or disability.

        b. Employee turns age 59½.

        c. Employee is separated from service.

        d. All of the above.

        e. None of the above.

25. Which of the following entities cannot establish 457(b) plans?

        a. Churches.

        b. Private Hospitals.

        c. Farmers' Cooperatives.

        d. Labor Unions.

QUICK QUIZ EXPLANATIONS

QUICK QUIZ 10.1
1. False. SIMPLE plans may only operate on a calendar year basis.
2. True.
3. True.

QUICK QUIZ 10.2
1. True.
2. True.
3. False. An employer may, but is not required to, allow for catch-up contributions for participants age 50 and older.

QUICK QUIZ 10.3
1. False. Only employers may establish 403(b) plans. Individuals may not establish 403(b) plans.
2. True.
3. False. Catch-up contributions may not be made with employee after-tax contributions.

QUICK QUIZ 10.4
1. False. The most recent year of service is not necessarily equal to a calendar year.
2. True.
3. True.

QUICK QUIZ 10.5
1. False. Churches may not establish 457 plans.
2. False. After-tax contributions to 457 plans are not permitted.
3. True.
4. False. The final three year catch-up provision essentially allows participants to double their contributions in the last three years, but is limited by the deferrals not taken in prior years.

QUICK QUIZ 10.6
1. False. The 457 contribution limit includes both employee contributions and employer matching contributions.
2. True.

SOCIAL SECURITY

LEARNING OBJECTIVES

After reading this chapter, you should be able to:

1. Understand the history and purpose of the Social Security program and the conditions under which it was enacted.
2. Provide an overview of the Social Security system, including payroll taxes, benefits, and qualifications.
3. Identify possible beneficiaries under the Social Security system and the types of benefits they may be entitled to receive.
4. Explain the computation of the Average Indexed Monthly Earnings (AIME) and the Primary Insurance Amount (PIA) and the impact on benefits relative to historical earnings.
5. Explain disability benefits, survivor benefits, and maximum family benefits under the Social Security system.
6. Advise clients in choosing the optimal date to begin receiving Social Security benefits, considering the impact of taxation, benefit reductions and credits, as well as life expectancy.
7. Understand proposed or possible changes to the Social Security system and the possible impact on retirement and other financial planning.
8. Understand and describe the taxation of Social Security benefits.

HISTORY

Social Security and other forms of social insurance were born out of changes in economies and in families. For centuries, farming and agriculture provided families with the foundation of their economic security. Farms provided food, shelter, and resources for families to survive. As family members aged, they were cared for on the farms. However, as economies changed as part of the industrial revolution, more and more people became employees working for someone else. This demographic shift continued such that a higher percentage of people began moving from the farms to the cities. As a result, people were less capable of providing for their own welfare as they aged, especially in difficult economic times.

These demographic shifts and the Great Depression set the stage for the Social Security system, which was signed into law by Franklin D. Roosevelt on August 14, 1935. At the signing of the law, President Roosevelt made the following statement:

> "Today a hope of many years' standing is in large part fulfilled. The civilization of the past hundred years, with its startling industrial changes, has tended more and more to make life insecure. Young people have come to wonder what would be their lot when they came to old age. The man with a job has wondered how long the job would last.
>
> This Social Security measure gives at least some protection to thirty millions of our citizens who will reap direct benefits through unemployment compensation, through old-age pensions and through increased services for the protection of children and the prevention of ill health.

We can never insure one hundred percent of the population against one hundred percent of the hazards and vicissitudes of life, but we have tried to frame a law which will give some measure of protection to the average citizen and to his family against the loss of a job and against poverty-ridden old age."

Today, the Social Security system is significantly different than what it was envisioned to be almost 80 years ago in terms of the programs offered and the size of the program. The system provides tremendous benefits to millions of Americans, as indicated in Exhibit 11.1. However, the system also has significant fiscal problems that must be addressed and resolved if there is any chance that it continues for generations to come. Two of the primary issues with the program are the number of workers paying into the system relative to the number of retirees and other beneficiaries and the significant increase in the life expectancy of our current and future population.

SOCIAL SECURITY BASIC FACTS[1]

EXHIBIT 11.1

1. In 2015, over 59 million Americans received $870 billion in Social Security benefits.

2. An estimated 165 million workers, 94% of all workers, are covered under Social Security.
    - 51% of the workforce has no private pension coverage.
    - 34% of the workforce has no savings set aside specifically for retirement.

3. Social Security is the major source of income for most of the elderly.
    - Nine out of ten individuals age 65 and older receive Social Security benefits.
    - Social Security benefits represent about 39% of the income of the elderly.
    - Among elderly Social Security beneficiaries, 53% of married couples and 74% of unmarried persons receive 50% or more of their income from Social Security.
    - Among elderly Social Security beneficiaries, 22% of married couples and about 47% of unmarried persons rely on Social Security for 90% or more of their income.

4. In 1940, the life expectancy of a 65-year-old was almost 14 years; today it is almost 21 years.

5. By 2035, there will be almost twice as many older Americans as today - from 48 million today to 79 million.

6. There are currently 2.8 workers for each Social Security beneficiary. By 2035, there will be 2.1 workers for each beneficiary.

---

1. Social Security Basic Facts, October 2015.

KNOW THE NUMBERS (2016)

Social Security Wage Base	$118,500
Social Security Quarter of Coverage	$1,260
Social Security Bottom Bend Point	$856
Social Security Top Bend Point	$5,157
Social Security Maximum Monthly Benefit	$2,639
Social Security Medicare Part A Deductible Days 1-60	$1,288 per benefit period
Social Security Medicare Part A Deductible Days 61-90	$322 per day
Social Security Medicare Part A Deductible Days 91 and Over	$644 per day
Social Security Medicare Part B Deductible	$166
Social Security Skilled Nursing Care Deductible Days 21-100	$161 per day
Social Security Disability Monthly Earnings Limit	$1,130
Social Security Disability Monthly Earnings Limit if Blind	$1,820
Social Security Death Benefit	$255
Social Security Earnings Limitation (under full retirement age)	$15,720
Social Security Earnings Limitation (full retirement age)	$41,880

INTRODUCTION

Social Security benefits were never intended to provide total pre-retirement wage replacement upon retirement. Social Security was created to supplement a covered worker's pension, savings, investments, and other earnings from assets to make up an appropriate wage replacement ratio (e.g., 70 percent). As illustrated in Chapter 2, individuals who retire may need 70 to 80 percent of their pre-retirement income during their retirement to maintain their pre-retirement standard of living.

Low wage earners receive Social Security retirement benefits averaging 60 percent of pre-retirement income. Average wage earners receive an average of 42 percent of pre-retirement income from Social Security benefits, whereas high wage earners receive an average of 26 percent of pre-retirement income (see Exhibit 11.2).

From a financial planning standpoint, it is important to understand Social Security law and the various benefits that are available from Social Security. This chapter provides an overview of the Social Security system and its benefits. The six major categories of benefits administered by the Social Security Administration are:
1. Retirement benefits
2. Disability benefits
3. Family benefits
4. Survivors' benefits
5. Medicare

6. Supplemental Security Income (SSI) benefits. SSI benefits are not funded by Social Security taxes but are funded by general funds from the Treasury.

The **retirement benefit** is the most well-known benefit from Social Security. Full retirement benefits are payable at "full retirement age" (reduced benefits are available as early as age 62) to anyone who has obtained a minimum amount (40 quarters) of Social Security credits. Based on the Social Security law in 1983, the age when full retirement benefits are paid began to rise from age 65 in the year 2000, and increases to age 67 by the year 2027. Workers who delay retirement beyond the full retirement age receive a special scheduled increase (Exhibit 11.14) in benefits for each delayed year extending until age 70.[2]

SOCIAL SECURITY BENEFITS AS A PERCENTAGE OF PRE-RETIREMENT INCOME

EXHIBIT
11.2

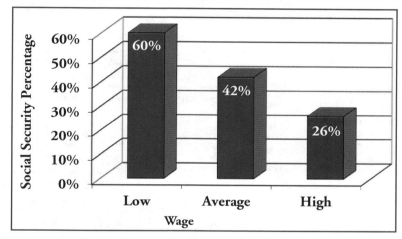

The **disability benefit** is payable at any age to workers who have sufficient credits under the Social Security system to qualify for disability benefits. Recipients must have a severe physical or mental impairment that is expected to prevent them from performing "substantial" work for at least a year or to result in their death. Monthly earnings of $1,130 for 2016 (if the individual is blind, then the amount is increased to $1,820 per month for 2016) or more is considered substantial. The disability insurance program has built-in incentives to smooth the transition back to the workforce including continuation of benefits and health care coverage.

---

2. The increases are not compounded, and there are no increases for delay past age 70.

EXHIBIT
11.3

SOCIAL SECURITY DISABILITY BENEFITS

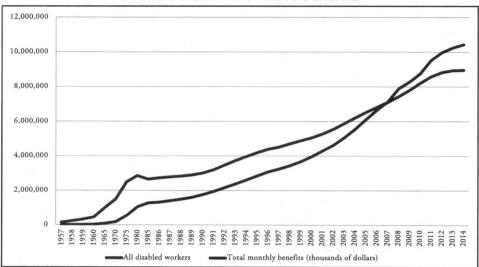

All disabled workers ▬▬ Total monthly benefits (thousands of dollars)

The **family benefit** is provided to certain family members of workers eligible for retirement or disability benefits. Such family members include spouses age 62 or older, spouses under age 62 but caring for a child under age 16, unmarried children under 18, unmarried children under age 19 and full-time students, and unmarried children of any age who were disabled before age 22.

Survivors' benefits apply to certain members of the deceased worker's family if the worker earned sufficient Social Security credits. Family members entitled to survivors' benefits include those listed for family benefits and may also include the worker's dependant parents if the worker was their primary means of support. A special one-time payment of $255 may be made to the spouse or minor children upon the death of a Social Security covered worker.

Medicare provides hospital and medical insurance. Those who have attained age 65 or those who receive disability benefits for at least two years automatically qualify for Medicare. Others must file an application to become qualified.

Finally, **Supplemental Security Income (SSI)** (funded by general tax revenues and not by Social Security taxes) is another benefit that provides monthly payments to those disabled or at full retirement age who have a low income and few assets. Generally, those who receive SSI also qualify for **Medicaid**, food stamps, and other governmental assistance.

KEY CONCEPTS

1. What are the six major categories of benefits administered by the Social Security Administration?

2. How are funds collected for Social Security?

SOCIAL SECURITY TAXES AND CONTRIBUTIONS

Although the Social Security retirement benefits program is thought by many to be one of the most complicated and confusing programs created, the basic concept is quite simple. Employees, employers, and self-employed individuals pay Social Security taxes, known as FICA taxes, during their working years. These payments are pooled in special trust funds. Contributing workers become "covered" workers, meaning that they will fall under the Social Security umbrella of benefits after contributing for approximately 10 years (40 quarters) and will receive retirement benefits based on those contributions and the Social Security benefits formula.

The **Federal Insurance Contributions Act (FICA)** is the law allowing Social Security taxes, including Medicare taxes, to be deducted from paychecks. A portion of these FICA taxes pays part of the Medicare coverage. Both employers and employees pay the taxes for Social Security and Medicare. For the year 2016, an employer and employee each pay 6.2 percent of the employee's gross salary up to a limit of $118,500 for **OASDI (Old Age, Survivor, and Disability Insurance)**. The salary limit rises annually based on annual increases in average wages. Self-employed workers pay 12.4 percent (6.2 percent x 2) of their taxable income up to the same salary limit. The Medicare portion of the Social Security tax is 1.45 percent for both employers and employees and is 2.9 percent for self-employed workers with no limit on the amount of compensation taxed.

EXAMPLE 11.1

If an employee earns a salary of $150,000 in 2016, the first $118,500 of the employee's salary will be subject to a tax of 7.65 (6.2 + 1.45) percent while the remaining $31,500 will be subject to a tax of only 1.45 percent. The employer pays the same amount as the employee.

	Taxable Amount	x	Tax Rate	Total Tax
Employee - Social Security	$118,500		6.20%	$7,347.00
Employee - Medicare	$150,000		1.45%	$2,175.00
Total Tax				$9,522.00

ADDITIONAL MEDICARE TAXES BEGINNING IN 2013

The Affordable care act created two additional Medicare taxes that impact wealthier taxpayers. The first is an additional Medicare tax of 0.9 percent on wages or self-employment income. The second is a 3.8 percent tax on certain amounts of net investment income.

The additional Medicare tax equal to 0.9 percent applies to wages or self-employment income that is above the following threshold amounts:

Married Filing Jointly	$250,000
Married Filing Separately	$125,000
Single	$200,000
Head of Household	$200,000

Employees pay this Medicare tax only. Employers do not pay this tax, but must withhold the tax from wages if the taxpayer has income in excess of $200,000.

Carlos, a single filer, has $130,000 in wages and $145,000 in self-employment income. His wages are not in excess of the $200,000 threshold for single filers, so Carlos is not liable for Additional Medicare Tax on these wages.

Before calculating the Additional Medicare Tax on self-employment income, the $200,000 threshold for single filers is reduced by his $130,000 in wages, resulting in a reduced self-employment income threshold of $70,000. Carlos is liable to pay Additional Medicare Tax on $75,000 of self-employment income ($145,000 in self-employment income minus the reduced threshold of $70,000). Carlos has total earnings of $275,000, which is $75,000 over the $200,000 threshold.

Dave and Dana are married and file jointly. Dave has $150,000 in wages and Dana has $175,000 in self-employment income. Dave's wages are not in excess of the $250,000 threshold for joint filers, so Dave and Dana are not liable for Additional Medicare Tax on Dave's wages.

Before calculating the Additional Medicare Tax on Dana's self-employment income, the $250,000 threshold for joint filers is reduced by Dave's $150,000 in wages resulting in a reduced self-employment income threshold of $100,000. Dave and Dana are liable to pay Additional Medicare Tax on $75,000 of self-employment income ($175,000 in self-employment income minus the reduced threshold of $100,000). Dave and Dana have total earnings of $325,000, which is $75,000 over the $250,000 threshold.

The 3.8 percent Medicare tax is imposed on the lesser of net investment income or modified AGI over the following threshold amounts:

Married Filing Jointly	$250,000
Married Filing Separately	$125,000
Single	$200,000
Head of Household	$200,000

Net investment income is a broadly defined term that includes gross income from interest, dividends, annuities, royalties, and rents other than such income derived from the ordinary course of a trade or business, **plus** other trade or business income, for which the entity is a passive activity (or if the entity is trading financial instruments or commodities), **plus** net gain attributable to the disposition of property other than property held in a trade or business. It should be noted that net investment income does not include any distribution from a 401(k), 403(b), 457(b) plan or an IRA or Roth IRA. However, such distributions may cause a taxpayer to exceed the threshold amounts.

In 2016, Dan and Mary (MFJ) have $250,000 of dividend income. In this case, they are not subject to the 3.8% surtax.

Same as Example 11.4, but Dan and Mary convert a traditional IRA to a Roth IRA. The taxable amount of the conversion is $100,000. Thus, they will have AGI of $350,000, and $100,000 will hence be subject to the 3.8% surtax.

Same as Example 11.4, but Dan and Mary also take minimum distributions of $50,000. They will be subject to the 3.8% tax on $50,000, which is the lesser of Net Investment Income and the AGI above $250,000.

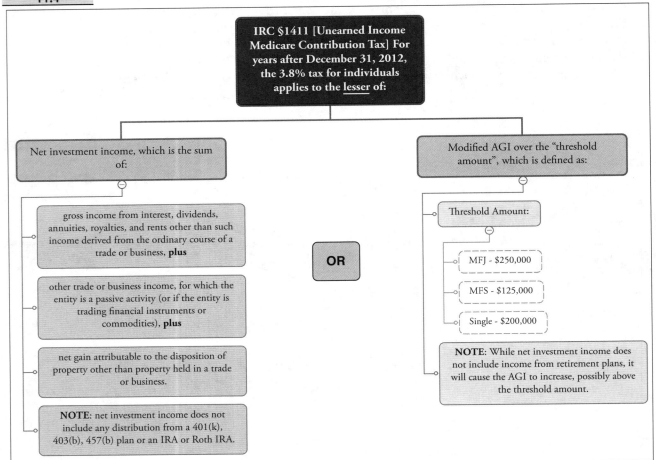

EXHIBIT 11.4 — 3.8% MEDICARE TAX

IRC §1411 [Unearned Income Medicare Contribution Tax] For years after December 31, 2012, the 3.8% tax for individuals applies to the lesser of:

Net investment income, which is the sum of:

- gross income from interest, dividends, annuities, royalties, and rents other than such income derived from the ordinary course of a trade or business, **plus**
- other trade or business income, for which the entity is a passive activity (or if the entity is trading financial instruments or commodities), **plus**
- net gain attributable to the disposition of property other than property held in a trade or business.
- **NOTE:** net investment income does not include any distribution from a 401(k), 403(b), 457(b) plan or an IRA or Roth IRA.

OR

Modified AGI over the "threshold amount", which is defined as:

Threshold Amount:

- MFJ - $250,000
- MFS - $125,000
- Single - $200,000

NOTE: While net investment income does not include income from retirement plans, it will cause the AGI to increase, possibly above the threshold amount.

EXAMPLE 11.7

In 2016, Steve and Ashley (MFJ) have $100,000 of dividend income and $100,000 of wages. In this case, they are not subject to the 3.8% surtax because they are not over the $250,000 limit.

EXAMPLE 11.8

Same as Example 11.7, but Steve and Ashley convert a traditional IRA to a Roth IRA. The taxable amount of the conversion is $100,000. Thus, they will have AGI of $300,000. The lesser of $50,000 or $100,000 will be subject to the 3.8% surtax.

EXAMPLE 11.9

Jack and Jill (MFJ) each earn $250,000 and have interest income of $1,000. The $1,000 would be subject to the 3.8% tax.

TRUST FUNDS

The United States Social Security system operates on a "pay-as-you-go" basis. Social Security taxes are collected and divided among several trust funds. The federal **Old Age and Survivors Insurance ("OASI")** **Trust Fund** pays retirement and survivors' benefits. The OASI Trust Fund receives 5.30 percent of the FICA tax. The federal **Disability Insurance ("DI")** **Trust Fund** pays benefits to workers with disabilities and their families. The DI Trust Fund receives 0.90 percent of the FICA tax. OASI and DI are the two trust funds used for payment of Social Security benefits (total 6.2 percent).

The two Medicare trust funds are the federal **Hospital Insurance ("HI") Trust Fund**, which pays for services covered under the hospital insurance provisions of Medicare (Part A), and the federal **Supplementary Medical Insurance ("SMI") Trust Fund**, which pays for services covered under the medical insurance provisions of Medicare, known as Part B and the new prescription drug provisions known as Part D.[3] The SMI Trust Fund is partially funded by the general fund of the Treasury with the remaining funding coming from monthly premiums paid by the individuals enrolled in Part B.

QUICK QUIZ 11.1

1. Social Security benefits are not payable until an individual reaches full retirement age.
   a. True
   b. False

2. Social Security contributions are placed in the following trust funds: OASI, DI, and SMI.
   a. True
   b. False

False, False.

EXHIBIT 11.5

SOURCES OF FUNDING TO SOCIAL SECURITY TRUST FUNDS

OASI Trust Fund	5.30 percent (limited to the maximum taxable earnings)
DI Trust Fund	0.90 percent (limited to the maximum taxable earnings)
HI Trust Fund	1.45 percent (all earnings are taxed) (In 1993, the Omnibus Budget Reconciliation Act of 1993 abolished the ceiling on taxable earnings for Medicare.)
SMI Trust Fund	-0- (no FICA taxes used; funded by general federal tax revenues and monthly premiums paid by enrollees)

---

3. Medicare Prescription Drug. Improvement and Modernization Act of 2003 (PL 108-173).

Case Study 11.1

The case of **_Veterinary Surgical Consultants, P.C. v. C.I.R._**, involved an owner of an S corporation who attempted to avoid FICA and FUTA taxes by declaring his remuneration as a K-1 distribution of corporate net income and not W-2 wages.[1] Dr. Sadanaga performed substantial services for the S corporation, Veterinary Surgical Consultants, P.C. ("VSC"). Dr. Sadanaga worked approximately 33 hours per week for VSC. He was the only individual working for VSC. Tellingly, all of VSC's income was generated from the consulting and surgical services provided by Dr. Sadanaga. As officer and sole shareholder, Dr. Sadanaga declared all remuneration he received on a K-1 form, not on a W-2 form, thus avoiding FICA and FUTA taxes.

VSC claimed that the amounts paid to Dr. Sadanaga were distributions of its corporate net income, rather than wages, and that as an S corporation it passed its net income to Dr. Sadanaga as its sole shareholder. Not surprisingly, the Court disagreed with VSC, i.e., Dr. Sadanaga, and concluded that an S corporation cannot avoid federal FICA and FUTA employment taxes by characterizing compensation paid to its sole director and shareholder as distributions of the S corporation's net income rather than wages. The Court's analysis focused on whether payments represented remuneration for services rendered. To characterize the payments to Dr. Sadanaga as distributions of VSC's net income was "but a subterfuge for reality." The payments constituted remuneration for services performed by Dr. Sadanaga on behalf of VSC. Regardless of how an employer may choose to characterize payments made to its employees, the true analysis is whether the payments represent remuneration for services rendered.[2] Dr. Sadanaga's reporting of the distributions as non-passive income from an S corporation had no bearing on the Federal employment tax treatment of those wages. He was VSC's sole source of income, thereby requiring treatment as an employee.[3] In short, while an S corporation is permitted to pass through items of income in calculating its income tax liability, it may not pass through its tax liability for federal employment taxes.

---

1. **_Veterinary Surgical Consultants, P.C. v. C.I.R._**, 117 T.C. No. 14, 117 T.C. 141, 2001 WL 1242120 (U.S.Tax Ct.), Tax Ct. Rep. (CCH) 54,527, Tax Ct. Rep. Dec. (RIA) 117.14 (U.S.Tax Ct. 2001).
2. See also **_Spicer Accounting, Inc. v. United States_**, 918 F.2d 90 (9th Cir. 1990); **_Joseph Radtke, S.C. v. United States_**, 895 F.2d 1196 (7th Cir. 1990).
3. Id., at 94-95.

SOCIAL SECURITY BENEFITS – ELIGIBILITY AND CALCULATIONS

COVERED WORKERS AND INSURED STATUS

To qualify for retirement benefits, a worker must be "**fully insured,**" which means that a worker has earned a certain number of quarters of coverage under the Social Security system. Since 1978, quarters of coverage have been determined based on annual earnings. In other words, earning a designated amount of money, regardless of when it was earned during the year, will credit the worker with a quarter of coverage for that year. In 2016, the designated amount for a quarter of coverage is $1,260. Thus, workers who earn at least $5,040 are credited with four quarters of coverage for 2016. No worker may earn more than four quarters in one year, regardless of earnings. The following is a list of the designated amounts for a quarter of coverage dating back to 1985:

KEY CONCEPTS

1. Who are covered workers with regard to Social Security?

2. Who are beneficiaries of Social Security benefits?

DESIGNATED AMOUNTS FOR A QUARTER OF SOCIAL SECURITY COVERAGE

EXHIBIT 11.6

Year	Amount Needed to Receive a Credit for One Quarter	Year	Amount Needed to Receive a Credit for One Quarter
1987	$460	2002	$870
1988	$470	2003	$890
1989	$500	2004	$900
1990	$520	2005	$920
1991	$540	2006	$970
1992	$570	2007	$1,000
1993	$590	2008	$1,050
1994	$620	2009	$1,090
1995	$630	2010	$1,120
1996	$640	2011	$1,120
1997	$670	2012	$1,130
1998	$700	2013	$1,160
1999	$740	2014	$1,200
2000	$780	2015	$1,220
2001	$830	2016	$1,260

For most persons, 40 quarters of coverage (10 years of work in employment covered by Social Security) or one quarter per year from age 21 to age 62 will fully insure a worker for life. Fully insured workers are entitled to the benefits under the Social Security system. Some benefits, like survivors' benefits, are available to "currently" (although not necessarily fully) insured individuals. **"Currently" insured workers** are those individuals who have at least six quarters of coverage out of the previous 13 quarters.

EXAMPLE 11.10

In 2016, William earned $10,000 from employment subject to Social Security between January 1 and March 31. He was then unemployed for the remainder of the year. How many quarters of coverage did he earn for Social Security?

For 2016, a worker receives one quarter credit for each $1,260 in annual earnings on which Social Security taxes are withheld up to a maximum of four quarters. It is irrelevant that William earned the $10,000 all in the first quarter. William has earned four quarters for the year.

EXAMPLE 11.11

How is a worker's insured status determined under Social Security?

It is determined by the number of quarters of coverage received. To achieve currently insured status under Social Security, a worker must have at least six quarters of coverage out of 13 calendar quarters prior to retirement, disability, or death. Any worker with 40 covered quarters is fully insured.

SOCIAL SECURITY BENEFICIARIES

Social Security benefits are paid upon retirement, disability, or death if the eligibility requirements are satisfied. The worker's spouse and children may also be eligible to receive benefits when the worker satisfies eligibility requirements. Generally, monthly Social Security benefits can be paid to:

- A disabled insured worker under age 65.
- A retired insured worker at age 62 or older.
- The spouse of a retired or disabled worker entitled to benefits who:
    - is at least 62 years old, or
    - is caring for a child who is under age 16 or disabled.
- The divorced spouse of a retired or disabled worker entitled to benefits if the divorced spouse is age 62 or older and was married to the worker for at least 10 years.
- The divorced spouse of a fully insured worker who has not yet filed a claim for benefits if both are at least age 62, were married for at least 10 years, and have been finally divorced for at least two continuous years.

QUICK QUIZ 11.2

1. "Fully insured" means that a worker has earned a certain number of quarters (generally 40) of coverage under the Social Security system.
    a. True
    b. False

2. Social Security benefits can be paid to the dependent parents of a deceased insured worker at age 62.
    a. True
    b. False

True, True.

- The dependent, unmarried child of a retired or disabled worker entitled to benefits or of a deceased insured worker if the child is:
  - under age 18;
  - under age 19 and a full-time elementary or secondary school student; or
  - age 18 or over but disabled (if the disability began before age 22).
- The surviving spouse (including a surviving divorced spouse) of a deceased insured worker if the widow(er) is age 60 or older.
- The disabled surviving spouse (including a surviving divorced spouse in some cases) of a deceased insured worker if the widow(er) is age 50 or older.
- The surviving spouse (including a surviving divorced spouse) of a deceased insured worker, regardless of age, if caring for an entitled child of the deceased who is either under age 16 or disabled before age 22.
- The dependent parents of a deceased insured worker at age 62 or older.

In addition to monthly survivors' benefits, a lump-sum death payment of $255 is payable upon the death of an insured worker. Exhibit 11.7 provides a summary of those eligible for OASDI benefits and the percentages of the worker's primary insurance amount ("PIA") that each beneficiary will receive. The PIA is the retirement benefit that the worker would receive if the worker retires at full retirement age.

Steve, age 38, has just died. He has been credited with the last 35 consecutive quarters of Social Security coverage since he left college. He did not work before leaving college. Which of the following persons are eligible to receive Social Security survivor benefits as a result of Steve's death?

1. Tim, Steve's 16-year-old son
2. Grace, Steve's 18-year-old daughter
3. Olivia, Steve's 38-year-old widow
4. Arline, Steve's 60-year-old dependent mother

Answer: Grace is too old; Olivia does not have a child under 16 and she is too young; and Arline is not eligible because she is too young. Thus, only Tim is eligible.

EXHIBIT
11.7

SUMMARY OF SOCIAL SECURITY OASDI BENEFITS (AS A PERCENTAGE OF PIA)

| | Assuming Full Retirement Age of the Worker | | | |
| | Retirement | Survivorship | | Disability[4] |
	Fully Insured[2]	Fully Insured[2]	Currently Insured[3]	
Participant	100%	Deceased	Deceased	100%
Child Under 18[6]	50%	75%	75%	50%
Spouse with child under 16[7]	50%	75%	75%	50%
Spouse - Full Age Retirement[1]	50%	100%	0%	50%
Spouse - Age 62[1, 8]	32.5% to 35%	80% to 81%[9]	0%	32.5% to 35%
Spouse - Age 60[1]	N/A	71.5%	0%	N/A
Dependent Parent (age 62)	0%	75/82.5%[5]	0%	0%

1. Includes divorced spouse if married at least 10 years (unless they have remarried). Survivorship benefits are also available to divorced spouse if remarried after age 60.
2. Fully insured is 40 quarters of coverage or one quarter for each year after age 21 but before age 62 (with at least six quarters of coverage).[1]
3. Currently insured is at least six quarters of coverage in the last 13 quarters.
4. Disability insured is based on age as follows:
   - Before age 24 - Must have 6 quarters of coverage in the last 12 quarters.
   - Age 24 through 30 - Must be covered for half of the available quarters after age 21.
   - Age 31 or older - Must be fully insured and have 20 quarters of coverage in the last 40 quarters.
5. Parent benefit is 82.5 percent for one parent and 75 percent for each parent if two parents.
6. Child under age 19 and a full-time student or of any age and disabled before age 22 also qualifies.
7. Spouse with child disabled before age 22 also qualifies.
8. A spouse can choose to retire as early as age 62, but doing so may result in a benefit as little as 32.5 percent of the worker's primary insurance amount. A spousal benefit is reduced 25/36 of one percent for each month before normal retirement age, up to 36 months. If the number of months exceeds 36, then the benefit is further reduced 5/12 of one percent per month.
9. The reduction for a widow(er) is 28.5 percent at age 60. It is prorated for months between full retirement age and age 60.

Note: Notice that when the participant worker is alive (retirement and disability), beneficiaries who qualify for a benefit, qualify for 50% of PIA. When the participant dies, all qualified beneficiaries generally receive 75% of PIA with the exceptions being the spouse who replaces the participant at 100% and any qualified dependent parents. See note 5.

1. 42 U.S.C.414.

> Under Social Security (OASDI), what benefits are available to the survivors of a deceased but only currently insured worker?
>
> A $255 lump-sum death benefit, which is generally payable to the insured's spouse, and 75 percent of the worker's PIA is available to a child under 18 or to a surviving spouse with a dependent child under the age of 16.

**EXAMPLE
11.13**

SOCIAL SECURITY RETIREMENT BENEFITS - A CLOSER LOOK

The most well known Social Security benefit is the Retirement Benefit. Until 2000, normal age retirement, the age where full retirement benefits are available to the retiree, was 65 years. The age at which full benefits are paid began to rise in the year 2000. Exhibit 11.8 illustrates the new law, which eventually raises normal age retirement with full benefits to age 67.

AGE FULL RETIREMENT BENEFITS BEGIN (NORMAL AGE RETIREMENT)

**EXHIBIT
11.8**

Full Retirement Age With Full Benefits	Year Born
65 years	Before 1938
65 years, 2 months	1938
65 years, 4 months	1939
65 years, 6 months	1940
65 years, 8 months	1941
65 years, 10 months	1942
66 years	1943-1954
66 years, 2 months	1955
66 years, 4 months	1956
66 years, 6 months	1957
66 years, 8 months	1958
66 years, 10 months	1959
67 years	1960-present

People who delay receiving Social Security retirement benefits beyond full retirement age receive an increase in their benefit when they do retire. People who take early retirement, currently as early as age 62, receive an actuarially reduced monthly benefit. (Early and late retirement options are discussed later in this chapter.)

When planning for an individual, it may be appropriate to calculate the individual's expected Social Security retirement benefit or to ask the client to request a Social Security statement and consider the benefit in that individual's retirement plan. Some advisors, however, choose not to consider the estimated retirement benefit in order to be conservative in developing a retirement plan. Others justify the exclusion of Social Security retirement benefits from retirement planning based on the belief that there will be drastic changes to the Social Security system through legislative action or through economically-driven forces.

THE RETIREMENT BENEFIT CALCULATION

Determining a worker's Social Security retirement benefit requires specific, detailed information pertaining to the person's age, actual earnings history that was subject to Social Security taxes, and the worker's retirement date. Social Security benefits are based on earnings averaged over most of a worker's lifetime. Actual earnings, in historical dollars, are first adjusted or "indexed" to current dollars to account for changes in average wages and inflation since the year the earnings were received. Then, the Social Security Administration calculates **average indexed monthly earnings ("AIME")** during the 35 years in which the applicant earned the most. The Social Security Administration applies a formula to these earnings and arrives at a basic benefit, which is referred to as the **primary insurance amount (PIA)**. The Social Security retirement benefit is based on the worker's PIA. The PIA determines the amount the applicant will receive at his full retirement age, but the dollar amount of the benefit depends on the year in which the worker retires. The PIA is indexed to the consumer price index (CPI) annually.

KEY CONCEPTS

1. How is a person's Social Security retirement benefit calculated?

2. How does retiring early or retiring late affect Social Security retirement benefits?

Figuring the Worker's Average Indexed Monthly Earnings (AIME)

To determine a worker's AIME, the worker's actual annual earnings from age 22 to 62 must be converted into current dollars by multiplying the worker's total annual earnings for each year by an indexing factor. The indexing factor is the result of dividing the national average wage for the year in which the worker attains age 60 by the national average wage for the actual year being indexed. Exhibit 11.9 provides national average wages from 1954 to 2014.

NATIONAL AVERAGE WAGE INDEXING SERIES, 1955-2014

EXHIBIT
11.9

Year	Amount	Year	Amount	Year	Amount
1955	$3,301.44	1975	$8,630.92	1995	$24,705.66
1956	$3,532.36	1976	$9,226.48	1996	$25,913.90
1957	$3,641.72	1977	$9,779.44	1997	$27,426.00
1958	$3,673.80	1978	$10,556.03	1998	$28,861.44
1959	$3,855.80	1979	$11,479.46	1999	$30,469.84
1960	$4,007.12	1980	$12,513.46	2000	$32,154.82
1961	$4,086.76	1981	$13,773.10	2001	$32,921.92
1962	$4,291.40	1982	$14,531.34	2002	$33,252.09
1963	$4,396.64	1983	$15,239.24	2003	$34,064.95
1964	$4,576.32	1984	$16,135.07	2004	$35,648.55
1965	$4,658.72	1985	$16,822.51	2005	$36,952.94
1966	$4,938.36	1986	$17,321.82	2006	$38,651.41
1967	$5,213.44	1987	$18,426.51	2007	$40,405.48
1968	$5,571.76	1988	$19,334.04	2008	$41,334.97
1969	$5,893.76	1989	$20,099.55	2009	$40,711.61
1970	$6,186.24	1990	$21,027.98	2010	$41,673.83
1971	$6,497.08	1991	$21,811.60	2011	$42,979.61
1972	$7,133.80	1992	$22,935.42	2012	$44,321.67
1973	$7,580.16	1993	$23,132.67	2013	$44,888.16
1974	$8,030.76	1994	$23,753.53	2014	$46,481.52

Source: Social Security Administration (www.ssa.gov)

For a worker age 62 in 2014, the indexing factor for the year 1980 is determined by dividing the national average wage for 2012 (when the worker attained age 60), which was $44,321.67, by the national average wage for 1980 (the year being indexed), which was $12,513.46, yielding a factor of 3.5419.

EXAMPLE
11.14

		Age 62 in 2014		Age 65 in 2014	
Year	AWI	Age	Factor	Age	Factor
1972	7,133.80	20	6.2129	23	5.7069
1973	7,580.16	21	5.8471	24	5.3708
1974	8,030.76	22	5.5190	25	5.0695
1975	8,630.92	23	5.1352	26	4.7169
1976	9,226.48	24	4.8037	27	4.4125
1977	9,779.44	25	4.5321	28	4.1630
1978	10,556.03	26	4.1987	29	3.8567
1979	11,479.46	27	3.8610	30	3.5465
1980	12,513.46	28	3.5419	31	3.2534
1981	13,773.10	29	3.2180	32	2.9559
1982	14,531.34	30	3.0501	33	2.8016
1983	15,239.24	31	2.9084	34	2.6715
1984	16,135.07	32	2.7469	35	2.5232
1985	16,822.51	33	2.6347	36	2.4201
1986	17,321.82	34	2.5587	37	2.3503
1987	18,426.51	35	2.4053	38	2.2094
1988	19,334.04	36	2.2924	39	2.1057
1989	20,099.55	37	2.2051	40	2.0255
1990	21,027.98	38	2.1077	41	1.9361
1991	21,811.60	39	2.0320	42	1.8665
1992	22,935.42	40	1.9325	43	1.7751
1993	23,132.67	41	1.9160	44	1.7599
1994	23,753.53	42	1.8659	45	1.7139
1995	24,705.66	43	1.7940	46	1.6479
1996	25,913.90	44	1.7103	47	1.5710
1997	27,426.00	45	1.6160	48	1.4844
1998	28,861.44	46	1.5357	49	1.4106
1999	30,469.84	47	1.4546	50	1.3361
2000	32,154.82	48	1.3784	51	1.2661
2001	32,921.92	49	1.3463	52	1.2366
2002	33,252.09	50	1.3329	53	1.2243
2003	34,064.95	51	1.3011	54	1.1951
2004	35,648.55	52	1.2433	55	1.1420
2005	36,952.94	53	1.1994	56	1.1017
2006	38,651.41	54	1.1467	57	1.0533
2007	40,405.48	55	1.0969	58	1.0076
2008	41,334.97	56	1.0723	59	1.0000
2009	40,711.61	57	1.0887	60	1.0000
2010	41,673.83	58	1.0635	61	1.0000
2011	42,979.61	59	1.0312	62	1.0000
2012	44,321.67	60	1.0000	63	1.0000
2013	███████	61	1.0000	64	1.0000
2014	███████	62	1.0000	65	1.0000

Next, each year's annual earnings must be multiplied by its indexing factor to arrive at the indexed earnings for the years from age 22 to 60. Note that the indexing factor will always equal one for the years in which the worker is 60 or older. After all annual earnings are indexed, or converted to current dollar amounts, the highest 35 years of indexed earnings are added together for a total. The sum of the highest 35 years is then divided by 420 (which represents 35 years multiplied by 12 months per year). This calculation yields the average amount of monthly earnings for all indexed years, hence the name Average Indexed Monthly Earnings (AIME). Once the worker's AIME is determined, the next step in determining the worker's retirement benefit is to calculate the primary insurance amount (PIA) for the worker.

EXAMPLE
11.15

Assume Ronnie and Karen both retire in 2014. Ronnie retires at age 62. Karen retires at her normal (or full) retirement age. Assume Karen has covered earnings from 1972 through 2014, as shown in columns labeled "nominal earnings" and Ronnie has covered earnings from 1972 through 2014.

Indexing adjusts nominal earnings to near-current wage levels. For each case, the table shows columns of earnings before and after indexing. Between these columns is a column showing the indexing factors. A factor will always equal one for the year in which the person attains age 60 and all later years. The indexing factor for a prior year Y is the result of dividing the average wage index for the year in which the person attains age 60 by the average wage index for year Y. For example, Ronnie's indexing factor for 1972 (6.2129) is the average wage for 2012 ($44,321.67) divided by the average wage for 1972 ($7,133.80).

The highest 35 years of indexed earnings are used in the benefit computation. The selected indexed amounts are bold. Below the indexed earnings are the sums for the highest 35 years of indexed earnings and the corresponding average monthly amounts of such earnings. (The average is the result of dividing the sum of the 35 highest amounts by the number of months in 35 years.) Such an average is called the "Average Indexed Monthly Earnings" (AIME).

As reflected in the following chart, Ronnie's AIME is $3,027 and Karen's AIME is $4,011.

		Ronnie					Karen			
Year	Age	Nominal earnings	Indexing factor	Indexed earnings	Top 35	Age	Nominal earnings	Indexing factor	Indexed earnings	Top 35
1972	20	$5,167	6.2129	**$32,102**	✓	23	$5,194	5.7069	$29,641	
1973	21	$5,525	5.8471	**$32,305**	✓	24	$5,747	5.3708	$30,866	
1974	22	$5,847	5.5190	**$32,270**	✓	25	$6,262	5.0695	$31,745	
1975	23	$6,140	5.1352	$31,530		26	$6,746	4.7169	$31,821	
1976	24	$6,452	4.8037	$30,994		27	$7,253	4.4125	$32,004	
1977	25	$7,088	4.5321	**$32,124**	✓	28	$8,135	4.1630	**$33,866**	✓
1978	26	$7,535	4.1987	**$31,637**	✓	29	$8,815	3.8567	**$33,997**	✓
1979	27	$7,988	3.8610	$30,841		30	$9,511	3.5465	$33,731	
1980	28	$8,589	3.5419	$30,422		31	$10,396	3.2534	$33,823	
1981	29	$9,186	3.2180	$29,560		32	$11,293	2.9559	$33,381	
1982	30	$9,742	3.0501	$29,714		33	$12,151	2.8016	**$34,043**	✓
1983	31	$10,521	2.9084	$30,599		34	$13,305	2.6715	**$35,544**	✓
1984	32	$11,447	2.7469	$31,444		35	$14,667	2.5232	**$37,007**	✓
1985	33	$12,485	2.6347	**$32,894**	✓	36	$16,197	2.4201	**$39,198**	✓
1986	34	$13,748	2.5587	**$35,177**	✓	37	$18,051	2.3503	**$42,425**	✓
1987	35	$14,513	2.4053	**$34,908**	✓	38	$19,273	2.2094	**$42,582**	✓
1988	36	$15,228	2.2924	**$34,909**	✓	39	$20,445	2.1057	**$43,051**	✓
1989	37	$16,131	2.2051	**$35,571**	✓	40	$21,887	2.0255	**$44,332**	✓
1990	38	$16,827	2.1077	**$35,467**	✓	41	$23,063	1.9361	**$44,652**	✓
1991	39	$17,335	2.0320	**$35,225**	✓	42	$23,994	1.8665	**$44,785**	✓
1992	40	$18,450	1.9325	**$35,654**	✓	43	$25,779	1.7751	**$45,759**	✓
1993	41	$19,369	1.9160	**$37,111**	✓	44	$27,311	1.7599	**$48,065**	✓
1994	42	$20,146	1.8659	**$37,590**	✓	45	$28,659	1.7139	**$49,119**	✓
1995	43	$21,087	1.7940	**$37,830**	✓	46	$30,257	1.6479	**$49,859**	✓
1996	44	$21,884	1.7103	**$37,429**	✓	47	$31,663	1.5710	**$49,744**	✓
1997	45	$23,024	1.6160	**$37,208**	✓	48	$33,582	1.4844	**$49,850**	✓
1998	46	$23,234	1.5357	**$35,680**	✓	49	$34,155	1.4106	**$48,179**	✓
1999	47	$23,869	1.4546	**$34,720**	✓	50	$35,360	1.3361	**$47,245**	✓
2000	48	$24,839	1.3784	**$34,238**	✓	51	$37,071	1.2661	**$46,936**	✓
2001	49	$26,067	1.3463	**$35,093**	✓	52	$39,188	1.2366	**$48,460**	✓
2002	50	$27,602	1.3329	**$36,791**	✓	53	$41,790	1.2243	**$51,165**	✓
2003	51	$29,061	1.3011	**$37,811**	✓	54	$44,305	1.1951	**$52,950**	✓
2004	52	$30,696	1.2433	**$38,164**	✓	55	$47,115	1.1420	**$53,807**	✓
2005	53	$32,410	1.1994	**$38,873**	✓	56	$50,076	1.1017	**$55,169**	✓
2006	54	$33,200	1.1467	**$38,071**	✓	57	$51,629	1.0533	**$54,381**	✓
2007	55	$33,551	1.0969	**$36,803**	✓	58	$52,503	1.0076	**$52,901**	✓
2008	56	$34,388	1.0723	**$36,873**	✓	59	$54,148	1.0000	**$54,148**	✓
2009	57	$36,400	1.0887	**$39,628**	✓	60	$56,092	1.0000	**$56,092**	✓
2010	58	$37,900	1.0635	**$40,308**	✓	61	$56,408	1.0000	**$56,408**	✓
2011	59	$38,113	1.0312	**$39,303**	✓	62	$57,103	1.0000	**$57,103**	✓
2012	60	$39,551	1.0000	**$39,551**	✓	63	$59,955	1.0000	**$59,955**	✓
2013	61	$40,000	1.0000	**$40,000**	✓	64	$60,000	1.0000	**$60,000**	✓
2014	62	$42,000	1.0000	**$42,000**	✓	65	$62,000	1.0000	**$62,000**	✓
		Highest-35 total		$1,271,316			Highest-35 total		$1,684,777	
	Total 420 Months		AIME	$3,027				AIME	$4,011	

Calculating the Worker's Primary Insurance Amount (PIA)

Generally, the PIA is the actual Social Security retirement benefit for the single retiree who retires at full retirement age. For those who retire early or late and for family or surviving beneficiaries, the PIA is not the actual amount of the benefit but the PIA is used to determine their actual benefit.

The PIA is a result of applying the AIME to the PIA formula. This benefit formula changes the dollar amounts (by CPI), but not the percentages, from year to year and depends on the worker's first year of eligibility, that is, when the worker turns 62, becomes disabled, or dies.

The PIA is the sum of three separate percentages of portions of the AIME. These portions are also known as "bend points." For the year 2016, these portions are the first $856 of AIME, the amount of AIME between $856 and $5,157, and the AIME over $5,157. The bend points for

2016 are thus $856 and $5,157. For individuals who first become eligible for retirement benefits or disability insurance benefits in 2016 or who die in 2016 before becoming eligible for benefits, their PIA will be the sum of:

    90 percent of the first $856 of their AIME, *plus*

    32 percent of their AIME over $856 up to $5,157, *plus*

    15 percent of their AIME that exceeds $5,157.

    (Maximum PIA for 2016 is $2,639)

The sum of these three calculations is rounded down to the next lower multiple of $0.10 (if it is not already a multiple of $0.10). For calculations in subsequent years, it is useful to know how to determine a given year's bend points. Exhibit 11.10 shows the established bend points from 1981 through 2016.

BEND POINT TABLE

EXHIBIT
11.10

Dollar Amounts (bend points) in PIA Formula		
Year	First	Second
1982	$230	$1,388
1982	$230	$1,388
1983	$254	$1,528
1984	$267	$1,612
1985	$280	$1,691
1986	$297	$1,790
1987	$310	$1,866
1988	$319	$1,922
1989	$339	$2,044
1990	$356	$2,145
1991	$370	$2,230
1992	$387	$2,333
1993	$401	$2,420
1994	$422	$2,545
1995	$426	$2,567
1996	$437	$2,635
1997	$455	$2,741
1998	$477	$2,875
1999	$505	$3,043
2000	$531	$3,202
2001	$561	$3,381
2002	$592	$3,567
2003	$606	$3,653
2004	$612	$3,689
2005	$627	$3,779
2006	$656	$3,955
2007	$680	$4,100
2008	$711	$4,288
2009	$744	$4,483
2010	$761	$4,586
2011	$749	$4,517
2012	$767	$4,624
2013	$791	$4,768
2015	$826	$4,980
2016	$856	$5,157

Source: Social Security Administration (www.ssa.gov)

These figures for the PIA rise each year based on a cost-of-living adjustment (**COLA**) that is applied to reflect changes in the cost of living. Recent COLAs, which are based on inflation, are shown in Exhibit 11.11.

EXHIBIT
11.11

COST-OF-LIVING ADJUSTMENT (COLA) PER YEAR*

Year	COLA	Year	COLA	Year	COLA
1992	3.0%	2000	3.5%	2008	5.8%
1993	2.6%	2001	2.6%	2009	0.0%
1994	2.8%	2002	1.4%	2010	0.0%
1995	2.6%	2003	2.1%	2011	3.6%
1996	2.9%	2004	2.7%	2012	1.7%
1997	2.1%	2005	4.1%	2013	1.5%
1998	1.3%	2006	3.3%	2014	1.7%
1999	2.5%	2007	2.3%	2015	0.0%

* Source: www.ssa.gov/oact/cola/colaseries.html

As mentioned, the calculation of the Social Security retirement benefit skews benefits toward the low-income worker. This design is evident in the PIA calculation with a 90 percent wage replacement for extremely low income and only a 15 percent wage replacement for higher income. The following exhibit illustrates the wage replacement ratio provided by Social Security at full retirement age based on the annualized income, which is AIME multiplied by 12 months.

EXHIBIT
11.12

WAGE REPLACEMENT RATIO FROM SOCIAL SECURITY

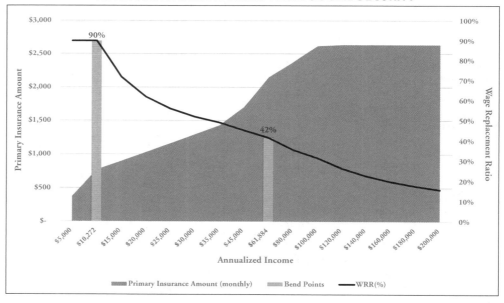

Annual COLA increases are determined by October of each year and go into effect in time so that they first appear on monthly benefit checks received in the following January. In 2016, the maximum monthly retirement benefit for retirees at full retirement age is $2,639, compared to $2,663 in 2015.

Early and Late Retirement Options

Workers entitled to retirement benefits can currently take early retirement benefits as early as age 62. The worker will receive a reduced benefit because he will receive more monthly benefit payments than if the worker had waited and retired at full retirement age. The reduction to one's monthly benefit for early retirement is permanent. Conversely, a delayed or postponed retirement will permanently increase the monthly retirement benefit for a worker.[4]

For each month of early retirement, workers will receive a reduction in their monthly retirement benefit of 5/9 of one percent for up to the first 36 months. For subsequent months of early retirement, the permanent reduction percentage is 5/12 of one percent per month.

Assume Robin begins receiving benefits at the earliest possible age, which is age 62. Then, the benefit amount for Robin is reduced for 48 months of retirement before Robin's normal retirement age, which is 66 years. Assume Robin's PIA before reduction is $1,421.90. The PIA is thus reduced to a monthly benefit of $1,066.43 (rounded to $1066.40).

EXAMPLE 11.16

PIA	$1,421.90
5/9 x 1% x 36 months	Less 20% reduction
5/12 x 1% x 12 months	Less 5% reduction
Monthly Benefit	$1,066.43

Although the full retirement age will increase to age 67, workers will still have the option of taking early retirement at age 62. However, the reduction percentage that is applied to the monthly retirement benefit will increase until 2027. Before 2000, those who retired at age 62 received 80 percent of their retirement benefit, but the increase in full retirement age has increased the number of months from 62 until full retirement age. For instance, in the year 2009, covered workers who retired at age 62 received 75 percent of their monthly retirement benefit, or 25 percent less than their full retirement benefit. By 2027, covered workers retiring at age 62 (full retirement age would be 67) will receive only 70 percent of their monthly retirement benefit. Exhibit 11.13, which was compiled by the Social Security Administration, shows the phase-in of the Social Security full retirement age and accompanying reductions for early retirement at age 62.

---

4. A spouse can choose to retire as early as age 62, but doing so may result in a benefit as little as 32.5 percent of the worker's primary insurance amount. A spousal benefit is reduced 25/36 of one percent for each month before normal retirement age, up to 36 months. If the number of months exceeds 36, then the benefit is further reduced 5/12 of one percent per month. Source: SSA.gov.

EXHIBIT
11.13

SOCIAL SECURITY FULL RETIREMENT AND REDUCTIONS* BY AGE

Year of Birth	Full Retirement Age	Age 62 Reduction Months	Monthly Percent Reduction	Total Percent Reduction
1937 or earlier	65	36	0.555	20.00
1938	65 & 2 months	38	0.548	20.83
1939	65 & 4 months	40	0.541	21.67
1940	65 & 6 months	42	0.535	22.50
1941	65 & 8 months	44	0.530	23.33
1942	65 & 10 months	46	0.525	24.17
1943-1954	66	48	0.520	25.00
1955	66 & 2 months	50	0.516	25.84
1956	66 & 4 months	52	0.512	26.66
1957	66 & 6 months	54	0.509	27.50
1958	66 & 8 months	56	0.505	28.33
1959	66 & 10 months	58	0.502	29.17
1960 and later	67	60	0.500	30.00

*Percentage monthly and total reductions are approximate due to rounding. The actual reductions are 0.555 or
5/9 of 1 percent per month for the first 36 months and 0.416 or 5/12 of 1 percent for subsequent months.
Source: Social Security Administration (www.ssa.gov)

No matter what the full retirement age is, a worker may start receiving benefits as early as age 62 and can also retire at any time between age 62 and full retirement age. However, if a worker starts benefits at one of these early ages, the benefits are reduced a fraction of a percent for each month before the full retirement age.

EXAMPLE
11.17

Assume that Josephine, a worker born in 1939, decided to retire on her 62nd birthday. Assume that her full retirement benefit would have been $1,429.20 at age 65 and four months, her full retirement age. If she retires at age 62, what is her monthly retirement benefit?

The answer is $1,119. Josephine retired 40 months early. The monthly retirement benefit reduction percentage is 1/180 (5/9 x 1% = 1/180 = 0.0056) for the first 36 months (1/180 x 36 = 20 percent) and 1/240 (5/12 x 1% = 1/240 = 0.0042) for the 4 subsequent months of early retirement (1/240 x 4 = 1.6668 percent), yielding a total permanent reduction to Josephine's monthly retirement benefit of 21.6667 percent. 21.6667 percent x $1,429.20 = $309.66. $1,429.20 - $309.66 = $1,119.50 (rounded).

What if Josephine retired at age 64 and six months? What is her permanent monthly retirement benefit (subject to COLA increases)? Note she retired 10 months early from normal retirement age.

EXAMPLE 11.18

The answer is $1,349. 1/180 x 10 = 5.5556 percent. 5.5556 percent x $1,429.20 = $79.40. $1,429.20 - $79.40 = $1,349.80 (rounded).

For those covered individuals who take late retirement, or when benefits are lost due to the earnings limitation, the monthly retirement benefit and the benefit paid to the surviving spouse will increase each year (until age 70) as follows:

PERCENTAGE INCREASES FOR DELAYED RETIREMENT

EXHIBIT 11.14

Increase For Year Born	Annual Percentage Increase Each Year Of Late Retirement	After Age
1917-1924	3.0%	65
1925-1926	3.5%	65
1927-1928	4.0%	65
1929-1930	4.5%	65
1931-1932	5.0%	65
1933-1934	5.5%	65
1935-1936	6.0%	65
1937	6.5%	65
1938	6.5%	65 and 2 months
1939	7.0%	65 and 4 months
1940	7.0%	65 and 6 months
1941	7.5%	65 and 8 months
1942	7.5%	65 and 10 months
1943 or later	8.0%	66

Jeanette will turn 66 in 2016 (thus she was born after 1942). She is considering taking Social Security retirement benefits at age 62, 66, or 70. Assume her monthly expected benefit is $1,000 at full retirement age, expected inflation is 4%, and her life expectancy is 90. Calculate the present value of her benefits at ages 62, 66, and 70 (A, B, or C).

EXAMPLE 11.19

Choice A – Begin Benefits at age 62.

PMT	$750	($1,000 less 25% reduction)
N	336	(90-62) x 12
i	0.3333	4/12
FV	0	
PV$_{@62}$	**$151,450.19**	

Choice B – Begin Benefits at age 66.

PMT	$1,000	Full benefit at full retirement age
N	288	(90-66) x 12
i	0.3333	4/12
FV	0	
PV$_{@66}$	$184,948.61	

Discount to age 62 for comparison.

PMT	$0	
N	4	(66-62)
i	4	
FV	$184,948.61	
PV$_{@62}$	**$158,094.84**	

Choice C – Begin Benefits at age 70.

PMT	$1,320	($1,000 plus 8% x 4 years increase)
N	240	(90-70) x 12
i	0.3333	4/12
FV	0	
PV$_{@70}$	$217,828.85	

Discount to age 62 for comparison.

PMT	$0	
N	8	(70-62)
i	4	
FV	$217,828.85	
PV$_{@62}$	**$159,165.41**	

As you can see, even though the benefit is reduced if Jeanette begins her benefit early, the PV of the total benefit at age 62 is not much less than if she took the benefit at age 66. Similarly, if she begins her payments later, her yearly payments will be higher but the PV of the benefit at age 62 is not much more than if she had taken benefits at age 66. The significance here is that all things being equal, the acceleration or delay of benefit generally has little impact on the PV of the benefit at age 62. However, the choice of retirement age is significant when considering the annual income needed to maintain one's standard of living.

Another critical factor in this analysis is the life expectancy of the worker. If the life expectancy is significantly less than what was assumed it might not make sense to delay benefits. Another factor that was not considered is the tax impact of benefits, which is discussed later in this chapter.

Although the calculations explained above can provide estimates of the Social Security benefits a retiring worker may receive, an advisor should have the client obtain his entire Social Security earnings history up to the moment of retirement from the Social Security Administration to get the most accurate benefit estimate.

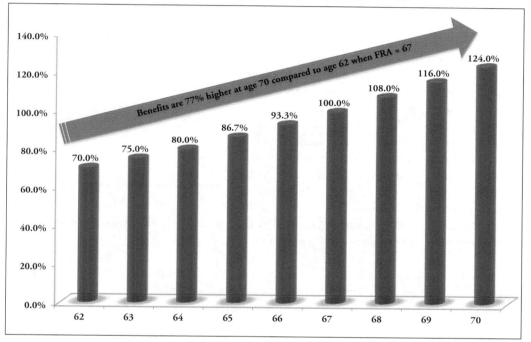

SOCIAL SECURITY BENEFITS AT DIFFERENT AGES

EXHIBIT
11.15

Reduction of Social Security Benefits

Besides early retirement, there are two other situations in which beneficiaries can have benefits reduced. The first instance is a reduction of benefits based on earnings, referred to as the **retirement earnings limitations test**. The other instance is through taxation of Social Security benefits. Both of these measures reduce one's net benefits.

A person may continue to work even though he is considered "retired" under Social Security. For a retiree who receives Social Security retirement benefits before normal retirement age, the earnings received by the beneficiary cannot exceed certain limitations without triggering a reduction in Social Security benefits. Beneficiaries can earn up to the limitation amount and receive all of their benefits, but if their earnings exceed the designated limit for the calendar year, then benefits will be reduced or eliminated. The law provides for earnings limitations of $15,720 for those under the full retirement age for 2016. The Social Security Administration reduces $1 in benefits for each $2 earned by those beneficiaries above $15,720. In the year that the retiree reaches full retirement age,

$1 in benefits will be deducted for each $3 earned above the given year's limit but only for earnings before the month the retiree reaches full retirement age. For 2016, the limit for earnings in the year the retiree reaches full retirement age is $41,880. The earnings limitation increases every year as median earnings nationwide increase. Once the retiree reaches normal retirement age, benefits will not be reduced regardless of the earnings limitations.

In the event that a beneficiary, who is younger than normal retirement age, has earnings that exceed the limitation, that beneficiary's benefits will be reduced depending on his or her age. The beneficiary must file an annual report of his earnings to the Social Security Administration by April 15 of the year following the year worked and must provide the exact earnings for that year and an estimate for the current year. The filing of a federal tax return with the IRS does not satisfy the filing requirement with the Social Security Administration. Also, the wages count toward the earnings limitation when they are earned, not when paid, whereas income for the self-employed normally counts when paid, not earned. If other family members receive benefits based on the beneficiary's Social Security record, then the total family benefits may be affected by the beneficiary's earnings that exceed the earnings limitation. In such a case, the Social Security Administration will withhold not only the worker's benefits but will withhold those benefits payable to family members as well.

QUICK QUIZ 11.3

1. Social Security benefits are based on the average of the three highest paid years for a covered worker.
   a. True
   b. False

2. Full retirement age for Social Security is decreasing because of the trend of individuals retiring early.
   a. True
   b. False

False, False.

EXAMPLE 11.20

Matthew is 64 years old and despite being retired from his occupation as an attorney, earned $20,000 in 2016 while working as a golf instructor at a local golf course. Matthew's monthly retirement benefit from Social Security is normally $1,200, which totals $14,400 for the entire year. Because Matthew exceeded the retirement earnings limitation, how much money will be reduced from Matthew's Social Security retirement benefit for 2016?

Matthew's total earnings in 2016	$20,000
Earnings limitation	($15,720)
Remainder excess	$4,280
One-half deduction	÷ 2
Benefits reduced by:	**$2,140**

The Social Security Administration will reduce Matthew's benefits for the year by $2,140. Matthew will receive $12,260 in retirement benefits ($14,400 annual retirement benefit less $2,140 reduction). Matthew's total income for 2016 will be $32,260, instead of $34,400.

> Mike is 67 years old. He has a full-time job working as a masseur. This year (2016) he anticipates earning $22,000 from his job. How much, in dollars, will Mike's Social Security benefits be reduced for the earnings test?

EXAMPLE 11.21

> None, because Mike is over normal retirement age.

Generally, only wages and net self-employment income count towards the retirement earnings limitation, whereas income from savings, investments, and insurance does not. The following is a nonexclusive list of sources of income that DO NOT count toward the earnings limitation:

- Pension or retirement income
- 401(k) plan and IRA withdrawals
- Dividends and interest from investments
- Capital gains
- Rental income
- Workers' compensation benefits (generally not payable after a worker has retired)
- Unemployment benefits
- Court-awarded judgments, less components of award that include lost wages
- Contest winnings

TAXATION OF SOCIAL SECURITY BENEFITS

Apart from the earnings limitation, some beneficiaries may be required to pay income tax on their Social Security benefits. For persons with substantial income in addition to Social Security benefits, up to 85 percent of their annual Social Security benefits may be subject to federal income tax. The Social Security Administration is concerned with a beneficiary's **modified adjusted gross income** (MAGI). For purposes of Social Security, MAGI is equal to the taxpayer's adjusted gross income plus tax exempt interest, including:

KEY CONCEPTS ✓

1. How are Social Security benefits taxed?
2. What benefits are available from Social Security other than retirement benefits?
3. What is the maximum family benefit?

- interest earned on savings bonds used for higher education;
- amounts excluded from the taxpayer's income for employer-provided adoption assistance;
- amounts deducted for interest paid for educational loans;
- amounts deducted as qualified tuition expense; and
- income earned in a foreign country, a U.S. possession, or Puerto Rico, that is excluded from income.

EXAMPLE 11.22

Last year Charlie and Eva had adjusted gross income of $40,000. They also had the following items:

- Eva spent 3 months during the year in Mexico visiting her mother. While she was there, she earned $5,000 that has been excluded from their AGI.

- While in Mexico, Eva fell in love with a little orphan girl. Luckily, Charlie's company has an Adoption Assistance Program. The program paid $8,000 towards the adoption and the amount was excluded from Charlie's AGI.

- Charlie has been attending night school for several years and has several student loans. Last year he paid and deducted $200 in student loan interest. He also took a qualified tuition expense deduction for $600 he paid to the school.

- Charlie and Eva had $900 in interest. $400 was from tax-exempt bonds and the remaining $500 was from corporate bonds.

Charlie and Eva's MAGI for last year is:

Adjusted Gross Income (AGI)	$40,000
+ Foreign Income Excluded	$5,000
+ Adoption Assistance Excluded	$8,000
+ Student Loan Interest Deduction	$200
+ Qualified Tuition Expense Deduction	$600
+ Tax-Exempt Bonds Interest	$400
= Modified Adjusted Gross Income (MAGI)	**$54,200**

Note that the $500 of corporate-bond interest has already been included in Charlie and Eva's AGI.

Generally, 50 percent of Social Security benefits may be subject to federal income taxes for beneficiaries who file a federal tax return as an "individual" and have a modified adjusted gross income between $25,000 and $34,000. For those with a modified adjusted gross income plus one-half of Social Security greater than $34,000, up to 85 percent of their Social Security benefits may be subject to federal income taxation. For those beneficiaries that file a joint federal tax return and have a modified adjusted gross income with their spouse between $32,000 and $44,000, 50 percent of their Social Security benefits will be subject to federal income taxes. Finally, if beneficiaries filing a joint tax return have a modified adjusted gross income plus one-half Social Security benefits that exceeds $44,000, 85 percent of their Social Security benefits may be subject to federal income taxation.

In summary, for persons with substantial income in addition to their Social Security benefits, up to 85 percent of their annual benefits may be subject to federal income tax.

SOCIAL SECURITY HURDLE AMOUNTS

EXHIBIT
11.16

	Married Filing Jointly	All Others Except MFS = 0
1st Hurdle	$32,000	$25,000
2nd Hurdle	$44,000	$34,000

If MAGI plus one half of Social Security benefits exceeds the first hurdle but not the second, the taxable amount of Social Security benefits is the lesser of:
- 50% Social Security Benefits, or
- 50% [MAGI + 0.50 (Social Security Benefits) - Hurdle 1].

A married couple has interest income of $18,000 and Social Security benefits of $20,000. What amount of their Social Security benefits must be included in their taxable income?

EXAMPLE
11.23

Lesser of:
- 0.50($20,000) = $10,000, or
- 0.50 [$18,000 + 0.50 (20,000) - 32,000] = Negative

They would have $0 inclusion due to a negative result.

A married couple has income of $30,000 and Social Security benefits of $20,000. What amount of their Social Security benefits must be included in their taxable income?

EXAMPLE
11.24

Lesser of:
- 0.50($20,000) = $10,000, or
- 0.50 [30,000 + 0.50 (20,000) - 32,000] = $4,000

They would have $4,000 of Social Security benefits included in taxable income.

If MAGI plus one-half the Social Security benefits exceeds the second hurdle, the taxable amount of Social Security benefits is the lesser of:
- 85% Social Security Benefits, or
- 85% [MAGI + 0.50 (Social Security Benefits) - Hurdle 2], plus the lesser of:
  - $6,000 for MFJ or $4,500 for all other taxpayers, or
  - The taxable amount calculated under the 50% formula and only considering Hurdle 1.

A married couple has income of $60,000 and Social Security benefits of $20,000. What amount of their Social Security benefits must be included in their taxable income?

0.85 ($20,000) = **$17,000**

0.85 [$60,000 + 0.50 ($20,000) - $44,000] = $22,100
   Plus the lesser of:
-   $6,000, or
-   0.50($20,000) = $10,000, or
-   0.50[$60,000+0.50($20,000)-$32,000] = $19,000

                                           $6,000
                                          $28,100

Therefore, **$17,000** must be included in their taxable income.

A married couple has income of $45,000 and Social Security benefits of $20,000. What amount of their Social Security benefits must be included in their taxable income?

0.85 ($20,000) = **$17,000**

0.85 [$45,000 + 0.50 ($20,000) - $44,000] = $9,350
   Plus the lesser of:
-   $6,000, or
-   0.50($20,000) = $10,000, or
-   0.50[$45,000+0.50($20,000)-$32,000] = $11,500

                                           $6,000
                                          $15,350

Therefore, **$15,350** must be included in their taxable income.

Last year Michelle, a single taxpayer, received $10,400 in Social Security benefits. For the entire year, she had an adjusted gross income of $28,000. How much, if any, of her Social Security benefit is taxable?

First, determine Michelle's modified adjusted gross income. Modified adjusted gross income is the sum of adjusted gross income, nontaxable interest, and foreign-earned income. One-half of Michelle's Social Security benefits must then be added to her MAGI. For Michelle, the equation is as follows: $28,000 + [$10,400 x 0.50] = $33,200. Since Michelle's modified adjusted gross income plus one-half of her Social Security benefits is between the two base amounts for a single individual of $25,000 and $34,000, we can use the following formula to determine her taxable amount. The income tax base will be the lesser of 50% of her Social Security benefits _OR_ 50% of the difference between Michelle's modified adjusted gross income plus one-half of her Social Security benefits less the base amount of $25,000. Based on this formula, Michelle will be subject to income tax on $4,100 of her Social Security benefit.

- 0.50($10,400) = $5,200
- 0.50($33,200 - $25,000) = $4,100 (the LESSER amount)

EXAMPLE 11.28

A married couple files jointly and has an adjusted gross income of $38,000, no tax-exempt interest, and $11,000 of Social Security benefits. How much, if any, of their Social Security benefits is included in gross income?

The lesser of the following:

- 0.50 ($11,000) = $5,500, or
- 0.50 [$38,000 + 0.50 ($11,000) - $32,000] = 0.50 ($11,500) = $5,750

They will include $5,500 in gross income. If the couple's adjusted gross income was $15,000 and their Social Security benefits totaled $5,000, none of the benefits would be taxable since 0.50 [$15,000 + 0.50 ($5,000) - $32,000] is negative.

EXAMPLE 11.29

Frank and Lois, married filing jointly, have tax-free municipal bond interest of $2,000. Assuming that Frank and Lois have differing AGI amounts ranging from $20,000 to $50,000, the Social Security amount includable in taxable income is shown below. Thus, if Frank and Lois have $20,000 in AGI, then only $1,000 of the Social Security benefit is included (4% of the benefit is included), but if they have AGI of $50,000 then $20,400 is includable (85% of the benefit is included). Notice that once an individual is substantially over the second hurdle they can expect to include 85% of the Social Security benefit.

	$20,000	$25,000	$30,000	$35,000	$40,000	$45,000	$50,000
Preliminary AGI	$20,000	$25,000	$30,000	$35,000	$40,000	$45,000	$50,000
Tax free bond interest	$2,000	$2,000	$2,000	$2,000	$2,000	$2,000	$2,000
MAGI	$22,000	$27,000	$32,000	$37,000	$42,000	$47,000	$52,000
50% of Social Security	$12,000	$12,000	$12,000	$12,000	$12,000	$12,000	$12,000
MAGI plus 1/2 Social Security	$34,000	$39,000	$44,000	$49,000	$54,000	$59,000	$64,000
First hurdle	$32,000	$32,000	$32,000	$32,000	$32,000	$32,000	$32,000
Second hurdle	$44,000	$44,000	$44,000	$44,000	$44,000	$44,000	$44,000
Excess of income over first hurdle	$2,000	$7,000	$12,000	$17,000	$22,000	$27,000	$32,000
Excess of income over second hurdle	$0	$0	$0	$5,000	$10,000	$15,000	$20,000
1. 50% of SSB	$12,000	$12,000	$12,000				
2. 50% [MAGI + 0.50 (SSB) - Hurdle 1)	$1,000	$3,500	$6,000				
3. 85% of SSB				$20,400	$20,400	$20,400	$20,400
4. [85% [MAGI + 0.5 (SSB)- Hurdle 2]] + 6000				$10,250	$14,500	$18,750	$23,000
5. [85% [MAGI + 0.5 (SSB)- Hurdle 2]] + 50% [MAGI + 0.50 (SSB) - Hurdle 1]				$14,450	$18,700	$22,950	$27,200
6. [85% [MAGI + 0.5 (SSB)- Hurdle 2]] + 50% of SSB				$16,250	$20,500	$24,750	$29,000
Includable portion of Social Security	$1,000	$3,500	$6,000	$10,250	$14,500	$18,750	$20,400
Percent of SS Taxed	4%	15%	25%	43%	60%	78%	85%

OTHER SOCIAL SECURITY BENEFITS

DISABILITY BENEFITS AND DISABILITY INSURED

Benefits are payable at any age to workers who have enough Social Security credits and who have a severe physical or mental impairment that is expected to prevent them from doing "substantial" work for a year or more or who have a condition that is expected to result in death. Workers are insured for disability if they are fully insured and, except for persons who are blind or disabled at age 31 or older, have a total of at least 20 quarters of coverage during the 40-quarter period ending with the quarter in which the worker became disabled. Workers who are disabled before age 31 must have total quarters of coverage equal to one-half the calendar quarters that have elapsed since the worker reached age 21 ending in the quarter in which the worker became disabled. However, a minimum of six quarters is required.

WORK CREDITS FOR DISABILITY BENEFITS

EXHIBIT
11.17

Born After 1929, Become Disabled at Age:	Number of Credits You Need:
31 through 42	20
44	22
46	24
48	26
50	28
52	30
54	32
56	34
58	36
60	38
62 or older	40

- Before age 24 - The disabled individual may qualify if they have 6 credits earned in the 3-year period ending when the disability starts.
- Age 24 to 31 - The disabled individual may qualify if they have credit for working half the time between age 21 and the time they become disabled. For example, if they become disabled at age 27, they would need credit for 3 years of work (12 credits) out of the past 6 years (between ages 21 and 27).
- Age 31 or older - In general, the disabled individual needs to have the number of work credits shown in the chart. Unless they are blind, they must have earned at least 20 of the credits in the 10 years immediately before they became disabled.

In 2016, earnings of $1,130 or more per month are considered substantial; therefore, a worker earning more than $1,130 per month would not be eligible for Social Security disability benefits. (If the individual is blind, then the amount is increased to $1,820.) The disability program includes incentives to smooth the disabled individual's transition back into the workforce, including continuation of benefits and healthcare coverage. Disability under the Social Security system is defined as an inability to engage in substantial gainful activity by reason of a physical or mental impairment expected to last at least 12 months or result in death. The impairment must be of such severity that the applicant is not only unable to do his previous work but cannot, considering age, education, and work experience, engage in any other kind of substantial gainful work that exists in the national economy.

FAMILY BENEFITS

If an individual is eligible for retirement or disability benefits, other members of the individual's family might receive benefits as well. Family members who may receive retirement or disability benefits include the following:

- A spouse, if the spouse is 62 years old, caring for a child under age 16, or caring for a child who was disabled before age 22.
- A child, if the child is unmarried and under age 18, under age 19 but still in school, or age 18 or older but disabled.

For those workers who are entitled to retirement or disability benefits, an ex-spouse who was married to the worker for more than 10 years could also be eligible for retirement benefits based on the worker's record.

A child's benefit stops the month before the child reaches 18, unless the child is unmarried and is either disabled or is a full-time elementary or secondary school student. Approximately five months before the child's 18th birthday, the person receiving the child's benefits will get a form explaining how benefits can continue. A child whose benefits stop at 18 can have them started again if the child becomes disabled before reaching 22 or becomes a full-time elementary or secondary school student before reaching 19. If the child continues to receive benefits after age 18 due to a disability, the child also may qualify for SSI disability benefits. When a student's 19th birthday occurs during a school term, benefits can be continued up to two months to allow completion of the school term.

SURVIVORS' BENEFITS

If a worker earned enough Social Security credits during his lifetime, certain members of the worker's family may be eligible for benefits when the worker dies. The family members of the deceased worker who may be entitled to survivors' benefits include:

- A widow or widower age 60, age 50 if disabled, or any age if caring for a child under age 16 or a disabled child.
- A child of the deceased worker, if the child is unmarried and under age 18, under age 19 but still in school, or age 18 or older but disabled.
- Parents of the deceased worker, if the deceased worker was their primary means of support.

A special one-time payment of $255 may be made to a deceased worker's spouse or minor children upon death. If a spouse was living with the beneficiary at the time of death, the spouse will receive a one-time payment of $255. The payment may be made to a spouse who was not living with the beneficiary at the time of death or an ex-spouse if the spouse or ex-spouse was receiving Social Security benefits based on the deceased's earnings record. If there is no surviving spouse, a child (or children) who is eligible for benefits on the deceased's work record in the month of death may claim the payment.

THE MAXIMUM FAMILY BENEFIT

When a person dies, the deceased's survivors receive a percentage of the worker's Social Security benefits ranging from 75 percent to 100 percent each. There is a limit on the amount of monthly Social Security benefits that may be paid to a family. This limit is called the **maximum family benefit** and it is determined through a formula based on the worker's PIA. While the limit varies, it is equal to roughly 150 to 180 percent of the deceased worker's PIA. If the sum of the family members' benefits exceeds the limit, the family members' benefits are proportionately reduced. For old-age and survivor family benefits, the formula computes the sum of four separate percentages of portions of the worker's PIA. For 2016, these portions are the first $1,093 of PIA, the amount between $1,093 and $1,578, the amount between $1,578 and $2,058 and the amount over $2,058. These are the bend points for the maximum family benefit formula for the year 2016, with the following percentage calculations:

> 150 percent of the first $1,093 of the worker's PIA, *plus*
> 272 percent of the worker's PIA over $1,093 through $1,578, *plus*
> 134 percent of the worker's PIA over $1,578 through $2,058, *plus*
> 175 percent of the worker's PIA over $2,058.
> This number is rounded to the next lower $0.10.

QUICK QUIZ 11.4

1. Up to 85% of an individual's Social Security benefits may be included in their taxable income.
   a. True
   b. False

2. Once divorced, non-working ex-spouses will not receive Social Security benefits.
   a. True
   b. False

3. The maximum family benefit establishes a limit on the benefits that can be received by one family.
   a. True
   b. False

True, False, True.

If an individual has the maximum PIA for 2016, $2,639 per month, this would provide a maximum family benefit of $4,660.30 per month as shown by the calculation below:

EXAMPLE 11.30

$1,093 x 1.50 =	$1,639.50
($1,578 - $1,093) x 2.72 =	$1,319.20
($2,058 - $1,578) x 1.34 =	$643.20
($2,639 - $2,058) x 1.75 =	$1,016.75
	$4,618.65
Rounded to	**$4,618.60**

**EXAMPLE
11.31**

Natalie and Brian, both age 50, are married and have two children, Ashley (age 15) and Kayli (age 5). Brian is disabled and has a PIA amount equal to the maximum PIA ($2,639). As seen in the example above, the maximum family benefit is $4,618.60. Because Brian is disabled, Natalie, Ashley, and Kayli are each entitled to receive a benefit equal to 50% of Brian's PIA, subject to the maximum family benefit limit, because the two children are under 18 and Natalie is a spouse/caretaker of a child under 18. Without regard to the maximum family benefit, they would each receive:

Brian	$2,639.00	100% of PIA
Natalie	$1,319.50	50% of Brian's PIA
Ashley	$1,319.50	50% of Brian's PIA
Kayli	$1,319.50	50% of Brian's PIA
Total	$6,597.50	

Because the benefit exceeds the maximum family benefit, the amounts for Natalie, Ashley, and Kayli must be prorated. Therefore, they will each receive $659.87 [($4,618.60 - $2,639)÷3].

Brian	$2,639.00	100% of PIA
Natalie	$659.87	50% of Brian's PIA subject to maximum family benefit
Ashley	$659.87	50% of Brian's PIA subject to maximum family benefit
Kayli	$659.87	50% of Brian's PIA subject to maximum family benefit
Total	$4,618.60	

Assume instead that Ashley is 19 and no longer eligible to receive benefits under Brian. The maximum family benefit would be calculated as follows:

Brian	$2,639.00	100% of PIA
Natalie	$989.80	50% of Brian's PIA subject to maximum family benefit
Ashley	$0.00	Not eligible
Kayli	$989.80	50% of Brian's PIA subject to maximum family benefit
Total	$4,618.60	

Now assume Ashley is 19 and Kayli is 17. In this case, Natalie is no longer eligible because she is not caring for a child under 16. The family benefit would be calculated as follows:

Brian	$2,639	100% of PIA
Natalie	$0	Not eligible
Ashley	$0	Not eligible
Kayli	$1,320	50% of Brian's PIA
Total	$3,959	

Notice that Kayli is limited to 50% of Brian's PIA, thus they do not reach the maximum family benefit.

CHOOSING WHEN TO BEGIN SOCIAL SECURITY RETIREMENT BENEFITS

There are many issues in deciding when to begin receiving Social Security retirement benefits. As discussed earlier in this chapter, Social Security retirement benefits may be reduced if other income is earned before full retirement age, benefits may or may not be subject to income tax, and benefits may be increased or decreased depending on the start date of benefits relative to full retirement age. In addition to these issues, there are other considerations that may impact the total benefits collected by the worker and the worker's spouse.

Ideally, the present value of the total lifetime benefits for a person with an average life expectancy would be the same whether the beneficiary takes a smaller benefit at age 62 or a larger benefit at 70, as the calculations are actuarially based. However, that is not the case. Decisions that are made by a worker can greatly impact both the present value of benefits and total lifetime benefits collected. In fact, even if a retiree's life span is cut short, delaying retirement benefits past age 62 may make sense.

> ## KEY CONCEPTS ✓
>
> 1. How are retirement benefits impacted by cost-of-living adjustments and by delayed credits?
>
> 2. What strategies can be used to potentially increase total lifetime benefits under Social Security?
>
> 3. How can a divorced spouse use "file and suspend?"

As discussed earlier in the chapter, delaying retirement benefits increases the annual benefit when it is received. However, delaying commencement of receipt of retirement benefits should not be confused with a cost-of-living adjustment (COLA). cost-of-living adjustments are averaging about 1.6 percent or 1.7 percent increases over recent years, but once retirement benefits are being paid to a retiree, those benefits only increase based on the COLA. Nonetheless, by delaying benefits from age 62 to 63, the yet-to-be-received benefit increases approximately seven percent for that one year. Delaying benefits for anyone born in or after 1943 beyond full retirement age increases benefits by eight percent per year. That return is large for what is considered to be a very secure investment. Once the Social Security benefit is adjusted for inflation through application of the COLA, the rate is even more attractive.

Is the eight percent increase worth delaying the start of benefits? That question is more complicated than it appears. Some of the important factors in this question are based on an individual's thoughts regarding wealth, cash flow needs, life expectancy, perception of the solvency of the Social Security program, as well as others.

An easy way to estimate a breakeven point for delayed benefits is to consider the benefit that is given up compared to the increase in future benefits. For example, assume a benefit of $1,000 per month or $12,000 per year at full retirement age. If the worker delayed benefits by one year, the benefits would increase by eight percent to $12,960 (without regard to a COLA). Therefore, the benefits that are received are $960 higher, but $12,000 had to be forfeited. Dividing what was given up ($12,000) by the increase ($960) results in a simple breakeven of 12.5 years. This calculation is very simplistic and does not consider the time value of money or other implications, such as taxation of benefits. However, it does provide basic guidance about how long one needs to live to justify giving up current benefits for higher future benefits.

The simplified breakeven analysis can be modified to include a COLA and a discount rate. As the spread between the COLA and the discount rate increases, so does the time it takes for the present value of the delayed benefits to exceed the present value of the benefits commencing immediately. For example, using a discount rate of four percent and a COLA of two percent (a spread of 2 percent) increases the breakeven point from 12.5 years to approximately 14 years. Thus, for someone to delay benefits until age 70 based solely on payback or breakeven, the person would have to live to at least age 82½, without considering the time value of money. However, there are other reasons that delaying benefits may be beneficial to the worker or their family members.

For non-married, lower wage earners who will not qualify for the maximum retirement benefit, it is important to keep in mind that the retirement benefit formula is based on the highest 35 years of work. If a non-married worker had historically lower earnings compared to earnings today, that worker might consider working longer to not only allow the automatic increase or growth of delaying the retirement benefit, but to also serve to increase the 35 year base, which is the basis for determining the retirement benefit. Delaying is especially helpful to those who do not work all 35 years, as that situation tends to have a more noticeable effect on the retirement benefit.

QUICK QUIZ 11.5

1. Delaying benefits to age 70 may be beneficial even if a person does not live beyond age 80.
   a. True
   b. False

2. A worker, who reaches full retirement age at age 67, can increase their benefit, without regard to a COLA, by 32 percent by delaying benefits until age 70.
   a. True
   b. False

3. Surviving spouses are entitled to 100 percent of the deceased worker's benefits after the worker dies.
   a. True
   b. False

True, False, True.

There has been much written on the topic of maximizing Social Security benefits over the last ten years. Strategies, such as "file-and-suspend," have been used to increase the total dollars that retirees would be receive over their lifetime. However, in 2015 Congress chose to eliminate the benefits of this strategy as they were seen by some as taking advantage of the system. In fairness, the file-and-suspend strategy did provide greater benefits to many seniors. However, the Bipartisan Budget Act (BBA) of 2015 eliminates file and suspend after April 29, 2016.

Married individuals are entitled (1) to a worker-determined retirement benefit based on their own earnings and/or (2) to a spousal benefit equal to one half of their spouse's benefit claimed at normal retirement age. If a married individual files a claim prior to attaining normal retirement age, the laws governing Social Security deem the individual as claiming both types of benefits and the benefits will be permanently reduced.

> Stacy Lynn qualifies for a retirement benefit of $250 and a spouse's benefit of $400. At her full retirement age, she will receive her own $250 retirement benefit, and $150 from her spouse's benefit, for a total of $400. If she takes her retirement benefit before her full retirement age, both amounts will be reduced.

EXAMPLE 11.32

Surviving spouses are entitled to 100 percent of the deceased worker's benefit amount after the worker dies. If the spouse with the higher benefits delays benefits until age 70 and then dies, it will increase the surviving spouse's benefit. This approach was one element of the file-and-suspend strategy. However, it does not appear that the new legislation impacts how this works.

Divorced spouses can also claim benefits based on their ex-spouse's record if they were married ten years or longer. Generally, the divorced spouse can collect based on their ex-spouse's record as long as they are unmarried, they are age 62 or older, and the ex-spouse is entitled to Social Security retirement or disability benefits. If a divorced spouse has reached full retirement age and is eligible for a spouse's benefit, then he or she can choose to receive only the divorced spouse's benefits and delay receiving their own retirement benefits until a later date. If retirement benefits are delayed, a higher benefit may be received at a later date based on the effect of delayed retirement credits. Thus, in effect, the spouse is able to receive a benefit from the ex-spouse's working history and let their own benefit increase until age 70.

> Jimmy and Cindy were happily married and raised four wonderful children, who went on to become contributing members of society: a butcher, a baker, a dancer, and a home maker. However, once the children left the home, Jimmy and Cindy grew apart and finally divorced after 25 years of marriage. They both were professionals early in their career and became college professors. As a result, their retirement benefits are comparable. While Jimmy has remarried, Cindy remains single. At full retirement age, Cindy could claim a spouse's benefit and let her retirement benefits increase until she turns age 70.

EXAMPLE 11.33

Deciding when to begin taking Social Security benefits should be planned as it can greatly impact the total benefits received over the life of a a worker and the worker's spouse. The planning should take into consideration the health and longevity of the spouses, as well as the need for income now and into the future.

MEDICARE BENEFITS

Medicare is a federal health insurance plan for people who are 65 and older, whether retired or still working. People who are disabled or have permanent kidney failure are entitled to Medicare at any age. The Health Care Financing Administration, now known as Centers for Medicare and Medicaid Services (or CMS), part of the United States Department of Health and Human Services, administers Medicare. Medicare is the nation's largest health insurance program, covering over 50 million individuals. There are three parts to Medicare: Hospital Insurance (Part A), Medical Insurance (Part B), and Prescription Drug Coverage (Part D).

KEY CONCEPTS

1. What benefits are provided by Medicare?

2. What benefits are provided by Supplemental Security Income?

3. How does marriage or divorce affect Social Security benefits?

Generally, individuals who are over age 65 and receive Social Security benefits automatically qualify for Medicare. Also, individuals who have received Social Security disability benefits for at least two years automatically qualify for Medicare. All other individuals must file an application for Medicare.

EXHIBIT 11.18

MEDICARE PARTS

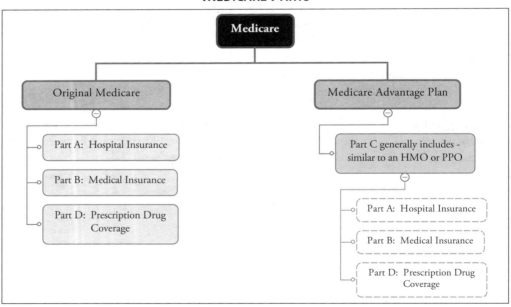

Part A, Hospital Insurance, is paid for by a portion of the Social Security tax. Part A helps pay for necessary medical care furnished by Medicare-certified providers, including inpatient hospital care, skilled nursing care, home health care, hospice care, and other care. The number of days that Medicare covers care in hospitals and skilled nursing facilities is measured in what is termed **benefit periods.** A benefit period begins on the first day a patient receives services in a hospital or skilled nursing facility and ends after 60 consecutive days without further skilled care. There is no limit to the number of benefit periods a beneficiary may have.

Benefit periods are identified because deductibles, coinsurance, and premiums relate to a benefit period instead of a calendar year. For instance, coverage under Medicare Part A for 2016 requires a deductible of $1,288 per benefit period. For the 61st through the 90th day of each benefit period, the insured individual must pay $322 per day in the form of coinsurance. Any days over 90 in a benefit period are considered lifetime reserve days. There are 60 lifetime reserve days available with coinsurance of $644 per day. Lifetime reserve days do not renew with each benefit period. It is important, therefore, to determine the number of days used in each benefit period.

MEDICARE TIME LINE

EXHIBIT 11.19

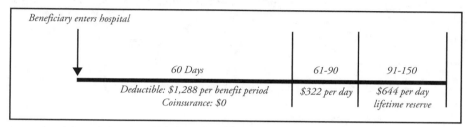

SKILLED NURSING FACILITY TIME LINE

EXHIBIT 11.20

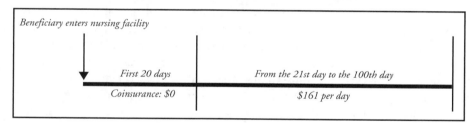

EXHIBIT
11.21

MEDICARE DEDUCTIBLE, COINSURANCE, AND PREMIUM AMOUNTS (2016)

Hospital Insurance (Part A)
• **Deductible** - $1,288 per Benefit Period
• **Coinsurance**
• $322 a day for the 61st through the 90th day
• $644 a day for the 91st through the 150th day for each lifetime reserve day (total of 60 lifetime reserve days – nonrenewable)
• **Skilled Nursing Facility coinsurance** - $161 a day for the 21st through the 100th day per Benefit Period
• **Hospital Insurance Premium** - $411 per month (Note: This premium is paid only by individuals who are not otherwise eligible for premium-free hospital insurance and have less than 30 quarters of Medicare covered employment.)
Medical Insurance (Part B)
• **Deductible** - $166 per year
• **Standard Monthly Premium** - $121.80 for new enrollees in 2016. The premium may be higher if income exceeds certain limits. However, most people who receive Social Security benefits will pay the same price as in 2015, which is $104.90.

Source: Social Security Administration (www.ssa.gov)

Medicare Part A helps pay for up to 90 days of inpatient hospital care during each benefit period. Covered services for inpatient hospital care include: semiprivate room and meals, operating and recovery room costs, intensive care, drugs, laboratory tests, x-rays, general nursing services, and any other necessary medical services and supplies. Convenience items such as television and telephones provided by hospitals in private rooms (unless medically necessary) are generally not covered. Medicare does not pay for custodial services for daily living activities such as eating, bathing, and getting dressed. Medicare does, however, pay for skilled nursing facility care for rehabilitation, such as recovery time after a hospital discharge. Part A may help pay for up to 100 days in a participating skilled nursing facility in each benefit period. Medicare pays all approved charges for the first 20 days relating to skilled nursing facility care, and the patient pays a coinsurance amount for days 21 through 100. Medicare may also pay the full, approved cost of covered home healthcare services, which includes part-time or intermittent skilled nursing services prescribed by a physician for treatment or rehabilitation of home-bound patients. Normally, the only cost to the insured for home health care is a 20 percent coinsurance charge for medical equipment, such as wheelchairs and walkers.

Medicare Part B, Medical Insurance, is optional and is subject to a monthly premium. Part B is financed by the monthly premiums paid by those who are enrolled and out of the general revenues from the U.S. Treasury. Medicare Part B is used to pay for doctors' services; ambulance transportation; diagnostic tests; outpatient therapy services; outpatient hospital services, including emergency room visits; X-rays and laboratory services; some preventative care; home healthcare services not covered by Part A; durable medical equipment and supplies; and a variety of other health services.

Medicare Part B pays for 80 percent of approved charges for most covered services. Unless an individual declines Part B medical insurance protection, the premium will automatically be deducted from their Social Security benefits. The standard Part B premium amount is $121.80 (or higher depending on your income). However, most people who get Social Security benefits will continue to pay the same Part B premium amount in 2016 as they paid in 2015, which is $104.90.

The deductible for Part B is $166 per year. The insured is responsible for paying a $166 deductible per calendar year and the remaining 20 percent of the Medicare-approved charges. Medicare Part B usually does not cover charges for prescription drugs, routine physical examinations, or services unrelated to treatment of injury or illness. Dental care, dentures, cosmetic surgery, hearing aids, and eye examinations are not covered by Part B.

MEDICARE PART B PREMIUMS (2016)

EXHIBIT
11.22

Premium	Filing Status: Single	Filing Status: MFJ
$121.80	$85,000 or less	$170,000 or less
$170.50	$85,001-$107,000	$170,001-$214,000
$243.60	$107,001-$160,000	$214,001-$320,000
$316.70	$160,001-$214,000	$320,001-$428,000
$389.80	Above $214,000	Above $428,000

Various plans under Medicare are available to insureds. The original Medicare Plan is the way most individuals get their Medicare Part A and Part B benefits. This is the traditional payment-per-service arrangement where the individual insured may go to any doctor, specialist, or hospital that accepts Medicare, and Medicare pays its share after services are rendered. Medicare carriers and fiscal intermediaries are private insurance organizations that handle claims under the original Medicare Plan. Carriers handle Part B claims while fiscal intermediaries handle Part A plans. The Social Security Administration does not handle claims for Medicare payments.

Many private insurance companies sell Medicare supplemental insurance policies, such as Medigap and Medicare SELECT. These supplemental policies help bridge the coverage gaps in the original Medicare Plan. These supplemental policies also help pay Medicare's coinsurance amounts and deductibles, as well as other out-of-pocket expenses for health care.

When a worker is first enrolled in Part B at age 65, there is a six-month open enrollment period in Medigap. During the time of open enrollment, the health status of the applicant cannot be used as a reason to refuse a Medigap policy or to charge more than other open enrollment applicants. The insurer may require a six-month waiting period for coverage of pre-existing conditions. If, however, the open enrollment period has expired, the applicant may be denied a policy based on health status or may be charged higher rates.

MEDICARE PART D SUBSIDY

Medicare prescription drug plans, known as the Medicare Part D Subsidy (Part D or Medicare Prescription Drug Plan), became available beginning January 1, 2006, to individuals with Medicare. Part D is intended to save participants money on prescription drug costs and help protect against higher drug costs in the future. Insurance companies and other private companies work with Medicare to offer these drug plans by negotiating discounts on drug prices. These plans are different from the Medicare-approved drug discount cards, which were phased out by the earlier of May 15, 2006 or when an individual's enrollment in a Medicare prescription drug plan took effect.

Medicare prescription drug plans provide insurance coverage for prescription drugs. Part D covers both brand-name and generic prescription drugs at certain pharmacies in a Part D participant's area. If an individual is enrolled in Medicare, then that individual is eligible under Part D regardless of income, assets, health status, or current prescription expenses. Like other insurance, if an individual joins, they pay a monthly premium and pay a share of the cost of their prescriptions. As with Part B, higher income taxpayers will pay higher premiums. In addition, the premiums increase for delayed enrollment into the program by a factor of the "national base beneficiary premium" times the number of full, uncovered months that a senior was eligible but did not join a Medicare drug plan and went without other creditable prescription drug coverage. This premium increase may have to be paid for as long as the Medicare drug plan is maintained.

> **EXAMPLE 11.34**
>
> Mrs. Jones did not join Part D when she was first eligible - by May 15, 2011. She joined a Medicare drug plan with an effective date of January 1, 2016. Since Mrs. Jones did not join when she was first eligible and went without other creditable drug coverage for 55 months (June 2011 to December 2015), she will be charged a monthly penalty of $19.25 in 2016 ($35 x 0.01 = $0.35 x 55 = $19.25) in addition to her plan's monthly premium.[5]

Individuals may enroll in Part D when they first become eligible for Medicare, which is three months before the month the applicant turns age 65 until three months after the applicant turns age 65. If Medicare was available due to a disability, the applicant can join from three months before to three months after the 25th month of cash disability payments. There are two ways to obtain Medicare prescription drug coverage. The individual can either join a Medicare prescription drug plan or join a Medicare Advantage Plan or other Medicare Health Plan that offers drug coverage. Whichever plan is chosen, Medicare drug coverage helps the participant by covering brand name and generic drugs at pharmacies.

Drug plans may vary as to what prescription drugs are covered, how much the individual must pay, and which pharmacies they can use. All drug plans will have to provide at least a standard level of coverage, which Medicare will set. The premium, deductible, co-payment/co-insurance, and coverage may vary from plan to plan. However, some plans might offer more coverage and additional drugs for a higher monthly premium. When an individual joins a drug plan, it is important for them to choose one that meets their prescription drug needs. A list of drugs that a Medicare drug plan covers is called a formulary, which includes generic drugs and brand name drugs. Most prescription drugs used by those with Medicare will be on the given plan formulary, whether it is in brand name or generic form. To insure coverage of an appropriate amount of drugs, a formulary must include at least two drugs in categories and classes of most commonly prescribed drugs to those individuals with Medicare. This helps to insure that people with varying medical conditions can get the medication or treatment they need.

---

5. The "national base beneficiary premium" of $35 is assumed for this example. The 2016 premium is actually $34.10.

Even individuals who do not use a lot of prescription drugs should consider joining Part D because aging people often need prescription drugs to stay healthy. For a relatively low premium, Medicare prescription drug coverage can protect the individual from unexpected drug expenses in the future.

Part D consists of four phases of coverage: the deductible, the coinsurance phase, the coverage gap, and the catastrophic phase. The deductible must be satisfied prior to any benefits being provided from the plan. In the initial phase, sometimes referred to as the coinsurance phase, beneficiaries pay a portion of the expenses up to an annual limit. The coverage gap is often referred to as "donut hole" because in this phase, beneficiaries pay most of the costs of prescription drugs, but may receive discounts depending on the plan. The catastrophic phase covers all but a small coinsurance amount for the remainder of the year.

OTHER MEDICARE HEALTH PLAN CHOICES

Medicare offers alternative methods of obtaining Medicare benefits through other health plan choices. Choices that vary by area include coordinated-care or Medicare managed care plans such as Health Maintenance Organizations (HMOs), HMOs with a point of service option, Provider Sponsored Organizations (PSOs), and Preferred Provider Organizations (PPOs). These plans involve specific groups of doctors, hospitals, and other providers who provide care to the insured as a member of the plan, like many employer-sponsored plans throughout the country. Medicare managed-care plans not only provide the same services that are covered by Part A and Part B, but most Medicare managed plans offer a variety of additional benefits like preventative care, prescription drugs, dental care, eyeglasses, and other items not covered by the original Medicare Plan. The cost of these extra benefits varies among the plans.

For those who receive Medicare and have low income and few resources, states may pay Medicare premiums and, in some cases, other out-of-pocket Medicare expenses, such as deductibles and coinsurance. The respective state decides if individuals qualify. For more general information about Medicare, the Social Security Administration's leaflet *Medicare Savings for Qualified Beneficiaries* (HCFA Publication No. 02184) is helpful, as are the websites *www.ssa.gov* and *www.medicare.gov*.

SUPPLEMENTAL SECURITY INCOME BENEFITS

Supplemental Security Income (SSI) makes monthly payments to individuals with low incomes and few assets. In order to obtain SSI benefits, an individual must be age 65, disabled, or blind. The definition of disability is satisfied when the individual is unable to engage in any substantial gainful activity due to a physical or mental problem expected to last at least a year or expected to result in death. Children as well as adults qualify for SSI disability payments. As its name implies, Supplemental Security Income supplements the beneficiary's income up to various levels depending on where the beneficiary lives. If an otherwise eligible SSI applicant lives in another's household and receives support from that person, the federal SSI benefit is reduced by one-third.

The federal government pays a basic rate. The basic monthly SSI check for 2016 is $733 per month for one person and $1,100 per month for married couples. Some states supply additional funds to qualified individuals. To ascertain the SSI benefit rates in a certain state, the advisor or client can contact a local Social Security office in that state or visit the Social Security

Administration's website. Generally, individuals who receive SSI benefits also qualify for Medicaid, food stamps, and other government assistance.

To be eligible for the monthly SSI benefit, the beneficiary must not have assets that exceed $2,000 for one person or $3,000 for married couples. This asset determination does not include the value of the home and some personal belongings, such as one car. If the potential beneficiary does not work, he may be eligible for SSI benefits if monthly income is less than $733 for one person and $1,100 for a couple. If the potential beneficiary works, more monthly income is allowed. SSI benefits are not paid from Social Security trust funds and are not based on past earnings of the beneficiary. Rather, SSI benefits are financed by general tax revenues and assure a minimum monthly income for needy elderly, disabled, or blind persons.

FILING FOR SOCIAL SECURITY CLAIMS

The Social Security Administration reports that many people fail to file claims with the Social Security Administration or fail to do so in a timely fashion. Individuals should file for Social Security or SSI disability benefits as soon they become too disabled to work or for survivors' benefits, when a family breadwinner dies. Social Security benefits do not start automatically. Social Security will not begin payment of benefits until the beneficiary files an application. When filing for benefits, applicants must submit documents that show eligibility, such as a birth certificate for each family member applying for benefits, a marriage certificate if a spouse is applying, and the most recent W-2 forms or tax returns.

To file for benefits, obtain information, or to speak to a Social Security representative, individuals must call the Social Security Administration's toll-free number, 800-772-1213, or visit the Social Security Administration's website. The toll-free number can be used to schedule an appointment at a local Social Security office. The Social Security Administration treats all calls confidentially. Periodically, a second Social Security representative will monitor incoming and outgoing telephone calls to ensure accurate and courteous service.

OTHER ISSUES

EFFECT OF MARRIAGE OR DIVORCE ON BENEFITS

Marriage or divorce may affect one's Social Security benefits, depending on the kind of benefits received. If a worker receives retirement benefits based on his own earnings record, the worker's retirement benefits will continue whether married or divorced. If an individual receives benefits based on his spouse's record, the individual's benefits will cease upon divorce unless the individual is age 62 or older and was married longer than 10 years. Widows and widowers, whether divorced or not, will continue to receive survivors' benefits upon remarriage if the widow or widower is age 60 or older. Disabled widows and widowers, whether divorced or not, will continue to receive survivors' benefits upon remarriage if the disabled widow or widower is age 50 or older.

Larry was married at the following ages and to the following wives. Larry is now 62 and married to Dawn.

EXAMPLE
11.35

	Wife	Current Age	Larry's Age at Marriage	Current Marital Status	Length of Marriage
1	Alice	62	20	Single	10 years, 1 month
2	Betty	63	31	Single	10 years, 1 month
3	Claire	64	42	Single	9 years
4	Dawn	65	53	Married	9 years

Who, among the wives, may be eligible to receive Social Security retirement benefits based upon Larry's earnings if Larry is retired or not retired?

Any divorced spouse, age 62 and married to Larry for 10 years or longer is eligible to receive benefits. If Larry is retired, then his current wife is also eligible to receive benefits. However, she cannot collect benefits if he is not retired.

If Larry is retired: Alice, Betty, and Dawn.

If Larry is not retired: Alice and Betty.

For all other forms of Social Security benefits, benefits will cease upon remarriage, except in special circumstances. When a person marries, it is presumed that at least one person in the marriage can provide adequate support. Likewise, Social Security benefits may recommence based on the previous spouse's benefits if the marriage ends.

CHANGE OF NAME

If an individual changes their name due to marriage, divorce, or a court order, that individual must notify the Social Security Administration of the name change so the Social Security Administration will be able to show the new name in their records and properly credit that individual for earnings. This notice will ensure that the individual's work history will be accurately recorded and maintained.

LEAVING THE UNITED STATES

Beneficiaries who are United States citizens may travel or live in most foreign countries without affecting their eligibility for Social Security benefits. However, there are a few countries where Social Security checks cannot be sent. These countries currently include Cuba, and North Korea.

Also, beneficiaries that go to any of the following countries can receive Social Security benefits only if they meet and agree to certain restricted conditions. These countries are:

- Azerbaijan
- Belarus
- Georgia
- Kazakhstan
- Kyrgyzstan
- Moldova
- Tajikistan
- Turkmenistan
- Ukraine
- Uzbekistan
- Vietnam

QUICK QUIZ 11.6

1. Medicare Part A generally pays for "Places" while Part B pays for "Services."
   a. True
   b. False

2. In order to obtain Supplemental Social Security benefits, the individual must be 62, disabled, or blind.
   a. True
   b. False

3. Social Security beneficiaries who are United States citizens may live in most foreign countries without affecting their eligibility for Social Security benefits.
   a. True
   b. False

True, False, True.

Beneficiaries should inform the Social Security Administration of their plans to go outside the United States for a trip that lasts 30 days or more. By providing the name of the country or countries to be visited and the expected departure and return dates, the Social Security Administration will send special reporting instructions to the beneficiaries and arrange for the delivery of their checks while they are abroad.

2016 SOCIAL SECURITY FACT SHEET

EXHIBIT
11.23

Fact Sheet

SOCIAL SECURITY

2016 SOCIAL SECURITY CHANGES

o   **Cost-of-Living Adjustment (COLA):**

Monthly Social Security and Supplemental Security Income (SSI) benefits will not automatically increase in 2016 as there was no increase in the Consumer Price Index (CPI-W) from the third quarter of 2014 to the third quarter of 2015. Other important 2016 Social Security information is as follows:

	2015	2016
o **Tax Rate:**		
Employee	7.65%	7.65%
Self-Employed	15.30%	15.30%

NOTE: The 7.65% tax rate is the combined rate for Social Security and Medicare. The Social Security portion (OASDI) is 6.20% on earnings up to the applicable taxable maximum amount (see below). The Medicare portion (HI) is 1.45% on all earnings. Also, as of January 2013, individuals with earned income of more than $200,000 ($250,000 for married couples filing jointly) pay an additional 0.9 percent in Medicare taxes. The tax rates shown above do not include the 0.9 percent.

o   **Maximum Taxable Earnings:**

Social Security (OASDI only)	$118,500	$118,500*
Medicare (HI only)	No Limit	

o   **Quarter of Coverage:** $1,220 $1,260

o   **Retirement Earnings Test Exempt Amounts:**

Under full retirement age	$15,720/yr.	$15,720/yr.*
	($1,310/mo.)	($1,310/mo.)

> NOTE: One dollar in benefits will be withheld for every $2 in earnings above the limit.

The year an individual reaches full retirement age	$41,880/yr.	$41,880/yr.*
	($3,490/mo.)	($3,490/mo.)

> NOTE: Applies only to earnings for months prior to attaining full retirement age. One dollar in benefits will be withheld for every $3 in earnings above the limit.

SSA Press Office 440 Altmeyer Building 6401 Security Blvd. Baltimore, MD 21235 410-965-8904 FAX 410-966-9973

There is no limit on earnings beginning the month an individual attains full retirement age.

o **Social Security Disability Thresholds:**

Substantial Gainful Activity (SGA)

Non-Blind	$1,090/mo.	$1,130/mo.
Blind	$1,820/mo.	$1,820/mo.*
Trial Work Period (TWP)	$ 780/mo.	$ 810/mo.

o **Maximum Social Security Benefit:** Worker Retiring at Full Retirement Age:

$2,663/mo.	$2,639/mo.**

o **SSI Federal Payment Standard:**

Individual	$ 733/mo.	$ 733/mo.*
Couple	$1,100/mo.	$1,100/mo.*

o **SSI Resources Limits:**

Individual	$2,000	$2,000
Couple	$3,000	$3,000

o **SSI Student Exclusion:**

Monthly limit	$1,780	$1,780*
Annual limit	$7,180	$7,180*

o **Estimated Average Monthly Social Security Benefits Payable in January 2016:**

All Retired Workers	$1,341
Aged Couple, Both Receiving Benefits	$2,212
Widowed Mother and Two Children	$2,680
Aged Widow(er) Alone	$1,285
Disabled Worker, Spouse and One or More Children	$1,983
All Disabled Workers	$1,166

* Because there is no COLA, by law these amounts remain unchanged in 2016.

** A decrease in full maximum benefits occurs when there is no COLA, but there is an increase in the national average wage index.

KEY TERMS

AIME (Average Indexed Monthly Earnings) - A worker's highest 35 years of earnings adjusted for inflation and averaged on a monthly basis. AIME is used as the basis for the PIA calculation.

Benefit Periods - Begins on the first day an individual receives services as a patient in a hospital or skilled nursing facility and ends after 60 consecutive days without further skilled care.

Cost-of-Living Adjustment (COLA) - The cost-of-living adjustments applied to Social Security benefits.

Currently Insured Workers - A worker who has earned at least six quarters of coverage out of the previous 13 quarters for Social Security.

Disability Benefit - A Social Security benefit available to recipients who have a severe physical or mental impairment that is expected to prevent them from performing "substantial" work for at least a year or result in death. To qualify for these benefits, the recipient must have the sufficient amount of Social Security credits.

Disability Insurance (DI) Trust Fund - The trust fund that pays benefits to workers with disabilities and their families. It is funded by 0.90 percent of an individual's taxable earnings up to $118,500 (2016).

Family Benefit - A Social Security benefit available to certain family members of workers eligible for retirement or disability benefits.

FICA (Federal Insurance Contributions Act) - A law allowing Social Security taxes, including Medicare taxes, to be deducted from employee's paychecks.

Fully Insured - A worker who has earned 40 quarters of coverage under the Social Security system.

Hospital Insurance (HI) Trust Fund - The trust fund that pays for services covered under the hospital insurance provisions of Medicare (Part A). It is funded by 1.45 percent of an individual's taxable earnings (no limitation).

Maximum Family Benefit - The limit on the amount of monthly Social Security benefits that may be paid to a family.

Medicaid - Provides medical assistance for persons with low incomes and resources.

Medicare - A federal health insurance plan for those who have attained full retirement age or have been disabled whether retired or still working.

KEY TERMS

MODIFIED ADJUSTED GROSS INCOME (WHEN CALCULATING TAXABLE SOCIAL SECURITY) - The sum of an individual's adjusted gross income plus tax exempt interest, including interest earned on savings bonds used for higher education; amounts excluded from the taxpayer's income for employer provided adoption assistance; amounts deducted for interest paid for educational loans; amounts deducted as qualified tuition expense; and income earned in a foreign country, a U.S. possession, or Puerto Rico that is excluded from income.

OLD AGE, SURVIVOR, AND DISABILITY INSURANCE (OASDI) - An inclusive title given to the Social Security benefit system.

OLD AGE AND SURVIVORS INSURANCE (OASI) - The trust fund that pays retirement and survivors' benefits funded by 5.30 percent of an individual's taxable earnings up to $118,500 (2016).

PIA (PRIMARY INSURANCE AMOUNT) - The amount on which a worker's retirement benefit is based; the PIA determines the amount the applicant will receive at his full retirement age based on the year in which the retiree turns 62. The PIA is indexed to the Consumer Price Index (CPI) annually.

RETIREMENT BENEFIT - The most familiar Social Security benefit, full retirement benefits are payable at normal retirement age and reduced benefits as early as age 62 to anyone who has obtained at least a minimum (40 quarters) amount of Social Security credits.

RETIREMENT EARNINGS LIMITATIONS TEST - A test that may reduce the Social Security benefit paid to an individual based on their other income.

SSI (SUPPLEMENTAL SECURITY INCOME) - A program administered by the Social Security Administration and funded by the general Treasury that is available to those at full retirement age or the disabled who have a low income and few assets.

SUPPLEMENTARY MEDICAL INSURANCE (SMI) TRUST FUND - The trust fund that pays for services covered under the medical insurance provisions of Medicare, known as Part B. The coverage is funded by general federal tax revenues and monthly medicare premiums paid by enrollees.

SURVIVORS' BENEFIT - Social Security benefit available to surviving family members of a deceased, eligible worker.

DISCUSSION QUESTIONS

1. List and describe the six major categories of benefits administered by the Social Security Association.

2. How are Social Security funds collected?

3. Which individuals are covered workers under the Social Security system?

4. List the beneficiaries of Social Security benefits.

5. How is a person's Social Security retirement benefit calculated?

6. How does retiring early or retiring late affect the calculation of Social Security benefits?

7. How are Social Security benefits taxed?

8. What other benefits are available from Social Security other than retirement benefits?

9. Discuss the maximum family benefit.

10. What Social Security benefits does Medicare provide?

11. Describe Supplemental Security Income benefits and when they are available.

12. How does marriage or divorce affect Social Security benefits?

MULTIPLE CHOICE PROBLEMS

1. Social Security is funded through all of the following except:

    a. Employee payroll tax.

    b. Employer payroll tax.

    c. Sales tax.

    d. Self-employment tax.

2. Brisco, now deceased, was married for 12 years. He had two dependent children, ages 10 and 12, who are cared for by their mother age 48. His mother, age 75, was his dependent and survived him. At the time of his death, he was currently but not fully insured under Social Security. His dependents are entitled to all of the following benefits except:

    a. A lump-sum death benefit of $255.

    b. A children's benefit equal to 75% of Brisco's PIA.

    c. A caretaker's benefit for the children's mother.

    d. A parent's benefit.

3. Medicare Part A provides hospital coverage. Which of the following persons is not covered under Part A?

    a. A person 62 or older and receiving railroad retirement.

    b. Disabled beneficiaries regardless of age that have received Social Security for two years.

    c. Chronic kidney patients who require dialysis or a renal transplant.

    d. A person 65 or older entitled to a monthly Social Security check.

4. Part B of Medicare is considered to be supplemental insurance and provides additional coverage to participants. Which of the following is true regarding Part B coverage?

    a. The election to participate must be made at the time the insured is eligible for Part A Medicare and at no time after.

    b. The premiums for Part B are paid monthly through withholding from Social Security benefits.

    c. Once a participant elects Part B, he must maintain the coverage until death.

    d. Coverage under Part B does not include deductibles or coinsurance.

5. A person receiving Social Security benefits under the age of 65 can receive earned income up to a maximum threshold without reducing Social Security benefits by the earnings test. Which of the following count against the earnings threshold?

    a. Dividends from stocks.

    b. Rental income.

    c. Pensions and insurance annuities.

    d. Gambling winnings.

6. Betty Sue, age 75, is a widow with no close relatives. She is very ill, unable to walk, and confined to a custodial nursing home. Which of the following programs is likely to pay benefits towards the cost of the nursing home?

    1. Medicare may pay for up to 80 additional days of care after a 20-day deductible.

    2. Medicaid may pay if the client has income and assets below state-mandated thresholds.

    a. 1 only.

    b. 2 only.

    c. Both 1 and 2.

    d. Neither 1 nor 2.

7. Which of the following concerning the Social Security system is correct?

    a. SSI benefits are funded by the Treasury, not Social Security taxes, as are the other benefits.

    b. The Social Security retirement benefit is payable at full retirement age with reduced benefits as early as age 59 to anyone who has obtained at least a minimum amount of Social Security benefits.

    c. The two Medicare trust funds are the federal Medical Insurance Trust Fund for Part A and the Supplementary Hospital Insurance Trust Fund for Part B of Medicare benefits.

    d. Benefits can be paid to the dependent parents of a deceased insured worker at age 59 or over.

8. Which of the following concerning the Social Security system is correct?

    a. Workers entitled to retirement benefits can currently take early retirement benefits as early as age 59.

    b. A worker who takes early retirement benefits will receive a reduced benefit because he will receive more monthly benefit payments as payments commence earlier than if the worker had waited and retired at full retirement age.

    c. Family members of an individual who are eligible for retirement or disability benefits include a spouse if the spouse is at least 59 years old or under 59 but caring for a child under age 16.

    d. Generally, individuals who are over the age of 59 and receive Social Security benefits automatically qualify for Medicare benefits.

9. All of the following statements concerning the Social Security system are correct except:

    a. If a worker receives retirement benefits based on his own earnings record, the worker's retirement benefits will continue whether married or divorced.

    b. Widows and widowers, whether divorced or not, will continue to receive survivors' benefits upon remarriage if the widow or widower is age 60 or older.

    c. By providing the name of a country or countries to be visited and the expected departure and return dates, the Social Security Administration will send special reporting instructions to the beneficiaries and arrange for delivery of checks while abroad.

    d. A special one-time payment of $1,000 may be made to a deceased worker's spouse or minor children upon death.

10. All of the following statements concerning Social Security benefits are correct except:

    a. The maximum family benefit is determined through a formula based on the worker's PIA.

    b. If a worker applies for retirement or survivors' benefits before his 65th birthday, he must also file a separate application for Medicare.

    c. People who are disabled or have permanent kidney failure can get Medicare at any age.

    d. The Social Security Administration is concerned with beneficiaries' combined income, which, on the 1040 federal tax return, includes adjusted gross income and nontaxable interest income.

11. All of the following statements concerning Social Security benefits are correct except:

    a. In order to obtain SSI benefits, an individual must be age 65 or older and must be disabled.

    b. The number of days that Medicare covers care in hospitals and skilled nursing facilities is measured in what is termed benefit periods.

    c. The definition of disability is that the individual is unable to engage in any substantial gainful activity due to a physical or mental problem expected to last at least a year or expected to result in death.

    d. Benefits are payable at any age to workers who have enough Social Security credits and who have a severe physical or mental impairment that is expected to prevent them from doing "substantial" work for a year or more or who have a condition that is expected to result in death.

12. Joyce and Melvin have been married for 30 years. In 2016, they received $22,000 of Social Security benefits and had $12,000 of interest income. What portion of the Social Security benefit is taxable?

    a. $0.

    b. $6,000.

    c. $10,200.

    d. $11,500.

13. Emile is single and received $28,000 of dividend income during the year. He also received $18,000 of Social Security benefits. What portion of his Social Security benefits are taxable?

    a. $0.

    b. $7,050.

    c. $9,000.

    d. $15,300.

14. Antoine immigrated from Italy last century, became a citizen and has worked the better part of his life in the United States, for which he is truly thankful. His full retirement age (normal retirement age) for Social Security benefits is age 66, but after a hard life working he wants to retire at age 63 and travel throughout America and back to his homeland. If his benefit at age 66 is $1,000 per month, how much will he receive in Social Security retirement benefits if he begins receiving benefits at age 63?

    a. $700.00.

    b. $800.00.

    c. $812.50.

    d. $1,000.00. The same benefit, he will simply not receive it for as long.

15. Antoine immigrated from Italy last century, became a citizen and has worked the better part of his life in the United States, for which he is truly thankful. His full retirement age for Social Security benefits is age 66, but after a hard life working he wants to retire at age 63 and travel in America and back to his homeland. After contacting the Social Security administration, they informed him that his benefit at age 63 would be $1,200 per month. Just prior to retiring, he sold his business for $100,000. Which of the following statements is correct?

    a. The sale of the business will not impact the amount of his retirement benefits from Social Security.

    b. The sale of the business will cause his benefits to be reduced by $1 for every $2 over the annual limit.

    c. The sale of the business will definitely increase the portion of his Social Security benefits that are subject to income tax.

    d. The sale of the business may cause him to pay a higher Medicare Part B premium in the year of the sale due to his higher income.

16. Antoine immigrated from Italy last century, became a citizen and has worked the better part of his life in the United States, for which he is truly thankful. His full retirement age for Social Security benefits is age 66, but after a hard life working he wants to retire at age 63 and travel in America and back to his homeland. He sold his restaurant for $150,000 and was retained by the acquiring company as a consultant for a one-year period. His consulting fee this year will be $50,000 and the benefit he expects to receive from Social Security is $2,000 per month. Which of the following statements is correct?

    a. He should delay receiving Social Security retirement benefits until after this year because he will be in a high tax bracket due to the sale of his business.

    b. He should delay receiving Social Security retirement benefits until after this year because there will be such a large reduction in benefits due to his consulting income and the sale of the business.

    c. He should begin receiving Social Security benefits today because although there is a reduction in benefits today, there will be an increase after full retirement age.

    d. He would be better off beginning Social Security benefits next year.

17. Kathryn taught at Fun Academic University for 25 years and is filing for Social Security retirement benefits this year, when she turns age 72. Her PIA is $1,000 per month as adjusted for inflation. How much in benefits will she receive assuming her full retirement age was 66?

    a. $1,320.

    b. $1,360.

    c. $1,480.

    d. $1,587.

18. A worker's AIME:

    a. Must be determined by converting actual earnings into current dollars through an indexing factor.

    b. Is determined from wage information over prior years' work.

    c. Uses the highest 35 years of indexed earnings (for workers that worked at least that long).

    d. Yields an average amount of monthly earnings for all indexed years.

    e. All of the above.

19. Robin Elizabeth qualifies for a retirement benefit of $250 and a spouse's benefit of $400. At her full retirement age, she will receive which of the following?

    a. Both $250 and $400

    b. The higher of her benefit or her spouse's benefit.

    c. Her spouse's benefit of $400.

    d. Her benefit of $250 plus $150 from her spouse's benefit.

20. Which of the following are correct?

    a. Surviving spouses are entitled to 100 percent of the worker's benefit amount after the worker dies.

    b. Divorced spouses can also claim benefits based on their ex-spouse's record if they were married 8 years or longer.

    c. For someone to delay benefits until age 70 based solely on payback or breakeven, the person would have to live to at least age 92, without considering the time value of money.

    d. All of the above are false.

QUICK QUIZ EXPLANATIONS

QUICK QUIZ 11.1
1. False. Reduced Social Security benefits can be withdrawn as early as age 62.
2. False. Social Security contributions are placed in the following trust funds: OASI, DI, and HI. The SMI Trust Fund is not funded by Social Security contributions.

QUICK QUIZ 11.2
1. True.
2. True.

QUICK QUIZ 11.3
1. False. The Social Security retirement benefit is based on the worker's PIA. A worker's PIA is based on the worker's average indexed monthly earnings during the 35 years in which the worker earned the most.
2. False. Full retirement age for Social Security is increasing because of increasing life expectancies.

QUICK QUIZ 11.4
1. True.
2. False. Once divorced, a non-working ex-spouse who was married to the worker for more than ten years can still receive Social Security benefits based on the worker's record.
3. True.

QUICK QUIZ 11.5
1. True.
2. False. The increase equals 8 percent per year times three years, which is a 24 percent increase.
3. True.

QUICK QUIZ 11.6
1. True.
2. False. In order to obtain SSI benefits, an individual must be 65, disabled, or blind.
3. True.

DEFERRED COMPENSATION AND NONQUALIFIED PLANS

LEARNING OBJECTIVES

After reading this chapter, you should be able to:
1. Explain the general characteristics of a deferred compensation plan and when it is appropriate.
2. Understand the significance of IRC §409A.
3. Describe the tax benefits of a deferred compensation plan available to employees and employers.
4. Discuss the tax issues of constructive receipt, substantial risk of forfeiture, economic benefit doctrine and income and payroll tax implications of a deferred compensation plan.
5. Analyze the benefits and risks of filing an 83(b) election.
6. Describe the various types of deferred compensation arrangements.
7. Calculate the income attributable to the exercise of ISOs and NQSOs as well as the gain from the subsequent sale of the acquired stock.
8. Explain the mechanics of restricted stock and ESPPs.

INTRODUCTION

Employers establish **deferred compensation arrangements** to provide benefits to a select group of employees without the limitations, restrictions, and rules of a qualified plan. These types of arrangements, usually in the form of **nonqualified plans** or other executive compensation, often discriminate in favor of key employees and can exceed the dollar limits imposed on qualified plans. These arrangements may take many forms but the ultimate objective is usually to recruit and/or retain key executives. While qualified plans and the other tax-advantaged plans are effective with respect to mid and lower-paid employees, the limitations imposed by these plans, especially the dollar limits and testing requirements, do not provide sufficient retirement resources for key executives who earn in excess of $265,000, the covered compensation limit for qualified plans for 2016.

The general characteristics of the deferred compensation arrangements presented in this chapter are:
1. They do not have the tax advantages of qualified plans.
2. They usually involve some deferral of income to the executive.
3. The employer generally does not receive an income tax deduction until the key employee receives the payment and it becomes recognizable as taxable income, thus following the traditional income tax matching principle of deduction by one party only upon inclusion by another party.
4. There is generally a requirement that the employee/executive have a "substantial risk of forfeiture" or else the government will claim that the executive, while perhaps not having actual receipt of the money, has "constructive receipt" of the money and, therefore, current income subject to income tax.

Correspondingly, deferred compensation arrangements are most often used for one or all of the three following reasons:

1. to increase the executive's wage replacement ratio,
2. to defer the executive's compensation, or
3. in lieu of qualified plans.

Some different arrangements include:

1. Golden Handshakes - severance package, often designed to encourage early retirement
2. Golden Parachutes - substantial payments made to executives being terminated due to changes in corporate ownership
3. Golden Handcuffs - designed to keep the executive with the company

It is also important to understand that employers also use deferred compensation arrangements as a method of retaining key employees. This can be done either by vesting schedules or through increased benefits with additional years of service.

WAGE REPLACEMENT RATIO

An individual may need approximately 70-80 percent of his pre-retirement income during his retirement years to maintain his pre-retirement lifestyle. Most low-income and middle-income employees are capable of accumulating the amounts necessary to attain their target **wage replacement ratio** utilizing qualified plans offered by their employer in conjunction with Social Security and their own savings. However, executives who earn substantially more than the qualified plan covered compensation limit, $265,000 for 2016, cannot attain a significant

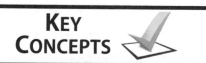

KEY CONCEPTS

1. What are deferred compensation arrangements?

2. What are the three common reasons employers use deferred compensation arrangements?

wage replacement ratio from qualified plans because qualified plans adhere to strict limits on either contributions (e.g., $53,000 per year in 2016 for defined contribution plans) or benefits (e.g., a defined benefit limit of $210,000 in 2016).

Consider the following employer data from Meyer Group.

EXAMPLE 12.1

QUALIFIED SAVINGS AS A PERCENTAGE OF GROSS PAY FOR 2016

Person	Current Compensation	Covered Compensation	Contribution to Qualified Plan (Limit)*	Savings Rate (As a % of Gross Compensation)
Al	$400,000	$265,000	$53,000	13.3%
John	$265,000	$265,000	$53,000	20.0%
Kelly	$40,000	$40,000	$20,000**	50.0%

Kelly could have a larger contribution under IRC 415(c) under certain scenarios.
** Assumed*

Each employee's final compensation can be projected using a 3.5 percent assumed wage rate increase and assuming that each employee is 20 years from retirement.

PROJECTED FUTURE COMPENSATION

Person	Current Compensation	Compensation 20 Years from Today (Assume 3.5% Raises)
Al	$400,000	$795,916
John	$265,000	$527,294
Kelly	$40,000	$79,592

Assuming that each employee saves the stated contribution amount each year at year end and the funds earn eight percent per year, determine the accumulated account balance and the dollar size of a 20-year annuity paid in arrears on an annual basis.

PROJECTED ACCUMULATION AT RETIREMENT AND A 20-YEAR ANNUITY

Person	Savings from Qualified Plan Today	Future Accumulated Balance at 8% in 20 Years	Accumulation 20-Year Annuity
Al	$53,000	$2,425,384	$247,031
John	$53,000	$2,425,384	$247,031
Kelly	$20,000	$915,239	$93,219

The wage replacement ratio that the annuity provides can then be calculated as a fraction of each employee's final pre retirement compensation.

WAGE REPLACEMENT RATIO

Person		Wage Replacement (Annuity/Future Compensation)
Al	31%	($247,031 ÷ $795,916)
John	47%	($247,031 ÷ $527,294)
Kelly	117%	($93,219 ÷ $79,592)

As illustrated, Al saves 13.3 percent of his gross compensation in the qualified plan, resulting in a wage replacement ratio from that qualified plan at retirement of 31 percent. This amount is substantially less than the 70-80 percent recommended wage replacement ratio that he will need.

The qualified plan restricted Al to this wage replacement ratio of 31 percent because the maximum contribution to the plan each year was limited ($53,000 for 2016).

The establishment of a deferred compensation plan allows an employer to provide nonqualified benefits to an executive without having to provide benefits to other rank and file employees. The purpose is to increase the executive's wage replacement ratio to a level commensurate with the executive's actual compensation instead of a wage replacement ratio limited by the qualified covered compensation limit of $265,000 for 2016 and the other limits of qualified plans (defined contributions of $53,000 and defined benefits of $210,000 for 2016). A common application of deferred compensation plans is to supplement qualified retirement plans.

IRC Section 409A

The American Jobs Creation Act of 2004 was signed into law on October 22, 2004 and created IRC §409A, which deals with nonqualified deferred compensation plans. The purpose of this section is to provide clear structure and guidance for these types of plans. These rules also enact harsh penalties for those plans that do not comply with §409A. Plans failing to meet the requirements of this section are subject to acceleration of prior deferrals, interest, penalties, and a 20 percent additional tax on the amount of the deferrals. These are serious ramifications for plans that fail to comply with the new rules.

The law attempts to define nonqualified deferred compensation plans as any plan that provides for "deferral of compensation." However, it excludes most qualified plans, incentive stock option plans, nonqualified stock option plans, employee stock purchase plans, stock appreciation rights plans, and standard type bonuses that are paid within 2½ months after the close of the taxable year. Eligible plans under IRC §457(b) are also excluded. However, the new rules do apply to plans under IRC §457(f) (as discussed in Chapter 10).[1]

If deferred compensation plans meet the requirements of §409A, then IRC §409A has no effect on the employee's gross income and taxes. If the arrangement does not meet the requirements of §409A, however, §409A generally provides that all amounts deferred under a nonqualified deferred compensation plan are currently includible in gross income to the extent that the amounts are not subject to a substantial risk of forfeiture and to the extent that the amounts have not been previously includible in gross income.[2] Compensation is subject to a substantial risk of forfeiture if entitlement to the amount is conditioned on the performance of substantial future services by any person or the occurrence of an event related to a purpose of the compensation, such as the attainment of certain earnings or equity value.[3]

In order to comply with §409A, the regulations require that the plan be established and maintained in accordance with the requirements of §409A. As part of these requirements, the material terms of the plan must be set forth in writing. In addition, §409A generally provides that payments may only be made at certain times or upon certain events, including:
- separation from service
- disability
- death
- at a specified time or pursuant to a fixed schedule
- upon a change in control[4]
- upon an unforeseeable emergency

IRC §409A greatly restricts the conditions under which a plan may permit the acceleration of the time or schedule of payments under the plan. The exceptions that the law provides are minimal but include domestic relations orders, distributions for paying income tax for 457(f) plans, and the payment of employment taxes.

---

1. IRC §409A(d)(1).
2. Internal Revenue Bulletin 2006-29.
3. IRC §409A(d)(4).
4. Treas. Reg. §1.409A-3(i)(5)(vi).

DEFERRED EXECUTIVE COMPENSATION

Deferred compensation arrangements may also be established simply to defer an executive's compensation to a future year. When an executive agrees to defer his compensation, the executive is agreeing to defer receipt of current income for a promise from the employer to pay that compensation at some later date. It is important to note that an agreement to defer compensation into the future must be made prior to the compensation being earned. Deferred compensation arrangements usually create income tax benefits for both the executive and the employer.

Employee Tax Benefit

An executive who elects to defer compensation generally earns a significantly greater amount than the covered compensation limit, is usually in the highest marginal income tax bracket, and does not currently need the deferred income to sustain his current standard of living. If the executive chooses to defer the compensation, the executive generally defers the compensation to a time when he expects to be in a lower marginal income tax bracket and thus, at the date of receipt, expects to pay less income tax on the compensation than would have been paid currently.

Employer Tax Benefit

The IRC places a $1,000,000 limit on a public company's deduction for compensation payable to any one of the top five executives of a publicly traded company.[5] For example, when a CEO is paid $1,250,000 per year, the employer can only deduct $1,000,000 for income tax purposes. In this case, if the executive elects to defer any income over the $1,000,000 limit to a year in which the executive earns less than the limit, the employer would be able to deduct the total compensation over the period of deferral and subsequent payment.

QUICK QUIZ 12.1

1. Deferred compensation plans allow the employer to take a current deduction for compensation expense while the employee can defer the income tax on the compensation.
   a. True
   b. False

2. Public companies are limited to a $1,000,000 compensation deduction for some executives.
   a. True
   b. False

False, True.

EXAMPLE 12.2

Josephine, the CFO of Eighteen Corporation, a publicly traded company, earns $1,250,000 per year. Without an election to defer any of her compensation, Eighteen Corporation will only be able to deduct $1,000,000 in relation to Josephine's compensation.

If, however, Josephine elected to defer $250,000 of her compensation until her retirement, Eighteen Corporation would be able to deduct $1,000,000 in the current year as Josephine's compensation, and upon Josephine's retirement, would be able to deduct the additional $250,000 payment to Josephine as deferred compensation.

---

5. IRC §162(m)(1) and Treas. Reg. §1.162-27. For the purposes of this section, covered employees are the CEO and the four highest paid executives other than the CEO.

Alternative to Qualified Plans

Deferred compensation plans are also used where the employer does not have a qualified plan because the employer does not desire to cover a broad group of employees. The employer may nonetheless be compelled to provide retirement benefits to certain key executives and can accomplish this goal by utilizing a deferred compensation plan. Nonqualified plans can discriminate in favor of key employees and are not subject to the limits imposed on qualified plans.

INCOME TAX ISSUES

Deferred compensation arrangements are typically used to benefit the highly compensated and key executives in an organization. One of the primary benefits to these types of plans is the deferral of income taxation for the key executive. For deferral of income tax to be realized, the deferred compensation plan must comply with certain income tax provisions.

CONSTRUCTIVE RECEIPT

Constructive receipt is an income tax concept that establishes when income is includible by a taxpayer and therefore subject to income tax. The rules for constructive receipt are found in Treasury Regulation §1.451-2.

Income, although not actually in a taxpayer's possession, is nonetheless constructively received by the taxpayer in the taxable year during which it is credited to his account, set apart for him, or otherwise made available so that he may draw upon it at any time, or so that he could have drawn upon it during the taxable year if notice of intention to withdraw had been given. Generally, an individual will be deemed to have constructive receipt of income if he can choose to receive the income today or in the future. However, income is not constructively received if the taxpayer's control of its receipt is subject to substantial limitations or restrictions. Thus, if a corporation credits its employees with stock as a bonus but the stock is not available to the employees until some future date, the mere crediting of the stock on the books of the corporation does not constitute constructive receipt of the stock.

> ## KEY CONCEPTS ✓
>
> 1. What is constructive receipt and how does it affect deferred compensation plans?
>
> 2. What is a substantial risk of forfeiture and how does it affect deferred compensation plans?
>
> 3. What is the Economic Benefit Doctrine and how does it affect deferred compensation plans?

Examples of Constructive Receipt

Amounts payable with respect to interest coupons that have matured and are payable, but which have not been cashed, are constructively received in the taxable year during which the coupons mature, unless it can be shown that there are no funds available for payment of the interest during such year. Dividends on corporate stock are constructively received when made subject to the demand of the shareholder without qualifications. However, if a dividend is declared payable on December 31 and the corporation followed its normal practice of paying the dividends by mailing checks so that the shareholders would not receive them until January of the following year, such dividends are not considered to have been constructively received in December. Generally, the amount of dividends or interest credited on savings bank deposits or to shareholders of organizations, such as building and loan associations or cooperative banks, is income to the depositors or shareholders for the taxable year when credited. However, if any portion of such dividends or interest is not subject to withdrawal at the time credited, that portion is not constructively received and does not constitute income to the depositor or shareholder until the taxable year in which the portion first may be withdrawn.

Deferred compensation plans are structured so that employees benefiting under the plan will avoid constructive receipt and will therefore be allowed the deferral of income taxation.

As mentioned, an employee who elects to defer compensation, such as a bonus, into the future under a deferred compensation arrangement must do so prior to the compensation being earned. Otherwise, the employee would effectively have the choice of receiving current income or deferring. This choice would result in the income being considered constructively received whether or not there was a subsequent substantial risk of forfeiture.

The following are some examples of what is not considered constructive receipt:

- an unsecured promise to pay
- the benefits are subject to substantial limitations or restrictions
- the triggering event is beyond the recipient's control (i.e., company is acquired)

SUBSTANTIAL RISK OF FORFEITURE

Substantial risk of forfeiture is another income tax concept that relates to when income is subject to income tax. The rules for substantial risk of forfeiture are found in Treasury Regulation §1.83-3(c).

QUICK QUIZ 12.2

1. Deferred compensation plans are generally structured so that employees benefiting under the plan will avoid constructive receipt.
   a. True
   b. False

2. A substantial risk of forfeiture is the risk that the employee will leave the corporation prematurely and take the plan assets with them.
   a. True
   b. False

3. For contributions to a deferred compensation plan to be taxed because of the economic benefit doctrine, there must be no restrictions or risks that the funds would not be paid to the employee.
   a. True
   b. False

True, False, True.

A substantial risk of forfeiture exists when rights in property that are transferred are conditioned, directly or indirectly, upon the future performance (or refraining from performance) of substantial services by any person, or the occurrence of a condition related to a purpose of the transfer and the possibility of forfeiture is substantial if the condition is not satisfied. The issue of whether a risk of forfeiture is substantial remains a matter of facts and circumstances. When there is a substantial risk of forfeiture, the taxpayer is not required to include the income as taxable income. When there is not a substantial risk of forfeiture, the taxpayer is required to recognize the income currently as taxable income.

Often, a deferred compensation agreement is structured as a simple contractual promise from the employer to a key employee. Generally, this puts the employee at risk that the employer might default or breach the contract and not pay. The obligation of a deferred compensation agreement is reflected on the balance sheet of the organization as a liability. However, in terms of the ranking of creditors in the case of liquidation, all secured and unsecured creditors would be fully paid prior to paying the deferred compensation obligation. In liquidation, a participant in a deferred compensation plan is paid before both preferred and common shareholders. Thus, it can be said that for an unfunded deferred compensation arrangement based on a simple contractual promise to pay, the employee is at a "substantial risk of forfeiture." Most deferred compensation arrangements are unfunded and, therefore, subject to the risk of nonpayment. Deferred compensation arrangements can, however, be funded.

> On November 25, 2016, Carb Corporation gives Edward, an employee, a bonus of 100 shares of Carb Corporation stock. The terms of the bonus arrangement obligate Edward to return the stock to Carb Corporation if he terminates his employment for any reason. However, for each year occurring after November 25, 2016, during which Edward remains employed with Carb Corporation, Edward ceases to be obligated to return 10 shares of the Carb Corporation stock. Therefore, each year occurring after November 25, 2016 that Edward remains employed, his rights in 10 shares of stock cease to be subject to a substantial risk of forfeiture. Thus, the value of 10 shares of stock will be included in Edward's income each year when the substantial risk of forfeiture expires. The value of this income is equal to the value of the stock on each November 25th, when the substantial risk of forfeiture expires.

EXAMPLE 12.3

Since one of the primary purposes of deferred compensation arrangements is to avoid current taxation for the key executive, these plans will almost always include a substantial risk of forfeiture so that the executive can defer payment of income tax. Employers may simply promise to pay the employee or may use some form of vesting schedule in an attempt to meet the substantial risk of forfeiture standard.

ECONOMIC BENEFIT DOCTRINE

The **economic benefit doctrine** provides that an employee will be taxed on funds or property set aside for the employee if the funds or property are unrestricted and nonforfeitable, even if the employee was not given a choice to receive the income currently. In other words, if an employer sets aside funds for an employee and there is no risk that the employee will not receive the funds, then the funds are taxable under this doctrine at the point in time at which there are no longer any restrictions attached to the property.

Deferred compensation plans may provide for a trust to hold the funds for the employee prior to retirement or termination. Contributions to an employee's trust made by an employer will generally be included in the gross income of the employee in accordance with IRC §83 (discussed below, except that the value of the employee's interest in the trust shall be substituted for the fair market value of the property for purposes of applying such section). This means that contributions to a trust are taxable to the employee even if there is not a distribution from the trust. To be subject to income tax, the funds simply have to be unrestricted and nonforfeitable, which could occur once the employee becomes partially or fully vested.[6] An exception to this rule can be achieved through use of a rabbi trust, discussed later in this chapter.

---

6. IRC §402(b).

Under no circumstances would a simple promise to pay be subject to current income tax since there are substantial risks as to whether the payments will be made. To be taxable under the economic benefit doctrine, there must be no restrictions or risks that the funds would not be paid to the employee.

IRC SECTION 83: PROPERTY TRANSFERRED IN CONNECTION WITH PERFORMANCE OF SERVICE

When an employer transfers property to an employee in connection with the performance of service, the employee will be taxed on the difference between the fair market value of the property and the amount paid for that property. For example, if an employer transferred stock worth $10 to an employee and the employee paid $3 for the stock, then the employee would be taxed on the difference of $7.

The fair market value of the property is determined at the time the rights of the person having the beneficial interest in the property are transferable or are not subject to a substantial risk of forfeiture, whichever occurs earlier. For example, if a company grants

KEY CONCEPTS

1. What is the Section 83(b) election with regard to a deferred compensation plan?

2. When are payroll taxes due on compensation placed into a deferred compensation plan?

3. When does the employer receive an income tax deduction for assets contributed to a deferred compensation plan?

$50,000 worth of company stock to Randy, a key executive, and provides that he can only receive it if he is employed for five additional years, then there is clearly a substantial risk of forfeiture that he will not be paid during that five year vesting period. Once Randy has completed the five years he will be taxed based on the value of the stock at that time, which may be greater or lower than $50,000.

Generally, the gain or difference between the fair market value of the property and any amounts paid by the employee is taxed as ordinary income to the employee. Usually, this amount is included in the employee's Form W-2 and is also subject to both withholding and payroll taxes. Any further appreciation from the point at which the income is included in taxable income is capital gain (assuming that the property is of a capital nature).

These rules are typically applicable to grants of stock, especially restricted stock, and employee stock options but can also be applied to other transfers of property to an employee. The Section 83(b) election allows an employee to include into income the net value of a transfer from an employer for the purpose of establishing a basis in a capital asset. This election is discussed in greater detail later in this chapter.

PAYROLL TAX

Deferred compensation is considered to be earned income at the time a substantial risk of forfeiture expires and, therefore, is subject to payroll taxes at that time even though the employee may not receive payment until sometime in the future. The general rule is that payroll tax will apply at the later of the time at which the deferred income is earned or the point at which the deferred income becomes nonforfeitable.[7] Restricted stock or other benefits may be subject to vesting or other restrictions that would result in an employee forfeiting benefits if employment was terminated prior to a specific point in time. Once the restrictions are lifted, the benefits are deemed nonforfeitable and payroll taxes are due. Benefits from these plans are reported on Form W-2 since it is literally deferred compensation. The taxable event occurs when there is no longer a substantial risk of forfeiture.

EXAMPLE 12.4

Employer C establishes a nonqualified deferred compensation plan for Employee A on January 1, 2016. Under the plan, which is an account balance plan, Employee A obtains a legally binding right on the last day of each calendar year (if Employee A is employed on that date) to be credited with a principal amount equal to 10 percent of compensation for the year. In addition, a reasonable rate of interest is credited quarterly. Employee A's account balance is nonforfeitable and is payable upon Employee A's termination of employment. For 2016, the principal amount credited to Employee A under the plan is $25,000.

The services creating the right to the $25,000 amount deferred are considered performed as of December 31, 2016, the date on which Employee A has performed all of the services necessary to obtain a legally binding right to the amount deferred. Thus, the $25,000 amount deferred must be taken into account as of December 31, 2016, which is the later of the date on which services creating the right to the amount deferred are performed or the date on which the right to the amount deferred is no longer subject to a substantial risk of forfeiture.

EXAMPLE 12.5

The facts are the same as in Example 12.4, except that the principal amount credited under the plan on the last day of each year (and attributable interest) is forfeited if the employee terminates employment within five years of that date.

Because Employee A's right to receive the $25,000 principal amount (and attributable interest) is conditioned on the performance of services for five years, a substantial risk of forfeiture exists with respect to that amount deferred until December 31, 2021.

EXAMPLE 12.6

The facts are the same as in Example 12.5, except that the principal amount credited under the plan on the last day of each year (and attributable interest) becomes nonforfeitable according to a graded vesting schedule under which 20 percent is vested after one year, 40 percent after two years, 60 percent after three years, 80 percent after four years, and 100 percent after five years.

Each 20 percent (of which there are five) is treated separately and a substantial risk of forfeiture exists with respect to that amount deferred until the point at which it is fully vested. Therefore, $5,000 plus attributable interest will vest on December 31, 2017, 2018, 2019, 2020, and 2021.

---

7. Treas. Reg. §31.3121(v)(2)-1(e)(1) states that except as otherwise provided in this paragraph (e), an amount deferred under a nonqualified deferred compensation plan must be taken into account as wages for FICA tax purposes as of the later of the date on which services creating the right to the amount deferred are performed or the date on which the right to the amount deferred is no longer subject to a substantial risk of forfeiture.

Executives and key employees who participate in deferred compensation plans generally have current earnings in excess of the Social Security wage base of $118,500 for 2016 and, therefore, only pay the 1.45 percent Medicare portion on income that is deferred in the deferred compensation plan. They will also be subject to the additional Medicare taxes for deferral income above certain limits.[8] While the funds are subject to payroll tax in the year earned, the employee is better off since the OASDI portion at 6.2 percent does not have to be paid. Likewise, the employer will also avoid paying the 6.2 percent for OASDI.

The Affordable care act created two additional Medicare taxes that will impact wealthier taxpayers and executives. The first is an additional Medicare tax of 0.9 percent on wages or self-employment income above specified thresholds. The second is a 3.8 percent tax on certain amounts of net investment income. Both of these are more fully discussed in Chapter 11.

The additional Medicare tax equal to 0.9 percent applies to wages or self-employment income that is above the following threshold amounts:

Married filing jointly	$250,000
Married filing separately	$125,000
Single	$200,000
Head of household	$200,000

The wages for an executive that are subject to FICA would also be subject to the additional Medicare tax of 0.9 percent, to the extent that the wages exceed the threshold amount.[9]

When the income is later paid to the executive, it will be subject to income tax. However, the payments will not constitute "earned income" in the period received and, therefore, will not be subject to payroll taxes and will not qualify for the earned income test for IRAs and other qualified plans.

EMPLOYER INCOME TAX DEDUCTION

As discussed in the first chapters of the book, one of the greatest benefits of qualified plans is that the employer receives a current income tax deduction for contributions to a qualified plan and the employee is not taxed on those contributed amounts until they are received as a distribution from the plan. This tax benefit does not extend to deferred compensation arrangements. In deferred compensation plans, the employer is entitled to receive an income tax deduction for contributions to the plan only when the employee is required to include the payments as taxable income. This concept is referred to as the matching principle - the employer's deduction follows the employee's inclusion into taxable income.

---

8. See Chapter 11 for a complete discussion.
9. See Treas. Reg §31.3121(v)(2)-1.

EXAMPLE
12.7

On January 1, 2016, the taxpayer and corporation X executed an employment contract under which the taxpayer is to be employed by the corporation in an executive capacity for a period of five years. Under the contract, the taxpayer is entitled to a stated annual salary and to additional compensation of 10x dollars for each year. The additional compensation will be credited to a bookkeeping reserve account and will be deferred, accumulated, and paid in annual installments equal to one-fifth of the amount in the reserve as of the close of the year immediately preceding the year of first payment. The payments are to begin only upon:

- termination of the taxpayer's employment by the corporation,
- the taxpayer's becoming a part-time employee of the corporation, or
- the taxpayer's becoming partially or totally incapacitated. Under the terms of the agreement, corporation X is under a merely contractual obligation to make the payments when due, and the parties did not intend that the amounts in the reserve be held by the corporation in trust for the taxpayer.

The contract further provides that if the taxpayer should fail or refuse to perform his duties, the corporation will be relieved of any obligation to make further credit to the reserve (but not of the obligation to distribute amounts previously contributed); but, if the taxpayer should become incapacitated from performing his duties, then credits to the reserve will continue for one year from the date of the incapacity, but not beyond the expiration of the five-year term of the contract.

The additional compensation to be received by the taxpayer under the employment contract concerned will be includible in his gross income only in the taxable years in which the taxpayer actually receives installment payments in cash or other property previously credited to his account.

EXAMPLE 12.8

Assume that in June 2016, Drew Brees entered into a five-year standard player's contract with the New Orleans Saints in which he agreed to play football and engage in activities related to football during the five-year term only for the Saints. In addition to a specified salary for the two-year term, it was mutually agreed that as an inducement for signing the contract the taxpayer would be paid a bonus of $10 million. He could have demanded and received payment of this bonus at the time of signing the contract, but at his suggestion there was added to the standard contract form a paragraph providing substantially as follows:

The player shall receive the sum of $10 million upon signing of this contract, contingent upon the payment of this $10 million to an escrow agent designated by him. The escrow agreement shall be subject to approval by the legal representatives of the player, the Saints, and the escrow agent.

QUICK QUIZ 12.3

1. A §83(b) election allows the employer to elect to include contributions to the deferred compensation plan into the employee's income.
   a. True
   b. False

2. Deferred compensation will never be subject to payroll taxes until the employee receives distributions from the plan.
   a. True
   b. False

3. An employer receives a current income tax deduction for contributions to a qualified plan.
   a. True
   b. False

False, False, True.

Pursuant to this added provision, an escrow agreement was executed on June 25, 2016, in which the Saints agreed to pay $10 million on that date to the Y bank, as escrow agent; and the escrow agent agreed to pay this amount, plus interest, to the taxpayer in installments over a period of five years, beginning at the end of this contract. The escrow agreement also provides that the account established by the escrow agent is to bear the taxpayer's name; that payments from such account may be made only in accordance with the terms of the agreement; that the agreement is binding upon the parties thereto and their successors or assigns; and that in the event of the taxpayer's death during the escrow period the balance due will become part of his estate.

Applying the principles stated in the Sproull decision[10] to the facts here, the $10 million bonus is includible in the gross income of Drew Brees in 2016, the year in which the club unconditionally paid such amount to the escrow agent. The taxpayer controlled when the funds would be received and the structure allowed for no risk of forfeiture.

---

10. E. T. Sproull v. Commissioner, 16 T.C. 244

SUMMARY OF DEFERRED COMPENSATION

EXHIBIT
12.1

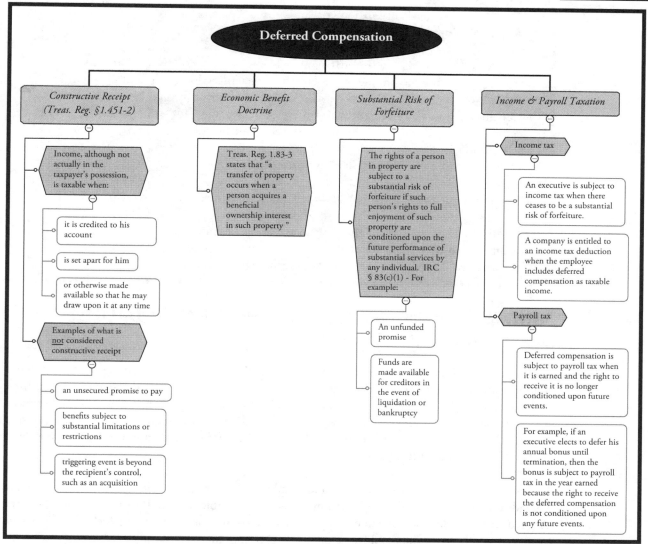

FUNDING ARRANGEMENTS AND TYPES OF NONQUALIFIED DEFERRED COMPENSATION PLANS

A **nonqualified deferred compensation plan (NQDC)** is a contractual arrangement between an employer and an executive whereby the employer promises to pay the executive a predetermined amount of money sometime in the future. In the future may mean at or during retirement or at or after termination of employment. These types of plans are neither required nor intended to meet the ERISA or IRC requirements to be a qualified plan. Therefore, the employer does not realize the tax advantages of a qualified plan.

There are certain benefits to employers and employees in setting up deferred compensation plans. The advantages of deferred compensation plans to the employer are: (1) cash outflows are often deferred until the future, (2) the employer will save on payroll taxes except for the 1.45 percent Medicare match (since the employee's income is probably over the Social Security wage base), and (3) the employer can discriminate and provide these benefits exclusively to a select group of key employees. The employee benefits from a deferred compensation plan by deferring the receipt of income, thus increasing the possibility of lower federal income taxes at the time of the actual payment and avoiding Social Security taxes (except the 1.45 percent for Medicare) at the time it was earned. In addition, both the employee and employer benefit in these types of plans because the total compensation, including deferred compensation, may exceed the $1 million annual limit on deductible compensation.

Although the characteristics discussed above apply to most NQDC plans, there are a variety of funding arrangements and types of plans to be discussed. These include unfunded promises to pay, secular trusts, rabbi trusts, phantom stock plans, and other types of deferred compensation arrangements.

UNFUNDED PROMISE TO PAY

Deferred compensation may take any form due to the flexibility and lack of requirements under ERISA and the IRC. An unfunded promise to pay falls within the spectrum of deferred compensation. This type of arrangement will meet the standards of a substantial risk of forfeiture and will, therefore, meet the objective of tax deferral. However, the employee is at some risk of not being paid. The employer may choose not to pay, or claim that the employee did not meet the conditions of the contract, or the employer may not have sufficient funds to pay the obligation. Obviously, the employee has the right to claim that the employer is in violation of the agreement, which may or may not yield any tangible benefit. To mitigate against such risk, employees would prefer that the employer set funds aside for the purpose of providing for the payment of the deferred obligation. However, as discussed, if there are no restrictions on the set aside funds or there is not a risk of forfeiture, then the funds become immediately taxable, thereby defeating the tax-deferral objective.

> ## KEY CONCEPTS ✓
>
> 1. What funding arrangements are available for deferred compensation plans?
>
> 2. What impact does Title I of ERISA have on deferred compensation plans?
>
> 3. What types of deferred compensation plans are available?
>
> 4. What are 401(k) wraps?

SECULAR TRUST

Secular trusts are irrevocable trusts designed to hold funds and assets for the purpose of paying benefits under a nonqualified deferred compensation arrangement. This type of plan provides protection for the assets in the trust. The funds are set aside for the benefit of employees and are not available to the employer or subject to the claims of the employer's creditors. Since a secular trust does not create a substantial risk of forfeiture for the employee, assets set aside in a secular trust result in immediate taxation to the employee.[11] This tax consequence is the cost of eliminating the risk that the funds will not be paid in the future.

Secular trusts are generally subject to Title I of ERISA and, therefore, have to comply with certain reporting, disclosure, vesting, and other requirements. Secular trusts may use a graduated vesting schedule, and the vesting of benefits will trigger the recognition of income for purposes of income tax. Once the funds are vested, the employee is required to include the value of the vested benefit in income and the employer will have an income tax deduction of an equal amount.

Treasury Regulation §1.402(b)-1 provides that any employer contribution made to a trust that is not exempt from taxation[12] shall be included as compensation in the gross income of the employee for his taxable year during which the contribution is made, but only to the extent that the employee's interest in such contribution is substantially vested at the time the contribution is made. Thus, the secular trust can be effectively used in combination with a vesting schedule to defer tax for the executive.

---

11. IRC §402(b) and the Economic Benefit Doctrine.
12. Such as a trust under IRC §501(a).

To compensate for the increased taxable income without necessarily having an increase in cash distributions, secular trusts may provide for distributions to the participants for the purpose of paying the income tax attributable to the taxability of the benefits in the trust.

The funds contributed to the trust will be invested and will generate income. The income will usually be taxable to the employee as it is earned if it is not subject to a substantial risk of forfeiture.

Oxford Corporation has created a deferred compensation plan (Plan) for 50 key executives (participants), all of whom are highly compensated employees. Oxford contributes each year on behalf of each participant to a trust, T. The trust is not and never has been a qualified trust under §401(a) and is not exempt from taxation under §501(a).

T's assets are not subject to the claims of Oxford's creditors. Separate accounts that reflect the participant's share of the net trust assets and income are maintained for each participant.

A participant's entire interest in T becomes vested upon completion of three years of service with Oxford beginning on the date the individual first becomes a participant in the Plan. Participants or their beneficiaries are entitled to receive their vested interest in the net assets of T, net of applicable withholding and other taxes, on death, disability, or termination of employment. In addition, T is required to distribute to each participant each year an amount that the trustee reasonably estimates will be equal to the amount of Federal, state, and local income and employment taxes payable by the participant with respect to the increase in the participant's vested accrued benefit in T during such year. T is permitted to make the distribution in part as a distribution of cash to the participant, and in part in the form of applicable employment tax withholding under Federal, state, or local law.

This arrangement is an example of a secular trust, in which assets cannot be seized by creditors, but tax is only deferred until the participant is vested.

RABBI TRUST

Rabbi trusts strike a balance between the risk of an unfunded promise to pay and the lack of substantial risk of forfeiture in a secular trust. Like a secular trust, a rabbi trust is an irrevocable trust that is designed to hold funds and assets for the purpose of paying benefits under a nonqualified deferred compensation arrangement. However, there are certain critical differences between rabbi trusts and secular trusts. Although the assets in a rabbi trust are for the sole purpose of providing benefits to employees and may not be accessed by the employer, they may be seized and used for the purpose of paying general creditors in the event of the liquidation of the company. In this regard, they do not protect the executive employee from bankruptcy of the employer. Because of this possibility, the IRS has ruled that rabbi trusts that are established and follow specific guidelines will create a substantial risk of forfeiture. When these guidelines are followed, any assets within a rabbi trust are not currently taxable to the employee yet provide significantly more protection to the employee than a simple unfunded promise to pay.

Even though assets are set aside in a trust, rabbi trusts are treated as unfunded (also can be informally funded) for purposes of Title I of ERISA due to the presence of a substantial risk of forfeiture. As a result, these plans do not have to comply with as many rules as secular trusts.

The income generated from the assets within the trust is taxed to the employer. However, the employer will receive an income tax deduction upon distribution from the trust. Many deferred compensation plans will use life insurance products to avoid taxation of income to the employer.

The American Jobs Creation Act of 2004 and the creation of IRC §409A had an impact on rabbi trusts. Section 409A(b) states that in most cases, assets set aside in a trust outside of the United States (i.e., an offshore trust account) are treated as property transferred in connection with the performance of service whether or not such assets are available to satisfy claims of general creditors. Thus, any such assets will be taxed to the executive as constructively received at the date of transfer.

The Pension Protection Act of 2006 further amended the rules regarding rabbi trusts. Under the PPA 2006, employers are prohibited from setting aside or transferring assets for the purpose of paying deferred compensation of an "applicable covered employee" under a nonqualified deferred compensation plan during a "restricted period" with respect to a qualified defined benefit plan. The term "applicable covered employee" includes certain current and past executives of the plan sponsor. The term "restricted period" means:

1. any period where the sponsor of a defined benefit plan is a debtor in a Chapter 11 proceeding;
2. the six month period prior to, and the six month period following, a qualified defined benefit plan's termination if the plan does not have sufficient assets to satisfy its liabilities upon termination; or
3. any plan year, beginning in 2008, during which a qualified defined benefit pension plan of the employer fails to meet certain minimum funding levels and is in "at-risk" status.[13]

Model Rabbi Trust

The IRS provided clear and specific rules defining a model rabbi trust in Revenue Procedure 92-64 that must be followed to make certain that the plan will result in the desired outcome. The Revenue Procedure provides for many rules, some of which are listed below:
- the model language must be adopted almost verbatim
- the trust must be valid under state law
- the trust must state that the assets are subject to the claims of creditors in the case of insolvency
- the trustee must be an independent third party, such as a bank
- the trustee must be given some level of discretion over investment of plan assets

---

13. Pension Protection Act of 2006.

EXHIBIT
12.2

CHARACTERISTICS OF ALTERNATIVE DEFERRED COMPENSATION ARRANGEMENTS

	Unfunded Promise to Pay	Rabbi Trust	Secular Trust
Funded with assets	No	Yes	Yes
Funded (for purposes of ERISA)	No	No	Yes
Risk of forfeiture without employer financial instability	Yes	No	No
Risk of forfeiture if employer is insolvent	Yes Claim is below general creditors	Yes Claim is below general creditors	No
When is there taxable income to the executive?	When actual or "constructively received"	When actually or "constructively received"	Immediately upon funding by employer or vesting
When is the payment deductible to employer?	Deferred until payment is made to executive	Deferred until payment is made to executive	When "constructively received" and taxable to executive
Accomplishes the objective of deferral	Yes	Yes	If vesting is required

Case Study 12.2

Bank of America, N.A. v. Moglia addressed creditors' interests in a "rabbi trust" that a Chapter 7 debtor established before filing for bankruptcy to create a source of funding for its otherwise unfunded employee benefit plans.[1] The Chapter 7 debtor, Outboard Marine Corporation ("Outboard"), had approximately $14 million in assets in a "rabbi trust." Bank of America, the agent of Outboard's secured creditors, claimed rights in those assets, while the trustee in bankruptcy claimed them for the unsecured creditors. The security agreement on which Bank of America relied covers all Outboard's "general intangibles," a term of great breadth in commercial law and broadly defined in the agreement as well to include "all other intangible personal property of every kind and nature."

The Court defined a "rabbi trust" as a form of trust whose tax treatment was first addressed in an IRS letter ruling on a trust for the benefit of a rabbi.[2] Under a rabbi trust, a trust is created by a corporation or other institution for the benefit of one or more of its executives (the rabbi in the IRS's original ruling).[3]

1. ***Bank of America, N.A. v. Moglia***, 330 F.3d 942 (7th Cir. 2003).
2. See Private Letter Ruling 8113107 (Dec. 31, 1980); see also ***IRS General Counsel Memorandum***, 39230 (Jan. 20, 1984).
3. See, for example, ***Westport Bank & Trust Co. v. Geraghty***, 90 F.3d 661, 663-64 (2nd Cir. 1996).

Case Study 12.2 Continued

According to the Court, the main reason for a rabbi trust is that should the control of the institution change, the trust could then be funded to cushion the fall of the old executives if the new management intends to reduce the compensation of, or even fire, the old executives. However, as the IRS explained in the letter ruling, unless an executive's right to receive money from the trust is "subject to substantial limitations or restrictions" rather than being his to draw on at any time (making it income to him in a practical sense), the executive must include any contribution to the trust and any interest or other earnings of the trust in his gross income in the year in which the contribution was made or the interest obtained.[1] Bank of America conceded that Outboard established a bona fide rabbi trust, so that its contributions to the trust and the income that those contributions generated were not includible in the executives' gross income.

The "substantial limitations or restrictions" condition was satisfied in the transaction on which the IRS ruled. The trust agreement provided that the rabbi would not receive the trust assets until he retired or otherwise ended his employment with the congregation. Until then, the corpus of the trust and any interest on it would be owned by the congregation, so the rabbi would have no right to the money.[2]

What was also key in the Moglia case, was that the trust instrument provided that "the assets of the trust estate shall be subject to the claims of [the congregation's] creditors as if the assets were the general assets of [the congregation]," thus reserving those assets for the unsecured creditors and preventing Outboard from creating a security interest in favor not only of the executives but also of any creditor.

The United States Seventh Circuit Court of Appeals concluded that the creditor's security interest in general intangibles of the debtor did not extend to the corpus of the rabbi trust and that the clause in the trust agreement creating the rabbi trust that prohibited the settlor from granting any creditor a security interest in trust corpus was enforceable. The Court explained that the creditors' security interest in general intangibles of Outboard did not extend to the corpus of "rabbi trust" because the corpus was to remain available at all times for payment of the debtor's general creditors pursuant under the terms of trust agreement and because Outboard was barred from creating any security interest in the trust corpus in favor of beneficiaries or creditors.

---

1. ***McAllister v. Resolution Trust Corp.***, 201 F.3d 570, 572-73, 575 (5th Cir. 2000).
2. Maher v. Harris Trust & Savings Bank, 75 F.3d 1182, 1185 (7th Cir.1996); Goodman v. Resolution Trust Corp., 7 F.3d 1123, 1125 (4th Cir.1993).

FUNDING WITH INSURANCE

For NQDC plans that have funds set aside to pay obligations under the plan, the employer will be responsible for paying income tax attributable to earnings on assets held in the plan. As assets accumulate for executives and remain "at risk," earnings will be subject to taxation by the employer. Ultimately, the employer will receive an income tax deduction when the funds are distributed to the executives. However, employers will often use insurance products because the increase in cash surrender value is not taxed if payments are not made from the policy. A permanent life insurance policy provides the cash value that can be used to fund the deferred compensation and it provides a death benefit that can be paid to the employer to offset some of the costs of the deferred compensation arrangement.

PHANTOM STOCK PLANS

A **phantom stock plan**[14] is a nonqualified deferred compensation arrangement where the employer gives fictional shares of stock to a key employee that is initially valued at the time of the grant. The stock is later valued at some terminal point (usually at termination or retirement), and the executive is then paid the differential value of the stock in cash. Phantom stock provides the same benefit as stock ownership except the final payment is made in cash. The employer has a deductible compensation expense equal to the payment made to the employee. The goal of phantom stock plans is to align the economic incentives of the executive with those of the company. Actual stock is not issued, usually because the current stockholders do not want to dilute their equity position (e.g., no non-family shareholders). This is particularly important in family and closely held business situations.

Mike became the president of Tantalus, a closely held family business. At the time of Mike's employment, the value of the company is $2 million and there are 2,000,000 shares of stock outstanding. Mike is granted phantom stock at the end of the first year valued at $100,000 because the value of the company has increased to $3 million or $1.50 per share. When Mike terminates, the value of the company is $5 million and he has phantom stock representing 300,000 shares at $2.50 per share. Tantalus will pay Mike $750,000 at termination as a result of the phantom stock plan. However, at no time did Mike actually own any shares or their voting rights.

TITLE I OF ERISA

Most NQDC plans do not have to meet the coverage, participation, funding, and discrimination requirements of ERISA imposed on qualified plans. Top-hat plans and unfunded excess benefit plans are statutorily exempted from **Title I of ERISA**. As such, these plans have minimal compliance requirements. There are, however, some reporting and disclosure requirements even for nonqualified plans (including SERP and top-hat plans). These include an initial, one-time filing of a Form 5500 disclosing that the company has such a plan. This "Alternative Reporting and Disclosure Statement" must be filed within 120 days of plan inception date. Additionally, the employer must be fair to all those in that plan and have disclosure requirements to them. Most employers establishing these types of plans will attempt to have the plan classified as a top-hat plan so that the plan is exempt from Title I.

---

14. Phantom stock plans are sometimes referred to as shadow stock plans.

TYPES AND APPLICATIONS OF NQDC PLANS

There are several types of nonqualified deferred compensation plans that can be established to benefit key executives. Salary reduction plans allow employees to elect to reduce their current salary and defer it until future years, generally until retirement or termination. Salary continuation plans typically provide benefits after retirement on an ongoing basis or for a predetermined period of time.

Supplemental executive retirement plans (generally referred to as SERPs) are nonqualified deferred compensation arrangements designed to provide additional benefits to an executive during retirement. These plans are also referred to as **top-hat plans** since they are designed to benefit a select group of top management or key employees. **Excess-benefit plans** are a type of SERP that is designed solely to provide benefits in excess of the benefits available in qualified plans based on the limits under IRC §415. As mentioned, unfunded excess benefit plans are not subject to Title I of ERISA while funded excess benefit plans are generally subject to these provisions.

QUICK QUIZ 12.4

1. A rabbi trust is a special trust used only by nonprofit organizations to fund deferred compensation plans.
   a. True
   b. False

2. Some nonqualified plans require governmental reporting even though they are exempt from Title I of ERISA.
   a. True
   b. False

3. A 401(k) wrap plan eliminates the substantial risk of forfeiture common in deferred compensation plans.
   a. True
   b. False

False, True, False.

EXAMPLE 12.11

People's Bank and Dorothy, the vice-president and a cash-basis employee, enter into an employment agreement providing an annual total salary of $300,000 to Dorothy. People's promises to pay Dorothy $100,000 of the $300,000 in ten equal annual installments beginning at Dorothy's retirement or to her heirs beginning at her death. The agreement is a nonfunded, nonqualified deferred compensation agreement. The $100,000 is not constructively received by Dorothy and is not deductible to People's Bank until actually paid. The entire $300,000 is currently subject to the 1.45 percent Medicare tax. When ultimately received, the $100,000 will be subject to income tax, but not subject to Social Security taxes. Likewise, the payment will then be deductible by People's Bank as compensation. This plan could be an excess benefit plan or a SERP/top-hat plan depending on the purpose. If the only purpose is to provide excess benefits over qualified plan limits, it is an excess benefit plan. However, most plans have additional purposes and are, therefore, SERPs/top-hat plans.

Salary-reduction plans are common with professional athletes. A large signing bonus, or a part thereof, is frequently transferred to an escrow agent, subject to general creditors of team or owner, to defer the receipt of taxable income until such time as the athlete is beyond his peak earning period, thereby helping to assure the athlete's future financial security.

401(k) WRAP PLAN

401(k) wrap plans are a form of salary reduction plans that enable executives who are subject to salary deferral limitations due to the nondiscrimination rules to contribute higher amounts than otherwise permitted under a 401(k) plan. From the executive's perspective, there is not a significant difference between funds being contributed in these plans and 401(k) plans. The contribution to both plans are subject to payroll tax and income tax is deferred. However, there is a risk that the funds within the wrap plan might not be paid. Otherwise, there would not be substantial risk of forfeiture and the funds would then be taxable.

The usual motivation for use of a nonqualified deferred compensation plan where a qualified plan is in existence is to increase the wage replacement ratio (WRR) for key employees. Recall that qualified plans have compensation limits ($265,000 for 2016). If a key executive makes exactly $265,000, the qualified plan may deliver a suitable wage replacement ratio at retirement. However, for a key employee whose compensation is $400,000, the qualified plan will deliver benefits as if that employee earned $265,000, not $400,000. Thus, the greater the current compensation in excess of the qualified plan limit, the smaller the wage replacement ratio delivered by the qualified plan. Nonqualified plans are used to make up for this inequity.

<table>
<tr><td>**EXAMPLE**
12.12</td><td>Rob, age 50 (president), and Joe, age 50 (vice-president), are the top two executives in AFA, Inc. Joe's compensation is $265,000 and Rob's is $400,000. Joe is expected to receive $120,000 per year in retirement from AFA's qualified plan, thus achieving a wage replacement ratio of 45.28% ($120,000/$265,000). Unfortunately for Rob, he will also receive the same $120,000 from the qualified plan, thus producing a WRR of 30% ($120,000/$400,000). To make their retirement WRRs equal, AFA might use a NQDC arrangement to pay Rob an additional $61,000 per year in retirement [($120,000 + $61,000) ÷ 400,000 = 45%]. This is an example of an excess benefits plan.</td></tr>
</table>

NQDC plans may be established for a wide variety of key employees, shareholder employees, officers, highly compensated employees, or any particular person. Their disadvantage, when compared to qualified plans, is the lack of a current income tax deduction for the employer. Despite this fact, there is widespread use of NQDCs due to their great flexibility and the fact that they have none of the disadvantages of qualified plans.

EXHIBIT 12.3	**NQDC CONCEPT SUMMARY**

Employer Viewpoint	**Employee Viewpoint**
• Unfunded promise to pay • Not a qualified plan • Cash outflows are deferred • Employer saves on payroll taxes • Income tax deduction deferred until paid • Sometimes used if compensation exceeds $1 million and, therefore, non-deductible • May discriminate among employees	• Employee is at risk for nonpayment • Fund by using a rabbi trust; if unfunded, best with a financially secure company • No current taxable income • Employee saves on payroll taxes • May provide future cash flow at lower income tax rate

EMPLOYER STOCK OPTIONS AND STOCK PLANS

STOCK OPTIONS

An employee **stock option** gives the employee a right to buy stock at a specified price for a specified period of time. As part of an employer's overall compensation package, an employee's stock option program can be used to attract or retain talented management and to tie the financial compensation of selected key executives to the performance of the company, thus aligning the interest of management executives with outside shareholders.

Through the technology bubble and the accounting scandals of the recent past, stock options were extremely popular with publicly-traded companies and "start-ups." However, with the financial accounting requirement that options be expensed, the use of options is on a decline. Companies are choosing to reward executives in other ways that do not have the same negative impact on a firm's financial statements.

Stock options are usually granted to select employees for the purchase of stock of the employer or a subsidiary. The option agreement must be in writing, and the option holder has no obligation to exercise the option. The terms of the option agreement must be stated (e.g., 10 years) in the agreement.

KEY CONCEPTS ✓

1. What are stock options?

2. What are Incentive Stock Options, and what are the tax consequences associated with the grant, exercise, and sale of ISOs?

3. What are Nonqualified Stock Options and what are the tax consequences associated with the grant, exercise, and sale of NQSOs?

Option Price

Generally, the **option price (exercise price)** is equal to the fair market value at the **grant date** (the date of issuance). If the option does not have a readily ascertainable fair market value at the grant date, there is no taxable income to the option holder as of the grant date. Employee stock options usually have substantial restrictions and vesting requirements such that a readily ascertainable fair market value for the options is not available. If values were available and the value was ascertainable, it would be taxable income to the recipient. An option is a form of deferred compensation if the price of the stock increases. If the stock price declines, the option holder will simply allow the option to lapse.

It is important to note that options granted at fair market value are not subject to the rules under IRC §409A. However, options issued at a discount from fair market value are subject to IRC §409A and its harsh tax results.

Vesting

Generally, stock options vest over time, thus continuing to provide an incentive to the executive who is receiving the option to remain with the employer and to be productive. As the fortunes of the company improve, it is common for more options to be granted. A common vesting schedule is 20 percent per year of service after the grant. However, the vesting schedule could take any form, even immediate 100 percent vesting, although that is uncommon.

Types of Options

There are two standard types of employer stock options: **Incentive Stock Options** (ISOs) and **Nonqualified Stock Options** (NQSOs). The goal of utilizing either type of option is to motivate employees by providing them with employer stock at a price that is expected to appreciate. From a tax perspective, however, ISOs can have more favorable tax treatment than NQSOs. The cost of this tax benefit is that ISOs have more restrictions.

INCENTIVE STOCK OPTIONS (ISOS)

An incentive stock option (ISO) is a right given to an employee to purchase an employer's common stock at a stated exercise price. If the requirements of IRC §422 are met when the incentive stock option is granted (provided the exercise price is equal to the fair market value of the stock), the employee will not recognize any taxable income at the date of grant. Further, at the date of exercise, the employee will also not be subject to ordinary income tax on the difference between the fair market value of the stock and the exercise price. However, this difference is a positive adjustment for the alternative minimum tax calculation. When the employee sells the stock subsequent to the exercise, the difference between the sales price of the stock and the original exercise price is considered long-term capital gain and there is a negative adjustment for the alternative minimum tax calculation. For an employee in the 39.6 percent ordinary income tax bracket, the long-term capital gain rate of 20 percent is very attractive, but to attain this tax benefit, ISOs have strict requirements.

REQUIREMENTS FOR INCENTIVE STOCK OPTION

EXHIBIT 12.4

1. ISOs can only be granted to an employee of the corporation issuing the ISOs.

2. The ISO plan must be approved by the stockholders of the issuing corporation.

3. The ISOs must be granted within 10 years of the ISO plan date.

4. The exercise of the ISO is limited to a 10-year period (5 years for 10% + owners).

5. At the date of the ISO grant, the exercise price must be greater than or equal to the fair market value of the stock.

6. An ISO cannot be transferred except at death.

7. An owner of more than 10% of a corporation cannot be given ISOs unless the exercise price is 110% of the fair market value at the date of grant and the option term is less than 5 years.

8. To the extent that the aggregate fair market value of stock with respect to which ISOs are exercisable for the 1st time by any individual during any calendar year exceeds $100,000, such options shall be treated as NQSOs.

9. To qualify as an ISO, the executive must hold the stock for the greater of two years from the grant of the ISO or one year from the date of exercise of the ISO.

10. The executive must be an employee of the corporation continuously from the date of the grant until at least three months prior to the exercise.

Taxation

Grant Date

At the date of the ISO grant there is no taxable income to the employee if the exercise price is greater than or equal to the fair market value of the employer stock. If the exercise price is less than the fair market value of the employer stock, the executive will have W-2 income equal to the difference and the employer will have compensation expense for the same amount. In addition, this would cause the option to fall within IRC §409A.

Exercise of the ISO

Once the ISO is exercisable, the executive purchases the employer stock at the exercise price. At the date of exercise in a qualifying ISO transaction, the executive will purchase the stock with his own funds with an intent to hold the stock for at least the holding period requirement (as discussed below). The exercise of the ISO in a qualifying transaction will not create any regular tax impact for either the employee or the employer but will create an alternative minimum tax (AMT) adjustment for the executive equal to the difference between the exercise price and the fair market value of the stock at the exercise date.

The exercise price of the ISO creates the executive's adjusted basis in the employer stock for regular tax purposes since the executive used after-tax dollars to purchase the stock under the ISO. However, the executive's AMT adjusted basis is the fair market value at the date of exercise.

Sale of the Stock from the ISO Exercise After Holding Period Requirement

An executive will receive favorable gain treatment on the appreciation of employer stock above the exercise price provided the executive does not sell the employer stock before two years from the date of grant and one year from the date of exercise, referred to as the holding period requirement. If the holding period requirement is met, the employer will never receive a tax deduction in relation to the ISO.

If the executive meets this holding period requirement and the value of the stock is greater than the exercise price of the ISO, the executive will have long-term capital gain treatment on the appreciation above the exercise price and a negative AMT adjustment equal to the AMT adjustment at the date of the exercise.

EXAMPLE 12.13

On January 5, 2016, Bob, vice president of XYZ Corporation, is granted 10,000 ISOs at an exercise price of $10. On February 6, 2017, he exercises all of the options when the price of XYZ stock is $42. Bob subsequently sells the stock at $60 on February 14, 2018. What are his tax consequences?

At the date of exercise, Bob has no W-2 income, or ordinary income, but does have an AMT adjustment of $320,000 ($420,000 - $100,000) which may cause Bob to pay AMT. For regular tax, he has an adjusted basis of $100,000. When he subsequently sells the stock for $600,000, he has a long-term capital gain of $500,000 subject to a capital gains rate of 20% and a negative AMT adjustment equal to $320,000.

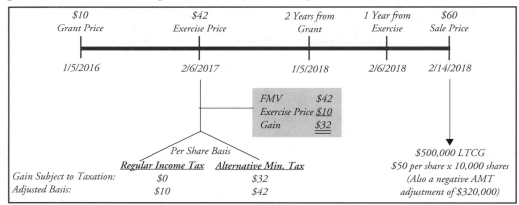

Keep in mind that presuming the holding period rules are met, the gain at exercise is deferred and treated as capital gain upon sale of the ISO stock. However, for AMT purposes there is no deferral of gain, which results in a timing difference between regular tax and AMT.

If the executive meets the holding period requirement but the value of the stock is less than the exercise price, the executive has a long-term capital loss equal to the difference between the exercise price and the sales price. The executive also has a negative AMT adjustment equal to the AMT adjustment at the exercise date.

Case Study 12.3

In *Speltz v. Commissioner of Internal Revenue,* 124 Tax Ct. No. 9 (15382-036, March 23, 2005 Ronald and June Speltz incurred AMT liability as a result of their exercise of incentive stock options in 2000. The stock declined precipitously in value after the date of exercise. Mr. and Mrs. Speltz partially paid the tax liability and submitted an offer in compromise with respect to the unpaid balance. The IRS rejected the offer in compromise and filed a lien on their property. The tax court held it was not an abuse of the IRS's discretion to reject Mr. and Mrs. Speltz's offer in compromise and to continue the lien. Mr. and Mrs. Speltz reasoned that their offer in compromise should have been accepted because of the unfair application of the alternative minimum tax (AMT).

Ronald Speltz was employed by McLeodUSA as a senior manager earning wages over $75,000 in 2000 and over $90,000 in 2004. As part of his compensation package he received ISOs for acquisition of McLeod Stock. In 2000, Mr. Speltz exercised some of the ISOs. Mr. and Mrs. Speltz filed their 1040 and the ISOs resulted in "excess of AMT income over regular tax income" of $711,118.

On their Form 1040, petitioners reported that their "regular" adjusted gross income was $142,070. Their taxable income was $105,461, and their "regular" tax was $18,678. They reported AMT of $206,191 for a total tax liability of $224,869. After application of Federal income tax withheld, the balance owed on Speltz's tax liability for 2000 was $210,065. The value of their McLeod stock dropped precipitously. On their tax return for 2000, the Speltzs reported that they sold 200 shares of McLeod stock on January 14 for a total of $14,011 and 500 shares of McLeod stock on March 10 for a total of $52,282. On their tax return for 2002, they reported that they sold 2,070 shares of McLeod stock on December 30 for a total of $1,647. The Speltzs partially paid the liability reported on their 2000 Form 1040 at the time that it was filed and paid an additional $75,000 in installments prior to November 2, 2001.

In November of 2001, they submitted to the Internal Revenue Service (IRS) a Form 656, Offer in Compromise. The Speltzs offered a cash payment of $4,457, the cash value of Mr. Speltz's life insurance policy, against the liability that then exceeded $125,000. On the Form 656, petitioners checked the box for "Doubt as to Collectibility" stating they had insufficient assets and income to pay the full amount.

Petitioners also attached to Form 656 a statement in which they explained that an offer in compromise was necessary because of the impact the AMT in 2000 had on their finances and their lifestyle.

Specifically, petitioner's income in 2000 was at a comfortable level for a family of five including three young daughters; the McLeod stock they held was nearly worthless and declining and had been used to secure a $134,000 loan with a bank to pay part of the 2000 Federal and State taxes; and, in the event of a sale of the stock (forced or otherwise), petitioners would be unable to carry back the capital loss to offset their 2000 gain.

They began building a new home in 2000 and sold their prior home in 2001, using the proceeds of sale to repay the bank. Lifestyle changes were necessary, including: Petitioner June M. Speltz had to get a job instead of staying home with the children; the oldest daughter had to switch schools; petitioners were unable to contribute to their retirement and to their children's education fund; and they had to reduce their charitable donations. Finally, they could not afford to have a fourth child, which they had wanted.

In the statement, petitioners expressed their mental anguish and frustration with the unfairness of their situation. The offer was ultimately rejected because the IRS believed the Speltzs did have the ability to pay.

The Speltzs did not actually dispute the AMT, instead they claimed that the IRS abused its discretion by not allowing them to pay less because of the decline in stock. While the Tax Court was sympathetic, it found that the IRS did not abuse its discretion.

Disqualifying Disposition

If stock acquired after exercising an ISO is disposed of before either two years from the date of the grant or one year from the date of exercise, the sale is known as a **disqualifying disposition** and some of the favorable tax treatment is lost. For such a sale, any gain on the sale of the stock attributable to the difference between the exercise price and the fair market value at the date of exercise is considered ordinary income and, reported on the executive's W-2, but not subject to payroll tax or federal income tax withholding.[15] Any gain in excess of the amount reported on the W-2 is short or long-term capital gain considering the executive's holding period. Any AMT adjustment created at the date of exercise is reversed at the date of the disqualifying disposition. Also, at this time, the employer has a tax deductible expense equal to the amount reported on the executive's W-2.

---

15. See IRC Section 3121(a)(22).

On October 12, 2016, Donald was granted 15,000 ISOs at an exercise price of $2 per share when the fair market value of the stock was also $2. On November 14, 2017, Donald exercised the stock when the fair market value was $8 per share. Subsequently, on January 1, 2018, Donald sold all the stock for $6 per share.

EXAMPLE 12.14

At the date of grant there was no taxable income because the exercise price of the stock was equal to the fair market value of the stock. At the date of exercise, there was no regular income tax but there was AMT income equal to $6 per share ($8 - $2). Because Donald did not hold the stock for at least two years from the date of the grant and one year from the date of exercise, Donald has a disqualifying disposition at the date of sale. The gain on the stock of $4 per share ($6 - $2) is ordinary income, and Donald's employer will receive a tax deduction for the same amount ($60,000). Donald will also have a negative AMT adjustment equal to $6 per share at the date of sale to reverse the adjustment at the date of exercise.

Assume the same facts as above, except that the stock price at the time of sale is $11 instead of $6. There is still a disqualifying disposition since the holding period was not met. However, in this case, there will be ordinary income equal to $6 ($8 - $2) per share and a short-term capital gain of $3 per share ($11 - $8). As before, Donald has a negative AMT adjustment equal to $6 per share.

EXAMPLE 12.15

Cashless Exercise

A **cashless exercise** is an exercise of an option where the executive does not utilize any cash. Cashless exercises are quite common as many executives do not have the additional cash to exercise the option. At the time of a cashless exercise, a third-party lender lends the executive the cash needed to exercise the option and the lender is immediately repaid with the proceeds of the almost simultaneous sale of the stock. A cashless exercise of incentive stock options automatically triggers a partial disqualifying disposition since the holding period requirements will not be met.

Because the executive does not hold the stock for at least two years from grant and one year from exercise, the disposition of the stock is a disqualifying disposition and any gain recognized from the transaction will be treated as ordinary income (reportable on the W-2) not subject to payroll taxes. From the executive's perspective, the entire transaction is a form of cash bonus. Like a disqualifying disposition when the executive recognizes the ordinary income, the employer will have a tax deductible compensation expense.

Jason, an executive, has 10,000 ISOs with an $8 exercise price. When the value of the stock increases to $32, the stock has a total value of $320,000. If Jason exercised today, he would need $80,000 to exercise the option (ignoring any potential AMT consequence). Like many individuals, Jason does not have the $80,000 cash available to exercise the option. Therefore, Jason makes a cashless exercise of the option and receives $240,000 (the proceeds from the sale of the stock less the exercise price of $80,000). In reality, the proceeds Jason actually receives are reduced for transaction fees.

EXAMPLE 12.16

Since the sale of the stock did not meet the holding period requirements of an ISO, $240,000 is subjected to ordinary income tax.

NONQUALIFIED STOCK OPTIONS (NQSOs)

An NQSO is an option that does not meet the requirements of an incentive stock option or it is explicitly identified as nonqualified. As such, the exercise of an NQSO does not receive favorable capital gains treatment but also does not require the holding period associated with ISOs. A NQSO is designed to tie a benefit given to an executive to the stock price of the company, but unlike an ISO, it does not provide the executive or the employer with substantial tax benefits.

From a risk perspective, the executive takes no risk in an NQSO. If the stock price falls below the exercise price, the executive simply does not exercise. If the stock appreciates, the executive may choose to exercise and may immediately sell the stock or hold it (there is investment risk to holding the stock).

Taxation
Grant Date
The grant of an NQSO will not create a taxable event assuming that there is no readily ascertainable value for the NQSO. Generally an option will not have a readily ascertainable value if the exercise price of the option is greater than or equal to the fair market value of the underlying stock. If, however, the option does have a readily ascertainable value at the date of grant or at anytime after the grant, the executive will otherwise have W-2 income equal to the value and the employer will have an income tax deduction.

Exercise of the NQSO
At the exercise date of the NQSO, the executive will deliver to the employer both the option and the exercise price per share. The executive will recognize W-2 income for the appreciation of the fair market value of the stock over the exercise price (often referred to as the bargain element), income tax withholding will apply, and the employer will have an income tax deduction for the same amount.

The fair market value of the stock at the exercise date (which is equal to the sum of the exercise price plus the appreciation of the stock after the date of grant) is the executive's adjusted basis in the employer stock. The executive's holding period for calculation of subsequent gains and losses also begins on the exercise date.

Sale of the Stock from the NQSO Exercise
Stock acquired through the exercise of an NQSO does not have a specified holding period requirement. When the stock is sold, the executive's gain or loss will be considered capital gain or loss and will receive short or long-term capital gain treatment according to the elapsed time between the date of the sale and the exercise date. The employer corporation does not have a tax effect at the sale date.

On January 2, 2016 (the grant date), Ned, an executive with ABC Corporation, is issued one nonqualified stock option from ABC Corporation with an exercise price of $10 (the current market price). On January 3, 2017, Ned exercises his option when the ABC stock price is $35. Ned brings the option and $10 to ABC. ABC issues the stock and Ned recognizes $25 in W-2 income from ABC. Ned's new basis in the stock is $35. He later sells the stock, on March 4, 2017 for $50, which creates a short-term capital gain of $15. If instead, Ned had sold the stock on or after January 4, 2018, the gain would be long term.

EXAMPLE 12.17

On January 5, 2016, Gerry was issued 10,000 nonqualified stock options of L&O Corporation, his employer. At the date of the grant, the fair market value of the stock was $35 and the exercise price was $35. Due to the time, vesting, and transferability provisions, there was no readily ascertainable value for the options at the time of the grant. The options vest 20% per year and are exercisable as vested. On January 5, 2017, Gerry exercised 2,000 options when the fair market value of the stock was $48. Gerry surrenders 2,000 options and $70,000 to L&O Corporation. He will receive 2,000 shares of L&O having a current fair market value of $96,000. He has W-2 income of $26,000 and has an adjusted basis in the stock of $96,000. If Gerry subsequently sells the stock, he will have a capital gain or loss, depending on the sale price of the stock. L&O Corporation will deduct $26,000 as compensation expense at the time of exercise.

EXAMPLE 12.18

Cashless Exercise

As discussed above, a cashless exercise is the exercise of an option when the executive does not utilize any cash. A NQSO can be exercised with a cashless exercise just as described above with the ISO, and the executive will receive the difference between the exercise price and the fair market value of the stock at the date of the cashless exercise as W-2 income.

Gifting of ISOs and NQSOs

Lifetime transfers of unexercised ISOs by the employee are not permitted. The requirement to obtain long-term capital gain treatment for the stock received upon exercise is that the stock must be transferred only after the holding period requirement. Any transfer of ISO stock before the completion of the holding period may cause the appreciation on the stock to be taxed as ordinary income rather than capital gain.

A NQSO can be gifted provided the NQSO plan permits transfer of ownership. There are no immediate income tax consequences on the transfer.

QUICK QUIZ 12.5

1. A stock option agreement must be in writing and must state an option term.
   a. True
   b. False

2. The exercise of an ISO triggers W-2 income for the employee.
   a. True
   b. False

3. At the exercise date of an NQSO, the employee will recognize W-2 income for the appreciation of the fair market value of the stock over the exercise price.
   a. True
   b. False

True, False, True.

Upon exercise of the NQSO by the donee, the employee will have W-2 income for the difference between the exercise price and the fair market value on the date of exercise. The donee's basis after the exercise will be equal to the fair market value on the date of exercise (exercise price plus employee's tax recognition). If the employee also pays the exercise price, it is an additional gift to the donee. Any gift of a NQSO that is neither vested nor exercisable is an incomplete gift. Valuation of options is determined using the **Black Scholes Method**. NQSOs are not good items to transfer to charities except after the option has been exercised and the stock held for more than a year and a day, which is when the stock can qualify as long-term capital gain property and is then available for a higher charitable deduction.

EXHIBIT
12.5

NQSO AND ISO SUMMARY

	NQSO	ISO
At Grant Date	No taxable income to holder if issued at the current or greater share price.	No taxable income to holder if issued at current or greater share price.
At Exercise	Executive gives options and exercise price to company. Company issues stock to executive to replace option.	Executive gives options and exercise price to company. Company issues stock to executive to replace option.
Employee Taxation	At exercise, executive recognizes W-2 income to extent of difference between current stock price and exercise price.	At exercise, executive does not recognize any regular taxable income but will have an AMT adjustment for the appreciation over the exercise price.
Employer Tax Deduction	Employer's income tax deduction equals the executive's taxable income.	The employer will not receive a tax deduction unless the stock is disposed of in a disqualifying disposition.
Adjustable Basis	Executive's adjusted basis in stock is equal to the fair market value of stock (exercise price in cash plus the recognition of W-2 income).	Executive's adjusted basis in stock is equal to the exercise price.
When Stock is Sold	Capital gain or loss treatment.	Capital gain or loss treatment.

STOCK APPRECIATION RIGHTS

Stock Appreciation Rights (SARs) are rights that grant to the holder cash in an amount equal to the excess of the fair market value of the stock over the exercise price.

EXAMPLE
12.19

Jamie is a key executive in NT Company. She is granted 1,000 SARs at $10, the current trading price of NT. If Jamie exercises the SARs two years from the grant when NT's stock price is $32, she will receive $22,000 as W-2 income subject to both income and payroll taxes.

The SAR is essentially a way to achieve a "cashless exercise." Notice in the above example, Jamie did not have to come up with the exercise price of $10,000 (1,000 x $10). The rights cannot be exercised before one year, and if they are not exercised within five years, they are deemed exercised on the fifth anniversary of the grant. At that time, the employee will be paid the amount of the appreciation. Payments received for the stock appreciation rights are includable in gross income in the year the rights are exercised.

An employee who possesses stock appreciation rights is not in constructive receipt of income by virtue of the appreciation of the employer's stock. The cash payment to which the employee is entitled is includible in gross income in the year a stock appreciation right is exercised.

The grant of the SAR does not constitute constructive receipt, even if immediately exercisable, because of the future potential appreciation of the SAR. If, however, the SAR has a cap or limit, there is constructive receipt when the stock reaches that limit price, unless the SAR is issued in tandem with the option and the option is terminated if not exercised simultaneously with the SAR. In such case, there is no constructive receipt.[16]

Generally, SARs are granted with NQSOs or ISOs and may be used to provide cash to the executive, which is necessary to exercise the NQSO or ISO. Usually, the number of NQSOs or ISOs is reduced by any exercised SARs.

KEY CONCEPTS

1. What are stock appreciation rights?

2. Explain the characteristics of restricted stock plans.

3. What are the benefits of an 83(b) election?

4. What are employee stock purchase plans?

SARs are generally subject to the requirements of §409A. However, there are certain circumstances under which SARs are excluded from coverage under §409A because the Internal Revenue Service has determined that these circumstances do not present the potential for abuse or intentional circumvention of the purposes of 409A. Specifically, a SAR will not constitute a deferral of compensation if (1) compensation payable under the SAR is not greater than the difference between the fair market value of the stock on the date of grant and the fair market value of the stock on the exercise date, with respect to a number of shares fixed on or before the date of grant; (2) the SAR exercise price is not less than the fair market value of the underlying stock on the date of grant; and (3) the SAR does not include any feature for the deferral of compensation other than the deferral of recognition of income until the exercise of the right.[17]

16. Revenue Ruling 82-121.
17. Proposed Treas. Reg. §1.409A-1(b)(5)(i)(B).

RESTRICTED STOCK PLANS

A **restricted stock plan** is an employer-provided plan designed to increase retention and compensate employees with a non-cash outflow. The plan pays executives with shares of the employer's stock. The executive does not pay any amount towards the allocation of the stock and is restricted by the employer from selling or transferring the stock. The restriction most often gives the employer the ability to repurchase the stock during a set period of years or prohibits the executive from selling the stock during a set number of years or until a defined occurrence or event (i.e., the executive attains 10 years of service with the company).

At receipt of the restricted stock, the executive will generally not recognize any taxable income (see §83(b) discussion below) as the restrictions generally create a substantial risk of forfeiture. In addition the employer will not have a deductible expense. However, when this substantial risk of forfeiture is eliminated the executive recognizes W-2 income equal to the value of the stock at that date and the employer will have a tax deductible expense for an equal amount. The amount recognized by the executive becomes the executive's adjusted basis in the stock for purposes of any subsequent gain or loss calculation. The executive's holding period of the stock also begins at the date the restrictions are lifted.

EXAMPLE 12.20	Dana was entitled to a $100,000 incentive bonus from Significant Corp. in 2016. However, Significant was short on cash due to poor planning and instead paid Dana $25,000 and gave her $75,000 worth of restricted stock (5,000 shares at $15 per share). In 2019, after all of the restrictions were lifted, Dana's shares are worth $30 per share. In 2019, Dana has W-2 income of $150,000 and Significant has a deduction of $150,000. Dana now has an adjusted basis in the Significant stock of $150,000.

The Section 83(b) Election

If property is transferred in connection with the performance of services, the person performing such services may elect to include in gross income under **IRC Section 83(b)** the excess (if any) of the fair market value of the property at the time of transfer over the amount (if any) paid for such property as compensation for services. The fact that the transferee has paid full value for the property transferred, realizing no bargain element in the transaction, does not preclude the use of the election as provided for in this section. If this election is made, any subsequent appreciation in the value of the property is not taxable as compensation to the person who performed the services but as capital gain at the date of sale. Thus, property with respect to which this election is made shall be includible in gross income as of the time of transfer even though such property is substantially nonvested at the time of transfer and no compensation will be includible in gross income when such property becomes substantially vested.

In computing the gain or loss from the subsequent sale or exchange of such property, its basis shall be the amount paid for the property increased by the amount included in gross income under §83(b). Its holding period shall be determined based upon the date the value was included in gross income. If property for which a §83(b) election is in effect is forfeited while substantially nonvested, such forfeiture shall be treated as a sale or exchange upon which there is realized a loss equal to the excess (if any) of the amount paid (if any) for such property over the amount realized (if any) upon such forfeiture. Therefore, the taxpayer would not receive any loss for the amount included in income, only a loss for the amount paid.

The economic benefit of this election is that the appreciation from the time of the grant through the vesting period will be treated as capital gain instead of W-2 income. However, the taxpayer must consider not only the tax issues of such an election but also other issues in deciding whether or not to make the election. For example, it is important to consider the investment characteristics of the property or stock. Another important consideration is whether the restrictions will be met. If, for example, an employee is issued restricted stock that vests over five years, it would not make sense for the employee to make the 83(b) election if there is a risk he would leave his employer within five years.

> Assume SARs Inc. has a restricted stock plan. Stock granted to employees of SARs under this plan vest after a 5-year period. Kristi, a new executive, was granted restricted stock worth $10,000 on January 5, 2016. Kristi believes that the value of the stock will increase significantly over the next five years. Kristi can make an 83(b) election and include the $10,000 into her current income.
>
> Assuming the stock is worth $25,000 at the end of five years, Kristi will not recognize any gain upon vesting of the stock. When the stock is sold, Kristi will have capital gain equal to the difference between the sale proceeds and the value of the stock at the time of the grant. Kristi has effectively converted ordinary income into capital gain income.
>
> If Kristi had not filed the election, then she would include the $25,000 in taxable income as ordinary income for the year in which the vesting was complete. Any future appreciation above $25,000 would be treated as a capital gain.

EXAMPLE 12.21

> Assume the same facts as above, including the fact that Kristi made the 83(b) election, except that Kristi quit two years after the grant. In this case, at the date of 83(b) election, Kristi would have ordinary income of $10,000 but at termination would not have a loss since she did not pay for the stock.

EXAMPLE 12.22

Making the Election

The 83(b) election must be filed no later than 30 days after the date the property is transferred and may be filed prior to the date of transfer. The election is made by filing one copy of a written statement with the internal revenue office with whom the person who performed the services files his return. Historically, one copy of such statement had to be submitted with his income tax return for the taxable year in which such property was transferred. However, the IRS issued proposed regulations in 2015 that eliminate the requirement that taxpayers must submit a copy of a section 83(b) election with their tax return for the year in which the property subject to the election was transferred.

The statement shall be signed by the person making the election, shall indicate that it is being made under §83(b) of the Code, and shall contain the following information:
- the name, address, and taxpayer identification number of the taxpayer,
- a description of each property with respect to which the election is being made,
- the date or dates on which the property is transferred and the taxable year (for example, "calendar year 2016" or "fiscal year ending May 31, 2017") for which such election was made,
- the nature of the restriction or restrictions to which the property is subject,

- the fair market value at the time of each property with respect to which the election is being made,
- the amount (if any) paid for such property, and
- a statement to the effect that copies have been furnished to other persons as provided in the regulations.

EMPLOYEE STOCK PURCHASE PLANS (ESPP)

Intended to benefit all or a large portion of an employer's employees (the plan cannot be discriminatory), per IRC §423, an **employee stock purchase plan** (ESPP) gives employees an incentive to buy employer stock by allowing the employees to purchase the stock at a discounted price and receive favorable tax treatment for any gains if the stock meets certain holding period requirements. As discussed in other areas of the text, an employee who owns stock in his employer is connected to the productivity of the company and, in most cases, will work more efficiently and effectively towards the goals of the company.

Generally, an employee elects to defer after-tax compensation throughout the plan year through payroll deductions to the ESPP established by the employer. The employee is able to purchase the employer stock through the ESPP for a price equal to no less than 85 percent of a date determined stock price or an average stock price.[18] An example of a date determined price is the lesser of fair market value (1) at the beginning of the plan period, grant date, or (2) the end of the plan period, exercise date. An example of an average price is the average price for the quarter. The grant date and exercise date generally coincide with the beginning and end of the calendar year, but either could follow quarters, months, or any other time period that the employer selects.

DTY Corporation's ESPP has a plan year of December 1, 2016 to November 30, 2017. DTY's employees are permitted to defer after-tax compensation into the plan from December 1, 2016 to November 30, 2017, and the ESPP will purchase the DTY stock for 85% of the lesser of the fair market value on December 1, 2016 or the fair market value on November 30, 2017. The fair market value of the stock at December 1, 2016 was $20, and the fair market value of the stock at November 30, 2017 was $28. The employee would be able to purchase the employer stock through the ESPP for $17 (85% of $20).

---

18. IRC §423(b)(6)(A). Most ESPPs utilize the 85% of the date determined price or average price; although, it may be any amount or percentage greater than 85%.

Tribro's ESPP operates four plan periods during the year following the normal quarters of the calendar year. Employees must elect to defer their after-tax compensation prior to the beginning of each period to participate in the ESPP. After the end of each quarter, the employee purchases the employer stock for 85% of the average price during the quarter.

EXAMPLE
12.24

At the date of purchase, the employee will not have any taxable consequences but will immediately have an unrealized gain at least equal to the price discount off the fair market value of the stock. Consider an employee who was able to purchase the stock of his employer through the ESPP for $11.05, 85% of the fair market value on the date of exercise ($13.00). This employee would have $1.95 ($13.00-$11.05) or a 17.6% ($1.95÷$11.05) immediate pre-tax gain. Even with a 30% marginal tax rate, the gain would be 12.32% (17.6% x (1 - 30%)) without considering the benefits of future appreciation and lower tax rates (discussed below).

Employee Dollar Limit

An employee is statutorily limited to purchasing $25,000 of employer stock per year as determined based on the fair market value at the date of grant of the employer stock through the ESPP.[19] For example, if at the grant date the fair market value of the stock was $31.25 and at the exercise date the stock had a fair market value of $28.00, the employee could only purchase 800 shares ($25,000 ÷ $31.25) for $23.80 (85% of $28.00) for a total of $19,040 (800 x $23.80). If the employee deferred more to the ESPP than necessary, the difference would be returned to him. The refund would not create any taxable consequences as the funds in the ESPP are post-tax. Some employers may place additional limitations on their employees by restricting the amount of stock they may purchase (i.e., 15% of compensation or 2,500 shares) through the ESPP. Such restrictions cannot be applied on a discriminatory basis.

---

19. IRC §423(b)(8).

Qualifying Disposition

If the employee holds the stock purchased through the ESPP for two years from the date of grant and one year from the date of exercise, any subsequent sale is a qualifying disposition of the stock. The employee's gain on the sale of the stock will be ordinary income to the extent the gain is attributable to the discount at the date of purchase. Any gain in excess of the ordinary income portion will be long-term capital gain. For example, if the employees were able to purchase the employer stock for $85.00 (85% of fair market value) and after meeting the required holding period requirements sold the stock for $90.00, then $5.00 ($90.00 - $85.00) would be considered as ordinary gain. This treatment occurs because the $5 represents part of the original discount. However, if after meeting the holding period requirement the employee sold the stock for $110.00, the total gain would be $25.00 ($110.00 - $85.00) and $15.00, the amount attributable to the discount, would be treated as ordinary income and the remaining $10.00 would be treated as long-term capital gain.

EXAMPLE 12.25

Stanley, Inc. has an ESPP, and the stock traded on January 2, 2016 for $12.00 and on December 31, 2016 for $15.00. The plan permitted Cline, an employee, to buy at 85% of the lesser of the two prices ($12.00 x 0.85 = $10.20 per share). Cline, who contracted to purchase $25,000 worth of stock, will receive 2,083 shares of Stanley, Inc. stock ($25,000 ÷ $12.00). Note that since the stock price has risen to $15.00 per share, Cline has a portfolio worth $31,245 for which he paid $21,247. If he holds the stock 2 years from the date of the original purchase before selling at $20 per share, Cline will have ordinary income of $3,749 ($12.00-$10.20 x 2,083) and long-term capital gain of $16,664 ($8.00 x 2,083).

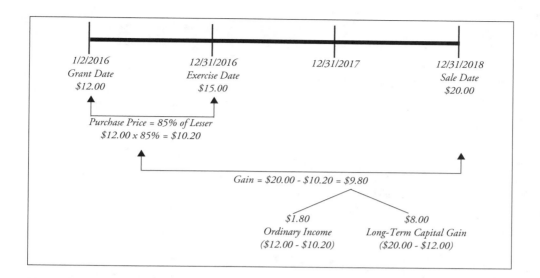

Assume the same facts as above, except that Cline sells the stock for $11.00. In this case, since the entire gain, $0.80 per share ($11.00 - $10.20), is less than Cline's purchase discount, ($1.80 per share), Cline will have ordinary income equal to $1,666 ($0.80 x 2,083).

Disqualifying Disposition

If an employee does not hold the stock purchased through the ESPP for at least two years from the date of grant and one year from the exercise date, any sale is a disqualifying disposition. The primary difference as compared to a qualifying disposition is that the gain attributable to the discount will be W-2 income rather than ordinary income and therefore subject to FICA. The employee's gain on the sale will be W-2 income to the extent the gain is attributable to the purchase discount. Any gain in excess of the ordinary income portion will be long or short-term capital gain dependent upon the holding period, which begins on the exercise date. For example, if an employee were able to purchase employer stock for $85.00 or 85 percent of fair market value, and before meeting the required holding period, sold the stock for $90.00, $5.00 ($90.00-$85.00) would be W-2 income. However, if the employee had sold the stock six months after the exercise date for $110.00, the total gain would be $25.00 ($110.00 - $85.00) and $15.00, the amount attributable to the discount, would be W-2 income and the remaining $10.00 would be short-term capital gain.

EXAMPLE
12.27

Timer, Inc. has an ESPP and its stock traded on June 30, 2016 for $30.00 and July 31, 2016 for $25.00. Rhonda had elected to defer after-tax income to the ESPP and purchased 400 shares of the stock at 85% of the lower of the two values. Rhonda purchased 400 shares of the Timer, Inc. stock for $8,500 ($21.25 x 400 shares). Six months later, Rhonda sold the 400 shares at $27 per share. Since Rhonda did not hold the stock for the required holding period, Rhonda will have W-2 income at the date of sale of $1,500 [($25.00 - $21.25) x 400] and a short-term capital gain of $800 [($27.00 - $25.00) x 400].

Loss

If the employee sells the stock purchased through the ESPP at a price less than the exercise price, the employee will have a short or long-term capital loss as determined based upon the holding period beginning at the date of exercise and the difference between the exercise price and the sales price.

EXHIBIT
12.6

ESPP SUMMARY

- Employee usually buys employer stock at 85% of fair market value.
- When the stock is sold, the price discount of 15% is ordinary income.
- The excess of the sales price over the undiscounted purchase price is long-term capital gain if a qualifying disposition.
- The stock purchase has a built-in return of 17.6% pretax.
- There is a $25,000 limit for purchases.

KEY TERMS

BLACK SCHOLES METHOD - An option valuation model.

CASHLESS EXERCISE - An exercise of an option where the option holder does not utilize any cash.

CONSTRUCTIVE RECEIPT - An income tax concept that establishes when income is includible by a taxpayer and therefore subject to income tax. Income is constructively received in the taxable year during which it is credited to the employee's account, set apart for him, or otherwise made available so that he may draw upon it at any time or so that he could have drawn upon it during the taxable year if notice of intention to withdraw had been given.

DEFERRED COMPENSATION ARRANGEMENTS - An arrangement to pay an executive compensation in a future year.

DISQUALIFYING DISPOSITION - If stock acquired after exercising an ISO is disposed before either two years from the date of the grant or one year from the date of exercise.

ECONOMIC BENEFIT DOCTRINE - An employee will be taxed on funds or property set aside for the employee if the funds or property are unrestricted and nonforfeitable even if the employee was not given a choice to receive the income currently.

EMPLOYEE STOCK PURCHASE PLAN - A plan designed to benefit all or a large portion of an employer's employees that gives employees an incentive to buy employer stock by allowing the employees to purchase the stock at a discounted price (up to a 15% discount) and receive favorable tax treatment for any gains if the stock meets certain holding period requirements.

EXCESS BENEFIT PLANS - A type of SERP that is designed solely to provide benefits in excess of the benefits available in qualified plans based on the limits under IRC §415.

401(k) WRAP PLANS - A form of salary reduction plan that enables executives, who are subject to salary deferral limitations due to the nondiscrimination rules, to contribute higher amounts than otherwise permitted under a 401(k) plan.

GRANT DATE - The date of issuance of a stock or option.

INCENTIVE STOCK OPTIONS (ISOs) - A right given to an employee to purchase an employer's common stock at a stated exercise price. If the requirements of IRC §422 are met, the employee will not recognize any taxable income at the date of grant. Further, at the date of exercise, the employee will also not be subject to ordinary income tax on the difference between the fair market value of the stock and the exercise price. This difference is a positive adjustment for the alternative minimum tax calculation. When the employee sells the stock subsequent to the exercise, the difference between the sales price of the stock and the original exercise price is considered long-term capital gain and there is a negative adjustment for the alternative minimum tax calculation.

KEY TERMS

IRC SECTION 83(b) ELECTION - Election to include in gross income the difference between the fair market value of restricted stock and its purchase price.

NONQUALIFIED DEFERRED COMPENSATION PLAN (NQDC) - A contractual arrangement between the employer and an executive, whereby the employer promises to pay the executive a predetermined amount of money sometime in the future.

NONQUALIFIED PLANS - Plans that do not meet the requirements of the IRC §401(a) and therefore do not have the benefits of qualified plans.

NONQUALIFIED STOCK OPTIONS (NQSOs) - An option that does not meet the requirements of an incentive stock option. The exercise of an NQSO does not receive favorable long-term capital gains treatment but also does not require the holding period associated with ISOs.

OPTION PRICE (EXERCISE PRICE) - Usually the fair market value at the grant date.

PHANTOM STOCK PLAN - A nonqualified deferred compensation arrangement where the employer gives fictional shares of stock to a key employee that are initially valued at the time of the grant. The stock is later valued at some terminal point and the executive is then paid in cash the differential value of the stock as compensation.

RABBI TRUST - An irrevocable trust that is designed to hold funds and assets for the purpose of paying benefits under a nonqualified deferred compensation arrangement. The assets in a rabbi trust are for the sole purpose of providing benefits to employees and may not be accessed by the employer, but they may be seized and used for the purpose of paying general creditors in the event of a liquidation of the company. Assets within a rabbi trust are not currently taxable to the employee.

RESTRICTED STOCK PLAN - An employer provided plan designed to increase retention and compensate employees with a non-cash outflow. The plan pays executives with shares of the employer's stock. The executive does not pay any amount towards the allocation of the stock and, in fact, is restricted by the employer from selling or transferring the stock.

SALARY REDUCTION PLANS - A nonqualified plan designed to receive deferral contributions from executives to reduce their current taxable income.

SECULAR TRUSTS - Irrevocable trusts designed to hold funds and assets for the purpose of paying benefits under a nonqualified deferred compensation arrangement. A secular trust does not create a substantial risk of forfeiture for the employee. Assets set aside in a secular trust results in immediate inclusion of income to the employee.

STOCK APPRECIATION RIGHTS (SARs) - Rights that grant to the holder cash in an amount equal to the excess of the fair market value of the stock over the exercise price.

KEY TERMS

STOCK OPTION - A right to buy stock at a specified price for a specified period of time.

SUBSTANTIAL RISK OF FORFEITURE - An income tax concept that relates to when income is subject to income tax. A substantial risk of forfeiture exists when rights in property that are transferred are conditioned, directly or indirectly, upon the future performance (or refraining from performance) of substantial services by any person, or the occurrence of a condition related to a purpose of the transfer and the possibility of forfeiture is substantial if the condition is not satisfied.

SUPPLEMENTAL EXECUTIVE RETIREMENT PLANS (SERP) - Nonqualified deferred compensation arrangements designed to provide additional benefits to an executive during retirement.

TITLE I OF ERISA - Coverage, participation, funding, and discrimination requirements of ERISA imposed on qualified plans.

TOP HAT PLANS - Plans designed to benefit a select group of top management or key employees.

WAGE REPLACEMENT RATIO (WRR) - An estimate of the percent of income needed at retirement compared to income just prior to retirement.

DISCUSSION QUESTIONS

1. Why are deferred compensation arrangements established?

2. List three common reasons deferred compensation arrangements are used.

3. Define "constructive receipt" and how it affects deferred compensation plans.

4. What is a substantial risk of forfeiture, and how does it affect deferred compensation plans?

5. Describe the Economic Benefit Doctrine and how it affects deferred compensation plans.

6. How is the 83(b) election used with regard to deferred compensation plans?

7. When are payroll taxes due on compensation contributed to a deferred compensation plan?

8. When will the employer receive an income tax deduction for assets contributed to a deferred compensation plan?

9. Discuss the funding arrangements available for deferred compensation plans.

10. What is the impact of Title I of ERISA on deferred compensation plans?

11. List and describe the types of deferred compensation plans available.

12. Describe 401(k) wrap plans.

13. What is an incentive stock option and what are the tax consequences associated with the grant, exercise and sale of ISOs?

14. What is a nonqualified stock option and what are the tax consequences associated with the grant, exercise, and sale of NQSOs?

15. What are stock appreciation rights?

16. What are restricted stock plans?

17. What is an employee stock purchase plan?

MULTIPLE CHOICE PROBLEMS

1. All of the following are reasons that an employer might favor a nonqualified plan over a qualified retirement plan except:

    a. There is more design flexibility with a nonqualified plan.

    b. A nonqualified plan typically has lower administrative costs.

    c. Nonqualified plans typically allow the employer an immediate income tax deduction.

    d. Employers can generally exclude rank-and-file employees from a nonqualified plan.

2. Rick has an 18% nonqualified deferred compensation plan that is funded annually by his employer. Payments are made to a separate trustee of a secular trust who was selected by Rick and his employer. The employer contributions are discontinued at Rick's death, disability, or employment termination. When Rick retires or terminates employment, he will receive the proceeds from the trust.

    Which of the following is/are correct regarding the deferred compensation plan?

    1. The contributions are not currently taxable to Rick because they are subject to a substantial risk of forfeiture.

    2. The contributions to the plan are currently subject to payroll taxes.

    3. The employer can deduct the contributions to the plan at the time of the contribution.

    a. 3 only.

    b. 1 and 3.

    c. 2 and 3.

    d. 1, 2, and 3.

3. Which of the following is false regarding a deferred compensation plan that is funded utilizing a rabbi trust?

    1. Participants have security against the employer's unwillingness to pay.

    2. Rabbi trust provide the participant with security against employer bankruptcy.

    3. Rabbi trusts provide tax deferral for participants.

    4. Rabbi trusts provide the employer with a current tax deduction.

    a. None, they are all true.

    b. 2 and 4.

    c. 1, 2, and 4.

    d. 1, 2, 3, and 4.

4. Which of the following is true regarding employer contributions to secular trusts for employee-participants of a nonqualified deferred compensation agreement?

    1. Participants have security against an employer's unwillingness to pay at termination.

    2. Participants have security against an employer's bankruptcy.

    3. Secular trusts provide tax deferral for employees until distribution.

    4. Secular trusts provide employers with a current income tax deduction.

      a. 3 only.

      b. 1 and 2.

      c. 1, 2, and 4.

      d. 1, 2, 3, and 4.

5. Ricky receives stock options for 12,000 shares of XYZ Corporation with an exercise price of $10 when the stock is trading on the national exchange for $10 per share. The XYZ company plan is an Incentive Stock Option Plan. Which of the following statements are true regarding the options?

    1. Ricky will be required to hold any ISOs for more than a year after exercise and more than two years from the grant date to have long-term capital gains.

    2. 2,000 of the options are NQSOs.

      a. 1 only.

      b. 2 only.

      c. Both 1 and 2.

      d. Neither 1 nor 2.

6. Joe Bob receives stock options (ISOs) with an exercise price of $18 when the stock is trading at $18. Joe Bob exercises these options two years after the date of the grant when the stock price is $39 per share. Which of the following statements is correct?

    a. Upon exercise Joe Bob will have no regular income for tax purposes.

    b. Joe Bob will have W-2 income of $21 per share upon exercise.

    c. Joe Bob will have $18 of AMT income upon exercise.

    d. Joe Bob's adjusted basis for regular income tax will be $39 at exercise.

7. Mary Jane received 1,000 NQSOs with an exercise price of $25 per share when the stock was $25 on the market. Two years from the date of grant Mary Jane exercises when the stock price is $102. At exercise, Mary Jane:

    a. Has W-2 income of $25,000.

    b. Has an AMT adjustment of $77,000.

    c. Has W-2 income of $77,000.

    d. Has an AMT adjustment of $25,000.

8. Which of the following are characteristics of a phantom stock plan?

    1. Benefits are paid in cash.

    2. There is no equity dilution from additional shares being issued.

      a. 1 only.

      b. 2 only.

      c. Both 1 and 2.

      d. Neither 1 nor 2.

9. ABC has an Employee Stock Purchase Plan (ESPP). Which statement(s) regarding an ESPP is/are correct?

    1. The purchase price of the stock may be as low as 85% of the stock value.

    2. When an employee sells ESPP stock at a gain in a qualifying disposition, all of the gain is capital gain.

    3. There is an annual limit of $25,000 per employee for ESPPs.

      a. 1 only.

      b. 1 and 2.

      c. 1 and 3.

      d. 2 and 3.

10. Arnie, the CEO of The Producers Inc., was awarded the following stock options from The Producers Inc.

Option	Grant Date	Type	Exercise Price	FMV	Number of Shares
1	1/1/2012	NQSO	$15	$15	1,000
2	1/1/2016	NQSO	$25	$25	1,000

During 2016 Arnie had the following transactions regarding the above options.

Option	Date	Action	Number of Options (O)/ Shares (S)	Market Price on Date
1	2/1/2016	Exercised	1,000 (O)	$27
1	2/1/2016	Sold	1,000 (S)	$27
2	12/12/2016	Exercised	1,000 (O)	$36

Which of the following is correct?

    a. Arnie has $11,000 of W-2 income and a $12,000 capital gain.

    b. Arnie has $23,000 of W-2 income.

    c. Arnie has capital gain of $12,000.

    d. Arnie has $66,000 of W-2 income.

11. Mike was awarded 1,000 shares of restricted stock of B Corp at a time when the stock price was $14. Assume Mike properly makes an 83(b) election at the date of the award. The stock vests 2 years later at a price of $12 and Mike sells it then. What are Mike's tax consequences in the year of sale?

    a. Mike has W-2 income of $12,000.

    b. Mike has a long-term capital loss of $2,000.

    c. Mike has W-2 income of $14,000.

    d. Mike has a $12,000 long-term capital gain.

12. Cindy Sue has been with CS Designs, Inc. for five years. CS Designs has a deferred compensation plan to provide benefits to key executives only. CS Designs contributed $400,000 into a trust for Cindy Sue's benefit under the company's deferred compensation plan. The plan requires that executives must work for the company for 10 years before any benefits can be obtained from the plan. Cindy Sue has come to you to determine when she will be subject to income tax on the contribution by the employer. Which of the following is correct?

    a. Since the assets were placed into a trust, the economic benefit doctrine will require inclusion in income for the current year contributions made by the employer.

    b. Since Cindy Sue cannot receive the benefits until she has been with the employer for 10 years, the substantial risk of forfeiture doctrine will not require inclusion in income for the current year contributions made by the employer.

    c. Since the assets were placed into a trust, the constructive receipt doctrine will require inclusion in income for the current year contributions made by the employer.

    d. Cindy Sue is subject to income tax in the current year because the plan is discriminatory.

13. In 2016, Chip, an accomplished professional race car driver, is to receive a signing bonus for agreeing to drive for Hot-Lap International, a racing team. Hot-Lap agrees to establish a NQDC agreement with Chip to defer the bonus beyond Chip's peak income producing years. Hot-Lap transfers the bonuses to an escrow agent, subject to the risk of forfeiture to team creditors in bankruptcy, who invests the funds in securities acting as a hedge against inflation. The bonus is deferred until 2017 and is then paid to Chip in years 2017-2026. When is the income deductible by the employer and includible by Chip?

Option	Employer Deduction	Employee Inclusion
A	2016	2016
B	2017	2017
C	2017-2026	2017
D	2017-2026	2017-2026

14. On July 31, 2011, B Corp sold 1,000 shares of its stock to Mike, an employee, for $12 per share. At the time of the sale, B stock was trading for $30 per share. The stock was to vest in 7 years on July 31, 2018. This restriction was stamped on the certificates. On July 31, 2018, the B stock was trading for $125 per share. Mike sold the stock in 2019 for $125 per share. Assuming no special elections, how much must Mike include in income and in what year?

Option	Year	Amount
A	2011	$18,000
B	2011 - 2018	$18,000 ratably
C	2018	$113,000
D	2019	$113,000

15. Jennifer received 1,000 SARs at $22, the current trading price of Clippers, Inc., her employer. If Jennifer exercises the SARs three years after the grant and Clipper's stock is $34 per share, which of the following statements is true?

    a. Jennifer will have an adjusted basis of $22,000 in the Clippers, Inc. stock.
    b. Jennifer will have W-2 income equal to $12,000.
    c. Jennifer will have long-term capital gain of $12,000.
    d. Jennifer will have ordinary income equal to $22,000.

QUICK QUIZ EXPLANATIONS

QUICK QUIZ 12.1
1. False. With a deferred compensation plan, the employer may take a compensation deduction when the deferred compensation is taxable to the employee.
2. True.

QUICK QUIZ 12.2
1. True.
2. False. A substantial risk of forfeiture exists when rights in property that are transferred are conditioned, directly or indirectly, upon a future performance or occurrence.
3. True.

QUICK QUIZ 12.3
1. False. A §83(b) election allows the employee to include in income the net value of a transfer from the employer in order to create basis in a capital asset.
2. False. Deferred compensation is subject to payroll taxes at the time the substantial risk of forfeiture expires.
3. True.

QUICK QUIZ 12.4
1. False. The use of rabbi trusts is not restricted to nonprofit organizations.
2. True.
3. False. A 401(k) wrap plan does not eliminate the substantial risk of forfeiture.

QUICK QUIZ 12.5
1. True.
2. False. The exercise of an ISO does not trigger W-2 income, but does create an AMT adjustment.
3. True.

QUICK QUIZ 12.6
1. True.
2. False. An Employee Stock Purchase Plan allows employees to use after-tax dollars to purchase company stock. An ESPP does not allow employees to use pre-tax dollars to purchase company stock.

EMPLOYEE BENEFITS: FRINGE BENEFITS

LEARNING OBJECTIVES

After reading this chapter, you should be able to:
1. State the rule that, unless an employer provided fringe benefit is specifically excluded by the IRC, it is taxable income.
2. Provide a general definition or description of a fringe benefit.
3. Identify the most important fringe benefits.
4. Know that, if a fringe benefit is provided by the employer to the employee, and it is not excludable, it is compensation and generally subject to both income and payroll taxes.
5. Be aware that most excludable fringe benefits have a non-discrimination requirement.
6. Be aware that employer provided fringe benefits can benefit a wide range of persons beyond the employee, including spouse, dependents, retired persons, directors, and in some cases independent contractors.
7. State the rules for exclusion of meals, lodging, athletic facilities, dependent care programs, no additional cost services, qualified employee discounts, working condition fringes, de minimus fringes, qualified moving expenses, adoption assistance, prizes and awards, and other fringe benefits when provided by employer to employee.
8. Know how fringe benefits are valued.

INTRODUCTION

When an employee provides services to an employer in return for compensation, the employee will often receive certain benefits, known as fringe benefits, that otherwise would be taxable income if the Internal Revenue Code (IRC) did not statutorily exclude the value of these benefits from the employee's gross income. Many employees do not even consider using the office copier or fax machine for personal reasons as an employer-provided fringe benefit, whereas other fringe benefits are more obvious, such as employer-provided health insurance.

Generally, when a fringe benefit is provided as a requirement of employment or is for the convenience of the employer (i.e., meals, lodging), the value of the benefits will not be included in the employee's gross income. However, this general statement is not always correct as the value of some fringe benefits are excluded from an employee's gross income merely based on statutory provisions that focus on social goals, fitness, and education (i.e., health insurance, fitness center use, tuition). In order for the value of a fringe benefit to be excluded from the employee's gross income, the fringe benefit must be provided to the employees following a specific set of rules and qualifications as set forth in the IRC.

FRINGE BENEFITS DEFINED

A "**fringe benefit**" is a form of compensation where a benefit other than customary taxable wages is provided by the employer to the employee for the performance of services. These benefits are considered on the "fringe" because such benefits merely accompany, or are in addition to, an employee's salary, wages, or other compensation. Broadly, fringe benefits include paid vacation, sick leave, family leave, health insurance, life insurance, pension plans, profit sharing plans, the use of recreational facilities, personal use of employer's property, holidays, parking, prizes and awards, discounted products and services, and many others. When any of these fringe benefits are provided in return for the performance of services, the value of the fringe benefit is initially deemed compensation for those services. However, not all of the value of all fringe benefits will be included in the employee's current gross pay even though the employer has a current income tax deduction. The existence of an employer's income tax deduction with no current taxable income to the employee is similar to some benefits of qualified retirement plans.

KNOW THE NUMBERS		
	2015	**2016**
Achievement Awards: Nonqualified[1]	$400	$400
Achievement Awards: Qualified[1]	$1,600	$1,600
Adoption Assistance[2]	$13,400	$13,460
Adoption Assistance Beginning Phaseout	$201,010	$201,920
Adoption Assistance Ending Phaseout	$241,010	$241,920
Business Miles Expense[3]	57.5 cents per mile	54 cents per mile
Dependent Care Assistance[4]	$5,000	$5,000
Educational Assistance Program[5]	$5,250	$5,250
Group Term Insurance	$50,000	$50,000
Moving Expense (Mileage)[6]	23 cents per mile	19 cents per mile
Qualified Bicycle Commuting[7]	$20 per month	$20 per month
Qualified Parking	$250 per month	$255 per month
Transit Passes	$250 per month	$255 per month

1. IRC §274(j)(2).
2. Rev. Proc.2014-61.
3. Notice 2014-79.
4. IRC §129(9)(2).
5. IRC §127(a).
6. Notice 2014-79.
7. IRC §132(f)(5)(F).

TAXATION OF FRINGE BENEFITS

Under IRS Treasury Regulations, all fringe benefits provided by an employer to an employee are taxable as wages unless a specific provision of the IRC excludes the benefit from taxation or unless the employee pays the fair value for the fringe benefit. Although a fringe benefit may not be specifically excluded by the regulations, the value of the fringe benefit is not taxable if it is fully paid for by the employee. The IRC and regulations, while providing no definition for the phrase "fringe benefit," list various examples of fringe benefits. Of paramount importance with fringe benefits is the issue of whether the fringe benefit is subject to income taxation and withholding requirements by the employer and employee.

> ## KEY CONCEPTS ✓
>
> 1. Define "fringe benefit."
>
> 2. In general, what are the tax consequences with regard to employee fringe benefits?
>
> 3. What are the nondiscrimination rules that apply to employee fringe benefits?

The value of a fringe benefit provided to an employee is deductible as compensation expense by the employer unless the fringe benefit is excludable from the employee's taxable income. Even if the expenditure by the employer is not deductible as compensation expense, it may very well be deductible under ordinary and necessary business expense. Employers should be aware that providing certain fringe benefits may trigger reporting requirements on W-2s for employees, K-1s for partners, or 1099s for independent contractors. The employer may also be required to withhold monies as a result of any taxable amount for FICA, FUTA, SUTA, or federal and state income taxes. Other issues that arise with fringe benefits are whether any exclusion has a limit, the amount of any such limit, who is eligible for the fringe benefit, and whether nondiscrimination requirements apply to the provision of the fringe benefit.

NONDISCRIMINATION OF FRINGE BENEFITS

A vital area of concern with some fringe benefits is the requirement that the employer not discriminate against different classes of employees. When these "nondiscrimination requirements" apply, and the fringe benefit is provided only to a "highly compensated employee," and is not available on substantially the same terms to all employees, then the fringe benefit is deemed discriminatory. If the provision of a fringe benefit is discriminatory, then the exclusion may be lost, resulting in the value of the fringe benefit being included or added to an employee's income. As discussed below, some fringe benefits have nondiscrimination requirements while others do not.

BENEFITING INDIVIDUALS

An employee performing services in return for a fringe benefit need not be the person who actually uses or enjoys the fringe benefit. For instance, a spouse or child of an employee may receive or use the fringe benefit of an employer-provided athletic facility. Other individuals beyond current employees who may be taxed on the value of the fringe benefit or who may be eligible to receive the fringe benefit without taxable income include retired employees, spouses of employees, dependent children, spouses of deceased employees, partners, directors, and independent contractors. The description of each fringe benefit includes a detail of those individuals who may receive or benefit from the fringe benefit.

SUMMARY OF AVAILABLE FRINGE BENEFITS

The fringe benefits that will be addressed in this chapter are those that are normally addressed in the regulations and are as follows:

1. Meals and lodging furnished for the convenience of the employer[1]
2. Athletic facilities furnished by the employer[2]
3. Educational assistance programs[3]
4. Dependent care programs[4]
5. No additional cost services (airlines/hotels/line of business)[5]
6. Qualified employee discounts (products versus services)[6]
7. Working condition fringe benefits[7]
8. *de minimis* fringe benefits[8]
9. Qualified moving expense reimbursement (W-2) for AGI[9]
10. Qualified transportation and parking[10]
11. Adoption assistance programs[11]
12. Prizes and awards[12]
13. Qualified tuition reduction plans[13]

QUICK QUIZ 13.1

1. An employee fringe benefit is not a form of compensation; rather, a fringe benefit is merely an extra that is given to employees.
   a. True
   b. False

2. Employee fringe benefits are taxable as wages unless specifically excluded by the IRC.
   a. True
   b. False

3. If an employee fringe benefit is discriminatory then it will always cause inclusion in the employee's income.
   a. True
   b. False

False, True, False.

SPECIFIC FRINGE BENEFITS

MEALS AND LODGING PROVIDED BY THE EMPLOYER TO THE EMPLOYEE

Meals

In general, an employee may exclude from gross income the value of all meals provided in-kind (not as cash reimbursement) to the employee, the employee's spouse, or any dependents. Meals are provided in-kind when the meal is actually served or supplied to the employee, as opposed to

---

1. IRC §119.
2. IRC §132(j)(4).
3. IRC §127.
4. IRC §129.
5. IRC §132(b).
6. IRC §132(c).
7. IRC §132(d).
8. IRC §132(e).
9. IRC §132(g).
10. IRC §132(f).
11. IRC §137.
12. IRC §274.
13. IRC §117.

providing a cash reimbursement for food. In addition, the in-kind meals must meet the following two conditions:

- the meals are furnished for the convenience of the employer, and
- the meals are furnished on the employer's business premises.

The Convenience of the Employer

Meals furnished by an employer without charge to the employee will be regarded as furnished for the convenience of the employer if the meals are furnished for a substantial business reason of the employer, not just as a means of providing additional compensation to the employee. The determination of "for the convenience of the employer" is made based on all of the surrounding facts and circumstances. The IRS provides some of the following examples as guidance when determining which meals provided by an employer would qualify, or be deemed, as furnished for the convenience of the employer.

> **KEY CONCEPTS** ✓
>
> 1. What requirements are necessary for meals to be excluded from income?
>
> 2. What requirements are necessary for lodging to be excluded from income?

EXHIBIT 13.1

MEALS DEEMED FOR THE CONVENIENCE OF THE EMPLOYER

- Meals furnished to the employee during working hours so that the employee will be available for emergency calls. It must be shown that emergencies have actually occurred or can reasonably be expected to occur in the employer's business during mealtime. For example, when a hospital provides a meal to an on-call doctor.

- Meals furnished to the employee during working hours because the employer's business requires restricted short meal periods, 30 or 45 minutes, and the employee could not be expected to eat elsewhere in such a short meal period.

- Meals furnished to the employee during working hours because the employee could not otherwise secure proper meals within a reasonable meal period and when there may be insufficient eating facilities in the vicinity of the employer's premises.

- Meals furnished to restaurant employees for each meal period in which the employee works, despite whether the meal is furnished during, immediately before, or immediately after the employee's working hours.

- If the employer furnishes a meal to all employees, and the reason for furnishing the meal for more than 50% of the employees is deemed for the convenience of the employer, 100% of the meals are deemed to be for the convenience of the employer.

- If the employer would have furnished a meal to an employee for any reason deemed to be for the convenience of the employer during the employee's working hours, but the employee's duties prevented him from obtaining a meal during those working hours, a meal provided by the employer immediately after the employee's working hours is deemed for the convenience of the employer.

> - If an employer charges the employee a fixed amount for the meal, the meal will be regarded as furnished for the convenience of the employer if the employee pays the fixed charge regardless of whether he accepts the meal or provides his own meal.

The IRS also provides specific examples as to what is not considered "for the convenience of the employer."

MEALS DEEMED NOT FOR THE CONVENIENCE OF THE EMPLOYER

EXHIBIT 13.2

> - Any meal provided to promote the morale or goodwill of the employee or to attract prospective employees does not qualify for the exclusion.
>
> - If the employer charges the employee for the meal, the meal will not be regarded as furnished for the convenience of the employer if the employee has a choice of accepting the meal and paying for it or of not paying for it and providing his own meals.

The Employer's Business Premises

The term "**business premises of the employer**" is defined as the place of employment of the employee. For example, meals provided in the employer's home to a domestic servant would constitute meals furnished on the business premises of the employer. Similarly, meals furnished to cowhands while herding their employer's cattle on leased land would be regarded as furnished on the business premises of the employer.[1]

> Barbara, a waitress at Circle Bar and Grill, works from 7 a.m. to 4 p.m. five days a week. Each workday she is furnished, without charge, two meals. The manager of Circle Bar and Grill encourages her to eat breakfast in the employee break room each day before 7 a.m. but does not expressly require her to do this. The manager does, however, require her to eat her lunch in the employee break room. Since Barbara is a food service employee and works during the normal breakfast and lunch periods, she can exclude the value of the breakfast and lunch from her gross income.

EXAMPLE 13.1

---

1. Treas. Reg. §1.119-1(c)(1).

Case Study 13.1

Dr. Walter Jacob was the executive director of the Training School Unit of the American Institute for Mental Studies. He was required, as a condition of his employment, to reside on the premises of Institute and be available 24 hours a day. Because of this requirement, the Institute provided his family housing and free groceries from the Institute's commissary. The provision of groceries to Mr. Jacob's family is excluded from his gross income as in-kind because the groceries were prepared into meals and consumed by Mr. Jacobs and his family on the Institute's premises.[1] In addition, the court held that the value of non-food items such as napkins, toilet tissue, and soap was an integral part of either lodging or meals and was excluded from gross income.

1. 74-1 USTC 9316.

 EXAMPLE 13.2

Mobile Processing and Manufacturing (MPM) built a cafeteria in its main building. Mark, a foreman at MPM, can purchase his lunch in the cafeteria or bring his lunch from home, but there are no other dining facilities nearby. Mark cannot exclude the value of any meals purchased in the cafeteria from his gross income because Mark has the choice to pay for and eat the cafeteria meal or to not pay for the cafeteria meal and bring his lunch from home.

EXAMPLE 13.3

In the above example, had MPM required Mark to pay $40 each month for food from the cafeteria whether he ate the food or not, the $40 would be excludable from Mark's gross income. This exclusion only applies because Mark is required to pay for the meal whether he eats it or not. The payment of $40 for the meal can be through payroll withholding or can be a cash payment by Mark. In either case, the payment will be excluded from Mark's gross income.

Lodging

The IRC also provides an exclusion from an employee's gross income for the value of lodging furnished by an employer to an employee if all three of the following qualifications are met:

1. The lodging is furnished on the employer's business premises,
2. The lodging is furnished for the convenience of the employer, and
3. The employee is required to accept the lodging as a condition of employment.

If all three elements of this test are satisfied, the exclusion applies regardless of whether the employee is charged a fee for the lodging.

The Employer's Business Premises

The requirement that lodging be provided on the employer's premises is similar to the requirement that meals be provided on the employer's business premises. Generally, the business premises of the employer means the place of employment of the employee. Lodging furnished in the home of an employer to a domestic servant constitutes lodging furnished on the business premises of the employer.[1] Likewise, lodging for cowhands while herding their employer's cattle on leased land is deemed lodging furnished on the business premises of the employer.

The Convenience of the Employer

Similar to the rules concerning meals above, lodging furnished by an employer without charge to the employee will be regarded as furnished for the convenience of the employer if the lodging is furnished for a substantial business reason of the employer, not just as a means of providing additional compensation to the employee. The determination of "for the convenience of the employer" is made based on all of the surrounding facts and circumstances of each employer.

Condition of Employment

The value of lodging is not includable in an employee's gross income if the employee is required to accept the lodging as a condition of employment. Requiring the employee to accept the lodging as a condition of employment is defined as the employee being required to accept the lodging to "enable him to perform the duties of his employment." In other words, the lodging is furnished because the employee is required to be available for duty at all times or because the employee could not perform the services required unless the employee is furnished such lodging.[1] If the employer provides lodging to the employee and the employee is charged a fixed amount whether or not the employee actually accepts the lodging, then the amount of the charge by the employer is not included in the employee's gross income.

Includable Lodging

If the lodging is not furnished on the business premises of the employer, or the lodging is not furnished for the convenience of the employer, or the employee is not required to accept the lodging as a condition of the employment, then the employee must include the value of the lodging in gross income irrespective of whether the value exceeds or is less than the amount charged. Unless evidence is shown to the contrary, the value of the lodging is considered to be equal to the amount charged.[2]

QUICK QUIZ 13.2

1. If a meal is provided to more than 50% of the employees for the convenience of the employer, then all of the meals are considered to be for the convenience of the employer.
   a. True
   b. False

2. In order for lodging to qualify for the exclusion from the employee's gross income, the employee must be required to accept lodging as a condition of employment.
   a. True
   b. False

True, True.

---

1. IRC §119(c).
1. IRC §119(b).
2. IRC §119(b).

EXAMPLE 13.4

An employee of an institution is given the choice of residing at the institution free of charge or of residing elsewhere and receiving a cash allowance in addition to his regular salary. If he elects to reside at the institution, the value to the employee of the lodging furnished by the employer will be includible in the employee's gross income because his residence at the institution is not required in order for him to perform properly the duties of his employment.

EXAMPLE 13.5

A construction worker is employed at a construction project at a remote job site in Alaska. Due to the inaccessibility of facilities for the employees who are working at the job site to obtain food and lodging in the prevailing weather conditions, the employer is required to furnish meals and lodging to the employee at the camp site in order to carry on the construction project. The employee is required to pay $40 a week for the meals and lodging. The weekly charge of $40 is not part of the compensation includible in the gross income of the employee, and the value of the meals and lodging is excludable from his gross income.

There has been significant litigation concerning what constitutes the business premises of the employer. The courts have been somewhat flexible on this issue and consider all facts and circumstances.[1]

---

1. This flexible position was seen in the case of Saunders v. Commissioner, 215 F.2d 768, 771 (3rd Cir. 1954), where the court articulated: " . . . (T)he rationale of the rule should make it applicable to determine the extent of gross income either when quarters and meals are furnished in kind or cash is paid in lieu thereof . . . Admittedly, the payment of cash to an employee is normally compensatory and probably more obviously so than payment in kind. Nevertheless, just as an employee is often furnished tangible property which cannot be regarded as compensation, an employee may be furnished cash which is not compensation . . ."

Case Study 13.3

In the case of **Erdelt v. United States,** 715 F.Supp. 278 (D.N.D. 1989), the school district purchased a house that was occupied by the district's superintendent. The house was located one block from the school facility. The fact that the house was not on the same contiguous piece of real estate as the school facility did not prevent the house from being considered on the district's business premises. The house was a "residence required as a condition of employment." The nature of the superintendent's position and uniqueness of the school district itself, the court reasoned, required that the superintendent be available to the community at all times through his presence and availability near the school. As such, the reasonable rental value of the house was not includable in his gross income for income tax purposes.

Nonetheless, some exclusions have been found to not apply under somewhat similar circumstances, like in **Wilson v. United States**, 412 F.2d 694 (1st Cir. 1969). There, a state trooper was reimbursed for "mid-shift" meals or lunches if he was more than 10 miles from his home. The court considered this to be includable in gross income of the state trooper.

Case Study 13.4

In Coyner v. Bingler, 344 F.2d 736, 738 (3rd Cir. 1965), a park foreman for the City of Pittsburgh volunteered to become a resident caretaker at a community cultural center while still working and receiving his salary as a park foreman. Mr. Coyner lived free of charge at the cultural center where he acted as caretaker. The Tax Court ruled that the value of the lodging should have been included in gross income, but the United States Third Circuit Court of Appeals disagreed, overturning the Tax Court and finding that the value of the lodging was excludable from gross income because Mr. Coyner had to live there in proper performance of his duties as caretaker. Mr. Coyner's occupancy of the apartment was not simply for his convenience and benefit, but was of distinct benefit to the City and, therefore, "for the convenience of the employer" within the terms of the statute.

The Court recognized the facts that his presence was required to prevent vandalism, to perform certain janitorial services, to be present to admit persons entitled to use the facilities and to secure and lock the building at night. Because the cultural center was almost constantly in use, Mr. Coyner could exclude the lodging from his gross income because it related to the practical working necessity of performing his duties with any sort of efficiency.[1] The Court did acknowledge that, had the commissioner introduced any evidence that Mr. Coyner was not required to be available for duty at all times, a different result may have been in order.

---

1. Excluding the value of lodging for officers and employees of a family owned funeral business was allowed where the lodging was furnished as a matter of company policy and the nature of the business required that close personal contact be made available on a 24-hour per day basis. **In the Matter of Harry Schwartz**, 22 T.C.M. 835 (1963).

ATHLETIC FACILITIES FURNISHED BY THE EMPLOYER

Under the regulations, the value of any "on premises athletic facility" provided by an employer to an employee is not included in the employee's gross income.[1] An "**on premises athletic facility**" is defined as a gym or other athletic facility such as a tennis court, pool, or golf course that meets all of the following requirements:

1. Operated by the employer,
2. Located on the employer's premises, and
3. "Substantially all" of the use of the facility is by employees of the employer, their spouses or their dependent children.[2]

Operated by the Employer

The employer is deemed to operate an athletic facility when the employer operates the facility by hiring its own employees or hires an independent contractor to operate the athletic facility. If the athletic facility is operated by an unpaid separate unrelated entity, then the exclusion does not apply and the value of the athletic facility will be included in an employee's taxable income. Also, the facility may be operated by more than one employer, and as long as an employer pays rent either directly to the owner of the premises or to a sub-lessor of the premises, that employer is eligible for the exclusion.[3]

KEY CONCEPTS

1. What requirements are necessary for athletic facilities provided to an employee as a fringe benefit to be excluded from income?

2. What requirements are necessary for education assistance programs provided to an employee as a fringe benefit to be excluded from income?

Located on the Employer's Premises

The requirement that the athletic facility be located on the employer's "premises" does not necessarily mean that the employer must own the facility or that the facility be located on the employer's *business* premises.[4] In other words, the premises could be leased or rented by the employer. As long as the employer pays reasonable rent for the premises, the facility may be considered the employer's premises. If the athletic facility is for "residential use" (like a tennis court, pool, or gym that are part of a resort), then this exclusion is lost (unless, of course, if the resort is owned by the employer).[5]

---

1. Treas. Reg. §1.132-1(e)(1).
2. Treas. Reg. §1.132-1(e). See also Treas. Reg. §1.132-1(b)(5) for the definition of dependent children. A dependent child or children of an employee under this § is a child or step-child who is a dependent of the employee or who is twenty-four years of age or younger whose parents are both deceased.
3. Treas. Reg. §1-132.1(e)(4).
4. Treas. Reg. §1.132-1(e)(2).
5. Treas. Reg. §1.132-1(e)(2).

Use by Employees
General Public

The exclusion for on-premises athletic facilities[1] is inapplicable to any athletic facilities made available to the general public through the sale or rental of memberships or similar arrangements.[2] For example, if the on-premises facility is a health club where others from the general public pay monthly membership dues, then the value of the use of the facility is included in an employee's gross income.

Discriminatory

Nondiscrimination requirements[3] do not apply to on-premises athletic facilities.[4] Thus, the employer has discretion to determine who may or may not have access to on-premises athletic facilities without jeopardizing the eligibility for the exclusion from the employee's gross income.

Covered Employees

The following individuals are treated as employees for the purposes of the athletic facility exclusion:
- current employees;
- former retired or disabled employees;
- widow(er)s of those who died while employed;
- widow(er)s of former retired or disabled employees;
- partners; or
- leased employees providing services to an employer on a substantially full-time basis for at least a year where the services are performed under the employer's primary control.

> Thomas works at ABC Insurance Company in a high rise building in downtown Austin, Texas. Adjacent to the main office, ABC rents out a gym from the building management. Under these circumstances, as long as the general public does not use the gym, the ABC employees may exclude the value of the use of the on-premises gym from their gross income. However, if the high rise building was a resort for residential use, then the value of the use of the athletic facility would need to be included in each employee's gross income.

EDUCATIONAL ASSISTANCE PROGRAMS

The value of an educational assistance program provided by an employer for the benefit of an employee is excluded from the employee's gross income subject to certain limitations and requirements.[5] Under the regulations, a **qualified educational assistance program** is a plan established and maintained by an employer that provides employees with educational assistance.[6] The program need not be funded, nor must the employer apply to the IRS for a determination of whether the plan is qualified.[7] The program must be a separate written plan of the employer set forth in a separate document and must only provide educational assistance.[8]

---

1. Treas. Reg. §1.132-1(e).
2. Treas. Reg. §1.132-1(e)(1).
3. The nondiscrimination requirements of §132 and §1.132-A do not apply to the on-site athletic facility.
4. Treas. Reg. §1.132-1(e)(5).
5. IRC §127.
6. Treas. Reg. §1.127-2.
7. Nonetheless, an employer may request that the IRS determine whether a plan is a qualified program.

The gross income exclusion for educational assistance is limited to the value of $5,250.[1] Nonetheless, as discussed below, an employer may exclude part or all of the excess of educational assistance over $5,250 from an employee's taxable income as a working condition benefit, assuming that the working condition benefit tests apply. Amounts above $5,250 that do not qualify as a working condition fringe benefit are treated as W-2 income.

Note that any educational expense reimbursed by an employer or paid for by an employer cannot be used as the basis for the American opportunity credit or lifetime learning credit.

Educational Assistance

"Educational assistance" is defined as either:

1. the employer's payment of expenses incurred on behalf of an employee for education, or
2. the employer's provision of education to an employee.[2]

If the program provides the employee with a choice between the employer providing educational assistance or the employer providing other remuneration to the employee that is includible in the employee's gross income, the value of any benefit received from the plan is taxable to the employee.[3] More particularly, educational assistance does not include:

- the employer's payment for tools or supplies other than textbooks that the employee may retain after completion of the course,
- the employer's payment for meals, lodging, or transportation, or
- the employer's payment for education involving sports, games, or hobbies, *unless* the education involves the employer's business or is a required part of a degree program.

The value of any of the above are included in the employee's gross income if provided by the employer.

Eligible Individuals

An educational assistance program must be an exclusive benefit for employees (defined below) of the employer. An educational assistance program must also be nondiscriminatory. Any educational assistance program for an employee's spouses or dependents does not apply to this exclusion.

Nondiscrimination

The IRC prohibits discrimination in the provision of the educational assistance program. If the program discriminates in favor of officers, shareholders, self-employed, or highly compensated employees, then the exclusion from gross income is lost. In other words, if the program is discriminatory, then the value of any benefit paid from the plan on behalf of an employee will be taxable to the employee. Specifically, the program meets the nondiscrimination requirements if the following conditions are met:

- the program benefits employees and does not favor highly compensated employees (as defined in Chapter 3);
- the program does not provide more than 5% of its benefits during the year to shareholders or owners (or their spouses or dependents) who own more than 5% of the stock, of the capital, or of the profit interest in the employer;

---

8. Treas. Reg. §1.127-2(b).
1. IRC §127(a).
2. Treas. Reg. §1.127-2(c)(1).
3. Treas. Reg. §1.127-2(c)(2).

- the employees are not allowed to choose cash that must be included in gross income in lieu of educational assistance; and
- reasonable notice is given to the employees that the program is provided to eligible employees.

Covered Employees

The following individuals are considered employees under this exclusion:

- current employees
- former employees who are retired, disabled, or laid off
- leased employees who provide services on a substantially full-time basis for at least a year and the services are performed under the employer's primary control
- sole proprietors
- partners performing services for the partnership

Todd is a covered employee of Toys, Toys & More Toys. The company implemented a qualified educational assistance program and offered educational assistance to Todd and all other employees. Todd incurred $5,000 of educational expenses that were paid for by the company. Todd and other employees had a choice between the company providing educational assistance or the company providing other remuneration that would be includable in employees' gross income. In this case, any benefit paid from the plan is taxable to Todd because the plan offered a choice between the company providing educational assistance or the company providing other remuneration that would be includable in the employees' gross income. If Todd's only choice was to either receive educational assistance or nothing at all, then the full $5,000 would be excluded from Todd's gross income.

QUALIFIED TUITION REDUCTION PLANS

An employee may exclude from gross income any amount representing a qualified tuition reduction.[1] **Qualified tuition reduction** is defined in the IRC as the amount of any reduction in tuition provided to an employee of an educational organization for education below the graduate level of:[2]

- current employees,
- former employees who retired or left on disability,
- widow(er)s of a person who died while employed,
- widow(er)s of former employees who retired or left on disability, or
- dependent children or spouses of any of the above.

---

1. IRC §117(d)(1).
2. IRC §117(d)(2).

Qualified Educational Organizations

Although this exclusion normally does not apply to the graduate level, if the individual is a graduate student teaching or performing research activities for an educational organization, then that individual may be eligible if he or she meets all other requirements of this exclusion.[1] To be qualified, an educational organization must normally maintain a regular faculty and curriculum and have a regularly enrolled body of students in attendance at the place where its educational activities are carried out in the normal course of business. This educational organization can be elementary, secondary, a college, or university.

Nondiscriminatory

For the exclusion to apply, the tuition reduction must not discriminate in favor of highly compensated employees, or stated differently, the reduction must be made available on substantially the same terms to each member of a group of employees defined under a reasonable classification set up by the employer that does not discriminate in favor of highly compensated employees.[2]

EXAMPLE 13.8

Dr. Bob is a professor of Ancient Roman History at Cool University. His daughter, Ainsley, decided she would pursue her undergraduate degree in journalism at CU. The waiver of her tuition by the university can be excluded from income. However, if Ainsley were pursuing a graduate degree, then the tuition waiver would be included in income.

DEPENDENT CARE ASSISTANCE

The IRC allows an employee to exclude the value of dependent care assistance[3] (as defined below) provided by an employer from the employee's gross income. This exclusion for **dependent care assistance** applies to household and dependent care services paid for or provided by the employer to an employee under a dependent care assistance program. The services must be provided under the following conditions:

---

1. IRC §117(d)(5).
2. IRC §117(d)(3).
3. These are programs under IRC §129.

1. The services must be provided for one of the following qualifying persons:[1]
   - dependent children under 13 years of age,
   - dependent children who are physically or mentally incapable of caring for themselves, or
   - an employee's spouse if the spouse is physically or mentally incapable of caring for himself.
2. The services must also allow an employee to work.
3. An employee may exclude up to the lesser of:
   - $5,000[2] annually ($2,500 for married couples filing separate returns) in benefits received through a dependent care assistance program from his gross income, or
   - the earned income of the employee or his spouse.
4. The plan must provide beneficiaries with advance notice of the program to permit them to make informed decisions about dependent care.[3]

Nondiscrimination

Nondiscrimination requirements apply to the dependent care assistance exclusion. Highly compensated employees may not exclude any benefits paid as dependent care assistance from their taxable wages unless the benefits provided under the program do not favor highly compensated employees and are not discriminatory as to the other employees. In addition, not more than 25 percent of the amounts paid or incurred by the employer for dependent care assistance during the year may be provided for the class of individuals who are shareholders or owners. In the event that the plan fails to meet certain requirements, it may be treated as a valid dependent care assistance program for employees who are not highly compensated.

Excluded Employees

The plan must define eligible employees. Similar to a qualified plan, a company does not have to include employees who have not attained age 21 and completed 1 year of service. In addition, employees who are covered by a collective bargaining agreement may be excluded if there is evidence that dependent care was part of the bargaining between the employer and the employee representatives.[4]

---

1. IRC §21(b).
2. IRC §129(9)(2).
3. This was the precise situation in ***American Family Mut. Ins. Co. v. United States***, 815 F.Supp. 1206 (W.D.Wis.1992), where the Court found that the exclusion was unavailable because the plan did not provide the beneficiaries with advance notice.
4. IRC §129(d)(9).

"NO-ADDITIONAL-COST SERVICES"

The exclusion for **no-additional-cost services** applies to any service provided by an employer to an employee that does not cause the employer to incur any substantial additional cost or lose revenue. The service provided as a fringe benefit must be offered to customers in the ordinary course of the line of business in which the employee performs substantial services. Examples of no-additional-cost services include providing free airline, bus, or train tickets, and hotel accommodations or telephone services either free or at reduced prices to employees working in those lines of business.[1] Also, an employee working as a parking lot attendant would have parking provided as a no-additional-cost service if the parking lot is not at capacity on a given day.[2]

> ### KEY CONCEPTS
>
> 1. What requirements are necessary for dependent care assistance programs provided to an employee as a fringe benefit to be excluded from income?
>
> 2. What are no-additional-cost services, and when are they excluded from income?
>
> 3. What are qualified employee discounts, and when are they excluded from income?

Lost or Forgone Revenue

One of the most important distinctions in determining whether a no-additional-cost service is excludable from an employee's gross income involves whether the employer loses revenue or incurs an opportunity cost by providing the fringe benefit to the employee. Stated differently, any lost or **forgone revenue** is deemed to be a cost when determining whether the employer has incurred substantial additional costs when providing a service to an employee. The employer is considered to incur substantial additional cost if the employer or the employee spends a substantial amount of time providing the service even if the time spent would otherwise be inactive or idle or if the services are provided outside normal business hours.

Covered Employees

The following individuals are considered employees under the no-additional-cost service exclusion:
- current employees,
- former employees retired or on disability,
- widow(er)s of an individual who died while employed,
- widow(er)s of a former employee who retired or left on disability,
- leased employees providing services to the employer on a substantially full-time basis for at least a year if the services were performed under the primary control of the employer, or
- a partner.

Providing this service to an employee's spouse or dependent child is viewed as being provided to the employee individually. Use of air transportation by an employee's parents is also considered use by the employee.

---

1. Treas. Reg. §1.132-2(a)(2).
2. Note that other exclusions could apply to this as well, such as a working condition fringe or de minimis fringe benefit if applicable.

Exception - Special Flight Rule

Airlines frequently provide personal flights at no charge, or at reduced costs, for employees or family members of employees. Whether the no-additional-cost exclusion is available depends upon seat availability to other customers and if reserved seating is provided to the employee. The key distinction is that the airline must not forego revenue in order to provide the excludable fringe benefit.

> Commercial Airline permits its employees to take personal flights on the airline at no charge and receive reserved seating. Because Commercial Airline foregoes potential revenue by permitting the employees to reserve seats, employees receiving such free flights are not eligible for the no-additional-cost exclusion and must include the value of the flight in their gross income.[1] However, if the employees are not allowed to reserve seats and only board the flight if there is available capacity, then employees receiving those flights are eligible for the no-additional-costs exclusion and may exclude the value of the flight from their gross income.

Unrelated Employers - Reciprocal Agreements

There is an exception for reciprocal agreements that meet certain requirements between unrelated employers. These written agreements are between unrelated entities within in the same type of business or industry and there is no substantial cost in providing these services to employees of the other business. These agreements are common in the airline industry.

A no-additional-cost service provided to an employee by an unrelated employer may qualify as an excludable benefit if the following requirements are met:
1. the service is the same type of service provided generally to customers in both the line of business of the employee and of the service provided;
2. the employer of the employee and the employer providing the service have a written reciprocal agreement whereby a group of employees of each employer in the same line of business receive no additional cost services from the other employer; and
3. the employer of the employee and the unrelated employer do not incur any substantial additional cost in providing this service or because of the written agreement.[2]

> Assume that commercial airline A and B have a reciprocal agreement that permits employees of A to fly on B's airlines subject to space available and allows B's employees to fly on A's airlines subject to space available. Because neither employer forgoes revenue or incurs substantial cost in offering this benefit, employees receiving these free flights are eligible for the no-additional-cost exclusion.

---

1. Treas. Reg. §1.132-2(c).
2. Treas. Reg. §1.132-2(b). If one employer receives a substantial payment from the other employer with respect to the reciprocal agreement, the paying employer will be considered to have incurred a substantial additional cost pursuant to the agreement, and consequently services performed under the reciprocal agreement will not qualify for exclusion as no-additional-cost services.

Case Study 13.5

In ***Charley v. Commissioner of Internal Revenue Service***,[1] Dr. Philip Charley, in his capacity as an employee of Truesdail Laboratories, traveled to various accident sites to inspect machinery. Truesdail had an "unwritten policy" that frequent flyer miles earned during employee travel became the sole property of the employee. If Dr. Charley chose to travel to an inspection by air, Truesdail would bill the client for round-trip, first class air travel. However, Dr. Charley would instruct the travel agent to arrange for coach service to and from the site but to charge Truesdail for first class travel. Dr. Charley would then use his frequent flyer miles (largely earned in connection with his business travel for Truesdail) to upgrade the coach ticket to first class and would instruct the travel agent to transfer funds equal to the difference in price between the first class ticket for which Truesdail was charged and the coach ticket to his personal travel account. Over the course of the taxable year, the travel agent maintained separate travel accounts for Dr. Charley and Truesdail. Dr. Charley took four business trips that year and using the procedures outlined above, received $3,149.93 in his personal travel account from his "sale" of the frequent flyer miles.

The IRS argued that Dr. Charley was wealthier after the transaction than before, showing that he received income. While the travel credits converted to cash can be characterized as additional compensation, Dr. Charley received property from his employer in the account upon which he could draw up to $3,149.93. Truesdail paid for first class airfare and allowed the travel agent to credit Philip's account with the difference between the first class price and the coach price. The funds constituting the difference therefore came from Truesdail, and the fact that travel credits were exchanged for frequent flyer miles was, according to the Court, irrelevant to their analysis. Dr. Charley asserted that the credits were "no-additional-cost services" that should be excluded under the IRC. However, the service in question must, among other things, be "offered for sale to customers in the ordinary course of the line of business of the employer in which the employee is performing services."[2] Truesdail did not offer frequent flyer miles to customers in the ordinary course of its business; thus, the travel credits at issue could not be deemed an excludable no-additional-cost service.

---

1. ***Charley v. Commissioner of Internal Revenue Service***, 91 F.3d 72 (9th Cir. 1996).
2. IRC §132(b).

Nondiscrimination

Employers may not exclude the value of the services to highly compensated employees if the value of the no-additional-cost service is not available on the same terms to all employees or at least to a group of employees defined under a reasonable classification that does not favor highly compensated employees. If the provision of the no-additional-cost service is discriminatory, then no aspect or portion of the exclusion applies to highly compensated employees. Therefore, the entire value of the exclusion is disallowed with the amount of the benefit included in the highly compensated employees' gross income.[1]

QUALIFIED EMPLOYEE DISCOUNTS

Under the regulations, the value of "**qualified employee discounts**" on property or services offered to an employer's customers in the ordinary course of the employer's business may be excluded from an employee's income (subject to certain limits).[2] However, this exclusion does not apply to discounts on real property or on personal property commonly held for investment purposes.[3]

QUICK QUIZ 13.4

1. Dependent care assistance can be excluded up to $2,500 for single individuals and $5,000 for married individuals filing jointly.
   a. True
   b. False

2. No-additional-cost services provided to employees may be discriminatory.
   a. True
   b. False

3. Qualified employee discounts are discounts given to the employees on property or services offered to an employer's customer in the ordinary course of business.
   a. True
   b. False

False, False, True.

Limits

The exclusion for an employee discount is limited based on whether the discount is for a service or merchandise:

- twenty percent of the price at which the service is offered to nonemployee customers, or
- for merchandise or other property, the employer's gross profit percentage[4] multiplied by the price the employer charges nonemployee customers for the property.

Covered Employees

The following individuals are treated as employees for the purposes of the qualified employee discount exclusion:

- current employees,
- former retired or disabled employees,
- widow(er)s of those who died while employed,
- widow(er)s of former retired or disabled employees,
- partners performing services for the partnership, or

---

1. Treas. Reg. §1.132-8(a)(2).
2. Treas. Reg. §1.132-3.
3. For instance, stocks and bonds are personal property commonly held for investment purposes.
4. An employer's gross profit percentage is determined based on all property offered to customers during the year preceding the year the discount is available, by subtracting the total cost of the property from the total sales price, and dividing the result by the total sales price of the property.

- leased employees providing services to an employer on a substantially full-time basis for at least a year where the services are performed under the employer's primary control.

Nondiscrimination

Nondiscrimination rules apply to the exclusion for qualified employee discounts. The discount must be made available to all employees or to a group of employees defined under a reasonable classification designated by the employer that does not favor highly compensated employees.

Randy's Parts Depot sells radiators for $100 to its customers. The radiator cost Randy's $80. If Randy's allows its employees to purchase the radiator for $90, the employees can exclude the $10 discount from gross income. If, however, Randy's sold the radiator to the employees at $75, then they would be required to include $5 in their gross income. The maximum excludable discount in this situation is $20 (20% x $100).

WORKING CONDITION FRINGE BENEFITS

The value of "**working condition fringe benefits**"[1] provided by an employer are excluded from an employee's gross income. Working condition fringes are defined as any property or service provided to an employee that enables the employee to perform his work and, if paid for by the employee, would be deductible as a trade or business expense.[2]

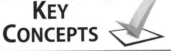

KEY CONCEPTS

1. What are working condition employee fringe benefits, and when are they excluded from income?

2. What are "de minimis" employee fringe benefits, and when are they excluded from income?

Covered Employees

Under the regulations, the following individuals are considered to be employees under the working conditions fringe exclusion:

- a current employee,
- a partner who performs services for a partnership,
- a director of the company, and
- an independent contractor performing services for the employer.[3]

Discriminatory

Working condition fringes are not subject to nondiscrimination requirements; therefore, the exclusion applies even if they favor highly compensated employees.

Eligible Benefits

The working condition fringe exclusion applies to cash payments provided for an employee's expenses for a business activity as long as the employee may deduct the expenses had the employee paid for the expenses without reimbursement. It is imperative that the employee keep sufficient documentation to verify the payment is actually used for those expenses and any unused portion of the payment is returned to the employer.

---

1. IRC §132.
2. IRC §162 or §167.
3. Treas. Reg. §1.132-1(b)(2).

The exclusion will not apply to:
- a service or property provided under a flexible spending account that provides the employee a certain level of unspecified non-cash benefits with a pre-determined cash value,
- a physical examination program provided by the employer, and
- any employee expense the employee may deduct as an expense for a trade or business other than the employer's trade or business.[1]

The property or service must be received by the employee, and there must be a legitimate business expense that relates to the employee's work. Business-related security devices, job-related education, parking, and use of company cars are some examples of working condition fringes.[2]

Company Car as a Working Condition Fringe Benefit

As listed above, a common working condition fringe benefit is the provision of a company car. If the employee utilizes the car for both personal and business purposes, the portion used for business is considered the value of the working condition fringe benefit, whereas the personal use value of the car will be included in the employee's gross income. Also, use of a demonstration car by full-time automobile salespersons qualifies as a working condition fringe benefit if the demonstration car is predominately used to facilitate the services the sales person provided to the employer and there are restrictions on personal use of the automobile.[3]

> Assume that an employer makes available to an employee an automobile and a chauffeur. Assume further that the value of the chauffeur services is $30,000 and that the chauffeur spends 30 percent of each workday driving the employee for personal purposes. There may be excluded from the employee's income 70 percent of $30,000, or $21,000, leaving an income inclusion with respect to the chauffeur services of $9,000.

EXAMPLE 13.12

Qualified Vehicles for "Non-Personal Use"

A **qualified non-personal use vehicle** is a vehicle that the employee does not use more than a minimal amount for personal reasons due to the design of the vehicle. If an employee is provided a vehicle that is deemed to be a qualified non-personal use vehicle, the value of the provision will be excluded from his gross income. Qualified non-personal use vehicles may include:
- clearly marked police and fire vehicles
- unmarked vehicles utilized by law enforcement individuals if the use is officially authorized
- an ambulance or hearse
- any vehicle designed to carry cargo with a loaded gross weight over 14,000 pounds
- delivery trucks with seating for the driver only or the driver with a folding jump seat
- a passenger bus with the capacity of at least 20 passengers
- school buses
- tractors or other farm-type vehicles

---

1. Treas. Reg. §1.132-5(a)(1).
2. Treas. Reg. §1.132-5.
3. Treas. Reg. §1.132-5(o).

Pickup truck: A pickup truck with a loaded gross vehicle weight of 14,000 pounds or less may be a qualified non-personal use vehicle if it has been modified so that it will unlikely be used more than for minimal personal use. Such pickup trucks that are clearly marked with decals, special painting, or other advertising associated with the function of the business may qualify if the pickup truck is equipped with a hydraulic lift tank, permanent tank or drum, permanent side boards that materially raise the level of the sides of the truck or the bed, or other heavy equipment are part of the vehicle. Also, if the pickup truck is primarily used to transport a particular type of load in construction, manufacturing, farming, drilling, timbering, or other similar operation for which it was specially designed, it will be considered a qualified non-personal use vehicle.

Vans: A van with a loaded gross vehicle weight of 14,000 pounds or less is a qualified nonpersonal-use vehicle if it has been specially modified so it is not likely to be used more than minimally for personal purposes. For example, a van qualifies if it is clearly marked with permanently affixed decals, special painting, or other advertising associated with the business and has a seat for the driver only (or the driver and one other person) and either of the following items: (1) permanent shelving that fills most of the cargo area, or (2) an open cargo area and the van always carries merchandise, material, or equipment used in the trade or business.

Education: Certain job-related education provided to an employee may qualify for exclusion as a working condition benefit. To qualify, the education must meet the same requirements that would apply for determining whether the employee could deduct the expenses had the employee paid the expenses. The education must meet at least one of the following tests:
1. The education is required by the employer or by law for the employee to keep his present salary, status, or job. The required education must serve a bona fide business purpose of the employer, or
2. The education maintains or improves skills needed in the job.

However, even if the education meets one or both of the above tests, it is not qualifying education if it is needed to meet the minimum educational requirements of the employee's present trade or business, or is part of a program of study that will qualify the employee for a new trade or business.

Employer provided transportation for security reasons:[1] The employee may not generally exclude the value of employer-provided transportation as a working condition fringe if such transportation is primarily personal. If, however, for bona fide business-oriented security concerns, the employee purchases transportation that provides him with additional security, the employee may generally deduct the excess of the amount actually paid for the transportation over the amount the employee would have paid for the same mode of transportation absent the bona fide business-oriented security concerns.

A bona fide business-oriented security concern exists only if the facts and circumstances establish a specific basis for concern regarding the safety of the employee. A generalized concern for an employee's safety is not a bona fide business-oriented security concern. Once a bona fide business-oriented security concern is determined to exist with respect to a particular employee, the employer must periodically evaluate the situation for purposes of determining whether the bona fide

---

1. Treas. Reg. §1.32-5(m).

business-oriented security concern still exists. Example(s) of factors indicating a specific basis for concern regarding the safety of an employee are:

1. A threat of death or kidnapping of, or serious bodily harm to, the employee or a similarly situated employee because of either employee's status as an employee of the employer, or

2. A recent history of violent terrorist activity (such as bombings) in the geographic area in which the transportation is provided, unless that activity is focused on a group of individuals which does not include the employee (or a similarly situated employee of an employer), or occurs to a significant degree only in a location within the geographic area where the employee does not travel.

In addition, the employer must establish an overall security program with respect to the employee involved. This program must include 24-hour protection and must be provided at the employee's residence and work place. However, an employer may make use of an independent security study and follow such recommendations, even if the security is not provided on a 24-hour basis. For example, the security concerns may simply involve travel to a specific geographic area.

> Assume that in response to several death threats on the life of A, the president of X a multinational company, X establishes an overall security program for A, including an alarm system at A's home and guards at A's workplace, the use of a vehicle that is specially equipped with alarms, bulletproof glass, and armor plating, and a bodyguard/chauffeur. Assume further that A is driven for both personal and business reasons in the vehicle. Also, assume that but for the bona fide business-oriented security concerns, no part of the overall security program would have been provided to A. With respect to the transportation provided for security reasons, A may exclude as a working condition fringe the value of the special security features of the vehicle and the value attributable to the bodyguard/chauffeur. Thus, if the value of the specially equipped vehicle is $40,000, and the value of the vehicle without the security features is $25,000, A may determine A's inclusion in income attributable to the vehicle as if the vehicle were worth $25,000. A must include in income the value of the availability of the vehicle for personal use.

EXAMPLE 13.13

> Assume that company Z retains an independent security consultant to perform a security study with respect to its chief executive officer. Assume further that, based on an objective assessment of the facts and circumstances, the security consultant reasonably recommends that 24-hour protection is not necessary but that the employee be provided security at his workplace and for ground transportation, but not for air transportation. If company Z follows the recommendations on a consistent basis, an overall security program will be deemed to exist with respect to the workplace and ground transportation security only.

EXAMPLE 13.14

"DE MINIMIS" FRINGE BENEFITS

The term **"de minimis" fringe benefit** is defined in IRC §132(e) as any property or service provided by an employer to an employee that is so small in value that it makes accounting for it unreasonable or administratively impracticable when taking into account the frequency that similar fringes are provided by the employer to employees. "De minimis" is a term that means minimal, very trifling, or small.

Examples of De Minimis Fringe Benefits

The following is an illustrative, but not exclusive, list of de minimis fringe benefits as discussed in the regulations:[1]

- occasional typing of personal letters by a secretary hired by an employer
- occasional personal use of an employer's copying machine, providing that the employer exercises sufficient control and imposes significant restrictions on the personal use of the machine so that at least 85% of the use of the machine is for business purposes
- occasional cocktail parties, group meals, or picnics for the employees and their guests
- traditional birthday or holiday gifts or property (not cash) with a low fair market value
- occasional theater or sporting event tickets
- coffee, donuts, or soft drinks
- local telephone calls
- flowers, fruit, or books, or similar property provided to employees under special circumstances (i.e., on account of illness, outstanding performance or family crisis)[2]

Examples of Fringe Benefits that are not De Minimis

The regulations also discuss examples of benefits that are not excludable as de minimis benefits:

- season tickets for sporting or theatrical events
- the commuting use of an employer-provided automobile or other vehicle more than one day a month
- membership in a private country club or athletic facility, regardless of the frequency with which the employee uses the facility
- employer-provided group term life insurance on the life of the spouse or child of an employee
- use of employer-owned or leased facilities (such as an apartment, hunting lodge, boat, etc.) for a weekend, unless required for work[3]

The Exclusion

The value of some or all of de minimis fringe benefits may be excluded from an employee's gross income under other statutory provisions or regulations such as the exclusion for meals furnished for the convenience of the employer discussed later in this section.[4]

The frequency of which similar fringes are furnished by the employer to the employee is generally calculated by reference to the frequency of which the employer furnishes the fringes to each individual employee.[5] An example of this employee-measured frequency is where an employer provides a free meal to one employee on a daily basis but not to any other employee, and the value of such meals is not de minimis concerning that one employee even though the meals are infrequently furnished to the employer's entire work force.[6]

---

1. Treas. Reg. §1.132-6.
2. Treas. Reg. §1.132-6(e)(1).
3. Treas. Reg. §1.132-6(e)(2).
4. Treas. Reg. §1.132-6(e)(2).
5. Treas. Reg. §1.132-6(b)(1).
6. Treas. Reg. §1.132-6(b)(1).

EXAMPLE 13.15

Make You Well Hospital provides meals in the hospital cafeteria free of charge to nurses that work shifts greater than 24 hours. On average, each nurse receives one free meal every two weeks. The hospital also provides the director of the hospital a free meal in the hospital cafeteria every day. While the free meals to the nurses may be de minimis because they are infrequent, the meals to the director are not because they are provided everyday.

Irrespective of the "employee-measured frequency" rule above, the frequency with which the benefits are furnished in the aggregate to the entire work force is used where it would be administratively difficult to determine frequency considering individual employees. [1]

A cash fringe benefit is never excludable[2] unless the cash is for reasonable, occasional meal money or local transportation fare.[3] The "occasional" requirement depends on the frequency, availability, and regularity of the benefit. The furnishing of meals, money, or local transportation fare on a regular or routine basis is not considered to be "occasional."[4] Further, the meals, meal money, or local transportation fare must be provided due to overtime work necessitating an extension of the employee's normal work schedule.[5] The meals or meal money are excludable if they are provided to allow the employee to work overtime. For instance, meal money given to the employee for meals consumed during overtime work satisfies this test.[6]

EXAMPLE 13.16

MAD Dog LLC is a well respected publisher of financial planning materials. MAD Dog requires its employees to work overtime when projects have to be completed by certain deadlines. When employees work overtime, MAD Dog often brings in food for the staff. As long as the overtime is deemed occasional and the meals are provided to allow employees to work longer hours, it will not be included in the income of the employees.

De Minimis Meals

When meals or meal money furnished is so small in value that accounting for it is unreasonable or administratively impractical, the de minimis fringe benefits exclusion will apply. There is some overlap between de minimis meals and meals furnished for the "convenience of the employer" under IRC §119. In numerous lawsuits, employers attempt to argue that meals furnished satisfy both de minimis fringe benefit requirements and meals for the convenience of the employer.[7] Aside from coffee, donuts, soft drinks, occasional meals or meal money to enable the employee to work overtime, and occasional picnics and parties, this exclusion deals largely with employer-operated eating facilities.[8] Employer-operated eating facilities for employees qualify for this exclusion if:
- the facility is located on or near the business premises of the employer, and

1. Treas. Reg. §1.132-6(b)(2).
2. IRC §132(a).
3. Treas. Reg. §1.132-6(d)(2).
4. Treas. Reg. §1.132-6(d)(2)(i)(A).
5. Treas. Reg. §1.132-6(d)(2)(i)(B).
6. Treas. Reg. §1.132-6(d)(2)(i)(C).
7. See ***Boyd Gaming Corp. v. Commissioner of Internal Revenue Service***, 17 F. 3d. 1096 (9th Cir. 1999), discussed later in this Chapter. See also IRC §119.
8. The facility may be operated "directly or through a hired third party" by the employer and owned or leased by the employer as well.

- the annual revenue of the facility is equal to or greater than the direct operating costs of the facility.[1]

If access to the facility is available on substantially the same terms to all members of a group of employees defined under a reasonable classification set up by the employer that does not discriminate in favor of highly compensated employees, then this de minimis fringe benefit is excludable from the gross income of all employees including highly compensated employees.[2] The revenue from furnishing a meal is presumed to be equal to the facility's direct operating costs if its value can be excluded from an employee's gross income.[3] It is here where the de minimis meal rule overlaps with meals furnished for the convenience of the employer rule.[4] Under §119, an employee may exclude meals furnished on the business premises of the employer for the convenience of the employer.[5]

QUICK QUIZ 13.5

1. Working condition fringe benefits may be discriminatory and still maintain the favored tax treatment.
   a. True
   b. False

2. A de minimis employee fringe benefit is property or service provided to an employee that is so small in value that accounting for it is unreasonable.
   a. True
   b. False

True, True.

One attractive feature of de minimis meals is that they are fully deductible for income tax purposes by the employer without the 50 percent statutory limit on deductions for cost of meals yet excludable from the employee's gross income.

De Minimis Transportation

Transportation provided with minimal value may also qualify as a de minimis" fringe benefit. If an employer furnishes an employee with taxi fare based on unusual circumstances and due to unsafe alternative transportation, the excess of the value of each one way trip over $1.50 is excluded from the employee's gross income.[6] Unusual circumstances are determined by consideration of all facts and circumstances relating to the situation, like a temporary change in employee's work schedule or being called to the work place at 1:00 a.m. when an employee usually works from 8:00 a.m. to 4:00 p.m.[7]

A public transit pass, tokens, or fare cards provided to the employee at a discount to defray commuting costs may be excluded from the employee's gross income as a de minimis fringe benefit if the discount or net value of the employee's costs does not exceed $21.00 per month.[8] Reimbursement of such expenses are excludable if the employee receives no more than $21.00 per month under a bona fide reimbursement arrangement.[9]

---

1. IRC §132(e).
2. IRC §132(e)(2).
3. *Id.*
4. See also ***Boyd Gaming Corporation, supra***, at page 1099.
5. IRC §119(a).
6. Treas. Reg. §1.132-6(d)(2)(iii).
7. Treas. Reg. §1.132-6(d)(2)(iii)(B).
8. Treas. Reg. §1.132-6(d)(1).

Benefits Exceeding Value and Frequency Limits - All or Nothing

If a benefit is provided to an employee that is not deemed de minimis due to excess value or excess frequency, then no amount is considered a de minimis fringe.[10] If, for example, an employer reimburses an employee $40.00 per month for taxi fare, then the entire $40.00 per month will be included in the employee's gross income, not merely the $19.00 ($40 minus the $21 total cost threshold) per month excess value.

Jane works for ABC Company. ABC reimburses Jane $15 per month for a ferry pass. The ferry pass costs Jane $40 per month. In this situation, $15 is excluded from Jane's gross income. If in the same example, ABC reimburses Jane $21 per month for the ferry pass, $21 is excluded from Jane's income. If in the same example, ABC reimburses Jane $25 per month, then none of the $25 could be excluded from Jane's income.

EXAMPLE 13.17

Case Study 13.6

The issues of de minimis meals for the convenience of the employer were presented to the United States 9th Circuit Court of Appeals in ***Boyd Gaming Corp. v. Commissioner of Internal Revenue Service.***[1]

Although decided in 1999, the Boyd Gaming case dealt with facts occurring in the 1987 - 1988 taxable years when 26 U.S.C. §274(n) provided for an 80% cap on meal and entertainment expenses. Concerned with tax laws that purportedly "unfairly allowed high income taxpayers to structure their business affairs in a manner that generated deductions for personal living expenses," Congress imposed a cap on the amount of deductions for business meals and entertainment.[2] Boyd Gaming Corporation and California Hotel and Casino and their subsidiaries were hotel and casino operators that required their employees to stay on the business premises throughout their work shift, resulting in the employees receiving free meals at onsite cafeterias. Boyd asserted that it was exempt from the then 80% cap on deductions because the meals provided were "de minimis fringe benefits".[3] The Tax Court rejected Boyd's argument and ruled that Boyd's deductions were limited to 80% under §274(n). The United States Ninth Circuit disagreed and reversed the Tax Court, finding that Boyd's stay-on-the-premises policy rendered the employee's meals furnished for the convenience of the employer and the meals constituted de minimis fringe benefits under 26 U.S.C. §132(e)(2).[4]

---

1. ***Boyd Gaming Corp. v. Commissioner of Internal of Revenue***, 177 F. 3d 1096 (9th Cir. 1999).
2. 177 F. 3d at 1097.
3. Id. (citing 26 U.S.C. §274(n)(2)); 26 U.S.C. §132 (e)).
4. ***Boyd Gaming***, 177 F. 3d at 1097.

---

9. Note that an employer who provides de minimis transportation benefits may also be eligible to establish a qualified transportation and parking benefits program. However, a qualified transportation and parking benefits program would have a greater administrative burden and the employer may not provide benefits under both a qualified program and the de minimis rule.

10. Treas. Reg. §1.132-6(d)(4).

Case Study 13.6 Continued

More specifically, Boyd offered reasons for its stay-on-the-premises policy, including security and efficiency concerns,[1] maintaining work force control,[2] handling business emergencies and continuous customer demands, and the impracticability of obtaining meals within a reasonable proximity. The Court analyzed the statutes that dealt with the test of deductibility and indicated that §132(e)(2) defined de minimis fringe benefits as an employer's operation of an eating facility for employees if the facility was located on or near the business premises of the employer and the revenue derived from the facility met or exceeded the direct operating costs of the facility.

Because there was no evidence as to the revenue derived, Boyd had to rely on the statutory presumption in §132(e)(2) that treats revenue as equal to operating costs if employees are entitled to exclude the value of the meals under IRC §119. Thus, in order to determine the applicability of the 80% cap on deductions, the Court resorted to §132(e)(2), which in turn required an analysis of §119's "convenience of the employer" test.[3] Boyd asserted that the stay-on-the-premises requirement constituted a "substantial non-compensatory business reason" for furnishing meals. The Court reasoned that Boyd furnished meals as a consequence of its stay-on-the-premises policy, as employees could not leave the premises during their shifts. The Court articulated that common sense dictated that, once the policy was embraced, the employees had no choice but to eat on the premises and were "indispensable to the proper discharge of the employee's duties."[4] Because Boyd supported its "closed campus policy" with adequate evidence of legitimate business reasons, the Court found that non-compensatory business reasons existed, and thus the employees could exclude the meals under §119, which consequently meant that the presumption in §132(e)(2) applied. Once the presumption of §132(e)(2) applied, the cap on deductions was inapplicable and Boyd was allowed to deduct all meal expenses from its income.

1. The Court described the facts behind Boyd's stay on the premises policy. The casino environment is one in which vast amounts of cash flow in fast-moving transactions and special security precautions are imposed by state regulations, and many of Boyd's employees handle or have easy access to cash and gambling chips. Consequently, each property performs special check-out procedures for certain employees before they are permitted to leave the premises. The "stay-on-premises" policy minimizes the number of entries and departures during each work shift, thereby reducing security risks and the costs of security measures.
2. Boyd contends that the "stay-on-premises" requirement allows it to maintain tight control over its workforce, thereby reducing the chances of employees succumbing to the distractions and temptations of the "festive" Las Vegas atmosphere.
3. IRC §119 (B) (4) considers meals to be furnished for the convenience of the employer if they are provided to more than half of the employees for a "substantial non-compensatory business reason." *Boyd Gaming*, 177 F.3d at 1099-1100.
4. *Boyd Gaming*, 177 F.3d at 1100.

Rules for Selected Fringe Benefits (2016)

EXHIBIT 13.3

Type of Fringe Benefit	Treatment Under Employment Taxes		
	Income Tax Withholding	Social Security and Medicare (including Additional Medicare Tax when wages are paid in excess of $200,000)	Federal Unemployment (FUTA)
Accident and health benefits	Exempt[1,2], except for long-term care benefits provided through a flexible spending or similar arrangement.	Exempt, except for certain payments to S corporation employees who are 2% shareholders.	Exempt
Achievement awards	Exempt[1] up to $1,600 for qualified plan awards ($400 for nonqualified awards).		
Adoption assistance	Exempt[1,3]	Taxable	Taxable
Athletic facilities	Exempt if substantially all use during the calendar year is by employees, their spouses, and their dependent children and the facility is operated by the employer on premises owned or leased by the employer.		
De minimis (minimal) benefits	Exempt	Exempt	Exempt
Dependent care assistance	Exempt[3] up to certain limits, $5,000 ($2,500 for married employee filing separate return).		
Educational assistance	Exempt up to $5,250 of benefits each year.		
Employee discounts	Exempt[3] up to certain limits.		
Employee stock options	Discussed in Chapter 12.		
Employer-provided cell phones	Exempt if provided primarily for noncompensatory business purposes.		
Group-term life insurance coverage	Exempt	Exempt[1,4,7] up to cost of $50,000 of coverage. (Special rules apply to former employees.)	Exempt
Health savings accounts (HSAs)	Exempt for qualified individuals up to the HSA contribution limits.		
Lodging on your business premises	Exempt[1] if furnished for your convenience as a condition of employment.		
Meals	Exempt if furnished on your business premises for your convenience.		
	Exempt if de minimis.		
Moving expense reimbursements	Exempt[1] if expenses would be deductible if the employee had paid them.		
No-additional-cost services	Exempt[3]	Exempt[3]	Exempt[3]
Retirement planning services	Exempt[5]	Exempt[5]	Exempt[5]
Transportation (commuting) benefits	Exempt[1] up to certain limits if for rides in a commuter highway vehicle and/or transit passes ($255), qualified parking ($255) or qualified bicycle commuting reimbursement[6] ($20).		
	Exempt if de minimis.		
Tuition reduction	Exempt[3] if for undergraduate education (or graduate education if the employee performs teaching or research activities).		
Working condition benefits	Exempt	Exempt	Exempt

[1] Exemption doesn't apply to S corporation employees who are 2% shareholders.

[2] Exemption doesn't apply to certain highly compensated employees under a self-insured plan that favors those employees.

[3] Exemption doesn't apply to certain highly compensated employees under a program that favors those employees.

[4] Exemption doesn't apply to certain key employees under a plan that favors those employees.

[5] Exemption doesn't apply to services for tax preparation, accounting, legal, or brokerage services.

[6] If the employee receives a qualified bicycle commuting reimbursement in a qualified bicycle commuting month, the employee can't receive commuter highway vehicle, transit pass, or qualified parking benefits in that same month.

[7] You must include in your employee's wages the cost of group-term life insurance beyond $50,000 worth of coverage, reduced by the amount the employee paid toward the insurance. Report it as wages in boxes 1, 3, and 5 of the employee's Form W-2. Also, show it in box 12 with code "C." The amount is subject to social security and Medicare taxes, and you may, at your option, withhold federal income tax.

Source: 2016 IRS Publication 15-b, Table 2-1 "Special Rules for Various Types of Fringe Benefits"

Nondiscrimination Rules

The nondiscrimination rules do not apply in determining the amount of a de minimis fringe benefit or working condition fringe benefit.[1] However, the nondiscrimination rules do apply to most other types of fringe benefits. Thus, the ability to classify a benefit that would ordinarily not allow discrimination as a de minimis fringe benefit may allow the employer to in effect discriminate.

QUALIFIED MOVING EXPENSE REIMBURSEMENT

A "**qualified moving expenses reimbursement**" may be excluded from an employee's gross income as a fringe benefit whether provided through services in kind, direct payment or reimbursement. Generally, employers may exclude qualified moving reimbursement expenses that are provided to an employee from the employee's wages. This exclusion applies to reimbursement of moving expenses that the employee could have deducted on his or her income tax return if the employee paid or incurred them without reimbursement, provided the employee did not deduct the moving expenses.[2]

KEY CONCEPTS

1. What is a qualified moving expense reimbursement, and when is it excluded from income?

2. What is qualified transportation and parking, and when is it excluded from income?

3. What requirements are necessary for adoption assistance programs to be excluded from income?

Qualifying Move

A move will be considered a qualifying move if the move is closely related to the start of work and both the distance test and the time tests are met.

Distance Test: The distance between the old home and the new job location must be at least 50 miles greater than the distance between the old home and the old job location.

EXAMPLE 13.18

Albert moved to a new home less than 50 miles from his former home because he changed main job locations. His old main job location was 3 miles from his former home. Albert's new main job location is 60 miles from that home. Because his new main job location is 57 miles farther from his former home than the distance from his former home to his old main job location, he meets the distance test.

Time Test: The employee needs to be either: (1) full time in the new location for no less than 39 weeks during the 12 month period immediately after arrival, or (2) full time or self employed at least 78 weeks during the 24 month period immediately after arrival and at least 39 weeks during the 12 month period immediately after arrival.

---

1. Treas. Reg. §1-132-5(q).
2. IRC §217.

EXAMPLE
13.19

Jacque quit his job and moved from the east coast to the west coast to begin a full-time job as a wine-maker for Dalton Family Winery. He generally worked at the winery about 40 hours each week. Shortly after the move, Jacque also began operating a custom furniture business from his home for several hours each afternoon and all day on weekends. Because Jacque's principal place of business is the winery, he can satisfy the time test by meeting the 39-week test.

If Jacque is unable to satisfy the requirements of the 39-week test during the 12-month period immediately following his arrival in the general location of his new principal place of work, he may be able to satisfy the 78-week test.

This exclusion for the qualified moving expense reimbursement applies to current employees and leased employees who provided services substantially full time for at least a year and perform under the employer's primary control. Those who own two percent or more of the corporation's stock are not considered employees under the rules for this exclusion.

DISTANCE TEST

EXHIBIT
13.4

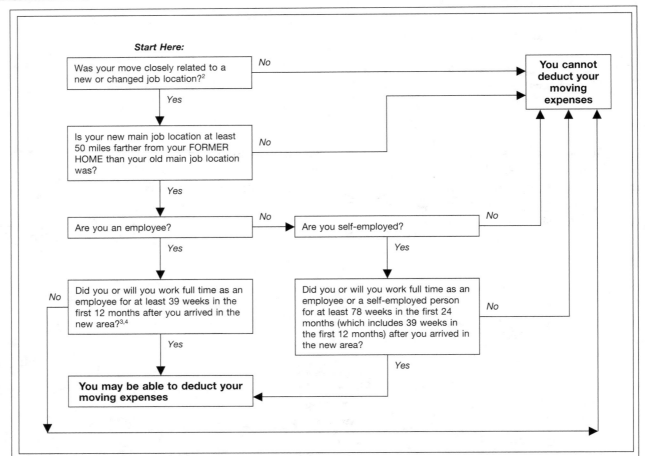

[1] Military persons should see *Members of the Armed Forces,* later, for special rules that apply to them.

[2] Your move must be closely related to the start of work at your new job location. See *Move Related to Start of Work,* earlier.

[3] If you deduct expenses and do not meet this test later, you must either file an amended tax return or report your moving expense deduction as other income. See *Time test not yet met,* later.

[4] If you became self-employed during the first 12 months, answer YES if your time as a full-time employee added to your time as a self-employed person equals or will equal at least 78 weeks in the first 24 months (including 39 weeks in the first 12 months) after you arrived in the new area.

Deductible Moving Expenses

Deductible moving expenses are confined to reasonable expenses for the following:

- moving household goods and personal effects from the former home to the new home (19 cents per mile for 2016), and
- traveling and associative lodging during the move from the former home to the new home.[2]

---

1. IRS Publication 521, Figure B.
2. IRC §217(b).

EXAMPLE
13.20

Thomas, an employee of MC Corp., works and maintains his principal residence in Pittsburgh, Pennsylvania. Upon receiving orders from his employer that he is to be transferred to the corporation's San Francisco, California office, Thomas drives to San Francisco with his family with stopovers at various cities between Pittsburgh and San Francisco to visit friends and relatives. In addition, Thomas detours into Texas for sight-seeing. Because of the stopovers and tour into Texas, Thomas' travel time and distance are increased over what they would have been had he proceeded directly to San Francisco. To the extent that Thomas' route of travel between Pittsburgh and San Francisco is in a generally southwesterly direction, it may be said that he is traveling by the shortest and most direct route available by motor vehicle. Since Thomas' excursion into Texas is away from the usual Pittsburgh-San Francisco route, the portion of the expenses paid or incurred attributable to the Texas excursion is not deductible. Likewise, that portion of the expenses attributable to Thomas' delays en route not necessitated by reasons of rest or repair of his vehicle is not deductible.

Any portion or amount of deductible expenses that are not reimbursed by an employer may be deducted on the employee's individual tax return as an "above-the-line" (or "For AGI") deduction.

Nondeductible Moving Expenses

Examples of items nondeductible as moving expenses include, but are not limited to, the following:[1]
- storage charges (other than in-transit)
- costs incurred in the acquisition of property
- costs incurred and losses sustained in the disposition of property
- penalties for breaking leases
- mortgage penalties
- expenses of refitting rugs or draperies
- expenses of connecting or disconnecting utilities
- losses sustained on the disposal of memberships in clubs, tuition fees, and similar items
- meals while in-route
- pre-move house hunting expenses
- temporary living expenses

If an employer reimburses an employee for any nondeductible expense, the employee must include that portion of the reimbursement in his gross income.

QUALIFIED TRANSPORTATION AND PARKING

The regulations provide for an exclusion of the value of qualified transportation benefits from an employee's gross income.[2] This exclusion for transportation benefits is subject to the following limitations:
- $255 per month (2016) for commuter highway transportation and transit passes combined.
- $255 per month (2016) for qualified parking.

1. Treas. Reg. §1.217-1(b)(3).
2. Treas. Reg. §1.132-9.

For any given month, if the value of a benefit is more than the limit, then any excess amount above the limit, less any amount the employee paid, is included in the employee's income. The excess may not qualify as a de minimis benefit.

After 2008, an employee who does not receive any of the transportation fringe benefits explained above, may exclude up to $20 per month of qualified bicycle commuting reimbursements from an employer. Qualified bicycle commuting reimbursements are employer reimbursements for the purchase, improvement, repair, or storage of a bicycle that is regularly used for travel between the employee's residence and place of employment. The $20 per month limit is not adjusted for inflation.

Covered Employees

The provision of the benefit may be discriminatory. Current employees and leased employees providing services substantially full time for at least a year under the employer's control are considered employees under this exclusion. Nonetheless, those who own two percent or more of the stock of an S corporation are not considered employees.

Excludable Transportation and Parking Benefits

The following examples are excludable transportation and parking benefits:

- a transit pass
- a ride in a commuter highway vehicle between the home of the employee and the workplace
- qualified parking[1]

QUICK QUIZ 13.6

1. Deductible moving expenses include moving household goods, lodging, and meals during the move.
   a. True
   b. False

2. Qualified transportation benefits may be given by the employer directly or through a bona fide reimbursement arrangement.
   a. True
   b. False

False, True.

The value of each one of these benefits are excludable from an employee's gross income without regard to whether one or all are provided by the employer to the employee. **Qualified parking** is parking provided by the employer on or near the employer's business premises. It also includes parking on or near the location where employees commute to work using mass transit, carpools, or commuter highway vehicles but not at the employee's home.

Qualified transportation benefits may be given by the employer directly or through a bona fide reimbursement arrangement. However, cash reimbursements for transit passes may qualify only when a voucher is not readily available for direct distribution by the employer.

ADOPTION ASSISTANCE PROGRAMS

Ordinarily, an employee may exclude from an employee's gross income amounts paid for, or expenses incurred, by the employer for qualified adoption expenses[2] concerning the adoption of a child by an employee if these amounts are furnished according to a written adoption assistance program.[3] An employer may establish a written **adoption assistance program** intended to

---

1. Treas. Reg. §1.132-9.
2. IRC §137.

promote adoption and that will pay expenses related to an adoption not exceeding $13,460 for 2016 to an employee.[1] The limitation of $13,460 for 2016 applies to an adoption for each child (there is no longer an increased amount for special needs adoptions). The amount paid is excluded from the employee's income, but there is a phaseout of this exclusion starting at $201,920 of adjusted gross income (AGI) for 2016 through $241,920. If the employee's AGI is greater than or equal to $241,920 for 2016, then the exclusion is eliminated.

The plan must comply with nondiscrimination requirements. The plan may pay for qualified adoption expenses consisting of adoption fees and related charges, court costs, attorney's fees, and other expenses directly tied to the adoption of a child under age 18 or who is physically or mentally incapable of caring for themselves.[2] While the payments or reimbursements made under the program are excluded from an employee's gross income, such payments continue to be subject to Social Security, Medicare, and federal unemployment taxes.

Taxpayers are also able to claim a credit for expenses incurred that are associated with adopting an eligible child. The credit, which is no longer refundable for years after December 31, 2011, has the same limits and income phase out ranges as discussed above with adoption assistance programs. Taxpayers may be able to make use of both the exclusion and the credit in certain circumstances.

Madelyn paid $10,000 in qualified adoption expenses for the adoption of an eligible child. Under a qualified adoption assistance program, Madelyn's employer reimbursed her for $4,000 of those expenses. Madelyn may exclude the $4,000 reimbursement from her income. However, because of the employer reimbursement, $4,000 of her expenses no longer meets the definition of qualified adoption expenses. As a result, Madelyn's maximum adoption credit is limited to $6,000 ($10,000 - $4,000).

EXAMPLE 13.21

Haylee paid $10,000 in qualified adoption expenses for the adoption of an eligible child. Under a qualified adoption assistance program, Haylee's employer paid an additional $6,000 of qualified adoption expenses on her behalf. Her total qualified adoption expenses are $16,000 ($10,000 + $6,000). Because the expenses paid by Haylee were different from the expenses paid by her employer, Haylee may exclude the $6,000 that her employer paid from her income and may claim a credit for the $10,000 of qualified adoption expenses she paid.

EXAMPLE 13.22

Paul paid $30,000 in qualified adoption expenses to adopt an eligible foreign child, and the adoption became final in 2016. Under a qualified adoption assistance program, Paul's employer reimbursed him for $13,460 of those expenses. Paul may exclude the $13,460 reimbursement from his income. The remaining $16,540 of expenses ($30,000 - $13,460) continue to be qualified adoption expenses that are eligible for the credit. However, Paul's credit is dollar-limited to $13,460. The remaining amount of expenses may never be claimed as a credit or excluded from gross income.

EXAMPLE 13.23

---

3. IRC §137(a).

1. The employer may institute a program providing $6,000 for children with special needs. See IRC §137.

2. IRC §23(d)(2).

According to a report by the GAO released in October 2011, the IRS has audited a significantly high number of returns on which the adoption credit was claimed by a taxpayer. The following is an excerpt from that report.

> "As of August 2011, 68 percent of the nearly 100,000 returns on which taxpayers claimed the adoption credit were sent to correspondence audit. However, of the approximately 35,000 returns on which audits have been completed as of August, IRS only assessed additional tax about 17 percent of the time. The equivalent rate for all correspondence audits in 2010 was 86 percent. The time it has taken IRS to audit these predominantly legitimate adoption credit claims has resulted in considerable delays in the payment of the related refunds. For the 2012 filing season, IRS has options that might allow it to reduce the number of costly audits and issue refunds faster while still maintaining a robust enforcement strategy. One option is for IRS to immediately send a letter to taxpayers who submit returns without any documentation requesting it before initiating an audit."[1]
>
> 1. GAO Report, October 2011, Adoption Tax Credit: IRS Can Reduce Audits and Refund Delays.

AWARDS AND PRIZES

Certain prizes and awards (as defined below) given to employees by their employer may be excluded from the employees' gross income.[1] An employee achievement award is defined in the IRC as an item of tangible personal property that is:

- transferred by an employer to an employee for length of service achievement or safety achievement,
- awarded as part of a meaningful presentation, and
- awarded under conditions and circumstances that do not create a significant likelihood of the payment of disguised compensation.[2]

KEY CONCEPTS

1. What requirements are necessary for awards and prizes to be excluded from income?

2. What requirements are necessary for qualified tuition reduction plans to be excluded from income?

For purposes of this section, the term "tangible personal property" does not include cash. Other items that will not be considered tangible personal property include vacations, meals, lodging, tickets to theater and sporting events, and stocks, bonds, and other securities.

Limits on Value of Awards

An employee is allowed to exclude from gross income the value of any employee achievement awards insofar as the cost of the award does not exceed the following limitations:[3]

1. IRC §274.
2. IRC §§274(j)(3)(A) and 74(c).
3. IRC §§274(j)(1) and (2).

- $400 for all nonqualified plan awards when added to the employer's cost for all other employee achievement awards made to such employee during the taxable year that are not qualified plan awards, and
- $1,600 for all qualified plan awards when added to the employer's cost for all other employee achievement awards made to such employee during the taxable year (including employee achievement awards that are not qualified plan awards).[1]

Only the excess amount over the $400 and $1,600 limitations is included in the employees income (but not deductible by the employer); the initial $400 or $1,600 limitations are not included in the employees' income (and deductible by the employer). In other words, if an employee achievement award exceeds the $1,600 limit and constitutes a qualified plan award, then only the excess amount above $1,600 is included in the employee's gross income and no penalty occurs that would render the entire amount taxable.

If the cost of the award provided to an employee is more than the employer's allowable deduction, then the larger of the following amounts must be included in the employee's wages: (a) the portion of the cost that is more than the employer's allowable deduction (up to the value of the award), (b) the amount of the value of the award that exceeds the employer's allowable deduction.

Qualified Plan Award

A "**qualified plan award**" is defined as an employee achievement award bestowed as part of an established written plan of the taxpayer that does not discriminate in favor of highly compensated employees (within the meaning of §414(q)) for eligibility or benefits.[2] However, there are limitations on this exclusion. If the "average cost"[3] of all employee achievement awards provided by the employer during the year exceeds $400, then such employee achievement award shall not be treated as a qualified plan award for any taxable year.

EXAMPLE 13.24

In 2016, J Company presents employee length of service awards to seven employees for a total cost to the employer of $2,100. The average cost of all awards is $300 ($2,100÷7). Since the average cost of all awards does not exceed $400, the awards are considered qualified plan awards provided there is a written plan that does not discriminate in favor of highly paid employees.

---

1. IRC §274(j)(2).
2. IRC §274(j)(3)(B)(i).
3. IRC §274(J)(3)(ii). For purposes of this provision, average cost shall be determined by including the entire cost of all qualified plan awards given by the employer without taking into account employee achievement awards of nominal value (less than $50).

Special Rules

In the event that an employee achievement award is granted by a partnership, the deduction limitations apply to the partnership as well as to each member.[1] For length of service awards, an award is not deemed as being provided for length of service achievement if it is accepted during the recipient's first five years of employment, or within any other five year period.[2] Meanwhile, an item is not considered a safety achievement award if:

- such safety achievement awards have been granted to more than 10 percent of the employees of the employer during the taxable year, or
- such item is awarded to a manager, administrator, clerical employee, or other professional employee.[3]

Covered Employees

Under this exclusion, employees are considered (1) current employees, or (2) leased employees providing services to an employer on a substantially full-time basis for at least a year if the services performed are under the employer's primary control. Two percent shareholders of S corporation are not considered employees of the corporation for this exclusion.

EXAMPLE 13.25

Kathleen is a professor at the University of Georgia. She receives an employee achievement award for her work during the year. She is given a crystal trophy and matching serving dishes for a total value of $1,500. The award is a qualified plan award. Is this amount excluded from her income for that taxable year?

Answer: Yes. In this scenario, Kathleen can exclude from her income $1,500 because it is a qualified plan award. If the plan was not qualified, then Kathleen could only exclude up to $400.

VALUATION RULES APPLYING TO FRINGE BENEFITS

In determining whether a fringe benefit is excludable from taxation, a common problem is the valuation of the fringe benefit in the event that the entire fringe benefit is taxable or a portion of the fringe benefit is taxable. Various taxation rules apply in determining the value of a fringe benefit. Ordinarily, the general valuation rule applies to the value of a fringe benefit. However, there are special valuation rules for certain benefits, which are discussed in this section. Aside from the general valuation rule, there are special valuation rules for employee transportation benefits,

---

1. IRC §274(j)(4)(A).
2. IRC §274(j)(4)(B).
3. IRC §274(j)(4)(C).

which include the cents per mile rule, the commuting rule, the lease value rule, and the unsafe conditions commuting rule.

THE GENERAL VALUATION RULE

Most fringe benefits are valued under the general valuation rule. Basically, the fair market value should be the value assigned to a fringe benefit. Under the regulations, the amount that an employee would be required to pay a third party in an arm's-length transaction to purchase or lease the benefit, or what one would pay in the market place, is considered the fair market value of a fringe benefit. This figure is different than the cost an employer may incur in providing the benefit to an employee. Likewise, this figure is not what an employee considers to be the value or the amount the employer would be willing to pay for the fringe benefit. Instead, the amount that is determined to be fair market value depends on the facts and circumstances of the particular situation.

For instance, with employer-provided vacations, the fair market value of an employer-provided vacation is the amount the employer would have to pay a third party, travel agent, or directly to the service provider for the same or similar vacation on the same or comparable terms in the geographic area where the vacation is taking place. Additionally, when ascertaining the value of an employer-provided vehicle, the fair market value is the amount the employee would need to pay a third party or dealership to lease the same or similar vehicle in the same or similar terms in the geographic area where the employer uses the vehicle. The duration of the lease is also relevant in this determination, so the comparable lease term should be a similar period as the period

> ## KEY CONCEPTS
>
> 1. How are employee fringe benefits valued under the general rule?
> 2. What is the cents per mile rule?
> 3. What is the commuting rule?
> 4. What is the lease value rule?
> 5. What is the unsafe conditions commuting rule?

provided by the employer-provided vehicle. In other words, if the employer is providing the vehicle to the employee for a two year period, then comparable lease terms of two years should be used in determining the fair market value.

THE CENTS PER MILE RULE

Valuation under the **cents per mile rule** requires multiplying the standard mileage rate by the total miles the employee drives the vehicle for personal purposes. Personal use is any use of the vehicle other than use in the employer's trade or business. The standard business mileage rate is 54 cents per mile (2016). Of course, the vehicle must be provided by an employer to the employee for both business use and personal use. Under the regulations, a vehicle is considered to be any motorized wheeled vehicle, which would include those manufactured primarily for use on public roads, streets, and highways.[1] One important issue in using this valuation is whether the vehicle is used regularly in the employee's business.[2]

The test for determining whether the vehicle is used regularly in the employee's business requires that any of the following conditions are satisfied:

---

1. Treas. Reg. §1.61-21(f)(4).
2. Treas. Reg. §1.61-21(f).

- 50% or more of the total annual mileage of the vehicle is for the employer's trade or business,
- the employer sponsors a commuting pool that uses the vehicle each work day to transport no less than three employees to and from work, or
- the vehicle is "regularly used," and not subject to infrequent business use such as occasional trips between multiple business premises, and this regular use is in the employer's business based on all the facts and circumstances.[1]

The employer cannot use the cents per mile rule for an automobile if its value when first made available to any employee for personal use is more than an amount determined by the IRS as the "maximum automobile value" for the year. The cents per mile rule can be utilized, however, if the employer reasonably expects the vehicle to be regularly used in its business during the calender year or if the vehicle meets the mileage test.

The "mileage test" is satisfied if: (1) the vehicle is driven at least an annual rate of 10,000 miles per year,[2] and (2) where the vehicle is used "primarily" during the year by employees. However, use of the vehicle by another individual who is not an employee should not be treated as use by an employee.

Notably, the value of maintenance and insurance for the vehicle are "built in" the cents per mile rate. The rate of any other service provided by the employer to the employee for a vehicle is not included in the cents per mile, and therefore use of the general valuation rule should be utilized to value those services.

THE COMMUTING RULE

The value of this fringe benefit is determined by multiplying each one way commute from home to work or from work to home by $1.50. This value applies to more than one employee irrespective of whether one or more employees ride in the vehicle during the commute. The **commuting rule** is allowed if all of the following requirements are satisfied:
- the employer provides the employee the vehicle for use in the employer's business and the employer requires the employee to commute in the vehicle for bona fide noncompensatory business reasons,[3]
- a written policy is established and implemented whereby the employer does not permit the employee to use a vehicle for personal use other than for commuting or minimal personal use,[4]
- other than de minimis personal use and commuting, the employee does not use the vehicle for personal use, and[5]

---

1. Treas. Reg. §1.61-21(e)(1)(iv).
2. For instance, if the vehicle was owned or leased only during a portion of the year, the 10,000 mile requirement is reduced proportionately.
3. As a general rule this requirement is satisfied if the vehicle is used each work day to carry no less than three employees to and from work in a commuting pool sponsored by the employer.
4. Minimal, or de minimis, personal use is considered use of the vehicle for a personal errand either going to and from work or between employee's home and a business delivery.
5. This is the essential difference between commuting rule and the cents per mile rule. Under the cents per mile rule, valuation is determined by taking a snap shot of the miles used for personal miles v. the miles used for work-related business. However, the commuting rule zeroes in simply on the commuting and de minimis personal use, and therefore prohibits significant or more than minimal personal use of the vehicle.

- if the vehicle used is an automobile, the employee who uses the automobile for commuting must not be a control employee.[1] Rather than using the definition of a control employee, an employer may choose to define a control employee as a highly compensated employee.[2]

THE LEASE VALUE RULE

According to the **lease value rule**, the value of an employer-provided automobile is determined by using the automobile's annual lease value. According to the general rule, the lease value of the automobile used by the employee in the employer's business is reduced by the amount excluded from the employee's wages as a working condition fringe benefit. Notably, the employer may choose to include the entire lease value in the employee's wages. The annual lease value of an automobile is determined by first ascertaining the automobile's fair market value on the first day it is available to any employee for personal use. Next, through reference to the Annual Lease Value Table (Exhibit 13.6), the annual lease value is provided by the applicable fair market value of the automobile. Automobiles with a fair market value exceeding $59,999 will have an annual lease value that is equal to 25 percent of the automobile's fair market value plus $500.

> $60,000 automobile (25% x $60,000) = $15,000, plus $500 = $15,500. Under this example, the annual lease value of a $60,000 vehicle would be $15,500.

EXAMPLE
13.26

As discussed earlier in this section, the fair market value of an automobile is the amount an individual would pay to purchase the automobile in an arm's-length transaction from a third party in the geographic area that the same automobile is bought or leased. The fair market value would therefore include an amount for all expenses related to the sale including tax, title and license, sales tax, and applicable fees. Only under these circumstances would a true fair market value be provided.

Importantly, safe harbor provisions apply to the determination of fair market value of an automobile. The safe harbor value may be used for an automobile purchased at arm's-length by utilizing the employer's costs (including tax, title, license, and other purchase expenses) as long as the employer is not the manufacturer of the automobile.

If the automobile is leased, safe harbor value for the lease can be any of the following:
- Invoice price including options and additions of the manufacturer, plus four percent,
- The suggested retail price of the manufacturer, minus eight percent, or
- The nationally recognized retail value of the automobile if that retail value is reasonable for the automobile.

Similar to the commuting rule, the annual lease value in the table provided includes, and has built in, the value of maintenance and insurance on the automobile. The annual lease value should not be reduced by the value of any services that were not provided by the employer. For instance, annual lease value should not be reduced by the value of a maintenance service contract or

---

1. A control employee is defined by the Treasury Regulations for the year 2016, as (1) an officer whose pay is more than $105,000, (2) a director, (3) an employee who makes $215,000 or more, (4) an employee owning 1% interest or more in the employer's business, or (5) an elected official. See IRS Publication 15-b.

2. Under the Treasury Regulations, a highly compensated employee for 2016 is an employee who (1) was a 5% owner at any time during the year or preceding year, or (2) the employee was paid more than $120,000 for the preceding year unless the employee was not also in the top 20% for employee compensation the preceding year.

insurance if the employer did not provide the maintenance or insurance. Conversely, the annual lease value does not include the value of fuel provided to an employee for personal use. The value of the fuel must be included separately in the employee's wages. If any other service other than maintenance and insurance is provided by the employer to the employee for an automobile, the fair market value of that service must be determined based on the fair market value of that service.

The annual lease values that are determined on an automobile may be prorated if an employee was provided an automobile for a period of 30 or more days but less than the entire calender year. The annual lease value is prorated by multiplying the annual lease value by a percentage derived by dividing the number of days of availability by 365 days. Treasury Regulations prohibit use of a prorated annual lease value if the reduction of federal taxes is the main reason the automobile is unavailable during the remainder of the calender year. Nonetheless, if the employer provides an automobile to an employee for a period continuously that is less than 30 days, a daily lease value is assigned. The daily lease value is determined by multiplying the annual lease value by the percentage derived by dividing four times the number of days of availability by 365.[1] The equation is as follows:

$$\text{Daily Lease Value} = \text{Annual Lease Value} \times \frac{(4 \times \text{Number of Days of Availability})}{365}$$

For instance, if the employee used the automobile continuously for 25 days and the annual lease value was $5,100, the daily lease value is calculated as follows.

$$\$5,100 \times \frac{(4 \times 25)}{365} = \$1,397 \text{ Daily Lease Value}$$

---

1. Treas. Reg. §1.61-21(d)(4)(ii).

ANNUAL LEASE VALUE TABLE

EXHIBIT
13.6

Automobile fair market value	Annual Lease Value
$0 to 999	$ 600
1,000 to 1,999	850
2,000 to 2,999	1,100
3,000 to 3,999	1,350
4,000 to 4,999	1,600
5,000 to 5,999	1,850
6,000 to 6,999	2,100
7,000 to 7,999	2,350
8,000 to 8,999	2,600
9,000 to 9,999	2,850
10,000 to 10,999	3,100
11,000 to 11,999	3,350
12,000 to 12,999	3,600
13,000 to 13,999	3,850
14,000 to 14,999	4,100
15,000 to 15,999	4,350
16,000 to 16,999	4,600
17,000 to 17,999	4,850
18,000 to 18,999	5,100
19,000 to 19,999	5,350
20,000 to 20,999	5,600
21,000 to 21,999	5,850
22,000 to 22,999	6,100
23,000 to 23,999	6,350
24,000 to 24,999	6,600
25,000 to 25,999	6,850
26,000 to 27,999	7,250
28,000 to 29,999	7,750
30,000 to 31,999	8,250
32,000 to 33,999	8,750
34,000 to 35,999	9,250
36,000 to 37,999	9,750
38,000 to 39,999	10,250
40,000 to 41,999	10,750
42,000 to 43,999	11,250
44,000 to 45,999	11,750
46,000 to 47,999	12,250
48,000 to 49,999	12,750
50,000 to 51,999	13,250
52,000 to 53,999	13,750
54,000 to 55,999	14,250
56,000 to 57,999	14,750
58,000 to 59,999	15,250

For vehicles having a fair market value in excess of $59,999, the annual lease value is equal to: (0.25 x the fair market value of the car) + $500.

THE UNSAFE CONDITIONS COMMUTING RULE

The **unsafe conditions commuting rule** determines the value of commuting transportation provided by an employer to a qualified employee solely because of unsafe conditions as $1.50 for a one-way commute.[1] The excess of the value of each one-way trip over $1.50 per one-way commute is excluded from gross income. The unsafe conditions commuting rule requires that a "qualified employee" be provided with the subject commuting transportation. If, however, the employer does not comply with record keeping requirements concerning the wages of the employee, as well as the employee's hours and other conditions and practices, then the employee may not be deemed a qualified employee. For the unsafe conditions commuting rule to apply, the employee must ordinarily walk or use public transportation; the employer must have a written policy against transportation for personal purposes other than commuting because of unsafe conditions; and the employee does not use the transportation for personal reasons beyond commuting due to unsafe conditions.

QUICK QUIZ 13.8

1. Employee fringe benefits are generally valued at the fair market value of the benefit provided.
   a. True
   b. False

True.

Finally, whether other "unsafe conditions" exist is determined based on the facts and circumstances of each individual situation. Unsafe conditions exist if a reasonable person would consider it unsafe for the employee to walk or use public transportation at the time of day that the employee is required to commute. Another factor used in determining whether conditions are unsafe is the history of criminal activity in the area surrounding the workplace or home of the employee at the time of day that the employee commutes.

---

1. Treas. Reg. §1.132-6(d)(2)(iii)(C).

SUMMARY CHART

EXHIBIT
13.7

Fringe Benefits	Key Aspects
Meals for the Convenience of the Employer	• The meals are for the convenience of the employer, and • The meals are furnished on the employer's business premises.
Lodging for the Convenience of the Employer	• The lodging is furnished on the employer's business premises, • The lodging is furnished for the convenience of the employer, and • The employee is required to accept the lodging as a condition of employment.

Athletic Facilities Furnished by the Employer*	• The facility must be:
	  • Operated by the employer,
	  • Located on the employer's premises, and
	  • Substantially all of the use of the facility is by employees or spouses or dependants.
	• Could be gym, pool, tennis court or golf course.
	• Cannot be operated by unrelated entity.

Educational Assistance	• Must be a separate written plan. • Must not be discriminatory. • Not more than 5% of the benefits can go to owners. • Employees cannot have a choice of cash or the education. • Limit: $5,250. • Amounts above the limit are generally W-2 income.
Qualified Tuition Reduction Plan	• Tuition reduction for education below the graduate level. • For an employee, spouse or dependant of the employee. • Must be an eligible educational institution - regular faculty with a regular student body.
Dependant Care Assistance	• Qualifying persons - include children under 13, children who are unable to care for themselves or a spouse who is unable to care for himself. • Services must allow employee to work. • Limit of $5,000.
No Additional Cost Services	• The service is offered to customers in the ordinary course of business, and • The employer incurs no additional cost (including foregone revenue).
Qualified Employee Discount	• Value of discounts on services or property offered to customers may be excluded. • Limit is 20% for services or the gross profit percentage for merchandise or other property. • Does not apply to real property or investment property.

Fringe Benefits	Key Aspects
Working Condition Fringe*	• Property or service provided to an employee that enables the employee to perform his work and if paid for by the employee would be deductible as a trade or business expense. • Examples: company car or chauffeur, security.
De Minimis Fringe*	• Any property or service provided to an employee that is so small in value that it makes accounting for it impracticable. • Examples of de minimis: occasional typing of personal letters by a secretary, occasional use of a copy machine, overtime meals, etc. • Examples of what is not de minimis: season tickets to sporting events, membership to a country club, group term life insurance on life of a non employee spouse or child.

Qualified Moving Expense Reimbursement	• Distance test: new main job location is at least 50 miles farther from your former home than your old main job location was from your former home.
	• Time test (employee or self-employed).
	  • Employee - you must work full time for at least 39 weeks during the first 12 months after you arrive in the general area of your new job location (39-week test).
	  • Self-employed - you must work full time for at least 39 weeks during the first 12 months and for a total of at least 78 weeks during the first 24 months after the move.

Qualified Transportation and Parking*	• Includes transportation in a commuter highway vehicle, transit passes and qualified parking. • 2016 limit of $255 for commuter highway transportation and transit passes combined. • 2016 limit of $255 for qualified parking. • $20 monthly limit for qualified bicycle commuting.
Adoption Assistance Programs	• Must be a written plan. • Expenses of up to $13,460 for 2016 can be paid by the employer. • Applies to the adoption of a child under the age of 18 or who is physically or mentally unable to care for themselves.
Awards and Prizes	• An employee can exclude the value of an award as long as it does not exceed $400 for nonqualified awards and $1,600 for qualified plan awards. • A qualified plan award requires that the average cost of all employee achievement awards does not exceed $400.

The fringe benefit can be discriminatory.

KEY TERMS

ADOPTION ASSISTANCE PROGRAM - An employee-provided program that pays adoption expenses up to $13,460 in 2016. The employee is not taxed on the payments or reimbursements made on his behalf.

BUSINESS PREMISES OF THE EMPLOYER - The employee's place of employment.

CENTS PER MILE RULE - To determine the value of the personal use of an employer-provided automobile, multiply the standard mileage rate (54 cents for 2016) by the total miles the employee drives the vehicle for personal purposes.

COMMUTING RULE - To determine the value of the personal use of an employer-provided vehicle, multiply each one way commute from the employee's home to work or from work to home by $1.50.

"DE MINIMIS" FRINGE BENEFIT - A benefit of any property or service provided by an employer to an employee that is so small in value that it makes accounting for it unreasonable or administratively impracticable when taking into account the frequency with which similar fringes are provided by the employer to all employees.

DEPENDENT CARE ASSISTANCE - Assistance that applies to household and dependent care services paid for or provided by the employer to an employee under a dependent care assistance program covering employees. The employee is not taxed on the value of the program or service paid on his behalf under the program (up to $5,000 per year).

FORGONE REVENUE - The lost revenue or opportunity cost incurred by an employer for providing the fringe benefit to the employee.

FRINGE BENEFIT - A benefit, other than customary taxable wages, provided by an employer to an employee for the employee's performance (in most instances) of services for the employer.

LEASE VALUE RULE - To determine the value of an employer-provided automobile, use the automobile's annual lease value.

NO-ADDITIONAL-COST SERVICES - Services provided by an employer to an employee that do not cause the employer to incur any substantial additional cost or lost revenue.

ON-PREMISES ATHLETIC FACILITY - A gym or other athletic facility such as a tennis court, pool, or golf course that is operated by the employer, located on the employer's business premises, and "substantially all" of the use of the facility is by employees of the employer, their spouses, or their dependent children. The value of the use of on premises athletic facilities is not taxable to the employee as long as its availability is nondiscriminatory.

KEY TERMS

QUALIFIED EDUCATIONAL ASSISTANCE PROGRAM - A plan established and maintained by an employer that provides employees with educational assistance. The employer may exclude $5,250 of benefits from an employee's taxable income.

QUALIFIED EMPLOYEE DISCOUNTS - A discount on the value of property or services offered to an employer's customers in the ordinary course of the employer's business may be excluded from an employee's income (subject to certain limitations).

QUALIFIED MOVING EXPENSES REIMBURSEMENT - Qualified moving expenses paid by an employer on behalf of an employee may be excluded from the employee's gross income. This exclusion applies to the reimbursement of moving expenses that the employee could have deducted on his income tax return if the employee had paid, or incurred, the costs without reimbursement.

QUALIFIED NON-PERSONAL USE VEHICLE - A vehicle that the employee does not use more than a minimal amount for personal reasons due to the design of the vehicle. The value of a qualified non-personal use vehicle is excluded from an employee's gross income.

QUALIFIED PARKING - Parking provided by the employer on or near the employer's business premises. An employee may exclude up to $255 per month (for 2016) from his gross income for employer provided parking.

QUALIFIED PLAN AWARD - An employee achievement award bestowed as part of an established written plan of an employer that does not discriminate in favor of highly compensated employees (within the meaning of §414(q)) for eligibility or benefits. The value of an award provided under the plan, up to $400 for a nonqualified award and $1,600 for a qualified award, is excluded from the employee's gross income.

QUALIFIED TUITION REDUCTION - The amount of any reduction in tuition provided to an employee of an educational organization for education below the graduate level is excluded from the employee's gross income.

UNSAFE CONDITIONS COMMUTING RULE - The value of commuting transportation provided by an employer to a qualified employee solely because of unsafe conditions is $1.50 for each one way commute.

WORKING CONDITION FRINGE BENEFITS - Any property or service provided to an employee that enables the employee to perform his work and, if paid for by the employee, is deductible as a trade or business expense (i.e., parking).

DISCUSSION QUESTIONS

1.   Define the term "employee fringe benefits" and identify common types of fringe benefits.

2.   What are the normal tax consequences to the employer and to the employee of employee fringe benefits?

3.   Describe the nondiscrimination rules that apply to employee fringe benefit plans.

4.   List the requirements necessary for the value of meals provided by an employer to be excluded from the employee's gross income.

5.   List the requirements necessary for the value of lodging provided by an employer to an employee to be excluded from the employee's gross income.

6.   List the requirements necessary for the value of athletic facilities provided by an employer to an employee to be excluded from the employee's income.

7.   List the requirements necessary for the value of an educational assistance program provided by an employer to an employee to be excluded from the employee's gross income.

8.   Describe the requirements necessary for the value of a dependent care assistance program provided by an employer to an employee to be excluded from the employee's gross income.

9.   What are employer-provided no-additional-cost services and identify when the value of this fringe benefit may be excluded from an employee's gross income?

10.   What are employer-provided qualified employee discounts and identify the requirements for excluding the value of this fringe benefit from an employee's gross income?

11.   List the requirements necessary for the value of working condition fringe benefits to be excluded from an employee's gross income.

12.   List the requirements necessary for the value of employer provided "de minimis" fringe benefits to be excluded from an employee's gross income.

13.   What is an employer provided qualified moving expense reimbursement and what are the requirements for the value of this fringe benefit to be excluded from an employee's gross income?

14.   Describe employer provided qualified transportation and parking and identify the requirements for the value of the fringe benefit to be excluded from an employee's gross income.

15.   Explain the limitations of excluding the value of employer-provided adoption assistance programs to an employee's gross income.

16. Describe the requirements necessary for the value of employer-provided awards and prizes to be excluded from an employee's gross income.

17. Describe the requirements necessary for employer-provided qualified tuition reduction plans to be excluded from an employee's income.

18. How are employee fringe benefits generally valued?

19. Describe the cents per mile rule.

20. Describe the commuting rule.

21. Describe the lease value rule.

22. Describe the unsafe conditions commuting rule.

MULTIPLE CHOICE PROBLEMS

1. Which of the following benefits provided by an employer to its employees is currently taxable to the employee?

    a. Employees of the DEF Department Store are allowed a 15% discount on store merchandise. DEF's normal gross profit percentage is 20%.

    b. On a space-available basis, undergraduate tuition is waived by Private University for the dependent children of employees (value of $15,000 per semester).

    c. Fly Airline allows its employees to fly free when there are open seats available on a flight (average value of $200).

    d. Incidental personal use of a company car.

2. Isse Peking is the manager of Airline Highway Motel. Isse lives in Unit 12. He was given the option to live at the motel if he would also look after the night auditing (the value of his reviews is $400 per month) responsibilities. The value of the motel unit on a monthly basis is $800, but Unit 12 rents on a daily basis for $100 per day. How much, if any, does Isse have to include in his gross income for living on the premises of his employer?

    a. $0 lodging for the convenience of the employer.

    b. $400 per month.

    c. $800 per month.

    d. $3,000 per month.

3. Meredith is an employee of a large company. The company has a health facility on its premises for the exclusive use of its employees and their dependents. A comparable private health club membership at a public facility would cost $2,400 per year. How much, if any, must Meredith include in her gross income if her 10-year old daughter uses the facilities for one-half of the year?

    a. $0.

    b. $600.

    c. $1,200.

    d. $2,400.

4. Which of the employee fringe benefits listed below, if provided by the employer, would be included in an employee's gross income?

    1. Business periodical subscriptions.

    2. Season tickets to professional football games.

    3. Free parking provided near its business (value of $90 per month).

    4. The use of an on-premises athletic facilities (value of $180 per month).

      a. 2 only.

      b. 1 and 2.

      c. 1, 2, and 3.

      d. 1, 2, 3, and 4.

5. Kohler Company allows a 25% discount to all nonofficer employees. Officers are allowed a 30% discount on company products. Kohler's gross profit percent is 35%. Which of the following is true?

      a. An officer who takes a 30% discount must include the extra 5% (30%-25%) in his gross income.

      b. Any discounts taken by any employee is includible in the employee's gross income because the plan is discriminatory.

      c. All discounts taken by officers (30%) are includible in their gross income because the plan is discriminatory.

      d. None of the discounts taken by any employee are includible in their gross income because the discount, in all cases, is less than the company's gross profit percentage.

6. Kenny holds two jobs - a full-time job with R Corporation and a part-time job with Z Corporation. Kenny uses his car to drive to work. The mileage is as follows: from Kenny's home to R is 70 miles; from R to Z is 10 miles; and from Z to Kenny's home is 70 miles. Kenny's deductible mileage for each work day is:

      a. 10 miles.

      b. 70 miles.

      c. 80 miles.

      d. 150 miles.

7. Robbin is married to Robert and they have one child Angel, age 14, who is in the 6th grade. Angel is a difficult child and she is cared for in the afternoon by the Sisters of Reformation, a group of Catholic nuns. Robbin pays $6,000 per year for the child care. Robbin's company has a dependent care assistance program. If Robbin makes the maximum use of the dependent care assistance program, how much can she exclude from her income if she files a joint return with Robert?

    a. $0.
    b. $2,500.
    c. $5,000.
    d. $6,000.

8. Professor Stabler has one child, Benson, who is 18 years old and a full-time student at Disc University, a private university where Professor Stabler is the chairman of the Finance Department and a full-time employee. The cost of undergraduate tuition at Disc University is $15,000 per semester, but the children of all full-time employees may attend Disc University for free. Last semester Benson took a Russian history class that was oversubscribed. Twenty-five students were on the waiting list, but Benson was number two. Three students got into the full class. Which of the following are correct?

    1. Professor Stabler has to include the value of the tuition remission in his income for last semester.

    2. Professor Stabler would not have to include the value of the tuition remission in his income if it was a graduate program that Benson was enrolled in.

    a. 1 only.
    b. 2 only.
    c. Both 1 and 2.
    d. Neither 1 nor 2.

9. ABC Corp. provides employees with discounts on the flat panel televisions they manufacture. The discounts were established using a length of service and employee status methodology.

Length of Service	Employee Discount	Officer Discount
1 - 5 years	10%	20%
> 5 - 10 years	15%	30%
> 10 years	20%	40%

The gross profit percentage for ABC is 40%.

George is an officer employee who has been with ABC Corp. for 13 years. For Christmas this year, George bought a 56 inch flat panel television that retails for $8,800 and he received a discount appropriate to the schedule discounts listed above. For this year, how much, if any, does George have to include in gross income as a result of this transaction?

    a. $0.

    b. $1,760.

    c. $2,640.

    d. $3,520.

10. Baldwin is the president of ZZZ Best Carpet Cleaners. Baldwin has a home with 18,000 square feet of floor space. Every week, Baldwin has the cleaning crew of ZZZ Best Carpet Cleaners clean his carpets. He theorizes that this is good training for the crew. Baldwin's CPA tells him that he can avoid the inclusion of the value of the services in his gross income if he offers to have any employees carpet cleaned at a reduction from retail. Baldwin establishes such a plan and allows a 50% reduction for all employees including himself. This year, the total retail value of the cleaning at Baldwin's house was $20,000, of which he paid $10,000. How much, if any, must Baldwin include in gross income resulting from the discount?

    a. $5,000.

    b. $6,000.

    c. $8,000.

    d. $10,000.

11. Jean works for A&R Law Firm and lives on the west bank of the city. A&R does not have a qualified transportation and parking benefits program, but it pays (reimburses) Jean $10 per month for riding the river taxi to work. The monthly pass to ride the river taxi is $50. How much does Jean need to include in gross income related to this river taxi pass?

    a. $0.

    b. $5.

    c. $10.

    d. $50.

12. ProLife Inc. has a written adoption assistance program that pays adoption expenses including fees, attorney fees, and other normal expenses. ProLife paid adoption expenses for the following employees during 2016.

Employee and Age	Employee AGI	Adoptee and Age	Amount Paid	Health of Adoptee
Joe (34)	$150,000	Cindylou (18)	$13,460	Excellent
James (34)	$250,000	Randi (6)	$13,460	Excellent
Donna (34)	$80,000	Brooke (3)	$13,460	Excellent
Connie (32)	$100,000	Silky (5)	$13,460	Excellent

Which of the following have income inclusions resulting from the employer adoption plan?

    a. No one, $13,460 is the maximum excludable limit for 2016.

    b. Joe.

    c. James.

    d. Joe and James.

13. Greg is employed by a large corporation with 400 employees. The corporation provides its employees with a no-cost gym membership at a local YMCA. The cost of the membership is $60 per month, which is completely paid for by Greg's employer. How much must Greg include in his yearly gross income related to this no-cost fringe benefit?

    a. $0.

    b. $60.

    c. $600.

    d. $720.

14. Eric moved from Houston to New Orleans. His expenses for the move included $400 for truck rental, $100 for lodging, and $200 of pre-move house-hunting expenses. If Eric's employer reimbursed him $600, how much of the reimbursement is included in his gross income?

    a. $0.

    b. $100.

    c. $200.

    d. $600.

15. Natalie is a secretary at JKL Law Firm. JKL provides her with free sodas at her discretion. Natalie estimates that she drinks $20 worth of sodas per month. How much must Natalie include in her annual gross income related to the sodas?

    a. $0.

    b. $20.

    c. $200.

    d. $240.

16. Which of the following are examples of fringe benefits that are not de minimus?

    a.   The commuting use of an employer-provided automobile or other vehicle more than one day per month.

    b.   Membership in a private country club.

    c.   Season tickets to theatrical events.

    d.   Employer-provided group term life insurance on the life of the spouse of an employee.

    e.   All of the above.

17. Which of the following is true concerning the qualified moving expense reimbursement?

    1.   The distance between the old home and the new job location must be at least 50 miles.

    2.   The distance between the old home and the new job location must be at least 50 miles greater than the distance between the old home and the old job location.

    3.   A qualifying move must be closely related to the start of work.

    a.   3 only.

    b.   1 and 3.

    c.   2 and 3.

    d.   All of the above.

    e.   None of the above.

18. Patrick works for the Atlanta Falcons in marketing. The Falcons have an athletic facility on the premises for employees other than football players. The value provided by the Falcons to Patrick of this fringe benefit is not included in Patrick's gross income if:

    a.   Substantially all of the use of the facility is be employees of the Falcons, their spouses or their dependent.

    b.   The facility is operated by a separate entity from the Falcons, called Super Sets.

    c.   The facility is five miles away from the Falcons premises.

    d.   None of the above.

19. The qualified tuition reduction does not apply to:

    a.   Current employees.

    b.   Former employees who retired or left on disability.

    c.   Widow(er)s of a person who died within three years of the employee's retirement.

    d.   Non-dependent children of current employees.

20. Which phrase best completes this sentence: "The exclusion for no-additional-cost services applies to any service provided by the employer to an employee that _____."

    a. Causes the employer to lose significant revenue.

    b. Does not cause the employee to incur substantial additional cost.

    c. Does not cause the employer to incur any substantial additional costs or lose revenue.

    d. Does not cause the employer to incur any additional costs but causes the employer to lose revenue.

21. Which of the following is false as to adoption assistance programs?

    1. The amount paid is excluded from the employee's income regardless of the employee's income level.

    2. The unlimited amount paid is excluded from the employee's income with an phaseout of AGI at certain levels.

    3. Up to $13,460 for 2016 is excluded from the employee's income with a phaseout of AGI at certain levels.

    a. 1 only.

    b. 3 only.

    c. 1 and 2.

    d. All of the above.

    e. None of the above.

QUICK QUIZ EXPLANATIONS

QUICK QUIZ 13.1
1. False. An employee fringe benefit is a form of compensation, and as a result, it is taxable as compensation unless specifically exempted from taxation under the Internal Revenue Code.
2. True.
3. False. Not all employee fringe benefits are subject to nondiscrimination requirements.

QUICK QUIZ 13.2
1. True.
2. True.

QUICK QUIZ 13.3
1. False. Only the value of an on-premises athletic facility furnished by the employer may be excluded from the employee's gross income.
2. True.
3. False. If a student is a graduate student and is teaching or performing research activities for an educational organization, then the student may be eligible for a qualified tuition reduction plan.

QUICK QUIZ 13.4
1. False. Dependent care assistance can be excluded up to (1) $2,500 for married filing separately individuals and $5,000 for married individuals filing jointly and single individuals, or (2) the earned income of the employee or the employee's spouse.
2. False. No-additional-cost services must be provided to all employees in a nondiscriminatory manner in order to avoid inclusion in the employee's gross income.
3. True.

QUICK QUIZ 13.5
1. True.
2. True.

QUICK QUIZ 13.6
1. False. Meals during the move are not a deductible moving expense.
2. True.

QUICK QUIZ 13.7
1. False. Cash awards may not be excluded from gross income.
2. False. Adoption assistance benefits may be excluded from the employee's gross income, but are subject to Social Security, Medicare, and federal unemployment taxes.

QUICK QUIZ 13.8
1. True.

EMPLOYEE BENEFITS: GROUP BENEFITS

LEARNING OBJECTIVES

After reading this chapter, you should be able to:

1. Understand that group insurance plans, if paid for by the employer, are generally considered by that employer as part of an overall compensation plan.
2. Explain the rules regarding the various insurance and other group benefit plans.
3. Describe the rules related to COBRA.
4. Explain the income tax treatment of group life insurance provided to an employee in excess of $50,000.
5. Describe a cafeteria plan and articulate its benefits.
6. Describe a flexible spending account (FSA) and articulate its benefits and rules.
7. Compare and contrast medical savings accounts (MSAs) and health savings accounts (HSAs).
8. Explain the major benefits that a Voluntary Employees' Beneficiary Association (VEBA) can and cannot provide.
9. Describe other employer / employee insurance arrangements such as buy/sell agreements, business disability, split dollar, and key person life and disability insurance.

INTRODUCTION

Most employees value fringe benefits, especially insurance benefits such as medical, life, and disability. With a large number of employees, employers can negotiate lower group insurance premiums and better coverage than an individual employee is able to negotiate in the open market. Thus, where insurance coverage is desired by a large number of employees, the employer may adopt an insurance plan as part of an overall compensation package. This may also enable the employer to be more competitive in the labor market. The federal government, in the case of some fringe benefits and insurance plans, also promotes employer insurance arrangements by allowing the employer to pay the premiums for employees and immediately deduct the cost for income tax purposes without requiring the participant employee to include such premium cost in their taxable income.

Most employer-provided health and other insurance is provided under group insurance coverage that is usually paid, at least in part, by the employer. Any premiums paid by the employer are generally deductible by the employer or included in the employee's gross income. It is not a requirement that the employer pay any of the premium of the group insurance; the employee may still benefit through a pretax payment of the insurance premium or through better rates. To receive the potential tax benefits for the employer or the employee, each type of group benefit has specific requirements.

This chapter addresses the following group benefits and details the benefits, requirements, and exemptions of each:

- Group medical plans
- Group term life insurance
- Group disability insurance
- Cafeteria plans used to provide diverse employee groups with a greater selection of employee benefits
- Flexible spending accounts

- Medical savings accounts
- Health savings accounts
- Voluntary Employee's Beneficiary Association
- Salary continuation plans
- Group long-term care insurance
- Group retirement planning services
- Business continuation plans
- Business overhead disability plans
- Split-dollar life insurance
- Key person life insurance

KNOW THE NUMBERS

	MSA		HSA	
Established	Before 2006		2004 and Later	
	Single	Family	Single	Family
Health Insurance Deductible	$2,250 - $3,350	$4,450 - $6,700	At least $1,300	At least $2,600
Maximum Out-of-Pocket	$4,450	$8,150	$6,550	$13,100
Maximum Contribution	65% of deductible	75% of deductible	100% of deductible limited to $3,350	100% of deductible limited to $6,750
Catch-Up Contribution Available	No		Yes $1,000 for 2016	

MEDICAL PLANS

There are several ways that employers can provide employees with benefits for medical expenses that result from personal injury or sickness. Many employers use these types of group health insurance plans as a part of the overall compensation package provided to their employees. Included in these health insurance plans are both private insurance plans and self-insurance plans. Any premium payments or costs made to or for these plans are deductible for federal income taxes by the employer and excluded from the employee's gross income.

GROUP MEDICAL INSURANCE

A group accident or health plan is an arrangement that provides benefits for employees, their spouses, and their dependents in the event of personal injury or sickness. The plan may be insured or noninsured and does not need to be in writing. The premiums paid by the employer for health insurance are not includable in the employee's taxable income but are a deductible business expense for the employer under IRC §162. Group medical insurance includes hospitalization coverage, major medical, indemnity coverage, health maintenance organization, preferred provider organizations, point of service plans, and dental and vision plans.

INCOME TAX IMPLICATIONS

The employer can generally exclude the value of accident or health benefits provided to an employee from the employee's gross income. Because the employer cannot treat a two percent shareholder of an S corporation as an employee for this exclusion, the employer must include the value of accident or health benefits it provides to the two percent shareholder in wages subject to federal income tax withholding.

KEY CONCEPTS

1. What are the tax implications of employer provided group medical plans?

2. What is COBRA?

However, the employer can exclude the value of these benefits (other than payments for specific injuries or illnesses) from the regular employee's wages, which are subject to Social Security, Medicare, and **FUTA** (Federal Unemployment Tax Act) taxes.

If the employer's plan is a self-insured medical reimbursement plan that favors highly compensated employees, the employer must include all or part of the amounts the employer pays to these employees as benefits in the employee's wages subject to federal income tax withholding. However, the employer can exclude these amounts (other than payments for specific injuries or illnesses) from the employee's wages subject to Social Security, Medicare, and FUTA taxes.

A **self-insured plan** is a plan that reimburses employees for medical expenses not covered by an accident or health insurance policy. For this exception, a highly compensated employee is any individual who is one of the five highest paid officers of the company or an employee who owns (directly or indirectly) more than 10 percent in value of the employer's stock. In addition, an employee who is among the highest paid 25 percent of all employees (other than those who can be excluded from the plan) is also considered a highly compensated employee for this exception.

When insurance benefits are paid, they are includible in the employee's income with the exception of payments received for medical care of the employee, spouse, and dependents, and payments for permanent loss or the loss of the use of a member or function of the body or permanent disfigurement of the employee, spouse, or dependent.

ELIGIBILITY

To be eligible to purchase group health insurance, an individual has to be affiliated with a group that is covered by a group health insurance policy. Typically, all individuals who are employed on a full-time basis (or are a member of a qualifying group) at a company that provides group health coverage are eligible to participate in the group plan. Sometimes non-employer groups provide coverage for their members as well. Common examples are local Chambers of Commerce (which may offer a group plan that can cover the employees of all member companies), labor unions, and professional associations (such as The American Bar Association or the American Institute of Certified Public Accountants). However, the Patient Protection and Affordable Care Act (ACA) has changed the way heath care is purchased and made available to individuals. As a result, some groups have ceased offering health insurance.

FEATURES OF GROUP HEALTH INSURANCE

Group policies are underwritten based on the characteristics of the group to be covered as a whole and include factors such as the average age of the group, and the type of work performed at the company. Most group contracts require that either all full-time employees or all members of a qualifying group be automatically covered (enrolled) under the plan. This requirement helps to prevent adverse selection risk for the insurer, which is the risk that healthy members of the group will opt out of coverage, leaving only those with greater expected health care needs covered in the plan.

The employer typically enrolls all eligible employees in the plan, and pays some or all of the premiums for coverage. If the employee pays part of the health insurance costs, those costs are typically paid through payroll deduction. Since the employer shoulders a large part of the administrative burden by enrolling employees and paying premiums, part of the administrative cost savings realized by the insurer is passed on to the employer in the form of lower group-health insurance premiums.

The ACA has also impacted how larger companies provide health benefits to their employees. Companies that have 50 or more full-time employees are required under the ACA to provide health coverage to employees or pay a penalty.

Types of Group Health Insurance

There are two primary types of group health insurance:
- group basic medical insurance
- group major medical insurance

When the features of these plans are combined into one policy, the policy is referred to as a Group Comprehensive Major Medical Insurance plan.

Group Basic Medical Insurance

Group basic medical insurance covers hospital and physician bills, and surgical bills, but typically has low policy limits. Due to the low policy limits, group basic medical coverage is often used in conjunction with group major medical insurance.

Group Major Medical Insurance

Group major medical insurance coverage supplements basic medical coverage by permitting a wider array of services and increasing policy maximums. Sometimes these policies are referred to as group supplemental insurance plans.

Group Comprehensive Major Medical Insurance

Group comprehensive major medical insurance plans combine the benefits of basic medical coverage and major medical coverage. Typically, plan deductibles are low, and the employee may be required to make a co-payment when receiving services. After the plan deductible has been met for the year, the insurance company often pays 80 percent of the cost of health care and the participant pays the remaining 20 percent until a maximum annual out-of-pocket limit is reached. The coinsurance percentage could be 70/30 or even 60/40 and still be adequate as long as the stop loss is reasonable. Once the annual out-of-pocket limit is reached, the insurance company pays 100 percent of the costs of care for that year.

EXAMPLE
14.1

Dylan is a participant in his employer's Group Comprehensive Major Medical Insurance Plan. The plan has a $200 deductible, and a $1,500 out-of-pocket maximum. If Dylan is injured in an accident and his medical costs total $2,000, Dylan will have to pay the first $200 to cover the deductible, and will pay $360 (20% of the remaining $1,800 in medical costs), for a total of $560. The plan will pay the remaining portion of the cost, or a total of $1,440. The next time that Dylan needs medical attention within the same year, he will pay 20% of those costs (but he would not have to pay another deductible, since the deductible has to be satisfied only once per year) until his total out-of-pocket costs for the year (including the deductible) is $1,500. In other words, Dylan will have to pay a maximum of $940 more for the year before the insurer pays 100% of future costs for the year.

Traditionally, comprehensive major medical plans were not favored by employees, since they resulted in the employee paying up to the out-of-pocket maximum each year. Many employees and unions favored first-dollar pay type plans, where the employee would make a small co-payment (of, perhaps $5 or $10) each time they visited a physician, and the insurance company would pay for the balance of the bill. First-dollar-pay type plans have higher premiums than comprehensive plans due to the increase in benefit payments made by the insurance company, and the increased administrative costs incurred. More recently, however, with the creation of Health Savings Accounts (HSAs) and the new federal requirements concerning health insurance coverage for employees, high deductible plans have enjoyed a renaissance as a means to provide adequate healthcare coverage while lowering premium costs for employers.

The Patient Protection and Affordable Care Act of 2010 and the Health Care and Education Reconciliation Act of 2010 require large employers (an employer that, at any time during the year, employs at least 50 people) to provide a minimum level of health insurance coverage to employees or face significant tax penalties. Small Employers (employers who, at all times during the year, employ less than 50 workers) are encouraged to provide health insurance to employees through the creation of tax credits for small businesses. The 2010 Health Care legislation also requires all U.S. citizens and residents to obtain health insurance, or face tax penalties for failing to comply. The constitutionality of mandating health coverage has already been challenged in the Supreme Court and has been ruled constitutional.[1] As a consequence of the 2010 legislation, it is likely that even more individuals than ever will be covered by Group Health Insurance Policies.

INDEMNITY HEALTH INSURANCE

Indemnity health insurance is also referred to as a traditional health insurance plan. Indemnity health insurance plans allow participants the benefit of having a whole range of health care practitioners at their disposal and not be locked into a service network system for medical care. Indemnity health insurance is the most flexible type of insurance policy, but participants also pay some of the highest premiums in order to have the flexibility of choosing their own health care providers. Typically, indemnity plans have deductibles, no co-pays, and coinsurance for major medical.

---

1. The debate continues regarding this legislation and there are various court challenges that are ongoing. These may or may not impact the law.

MANAGED CARE INSURANCE

Managed care insurance emerged from a desire to reduce the costs of health care while increasing competition among service providers. When compared to major medical plans, managed care approaches to health care restrict participant choice of health care providers, and often require participants to obtain pre-approval from insurance company representatives (who are not always medically trained) as a condition of obtaining covered treatment that is not considered emergency care. Companies offering

managed care have also been criticized for prohibiting physicians from discussing alternative options to care with the patients, creating an ethical dilemma for the health care provider who is determined to act in the best interest of the patient. Despite their shortcomings, managed care approaches to health insurance have assisted in somewhat containing the cost of medical services over time.

There are three main types of managed care approaches to health insurance coverage:
- Health Maintenance Organization (HMO)
- Preferred Provider Organization (PPO)
- Point-of-Service Plans (POS)

Health Maintenance Organizations (HMOs)

Health Maintenance Organizations (HMOs) were authorized by the HMO Act of 1973. HMOs consist of a group of physicians who provide comprehensive care for their patients, and are organized in an effort to control the rising cost of healthcare. Physicians are employed by the HMO directly or may be physicians in private practice who have chosen to participate in the HMO network. The independent physicians are paid a fixed amount for each HMO member that uses them as a **primary care physician**. Some HMOs require medical services be performed by the pre-approved physicians who are either employees or independent contractors of the HMO, and will not pay for health care services obtained outside of the HMO's physician network. Other HMOs permit their members to obtain coverage outside of the insurance company's provider network, but claim payments made for services performed by an out-of-network provider will typically be smaller than claims allowed for similar services provided within the network (which effectively increases the cost to the participant).

One major disadvantage of HMOs is that patient choice is limited by establishing a network of approved health care providers. Americans, as a group, do not like having their options limited, which may explain why HMOs never became popular vehicles for providing health care services.

EXHIBIT 14.1

ADVANTAGES AND DISADVANTAGES OF HMOs

ADVANTAGES

- Fixed fee for health care
- Low co-payments
- Total health care costs is generally lower and more predictable than with PPO or POS

DISADVANTAGES

- Gatekeeper for specialists services so it is often difficult and complicated to get specialized care
- Longer waits for non-emergency doctor appointments
- Any health care costs from out-of-network providers, except in emergencies, is not covered much or at all

Preferred Provider Organizations (PPOs)

A **Preferred Provider Organization** is an arrangement between insurance companies and health care providers that permits members of the PPO to obtain discounted health care services from the preferred providers within the network. Unlike an HMO, which limits choice of physicians and other health care providers, a PPO typically has a larger provider pool for participants from which to choose. Participants are not required to receive services from preferred providers, but higher deductibles and coinsurance payments may apply when services are obtained from providers outside of the network. Health care providers are not employed by the PPO, but do receive a fee for serving as primary health care provider for a member of the PPO.

EXHIBIT 14.2

ADVANTAGES AND DISADVANTAGES OF PPOs

ADVANTAGES

- Health care costs are low when using in-network providers
- Consultations with any specialists, including out-of-network providers
- Primary care physician is not required
- Yearly out-of-pocket costs are limited

DISADVANTAGES

- Out-of-network treatment is more expensive
- Co-payments are generally larger than with HMOs
- May need to satisfy a deductible, especially with out-of-network providers

Point of Service Plans (POS)

A **point of service plan (POS)** is considered a managed care/indemnity plan hybrid, as it mixes aspects of in-network and fee-for-service, for greater patient choice. Members choose which option that they will use each time they seek health care.

Like an HMO and a PPO, a POS plan has a contracted provider network. POS plans encourage members to choose a primary care physician from within the health care network. This physician becomes the patient's "point of service." The in-network, primary care physician may make referrals outside of the network, if the patient prefers an out-of-network provider, but higher deductibles and coinsurance payments may apply if the insured is receiving services on the indemnity side. The patient does not require permission to go out of network care but, similar to an indemnity plan, will have a deductible and coinsurance up to the stop loss.

POS plans are becoming more popular because they offer more flexibility, lower costs, and freedom of choice than standard HMOs, PPOs, or indemnity plans.

ADVANTAGES AND DISADVANTAGES OF POS PLANS

EXHIBIT
14.3

ADVANTAGES
• Freedom of choice for managed care
• Not limited to only HMO or PPO network providers
• Costs are minimal for in-network care
• Annual out-of-pocket costs are limited
• No referral is needed for choosing an out of network doctor

DISADVANTAGES
• Copays for out-of-network providers are high
• There are deductibles for out-of-network providers
• It is sometimes difficult and complicated to get specialized care within network providers

HEALTH REIMBURSEMENT ARRANGEMENT (HRA)

Health reimbursement arrangements, also known as "health reimbursement accounts" or "personal care accounts," are a type of health insurance plan that reimburses employees for qualified medical expenses. An HRA is an arrangement that: (1) is paid for solely by the employer and not provided pursuant to salary reduction election or otherwise under a §125 cafeteria plan, (2) reimburses the employee for medical care expenses incurred by the employee and the employee's spouse and dependents, and (3) provides reimbursements up to a maximum dollar amount for a coverage period. Any unused portion of the maximum dollar amount at the end of a coverage period is carried forward to increase the maximum reimbursement amount in subsequent coverage periods. To the extent that an HRA is an employer-provided accident or health plan, coverage and reimbursements of medical care expenses of an employee and the employee's spouse and dependents are generally excludable from the employee's gross income under IRC §106 and IRC §105.

QUICK QUIZ 14.1

1. PPOs typically have a wider network of health care providers, from which to choose, than HMOs.
   a. True
   b. False

2. The emergence of managed care plans was born from a desire to decrease competition amongst health care providers.
   a. True
   b. False

True, False.

Medical care expenses submitted for reimbursement must be substantiated under the HRA and the HRA may not reimburse a medical care expense that is attributable to a deduction allowed for medical expenses for any prior taxable year. Additionally, an HRA may neither reimburse a medical care expense that is incurred before the date the HRA is in existence nor reimburse a medical care expense that is incurred before the date an employee first becomes enrolled under the HRA.

The objective of these plans, like many other fringe and group benefits, is to provide benefits to employees that are excludible from the employee's taxable income. As long as the plan is not discriminatory and as long as the expenses are valid under IRC §213 (medical expenses), then the expense will be deductible and the benefit received will not be subject to taxation.

While these plans are relatively new, they may be implemented by small or large companies and as stand-alone plans or in conjunction with other health plans of the employer.

THE HEALTH INSURANCE PORTABILITY AND ACCOUNTABILITY ACT OF 1996 (HIPAA)

President Clinton signed HIPAA into law in 1996. The law offers protections for millions of American workers that improve portability and continuity of health insurance coverage in addition to insuring that the privacy of individual's health information is maintained.

HIPAA includes protections for coverage under group health plans that:
- Limit exclusions for preexisting conditions
- Prohibit discrimination against employees and dependents based on their health status
- Allow a special opportunity to enroll in a new plan to individuals in certain circumstances
- Provide privacy of medical information

One of the most important protections under HIPAA is that it assists those with preexisting conditions in obtaining health coverage. In the past, some employers' group health plans limited, or even denied coverage if a new employee had such a condition prior to enrolling in the plan. Under HIPAA, that is not permitted. If the plan generally provides coverage but denies benefits to an employee because that employee had a condition before the coverage began, then HIPAA applies.

Under HIPAA, a plan is allowed to look back only six months for a condition that was present prior to the start of coverage in a group health plan. Specifically, the law says that a preexisting condition exclusion may be imposed on a condition only if medical advice, diagnosis, care, or treatment was recommended or received during the six months occurring just prior to the enrollment date in the plan.

A major goal of the Privacy Rule is to assure that individuals' health information is properly protected while allowing the flow of health information needed to provide and promote high quality health care and to protect the public's health and well being. The Rule strikes a balance that permits important uses of information, while protecting the privacy of people who seek care and healing. Given that the health care marketplace is diverse, the Rule is designed to be flexible and comprehensive to cover the variety of uses and disclosures that need to be addressed.

THE PATIENT PROTECTION AND AFFORDABLE CARE ACT (ACA) OF 2010

The ACA was enacted in 2010 and survived a Supreme Court challenge. The act sets out to:

- End pre-existing conditions.
- End lifetime limits on coverage.
- Increase the age that children can remain on their parent's heath insurance policy to age 26.
- Require that insurance providers offer a Summary of Benefits and Coverage (SBC) document that provides individuals with easy-to-understand information about their policy and make it easier to compare to other policies.
- Create federal and state exchanges that permit individuals to purchase insurance.

Although the law was signed into law on March 23, 2010, it is not fully implemented at this point and will likely continue to change over the next few years. It will certainly have many changes on the heath system.

COBRA PROVISIONS

Under the **Combined Omnibus Budget Reconciliation Act of 1986 (COBRA)**,[2] an employer that maintains a group health plan and employs 20 or more people on more than 50 percent of the calendar days in a year is required to continue to provide coverage under the plan to covered employees and qualified beneficiaries following the occurrence of a statutorily defined qualifying event as depicted in the following exhibit.[3]

SUMMARY OF COBRA PROVISIONS

EXHIBIT 14.4

Event	Beneficiary (Qualifying)			Period of Coverage
	Worker	Spouse	Dependant	
Normal termination (resigned, laid off, or fired; except gross misconduct) *(29 USCA 1163(2))*	✓	✓	✓	18 months
Full time to part time *(29 USCA 1163(2))*	✓	✓	✓	18 months
Disabled employee or dependent (must meet Social Security definition of disabled) *(29 USCA 1162(2)(A))*	✓	✓	✓	29 months
Qualified dependent (child reaches age no longer eligible for plan) *(29 USCA 1163(5))*			✓	36 months
Death of employee *(29 USCA 1163(1))*		✓	✓	36 months
Employee reached Medicare age *(29 USCA 1163(4))*		✓	✓	36 months
Divorce *(29 USCA 1163(3))*		✓	✓	36 months
Plan terminates *(29 USCA 1163(6))*	✓	✓	✓	36 months

2. Public Law 99-272 (April 7, 1986).
3. 29 USCA §1161.

COBRA Premiums

The employer may pay for the COBRA coverage either directly or by reimbursing the employee; or the employer may shift the burden of paying the premium for the benefit to the beneficiaries. If the employer pays for the medical coverage, then the exclusion from the employee's income for accident and health benefits applies to amounts the employer pays to maintain medical coverage under COBRA. The exclusion applies regardless of the length of employment, whether the employer pays the premiums directly or reimburses the former employee for premiums paid, and whether the employee's separation is permanent or temporary.

During the statutory COBRA period, the premium charged to the employee cannot exceed 102 percent of the cost to the plan for similarly situated individuals who have not incurred a qualifying event.[4] The 102 percent includes both the portion paid by beneficiary employees and any portion paid by the employer before the qualifying event plus two percent for administrative costs. If a qualified beneficiary receives the 11 month disability extension of coverage, the premium for the additional 11 months may be increased to 150 percent of the plan's total cost of coverage. COBRA premiums may be increased if the costs to the plan increase, but generally must be fixed in advance of each 12-month premium cycle.

QUICK QUIZ 14.2

1. The value of health benefits provided to all employees or owners can be excluded from the employee or owner's income.
   a. True
   b. False

2. COBRA premiums paid by the employer on behalf of a former employee can be excluded from the employee's taxable income.
   a. True
   b. False

False, True.

EXAMPLE 14.2

Brandy recently terminated her employment. Her major medical insurance ended on her last day of employment. She will begin work at her new job in two weeks. Should she elect COBRA? Yes, in this instance it is probably a good idea because she does not want to have a period of non-coverage.

EXAMPLE 14.3

Assume the facts above except Brandy is going to take 18 months off to find herself in Africa. Now is COBRA an appropriate election? In this instance, the answer is maybe. On one hand, she may find that an individual policy is quite expensive. The risk is that if she elects COBRA, it will end after 18 months. Should she contract a serious disease overseas, then she would become uninsurable and may not be able to get an affordable policy at that time. She may be better off spending the extra money on an individual policy in order to ensure future coverage. Assuming she elects COBRA, she should also purchase a high deductible major medical policy to reduce her overall risk.

---

4. 29 USCA 1162(3).

GROUP TERM LIFE INSURANCE

Amounts paid by the employer for group term life insurance also receive favorable tax treatment. The employer can deduct the amounts paid for the insurance, and the employee can exclude a portion, if not all, of the value from the employee's income (discussed below). To receive such favorable treatment, the life insurance must provide a general death benefit to a group of employees, and the coverage must provide an amount of insurance to each employee based on a formula that prevents individual selection. This formula must use factors such as the employee's age, years of service, pay, or position.

Group term life insurance is pure insurance protection that pays a predetermined sum if the insured dies during a specified period of time (i.e., the term, which may be 1, 5, 10, 20 years or longer). Term insurance generally has no cash value savings or investment component and essentially states, "If you pay *x*, we will pay *y* if you die during the term." The protection ceases at the end of the term unless renewed. Term insurance is very inexpensive at young ages (substantially less than whole life). The premium pattern may be level or increasing on an annual or set period basis (i.e., five-year renewable term). The face amount may be level, decreasing, or increasing (i.e., there may be a cost of living provision that increases the face).

Group term life insurance is usually renewable on an annual term, and does not include the following types of insurance:
- Insurance without general death benefits, such as travel insurance or a policy providing only accidental death benefits;
- Life insurance on the life of the employee's spouse or dependent. However, the employer may be able to exclude the cost of this type of insurance from the employee's wages as a de minimis fringe benefit (as discussed in Chapter 13);
- Permanent life insurance; or
- Life insurance where the employer is the beneficiary of the policy.

DEFINITION OF EMPLOYEE AND REQUIREMENTS

Generally, life insurance provided by the employer is not considered group term life insurance unless the employer provides it to at least 10 full-time employees at some time during the year. For this purpose, employees are typically defined as current common-law employees, full-time life insurance agents who are current statutory employees, and leased employees who have provided services to the employer on a substantially full-time basis for at least a year (if the services are performed under the employer's primary direction and control).

The employer should count employees who choose not to receive the life insurance unless, to receive the coverage, the employee must pay for benefits other than group term life insurance. For example, the employer should count an employee who is eligible to benefit from the group term life insurance by paying part of the premium, even if that employee chooses not to receive the life insurance coverage. However, the employer does not count an employee who must pay part or all of the cost of permanent benefits to benefit from the group life insurance unless that employee chooses to pay the costs and benefit from the life insurance coverage.

If the employer does not meet the general 10-employee-rule, the employer may still be eligible to receive the benefits of the group term life insurance coverage if the employer's provision of the coverage meets the following three requirements:

1. The employer provides coverage under the plan to all of its full-time employees who provide evidence of insurability.
2. The coverage provided under the plan must be based on either a uniform percentage of pay or a set amount of coverage depending upon age, years of service, compensation, or position.
3. The required evidence of insurability must be limited to a medical questionnaire (completed by the employee) that does not require a physician.

When applying this exception, employers should not consider employees who were denied insurance for any of the following reasons:
1. The employees were 65 or older;
2. The employees customarily work 20 hours or less a week or five months or less in a calendar year; or
3. The employees have not been employed for a waiting period stated in the policy (which cannot exceed six months).

S CORPORATION SHAREHOLDERS

When an employer provides group term life insurance coverage for a more than two percent shareholder of an S Corporation, the cost of the coverage is included in the shareholder's gross income and is subject to Social Security and Medicare taxes. However, the employer does not pay federal unemployment tax (FUTA) on the cost of any group term life insurance coverage provided to a more than two percent shareholder.

INCOME TAX TREATMENT

Group term life insurance premiums paid by the employer on the first $50,000 of death benefits are deductible by the employer and are excludable from an employee's gross income. The cost, as determined under the Uniform Premium Table provided by the IRS, of any death benefit coverage in excess of $50,000 is taxable to the employee. The monthly cost of the insurance to include in the employee's gross income is determined by multiplying the number of thousands of dollars of insurance coverage over $50,000 (rounded to the nearest $1,000) by the cost shown in the following table. The table corresponds with the employee's age as of the last day of the tax year and the includable amount is reduced by any contribution payments made by the employee.

UNIFORM PREMIUM TABLE: COST PER $1,000 OF PROTECTION FOR 1 MONTH[5]

EXHIBIT
14.5

Age	Cost
Under 25	$0.05
25 through 29	$0.06
30 through 34	$0.08
35 through 39	$0.09
40 through 44	$0.10
45 through 49	$0.15
50 through 54	$0.23
55 through 59	$0.43
60 through 64	$0.66
65 through 69	$1.27
70 and older	$2.06

The employee can always receive the first $50,000 of death benefit coverage tax-free. Thus, if an employee's death benefit under the employer-provided term life insurance is $90,000, the employee will be taxed (as determined above) on $40,000 ($90,000 - $50,000) of the coverage. Also, if an employee pays an amount towards the cost of the taxable death benefit coverage, the taxable amount is decreased by the employee's payment.

BigBully Corp provides all of its employees with group term life insurance coverage equal to their salary. Steve earns $40,000 per year and is 40 years old. Steve is not considered a key employee. In this instance, Steve's term policy will provide a death benefit of $40,000. Since the benefit is below the taxable limit, Steve's benefit will be excluded from his income.

EXAMPLE
14.4

BigBully Corp provides all of its employees with group term life insurance coverage equal to their salary. Fred earns $100,000 per year and is 40 years old. Fred is not considered a key employee. The cost of the insurance that must be included in Fred's compensation is calculated as follows:

EXAMPLE
14.5

5. Treas. Reg. 1.79-3(d).

Salary	$100,000
Less exclusion	- $50,000
	$50,000
Divided by 1,000	÷ 1,000
	50
Times cost (as provided in table)	X 0.10
	$5.00
Times 12 months	X 12
Yearly inclusion in employee's income (W-2)	$60.00

EXAMPLE 14.6

BigBully Corp provides all of its employees with group term life insurance coverage equal to their salary. Ralph earns $100,000 per year and is 40 years old. Ralph is not considered a key employee and pays $50 per year toward the cost of the insurance. The cost of the insurance that must be included in Ralph's compensation is calculated as follows:

Salary	$100,000
Less exclusion	- $50,000
	$50,000
Divided by 1,000	÷ 1,000
	50
Times Cost (as provided in table)	X 0.10
	$5.00
Times 12 months	X 12
Yearly premium cost	$60.00
Premium paid by employee	- $50.00
Yearly inclusion in employee's income (W-2)	$10.00

KEY EMPLOYEES

To qualify for favorable tax treatment, a group term life insurance plan must be nondiscriminatory. To be nondiscriminatory, the plan must cover either:[6]
- 70% or more of all eligible employees, or
- 85% of the non-key employees.

If the plan does not meet either of the two tests, the plan is considered discriminatory and the key employee must include the greater of either the cost as determined in the Uniform Premium Table or the actual cost of the life insurance coverage to the employer in the employee's gross income. In addition, if the plan is discriminatory, there is no exclusion for the first $50,000 of coverage.

6. IRC §79(d)(3).

COVERAGE FOR DEPENDENTS

The cost of group term life insurance coverage paid by the employer for the spouse or dependents of an employee may be excludable from an employee's gross income as a de minimis fringe benefit. The cost of the coverage is determined by the Uniform Premium Table.

GROUP DISABILITY INSURANCE

Disability insurance provides benefits in the form of periodic payments to a person who is unable to work due to sickness or accidental injury. The cost of disability insurance varies depending on occupation, age, and sex of the insured, as well as the benefit term, coverage, and the length of the waiting period (elimination period) provided under the policy.

Disability insurance can be provided under a group or individual plan. Group disability policies are often cheaper than individual polices but may actually have additional restrictions as compared to individual policies.

KEY CONCEPTS

1. What are the tax implications of employer-provided group disability insurance?

2. What are cafeteria plans and how are they used?

3. What are the tax implications of employer-provided cafeteria plans?

In addition, there is a clear difference between **group short-term disability policies** and **group long-term disability policies**. Short-term disability will generally begin after a very brief period of time (1-14 days), often corresponding to the employer's sick leave. Long-term disability benefits typically begin after short-term and will often continue for a fixed period of time, until retirement or in some cases for life. Many of the differences between short and long-term group disability plans, including coverage period, elimination periods, eligible employees, and definition of disability, are identified in the following exhibit.

EXHIBIT
14.6

GROUP SHORT-TERM DISABILITY VS. GROUP LONG-TERM DISABILITY

	Short-Term Disability	Long-Term Disability
Definition of Disability	Generally more liberal than long-term disability	May be any occupation, own occupation, or split-definition
Begins	After sick-leave - usually a short period of time (may be 0-14 days)	After elimination period - often 6 months (but may be from 90 - 180 days)
Benefit Period	• Generally 3-6 months for group policies • Will often tie to the elimination period for the long-term policy • Range: 3, 6, 12, 24 months	• May be a term of years (5, 10), or: • To an age 65, 67, 70 (or other) • For life (benefits may be shorter for blue collar workers and longer for white collar workers)
Benefit	Up to 100% of income but usually 40-65% of salary and usually with a dollar cap and a time cap	Generally up to 60% - 70% of income

EXHIBIT
14.7

DISABILITY COVERAGE PHASES

TAXATION OF DISABILITY BENEFITS

Premiums paid by the employer are deductible by the employer and are not included in the employee's gross income. However, when the employer pays the premium and the value is excluded from the employee's gross income, any disability income benefit received by the employee is taxable to the employee. If the employee pays the entire premium with after-tax income or the employer pays the premium and the employee includes the premium payment in income, any benefits received will be considered tax-exempt. As such, many employees choose to include the cost of the premiums in their taxable income even when paid by the employer because any disability benefits paid from such a plan would then be received tax-free. If the employer and employee each pay part of the premium, the prorated part of the benefits associated with the employer's contribution is taxable to the employee.

TYPES OF DISABILITY INSURANCE POLICIES

Disability insurance policies typically cover periods when the insured is unable to work due to suffering an accident or sickness. There are three primary types of disability policies, as determined by the definition of disability:

- own occupation policies,
- any occupation policies, and
- split definition policies.

TYPES OF DISABILITY POLICIES

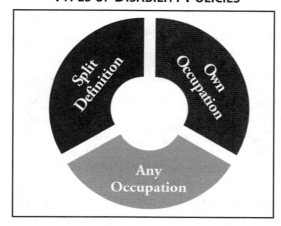

EXHIBIT 14.8

An **own occupation** policy states that if the insured is unable to perform each and every duty associated with his own occupation (specified e.g., orthopedic surgeon) the insured is deemed to be disabled and the policy will provide benefits.

> Rosemary is a concert pianist and has spent her lifetime practicing and performing piano concertos around the world. She recently contracted a disease which affected the dexterity of her hands and prevented her from being able to perform at concerts. She purchased an own occupation disability insurance policy 25 years ago so the insurance policy will pay disability benefits to Rosemary since she can no longer perform the duties of her own occupation as a pianist.

EXAMPLE 14.7

Own occupation policies were popular disability tools in the late 1980s and early 1990s, particularly with physicians, musicians, and other professionals whose income was dependent on their ability to perform specific tasks. Over time insurance companies recognized that there was a large adverse selection risk associated with these policies, which are now less available. When an own-occupation policy (as they are referred to) is issued, the premium is high due to the risks undertaken by the insurance company.

An **any occupation** disability insurance policy provides benefits to a policy owner if the policy owner is unable to perform the duties of any occupation. This type of policy is not attractive to individuals in high-skill professions. The surgeon, for example, would probably not want a policy that will not pay benefits unless the surgeon could not perform telemarketing services. The courts have limited the interpretation of this definition of disability to mean that the insured can collect benefits if the insured is unable to perform any occupation for which he is suited based on training, experience, and educational degrees. Continuing our example, if the surgeon is unable to perform surgery due to an injury to his hands, but could teach medical school to new physicians, he would be expected to earn income in that fashion, and would not receive benefits under the policy. The surgeon would not, however, be required to perform telemarketing services as a means of minimizing benefits received under the policy.

Many disability insurance policies today use a **split definition** of disability in their disability insurance policies. Under a split definition policy, an insured is covered against the risk of not performing his own occupation for a period of time and, after that period expires, an any-occupation definition of disability is used. This gives the insured a period to adjust to his new reality and perhaps get the training necessary to perform other occupations that will allow him to replace the lost income from the old occupation.

CAFETERIA PLANS

A **cafeteria plan** is a written plan, under which the employee may choose to receive cash as compensation or tax-free fringe benefits. Provided the cafeteria plan meets the requirements defined below, the value of the fringe benefit, if chosen by the employee, will be a deductible expense for the employer and will not be included in the employee's gross income. These plans are referred to as §125 plans because they are permitted by IRC §125, which requires a cafeteria plan to offer at least one taxable benefit, usually cash, and one qualified nontaxable benefit. The usual nontaxable benefits include group term life insurance in any amount, medical reimbursements or insurance plans, accident and disability benefits, dependent care assistance, and paid vacation.

USES AND APPLICATIONS

A cafeteria plan is appropriate when employee benefit needs vary within the employee group; the employee mix includes young, unmarried people with minimal life insurance and medical benefits needs, as well as older employees with families who need maximum medical and life insurance benefits. A cafeteria plan is also appropriate when employees want to choose the benefit package most suited to their individual needs, and when an employer seeks to maximize employee satisfaction with the benefit package, thereby maximizing the employer's benefit from its compensation expenditures. A cafeteria plan is also appropriate when the employer is large enough to afford the expense of such a plan. A cafeteria plan is a way of managing fringe benefit costs to the employer by individually pricing each benefit, and providing a total dollar equivalency to each employee to effectively shop for the best mix of benefits for that employee.

Cafeteria plans help give employees an appreciation of the value of their benefit package by allowing them to choose the cash or purchase the benefit. Cafeteria plans can also help control employer costs of providing benefit packages because the employer does not pay for benefits that are not used by the employees. Cafeteria plans are more complex and expensive to design and administer and usually include some insured benefits such as medical and life insurance.

CAFETERIA PLANS

EXHIBIT
14.9

Qualified Benefits	Benefits Not Allowed
• Accident and health benefits (but not medical savings accounts or long-term care insurance) • Adoption assistance • Dependent care assistance • Group term life insurance up to $50,000 • Group term life insurance above $50,000 can be provided, but is includible in an employee's gross income • Long-term or short-term disability coverage • A qualified cash or deferred arrangement (401(k) plan) • Contributions to Health Savings Accounts (HSAs)	• Archer Medical Savings Accounts (see accident and health benefits) • Athletic facilities • De minimis (minimal) benefits • Deferred compensation arrangements • Educational assistance • Employee discounts • Lodging on employer's business premises • Meals • Moving expense reimbursements • No-additional-cost services • Transportation benefits • Tuition reduction • Working condition benefits

BENEFITS PROVIDED

Qualified benefits include benefits that the employer could provide tax-free to the employee (except for the items listed above). More specifically, qualified benefits include accident and health insurance benefits (but not medical savings accounts or long-term care insurance), adoption assistance, dependent care assistance, and group term life insurance coverage (including costs that cannot be excluded from wages). A cafeteria plan cannot include an Archer medical savings account, the payment of athletic facilities dues, de minimis (minimal) benefits, educational assistance, employee discounts, lodging on the employer's business premises, meals, moving expense reimbursements, no-additional-cost services, transportation (commuting) benefits, tuition reduction, working condition benefits, and scholarships or fellowships.

Generally, a cafeteria plan can not include any plan that offers a benefit that defers an employee's compensation, like a contribution to a retirement plan. However, a cafeteria plan can include a qualified 401(k) plan as an available nontaxable benefit.

The flexible spending account (FSA) is a cafeteria plan funded through employee salary reductions. FSAs are discussed in detail in the next section.

EXAMPLE 14.8

Employer NR provides group-term life insurance coverage to its employees only through its cafeteria plan. Employer NR's cafeteria plan allows employees to elect salary reduction for group-term life insurance. Bambi, age 42, elected salary reduction of $200 for $150,000 of group-term life insurance. None of the group-term life insurance is paid through after-tax employee contributions. Implications:

- Bambi's $200 of salary reduction for group-term life insurance is excludible from her gross income.
- Bambi has a total of $150,000 of group-term life insurance. The group-term life insurance in excess of the dollar limitation of section 79 is $100,000 (150,000 - 50,000).
- The Table I cost is $120 (100 x $0.10 x 12 months) for $100,000 of group-term life insurance for an individual between ages 40 to 44. The Table I cost of $120 is reduced by zero (because Bambi paid no portion of the group-term life insurance with after-tax employee contributions).
- The amount includible in Bambi's gross income for the $100,000 of excess group-term life insurance is $120 for the year.

INCOME TAX IMPLICATIONS

Because the employee who benefits from a cafeteria plan has the choice to either receive cash as compensation or use the value to "purchase" fringe benefits tax-free within the cash balance pension plan, the cafeteria plan must meet the rules of IRC §125. Under this section, the IRC provides the benefits payable from a fringe benefit plan with an exclusion from the constructive receipt rule, which would otherwise require the employee to include the value of the benefits purchased in his taxable income.

A cafeteria plan meets the qualifications of the IRC if the benefits provided under the plan are qualified (as discussed above), the plan does not favor the highly compensated employees, and the nontaxable benefits provided to key employees is less than 25 percent of the total nontaxable benefits provided under the plan to all employees.

Benefits under the plan cannot discriminate in favor of highly compensated employees or key employees. Cafeteria plans cannot discriminate in favor of highly compensated individuals as to eligibility to participate, or highly compensated participants as to contributions and benefits. If benefits provided to key employees exceed 25 percent of the aggregate of nontaxable benefits provided for all employees through the cafeteria plan, each key employee must include in gross income an amount equal to the maximum taxable benefits that he could have elected for the plan year.

Highly compensated employees for purposes of cafeteria plans are defined as an officer, a greater than five percent owner, or an employee with income in excess the annual limit ($120,000 for 2016).

Key employees are defined in the same manner as for qualified plans. A **key employee** is any employee who is any one or more of the following:

- A greater than five percent owner,[7] or
- A greater than one percent owner with compensation in excess of $150,000 (not indexed), or
- An officer (defined below) with compensation in excess of $170,000 for 2016 as determined last year.[8]

When a cafeteria plan meets the requirements of the IRC, the employee will not be taxed on the value of the nontaxable fringe benefits chosen, and the employer can deduct the value of the nontaxable fringe benefits chosen by the employee. In the case where the plan provides a benefit that is not qualified, the value of the benefit will be included in the employee's gross income. Also, in the case where the plan is deemed discriminatory by favoring the highly compensated or providing more than 25 percent of the benefit to key employees, the value of the nontaxable benefits chosen by the key employees or highly compensated will be included in their gross income.

QUICK QUIZ 14.4

1. If an employer pays for and provides disability insurance to an employee, the benefits received from such a policy will be tax-free.
   a. True
   b. False

2. Cafeteria plans allow an employee to exclude from income the value of the nontaxable fringe benefits selected.
   a. True
   b. False

False, True.

SIMPLE CAFETERIA PLANS FOR SMALL BUSINESSES

After December 31, 2010, small employers meeting contribution requirements and eligibility and participation requirements can establish a simple cafeteria plan. Simple cafeteria plans do not have to meet the same nondiscrimination rules that a regular cafeteria plan generally must meet. Simple cafeteria plans are treated as meeting the nondiscrimination requirements of a cafeteria plan and certain benefits under a cafeteria plan.

Eligible employers will generally have 100 or fewer employees. The test for this rule is that the employer had an average of 100 or fewer employees on business days during either of the two preceding years. In addition, small companies that increase in size retain small employer status until such time as the average number of employees equals or exceeds 200.

Employers must make a contribution to provide qualified benefits on behalf of each qualified employee in an amount equal to:
1. A uniform percentage (not less than 2%) of the employee's compensation for the plan year, or
2. An amount which is at least six percent of the employee's compensation for the plan year or twice the amount of the salary reduction contributions of each qualified employee, whichever is less.

---

7. The definition of a five-percent owner under top-heavy rules is the same as it is for determining whether an employee is highly compensated and includes family attributions.
8. IRC §416(i)(1).

If the contribution requirements are met using option (2) above, the rate of contribution to any salary reduction contribution of a highly compensated or key employee can not be greater than the rate of contribution to any other employee.

Employers must generally cover any employee who has attained the age of 21, has one year of service and works at least 1,000 hours during the year.

FLEXIBLE SPENDING ACCOUNTS

A **flexible spending account (FSA)** is a cafeteria plan under which employees can choose between receiving cash or deferring income tax-free to fund the cost of certain employee selected benefits. Because of the consequences of forfeiture of unused benefits, these are often referred to as "Use It or Lose It" accounts.

A flexible spending account is appropriate in any of the following situations:
1. An employer wants to expand employee benefit choices without significant employer out-of-pocket costs (or possibly realize some actual dollar savings).
2. Many employees have employed spouses with duplicate medical coverage.
3. Employees contribute to health insurance costs.
4. The employer's medical plans have large deductibles or coinsurance (co-pay) provisions.
5. There is a need for benefits that are difficult to provide on a group basis, such as dependent care.
6. The costs of employee benefit plans, such as health insurance, have increased, and the employer must impose additional employee cost sharing in the form of increased employee contributions and deductibles.

The FSA approach minimizes employee outlay since the FSA converts what would have been after-tax employee expenditures for the benefits selected to pretax expenditures. The plan provides employees a degree of choice to receive either cash as compensation or the cash to pay for the costs of certain benefits. The FSA is funded entirely through employee salary reductions, only requiring the employer to bear the administrative costs. Salary reductions elected by employees to fund the nontaxable benefits available under the plan are not subject to income taxes or payroll taxes. There are many nontaxable benefits available from a FSA, which include many benefits that employers might not otherwise provide to their employees such as dependent care, dental, etc.

> ### KEY CONCEPTS ✓
> 1. What are flexible spending accounts, and when are they appropriate?
> 2. What are the tax implications of employer provided flexible spending accounts?

FLEXIBLE SPENDING ACCOUNT LIMIT (POST 2012)
As a result of the Affordable Care Act of 2010, flexible spending accounts now have a limit on the amount that employees can contribute in 2013 and beyond. That limit is $2,550 for 2016. While this limit is indexed for inflation beyond 2013, it reduces the amount that could be contributed from an employees salary and spent tax free on health care.[9]

USE IT OR LOSE IT RULE

FSAs must comply with the use-or-lose rule since cafeteria plans cannot defer compensation. In 2005, the IRS modified the "use it or lose it" rules to extend the time period through which employees can use FSA funds.[10] This extension of time, referred to as a grace period, must apply to all participants in the FSA cafeteria plan. Expenses for qualified benefits incurred during the grace period may be paid or reimbursed from benefits or contributions remaining unused at the end of the immediately preceding plan year. The grace period must not extend beyond the fifteenth day of the third calendar month after the end of the immediately preceding plan year to which it relates (i.e., "the 2½ month rule"). The effect of the grace period is that the participant may have as long as 14 months and 15 days (the 12 months in the current cafeteria plan year plus the grace period) to use the benefits or contributions for a plan year before those amounts are "forfeited" under the "use-it-or-lose-it" rule.

> Employee A plans to have eye surgery in 2016. For the 2016 plan year, Employee A timely elects salary reduction of $2,550 for a health FSA. During the 2016 plan year, Employee A learns that she cannot have the eye surgery performed, but incurs other medical expenses totaling $1,250. As of December 31, 2016, she has $1,300 of unused benefits and contributions in the health FSA. Consistent with the use-it-or-lose-it rules she would forfeit the $1,300 if it is not used by March 15, 2017.

EXAMPLE 14.9

The Affordable Care Act, enacted in March 2010, established a new uniform standard that, effective January 1, 2011, applies to FSAs. Under the new standard, the cost of an over-the-counter medicine or drug cannot be reimbursed from the FSA account unless a prescription is obtained. The change does not affect insulin, even if purchased without a prescription, or other health care expenses such as medical devices, eye glasses, contact lenses, co-pays and deductibles. The new standard applies only to purchases made on or after January 1, 2011.

Over the last several years, the IRS has considered various methods of relief for taxpayers using FSAs. In October 2013, the IRS issued Notice 2013-71, which contains modifications to the "use-or-lose" rule for FSA. This modification allows §125 cafeteria plans to be amended to allow up to $500 of unused amounts remaining at the end of a plan year in a health FSA to be paid or reimbursed to plan participants for qualified medical expenses incurred during the following plan year, provided that the plan does not also incorporate the grace period rule discussed above. This carryover of up to $500 does not affect the maximum amount of salary reduction contributions that the participant is permitted to make to the FSA for the year. This carryover option provides an alternative to the current grace period rule.

---

9. IRC §125(i).
10. IRS Notice 2005-42.

EXAMPLE 14.10

Employer sponsors a §125 cafeteria plan and health FSA with a calendar plan year, an annual run-out period from January 1 through March 31 in which participants can submit claims for expenses incurred during the preceding plan year, and an annual open enrollment season in November in which participants elect a salary reduction amount (not to exceed $2,550) for the following plan year. The plan is timely amended to provide for a carryover that allows all participants to apply up to $500 of unused health FSA amounts remaining at the end of the run-out period to the health FSA for expenses incurred at any time during that plan year. The plan does not provide for a grace period with respect to the health FSA.

In November 2016, Participant A elects a salary reduction amount of $2,550 for 2017. By December 31, 2016, A's unused amount from the 2016 plan year is $800. On February 1, 2017, A submits claims and is reimbursed with respect to $350 of expenses incurred during the 2016 plan year, leaving a carryover on March 31, 2017 (the end of the run-out period) of $450 of unused health FSA amounts from 2016. The $450 amount is not forfeited; instead, it is carried over to 2017 and available to pay claims incurred in that year so that $3,000 (that is, $2,550 + $450) is available to pay claims incurred in 2017. A incurs and submits claims for expenses of $2,700 during the month of July 2017, and does not submit any other claims during 2017. A is reimbursed with respect to the $2,700 claim, leaving $300 as a potential unused amount from 2017 (depending upon whether A submits claims during the 2017 run-out period in early 2018).

UNIFORM COVERAGE RULES APPLICABLE TO HEALTH FSAS

The maximum amount of reimbursement from a health FSA must be available at all times during the year (properly reduced as of any particular time for prior reimbursements for the same period of coverage). Thus, the maximum amount of reimbursement at any particular time during the year cannot relate to the amount that has been contributed to the FSA at any particular time prior to the end of the plan year. Similarly, the payment schedule for the required amount for coverage under a health FSA may not be based on the rate or amount of covered claims incurred during the coverage period. Employees' salary reduction payments must not be accelerated based on employees' incurred claims and reimbursements. The uniform coverage rule applies only to health FSAs and does not apply to FSAs for dependent care assistance or adoption assistance.

EXAMPLE 14.11

Employer C maintains a calendar year cafeteria plan, offering an election between cash and a health FSA. The cafeteria plan prohibits accelerating employees' salary reduction payments based on employees' incurred claims and reimbursements.

For 2016, Employee N timely elects salary reduction of $2,550 for a health FSA. Employee N pays the $2,550 salary reduction amount through salary reduction of $212.50 per month throughout the year. Employee N is eligible to receive the maximum amount of reimbursement of $2,550 at all times throughout the year (reduced by prior reimbursements).

N incurs $2,550 of medical expenses in January of the current year. The full $2,550 is reimbursed although Employee N has made only one salary reduction payment of $212.50. After Employee N submits a claim for reimbursement and substantiates the medical expenses, the cafeteria plan reimburses N for the $2,550 of medical expenses. Employer C's cafeteria plan satisfies the uniform coverage rule.

DEPENDENT CARE EXPENSES: FSA VS CHILD AND DEPENDENT CARE CREDIT

Using a flexible spending account to pay for dependent care expenses (if provided) may provide more tax savings than utilization of the Child and Dependent Care Credit. In general, an employee is better off using an FSA unless the employee's income (AGI) is less than $43,000.

Sue is a single parent with three children. Sue's income is $25,000 per year. She has $2,550 in child care expenses. In this instance using the dependant care credit will provide a greater tax savings than a flexible spending account. The calculation is as follows:

Dependent Child Care Credit		Flexible Spending Account	
$2,550	Expenses (limit is $3,000)	$2,550	Expense
x 0.30	Rate for $25,000 of income	x 0.15	Tax bracket
$765	Tax savings (Credit)	$382.50	Tax savings
		+ 191	7.65 Payroll tax saved by Sue
		$573.50	Total taxes saved

Assume Sue marries Derek, whose income is $125,000. Sue's income is $25,000 per year and she still has $2,550 in expenses for the three children. In this instance using the flexible spending account would be more beneficial because of the income tax rate differential on the dependant care credit. The calculation is as follows:

Dependent Child Care Credit		Flexible Spending Account	
$2,550	Expenses	$2,550	Expense
x 0.20	Rate for $125,000 of income	x 0.28	Tax bracket
$510	Tax savings (Credit)	$714	Tax savings
		+ 191	7.65 Social Security saved by Sue[1]
		$905	Total taxes saved

1. Assume entire $125,000 is subject to the full FICA of 7.65 percent.

An FSA must meet the nondiscrimination requirements as previously discussed for cafeteria plans. FSAs also require that employees evaluate their personal and family benefit situations, and file a timely election form each year indicating their deferral choice. The plan could result in adverse selection that would ultimately raise benefit costs. The employer is at risk for the total annual amount an employee elects to allocate to health benefits under his FSA even if the employee terminates employment before funding the amount used from the plan. In addition, if the employee fails to use all contributed amounts within a certain time period, contributions are forfeited back to the employer (use it or lose it).

INCOME TAX IMPLICATIONS

Employee salary reductions applied to nontaxable benefits are not subject to income taxes or payroll taxes. The employer gets a tax deduction for any amounts it pays under the plan coverage.

QUICK QUIZ
14.5

1. An employee should consider carefully whether to use a flexible spending account for child care expenses as the FSA is usually more beneficial than the child and dependent care credit.
   a. True
   b. False

2. An employee who contributes to a FSA reduces his taxable income but must still pay payroll taxes on the contributed amount.
   a. True
   b. False

True, False.

Case Study 14.1

FSA contributions not only affect taxes, but may affect disability benefit calculations. In *Brosted v. Unum Life Ins. Co. of America*,[1] Mr. Daniel Brosted was employed by Dreisilker Electric Motors, Inc., which was also the plan administrator for Dreisilker Electric Motors, Inc. Group Long Term Disability Income Plan, a single-employer employee benefit plan. Mr. Brosted was employed by Dreisilker as a purchasing manager from 1974 until January 3, 2000, and was a member of the Plan from its inception. Another defendant, Unum Life Insurance Company of America, provided the insurance coverage for the Plan. Mr. Brosted sought to recover $22,086.09 for past benefits he felt were wrongfully not paid, as well as an increase of his current benefits by $513.63 per month.

Mr. Brosted was diagnosed with multiple sclerosis at age thirty-two. In 2000, Mr. Brosted was hospitalized for his illness and subsequently was prevented from returning to work by Dreisilker. In June 2000, Mr. Brosted applied for long-term disability benefits under the Plan, and by August 1st, Mr. Brosted reached an agreement with Dreisilker concerning his severance from the company. Shortly thereafter, an Unum accountant reviewed Mr. Brosted's file and discovered that his disability benefits had been improperly calculated. According to the policy, benefits were to be either sixty percent of the claimant's monthly earnings prior to disability or $6,000, whichever was less. The monthly earnings used to calculate the benefit were not to include "pre-tax contributions to a qualified deferred compensation plan, §125 plan, or other flexible spending account." Unum's original calculations neglected to take into account Mr. Brosted's pre-tax contributions to his §125 flexible spending account and to his deferred compensation plan. As a result, his monthly benefits were reduced by $513.

Mr. Brosted argued that the Plan and Unum were legally prevented from changing his benefit amount and that Unum breached its fiduciary duty to him under ERISA. The Court disagreed, and granted the defendants' pretrial motion to dismiss because the pre-tax contributions to his §125 flexible spending account and to his deferred compensation plan should not have been included in calculating his disability benefits.

---

1. *Brosted v. Unum Life Ins. Co. of America*, 349 F.Supp.2d 1088, 34 Employee Benefits Cas. 1523 (N.D.Ill. 2004).

OTHER EMPLOYEE BENEFITS

MEDICAL SAVINGS ACCOUNTS

The Health Insurance Portability and Accountability Act (HIPAA) established a tax-favored savings account for medical expenses called an **Archer Medical Savings Account (MSA)**.[11] The MSAs could be established after 1996 and before 2006 for employers with 50 or less employees and self-employed individuals. Employees could not establish the MSA but could contribute (subject to the limitations discussed below) to the account if their employer established an MSA on their behalf. After 2005, an MSA cannot be established and has been replaced by the Health Savings Account (HSA), which is discussed later. However, the MSAs that were established prior to 2006 are still in existence, may still be maintained, and retain their tax-favored status.

KEY CONCEPTS

1. What are the tax implications of employer-provided Archer MSAs, and when can they be established?

2. What are the tax implications of employer-provided HSAs, and when can they be established?

3. What are VEBAs, and what are the tax implications of payments made by the employer to the VEBA?

For MSAs to be established, the employer must have provided its employees with a high-deductible health plan with a maximum out-of-pocket cost.[12] A high deductible plan for purposes of meeting the requirements of the MSA is a major medical health insurance plan with a deductible between $2,250 and $3,350 (2016) for individual coverage and between $4,450 and $6,700 for 2016 for family coverage. The maximum out-of-pocket costs for the plan is $4,450 for individual coverage and $8,150 for family coverage. These same limitations apply for self-employed individuals.

Contributions can be made to the MSA by the employee or the employer. Employee contributions are deductible from the employee's gross income. In addition, employer contributions are tax deductible by the employer, not subject to payroll taxes, and not taxable income to the employee. The aggregate contributions to the plan by the employee and the employer cannot exceed 65 percent of the deductible for individual coverage and 75 percent of the deductible for family coverage.

The earnings on the assets within an MSA are tax deferred until a distribution is taken from the account. If a distribution is for qualified medical expenses, the distribution, including any earnings, is not taxable. If the distribution is not for qualified medical expenses, the entire distribution is taxable as ordinary income. In addition, if the distribution is taken before the owner of the account is age 65, the distribution is subject to an additional 20 percent excise penalty tax.

11. Public Law 104-191 (August 21, 1996); IRC §220.
12. IRC §220(c)(2)(A); Rev. Proc. 2004-71.

HEALTH SAVINGS ACCOUNTS

The Medicare Act of 2003 created **Health Savings Accounts (HSAs)**, which are very similar to MSAs but less restrictive. Specifically, HSAs can be established by anyone with a high deductible health insurance plan (see below), allow a higher contribution amount, and reduce the penalty for non-medical distributions.

To qualify for an HSA, the individual's health insurance plan's deductible must be at least $1,300 for single coverage and the annual out-of-pocket costs cannot exceed $6,550 for 2016.[13] For family coverage under an HSA, the health insurance plan deductible must be at least $2,600, and the annual out-of-pocket costs cannot exceed $13,100 for 2016.

Contributions to the HSA can be made by the individual or by the individual's employer. In either case, the aggregate contributions cannot exceed the health insurance plan deductible subject to a maximum contribution of $3,350 for individuals and $6,750 for families for 2016. However, individuals between 55 years old and 64 years old can make additional catch-up contributions of $1,000 over these limits for 2016.[14]

Earnings within the HSA are not taxable, and amounts distributed from an HSA are also not taxable provided the distributions are used to pay for qualified medical expenses. If a distribution is not for qualified medical expenses, the entire distribution is taxable as ordinary income. If the distribution is taken before the owner of the account is 65, the distribution is subject to an additional 20 percent excise penalty tax.[15]

DEATH OF AN HSA OWNER

Owners of HSAs need to establish beneficiaries for their accounts when they are set up. Upon death, an HSA will become the spouse's HSA if left to the spouse. If the beneficiary is someone other than the spouse, then the account ceases being an HSA and is taxable in the year of death to the beneficiary.

---

13. IRC §§223(b) and (c); Rev. Proc. 2004-71.
14. IRC §223(b)(3)(B).
15. IRC §223(f)(4).

EXHIBIT
14.10

COMPARISON OF MSA (ARCHER) AND HSA FOR 2016

	MSA (ARCHER)		HSA	
Established	Before 2006		2004 and Later	
Creators	• Employers with less than 50 employees • Self-employed individuals		Any individual	
	Single	**Family**	**Single**	**Family**
Health Insurance Deductible	$2,250- $3,350	$4,450 - $6,700	At least $1,300	At least $2,600
Maximum Out-of-Pocket	$4,450	$8,150	$6,550	$13,100
Maximum Contribution	65% of deductible	75% of deductible	100% of deductible limited to $3,350	100% of deductible limited to $6,750
Catch-Up Contribution Available	No		Yes $1,000 for 2016	
Penalty for Nonqualified Expenditures	Ordinary income tax on earnings and 20% penalty if owner is < 65		Ordinary income tax on earnings and 20% penalty if owner is < 65	

VOLUNTARY EMPLOYEES' BENEFICIARY ASSOCIATION (VEBA)

A **Voluntary Employees' Beneficiary Association (VEBA)** is a welfare benefit plan, into which an employer deposits funds that will be used to provide specified employee benefits in the future. Technically, the VEBA is either a trust or a corporation set up by an employer to hold funds used to pay benefits under an employer benefit plan. However, generally they are trusts that are exempt from tax under the provisions of IRC §501(c)(9) and subject to the "welfare benefit fund" rules under §419 and §419A. While welfare benefit funds can also be taxable trusts, most welfare benefit funds apply for exempt status as VEBAs in order to reduce or eliminate income taxes at the trust level. VEBA's file Form 990, whereas taxable trusts file Form 1041.

VEBAs must meet all of the following requirements:
1. The organization is an employees' association,
2. Membership in the association is voluntary,
3. The organization provides for the payment of life, sick, accident, or other benefits to its members or their dependents or designated beneficiaries, and substantially all of its operations are in furtherance of providing such benefits, and
4. No part of the net earnings of the organization inures, other than by payment of the benefits referred to above, to the benefit of any private shareholder or individual.

Generally, all ordinary and necessary expenses are deductible under IRC §162. However, expenses for deferred compensation are not deductible until included into income by the employee as discussed in Chapter 12.

Welfare benefit plans provide for deferral of funds used for the purpose of providing future benefits to employees and are not subject to the same taxation rules as deferred compensation plans. This exception is largely because it is society's interest to provide these type of benefits to employees. IRC §404(a), which governs the taxation of qualified plans and deferred compensation, does not apply to a plan that does not defer the receipt of compensation. Furthermore, §404(a) does not apply to deductions for contributions under a plan which is solely a dismissal wage or unemployment benefit plan, or a sickness, accident, hospitalization, medical expense, recreation, welfare, or similar benefit plan, or a combination thereof. For example, if under a plan an employer contributes five percent of each employee's compensation per month to a fund out of which employees who are laid off will be paid benefits for temporary periods, but employees who are not laid off have no rights to the funds, such a plan is an unemployment benefit plan, and the deductibility of the contributions to it is determined under section 162.

QUICK QUIZ 14.6

1. Archer MSAs cannot be established after April 15, 2004.
   a. True
   b. False

2. Distributions from an HSA that are not used for medical expenses are taxed as ordinary income and subject to a 10% penalty if the owner of the HSA has not reached age 59½.
   a. True
   b. False

3. A VEBA allows an employer to take a current deduction for future benefits that will be provided to employees.
   a. True
   b. False

False, False, True.

Under IRC §419 and §419A, employers can make contributions to welfare benefit plans without the benefits being currently distributed and avoiding current taxation. These sections limit the amount of deductions for contributions to these type of plans. However, there is an exception to these limits for plans with ten or more employers contributing to the plan.

As with other areas of the Code that allow for current deductions and no corresponding current income, the exception for these plans has been subject to abuse and the current rules are much less favorable then in the past. The IRS Notice 95-34 discusses tax problems raised by certain trust arrangements seeking to qualify for exemption from IRC §419. Additionally, it puts taxpayers on notice that deductions for contributions to some of these arrangements are disallowable for any one of several reasons (e.g., the arrangements may provide deferred compensation, the arrangements may be separate plans for each employer, the arrangements may be experience rated in form or operation, or the contributions may be nondeductible prepaid expenses).

Despite the abuses with these types of plans, VEBAs and other welfare benefit plans continue to be beneficial to some companies and employees.

Application and Benefits

By creating and funding a VEBA, an employer can reduce the employer's income tax burden by accelerating an income tax deduction for the payment of welfare type benefits that would have been funded by the employer in the future. An employer can also potentially reduce future cash flow and the total cost of the benefits as the earnings within the VEBA are not taxed, which will provide the employer with additional funds to pay the benefit' costs.

VEBAs also provide employees with benefit security, because after the funds are deposited into the VEBA, the funds can only be used for the exclusive benefit of the employees, are beyond the reach of the employer's creditors, and generally cannot revert to the employer.

Life insurance benefits provided by a VEBA will generally be subject to current taxation, similar to the tax treatment for life insurance. However, the proceeds are generally tax-free and are not included in the gross estate of the decedent since the decedent had no incidents of ownership.

CONTRIBUTIONS

The level of annual contributions to the VEBA in order to fund benefits is determined actuarially. This amount is paid annually or in more frequent installments if the employer desires and, provided the plan meets the qualification requirements, is fully deductible by the employer in the year of the contribution.

EXHIBIT 14.11

VEBA BENEFITS THAT CAN AND CANNOT BE PROVIDED

VEBAs Can Provide	VEBAs Cannot Provide
• Life insurance before and after retirement • Other survivor benefits • Sickness and accident benefits • Other benefits including vacation and recreation benefits • Severance benefits paid through a severance pay plan • Unemployment and job training benefits • Disaster benefits • Legal service payment for credits	• Savings • Retirement • Deferred compensation • Coverage of expenses such as commuting expenses • Accident or homeowners insurance covering damage to property • Other items unrelated to the maintenance of the employee's earning power

SALARY CONTINUATION PLANS

A **salary continuation plan** is an arrangement between an employer and an employee where the employer agrees to continue to pay an employee after retirement or to the employee's spouse if the employee dies prior to retiring. A salary continuation plan can be provided on a discriminatory basis and provides the benefit of shifting the income to the employee to a period when the tax burden is not as heavy (i.e., retirement).

When the payments are made from the salary continuation plan, the value is included in an employee's gross income, is subjected to payroll tax,

KEY CONCEPTS

1. What are the tax implications of employer-provided salary continuation plans?

2. What are the tax implications of employer-provided group long-term care insurance?

3. What are the tax implications of employer-provided group retirement planning services?

and is deductible by the employer. Some employers fund the salary continuation plan through the use of a permanent life insurance policy on the employee. Premiums for this type of insurance are not deductible by the employer, but amounts paid to the employee or to the employee's dependents are deductible by the employer at the time of payment.

GROUP LONG-TERM CARE INSURANCE

The premium payments for qualified group long-term care insurance are tax deductible if paid by the employer and tax-free to the employee (see below for a discussion of self-employed individuals). In addition to the tax advantages, group long-term care insurance generally also provides the following advantages:
- lower rates than individual policies (generally 30% - 60% less)
- guaranteed coverage for all employees, even those who might not be insurable under an individual policy
- increase eligibility for extended family members including parents, grandparents, and in-laws
- the policy must be guaranteed renewable
- the average can be provided in a discriminatory manner
- "qualified" benefits are non-taxable to the recipient of the care

To be a qualified long-term care insurance plan, the plan must meet the provisions of the IRC, specifically the plan must:
- only provide long-term care insurance coverage
- not duplicate benefits paid by Medicare
- the plan must be guaranteed renewable
- only pay benefits when the employee or beneficiary of the plan is certified by a licensed health care practitioner as chronically ill

Long-term care premiums cannot be paid for within a cafeteria plan or flexible spending account nor can the premium payment be made with pretax employee salary deferrals. If, however, the employee pays the premiums with after-tax dollars, the employee may deduct, as an itemized medical expense deduction (subject to the 10% hurdle), the costs on the employee's income tax return for the year. The deduction limit is the lesser of the premium paid or the amount corresponding to the employee's age in the table below.[16]

ELIGIBLE LONG-TERM CARE PREMIUMS FOR 2016

EXHIBIT 14.12

Age	Maximum Deductible Amount for 2016
≤ 40	$390
41 - 50	$730
51 - 60	$1,460
61 - 70	$3,900
≥ 71	$4,870

16. IRC §213(d)(10) adjusted for inflation. See Rev. Proc. 2004-71.

Self-Employed Individuals

Self-employed individuals as well as individuals that are considered self employed, including partners of partnerships and members of limited liability companies that are taxed as partnerships, must include the cost of long-term care insurance paid by the employer in their gross income. The individual will be eligible for the income tax deduction as discussed above. The premiums paid for by the plan for any other employees who are not considered self-employed will continue to be a deductible business expense for the employer that is not included in the employee's income.

GROUP RETIREMENT PLANNING SERVICES

An employer may exclude from an employee's gross income the value of any retirement planning advice or information the employer provides to the employee or his spouse if the employer maintains a qualified retirement plan.[17] In addition to employer plan advice and information, the services provided may include general advice and information on retirement. However, the exclusion does not apply to the value of services for tax preparation, accounting, legal, or brokerage services.

QUICK QUIZ 14.7

1. A salary continuation plan allows employees to shift income to future years.
   a. True
   b. False

2. Long-term care plans are frequently a benefit option of a cafeteria or FSA plan.
   a. True
   b. False

3. An employer can exclude from an employee's gross income the value of any retirement planning advice provided to an employee whether or not the employer has a retirement plan.
   a. True
   b. False

True, False, False.

The employer may not discriminate in favor of highly compensated executives. The nondiscrimination rule states that the exclusion is allowable for highly compensated employees only if the retirement planning services are available on substantially the same terms to each member of the group of employees normally provided education and information regarding the employer's qualified employer plan.

PREPAID LEGAL SERVICES

A prepaid legal services plan provides broader access to legal services for an employee base at a discounted rate.These plans can be funded by employees, employers or partially paid by both the employee and employer. These plans work in a similar fashion to group life, health, or disability insurance. The risk of needing a lawyer is pooled together and costs are reduced. However, these plans no longer receive favorable tax treatment.

Under IRC §120, qualified group legal services plans received special tax treatment prior to July 1992. Employer contributions to the plan were deductible by the employer if the plan provided personal legal services for its employees, their spouses, and their dependents and the plan met the requirements of IRC §120. In addition, the value of the legal services provided under the plan was not subject to taxation for the employee receiving the benefits. However, this benefit is no longer available.

---

17. IRC §132(m).

SUCCESSION PLANNING AND INSURANCE ARRANGEMENTS

SUCCESSION PLANNING

Companies use succession planning to ensure leadership continuity, which helps to ensure effective future operations. Through this process, current leaders identify and develop employees who have the potential to be trained to take on additional leadership roles in the future. While succession planning is routinely conducted in the corporate world, it is also conducted in the small business setting, and there are clear differences.

For large private and publically-traded companies, succession planning is often an ongoing process that happens at many levels of the organization. It is often a part of the annual review process, in which a manager seeks out individuals who have the requisite skills, desire, work ethic, and experience to take over the manager's own role. Employees who have been identified to advance in the organization are often selected for continued development, which may involve internal or external leadership training. In addition, these individuals may often change leadership roles within the organization periodically to increase exposure to other functions within the company.

> Dennis has worked for N-ergy for the last 25 years in various roles. He was moved to a management role in the IT department five years ago and has continued to be one of the top performers in the organization. He has been reporting to the Chief Information Officer (CIO) for the past two years. The CIO has moved Dennis several times to run different departments within the IT organization. Dennis is being groomed to take over the CIO position in the future.

EXAMPLE
14.14

In large organizations, leadership positions are often vacated when leaders advance within the organization or leave the organization entirely. For example, talented managers may be enticed to go to work for competitors with higher compensation packages. To avoid the leadership gaps this practice can cause, successful companies have formalized programs to identify and develop leadership so that there is continuity of management. These programs also help mitigate the risk of losing talented employees.

In the small business setting, especially ones in which the original entrepreneur(s) function as senior leadership, the major business functions tend to reside with a small group of people. These companies may have less risk of an owner leaving to work for a competitor, as they are vested in the business; however, these organizations often have significant challenges filling leadership roles.

Owners of small businesses should consider their long-term objectives for the business. These options are usually:
- Close the business and walk away
- Sell the business to a third-party buyer (or go public)
- Sell the business to employees
- Transfer the business to family members
- Continue to own the business but transition out of management
- Transfer the business to the other owners in the event of an untimely death

Closing the Business

Closing the business is not a commonly considered choice, as most entrepreneurs believe there is a significant amount of value in their businesses. The owners have often worked for years in their businesses and have a vested interest in them. However, for some owners, simply closing the business is the best option regardless of value.

It often takes decades for a small business to become successful. During this time, entrepreneurs often sacrifice many aspects of their lives. Once successful, many entrepreneurs, who have worked in their businesses for much of their lives, look to their businesses as sources of funding for retirement. This funding could be from the sale of the businesses or from distributions from the businesses as they continues to operate.

Owners who want to sell their businesses have a few choices in terms of potential buyers. However, selling a business is not always easy or guaranteed. Owners can sell to a third party, employees, current owners, or to family members.

Selling to a Third Party

Selling to a third party is not always an option but may be quite lucrative. Third-party buyers include strategic buyers and private equity firms. Strategic buyers make acquisitions for a variety of purposes, including:

- Acquiring a new, innovative process or product
- Expanding its product offering through the acquisition
- Eliminating a competitor, which may result in a better product offering and costs savings
- Other reasons, such as gaining competent management or research and development

Private equity (PE) firms generally make acquisitions to earn a return on invested capital. PEs attempt to purchase companies at a relatively low multiple (price to EBITA or net income), grow net income, and sell at a higher multiple.

> Hyper Growth Horizons Firm (HGH) is a private equity firm. They just purchased Muscle Chem, Inc., which is a nutritional supplements company, for $7 million. Muscle Chem's net income is $1 million, so HGH paid seven times net income for the company. HGH believes that they can help management double the net income over the next three-to-five years and can sell to a larger nutritional supplements company for 14 times net income. Based on those assumptions, HGH expects to quadruple its money.

Typically, an acquiring company wants key employees to remain with the company for a minimum period of time. This aspect of an acquisition agreement normally applies to the owners, also, which means that the owners should be open to staying employed after the purchase for a period of time. However, in some acquisitions, the acquiring company has less interest in personnel and more interest in a company's products, services, or cash flows.

Another option is to take the company public and hold an initial public offering. This choice is more appropriate and realistic for larger companies and requires significant cost and, usually, the assistance of an investment banker.

In some cases, finding a company to purchase a business is difficult or even impossible. In these cases, an owner may attempt to sell the business to an individual or an employee. The challenge with this approach is often that the buyer does not have the funds to purchase the company and wants to finance the purchase with the internally-generated future cash flows of the business. This approach is usually a bad idea for the owner, as the owner effectively continues to retain the risk of operating the business after the sale with little or no upside potential. If the business declines, the owner may not be repaid. However, if the business succeeds, he is repaid but does not participate in the growth. It's not advisable to retain the risk side of a transaction without the return side.

Selling to Employees
The final selling option is to sell it to the employees. As discussed above, the employees do not always have enough funds to acquire the company. In this situation, the owner can use a leveraged ESOP, which was discussed earlier in the text and involves using borrowed funds to finance the purchase.

In many cases, owners are concerned about ensuring the continuing operation of the business in the event of an untimely death of one of the owners. This risk can often be managed with buy-sell agreements, discussed earlier in this chapter.

Transferring to Family Members
Small businesses are often family businesses, meaning that various family members work in the business. In these situations, as an owner gets older, it is common to want to transfer the business to a child or to children. This process of transferring the business, if done correctly, requires a great deal of planning. This type of planning attempts to ensure that the business continues to operate effectively and that the transferee (often a child) has the requisite skills and experience to effectively manage the business. One of the biggest problems occurs when parents put their adult children in roles for which they are inexperienced and ill-equipped to successfully manage.

To successfully run a small business, a successor must have an understanding of:
* Basic aspects of accounting and finance (including some tax law)
* The company's product offerings, industry and competitors
* The company's operations, including supply chain management and distribution
* Basic human resources, including hiring, managing, inspiring, and firing
* Basic strategic planning

Because running a small business requires an enormous number of skills, many small businesses fail in the first or second generation. Large businesses have the resources to hire personnel who can specialize in one or a few of these areas, while a small business owner must have a basic understanding of most of these skills.

Once the decision to transfer the business has been made, the method must be chosen. The owner has the option to either sell or donate the business to a child immediately or over time. This choice and its implications are discussed in more detail in the Money Education Estate Planning Text.

In the event that the owner/transferor of a small business is dependent on the future cash flows from the business, there will have to be simultaneous financial planning for the transferor and strategic planning for the transferee. This requirement is one of the reasons that successful planning in a small business can take a significant number of years to complete.

Transition Out

In some cases, owners may want to continue to own the business but transition out of management. The objective of this approach is to continue to benefit from the fruits of prior labor. The owner has worked for years building a company and often has an emotional attachment to the business. Often the idea of selling the business is somewhat frightening, as it signifies an abrupt change in the owner's life, as opposed to a more gradual change by "transitioning out". The transitioning out option allows the owner to maintain ownership and control while continuing to receive income from the business.

Transitioning is a nice compromise between continuing to run the business and selling. However, it has potential issues for the owner that range from working too much to not paying enough attention to what is going on in the business. In some cases, owners may have a hard time not going into the office and may end up working more than they had imagined. In other cases, they are so far removed from the business that they miss potential issues that could be devastating to the business. It often takes a lifetime to build a great reputation and only a short time to tarnish it. This option of transitioning out absolutely does not work unless a succession plan is successfully executed, resulting in a competent leadership team that can run the business with little or no input from the owner. Without a reliable leadership team, it is only a matter of time before the company goes out of business.

Untimely Death of a Business Owner

The untimely death of a business owner can be devastating to the business, the remaining owners, as well as the family of the deceased owner. The section below discusses how buy-sell agreements can provide needed liquidity for the business as well as for the deceased owner's family.

BUSINESS CONTINUATION (BUY/SELL) AGREEMENTS

Closely-held business interests often represent a considerable portion of business owner's net worth and gross estate at the death of the owner. These business interests are generally illiquid, which creates a need for liquidity within the estate and often for a surviving spouse. Life insurance can be used to fund buy-sell agreements for closely held and family-owned business owners. While a complete discussion of buy-sell agreements and their tax consequences is beyond the scope of this chapter, an overview of this common planning technique is warranted.

KEY CONCEPTS

1. Highlight the parties to an entity agreement versus a cross-purchase agreement.

2. Distinguish between an entity agreement, a cross-purchase agreement, and wait-and-see buy-sell agreement.

3. Explain why life insurance is a perfect hedge for buy-sell agreements that are triggered on the death of the owner.

Buy-sell agreements are legal arrangements that require the sale of securities owned by one individual to another individual or entity upon a specified triggering event. Buy-sell agreements are commonly used by business owners to plan for the orderly transfer and control of a business interest, to create a market for stock that is not traded on securities exchanges, and to plan for liquidity in the estate of a deceased business owner.

The most common triggering event that invokes obligations under a buy-sell agreement is the death of the business owner. A properly structured buy-sell agreement requires the estate of the business owner to sell the decedent's business interest to another entity or person, who is often a family member or close business associate of the decedent. Since an obligation to purchase a business interest is triggered at the death of the owner, life insurance is an ideal funding vehicle for buy-sell agreements triggered at death. Typically, either the business itself, or the individual or entity who is obligated to purchase the decedent's business interest will hold a life insurance policy on the decedent's life that has a death benefit sufficient to cover the purchase price of the decedent's business interest.

Other triggering events for buy-sell agreements include disability, divorce, retirement, and withdrawal from the business, but a full discussion of these is beyond the scope of this chapter.

Buy-sell agreements generally are of one of three types:
- entity purchase (sometimes referred to as redemption agreements)
- cross-purchase agreements
- wait-and-see agreements

Entity (Redemption) Agreements

The simplest form of buy-sell agreement is the **entity purchase**, or redemption, agreement. This type of buy-sell agreement obligates the business entity to purchase an owner's interest in the entity upon that owner's death. This type of buy-sell agreement works well for organizations that have a separate legal existence from their owners but would not be appropriate for a sole proprietorship. Sole proprietorships are wholly owned by one person, and when that person dies, so does the proprietorship. The business of a sole proprietor may be transferred to another person or entity at the death of the sole proprietorship through a cross-purchase agreement (discussed below), but the proprietorship cannot purchase itself.

> Cecil is part owner of a luxury resort hotel, Fawlty Towers. Fawlty Towers is organized as a C corporation, and the corporation is wholly owned by members of Cecil's family. To ensure that the ownership of the hotel stays within the family and to make sure that Cecil's estate has sufficient liquidity to cover its expenses at his death, Cecil enters into a buy-sell agreement with Fawlty Towers, Inc. whereby Cecil (through his estate) agrees to sell, and Fawlty Towers agrees to purchase his stock when he dies. The agreement between Cecil and Fawlty Towers is an entity purchase buy-sell agreement.

EXAMPLE 14.16

To fund the purchase obligation under an entity-purchase buy-sell agreement, the business can acquire a life insurance policy on the owner's life with a death benefit sufficient to cover the purchase amount. Life insurance is an ideal vehicle to use for this purpose, since it provides funds at the exact time they are needed (the death of the insured). Furthermore, using the death benefit to meet the purchase obligation under the buy-sell agreement does not affect cash holdings or other assets that the company may need for continued business operations.

What type of life insurance policy should be purchased to fund the buy-sell agreement? The answer, of course, depends on the facts. If the business is family owned, and the owner of the interest is a family member, or if there has been a long-term relationship between the owner and the business with no definitive date when that relationship will end (such as a retirement date), a permanent life insurance policy should be considered. Permanent life insurance costs more up front but provides protection for longer periods of time with guarantees from the insurance company. Using term life, universal life, or variable universal life may be risky, since those policies will only remain in force as long as there is money to pay premiums or in the policy cash value to pay the annual mortality and expense charges. Permanent life insurance guarantees that the money needed to buy the business interest will be there no matter how long the owner lives or continues to be involved in the operation of the business activity.

Disadvantages

While entity buy-sell agreements have the advantage of simplicity, there is at least one disadvantage to using this structure.

If an entity buy-sell agreement is used, and the surviving owners plan to sell their business interests after the death of the first owner but prior to their own deaths, the entity buy-sell agreement will increase their taxable gain upon sale of their interests. Of course, this would not be an issue for family businesses that are not sold during the lifetimes of the family members. This first disadvantage of entity buy-sell agreements is easily remedied by using a cross-purchase buy-sell agreement.

Cross-Purchase Agreements

A **cross-purchase buy-sell agreement** is an arrangement between individuals who agree to purchase the business interest of a deceased owner. Unlike an entity-type agreement, which involves the business itself, a cross-purchase agreement only involves the owners of the business.

EXAMPLE 14.17

> Cecil and his sister, Sybil, are equal owners of a luxury resort hotel, Fawlty Towers. Fawlty Towers is organized as a C corporation, and the corporation has been wholly owned by members of Cecil & Sybil's family since it began. Neither Cecil nor Sybil are married, and neither has any children. To ensure that the ownership of the hotel stays within the family, and to make sure that their estates have sufficient liquidity to cover expenses at death, Cecil and Sybil enter into a buy-sell agreement whereby the first sibling to die agrees to sell (through her estate), and the surviving sibling agrees to purchase the decedent's interest when she dies. The agreement between Cecil and Sybil is a cross-purchase buy-sell agreement.

To fund a cross-purchase buy-sell agreement with life insurance, each party to the agreement purchases a life insurance policy on the life of all of the other parties to the agreement so that the death benefit is sufficient to purchase the interest of any deceased owner. If there are only two parties, this approach is relatively straightforward – each party purchases one policy on the life of the other. When more than two owners are involved, however, things can get complicated, and as the number of owners grows, so does the complexity of the arrangement and the number of life insurance policies that must be purchased.

> Bertie, Claude, and Eustice are equal owners of Wooster Enterprises, Ltd. They have entered into a cross-purchase buy-sell agreement triggered upon death. If Bertie dies first, his 1/3 interest would have to be purchased by Claude and Eustice in equal shares. To fund the agreement, both Claude and Eustice should purchase a life insurance policy on Bertie's life that will pay a death benefit equal to 1/6 (1/3 x 1/2) of the value of the company. Bertie and Claude should each purchase a life insurance policy on Eustice's life for the same amount (in case Eustice dies first), and Eustice and Bertie should purchase a life insurance policy on Claude's life in case Claude dies first. As this example illustrates, for a three-owner agreement, six life insurance policies would have to be purchased to fund this buy-sell agreement.

The number of cross purchase policies needed to fully fund the buy-sell agreement can be calculated by using the formula:

$$\text{Number of policies} = N(N-1)$$

Where N = the number of owners subject to the agreement. The greater the number of owners, the greater the number of life insurance policies that should be purchased. For example, four owners would require twelve policies or 4(4-1).

While applying for a large number of life insurance policies does somewhat complicate the administration of a cross-purchase agreement, the real issues emerge in the annual maintenance of the agreement. Each year, each of the owners will pay the premiums on policies they own covering the lives of other owners in order to keep those policies in force. If just one owner fails to pay the premium and another owner dies, the benefits of entering into the buy-sell agreement may be in jeopardy.

An entity agreement is a simple arrangement in which only one policy is purchased on the life of each owner and the premiums are paid by the entity. A cross-purchase agreement is much more complex than an entity agreement.

One of the advantages to a cross-purchase agreement is the ability to increase the surviving owner's basis in his or her shares of the business entity. When life insurance death benefits are received (on a tax-free basis), and are used to purchase the business interest of a deceased owner, each surviving owner's share of the business increases, but so does his or her basis in the business entity. Basis is that portion of the sale proceeds not subject to income tax, so a higher basis results in a higher after-tax benefit to the taxpayer. This benefit is unavailable with entity buy-sell agreements and is often the reason that financial advisors prefer cross-purchase arrangements.

Bertie, Claude, and Eustice are equal owners of Wooster Enterprises, Ltd. The adjusted basis for each 1/3 interest is $100,000. They have entered into a cross-purchase buy-sell agreement triggered upon death. Bertie passed away, and his 1/3 interest in Wooster enterprises was valued at $334,000. The entire business was worth $1 million, leaving $333,000 each for Claude and Eustice. As specified in the buy-sell agreement, Claude and Eustice each purchase half of Bertie's 1/3 interest in Wooster Enterprise, Ltd. for $167,000. After the purchase, Claude's and Eustice's ownership percentages increased from 33% to 50%. Their basis in the ownership interests increased from $100,000 to $267,000 each ($100,000 original adjusted basis + $167,000 paid for acquisition of the interest from Bertie's estate). If Claude and Eustice immediately sold Wooster Enterprises, Ltd. for $1 million, each of them would receive $500,000 (1/2 the proceeds) and would have to pay income tax on a capital gain of $233,000 ($500,000 amount realized - $267,000 adjusted basis).

How would this result differ if the buy-sell agreement was structured as an entity buy-sell, and Claude and Eustice sold the business after Bertie died? As described above, Claude and Eustice would each receive $500,000 (1/2 the proceeds) but would have to pay income tax on a capital gain of $400,000 ($500,000 amount realized - $100,000 adjusted basis). In this instance, the basis of the surviving shareholders is not affected because the corporation, not the individual shareholders, purchased the shares from Bertie's estate.

Cross-purchase agreements are typically preferred from a tax planning standpoint because:
1. they permit the surviving shareholders to increase their basis in the business interest;
2. the death benefit on life insurance owned by individuals is not subject to the possible imposition of the alternative minimum tax; and
3. life insurance owned by business owners outside of a corporation does not trigger any potential accumulated earnings tax.

Wait-and-See Buy-Sell Agreements

Wait-and-see buy-sell agreements are a cross between entity and cross purchase buy-sell agreements. Using this approach, the business has the first option to purchase the interest of a deceased owner. If the business entity chooses not to purchase the interest, the surviving owners of the company are given the opportunity to purchase the deceased owner's interest in proportion to his or her ownership interest. If the surviving owners do not exercise their right to purchase the interest, any interest remaining is purchased by the business.

By giving both the company and the owners the right to purchase an interest, the wait-and-see buy-sell maintains flexibility between the simplicity of the entity agreement and the tax advantages of the cross-purchase agreement. Both the company and the surviving owners can assess their respective situations when the death of an owner occurs and act in a way that maximizes their combined benefits.

Wait-and-see buy-sell agreements are very useful for C corporations with large amounts of retained earnings. When retained earnings are distributed to shareholders, they are usually treated as dividend distributions and are subject to income tax. If a corporation redeems shares from the estate of a deceased owner, and the redemption does not exceed the estate and inheritance taxes plus funeral expenses incurred by the deceased owner's estate, the redemption is typically exempt from income tax. This approach results in a reduction in retained earnings at the corporate level (IRC Sec. 303). The reduction in retained earnings reduces the amount of future corporate distributions that are subject to taxes as dividends, which is a significant benefit for C corporations and their surviving shareholders. Under a wait-and-see buy-sell agreement, the corporation will typically exercise its first option to purchase the number of shares necessary to effectuate a Sec. 303 redemption (thereby reducing its retained earnings) and give the surviving shareholders the option to purchase the remaining interest. If the surviving shareholders exercise this option, they will receive an increase in their basis in the business interest, which will reduce their taxable gain in the business entity should they decide to sell their interests before their deaths.

While wait-and-see buy-sell agreements are often used for C corporations, they are not frequently used for S corporations, partnerships, limited liability companies, or limited liability partnerships. Only C corporations issue taxable dividends, so the tax features of the wait-and-see buy-sell agreements are applicable only to C corporations. Wait-and-see buy-sell agreements could still be used with other types of business entities if the primary objective is to maintain flexibility in the repurchase of interests.

Life Insurance is the Perfect Hedge for a Buy-Sell Agreement Triggered at Death

As illustrated in the discussion above, life insurance is a perfect hedge for buy-sell agreements that are triggered on the death of the owner. If life insurance is purchased on the owner's life, the proceeds can be used to purchase the business interest from the decedent owner's estate. This facilitates effective transfer of ownership and control of the business entity and provides liquidity for the deceased owner's estate so that estate and inheritance taxes, funeral expenses, and end-of-life medical care costs can be paid.

QUICK QUIZ 14.8

1. A cross purchase agreement will increase the income tax basis of survivors/owners.
   a. True
   b. False

2. The number of policies for 5 equal partners in an entity approach to buy/sell is 20.
   a. True
   b. False

3. The number of policies for 5 equal partners in cross-purchase arrangement to buy/sell is 20.
   a. True
   b. False

True, False, True.

BUSINESS DISABILITY PLANS

Disability overhead insurance is designed to cover the expenses that are usual and necessary expenses in the operation of a business should the owner become disabled. Premiums are deductible as a business expense, and benefits payable from the plan are taxable income to the entity. Disability buyout policies are policies to cover the value of an individual's interest in the business should they become disabled.

SPLIT-DOLLAR LIFE INSURANCE ARRANGEMENT

A split-dollar arrangement is a discriminatory benefit plan using life insurance. The employer and employee share the cost of a life insurance policy on the employee (usually permanent insurance such as whole life insurance or variable universal life insurance). Such arrangements are typically used by businesses to provide low cost insurance to key employees. A **split-dollar life insurance arrangement** is generally structured in one of either of the two following ways:

1. The endorsement method, or
2. The collateral assignment method.

The Endorsement Method

Under a split-dollar life insurance plan using the endorsement method, the employer owns the life insurance policy on the employee and the employer pays the policy premium. The employer withholds the right in the plan to be repaid for all of its premium either at the employee's death or the surrender of the life insurance policy. Usually any death benefit or cash surrender value in excess of the employer's refund is paid to the policy beneficiaries.

The Collateral Assignment Method

Under a split-dollar life insurance plan using the collateral assignment method, the employee owns the life insurance policy and the employer makes a loan to the employee to pay the policy premiums. In this case, at the employee's death or at the surrender of the policy, the employer loan will be repaid and any excess will be paid to the policy beneficiaries.

Uses of Split-Dollar Life Insurance

A split-dollar life insurance policy is appropriate when an employer wishes to provide an executive with life insurance benefits at a low cost and low cash outlay to the executive (the premiums are essentially paid for by the employer). Split-dollar life insurance plans are best suited for executives in their 30s, 40s, and early 50s since the plan requires a reasonable duration to build adequate policy cash value and the cost to the executive at later ages is usually prohibitive. Split-dollar life insurance can be used as an alternative to an insurance-financed nonqualified deferred compensation plan or in conjunction with a nonqualified, unfunded, deferred compensation plan. A split-dollar policy is also effective when an employer is seeking a totally selective executive fringe benefit as the nondiscrimination rules do not apply.

> ## KEY CONCEPTS
>
> 1. What are the tax implications of business overhead disability plans?
>
> 2. What is split-dollar life insurance, and what are the income tax consequences associated with such plans?
>
> 3. What is key person insurance, and what are the income tax consequences associated with such plans?

A split-dollar plan allows an executive to receive the benefit of current value using employer funds with minimal or no tax cost to the executive. In most types of split-dollar plans, the employer's outlay is at all times fully secured. Upon the employee's death or termination of employment, the employer is reimbursed from policy proceeds for its premium outlays. The net cost to the employer for the plan is merely the loss of the net after-tax income the funds could have earned while the plan was in effect.

Income Taxation Issues

The income tax treatment of split-dollar life insurance arrangements will be determined under one of two sets of rules depending on who owns the policy. If the executive, or someone designated by the executive, owns the life insurance policy, then the loan taxation rules apply. If the employer owns the policy, the economic benefit rules apply.

If the executive owns the policy, the employer's premium payments are treated as below-market loans from the employer to the executive. Consequently, unless the executive is required to pay the employer market-rate interest on the loan, the executive will be taxed on the difference between market-rate interest and the actual interest charged.

If the employer is the owner of the policy, the employer's premium payments are treated as providing taxable economic benefits to the executive. The executive recognizes as taxable income the value of life insurance coverage, as well as any increase in equity currently accessible to the executive. By taxing the executive on the increase in equity each year, this arrangement is discouraged.

Death Benefit - Transfer for Value
Death benefits payable from a split-dollar life insurance plan including both the employer's share and the employee/beneficiary's share are generally received income tax-free. However, the tax-free nature of the death proceeds is lost if the policy has been transferred for value. The transfer of an insurance policy is exempt from the transfer for value rules and will not cause the loss of the death proceeds' tax-free nature if the transfer is one of the statutorily defined exceptions. Examples of exceptions to the transfer-for-value rule are:
- A transfer of the policy to the insured.
- A transfer to a partner of the insured or to a partnership of which the insured is a partner.
- A transfer to a corporation of which the insured is a shareholder or officer.
- A transfer in which the transferee's basis is determined, in whole or in part, by reference to the transferor's basis (e.g., a substituted or carryover basis).

QUICK QUIZ 14.9

1. The premiums paid for a cross purchase life insurance policy are deductible by the payor.
   a. True
   b. False

2. An entity must include in income any benefits received from a business overhead disability plan.
   a. True
   b. False

3. Key person insurance premiums are not deductible by the employer until the death benefit is paid.
   a. True
   b. False

False, True, False.

Estate Consequences of Split-Dollar Life Insurance

Incidents of ownership will cause inclusion in the gross estate if the decedent retained the ownership or had the right to name or change the beneficiary. Inclusion in the gross estate could result from a policy transferred or assigned with the three year period prior to the insured/owner's death.

KEY PERSON LIFE AND DISABILITY INSURANCE

Key person life and disability insurance covers employees who are considered critical to the success of a business; and whose death or disability might cause financial loss to the company. The company has an insurable interest in the person. Therefore, the company pays the premiums and is the beneficiary of the insurance policy. The premiums are not deductible, and the benefits are not taxable.

KEY TERMS

ANY OCCUPATION - Type of disability insurance policy that provides benefits to a policy owner if he is unable to perform the duties of any occupation.

ARCHER MEDICAL SAVINGS ACCOUNT (MSA) - A medical savings account available for employers with 50 or less employees and self-employed individuals (must have been established by 12/31/05). The account allows participants to make pretax contributions (subject to limitations) to the account and benefit from tax-free earnings provided they are covered under a high deductible health insurance policy. Further, if the funds are utilized for qualified medical expenses, the distributions from the plan will not be taxable.

BUY-SELL AGREEMENTS - Legal arrangements that require the sale of securities owned by one individual to another individual or entity upon a specified triggering event.

CAFETERIA PLAN - A written plan where the employee may choose to receive cash as compensation or, alternatively, the employee may choose from among a range of tax-free fringe benefits.

COMBINED OMNIBUS BUDGET RECONCILIATION ACT OF 1986 (COBRA) - Requires an employer that employes 20 or more people in a typical business day and has a health insurance plan to continue to provide health insurance coverage under that health insurance plan to covered employees and qualified dependants following the occurrence of a statutorily defined qualifying event.

CROSS PURCHASE BUY-SELL AGREEMENT - A partner or shareholder purchases a sufficient amount of life insurance on the lives of each other partner or shareholder to assure sufficient liquidity to buyout a deceased partner or shareholder's interest.

DISABILITY INSURANCE - Insurance that provides benefits in the form of periodic payments for a person who is unable to work due to sickness or accidental injury.

DISABILITY OVERHEAD INSURANCE - Insurance that is designed to cover the expenses that are usual and necessary expenses in the operation of a business should the insured owner or key employee become disabled.

ENTITY PURCHASE AGREEMENT - Insurance in which the entity purchases a life insurance policy on the life of each partner or shareholder that is used for buyouts triggered by death of a shareholder or partner.

FLEXIBLE SPENDING ACCOUNT (FSA) - A cafeteria plan under which employees can choose between receiving cash or deferring income tax-free to fund the cost of certain employee selected benefits. If the participant does not utilize the money in the account by the end of the year, the participant forfeits the deferred funds.

FEDERAL UNEMPLOYMENT TAX ACT (FUTA) - A tax on an employee's wages.

KEY TERMS

GROUP LONG-TERM DISABILITY POLICIES - Benefits typically begin after short-term disability and will often continue for a fixed period of time, until retirement or for life.

GROUP SHORT-TERM DISABILITY POLICIES - Benefits generally begin after a short period of time, often corresponding to the employer's sick leave.

GROUP TERM LIFE INSURANCE - Pure insurance protection purchased as a group that pays a predetermined sum if the insured dies during a specified period of time (i.e., the term, which may be 1, 5, 10, 20 years or longer). The value of the premiums, up to $50,000 of death benefit coverage, provided by an employer may be excluded from an employee's gross income.

HEALTH MAINTENANCE ORGANIZATIONS (HMOs) - A form of managed care in which participants receive all of their care from participating providers. Physicians are employed by the HMO directly, or may be physicians in private practice who have chosen to participate in the HMO network. The independent physicians are paid a fixed amount for each HMO member that uses them as a primary care physician.

HEALTH REIMBURSEMENT ARRANGEMENT (HRA) - A type of health insurance plan that reimburses employees for qualified medical expenses.

HEALTH SAVINGS ACCOUNTS (HSAs) - A medical savings account, similar to an MSA but less restrictive, that allows anyone with a high deductible health insurance plan to make pretax contributions (subject to limitations). The earnings within the account and the value of the contributions will not be taxed to the extent they are used to pay for qualifying medical expenses.

INDEMNITY HEALTH INSURANCE - Traditional, fee-for-service health insurance that does not limit where a covered individual can get care.

KEY EMPLOYEE - Any employee who is any one or more of the following: a greater than five percent owner, or greater than one percent owner with compensation in excess of $150,000 (not indexed), or an officer with compensation in excess of $170,000 for 2016 as determined last year.

KEY PERSON LIFE AND DISABILITY INSURANCE - Life insurance coverage for employees who are considered critical to the success of a business and whose death might cause financial loss to the company.

MANAGED CARE INSURANCE - Health-care delivery systems that integrate the financing and delivery of health care. Managed care plans feature a network of physicians, hospitals, and other providers who participate in the plan. Managed care includes HMOs, PPOs, and POS plans.

OWN OCCUPATION - Type of disability policy which states that if the insured is unable to perform the duties associated with his own occupation, the insured is deemed to be disabled and the policy will provide benefits.

KEY TERMS

POINT OF SERVICE PLAN (POS) - A form of managed care that is considered a managed care/indemnity plan hybrid, as it mixes aspects of HMOs, PPOs, and indemnity plans for greater patient choice. A primary care physician coordinates patient care, but there is more flexibility in choosing doctors and hospitals than in an HMO.

PREFERRED PROVIDER ORGANIZATION - A form of managed care in which participants have more flexibility in choosing physicians and other providers than in an HMO. The arrangement between insurance companies and health care providers permits participants to obtain discounted health care services from the preferred providers within the network.

PRIMARY CARE PHYSICIAN - A physician that is designated as a participant's first point of contact with the health care system, particularly in managed care plans.

SALARY CONTINUATION PLAN - An arrangement between an employer and an employee where the employer agrees to continue to pay an employee after his retirement or to the employee's spouse if the employee dies prior to retirement.

SELF-INSURED PLAN - A plan that reimburses employees for medical expenses not covered by an accident or health insurance policy.

SPLIT DEFINITION - Type of disability policy where an insured is covered against the risk of not performing his own occupation for a period of time, and after that period expires, an any-occupation definition of disability is used.

SPLIT-DOLLAR LIFE INSURANCE ARRANGEMENT - A single life insurance policy in which two parties, employer and employee, have an ownership interest. The two parties generally split ownership, premiums, and beneficiaries any way they wish.

VOLUNTARY EMPLOYEES' BENEFICIARY ASSOCIATION (VEBA) - A welfare benefit plan into which employers deposit funds that will be used to provide specified employee benefits in the future. The deposits are deductible for the employer at the date of the contribution rather than at the date when the employee benefits are provided.

DISCUSSION QUESTIONS

1. Discuss the tax implications of employer-provided group medical plans.

2. Describe COBRA and discuss the tax implications of employer-paid premiums.

3. Describe the requirements for a life insurance policy to be considered group term life insurance.

4. Discuss the tax implications of employer-provided group term life insurance.

5. Discuss the tax implications of employer-provided group disability insurance.

6. Describe cafeteria plans and discuss how are they used to provide employer benefits.

7. Discuss the tax implications of employer-provided cafeteria plans.

8. Describe flexible spending accounts (FSAs). Discuss the tax implications of employer provided Flexible Spending Accounts.

9. Discuss the tax implications of employer provided Archer MSAs, and when they can be established.

10. Describe VEBA's and discuss the tax implications of payments made by the employer.

11. Discuss the tax implications of employer-provided salary continuation plans.

12. Discuss the tax implications of employer-provided group long-term care insurance.

13. Discuss the tax implications of employer-provided group retirement planning services.

14. Describe buy-sell agreements and describe the income tax consequences associated with such plans.

15. Discuss the tax implications of business overhead disability plans.

16. Describe split-dollar life insurance and discuss the income tax consequences associated with such plans.

17. Describe key person insurance and discuss the income tax consequences associated with such plans.

MULTIPLE CHOICE PROBLEMS

1. Medical Trials Inc. has a cafeteria plan. Full-time employees are permitted to select any combination of the benefits listed below, but the total value received by each employee must be $6,500 a year or less.

    1. Group medical and hospitalization insurance for employee only, $3,600 a year.
    2. Group medical and hospitalization insurance for employee's spouse and dependents, $1,200 additional a year.
    3. Child-care payments, actual cost not to exceed $5,000.
    4. Cash required to bring the total of benefits and cash to $6,500.
    5. Universal variable life insurance $1,000.

    Which of the following statements is true? (All employees are full time)

    a. James chooses to receive $6,500 cash because his wife's employer provides medical benefits for him. James has $2,900 of taxable income ($6,500 - $3,600).
    b. Matt chooses 1, 2, 5, and $700 cash. He must include $700 in taxable income.
    c. Randy chooses 1 and 2 and $1,700 in child care. He must include the $1,700 in gross income.
    d. Robin chooses 1 and 2 and $1,700 cash. Robin must include $1,700 in taxable income.

2. Which of the following circumstances suggest the use of a cafeteria plan?

    1. A cafeteria plan is appropriate when the employee mix is comprised only of older employees with families who need maximum medical and life insurance benefits.
    2. A cafeteria plan is appropriate when employers want to choose the benefit package most suited to their employee's individual needs.
    3. A cafeteria plan is appropriate when an employer seeks to maximize employee satisfaction with the benefit package, thereby maximizing the employer's benefit from its compensation expenditures.
    4. A cafeteria plan is appropriate for a small employer who does not have much money to spend on benefits.

    a. 3 only.
    b. 4 only.
    c. 1, 2, and 4.
    d. 1, 2, 3, and 4.

3. Which of the following is/are advantages of cafeteria plans?

   1. Cafeteria plans help to give employees an appreciation of the value of their benefit package.
   2. The flexibility of a cafeteria benefit package helps to meet varied employee needs.
   3. Cafeteria plans can help control employer costs for the benefit package because the cost of benefits that employees do not need is minimized.
   4. Cafeteria plans are less complex and less expensive to design and administer than general group benefit plans.

   a. 2 only.
   b. 1 and 2.
   c. 1, 2, and 3.
   d. 1, 2, 3, and 4.

4. Jane is covered by a $90,000 group-term life insurance policy, her daughter is the sole beneficiary. Jane's employer pays the entire premium for the policy; the uniform annual premium is $0.60 per $1,000 per month of coverage. How much, if any, is W-2 taxable income to Jane resulting from the insurance?

   a. $0.
   b. $24.
   c. $288.
   d. $648.

5. What is the maximum number of employees that a company with a health plan can have and not be subject to the COBRA rules?

   a. 10.
   b. 15.
   c. 19.
   d. 20.

6. Which of the following premiums for health insurance provided by an employer is/are excludable from income tax by the employee?

   1. Premiums for the employee if currently employed.
   2. Premiums for the employee's spouse.
   3. Premiums for the employee's dependents other than a spouse.
   4. Premiums for the employee if retired.

   a. 1 only.
   b. 1 and 2.
   c. 1, 2, and 3.
   d. 1, 2, 3, and 4.

7. Employer-sponsored life insurance is usually referred to as group life insurance. Which type of life insurance (offered as group life) is beneficial to both the employer and the employee from a tax standpoint?

    a. Term life insurance.
    b. Ordinary life insurance.
    c. Universal life.
    d. Single premium whole life insurance.

8. Life insurance used to fund a three person partnership buy/sell agreement using a cross purchase technique:

    a. Will have the same number of policies as an entity plan.
    b. Will be paid for with tax-deductible dollars.
    c. Will require three policies.
    d. Will require six policies.

9. Split-dollar life insurance is:

    a. An insurance arrangement in which the employee pays the cost of the premium and the employee names the employer as the beneficiary.
    b. An insurance arrangement in which the employer and the employee share the cost of the life insurance on the employee and the portion of the premium that is paid by the employer is the value of the term life portion of the policy.
    c. An insurance arrangement in which the employee pays the majority of the premium while the employer names the beneficiary.
    d. An insurance arrangement in which the employer is the owner of the policy and is also the beneficiary to the extent of the premiums paid by the employer.

10. The beneficiary of key person life insurance is usually:

    a. The spouse of the employee.
    b. The employee's spouse and dependants.
    c. The company.
    d. The estate of the employee.

11. A business valued at $3,000,000 has 3 partners. Each of the 3 partners buys a $500,000 life insurance policy for purposes of a buy/sell agreement on each of the other partners. Which of the following is/are true?

    1.   This is an example of an entity purchase plan.

    2.   This is an example of a cross purchase plan.

    3.   The buy/sell agreement is under funded.

        a.   1 only.

        b.   2 only.

        c.   1 and 3.

        d.   2 and 3.

12. NOTCM partnership has 5 partners who have entered into a binding buy/sell agreement that requires any surviving partners to purchase the partnership interest of any partner to die. The partnership uses an entity approach to fund this arrangement. How many insurance policies are required to satisfy this arrangement?

        a.   1.

        b.   5.

        c.   10.

        d.   20.

13. Wallace and Associates is considering implementing a buy/sell agreement where each partner purchases a life insurance policy on each of the other partners. Which one of the following statements is correct given this information?

    a.   The partners are entering into an entity redemption agreement.

    b.   Upon the death of an owner, the life insurance proceeds will be used to buy out the decedent's share of the partnership. Those life insurance proceeds are taxable as ordinary income.

    c.   The amount of insurance per policy will equal the value of the partnership.

    d.   The partners are entering into a cross-purchase agreement.

14. HMO Inc. is paying the premium for long-term care policies for their 250 employees. How are these payments treated for federal income tax purposes?

    a.   Payments for group premiums for long-term care are tax deductible to the employer and not taxable income to the employee.

    b.   Payments for group premiums for long-term care are tax deductible to the employer but are taxable income to the employee based on the coverage schedule.

    c.   Payments for the group premiums for long-term care are not tax deductible to the employer and not taxable income to the employee.

    d.   Payments for the group premiums for long-term care are not tax deductible to the employer but are taxable income to the employee based on the coverage schedule.

QUICK QUIZ EXPLANATIONS

QUICK QUIZ 14.1
1. True.
2. False. Managed care plans emerged from a desire to decrease health care costs and increase completion amongst health care providers.

QUICK QUIZ 14.2
1. False. Health benefits provided to employees can be excluded from income. Employees who are also greater than two percent owners of S corporations must include the benefit into their income. However, they may be entitled to an above-the-line deduction for the amount paid to them.
2. True.

QUICK QUIZ 14.3
1. False. To be considered a group term life insurance policy, the employer must provide life insurance benefits to at least 10 employees.
2. False. If an employer provides a group term policy with a benefit over $50,000, then the employee must include in income an amount determined by multiplying the number of thousands of dollars of insurance coverage over $50,000 (rounded to the nearest $1,000) by the cost shown in the Uniform Premium Table provided by the IRS.

QUICK QUIZ 14.4
1. False. When the employer pays the premium and the premium value is excluded from the employee's gross income, any disability income benefit received by the employee is taxable to the employee.
2. True.

QUICK QUIZ 14.5
1. True.
2. False. Salary reductions elected by employees to fund nontaxable benefits available under the plan are not subject to income taxes or payroll taxes.

QUICK QUIZ 14.6
1. False. An MSA cannot be established after 2005.
2. False. Distributions from an HSA that are not used for medical expenses are taxed as ordinary income and subject to a 20 percent penalty if the owner of the HSA has not reached age 65.
3. True.

QUICK QUIZ EXPLANATIONS

QUICK QUIZ 14.7
1. True.
2. False. Long-term care premiums cannot be paid for within a cafeteria plan or flexible spending account nor can the premium payment be made with pretax employee salary deferral.
3. False. An employer may exclude from an employee's gross income the value of any retirement planning advice or information the employer provides to the employee or his spouse if the employer maintains a qualified retirement plan.

QUICK QUIZ 14.8
1. True.
2. False. An entity approach buys one policy per owner, therefore 5 policies not 20.
3. True.

QUICK QUIZ 14.9
1. False. The premiums for a cross-purchase life insurance policy are not deductible.
2. True.
3. False. Key person insurance premiums are not deductible, and the benefits of such a policy are not taxable.

ITEM SETS AND THE MIKE & MARIA ROMAN CASE

ITEM SET 1: RETIREMENT PLAN DISTRIBUTIONS

Chad Boudreaux is a 58-year old riverboat captain. He grew up in New Orleans and has worked on the Mississippi River his entire life. He works for a private company in New Orleans called Crescent River Pilots Inc. (CRP) and is married to Patricia, who is 35 years old. They have a seven-year-old son, named River. CRP sponsors a 401(k) plan that offers a Roth account and a separate ESOP. Chad has the following retirement plan accounts:

Account Description	Current FMV	Beneficiary
ESOP account from CRP - consists of CRP shares. The cost basis for the shares is $75,000.	$400,000	Patricia
401(k) Plan From CRP Inc.	$800,000	Patricia
401(k) Plan from Schlumberger, where he worked in his thirties	$90,000	Patricia
Roth IRA (established in 2000 with a $2,000 initial contribution; three years ago he rolled over a traditional IRA with a balance of $10,000	$45,000	Patricia
Traditional IRA (established twenty years ago with $15,000 of after-tax contributions)	$90,000	River
Inherited IRA from the death of his Mama. She died in the same year Chad turned 50 years old.	$120,000	River

1. Chad plans on retiring in March of this year, and he and his wife would like to go to Rome for an extended vacation. He wants to take a distribution of $20,000 from one of his retirement accounts to pay for the vacation. Which of his retirement plans would allow him to take a penalty-free withdrawal to fund his vacation?

Answer:

_____

_____

_____

_____

_____

_____

_____

_____

2. Can Chad change the beneficiary designations on his IRAs without spousal consent?

Answer:

_____

_____

_____

_____

_____

_____

_____

_____

3. Can Chad change the beneficiary designations on his non-IRA retirement plans without spousal consent?

Answer:

_____

_____

_____

_____

_____

_____

_____

_____

4.   If the balance in Chad's Mom's IRA was $120,000 at the end of last year and $140,000 at the end of this year, how much, if any, must he take out from this account to satisfy the minimum distribution rules?

Answer:

_____

_____

_____

_____

_____

_____

_____

_____

5.   If Chad were to die and River was to inherit the inherited IRA, how would he comply with the minimum distribution rules?

Answer:

_____

_____

_____

_____

_____

_____

_____

_____

6. Assuming Chad decided to take out the entire balance in the Roth IRA to purchase a new fishing boat, how would the distribution be taxed?

Answer:

_____

_____

_____

_____

_____

_____

_____

_____

7. If Chad took a $20,000 distribution from his traditional IRA to pay for the vacation, what are the tax implications?

Answer:

_____

_____

_____

_____

_____

_____

_____

_____

8. If Chad retires, what should he do with the CRP shares and why?

Answer:

_____

_____

_____

_____

_____

_____

_____

_____

9. If Chad were to die, what options would Patricia have for satisfying the minimum distribution rules on the Roth IRA account?

Answer:

_____

_____

_____

_____

_____

_____

_____

_____

ITEM SET 2: REQUIRED MINIMUM DISTRIBUTIONS (RMDs)

Mit, who turned age 70½ on June 10th of Year 2, owns 32% of Big Company and is its current CEO. He has amassed $15 million in his qualified plan account as of December 31st of Year 1 and $17 million as of December 31st of Year 2. He has named his grandson Colin (age 9 at the end of Year 2) as his beneficiary.

1. What is the minimum distribution that Mit must receive for Year 2?

Answer:

_____

_____

_____

_____

_____

_____

_____

_____

2. If he only receives a distribution of $200,000 during the current year, then how much in penalties will he be required to pay for Year 2?

Answer:

_____

_____

_____

_____

_____

_____

_____

_____

_____

3. Assume that the market crashes in Year 3 and the value of the qualified plan drops to $1 million. As a result of the market drop, Mit dies in September of Year 3 and Colin inherits the IRA. If the value of the IRA is $1 million at the end of Year 3, $1.2 million at the end of Year 4, and $1.5 million at the end of Year 5, how much, if any, must Colin take out to satisfy the minimum distributions in Years 3, 4, and 5?

Answer:

_____

_____

_____

_____

_____

_____

_____

_____

4. Can Mit delay taking minimum distributions from his Big Company Plan since he is still employed? Explain why or why not.

Answer:

_____

_____

_____

_____

_____

_____

_____

_____

_____

ITEM SET 3: ISOs AND NQSOs

Nick Icamina is the CEO of Chaos Baseball Equipment, Inc. (Chaos). It is a rapidly growing publicly traded company. He was awarded the following stock options from his company:

Option Grant	Grant Date	Type	Exercise Price	# Shares
A	February 1, Year 1	ISO	$20	100
B	July 1, Year 2	NQSO	$25	100
C	August 1, Year 3	ISO	$30	100
D	May 1, Year 4	NQSO	$30	100

During Year 5, Nick had the following transactions regarding the above stock options:

Option Grant	Date	Action	# Shares	Market Price on Action Date
A	February 1	Exercised	100	$42
A	February 1	Sold	100	$42
B	February 14	Exercised	100	$45
C	February 14	Exercised	100	$45
D	May 1	Exercised	100	$50
D	June 1	Sold	100	$60

1.   What are the tax implications for the A options during Year 5?

Answer:

_____

_____

_____

_____

_____

_____

_____

_____

_____

_____

2.   What are the tax implications for the B options during Year 5?

Answer:

_____

_____

_____

_____

_____

_____

_____

_____

3.   What are the tax implications for the C options during Year 5?

Answer:

_____

_____

_____

_____

_____

_____

_____

_____

4.   What are the tax implications for the D options during Year 5?

Answer:

_____

_____

_____

_____

_____

_____

_____

_____

_____

ITEM SET 4: QUALIFIED PLAN RULES

Bubbles LLC is a web design company that operates out of Boulder, Colorado. Mark and Jeff started Bubbles twenty years ago and it has grown to be one of the more sizable web development firms in Colorado. Bubbles offers a 401(k) /profit sharing plan with a Roth account option. The plan has the following characteristics:

- Eligibility: age 21 and one-year of service
- Match: dollar for dollar match
- Vesting: 20% per year (years 1 through 5)
- Highly compensated definition: uses top 20% election
- Profit-sharing contribution: Bubbles generally makes a sizeable contribution, but the percentage varies.
- The plan has been amended to permit in-plan Roth rollovers.
- The plan permits rollovers from other qualified plans and IRAs.

EE#	Employee	Ownership	Age	Tenure	Salary	Deferral
1	Mark	60%	48	20 Years	$200,000	$10,000
2	Jeff	30%	49	20 Years	$150,000	$15,000
3	Chad	6%	33	15 Years	$75,000	$5,250
4	Josh	4%	42	10 Years	$85,000	$5,100
5	Alex	0%	58	8 Years	$60,000	$0
6	Shay	0%	29	6 Years	$75,000	$4,500
7	Lisa	0%	53	4 Years	$50,000	$0
8	Alison	0%	19	2 Years	$60,000	$0
9	Chung	0%	25	8 Months	$24,000	$0
10	Chau	0%	19	6 Months	$18,000	$0

Note: Shay is Jeff's daughter. She graduated from the art institute five years ago.

1. Who is not eligible for the 401(k) plan?

Answer:

_____

_____

_____

_____

_____

_____

_____

_____

_____

2.   Who is highly compensated?

Answer:

_____

_____

_____

_____

_____

_____

_____

3.   What is the most that Bubbles could contribute to the profit-sharing plan for the current year assuming the salary deferrals stay constant?

Answer:

_____

_____

_____

_____

_____

_____

_____

_____

4.   What is the actual deferral percentage for the highly compensated employees?

Answer:

_____

_____

_____

_____

_____

_____

_____

_____

5.   What is the actual deferral percentage for the non-highly compensated employees?

Answer:

_____

_____

_____

_____

_____

_____

_____

_____

6. Does the plan pass the ADP test? Why or why not and what can the company do if the plan does not pass the test?

Answer:

_____

_____

_____

_____

_____

_____

_____

_____

_____

7. Assume the company decided to make a profit-sharing contribution that was integrated with Social Security, with an integration level equal to the Social Security wage base. If the base percentage was 9% with a maximum excess percentage, how much would be contributed to the plan on behalf of Mark (disregard the salary deferral)?

Answer:

_____

_____

_____

_____

_____

_____

_____

_____

8. How many years of service does Alison currently have for purposes of vesting?

Answer:

_____

_____

_____

_____

_____

_____

_____

_____

ITEM SET 5: 403(b) PLANS

Roger Rogers, 46, works for the local public school teaching Physics to advanced science high school students. Roger has been with the school for 21 years, earns $65,000 per year, and has never contributed to the 403(b) retirement plan that is offered. The 403(b) plan offers dollar for dollar matching on all contributions. The school district is considering adopting a 457 plan.

1.   Which plan will offer Roger the highest tax deferral in 2016?

Answer:

_____

_____

_____

_____

_____

_____

_____

_____

_____

2.   If Roger's wife makes enough money for them to live on and they decide to save as much of his income as possible, how much is the maximum that he can defer in tax-deferred retirement savings vehicles assuming the school adopts the 457 plan?

Answer:

_____

_____

_____

_____

_____

_____

_____

_____

_____

3. What type of investments is Roger permitted to make in the 403(b) plan?

Answer:

_____

_____

_____

_____

_____

_____

_____

_____

4. What type of employers may adopt a 403(b) plan?

Answer:

_____

_____

_____

_____

_____

_____

_____

_____

_____

5. What types of employees benefit the most from the implementation of a 403(b) plan?

Answer:

_____

_____

_____

_____

_____

_____

_____

_____

_____

ITEM SET 6: SIMPLE IRAs

Paul's Paint -N- Plumbing, Inc. (3P) has been in business since for 33 years. Paul is retiring and passing the business on to his two children in equal shares to manage and operate according to their skills and experience. The children, Paula and Prescott, decide to adopt a retirement plan for both current and future employees in an attempt to attract and retain talent. They have decided to adopt a SIMPLE IRA, funded by both employee and employer contributions.

1. What are the advantages and disadvantages of offering a SIMPLE IRA over a qualified plan, such as a 401(k) plan?

Answer:

_____

_____

_____

_____

_____

_____

_____

_____

2. If Philip (age 55), a long-time employee of 3P, wants to contribute both to the SIMPLE IRA at work and to a traditional IRA, what are the limits on his contributions and deductibility regarding the traditional IRA?

Answer:

_____

_____

_____

_____

_____

_____

_____

_____

_____

3. What are the annual dollar limits for contributing to a SIMPLE IRA and Traditional IRA? Also what are the phase-out levels for making these contributions, including spousal IRA contributions?

Answer:

_____

_____

_____

_____

_____

_____

_____

4. Pete has been with 3P for a year and a half. He has deferred some of his compensation and has received a company match in the SIMPLE. Pete's daughter is about to attend college, however, he has not saved any money for her education. What are the tax implications if Pete takes a distribution from his SIMPLE IRA with 3P to pay for her college education expenses?

Answer:

_____

_____

_____

_____

_____

_____

_____

_____

ITEM SET 7: SEPs

Robert "Bubba" Boudreaux, 32, owns and operates a po'boy shop in New Orleans, called Ya Mama's Po Boys. It is a family business that sells authentic New Orleans fare, just like "ya mama would serve," assuming she was from New Orleans. Bubba wants to establish a retirement plan so he can save for his retirement and the retirement of his employees on a tax-deferred basis. He has recruited you to assist in making a plan selection.

Bubba only wants to contribute in years that he makes a profit and does not want to incur much if anything on administrative expenses. Since the employees of Ya Mama's are all family members, Bubba is happy to contribute on behalf of the employees when the restaurant is doing well.

1.   Based on Bubba's objectives, what type of retirement plan is most suited for his needs?

Answer:

_____

_____

_____

_____

_____

_____

_____

_____

_____

2.   Why might you recommend that Bubba utilize a qualified profit sharing plan with a CODA in lieu of the suggestion in question 1? (If you suggested a profit sharing plan with a CODA for question 1, reconsider.)

Answer:

_____

_____

_____

_____

_____

_____

_____

_____

_____

3. Bubba employs the following individuals. Which employees may he exclude if the plan was a SIMPLE, SEP, or 401(k) profit-sharing plan?

Name	Age	Years of Service	Full-Time / Part-Time (< 1,000 hours)	Annual Income
Bubba	32	13	Full-Time	$160,000
Mama	49	4	Full-Time	$35,000
Trey	22	2	Full-Time	$32,000
Chad	28	4	Part-Time	$26,000
Rice	18	1	Part-Time	$12,000

Answer:

ITEM SET 8: REQUIRED MINIMUM DISTRIBUTIONS (RMDs)

Mary and Larry have been married for 40 years and have three children together. They are currently semi-retired and enjoying life at the beach in Florida. Mary turned 70 on February 14th Year 2 and Larry turned 70 on October 15th Year 2. Mary is fully retired as a lingerie model from Burl's Boutique, which marketed to older customers. Larry still works part-time for a company that rents sailboats and provides sailing guides for customers renting boats. The company, called Set Sail, sponsors a 401(k) plan, in which Larry continues to make contributions. Larry gave up his corporate job at IBM several years ago and plans to continue working at Set Sail because he loves it.

Larry's rich uncle Juan died earlier during Year 2 and left his Roth IRA to Larry. Larry is sad about Juan, but happy about the IRA and even happier that it is a Roth IRA. Juan started the Roth IRA over ten years ago.

They need to know whether they need to take minimum distributions and if so, how much and from what accounts. The balances in the accounts are shown below.

Plan Owner	Plan #	Account /Plan Type	December 31 Year 1 Balance	December 31 Year 2 Balance	December 31 Year 3 Balance
Mary	1	Self Directed IRA	$22,000	$23,500	$20,500
Mary	2	Self Directed Roth IRA	$58,000	$67,000	$68,000
Mary	3	Self Directed IRA	$45,000	$51,300	$50,300
Mary	4	Burl's MPPP	$270,000	$267,000	$260,000
Larry	5	Inherited Roth IRA	$180,000	$200,000	$220,000
Larry	6	Self Directed IRA	$17,000	$18,000	$20,000
Larry	7	IBM 401(k) Roth Account	$40,000	$41,500	$49,000
Larry	8	IBM MPPP	$600,000	$650,000	$700,000
Larry	9	Set Sail 401(k) Roth Account	$80,000	$89,000	$92,000

1. What is the required beginning date (RBD) for Mary and Larry?

Answer:

_____

_____

_____

_____

_____

_____

_____

_____

_____

2.   What is the factor for Mary and for Larry's first required minimum distribution (RMD)?

Answer:

_____

_____

_____

_____

_____

_____

_____

_____

3.   Which plans must they take a distribution from during Year 3 (without regard to the ability to delay a distribution)?

Answer:

_____

_____

_____

_____

_____

_____

_____

_____

_____

4.   What is the total amount of Larry's RMD for Year 3?

Answer:

_____

_____

_____

_____

_____

_____

_____

_____

5.   What is the minimum number of RMDs Mary has to take each year?

Answer:

_____

_____

_____

_____

_____

_____

_____

_____

6.   If Mary delays her first RMD to April 1st of Year 3, how much is the total amount of her RMDs for next year?

Answer:

_____

_____

_____

_____

_____

_____

_____

_____

7.   How is the life expectancy factor for the inherited Roth IRA determined for the second year compared to the life expectancy factor for Larry's other accounts?

Answer:

_____

_____

_____

_____

_____

_____

_____

_____

_____

ITEM SET 9: 401(k) PLANS

Kryptonite is a telecommunications provider located in Iowa with hundreds of thousands of employees. Their CEO, Clark Kline, is considering the replacement of their expensive defined benefit (DB) pension plan with a 401(k) where the employees will bear the investment risk. The majority of the workforce is young and the top executives are all in their 50's and 60's.

1. As Clark's top financial advisor, what type of qualified retirement plan would you recommend instead of the 401(k) if he wants the majority of the benefits to accrue to the top executives?

Answer:

_____

_____

_____

_____

_____

_____

_____

_____

2. An intern who works for you recommends utilizing a DB/K plan. What is your opinion of using such a plan in this case?

Answer:

_____

_____

_____

_____

_____

_____

_____

_____

3. Who would benefit the most from the change away from the DB plan to a 401(k)?

Answer:

_____

_____

_____

_____

_____

_____

_____

_____

4. What is the maximum contribution to a 401(k) of a worker age 56, who earns $20,000 per year as a factory worker with Kryptonite?

Answer:

_____

_____

_____

_____

_____

_____

_____

_____

_____

_____

5. Lois Kent has been with Kryptonite for 10 years but is nervous now that Clark has taken over operations. She wants to know her options regarding taking money out of the 401(k) at a later date. You correctly tell her that she can access her 401(k) funds without penalty under what 7 circumstances?

Answer:

_____

_____

_____

_____

_____

_____

_____

_____

6. Clark has heard that the ADP testing is an issue for 401(k) plans. What are three ways to minimize this issue?

Answer:

_____

_____

_____

_____

_____

_____

_____

_____

_____

_____

ITEM SET 10: MEDICARE

Gaye Davis is a 68-year old individual who retired from Yosimiti Corporation last year. Yosimiti is a multi-national corporation employing over 10,000 employees. She worked for the company for over 20 years, and was fully insured for purposes of Social Security retirement benefits, which she began receiving at age 63. At age 65, her Medicare Part A coverage began, and she opted to receive Medicare Part B coverage. Gaye has come to you with the following questions regarding her Medicare coverage.

1. What types of costs are covered under Medicare Part A?

Answer:

_____

_____

_____

_____

_____

_____

_____

_____

2. What types of costs are covered under Medicare Part B?

Answer:

_____

_____

_____

_____

_____

_____

_____

_____

_____

3. Assume that Gaye suffered a severe fall and spent 100 days in the hospital. How much would she have to pay under Medicare for 2016?

Answer:

_____

_____

_____

_____

_____

_____

_____

_____

CASE EXAMPLE

MIKE & MARIA ROMAN CASE

MIKE AND MARIA ROMAN

Mike and Maria have come to you, a financial planner, for help in developing a plan to accomplish their financial goals. From your initial meeting together, you have gathered the following information.

PERSONAL BACKGROUND AND INFORMATION COLLECTED

THE FAMILY

Mike and Maria Roman live in the country and operate a baseball academy on their property. They have a quaint home with a baseball field to the left of their house and two covered baseball batting and pitching cages. Mike played professional baseball for 15 years and now provides baseball instruction through RBI to children ages six to the early twenties. Mike currently coaches several college baseball players and is one of the most respected hitting and pitching coaches in the area. He also coaches a 9-year old team and a 14-year old team, both competing at the major division level. Maria has the tireless job of scheduling all of the lessons.

Mike and Maria Roman

Mike is 44 years old and loves his job. He is also an avid hunter and fisherman. Maria is also 44 years old and has done a wonderful job of raising their two kids, while helping with the family business.

The Children

Emily is 20 years old and is a Junior at Florida State University where she is double majoring in anthropology and communications. She has always been an excellent student and has a full academic scholarship. She also works part time to earn additional spending money. Her brother, Michael, is 17 years old and is a junior at Mission High School, where he plays shortstop on the baseball team and is hitting over 300 for the year.

Roman's Baseball Institute (RBI)

Mike started RBI seven years ago after he left professional baseball. He has built his reputation, as well as that of RBI over that time period. RBI is one of the premier baseball academies in the area.

The primary source of income for RBI is fees from baseball lessons. Lessons are priced at $70 per hour. Mike has three other coaches who help him provide lessons (Mickey, Mr. Joe, and Joey). His dad, Mickey, who is now retired from the Post Office, taught him how to play baseball, coached him growing up, and works with him now that he is retired. Mr. Joe also coached Mike as a child and now coaches for Mike. Joey is 20 years old, played baseball for Mike growing up and played in college during his freshman year before getting injured.

RBI generates $245,000 in gross annual revenue and has the following expenses:

Coaching fees to his coaches	$60,000
Utilities	$2,500
Field Maintenance	$7,000
Equipment (balls, etc.)	$1,000
Other Expenses	$3,000

Mike works 1,500 hours and the other coaches total 2,000 hours. His three coaches work the following number of hours and are paid $30 per hour:

Mickey	1,100
Joey	500
Mr. Joe	400

Mike's coaches have worked with him for at least five years. Mike's net income equals the fees less the expenses listed above. He reports his revenue and expenses on Schedule C of his personal income tax return.

PERSONAL AND FINANCIAL OBJECTIVES FOR MIKE AND MARIA ROMAN

1. Provide for retirement. They would like to retire when Mike is age 60. They want to plan on $100,000 of retirement income in today's dollars. They expect to receive Social Security and Mike has a pension with Major League Baseball (MLB). They would like to plan on funding potential retirement expenditures until they turn age 95 and would like to maintain the same level of spending, even if Mike or Maria died early.
2. Provide for the cost of Michael's college education. They expect Michael to receive a partial baseball scholarship, but they plan on paying $15,000 per year for each of his five years for college.
3. Establish a retirement plan for the income he earns at RBI.

EXTERNAL INFORMATION

ECONOMIC INFORMATION
- Inflation is expected to be 3.0% annually.
- There is no state income tax.
- The yield curve is slightly upward sloping, but relatively flat.
- The historic and expected correlation between the equity markets in the modernized countries is relatively high. The correlation between these markets increase especially during economic crisis.
- They have a required rate of return of 9 percent.
- The economy is in a steady slow growth expansion phase with moderate unemployment.

BANK LENDING RATES

- 15-year mortgage rate is 5.0%.
- 30-year mortgage rate is 6.0%.
- Secured personal loan rate is 10.0%.

EDUCATION INFORMATION

- Mike and Maria believe strongly in education. They want Michael to attend a college for learning, as well as baseball. As mentioned, they expect to fund $15,000 per year for five years in today's dollars for Michael's education. Tuition has been increasing at a 7 percent rate, which is expected to continue indefinitely.

INTERNAL INFORMATION

INSURANCE INFORMATION

Life Insurance

	Policy A	Policy B
Insured	Mike	Maria
Face Amount	$150,000	$40,000
Type	Term	Term
Cash Value	$0	$0
Annual Premium	$156	$50
Who pays premium	Mike	Mike
Beneficiary	Maria	Mike
Policy Owner	Mike	Maria
Settlement options clause selected	None	None

Health Insurance

Mike and Maria are covered under the Major League Baseball policy. The plan includes a family deductible of $12,600 at a cost of $500 per month.

Long-Term Disability Insurance

- Neither Mike nor Maria are covered by any disability insurance.

Homeowners Insurance

- The Romans have a HO3 policy with endorsements for replacement value and open perils for personal property. The current dwelling coverage is 100% replacement value with an inflation rider.

Automobile Insurance
- Both of their cars are covered.

Type	PAP
Bodily Injury	$100,000/$300,000
Property Damage	$50,000
Medical Payments	$5,000 per person
Physical Damage	Actual Cash Value
Uninsured Motorist Bodily Injury	$100,000/$300,000
Uninsured Motorist Property Damage	$50,000
Comprehensive Deductible	$1,000
Collision Deductible	$1,000
Premium (annual)	$3,300

Personal Liability Insurance
- Neither Mike nor Maria have PLUP coverage.

INCOME TAX INFORMATION
The Romans filing status for their federal income tax return is married filing jointly.

RETIREMENT INFORMATION
Mike would like to retire at age 60 and quit working. Mike met the requirements for the MLB minimum pension of $34,000 per year, which is what he expects to receive. This pension begins at age 62 and the amount is fixed for life (both his and his spouse's life). It is not inflation adjusted from today or during retirement. Mike expects his Social Security benefits will equal $30,000 in today's dollars at full retirement age, which is age 67. Maria does not have 40 quarters of Social Security coverage.

GIFTS, ESTATES, TRUSTS, AND WILL INFORMATION
Neither Mike nor Maria have prepared a will or any other estate planning documents.

MICKEY ROMAN
Mickey is Mike's dad and is an "old school" baseball coach. He turned 70 on December 22nd last year. He has a pension payment from the USPS of $2,000 per month and he and his wife receives a monthly payment from Social Security of $2,200. He also has an IRA with a balance of $85,000 as of December 31st 2014. Since his wife will continue to receive Social Security and his pension in the event he dies, he has named his grandson Michael as the beneficiary of his IRA.

Mickey also has Exxon stock that was distributed from a qualified plan 30 years ago. The distribution was a lump-sum distribution in which the FMV of the stock from the plan was $100,000. Mickey deposited the stock in his brokerage account and included $20,000 in his taxable income in the year of the distribution, based on the Form 1099-R. Mickey still owns the stock, which is now worth $324,340 and is held in the same brokerage account. He is hoping to leave it to Mike when he dies.

FINANCIAL STATEMENTS

Statement of Income and Expenses

Statement of Income and Expenses Mike and Maria Roman Statement of Income and Expenses for 2015 and Expected (Approximate) For 2016		
CASH INFLOWS		**Totals**
Salaries		
RBI Gross Revenue	$245,000	
Total Cash Inflows		$245,000
CASH OUTFLOWS		
Taxes		
Federal Estimated Tax Payments	$40,000	
Property Tax Principal Residence & Land	$10,000	
		$50,000
Debt Payments		
Principal Residence	$22,547	
Auto Loan - Jeep	$3,488	
Auto Loan - Ram	$7,968	
Credit Card Payments	$13,000	
Total Debt Payments		$47,002
Living Expenses		
Utilities Principal Residence	$3,900	
Gasoline for Autos	$3,500	
Gifts	$1,000	
Entertainment	$1,750	
Vacations	$2,000	
Church Donations	$500	
Clothing	$2,000	
Auto Maintenance	$2,000	
Satellite TV	$2,000	
Food	$4,650	
Total Living Expenses		$23,300
RBI Expenses		
Fees Paid to the Three RBI Coaches	$60,000	
Utilities for Batting Cages	$2,500	
Baseball Field Maintenance	$7,000	
Baseball Equipment	$1,000	
Other Baseball Business Expenses	$3,000	
Total RBI Expenses		$73,500
Insurance Payments		
MLB Health Insurance Premium	$6,000	
HO Insurance Principal Residence	$3,000	
Auto Insurance Premiums	$3,300	
Life Insurance Premiums (Policy A &B)	$2,472	
Total Insurance Payments		$14,772
Total Cash Outflows		$208,574
NET DISCRETIONARY CASH FLOWS		$36,426

ASSETS[1]			LIABILITIES AND NET WORTH		
Cash and Cash Equivalents			**Liabilities[2]**		
Cash	$5,000		Home Mortgage[3]	$307,808	
Savings Account	$25,000		Credit Card Balance Visa[4]	$2,000	
Total Cash and Cash Equivalents		$30,000	Credit Card Balance MC	$1,200	
Investment Assets			Auto Loan - Mike[5]	$26,444	
Brokerage Account[6]	$70,000		Auto Loan - Maria[7]	$9,918	
Municipal Bond Portfolio[8]	$20,000		**Total Liabilities**		$344,170
Education Portfolio	$10,000				
IRA	$20,000				
Total Investment Assets		$120,000	**Total Net Worth**		$335,630
Personal Use Assets					
Personal Residence	$200,000				
Land for Home & Baseball Field	$200,000				
Jeep - Maria	$18,000				
Ram Truck - Mike	$35,000				
Furniture & Personal Property	$80,000				
Total Personal Use Assets		$533,500			
Total Assets		**$683,000**	**Total Liabilities & Net Worth**		**$683,000**

Statement of Financial Position
Mike and Maria Roman
Balance Sheet as of 1/1/2016

1. Assets are stated at fair market value.
2. Liabilities are stated at principal only as of January 1, 2016 (prior to January payments).
3. The home and land were financed with a $350,000 loan, seven years ago at 5 percent over 360 months.
4. They typically spend about $1,000 per month on each credit card, but the balances are higher after the holidays. They do not maintain these balances.
5. The Ram truck was financed with a loan of $30,000, six months ago at 3 percent over 48 months.
6. Mike's brokerage account is highly correlated to the market. In fact the account has a correlation with the market of about 99 percent. However, because Mike has some leveraged mutual funds in the account, the beta of the portfolio is approximately 20 percent greater than the market. Mike's brokerage account is a margin account, which has an initial margin of 50 percent and a maintenance margin of 35 percent.
7. The Jeep was financed with a loan of $13,000, 12 months ago at 3.5 percent over 48 months.
8. The municipal bond portfolio has a modified duration of 5 and a current YTM of 7 percent.

CASE ASSUMPTIONS

- Required return - use the required return as stated in the case.
- For retirement and other long-term goals, assume cash and cash equivalents are added to investment accounts for purposes of projections and asset allocation decisions.
- Assume Social Security benefits begin at age 67.

Appendix

A

GLOSSARY

A

ACTIVE PARTICIPANT - Individuals who participate in a qualified plan under IRC 401(a), a 403(b) plan, a government retirement plan, a SEP, or a SIMPLE. Participating means receiving a benefit under the plan.

ACTUAL CONTRIBUTION PERCENTAGE TEST (ACP) - A nondiscrimination test that limits the sum of employee after-tax contributions and employer matching contributions for the HC based on the sum of employee after-tax contributions and employer matching contributions for the NHC.

ACTUAL DEFERRAL PERCENTAGE TEST (ADP) - A nondiscrimination test that limits employee elective deferrals for the highly compensated employees (HC) based on the elective deferrals of non- highly compensated employees (NHC).

ACTUARY - An expert professional who makes quantitative calculations and assumptions about inflation, wage increases, life expectancy of the assumed retirees, investment returns on plan assets, mortality rates for retirees, and forfeitures resulting from termination in order to determine funding for a retirement plan.

ADEQUATE CONSIDERATION STANDARD - Fair market value determined in good faith.

ADJUSTED BASIS (AB) - The portion of a distribution that is not subject to income tax. Usually, the return of after-tax contributions or nondeductible contributions.

ADJUSTED GROSS INCOME (AGI) - A tax return amount that includes an individual's income less certain deductions, known as "above-the-line" deductions. AGI is calculated before subtracting the standard or itemized deductions and the personal and dependency exemptions. The calculated AGI affects the deductibility of traditional IRA contributions and the ability to make Roth IRA contributions.

ADOPTION ASSISTANCE PROGRAM - An employee-provided program that pays adoption expenses up to $13,400 in 2016. The employee is not taxed on the payments or reimbursements made on his behalf.

AGE-BASED PROFIT SHARING PLAN - A qualified profit sharing plan that uses a combination of age and compensation as the basis for allocating the contribution to a participant's account.

AIME (AVERAGE INDEXED MONTHLY EARNINGS) - A worker's highest 35 years of earnings adjusted for inflation and averaged on a monthly basis. AIME is used as the basis for the PIA calculation.

ALIMONY - Support payments from one ex-spouse to the other. Alimony received is considered earned income for purposes of making IRA contributions.

ANNUITY CONTRACTS - While the contracts are not specifically defined in the Internal Revenue Code, an annuity contract must be purchased for the employee from an insurance company and may give a fixed benefit or a variable benefit depending on the performance of the investment. Any contract or certificate that is transferable to a person other than a trustee is not an annuity contract.

ANNUITY METHOD - Determines how much a client needs to fund their retirement based on the assumption that the person will die exactly at the assumed life expectancy with a retirement account balance of zero.

ANTI-ALIENATION PROTECTION - An ERISA-afforded protection for qualified plans that prohibits any action that may cause a qualified plan's assets to be assigned, garnished, levied, or subjected to bankruptcy proceedings. Exceptions to the anti-alienation rule apply for tax levies and QDROs.

ANY OCCUPATION - Type of disability insurance policy that provides benefits to a policy owner if he is unable to perform the duties of any occupation.

ARCHER MEDICAL SAVINGS ACCOUNT (MSA) - A medical savings account available for employers with 50 or less employees and self-employed individuals (must have been established by 12/31/05). The account allows participants to make pretax contributions (subject to limitations) to the account and benefit from tax-free earnings provided they are covered under a high deductible health insurance policy. Further, if the funds are utilized for qualified medical expenses, the distributions from the plan will not be taxable.

AVERAGE BENEFITS PERCENTAGE TEST - One part of the average benefits coverage test that requires the average benefit percent of the nonhighly compensated employees to be at least 70 percent of the average benefit percentage of the highly compensated employees.

AVERAGE BENEFITS TEST - A qualified plan coverage test that determines whether the plan adequately benefits the nonhighly compensated employees by comparing the benefits received by the nonhighly compensated to the benefits of the highly compensated employees and also determines whether the employee classification is nondiscriminatory. The test consists of the Average Benefits Percentage Test and the Nondiscriminatory Classification Test.

B

BACK LOADING - A practice of delaying the accrual of benefits until late in someone's career so that if they were to leave the company they would forfeit all or a large portion of their benefits.

BENEFIT PERIODS - Begins on the first day an individual receives services as a patient in a hospital or skilled nursing facility and ends after 60 consecutive days without further skilled care.

BLACK SCHOLES METHOD - An option valuation model.

BUSINESS PREMISES OF THE EMPLOYER - The employee's place of employment.

BUY-SELL AGREEMENTS - Legal arrangements that require the sale of securities owned by one individual to another individual or entity upon a specified triggering event.

C

CAFETERIA PLAN - A written plan where the employee may choose to receive cash as compensation or, alternatively, the employee may choose from among a range of tax-free fringe benefits.

CAPITAL NEEDS ANALYSIS - The process of calculating the amount of investment capital needed at retirement to maintain the pre-retirement lifestyle and mitigate the impact of inflation during the retirement years.

CAPITAL PRESERVATION MODEL (CP) - A capital needs analysis method that assumes that at client's life expectancy, the client has exactly the same account balance as he did at the beginning of retirement.

CASH BALANCE PENSION PLAN - A defined benefit pension plan that shares many of the characteristics of defined contribution plans but provides specific defined benefits based on a mandatory contribution and earnings rate.

CASH OR DEFERRED ARRANGEMENT (CODA) - Permits an employee to defer a portion of his salary on a pretax basis to a qualified plan or receive the salary as current taxable income.

CASHLESS EXERCISE - An exercise of an option where the option holder does not utilize any cash.

CATCH-UP CONTRIBUTION - A contribution that allows those nearing retirement to increase their deferral contributions to improve their financial situation for retirement. An elective contribution for employees 50 and over that allows the employee to increase their elective deferral limit by up to $6,000 for 2016.

CENTS PER MILE RULE - To determine the value of the personal use of an employer-provided automobile, multiply the standard mileage rate (54 cents for 2016) by the total miles the employee drives the vehicle for personal purposes.

CLIFF VESTING SCHEDULE - A vesting schedule that provides the participant's full rights to the plan's assets immediately upon the passage of a certain number of years.

COMBINED OMNIBUS BUDGET RECONCILIATION ACT OF 1986 (COBRA) - Requires an employer that employees 20 or more people in a typical business day and has a health insurance plan to continue to provide health insurance coverage under that health insurance plan to covered employees and qualified dependants following the occurrence of a statutorily defined qualifying event.

COMMUTING RULE - To determine the value of the personal use of an employer-provided vehicle, multiply each one-way commute from the employee's home to work or from work to home by $1.50.

CONDUIT IRAS - Accounts that hold rollover funds are often referred to as IRA rollover accounts.

CONSTRUCTIVE RECEIPT - An income tax concept that establishes when income is includible by a taxpayer and therefore subject to income tax. Income is constructively received in the taxable year during which it is credited to the employee's account, set apart for him, or otherwise made available so that he may draw upon it at any time or so that he could have drawn upon it during the taxable year if notice of intention to withdraw had been given.

CONTRIBUTIONS - Payments to an IRA.

CONVERSION - When a traditional IRA is converted to a Roth IRA. At the date of conversion, an individual includes the fair market value of the traditional IRA into his adjusted gross income.

CORRECTIVE DISTRIBUTION - A distribution to satisfy the ADP or ACP test that reduces the elective deferrals or contributions of the HC employees by distributing or returning the funds to the HC employees.

COST OF LIVING ADJUSTMENT (COLA) - The cost-of-living adjustments applied to Social Security benefits.

COVERED COMPENSATION LIMIT - The maximum employee compensation that may be considered for contributions to qualified plans or the accrual of benefits to a qualified plan. For 2016, the covered compensation limit is $265,000.

COVERED EMPLOYEE - An employee who benefits from a qualified plan during the year.

CREDIT FOR PRIOR SERVICE - To give employees credit for years of service (with the plan sponsor) prior to the establishment of the qualified plan.

CROSS PURCHASE LIFE INSURANCE - A partner or shareholder purchases a sufficient amount of life insurance on the lives of each other partner or shareholder to assure sufficient liquidity to buyout a deceased partner or shareholder's interest.

CURRENTLY INSURED WORKERS - A worker who has earned at least six quarters of coverage out of the previous 13 quarters for Social Security.

CUSTODIAL ACCOUNTS - Accounts generally maintained by a bank or other financial institution for the benefit of participants.

CUSTODIANS - Brokerage company, bank, or mutual fund company that holds an individual's IRA.

D

DB(k) RETIREMENT PLAN - For plan years beginning in 2010 and later, a DB(k) retirement plan incorporates, under one single plan with a single trust, a defined benefit plan combined with a 401(k) arrangement.

DEFERRED COMPENSATION ARRANGEMENTS - An arrangement to pay an executive compensation in a future year.

DEFINED BENEFIT PLAN - A qualified retirement plan that provides its participants with pre-determined formula-based benefits at retirement.

DEFINED CONTRIBUTION PLAN - A qualified retirement plan that provides its participants with either a contributory or noncontributory retirement account which benefits from tax-deferred growth for contributions and earnings in the plan.

"DE MINIMIS" FRINGE BENEFIT - A benefit of any property or service provided by an employer to an employee that is so small in value that it makes accounting for it unreasonable or administratively impracticable when taking into account the frequency with which similar fringes are provided by the employer to all employees.

DEPARTMENT OF LABOR - Governmental department charged with enforcing the rules governing the conduct of plan managers, investment of plan assets, reporting and disclosure of plan information, enforcement of the fiduciary provisions of the law, and workers' benefit rights as regulated by ERISA.

DEPENDENT CARE ASSISTANCE - Assistance that applies to household and dependent care services paid for or provided by the employer to an employee under a dependent care assistance program covering employees. The employee is not taxed on the value of the program or service paid on his behalf under the program (up to $5,000 per year).

DETERMINATION LETTER - A request filed with the IRS requesting a determination on a particular topic. In the case of a retirement plan, they are used when a plan is adopted, amended, or terminated to assure the plan sponsor that the qualified plan complies with applicable provisions.

DILUTION - The reduction in the monetary value or voting power of an owner's stock as a result of contributions to stock bonus plans and ESOPs.

DIRECT ROLLOVER - Occurs when the plan trustee distributes the account balance directly to the trustee of the recipient account.

DISABILITY BENEFIT - A Social Security benefit available to recipients who have a severe physical or mental impairment that is expected to prevent them from performing "substantial" work for at least a year or result in death. To qualify for these benefits, the recipient must have the sufficient amount of Social Security credits.

DISABILITY INSURANCE - Insurance that provides benefits in the form of periodic payments for a person who is unable to work due to sickness or accidental injury.

DISABILITY INSURANCE (DI) TRUST FUND - The trust fund that pays benefits to workers with disabilities and their families. It is funded by 0.90 percent of an individual's taxable earnings up to $118,500.

DISABILITY OVERHEAD INSURANCE - Insurance that is designed to cover the expenses that are usual and necessary expenses in the operation of a business should the insured owner or key employee become disabled.

DISCRETIONARY - The choice for a plan sponsor of a profit sharing plan as to the amount and frequency of a contribution.

DISCRETIONARY CONTRIBUTIONS - Allows an employer to decide each year whether to make a matching contribution and then inform the plan participants.

DISQUALIFIED PERSONS - any person who owns with other family members 20 percent or more of the stock of the company, or in the case of someone without other family ownership, owns 10 percent or more of the stock of the company.

DISQUALIFYING DISPOSITION - If stock acquired after exercising an ISO is disposed before either two years from the date of the grant or one year from the date of exercise.

DISTRESS TERMINATION - Termination that occurs when the employer is in financial difficulty and is unable to continue with a defined benefit plan.

DIVERSIFIED INVESTMENT PORTFOLIOS - An investment portfolio invested in a broad range of investment classes to reduce investment risk.

E

EARLY WITHDRAWAL PENALTY - A 10 percent penalty on distributions made before the participant attains the age of 59½ (exceptions apply).

EARNED INCOME - Any type of compensation where the individual has performed some level of service for an employer or is considered self-employed, plus alimony received.

ECONOMIC BENEFIT DOCTRINE - An employee will be taxed on funds or property set aside for the employee if the funds or property are unrestricted and nonforfeitable even if the employee was not given a choice to receive the income currently.

EMPLOYEE CENSUS - A matrix of information that is used in plan selection and identifies each employee, their age, compensation, number of years of employment, and any ownership interest in the plan sponsor.

EMPLOYEE ELECTIVE DEFERRAL CONTRIBUTIONS - Pretax employee contributions to a qualified retirement plan with a CODA. The employee must choose to defer the compensation before earning the compensation.

EMPLOYEE PLANS COMPLIANCE RESOLUTION SYSTEM (EPCRS) - The system provided by the IRS that allows plan sponsors to voluntarily correct any disqualifying actions within two years of the plan year end in which the problem occurred.

EMPLOYEE RETIREMENT INCOME AND SECURITY ACT (ERISA) - Legislation enacted by Congress in 1974 as a result of various abuses by plan sponsors to provide protection for an employee's retirement assets, both from creditors and from plan sponsors.

EMPLOYEE STOCK OWNERSHIP PLAN (ESOP) - A qualified profit sharing plan that utilizes employer contributions to the plan to purchase the stock of the employer's company and allocates the ownership to the plan participants.

EMPLOYEE STOCK PURCHASE PLAN - A plan designed to benefit all or a large portion of an employer's employees that gives employees an incentive to buy employer stock by allowing the employees to purchase the stock at a discounted price and receive favorable tax treatment for any gains if the stock meets certain holding period requirements.

EMPLOYER MATCHING CONTRIBUTIONS - Employer-provided contributions to a qualified retirement plan, usually a 401(k) plan, that are based on the employee contributions.

ENTITY INSURANCE - Insurance in which the entity purchases a life insurance policy on the life of each partner or shareholder that is used for buyouts triggered by death of a shareholder or partner.

ERISA ATTORNEY - An attorney who specializes in ERISA law.

EXCESS BENEFIT PLANS - A type of SERP that is designed solely to provide benefits in excess of the benefits available in qualified plans based on the limits under IRC §415.

F

FAIR MARKET VALUE - The price that a willing buyer would pay a willing seller, both having reasonable knowledge of the pertinent facts and neither under duress.

FAMILY BENEFIT - A Social Security benefit available to certain family members of workers eligible for retirement or disability benefits.

FICA (FEDERAL INSURANCE CONTRIBUTIONS ACT) - A law allowing Social Security taxes, including Medicare taxes, to be deducted from employee's paychecks.

FIDUCIARY - An individual that has a special relationship of trust, confidence, and responsibility in certain financial obligations.

15-YEAR RULE - A special catch-up provision for 403(b) plan participants that have worked for the plan sponsor for 15 years. The catch-up allows them to defer up to an additional $15,000 during the plan year.

50/40 COVERAGE TEST - A coverage test applicable only to a defined benefit pension plans that requires the plan to cover for every day during the plan year the lesser of 50 employees or 40% of all eligible employees.

FINAL 3-YEAR CATCH-UP PROVISION - A special catch-up provision for public and private 457(b) plans that allows an individual to defer an additional $18,000 for 2016 to the plan in their final three years before the plan's normal retirement age.

501(c)(3) ORGANIZATIONS - Nonprofit tax-exempt organizations that are established under IRC §501(c)(3) of the Internal Revenue Code.

FIXED AMORTIZATION METHOD - The payment is calculated over the participant's life expectancy if single, or the joint life expectancy if married, and the interest rate is reasonable.

FIXED ANNUITIZATION METHOD - The participant takes distributions of the account over a number of years determined by dividing the account balance by an annuity factor using a reasonable interest rate and mortality table.

FLAT AMOUNT FORMULA - A benefit formula of a defined benefit pension plan that provides each of its participants with an equal dollar benefit at retirement.

FLAT PERCENTAGE FORMULA - A benefit formula of a defined benefit pension plan that provides all plan participants with a benefit equal to a fixed percentage of the participant's salary, usually the final salary or an average of the participant's highest salaries.

FLEXIBLE SPENDING ACCOUNT (FSA) - A cafeteria plan under which employees can choose between receiving cash or deferring income tax-free to fund the cost of certain employee selected benefits. If the participant does not utilize the money in the account by the end of the year, the participant forfeits the deferred funds.

FORFEITURES - The percentage or amount of a participant's accrued benefit that was not vested to the employee at the employee's termination from the plan sponsor. The forfeited amount stays in the plan and may be allocated to the other plan participants (defined contribution plan) or reduce future plan costs (defined contribution plan or defined benefit plan).

FORGONE REVENUE - The lost revenue or opportunity cost incurred by an employer for providing the fringe benefit to the employee.

FORM 5304-SIMPLE - The IRS form used to establish a SIMPLE IRA plan when the employees choose the financial institution.

FORM 5305-SIMPLE - The IRS form used to establish a SIMPLE IRA plan when the employer chooses the financial institution.

401(k) WRAP PLANS - A form of salary reduction plan that enable executives who are subject to salary deferral limitations due to the nondiscrimination rules to contribute higher amounts than otherwise permitted under a 401(k) plan.

457 PLAN - A nonqualified deferred compensation plan for employees of state and local government and tax-exempt entities.

457(b) PLANS - 457(b) plans for governmental and tax- exempt organizations under 501(c) that allow employees to defer income taxation on savings for retirement into future years. Eligible plans are available to most of an employer's employees.

457(f) PLANS - 457(f) plans for employees of governmental entities and tax-exempt entities under 501(c)(3). Ineligible plans are only available to highly compensated and management employees.

FRINGE BENEFIT - A benefit, other than customary taxable wages, provided by an employer to an employee for the employee's performance (in most instances) of services for the employer.

FULLY INSURED - A worker who has earned 40 quarters of coverage under the Social Security system.

FUTA (FEDERAL UNEMPLOYMENT TAX ACT) - A tax on an employee's wages.

G

GRACE PERIOD - If an employer meets the 100-employee limitation in a given year, then the employer will have a two-year "grace period" when the employer can exceed the limitation without losing eligibility to maintain the SIMPLE.

GRADUATED VESTING SCHEDULES - A vesting schedule that provides an employee with full rights to a certain percentage (less than 100%) of benefits after completing a number of years of service and provides the employees with an additional percentage for each additional years of service.

GRANT DATE - The date of issuance of a stock or option.

GROUP LONG-TERM DISABILITY POLICIES - Benefits typically begin after short-term disability and will often continue for a fixed period of time, until retirement or for life.

GROUP SHORT-TERM DISABILITY POLICIES - Benefits generally begin after a short period of time, often corresponding to the employer's sick leave.

GROUP TERM LIFE INSURANCE - Pure insurance protection purchased as a group that pays a predetermined sum if the insured dies during a specified period of time (i.e., the term, which may be 1, 5, 10, 20 years or longer). The value of the premiums, up to $50,000 of death benefit coverage, provided by an employer may be excluded from an employee's gross income.

H

HARDSHIP DISTRIBUTIONS - A distribution from a 401(k) plan because the employee has an immediate and heavy financial need and the withdrawal is necessary to satisfy the need. The distribution is taxable and subject to penalties to the extent the participant has other resources to have satisfied the financial need.

HEALTH SAVINGS ACCOUNTS (HSAS) - A medical savings account, similar to an MSA but less restrictive, that allows anyone with a high deductible health insurance plan to make pretax contributions (subject to limitations). The earnings within the account and the value of the contributions will not be taxed to the extent they are used to pay for qualifying medical expenses.

HEALTH MAINTENANCE ORGANIZATIONS (HMOS) - A form of managed care in which participants receive all of their care from participating providers. Physicians are employed by the HMO directly, or may be physicians in private practice who have chosen to participate in the HMO network. The independent physicians are paid a fixed amount for each HMO member that uses them as a primary care physician.

HEALTH REIMBURSEMENT ARRANGEMENT (HRA) - A type of health insurance plan that reimburses employees for qualified medical expenses.

HIGHLY COMPENSATED EMPLOYEE - An employee who is either a more than 5 percent owner at any time during the plan year or preceding plan year, or had compensation in excess of $120,000 for the prior plan year. A special election can be made to count only those employees whose compensation is in excess of $120,000 and are in the top 20% of employees as ranked by compensation.

HOSPITAL INSURANCE (HI) TRUST FUND - The trust fund that pays for services covered under the hospital insurance provisions of Medicare (Part A). It is funded by 1.45 percent of an individual's taxable earnings (no limitation).

HYPOTHETICAL ACCOUNT - The account statement that displays hypothetical allocations and hypothetical earnings. The accounts are hypothetical because the cash balance pension plan assets are managed by the plan sponsor in the same manner as a defined benefit pension plan.

I

INCENTIVE STOCK OPTIONS (ISOS) - A right given to an employee to purchase an employer's common stock at a stated exercise price. If the requirements of IRC §422 are met, the employee will not recognize any taxable income at the date of grant. Further, at the date of exercise, the employee will also not be subject to ordinary income tax on the difference between the fair market value of the stock and the exercise price. This difference is a positive adjustment for the alternative minimum tax calculation. When the employee sells the stock subsequent to the exercise, the difference between the sales price of the stock and the original exercise price is considered long-term capital gain and there is a negative adjustment for the alternative minimum tax calculation.

INCLUDIBLE COMPENSATION - An employee's taxable wages and benefits for the most recent year of service.

INDEMNITY HEALTH INSURANCE - Traditional, fee-for-service health insurance that does not limit where a covered individual can get care.

INDIRECT ROLLOVER - A distribution to the participant with a subsequent transfer to another qualified account.

INDIVIDUAL 401(k) PLAN - An easy-to-administer, low-cost retirement plan designed for self-employed individuals and owner-only businesses.

INDIVIDUAL RETIREMENT ACCOUNT (IRA) - Two general types under present law: traditional IRAs, to which both deductible and nondeductible contributions may be made, and Roth IRAs, to which only nondeductible contributions may be made.

INDIVIDUAL RETIREMENT ANNUITY - An annuity contract or endowment contract issued by an insurance company that follows many of the same rules for deductibility of premium payments and the limits for premium payments as a traditional IRA.

IN-SERVICE WITHDRAWAL - Any withdrawal from a qualified retirement plan other than a loan while the employee is a participant in the plan.

INTERESTED PARTIES - Present employees who are eligible to participate in the plan and present employees who are not eligible for the plan but whose principal place of employment is the same as the principal place of employment of any employee who is eligible to participate.

INVOLUNTARY TERMINATION - Termination initiated by the PBGC for a defined benefit plan that is unable to pay benefits from the plan.

IRA ANNUITY - An annuity contract or endowment contract issued by an insurance company that follows many of the same rules for deductibility of premium payments and the limits for premium payments as a traditional IRA.

J

JOINT LIFE EXPECTANCY TABLE - The life expectancy table used to determine a participant's RMD when the participant's sole designated beneficiary is the participant's spouse and that spouse is more than 10 years younger than the participant.

K

KEOGH PLAN - A qualified plan for a self-employed individual.

KEY EMPLOYEE - Any employee who is a greater than five percent owner, a greater than one percent owner with compensation in excess of $150,000 (not indexed), or an officer with compensation in excess of $170,000 (2016).

KEY PERSON LIFE AND DISABILITY INSURANCE - Life insurance coverage for employees who are considered critical to the success of a business and whose death might cause financial loss to the company.

L

LEASE VALUE RULE - To determine the value of an employer-provided automobile, use the automobile's annual lease value.

LEPTO-KURTIC - A distribution that appears to be normal but has more area under the two tails than a normal distribution (i.e., fat tails).

LEVERAGED ESOP - An ESOP that borrows the funds necessary to purchase the employer's stock. The interest and principal repayments on the loan are tax deductible for the employer.

LUMP-SUM DISTRIBUTION - A complete distribution of a participant's account balance within one taxable year on account of death, disability, attainment of age 59½, or separation from service. Lump- sum distributions from qualified plans are eligible for special taxation options.

M

MANAGED CARE INSURANCE - Health-care delivery systems that integrate the financing and delivery of health care. Managed care plans feature a network of physicians, hospitals, and other providers who participate in the plan. Managed care includes HMOs, PPOs, and POS plans.

MANDATORY FUNDING REQUIREMENT - An amount or percentage that must be contributed to a qualified pension plan by the employer each plan year.

Master Plan - Provides a single trust or custodial account that is jointly used by all adopting employers.

Maximum Family Benefit - The limit on the amount of monthly Social Security benefits that may be paid to a family.

Medicaid - Provides medical assistance for persons with low incomes and resources.

Medicare - A federal health insurance plan for those who have attained full retirement age or have been disabled whether retired or still working.

Modified Adjusted Gross Income - When calculating taxable Social Security, it is the sum of an individual's adjusted gross income plus tax exempt interest, including interest earned on savings bonds used for higher education; amounts excluded from the taxpayer's income for employer provided adoption assistance; amounts deducted for interest paid for educational loans; amounts deducted as qualified tuition expense; and income earned in a foreign country, a U.S. possession, or Puerto Rico that is excluded from income.

Money Purchase Pension Plan - A defined contribution pension plan that provides for mandatory employer contributions to the plan each year of a fixed percentage of the employees' compensation. The employer does not guarantee a specific retirement benefit.

Monte Carlo Analysis - A mathematical tool used to calculate the success of an individual's retirement portfolio using changing variables.

myRA (my Retirement Account) - a new type of Roth IRA with an investment fund that is backed by the United States Treasury and the account carries no risk of losing money.

N

Net Unrealized Appreciation (NUA) - A special taxation treatment for a lump-sum distribution from a qualified plan that treats part of the distribution as capital gain.

New Comparability Plan - A qualified profit sharing plan in which contributions are made to employees' accounts based on their respective classification in the company as defined by the plan sponsor.

No-Additional-Cost Services - Services provided by an employer to an employee that do not cause the employer to incur any substantial additional cost or lost revenue.

Nonallocation Year - Any plan year of an employee stock ownership plan that holds employer securities consisting of stock in an S corporation, and disqualified persons own at least 50 percent of the number of shares of stock in the S corporation.

NONCONTRIBUTORY PLANS - Qualified retirement plans that do not include employee contributions.

NONDISCRIMINATORY - A requirement of all qualified plans. The eligibility rules, coverage requirements, and contributions allocations of a qualified plan cannot discriminate against the rank-and-file employees for the benefit of shareholder, officers, and highly compensated employees.

NONDISCRIMINATORY CLASSIFICATION TEST - As the second requirement of the average benefits test, it helps to determine whether a plan adequately benefits nonhighly compensated employees.

NONELECTIVE CONTRIBUTIONS - Contributions to a qualified plan on behalf of all eligible employees.

NONEXCLUDABLE - An employee who must be considered as eligible to participate in a qualified plan.

NONQUALIFIED DEFERRED COMPENSATION PLAN (NQDC) - A contractual arrangement between the employer and an executive whereby the employer promises to pay the executive a predetermined amount of money sometime in the future.

NONQUALIFIED PLANS - Plans that do not meet the requirements of the IRC §401(a) and therefore do not have the benefits of qualified plans.

NONQUALIFIED STOCK OPTIONS (NQSOs) - An option that does not meet the requirements of an incentive stock option. The exercise of an NQSO does not receive favorable long- term capital gains treatment but also does not require the holding period associated with ISOs.

NONRECOGNITION OF GAIN TREATMENT - A delay in the recognition of gain available to owners of a company that sell company stock to an ESOP. The transaction must meet the stated requirements of the IRC and the owner must reinvest the proceeds from the sale within 12 months of the sale into qualified domestic replacement securities.

O

OFFICER - An administrative executive who is in regular and continued service and has the executive authority normally associated with an officer.

OLD AGE, SURVIVOR, AND DISABILITY INSURANCE (OASDI) - An inclusive title given to the Social Security benefit system.

OLD AGE AND SURVIVORS INSURANCE (OASI) - The trust fund that pays retirement and survivors' benefits funded by 5.30 percent of an individual's taxable earnings up to $118,500 (2016).

ON-PREMISES ATHLETIC FACILITY - A gym or other athletic facility such as a tennis court, pool, or golf course that is operated by the employer, located on the employer's business premises, and "substantially all" of the use of the facility is by employees of the employer, their spouses, or their dependent children. The value of the use of on premises athletic facilities is not taxable to the employee as long as its availability is nondiscriminatory.

ONE YEAR OF SERVICE - 1,000 hours of service with an employer within a 12-month period.

OPTION PRICE (EXERCISE PRICE) - Usually the fair market value at the grant date.

OWN OCCUPATION - Type of disability policy which states that if the insured is unable to perform the duties associated with his own occupation, the insured is deemed to be disabled and the policy will provide benefits.

P

PASS THROUGH VOTING RIGHTS - The voting rights of the stock pass through from the ESOP or the stock bonus plan to the participant.

PAYROLL TAXES - The combination of OASDI and Medicare tax paid by an employee and employer on an employee's compensation.

PENSION BENEFIT GUARANTY CORPORATION (PBGC) - Established in 1974 when President Gerald R. Ford signed the Employee Retirement Income Security Act (ERISA) into law. The PBGC guarantees qualified pension benefits. It is a federal corporation that acts as an insurance provider to maintain the benefits promised to employees by their defined benefit pension plans.

PENSION PLAN - A qualified retirement plan that pays a benefit, usually determined by a formula, to a plan participant for the participant's entire life during retirement.

PERMITTED DISPARITY (SOCIAL SECURITY INTEGRATION) - A technique or method of allocating qualified plan contributions to an employee account that provides a higher contribution to those employees whose compensation is in excess of the Social Security wage base ($118,500 for 2016) or selected integration level for the plan year.

PHANTOM STOCK PLAN - A nonqualified deferred compensation arrangement where the employer gives fictional shares of stock to a key employee that are initially valued at the time of the grant. The stock is later valued at some terminal point and the executive is then paid in cash the differential value of the stock as compensation.

PHASEOUT - The AGI range that will affect the deductibility of IRA contributions and an individual's ability to make contributions to a Roth IRA.

PIA (PRIMARY INSURANCE AMOUNT) - The amount on which a worker's retirement benefit is based; the PIA determines the amount the applicant will receive at full retirement age based on the year in which the retiree turns 62. The PIA is indexed to the Consumer Price Index (CPI) annually.

PLAN ENTRANCE DATE - The date an eligible employee becomes a participant in a qualified plan.

PLAN FREEZE - Employer will no longer make any contributions to the plan, but does not want to fully terminate the plan.

PLAN LOANS - Loans from a qualified plan made available to all participants on an effectively equal basis that are limited in amount, are repaid within a certain time period, bear a reasonable rate of interest, are adequately secured, and require the administrator to maintain a proper accounting.

POINT OF SERVICE PLAN (POS) - A form of managed care that is considered a managed care/indemnity plan hybrid, as it mixes aspects of HMOs, PPOs, and indemnity plans for greater patient choice. A primary care physician coordinates patient care, but there is more flexibility in choosing doctors and hospitals than in an HMO.

PRE-1974 CAPITAL GAIN TREATMENT - A special taxation treatment for lump-sum distributions from qualified plans that treat the distribution attributable to pre-1974 participation in the plan as long-term capital gain.

PREFERRED PROVIDER ORGANIZATION - A form of managed care in which participants have more flexibility in choosing physicians and other providers than in an HMO. The arrangement between insurance companies and health care providers permits participants to obtain discounted health care services from the preferred providers within the network.

PRIMARY CARE PHYSICIAN - A physician that is designated as a participant's first point of contact with the health care system, particularly in managed care plans.

PROFIT SHARING PLAN - A qualified retirement plan established and maintained by an employer where the employer makes deductible contributions on behalf of the employees, the assets grow tax-deferred, and if there is a CODA feature, the employee also makes pretax contributions.

PROHIBITED TRANSACTIONS - Transactions between the plan and a disqualified person that are prohibited by law.

PROTOTYPE PLAN - A prepackaged plan that allows the sponsor to use a check the box approach to plan choices.

PURCHASING POWER PRESERVATION MODEL (PPP) - A capital needs analysis method that assumes that at a client's life expectancy, the client will have a capital balance with purchasing power equal to the purchasing power at the beginning of retirement.

PURE ANNUITY CONCEPT - The basic capital needs analysis approach, which is generally prepared on a pretax basis.

Q

QUALIFIED AUTOMATIC CONTRIBUTION ARRANGEMENT (QACA) - A plan that contains a "qualified automatic enrollment feature" and is eligible for a new nondiscrimination safe harbor under PPA 2006.

QUALIFIED DISTRIBUTION - A distribution from a Roth IRA that is made after a five-taxable-year period and on account of the account owner's death, disability, attainment of age 59½, or first time home purchase.

QUALIFIED DOMESTIC RELATIONS ORDER (QDRO) - A court order related to divorce, property settlement, or child support that can divide a participant's interest in a qualified plan.

QUALIFIED EDUCATIONAL ASSISTANCE PROGRAM - A plan established and maintained by an employer that provides employees with educational assistance. The employer may exclude $5,250 of benefits from an employee's taxable income.

QUALIFIED ELECTION PERIOD - The term "qualified election period" means the 6-plan-year period beginning with the first plan year in which the individual first became a qualified participant.

QUALIFIED EMPLOYEE DISCOUNTS - A discount on the value of property or services offered to an employer's customers in the ordinary course of the employer's business may be excluded from an employee's income (subject to certain limitations).

QUALIFIED JOINT AND SURVIVOR ANNUITY (QJSA) - The QJSA pays a benefit to the participant and spouse as long as either lives; although, at the death of the first spouse, the annuity may be reduced.

QUALIFIED MATCHING CONTRIBUTION (QMC) - Additional matching contributions made by the employer to satisfy the ADP or ACP test that increases the ACP or ADP of the NHC employees by who had deferred compensation during the plan year.

QUALIFIED MOVING EXPENSES REIMBURSEMENT - Qualified moving expenses paid by an employer on behalf of an employee may be excluded from the employee's gross income. This exclusion applies to the reimbursement of moving expenses that the employee could have deducted on his income tax return if the employee had paid, or incurred, the costs without reimbursement.

QUALIFIED NONELECTIVE CONTRIBUTION (QNEC) - A contribution made by the employer to satisfy the ADP or ACP test that increases the ADP or ACP of the NHC employees by making additional contributions to all NHC eligible employees without regard to any elective deferral election made by the employees.

QUALIFIED NON-PERSONAL USE VEHICLE - A vehicle that the employee does not use more than a minimal amount for personal reasons due to the design of the vehicle. The value of a qualified non-personal use vehicle is excluded from an employee's gross income.

QUALIFIED OPTIONAL SURVIVOR ANNUITY (QOSA) - An annuity for the life of a participant with a survivor annuity for the life of the participant's spouse that is equal to a specified applicable percentage of the amount of the annuity that is payable during the joint lives of the participant and the spouse (and that is actuarially equivalent to a single life annuity for the life of the participant).

QUALIFIED PARKING - Parking provided by the employer on or near the employer's business premises. An employee may exclude up to $255 per month (for 2016) from his gross income for employer provided parking.

QUALIFIED PARTICIPANT - The term "qualified participant" means any employee who has completed at least 10 years of participation under the plan and has attained age 55.

QUALIFIED PLAN - A retirement plan that meets the qualifications of IRC §401(a).

QUALIFIED PLAN AWARD - An employee achievement award bestowed as part of an established written plan of an employer that does not discriminate in favor of highly compensated employees (within the meaning of §414(q)) for eligibility or benefits. The value of an award provided under the plan, up to $400 for a nonqualified award and $1,600 for a qualified award, is excluded from the employee's gross income.

QUALIFIED PRE-RETIREMENT SURVIVOR ANNUITY (QPSA) - Provides a benefit to the surviving spouse if the participant dies before attaining normal retirement age.

QUALIFIED REPLACEMENT SECURITIES - Securities in a domestic corporation, including stocks, bonds, debentures, or warrants, which receive no more than 25% of their income from passive investments.

QUALIFIED TRUST - A trust established or organized in the U.S. that is maintained by the employer for the exclusive benefit of employees.

QUALIFIED TUITION REDUCTION - The amount of any reduction in tuition provided to an employee of an educational organization for education below the graduate level is excluded from the employee's gross income.

R

RABBI TRUST - An irrevocable trust that is designed to hold funds and assets for the purpose of paying benefits under a nonqualified deferred compensation arrangement. The assets in a rabbi trust are for the sole purpose of providing benefits to employees and may not be accessed by the employer, but they may be seized and used for the purpose of paying general creditors in the event of a liquidation of the company. Assets within a rabbi trust are not currently taxable to the employee.

RANK-AND-FILE EMPLOYEES - The non-key, non-highly compensated employees.

RATIO PERCENTAGE TEST - A coverage test that compares the ratio of nonhighly compensated covered by a retirement plan to the ratio of highly compensated covered by the plan. The comparative ratio must be at least 70%.

RECHARACTERIZATION OF DEFERRALS - To change the nature of any excess employee deferrals from pretax employee contributions to after-tax employee contributions.

RECHARACTERIZE - Transferring a contribution and its attributable earnings from a traditional IRA to a Roth IRA or vice versa. The recharacterization must occur by the tax return filing date including extensions for the year of the recharacterization.

REMAINING WORK LIFE EXPECTANCY (RWLE) - The work period that remains at a given point in time before retirement.

REPURCHASE OPTION (PUT OPTION) - An option that allows a terminating employee to receive in cash the fair market value of the employer's stock within a stock bonus plan or ESOP if the employer stock is not readily tradable on an established market. An option to sell to the employer.

REQUIRED MINIMUM DISTRIBUTION - A minimum amount that must be withdrawn from a qualified plan each year after the participant attains the age of 70½. The amount is calculated using the uniform distribution table, the single life expectancy table, or the joint life expectancy tables.

REQUIRED MINIMUM DISTRIBUTION METHOD - The payment is calculated in the same manner as required under minimum distribution rules. Note that payments are recalculated annually.

RESTRICTED STOCK PLAN - An employer provided plan designed to increase retention and compensate employees with a non-cash outflow. The plan pays executives with shares of the employer's stock. The executive does not pay any amount towards the allocation of the stock and, in fact, is restricted by the employer from selling or transferring the stock.

RETIREMENT BENEFIT - The most familiar Social Security benefit, full retirement benefits are payable at normal retirement age and reduced benefits as early as age 62 to anyone who has obtained at least a minimum (40 quarters) amount of Social Security credits.

RETIREMENT EARNINGS LIMITATIONS TEST - A test that may reduce the Social Security benefit paid to an individual based on their other income.

RETIREMENT LIFE EXPECTANCY (RLE) - The time period beginning at retirement and extending until death; the RLE is the period of retirement that must be funded.

ROLLOVER - To elect to transfer funds from one tax-advantaged account to another tax-advantaged account to continue to defer the recognition of income taxes until the ultimate distribution of the assets.

ROTH IRA - An IRA created by the Taxpayer Relief Act of 1997. Contributions to a Roth IRA are nondeductible and qualified distributions are excluded from an individual's taxable income.

S

S CORPORATIONS - Small corporations taxed as pass-through entities that cannot have more than 100 individual shareholders and have only one class of stock.

SAFE HARBOR COVERAGE TEST - A coverage test that requires the employer to cover at least 70% of the nonhighly compensated employees.

SAFE HARBOR 401(k) PLANS - A 401(k) plan that satisfies a minimum contribution or matching test and allows the plan sponsor to bypass the ADP test, the ACP test, and the top-heavy tests.

SALARY CONTINUATION PLAN - An arrangement between an employer and an employee where the employer agrees to continue to pay an employee after his retirement or to the employee's spouse if the employee dies prior to retirement.

SALARY REDUCTION PLANS - A nonqualified plan designed to receive deferral contributions from executives to reduce their current taxable income.

SALARY REDUCTION SIMPLIFIED EMPLOYEE PENSION (SARSEP) - A plan that can no longer be established but allowed employees to elect to defer a portion of their current salary into a SEP-IRA in a similar fashion to a 401(k) plan.

SAVERS CREDIT (RETIREMENT SAVINGS CONTRIBUTIONS CREDIT) - A tax credit for making eligible contributions to an IRA or employer-sponsored retirement plan.

SAVINGS INCENTIVE MATCH PLANS FOR EMPLOYEES (SIMPLEs) - Retirement plans for small employers with 100 or fewer employees who earn more than $5,000 in a year. SIMPLEs may be established as SIMPLE 401(k)s or SIMPLE IRAs.

SAVINGS RATE - The average savings amount in the U.S. based on consumption.

Section 83(b) Election - Election to include in gross income the difference between the fair market value of restricted stock and its purchase price.

Secular Trusts - Irrevocable trusts designed to hold funds and assets for the purpose of paying benefits under a nonqualified deferred compensation arrangement. A secular trust does not create a substantial risk of forfeiture for the employee. Assets set aside in a secular trust results in immediate inclusion of income to the employee.

See-Through Trust – A trust that is the beneficiary of a custodial IRA. It provides for more control over distribution of IRA assets after the owner's death, as well as providing increased creditor protection for the beneficiaries of the trust.

Self-Insured Plan - A plan that reimburses employees for medical expenses not covered by an accident or health insurance policy.

Sensitivity Analysis - A tool used to understand the range of outcomes for each variable in a retirement plan by rotating each variable toward the undesirable side of the risk to determine the impact of a small change in that variable on an overall plan.

Separate Interest Approach - Divides the participant's retirement benefit into two separate portions: one for the alternate payee and one for the participant.

Shared Payment Approach - Splits the actual benefit payments made between the participant and the alternate payee.

SIMPLE 401(k) - A SIMPLE plan that utilizes a 401(k) plan as the funding vehicle of the plan.

SIMPLE IRA - A SIMPLE plan that utilizes an IRA account as the funding vehicle of the plan.

Simplified Employee Pension (SEP) - A practical retirement plan alternative to a qualified plan that can be used by small businesses and sole proprietors. It follows many of the same limits as qualified plans but may require the employer to cover more employees.

Single Life Expectancy Table - Tables used to calculate the required minimum distribution for beneficiaries.

Social Security Integration (Permitted Disparity) - A technique or method of allocating qualified plan contributions to an employee account that provides a higher contribution to those employees whose compensation is in excess of the Social Security wage base ($118,500 for 2016) or selected integration level for the plan year.

Split Definition - Type of disability policy where an insured is covered against the risk of not performing his own occupation for a period of time, and after that period expires, an any-occupation definition of disability is used.

SPLIT-DOLLAR LIFE INSURANCE ARRANGEMENT - A single life insurance policy in which two parties, employer and employee, have an ownership interest. The two parties generally split ownership, premiums, and beneficiaries any way they wish.

SPOUSAL IRA - An IRA created on behalf of a spouse who does not have the necessary earned income to make a contribution to an IRA of their own but can borrow earned income from their spouse.

SSI (SUPPLEMENTAL SECURITY INCOME) - A program administered by the Social Security Administration and funded by the general Treasury that is available to those at full retirement age or the disabled who have a low income and few assets.

STANDARD ELIGIBILITY - The general eligibility requirement that requires an employer to consider an employee eligible when he attains 21 years of age and has completed one-year of service (defined as 1,000 hours of service with an employer within a 12-month period).

STANDARD ELIGIBILITY REQUIREMENTS - IRC eligibility rules for participation in a qualified plan. Provides that an employee must be considered eligible to participate in the plan after completing a period of service with the employer extending beyond the later of the date on which the employee attains the age of 21 or the date on which the employee completes one year of service (1,000 hours of service within 12 months).

STANDARD TERMINATION - Termination in which the employer has sufficient assets to pay all benefits (liabilities) at the time of final distribution.

STOCK APPRECIATION RIGHTS (SARs) - Rights that grant to the holder cash in an amount equal to the excess of the fair market value of the stock over the exercise price.

STOCK BONUS PLAN - A qualified profit sharing plan funded solely with employer stock.

STOCK OPTION - A right to buy stock at a specified price for a specified period of time.

SUBSTANTIAL AND RECURRING - IRC standard defining the frequency requirement of contributions by employers to profit sharing plans.

SUBSTANTIAL RISK OF FORFEITURE - An income tax concept that relates to when income is subject to income tax. A substantial risk of forfeiture exists when rights in property that are transferred are conditioned, directly or indirectly, upon the future performance (or refraining from performance) of substantial services by any person, or the occurrence of a condition related to a purpose of the transfer and the possibility of forfeiture is substantial if the condition is not satisfied.

SUITABILITY - Having a reasonable basis to believe that a recommended transaction or investment strategy is appropriate for a client, after considering the client's age, other investments, financial situation and needs, tax status, investment objectives, investment experience, investment time horizon, liquidity needs, risk tolerance and other relevant issues. See FINRA Rule 2111

SUMMARY OF MATERIAL MODIFICATIONS - Document that provides in plain language the modifications made to a qualified plan.

SUMMARY PLAN DESCRIPTION - Document that explains in plain language the details of a retirement plan and how it operates. It provides information on when an employee can begin to participate in the plan, how service and benefits are calculated, when benefits become vested, when and in what form benefits are paid, and how to file a claim for benefits.

SUPPLEMENTAL EXECUTIVE RETIREMENT PLANS (SERP) - Nonqualified deferred compensation arrangements designed to provide additional benefits to an executive during retirement.

SUPPLEMENTARY MEDICAL INSURANCE (SMI) TRUST FUND - The trust fund that pays for services covered under the medical insurance provisions of Medicare, known as Part B. The coverage is funded by general federal tax revenues and monthly Medicare premiums paid by enrollees.

SURVIVORS' BENEFIT - Social Security benefit available to surviving family members of a deceased, eligible worker.

T

TANDEM PLAN - A 10% money purchase pension plan combined with a 15% profit sharing plan. These were popular prior to TRA 2001.

TARGET BENEFIT PENSION PLAN - A special type of money purchase pension plan that determines the contribution to the participant's account based on the benefit that will be paid from the plan at the participant's retirement rather than on the value of the contribution to the account. Requires an actuary at inception.

TAX SHELTERED OR DEFERRED ANNUITIES (403(b) PLANS) - Retirement plans for certain qualified non- profit organizations or employees of public educational systems – often called 401(k)s for nonprofit organizations.

10-YEAR FORWARD AVERAGING - A method of income tax calculation for certain lump-sum distribution from qualified plans that divides the taxable portion of the lump-sum distribution by 10 and applies the result to the 1986 individual income tax rates. The resulting calculation is then multiplied by 10 to determine the total income tax due on the distribution.

TERM INSURANCE POLICY - A life insurance contract which states if the insured dies within the term of the contract, the insurance company will pay a stated death benefit.

THIRD PARTY ADMINISTRATOR - An organization unrelated to the plan sponsor who is paid to administer the plan sponsor's qualified or other retirement plan.

THRIFT PLAN - A qualified retirement plan that permits employees to make after-tax contributions to the plan. Although the contributions are taxable before being contributed to the plan, the account still benefits from tax-deferred growth on earnings.

THRIFT SAVINGS PLAN (TSP) - A retirement savings and investment plan for Federal employees and members of the uniformed services, including the Ready Reserve.

TITLE I OF ERISA - Coverage, participation, funding, and discrimination requirements of ERISA imposed on qualified plans.

TOP HAT PLANS - Plans designed to benefit a select group of top management or key employees.

TOP-HEAVY - Rules that were designed to ensure that plans established primarily to benefit the owners and executives of the company also provided some minimum level of benefits for the rank-and-file employees.

TRADITIONAL IRA - An IRA that may accept deductible and nondeductible contributions and whose assets grow tax-deferred until distribution.

TRUSTEED IRA – A trust established within the United States that holds IRA assets, which is an alternative to a custodial IRA. It allows for ultimate control over the distribution of the IRA assets by the owner after his or her death and provides creditor protection for the beneficiaries.

TWO-YEAR ELIGIBILITY ELECTION - A special election that overrides the standard eligibility requirements and permits the employer to only consider those employees who have two years of service as eligible to participate in a plan. If the employer elects the two-year requirement, than the employer must also provide 100% vesting at the completion of two years of service.

U

UNIFORM LIFETIME TABLE - A table used to calculate the RMD for the plan participant unless the participant's sole designated beneficiary is the participant's spouse and that spouse is more than 10 years younger than the participant.

UNIT CREDIT FORMULA - A benefit formula of a defined benefit pension plan that utilizes a combination of the participant's years of service and salary to determine the participant's accrued benefit.

UNIVERSAL LIFE INSURANCE - A term insurance policy with a cash accumulation account attached to it.

UNSAFE CONDITIONS COMMUTING RULE - The value of commuting transportation provided by an employer to a qualified employee solely because of unsafe conditions is $1.50 for each one way commute.

V

VEST - To give an employee rights to employer contributions and earnings in their retirement plan benefits.

VOLUME SUBMITTER PLAN - A plan that is designed by a professional, such as an attorney, CPA or third party administrator, which contains language that has been pre-approved by the IRS. This type of plan allows for more customization than a standard prototype plan, but is generally much less costly than an individualized plan.

VOLUNTARY EMPLOYEES' BENEFICIARY ASSOCIATION (VEBA) - A welfare benefit plan into which employers deposit funds that will be used to provide specified employee benefits in the future. The deposits are deductible for the employer at the date of the contribution rather than at the date when the employee benefits are provided.

W

WAGE REPLACEMENT RATIO (WRR) - An estimate of the percent of income needed at retirement compared to earnings prior to retirement.

WHOLE LIFE INSURANCE POLICY - A permanent life insurance policy that guarantees that the policy will remain in force as long as the premium is paid. The life insurance policy has a cash account that grows tax deferred.

WORK LIFE EXPECTANCY (WLE) - The period of time a person is expected to be in the work force, generally 30-40 years.

WORKING CONDITION FRINGE BENEFITS - Any property or service provided to an employee that enables the employee to perform his work and, if paid for by the employee, is deductible as a trade or business expense (i.e., parking).

Y

YEAR OF SERVICE - At least 1,000 hours of service for an employer and 12 months of continuous employment.

Appendix

B

INDEX

Numerics

A